S0-AVQ-270

Contemporary
Theatre, Film,
and Television

A Note About
Contemporary Theatre, Film, and Television
and
Who's Who in the Theatre

Contemporary Theatre, Film, and Television is a continuation of *Who's Who in the Theatre,* expanded to include film and television personalities. The editors believe this change in coverage of the series makes for a more representative and useful reference tool.

To provide continuity with *Who's Who in the Theatre,* the cumulative index at the back of this volume interfiles references to *Contemporary Theatre, Film, and Television,* Volumes 1-2, with references to *Who's Who in the Theatre,* 1st-17th Editions. Only those deceased or inactive individuals whose *Who's Who in the Theatre* entries are included in Gale's *Who Was Who in the Theatre* are not listed in the cumulative index.

ISSN 0749-064X

Contemporary Theatre, Film, and Television

A Biographical Guide Featuring Performers,
Directors, Writers, Producers, Designers, Managers,
Choreographers, Technicians, Composers, Executives,
Dancers, and Critics in the United States and Great Britain

A Continuation of
Who's Who in the Theatre

Monica M. O'Donnell, Editor

Foreword by Edwin Sherin

R
791.092
C761

Volume 2

Includes Cumulative Index Containing References to
Who's Who in the Theatre

COLLEGE OF THE SEQUOIAS

LIBRARY

GALE RESEARCH COMPANY • BOOK TOWER • DETROIT, MICHIGAN 48226

STAFF

Monica M. O'Donnell, *Editor*

J. Peter Bergman, Mel Cobb, James R. Kirkland, *Sketchwriters*
Thomas W. Bachmann, Darryl W. Bridson, Vincent Henry, Susan Reu, Timothy L. Schuman, *Editorial Assistants*

Linda S. Hubbard, *Consulting Editor*
Hank Hubbard, Peter Ruffner, *Program Designers*

Carol Blanchard, *Production Director*
Mary Beth Trimper, *Senior Production Associate*
Jay Lander, Paula Lander, *Layout Artists*
Arthur Chartow, *Art Director*

Special acknowledgment is due to the
Contemporary Authors staff members who
assisted in the preparation of this volume.

Frederick G. Ruffner, *Publisher*
James M. Ethridge, *Executive Vice-President/Editorial*
Dedria Bryfonski, *Editorial Director*
Christine Nasso, *Director, Literature Division*

Copyright © 1986 by GALE RESEARCH COMPANY

Library of Congress Catalog Card Number 84-649371
ISBN 0-8103-2065-7
ISSN 0749-064X

No part of this book may be reproduced in any form without permission in
writing from the publisher, except by a reviewer who wishes to quote brief
passages or entries in connection with a review written for inclusion in a
magazine or newspaper. Manufactured in the United States of America.

Computerized photocomposition by
Roberts/Churcher
Brooklyn, New York

Contents

Foreword
By Edwin Sherin

Nowadays it's more a question of which coast you call home, rather than whether you work in theatre, film, or television. The trend in our business is clearly toward doing it all—being involved with more than one aspect of the various performing arts.

Nearly thirty years ago, I worked as an extra with the American Shakespeare Festival. John Houseman was directing this permanent company of twenty-five or more actors performing on seasonal contracts in rotating repertory. I doubt that any performer in that company thought much beyond the size and challenge of his next role. On Broadway during the same 1957 season, more than two hundred plays and musicals opened, and the list of credible Broadway producers from whom actors could reasonably seek out work exceeded five pages in the *Theatrical Index.*

Broadway no longer provides sufficient opportunity for the people who might otherwise choose to work there. A bicoastal crisscrossing of careers, now commonplace, has peppered Los Angeles with talent from the East. The film, television, and theatre industries of the West Coast create a diversified marketplace that allows performers, directors, producers, and writers to express themselves in a variety of media while reaching a variety of audiences.

These artists and those who remain in New York have substantially changed their approach to developing their craft. Performers energetically seek commercials, television soap operas, industrial films, and Equity waiver showcases (showcases that Equity allows its members to work in for no money), as well as more traditional Broadway plays and musicals, films, and television; they study dancing, singing, juggling, gymnastics, mime, and puppetry, as well as acting, voice, and speech. Actors, singers, and dancers, once specialists, are now called upon to excel in all disciplines. Performers in increasing numbers also write plays, popular music, comedy routines, and commercials while working at other crafts and trades. To keep their offices open and cash flow sustained, Broadway producers have formed companies operating in all media. Many directors and stars have established their own production organizations, mastering such concepts as "down-side protection," "rolling break-even points," "negative depreciation," and "ancillaries." Agents, managers, lawyers, and accountants, aware of the dissolving boundaries between producers, performers, directors, and even writers, have become more directly involved in the creative side of the entertainment media. Never in the history of entertainment has so much been done by so many.

Computers, microdish antennae technology, and video cassette marketing secure a future for the burgeoning television and film businesses while the growth of the cable television and video cassette industries is changing our concept of home entertainment. Cable networks and video cassette recorders extend the life of a theatrical film by attracting an entirely new viewing audience amounting to millions of people, and bringing in millions of dollars in revenue; a film considered a "box office failure" in the past is now termed successful, both financially and artistically, if it reaches these wider home audiences.

In filmmaking, technological advances, particularly in visual and aural effects, have brought millions of delighted moviegoers out of their homes and into the movie theatres. A review of the top-grossing films of the last decade attests to this. *The Exorcist,* the "Star Wars" trilogy, and the "Indiana Jones" movies (in fact, all of Steven Spielberg's films, including *Jaws, Close Encounters of the Third Kind, E.T., Gremlins,* and *The Goonies*) all rely heavily on special effects and have all done extremely well at the box office.

Independent filmmakers now more than ever are breaking through to larger markets with major features, and breaking box office records as well. And while these filmmakers retain their production independence, their films are often released by major studios, insuring wide distribution.

But what about theatre? In the last three decades Broadway has undergone irreversible change. Actors of national stature who learned their craft on the "boards" do not return to Broadway. Writers who contributed a play a year throughout most of their careers and were numerous earlier this century are nonexistent now. Within one season producers appear, then disappear, never to be heard from again. Directors seek other stages or other media, and choreographers, designers, and technicians look elsewhere for survival and growth.

Can the theatre overcome spiralling production costs and increasing ticket prices? And are the problems only cost overruns? Will the producers, writers, directors, and actors who might bring excitement back to Broadway be willing to forgo the security of film and television, which provides more dollars for fewer aesthetic and economic risks? (Remember, there is no greater horror in show business than participating in a Broadway play that closes during its first few days and brings to an end a production that took profitless years to prepare.)

The answers are uncertain, yet theatre continues and is flourishing elsewhere. Men and women still are sustained by the collective need for its ritual—Off, Off-Off, and far from Broadway. Companies exist from New Haven to San Francisco, from Houston to Seattle, from Minneapolis to Providence, which offer a rich variety of plays and dare to take chances. Several hundred of these "resident" theatres now thrive in our country, serving an audience of over fifteen million people.

When Zelda Fichandler founded Washington's Arena Stage in 1950, there was no appreciable resident theatre movement. She said recently, "Once we made the choice to produce our plays, not to recoup an investment, but to recoup some corner of the universe for our understanding and enlargement, we entered into the same world as the university, the library, the museum, the church, and became, like them, an instrument of civilization." These resident companies, more than any other resource, insure the theatre's growth.

As the disciplines of theatre, film, and television converge, we have had to become jacks of all trades, bringing special skills learned in one medium and adapting them for use in the others. We will have many diverse opportunities in the world of entertainment, and we must all be prepared to take advantage of them. And as the trend toward doing it all continues, one can envision, a hundred years from now, a *Contemporary Theatre, Film, and Television* biographical guide with as many names in it as the combined New York and Los Angeles telephone directories.

Edwin Sherin began his career as an actor. Since his directorial debut in 1959, he has been associate producing director at the Arena Stage in Washington, DC, producing artistic director at the Hartman in Stamford, CT, and has directed on Broadway, in London, and in major regional theatres throughout the United States.

Preface

The worlds of theatre, film, and television hold an undeniable appeal, and the individuals whose careers are devoted to these fields are subjects of great interest. The people both behind the scenes and in front of the lights and cameras—writers, directors, producers, performers, and others—all have a significant impact on our lives, for they enlighten us as they entertain.

Contemporary Theatre, Film, and Television
Continues and Improves
Who's Who in the Theatre

Contemporary Theatre, Film, and Television (CTFT), a comprehensive new biographical guide, is designed to meet the need for information on theatre, film, and television personalities. Existing biographical sources covering entertainment figures are generally limited in scope, focusing only on theatre, for example, as was the case with *Who's Who in the Theatre (WWT)*. For more than seventy years *WWT* provided reliable information on theatre people. However, when the editors began reviewing names for inclusion in a proposed supplement to the seventeenth edition of *WWT*, they recognized that they were eliminating large numbers of people who, though not active in the theatre, make significant contributions to other entertainment media. Thus, the editors believe that expanding the scope of *WWT* to encompass not only theatre notables but film and/or television figures as well provides a more useful reference tool.

In addition to its expanded scope, *CTFT* improves upon *WWT* in other important ways. *WWT* was published in *editions*, with the majority of the biographies in every edition being updated and included in subsequent editions. Since entries were dropped from one edition to the next only when listees had been inactive for a sustained period or when active listees died, the number of new entries it was possible to include in each *WWT* edition was governed in part by how many old ones were dropped. *CTFT*, however, will be published annually in *volumes*, and each volume will cover primarily new, entirely different personalities. Thus *CTFT*'s coverage will not be limited by the number of entries that can be listed in a single volume, and cumulative indexes will make the entries in all *CTFT* volumes easily accessible.

Entry format, discussed in greater detail later in this preface, has also been improved in *CTFT*. Instead of presenting information with minimal paragraphing, as was the case in *WWT*, the editors have divided *CTFT* entries into numerous clearly labeled sections to make it easier to locate specific facts quickly. And the inclusion of hundreds of photographs of the personalities listed in *CTFT* adds a useful visual dimension to *CTFT* missing from *WWT*.

Scope

CTFT is a biographical series covering not only performers, directors, writers, and producers but also designers, managers, choreographers, technicians, composers, executives, dancers, and critics from the United States and Great Britain. With nearly 700 entries in *CTFT*, Volume 2, the series now provides biographies for over 1,800 people involved in all aspects of the theatre, film, and television industries.

Primary emphasis is given to people who are currently active. *CTFT* includes major, established figures whose positions in entertainment history are assured, such as actor and director Jackie Cooper, producer and director Roger Corman, actress and director Marsha Mason, and actress Mary Wickes. New and highly promising individuals who are beginning to make their mark are represented in *CTFT* as well—people such as film and television actor Hart Bochner, who appeared recently in a television presentation of *The Sun Also Rises;* stage and television actress Kate Burton, known for her portrayal of *Alice in Wonderland* and seen in television's *Ellis Island;* actor Steve Guttenberg, star of the *Policy Academy* films, *Cocoon,* and several made-for-television movies; and Caroline Lagerfelt, who was most recently seen in the Broadway production of *The Real Thing.*

CTFT also includes sketches on people no longer professionally active who have made significant contributions to their fields and whose work remains of interest today. This volume, for example, contains entries on actress and businesswoman Arlene Dahl, director Gordon Douglas, actor John Gavin, who is now the American ambassador to Mexico, and stage and film star Hermione Gingold. Selected sketches also record the achievements of theatre, film, and television personalities deceased since 1960. Among such notables with sketches in this volume are Abe Burrows, Richard Burton, Selma Diamond, and Margaret Hamilton.

With its broad coverage and detailed entries, *CTFT* is designed to assist a variety of users—a student preparing for a class, a teacher drawing up an assignment, a researcher seeking a specific fact, a librarian searching for the answer to a question, or a general reader looking for information about a favorite personality.

Compilation Methods

Every effort is made to secure information directly from biographees. The editors consult industry directories, biographical dictionaries, published interviews, feature stories, and film, television, and theatre reviews to identify people not previously covered in *WWT* or *CTFT*. Questionnaires are mailed to prospective listees or, when addresses are unavailable, to their agents, and sketches are compiled from the information they supply. The editors also select major figures included in *WWT* whose entries require updating and send them copies of their previously published entries for revision. *CTFT* sketches are then prepared from the new information submitted by these well-known personalities or their agents. Among the notable figures whose *WWT,* seventeenth edition, entries have been completely revised for this volume of *CTFT* are Garson Kanin, Marian Seldes, Martin Sheen, and Patricia Zipprodt. If people of special interest to *CTFT* users are deceased or fail to reply to requests for information, materials are gathered from reliable secondary sources. Sketches prepared solely through research are clearly marked with an asterisk (*) at the end of the entries.

The emphasis in future volumes will remain on people currently active in theatre, film, and television who are not already covered in *WWT* or *CTFT*. To insure *CTFT*'s timeliness and comprehensiveness, future volumes will continue to include updated *WWT* entries and will also provide revisions of *CTFT* sketches that have become outdated.

Format

CTFT entries, modeled after those in the Gale Research Company's highly regarded *Contemporary Authors* series, are written in a clear, readable style with few abbreviations and no limits set on length. So that a reader needing specific information can quickly focus on the pertinent portion of an entry, typical *CTFT* listings are clearly divided into the following sections:

> **Entry heading**—Cites the form of the name by which the listee is best known followed by birth and death dates, when available.

> **Personal**—Provides the biographee's full or original name if different from the entry heading, date and place of birth, family data, and information about the listee's education (including professional training), politics, religion, and military service.

> **Vocation**—Highlights the individual's primary fields of activity in the entertainment industry.

> **Career**—Presents a comprehensive listing of principal credits or engagements. The career section lists theatrical debuts (including New York and London debuts), principal stage appearances, and major tours; film debuts and principal films; television debuts and television appearances; and plays, films, and television shows directed and produced. Related career items, such as professorships and lecturing, are also included as well as non-entertainment career items.

> **Writings**—Lists published and unpublished plays, screenplays, and scripts along with production information. Published books and articles, often with bibliographical data, are also listed.

> **Awards**—Notes theatre, film, and television awards and nominations as well as writing awards, military and civic awards, and fellowships and honorary degrees received.

> **Sidelights**—Cites memberships, recreational activities, and hobbies. Frequently this section provides portions of agent-prepared biographies or personal statements from the listee.

> **Address**—Notes home, office, and agent addresses, when available.

Enlivening the text in many instances are large, clear photographs. Often the work of theatrical photographers, these pictures are supplied by the biographees to complement their sketches.

New Feature: Brief Entries

CTFT users have indicated that having some information, however brief, on individuals not yet in the series would be preferable to waiting until full-length sketches can be prepared as outlined above under "Compilation Methods." Beginning with this volume, therefore, *CTFT* introduces abbreviated listings on notables who presently do not have sketches in *CTFT*. These short profiles, identified by the heading "Brief Entry," highlight the person's career in capsule form.

Brief entries are not intended to replace sketches. Instead, they are designed to increase *CTFT*'s comprehensiveness and thus better serve *CTFT* users by providing pertinent and timely information about well-known people in the entertainment industry, many of whom will be the subjects of full sketches in forthcoming volumes.

This volume, for example, includes brief entries on such up-and-coming people as Jennifer Beals, Emilio Estevez, Tom Hanks, and Ally Sheedy.

Cumulative Index

To facilitate locating sketches on the thousands of notables profiled in *CTFT* as well as in *WWT*, the *CTFT* cumulative index at the back of this volume interfiles references to *CTFT*, Volumes 1 and 2, with references to *WWT*, first through seventeenth editions. Deceased or inactive individuals drawn from the first fifteen editions of *WWT* and included in Gale's *Who Was Who in the Theatre*, published in 1978, are not listed in the *CTFT* cumulative index; all other *WWT* biographees are cited with references to the latest edition of *WWT* containing their entries. Thus by consulting only two sources—the *CTFT* cumulative index and *Who Was Who in the Theatre*—users have easy access to the tens of thousands of biographical sketches in *CTFT* and all previous editions of *WWT*.

Acknowledgments

The editors would like to extend special and sincere thanks to Sir Peter Saunders for recommending British names for inclusion in this volume of *CTFT*.

Suggestions Are Welcome

If readers would like to suggest people to be covered in future *CTFT* volumes, they are encouraged to send these names (along with addresses, if possible) to the editor. Other suggestions and comments are also most welcome and should be addressed to: The Editor, *Contemporary Theatre, Film, and Television,* 150 East 50th St., New York, NY 10022.

Contemporary Theatre, Film, and Television

Contemporary Theatre, Film, and Television

* Indicates that a listing has been compiled from secondary sources believed to be reliable.

BROOKE ADAMS

ADAMS, Brooke   1949-

PERSONAL: Born February 8, 1949, in New York City; daughter of Robert K. (an actor and producer) and Rosaland (an actress; maiden name, Gould) Adams. EDUCATION: High School of Performing Arts; Institute of American Ballet; studied acting with Lee Strasberg.

VOCATION: Actress.

CAREER: NEW YORK DEBUT—Gabrielle, *The Petrified Forest,* St. Clements. PRINCIPAL STAGE APPEARANCES—Carol, *Split,* Second Stage, NY, 1980; Lisa, *Key Exchange,* WPA, NY, 1982; Julia, *The Philanderer,* Yale Repertory, New Haven, CT, 1983; Carol, *Linda Hur,* Second Stage, NY, 1984.

FILM DEBUT—*Car Wash,* Universal, 1976. PRINCIPAL FILM AP-PEARANCES—*Shockwaves* (a.k.a. *Death Corps*), 1977; *Days of Heaven,* Paramount, 1978; *Invasion of the Body Snatchers,* United Artists, 1978; *A Man and a Woman and a Bank,* Avco Embassy, 1979; *Cuba,* United Artists, 1979; *Tell Me a Riddle,* 1980; *The Dead Zone,* Paramount, 1983; Erica Bayer, *Almost You,* Twentieth Century-Fox, 1985; *Key Exchange* (forthcoming); *Utilities* (forthcoming).

PRINCIPAL TELEVISION APPEARANCES—*The Daughters of Joshua Cabe,* 1972; *The Daughters of Joshua Cabe Return,* 1975; *Murder on Flight 502,* 1975; *James Dean: Portrait of a Friend,* 1976; *Last of the Belles; The Lords of Flatbush; Special People; Lace,* ABC; *Lace II,* ABC; *Haunted,* PBS; *The Bob Newhart Show; Police Woman.*

ADDRESS: OFFICE—MSI, 250 W. 57th Street, New York, 10019. AGENT—William Morris, 1350 Avenue of the Americas, New York, NY 10019.

*   *   *

ADAMS, Molly

VOCATION: Actress.

CAREER: STAGE DEBUT—Susan, *The Little Hut,* Pineville Country Dinner Theatre, Charlotte, NC, 1967. NEW YORK DEBUT—Rosemary, *Are You Prepared to Be a United States Marine,* Cubiculo, 1968, for sixteen performances. PRINCIPAL STAGE APPEAR-ANCES—Gertrude, *Hamlet,* A.M.D.A., NY, 1969; Waiting Gentlewoman and Lady Macbeth standby, *Macbeth,* Madison Avenue Baptist Church, 1971; Jewish Wife, *Jesus, As Seen by His Friends,* Manhattan Theatre Club, NY, 1971; Babe, *Home Again, Home Again, Jiggetty Jig,* Tosos, NY, 1972; Irene, *When We Dead Awaken,* Circle Repertory, NY, 1973; Howardina, et al., *Older People,* New York Shakespeare Festival at the Anspacher, NY, 1974; Howardina, et al., *Lost Jazz,* Ensemble Studio, NY, 1974; Lorraine, *The Steak Palace,* Open Space in Soho, NY, 1975; Dee, *Seed from the East,* Theatre for the New City, NY, 1976; Judith Bliss, *Hay Fever,* Tosos, NY, 1977; Governor's Wife, *The Unicorn in Captivity,* Impossible Ragtime Theatre (IRT), NY, 1978.

Hallie, *Buried Child,* Circle Repertory, NY, 1979; Fran, *Did You See the Elephant,* American Renaissance Theatre Co., NY, 1980; Laura's Mother, *The Father,* Circle in the Square, NY, 1980; Defenseless Creature, et al., *The Good Doctor,* American Renaissance Theatre Co., NY, 1983; Paulina, *The Seagull,* Saratoga Performing Arts Center, Little Theatre, Saratoga Springs, NY, 1983.

FILM DEBUT—Young grandmother, *Voyeur,* Yale School of Drama film, c. 1974.

TELEVISION DEBUT—*Love Is a Many Splendored Thing*, CBS, 1968.

ADDRESS: AGENT—Don Buchwald & Associates, Ten E. 44th Street, New York, NY 10017.

*   *   *

ADAMS, Tony   1953-

PERSONAL: Born Anthony Patrick Adams, February 15, 1953, in Dublin, Ireland; son of Charles (a contractor) and Teresa (Fitzsimons) Adams; married; children: Andrew, Alister. EDUCATION: Atlantic College, FL; Pepperdine University, CA; special training at the Dublin Communication Centre.

VOCATION: Producer.

CAREER: PRINCIPAL FILM WORK—Associate producer, *Return of the Pink Panther*, United Artists, 1975; associate producer, *The Pink Panther Strikes Again*, United Artists, 1976; executive producer, *Revenge of the Pink Panther*, United Artists, 1978; producer, *"10"*, Warner Bros., 1979; producer, *S.O.B.*, Paramount, 1981; producer, *Victor/Victoria*, Metro-Goldwyn-Mayer/United Artists, 1982; producer, *Trail of the Pink Panther*, Metro-Goldwyn-Mayer/United Artists, 1982; producer, *Curse of the Pink Panther*, Metro-

TONY ADAMS

Goldwyn-Mayer, 1983; producer, *The Man Who Loved Women*, Columbia, 1983; producer, *Micki & Maude*, Columbia, 1984.

PRINCIPAL TELEVISION WORK—Producer, *Because We Care*.

MAJOR TOURS—Producer: Julie Andrews' London concert; Julie Andrews' U.S. and Japan tours, 1972-1975.

RECORDINGS—Producer, *Julie Andrews Live in Concert*, 1980.

WRITINGS: PLAYS, PRODUCED—*The English Can't Remember . . . The Irish Can't Forget*, Pepperdine University, 1972.

AWARDS: Golden Globe Award nomination, 1979, for *"10"*; Golden Globe Award nomination, 1981, for *S.O.B.*; Golden Globe Award, 1982, for *Victor/Victoria;* French Academy of Cinema Arts and Techniques "Cesar" Award, 1982, for *Victor/Victoria;* David Di Donatello "Golden David" Award, 1982, for *Victor/Victoria;* Premio "Sant Jordi" de cinematografia de R.N.E., 1983, for *Victor/Victoria*, President's Volunteer Action Award, 1983; Golden Globe, 1984, for *Micki and Maude;* Academy of Motion Picture Arts and Sciences Jean Hersholt Humanitarian Award, nominee.

SIDELIGHTS: MEMBERSHIPS—Academy of Motion Picture Arts and Sciences, American Film Institute, Producers Guild of America, International Institute of Kidney Diseases (former chairman), Operation California (board of trustees), Committee of Concern for Central America.

Adams has travelled extensively throughout the world, including tours of refugee camps in Southeast Asia and the Middle East.

ADDRESS: OFFICE—Blake Edwards Enterprises, 1888 Century Park East, Suite 1616, Los Angeles, CA 90067.

*   *   *

ADDAMS, Dawn   1930-85

PERSONAL: Born September 21, 1930, in Felixstowe, Suffolk, England; died May 7, 1985, in London, of cancer; daughter of James Ramage and Ethel Mary (Hickie) Addams; married Vittorio Massimo (divorced; since has died); married James White; children: (first marriage) one son.

VOCATION: Actress.

CAREER: STAGE DEBUT—Amy Spettigue, *Charley's Aunt*, Piccadilly, London, 1949. PRINCIPAL STAGE APPEARANCES—Title role, *Peter Pan*, Scala, London, 1964; Annabelle West, *Cat and the Canary*, King's Edinburgh, London, 1966; Elle, *Sleeping Partner*, 1967; Bromley Mar, New, London, 1970; Jemima, *The Coming Out Party*, 1970; Susan, *The Little Hut*, Richmond, London, 1970.

MAJOR TOURS—Title role, *Peter Pan*, 1972.

PRINCIPAL FILM APPEARANCES—*Night into Morning*, 1951; *The Robe*, 1953; *The Moon Is Blue*, 1953; *A King in New York*, Classic Entertainment, 1957; *The Silent Enemy*, Universal, 1958; *Where the Bullets Fly*, Embassy, 1966; *Vampire Lovers*, 1971; *The Vault of Horror*, Cinerama, 1973.*

ADLER, Luther   1903-84

PERSONAL: Born Lutha Adler, May 4, 1903, in New York City; died December 8, 1984, in Kutztown, PA; son of Jacob and Sarah (Lewis) Adler; married Sylvia Sidney (divorced); married Julia Roche; children: one son. EDUCATION: Lewis Institute, Chicago.

VOCATION: Actor.

CAREER: STAGE DEBUT—*Schmendrick*, Thalia, NY, 1908. PRINCIPAL STAGE APPEARANCES—Joe and Samuel Elkas, *The Hand of the Potter*, Provincetown, NY, 1921; Leon Kantor, *Humoresque*, Vanderbilt, NY, 1923; Zizi, *The Monkey Talks*, Sam H. Harris, NY, 1925; Sam Madorsky, *Money Business*, National, NY, 1926; Phil Levine, *We Americans*, Sam H. Harris, NY, 1926; Old Man, *John*, Klaw, 1927; *The Music Master*, 1927; *Is Zat So?*, NY, 1927; *Give and Take*, 1927; Sam, *Street Scene*, Playhouse, NY, 1929; Piotr, *Red Rust*, Martin Beck, NY, 1929; Don Fernando, *Night Over Taos*, 48th Street, NY, 1932; Sol Ginsberg, *Success Story*, Maxine Elliott, NY, 1932; Julian Vardaman, *Alien Corn*, Belasco, NY, 1933; Dr. Gordon, *Men in White*, Broadhurst, NY, 1933; Emperor Norton and Tang Sing, *Gold Eagle Guy*, Morosco, NY, 1934; Moe Axelrod, *Awake and Sing*, Belasco, NY, 1935; Marcus Katz, *Paradise Lost*, Longacre, NY, 1935.

Doctor, *The Case of Clyde Griffiths*, Barrymore, NY, 1936; Joe Bonaparte, *Golden Boy*, Belasco, NY, 1937; Mr. Prince, *Rocket to the Moon*, Belasco, NY, 1938; Chatterton, *Thunder Rock*, Mansfield, NY, 1939; Lawrence Ormont, *Two on an Island*, Broadhurst, NY, 1940; Golba, *The Russian People*, Guild, NY, 1942; Mr. Rochester, *Jane Eyre*, 1943; Harry, *Uncle Harry*, Chicago, 1944; Captain Angelini, *Common Ground*, Fulton, NY, 1945; Noll Turner, *Beggars Are Coming to Town*, Coronet, NY, 1945; Miguel Riachi, *Dunnigan's Daughter*, Golden, NY, 1945; Tevya, *A Flag Is Born*, Music Box, NY, 1946; Commissar Corotchenko, *Tovarich*, City Center, NY, 1952; *The Play's the Thing*, Boston, 1952; Shylock, *The Merchant of Venice*, City Center, NY, 1953; Shpichelsky, *A Month in the Country*, Phoenix, NY, 1956; Casale, *A Very Special Baby*, Playhouse, NY, 1956.

A View from the Bridge, 1960; Lenin, *The Passion of Josepf D*, Barrymore, NY, 1964; Chebutykin, *The Three Sisters*, Morosco, NY, 1964; Tevye, *Fiddler on the Roof*, Imperial, NY, 1965; *The Tenth Man*, 1966; General St. Pe, *Waltz of the Toreadors*, Ivanhoe, Chicago, 1969; Gregory Solomon, *The Price*, Theatre on the Mall, Paramus, NJ, 1970.

FILM DEBUT—*Cornered*, 1945. PRINCIPAL FILM APPEARANCES—*Saigon*, 1948; *The Loves of Carmen*, 1948; *House of Strangers*, 1949; *D.O.A.*, 1949; *South Sea Sinner*, 1950; *Under My Skin*, 1950; *Kiss Tomorrow Goodbye*, 1950; *M*, 1951; *Hoodlum Empire*, 1952; *The Miami Story*, 1954; *Crashout*, 1955; *The Girl in the Red Velvet Swing*, 1955; *Hot Blood*, Columbia, 1956; *The Last Angry Man*, Columbia, 1959; *Cast a Giant Shadow*, United Artists, 1966; *The Brotherhood*, Paramount, 1968; *Crazy Joe*, Columbia, 1974; *Murph the Surf*, American International, 1975; *The Man in the Glass Booth*, 1975; *Voyage of the Damned*, Avco-Embassy, 1976.*

*   *   *

AGUTTER, Jenny   1952-

PERSONAL: Emphasis is on the first syllable; born December 20, 1952, in Taunton, England; daughter of Derek Brodie (a live entertainment organizer) and Catherine (Lynam) Agutter. EDUCATION: Trained for the stage at the Elmhurst Ballet School.

VOCATION: Actress.

CAREER: STAGE DEBUT—Lady Teazle, *The School for Scandal*, Castle Theatre, Farnham, Surrey, 1972. LONDON DEBUT—*Rooted*, Hampstead Theatre Club, 1973. PRINCIPAL STAGE APPEARANCES—Raina, *Arms and the Man*, Manchester '73 Festival, 1973; *The Ride Across Lake Constance*, Hampstead Theatre Club, 1973; Miranda, *The Tempest*, Thea, *Spring's Awakening*, National Theatre, 1974; Hedda, *Hedda Gabler*, Round House, London, 1980; Emma, *Betrayal*, Charles Playhouse, Boston, MA, 1980; Alice Arden, *Arden of Faversham*, Royal Shakespeare Company, 1982; Fontanelle, (Edward Bond's) *Lear*, Royal Shakespeare Company, 1982; *The Other Place*, Royal Shakespeare Company, 1982; Regan, *King Lear*, Royal Shakespeare Company, 1982-83; Grace, *The Body*, Royal Shakespeare Company, 1983.

FILM DEBUT—An Arab child, *East of Sudan*, 1963. PRINCIPAL FILM APPEARANCES—*Ballerina;* Maud, *Gates of Paradise;* Pamela, *Star!*, Twentieth Century-Fox, 1968; Wynne, *I Start Counting*, United Artists, 1970; *Walkabout*, Twentieth Century-Fox, 1971; Roberta, *The Railway Children*, Universal, 1971; Jessica, *Logan's Run*, United Artists, 1976; Molly, *The Eagle Has Landed*, Columbia, 1977; Jill Mason, *Equus*, Warner Brothers, 1977; Anne, *Dominique*, 1978; Catherine, *Clayton and Catherine*, 1978; Clara Dollman, *The Riddle of the Sands*, 1979; Ann, *Sweet William*, 1980; Miss Hobbs, *The Survivor*, 1980; Amy, *Amy*, 1981; Nurse Alex Price, *An American Werewolf in London*, 1981.

PRINCIPAL TELEVISION APPEARANCES—Grace Hubbard, *Alexander Graham Bell;* Johanna, *Long after Summer;* Kristy Kerr, *The Newcomers; The Great Mr. Dickens*, 1970; Hedvig, *The Wild Duck*, BBC, 1971; Anya, *The Cherry Orchard*, BBC, 1971; Fritha, *The Snow Goose*, 1971; Beth, "As Many As Are Here Present," *The Ten Commandments*, Yorkshire TV, 1971; Mary Shelley, *Omnibus*, BBC, 1971; *A War of Children*, BBC, 1972; nurse, *A House in Regent Place;* "Kiss Me and Die," *Thriller*, 1973; Melanie, *A Legacy*, BBC, 1975; Sue, *The Waiting Room*, Thames TV, 1975; *The Man in the Iron Mask*, 1976; Dr. Leah Russell, *Six Million Dollar Man*, 1977; Pricilla Mullins, *The Mayflower, Voyage of the Pilgrims*, 1979; Poppy Jackson, *School Play*, BBC, 1979; an English prostitute, *Beulah Land*, 1980; *A Dream of Alice*, BBC, 1982; Rosline, *Love's Labours Lost*, BBC, 1984; Pam Fawce, *This Office Life*, BBC, 1984.

RADIO DEBUT—*There's Love and Love*, BBC, 1973.

WRITINGS: NON-FICTION—*Snap: Observations of Los Angeles and London*, Quartet Books, 1983.

AWARDS: Most Promising Artiste Award, 1971, Variety Club of Great Britain; Emmy, Best Supporting Actress, 1971, for Jenny, *The Snow Goose;* Best Actress nomination, 1972, New York British TV Scout, for *A War of Children;* Best Supporting Actress, 1976, British Academy of Film and Television Arts and Sciences, for Jill Mason, *Equus*.

SIDELIGHTS: MEMBERSHIPS—British American Academy of Dramatic Art.

ADDRESS: AGENT—William Morris Agency, 151 El Camino Drive, Beverly Hills, CA 90212.

AIMEE, Anouk   1934-

PERSONAL: Born Francoise Dreyfus, April 27, 1934, in Paris, France. EDUCATION: Attended Bauer-Therond Dramatic School, Paris.

VOCATION: Actress.

CAREER: STAGE DEBUT—*La Maison Sous La Mar*, Paris, 1946.

PRINCIPAL FILM APPEARANCES—*Les Amants De Verone; The Golden Salamander; Le Rideau Cramoisi; Nuit D'Orage; La Bergere et Le Ramoneur; Mauvais Rencontres; Nina Stresemann; Tous Peuvent Me Tuer; Pot Bouille; Modigliani of Monparnasse; Le Tete Contres Les Murs; Les Dragueurs; La Dolce Vita; Le Farcuer; Lola; Les Amours De Paris L'Imprevu; 8 1/2; Sodom and Gormorrah; La Fuga; A Man and a Woman; Un Soir; Un Train; The Appointment; The Model Shop; Justine; The Mandarians; Tragedy of a Ridiculous Man; Leap into the Void; Success Is the Best Revenge* (upcoming); *Flagrant Desire* (upcoming); *A Man and a Woman, Twenty Years Later* (upcoming).

AWARDS: Studios International Circle of Achievement, 1985.*

*   *   *

AKINS, Claude   1918-

PERSONAL: Born May 25, 1918, in Nelson, GA; married Therese Fairfield, 1952; children: Claude, Wendy, Michelle. EDUCATION—Northwestern University, B.S.

VOCATION: Actor.

CAREER: PRINCIPAL STAGE APPEARANCES—Appeared at the Barter Theatre, Abingdon, VA; *The Rose Tatoo*, Broadway production; Everett, *Traveler in the Dark*, Mark Taper, Los Angeles, 1985.

PRINCIPAL FILM APPEARANCES—*From Here to Eternity*, Columbia, 1953; *The Caine Mutiny*, 1954; *Sea Chase*, Warner Brothers, 1955; *Johnny Concho*, United Artists, 1956; *Defiant Ones*, United Artists, 1958; *Onionhead*, Warner Brothers, 1958; *Rio Bravo*, Warner Brothers, 1959; *Porgy and Bess*, Columbia, 1959; *Inherit the Wind*, United Artists, 1960; *How the West Was Won*, Metro-Goldwyn-Mayer, 1962; *The Devil's Brigade*, United Artists, 1968; *The Great Bank Robbery*, 1969; *Skyjacked*, Metro-Goldwyn-Mayer, 1972; *Timber Tramps*, 1977.

PRINCIPAL TELEVISION APPEARANCES—Sonny Pruitt, *Movin' On*, NBC, 1974-76; *Nashville 99*, CBS, 1977; Sheriff Lobo, *Sheriff Lobo*, NBC, 1979-81; *Police Story; Medical Story; Mannix; McCloud; Cannon; The Streets of San Francisco; Fantasy Island; B.J. and the Bear.*

SIDELIGHTS: MEMBERSHIPS—Actors' Equity Association, American Federation of Television Arts and Sciences, Screen Actors Guild, Hollywood Hackers.

Akins hosted the Claude Akins/Julius Brothers Kansas City Shrine Classic in 1978, the $100,000 Ladies Professional Golf Association Sunstar Classic, held in Los Angeles in 1979, and the $150,000 Olympia Gold Ladies Professional Golf Association Classic, held in Industry Hills, CA.

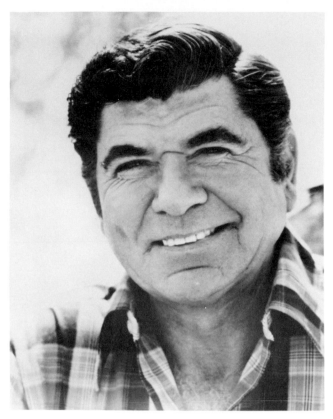

CLAUDE AKINS

ADDRESS: HOME—Pasadena, CA. AGENT—Mishkin Agency, Inc., 9255 Sunset Blvd., Los Angeles, CA 90069.

*   *   *

ALBERT, Eddie   1908-

PERSONAL: Born Edward Albert Heimberger, April 22, 1908, in Rock Island, IL; son of Frank Daniel and Julia (Jones) Heimberger; married Margo (an actress; full name, Maria Margarita Guadalupe Bolado Castilla y O'Donnell); children: Edward, Maria. EDUCATION: Attended University of Minnesota. MILITARY: U.S. Navy, World War Two.

VOCATION: Actor.

CAREER: FILM DEBUT—*Brother Rat*, 1938. PRINCIPAL FILM APPEARANCES—*On Your Toes*, 1939; *Roman Holiday*, 1953; *Oklahoma!*, Magna, 1955; *The Teahouse of the August Moon*, Metro-Goldwyn-Mayer, 1956; *Sun Also Rises*, Twentieth Century-Fox, 1957; *Roots of Heaven*, Twentieth Century-Fox, 1958; *Attack*, United Artists, 1958; *Longest Day*, Twentieth Century-Fox, 1962; *Miracle of the White Stallions*, Buena Vista, 1963; *Captain Newman, M.D.*, Universal, 1964; *Heartbreak Kid*, Twentieth Century-Fox, 1972; *The Longest Yard*, Paramount, 1974; *Escape to Witch Mountain*, Buena Vista, 1975; *Carrie*, United Artists, 1976; *Yes, Giorgio*, Metro-Goldwyn-Mayer/United Artists, 1982; *Dreamscapes*, 1983; *Head Office*, 1985.

PRINCIPAL TELEVISION APPEARANCES—*Green Acres*, CBS, 1965-71; *Switch*, CBS, 1975-78; also: *Studio One*, 1948-57; *Your Show of Shows; Outer Limits; The Chocolate Soldier; Turandot*, 1982.

STAGE DEBUT—Singer and stage manager, Minneapolis, MN, 1933. NEW YORK DEBUT—*O Evening Star*, Empire, 1935. PRINCIPAL STAGE APPEARANCES—*The Honeymooners*, Chicago, NY, Cincinnati, OH, St. Louis, MO; Bing Edwards, *Brother Rat*, Biltmore, NY, 1936; Leo Davis, *Room Service*, Cort, NY, 1937; Antipholus, *The Boys from Syracuse*, Alvin, NY, 1938; Horace Miller, *Miss Liberty*, Imperial, NY, 1949; Reuben, *Reuben, Reuben*, Shubert, Boston, MA, 1955; Jack Jordan, *Say Darling*, ANTA, NY, 1958; Harold Hill, *Music Man*, Majestic, NY, 1960; George Bartlett, *No Hard Feelings*, Martin Beck, NY, 1973.

RADIO APPEARANCES—*The Honeymooners*, 1935.

AWARDS: Academy Award nominations, 1955, for *Roman Holiday* and 1972, for *Heartbreak Kid;* honorary doctor of Fine Arts, Southern Illinois University, 1982; Presidential World without Hunger Award, 1984.

SIDELIGHTS: MEMBERSHIPS—Meals for Millions, 1963. RECREATION—Organic gardening, philosophy, guitar playing, making mobiles, glass painting.

ADDRESS: HOME—Pacific Palisades, CA.

EDDIE ALBERT

ALDRICH, Robert   1918-83

PERSONAL: Born August 9, 1918; died December 5, 1983; married Sibylle; children: (previous marriage) Adell, William, Alida, Kelly. EDUCATION: University of Virginia.

VOCATION: Director and writer.

CAREER: PRINCIPAL FILM WORK—Director: *Big Leaguer*, 1953; *Apache*, 1954; *Vera Cruz*, 1954; *Autumn Leaves*, Columbia, 1956; *Ten Seconds to Hell*, United Artists, 1959; *The Angry Hills*, Metro-Goldwyn-Mayer, 1959; *Last Sunset*, Universal, 1961; *Whatever Happened to Baby Jane?*, Warner Brothers, 1962; *Four for Texas*, Warner Brothers, 1963; *Hush . . . Hush Sweet Charlotte*, Twentieth Century-Fox, 1965; *The Flight of the Phoenix*, Twentieth Century-Fox, 1966; *The Dirty Dozen*, Metro-Goldwyn-Mayer, 1966; *Ulzana's Raid*, Universal, 1972; *Emperor of the North*, Twentieth Century-Fox, 1973; *The Longest Yard*, Paramount, 1974; *Hustle*, Paramount, 1975; *Twilight's Last Gleaming*, Allied Artists, 1977; *The Choirboys*, Universal, 1977.

Producer and director: *World for Ransom*, 1954; *Kiss Me Deadly*, United Artists, 1954; *The Big Knife*, United Artists, 1955; *Attack!*, United Artists, 1958; *The Legend of Lylah Clare*, Metro-Goldwyn-Mayer, 1968; *The Killing of Sister George*, Cinerama, 1968; *Too Late the Hero*, Cinerama, 1970; *The Grissom Gang*, National General, 1971; *The Frisco Kid*, Warner Brothers, 1979.

PRINCIPAL TELEVISION WORK—Director and writer: *The Doctor; China Smith*.

SIDELIGHTS: Aldrich's first job was as a production clerk for RKO Studios in 1941. He was vice president and later president of the Directors Guild in the 1970's.*

*   *   *

ALEANDRI, Emelise

PERSONAL: Born in Riva del Garda, Italy; daughter of John Baptista (a mail carrier) and Elodia Vladimira (a teacher; maiden name, Lutterotti) Aleandri. EDUCATION: College of New Rochelle, NY, A.B., French, 1965; Hunter College, M.A., theatre, 1975; City University of New York, Ph.D., 1983; studied Middle Eastern dance in New York City.

VOCATION: Director, teacher, dancer, choreographer, and actress.

CAREER: PRINCIPAL STAGE WORK—Director (unless otherwise stated): Assistant to producers, *As You Like It*, Broadway production; assistant director, *Onward Victoria*, Broadway production; *Not Every Thief Will Bring You Grief*, off Broadway; *Discovering Bodies*, New York Theatre Ensemble; *Schizzo Hey Ride*, Stage 73, NY; *Applejuice*, Joseph Jefferson Theatre Company; *Duo*, Forum; *Peanuts* (children's play), Boerum Hill Children's Theatre workshop; *Doctor's Duty*, Brooklyn College; *Superman*, Bennington College; *The Marriage Proposal*, College of New Rochelle; *Willpower*, New York City Community College; *The New Americans*, St. Patrick's Theatre, NY; assistant director, *Peep*, South Street, NY; assistant director, *Winning Hearts and Minds*, New York Shakespeare Festival, Public Theatre.

EMELISE ALEANDRI

Choreographer (Middle Eastern dance): *The Birds,* Drama Committee Repertory, NY; *Schizzo Hey Ride,* Stage 73, NY.

PRINCIPAL STAGE APPEARANCES—Italian model, *96A,* Eccentric Circles Theatre; Princess, *The Bandit Princess,* staged reading, Kikue Tashiro; Good Deeds, *Everyman,* Galaxy Theatre Company; Maria Antonia, *Mon Ami Angelique,* Provincetown Playhouse; Opal Jewel, *Power,* People's Performing Company.

As a dancer: As Scheherezade with the Serena Wilson Company: *Salute to King Tut,* Central Park Bandshell, NY; *Lincoln Center Gestical,* Damrosch Park, NY; Ninth Avenue Food Fair, NY; *Gateway Showcase 80,* Gateway Community Restoration; *George White Ensemble,* Marymount Manhattan; featured dancer, Oceanic cruise ships.

MAJOR TOURS—Field director, International Pageant Systems.

PRINCIPAL FILM APPEARANCES—*All That Jazz; Raging Bull; Fort Apache; The World According to Garp; King of the Gypsies; The Night of the Juggler; King Kong; Defiance; Willy and Phil; Out to Lunch; This Is Videx.*

PRINCIPAL TELEVISION APPEARANCES—*Nurse,* CBS; *Eischeid,* NBC; *All My Children,* ABC.

RELATED CAREER—Teacher, voice and diction, New York City Technical College, 1973-present; speech tutor in English department, Fashion Institute of Technology, 1979 and 1983; dance and exercise instructor, DC37-AFSCME, 1980-present; teacher, Research and Description, Contemporary Playwrights, Ethnic Theatre,

Theatre Journalism, New York University School of the Arts, 1977-78; teacher, advanced directing, Bennington College, VT; adjunct professor, College of New Rochelle; teacher, public speaking, drama workshop, LaGuardia Community College, 1974-75; adjunct lecturer, Manhattan Community College; adjunct lecturer, Hunter College, 1971-72; medical social worker, New York State Department of Social Services.

AWARDS: Grant from CUNY-AIDART Program in Ethnic Theatre, 1970; grant from Immigration History Research Center, University of Minnesota, 1976; Certificate of Achievement from the New York State Commission on Historic Observances.

SIDELIGHTS: MEMBERSHIPS—Society of Stage Directors and Choreographers, Actors' Equity Association, Screen Actors Guild, American Guild of Variety Artists, American Federation of Television and Radio Artists, Goldin's Italian-American Advisory Council (comptroller), Italian Heritage and Culture Committee, American-Italian Historical Association, Coalition of Italian-American Associations.

ADDRESS: OFFICE—Center for Italian-American Studies, Brooklyn College, Brooklyn, NY 11210.

*   *   *

ALEXANDER, Robert A.   1929-

PERSONAL: Born March 17, 1929; son of Edward (an accountant) and Jean (Zomick) Alexander; married: Jane Quigley, 1962 (divorced, 1968); married Riki, 1970 (divorced, 1981); children:

ROBERT ALEXANDER

Jason, Taro. EDUCATION: Studied for the theatre with Nola Chilton, Uta Hagen, Mira Rostova, and Morris Carnovsky. POLITICS: Humanist.

VOCATION: Director.

CAREER: Director, the Young People's Theatre, Charles Playhouse, Boston, 1964-66; director, Living Stage Company, Arena Stage, Washington, DC, 1966-present.

WRITINGS: BOOKS, PUBLISHED—*Life, Death, and Creativity,* Sage, 1977; *What Are Children Doing When They Create,* Living Stage, 1981; *A Manual for Theatre as Applied in an Educational Setting,* Living Stage, 1984.

AWARDS: Washingtonian of the Year, 1982; Robert Alexander Day (declared by the mayor of Washington, DC), December, 1982.

SIDELIGHTS: MEMBERSHIPS—Actors' Equity Association, Screen Actors Guild, American Federation of Television and Radio Artists.

Alexander told *CTFT* that he was "nursed on the concepts and philosophies of the Group Theatre. I was inspired by Stanislavski, O'Casey, Lorca, Pete Seeger, Martha Graham, and Zelda Fichandler." He states further that "I have always been drawn to social justice ideas and am a strong advocate for the rights of children and youth."

*ADDRESS:*HOME—Washington, DC. OFFICE—Sixth and Maine Avenue, SW, Washington, DC 20024.

*　　*　　*

ALLEN, Nancy

PERSONAL: Born June 24, in New York City; married Brian De Palma, 1979 (divorced 1983). EDUCATION: High School of the Performing Arts, NY.

CAREER: FILM DEBUT—*The Last Detail,* Columbia, 1974. PRINCIPAL FILM APPEARANCES—*Carrie,* United Artists, 1976; *I Wanna Hold Your Hand,* Universal, 1978; *1941,* Universal, 1979; *Home Movies,* 1979; Liz Blake, *Dressed to Kill,* Filmways, 1980; *Blow Out,* Filmways, 1981; *Strange Invaders,* Orion, 1983; *The Buddy System,* Twentieth Century-Fox, 1984; *The Philadelphia Experiment,* New World Pictures, 1984; *The Last Victim* (aka *Forced Entry*), 1984; Lois, *Not for Publication,* Thorn-EMI, 1984.*

*　　*　　*

ALMBERG, John   1940-

PERSONAL: Born April 3, 1940, in Joliet, IL; son of Carl Albert (an engineer) and Arlotte Lillian (a teacher; maiden name, Wix) Almberg. EDUCATION: Augustana College, Rock Island, IL, M.A., business. MILITARY: U.S. Army, Sergeant, 1962-64.

VOCATION: Actor and singer.

CAREER: STAGE DEBUT—Sergei, *A Song for Anastasia,* Bruns-

wick Music Theatre, ME, 1967. NEW YORK DEBUT—Oscar, *Seesaw,* Mark Hellinger, 1973. PRINCIPAL STAGE APPEARANCES—El Gallo, *The Fantasticks,* Brunswick Music Theatre, 1972; Freddy, *My Fair Lady,* Chateau de Ville Dinner Theatre, 1972; Curly, *Oklahoma!,* Brunswick Music Theatre, 1972; Big John, *Mack & Mabel,* Majestic, NY, 1974; Brom Broeck, *Knickerbocker Holiday,* Bert Wheeler, NY, 1975; Frank Butler, *Annie Get Your Gun,* An Evening Dinner Theatre, 1976, Coachlight Dinner Theatre, 1977, Derby Dinner Theatre, 1981, Country Dinner Theatre, 1981-82.

Abner, *Li'l Abner,* An Evening Dinner Theatre, 1977, Music Theatre of Wichita, 1981; Leadville Johnny, *The Unsinkable Molly Brown,* An Evening Dinner Theatre, 1979, Music Theatre of Wichita, 1980; Billy, *Carousel,* Music Theatre of Wichita, 1979; Joe Hardy, *Damn Yankees,* St. Louis Municipal Opera, 1979; Sid, *Pajama Game,* Music Theatre of Wichita, 1979; Aristede, *Can-Can,* Derby Dinner Theatre, 1982; Beau, *Mame,* Northstage, 1983; Warbucks, *Annie,* Derby Dinner Theatre, 1983, Music Theatre of Wichita, 1984.

MAJOR TOURS—Jefferson, *1776,* bicentennial national tour, 1975-76; Steve, *Showboat,* National Company, 1979-80.

SIDELIGHTS: MEMBERSHIPS—Actors' Equity Association, American Federation of Television and Radio Artists.

Almberg has also worked as production coordinator for American Heritage Publishing Company, 1965-66 and as packaging engineer, for Weigh Right Automatic Scale Company.

ADDRESS: AGENT—Honey Sanders Agency Ltd. 229 W. 42nd Street, New York, NY 10036.

*　　*　　*

ALTMAN, Robert B.   1925-

PERSONAL: Born February 20, 1925, in Kansas City, MO; married Kathryn; children: (first marriage) Michael, Stephen, Christine; (second marriage) Robert, Matthew. EDUCATION: Attended University of Missouri. MILITARY: U.S. Army, 1943-47.

VOCATION: Director, producer, and writer.

CAREER: PRINCIPAL FILM WORK—Director, *The Delinquents,* United Artists, 1957; co-producer, *The James Dean Story,* Warner Brothers, 1957; director, *Countdown,* Warner Brothers-Seven Arts, 1968; director, *That Cold Day in the Park,* Commonwealth United, 1969; director, *M*A*S*H,* Twentieth Century-Fox, 1970; director and writer, *Brewster McCloud,* Metro-Goldwyn-Mayer, 1970; director and writer, *McCabe and Mrs. Miller,* Warner Brothers, 1970; director and writer, *Images,* Columbia, 1972; director and writer, *The Long Goodbye,* 1973; director and writer, *Thieves Like Us,* United Artists, 1974; director and writer, *California Split,* Columbia, 1974; director and writer, *Nashville,* Paramount, 1975; director and writer, *Buffalo Bill and the Indians,* United Artists, 1976; producer, *The Late Show,* Warner Brothers, 1977; producer, *Welcome to L.A.,* Lion's Gate, 1977.

Producer, director, and writer, *Three Women,* Twentieth Century-Fox, 1977; producer and director, *A Wedding,* Twentieth Century-Fox, 1978; producer and director, *Quintet,* Twentieth Century-Fox, 1979; *A Perfect Couple,* Twentieth Century-Fox, 1979; producer, director, and writer, *Health*, 1979; producer, *Rich Kids*, United Artists, 1979; director, *Popeye*, Paramount, 1980; director, *Come Back to the Five and Dime Jimmy Dean, Jimmy Dean*, 1982; director, *Streamers*, 1983; director, *Secret Honor* (upcoming); director, *Fool for Love*, 1986.

PRINCIPAL TELEVISION WORK—Writer, producer, and director, *Kraft Theatre;* writer and producer, *The Long Hot Summer;* director, *The Laundromat*, HBO, 1985.

FIRST STAGE WORK—Director, *Come Back to the Five and Dime, Jimmy Dean, Jimmy Dean*, Martin Beck, NY, 1982.

AWARDS: Grand Prize Award, Cannes Film Festival, National Society of Film Critics Award, Best Film, all 1970, for *M*A*S*H*.

SIDELIGHTS: MEMBERSHIPS—Directors Guild of America.

ADDRESS: OFFICE—Landscape Films, 12115 Magnolia Blvd., Suite 123, N. Hollywood, CA 91607. AGENT— International Creative Management, 40 W. 57th Street, New York, NY 10019.*

*   *   *

AMECHE, Don   1908-

PERSONAL: Born Dominic Felix Amici, May 31, 1908, in Kenosha, WI; son of Felix and Barbara Etta (Hertle) Amici; married Hortense Prendergast. EDUCATION: Attended Columbia Academy, Marquette University, Georgetown University, University of Wisconsin.

VOCATION: Actor.

CAREER: FILM DEBUT—*Sins of Man*, 1933. PRINCIPAL FILM APPEARANCES—*Ramona*, 1936; *Ladies in Love*, 1936; *You Can't Have Everything*, 1937; *Alexander's Ragtime Band, In Old Chicago*, both 1938; *Swanee River, The Story of Alexander Graham Bell*, both 1939; *Lillian Russell*, 1940; *Four Sons*, 1940; *That Night in Rio*, 1941; *Kiss the Boys Goodbye*, 1941; *Heaven Can Wait*, 1943; *So Goes My Love*, 1946; *That's My Man; Sleep My Love*, 1948; *Slightly French*, 1949; *A Fever in the Blood*, Warner Brothers, 1961; *Rings Around the World*, Columbia, 1966; *Picture Mommy Dead*, Embassy, 1966; *Suppose They Gave a War and Nobody Came*, Cinerama, 1970; *The Boatniks*, Buena Vista, 1970; *Trading Places*, Paramount, 1983; *Cocoon*, Twentieth Century-Fox, 1985.

STAGE DEBUT—Al Jackson Stock Company, Madison, WI, 1928. NEW YORK DEBUT—Perkins, *Jerry-for-Short*, Waldorf, 1929. PRINCIPAL STAGE APPEARANCES—*Excess Baggage*, Greenwich, CT, 1930; *Illegal Practice*, Chicago, IL, 1930; Steve Canfield, *Silk Stockings*, Imperial, NY, 1955; Robert Dean, *Holiday for Lovers*, Longacre, NY, 1957; Max Grady, *Goldilocks*, Lunt-Fontanne, NY, 1958; Chun, *13 Daughters*, 54th Street Theater, NY, 1961; Henry Orient, *Henry, Sweet Henry*, Palace, NY, 1967; Jimmy Smith, *No, No, Nanette*, State Fair Music Hall, Dallas, TX, 1972, Westbury Music Fair, Long Island, NY, 1974; *Never Get Smart with an Angel*, Country Dinner Playhouse, Austin, TX, 1976.

MAJOR TOURS   *Texas Guinan Vaudeville Show*, U.S. cities, 1930; Steve Canfield, *Silk Stockings*, U.S. cities, 1956; *I Married an Angel*, U.S. cities, 1964; Oscar Madison, *The Odd Couple*, U.S. cities, 1968; Jimmy Smith, *No, No, Nanette*, U.S. cities, 1973.

TELEVISION DEBUT—1950. PRINCIPAL TELEVISION APPEARANCES—*Frances Langford-Don Ameche Show; High Button Shoes; Junior Miss*, 1957.

RADIO DEBUT—1930. PRINCIPAL RADIO APPEARANCES—*The Chase and Sanborn Hour*, 1937-39; *The Old Gold Don Ameche Show; The Charlie McCarthy Show*, 1940; *The Morgan-Ameche-Langford Show*, 1947-48; *Don Ameche's Real-Life Stories*, 1958.

ADDRESS: AGENT—c/o Simon and Rosner, One S. Wacker Drive, Suite 2400, Chicago, IL 60606.*

*   *   *

ANDERSON, Lindsay   1923-

PERSONAL: Born 1923, in Bangalore, India. EDUCATION: Attended Chelternham College and Wadham College, Oxford.

VOCATION: Director and writer.

CAREER: PRINCIPAL STAGE WORK—Director: *The Waiting of Lester Abbs*, Royal Court Theatre, London, 1957; *The Long and the Short and the Tall; Progress to the Park; Jazzetry, Dispersal, Serjeant Musgrave's Dance*, all 1959; *The Lily-White Boys, Billy Liar, Trials by Logue*, all 1960; *Box and Cox, The Fire Raisers*, both 1961; *The Diary of a Madman*, 1963; *Andorra*, National, London, 1964; *Julius Caesar*, 1964; *The Cherry Orchard*, Chichester, 1966; *Inadmissible Evidence*, Contemporary Theater, Warsaw, 1966; *In Celebration, The Contractor*, both Royal Court, London, 1969.

Home, Royal Court, London, and NY, 1970; *The Changing Room*, Royal Court, London, 1971; *The Farm*, Royal Court, London, 1973; *Life Class*, Royal Court, London, 1974; *What the Butler Saw*, Royal Court, London, 1975; *The Seagull, The Bed Before Yesterday*, both Lyric, London, 1975; *The Kingfisher*, Lyric, London, 1977; *Alice's Boys*, Savoy, London, 1978; *The Kingfisher*, Biltmore, NY, 1978; *The Bed Before Yesterday*, Sydney, Australia, 1979; *Early Days*, National, London, 1980; *In Celebration*, Manhattan Theatre Club, NY, 1984.

PRINCIPAL STAGE APPEARANCES—Reg Parsons, *Miniatures*.

PRINCIPAL FILM WORK—Director: *Meet the Pioneers*, 1948; *Thursday's Children*, 1953; *Pleasure Garden; Wakefield Express; Every Day Except Christmas*, 1957; *This Sporting Life*, 1963; *The White Bus*, 1966; *If. . .*, 1968; *O, Lucky Man!*, 1973; *In Celebration*, 1975; *Britannia Hospital*, 1982.

PRINCIPAL FILM APPEARANCES—*Inadmissable Evidence*.

PRINCIPAL TELEVISION WORK—Director: Series—*Robin Hood; The Old Crowd*, 1979.

PRINCIPAL TELEVISION APPEARANCES—*The Parachute*.

WRITINGS: BOOKS—*Making a Film*, 1951; *About John Ford*, 1981.

AWARDS: Academy Award, 1953, for *Thursday's Children;* Grand Prix Award, Venice Film Festival, 1957, both for *Every Day Except Christmas;* Grand Prix Award, Cannes International Film Festival, 1969, both for *If. . . .*

ANDERSON, Loni

PERSONAL: Born August 5, in St. Paul, MN; daughter of Klaydon (a pharmaceutical executive) and Maxine (a former model) Anderson; married second husband, Ross Bickell (divorced, 1981); children: (first marriage) Deidre. EDUCATION: University of Minnesota, B.A., art and drama.

VOCATION: Actress.

CAREER: PRINCIPAL TELEVISION APPEARANCES—Jennifer, *WKRP in Cincinnati,* CBS; Sydney Kovac, *Partners in Crime,* NBC, 1984-85; *Three's Company,* ABC; *The Love Boat,* ABC; *Barnaby Jones,* CBS; *The Bob Newhart Show,* CBS; *Phyllis,* CBS; *The Magic of David Copperfield; Christmas in Opryland; Circus of the Stars,* CBS; *Alan Funt's Candid Camera Special; The Funtastic Funnies,* 1980; Bob Hope specials; *Three on a Date.* Movies: Title role, *Jayne Mansfield: A Symbol of the 50's,* 1980; *Sizzle,* 1981; *Country Gold,* 1982.

PRINCIPAL FILM APPEARANCE—*Stroker Ace,* Universal, 1983.

PRINCIPAL STAGE APPEARANCES—At regional and dinner theatres: Billie Dawn, *Born Yesterday;* Tzeitel, *Fiddler on the Roof; The Star Spangled Girl; Never Too Late; Any Wednesday; Can-Can; The Threepenny Opera.*

ADDRESS: OFFICE—8961 Sunset Blvd., Suite B, Los Angeles, CA 90069.*

* * *

ANDERSON, Melissa Sue 1962-

BRIEF ENTRY: Born September 26, 1962, in Berkeley, CA; educated in the Los Angeles public schools. She first appeared in a variety of television commercials and then made her dramatic debut in an episode of the television series *The Brady Bunch,* ABC. A star of the long-running series *Little House on the Prairie,* NBC, Anderson played the role of Mary Ingalls. Other television series work has included *Shaft* and *The Love Boat,* and non-series work has included *Very Good Friends, James at 15,* and *The Loneliest Runners.* Anderson's first feature film role was in *Happy Birthday to Me.**

* * *

ANDREWS, Eamonn 1922-

PERSONAL: Born December 19, 1922, in Dublin, Ireland; son of William and Margaret Andrews; married Grainne Bourke, November 7, 1951; children: Emma, Fergal, Niamh. EDUCATION: Irish Christian Brothers, Dublin; stage training at the Ria Mooney School of Acting, Dublin, Ireland.

VOCATION: Writer and television commentator and presenter.

CAREER: TELEVISION DEBUT—BBC-TV, 1961. PRINCIPAL TELEVISION APPEARANCES—*What's My Line; This Is Your Life; Eamonn Andrews Show; World of Sport; Top of the World;* children's programs; sports programs (boxing); independent television since 1964.

RELATED CAREER—Chairman, Radio Telefis Eireann (statutory authority charged with establishment of television in Ireland), 1960-66.

WRITINGS: PLAY—*The Moon Is Black,* 1941. AUTOBIOGRAPHY—*This Is My Life,* 1963; *Surprise of Your Life,* 1978. ARTICLES—For ''Punch,'' ''Catholic Herald,'' ''High Life,'' etc.

AWARDS: Knight of the Order of St. Gregory, 1964; Commander of the British Empire, 1970.

ADDRESS: AGENT—Sheelagh O'Donovan, 19 Russell Street, London WC2B 5HP, England.

* * *

ANDREWS, Harry 1911-

PERSONAL: Born November 10, 1911, in Tonbridge, Kent, England; son of Henry Arthur and Amy Diana Frances (Horner) Andrews. EDUCATION: Attended Wrekin College. MILITARY: Royal Artillery, 1939-45.

VOCATION: Actor.

CAREER: STAGE DEBUT—John, *The Long Christmas Dinner,* Liverpool Playhouse, 1933. LONDON STAGE DEBUT—John, *Worse Things Happen at Sea,* St. James, 1935. NEW YORK DEBUT—Horatio, *Hamlet,* Empire, 1936. PRINCIPAL STAGE APPEARANCES—

HARRY ANDREWS

Christopher, *Snow in Summer,* Whitehall, London, 1935; Lion, *Noah,* New Theatre, London, 1935; Abraham and Captain, *Romeo and Juliet,* London, 1935; Francis, *He Was Born Gay,* Queen's, London, 1937; Queen's Gentleman, *Victoria Regina,* Lyric, London, 1937; *Richard II, The School for Scandal, Three Sisters, The Merchant of Venice,* all with John Gielgud's Company, Queen's, London, 1937-38.

Diomedes, *Troilus and Cressida,* Westminster, London, 1938; Demetrius, *A Midsummer Night's Dream,* Old Vic, London, 1938; Charlie Glover, *Hundreds and Thousands,* Garrick, London, 1939; John, *We at the Cross Roads,* Globe, London, 1939; Laertes, *Hamlet,* Lyceum, London, then Elsinore, 1939; Sir Walter Blunt, *Henry IV, Part I,* Scroop, *Henry IV, Part II,* Creon, *Oedipus,* Sneer, *The Critic,* all at Old Vic, London, 1945, then at Century, NY, 1946; Cornwall, *King Lear,* Gerald Croft, *An Inspector Calls,* De Castel-Jaloux, *Cyrano de Bergerac,* Bolingbroke, *Richard II,* Hortensio, *The Taming of the Shrew,* Earl of Warwick, *St. Joan,* Osip, *The Government Inspector,* Tullus Aufidius, *Coriolanus,* Orsino, *Twelfth Night,* Lucifer, *Dr. Faustus,* Mirabel, *The Way of the World,* Epihodov, *The Cherry Orchard,* all at the New Theater, London, 1946-49.

Macduff, *Macbeth,* Don Pedro, *Much Ado About Nothing,* Theseus, *A Midsummer Night's Dream,* Pisanio, *Cymbeline,* Cardinal Wolsey, *King Henry VIII,* all at the Memorial Theater, Stratford-on-Avon, 1949; Vincentio, *Measure for Measure,* Brutus, *Julius Caesar,* Edgar, *King Lear,* Benedick, *Much Ado About Nothing,* all at the Memorial Theater, Stratford-on-Avon, 1950; Bolingbroke, *Henry IV,* Memorial Theater, Stratford-on-Avon, 1951; Lucius Septimus, *Caesar and Cleopatra,* Enobarbus, *Antony and Cleopatra,* both at Ziegfeld, NY, 1951; Antonio, *The Merchant of Venice,* Buckingham, *Richard III,* Enobarbus, *Antony and Cleopatra,* Kent, *King Lear,* all at the Memorial, Stratford-on-Avon, 1953; Claudius, *Hamlet,* Othello, *Othello,* Don Adriano de Armado, *Love's Labor's Lost,* Memorial, Stratford-on-Avon, 1956.

Casanova, *Camino Real,* Phoenix, London, 1957; Henry, *Henry VIII,* Old Vic, London, 1958; Menenius, *Coriolanus,* Memorial, Stratford-on-Avon, 1959; General Allenby, *Ross,* Haymarket, London, 1960; Robert Rockhart, *The Lizard on the Rock,* Phoenix, London, 1962; Ekart, *Baal,* Haymarket, London, 1963; Crampton, *You Never Can Tell,* Haymarket, London, 1966; Lear, *Lear,* Haymarket, London, 1971; Ivan Kilner, *A Family,* Haymarket, London, 1978; *Uncle Vanya,* Haymarket, London, 1982; *A Patriot for Me,* Haymarket, London, 1983, then Los Angeles, CA, 1984.

MAJOR TOURS—Macduff, *Macbeth,* Don Pedro, *Much Ado About Nothing,* Theseus, *A Midsummer Night's Dream,* Pisanio, *Cymbeline,* Cardinal Wolsey, *King Henry VIII,* all with Memorial Theatre Company, Australian cities, 1949; Henry, *Henry VIII,* Paris, Antwerp, Brussels, 1958.

FILM DEBUT—*The Red Beret,* 1952. PRINCIPAL FILM APPEARANCES—*The Black Knight,* 1954; *The Man Who Loved Redheads,* United Artists, 1955; *Alexander the Great,* United Artists, 1956; *Moby Dick,* Warner Brothers, 1956; *Devil's Disciple,* United Artists, 1959; *Solomon and Sheba,* United Artists, 1959; *Hell in Korea* (aka *A Hill in Korea*), Hal Roach, 1959; *Desert Attack* (aka *Ice Cold in Alex*), Twentieth Century-Fox, 1960; *In the Nick; Circle of Deception,* Twentieth Century-Fox, 1961; *Best of Enemies,* Columbia, 1962; *Cleopatra,* Twentieth Century-Fox, 1963; *Reach for Glory,* Royal, 1963; *The Inspector; 55 Days at Peking,* Allied Artists, 1963; *The Snout; The Girl Getters* (aka *The System*), American International Pictures, 1965; *The Agony and the Ecstasy,* Twentieth

Century-Fox, 1965; *Sands of Kalahari,* Paramount, 1965; *The Hill,* Metro-Goldwyn-Mayer, 1965; *Deadly Affair,* Columbia, 1967; *A Dandy in Aspic,* Columbia, 1968; *Charge of the Light Brigade,* United Artists, 1968; *Night They Raided Minsky's,* United Artists, 1968; *The Seagull,* Warner Brothers/Seven Arts, 1968.

A Nice Girl Like Me, Avco Embassy, 1969; *Too Late the Hero,* Cinerama, 1970; *The Gaunt Woman; Country Dance* (aka *Brotherly Love*), Metro-Goldwyn-Mayer, 1970; *Entertaining Mr. Sloane,* Continental, 1970; *Wuthering Heights,* American International, 1971; *Nicholas and Alexandra,* Columbia, 1971; *I Want What I Want,* Cinerama, 1972; *The Nightcomers,* Avco Embassy, 1972; *Ruling Class,* Avco Embassy, 1972; *Man of La Mancha,* United Artists, 1972; *Theatre of Blood,* United Artists, 1973; *Mackintosh Man,* Warner Brothers, 1973; *Man at the Top,* 1975; *Sky Riders,* Twentieth Century-Fox, 1976; *The Bluebird,* Twentieth Century-Fox, 1976; *Passover Plot; Superman,* Warner Brothers, 1978; *Medusa Touch,* Warner Brothers, 1978; *The Big Sleep,* United Artists, 1978; *Death on the Nile,* Paramount, 1978; *Seven Dials Mystery; Sound Machine; The Prince and the Pauper; Equus,* Warner Brothers, 1977; *Mesmerized,* 1984.

PRINCIPAL TELEVISION APPEARANCES—Series: *Clayhanger;* Tom Carrington, *Dynasty.* Specials: Tolstoy, *A Question of Faith;* Othello, *Othello; Affair of Honor; Two Gentle People.* Movies: *A Question of Guilt,* 1978; *SOS Titanic,* 1979; *Curse of King Tut's Tomb,* 1980.

SIDELIGHTS: FAVORITE ROLES—Bolingbroke, Enobarbus, Brutus, Buckingham, title role in *Richard III,* Duke in *Measure for Measure,* Kent, and title role in *King Lear.* RECREATION—Cricket, sailing, tennis, riding, and gardening.

ADDRESS: HOME—Church Farm Oasts, Saleshurst, Robertsbridge, Sussex.

*   *   *

ANTON, Susan   1951-

BRIEF ENTRY: Born October 12, 1951, in Yucaipa, CA; daughter of Wally (a detective) and Lou Anton; educated at Bernadino College. Anton was Miss California in 1969 and tied for second runner-up in the 1970 Miss America pageant. She began her professional entertaining career with a musical Las Vegas nightclub act, and she won the role of the "Muriel Cigar" girl in 1976, competing against 400 others. Musically, Anton recorded a country-and-western album, *The First Time,* and had two hit singles on the country and western charts: *Killin' Time* and *Foxy.* She made her movie debut in *Goldengirl,* Avco-Embassy, 1979, and has since appeared in the films *Cannonball Run II,* Twentieth Century-Fox, 1983, and *Spring Fever.* Anton has starred in four NBC television specials, including *Presenting Susan Anton* and *Cliffhangers,* and she joined Kenny Rogers on a national concert tour. On Broadway, she appeared in the play *Hurlyburly,* beginning in 1984-85, in the role of Darlene. She was seen on PBS's *Wonder Works.**

*   *   *

ARBEIT, Herman O.   1925-

PERSONAL: Born April 19, 1925; son of Max (a candystore keeper, packer, and sewing machine operator) and Katie (Zweibel) Arbeit;

HERMAN O. ARBEIT

married Sylvia Newfeld (a receptionist), February 16, 1958; children: Barbara Rachel. EDUCATION: City College of New York Business School, for three years; studied for the theatre at the Neighborhood Playhouse, Herbert Berghof Studios and the Shakespeare Festival, with Sanford Meisner, Morris Carnovsky, Aaron Frankel, and Bobby Lewis. MILITARY: U.S. Army, World War Two.

VOCATION: Actor.

CAREER: STAGE DEBUT—Doc, *Come Back, Little Sheba,* Playrads Drama Group, City College of New York, 1952. NEW YORK DEBUT—Reverend, *Climate of Eden,* Actors Playhouse, 1955. PRINCIPAL STAGE APPEARANCES—Tarleton, *Misalliance,* Kendall, *Little Scandal,* both at Cragsmoor, NY, 1954; Doctor, *Boy Meets Girl,* Equity Library, NY, 1955; Lawyer, *A Dream Play,* Minor Latham, NY, 1957; Paravicini, *The Mouse Trap,* Papa, *The Happy Time,* Sherriff Talbott, *Orpheus Descending,* Uncle Max, *A Hole in the Head,* Barney, *Summer of the Seventeenth Doll,* Bellhop, *The Girls in 509,* Otto Frank, *Diary of Anne Frank,* Noah, *The Flowering Peach,* all at Rockland County Playhouse, NY, 1959; Walter, *Time Remembered,* Milgrim, *The Disenchanted,* Rabbi David and Aaron, *The World of Sholom Aleichem,* Gant, *Look Homeward, Angel,* both at Woodstock Playhouse, NY, 1960; Hunk, *Dead End,* Equity Library, NY, 1960.

Professor, *The Lesson,* Center Stage, Baltimore, MD, 1963; Brabantio, *Othello,* Dodds, *Calculated Risk,* both at Corning Summer Theatre, NY, 1963; Sidney Black, *Light Up the Sky,* Chausable, *The Importance of Being Earnest,* Senator, *The Respectful Prostitute,* Bert, *The Room,* all at Center Stage, Baltimore, MD, 1963-64; Alonzo, *The Tempest,* Washington Theatre Club, Washington, DC,

1965; title role, *The Prisoner,* Erie Civic Theatre Association, Erie, PA, 1967; Peter Stockmann, *An Enemy of the People,* Equity Library, NY, 1968; Sgt. Carlino, *Wait Until Dark,* Gilbert, *Everything in the Garden,* both at Corning Summer Theatre, NY, 1968; the Merchant, *The Exception and the Rule,* Assembly, NY, 1970; Duncan, porter, and Hecate, *Macbeth,* North Shore Music Theatre, Beverly, MA, 1972; Harry Brock, *Born Yesterday,* Firehouse Dinner Theatre, Omaha, NE, 1973; Uncle Murry, *Moonchildren,* Charles St. Playhouse, Boston, MA, 1974; Reb Alter, *Yentl,* Chelsea, NY, 1974-75; Yekel, *God of Vengeance,* Masterworks Laboratory, Brooklyn, NY, 1975.

Reb Alter, *Yentl,* Eugene O'Neill, NY, 1975-76; Wiseman, Cohn, and understudy Abe, *Knock Knock,* Biltmore, NY, 1976; Dankel, *Marathon '33,* Lion, NY, 1976; Abe, *Knock Knock,* Center Stage, Baltimore, MD, 1977; Oscar Wolfe, *The Royal Family,* Loach, *The National Health,* both at Seattle Rep, Seattle, WA, 1977-78; Uncle Morty, *Awake and Sing,* Harry Edison, *The Prisoner of Second Avenue,* both at Playwrights Horizons, NY, 1978; Dodge, *Buried Child,* GeVa, Rochester, NY, 1979; Uncle David, *Me and Molly,* Jewish Repertory, NY, 1980; Soloway, *The Goodbye People,* PAF, NY, 1981; Dr. Edward Peller, *In the Matter of J. Robert Oppenheimer,* American Jewish Theatre, NY, 1981; Ranger Three, *Who Killed Johnny Granger,* Columbia University, NY, 1982; Zog, *The Seventh Day,* Quaigh, NY, 1983; Max Glass, *Taking Steam,* Jewish Repertory, NY, 1983; Judge, *Christopher Blake,* Quaigh, NY, 1983; Harpagon, *The Miser,* University of Maryland, College Park, MD, 1983.

MAJOR TOURS—Bellamy, *The Fantasticks,* Bermudiana Hotel, Bahamas, 1964; Mayor, *Never Too Late,* summer tour, Barnesville, PA, Detroit, MI, 1965; Doc, *West Side Story,* Beverly, Cohasset, and Hyannis, MA, 1968; understudy Gregory Solomon, *The Price,* national tour, 1969-70; Willy Loman, *Death of a Salesman,* National Theatre Co. tour, 1970-71; Murray, *The Odd Couple,* Chateau de Ville Dinner Theatre productions tour, MA and CT, 1973-74; Professor Lyman, *Bus Stop,* ACT tour, KY and IL, 1981.

FILM DEBUT—Detective, *Cop Haters,* 1964. PRINCIPAL FILM APPEARANCES—Desk clerk, *Headin' for Broadway,* 1980.

TELEVISION DEBUT—Waiter, *Concerning Miss Marlowe,* 1954. PRINCIPAL TELEVISION APPEARANCES—Juror, *Another World,* NBC, 1965; Scott Candless, *It's My Body, It's My Life,* WCVB, Boston, 1974; superintendent, *Edge of Night,* 1981; police sergeant, *As the World Turns,* CBS, 1982; desk sergeant, *The Guiding Light,* CBS, 1983.

SIDELIGHTS: Arbeit told *CTFT,* "In addition to learning and growing in a craft, acting proved to be enormous personal therapy, not only giving me insights to personal problems but challenging me to take the strength garnered onstage and incorporate it into my daily life."

ADDRESS: OFFICE—c/o L.L. Flippin, 1753 Caufield Avenue, Los Angeles, CA 90035.

*   *   *

ARCHER, John   1953-

PERSONAL: Born John William Archer, September 19, 1953; son of Thomas William (a farmer) and Constance Lillian (Hemson) Archer; married Jennifer McKay (a journalist), Febru14ry 10, 1979.

EDUCATION: University of Birmingham, B.A., 1974; University College, Cardiff, diploma in journalism, 1975.

VOCATION: Producer and director.

CAREER: TELEVISION DEBUT—Producer: *Nationwide,* BBC-1, 1975. PRINCIPAL TELEVISON WORK—Producer: *Did You See . . . ?; The Book Programme.* PRINCIPAL TELEVISION WORK—Producer and director: *Global Report, Writers and Places;* editor, *Saturday Review.*

AWARDS: BAFTA nominations, 1983, 1984, for *Did You See . . . ?*

SIDELIGHTS: MEMBERSHIPS—ACCT.

ADDRESS: OFFICE—BBC-TV, Wood Lane, London W12, England.

*   *   *

ARENAL, Julie

PERSONAL: Daughter of Luis (an artist) and Rose (a teacher and writer; maiden name, Beagle) Arenal; married Barry Primus (an actor and director). EDUCATION: Attended Bennington College.

VOCATION: Choreographer and director.

CAREER: FIRST LONDON STAGE WORK—Choreographer, *Hair,* Shaftsbury, 1968. PRINCIPAL STAGE WORK—Choreographer, *Hair,* Biltmore, NY, 1968; choreographer and co-director, *Isabel's a Jezebel,* Duchess, London, 1970; choreographer, *Gun Play,* Cherry Lane, NY, 1971; choreographer, *Siamese Connection,* Ann Arbor, MI, 1971; choreographer, *Hunger and Thirst,* Berkshire Theatre Festival, NY, 1972; choregrapher, *2008 1/2,* NY, 1974; choreographer, *Butterfinger's Angel,* Syracuse Stage, NY, 1974, 1978.

Choreographer, *Boccacio,* Edison, NY, 1975; choreographer, *Hair,* Biltmore, NY, 1977; choreographer, *I Took Panama,* Puerto Rican Traveling Theater, NY, 1977; choreographer, *The Sun Always Shines for the Cool,* NY, 1979; director and choreographer, *Funny Girl,* Toho Company, Tokyo, Japan, 1980; director, *Dog Lady,* INTAR, NY, 1983.

Ballets: Choreographer, *Fiesta,* Ballet Hispanico, NY, 1972; choreographer, *A Puerto Rican Soap Opera,* Ballet Hispanico, Delacorte, NY, 1973; choreographer, *A Private Circus,* New York Dance Ensemble, NY, 1975; choreographer, *An Afternoon of Music and Dance,* New York Dance Ensemble, NY, 1976; choreographer, *Doing Dances for Broadway,* Library of the Performing Arts, Lincoln Center, NY, 1977; choreographer, *The Referee,* San Francisco Ballet, CA, 1977; choreographer, *El Arbito,* Alicia Alonso's Ballet Nacional de Cuba, 1978; choreographer, *Hair,* American Dance Machine, NY, 1979; director and choreographer, *On the Move* and *The City,* Spoleto Festival, Italy and U.S., New York Express Company, NY, 1984.

PRINCIPAL FILM WORK—Choreographer, *King of the Gypsies,* Paramount, 1978; choreographer, *Four Friends,* 1980; choreographer, *Soup for One,* Warner Brothers, 1981; choreographer, *Once Upon a Time in America,* 1982; choreographer, *Winning a Better Life,* MCA, 1982; actress, *Beat Street,* Orion, 1983.

PRINCIPAL TELEVISION WORK—Choreographer: *Gypsy Fever,* ABC, 1978; *Song of Taste,* 1982; *Self Control,* MTV, 1984; *Breakout,* 1984.

RELATED CAREER—Dance teacher: Herbert Berghof Studio, 1962-present, Puerto Rican Traveling Theater, 1974-present.

AWARDS: Saturday Review Award, Swedish Government Award, both for Best Choreographer, 1968, for *Hair;* National Endowment Award, 1973, for *A Puerto Rican Soap Opera.*

ADDRESS: HOME—205 E. Tenth Street, New York, NY 10003.

*   *   *

ARKIN, Alan   1934-

PERSONAL: Born March 26, 1934, in Brooklyn, NY; son of David I. and Beatrice (Wortis) Arkin; married second wife, Barbara Dana (an actress and author), 1964; children: (first marriage) Adam, Matthew; (second marriage) Tony. EDUCATION: Los Angeles City College; Los Angeles State College; Bennington College.

VOCATION: Actor, director, author, and composer.

CAREER: STAGE DEBUT—In improvisation, *Compass Players,* Crystal Palace, St. Louis, MO, 1959. NEW YORK DEBUT—Revue player, *From the Second City,* Royale, 1961. PRINCIPAL STAGE APPEARANCES—*Second City,* Chicago, 1960; *Man Out Loud, Girl Quiet,* Cricket, NY, 1962; David Kolovitz, *Enter Laughing,* Henry Miller, NY, 1963; revue player, *A View from Under the Bridge,* Second City at Square East, 1964; Harry Berlin, *Luv,* Booth, NY, 1964.

MAJOR TOURS—David, *Enter Laughing,* national company, 1964.

PRINCIPAL STAGE WORK—Director: Revue material, dates uncertain; *Eh?* Circle in the Square, NY, 1966; *Hail Scrawdyke,* NY, 1966; *Little Murders,* Circle in the Square, NY, 1968; *The White House Murder Case,* Circle in the Square, NY, 1970; *The Sunshine Boys,* Booth, NY, 1972; *Molly,* NY, 1973; *Joan of Lorraine,* 1974; double bill, *Rubber Ducks* and *Yanks 3 Detroit 0, Top of the Seventh,* American Place, NY, 1975; *The Soft Touch,* Boston, MA, 1975; *Joan of Lorraine,* Hartman, Stamford, CT, 1976; *Precious Son,* NY.

FILM DEBUT—Rozanov, *The Russians Are Coming, the Russians Are Coming,* United Artists, 1966. PRINCIPAL FILM APPEARANCES—Various roles, *Woman Times Seven,* Embassy, 1967; Roat, *Wait Until Dark,* Warner Brothers-Seven Arts, 1967; Deaf-Mute, *The Heart Is a Lonely Hunter,* Warner Brothers-Seven Arts, 1968; title role, *Popi,* United Artists, 1969; *Catch-22,* Paramount, 1970; *Little Murders,* Twentieth Century-Fox, 1971; *Deadhead Miles,* 1972; *Last of the Red Hot Lovers,* Paramount, 1972; *Freebie and the Bean,* Warner Brothers, 1974; *Rafferty and the Gold Dust Twins,* Warner Brothers, 1975; *Hearts of the West,* United Artists, 1975; Sigmund Freud, *Seven Per Cent Solution,* Universal, 1976; *Fire Sale,* 1977; *The In-Laws,* Warner Brothers, 1979; *Simon,* Warner Brothers, 1980; Flash, *Chu Chu and the Philly Flash,* Twentieth Century-Fox, 1981; *The Return of Mr. Invisible; Improper Channels,* Canadian, 1981; *Joshua Then and Now; Bad Medicine,* Twentieth Century-Fox, 1985.

PRINCIPAL FILM WORK—Director: Two short films, *T.G.I.F.* and *People Soup,* Columbia, 1969; *Little Murders,* Twentieth Century-Fox, 1971; *Fire Sale,* 1977.

TELEVISION DEBUT—*The David Suskind Show,* 1962. PRINCIPAL TELEVISION APPEARANCES—*Busting Loose,* CBS, 1977; Simas Kudirka, *The Defection of Simas Kudirka,* 1978; *Escape from Hell; St. Elsewhere,* NBC; "The Emperor's New Clothes," for *Storytime Theatre,* PBS; *Sesame Street,* PBS; Flagg Purdy, "A Matter of Principle," for *American Playhouse,* PBS, 1984; *The Fourth Man,* ABC, 1985.

PRINCIPAL TELEVISION WORK—Director: *Twigs; Fay* (pilot), NBC, 1975.

RELATED CAREER—Folk-singer with his group *The Tarriers;* singer of children's songs with his group, *The Babysitters.*

WRITINGS: STAGE WORKS, PRODUCED—Musical compositions, *Man Out Loud, Girl Quiet,* Cricket, NY, 1962; sketches, music, lyrics, *A View from Under the Bridge,* Second City at Square East, 1964. BOOKS—*Tony's Hard Work Day* (juvenile), Harper & Row, 1972; *The Lemming Condition* (juvenile), Harper & Row, 1976; *Halfway Through the Door: First Steps on a Path of Enlightenment,* Harper & Row, 1979. SONGS—Over one hundred.

AWARDS: Antoinette Perry Award, Variety's New York Drama Critics Poll Award, Best Actor, 1963, for *Enter Laughing;* Academy Award nomination, Best Actor, 1966, for *The Russians Are Coming, the Russians Are Coming;* Academy Award nomination, New York Critics Award, Best Actor, 1968, for *The Heart Is a Lonely Hunter;* Obie, Best Director, *Little Murders,* 1969; Academy Award nomination, Best Live Action Short Subject, *People Soup,* 1969; New York Critics Award, Best Actor, *Hearts of the West,* 1975; Canadian Best Foreign Actor Award, *Improper Channels,* 1981.

SIDELIGHTS: In his publicity release, Arkin highlights his other musical accomplishments, including playing flute and guitar and dabbling in other instruments from the synthesizer to the nose whistle. He has often collaborated in his writing with his wife, Barbara Dana.

ADDRESS: AGENT—c/o Robinson, Luttrell, and Associates, 141 El Camino Real, Suite 110, Beverly Hills, CA 90212.

*   *   *

ARMEN, Rebecca   1957-

PERSONAL: Born April 24, 1957, in Norwood, MA; daughter of Seth Avakian (a retired CPA) and Eloise Sheldon (a former actress and producer; maiden name, Bullard) Armen. EDUCATION: Wesleyan University, B.A., theatre, 1979; trained for the stage at the Drama Studio, London (certificate of training with distinction) and with Eva LeGallienne.

VOCATION: Actress.

CAREER: DEBUT—The Girl, *Veronica's Room,* High Tor Summer Theatre, Fitchburg, MA, 1977. NEW YORK DEBUT—Perdita, *The Winter's Tale,* Manhattan Theatre Club, 1980. LONDON DEBUT—Marianne, *Scenes from a Marriage,* Theatre at New End, 1980.

PRINCIPAL STAGE APPEARANCES—Clarisse, *When You Comin'*

REBECCA ARMEN

Back, Red Ryder?, High Tor Summer Theatre, Fitchburg, MA, 1978; Olwen Peel, *Dangerous Corner,* Worcester Foothills, Worcester, MA, 1980; Jane, *The Admirable Crichton,* Long Wharf, New Haven, CT, 1980; Cecily, *The Importance of Being Earnest,* Lyric Stage, Boston, MA, 1981; Eaglet, Card, Duchess' Baby, and understudy to Red Queen, *Alice in Wonderland,* Virginia, NY, 1982; Helena, *A Midsummer Night's Dream,* New York Renaissance Festival, 1983; Viola, *Twelfth Night,* New York Renaissance Festival, 1984.

MAJOR TOURS—Poe's Women and Kid, *Tell Tale Poe/Mark Twain Sketches,* Chamber Repertory Theatre, two national tours, 1981, 1982; one woman educational show touring high schools nationally.

TELEVISION DEBUT—*One Life to Live,* ABC. PRINCIPAL RADIO WORK—First Witch, *Macbeth,* WESU-FM, CT; BBC Radio Competition finalist, England.

SIDELIGHTS: MEMBERSHIPS—Actors' Equity Association, American Federation of Television and Radio Artists, Screen Actors Guild.

ADDRESS: HOME—310 W. 56th Street, New York, NY 10019.

*   *   *

ARQUETTE, Rosanna

PERSONAL: Born in New York City; daughter of Lewis (a performer) and Madi (a poet and political activist) Arquette.

VOCATION: Actress.

CAREER: PRINCIPAL FILM APPEARANCES—*More American Graffiti,* Universal, 1979; *World According to Garp,* Warner Brothers, 1982; *Off the Wall; S.O.B.,* Paramount, 1981; *Baby It's You,* Paramount, 1983; *Desperately Seeking Susan,* Orion, 1985; *Silverado,* Columbia, 1985; *The Aviator* (upcoming); *After Hours* (upcoming); *Eight Million Ways to Die,* PSO/Tri-Star (upcoming).

PRINCIPAL TELEVISION APPEARANCES—*Harvest Home; The Long Way Home,* 1981; *The Wall,* 1982; *The Executioner's Song,* 1982; *Johnny Belinda,* 1982; *One Cooks, the Other Doesn't,* 1983; *The Parade,* 1984; *Survival Guides,* PBS.*

*   *   *

ASADE, Jim   1936-

PERSONAL: Born James W. Assad, September 12, 1936, in Denbo, PA; son of Rene (Seghi) Assad. EDUCATION: University of West Virginia, M.A., guidance and psychology, 1958; University of Missouri, M.A., theatre, 1967; University of Kansas, Ph.D. candidate; trained for the stage at the Royal Academy of Dramatic Art, London.

VOCATION: Director and actor.

CAREER: STAGE DEBUT—Rumpelstiltskin, *Rumpelstiltskin,* Brownsville Community Theatre, Brownsville, PA, for five performances. PRINCIPAL STAGE APPEARANCES—All at Missouri Repertory Theater, Kansas City, MO: Hamlet, *Hamlet:* Enrico, *Enrico IV;* Jimmy Porter, *Look Back in Anger;* Orgon, *Tartuffe;* Fool, *King Lear;* Becket, *Becket;* Feste, *Twelfth Night;* Tom, *The Glass Menagerie;* Sakini, *Teahouse of the August Moon;* Lachie, *The Hasty Heart;* Morgon, *The Corn Is Green;* Toby, *The Medium.*

PRINCIPAL STAGE WORK—Director: *The Cherry Orchard, Ah! Wilderness,* both at Pennsylvania State University Resident Theater Company; with the Missouri Repertory Company, Kansas City, MO: *Wings, The Shadow Box, Much Ado About Nothing, Old Times, Who's Afraid of Virginia Woolf?,* all 1976, *The Rainmaker, All My Sons, The Glass Menagerie, Six Characters in Search of an Author, Hamlet,* all 1980, *Catsplay, Nicholas Nickleby,* both 1983; *Jacques Brel Is Alive and Well and Living in Paris, A Day in the Death of Joe Egg, Dylan,* all at The Theatre; *Enrico IV, Storybook Tales,* both with Actors Prologue Company; *Romeo and Juliet,* Penn State Arts Company; *The Medium, Die Kluge,* both with Lyric Opera Company; *Hansel and Gretel,* Kansas City Philharmonic; *Crimes of the Heart,* Madison Repertory, Madison, WI, 1985.

MAJOR TOURS—Director, company manager, midwestern cities, 1974-76.

FILM DEBUT—Floyd Wells, *In Cold Blood,* Columbia, 1968.

PRINCIPAL TELEVISION APPEARANCES—Hamlet, *Hamlet,* Calvin Productions; performer number one, *Arts in Kansas City,* Centron Productions.

PRINCIPAL TELEVISION WORK—Director, *Watermelon Boats,* PBS affiliate, Kansas City, MO.

RELATED CAREER—Artistic director, Missouri Vanguard Theatre;

JIM ASADE

artistic director, Pennsylvania Arts Company; director of theatre, Avila College, Kansas City, MO, 1970-73; director of arts company, Pennsylvania State University, University Park, PA, 1978-79; assistant director, Missouri Repertory Theatre, Kansas City, MO, 1979-80; co-director, M.F.A. acting program, University of Missouri, Kansas City, MO, 1979-80.

AWARDS: House of Representatives Citation Award, for *Nicholas Nickleby;* Kansas City Trust and Foundations Grant.

SIDELIGHTS: MEMBERSHIPS—Actors' Equity Association, Society of Stage Directors and Choreographers, American Guild of Musical Artists, Alpha Psi Omega, Pi Sigma Phi.

Asade told *CTFT,* "My ultimate joy would be to see the establishment of a fully subsidized American national theatre company."

ADDRESS: HOME—5406 Harrison Street, Kansas City, MO 64110; 165 Christopher Street, Apt. 31, New York, NY 10014.

*   *   *

ASHER, Jane   1946-

PERSONAL: Born April 5, 1946, in London, England; daughter of Richard Alan John and Margaret (Eliot) Asher; married Gerald Scarfe; children: three. EDUCATION: North Bridge House; Miss Lambert's.

VOCATION: Actress and writer.

CAREER: STAGE DEBUT—*Housemaster,* Frinton Summer Thea-

JANE ASHER

tre, 1957. LONDON DEBUT—Muriel Webster, *Will You Walk a Little Faster,* Duke of York's, June, 1960. NEW YORK DEBUT— Julietta, *Measure for Measure,* Bristol Old Vic company, City Center, February, 1967. PRINCIPAL STAGE APPEARANCES—Alice, *Through the Looking Glass,* Playhouse, Oxford, 1958; Wendy, *Peter Pan,* Scala, London, 1961; Dinah, *Level Crossing,* Theatre Royal, Windsor, 1962; title role, *Cinderella* (in pantomime), New, Bromley, 1962; with Bristol Old Vic: *Cleo, Great Expectations, The Happiest Days of Your Life, Sixty Thousand Nights,* 1965.

Cassandra, *The Trojan Women,* Pop Theatre, Edinburgh Festival, 1966; Perdita, *The Winter's Tale,* Pop Theatre, Edinburgh Festival, 1966, then Cambridge, London, 1966; Juliet, *Romeo and Juliet,* Julietta, *Measure for Measure,* both with Bristol Old Vic, 1966-67; Lorette, *Summer,* Fortune, London, 1968; Alison, *Look Back in Anger,* Royal Court, then Criterion, 1968; Celia, *The Philanthropist,* Royal Court, London, then, May Fair, 1970, and Ethel Barrymore, NY, 1971; *Fifty* (gala performance), Oxford Playhouse, 1973; Sally, *Old Flames,* New Vic Studio, Bristol, 1975; Ann, *Treats,* Royal Court, then May Fair, 1976; Charlotte, *Strawberry Fields,* and *To Those Born Later,* National Theatre Company, Cottesloe, London, 1977; title role, *Ophelia,* Oxford Playhouse, 1977; Dr. Scott, *Whose Life Is It Anyway?,* Mermaid, London, then Savoy, 1978; title role, *Peter Pan,* Shaftesbury, London, 1978; *Before the Party,* Queens, London, 1981.

MAJOR TOURS—Wendy, *Peter Pan,* 1962; *Ophelia,* 1977.

PRINCIPAL STAGE WORK—Producer: *Before the Party,* Queens, London, 1981.

FILM DEBUT—As child actress, *Mandy* (a.k.a. *Crash of Silence*), 1953. PRINCIPAL FILM APPEARANCES—*The Greengage Summer,* Columbia, 1961; *The Girl in the Headlines,* 1963; *The Masque of the Red Death,* American International, 1964; *Alfie,* Paramount, 1966; Susan, *Deep End,* Paramount, 1971; *Henry VIII and His Six Wives,* Levitt-Pickman, 1973; *Runners; Dream Child;* others.

PRINCIPAL TELEVISION APPEARANCES—*The Mill on the Floss; Brideshead Revisited; Love Is Old, Love Is New; A Voyage Round My Father; Tales of the Unexpected; East Lynne; The Mistress; Bright Smiles,* Granada-TV.

WRITINGS: BOOKS—*Jane Asher's Party Cakes,* Pelham, 1982; *Jane Asher's Fancy Dress,* Pelham, 1983; *Silent Night for You and Your Baby,* Pelham, 1984.

SIDELIGHTS: MEMBERSHIPS—British Academy of Film and Television Arts, Bristol Old Vic, National Theatre Company, associate member of Royal Academy of Dramatic Arts. RECREATION— Music and cookery.

ADDRESS: AGENT—c/o Chatto & Linnit, Ltd., Prince of Wales Theatre, Coventry Street, London W1V 7FE, England.

*   *   *

ASKIN, Leon   1907-

PERSONAL: Born Leon Aschkenazy, September 18, 1907, in Vienna, Austria; son of Samuel and Malvine (Susman) Aschkenazy; married Annelies Ehrlich (a painter), April 12, 1955; children: Dr. Irene Hartzell (step-daughter). EDUCATION: New School for Dramatic Arts (Reinhardt-Seminar), Vienna, 1927; Columbia University, NY, 1951. MILITARY: U.S. Army Air Force, 1942-46 (top Sergeant).

VOCATION: Actor, director, producer, and writer.

CAREER: PRINCIPAL STAGE APPEARANCES—Dumont Playhouse, Dusseldorf, Germany, 1927; cabaret appearances, Paris, France, 1933-35; Shylock, *The Merchant of Venice,* 1952; various Broadway shows, 1946-1952; title role, *Othello,* Hamburg and Berlin, West Germany, 1957.

PRINCIPAL STAGE WORK—Director: Cabaret, Paris, France, 1933-35; *First Legion,* Linz, Austria, 1935; *Troilus and Cressida,* 1941; *The Apple Cart; The American Way; Faust,* Goethe Festival, 1948-49; *The Merchant of Venice,* 1952; *St. Joan,* 1954; *Julius Caesar,* 1960; *The Egg,* 1975; *Fever in the Brain.*

Artistic director, literary and political cabaret, *ABC,* Vienna, 1935-38; artistic director, Washington Civic Theatre, 1940-42.

PRINCIPAL FILM APPEARANCES—Ramayana, *The Road to Bali,* Paramount, 1952; *The Robe,* Twentieth Century-Fox, 1953; *Knock on Wood,* Goldwyn, 1954; *Son of Sinbad,* RKO Radio, 1955; *My Gun Is Quick,* United Artists, 1958; Peripetchikoff, *One, Two, Three,* United Artists, 1961; Langsdorf, *Do Not Disturb,* Twentieth Century-Fox, 1965; *Guns for San Sebastian,* Metro-Goldwyn-Mayer, 1968; *The Maltese Bippy,* Metro-Goldwyn-Mayer, 1969; Dr. Krodt, *Hammersmith Is Out,* Cinerama, 1972; *Going Ape,* Paramount, 1981; *Horror Star,* 1982; *Airplane II: The Sequel,* Paramount, 1982.

PRINCIPAL TELEVISION APPEARANCES—Pierre, *The Charlie Farrell Show,* CBS and NBC, 1956-1960; Gen. Burkhalter, *Hogan's*

Heroes, CBS, 1966-1971; Martin Luther, Karl Marx, *Steve Allen's Meeting of Minds,* independent network, 1970's.

WRITINGS: THEATRICAL, PERFORMED—Cabaret, Paris, France, 1933-35. ARTICLES, PUBLISHED—In the *Los Angeles Times.* ESSAYS, PUBLISHED—''Hamburg Arbeitstelle fur Exilliteratur.''

AWARDS: Most Outstanding Production of 1941, *Troilus and Cressida;* Medal of Honor, City of Vienna, 1983.

SIDELIGHTS: MEMBERSHIPS—Actors' Equity Association (director, West Coast Advisory Committee, 1952-55), Screen Actors Guild (director, 1973), American Federation of Television and Radio Artists, Academy of Motion Picture Arts and Sciences, Academy of Television Arts and Sciences, ANTA (national board), American National Theatre and Academy West (chairman of the board, 1976-76; president 1979-82; president emeritus, 1983-present).

Askin told *CTFT* that he founded the Actors' Equity Community Theatre in 1948, was chairman of several committees for Equity Library Theatre between 1947-52, and is an honorary life director of that organization. Askin also organized and presented the National Artist Award to Fred Astaire, Henry Fonda, Bob Hope, Jimmy Stewart and Roger Stevens and initiated the ANTA West/Hearst Discovery Theatre.

Askin emigrated to the U.S. in 1940 and was naturalized in 1943.

ADDRESS: HOME—625 N. Rexford Drive, Beverly Hills, CA 90210. OFFICE—ANTA West, 9777 Wilshire Boulevard, Suite 900, Beverly Hills, CA 90213.

*   *   *

ATKINS, Christopher   1961-

BRIEF ENTRY: Born February 21, 1961, in Rye, NY; educated at Dennison University, OH. Before acting he worked as a model. *The Blue Lagoon,* Columbia, 1980, marked his film debut, followed by *The Pirate Movie,* Twentieth Century-Fox, 1982, and *A Night in Heaven.* On television, Atkins played Peter Richards in the cast of the series *Dallas,* CBS, and he appeared in a television movie, *Raid on Short Creek.* He is scheduled to appear in the Broadway production of *The Rose Tatoo* in 1985.*

*   *   *

AUBERJONOIS, Rene   1940-

PERSONAL: Born June 1, 1940, in New York City; son of Fernand and Laura (Murat) Auberjonois; married Judith Mihalyi, October 19, 1963; children: Tessa Louise, Remy-Luc. EDUCATION: Attended Carnegie-Mellon University.

VOCATION: Actor.

CAREER: NEW YORK DEBUT—Fool, *King Lear,* Vivian Beaumont, 1968. PRINCIPAL STAGE APPEARANCES—Witch Boy, *Dark of the Moon,* Leslie, *The Hostage,* Edmund, *Long Day's Journey into Night,* all at Arena Stage, Washington, DC, 1962-64; *Beyond*

RENE AUBERJONOIS

the Fringe; title role, *Tartuffe,* title role, *King Lear, Charley's Aunt,* all at American Conservatory Theater, San Francisco, CA, 1965-67; three roles at the Mark Taper Forum, Los Angeles, CA, 1968; Ned, *A Cry of Players,* Vivian Beaumont, NY, 1968; Marco, *Fire,* Longacre, NY, 1969; *Chemin de Fer,* Mark Taper Forum, Los Angeles, CA, 1969; Sebastian Baye, *Coco,* Mark Hellinger, NY, 1969.

Malvolio, *Twelfth Night,* Vivian Beaumont, NY, 1972; Scapin, *Tricks,* Alvin, NY, 1973; Edgar, *King Lear,* Delacorte, NY, 1973; *The Good Doctor,* Eugene O'Neill, NY, 1973; *The Ruling,* American Conservatory Theater, San Francisco, CA, 1975; John Karslake, *The New York Idea,* Solynony, *Three Sisters,* both at Brooklyn Academy, NY, 1977; Sandor Turai, *The Play's the Thing,* Brutus, *Julius Caesar,* both at Brooklyn Academy, NY, 1978; Johann Schiml, *Break a Leg,* Palace, NY, 1979; Ivanov, *Every Good Boy Deserves Favour,* Metropolitan Opera House, NY, Kennedy Center, Washington, DC, 1979; *Richard III,* Alceste, *The Misanthrope, Flea in Her Ear,* Chekhov, *Yalta, Twelfth Night,* all at Mark Taper Repertory, Los Angeles, CA, 1980-83; the Duke, *Big River,* Eugene O'Neill, NY, 1985.

FILM DEBUT—*M*A*S*H,* 1969. PRINCIPAL FILM APPEARANCES—*Brewster McCloud,* Metro-Goldwyn-Mayer, 1970; *McCabe and Mrs. Miller,* Warner Brothers, 1971; *Pete n' Tillie,* Universal, 1972; *Images,* Columbia, 1972; *Hindenberg,* Universal, 1975; *King Kong,* Paramount, 1976; *Eyes of Laura Mars,* Columbia, 1978; *Where the Buffalo Roam,* 1980.

TELEVISION DEBUT—1971. PRINCIPAL TELEVISION APPEARANCES—*Mod Squad; McMillan and Wife;* Clayton, *Benson;* over one hundred television appearances.

AWARDS: Antoinette Perry Award, 1969, for *Coco;* Antoinette Perry Award nomination, 1973, for *The Good Doctor.*

SIDELIGHTS: FAVORITE ROLES—Tartuffe and Fancourt Babberley. RECREATION—Drawing, yoga.

ADDRESS: OFFICE—124 W. 79th Street, New York, NY 10024. AGENT—c/o Smith-Freedman Agency, 123 N. San Vicente, Beverly Hills, CA 90211.

*   *   *

AVNET, Jonathan   1949-

PERSONAL: Born November 17, 1949; son of Lester Francis (founded Avnet Electronics) and Joan Bertha (Grossman) Avnet; married Barbara Brody (a fabric designer), September 19, 1975; children, Alexandra, Jacob. EDUCATION: University of Pennsylvania, Wharton, two years; Sarah Lawrence College, B.A., film; studied at the American Film Institute.

VOCATION: Producer and manager.

CAREER: PRINCIPAL TELEVISION WORK—Producer: *No Other Love*, CBS, 1979; *Homeward Bound*, CBS, 1980; *Prime Suspect*, CBS, 1982; *Something So Right*, CBS, 1982; *The Burning Bed*, NBC, 1984; *Call to Glory* (pilot), ABC, 1984; *Silence of the Heart*, CBS, 1984.

PRINCIPAL FILM WORK—Producer: *Coast to Coast*, Paramount, 1980; *Risky Business*, Warner Brothers, 1983.

SIDELIGHTS: MEMBERSHIPS—Academy of Motion Picture Arts and Sciences, Academy of Television Arts and Sciences.

ADDRESS: OFFICE—515 N. Robertson Blvd., Los Angeles, CA 90048.

*   *   *

AZNAVOUR, Charles   1924-

PERSONAL: Born May 22, 1924, in Paris, France; son of Misha (a singer) and Knar (an actress; maiden name, Bagdassar) Aznavour; married Ulla, January 11, 1960; children: Seda, Katia, Misha, Nicolas. EDUCATION: Left school at ten years of age. RELIGION: Gregorian.

VOCATION: Singer, actor, composer, and writer.

CAREER: STAGE DEBUT—Siky, *Emil et les Detectives,* Studio Des Champs Elysee, Paris, France, 1933. NEW YORK DEBUT—One man show, *Charles Aznavour,* Carnegie Hall, 1963. LONDON DEBUT—One man show, *Charles Aznavour,* Royal Albert Hall, 1967. PRINCIPAL STAGE APPEARANCES—One man show, *Charles Aznavour,* Olympia and Alhambra in Paris, Paladium in London, Music Box, Minskoff, Ambassador, and Lunt-Fontanne in NY, and over 80 countries.

CHARLES AZNAVOUR

FILM DEBUT—Singing croupier, *Adieu Cherie,* 1947. PRINCIPAL FILM APPEARANCES—*C'est arrive a 36 Chandelles,* 1957; *Les dragueurs,* 1959; *Shoot the Piano Player,* 1959; *Le testament d'Orphee,* 1959; *Le passage du Rhin,* 1960; *Un taxi pour Tobrouk,* 1960; *Horace 62,* 1961; *Tempo di Roma,* 1962; *Les quatre verites,* 1962; *Le Rat d'Amerique,* 1962; *Le diable et les dix commandements,* 1962; *Alta infedelta,* 1963; *Les vierges,* 1963; *Cherchez l'idole,* 1964; *La metamorphose des cloportes,* 1965; *Paris au mois d'aout,* 1965; *Un facteur s'en va-t-en guerre,* 1966; *Caroline Cherie,* 1967; *Candy,* 1968; *The Games,* 1969; *Le temps des loups,* 1969; *Un beau monstre,* 1970; *La part des lions,* 1971; *Les intrus,* 1972; *Ein unbekannter rechnet ab,* 1974; *Sky Riders,* 1975; *Folies bourgeoises,* 1976; *Die Biechtrommel,* 1978; *Die Zauberberg,* 1981; *Edith et Marcel,* 1982; *Viva la vie of Claude Lelouche,* 1983.

PRINCIPAL TELEVISION APPEARANCES—Six hour mini series for French, Italian, and German television.

RELATED CAREER—S.P.A. Publishing company, Charles Aznavour.

AWARDS: Best actor of the year, 1958, *La tete contre les murs;* Best composer, Country Music Award, *Yesterday When I Was Young;* 37 Golden albums.

SIDELIGHTS: MEMBERSHIPS—Authors and Composers society in France and Switzerland.

ADDRESS: AGENT—G. Beaumc, 3 quai Malaquais 75006, Paris, France.

B

BACH, Barbara

PERSONAL: Born Barbara Goldbach in Flushing, NY; daughter of Howard and Marjorie Golbach; married Augusto Gregorini (an industrialist; divorced); married Ringo Starr, April 27, 1981; children: (first marriage) Francesca, Gian Andrea. EDUCATION—Queens College.

VOCATION: Actress.

CAREER: PRINCIPAL FILM APPEARANCES—The Spy Who Loved Me; The Humanoid; The Jaguar Lives; The Volcanic Islands; Force Ten from Navarone; The Unseen; Up the Academy; Caveman; Give My Regards to Broad Street; The Odyssey, Italy; and many European films.

PRINCIPAL TELEVISION APPEARANCE—Cordialemente, Italy.

RELATED CAREER—Model, appeared on covers of Mademoiselle, Glamour, and Seventeen.*

*   *   *

BACH, Catherine

BRIEF ENTRY: Actress. Grew up in South Dakota and Los Angeles, CA; married David Shaw (divorced). Catherine Bach moved to Los Angeles after completing high school in South Dakota. In Hollywood, she made occasional television appearances and had small roles in the films The Midnight Man, Universal, 1974; Thunderbolt and Lightfoot, United Artists, 1974; and Hustle, Paramount, 1975. She is best known for her television role as Daisy Duke, The Dukes of Hazzard, CBS, 1979-85. She also starred in the television movie White Water Rebels, CBS, 1982. In 1985, Bach appeared in Extremities at the Jupiter Theatre.*

*   *   *

BACON, Kevin

BRIEF ENTRY: Born in Philadelphia, PA; son of city planner Edmund Bacon, he began his training at Manning Street Actor's Theatre, then was an apprentice at New York's Circle in the Square, where at eighteen he was the youngest member of the repertory company. Bacon made his Broadway debut in Slab Boys with Sean Penn, and his other Broadway credits include Forty-Deuce, Poor

Little Lambs, and was seen off Broadway in Album and Getting Out. On television Bacon has worked on the daytime serials The Guiding Light, CBS, and Search for Tomorrow, NBC, and he acted in two television movies, The Gift and Enormous Changes at the Last Minute, which was later shown in movie theaters as well. In film he made his debut in National Lampoon's Animal House, Universal, 1978, and went on to appear in Friday the 13th, 1980; Hero at Large, United Artists, 1980; Only When I Laugh, Columbia, 1981; Diner, Metro-Goldwyn-Mayer/United Artists, 1982; Forty-Deuce (reprising his stage role), 1982; Footloose, 1984; Quicksilver, 1985.*

*   *   *

BAIO, Scott   1961-

BRIEF ENTRY: Born 1961, in Brooklyn, NY. Actor. Baio started his career at the age of nine, doing television commericials and voice-overs. He is best known for his role as Chachi on both Happy Days, ABC, 1977-84, and Joanie Loves Chachi, ABC, 1982-83. Other television credits include two ABC Afterschool Specials, ''Luke Was There'' and ''A House in the Woods,'' and CBS Schoolbreak Specials, ''All the Kids Do It,'' ''The Boy Who Drank Too Much,'' and ''Stoned.'' Baio also appeared in Blansky's Beauties, ABC, 1977; Who's Watching the Kids, NBC, 1978; and starred as Charles in Charles in Charge, CBS, 1984-85. He has also made guest appearances on The Mike Douglas Show, Dinah, Operation Runaway, Hollywood Squares, 20/20, Us Against the World, Kids Are People Too, Joe Namath Special, Bay City Rollers Variety Hour, Battle of the Network Stars (several appearances), and was host of both Hollywood Teen and Shorts. His film credits include Bugsy Malone, Paramount, 1976; Foxes, United Artists, 1980; and Zapped!, Embassy, 1982.

ADDRESS: AGENT—Phil Gersh, 222 N. Canon Drive, Beverly Hills, CA 90210.*

*   *   *

BALCH, Marston   1901-

PERSONAL: Full name Marston Stevens Balch; born November 21, 1901; son of Ernest Alanson (a history professor and mayor of Kalamazoo, MI) and Bertha Lou (a volunteer social worker; maiden name, Stevens) Balch; married Germaine Cornier (a French professor), September 6, 1927 (died July 18, 1969); married Roberta Newton Blanchard (an author, craftsman, and artist), September 8,

MARSTON BALCH

1976; children: (first marriage) Gabrielle. EDUCATION: Kalamazoo College, A.B. 1923; Harvard University, M.A., 1925, Ph.D., 1931, English literature, dramatic literature, theatre history. POLITICS: Independent. RELIGION: Anglican. MILITARY: Served in North Africa and France with the Office of War Information and the U.S. Information Service, 1943-46.

VOCATION: Educator, director, manager, producer, writer, and editor.

CAREER: Directed over 125 student productions at Tufts University.

RELATED CAREER: English instructor, Williams College, 1925-27; English instructor and modern languages tutor, Harvard University, 1928-33; assistant English professor, Tufts University, 1934-37; director, Tufts University Theatre, 1935-66; drama professor and Fletcher Professor of Oratory, Tufts, 1937-71; professor emeritus of drama, Tufts, 1971-present; secretary of the French Library, Boston, 1965-present.

WRITINGS: BOOKS—The Dramatic Legacy of Thomas Middleton, 2 vols. (unpublished); editor, *Modern Short Biographies*, 1935; co-author, *You and College*, 1936; co-editor, *The College Omnibus*, 1936; editor, *Modern Short Biographies and Autobiographies*, 1940; co-author, *Theatre in America: Appraisal and Challenge*, 1968. TRANSLATIONS, PLAYS—*The Steamship Tenacity; Beggars in Paradise; The Chief Thing; Doctor Knock; The Would-Be Gentleman.*

AWARDS: Medaille de la Reconnaissance Francaise, 1946; Chevalier, Legion d'Honneur, 1958; Margo Jones Award for aiding new playwrights, 1960; Doctor of Humane Letters, L.H.D., Kalamazoo College; Man of the Year, French Library in Boston, 1984; Distinguished Service Awards, Kalamazoo College and Tufts University, 1984.

SIDELIGHTS: MEMBERSHIPS—National Council of the Arts in Education (board member), Dramatists Guild, National Theatre Conference (executive secretary, 1960-68), College of Fellows, New England Theatre Conference (co-founder, board member, and vice president), American Society for Theatre Research, American Association of University Professors, Harvard Club of Boston, Boston Chapter of France Forever (vice president and co-founder), French Library in Boston (trustee and co-founder, 1946-), Boston Authors Club, Balch House Associates of the Beverly Historical Society, MA (president), Boston Athenaeum.

ADDRESS: HOME—32 Calumet Road, Winchester, MA 01890.

*   *   *

BALSAM, Martin   1919-

PERSONAL: Born November 4, 1919, in New York, City; son of Albert and Lillian (Weinstein) Balsam; married Pearl L. Somer, October, 1952 (divorced, 1954); married Joyce Van Patten, August, 1959 (divorced, 1962); married Irene Miller, November, 1963; children: (second marriage) a daughter. EDUCATION: Attended the New School for Social Research. MILITARY: U.S. Army, 1941-45.

VOCATION: Actor.

CAREER: FILM DEBUT—*On the Waterfront,* 1954. PRINCIPAL FILM APPEARANCES—*Twelve Angry Men,* United Artists, 1957; *Marjorie Morningstar,* Warner Brothers, 1957; *Time Limit,* United Artists, 1957; *Al Capone,* Allied Artists, 1959; *Middle of the Night,* Columbia, 1959; *Psycho,* Paramount, 1960; *All at Home,* 1960; *Breakfast at Tiffany's,* Paramount, 1961; *Ada,* Metro-Goldwyn-Mayer, 1961; *Cape Fear,* Universal, 1962; *The Captive City,* 1962; *Who's Sleeping in My Bed,* 1963; *Seven Days in May,* 1963; *Youngblood Hawke,* Warner Brothers, 1964; *The Carpetbaggers,* Paramount, 1964; *The Bedford Incident,* Columbia, 1965; *Harlow,* Paramount, 1965; *After the Fox,* United Artists, 1966; *A Thousand Clowns,* United Artists, 1966; *Hombre,* Twentieth Century-Fox, 1967; *Among the Paths to Eden,* 1967; *Me, Natalie,* National General, 1968; *2001: A Space Odyssey,* Metro-Goldwyn-Mayer, 1968; *The Good Guys and the Bad Guys,* Warner Brothers, 1969; *Trilogy,* Allied Artists, 1969.

Catch 22, Paramount, 1970; *Tora! Tora! Tora!,* Twentieth Century-Fox, 1970; *Little Big Man,* National General, 1970; *The Anderson Tapes,* Columbia, 1971; *The Commissioner,* 1972; *The Stone Killer,* Columbia, 1973; *Summer Wishes, Winter Dreams,* Columbia, 1973; *The Taking of Pelham 1,2,3,* United Artists, 1974; *Murder on the Orient Express,* Paramount, 1974; *Mitchell,* Allied Artists, 1975; *All the President's Men,* Warner Brothers, 1976; *Two-Minute Warning,* Universal, 1976; *The Sentinel,* Universal, 1977; *Silver Bears,* Columbia, 1978; *Cuba,* United Artists, 1979; *There Goes the Bride,* 1980; Max Silverman, *The Goodbye People,* 1984; *St. Elmo's Fire,* Columbia, 1985; *Death Wish Three,* Cannon (upcoming).

PRINCIPAL TELEVISION APPEARANCES—*Actors Studio Theatre; U.S. Steel Hour; Mr. Peepers; Alfred Hitchcock Presents; Arrest and Trial.* Series: Murray Klein, *Archie Bunker's Place,* CBS, 1979-81.

STAGE DEBUT—The Villain, *Pot Boiler,* Playground, NY, 1935. PRINCIPAL STAGE APPEARANCES—Johann, *The Play's the Thing,* Red Barn, Locust Valley, NY, 1941; Mr. Blow, *Ghost for Sale,*

Daly's, NY, 1941; with the Town Hall Players, Newbury, MA, 1947; Eddie, *The Wanhope Building,* Princess, NY, 1947; *A Sound of Hunting,* Equity Library, NY, 1947; Sizzi, *Lamp at Midnight,* New Stages, NY, 1947; Murderer, *Macbeth,* National, NY, 1948; Merle, *Sundown Beach,* Belasco, NY, 1948; Ambulance Driver, *The Closing Door,* Empire, NY, 1949.

Three Men on a Horse, Home of the Brave, A Letter from Harry, all 1949; Serving Man, *The Liar,* Broadhurst, NY, 1950; Man, *The Rose Tattoo,* Martin Beck, NY, 1951; *Camino Real,* National, NY, 1953; Bernie Dodd, *The Country Girl,* Gangster, *Detective Story,* 1953; *The Country Girl, Thirteen Clocks,* both 1954; Son-in-law, *Middle of the Night,* ANTA, NY, 1956; Eddie Carbone, *A View from the Bridge,* La Jolla Playhouse, CA, 1958; *The Iceman Cometh,* Theatre Group, University of California, Los Angeles, 1961; Moe Smith, *Nowhere to Go But Up,* Winter Garden, NY, 1962; Jules Walker, *The Porcelain Year,* Locust, Philadelphia, PA, 1965.

Richard Pawling, George, Chuck, *You Know I Can't Hear You When the Water's Running,* Ambassador, NY, 1967; Willy Loman, *Death of a Salesman,* Walnut Street Theater, Philadelphia, PA, 1974; Joseph Parmigian, *Cold Storage,* American Place, NY, Lyceum, NY, 1977.

MAJOR TOURS—Norman, *Wedding Breakfast,* U.S. cities, 1955.

AWARDS: Academy Award, 1964, for *A Thousand Clowns;* Antoinette Perry Award, Outer Critics Circle Award, both 1967, for *You Know I Can't Hear You When the Water's Running.*

SIDELIGHTS: RECREATION—Golf and photgraphy.

ADDRESS: AGENT—Robinson's Associates, Inc., 132 S. Rodeo Drive, Beverly Hills, CA 90212.*

*   *   *

BARBOUR, Elly 1945-

PERSONAL: Full name Eleanor Barbour; born January 23, 1945, in New York City; daughter of William and Jane (Muhlfeld) Barbour. EDUCATION—Hofstra University, B.A.; studied with Ed Dixon, Stella Adler, and Ron Forella in NY.

VOCATION: Actress.

CAREER: STAGE DEBUT—Gloria, *Everybody Loves Opal,* Colorado Music Hall Dinner Theatre, Denver, March, 1974. NEW YORK DEBUT—Singer, *Pat Carroll at Town Hall,* June, 1974. PRINCIPAL STAGE APPEARANCES—Young Phyllis, *Follies,* Equity Library, NY, 1976; Ensemble, *Under Milkwood,* the Lady, *Man with a Load of Mischief,* both at Theatre by the Sea, NH, 1977; Master of Ceremonies, *Incredible World of Magic,* Village Gate, NY, 1978; Ensemble, *Manhattan Breakdown,* Equity Library, 1978; Freddie, *The Club,* Player's State Theatre, FL, 1980; Bella, *Moony Shapiro "Songbook,"* Olney, Baltimore, MD, 1982; Denise Wilson, *Oliver Quade,* American Jewish Theatre, 1984.

MAJOR TOURS—Bobby, *The Club,* 1980; Helen McFudd, *Irene,* 1975-76.

RELATED CAREER—Orchestra, *The Drunkard, The Boyfriend,*

both at Parkway Casino, NY, 1974-75; cabaret singer, major New York City and Catskill hotels; taught flute and guitar, 1965-68.

SIDELIGHTS: MEMBERSHIPS—Actors' Equity Association.

ADDRESS: HOME—17 Columbia Place, Brooklyn, NY 11201. AGENT—Honey Sanders Agency Ltd., 229 W. 42nd Street, New York, NY 10036.

*   *   *

BARBOUR, Thomas 1921-

PERSONAL: Born July 25, 1921, in New York City; son of Frederick K. (president of a thread company) and Helen Alison (Carrere) Barbour. EDUCATION: Princeton University, B.A., 1943; Harvard University, M.A., 1948; trained for the stage at the Herbert Berghof Studio with Lee Grant. POLITICS: Independent. RELIGION: Episcopalian. MILITARY: American Field Service.

VOCATION: Actor and writer.

CAREER: STAGE DEBUT—Group Twenty Players, Wellesley, MA, 1953. NEW YORK DEBUT—*Twelfth Night,* Shakespearean Rights, off Broadway, 1954-55. PRINCIPAL STAGE APPEARANCES—Editor of the "Times" and Archbishop of Canterbury, *Portrait of a Queen,* Henry Miller, NY, 1968; *The Great White Hope,* Alvin, NY, 1968-70.

FILM DEBUT—Doctor, *Diary of a Mad Housewife,* Universal, 1970. PRINCIPAL FILM APPEARANCES—*The Taking of Pelham 1-2-3,* United Artists, 1974; Sanford Bach, *Arthur,* Warner Brothers, 1981.

TELEVISION DEBUT—"The Life of Samuel Johnson," *Omnibus,* 1958.

RELATED CAREER—Instructor: Emerson College, Boston, 1948-50, Columbia University, 1960-61.

WRITINGS: PLAYS, PRODUCED—*A Little Brown Bird* (aka *Champagne for Two*), Hilltop Theatre, Lutherville, MD, 1954; *The Smokeweaver's Daughter,* NY, 1959.

SIDELIGHTS: MEMBERSHIPS—Actors' Equity Association, Screen Actors Guild, American Federation of Television and Radio Artists, National Academy of Television Arts and Sciences, Dramatists Guild, Polaris Repertory Company (chairman), Players Club, Episcopal Actors Guild.

ADDRESS: HOME—60 Perry Street, New York, NY 10014. AGENT—Triad Associates, 888 Seventh Avenue, New York, NY 10019.

*   *   *

BARKER, Bob 1923-

PERSONAL: Full name Robert William Barker; born December 12, 1923, in Darrington, WA; son of Byron John and Matilda Kent (Tarleton) Barker; married Dorothy Jo Gideon, January 12, 1945. EDUCATION: Drury College, B.A., economics (summa cum laude), 1947. RELIGION: Protestant. MILITARY: U.S. Navy, 1943-45.

BOB BARKER

EVALYN BARON

VOCATION: Television host.

CAREER: TELEVISION DEBUT—Host, *Truth or Consequences*, NBC, 1956 (continued until 1975 in syndication). PRINCIPAL TELEVISION APPEARANCES—Host: *Price Is Right*, CBS, 1972-present; *Miss USA Beauty Pageant*, CBS, 1966-present; *Miss Universe*, CBS, 1966-present; *Pillsbury Bake-Off*, CBS, 1969-present; *Rose Parade*, CBS, 1969.

MAJOR TOURS—*Bob Barker Fun and Games Show*.

SIDELIGHTS: MEMBERSHIPS—American Guild of Variety Artists, American Federation of Television and Radio Artists, Screen Actors Guild, Society Against Vivisection, Fund for Animals (national chairman), Actors and Others for Animals (board of directors).

Barker has long been an animal rights activist.

ADDRESS: OFFICE—9201 Wilshire Blvd., Suite 201, Beverly Hills, CA 90210. AGENT—c/o William Morris Agency, 151 El Camino, Beverly Hills, CA 90212.

*   *   *

BARON, Evalyn   1948-

PERSONAL: Born April 21, 1948, in Atlanta, GA; daughter of Paul Hirsch (an art restorationist) and Sarah Lee (an educational administrator; maiden name, Meyer) Baron; married Paul S. Daniels (a theatrical manager), January 14, 1973. EDUCATION: Northwestern University, B.A., 1969; University of Minnesota, M.F.A., 1972;

trained for the stage at the Warren Robertson Studio with Larry Moss.

VOCATION: Actress and singer.

CAREER: STAGE DEBUT—Sally Cato, *Mame*, Theater of the Stars, Atlanta, GA, 1965. NEW YORK DEBUT—*Scrambled Feet*, Village Gate, 1979-80. PRINCIPAL STAGE APPEARANCES—Broadway: Mrs. Clayton, *Fearless Frank*, 1979-80; Evie, *Jerry's Girls*, 1981-82; Margaret, *Quilters*, 1984; Miss Watson, *Big River*, 1985.

Off-Broadway: Hochspitz, *Hijinks*, West Side Arts, 1980-81; Alice, *I Can't Keep Running in Place*, West Side Arts, 1981-82.

Regional: Kate, *Taming of the Shrew*, Guthrie, Minneapolis, MN, 1972-73; Duenna, *Cyrano de Bergerac*, Hartford Stage Company, CT, 1972-73; Gay, *You Can't Take It with You*, Hartford Stage, CT, 1974; Sister Woman, *Cat on a Hot Tin Roof*, Stage West, 1975; Doris, *Alms for the Middle Class*, Pittsburgh Public, PA, 1983.

MAJOR TOURS—Madame Pavlenko, *A Day in Hollywood/A Night in the Ukraine*, national, 1982-83.

TELEVISION DEBUT—Louise, *Edge of Night*, ABC, 1979. PRINCIPAL TELEVISION APPEARANCES—*Captain Kangaroo*, CBS, 1980-83; Eve, *Oh, Madeline*, ABC, 1983; Miss Devon, *Another World*, NBC, 1984.

AWARDS: Antoinette Perry Award nomination, 1985, for *Quilters*.

SIDELIGHTS: MEMBERSHIPS—Actors' Equity Association, Screen Actors Guild, American Federation of Television and Radio Artists.

Baron told *CTFT*, "To communicate the things common, real, humane in our lives is a privilege and special joy. *Quilters,* and the strength of those pioneer women changed my life."

ADDRESS: AGENT—c/o Don Buchwald Agency, Ten E. 44th Street, New York, NY 10017.

* * *

BARRY, Gene   1922-

PERSONAL: Born Eugene Klass, June 4, 1922, in New York City; son of Martin and Eva (Conn) Klass; married Betty Claire Kalb, October 22, 1944; children: Michael Lewis, Fredric James, Liza.

VOCATION: Actor.

CAREER: PRINCIPAL TELEVISION APPEARANCES—*Bat Masterson,* NBC, 1958; *Burke's Law,* 1968; *Name of the Game,* 1969.

PRINCIPAL FILM APPEARANCES—*Atomic City,* 1952; *Girls of Pleasure Island,* 1953; *War of the Worlds,* 1953; *Those Redheads from Seattle,* 1953; *Alaska Seas,* 1954; *Red Garters,* 1954; *Naked Alibi,* 1954; *Soldier of Fortune,* Twentieth Century-Fox, 1955; *Purple Mask,* Universal, 1955; *Houston Story,* Columbia, 1956; *Back from Eternity,* Universal, 1956; *China Gate,* Twentieth Century-Fox, 1957; *Twenty-Seventh Day,* Columbia, 1957; *Thunder Road,* United Artists, 1958; *Maroc Seven,* Paramount, 1968.

NEW YORK STAGE DEBUT—1942. PRINCIPAL STAGE APPEARANCES—*Rosalinda; Catherine Was Great; Happy Is Larry; Bless You All; The Perfect Setup,* 1962; Georges, *La Cage Aux Folles,* Palace, NY, 1983, then Patages, Los Angeles, 1985.

SIDELIGHTS: MEMBERSHIPS—Screen Actors Guild (former first vice-president), Boy Scouts of America.

ADDRESS: AGENT—International Creative Management, 40 W. 57th Street, New York, NY 10019.*

* * *

BARRY, Jack   1918-84

PERSONAL: Born March 20, 1918, in Lindenhurst, NY; died May 2, 1984, of heart failure in New York City; married Patte Preble; children: Jeffrey, Jonathan, Barbara, Douglas Curtis. EDUCATION: University of Pennsylvania, Wharton School of Finance and Commerce, B.S., economics.

VOCATION: Producer and television host.

CAREER: PRINCIPAL TELEVISION WORK—Producer and/or host: *Juvenile Jury* (began as a radio show in 1946), NBC, 1947; *Life Begins at 80,* 1947; *Tic-Tac-Dough; Concentration; Everybody's Talking; By the Numbers; 21; Generation Gap; Break the Bank; Hot Potato; Joker's Wild; Play the Percentages; Hollywood Connection; Way Out Games; The Peel Game.*

PRINCIPAL FILM WORK—Producer, *Private Lessons,* 1981.

SIDELIGHTS: Barry was president of Barry and Enright Productions. He also owned and operated the Barry Cable TV System in the Los Angeles area.*

* * *

BARRYMORE, Drew   1975-

BRIEF ENTRY: Born 1975; daughter of John and Jaid Barrymore. Actress. Drew Barrymore is a descendent of one of America's great theatrical families. She made her debut when she was eleven months, appearing in a television commercial. When she was two and one-half years old, she appeared in the television movie *Suddenly Love,* 1978, and has since appeared in another television movie, *Bogie,* 1980. In 1984, she was one of the stars on *Night of 100 Stars,* ABC. She made her film debut in *Altered States,* Warner Brothers, 1980, and has gone on to star in *E.T.: The Extra-Terrestrial,* Universal, 1982; *Irreconcilable Differences,* 1984; *Firestarter,* 1984; *Cat's Eye,* 1985. She will star in an *ABC Weekend Special* as Connie Sawyer in an updated version of Mark Twain's *Tom Sawyer* and *Huckleberry Finn* entitled *Con Sawyer and Hucklemary Finn,* 1985-86.*

* * *

BART, Peter   1932-

PERSONAL: Born August 24, 1932, in New York City; son of M.S. and Clara Bart; married Leslie; children: Colby, Dilys. EDUCATION: Swarthmore College; London School of Economics. POLITICS: Independent.

VOCATION: Writer and producer.

CAREER: PRINCIPAL FILM WORK—Producer, *Islands in the Stream,* Paramount, 1977; co-producer, *Fun with Dick and Jane,* Columbia, 1975. Producer and vice president, Paramount Pictures; president, Lorimar Film Company; senior vice president, Metro-Goldwyn-Mayer.

RELATED CAREER: Reporter, *The New York Times.*

WRITINGS: NOVELS—*Destinies* (co-author), 1980; *Thy Kingdom Come,* 1982.

ADDRESS: HOME—2270 Betty Lane, Beverly Hills, CA 90210.

* * *

BASEHART, Richard   1914-84

PERSONAL: Born August 31, 1914, in Zanesville, OH; son of Harry T. and Mae (Wetherald) Basehart; married Stephanie Klein, 1940 (died, 1950); married Valentina Cortesa (divorced); married Diana Lotery; children: (third marriage) Gayla, Jenna, John Autrey.

VOCATION: Actor.

CAREER: STAGE DEBUT—With the Wright Players Stock Company, Zanesville, OH, 1932. NEW YORK DEBUT—Weiler, *Counterattack*, Windsor, 1943. PRINCIPAL STAGE APPEARANCES—Member of the Hedgerow Theatre, Moylan, PA, 1938-42; Sgt. Hauptmann, *Land of Fame*, Belasco, NY, 1943; *Othello*, Shubert, 1943; Kip, *Take It as It Comes*, 48th Street Theatre, NY, 1944; Steven Ames, *Hickory Stick*, Mansfield, NY, 1944; Lachlan, *The Hasty Heart*, Hudson, NY, 1945; Steve Decker, *The Survivors*, Playhouse, NY, 1948; Charles Morrow, *The Day the Money Stopped*, Belasco, NY, 1958; title role, *Richard II*, American Shakespeare Festival, Stratford, CT, 1962; *Uncle Vanya*, Mark Taper Forum, Los Angeles, 1969.

FILM DEBUT—*Cry Wolf*, 1947. PRINCIPAL FILM APPEARANCES—*Repeat Performance*, 1947; *He Walked by Night*, 1948; *Roseanna McCoy*, 1948; *Tension*, 1948; *Outside the Wall*, 1949; *Reign of Terror*, 1949; *Fixed Bayonets*, 1951; *The House on Telegraph Hill*, 1951; *Decision Before Dawn*, 1951; *Titanic*, 1953; *The Good Die Young*, United Artists, 1954; *The Stranger's Hand*, Distributors Corp. of America, 1954; *La Strada*, Trans-Lux, 1954; *Canyon Crossroads*, United Artists, 1955; *Il Bidone*, 1955; *Finger of Guilt*, RKO, 1956; *Moby Dick*, Warner Brothers, 1956; *Time Limit*, United Artists, 1957; *The Brothers Karamazov*, Metro-Goldwyn-Mayer, 1958.

Five Branded Women, Paramount, 1960; *Portrait in Black*, Universal, 1960; *For the Love of Mike*, Twentieth Century-Fox, 1960; *Passport to China*, Columbia, 1961; *Hitler*, Allied Artists, 1962; *The Savage Guns*, Metro-Goldwyn-Mayer, 1962; *Kings of the Sun*, United Artists, 1963; *Cartouche*, RKO, 1964; *The Satan Bug*, United Artists, 1965; *Chato's Land*, 1972; *Rage*, Warner Brothers, 1972; *And Millions Will Die*, 1973; *Mansions of the Doomed*, 1977; *Shenanigans* (aka *The Great Bank Hoax*), 1977; *The Island of Dr. Moreau*, American International, 1977; *Being There*, United Artists, 1979. Also: *The Extra Day; L'Ambtieuse; The Climbers*.

PRINCIPAL TELEVISION APPEARANCES—Plays and movies: *Playhouse 90; So Soon to Die; City Beneath the Sea*, 1953; *Maneater*, 1969; *The Death of Me Yet*, 1971; *Assignment: Munich*, 1972; *The Bounty Man*, 1972; *Twenty-One Hours at Munich*, 1976; *Time Travellers*, 1976; *Flood*, 1976; *Stone Street*, 1977; *The Critical List*, 1978; *The Rebels*, 1979; *Marilyn: The Untold Story*, 1980; *Sole Survivor; The Andersonville Trial; The Trial of Lt. William Cally; Valley Forge; Knight Rider*.

Series: Voyage to the Bottom of the Sea, 1964-67; *Studio One; Naked City; Rawhide; Route 66; Twilight Zone; W.E.B.*

Narrator: *Four Days in November; Let My People Go; Masada; Vietnam: The 10,000 Day War; Vietnam: A Television History;* closing ceremonies of the 1984 Olympics.

AWARDS: Drama Critics Award, 1945, for *The Hasty Heart*; National Board of Review Award, Best Actor, 1951, for *Fourteen Hours*.

SIDELIGHTS: Basehart was co-founder of Actors and Others for Animals.*

*   *   *

BASINGER, Kim

BRIEF ENTRY: Born in Athens, GA; married Ron Britten. Actress

and former model. Basinger was listed with the Ford Model Agency in New York City when she was seventeen years old. Her film credits include *Hard Country; Mother Lode; Never Say Never Again*, Warner Brothers, 1983; *The Man Who Loved Women*, Columbia, 1983; *The Natural*, Tri-Star, 1984; *9 1/2 Weeks* (upcoming); *Fool for Love* (upcoming), Cannon. She has appeared in the television movies *Katie: Portrait of a Centerfold; The Ghost on Flight 401;* the miniseries *From Here to Eternity;* and on the series *Dog and Cat*, ABC, 1977.*

*   *   *

BATEMAN, Jason

BRIEF ENTRY: Son of Kent (an acting coach and theatrical manager) and Victoria (a flight attendant) Bateman. Actor. His television credits include Matthew Burton on *Silver Spoons*, NBC. This character was spun off to his own series, *It's Your Move*, NBC, 1984-85. He has also appeared on *Little House on the Prarie* and the game show, *Body Language*. With his sister Justine, he was seen in the play *Journey to the Day*, in Birmingham, AL.*

*   *   *

BATEMAN, Justine

BRIEF ENTRY: Daughter of Kent (an acting coach and theatrical manager) and Victoria (a flight attendant) Bateman. Actress. Bateman is best known for her role as Mallory Keaton on *Family Ties*, NBC, 1983-present. She also starred as Deborah Jahnke in the television movie *Right to Kill?*, ABC, 1985; and was in the play *Journey to the Day*, in Birmingham, AL, with her brother Jason.*

*   *   *

BATES, Alan   1934-

PERSONAL: Born February 17, 1934, in Derbyshire, England; son of Harold Arthur and Florence Mary (Wheatcroft) Bates; married Victoria Ward. EDUCATION: Studied at the Royal Academy of Dramatic Arts in London.

VOCATION: Actor.

CAREER: STAGE DEBUT—*You and Your Wife*, Midland Theatre Company, Coventry, England, 1955. LONDON DEBUT—Simon Fellowes, *The Mulberry Bush*, Royal Court, 1956. NEW YORK DEBUT—Cliff, *Look Back in Anger*, Lyceum, 1958. PRINCIPAL STAGE APPEARANCES—As member of the English Stage Company at the Royal Court Theatre: Hopkins, *The Crucible*, 1956, Cliff, *Look Back in Anger*, 1956, Stapleton, *Cards of Identity*, 1956, Mr. Harcourt, *The Country Wife*, 1956, Monsieur le Cracheton, *The Apollo de Bellac*, 1957, Dr. Brock, *Yes—and After*, 1957; Cliff, *Look Back in Anger*, World Youth Festival, Moscow, 1957, and Edinburgh Festival, 1958; Edmund, *Long Day's Journey into Night*, Edinburgh Festival and the Globe, London, 1958.

Mick, *The Caretaker*, Arts, also at the Duchess, London, and

Lyceum, NY, 1960-61; Richard Ford, *Poor Richard*, Helen Hayes, NY, 1964; Adam, *The Four Seasons*, Saville, London, 1965; Ford, *The Merry Wives of Windsor*, Richard, *Richard III*, both at Stratford Ontario Shakespeare Festival, 1967; Andrew, *In Celebration*, Royal Court, London, 1969; title role, *Hamlet*, Playhouse, Nottingham, Cambridge, England, 1971; title role, *Butley*, Criterion, London, 1971; Petruchio, *The Taming of the Shrew*, Stratford-on-Avon, 1973; Allott, *Life Class*, Royal Court, Duke of York's, London, 1974; Simon, *Otherwise Engaged*, Queen's, London, 1975; Trigorin, *The Seagull*, Derby Playhouse, Duke of York's, London, 1976; Robert, *Stage Struck*, Vaudeville, London, 1979; *A Patriot for Me*, Chichester Festival, 1983, London, 1983, Los Angeles, 1984.

FILM DEBUT—Frank Rice, *The Entertainer*, Continental, 1960. PRINCIPAL FILM APPEARANCES—*A Kind of Loving*, Governor, 1962; *Zorba the Greek*, International Classics, 1965; *Far from the Madding Crowd*, Metro-Goldwyn-Mayer, 1967; *The Fixer*, Metro-Goldwyn-Mayer, 1968; *Women in Love*, United Artists, 1970; *The Go-Between*, Columbia, 1971; *Royal Flash*, Twentieth Century-Fox, 1975; *An Unmarried Woman*, Twentieth Century-Fox, 1978; *Nijinsky*, Paramount, 1980.

PRINCIPAL TELEVISION APPEARANCES—Cliff, *Look Back in Anger*; Mick, *The Caretaker; The Wind and the Rain; The Mayor of Casterbridge; A Voyage Round My Father; Separate Tables; An Englishman Abroad; Dr. Fischer of Geneva.*

AWARDS: Clarence Derwent, 1959, for Mick, *The Caretaker*; *Evening Standard* Award, Best Actor, 1976; Best Actor, Variety Club of Great Britain and Best Actor in a Revival, Society of West End Theatre Managers, both 1983-84, for *A Patriot for Me*; Best Actor, British Academy of Film and Television Arts, 1983, for *An Englishman Abroad.*

ADDRESS: AGENT—c/o Chatto and Linnit, Prince of Wales Theatre, Coventry Street, London W1, England.

*   *   *

BAUGHMAN, Renee

VOCATION: Actress, dancer, and singer.

CAREER: PRINCIPAL STAGE APPEARANCES—*Peoples Lives*, Manhattan Theatre Club; *Li'l Abner*, Paper Mill Playhouse, NJ; featured dancer, *Smith*, Eden; understudy Betty from Boston, *No, No, Nanette*, Paper Mill Playhouse; original company, *Applause*, Palace, NY; understudy, *Music, Music*, City Center, NY; original company, Kristine, "Sing," *A Chorus Line*, Shubert, NY and Los Angeles.

PRINCIPAL TELEVISION APPEARANCES—*Ed Sullivan Specials: The Broadway Years, The Comedy Years; Antoinette Perry Awards Show*, 1970; *How to Survive the 70's; The David Letterman Show; World of Disney*, twenty-fifth anniversary show.

SIDELIGHTS: MEMBERSHIPS—Actors' Equity Association, Screen Actors Guild, American Federation of Television and Radio Artists.

ADDRESS: HOME—Hollywood, CA. AGENT—Honey Sanders Agency, 229 W. 42nd Street, New York, NY 10036.

RENEE BAUGHMAN

BAXLEY, Barbara   1927-

PERSONAL: Born January 1, 1927, in Stockton, CA; daughter of Bert and Emma (Tyler) Baxley; divorced, 1978. EDUCATION: Attended College of the Pacific; prepared for the stage at the Neighborhood Playhouse and the Actors Studio.

VOCATION: Actress.

CAREER: NEW YORK DEBUT—Sibyl Chase, *Private Lives*, Plymouth, 1948. LONDON DEBUT—Natalya, *The Three Sisters*, Aldwych, 1965. PRINCIPAL STAGE APPEARANCES—Peter, *Peter Pan*, Imperial, NY, 1950; Virginia Beamer, *Out West of Eighth*, Ethel Barrymore, NY, 1951; Sally Bowles, *I Am a Camera*, Empire, NY, 1952; Esmeralda, *Camino Real*, National, NY, 1953; Virginia Belden, *The Frogs of Spring*, Broadhurst, NY, 1953; Mildred Turner, *Oh Men! Oh Women!*, Henry Miller, NY, 1954; Goldie, *The Flowering Peach*, Belasco, NY, 1954; Cherie, *Bus Stop*, Music Box, NY, 1955; Beatrice, *Much Ado About Nothing*, Studebaker, Chicago, IL, 1956; Barbara Harris, *A Palm Tree in a Rose Garden*, Cricket, NY, 1957; Isabel Haverstick, *Period of Adjustment*, Helen Hayes, NY, 1960; *Brecht on Brecht*, Theatre de Lys, NY, 1962; Kate, *Taming of the Shrew*, University of Oklahoma, Norman, 1962.

Miss Ritter, *She Loves Me*, Eugene O'Neill, NY, 1963; Natalya, *The Three Sisters*, Morosco, NY, 1964; Celimene, *The Misanthrope*, University of Chicago, IL, 1966; Isabel, *Measure for Measure*, New York Shakespeare Festival, Delacorte, NY, 1966; Dollyheart Talbo, *The Grass Harp*, Trinity Square, Providence, RI, 1966; Portia, *The Merchant of Venice*, American Shakespeare Festival, Stratford, CT, 1967; *Plaza Suite*, Plymouth, NY, 1968; *To Be Young, Gifted, and Black*, Cherry Lane, NY, 1969; Juliet, *Oh, Pioneers*, Theatre de Lys, NY, 1969; Goody Rickby, *The Scare-*

BARBARA BAXLEY

crow, Eisenhower, Washington, DC, 1975; Annie, *Me Jack, You Jill,* John Golden, NY, 1976; Carolyn Parsky, *Best Friend,* Lyceum, NY, 1976; Elaine Thomas, *The Dream,* Forrest, Philadelphia, PA, 1977; Emily Michaelson, *Past Tense,* Hartford Stage, CT, 1977; Lillian Hellman, *Are You Now or Have You Ever Been . . . ?,* Promenade, NY, 1979.

Evy, *Gingerbread Lady* and one woman show, *Spooky Lady,* both at Portland State University, Cannon Beach, OR, 1980; *Spooky Lady,* Syracuse University, NY, Yale University Cabaret, CT, Circle Repertory, NY, Spirit Square, Charlotte, NC, 1981-82; Lillian Cornwall, *Isn't It Romantic,* Phoenix, NY, 1982; Mrs. Warren, *Mrs. Warren's Profession,* Yale Repertory, New Haven, CT, 1982; *Whodunnit?,* Barrymore, NY, 1982-83; Lady Britomart, *Major Barbara,* Yale Repertory, New Haven, CT, 1984; *Harvey,* Berkshire Festival, Stockbridge, MA, 1984; Princess, *Sweet Bird of Youth,* Portland State University, OR, 1984.

MAJOR TOURS—Cora Flood, *The Dark at the Top of the Stairs,* U.S. cities, 1959; Hortense, *Zorba!,* U.S. cities, 1972-73.

PRINCIPAL STAGE WORK—Director, *The Misanthrope,* Carnegie-Mellon University, Pittsburgh, PA, 1985.

TELEVISION DEBUT—1953. PRINCIPAL TELEVISION APPEARANCES—*Danger; Studio One; Philco Playhouse; Alfred Hitchcock Presents; Twilight Zone; Hawaii Five-0; U.S. Steel Hour; Dr. Kildare; Playhouse 90; The Law; Owen Marshall: Counselor at Law; The Defenders; All That Glitters; Hotel,* 1984; contract player, *Search for Tomorrow.*

FILM DEBUT—1954. PRINCIPAL FILM APPEARANCES—*East of Eden,* Warner Brothers, 1955; *The Savage Eye,* 1960; *All Fall Down,* Metro-Goldwyn-Mayer, 1962; *Norma Rae,* Twentieth Century-Fox, 1979; *The Last Resort.*

RELATED CAREER—Visiting professor of acting: Carnegie-Mellon University, Pittsburgh, PA, 1984, Portland State University, OR, 1984.

AWARDS: Philadelphia Drama Critics Award, Best Female Performance, 1960-61; American Television Commercials Festival Award, Best Off-Camera Spokesman, 1964; California Arts Commission Award, Highest Standards of Quality as Performer and Individual, 1979.

SIDELIGHTS: MEMBERSHIPS—Actors' Equity Association, Screen Actors Guild, American Federation of Television and Radio Actors. FAVORITE ROLES—Esmeralda, Peter Pan, Isabel Haverstick, Miss Ritter. RECREATION—Reading.

ADDRESS: HOME—New York, NY. AGENT—c/o Clifford Stevens and David Eidenberg, S.T.E., 888 Seventh Avenue, New York, NY 10019 or 211 S. Beverly Drive, Beverly Hills, CA 90212.

*   *   *

BEALS, Jennifer   1963-

BRIEF ENTRY: Born 1963, in Chicago, IL. Beals worked as a model and has made one television movie, *The Picture of Dorian Grey.* She achieved stardom with her theatrical film debut in *Flashdance,* Paramount, 1983, and then went on to star in *The Bride,* Columbia, 1985, with rock star Sting. She will be seen on cable television as the title character in *Faerietale Theatre*'s production of "Cinderella."*

*   *   *

BEATTY, John Lee   1948-

PERSONAL: Born April 4, 1948, in Palo Alto, CA; son of Shelton Lee and Caroline (Burtis) Beatty. EDUCATION: Brown University, B.A., 1970; Yale School of Drama, B.F.A., 1973.

VOCATION: Scenic designer.

CAREER: PRINCIPAL STAGE WORK—*Baal,* Yale Repertory, New Haven, CT, 1974; *Rebel Women,* 1976, *Ashes,* 1977, *The Woods,* 1979, all at New York Shakespeare Festival; *Catsplay,* 1978, *The Rear Column,* 1978, *Livin' Dolls,* 1982, *The Miss Firecracker Contest,* 1984, all at Manhattan Theater Club. On Broadway: *Knock, Knock,* 1976; *Innocents,* 1976; *The Water Engine,* 1978; *Ain't Misbehavin',* 1978; *Whoopee,* 1979; *Faith Healer,* 1979; *Talley's Folly,* 1980; *Hide and Seek,* 1980; *Fifth of July,* 1981; *Crimes of the Heart,* 1982; *Baby,* 1983; *Alice in Wonderland,* 1983; *Angels Fall,* 1983; and *Ain't Misbehavin',* London, 1979.

Also, work done in the following regional theatres: Goodman, Chicago, IL; Mark Taper Forum, Los Angeles, CA; Seattle Repertory, WA; Indiana Repertory; Arena Stage, Washington, DC; Goodspeed Opera House, CT; Los Angeles Civic Light Opera, CA; Hartford Stage Company, CT; Long Wharf, CT.

PRINCIPAL TELEVISION WORK—*The Mound Builders,* PBS, 1975; *Out of Our Father's House,* PBS, 1979.

RELATED CAREER—Teacher: Brooklyn College, 1979; North Carolina School of the Arts, 1985.

AWARDS: Obie Award, 1975; Antoinette Perry Award and Outer Critics Circle Award, 1980; Drama Desk Award, 1981.

ADDRESS: OFFICE—107 W. 86th Street, New York, NY 10024.

*   *   *

BEDFORD, Brian   1935-

PERSONAL: Born February 16, 1935, in Morley, Yorkshire; son of Arthur and Ellen (O'Donnell) Bedford. EDUCATION: Attended St. Bede's School, Bradford; trained for the stage at the Royal Academy of Dramatic Art.

VOCATION: Actor.

CAREER: STAGE DEBUT—Decius Brutus, *Julius Caesar,* Bradford Civic Theater, 1951. LONDON DEBUT—Travis de Coppet, *The Young and Beautiful,* Arts, 1956. NEW YORK DEBUT—Clive Harrington, *Five Finger Exercise,* Music Box, 1959. PRINCIPAL STAGE APPEARANCES—Liverpool Playhouse Company, 1956; Rodolpho, *A View from the Bridge,* Comedy, London, 1956; a Frenchman, Arviragus, *Cymbeline,* Memorial Theater, Stratford on Avon, 1957; Ariel, *The Tempest,* Memorial, Stratford, then Drury Lane, London, 1957; Clive Harrington, *Five Finger Exercise,* Comedy, London, 1958; David Roddingham, *Write Me a Murder,* Lyric, London, 1962; Derek Pengo, *Lord Pengo,* Royale, NY, 1962; Louis Dubedat, *The Doctor's Dilemma,* Haymarket, London, 1963.

Tchaik, *The Private Ear,* Morosco, NY, then Wimbledon, England, 1963; Tom, *The Knack,* New, London, 1964; James, *The Astrakhan Coat,* General, *The Unknown Soldier and His Wife,* Vivian Beaumont, NY, 1967; Edward Chamberlayne, *The Cocktail Party,* Lyceum, NY, 1968; Hamlet, *Hamlet,* Tusenback, *Three Sisters,* both American Shakespeare Festival, Stratford, CT, 1969; Elyot Chase, *Private Lives,* Billy Rose, NY, 1969; Charles, *Blithe Spirit,* Stranger, *The Tavern,* both Lake Forest, MI, 1970; Arnolphe, *School for Wives,* Lyceum, NY, 1971; General, *The Unknown Soldier and His Wife,* New, London, 1973; George Moore, *Jumpers,* Kennedy Center, Washington, DC, then Billy Rose, NY, 1974; Angelo, *Measure for Measure,* Malvolio, *Twelfth Night,* both Stratford Shakespeare Festival, Canada, 1975; Actor, *The Guardsman,* Ahmanson, Los Angeles, CA, 1976, then Stratford Shakespeare Festival, Canada, 1977; Richard, *Richard III,* Jacques, *As You Like It,* both Stratford Shakespeare Festival, Canada, 1977. Jacques, *As You Like It,* Leontes, *The Winter's Tale,* Astrov, *Uncle Vanya,* Elyot Chase, *Private Lives,* all Stratford Shakespeare Festival, Canada, 1978; Benedick, *Much Ado About Nothing,* Trigorin, *The Seagull,* Malvolio, *Twelfth Night,* all Stratford Shakespeare Festival, Canada, 1980; Alceste, *The Misanthrope,* Charles, *Blithe Spirit,* both Stratford Shakespeare Festival, *Blithe Spirit* then moved to Royal Alexandra Theater, Toronto, Canada, 1981; Isaaac Newton, *The Physicists,* Tartuffe, *Tartuffe,* both Kennedy Center, Washington, DC, 1982; Bluntschli, *Arms and the Man,* Stratford Shakespeare Festival, Canada, 1982; Richard, *Richard II,* Tartuffe, *Tartuffe,* both Stratford Shakespeare Festival, Canada, 1983; Alceste, *The Misanthrope,* Circle in the Square, NY, 1983; Tartuffe, *Tartuffe,* Bottom, *A Midsummer Night's Dream,* Vladimir, *Waiting for Godot,* all Stratford Shakespeare Festival, Canada, 1984; Henry,

The Real Thing, Citadel, Edmonton, Alberta, Canada, 1984.

MAJOR TOURS—Butley, *Butley,* U.S. cities, 1973; Martin Dysart, *Equus,* U.S. cities, 1975; Sidney Bruhl, *Deathtrap,* U.S. and Canadian cities, 1979-80; *Whose Life Is It Anyway,* U.S. and Canadian cities, 1980; Henry, *The Real Thing,* U.S. cities, 1985.

PRINCIPAL STAGE WORK—Director: *Coriolanus, Blithe Spirit,* both Stratford Shakespeare Festival, Canada, 1981; *Tartuffe, The Rivals,* both Stratford Shakespeare Festival, Canada, 1982.

TELEVISION DEBUT—1955. PRINCIPAL TELEVISION APPEARANCES—*Winterset; The Judge and His Hangman; The Secret Thread; Tartuffe,* 1984.

PRINCIPAL FILM APPEARANCES—*Man of the Moment,* 1955; *Miracle in Soho,* 1957; *The Angry Silence,* 1960; *Number Six,* 1961; *The Pad and How to Use It,* Universal, 1966; *Grand Prix,* Metro-Goldwyn-Mayer, 1966.

AWARDS: Antoinette Perry Award, Best Actor, 1971, for *School for Wives.*

SIDELIGHTS: FAVORITE ROLES—Arnolphe, Angelo. RECREATIONS—Living in the country, going to the movies, and eating.

ADDRESS: AGENT—STE Representation, 888 Seventh Avenue, New York, NY 10019.

*   *   *

BELGRADER, Andrei   1946-

PERSONAL: Born March 31, 1946, in Romania; son of Tiberiu (an economist) and Magdalena (a translator; maiden name, Gross) Belgrader; married Dora, 1976 (divorced, 1983). EDUCATION: Romanian Institute of Theatre and Film Arts, M.F.A., 1972. POLITICS: Conservative anarchist.

VOCATION: Director and writer.

CAREER: FIRST STAGE WORK—Director and writer, *Rhythms,* Performing Arts Center, Romania. FIRST NEW YORK STAGE WORK—Director, *Woyzeck,* Changing Space, 1978. PRINCIPAL STAGE WORK—Director: *As You Like It,* 1979, *Ubu Rex,* 1980, *About Face,* 1983, *What the Butler Saw,* 1985, all at Yale Repertory, New Haven, CT; *As You Like It,* 1981, *Waiting for Godot,* 1983, *Measure for Measure,* 1984, all at American Repertory, Cambridge, MA; *Troilus and Cresida,* Changing Space, NY.

PRINCIPAL TELEVISION WORK—Director: *Variety Show,* Romanian State Television, 1975; *Playboy of the Western World,* Romanian State Television, 1976; also works by Albert Camus, Oscar Wilde, Eugene Ionesco, Franz Kafka, S. Mrozeck, Moliere, Shakespeare, Chekhov, etc.

RELATED CAREER— Teacher: Bucharest Center for the Performing Arts, Romania, 1967-72; Yale School of Drama, 1979-present.

WRITINGS: PLAYS, PRODUCED—*Rhythms,* International Festival Theater, Wroclaw, Poland, 1968; *The Little Prince,* State Theatre of Consantsa, 1973. MUSICAL PLAYS—*The Gomorrah Post Cantata* (with Keith Reddin).

ANDREI BELGRADER

AWARDS: Constantza Festival Award, 1973, for *The Little Prince;* Boston Theatre Critics Circle Award, Best Director, Best Play, 1983, for *Waiting for Godot.*

SIDELIGHTS: MEMBERSHIPS—Society for Stage Directors and Choreographers.

ADDRESS: HOME—84 Charles Street, New York, NY 10014. OFFICE—c/o Yale School of Drama, New Haven, CT.

*   *   *

BELKNAP, Allen R.   1941-

PERSONAL: Born November 25, 1941, in New York City; son of Ellsworth (a stock manager) and Deane (a teacher) Belknap. EDUCATION: University of Pennsylvania, B.A., 1963; Carnegie-Mellon University, M.F.A., 1965.

VOCATION: Director and teacher.

CAREER: PRINCIPAL STAGE WORK—Director: *Electra; The Guardsman; On Borrowed Time; Beowulf; The Art Lovers; Anele; A Phoenix Too Frequent; A Sleep of Prisoners; Brechon-Brecht; Tango; The Bacchae; The Days Between; Under Milkwood; A Musical Timepiece; Brand; Arms and the Man; Peer Gynt; Room, Collection, Slight Ache; Dial M' for Murder; The Rose Tattoo; The Hostage; The Way of the World; Two for the Seesaw; A Streetcar Named Desire; The Little Foxes; Look Back in Anger; Picnic; After the Fall; Private Ear/Public Eye; A Taste of Honey; Barefoot in the Park; Who's Afraid of Virginia Woolf?; The Imaginary Invalid; My Fair Lady; Richard III; Threepenny Opera,* all 1965-72.

Pop, Players Theatre, NY, 1974; at the Direct Theatre, NY: *The Devils, Gilgamesh,* both 1975, *Columbus, Nature and Purpose of the Universe,* both 1976, *Lulu, Earth Spirit and Pandora's Box,* both 1977, *The Beasts, Modigliani,* both 1978; *Approaching Zero,* La MaMa, 1978; *Nature and Purpose of the Universe, Jaywalkin',* both at Direct Theater, NY, 1979; *Modigliani,* Astor Place, NY, 1979; *The Interview,* Direct, NY, 1980; *Blau and Pignoli,* Perry Street Theater, NY, 1980; *Beginner's Luck,* Tiffany's Attic, Kansas City, MO, 1981; *Almost an Eagle,* American Stage Festival, 1981; *Last of the Red Hot Lovers,* Tiffany's Attic, Kansas City, MO, 1982; *South Pacific,* Fredericksburg Theater Company, 1982.

Princess Grace, Wisdoms Bridge, Chicago, IL, 1982; *Blood Moon,* Production Company, NY, 1983; *Comedy of Errors,* Fort Worth Shakespeare Festival, TX, 1983; *The Taming of the Shrew,* Alabama Shakespeare Festival, 1983; *Without Apologies,* Pittsburgh Playhouse, 1983; *Blood Moon,* Actors and Directors, NY, 1983; *The Killing of Sister George,* Roundabout, NY, 1983; *School for Scandal,* Folger, Washington, DC, 1984; *The Flight of the Earls,* Westside Arts, NY, 1984; *They're Playing Our Song,* Toho Productions, Tokyo, Japan, 1984; *Philco Blues,* NY, 1984.

RELATED CAREER—Instructor, University of Washington, Seattle, 1965-68; associate professor, Hunter College, NY, 1968-74; founder and artistic director, Direct Theater, NY, 1974-80.

AWARDS: National Endowment Directing Award, 1984-85.

SIDELIGHTS: MEMBERSHIPS—Society of Stage Directors and Choreographers.

ADDRESS: HOME AND OFFICE—115 W. 77th Street, New York, NY 10024. AGENT—c/o Hesseltine-Baker, 165 W. 46th Street, New York, NY 10024.

*   *   *

BELUSHI, Jim

BRIEF ENTRY: Graduated Southern Illinois University. Actor and comedian. Belushi toured with the *Second City* troupe. His television credits include *Who's Watching the Kids,* NBC, 1978; *Working Stiffs,* CBS, 1979; *Saturday Night Live,* NBC, 1983-present. Stage appearances include *Baal in the Twenty-First Century,* at the Goodman, Chicago, 1980, and he portrayed the Pirate King at the Uris Theatre in *Pirates of Penzance,* 1982. Belushi has been featured in the films *Trading Places,* Paramount, 1983; *The Man with One Red Show,* Twentieth Century-Fox, 1985; and the upcoming *Salvador.*

ADDRESS: OFFICE—NBC, 30 Rockefeller Plaza, New York, NY 10020.*

*   *   *

BENNETT-GORDON, Eve

PERSONAL: Born Eve Gordon; daughter of Richard Bennett (a lawyer) and Mary (a historian; maiden name, McDougall) Gordon. EDUCATION: Brown University, B.A., 1978; Yale University, M.F.A., 1981; trained for the stage at the Yale School of Drama.

VOCATION: Actress and singer.

CAREER: STAGE DEBUT—*The Magnificent Cuckhold,* Yale Repertory, New Haven, CT, 1981, for 30 performances. NEW YORK DEBUT—Sophie Barger, *Baal,* Kozo, 1982, for fifteen performances. PRINCIPAL STAGE APPEARANCES—Lillian Holliday, *Happy End,* Yale; Charlene Loody, *Palace of Amateurs;* Marie, *The Workroom,* Longwharf, New Haven, CT, 1982; Melissa, *Herself as Lust,* Playwrights Horizons, NY, 1982; Bonnie, *What I Did Last Summer,* Cape Playhouse, 1982; Dixie Evans, *The Big Knife,* Berkshire Theatre Festival, NY, 1983; JoJo, *Doonesbury,* NY, 1983; *Hang on to Me,* Guthrie, Minneapolis, MN, 1984; Cunegonde, *Candide,* Goodman, Chicago, IL, 1984.

FILM DEBUT—Marge Tallworth, *The World According to Garp,* Warner Brothers, 1982. PRINCIPAL FILM APPEARANCES—Rita, *Dear Mr. Wonderful,* Vonvietinghoff Productions, 1982.

TELEVISION DEBUT—Judith Hastings, *Gemini,* Showtime, 1982.

SIDELIGHTS: FAVORITE ROLES—Lillian Holliday, *Happy End;* Dixie Evans, *The Big Knife;* Charlene Loody, *Palace of Amateurs;* Cunegonde, *Candide.*

ADDRESS: AGENT—Richard Schmenner, STE Representation, 888 Seventh Avenue, New York, NY 10019.

*   *   *

BERGER, Keith   1952-

PERSONAL: Born September 18, 1952, in Los Angeles, CA; son of Raymond M. (a playwright) and Frances R. (a psychologist; maiden name, Lucow) Berger. EDUCATION: American Academy of Dramatic Arts, NY, for two years; American Mime Theatre, for four years; trained for mime with Paul Curtis. RELIGION: Jewish.

VOCATION: Actor, director, writer, and mime performer and director.

CAREER: STAGE DEBUT—Silent actor, *The Advent,* Radio City West, Los Angeles. NEW YORK DEBUT—Rooty Kazooty, *Broken Toys,* Orpheum and Actors Playhouse, 1982. PRINCIPAL STAGE APPEARANCES—Solo mime, Palais D'Europe for Princess Grace, Monaco; solo mime, President Carter's inauguration.

MAJOR TOURS—Ten years of touring U.S. and Europe colleges and festivals performing solo mime.

FILM DEBUT—*Keith,* Billy Budd Films. FILM APPEARANCES—*Angels,* 1974; *Crossover,* Mambro Productions, 1984.

TELEVISION DEBUT—Mime, *Funny Faces/Red Skelton,* HBO, 1981.

WRITINGS: PLAYS, PRODUCED—*Dog and Pony Show,* Oberlin College; *Interuptions,* Silent Theatre; *Visitor from Space,* Silent Theatre; *Broken Toys,* Actors Playhouse, Orpheum, NY, 1982.

AWARDS: Joseph Papp Street Performer Award.

SIDELIGHTS: MEMBERSHIPS—Actors' Equity Association, American Federation of Television and Radio Artists, Screen Actors Guild, Oberlin Mime Company (director).

ADDRESS: OFFICE—579 Broadway, Third Floor N., New York, NY 10013. AGENT—Esther Eagels Associates, 305 E. 24th Street, New York, NY 10010.

*   *   *

BERK, Tony

PERSONAL: Born January 21, in Indianapolis, IN; son of Bernard Leo (a doctor of pharmacy) and Rosalind L. (a dancer; maiden name, Miceli) Berk. EDUCATION: Florida State University, B.A., theatre.

VOCATION: Director and stage manager.

CAREER: Directed Off-Broadway and stage managed for Broadway productions, industrial shows, Off-Broadway, and at Radio City Music Hall in NY.

SIDELIGHTS: MEMBERSHIPS—Actors' Equity Association, Society of Stage Directors and Choreographers, American Guild of Variety Artists, Stage Managers Association.

ADDRESS. HOME—360 W. 55th Street, New York, NY 10019.

*   *   *

BERNHARDT, Melvin

PERSONAL: Born Melvin Bernhard, February 26, in Buffalo, NY; son of Max and Kate (Benatovich) Bernhard. EDUCATION: University of Buffalo, B.A.; Yale University, M.F.A.

VOCATION: Director.

CAREER: PRINCIPAL STAGE WORK—Director: *Conerico Was Here to Stay,* Cherry Lane, NY, 1965; *Eh?,* Playhouse in the Park, Cincinnati, OH, 1966; *Father Uxbridge Wants to Marry, A View from the Bridge,* both at Hartford Stage Company, CT, 1967; *The Loves of Don Perlimplin and Belissa,* National Theater of the Deaf Repertory, 1968; *Honor and Offer,* Cincinnati, OH, 1968; *The Homecoming,* Hartford, CT, 1969; *Cop Out,* NY, 1969; *The Effect of Gamma Rays on Man-in-the-Moon Marigolds,* NY, 1970; *Early Morning,* La MaMa ETC, NY, 1970; *And Miss Reardon Drinks a Little,* NY, 1971; *The Effect of Gamma Rays on Man-in-the-Moon Marigolds,* Hampstead Theatre Club, London, 1972; *Echoes,* NY, 1973; *Other Voices, Other Rooms,* Buffalo Studio Arena, NY, 1973.

The Killdeer, Public, NY, 1974; *Children,* Manhattan Theater Club, NY, 1976; *The Middle Ages,* Hartman, Stamford, CT, 1978; *Da,* NY, 1978; *Hide and Seek,* NY, 1980; *Crimes of the Heart,* Manhattan Theatre Club then Broadway, NY, 1980-81; *Is There Life After High School?,* Hartford, CT, 1981; *Bedrock,* Hartman, Stamford, CT, 1983; *Dancing in the Endzone,* Ritz, NY, 1985.

MAJOR TOURS—Director: *Muzeeka, Who's Happy Now?,* U.S.

Photography by Jill Krementz

MELVIN BERNHARDT

cities, 1967; *Da,* U.S. cities, 1979; *What I Did Last Summer,* U.S. cities, 1982.

PRINCIPAL TELEVISION WORK—Director: *Another World,* NBC, 1974-80; *Mister Roberts,* NBC, 1984; *One Life to Live,* ABC, 1985.

AWARDS: Obie, 1970, for *The Effect of Gamma Rays on Man-in-the-Moon Marigolds;* Obie, 1976, for *Children;* Antoinette Perry Award and Drama Desk, 1978, for *Da;* Obie, 1980, for *Crimes of the Heart;* two Emmy Award nominations, for *Another World.*

ADDRESS: AGENT—c/o Steven C. Durham, 123 W. 74th Street, New York, NY 10023.

*   *   *

BEROZA, Janet

PERSONAL: Born in Muskegon, MI; married Renaud de Damcourt (a director and writer). EDUCATION: Michigan State University, M.F.A.

VOCATION: Production stage manager, designer, and properties.

CAREER: PRINCIPAL STAGE WORK—Property master, *Agamemnon,* McCarter, Princeton, NJ; assistant designer, *Babes in Arms,* Equity Library, NY; supervising stage manager, *Annie,* Victoria Palace, London, England, 1978; *La Cage Aux Folles,* Los Angeles.

MAJOR TOURS—Stage manager: *Annie,* Los Angeles, London, West coast; *Good; All's Well That Ends Well; Bette! Divine Madness; Peter Allen, Up in One; Bette Midler's Tour for the New Depression.*

PRINCIPAL FILM WORK—Stage manager, *Divine Madness,* Ladd Company, 1980.

SIDELIGHTS: MEMBERSHIPS—Actors' Equity Association, Dramatists Guild of America.

ADDRESS: HOME—600 West End Avenue, New York, NY 10024.

*   *   *

BERRY, David   1943-

PERSONAL: Full name David Adams Berry; born July 8, 1943, in Denver, CO; son of Richard Lambert (a chemist) and Mary Elizabeth (a real estate broker; maiden name, Adams) Berry; married Robin Graham, May 1, 1971 (divorced 1980); children: (step-daughter) Julia Lee Barclay. EDUCATION: Wesleyan University, B.A., history and theatre, 1968; Harvard University Business School, certificate, 1972. POLITICS: Independent. MILITARY: U.S. Army, 1968-69.

VOCATION: Playwright and teacher.

CAREER: Intern (stage manager, house manager, and actor), O'Neill Theatre Center, National Playwrights Conference, 1968; assistant director, O'Neill Theatre Center, 1971-74; playwright in residence, Assumption College, Worcester Polytechnic Institute, MA, 1977-78; theatre specialist, Rhode Island State Council on the Arts, 1975-76; playwriting instructor, National Theatre Institute, 1980-83.

WRITINGS: PLAYS, PRODUCED—*G.R. Point,* National Playwrights Conference, O'Neill Center, CT, 1976, Phoenix Theatre, NY, 1977, Center Stage, Baltimore, MD, 1979, Playhouse, NY, 1979, Chicago, 1979, Los Angeles, 1981, published 1981; *The Whales of August,* Center Stage, Baltimore, MD, 1980, Trinty Square Repertory, Providence, RI, 1981, WPA, NY, 1982, Victory Gardens, Chicago, 1983, published 1984, screenplay, 1984; *Tracers,* NY Shakespeare Festival, Public, 1985.

AWARDS: Obie Award, Distinguished Playwriting, 1977, for *G.R. Point;* Drama Desk Award nomination, Best New American Play, 1977, for *G.R. Point;* Creative Writing Fellowship, National Endowment for the Arts, 1978.

SIDELIGHTS: MEMBERSHIPS—Dramatists Guild, Vietnam Veterans of America.

Berry told *CTFT:* "My enduring passion is for exploring the entire matrix of the Vietnam war in American consciousness and experience in order to learn its lessons."

ADDRESS: AGENT—Luis Sanjurjo, International Creative Management, 40 W. 57th Street, New York, NY 10019.

*   *   *

BESSETTE, Denise   1954-

PERSONAL: Born August 25, 1954, in Midland, MI; daughter of A. Raymond (chairman, chemical corporation) and Doris Anne (Brodeur) Bessette; married Paul John Schneeberger (a stage manager

DENISE BESSETTE

and director), September 4, 1982. EDUCATION: Marymount, Tarrytown, NY, for two years, then Marymount, Manhattan, NY, B.A., theatre, 1976; studied for the theatre at Central School in London for one session, Royal Academy of Dramatic Art, London, for one year and with William Esper in NY for two years.

VOCATION: Actress.

CAREER: NEW YORK DEBUT—Little Miss, *La Ronde,* Spectrum, for 18 performances. LONDON DEBUT—Adela, *House of Bernarda Alba,* Royal Academy of Dramatic Art, 1975. PRINCIPAL STAGE APPEARANCES—Margery Pinchwife, *The Country Wife,* Royal Academy of Dramatic Art, London; Louise, *The Runner Stumbles,* Nancy, *Angel Street,* both at Cohoes Music Hall, Cohoes, NY, 1978; Amy, *Charley's Aunt,* Meadowbrook Theatre, MI; Juliet, *Romeo and Juliet,* Dorine, *Tartuffe,* Hermia, *A Midsummer Night's Dream,* Cecily, *The Importance of Being Earnest,* Cecily, *Travesties,* all at New Jersey Shakespeare Festival, Madison, NJ, 1980; Amy, *The Show-off,* Hermia, *A Midsummer Night's Dream,* both for Asolo State Theatre, Sarasota, Florida; Muriel, *Ah! Wilderness,* GeVa, Rochester, NY; Lady Anne, *Richard III,* American Shakespeare Theatre, Stratford, CT and Kennedy Center, Washington, DC; Actress Number Three, *The Dining Room,* Huntington, Boston, MA, 1982; Grazielle, *At 50, She Discovered the Sea,* Delilah, *The War Brides,* both for New Play Festival, Peoples Light and Theatre Co., Malvern, PA; Helen Keller, *Monday After the Miracle,* Playhouse in the Park, Cincinnati, OH, 1984.

Ellen Terry, *Freshwater,* Gene Frankel Theatre, NY; Natasha, *War and Peace,* Symphony Space, then New School for Social Research, and at the United Nations, all NY; Lady Agatha, *The Admirable Crichton,* Spectrum, NY; Nantelle, *Glory Hallelujah!,* Vandamm, NY; Ruthie, *The Desk Set,* Equity Library, NY; Ensemble, *The Tattler,* New Dramatists, NY; Jan, *The Art of Self-Defense,* Manhattan Punch Line One-Acts, NY.

FILM DEBUT—Sylvia Matera, *And Then You Die,* Louis and Clark Productions.

AWARDS: New Jersey Drama Critics Award, Best Supporting Actress, 1980, for Hermia, *A Midsummer Nights's Dream* and Cecily, *The Importance of Being Earnest.*

SIDELIGHTS: MEMBERSHIPS—Actors' Equity Association, Screen Actors Guild, Writers' Theatre, NY; former volunteer, "Under-21" home for runaways, NY. RECREATION—Piano, sewing, jogging, enjoys the country and being with her husband and family.

In her reply to *CTFT,* Bessette indicated that she has traveled extensively in the U.S. and Europe and is "very concerned about world peace and the condition of the world into which we are introducing the next generation."

ADDRESS: AGENT—Marje Fields, Inc., 165 W. 46th Street, New York, NY 10036.

*   *   *

BINUS, Judith   1944-

PERSONAL: Surname pronounced *Bi*-nus; born August 30, 1944, in Louisville, KY; daughter of Rudolph and Emily (Leibson) Binus. EDUCATION: Indiana University, B.S., education, 1966; New York University School of the Arts, 1967-69.

VOCATION: Stage manager and lighting designer.

CAREER: PRINCIPAL STAGE WORK—Stage manager: Joffrey Ballet, City Center, NY, 1969; Joffrey II Company, 1970; Niagara Frontier Ballet, Buffalo, NY, 1970; *What the Butler Saw,* Academy Festival Theatre, Lake Forest, IL, 1971; *Nutcracker,* Arie Crown, Chicago, IL, 1971-72; *The Boys from Syracuse,* Goodman, Chicago, IL, 1972; *Moonchildren,* Academy Playhouse, Lake Forest, IL, 1972; *Gallows Humor,* Academy Playhouse, Lake Forest, IL, 1973; Dallas Civic Opera, TX, 1975 season; *The Dybbuk,* Pearl Lang Dance Company, 92nd Street YMHA, NY, 1976; *Herzl,* Palace, NY, 1976; *Showboat,* Miami Beach and Parker Playhouse, FL, 1977; *Toller Cranston's Ice Show,* Palace, NY, 1977; *Hello, Dolly!,* Lunt-Fontanne, NY, 1977-78; *A Broadway Musical,* Riverside Church and Lunt-Fontanne, NY, 1978; *Children of a Lesser God,* Longacre, 1980-82; *Whodunnit,* Biltmore, 1982-83; Siobhan McKenna and the Chieftains, Felt Forum, NY, 1983.

MAJOR TOURS—Stage manager: *Don't Bother Me I Can't Cope,* 1975; *Ben Franklin, Citzen,* 1976; *West Side Story,* Bus & Truck, 1976; *Hello, Dolly!,* National Company, 1977-78; *Annie,* First National Company, 1979-80; *Children of a Lesser God,* Spoleto, Italy, 1982.

LIGHTING DESIGN—Served as assistant to Tom Skelton, Ken Billington, John Gleason, and David Segal on such shows as *Bad Habits, The Skin of Our Teeth, The King and I, A Streetcar Named Desire,* and *Lorelei,* and at the American Shakespeare Festival and New Phoenix Repertory Company.

Principal designer: *The Lower Depths,* Equity Library Theatre, 1969; Joffrey II Company, 1970; Niagara Frontier Ballet, Buffalo, NY, 1970; *Borstal Boy,* Academy Playhouse, Lake Forest, IL, 1971.

SIDELIGHTS: MEMBERSHIPS—Actors' Equity Association, United Scenic Artists, Local 829.

ADDRESS: HOME—New York, NY.

*   *   *

BISSET, Jacqueline   1946-

PERSONAL: Born September 13, 1946, in Weybridge, England. EDUCATION: Attended French Lycee, London.

VOCATION: Actress.

CAREER: FILM DEBUT—A girl, *The Knack,* United Artists, 1965. PRINCIPAL FILM APPEARANCES—*Cul De Sac,* Sigma III, 1966; *Two for the Road,* Twentieth Century-Fox, 1967; *Casino Royale,* Columbia, 1967; *The Detective,* Twentieth Century-Fox, 1968; *Bullitt,* Warner Brothers-Seven Arts, 1968; *The Sweet Ride,* Twentieth Century-Fox, 1968; *The First Time,* United Artists, 1969; *Airport,* Universal, 1970; *The Grasshopper,* National General, 1970; *The Mephisto Waltz,* Twentieth Century-Fox, 1971; *Believe in Me,* Metro-Goldwyn-Mayer, 1971; *Secrets,* 1971 (rereleased, 1978); *The Life and Times of Judge Roy Bean,* National General, 1972; *Stand Up and Be Counted,* Columbia, 1972; *The Thief Who Came to Dinner,* Warner Brothers, 1972; *Day for Night,* Warner Brothers, 1973; *Murder on the Orient Express,* Paramount, 1974; *The Spiral Staircase,* 1975; *End of the Game,* Twentieth Century-Fox, 1976; *St. Ives,* Warner Brothers, 1976; *Sunday Woman,* Twentieth Century-Fox, 1976; *The Deep,* Columbia, 1977; *Le Magnifique; The Greek Tycoon,* Universal, 1978; *Who Is Killing the Great Chefs of Europe?,* Warner Brothers, 1978; *When Time Ran Out,* Warner Brothers, 1980; *Rich and Famous,* 1981; *Inchon,* 1982; *Class,* Orion, 1983; *Under the Volcano,* Universal, 1984; *Forbidden* (upcoming).

PRINCIPAL TELEVISION APPEARANCE—*Anna Karenina,* CBS, 1985.

ADDRESS: AGENT—International Creative Management, 8899 Beverly Blvd., Los Angeles, CA 90048.*

*   *   *

BLACK, Dorothy   1913-85

PERSONAL: Born April 30, 1913, in Johannesburg, South Africa; died February 19, 1985, in London, England; daughter of Francis and Elizabeth Johanna (Albertyn) Black. EDUCATION: Roedean, Johannesburg, St. Albans, and Paris.

VOCATION: Writer and actress.

CAREER: PRINCIPAL STAGE APPEARANCES—Toured with a Shakespearean repertory company.

WRITINGS: PLAYS, PRODUCED—*The Prince of Bohemia* (adapted from Robert Louis Stevenson's story "The Suicide Club"), 1941; *Landslide* (with David Peel), 1943; *Men without Shadows,* 1947;

The Respectable Prostitute (adapted from Jean-Paul Sartre), 1947; *Crime Passionel* (adapted from Sartre), 1948; *Point of Departure* (adapted from Jean Anouilh), 1950; *The Untamed* (adapted from Anouilh), 1951; *Lucifer and the Lord* (adapted from Sartre), 1952; *The Public Prosecutor* (adapted from Fritz Hochwalder), 1953; *The Snow Was Black* (adapted from Simenon), 1953; *Kean* (adapted from Sartre), 1954; *Three Sisters* (with Micki Iveria), 1955; *Donadiu* (adapted from Hochwalder), 1956; *Wings of the Wind* (adapted from Alexander Rivemale), 1957; *The Innocent Man* (adapted from Hochwalder), 1958.

Love from Italy (adapted from Louis Ducreux), 1960; *The Rehearsal* (adapted from Jean Anouilh; with Pamela Hansford Johnson), 1961; *Bonne Soupe* (adapted from Felicien Marceau), 1961; *The Singing Dolphin* (original idea), 1963; *Isabelle* (adapted from Jacques Deval), 1964; *Maxibules* (adapted from Marcel Ayme), 1964; *The Soldier's Tale* (with Michael Flanders), 1970; *Sword of Vengeance* (adapted from Hochwalder), 1975; *Riding to Jerusalem* (adapted from Evelyn Coquet), 1978.*

*   *   *

BLACK, Noel   1937-

PERSONAL: Born June 30, 1937, in Chicago, IL; son of Samuel A. and Susan (Quan) Black; married Sandra MacPhail, December 2, 1967; children: Marco, Nicole. EDUCATION: Attended University of Chicago, 1954-1957; University of California, Los Angeles, B.A., 1959, M.A. 1964.

NOEL BLACK

VOCATION: Director, producer, and writer.

CAREER: PRINCIPAL FILM WORK—Writer and director, *Skater-dater*, United Artists; director and co-producer, *Pretty Poison*, Twentieth Century-Fox, 1968; director, *A Man, a Woman and a Bank*, Avco Embassy, 1979; director, *Heart and Soul*, 1985.

PRINCIPAL TELEVISION WORK—Writer and director, *Trilogy: The American Boy*, ABC; director for all of the following: "I'm a Fool," *American Short Story*, PBS; *Mulligan's Stew* (pilot), NBC, 1977; "The Golden Honeymoon," *American Short Story*, PBS; *The Electric Grandmother*, NBC; *The Other Victim*, CBS, 1981; *Prime Suspect*, CBS, 1981; *Happy Endings*, CBS, 1982; *Quarterback Princess*, CBS, 1983.

AWARDS: Grand Prix Short Subjects, Cannes XX Film Festival; Silver Medal, Moscow V Film Festival; Waterford Glass Award, Cork XI International Film Festival; Lion of St. Mark Award, Venice XVIII International Film Festival.

SIDELIGHTS: MEMBERSHIPS—Academy of Motion Picture Arts and Sciences, Directors Guild of America, Academy of Television Arts and Sciences, Writers Guild of America.

ADDRESS: OFFICE—Twentieth Century-Fox, 1201 W. Pico Blvd., Los Angeles, CA 90035. AGENT—Tom Chasin, International Creative Management, 8899 Beverly Blvd., Los Angeles, CA 90048.

*   *   *

ROBERT BLOCH

BLAIR, Pamela   1949-

PERSONAL: Born December 5, 1949, in Bennington, VT; daughter of Edgar Joseph and Geraldine Marie (Cummings) Blair; married Donald Scardino (an actor and director), September 14, 1984. EDUCATION: Presently studying at Morris County College; studied acting with Uta Hagen.

VOCATION: Actress.

CAREER: DEBUT—Dancer, *Promises, Promises*, Shubert, NY, 1968. PRINCIPAL STAGE APPEARANCES—Standby for lead, *Sugar*, Brooks Atkinson, NY, 1972; Curley's Wife, *Of Mice and Men*, Brooks Atkinson, NY, 1974; Val, *A Chorus Line*, New York Shakespeare Festival, then Shubert, NY, 1975; Amber, *The Best Little Whorehouse in Texas*, 46th Street, NY, 1978.

MAJOR TOURS—Jeunefille, *King of Hearts*, Boston, MA, Minskoff, NY, 1978.

TELEVISION DEBUT—Rita Mae Bristow, *Loving*, ABC, 1983. PRINCIPAL TELEVISION APPEARANCES—Trish, *Svengali*, CBS, 1983.

SIDELIGHTS: Blair tells *CTFT* that she "owns two standard mares which I am training in jumping and dressage."

ADDRESS: AGENT—Bret Adams, Ltd., 448 W. 44th Street, New York, NY 10036.

BLOCH, Robert   1917-

PERSONAL: Born April 5, 1917, in Chicago, IL; son of Raphael A. (a bank cashier) and Stella (a social worker; maiden name, Loeb) Bloch; married Marion Holcombe, October 2, 1940 (divorced, 1963); married Eleanor Alexander (a cosmetic representative), October 2, 1964; children: (first marriage) Sally Ann. EDUCATION: Graduated from Lincoln High School, Milwaukee, WI, 1934.

VOCATION: Writer.

WRITINGS: SCREENPLAYS—*The Couch*, Warner Brothers, 1962; *The Cabinet of Caligari*, Twentieth Century-Fox, 1962; *Strait-Jacket*, Columbia, 1964; *The Night Walker*, Universal, 1965; *The Psychopath*, Paramount, 1966; *The Deadly Bees* (with Anthony Marriot), Paramount, 1967; *Torture Garden*, Columbia, 1968; *The House That Dripped Blood*, Cinerama, 1971; *Asylum*, Cinerama, 1972.

TELEVISION—Movies: *The Cat Creature*, 1973; *The Dead Don't Lie*, 1975. Episodic: *Thriller*; *The Alfred Hitchcock Show*; *Star Trek*.

BOOKS—*The Opener of the Way; The Scarf; Spiderweb; The Will to Kill; The Kidnapper; Shooting Star; Terror in the Night; Psycho; The Dead Beat; Pleasant Dreams; Blood Runs Cold; Firebug; Nightmares; Terror; The Couch; Atoms and Evil; Yours Truly, Jack the Ripper; More Nightmares; The Eighth Stage of Fandom; Horror-7; Bogey Men; Tales in a Jugular Vein; The Skull of the Marquis de Sade; 15 Grusel Stories; The House of the Hatchet; Chamber of Horrors; The Living Demons; The Todd Dossier* (as Collier Young); *The Star Stalker; Ladies Day/Crowded Earth; Dragons and Nightmares; Bloch and Bradbury* (with Ray Bradbury); *Fear Today, Gone Tomorrow; Sneak Preview; It's All in Your*

Mind; Nightworld; Contes de Terreur; American Gothic; Cold Chills; The King of Terrors; The Best of Robert Bloch; Out of the Mouths of Graves; Strange Eons; Such Stuff as Screams Are Made Of; There Is a Serpent in Eden; La Boite a Malefices de Robert Bloch; Mysteries of the Worm; Psycho II; Twilight Zone, the Movie; The Night of the Ripper.

SHORT STORIES—Over four hundred short stories and articles.

AWARDS: World Science Fiction Convention Award, Best Short Story, 1958, for *The Hellbound Train;* E.E. Evans Memorial Award, 1958; Mystery Writers of America Edgar Allan Poe Special Scroll and Screen Writers Award for Writing Achievement, 1960, for *Psycho;* Third Festival di Fanta-Scienza, Trieste, 1964; Inkpot Award for Science Fiction, San Diego, 1964; Los Angeles Science Fantasy Society Award, Service to the Field of Science Fantasy, 1974; World Science Fantasy Convention Lifetime Career Award, 1975; Fritz Leiber Fantasy Award, 1978; Le Prix du Boucher de Cristal, Reims Festival du Roman et Film Policier, 1979; 50 Year Career Award, Fantasy Festival, 1984; World Science Fiction Convention Award, 1984.

SIDELIGHTS: MEMBERSHIPS—Academy of Motion Picture Arts and Sciences, Writers Guild of America West, Mystery Writers of America, Science Fiction Writers of America.

ADDRESS: AGENT—c/o Shapiro-Lichtman Talent Agency, 8827 Beverly Blvd., Los Angeles, CA 90048.

*   *   *

BLOCK, Larry   1942-

PERSONAL: Born October 30, 1942, in New York City; son of Harold (in the garment industry) and Sonia (a travel agent; maiden name, Kutcher) Block; married Jolly King (an actress), September 25, 1981; children: Zoe Lenna. EDUCATION: University of Rhode Island, B.A., English, 1964; studied for the theatre with Wynn Handman. POLITICS: Liberal Democrat. RELIGION: Ethical Culture. MILITARY: U.S. Army, Special Services, 1967-1969.

VOCATION: Actor.

CAREER: THEATRE DEBUT—Mercutio's page, *Romeo and Juliet,* American Shakespeare Festival, Stratford, CT, for eighty performances. NEW YORK DEBUT—Understudy (matinee performances) Malcom Scrawdyke, *Hail, Scrawdyke,* Booth, 1966. PRINCIPAL STAGE APPEARANCES—Roles in *Coriolanus, King Lear,* and *The Taming of the Shrew,* American Shakespeare Festival, Stratford, CT, 1965; the Boy, *La Turista,* American Place March, 1967; *Harry, Noon and Night* and *The Recruiting Officer,* Theatre of the Living Arts, Philadelphia, 1970; *Fingernails Blue as Flowers,* American Place, NY, 1972; Lucky, *Waiting for Godot,* St. Clements, NY, 1974; Dromio, *The Comedy of Errors,* New York Shakespeare Festival, 1975; *Where Do We Go from Here,* New York Shakespeare Festival, 1975; *The Last Days of British Honduras,* New York Shakespeare Festival, 1976.

Manny Alter, *Coming Attractions,* Playwrights Horizons, NY, 1980; Sir Toby Belch, *Twelfth Night,* Shakespeare and Co., Lee, MA, 1981; Leon, *The Workroom (L'Atelier),* Center Stage, Balti-

more, 1981; Godshill, *Henry IV, Part I,* New York Shakespeare Festival, 1981; Martin Borman, *The Fuhrer Bunker,* American Place, NY, 1981; *Manhattan Love Songs,* Actor's Studio, NY, 1982; *A Tantalizing* and Benny Silverman, *The Value of Names,* Actors Theatre of Louisville, KY, 1983; *Souvenirs,* Cubiculo, NY, 1984; *The Value of Names,* Hartford Stage Company, CT, 1984; *The Golem,* New York Shakespeare Festival, 1984; Sir Toby Belch, *Twelfth Night* and Mr. Fezziwig, *A Christmas Carol,* Guthrie, Minneapolis, 1984.

PRINCIPAL FILM APPEARANCES—Springy, *Shamus,* Columbia, 1973; referee, *Slap Shot,* Universal, 1977; Ted Peters, *Heaven Can Wait,* Paramount, 1978; Detective Anson, *Hardcore,* Columbia, 1979; Buddy, *After Hours,* 1985.

PRINCIPAL TELEVISION APPEARANCES—Cal Jamison, *General Hospital;* Mickey Potter, *Secret Storm;* Tom, *Sesame Street;* *M*A*S*H; Barney Miller; Charlie's Angels; The Lingbergh Kidnapping Case; Chips; Kojak; Baretta; Police Story; Ellery Queen; Rosetti and Ryan; Space Force,* others.

PRINCIPAL RADIO APPEARANCES—David Mamet's *Prairie du Chien,* Earplay, National Public Radio; "Pilot," *National Public Radio Playhouse; Under the Gun,* WBAI.

ADDRESS: HOME—484 W. 43rd Street, New York, NY 10036. AGENT—The Gage Group, 1650 Broadway, New York, NY 10019.

*   *   *

BOCHNER, Hart   1956-

VOCATION: Actor.

PERSONAL: Born December 3, 1956, in Toronto, Canada; son of Lloyd (an actor) Bochner. EDUCATION: University of California at San Diego, B.A.

HART BOCHNER

CAREER: FILM DEBUT—*Islands in the Stream*, Paramount, 1975. PRINCIPAL FILM APPEARANCES—*Breaking Away*, Twentieth Century-Fox, 1978; *Terror Train*, Twentieth Century-Fox, 1979; *Rich and Famous*, Metro-Goldwyn-Mayer, 1980; *Supergirl*, Tri-Star, 1984; *Wild Life*, Universal, 1984.

TELEVISION DEBUT—*Haywire*, Warner Brothers, CBS, 1979. PRINCIPAL TELEVISION APPEARANCES—Movies: *East of Eden*, ABC, 1980; *Having It All*, ABC, 1982; *The Sun Also Rises*, NBC, 1984.

STAGE DEBUT—*The Wager*, Cast Theatre, Los Angeles, CA, 1982.

AWARDS: Dramalogue Award, 1982, for *The Wager*.

ADDRESS: AGENT—International Creative Management, 8899 Beverly Blvd., Los Angeles, CA 90048.

*   *   *

BOHANNON, Judy

PERSONAL: Full name Judith Layton Bohannon; born June 30, in Louisville, KY; daughter of Russell Clay (a farmer and factory worker) and Nancy Melissa (a teacher; maiden name, Elliott) Bohannon; married Woodford Helm Fields, December 28, 1968 (divorced 1974). EDUCATION: Georgetown College, B.A., English, speech; Northwestern University, M.A., theatre; studied for the theatre with Uta Hagen and Michael Shurtleff at the Herbert Berghof Studios and the Corner Loft.

JUDY BOHANNON

VOCATION: Actress, director, writer, and acting teacher.

CAREER: STAGE DEBUT—A violet in a first grade play, Cropper Elementary School, Cropper, KY. NEW YORK DEBUT—Madge, *Summer Brave (Picnic)*, Equity Library, 1973, for sixteen performances. PRINCIPAL STAGE APPEARANCES—Susie, *Wait Until Dark*; Lu Ann, *Lu Ann Hampton Laverty Oberlander*; Eliza Doolittle, *Pygmalian*; Estelle, *No Exit*; Judy, *Double D*, Lincoln Center, NY; Rosalie, *Storytime*; Peggy, *Witness*, Lincoln Center, NY; also: *Born Yesterday*, 1971; *Secretary Bird*, 1971; *Love-Death Plays of William Inge*, 1975.

FILM DEBUT—Bus ticket sales girl, *Welcome Home, Soldier Boys*, Twentieth Century-Fox, 1972. FILM APPEARANCES—Lilly, *Rocket Man*, AFI, 1982; Ada, *Little Man*, Demille Productions, 1982.

TELEVISION DEBUT—Clara, *Man Under Cover*, NBC, 1978. TELEVISION APPEARANCES—Hostess, *Cinemax*, HBO, 1982; running role, *Capitol*, CBS, 1982-83; also over two hundred television commercials.

RELATED CAREER—Acting teacher, American Academy of Dramatic Arts, West Coast (Pasadena, CA), 1983-85.

WRITINGS: FILM SCRIPTS, UNPRODUCED—Circus World; The First Mrs. Gable; Paul.

SIDELIGHTS: RECREATION—Aerobics, horse-back riding, biking, rollerskating, speaking French.

Bohannon told *CTFT* that she has occasionally worked in the theatre under the name Judy Fields. She has studied French at the Universite de Montpelier and traveled extensively throughout Europe. She is fond of computers and has raised Irish Setters which she often shows.

ADDRESS: HOME—New York, NY; Los Angeles, CA. OFFICE—5629 Ensign Avenue, N. Hollywood, CA 91601. AGENT—Cunningham, Escott & Dipens, 260 S. Robertson, Los Angeles, CA 90211.

*   *   *

BORGNINE, Ernest   1917-

PERSONAL: Born January 24, 1917, in Hamden, CT; son of Charles B. and Anna (Bosselli) Borgnine; married Ethel Merman (divorced); married Tove Newman, 1972. MILITARY: U.S. Navy, World War Two.

VOCATION: Actor.

CAREER: FILM DEBUT—*China Cosair*, 1951. PRINCIPAL FILM APPEARANCES—*The Mob*, 1951; *From Here to Eternity*, 1953; *Bad Day at Black Rock*, 1954; *Demetrius and the Gladiators*, 1954; *Johnny Guitar*, 1954; *Vera Cruz*, 1954; *Run for Cover*, Paramount, 1955; *Violent Saturday*, 1955; *Marty*, United Artists, 1955; *Last Command*, Republic, 1955; *Square Jungle*, Universal, 1956; *The Catered Affair*, Metro-Goldwyn-Mayer, 1956; *Jubal*, Columbia, 1956; *The Best Things in Life Are Free*, Twentieth Century-Fox, 1956; *Three Brave Men*, Twentieth Century-Fox, 1957; *Badlanders*, Metro-Goldwyn-Mayer, 1958; *Rabbit Trap*, United Artists, 1959; *Man on a String*, Columbia, 1960; *Pay or Die*, Allied Artists, 1960;

Go Naked in the World, Metro-Goldwyn-Mayer, 1961; *Barrabas,* Columbia, 1962; *McHale's Navy,* Universal, 1964; *Flight of the Phoenix,* Twentieth Century-Fox, 1966; *Chuka,* Paramount, 1967; *The Dirty Dozen,* Metro-Goldwyn-Mayer, 1967; *Legend of Lylah Clare,* Metro-Goldwyn-Mayer, 1968; *The Wild Bunch,* Warner Brothers, 1969.

The Adventurers, Paramount, 1970; *Suppose They Gave a War and Nobody Came?,* Cinerama, 1970; *A Bullet for Sandoval,* UMC, 1970; *Bunny O'Hare,* American International, 1971; *Willard,* Cinerama, 1971; *Hannie Caulder,* Paramount, 1972; *The Revengers,* National General, 1972; *The Poseidon Adventure,* Twentieth Century-Fox, 1972; *The Emperor of the North,* Twentieth Century-Fox, 1973; *Law and Disorder,* Columbia, 1974; *Hustle,* Paramount, 1975; *The Devil's Rain,* Bryanston, 1975; *Shoot,* Avco-Embassy, 1976; *The Greatest,* Columbia, 1977; *Convoy,* United Artists, 1978; *Crossed Swords,* Warner Brothers, 1978; *The Black Hole,* Buena Vista, 1979; *The Double McGuffin,* 1979; *The Ravagers,* 1979; *When Time Ran Out,* Warner Brothers, 1980; *Escape from New York,* Avco-Embassy, 1981; *Deadly Blessing,* United Artists, 1981; *The Graduates of Malibu High.*

PRINCIPAL TELEVISION APPEARANCES—Quinton McHale, *McHale's Navy,* ABC, 1962-66; Dominic Santini, *Air Wolf,* CBS, 1984-85. Movie: *All Quiet on the Western Front;* Lion, *Alice in Wonderland,* CBS, 1986.

AWARDS: Academy Award, 1956, for *Marty.*

SIDELIGHTS: MEMBERSHIPS—Mason.*

*   *   *

BOSTWICK, Barry

BRIEF ENTRY: Born in San Mateo, CA; son of Henry and Betty Bostwick; graduated California Western University, B.A., acting. Actor. Bostwick's stage credits include: *Cock-a-Doodle Dandy* (Broadway debut); *Colette; Grease; The Robber Bridegroom* (won Antoinette Perry Award); a revival of *She Loves Me; L'Historie du Soldat; The Death of Von Richthofen as Witnessed from Earth; Pirates of Penzance.* His television appearances include the series *Foul Play,* ABC, 1981; the miniseries *George Washington,* 1984, and *Deceptions,* 1985-86; and the television movie *A Woman of Substance,* 1984. He appeared in the film *The Rocky Horror Picture Show.**

*   *   *

BOWERS, Faubion   1917-

PERSONAL: Born January 29, 1917, in OK; son of Powell Clayton and Emily (Robinson) Bowers; divorced; children: Jai Peter. EDUCATION: Columbia University; Universite de Poitier (France); Ecole Normale de Musique (France); Juilliard Graduate School of Music. MILITARY: U.S. Army, to 1948, major.

VOCATION: Writer and critic.

CAREER: PRINCIPAL TELEVISION WORK—Bowers has appeared in, produced, or written thirty television programs for *Camera*

Three, CBS, CBS Cable, ABC, and PBS, covering dance, drama, sociology, and travelogs through Europe and Asia, including *The Cruelty of Beauty,* PBS, the first full-length documentary of Kabuki and Bushido, 1981.

RELATED CAREER—Teacher: Hosei Daigaku, Tokyo; Taman Siswa, Indonesia; Groupe Estevale pour la Musique Moderne, Paris; New School for Social Research, New York; distinguished professor, Asian Studies, University of Kansas.

WRITINGS: PLAYS, UNPUBLISHED—The Daytime Moon, 1960. TELEVISION SCRIPT—*Portrait of Giselle,* 1982. BOOKS, PUBLISHED—*Japanese Theatre; Dance in India; Theatre in the East; Islands of the Rising Sun; Broadway: U.S.S.R.; Scriabin; The New Scriabin.* ARTICLES—On electronic music, avant-garde dance, and Asian theatre forms in various publications; music editor, *House and Garden;* regular critic, *Musical America.*

AWARDS: Golden Eagle, 1982, script, for *Portrait of Giselle;* Order of the Sacred Treasure, awarded by the Japanese Government for Culture, 1984; Bronze Star and Oak Leaf Cluster during World War Two for translation and interrogation services.

SIDELIGHTS: Bowers told *CTFT* that, in addition to his other published or produced works, he has translated the Egyptian *Book of the Dead* and the *Primer of Hinduism.* He provided simultaneous voice-over translations during performances of Jean-Louis Barrault's *Rabelais.* He has also performed this same service for *The Grand Kabuki* during its six tours of America, most recently in 1985, at the Metropolitan Opera House and Kennedy Center in Washington, DC.

It is of interest to note that during the 1946-48 occupation of Japan, Bowers was aide-de-camp to General MacArthur. After that, from 1948-49, he was the censor and sponsor at the Japanese Theatre, Tokyo.

ADDRESS: HOME—205 E. 94th Street, New York, NY 10128. OFFICE—William Morris Agency, 1350 Avenue of the Americas, New York, NY 10019.

*   *   *

BRADEN, William   1939-

PERSONAL: Born William C. McIlvride, June 2, 1939, in Red Deer, Alberta, Canada; son of William Dunn (a mechanic) and Mabel Alice (Kenney) McIlvride; married Debora J. Reuter, August 22, 1979; children: William D., Michelle G., Christine D., John-Paul C. EDUCATION: H.K.U. School of Continuing Education, M.A.

VOCATION: Producer and writer.

CAREER: PRINCIPAL FILM WORK—Production executive: *Farewell My Lovely,* Avco-Embassy, 1975, *Rancho Deluxe,* United Artists, 1975, *92 in the Shade,* United Artists, 1975, *Russian Roulette,* Avco-Embassy, 1975; associate producer and production supervisor, *The Pyramid,* Pyramid Movie Associates, 1975; *Breakheart Pass,* 1976; president, Dunatai Corporation, 1976-78; creator, supervising re-editor, *Dublin Murders, One Way Out;* script editor, *Price of Bones, Faraway Island, Last Resort,* 1978; director, co-producer, *America: Life in the Family*, Pyramid Films, 1978; production executive, *Goldengirl*, 1979; line producer, *Running Scared*, 1979; supervising producer, *Bigshot*, GMT Productions, 1980; assistant director, *Death Valley*, Universal, 1980.

Producer, *Rest in Peace*, RIP Company, 1981; production executive, Avco-Embassy Pictures, 1981, pictures include *The Seduction*, 1982, and *Swamp Thing*, 1982; production executive, *Slapstick*, Film Finance Ltd., London, 1982 (released, 1984); production executive and representative: *Undercover, Constance, Heart of the Stag, Razorback*, Completion Bond Company, 1982-83; managing director, Filmaker Completion: *Kalash, Harbour Pilots, Ghost of the Sky, Mountain Man, Kakadu, Fishing Down Under, Sylvia, False Door, Human Face Series, Leonski, God Doesn't Play Dice, Aussie Assault*, Australia, 1983-85; script editor, *Kamareuka*, 1984.

PRINCIPAL TELEVISION WORK—Producer, *If My People. . .*, 1975; for Dunatai Corporation, 1976-78: co-producer, *I Believe*, producer and creator, *Requiem for a Planet*, producer, *He Wants Her Back*, assistant director, *Waikiki* (pilot), ABC, 1979.

PRINCIPAL STAGE WORK—Producer, *If My People. . .*, toured U.S. cities, 1976.

WRITINGS: SCREENPLAYS—*Troubled Waters*, 1980; *Winds of Winter* (with J. Michael Smith), 1980; *Somebody! Love Me* (with J. Michael Smith), 1980; *Deep Cover*, 1984; *Birdie's Cowboys*, 1984.

SIDELIGHTS: MEMBERSHIPS—Directors Guild of America, Directors Guild of Canada, Producers and Directors Guild of Australia, Writers Guild of Australia.

ADDRESS: AGENT—c/o Tom Chasen, Gersh Agency, 222 N. Canon, Beverly Hills, CA, 90210.

*   *   *

BRADY, Scott   1924-85

PERSONAL: Born Jerry Tierney, September 13, 1924, in Brooklyn, NY; died April 17, 1985; married Lisa; children: Timothy, Terrance.

VOCATION: Actor.

CAREER: FILM DEBUT—*In This Corner*, 1947. PRINCIPAL FILM APPEARANCES—*He Walked by Night*, 1948; *Canon City*, 1948; *Port of New York*, 1949; *Undertow*, 1949; *The Gal Who Took the West*, 1949; *Kansas Raiders*, 1950; *I Was a Shoplifter*, 1950; *Undercover Girl*, 1950; *The Model and the Marriage Broker*, 1951; *Bronco Buster*, 1952; *Bloodhounds of Broadway*, 1952; *Montana Belle*, 1952; *Yankee Buccaneer*, 1952; *Untamed Frontier*, 1952; *Perilous Journey*, 1953; *El Alamien*, 1953; *White Fire; Johnny Guitar*, 1954; *The Law vs. Billy the Kid*, 1954; *Gentlemen Marry Brunettes*, United Artists, 1955; *The Vanishing American*, Republic, 1955.

Shotgun Slade, 1956; *Terror at Midnight*, Republic, 1956; *The Maverick Queen*, Republic, 1956; *The Restless Breed*, Twentieth Century-Fox, 1957; *Blood Arrow*, 1958; *Battle Flame*, Allied Artists, 1959; *Operation Bikini*, American International, 1963; *John Goldfarb, Please Come Home*, Twentieth Century-Fox, 1965; *Black Spurs*, Paramount, 1965; *Castle of Evil*, United Pictures, 1966; *Destination Inner Space*, Magna, 1966; *Journey to the Center of*

Time, 1967; *Marooned*, 1969; *Satan's Sadists*, 1970; *Hell's Bloody Devils*, 1970; *Dollars*, Columbia, 1972; *Wicked, Wicked*, Metro-Goldwyn-Mayer, 1973; *Law and Order*, 1976; *The China Syndrome*, Columbia, 1979; *Gremlins*, Warner Brothers, 1984.

PRINCIPAL TELEVISION APPEARANCES—*The Loretta Young Show; Lux Playhouse; The Last Ride of the Daltry Gang; Power; The American Dream; McClain's Law; Charlie's Angels; Shotgun Slade*.

PRINCIPAL STAGE APPEARANCES—Broadway: *The Moon Is Blue*, 1952; *The Best Man; Destry Rides Again.**

*   *   *

BREEN, Robert   1914-

PERSONAL: Born December 26, 1914; son of Henry James and Marie Therese (Cody) Breen; married Wilva Davis (an actress and executive), September 11, 1946; children: two sons. EDUCATION: Attended University of Iowa; College of St. Thomas.

VOCATION: Director, producer, and actor.

CAREER: STAGE DEBUT—Romaine, *Ten Nights in a Bar Room*, University of Iowa, 1931. PRINCIPAL STAGE APPEARANCES—Captain Hook, *Peter Pan*, Baptista, *The Taming of the Shrew*, Chancellor, *The Ivory Door*, Louis XI, *If I Were King*, Brian de Guilbert, *Ivanhoe*, Winterset, *Monsieur Beaucaire*, Antony, *Julius Caesar*, Osvald, *Ghosts*, all at Old Minneapolis Repertory Company, MN, 1931-32; Lord Dilling, *The Last of Mrs. Cheyney*, Gregers Werle, *The Wild Duck*, University of Minnesota, MN, 1932; Mephistopheles, *Urfaust*, College Art Theatre, St. Paul, MN, 1933; Hamlet, *Hamlet*, College Art, St. Paul, 1933, then Shubert,

Photography by Roy Schatt

ROBERT BREEN

Minneapolis, MN, 1933; *The Enemy, The Fool,* and *The Cat and the Canary,* Paramount and Grand Theatres, St. Cloud, MN, 1933-34; Chancellor, *The Ivory Door,* Mephistopheles, *Urfaust,* Chairman, *Amaco* (also directed), Hamilton Park, Chicago, IL, 1935; appeared as Mephistopheles, *Faust* (also directed), Great Northern, Chicago, IL, 1936; Mephistopheles, *Speak of the Devil* (also directed), Nora Bayes, NY, 1939.

PRINCIPAL STAGE WORK—Producer for ANTA Experimental Theater, NY: *The Wanhope Building, O'Daniel, As We Forgive Our Debtors, The Great Campaign, Virginia Reel,* all at the Princess, 1947; *Galileo,* 1947; *Skipper Next to God,* 1948; *A Long Way from Home,* 1948; *A Temporary Island, Celebration, Afternoon Storm, Hope Is a Thing with Feathers, Ballet Ballads, Talent '48, The Martha Graham Company,* all at Maxine Elliott's, 1948; *Seeds in the Wind,* Lenox Hill Playhouse, NY, 1948; *Danny Larkin; Battle for Heaven,* Educational Alliance, 1948; *These Tender Mercies,* Lenox Hill Playhouse, 1948; *E = MC,* Brander Matthews, Columbia University, 1948; *Hippolytus,* Lenox Hill Playhouse, 1948; *Uniform of Flesh, Cock-a-Doodle-Doo, The 19th Hole of Europe, Sister Oakes, Sleeper, The Fifth Horseman,* all at Lenox Hill Playhouse, 1949; *ANTA Album,* Ziegfeld, NY, 1950.

Organized for State of Utah Centennial: Orson Welles' *Macbeth,* Katherine Cornell's *The Barretts of Wimpole Street,* 1947.

Director: *Dr. Jekyll and Mr. Hyde, Romeo and Juliet,* Paramount and Grand Theaters, St. Cloud Theater Guild, MN, 1933-34; *Technique,* Los Angeles, CA, 1938; *The Zeal of Thy House,* NY, 1939, *Adam the Creator,* NY, 1940; *Winesburg, Ohio,* Irving Place, NY, 1940; *Porgy and Bess,* command performance at the White House, Washington, DC, 1957.

MAJOR TOURS—Appeared as Hamlet and directed, *Hamlet,* State Theater of Virginia, Kronberg Castle, Elsinore, Denmark, and cities in Germany, 1948-49; producer, *American Ballet Theater,* European cities, 1950; producer and director, *Porgy and Bess,* extensive tour of U.S., Canadian, African, Near Eastern, Latin American, and European cities, including: Dallas, Chicago, Washington, DC, Los Angeles, Toronto, London, Paris, Athens, Tel Aviv, Casablanca, Milan, Zurich, Brussels, Rio de Janeiro, Mexico City, Munich, Moscow, Prague, 1952-1956; director, *Free and Easy,* Amsterdam, Brussels, Utrecht, Paris, 1959-60.

PRINCIPAL FILM APPEARANCES—Bolus, *The Pentagram,* Kalmar Productions, Berlin Film Festival, 1964.

PRINCIPAL TELEVISION APPEARANCES—Cardinal-Inquisitor, "Lamp at Midnight," *Hallmark Hall of Fame,* NBC, 1966; Elijah, *Inherit the Wind,* NBC, 1966.

PRINCIPAL TELEVISION WORK—Producer, *ANTA Television Playhouse,* NBC, 1947-48; director, *Theater USA,* ABC, 1949-50.

PRINCIPAL RADIO APPEARANCES—Dr. Stockmann, *An Enemy of the People,* Metternich, *L'Aiglon,* KSTP, St. Paul, MN, 1931-33.

RELATED CAREER—Organized the WPA Federal Theater Project, serving as associate director and administrator, Chicago, IL, 1935; formulated, with Wilva Davis and Robert Porterfield, the plan that ended in the congressional chartering of the American National Theatre and Academy, 1935, and was appointed executive secretary; organized ANTA's first National Theatre Assembly, NY, 1951; arranged exchange programs between U.S. theatre productions and theaters in Germany; vice-president, Everyman Opera Inc., 1952-present.

AWARDS: Danish Hamlet Medal, 1949.

SIDELIGHTS: MEMBERSHIPS—American National Theatre and Academy (life member).

ADDRESS: HOME—139 W. 44th Street, New York, NY 10036.

*   *   *

BRENNER, David   1945-

PERSONAL: Born February 4, 1945, in Philadelphia, PA; son of Louis Yehuda (a vaudeville singer, dancer, and comedian) and Estelle Anne (Rosenfeld) Brenner; children: Cole Jay. EDUCATION: Temple University, B.S., mass communications. RELIGION: Jewish. MILITARY: U.S. Army, early 1960's, Corporal.

VOCATION: Comedian.

CAREER: DEBUT—Pips, Sheepshead Bay, Brooklyn, NY, for seven shows. PRINCIPAL APPEARANCES—Has appeared in concert halls, colleges, nightclubs, etc. since August, 1969.

TELEVISION DEBUT—*The Tonight Show,* January 8, 1971. PRINCIPAL TELEVISION APPEARANCES—*The Hollywood Squares;* guest host (more than 39 times), *The Tonight Show with Johnny Carson;* others. Also: commercials.

PRINCIPAL TELEVISION WORK—Producer: WBBM-TV, Chicago; WRCV, Philadelphia; KYW-TV, Philadelphia; WNEW-TV, NY; PBL-TV, NY. Also: Producer, director, writer, for television documentaries.

WRITINGS: BOOKS—*Soft Pretzels with Mustard,* Arbor House, 1983; *Revenge Is the Best Exercise,* Arbor House, 1985; *Nobody Sees You Eat Tuna Fish,* all Arbor House, 1985.

AWARDS: American Guild of Variety Actors Comedy Award, 1976; Las Vegas Entertainer of the Year Award, 1978; Atlantic City Comedian of the Year, 1984; College Campus Entertainer/Comedian of the Year, 1984.

SIDELIGHTS: Brenner told *CTFT* that he strives to "make as many persons laugh as heartily as they can for as long as I can and to be as funny, original, and honest a performer as possible."

He is mentioned in *Book of Lists 2* for having the most appearances as a talk show guest host in history.

ADDRESS: OFFICE—Sound Advice, 110 W. 57th Street, New York, NY 10019. AGENT—Artie Moscowitz, William Morris Agency, 1350 Avenue of the Americas, New York, NY 10019.

*   *   *

BROAD, Jay   1930-

PERSONAL: Born August 5, 1930, in Newcastle, PA; son of Henry and Celia Broad. EDUCATION: Attended Westminster College and Penn State University.

VOCATION: Director and playwright.

CAREER: PRINCIPAL STAGE WORK—*Are You Now or Have You Ever Been?*, NY, 1973; *Play Me a Country Song*, 1982; *Madness in Jerusalem*, 1984; *The Barclay Decision*, 1985.

RELATED CAREER—Director, Theater Atlanta, 1965-70; visiting lecturer, Yale School of Drama, New Haven, CT, 1978; director, PAF Playhouse, Huntington Station, NY, 1975-80; playwright in residence, Arizona State University, 1980-81; consultant, National Endowment for the Arts, 1981-82; visiting director and professor, University of Southern California, 1983-85.

WRITINGS: PLAYS, PRODUCED—*Red, White and Maddox* (with Don Tucker), Theatre Atlanta, 1968, Cort, NY, 1969; *The Great Big Coca-Cola Swamp in the Sky*, 1971; *Conflict of Interest*, 1972; *The Killdeer*, Public, NY, 1974; *To Kill a Mockingbird* (adaptation), 1975; *White Pelicans*, 1976, Theater de Lys, 1978; *Events from the Life of Ted Snyder*, 1977.

ADDRESS: HOME—895 West End Avenue, New York, NY 10025.

*   *   *

BROADHURST, Kent   1940-

PERSONAL: Born February 4, 1940, in St. Louis, MO. EDUCATION: University of Nebraska, B.F.A.; studied for the theatre with Stella Adler, Uta Hagen, Herbert Berghof, Michael Howard, Bill Hickey, Warren Robertson, Charles Nelson Reilly, and Kurt Reis.

VOCATION: Actor, playwright, artist, photographer, and inventor.

CAREER: PRINCIPAL STAGE APPEARANCES—Oz Valentine, *Circus Valentine*, Actors Theatre of Louisville Festival, KY, 1979; Gideon, *Sunset/Sunrise*, Actors Theatre of Louisville Festival, KY, 1981; Gelb, *Neutral Countries*, Running Joke, *Food from Trash*, Actors Theatre of Louisville Festival, KY, 1983; Challee, *The Caine Mutiny Court Martial*, Circle in the Square, NY, 1983; Harvey Milk, *Execution of Justice*, Actors Theatre of Louisville Festival, KY, 1984.

George, *Of Mice and Men*, Actors Theatre of Louisville, KY, Philadelphia Drama Guild, Cincinnati Playhouse, Playmakers Repertory Co; Brian, *The Shadow Box*, Actors Theatre of Louisville, KY; Dr. Michaelis, *Semmelweiss*, Buffalo Studio Arena, NY; Jamie, *Long Day's Journey into Night*, Missouri Repertory; Aston, *The Caretaker*, Nelson Gallery Series; Tom, *The Glass Menagerie*, Nebraska Repertory; Rupert Forster, *Marching Song*, Lion Theatre Co., NY; original group member, The Fourth Wall Improvisation, Theatre East, NY; Leo, *Design for Living*, Manhattan Theatre Club, NY; the Painter, *Vieux Carre*, Warren Robertson Studio, NY.

PRINCIPAL STAGE WORK—Director, *Lemons*.

FILM DEBUT—Bill Whitley, *Brubaker*, Twentieth Century-Fox, 1980. PRINCIPAL FILM APPEARANCES—Joseph Alito, *The Verdict*, Twentieth Century-Fox, 1982; Dave, *Lovesick*, Warner Brothers, 1983; Carl Browning, *Silkwood*, Twentieth Century-Fox, 1983; Sam Bass, *Solomon Northup's Odyssey*; Herb Kincaid, *Silver Bullet*.

PRINCIPAL TELEVISON APPEARANCES—D.A., *I Want to Live*, 1983; Pavlick, *Kennedy*, NBC; Frazier, *All My Children*; ABC; Don Goodman, *As the World Turns*, CBS; Phillip Monet, *One Life to*

KENT BROADHURST

Live, ABC; Dr. Morgan, *Search for Tomorrow*; Sgt. Dietrich, *The Guiding Light*.

WRITINGS: PLAYS, PRODUCED—*They're Coming to Make It Brighter*, Actors Theatre of Louisville, KY, 1980, Mixed Blood Theatre, Minneapolis, MN, 1981; *The Eye of the Beholder*, Actors Theatre of Louisville Shorts, KY, 1981, Actors Theatre of Louisville New Plays Festival, 1982, Actors Theatre of Louisville Budapest Tour, 1982, Australian tour, 1983, King's Head, London, 1982, Lunchbox, Calgary, Canada, 1982; *The Habitual Acceptance of the Near Enough*, Actors Theatre of Louisville Shorts, 1982, Actors Theatre of Louisville New Play Festival, 1983, Actors Theatre of Louisville Belgrade tour, 1983, People's Light and Theatre Co., Philadelphia, 1983; *Lemons*, Mixed Blood Theatre Co., Minneapolis, MN, 1982, Actors Theatre of Louisville New Play Festival, 1984, Group Theatre, Seattle, WA, 1984.

PLAYS, PUBLISHED—*The Eye of the Beholder; The Habitual Acceptance of the Near Enough; Lemons*.

SIDELIGHTS: Playwright in Residence, Actors Theatre of Louisville, 1981. In addition to his work as an actor and director, Broadhurst is also a professional photographer and an artist with over two thousand painting commissions to his credit in private and public collections across the United States.

ADDRESS: AGENT—Don Buchwald, Ten E. 44th Street, New York, NY 10017 (acting); Samuel Liff, William Morris Agency, 1350 Sixth Avenue, New York, NY 10019 (writing).

39

BROCKSMITH, Roy   1945-

PERSONAL: Born September 15, 1945, in Quincy, IL; son of Otis E. (a mechanic) and Vera A. (Hartwig) Brocksmith; married Adele M. Albright, December 25, 1963; children: Blake.

VOCATION: Actor, director, essayist.

CAREER: DEBUT—Jack in the Box, *A Christmas Pageant,* Quincy Junior Theatre, Quincy, IL, 1950. NEW YORK DEBUT—Cop, *The Whip Lady,* Hunter's Playwrights Project, for twelve performances, 1971. PRINCIPAL STAGE APPEARANCES, NEW YORK—Dr. Roy, *Doctor Selavy's Magic Theatre;* multiple roles, *Polly;* Ben Budge/Peachum, *The Beggar's Opera;* Varanushka, *The Master and Margarita;* Worm, *In the Jungle of Cities;* Sganarelle, *Don Juan, Delacorte; Green Father, The Leaf People;* multiple roles, *Stages;* Loyal, *Tartuffe;* ballad singer, *The Threepenny Opera;* Louis XIII, *The Three Musketeers,* 1984.

PRINCIPAL STAGE APPEARANCES, REGIONAL—Cauchon, *Joan of Lorraine,* Hartman, CT; Baron, *The Lower Depths,* Arena; Harry Donovan, *Swing,* Kennedy Center, Washington, DC; Petkoff, *Arms and the Man,* Sganarelle, *Don Juan,* Prof. Willard, *Our Town,* Touchstone, *As You Like It,* Semicolon, *Hang On to Me,* all at the Guthrie, Minneapolis, MN.

PRINCIPAL FILM APPEARANCES—*Rip Off,* J. Cinemax, 1972; *Rent Control; King of the Gypsies,* Paramount, 1978; *Killer Fish,* 1979; *Stardust Memories,* United Artists, 1980; *Tales of Ordinary Madness,* 1983.

TELEVISION APPEARANCES—*The Streets* (pilot), NBC; *Starstuck* (pilot), CBS; ''Tartuffe,'' *PBS Great Performances;* ''Charlie Smith and the Fritter Tree,'' *Nova,* PBS; *3-2-1 Contact,* PBS; *The Beggar's Opera,* cable.

WRITINGS: PLAYS, PRODUCED—*Paraplanta Verite,* La MaMa, NY, 1977. ARTICLES—''Protest from a Professional Liar,'' *Performing Arts Journal,* Vol. 22; satirical newsletters under the pseudonym Billy Breeze, 1975-84.

AWARDS: Kudos Award, Minneapolis, 1981, for Sganarelle in *Don Juan.*

SIDELIGHTS: Brocksmith was on the cover of *The New York Times Magazine,* on November 9, 1975.

ADDRESS: AGENT—Actor's Group Agency, 157 W. 57 Street, New York, NY 10036.

*   *   *

BROCKWAY, Amie   1938-

PERSONAL: Born Amarae Woodworth, December 13, 1938; daughter of Raymond H. (a farmer) and Amabelle V. (a teacher; maiden name, Willard) Woodworth; married Ronald F. Brockway, June 3, 1956 (divorced, 1980); married Richard G. Henson (a

ROY BROCKSMITH

AMIE BROCKWAY

teacher), June 30, 1984; children: (first marriage) Adrienne J., Virginia A. EDUCATION: State University of New York, B.F.A., 1975; Mason Gross School of the Arts, Rutgers University, M.F.A., 1978.

VOCATION: Director.

CAREER: FIRST STAGE WORK—Director, *Stop the World, I Want to Get Off,* Theater by the Lake, Hightstown, NJ, eight performances. NEW YORK DEBUT—Director, *Redeye,* Theater of the Open Eye, 1980, eighteen performances. PRINCIPAL STAGE WORK—Director: *The Sun Gets Blue,* 1981, *La Belle Au Bois,* 1982, *Behind a Mask,* 1983, *A Cricket on the Hearth,* 1984, *Scapin,* 1984, *She Also Dances,* 1985, all at Theater for the Open Eye, NY; *Rosalind, Light Up the Sky,* both at American Renaissance Theater, NY; *Whatever Happened to Amos 'n Andy?,* Theatre at St. Clements, NY; *The Happy Hour,* Vineyard Workshop, NY; *Oklahoma!,* Hofstra University; *Scenes from American Life, The Rimers of Eldritch, The Collection, The Veteran, The Understanding,* all at Rutgers University, NJ; *Look Back in Anger, The Long Stay Cut Short,* State University of New York, Purchase, NY; *Story Theater,* Mercer County College, NJ; *A Funny Thing Happened on the Way to the Forum, The Prisoner of Second Avenue,* both at Theatre by the Lake, NJ.

Children's theater: *Tales Alive,* Theater of the Open Eye, NY; *You, Alice, and Me;* Performance Troupe, Princeton, NJ; *If You've Seen One Dragon, The Great Cross-Country Race,* both at Performance Troupe, Princeton, NJ; *Beginnings, Dundor, The Ugly Duckling,* all at Princeton Street Theater, NJ.

AWARDS: Theater Communications Group Award, 1984.

SIDELIGHTS: MEMBERSHIPS—Society of Stage Directors and Choreographers.

ADDRESS: HOME—460 W. 49th Street, New York, NY 10019. OFFICE—c/o Theater of the Open Eye, 316 E. 88th Street, New York, NY 10128.

*   *   *

BROSTEN, Harve   1943-

PERSONAL: Born May 15, 1943, in Chicago, IL; son of Hy (an automobile salesman) and Roslyn (Rifkin) Brosten. EDUCATION: Art Institute, Goodman Memorial Theatre, Chicago, IL.

VOCATION: Writer and director.

WRITINGS: PRINCIPAL TELEVISION WORK—Episodes of *All in the Family,* CBS: "Archie's Missing, Part I," "Edith's Friend," "Cousin Liz;" premiere episode, *The Jefferson's,* CBS; pilots for Columbia, NBC.

AWARDS: Emmy, Comedy Writing, 1978, for *All in the Family,* "Cousin Liz."

SIDELIGHTS: MEMBERSHIPS—Directors Guild of America, Writers Guild of America.

ADDRESS: HOME—New York, NY. OFFICE—365 W. 52nd Street, New York, NY 10019.

ARVIN BROWN

BROWN, Arvin   1940-

PERSONAL: Born 1940, in Los Angeles, CA; married Joyce Ebert (an actress). EDUCATION: Stanford University, B.A.; Harvard University, M.A.; Bristol University; studied for the theatre at the Yale School of Drama.

VOCATION: Artistic director, director, and producer.

CAREER: FIRST STAGE WORK—Director, *Long Day's Journey into Night,* Long Wharf, New Haven, CT, 1966. PRINCIPAL STAGE WORK—Director: *Solitaire/Double Solitaire,* 1971; *The National Health,* 1974; *Ah! Wilderness!,* 1975; *Watch on the Rhine,* 1980; *A View from the Bridge,* 1982; *American Buffalo,* 1983; *Requiem for a Heavyweight,* 1985; *A Day in the Death of Joe Egg,* 1985. (All of the above opened at Long Wharf and later moved to Broadway).

Also directed at the Long Wharf: *Open Admission,* 1982; *Free and Clear,* 1983; *The Hostage,* 1983; *Tobacco Road,* 1984; *Albert Herring,* 1985. Also directed on and off Broadway: *A Whistle in the Dark,* 1968; *Hay Fever,* 1970; *Long Day's Journey into Night,* 1971; *27 Wagons Full of Cotton/A Memory of Two Mondays,* 1976; *Strangers,* 1979.

PRINCIPAL FILM WORK—Director, *Cold Sweat,* 1973.

PRINCIPAL TELEVISION WORK—Director: *Close Ties,* RCTV; *Amahl and the Night Visitors,* PBS; *The Widowing of Mrs. Holroyd,* PBS; *Ah! Wilderness!,* PBS; *Forget-Me-Not-Lane,* PBS; *Blessings,* PBS.

RELATED CAREER—Supervisor, apprentice program, Long Wharf Theatre, New Haven, CT, during its first season, 1965.

AWARDS: Vernon Rice Award; Variety Critics Poll for his off Broadway work; ''Fifty Faces of the Future'' Award, *Time* magazine; honorary degrees, University of New Haven, University of Bridgeport, Fairfield University; Antoinette Perry Award nomination, Best Revival, 1982, for *A View from the Bridge;* Antoinette Perry Award nomination, Best Revival, 1983, for *American Buffalo;* Antoinette Perry Award, Best Revival, 1985, for *Joe Egg.*

SIDELIGHTS: Arvin Brown was appointed artistic director of the Long Wharf Theatre in 1967 and has held that post, without break, since that date.

ADDRESS: OFFICE—Long Wharf Theatre, 222 Sargent Drive, New Haven, CT 06511.

*　　*　　*

BROWN, Kenneth H.　1936-

PERSONAL: Born March 9, 1936, in New York City; son of Kenneth F. (a policeman) and Helen (a bank manager; maiden name, Bella) Brown. EDUCATION: Attended Columbia University, 1957-58. MILITARY: U.S. Marine Corps, 1954-57, Corporal.

VOCATION: Writer.

CAREER: Resident playwright, Yale University, Graduate Drama School, 1966-69; visiting lecturer, Hollins College, VA, 1969-1970, Hunter College, NY, 1970-71, University of Iowa, 1971-72.

WRITINGS: PLAYS, PRODUCED—*The Brig,* Living Theatre, NY, 1963; *The Happy Bar,* 1967; *Blakes Design,* Yale School of Drama, CT, Theatre for the New City, NY; *Devices,* Actors Studio, NY, Judson Poets Theatre, NY, Yale School of Drama, CT; *The Green Room,* 1971; *Night Light,* Hartford Stage Company, CT, 1973; *The Cretan Bull,* Eugene O'Neill Theatre Center, Waterford, CT, 1972, Manhattan Theatre Club, 1974.

PLAYS, PUBLISHED—*The Brig,* Hill & Wang; *Night Light,* Samuel French; ''Blakes Design,'' *Best Short Plays of 1968,* Chilton Book Co.

ADDRESS: AGENT—Ellen Neuwald, 905 West End Avenue, New York, NY 10025.

*　　*　　*

BRYAN, Kenneth　1953-

PERSONAL: Born Kenneth Earle Adams, Jr., July 30, 1953, in Fort Monmouth, NJ; son of Kenneth Earl (a commercial artist) and Adella Geraldine (an administrative secretary; maiden name, Lowery) Adams. EDUCATION: Indiana University, B.S., 1976; trained for the stage with Janet Sarno and Eileen Swedish.

VOCATION: Actor, writer, and singer.

CAREER: STAGE DEBUT—Preacher John, *Finian's Rainbow,* Chanhassen Dinner Theatre, Chanhassen, MN, 1977. NEW YORK DEBUT—Simeon, Butler, *Joseph and the Amazing Technicolor Dreamcoat,* Entermedia then Royale, NY, 1981-82, 824 performances. PRINCIPAL STAGE APPEARANCES—Narrator, Death, *He*

KENNETH BRYAN

Lived the Good Life, Guthrie, Minneapolis, MN, 1978-79; Curly, *Oklahoma!,* Cortland Repertory, Cortland, NY, 1979; Soldier, *The Human Comedy,* New York Shakespeare Festival, Royale, NY, 1984-85.

MAJOR TOURS—Voice of Vernon, *They're Playing Our Song,* U.S. cities, 1979-81.

AWARDS: Member, Phi Kappa Lambda, honorary fraternity for excellence in academics in the field of music, Indiana University, 1975.

SIDELIGHTS: MEMBERSHIPS—Actors' Equity Association, Screen Actors Guild, American Federation of Television and Radio Actors.

ADDRESS: HOME—1851 Trinity Avenue, Apt. 218, Walnut Creek, CA 94596.

*　　*　　*

BUONO, Victor　1938-81

PERSONAL: Born February 3, 1938, in San Diego, CA; died January 1, 1981. EDUCATION: Attended Villanova University.

VOCATION: Actor.

CAREER: PRINCIPAL FILM APPEARANCES—*Whatever Happened to Baby Jane?,* Warner Brothers, 1962; *My Six Loves,* Paramount,

1963; *Four for Texas*, Warner Brothers, 1963; *The Strangler*, Allied Artists, 1964; *Robin and the Seven Hoods*, Warner Brothers, 1964; *Hush . . . Hush Sweet Charlotte*, Twentieth Century-Fox, 1965; *The Greatest Story Ever Told*, United Artists, 1965; *Who's Minding the Mint*, Columbia, 1967; *Target: Harry*, 1969; *Boot Hill*, 1969; *Beneath the Planet of the Apes*, Twentieth Century-Fox, 1970; *The Wrath of God*, Metro-Goldwyn-Mayer, 1972; *Arnold*, Cinerama, 1973; *The Evil*, 1978; *Trip to Terror; The Mad Butcher; The Toy Grabbers; The Savage Season; Big Daddy; Moon Child; The Man with Icy Eyes; In the Name of the Father; Northeast Seoul; Partisan; Savage in the City; Ciclon; The Man with Bogart's Face*, 1980; *Sam Marlow, Private Eye*, Twentieth Century-Fox, 1980.

PRINCIPAL TELEVISION APPEARANCES—Movies: *Goodnight, My Love; Crime Club; The Lie; The Ambassador; Benjamin Franklin; Brenda Starr; Trouble Shooters; Better Late Than Never; Murder Can Hurt You; More Wild, Wild West; Gamma Chronicles; Judgement Day*. Series: King Tut, *Batman;* Mr. Schubert, *Man from Atlantis; The Wild, Wild West; The Untouchables; The Detectives; Checkmate; The Corrupters; Thriller*.

SIDELIGHTS: Before the announcement of his death, Buono was scheduled to appear in Anthony Shaffer's *Whodunnit?* on Broadway.*

*　　　*　　　*

BURCH, Shelly   1959-

PERSONAL: Born March 19, 1959, in Tucson, AZ; daughter of Roy Dean (an attorney) and Patricia Ann (a businesswoman; maiden name, Meeks) Burch. EDUCATION: Carnegie-Mellon University, 1976-77; trained for the stage at Circle in the Square, NY with Nikos Psacharopolous. RELIGION: Presbyterian.

VOCATION: Actress and singer.

CAREER: STAGE DEBUT—Chorus roles, *Anything Goes, Gypsy, Finian's Rainbow, Oliver,* and *Company*, Pittsburgh Civic Light Opera, 1977. NEW YORK DEBUT—Jane, *Stop the World, I Want to Get Off*, New York State Theatre, Lincoln Center, NY, 1978. PRINCIPAL STAGE APPEARANCES—''Star-to-Be,'' *Annie*, Alvin, NY, 1979; Claudia, *Nine*, 46th Street Theatre, NY, 1981.

MAJOR TOURS—Jane, *Stop the World . . .* , Los Angeles, San Diego, Chicago, etc., 1977.

FILM DEBUT—Jane, *Stop the World, I Want to Get Off*, 1978 (possible cable-TV film). PRINCIPAL FILM APPEARANCES— Jerrilyn, *Cats Eye*, Metro-Goldwyn-Mayer/United Artists, 1985.

TELEVISION DEBUT—Delila, *One Life to Live*, ABC, 1981.

AWARDS: Drama Desk Award nomination, 1982, for *Nine*.

ADDRESS: OFFICE—888 Eighth Avenue, Suite 12-O, New York, NY 10036. AGENT—Dulcina Eisen Associates, 154 E. 61st Street, New York, NY 10021.

*　　　*　　　*

BURROWS, Abe   1910-84

PERSONAL: Born Abram Solman Borowitz, December 10, 1910,

in New York City; died May 17, 1984, in New York City; married Ruth Levinson, 1938 (divorced, 1948); married Caron Smith Kinzel, 1950; children: (first marriage) James, Laurie.

VOCATION: Librettist, director, author, and comic.

CAREER: PRINCIPAL STAGE WORK—Director: *Can-Can*, 1952; *Two on the Aisle*, 1952; *Reclining Figure*, 1954; *Happy Hunting*, 1956; *Say Darling*, 1958; *First Impressions* and *Golden Fleecing*, both 1959; *How to Succeed in Business without Really Trying* (also co-produced), 1961; *What Makes Sammy Run*, 1964; *Cactus Flower*, 1965; *Forty Carats*, 1968; *Four on a Garden*, 1971; *No Hard Feelings; Good News*, 1973.

WRITINGS: PLAYS, PRODUCED—*Guys and Dolls* (with Frank Loesser and Jo Swerling), 1950; *Three Wishes for Jamie* (with Charles O'Neal), 1952; *Can-Can*, 1953; *Silk Stockings* (with George S. Kaufman and Leueen McGrath), 1955; *Say Darling* (with Richard and Marian Bissell), 1958; *First Impressions*, 1959; *How to Succeed in Business without Really Trying* (with Loesser and Swerling), 1961; *Cactus Flower*, 1965; *Four on a Garden*, 1971; *Hellzapoppin*, 1976.

AUTOBIOGRAPHY—*Honest Abe*, 1980.

AWARDS: Drama Critics Circle, Antoinette Perry Award, both 1950, for *Guys and Dolls;* Pulitzer, Drama Critics Circle, Antoinette Perry Award, all 1961, for *How to Succeed in Business without Really Trying*.

SIDELIGHTS: Burrows began his career as a radio and television writer for *This Is New York*, 1938, *Rudy Vallee Program*, 1940, *Duffy's Tavern*, 1940-45, and *Abe Burrows' Show*, 1946-47.*

*　　　*　　　*

BURTON, Kate   1957-

PERSONAL: Full name Katherine Burton; born September 10, 1957, in Geneva, Switzerland; daughter of Richard (an actor) and Sybil (a producer; maiden name, Williams) Burton; married Michael Ritchie, June, 1985. EDUCATION: Brown University, history and Russian, 1979; Yale School of Drama, M.F.A., acting, 1982. POLITICS: Democrat.

CAREER: NEW YORK STAGE DEBUT—Daphne, *Present Laughter*, Circle in the Square, NY, 1982. PRINCIPAL STAGE APPEAR-ANCES—Alice, *Alice in Wonderland*, Virginia Theatre, NY, 1983; May, *Winners*, Roundabout, NY, 1983; JJ, *Doonesbury*, Biltmore, NY, 1983; Eva, *The Accrington Pals*, Hudson Guild, NY, 1984; Pegeen, *Playboy of the Western World*, Roundabout, NY, 1985; *Plough and the Stars*, Roundabout, NY, 1985.

TELEVISION DEBUT—Alice, *Alice in Wonderland*, PBS, 1983. PRINCIPAL TELEVISION APPEARANCES—Vanessa, *Ellis Island*, CBS, 1984; Agatha, *Evergreen*, NBC, 1985.

AWARDS: Theatre World Awards for *Present Laughter*, *Alice in Wonderland*, and *Winners*, 1982-83.

SIDELIGHTS: Burton told *CTFT:* ''My favorite role was May in *Winners*. I work with a group in New York called Artists in Action which involves itself in many political events, most notably, the

KATE BURTON

Mondale campaign and, most recently, America's involvement in Central America.''

ADDRESS: AGENT—Smith-Freedman, 850 Seventh Avenue, New York, NY 10019.

*   *   *

BURTON, Richard   1925-84

PERSONAL: Born November 10, 1925, in Wales; died August 5, 1984 in Switzerland; married Sybil Williams, 1949 (divorced, 1963); married Elizabeth Taylor, 1964 (divorced, 1974); married Elizabeth Taylor, 1975 (divorced, 1976); married Susan Hunt, 1976 (divorced 1982); married Sally Ann Hay, 1983; children: (first marriage) two daughters.

VOCATION: Actor.

CAREER: STAGE DEBUT—Glan, *Druid's Rest*, Royal Court Theatre, Liverpool, England, 1943. PRINCIPAL STAGE APPEARANCES— Angelo, *Measure for Measure*, 1944; Mr. Hicks, *Castle Anna*, Lyric Theatre, Hammersmith, 1948; Richard, *The Lady's Not for Burning*, Globe, 1949; Cuthman, *The Boy with a Cart*, Lyric, Hammersmith, 1950; Tegeus, *A Phoenix too Frequent*, Brighton, 1950; Musician, *Legend of Lovers*, Plymouth, 1951; Captain Montserrat, *Montserrat*, Lyric, Hammersmith, 1952; title role, *Hamlet*, Edinburgh Festival, 1953; Philip the Bastard, *King John;* Sir Toby Belch, *Twelfth Night;* Caius Martius, *Coriolanus;* Caliban, *The Tempest;* title role, *Henry V,* Old Vic, 1955; Prince Albert, *Time Remembered*, Morosco, NY, 1957; Arthur, *Camelot*, Majestic, NY, 1960; title role, Sir John Gielgud's production of *Hamlet*, Lunt-Fontaine, NY, 1964; title role, *Dr. Fastus*, Oxford Playhouse, 1966; Martin Dysart, *Equus*, Plymouth, NY, 1976; *Private Lives*, NY.

FILM DEBUT: *My Cousin Rachel*, 1952. PRINCIPAL FILM WORK— *The Robe*, 1953; *Prince of Players*, 1955; *Alexander the Great*, United Artists, 1956; *Rains of Ranchipur*, Twentieth Century-Fox, 1956; *The Bramble Bush*, Warner Brothers, 1960; *The Longest Day*, Paramount, 1960; *Cleopatra*, Twentieth Century-Fox, 1963; *Look Back in Anger*, Warner Brothers, 1959; *Becket*, Paramount, 1964; *Night of the Iguana*, Metro-Goldwyn-Mayer, 1964; *The Sandpiper*, Metro-Goldwyn-Mayer, 1965.

The Spy Who Came in from the Cold, Paramount, 1966; *Who's Afraid of Virginia Woolf*, Warner Brothers, 1966; *The Taming of the Shrew*, Columbia/Royal Films, 1967; *Doctor Faustus*, Columbia, 1968; *Boom*, Universal, 1968; *Candy*, Cinerama, 1968; *Where Eagles Dare*, Metro-Goldwyn-Mayer, 1969; *The Comedians*, Metro-Goldwyn-Mayer, 1969; *Staircase*, Twentieth Century-Fox, 1969; *Anne of the Thousands Days*, 1970; *Raid on Rommel*, Universal, 1971; *Villian*, Universal, 1971; *Under Milkwood*, 1973; *Hammersmith Is Out*, Cinerama, 1972; *Tito; The Assassination of Trotsky*, Cinerama, 1972; *Bluebeard*, Cinerama, 1972; *Massacre in Rome*, National General, 1973; *The Voyage*, 1973; *The Klansman*, Paramount, 1974; *Exorcist II: The Heretic*, Warner Brothers, 1977; *The Medusa Touch*, Warner Brothers, 1978; *The Wild Geese*, Allied Artists, 1978; *Absolution; Sergeant Steiner; Tristan and Zseult; Circle of Two*, 1980; *1984*.

PRINCIPAL TELEVISION APPEARANCES—*Wuthering Heights*, 1958; *Divorce His, Divorce Hers; Brief Encounter; Here's Lucy* (episode), 1970; *Wagner* (television movie), 1982; *Ellis Island* (mini-series), 1984; *Walk with Destiny*.

AWARDS: Received seven Oscar nominations for the following films: *My Cousin Rachel*, 1952; *The Robe*, 1953; *Becket*, 1964; *The Spy Who Came in from the Cold*, 1966; *Who's Afraid of Virginia Woolf?*, 1966; *Anne of the Thousand Days*, 1969; *Equus*, 1977; Golden Globe Award, *Equus*.*

*   *   *

BUZAS, Jason   1952-

PERSONAL: Born February 22, 1952; son of Joseph and H. Penelope (McConnell) Buzas. EDUCATION: Carnegie-Mellon University, B.F.A., 1973.

VOCATION: Director.

CAREER: STAGE DEBUT—*The Devil's Disciple*, Brooklyn Academy of Music Theater Company, NY, 1976.

PRINCIPAL STAGE WORK—Director: *The Prevalence of Mrs. Seal*, Manhattan Punch Line, NY, 1981; *Eileen, Rosalie, One Touch of Venus, Roberta, Music in the Air*, all at New Amsterdam Theatre Company, Town Hall, NY, 1982-85; *After You've Gone*, Actor's Repertory, NY, 1982; *All's Well That Ends Well*, Shakespeare Festival of Dallas, TX, 1982; *The Virgin Unmasked*, Kennedy Center Musical Theatre Lab, Washington, DC, 1983; *I Don't Want to be Zelda Anymore*, Actor's Repertory, NY, 1984.

RELATED CAREER—Artist training consultant, Affiliate Artists, Inc., 1979-81; guest director, State University of New York at Purchase, 1983-85; teaching artist, Lincoln Center Institute, NY, 1981-86.

SIDELIGHTS: MEMBERSHIPS—Actors' Equity Association, Society of Stage Directors and Choreographers.

ADDRESS: HOME—156 Franklin Street, New York, NY 10013.

C

CADELL, Simon   1950-

PERSONAL: Born Simon John Cadell, July 19, 1950, in London, England; son of John (a theatrical agent) and Gillian (a drama school principal; maiden name, Howell) Cadell. EDUCATION: Studied for the theatre at the Bristol Old Vic.

VOCATION: Actor.

CAREER: PRINCIPAL STAGE APPEARANCES—Zigger Zagger, National Youth Theatre; Major Barbara, Macbeth, School for Scandal, The Importance of Being Earnest, Arms and the Man, Bristol Old Vic; A Close Shave, Antigone, The Balcony, Nottingham Theatre; Geneva, Mermaid, London; Lloyd George Knew My Father, Savoy, London; Oswald, Ghosts, Birmingham Repertory; The Case in Question, Haymarket, London; Lies, Albery, London; Widower's Houses, How the Other Half Loves, The Amazons, Actors Company; Ernest, You Should See Us Now, Greenwich; Hamlet, Hamlet, Birmingham Repertory; Raffles, Raffles, Watford Place, Watford.

MAJOR TOURS—Elyot, Private Lives, British National Tour.

PRINCIPAL TELEVISION APPEARANCES—Plaintiff and Defendant, BBC; Two Sundays, BBC; The Glittering Prizes, BBC; The Dame of Sark, Anglia; The Promise, Anglia; She Fell among Thieves, BBC; The Trials of Oscar Slater, BBC; Name for the Day, BBC; Edward and Mrs. Simpson, Thames; Minder, Euston Films; When the Boat Comes In, BBC; Tales of the Unexpected, Anglia; Enemy at the Door, LWT; Bergerac, BBC; lead, Hi De Hi, BBC; Blott on the Landscape, BBC.

ADDRESS: AGENT—MLR, 200 Fulham Road, London SW 10, England.

*   *   *

CAGE, Nicholas

BRIEF ENTRY: Born Nicholas Coppola. Actor. He changed his name to avoid calling attention to his relation to Francis Ford Coppola (Coppola is Cage's uncle). At age fifteen, Cage was a member of the American Conservatory Theatre in San Francisco. His film credits include Valley Girl, Atlantic, 1983; Rumble Fish, Universal, 1983; Racing with the Moon, Paramount, 1984; Birdy, Tri-Star, 1984; Cotton Club, 1984; The Boy in Blue (upcoming).*

CANDY, John

BRIEF ENTRY: Born in Toronto, ON, Canada. Actor and comedian. Candy first found acclaim as a member of the Second City comedy troupe in Toronto and Chicago. He was a featured player in SCTV and Network 90, and starred in his own television show, Big City Comedy. He also co-wrote and starred in the television movie Drums over Malta. His motion picture credits include 1941, Universal, 1979; The Blues Brothers, Universal, 1980; Strips, Columbia, 1981; Night Shift, Warner Brothers, 1982; National Lampoon's Vacation, Warner Brothers, 1983; Splash, Touchstone, 1984; Brewster's Millions, 1985; Summer Rental, Paramount, 1985; and Volunteers (upcoming).*

*   *   *

CAPSHAW, Kate

BRIEF ENTRY: Born Kathy Sue Nail, in TX; married John Capshaw (divorced); children: Jessica. Former high school teacher and model. Capshaw appeared in the television daytime drama The Edge of Night, ABC. Her film credits include A Little Sex, Universal, 1982; Windy City, 1983; Indiana Jones and the Temple of Doom, Universal, 1984; Best Defense, Paramount, 1984; Dreamscape, 1984; Power, Lorimar (upcoming); SpaceCamp (upcoming).*

*   *   *

CARA, Irene   1960-

BRIEF ENTRY: Born 1960, in Bronx, NY. Actress and singer. Cara made her stage debut in the Broadway production of the musical Maggie Flynn when she was five years old. At age eleven, she won an Obie for her performance in The Me Nobody Knows. Other stage credits include the Broadway production of Via Galactica, 1972; she was part of the original off Broadway cast of Ain't Misbehavin'; and was seen in Got to Go Disco. Cara's first feature film was Aaron Loves Angela, Columbia, 1975. Since then, her credits include Sparkle, Warner Brothers, 1976; Fame, United Artists, 1980; The Man in 5A; D.C. Cab, 1983; City Heat, 1984; A Certain Fury, New World Pictures, 1985. On television: Electric Company, PBS, 1972; Roots: The Next Generation, ABC, 1979; The Guyana Tragedy: The Story of Jim Jones, 1980; Sisters, NBC; For Us the Living, PBS. Her song hits include "Flashdance . . . What a Feeling," for which she won a Grammy and an Oscar; "Fame," "Out Here on My Own," "Anyone Can See," "The Dream" (from D.C. Cab), and "Breakdance."

ADDRESS: OFFICE—104-60 Queens Blvd., Forest Hills, NY 11375.*

KEVIN CARLISLE

CARLISLE, Kevin   1935-

PERSONAL: Born December 24, 1935, in Brooklyn, NY; son of Theodore D. and Ruth (Bardell) Carlisle. EDUCATION: Graduate of Juilliard School of Music.

VOCATION: Director, producer, and choreographer.

CAREER: PRINCIPAL TELEVISION WORK—Producer, director, and choreographer: *Tony Awards Show,* 1970; *Academy Awards Show,* 1972; *Grammy Awards Show,* 1973; *Disney Golf Classic Variety Special; Disney Thanksgiving Special; Jim Nabors Show; Smothers Brothers Show; Nobody's Perfect; The Singers; Sonny and Cher Show; Music for a Winter's Night; Bing Crosby Special; Jonathan Winters Special; Tennessee Ernie Ford Christmas Special; Monty Hall Special; The Brass Are Coming; Don Ho Special;* (three) *Bob Hope Special; Jack Benny Specials; Dick Van Dyke Meets Bill Cosby; Doris Day Special; Jose Feliciano Special.*

Dinah Shore Telethon; Jerry Lewis Telthon, 1974, 1976; (four) *Bell Telephone Hour;* (four) *Chevrolet Special; Tony Bennett Special; Gypsy Fever; State Fair America,* 1977; *The Great American Music Celebration,* 1977; *The Junior Miss Pageant,* 1974-78; *Rich Little Christmas Carol,* 1978; *The Second Barry Manilow Special,* 1978; *The Third Barry Manilow Special,* 1979; *Tuscaloosa's Calling Me But I'm Not Going,* 1980; *Karen Morrow and Nancy Dussault Special,* 1980; *John Schneider Special,* 1980; *Bea Arthur Special,* 1980; *Barry Manilow, "One Voice,"* 1980; *Solid Gold,* 1979-82; *Solid Gold Christmas Special,* 1982; *Battle of the Beat,* 1983; *Pump Boys and Dinettes,* 1983; *Debbie Reynolds Exercise Show,* 1983; *Barry Manilow in Concert,* Showtime, 1983; *Barry in Japan,* TBS, 1983; *Barry at Blenheim,* BBC, 1983.

Series: *Garry Moore Show; Dean Martin Show; Coliseum Variety; Glen Campbell Show; What's It All About World Series; Cos,* 1977; *Peter Marshall Variety Show,* 1977; *Sha Na Na,* 1978; *The New Quiz Kids,* 1978; *The Little Show,* 1978; *Sold Gold,* 1980-83; *Alice,* 1984; *Benson,* 1984.

Foreign Specials: *A Christmas Carol,* Canadian Broadcasting System; *Vienna Ice Show, Carousel, Wonderful Town,* Belgium; *Krona Circus,* Germany; *The Modern Jazz Quartet,* France; (two) *Roy Castle,* England; *Sabato Serra,* Italy; *La Pelirroja, La tia de Carlos,* Mexico; *La Pelirroja,* Spain; *Tokyo Music Festival,* 1974, 1983, Japan.

PRINCIPAL STAGE WORK—Director, producer, and choreographer: Concerts—Ed Bruce; Charly McClain; Group with No Name; Shari Lewis; Holly Lipton; Lettermen; Hank Williams Jr.; Judy Garland; *An Evening with George Burns;* The Mike Curb Congregation; Joey Heatherton; Liberace; Steve Lawrence and Eydie Gorme; Connie Stevens; Shields and Yarnell; Karen Morrow and Nancy Dussault; Peter Marshall; Janie Fricke; *Kevin Carlisle's Sold Gold Dancers;* Paul Anka, 1983; *Barry Manilow-The Concert at Blenheim Palace;* Melissa Manchester, 1983, 1984; Tammy Wynette, 1984; *Solid Gold at Riviera Hotel, Las Vegas,* 1984, 1985; Marilyn McCoo and Billy Davis Jr., 1984; Marilyn McCoo, 1984, 1985; Robert Guillaume, 1985.

Choreographer (Broadway): *Happy Time; Hallelujah, Baby!; Harry Blackstone, Jr. on Broadway; Barry Manilow on Broadway,* 1983.

MAJOR TOURS—Barry Manilow's national tour, 1979-85; Barry Manilow's international tour, 1979-85; Shaun Cassidy's national tour, 1979-80; Harry Blackstone, Jr., 1980.

AWARDS: Antoinette Perry Award nomination, for *Hallelujah, Baby!;* Antoinette Perry Award, for *Happy Time;* Emmy Award, 1979, for *The Third Barry Manilow Television Special.*

SIDELIGHTS: MEMBERSHIPS—Society of Stage Directors and Choreographers, Actors' Equity Association, American Federation of Television and Radio Artists, Directors Guild of America, Association of Canadian Television and Radio Artists, American Society of Composers, Authors, and Publishers.

ADDRESS: OFFICE—1915 N. Crescent Heights Blvd., Los Angeles, CA 90069.

*   *   *

CARR, Martin   1932-

PERSONAL: Born Martin Douglas Conovitz, January 20, 1932, in Flushing, NY; son of Irving and Isabel (Hochdorf) Conovitz. EDUCATION: Williams College, B.A., 1953; studied at Neighborhood Playhouse School of Theatre with Sanford Meisner, 1956. MILITARY: U.S. Navy Reserve, 1953-55.

VOCATION: Producer, director, and writer.

CAREER: PRINCIPAL TELEVISION WORK—Producer: *CBS News* NY, 1957-69, *NBC News,* NY, 1969-71, *ABC News,* NY, 1973-75; producer, writer and director: *CBS Reports: Hunger in America; The Search for Ulysses; Gaugin in Tahiti; Five Faces of Tokyo; Dublin Through Different Eyes; NBC White Paper: Migrant; NBC*

White Paper: The Child Is Rated X; director: *ABC Close-Up: The Culture Thieves; 20/20; PBS Global Paper: Waging Peace;* executive producer, *Smithsonian World,* Washington, DC, PBS, 1981-present.

AWARDS: Emmy, National Academy of Television Arts and Sciences, 1966, 1967, 1968, 1971; Peabody, University of Georgia School of Journalism, 1968, 1970, 1971; Robert F. Kennedy Journalism Award, 1970; Sidney Hillman Foundation Award, 1971; DuPont/Columbia Journalism Award, 1971; Gavel Award, American Bar Association, 1972.

SIDELIGHTS: MEMBERSHIPS—Williams Club.

ADDRESS: HOME—1080 Wisconsin Avenue, N.W., Suite 3010, Washington, DC 20007. AGENT—Geller Media Management, Inc., 250 W. 57th Street, New York, NY 10019.

* * *

CARTER, Lynda

BRIEF ENTRY: Full name Lynda Jean Carter; born July 24, in Phoenix, AZ; married Ron Samuels (divorced); married Robert A. Altman. Attended Arizona State University. Carter toured for four years with the rock group Garfin Gathering. In 1973, she was named Miss World-USA. On television she starred as *Wonder Woman,* ABC, 1976-77; then again in *The New Adventures of Wonder Woman,* CBS, 1977-79. She also starred in the series *Partners in Crime,* NBC, 1984. Her television movies include *The Last Song,* 1980; *Born to Be Sold,* 1981. She also did several specials for CBS and appears regularly in Las Vegas.

ADDRESS: OFFICE—Lynda Carter Productions, P.O. Box 5973, Sherman Oaks, CA 91413.*

* * *

CARTWRIGHT, Veronica

BRIEF ENTRY: Actress. Cartwright, like her sister Angela, began her career as a child actress. She portrayed Jemima Boone in *Daniel Boone,* NBC, 1964-66. She was also seen as Agatha in the *Twilight Zone* episode, "I Sing the Body Electric." Later television appearances include her portrayal of Ethel Kennedy in the CBS miniseries *Robert Kennedy and His Times,* 1984. Her film credits include *The Birds,* Universal, 1963; *Invasion of the Body Snatchers,* United Artists, 1978; *Alien,* Twentieth Century-Fox, 1979; *The Right Stuff,* Warner Brothers, 1983; *Nightmares,* 1983, and *Inside Adam Swit* Tri-Star, (upcoming). Most recently she was seen in the play "Mirror, Mirror," a segment of *The Triplet Connection* at the Matrix in Los Angeles, 1985.*

* * *

CATLETT, Mary Jo 1938-

PERSONAL: Born September 2, 1938; daughter of Robert J. and Cornelia M. Catlett. EDUCATION: B.A., 1960. RELIGION: Catholic.

VOCATION: Actress.

CAREER: STAGE DEBUT: *Shoemaker and the Elves,* school play, age 6. NEW YORK DEBUT: Ernestia, *Hello, Dolly!,* St. James, for three years. PRINCIPAL STAGE APPEARANCES—*Promenade,* NY, 1966; *The Canterbury Tales,* NY, 1967; *Lysistrata,* NY, 1969; *Different Times,* NY, 1970; *Fashion,* NY, 1973; *The Pajama Game,* NY, 1974; *Play Me a Country Song,* NY, 1981. Also: Lola, *Come Back, Little Sheba,* Los Angeles; Annie, *Annie Get Your Gun;* Gramma Briggs, *Greenwillow,* ELT, NY; Flora Meighan, *27 Wagons Full of Cotton,* Washington, DC; *Philadelphia, Here I Come,* Los Angeles, CA.

FILM DEBUT: Erlene, *Semi-Tough,* United Artists, 1977. PRINCIPAL FILM APPEARANCES: *The Champ,* United Artists, 1979; *The Best Little Whorehouse in Texas,* Universal, 1982.

TELEVISION DEBUT: Terrible Tessie, *Starsky and Hutch,* ABC, 1976. PRINCIPAL TELEVISION APPEARANCES: *The Bob Newhart Show,* CBS; *Diff'rent Strokes,* NBC; *Foul Play; Where the Ladies Go,* 1980.

AWARDS: Washington Drama Critics, 1970, for *27 Wagons Full of Cotton;* Los Angeles Drama Critics, for *Come Back, Little Sheba* and *Philadelphia, Here I Come.*

SIDLELIGHTS: MEMBERSHIPS—Actors' Equity Association, American Federation of Television and Radio Artists, American Guild of Variety Artists, Screen Actors Guild.

FAVORITE ROLES: Lola, *Come Back, Little Sheba* and Annie, *Annie Get Your Gun.*

Expressing her concerns to *CTFT,* Mary Jo Catlett said, "I feel animal experimentation must be stopped."

ADDRESS: AGENT—Marje Fields, Inc., 165 W. 46th Street, New York, NY 10036.

* * *

CHACKSFIELD, Frank
(Roger Senicourt, Martino Patacano)

PERSONAL: Born in England; son of Charles (an engineer) and Alice May (Evans) Chacksfield; married Jeanne Lehmann, October 19, 1946. EDUCATION: Battle and Langton School, Sussex.

VOCATION: Composer, conductor, and arranger.

CAREER: COMPOSITION, FILMS—*Meet Mr. Callahan; A Time to Kill; The Harrassed Hero.* COMPOSITION, ORCHESTRAL—*Sea Mist; Catalan Sunshine; Cuban Boy; Love by Starlight; Blue Train.*

PRINCIPAL RADIO WORK—*The Frank Chacksfield Hour,* BBC.

Conducted live concerts in London and Europe; conducted television concerts in Great Britain, Europe and Japan, and television and radio concerts in the U. S. Recorded more than 100 records for British Decca, 1953-1979.

RELATED CAREER—Publisher of Frank Chacksfield Music/Eros Music.

AWARDS: Golden Records for sales in excess of one million disks,

FRANK CHACKSFIELD

Limelight and *Ebb Tide;* Cash Box Award for the Most Promising New Orchestra of 1953.

SIDELIGHTS: MEMBERSHIPS—Performing Rights Society, MCPS. RECREATION—Classical music including Mozart and Grieg; good food and wine.

ADDRESS: OFFICE—''Allegro'', Elm Walk, Farnborough Park, Oppington, Kent, BR6 8LX England.

* * *

CHANDLER, Jeffrey Alan

PERSONAL: Born September 9, in Durham, NC; son of Druery Allen (a mailman) and Annie Louise (an office worker; maiden name, Weaver) Chandler. EDUCATION: Carnegie Institute of Technology, B.F.A., 1967. RELIGION: Methodist.

VOCATION: Actor.

CAREER: STAGE DEBUT—Matt, *The Fantasticks,* Pittsburgh Playhouse, PA, 1965. NEW YORK DEBUT—Phillip of Spain, *Elizabeth, I,* Lyceum, 1971. PRINCIPAL STAGE APPEARANCES—Over forty roles in eight seasons with the Tyrone Guthrie, Minneapolis, 1973-1979, including: Tom, *The Glass Menagerie,* Aston, *The Caretaker,* Scrooge, *A Christmas Carol,* Clov, *Endgame,* Rosencrantz, *Rosencrantz and Guildenstern Are Dead,* Claudio, *Measure*

for Measure, Leo, *Design for Living,* Flamino, *The White Devil,* Lucky, *Waiting for Godot,* Tony Lumpkin, *She Stoops to Conquer,* Swiss Cheese, *Mother Courage,* first voice, *Under Milkwood,* Foster, *The National Health,* Prince Florizel, *A Winter's Tale,* Boyet, *Love's Labor's Lost,* the Young Gentleman, *La Ronde,* Salario, *The Merchant of Venice,* Bobchinsky, *The Government Inspector,* Ed, *You Can't Take It with You.*

Algernon, *The Importance of Being Earnest,* Mercury, *Amphytrion '38,* Melville, *Mary Stuart, A Streetcar Named Desire,* all at the Milwaukee Repertory; Jacques, *As You Like It,* George, *Of Mice and Men,* both at the Hartford Stage Co.; Matthew, *An Attempt at Flying,* Yale Repertory, New Haven, CT; Sir Andrew Aguecheek, *Twelfth Night,* Roderigo, *Othello,* Dr. Einstein, *Arsenic and Old Lace,* the Priest, *Roshomon,* Leslie, *Taking Steps,* all at the Old Globe Theatre, San Diego, CA; Shylock, *The Merchant of Venice,* Antonio, *The Tempest,* Billings, *The Enemy of the People,* Dr. Serringe, *The Relapse,* St. Albans, *Hadrian VII,* all at A.C.T., San Francisco; Babyface, *Kid Twist,* Mark Taper Playworks, Los Angeles; Wally, *Alphabetical Order;* Danny, *Your Own Thing,* Orpheum, NY; Houdini, *Houdini,* NY; Singer, *The People vs. Ranchman,* NY; Penguin, *Penguin Touquet,* NY; Pilate, *Jesus Christ, Superstar,* Los Angeles Company; Kent, *The Dresser,* Brooks Atkinson, NY, 1981; Sergeant Standish, *Whodunit,* Broadhurst, NY, 1982 (also at A.C.T. and Hartford Stage Company).

TELEVISION DEBUT—*Lou Grant,* 1979. PRINCIPAL TELEVISION APPEARANCES—*Hill Street Blues; A School for Scandal; Camille; All the World's a Stage.*

SIDELIGHTS: MEMBERSHIPS—Actors' Equity Association, Ameri-

JEFFREY ALAN CHANDLER

can Federation of Television and Radio Artists, Screen Actors Guild.

ADDRESS: AGENT—The Gage Group, Inc., 1650 Broadway, New York, NY 10019.

* * *

CHARNIN, Martin 1934-

PERSONAL: Born November 24, 1934, in New York City; son of William and Birdie (Blakeman) Charnin; married Lynn Ross (divorced); married Genii Prior (divorced); married Jade Hobson. EDUCATION: Cooper Union, B.A., 1955.

VOCATION: Director, lyricist, producer, composer, author, and actor.

CAREER: NEW YORK DEBUT—Big Deal, *West Side Story,* Winter Garden, 1957. PRINCIPAL STAGE APPEARANCES— Performer, *The Boys Against the Girls,* Alvin, NY, 1960; Big Deal, *West Side Story,* Winter Garden, NY, 1960.

PRINCIPAL STAGE WORK—Producer and lyricist, *Kaleidoscope Revue,* Provincetown Playhouse, 1957; writer and lyricist, *Fallout Revue,* Renata, NY, 1959; lyricist, *Pieces of Eight,* Upstairs at the Downstairs, NY, 1959; lyricist, *Hot Spot,* Majestic, NY, 1963; writer, *Wet Paint,* Renata, NY, 1965; lyricist, *Mata Hari,* Washington, DC, 1967; lyricist and director, *Ballad for a Firing Squad,* Theatre de Lys, NY, 1968; lyricist, *Two by Two,* Imperial, NY,

MARTIN CHARNIN

1970; writer and director, *Nash at Nine,* 1973; director, *Music, Music,* 1974; lyricist and director, *Annie,* NY, 1977; director, *Barmitzvah Boy,* London, 1978; lyricist, *I Remember Mama,* NY, 1979; writer, lyricist, and director, *The First,* NY, 1981; lyricist, *Lena Horne: A Lady and Her Music,* NY, 1982; director, *A Little Family Business,* NY, 1983; writer, producer, and director, *Upstairs at O'Neals,* NY, 1983; director, *On the Swingshift,* Manhattan Theater Club, NY, 1984; director, *A Backer's Audition,* Manhattan Theatre Club, NY, 1984.

MAJOR TOURS—Lyricist, *Little Revue,* 1960; lyricist, *Zenda,* California cities, 1963; lyricist and director, *Annie,* U.S. cities, London, 1978.

PRINCIPAL TELEVISION WORK—Lyricist, *Feathertop,* 1961; lyricist, *Jackie Gleason Show,* 1961; producer, *Annie: The Women in the Life of a Man,* 1970; director, *George M!;* director, *'S Wonderful, 'S Marvelous, 'S Gershwin;* director, *Dames at Sea.*

WRITINGS: BOOKS—*The Giraffe Who Sounded Like Ol' Blue Eyes,* 1976; *Annie: A Theatre Memoir,* 1977.

AWARDS: Emmy Award, 1970, for *Annie: The Women in the Life of a Man.*

ADDRESS: OFFICE—c/o Richard Ticktin, 555 Fifth Avenue, New York, NY 10017.

* * *

CHER 1946-

BRIEF ENTRY: Born Cherilyn Sarkisian, May 20, 1946; daughter of John and Georgia (Holt) Sarkisian; married Sonny Bono, 1964 (divorced); married Gregg Allman, 1975 (divorced); children: (first marriage) Chastity; (second marriage) Elijah Blue. Studied drama with Jeff Corey. Cher began her career with her first husband as part of the duo Sonny and Cher. Some of their hits include "I Got You Babe," "Baby Don't Go," and "You Better Sit Down Kids." They appeared on *Shindig,* ABC, 1964, then starred in three variety shows: *The Sonny and Cher Comedy Hour,* CBS, 1971-74; *Cher,* CBS, 1975-76; and *The Sonny and Cher Show,* CBS, 1976-77. She made her Broadway debut in *Come Back to the Five and Dime, Jimmy Dean, Jimmy Dean.* Her film credits include *Good Times,* Columbia, 1967; *Chastity,* American International Pictures, 1969; *Come Back to the Five and Dime, Jimmy Dean, Jimmy Dean,* 1982; *Silkwood* (Academy Award nomination, Best Supporting Actress), Twentieth Century-Fox, 1983; *Mask,* 1985. Some of Cher's solo hits as a recording artist are "Gypsies, Tramps, and Thieves," "Dark Lady," "Take Me Home," and "Half Breed." She had two consecutive number one hits on the top forty pop chart.

ADDRESS: AGENT—International Creative Management, 8899 Beverly Blvd., Los Angeles, CA 90048.*

* * *

CHESTER, Nora

PERSONAL: Daughter of Leland Rucker (a banker and oil executive) and Alice Catherine (a singer and writer; maiden name,

NORA CHESTER

Collins) Chester. EDUCATION: Washington State University, B.A., speech, 1973; Florida State University, M.F.A., acting, 1976.

VOCATION: Actress, director, and writer.

CAREER: PRINCIPAL STAGE APPEARANCES—Pauline, *Four to Four*, Ubu Repertory, NY; June, *This Place Is Closed . . .* Production Company, NY; Pup, *Pup*, Theatre of the Open Eye, NY; Maddy, *Ornaments*, Direct Theatre, NY; Eleanor Bull, *Death by Misadventure*, N.E.T.W.O.R.K. Studios, NY; Louka, *Arms and the Man*, Dionysa, Bawd, *Pericles*, Belle Starr, *Jesse and the Bandit Queen*, all at University of Rochester Summer Theatre; Anise, *Watch on the Rhine*, Gertrude, *The Sea Horse*, Attic Theatre; Gertrude Stein, *A Conversation with Gertrude Stein*, Mrs. Drudge, *The Real Inspector Hound*, Josie, *A Moon for the Misbegotten*, all at Bergenstage, NJ; Ethel, *The Music Man*, Agatha, *Guys and Dolls*, Ann Mulcahy, *Hogan's Goat*, Gertrude, *The Sea Horse*, all at Asolo State Theatre; waitress, wife, *Put Them All Together*, courtesan, *A Comedy of Errors*, McCarter, Princeton, NJ; Kate, *The S.S. Glencairn*, Long Wharf, New Haven, CT; Eunice, *A Streetcar Named Desire*, Daughter Margaret, *Quilters*, both at Geva; April, *The Hot L Baltimore*, Nurse, *Wings*, Sue Bayliss, *All My Sons*, all at Alaska Repertory; Leatha, *Food from Trash*, Actors Theatre of Louisville, KY; Jessie, *night Mother*, Alley Theatre.

PRINCIPAL STAGE WORK—Director: *A Coupla White Chicks Sitting Around Talking*, Attic Theatre; *Nice People Dancing to Good Country Music*, Alaska Repertory.

PRINCIPAL TELEVISION APPEARANCES—*CBS Mystery Theatre*; *Texas*.

WRITINGS: PLAYS, PRODUCED—*A Conversation with Gertrude Stein*, Bergenstage, NJ.

SIDELIGHTS: MEMBERSHIPS—Actors' Equity Association, Screen Actors Guild, American Federation of Television and Radio Artists; volunteer with Cancer Care and the American Cancer Society.

ADDRESS: HOME—Five W. 95th Street, New York, NY 10025.

*   *   *

CHONG, Tommy   1938–

BRIEF ENTRY: Full name Thomas Chong; born May 24, 1938, in Edmonton, Alberta, Canada; son of Stanley and Lorna Jean (Gilchrist) Chong. Comedian, actor, writer, and director. Has been part of the music groups "The Shades" and "The Vancouvers." Founder of improvisational troupe "City Works." Chong is half of the comedy duo Cheech (Richard Marin) and Chong. They have performed in numerous nightclubs and have recorded comedy albums. As part of Cheech and Chong, Chong's film work includes: co-writer and actor, *Up in Smoke*, Paramount, 1978; co-writer, director, and actor, *Cheech and Chong's Next Movie*, Universal, 1980; co-writer, director, and actor, *Cheech and Chong's Nice Dreams*, Columbia, 1981; co-writer and actor, *Things Are Tough All Over*, Columbia, 1982; actor, *It Came from Hollywood*, Paramount, 1982; co-writer, director, and actor, *Still Smoking*, Paramount, 1983; co-writer, director, and actor, *The Corsican Brothers*, Orion, 1984; *After Hours* (upcoming).

ADDRESS: OFFICE—Monterey Peninsula Artists, P.O. Box, 7308, Carmel, CA 93921.*

*   *   *

CHRISTY, Donald

PERSONAL: Born September 9, in Brooklyn, NY; married Alice Field (an actress), September 21; children: Pamela. EDUCATION: Ohio University, B.F.A. MILITARY: U.S. Army.

VOCATION: Production stage manager, director, and writer.

CAREER: PRINCIPAL STAGE WORK—Production stage manager: *Eubie, Timbuktu, The Wiz, Ulysses in Nighttown, Applause, Mother Earth, Don't Call Back, Thieves*, all on Broadway; *Encore*, Radio City Music Hall; *America*, Radio City Music Hall.

Stock and dinner theater: American Music Theatre Festival; Mineola Theatre; Westport Country Playhouse; Parker Playhouse; Coconut Grove Playhouse; Royal Poinciana Playhouse; Sacramento Music Circus; Fresno Music Circus; Garden Court Dinner Theatre.

Director at St. Louis Municipal Theater, Dallas Summer Musicals, Kansas City Starlight, Music Fairs, Milwaukee Melody Top, Casa Manana Musicals, Kenley Players, Once Upon a Stage Dinner Theatre.

MAJOR TOURS—Production stage manager: *Star-Spangled Girl; Agnes DeMille Dance Theatre; Black Comedy; Cactus Flower; Irene; The Wiz; Your Arms Too Short to Box with God*, 1982-83; *Zorba; Dracula*, 1984-85.

PRINCIPAL TELEVISION WORK—Production stage manager, *Night of a Hundred Stars,* 1981; stage manager, *Antoinette Perry Awards Show,* 1971, 1975, 1976.

SIDELIGHTS: MEMBERSHIPS—Actors' Equity Association, Society of Stage Directors and Choreographers, American Guild of Musical Artists, American Guild of Variety Artists.

ADDRESS: OFFICE—58-34 215th Street, Bayside Hills, NY 11364.

*   *   *

CIMINO, Michael   1948-

VOCATION: Writer, director, and producer.

PERSONAL: Writer, director, and producer.

CAREER: PRINCIPAL FILM WORK—Writer, *Silent Running,* Universal, 1972; writer, *Magnum Force,* Warner Brothers, 1973; writer and director, *Thunderbolt and Lightfoot,* United Artists, 1974; producer, writer, and director, *The Deer Hunter,* Universal, 1979; writer and director, *Heaven's Gate,* United Artists, 1980; co-writer (with Oliver Stone) and director, *The Year of the Dragon,* Metro-Goldwyn-Mayer/United Artists, 1985; director, *The Yellow Jersey* (upcoming).

ADDRESS: AGENT—International Creative Management, 8899 Beverly Blvd., Beverly Hills, CA 90048.*

*   *   *

CLARK, China

PERSONAL: Born in PA; daughter of Elise Baldock; married David Bloomquist (an actor). EDUCATION: Attended Columbia University and Central State University; trained for the stage at the American Academy and Herbert Berghof Studio.

VOCATION: Writer and actress.

CAREER: Principally a writer (see below), but has also acted. PRINCIPAL STAGE APPEARANCES—*Perfection in Black,* Negro Ensemble Company, NY, 1972; *In Sorrow's Room,* Henry Street, 1973-74; *Neffie's Dance,* Urban Arts, NY, 1975; *The Chinese Screen,* La MaMa, NY, 1976; *In Sorrow's Room,* Grass Roots, San Francisco, CA, 1977.

RELATED CAREER—President, New York Writers Network, 1978-84; president, China Company, 1982-84.

WRITINGS: TELEVISION—*Bill Cosby Show,* ABC, 1976; *Joy; Inglewood Cliffs; Those Broad House Girls; Baker; Cos.* FILM—*Mary's Emmanuel.* BOOKS—*A Black Woman in Contemporary Drama.* PLAYS, PRODUCED—*In Sorrow's Room,* Henry Street, NY, 1973; *Neffie's Dance,* Urban Arts, NY, 1975.

AWARDS: Three Woolrich Foundation Fellowships, Columbia University; Hannah del Vecchio Award; Creative Artists Award.

SIDELIGHTS: MEMBERSHIPS—Writers Guild, National Society of

Arts and Letters, National Academy of Television Arts and Sciences.

ADDRESS: HOME—353 W. 57th Street, New York, NY 10019.

*   *   *

CLAVER, Bob   1928-

PERSONAL: Full name Robert E. Claver; born May 22, 1928, in Chicago, IL; son of Louis E. and Sara M. (Sosna) Claver; married Catherine T. Dowdalls (a script supervisor); children: Nancy Beth. EDUCATION: University of Illinois, Champaign, B.A., journalism, 1950. RELIGION: Jewish. MILITARY: U.S. Army, 1951-53.

VOCATION: Director, producer, and writer.

CAREER: PRINCIPAL TELEVISION WORK—Producer and director: *Here Come the Brides,* ABC, 1968-70; *The Interns,* CBS, 1970-71; *The Partridge Family,* ABC, 1970-74; *Gloria,* CBS, 1982-83.

Director: *All's Fair,* 1976-77, CBS; *Welcome Back, Kotter,* ABC, 1977-78; *House Calls,* CBS, 1979-80; *Mork and Mindy,* ABC, 1981-82.

WRITINGS: TELEVISION SCRIPTS—*Captain Kangaroo* (wrote and also produced the first one thousand shows), CBS, 1955-57.

AWARDS: Peabody and Sylvania Awards, *Captain Kangaroo.*

SIDELIGHTS: MEMBERSHIPS—Directors Guild of America.

ADDRESS: AGENT—Shapiro-Lichtman, 8827 Beverly Blvd., Los Angeles, CA 90048.

*   *   *

CLAYBURGH, Jill   1944-

PERSONAL: Born April 30, 1944, in New York City; daughter of Albert Henry and Julia (Door) Clayburgh; married David Rabe (a playwright), March, 1979. EDUCATION: Sarah Lawrence College, B.A., 1966.

VOCATION: Actress.

CAREER: PRINCIPAL FILM APPEARANCES—*Portnoy's Complaint,* Warner Brothers, 1972; *The Thief Who Came to Dinner,* Warner Brothers, 1972; *The Terminal Man,* Warner Brothers, 1974; *Gable and Lombard,* Universal, 1976; *Semi-Tough,* United Artists, 1977; *An Unmarried Woman,* Twentieth Century-Fox, 1978; *Luna,* Twentieth Century-Fox, 1979; *Starting Over,* Paramount, 1979; *It's My Turn,* Columbia, 1980; *First Monday in October,* Paramount, 1981; *I'm Dancing as Fast as I Can,* Paramount, 1982; *Hannah K.,* Universal, 1983; *Where Are the Children* (upcoming).

PRINCIPAL TELEVISION APPEARANCES—Movies: *Hustling,* 1975; *Griffin and Phoenix,* 1976.

NEW YORK STAGE DEBUT—*The Rothschilds,* 1970. PRINCIPAL STAGE APPEARANCES—*Design for Living,* Circle in the Square, NY, 1984; also, off Broadway: *The Nest; In the Boom Boom Room.*

COLLEGE OF THE SEQUOIAS

LIBRARY

AWARDS: Cannes Film Festival Award, Best Actress, 1978, for *An Unmarried Woman.*

ADDRESS: OFFICE—c/o Press Relations, Universal Pictures, 445 Park Avenue, New York, NY 10022.*

*   *   *

COCA, Imogene   1908-

PERSONAL: Born November 18, 1908, in Philadelphia, PA; daughter of Joe (an orchestra leader) and Sadie (a vaudevillian; maiden name, Brady) Coca; married Robert Burton (died); married King Donovan.

VOCATION: Actress.

CAREER: STAGE DEBUT—Dancer, Vaudeville Circuit, age nine. NEW YORK STAGE DEBUT—Chorus Girl, *When You Smile,* National, 1925. PRINCIPAL STAGE APPEARANCES—Jan, *Bubbling Over,* Werba's, Brooklyn, NY, 1926; *Snow and Columbus,* Palace, NY, 1927; *Garrick Gaieties,* Guild, NY, 1930; *Shoot the Works,* George M. Cohan Theater, NY, 1931; *Flying Colors,* Imperial, NY, 1932; *New Faces of 1934,* Fulton, NY, 1934; *Fools Rush In,* Playhouse, NY, 1934; *New Faces of 1936,* Vanderbilt, NY, 1936; *Calling All Men, Spring Dance,* 1936-39; *Straw Hat Revue,* Ambassador, NY, 1939; *All in Fun,* Majestic, NY, 1940; *Concert Varieties,* Ziegfeld, NY, 1945; Ruth, *Wonderful Town,* State Fair Music Hall, Dallas, TX, 1954; Jessica, *Janus,* Plymouth, NY, 1956; Mimsy, *The Girls in 509,* Belasco, NY, 1958; Agnes, *The Fourposter,* 1960.

The Queen, *Under the Sycamore Tree,* Pasadena Playhouse, CA, 1962; *You Can't Take It with You,* Repertory Theatre of St. Louis, MO, 1969; Mrs. Malaprop, *The Rivals,* Philadelphia Drama Guild, PA, 1972; Edna Edison, *The Prisoner of Second Avenue,* Arlington Park, Chicago, IL, 1973; *Double Take,* Arlington Park, IL, 1974; Letitia Primrose, *On the Twentieth Century,* St. James, NY, 1978. Dinner theater: *Send Me No Flowers; The Fourposter; The Solid Gold Cadillac.*

MAJOR TOURS—Jan, *Bubbling Over,* U.S. cities, 1926; *New Faces of 1934,* U.S. cities, 1934; *A Night at the Folies Bergere,* U.S. cities, 1940; Addie, *Happy Birthday,* U.S. cities, 1948; Essie, *The Great Sebastians,* U.S. cities, 1957; Mimsy, *The Girls in 509,* U.S. cities, 1959; Princess Winnifred, *Once Upon a Mattress,* U.S. cities, 1960-61; *A Thurber Carnival,* U.S. cities, 1961-62; Ella Peterson, *Bells Are Ringing,* U.S. cities, 1962; Ellen Manville, *Luv,* U.S. cities, 1967; Edna Edison, *The Prisoner of Second Avenue,* U.S. cities, 1973-74; *Cabaret,* U.S. cities, 1977; Letitia Primrose, *On the Twentieth Century,* U.S. cities, 1978.

TELEVISION DEBUT—*Buzzy Wuzzy,* 1948. PRINCIPAL TELEVISION APPEARANCES—Series: *Admiral Broadway Revue,* 1949; *Your Show of Shows,* NBC, 1950-54; *Imogene Coca Show,* NBC, 1954-55; *Sid Caesar Invites You,* ABC, 1958; *Grindl,* NBC, 1963-64; Shad, *It's About Time,* CBS, 1966-67; *Hollywood Palace,* ABC; *Fireside Theatre; Love, American Style,* ABC; Cook, *Alice in Wonderland,* CBS, 1986.

FILM DEBUT—*Bashful Ballerina,* 1937. PRINCIPAL FILM APPEARANCES—*Under the Yum-Yum Tree; Ten from Your Show of Shows,* 1973; *Rabbit Test; National Lampoon's Vacation.**

MICHAEL CODRON

CODRON, Michael   1930-

PERSONAL: Born June 8, 1930; son of Isaac and Lily (Morgenstern) Codron. EDUCATION: Worcester College, Oxford.

VOCATION: Producer.

CAREER: PRINCIPAL STAGE WORK—Producer or co-producer (all London unless otherwise indicated): *Ring for Catty,* 1956; *A Month of Sundays, Share My Lettuce,* both 1957; *Breath of Spring, Little Eyolf, The Dock Brief, What Shall We Tell Caroline?, The Birthday Party, Honour Bright, Valmouth,* all 1958; *Fool's Paradise, How Say You?, Pieces of Eight,* all 1959; *The Wrong Side of the Park, The Caretaker, The Golden Touch,* 1960; *Three* (triple bill), *Stop It Whoever You Are, One Over the Eight, The Tenth Man, Under Milkwood, Ducks and Lovers, Big Soft Nellie,* all 1961; *Two Stars for Comfort, Everything in the Garden, Infanticide in the House of Fred Ginger, Rattle of a Simple Man, Doctors of Philosophy, End of Day, A Cheap Bunch of Nice Flowers, Cindy Ella . . . or I Gotta Shoe, Three at Nine,* all 1962; *An Evening of British Rubbish, Next Time I'll Sing to You, License to Murder, Kelly's Eye, Private Lives, The Lover* and *The Dwarfs* (double bill), *Out of the Crocodile, Cockade, Cider with Rosie,* all 1963.

Poor Bitos, The Brontes (recital), *The Cloud, Hedda Gabler, Hang Down Your Head and Die, The Formation Dancers, The Subtopians, Entertaining Mr. Sloane, See How They Run, A Scent of Flowers, Busybody,* all 1964; *Travelling Light, The Killing of Sister George, Ride a Cock Horse, Anyone for England?, Entertaining Mr. Sloane,* NY, all 1965; *A Lily in Little India, Little Malcolm and His Struggle Against the Eunuchs, The Anniversary, There's a Girl in My Soup, When Did You Last See My Mother?, Public and Confidential, A Present from the Past, Big Bad Mouse, Four Degrees Over,* all

1966; *The Judge, Flip Side, Country Dance, Fill the Stage with Happy Hours, Wise Child, There's a Girl in My Soup,* NY, *Everything in the Garden, The Boy Friend, Fanghorn,* 1967; *Flip Side,* NY, *Not Now Darling, Mrs. Mouse Are You Within?, The Real Inspector Hound* and *The Audition* (double bill), *They Don't Grow on Trees, The Servant of Two Masters,* all 1968; *The Death and Resurrection of Mr. Roche, There'll Be Some Changes Made, The Bandwagon,* all 1969; *It's a Two Foot Six Inches Above the Ground World, Girlfriend, The Contractor, Slag, Not Now Darling,* NY, *The Two of Us, The Philanthropist,* all 1970.

A Game Called Arthur, The Philanthropist, NY, *The Foursome, Butley, A Voyage Round My Father, Slag, The Changing Room,* all 1971; *Butley,* NY, *Seige, Veterans, Me Times Me, Time and Time Again, Crown Matrimonial, Owners, My Fat Friend,* all 1972; *Crown Matrimonial,* NY, *Collaborators, Savages, Habeas Corpus, The Sea, Absurd Person Singular,* all 1973; *Absurd Person Singular,* NY, *Knuckle,* Comedy, *Flowers,* Regent, *My Fat Friend,* NY, *Golden Pathway Annual,* Mayfair, *The Norman Conquests,* Globe, *John, Paul, George, Ringo . . . and Bert,* Lyric, all 1974; *A Family and a Fortune,* Apollo, *Alphabetical Order,* Mayfair, *A Far Better Husband* (tour), *Ashes,* Young Vic, *Absent Friends,* Garrick, *Otherwise Engaged,* Queens, Comedy, *Stripwell,* Royal Court, *The Norman Conquests,* NY, *Habeas Corpus,* NY, all 1975; *Funny Peculiar,* Mermaid, Garrick, *Treats,* Royal Court, Mayfair, *Donkey's Years,* Globe, *Confusions,* Apollo, *Teeth n' Smiles,* Royal Court, Wyndham, *Yahoo,* Queens, 1976.

Dusa, Stas, Fish, and Vi, Hampstead, Mayfair, *Just Between Ourselves,* Queens, *Oh Mr. Porter,* Queens, *The Bells of Hell,* Garrick, *Breezeblock Park,* Mermaid, *The Old Country,* Queens, *Otherwise Engaged,* NY, all 1977; *The Rear Column,* Globe, *The Times Table,* Globe, *The Homecoming,* Garrick, *Alice's Boys,* Savoy, *The Unvarnished Truth,* Phoenix, *Night and Day,* Phoenix, all 1978; *Joking Apart,* Globe, *Tishoo,* Wyndham, *Stage Struck,* Vaudeville, *Night and Day,* NY, all 1979; *Dr. Faustus,* Lyric Hammersmith, *Make and Break,* Lyric Hammersmith, Haymarket, *The Dresser,* Queens, *Taking Steps,* Lyric, *Enjoy,* Vaudeville, *Hinge and Bracket at the Globe,* Globe, all 1980; *Rowan Atkinson in Revue,* Globe, *House Guest,* Savoy, *Quartermaine's Terms,* Queens, *The Dresser,* NY, all 1981; *Noises Off,* Lyric Hammersmith, Savoy, *Season's Greetings,* Apollo, *Funny Turns,* Duchess, *The Real Thing,* Strand, all 1982; *The Hard Shoulder,* Aldwych, *Noises Off,* NY, both 1983; *Look, No Hans!* (tour), *Benefactors,* Vaudeville, *The Real Thing,* Plymouth, NY, all 1984; *Why Me?,* Strand, *Jumpers,* Aldwych, both 1985.

ADDRESS: OFFICE—c/o Aldwych Theatre Offices, Aldwych, London WC2B 4DF England.

*   *   *

COHENOUR, Patti   1952-

PERSONAL: Full name Patricia Ann Cohenour; born December 17, 1952, in Albuquerque, NM; daughter of William Edward (a physician) and Suzanne (an opera singer; maiden name, Miller) Cohenour; married Thomas Edward Bliss (a film producer). EDUCATION: Attended University of New Mexico; trained for dance with George Zoritch, Patricia Stander, Suzanne Johnston, Stefan Wenta, Steve Merritt and Joey Sheck.

VOCATION: Actress and dancer.

CAREER: STAGE DEBUT—*A Bluebell,* Krasnoff School of Ballet Recital, Albuquerque Civic Auditorium, Albuquerque, NM, for two performances. NEW YORK STAGE DEBUT—Helga and understudy Nora, *A Doll's Life,* Mark Hellinger, 1982, for twenty-two performances. PRINCIPAL STAGE APPEARANCES—Chava, *Fiddler on the Roof,* Harlequin Dinner Theater, Costa Mesa, CA, 1979; *Let's Call the Whole Thing Gershwin Revue,* Westwood Playhouse, Los Angeles, CA, 1980; Julia Finsbury, *The Wrong Box,* Gene Dynarsky Theater, Los Angeles, CA, 1983; *La Boheme,* 1984; *Big River,* 1985; Rosa Bud and Deirdre Peregrine, *The Mystery of Edwin Drood,* Delacorte, NY, 1985.

MAJOR TOURS—*Pirates of Penzance,* U.S. cities; *The New Christy Minstrels,* U.S. and European cities, 1977, 1980.

TELEVISION DEBUT—Singer and dancer, *Music Hall America,* Viacom, Opryland Productions, 1976-77. PRINCIPAL TELEVISION APPEARANCES—*Powers of Matthew Starr,* Paramount; *Happy Days,* ABC.

AWARDS: Drama Desk Award nomination, Theater World Award, 1985, for *Big River;* Theatre World Award, 1984, for *La Boheme.*

SIDELIGHTS: RECREATION—Horseback riding, racehorse exerciser, guitar.

ADDRESS: HOME—New York, NY. AGENT—Abrams and Associates, 420 Madison Avenue, New York, NY 10017.

*   *   *

COLBERT, Claudette   1905-

PERSONAL: Born Lily Claudette Chauchoin, September 13, 1905, in Paris, France; daughter of Georges and Jeanne (Loew) Chauchoin; married Norman Foster (an actor), 1928 (divorced, 1935); married Joel Pressman (a physician) 1935 (died, 1968). EDUCATION: New York City public schools.

VOCATION: Actress.

CAREER: STAGE DEBUT—Sybil Blake, *The Wild Westcotts,* Frazee, NY, 1923. LONDON DEBUT—Lou, *The Barker,* Playhouse, 1928. PRINCIPAL STAGE APPEARANCES—Ginette, *A Kiss in the Taxi,* Ritz, NY, 1925; Peggy Murdock, *The Ghost Train,* Eltinge, NY, 1926; Pilgrim, *The Pearl of Great Price,* Century, NY, 1926; Lou, *The Barker,* Biltmore, NY, 1927; Sylvia Bainbridge, *The Mulberry Bush,* Republic, NY, 1927; Carlotta d'Astradente, *La Gringa,* Little, NY, 1928; Aggie Lynch, *Within the Law,* Cosmopolitan, NY, 1928; Patricia Mason, *Fast Life,* Ambassador, NY, 1928; Jill O'Dare, *Tin Pan Alley,* Biltmore, NY, 1928; Ada Fife, *Dynamo,* Martin Beck, NY, 1929; Nanette Dodge Kosloff, *See Naples and Die,* Vanderbilt, NY, 1929.

Island Fling, Westport Country Playhouse, CT, 1951; Jessica (replacing Margaret Sullavan), *Janus,* Plymouth NY, 1956; Content Lowell, *Marriage-Go-Round,* Plymouth, NY, 1958; Julia Ryan, *Jake, Julia, and Uncle Joe,* Booth, NY, 1961; Hedda Rankin, *The Irregular Verb to Love,* Ethel Barrymore, NY, 1963; Linda Marshall, *Diplomatic Relations,* Royal Poinciana Playhouse, Palm Beach, FL, 1965; Alix Carpenter, *A Community of Two,* New Locust, Philadelphia, PA, 1974; Lady Townsend, *The Kingfisher,* Biltmore, NY, 1978; Anne Royce McClain, *A Talent for Murder,* Biltmore,

1981; Lady Frinton, *Aren't We All,* Theatre Royal, Haymarket, London, 1984, Brooks Atkinson, NY, 1985.

MAJOR TOURS—*The Marionette Man, We've Got to Have Money, The Cat Came Back,* all 1924; *Leah Kleschna, High Stakes,* both 1925; *A Community of Two,* 1974; *Marriage-Go-Round,* 1978; *The Kingfisher,* 1979.

FILM DEBUT—*For the Love of Mike,* First National, 1927. PRINCIPAL FILM APPEARANCES—*The Hole in the Wall,* Paramount, 1929; *The Lady Lies,* Paramount, 1929; *Manslaughter,* Paramount, 1930; *The Big Pond,* Paramount, 1930; *Young Man of Manhattan,* Paramount, 1930; *L'Enigmatique Mr. Parkes* (French version of *Slightly Scarlet),* Paramount, 1930; *Honor Among Lovers,* Paramount, 1931; Franzi, *The Smiling Lieutenant,* Paramount, 1931; *Secrets of a Secretary,* Paramount, 1932; *His Woman,* Paramount, 1932; *The Wiser Sex,* Paramount, 1932; *The Misleading Lady,* Paramount, 1932; unbilled guest appearance, *Make Me a Star,* Paramount, 1932; *The Man from Yesterday,* Paramount, 1932; Poppaea, *The Sign of the Cross,* Paramount, 1932; *The Phantom President,* Paramount, 1932; *Tonight Is Ours,* Paramount, 1933; *I Cover the Waterfront,* Paramount, 1933; *Torch Singer,* Paramount, 1933; *Three-Cornered Moon,* Paramount, 1933; *Four Frightened People,* Paramount, 1934; Ellie Andrews, *It Happened One Night,* Columbia, 1934; Cleopatra, *Cleopatra,* Paramount, 1934; Beatrice (Bea) Pullman, *Imitation of Life,* Universal, 1934.

The Gilded Lily, Paramount, 1935; *Private Worlds,* Paramount, 1935; *She Married the Boss,* Columbia, 1935; *The Bride Comes Home,* Paramount, 1935; Cigarette, *Under Two Flags,* Twentieth Century-Fox, 1936; *Maid of Salem,* Paramount, 1937; *I Met Him in Paris,* Paramount, 1937; Grand Duchess Tatiana, *Tovarich,* Warner Brothers, 1937; *Bluebeard's Eighth Wife,* Paramount, 1938; Zaza, *Zaza,* Paramount, 1939; Eve, *Midnight,* Paramount, 1939; Lana (Magdelana) Martin, *Drums Along the Mohawk,* Twentieth Century-Fox, 1939; *It's a Wonderful World,* Metro-Goldwyn-Mayer, 1939; Betsy Bartlett, *Boom Town,* Metro-Goldwyn-Mayer, 1940; *Arise My Love,* Paramount, 1940; *Skylark,* Paramount, 1941; *The Palm Beach Story,* Paramount, 1942; *Remember the Day,* Twentieth Century-Fox, 1942; *No Time for Love,* Paramount, 1943; Lieutenant Janet Davidson, *So Proudly We Hail,* Paramount, 1943.

Anne Hilton, *Since You Went Away,* United Artists, 1944; *Practically Yours,* Paramount, 1944; *Guest Wife,* United Artists, 1945; *Without Reservations,* RKO, 1946; Elizabeth (MacDonald) Hamilton, *Tomorrow Is Forever,* RKO, 1946; *The Secret Heart,* Metro-Goldwyn-Mayer, 1946; Betty MacDonald, *The Egg and I,* Universal, 1947; *Sleep, My Love,* United Artists, 1948; *Family Honeymoon,* Universal, 1948; *Bride for Sale,* RKO, 1949; *Three Came Home,* Twentieth Century-Fox, 1950; *The Secret Fury,* RKO, 1950; *Thunder on the Hill,* Universal, 1951; *Let's Make It Legal,* Twentieth Century-Fox, 1951; *Outpost in Malaya* (a.k.a. *The Planter's Wife),* United Artists, 1952; *Destinees (Daughters of Destiny;* French), 1953; *Si Versailles m'etait Conte* (French), 1954; *Texas Lady,* RKO, 1955; Ellen McLean, *Parrish,* Warner Brothers, 1961.

TELEVISION APPEARANCES—Julie Cavendish, *The Royal Family,* Ruth Condomine, *Blithe Spirit,* The Actress, *The Guardsman,* on such popular drama anthology series as: *Ford Theatre* (all three networks), 1949-57; *Robert Montgomery Presents,* NBC, 1950-57; *Telephone Time,* CBS and ABC, 1956-58; others.

RADIO APPEARANCES—Fourteen different dramatizations between 1936 and 1945.

AWARDS: Academy Award, Best Actress, 1934, for *It Happened One Night;* Academy Award nominations, 1935, for *Private Worlds,*

1944, for *Since You Went Away.*

SIDELIGHTS: During the 1920's, Colbert was under personal contract to the legendary Broadway producer and manager Al Woods; during her last two appearances for Woods *(Dynamo* and *See Naples and Die),* Paramount negotiated successfully to buy her contract.

ADDRESS: HOME—Bellerive, St. Peter, Barbados, West Indies.

*   *   *

COLBIN, Rod   1923-

PERSONAL: Born J.H. Lichtenstein, December 23, 1923, in New Haven, CT; son of Samuel (made gravestones) and Bess (Silver-dollar) Lichtenstein; married Annemarie Polonyi, September 16, 1965 (divorced, 1978); children: Shana Rebecca, Kaila Johanna. EDUCATION: Attended Columbia University, New York City; studied acting with Stella Adler and at the Central School of Speech and Drama, London, England. MILITARY: U.S. Army Infantry, World War Two, Sargeant.

VOCATION: Actor, choreographer, and fencing master.

CAREER: DEBUT—Narrator, *Town Topics Revue,* New Haven CT, 1940. NEW YORK DEBUT—Tommy Artsuch, *Junior Miss,* Lyceum, 1941. LONDON DEBUT—*Oedipus.* PRINCIPAL STAGE APPEARANCES—Broadway: *A Patriot for Me, Cyrano de Bergerac, Twigs, Legend of Lizzie, The Physicists.*

ROD COLBIN

Repertory: *Angel Street, As You Like It, Room Service, Sound of Hunting, Ghosts, King John, Julius Caesar, Measure for Measure, The Importance of Being Earnest, Mister Roberts;* also *Henry IV, Part One* (a special recitation for the Royal Family), London.

MAJOR TOURS—*Maggie, South Pacific, West Side Story, The (Not So Very) Deadly Art of Swordplay* (one man show).

PRINCIPAL FILM APPEARANCES—*Gumball Rally,* Warner Brothers, 1976; *Change of Seasons,* Twentieth Century-Fox, 1980; *The Hand,* Warner Brothers, 1981; *Yes, Giorgio,* Metro-Goldwyn-Mayer/ United Artists, 1982; *Frances,* Universal, 1982; *The Falcon and the Snowman,* 1985; *Frankenstein's Great Aunt Tillie.*

PRINCIPAL TELEVISION APPEARANCES—Movies: *To Kill a Cop,* 1978; *Seduction of an Anatomy; Rape and Marriage: The Rideout Case,* 1980; *Jon Huss,* 1980; *R.I.P.; Hazzard's People; Ghost Dancing,* 1983. Series: *The Devlin Connection; Flo; The Ropers; Quincy; Barney Miller; Charlie's Angels; Alice; Lou Grant; The Jeffersons; Three's Company; Insight; Marcus Welby; The Edge of Night; Maude; Invisible Man; As the World Turns; Omnibus; CBS Family Classics; Greatest American Hero; Hallmark Shakespeare Series; Mary Hartman, Mary Hartman; A-Team; Hardcastle & McCormack; Tonight Show; Mike Douglas Show.*

RELATED CAREER: Duel choreography for Broadway productions: *The Fighting Cock, Hamlet, Henry IV, Julius Caesar.* For television: *Prisoner of Zenda, Macbeth, Monsieur Beaucaire, The Three Musketeers, Mork & Mindy.*

AWARDS: Christian Academy Award, Best Actor, 1980, for *Jon Huss.*

SIDELIGHTS: MEMBERSHIPS—Society of American Fight Directors (vice president), Screen Actors Guild, Actors' Equity Association, American Federation of Television and Radio Artists.

ADDRESS: AGENT—Mary Ellen White, 151 N. San Vincente Blvd., Beverly Hills, CA 90211.

*   *   *

COLE, Nora   1953-

PERSONAL: Full name Nora Marie Cole; born September 10, 1953, in Louisville, KY; daughter of Lattimore Wallis (a postal supervisor) and Mary Lue (an assembly line worker; maiden name, Bradford) Cole. EDUCATION: Attended Beloit College; Goodman School of Drama, B.F.A., 1978; studied acting with Wynn Handman at American Place Theatre, NY. RELIGION: Christian.

VOCATION: Actress.

CAREER: STAGE DEBUT—Duchess, *Alice in Wonderland,* Louisville Children's Theatre, KY, 1965. NEW YORK DEBUT—Obiah Woman, *The Ups and Downs of Theophilus Maitland,* Urban Arts Corporation, 1976. PRINCIPAL STAGE APPEARANCES—*I'm Laughin' but I Ain't Tickled,* Widow, *Boogie Woogie Rumble,* Duchess, *Alice in Wonderland,* all at Urban Arts, NY; Velma, *Movie Buff,* Actors Playhouse, NY; *El Hajj Malik,* Gene Frankel, NY; Mayda, *Cartoons for a Lunch Hour,* Perry Street, NY; Norene, *The Peanut Man* and Poet, *Beowolf,* both at AMAS Repertory, NY; Cassandra, *Trojan Women,* Black Theatre Alliance; Deidre and understudy Roby, *Runaways,* New York Shakespeare Festival,

1978; featured soloist, Radio City Music Hall, 1980-81; Carmen and understudy Sally Baby, *Inacent Black,* Biltmore, NY, 1981; Singing Mary, *Your Arms Too Short to Box with God,* Alvin, NY, 1982.

MAJOR TOURS—Addaperle, *The Wiz,* 1980-81; Singing Mary, *Your Arms Too Short to Box with God,* 1982-83; Rachael, *When Hell Freezes Over I'll Skate,* 1984; *The All Night Strut,* 1984-85.

SIDELIGHTS: MEMBERSHIPS—Actors' Equity Association, American Federation of Television and Radio Artists, Screen Actors Guild, American Guild of Variety Artists.

ADDRESS: OFFICE—Honey Sanders Agency, Ltd., 229 W. 42nd Street, New York, NY 10036.

*   *   *

COLLIER, Gaylan Jane   1924-

PERSONAL: Born July 23, 1924; daughter of Ben Vivian (a stock farmer) and Narcis Nura (Smith) Collier. EDUCATION: Abilene Christian University, B.A., speech and drama, 1946; University of Iowa, M.A., drama, 1949; University of Denver, Ph.D., theatre, 1957; advanced study at Cornell University, 1953. POLITICS: Democrat. RELIGION: Church of Christ.

VOCATION: Educator, director, and teacher.

CAREER: Instructor, drama, University of North Carolina, Greens-

GAYLAN JANE COLLIER

boro, 1947-48; assistant professor and acting chairperson, Greeensboro College, Greensboro, NC, 1949-50; assistant professor and director of theatre, 1950-57, associate professor, 1957-60, Abilene Christian University, TX; director of acting studies and associate professor, Idaho State University, Pocatello, 1960-63; associate professor, 1963-65, professor, 1967-76, Sam Houston State University, Huntsville, TX; professor of theatre and director of acting and the directing program, Texas Christian University, Ft. Worth, 1967-present.

Collier has directed over 135 theatrical productions in university and semi-professional theatres, including: *The Imaginary Invalid; You Can't Take It with You; Tartuffe; Vanities; Mornings at Seven; The Chalk Garden; When You Comin' Back Red Ryder?*

WRITINGS: BOOKS—*Assignments in Acting,* 1966. ARTICLES—In professional journals *Southern Speech; Western Speech.*

AWARDS: Best Actress, Abilene Christian University, 1943-46; directed *The Imaginary Invalid,* chosen to represent the U.S. in the American Festival in Britain, 1970 (also toured northern England); directed *You Can't Take It with You* at Texas Christian University, selected for regional representation, American Theatre Festival, 1979.

SIDELIGHTS: MEMBERSHIPS—American Theatre Association, Children's Theatre Association, Southwest Theatre Conference, Texas Educational Theatre Association, Alpha Psi Omega, National Honorary Drama Fraternity, Zeta Phi Eta, National Professional Speech Association for Women.

Writing to *CTFT,* Collier said, ''My motivation has been to train the aspiring actor through teaching and directing in such a way that he learns to use body, voice, and emotion successfully for any director or teacher.''

ADDRESS: OFFICE—Department of Theatre, Texas Christian University, Ft. Worth, TX 76129.

*   *   *

COLLINS, Joan   1935-

PERSONAL: Full name Joan Henreitta Collins; born May 3, 1935, in London, England; daughter of Joseph William and Elsa (Bessant) Collins; married Maxwell Reed (an actor; divorced); married Anthony Newley (actor, singer, and composer; divorced); married Ronald S. Kass (divorced); children: (second marriage) Tara, Sacha; (third marriage) Katyana. EDUCATION: Francis Holland School, London, England; Royal Academy of Dramatic Arts.

VOCATION: Actress and writer.

CAREER: DEBUT—*A Doll's House,* Arts Theatre, London, 1945. PRINCIPAL STAGE APPEARANCES—*Jassy; The Praying Mantis; The Skin of Our Teeth; Claudia and David; The Last of Mrs. Cheyney; Murder in Mind.*

PRINCIPAL FILM APPEARANCES—*I Believe in You, Lady Godiva Rides Again, The Woman's Angle, Decameron Nights, The Slasher, Judgement Deferred,* 1952; *The Square Ring, Turn the Key Softly, Our Girl Friday,* 1953; *The Good Die Young, Land of the Pharoahs,* 1954; *The Virgin Queen,* 1955; *The Girl in the Red Velvet Swing,* Twentieth Century-Fox, 1955; *The Opposite Sex,* Metro-Goldwyn-

Mayer, 1956; *Seawife,* Twentieth Century-Fox, 1957; *Island in the Sun,* Twentieth Century-Fox, 1957; *Stopover Tokyo,* Twentieth Century-Fox, 1957; *The Wayward Bus,* Twentieth Century-Fox, 1957; *The Bravados,* Twentieth Century-Fox, 1958; *Rally Round the Flag Boys,* Twentieth Century-Fox, 1958; *Seven Thieves,* Twentieth Century-Fox, 1960; *Esther and the King,* Twentieth Century-Fox, 1960; *The Road to Hong Kong,* United Artists, 1962; *La Conguntura,* 1964; *Warning Shot,* Paramount, 1967; *Subterfuge,* 1969; *If It's Tuesday, This Must Be Belgium,* United Artists, 1969; *The Executioner,* Columbia, 1970; *Up in the Cellar,* 1970.

Quest for Love, 1971; *Inn of the Frightened People* (aka *Revenge*), 1971; *Fear in the Night,* 1972; *Tales from the Crypt,* Cinerama, 1972; *The Man Who Came to Dinner,* 1972; *Tales That Witness Madness,* Paramount, 1973; *State of Siege,* Cinema V, 1973; *Dark Places,* 1974; *Alfie Darling, The Referee, Fallen Angels,* all 1974; *The Great Adventure,* 1975; *The Devil within Her,* 1975; *The Bawdy Adventures of Tom Jones,* Universal, 1976; *The Moneychangers,* 1976; *Poliziotto Senza Paula,* 1977; *The Big Sleep,* United Artists, 1978; *Zero to 60,* 1978; *The Stud,* 1978; *Game for Vultures,* 1978; *Sunburn,* Paramount, 1979; *The Bitch,* 1979; *Nutcracker,* 1982; *Hansel and Gretel,* 1982; *My Life as a Man,* 1983.

PRINCIPAL TELEVISION APPEARANCES—Alexis, *Dynasty,* ABC, 1981-present. Movies: *Drive Hard Drive Fast,* 1969; *Paper Dolls,* 1982; *Wild Women of Chasity Gulch,* 1982; *The Making of a Male Model,* 1983; *The Cartier Affair,* NBC, 1984; *Sins,* 1985. Guest appearances: *Batman, Mission: Impossible, The Bob Hope Show, Blondes vs. Brunettes, Baretta, Fantastic Journey, Ellery Queen, Switch, Starsky & Hutch, The Human Jungle, Tales of the Unexpected, Orson Welles Great Mysteries, Fantasy Island, Police Woman, Run for Your Life, The Virginian.*

VIDEO—*The Joan Collins Video Special,* 1981.

WRITINGS: BOOKS, PUBLISHED—*Past Imperfect,* 1978; *The Joan Collins Beauty Book,* 1981; *Katy—A Fight for Life,* 1982.

AWARDS: Golden Globe Award, *Dynasty.*

SIDELIGHTS: MEMBERSHIPS—Actors' Equity Association, American Federation of Television and Radio Artists, Screen Actors Guild.

ADDRESS: OFFICE—c/o Warner Hollywood, Formosa Avenue, Los Angeles, CA 90046. AGENT—William Morris Agency, 151 El Camino Drive, Beverly Hills, CA 90212.

*   *   *

COMDEN, Betty   1919-

PERSONAL: Born Betty Cohen, May 3, 1919, in Brooklyn, NY; daughter of Leo and Rebecca (Sadvoransky) Cohen; married Steven Kyle, January 4, 1942; children: Susanna, Alan. EDUCATION: New York University, B.S.

VOCATION: Lyricist, playwright, and actress.

CAREER: DEBUT—Cabaret act, *The Revuers,* 1944. PRINCIPAL STAGE APPEARANCES—Claire, *On the Town,* Adelphi, 1944; *A*

Party with Betty Comden and Adolph Green, Cherry Lane, NY, then Golden, NY, 1958; *An Evening with Betty Comden and Adolph Green*, 1971; *Lyrics and Lyricists*, Kaufman Auditorium, 1971; *A Party with Betty Comden and Adolph Green*, Juilliard School of Music, NY, 1971; *A Party . . .* , Morosco, NY, 1977 and tour; *Isn't It Romantic*, Playwrights Horizons, NY, 1983-84.

WRITINGS: PLAYS, PRODUCED—Sketches, principally in collaboration with Adolph Green and Judy Holliday, *The Revuers*, 1941; musical with Adolph Green and Leonard Bernstein, *On the Town*, 1944; musical with Adolph Green and Morton Gould, *Billion Dollar Baby*, 1945; musical with Adolph Green, *Bonanza Bound!*, 1947; sketches and lyrics with Adolph Green, *Two on the Aisle*, 1951; musical with Adolph Green and Leonard Bernstein, *Wonderful Town*, 1953; musical with Adolph Green and Jule Styne, *Peter Pan*, 1954; musical with Adolph Green and Jule Styne, *Bells Are Ringing*, 1956; musical with Adolph Green and Jule Styne, *Say, Darling*, 1958; with Adolph Green, *A Party with Betty Comden and Adolph Green*, 1960; lyrics with Adolph Green, *Do Re Mi*, 1960.

Musical with Adolph Green and Jule Styne, *Subways Are for Sleeping*, 1961; musical with Adolph Green, *On the Town*, 1963; musical with Adolph Green and Jule Styne, *Fade Out—Fade In*, 1964, revised 1965; *Leonard Bernstein's Theatre Songs* (some lyrics), 1965; musical with Adolph Green and Jule Styne, *Hallelujah, Baby!*, 1967; book for musical with Adolph Green, Charles Strouse, and Lee Adams, *Applause*, 1970; lyrics, revisions to book, direction with Adolph Green and Jule Styne, *Lorelei*, 1974; book with Adolph Green, *By Bernstein*, 1975; musical with Adolph Green and Jule Styne, *On the Twentieth Century*, 1978; *Peter Pan*, revived, 1979; musical with Adolph Green, *A Doll's Life*, 1982.

FILMS—(Screenplays and/or lyrics) *Good News*, Metro-Goldwyn-Mayer, 1947; *The Barkleys of Broadway*, Metro-Goldwyn-Mayer, 1949; *On the Town*, Metro-Goldwyn-Mayer, 1949; *Take Me Out to the Ball Game*, Metro-Goldwyn-Mayer, 1949; *Singin' in the Rain*, Metro-Goldwyn-Mayer, 1952; *The Band Wagon*, Metro-Goldwyn-Mayer, 1953; *It's Always Fair Weather*, Metro-Goldwyn-Mayer, 1955; *Auntie Mame*, Warner Brothers, 1958; *Bells Are Ringing*, Metro-Goldwyn-Mayer, 1960; *What a Way to Go*, Twentieth Century-Fox, 1964.

TELEVISION—*Wonderful Town; Peter Pan; Applause; A Party with Betty Comden and Adolph Green*.

AWARDS: Donaldson (with Adolph Green), 1953, for *Wonderful Town;* Academy Award nomination (with Adolph Green), Best Story and Screenplay, 1953, for *The Band Wagon;* Academy Award nomination (with Adolph Green), Best Story and Screenplay, 1955, for *It's Always Fair Weather;* Antoinette Perry Awards (with Adolph Green and Jule Styne), Best Score; Antoinette Perry Award (wtih Adolph Green and Jule Styne), Best Lyrics, *Hallelujah, Baby!*, 1968; Antoinette Perry Award (with Adolph Green, Charles Strouse, and Lee Adams), Best Musical, 1970, for *Applause;* Antoinette Perry Award, Best Book (with Adolph Green) and Best Score (with Adolph Green and Cy Coleman), 1978, for *On the Twentieth Century;* Outer Critics Circle Award; Screen Writers Guild Award.

SIDELIGHTS: MEMBERSHIPS—Dramatists Guild (council).

ADDRESS: OFFICE—c/o The Dramatists Guild, 234 W. 44th Street, New York, NY 10036.

CONAWAY, Jeff 1950-

BRIEF ENTRY: Born October 5, 1950, in New York City; married Rona Newton-John; they have a son, Emerson. Educated at North Carolina School of the Arts and New York University. Actor. Conaway made his Broadway debut in *All the Way Home* in 1960. He toured with the national company of *Critics Choice*, took over the role of Danny in the Broadway production of *Grease*, and was Billy in *Wanted* at the Judson Poet's Theatre. He is best known to television audiences as Bobby Wheeler on ABC's *Taxi*. He was also seen on *Berrenger's*, NBC, 1985. His film credits include *Jennifer on My Mind*, United Artists, 1971; *The Eagle Has Landed*, Columbia, 1977; *Pete's Dragon*, Buena Vista, 1977; *I Never Promised You a Rose Garden*, New World, 1977; and played Kenickie in *Grease*, Paramount, 1978.*

*   *   *

CONWAY, Gary

PERSONAL: Born Gareth Monello Carmody, in Boston, MA; son of John G. S. (a teacher) and Vera S. (a teacher; maiden name, Monello) Carmody; married Marian McKnight. EDUCATION: University of California, B.A. POLITICS: Democrat. RELIGION: Unitarian.

VOCATION: Actor, manager, and writer.

GARY CONWAY

CAREER: FILM DEBUT—Contract player, Warner Brothers, 1960.

PRINCIPAL FILM APPEARANCES—*Teenage Frankenstein; Young Guns of Texas*, Twentieth Century-Fox, 1962; *Black Gunn*, Paramount, 1972; *Once Is Not Enough*, Paramount, 1975; *The Farmer*, Columbia, 1977.

PRINCIPAL TELEVISION APPEARANCES—*Burke's Law*, ABC; *Land of the Giants*, ABC; *Columbo*, NBC; *Judge and Jake Wyler*, 1972, NBC; *Class of '55*, ABC.

STAGE DEBUT—Robroy Fruitwell, *Beauty Part*, Bucks County Playhouse. PRINCIPAL STAGE APPEARANCES—Robroy Fruitwell, *Beauty Part*, NY.

WRITINGS: SCREENPLAYS—*Over the Top; The Smuggler*.

ADDRESS: AGENT—c/o Ricky Barr, 9100 Sunset Blvd., Los Angeles, CA 90060; Creative Artists Agency, 1888 Century Park E., Los Angeles, CA 90067.

*   *   *

CONWAY, Kevin   1942-

PERSONAL: Born May 29, 1942, in New York City; son of James and Margaret (Sanders O'Brien) Conway; married Mila Quiros (an actress). EDUCATION: Studied for the theatre with Uta Hagen and at the Dramatic Workshop in New York.

VOCATION: Actor and director.

KEVIN CONWAY

CAREER: STAGE DEBUT—Andy, *The Impossible Years*, Elitch Gardens, Denver, CO, July, 1967. NEW YORK DEBUT—Number Two, *Muzeeka*, Provincetown Playhouse, 1968. PRINCIPAL STAGE APPEARANCES—Philly Cullen, *The Playboy of the Western World*, Leo Davis, *Room Service*, both at Long Wharf, New Haven, CT, 1967; Tom, *The Knack*, Stage West, Springfield, MA, 1968; Cliff, *Look Back in Anger*, First Messenger, *The Bacchae*, both at Charles Playhouse, Boston, MA, 1968; Black Hawk, *Indians*, Brooks Atkinson, NY, 1969; Fred, *Saved*, Chelsea Theatre Center, Brooklyn, NY, then Cherry Lane, NY, 1970; Mike, *Moonchildren*, Arena Stage, Washington, DC, 1971; various roles, *An Evening of Julie Bovasso Plays*, La MaMa, NY, 1971; Mike, *Moonchildren*, Royale, NY, 1972.

Covey, *The Plough and the Stars*, Vivian Beaumont, Lincoln Center, NY, 1973; McMurphy, *One Flew Over the Cuckoo's Nest*, Mercer-Hansberry, NY, then Eastside Playhouse, NY, 1973; Teddy, *When You Comin' Back, Red Ryder?*, Eastside Playhouse, NY, 1973, also at Berkshire Playhouse, Stockbridge, MA, summer, 1973; George, *Of Mice and Men*, Brooks Atkinson, NY, 1974; Teddy, . . . *Red Ryder?*, Westwood Playhouse, Los Angeles, CA, 1975; Allott, *Life Class*, Manhattan Theatre Club, NY, 1975; Jamie, *Long Day's Journey into Night*, Kennedy Center, Washington, DC, 1975, then Brooklyn Academy of Music, NY, January, 1976; Frederick Treves, *The Elephant Man*, St. Peter's Church, NY, then Booth, NY, 1979; *Other Places*, Manhattan Theatre Club, NY, 1984.

PRINCIPAL STAGE WORK—Director: *Mecca*, Quaigh, NY, 1980; *One Act Play Festival*, Lincoln Center, NY, 1982-83; *The Elephant Man*, Westport Playhouse, CT, 1983; *Short Eyes*, Second Stage, NY, 1984.

FILM DEBUT—*Slaughterhouse Five*, Universal, 1972. PRINCIPAL FILM APPEARANCES—*Portnoy's Complaint*, Warner Brothers, 1972; *F.I.S.T.*, United Artists, 1978; *Paradise Alley*, Universal, 1978; *The Funhouse*, 1980; *Flashpoint*, Tri-Star, 1984.

PRINCIPAL TELEVISION APPEARANCES—*Hogan's Goat; The Scarlet Letter*, PBS; *The Lathe of Heaven* (first film produced for Public Television), PBS; *Johnny, We Hardly Knew Ye; The Deadliest Season*; Treves, *The Elephant Man*, ABC, 1983; *Rage of Angels*, NBC mini-series, 1983; *Something About Amelia*, ABC, 1984; Eakins, *Life of Thomas Eakins*, PBS, 1985.

AWARDS: Obie, Drama Desk Award, 1973, for *When You Comin' Back, Red Ryder?*

SIDELIGHTS: MEMBERSHIPS—Friar's Club, Players Club.

According to information supplied to *CTFT*, Conway's favorite roles are McMurphy in *One Flew Over the Cuckoo's Nest*, Teddy in *When You Comin' Back, Red Ryder?*, and George in *Of Mice and Men*.

Conway worked for a time as an IBM sales analyst.

ADDRESS: OFFICE—Critter Productions, 25 Central Park West, New York, NY 10023.

*   *   *

COOPER, Jackie   1922-

PERSONAL: Born September 15, 1922, in Los Angeles, CA;

married Barbara Kraus (an advertising executive), 1954; children: (previous marriage) John; (second marriage) Russell, Julie, Cristina. EDUCATION: University of Notre Dame, three and one-half years; U.S. Navy, V-12 program, wartime accellerated program. MILITARY: U.S. Navy, World War Two, Captain (ret), U.S. Naval Reserve.

VOCATION: Actor, director, and producer.

CAREER: FILM DEBUT—A Lloyd Hamilton comedy, 1925. PRINCIPAL FILM APPEARANCES—*Our Gang,* comedies, beginning 1929; lead role, *Skippy,* 1930; *The Champ,* Metro-Goldwyn-Mayer, 1931; lead role, *Kilroy Was Here,* 1946; *The Love Machine,* Columbia, 1970; *The Chosen Survivors,* Columbia, 1973; Perry White, *Superman,* Warner Brothers, 1978; *Superman II,* Warner Brothers, 1981, *Superman III,* Warner Brothers, 1983.

PRINCIPAL TELEVISION APPEARANCES—*Kraft Theatre, Robert Montgomery Presents, Producer's Showcase, Philco Playhouse, U.S. Steel Hour,* all between 1947-1951; *The People's Choice* (also directed), NBC, 1955-58; *Hennessy* (also produced and directed), CBS, 1959-62; *Columbo,* 1973; *Kojak,* 1974; *Police Story,* 1974-75; *Hec Ramsay,* 1974; *Ironside,* 1975.

Television movies: *Shadow on the Land,* ABC, 1968; *Maybe I'll Come Home in the Spring,* ABC, 1970; *The Astronaut,* ABC, 1971; *Of Men and Women,* NBC, 1972; *The Day the Earth Moved,* ABC, 1974; *The Invisible Man,* NBC, 1975; *Mobile One,* ABC, 1975; *Mobile Two,* 1975; *Operation Petticoat,* 1977.

PRINCIPAL TELEVISION WORK—Director: *Stand Up and Be Counted,* 1971; *M*A*S*H* (episodes), 1972-73; *The Texas Wheelers,* 1974; *The Last Detail* (pilot), 1975; *The Rockford Files* (episodes), 1974-75; *Holmes and YoYo* (also producer), ABC, 1976; *Snafu* (pilot), NBC, 1976; *Blacksheep Squadron,* 1976; *Quincy,* 1977; *McMillan & Wife,* 1977; *The White Shadow* (pilot and first six episodes), 1978; *Paris* (pilot), 1978; *Trapper John* (pilot), 1979.

Television movies: *Perfect Gentleman* (also producer), 1977; *Having Babies,* 1977; *Rainbow,* NBC, 1978; *White Mama,* 1979; *Sex and the Single Parent,* CBS, 1979; *Rodeo Girl,* 1980; *Leave 'em Laughing,* 1981; *Rosie - The Rosemary Clooney Story* (also producer), 1982; *The Ladies* (also co-producer), NBC, 1983; *Glitter,* ABC, 1984; *The Night They Saved Christmas,* ABC, 1984; *Uncommon Courage.*

Producer (with Bob Finkel): *Bing Crosby Specials,* 1970-72; *Perry Como Specials,* 1970-72.

PRINCIPAL STAGE APPEARANCES—*Magnolia Alley,* NY, 1947-48; Ensign Pulver, *Mister Roberts,* NY, London, 1949-51; *Remains to Be Seen,* NY, 1951; *King of Hearts,* NY, 1955.

RELATED CAREER—Vice president in charge of Television Program Production, Columbia Pictures Corporation, 1964-69; producer and director with Bob Finkel, Cooper-Finkel Company, 1969-73.

WRITINGS: AUTOBIOGRAPHY—*Please Don't Shoot My Dog* (with Dick Kliener), William Morrow, 1981.

AWARDS: Two Emmy nominations, Academy of Television Arts and Sciences, Best Actor, special citation, American Medical Association, Distinguished Public Service Medal, United States

Navy, all for *Hennesey;* Emmy, National Academy of Television Arts and Sciences, Best Comedy Director, 1973, for episodes of *M*A*S*H;* Emmy, Best Dramatic Director, 1978, for *The White Shadow;* Film Advisory Board Award, as producer and director, 1982, for *Rosie - The Rosemary Clooney Story.*

Additional honors and awards from: National Academy of Motion Picture Arts and Sciences; United Funds and Community Chest; March of Dimes; Hollywood Radio and Television Society; American Center of Films for Children; Directors Guild of America; Writers Guild of America; Pearl Harbor Survivors Association; U.S. Navy Recruiting Service; Navy League; Association of Naval Aviation; Society of Experimental Test Pilots; Combat Pilots Association; American Academy of General Practice; University of Southern California; University of California at Los Angeles; Special Olympics; International Motor Sports of America; Center for Improvement of Child Caring; Cinema Circulus; Caucus for Writers, Producers, and Directors.

Military Awards: Letters of commendation from six secretaries of the United States Navy; Honorary Naval Aviator, Wings of Gold, 1970; Commendation Medal with citation and the Legion of Merit with citation upon retirement from U.S. Naval Reserve, 1974.

SIDELIGHTS: MEMBERSHIPS—Screen Actors Guild (former board member), American Federation of Television and Radio Artists, American Federation of Musicians, Directors Guild of America (council member and national board of directors), Cinema Circulus at USC (board of directors), Naval Aviation Society, Naval Reserve Association, Aircraft Owners and Pilots Association, VIVA to return MIAs and POWs from Vietnam (charter member).

From Cooper's publicity biography, we learn that "he began his acting career at age three. By age seven, he was a member of the *Our Gang* comedies, known to today's television audience as the *Little Rascals.* By the time he was twenty five, Cooper had worked at every major film studio, co-starring with such performers as Lana Turner, James Stewart, Judy Garland, and Henry Fonda.

"After his naval duties in World War Two, he tried film acting again in California, but moved to New York in 1947, where he became one of the first Hollywood actors to participate in live television performing. At this time, Cooper also began acting in summer stock and on Broadway, and started his directorial career.

"Cooper returned to California in 1955, where he continues to act in and direct television shows. His success at directing is reflected in the many awards and nominations for awards that the shows he has been involved with have garnered.

"Besides remaining an active commercial pilot, he is also an automobile enthusiast. Until 1956, he was a member of the Sports Car Club of America (SCCA), having driven in over two dozen SCCA sportscar races and been awarded nearly as many trophies. In 1953, along with three other drivers, he broke over twenty five world speed and endurance class D' records in specially prepared Austin-Healys at the Bonneville Salt Flats in Utah, supervised by the AAA."

ADDRESS: OFFICE—c/o David Licht Associates, 9171 Wilshire Blvd., Beverly Hills, CA 90210. AGENT—Creative Artists Agency, 1888 Century Park E., Suite 1400, Los Angeles, CA 90067.

Photography by Zoe Dominic

SUSAN COOPER

COOPER, Susan   1935-

PERSONAL: Born May 23, 1935, in England; daughter of John Richard and Ethel May (Field) Cooper; married Nicholas J. Grant, August 3, 1963 (divorced 1983); children: Jonathan, Katharine. EDUCATION: Oxford, M.A., 1956.

VOCATION: Writer.

WRITINGS: PLAYS, PRODUCED—*Foxfire* (with Hume Cronyn), Avon, Stratford, Ontario, Canada, 1980, Guthrie, Minneapolis, 1981, Ethel Barrymore, NY, 1982. SCREENPLAYS, PRODUCED—*The Dollmaker* (with Hume Cronyn), ABC, 1984 (released commercially in Europe). PLAYS, PUBLISHED—*Foxfire*, Samuel French, 1983.

JUVENILE BOOKS, PUBLISHED—"The Dark Is Rising" series: *Over Sea, Under Stone*, J. Cape, 1965, Harcourt, 1966; *The Dark Is Rising*, Atheneum, 1973; *Greenwitch*, Chatto & Windus, 1973, Atheneum, 1974; *The Grey King*, Chatto & Windus, 1974, Atheneum, 1975; *Silver on the Tree*, Atheneum, 1977. NOVELS, PUBLISHED—*Dawn of Fear* (illustrated by Margery Gill), Harcourt, 1970; *Jethro and the Jumbie* (illustrated by Ashley Bryan), Atheneum, 1979; *The Silver Cow* (illustrated by Warwick Hutton), Atheneum, 1983; *Seaward*, Atheneum, 1983.

AWARDS: Christopher, Emmy nomination, 1984, for *The Dollmaker;* numerous awards for fiction including the Newbery Medal, 1976, for *The Grey King*

SIDELIGHTS: MEMBERSHIPS—Society of Authors (U.K.), Authors League of America, Authors Guild, Writers Guild of America.

Cooper has also worked extensively as a journalist and essayist (for more complete information on this aspect of her career, please see *Contemporary Authors.)*

ADDRESS: AGENT—Sam Cohn, International Creative Management, 40 W. 57th Street, New York, NY 10019.

*   *   *

CONRAD, Michael   1925-83

PERSONAL: Born 1925, in New York City, died November 22, 1983; survived by his fourth wife, Sema. EDUCATION: Attended the City College of New York and the New School for Social Research. MILITARY: U.S. Army, Artillery, World War Two.

VOCATION: Actor.

CAREER: PRINCIPAL STAGE APPEARANCES—*Mrs. Warren's Profession*, Gate Theatre, 1958; *A Man's a Man*, Masque Theatre, 1962.

MAJOR TOURS—*A Streetcar Named Desire*, national tour; *Mr. Roberts*, national tour.

PRINCIPAL FILM APPEARANCES—*The Longest Yard; Cattle Annie and Little Britches; They Shoot Horses Don't They?; Castle Keep.*

PRINCIPAL TELEVISION APPEARANCES—*The Edge of Night;* Lieutenant Macavan, *Delvecchio*, 1976; Sergeant Phillip Esterhaus, *Hill Street Blues*, 1981-1983; also: *Naked City; The Defenders; Wagon Train; Gunsmoke; Rawhide.*

AWARDS: Emmy, for Sergeant Esterhaus, *Hill Street Blues.**

*   *   *

CONRAD, William   1920-

PERSONAL: Born September 27, 1920, in Louisville, KY. EDUCATION: Attended Fullerton Junior College. MILITARY: U.S. Air Force, 1943-45.

VOCATION: Actor, producer, and director.

CAREER: PRINCIPAL TELEVISION APPEARANCES—*The D.A.*, 1971-72; *O'Hara, U.S. Treasury*, 1971-72; *Cannon*, 1971-76; *Nero Wolfe*, 1981. Movies: *The Brotherhood of the Bell*, 1970; *Conspiracy to Kill*, 1970; *Night Cries*, 1978; *The Rebels*, 1979. Narrator, *Return of the King.*

PRINCIPAL TELEVISION WORK—Producer and director, *Klondike;* producer, *77 Sunset Strip;* director, *True;* producer, *Turnover Smith.*

FILM DEBUT—*The Killers*, 1946. PRINCIPAL FILM APPEARANCES—*Body and Soul*, 1947; *Sorry, Wrong Number*, 1948; *East Side, West Side*, 1949; *The Naked Jungle*, 1954; *—30—*, Warner Brothers, 1959; *Moonshine County Express*, 1977.

PRINCIPAL FILM WORK—Producer: *Two on a Guillotine*, Warner Brothers, 1965; *Brainstorm*, Warner Brothers, 1965; *An American*

Dream, Warner Brothers, 1966; *A Covenant with Death*, Warner Brothers, 1967; *First to Fight*, Warner Brothers, 1967; *The Cool Ones*, Warner Brothers, 1967; *The Assignment*.

PRINCIPAL RADIO APPEARANCES—*Gunsmoke*, 1949-60.

ADDRESS: AGENT—Creative Artists Agency, 1888 Century Park E., Suite 1400, Los Angeles, CA 90067.*

*   *   *

CONREID, Hans   1917-82

PERSONAL: Born March 15, 1917, in Baltimore, MD; died of a heart attack, January 5, 1982; son of Hans Jr. and Edith Conreid; married Margaret Grant; children: Hans Jr., Alexander, Trilby, Edith. EDUCATION: Columbia University.

CAREER: NEW YORK DEBUT—Boris Adzindzinade, *Can-Can*, Shubert, 1953. PRINCIPAL STAGE APPEARANCES—Professor Leon Solomon, *Tall Story*, Belasco, NY, 1959; Andrew Pilgrim, *The Absence of a Cello*, Huntington Hartford, Los Angeles, 1966; Walter Hollander, *Don't Drink the Water*, Coconut Grove Playhouse, Miami, FL, 1967; *70 Girls 70*, Broadhurst, NY, 1971; Madame Lucy, *Irene*, Minskoff, 1974; Samuel Jones, *Something Old, Something New*, Morosco, 1977. Stock productions: *How the Other Half Loves; My Fair Lady; The Pleasure of His Company; Not in the Book; Take Her, She's Mine*.

MAJOR TOURS—Jim Bolton, *Generation*, national tour, 1967; title role, *Spofford*, national tour, 1969-70; Ben Chambers, *Norman, Is That You?* national tour, 1971; Madame Lucy, *Irene*, national tour, 1974;

FILM DEBUT—*Dramatic School*. PRINCIPAL FILM APPEARANCES—*It's a Wonderful World; Crazy Horse; Dulcy; Journey into Fear; Hostages; The Big Street; Mrs. Parkington; Passage to Marseilles; The Senator Was Indiscreet; My Friend Irma; On the Town; Siren of Bagdad; Summer Stock; The World in His Arms; The 5000 Fingers of Dr. T; The Twonky; The Affairs of Dobie Gillis; Rockabye Baby; Bus Stop; Jet Pilot; The Patsy; The Brothers O'Toole; The Shaggy D.A.; The Cat from Outerspace; Oh God Book II*.

PRINCIPAL TELEVISION APPEARANCES—*My Friend Irma*, for seven years; *The Tony Randall Show*; Uncle Toonoose, *The Danny Thomas Show*; *Life with Wigi*; *The Love Boat*; *Alice*; *Laverne and Shirley*; host, *Fractured Flickers*; *Biography*; *Fantasy Island*; *Supertrain*.

SIDELIGHTS: MEMBERSHIPS—American Federation of Television and Radio Artists (founding member), Actors' Equity Association, Screen Actors Guild.

Conreid began his career as a radio actor, portraying Professor Kropothin in *My Friend Irma*, in the late 1930's.*

*   *   *

CORLETT, William   1938-

PERSONAL: Born October 8, 1938, in Great Britain. EDUCATION: Attended Fettes College, Edinburgh, Scotland; trained for the stage at the Royal Academy of Dramatic Art.

VOCATION: Writer.

WRITINGS: TELEVISION PLAYS—For ABC, ATV, BBC, 1964-77; *The Paper Lads*, Tyne Tees Television, 1978-79; *Going Back*, Yorkshire, 1979; *Kids*, London Weekend, 1979; *The Gate of Eden*, YTV, 1980; *Barriers*, Tyne Tees, 1980-81; *The Agatha Christie Hour*, Thames, 1982; *The Machine Gunners*, BBC, 1982; *Dearly Beloved*, YTV, 1983; *The Christmas Tree*, YTV, 1985.

PLAYS, PRODUCED—*The Gentle Avalance*, Royal Court, London, 1962; *Return Ticket*, Duchess, London, 1965; *Tinker's Curse*, Nottingham Playhouse, 1968.

BOOKS—*The Gate of Eden*, Hamish Hamilton, 1974; *The Land Beyond*, Hamish Hamilton, 1975; *Return to the Gate*, Hamish Hamilton, 1975; *The Dark Side of the Moon*, Hamish Hamilton, 1976; *The Question of Religion, The Christ Story, The Hindu Sound, The Judaic Law, The Buddha Way, The Islamic Space* (with John Moore), all Hamish Hamilton, 1978-80; *Bloxworth Blue*, Julia MacRae Books, 1984.

AWARDS: Pye Television Award, Children's Writer of the Year, 1979; Gold Medal Award, IFT Festival of New York, 1980; Pye Television Award, Children's Writer of the Year, 1981; Gold Medal Award, IFT Festival of New York, 1983.

ADDRESS: HOME—Essex, England. AGENT—Fraser and Dunlop Scripts, 91 Regent Street, London W1, England.

*   *   *

CORMAN, Roger   1926-

PERSONAL: Born April 5, 1926, in Chicago, IL; son of William (an engineer) Corman; married Julie Halloran (a film producer); children: Catherine, Roger Martin, Brian, Mary. EDUCATION: Stanford University, B.S., industrial engineering.

VOCATION: Director and producer.

CAREER: PRINCIPAL FILMS—Producer: *The Monster from the Ocean Floor*, 1954; *The Fast and the Furious*, 1954; *Highway Dragnet*, 1954; *Ride the Whirlwind* (uncredited executive producer), 1965; *The Shooting* (uncredited executive producer), 1967; *Battle Beyond the Stars*, 1981.

Producer and director: *Five Guns West*, American Releasing Corp., 1955; *Apache Woman*, American International, 1955; *The Day the World Ended*, American Releasing Corp., 1956; *Swamp Woman*, Woolner Bros., 1956; *Oklahoma Woman*, American International, 1956; *Gunslinger*, American International, 1956; *It Conquered the World*, American International, 1956; *Not of This Earth*, Allied Artists, 1957; *The Undead*, American International, 1957; *She-Gods of Shark Reef*, American International, 1957; *Naked Paradise*, American International, 1957; *Attack of the Crab Monsters*, Allied Artists, 1957; *Rock All Night*, American International, 1957; *Teenage Doll*, Allied Artists, 1957; *Carnival Rock*, 1957; *The Little Guy* (uncompleted), 1957; *Reception* (uncompleted), 1957; *Sorority Girl*, American International, 1958; *Viking Women and the Sea Serpent*, American International, 1958; *War of the Satellites*, Allied Artists, 1958; *Machine Gun Kelly*, American International, 1958; *Teenage Caveman*, American International, 1958; *I, Mobster*, Twentieth Century-Fox, 1958; *Bucket of Blood*, American International, 1959; *The Cry Baby Killer*, Allied Artists, 1959; *Wasp Woman*, Filmgroup, 1959.

ROGER CORMAN

Ski Troop Attack, Film Group, 1960; *The Fall of the House of Usher*, American International, 1960; *The Little Shop of Horrors*, 1960; *Last Woman on Earth*, 1960; *Creature from the Haunted Sea*, 1961; *Atlas*, 1961; *The Pit and the Pendulum*, American International, 1961; *The Intruder*, 1961; *The Premature Burial*, American International, 1962; *Tales of Terror*, 1962; *Tower of London*, United Artists, 1962; *The Young Racers*, American International, 1963; *The Raven*, 1963; *The Terror*, American International, 1963; *X—The Man with the X-Ray Eyes*, American International, 1963; *The Haunted Palace*, 1963; *The Secret Invasion*, United Artists, 1964; *The Masque of the Red Death*, American International, 1964; *The Tomb of Ligeia*, American International, 1965; *The Wild Angels*, American International, 1966; *The Saint Valentine's Day Massacre*, 1967; *The Trip*, American International, 1967; *What's in It for Harry?*, 1968; *Bloody Mama*, American International, 1969; *Gas!*, 1969; *The Red Baron*, 1971; *Spider Man* (upcoming).

SIDELIGHTS: MEMBERSHIPS—Academy of Motion Picture Arts and Sciences.

Corman's career has been assembled into a book, *The Films of Roger Corman* by Ed Naha. He has been celebrated as an independent filmmaker with a remarkable facility for shooting his low-budget films very quickly. *The Little Shop of Horrors*, for example, was shot in only two days; *Bucket of Blood* in five days.

ADDRESS: OFFICE—11600 San Vicente Blvd., Los Angeles, CA 90049.

CORWIN, Betty L.   1920-

PERSONAL: Born Betty Linkoff, November 19, 1920; daughter of Irving and Mae Linkoff; married Henry R. Corwin (a physician), June 13, 1943; children: John, Pamela, Tom. EDUCATION: Adelphi College, B.A., 1942.

VOCATION: Project director.

WRITINGS: MAGAZINE ARTICLES—"Theatre on Film and Tape," *Performing Arts Resources,* 1976; "Theatre on Film and Tape: Preserving Stage Performances," *Variety,* 1980.

RELATED CAREER—Songwriter, Bourne Music, Inc., 1960-69; director, Theatre on Film and Tape Project, Billy Rose Theatre Collection, New York Public Library at Lincoln Center, NY. Lecturer: American Theatre Association, 1973; American Society for Theatre Research, 1974; Long Island University; New York Library Association, 1981. Consultant: National Library of Canberra, Australia, 1979; East Midlands Arts Council, England, 1979; Dallas Theater Center, 1980; Skokie Fine Arts Council, IL, 1981; Dallas Public Library, Fine Arts Division, 1983; Wolf Trap Foundation, 1984; Elders Share the Arts, 1984.

AWARDS: The Villager Award, 1982; Women in Communications Award, 1984; Broadway on Showtime Award, 1985.

SIDELIGHTS: MEMBERSHIPS—American Theater Association, International Federation for Theatre Research, Theatre Library Association, American Society for Theatre Research, New Drama Forum (second vice-president and program chairman, 1983-84), Outer Critics Circle, American Society of Composers, Authors, and Publishers.

Corwin also held the following positions: advertising executive, Erwin Wasey Advertising Agency, 1942-43; Curtis Publishing Company, 1942-43; organizer, co-ordinator, Bookcenter for Civil and Human Rights, World Affairs Center, Fairfield County, CT, 1962-69.

ADDRESS: HOME—25 Huckleberry Lane, Weston, CT 06880. OFFICE—New York Public Library at Lincoln Center, 111 Amsterdam Avenue, New York, NY 10023.

*   *   *

COULLET, Rhonda

PERSONAL: Daughter of Horace Oglesby and Cecil (Hudson) Coullet. EDUCATION: Denver University for one year and University of Arkansas for two years; studied for the theatre at the University of Southern California at its Musical Comedy Workshop.

VOCATION: Actress and composer.

CAREER: PRINCIPAL STAGE APPEARANCES—Jeanie, *Hair*, Los Angeles, CA; Rosamond, *The Robber Bridegroom*, Biltmore, NY, 1977; Prudie, *Pump Boys and Dinettes*, NY; Blanche, *Shot Thru the Heart*, NY; Frances, *Frances Farmer*, Pennsylvania Stage Festival; lead, *National Lampoon's Lemmings*, Village Gate, NY; standby for Gilda Radner, *National Lampoon Revue*, NY; Fay Apple, *Anyone Can Whistle*, Berkshire Theatre Festival, Stockbridge, MA, 1981; company, *Jesus Christ, Superstar*, NY.

PRINCIPAL STAGE WORK—Choreographer: *Jesus Christ, Superstar,* Scandinavian tour; *Hair,* restaged for U.S. and Scandinavian tours.

PRINCIPAL FILM APPEARANCES—Princess Wahini, *Mr. Mike's Mondo Video; This Is Spinal Tap,* Embassy, 1984.

PRINCIPAL TELEVISION APPEARANCES—*Saturday Night Live,* NBC; *Video Tribute to John Belushi.*

RADIO APPEARANCES—Comedy roles, *The National Lampoon Radio Hour.*

CONCERTS, CLUBS, CABARETS—Rhonda Coullet and the Cows, have appeared at the Lone Star Cafe, Folk City, S.N.A.F.U., J.P., Reno Sweeney's, Central Falls, Le Select (St. Bart's).

RECORDINGS: Original cast recording, *The Robber Bridegroom;* background vocals for two Meatloaf albums, *Bat Out of Hell* and *Deadringer;* background vocals, Jimmy Buffet's *Riddles in the Sand;* comedy roles, National Lampoon recordings: *White House Missing Tapes, Goodbye Pop, That's Not Funny - That's Sick, The Best of National Lampoon.*

WRITINGS: SONGS, RECORDED—*Bigger Than Both of Us,* sung by Jimmy Buffet.

SIDELIGHTS: MEMBERSHIPS—Actors' Equity Association, Screen Actors Guild, American Federation of Television and Radio Artists, American Society of Composers, Authors, and Publishers.

Coullet informed *CTFT* that she has composed over one hundred songs as well as movie soundtracks, television background for *Saturday Night Live,* and jingles heard on *Sesame Street* and *Captain Kangaroo.*

ADDRESS: HOME—P.O. Box 99, Canady Hill Road, West Berne, NY 12023.

*   *   *

CRABE, James   1931-

PERSONAL: Born August 19, 1931, in Los Angeles, CA; son of Lyall Aubrey (a cartoon animator) and Carmel (Ricciardi) Crabe.

VOCATION: Director of photography and cinematographer.

CAREER: PRINCIPAL FILM WORK—*Zig Zag,* Metro-Goldwyn-Mayer, 1970; *The Honkers,* United Artists, 1972; *Save the Tiger,* Paramount, 1972; *Rhinoceros,* AFT Distributing, 1973; *W.W. and the Dixie Dance Kings,* Twentieth Century-Fox, 1974; *Rocky,* United Artists, 1977; *Sextette,* 1977; *Thank God It's Friday,* Columbia, 1978; *The China Syndrome,* Columbia, 1979; *Players,* Paramount, 1979; *The Baltimore Bullet,* AVCO Embassy, 1980; *How to Beat the High Cost of Living,* Filmways, 1980; *The Formula,* United Artists, 1980; *Night Shift,* Warner Bros., 1982; *The Karate Kid,* Columbia, 1983; *Police Academy II,* Warner Bros., 1984.

PRINCIPAL TELEVISION WORK—*Lost Flight,* 1969; *Sole Survivor,* 1969; *A Step Out of Line,* 1970; *Sweet, Sweet Rachel,* 1971; *The Autobiography of Miss Jane Pittman,* 1974; *The Dead Won't Die,* 1974; *The Entertainer,* 1975; *F. Scott Fitzgerald in Hollywood,* 1976; *The Disappearance of Aimee,* 1976; *Eleanor and Franklin, the White House Years,* 1977; *A Death in Canaan,* 1978; *Strangers:*

Photography by Robert A. de Stolfe

JAMES CRABE

The Story of a Mother and Daughter, 1979; *The Letter,* 1982; *Trauma Center,* 1982; *Concrete Beats,* 1983; *Two Kinds of Love,* 1983; *Family Secrets,* 1983; *More Than Murder,* 1983; *Paper Dolls,* 1984; *Long Time Gone,* 1984.

AWARDS: Emmy, 1982, for *The Letter,* 1983, for *More Than Murder;* Academy Award nomination, 1979, for *The Formula;* Emmy nominations, 1975, for *The Entertainer,* 1977, for *Eleanor and Franklin, the White House Years.*

SIDELIGHTS: MEMBERSHIPS—American Society of Cinematographers, Society of Motion Picture and Television Engineers, American Film Institute.

ADDRESS: AGENT—Mortie Guterman, 8150 Beverly Blvd., Los Angeles, CA 90048.

*   *   *

CRAIG, Carl   1954-

PERSONAL: Born August 1, 1954, in Tallahassee, FL; son of Walter O. (a music professor) and Ruth (a secretary; maiden name, Roper) Craig; married Angela E. Fong (an airline worker). EDUCATION: University of Rochester, B.A., 1976; studied with Stella Adler in New York City. RELIGION: Catholic.

VOCATION: Actor and singer.

CAREER: PRINCIPAL STAGE APPEARANCES—Shine, *The Great Mac Daddy,* Negro Ensemble Company, NY; *The Brownsville*

CARL CRAIG

Raid, Negro Ensemble Company, NY; Bubba, *Second Thoughts,* Afro American Total Theatre, NY; Universal Man, *Poets from the Inside,* Public, NY; Tony, *Black Sheep,* Billie Holiday, NY; Pierre, *Sister Racher and the Ton Ton Maconte,* La MaMa E.T.C., NY; *Ceremonies in Dark Old Men,* GEVA, Rochester, NY; Catesby, *Richard III,* U.R.S.T., Rochester, NY.

PRINCIPAL FILM APPEARANCES—Titons gang leader, *Warriors,* Paramount, 1979; street punk, *Fort Apache, the Bronx,* Twentieth Century-Fox, 1981; junkie, *Prince of the City,* Warner Brothers, 1981; mental patient, *Endless Love,* Universal, 1981.

PRINCIPAL TELEVISION APPEARANCES—*Hollow Image,* 1979; paramedic cop, *As the World Turns,* CBS; waiter, *All My Children,* ABC; "Lead Poisoning," *Black Dimensions,* PBS.

SIDELIGHTS: MEMBERSHIPS—Actors' Equity Association, American Federation of Television and Radio Artists, Screen Actors Guild.

ADDRESS: HOME—Orange, NJ. AGENT—Sara Packard, S.T.E. Representation Ltd., 888 Seventh Avenue, New York, NY 10106.

*   *   *

CRAVEN, Gemma   1950-

PERSONAL: Born June 1, 1950, in Dublin, Ireland; daughter of Bernard and Lillian Josephine (Byrne) Craven. EDUCATION: St. Bernard's Convent, Westcliff-on-Sea, Dublin; studied acting at the Bush Davies School.

VOCATION: Actress and singer.

CAREER: STAGE DEBUT—The maid, *Let's Get a Divorce,* Palace, Westcliff, Ireland. LONDON DEBUT—Anya, *Fiddler on the Roof,* Her Majesty's, 1970. PRINCIPAL STAGE APPEARANCES—(All England unless otherwise noted) Title role, *Audrey,* The Place, 1971; Jenny Bell, *Saturnalia,* Belgrade, Coventry, 1971; Sabrina, *Sabrina Fair,* Thorndike, Leatherhead, 1972; Rose Trelawny, *Trelawny of the Wells,* Sadler's Wells, Prince of Wales, 1972; Jasmin, *R Loves J,* Sheba, *Dandy Dick,* both at Chichester Festival, 1973; Sheba, *Dandy Dick,* Garrick, 1973; Corinna, *The Confederacy,* May and Katya, *A Month in the Country,* both at Chichester Festival, 1974; Elizabeth Snowden, *Underground,* Billingham Forum, 1974; Polly Peachum, *Threepenny Opera,* Theatre Royal, Bristol, 1975; Carol Melchett, *Black Comedy,* Shaw, 1976; Shelley Jones and Meatball Jones, *The Happiest Tears in Town,* Thorndike, Leatherhead, 1976; *Side by Side by Sondheim,* Gaiety, Dublin, 1977; Yvonne Arnaud, *Guilford,* Gaiety, Dublin, 1978; *Songbook,* Globe, 1979; Sonia, *They're Playing Our Song,* Shaftsbury Theatre, 1980-81; *Song and Dance,* Palace, 1984-85; Fay, *Loot,* Ambassador's, Lyric, 1985; *The Comeback,* 1985; *A Chorus of Disapproval,* National Theatre, 1985.

PRINCIPAL FILM APPEARANCES—*Kingdom of Gifts; Why Not Stay for Breakfast; The Slipper and the Rose,* Universal, 1976; *Wagner.*

PRINCIPAL TELEVISION APPEARANCES—*Pennies from Heaven; Must Wear Tights; She Loves Me; Song by Song by Noel Coward; Song by Song by Alan Jay Lerner; East Lynne; Robin of Sherwood; Treasure Hunt; Gemma Girls and Gershwin.*

AWARDS: Evening News, Most Promising New Actress in Films, 1976; Variety Club, Film Actress of 1976; Best Actress in a Musical, Society of West End Theatres, 1980, for *They're Playing Our Song.*

ADDRESS: AGENT—Stella Richards, 42 Hazlebury Road, London SW6 2ND, England.

*   *   *

CRAWLEY, Tom   1940-

PERSONAL: Born August 4, 1940, in Central Falls, RI; son of Thomas F. (a textile worker) and Eileen A. (Gibson) Crawley. EDUCATION: Providence College, RI, B.A., 1962; University of Nebraska, M.A., 1964, Ph. D., 1969; trained for the stage at the New York University School of the Arts.

VOCATION: Actor, director, and teacher.

CAREER: STAGE DEBUT—Dude, *Tobacco Road,* Lakes Region Playhouse, Laconia, NH, 1964. NEW YORK DEBUT—Troll, *Peer Gynt,* Delacorte, 1969.

MAJOR TOURS—Charlie, *Da,* U.S. cities, 1979-80.

TELEVISION DEBUT—Captain Orin, *Texas,* ABC, 1980.

FILM DEBUT—Detective Broder, *The Clairvoyant,* 1981.

RELATED CAREER—Teacher: John Jay College, NY, 1974-75, 1982-85; Fordham Graduate School of Business, 1983-85.

SIDELIGHTS: MEMBERSHIPS—Actors' Equity Association, Screen

credits include *Endless Love*, Universal, 1981; *Taps*, Twentieth Century-Fox, 1981; *Losin' It*, Embassy, 1983; *The Outsiders*, Warner Brothers, 1983; *Risky Business*, Warner Brothers, 1983; *All the Right Moves*, Warner Brothers, 1983; *Legend* (upcoming); *Top Gun* (upcoming).*

*   *   *

CULLITON, Joseph   1948-

PERSONAL: Born January 25, 1948, in Boston, MA; son of Daniel Joseph (an attorney) and Gertrude (a journalist; maiden name, Haworth) Culliton. EDUCATION: Attended California State University at Northridge, 1966-68; Academy of Dramatic Art at Oakland University, 1968-70; studied acting with Jeff Corey. POLITICS: Democrat. RELIGION: Roman Catholic.

VOCATION: Actor.

CAREER: STAGE DEBUT—Ferdinand, *The Tempest*, Guthrie Theatre, Minneapolis, MN, 1970. NEW YORK DEBUT—James Callifer, *The Potting Shed*, Malachy Theatre Company, 1974, 16 performances. PRINCIPAL STAGE APPEARANCES—Jeriah Jip, *A Man's a Man*, First Gang Leader, *A Play by Alexander Sozhenitsyn*, the Tramp, *Baal*, all at the Guthrie, 1970; Second Gentleman, *Othello*, Mark Taper Forum, Los Angeles, CA, 1971; Troilus, *Troilus and Cressida*, Trinity Square Repertory, RI, 1971; Bagot, *Richard III*, Kennedy Center, Washington, DC, 1972; Jean-Pierre, *13 Rue de L'Amour*, Peter Latham, *Forty Carats*, Jimmy, *There's a Girl in My Soup*, Joe Janke, *Everybody Loves Opal*, Desmond, *The Happy Time*, Paul Sevinge, *A Shot in the Dark*, David Hoylake-Johnson, *The Reluctant Debutante*, all at Showboat Dinner Theater, FL,

TOM CRAWLEY

Actors Guild, American Federation of Television and Radio Artists, Players Club, Writers and Directors Unit.

ADDRESS: AGENT—Kass-Woo, 156 Fifth Avenue, New York, NY 10013.

*   *   *

CROSBY, Mary Frances

BRIEF ENTRY: Daughter of Bing and Kathryn (Grandstaff) Crosby; married Ebb Lottimer, November, 1978. Actress. Attended University of Texas, Austin. Crosby was the youngest student ever to attend the advanced training program at the American Conservatory in San Francisco. Her television credits include Kristin in *Dallas*, CBS, the television movies *Midnight Lace*, 1980, and *Golden Gate*, ABC, 1981, and the NBC miniseries *Hollywood Wives*. She starred in the motion picture *The Ice Pirates*, Metro-Goldwyn-Mayer/United Artists, 1984.*

*   *   *

CRUISE, Tom

BRIEF ENTRY: Born in Syracuse, NY. Actor. Cruise made his stage debut in a dinner theatre production of *Godspell*. His film

JOSEPH CULLITON

1973; Jeffrey, *Here Today*, Igor Sullivan, *Cactus Flower*, Carousel Dinner Theater, OH, 1974.

Macheath, *Threepenny Opera*, George Street Playhouse, New Brunswick, NJ, 1976; Inspector Thomas, *The Unexpected Guest*, Tony, *Roman Conquest*, Matthew, *Late Love*, all at Wolfeboro Playhouse, NH, 1976; Limousine, *Georgie's Papa*, Stagelights Repertory, NY, 1977; File, *The Rainmaker*, Trotter, *The Mousetrap*, Manuel, *The Gingerbread Lady*, Cass, *Any Wednesday*, all at Wolfeboro Playhouse, NH, 1977; Chamberlain, *Cromwell*, Ansonia Studio One, NY, 1978; Orsino, *Twelfth Night*, George Street Playhouse, NJ, 1979; Macduff, *Macbeth*, American Shakespeare Festival, Stratford, CT, 1980; Morris Townsend, *The Heiress*, Barter, VA, 1980; Philip Berrigan, *Trial of the Catonsville Nine*, Baron, *The Lower Depths*, both at Vandamm, NY, 1981; Thomas Mendip, *The Lady's Not for Burning*, York Players, NY, 1981; Roger Calhoun, *Something for the Boys*, Bandwagon Productions, NY, 1981.

Elias, *Francis*, Theatre at St. Peters, NY, 1982; Charles Dickens, *Life and Times of Charles Dickens*, Kaufman Auditorium, NY, 1982; Trinidad Joe, *Girl of the Golden West*, Jack Chesney, *Charley's Aunt*, Asolo State Theatre, FL, 1982; Jack Worthing, *The Importance of Being Earnest*, New Globe, NY, 1982, Long Island Playhouse, NY, 1983; Albert Adams, *The Play's the Thing*, New Globe, NY, 1983; Coriolanus, *Coriolanus*, Shakespeare Marathon, NY, 1983; Arthur, *Porter's Brandy*, Company of St. Justus, NY, 1983; Martin, *Flirtations*, T.O.M.I., NY, 1983; George Kitteridge, *The Philadelphia Story*, Alaska Repertory, 1983; Joey Percival, *Misalliance*, New Globe, NY, 1984; Peter Quilpe, *The Cocktail Party*, New Globe, NY, 1984; Sergius, *Arms and the Man*, Hubert Stem, *Clarence*, both at Syracuse Stage, NY, 1984; Harry/Martin, *Cloud 9*, Virginia Museum, 1985.

MAJOR TOURS—Bagot, *Richard III*, Ahmanson, Los Angeles, Kennedy Center, Washington, DC, 1973; David Hoylake-Johnson, *The Reluctant Debutante*, 1974-75; *A Shakespeare Tryptch*, 1980; *The Life and Times of Charles Dickens*, 1983.

FILM DEBUT—Red, *Cahill, U.S. Marshall*, Warner Brothers, 1973. PRINCIPAL FILM APPEARANCES—Butler, *Pat Garrett and Billy the Kid*, Metro-Goldwyn-Mayer, 1973; Martin, *Somebody Killed Her Husband*, Columbia, 1978.

TELEVISION DEBUT—Peter Davis, *Ryan's Hope*, 1981.

SIDELIGHTS: Culliton told *CTFT*, "I am a third generation actor. My maternal grandfather, William Haworth, was an enormously successful playwright and actor in this country at the turn of the cetury. His plays *The Ensign*, *A Nutmeg Match*, and *On the Mississippi*, among others, were widely produced in New York, on the road, and in stock. His brother, Joseph Haworth, was a star classical actor and matinee idol. Joseph Haworth played Hamlet successfully in New York and on the road; he played Romeo opposite Julia Marlowe in her New York debut; and he played Macbeth to Helene Modjeska's celebated Lady Macbeth. Stage and film actor Wallace Ford was my uncle. Another uncle is Academy Award winning art director Ted Haworth. My brother, Patrick Culliton, has acted extensively in television and films. Representing the fourth generation is my niece, Sarah Tuttle Dirksen, who is presently a student at the Lee Strasberg Institute in Los Angeles. I am deeply proud to be part of a family that has participated in the American theatre for the past one hundred years."

ADDRESS: HOME—484 W. 43rd Street, New York, NY 10036. AGENT—c/o Fifi Oscard Associates, Inc., 19 W. 44th Street, New York, NY 10036.

KAREN CULLIVER

CULLIVER, Karen   1959-

PERSONAL: Born December 30, 1959, in FL; daughter of Robert Eugene (a tax auditor and licensed minister) and Melinda Jane (a reading teacher; maiden name, Jones) Culliver. EDUCATION: Attended Stetson University, FL, 1978-79; also attended the Orlando School of the Performing Arts; studied voice with Eric Stern and Michael Richardson, dance with Bob Audy, George Koller, and Stanley Kahn.

VOCATION: Actress and singer.

CAREER: STAGE DEBUT—Elaine Harper, *Arsenic and Old Lace*, Once Upon a Stage Dinner Theatre. NEW YORK DEBUT—Kim, *Showboat*, Gershwin, 1983. PRINCIPAL STAGE APPEARANCES—Linda Christie, *Play It Again, Sam*, Sarah Brown, *Guys and Dolls*, Daisy Mae, *Li'l Abner*, Laurey, *Oklahoma!*, all at Once Upon a Stage; Pegeen Ryan, *Mame*, Show Boat Dinner Theatre; Philia, *A Funny Thing Happened on the Way to the Forum*, Country Dinner Playhouse; Gwendolyn, *Little Mary Sunshine*, Burt Reynolds, FL; Gloria Upson, *Mame*, Coachlight Dinner Theatre; Mrs. Potiphar, *Joseph and the Amazing Technicolor Dreamcoat*, An Evening Dinner Theatre; Luisa, *The Fantasticks*, Sullivan Street, NY, 1984.

MAJOR TOURS—Chorus, *Camelot;* Kim and understudy Magnolia, *Showboat*, Houston, Los Angeles, San Francisco, Seattle, Denver, Baltimore, Chicago, Detroit, Washington, DC, and San Diego.

FILM DEBUT—*Preppie*, 1984. PRINCIPAL FILM APPEARANCES—*Flamingo Kid*, 1984; *Falling in Love*, 1984; Mayor's Aide, *Turk 182!*, 1985; *Whatever It Takes*, 1985.

RELATED CAREER—*Kids of the Kingdom,* Walt Disney World, Orlando, FL, 1978-79.

SIDELIGHTS: MEMBERSHIPS—Actors' Equity Association, Screen Actors Guild.

Culliver was voted Miss Orlando of 1980.

ADDRESS: HOME—160 W. 71st Street, 14E, New York, NY 10023.

*   *   *

CURTIS, Keene   1923-

PERSONAL: Born February 15, 1923, in Salt Lake City, UT; son of Ira Charles and Polley Francella (Holbrook) Curtis. EDUCATION: University of Utah, M.S., 1947.

VOCATION: Actor.

CAREER: NEW YORK DEBUT—Standby Archie, *The Shop at Sly Corner,* 1949. PRINCIPAL STAGE APPEARANCES—Franz, *Anatole,* Medvedenko, *The Seagull,* Straker, *Man and Superman,* all with Association of Producing Artists, Bermuda, 1960; Tyson, *The Lady's Not for Burning,* Scapin, *Scapin,* Stevens, *The Tavern,* Agazzi, *Right You Are If You Think You Are,* Lane, *The Importance of Being Earnest,* all at McCarter, Princeton, NJ, 1960; Bottom, *A Midsummer Night's Dream,* Player King, *Hamlet,* Feste, *Twelfth Night,* Oswald, *King Lear,* Sir Oliver, *The School for Scandal,* Sheriff, *The Tavern,* Dr. Dorn, *The Seagull,* Colonel Howard, *Fashion,* all at McCarter, 1961.

Selincourt, *Penny for a Song,* Sir Benjamin Backbite, *The School for Scandal,* both at APA Repertory, NY, 1962; IRA officer, *The Hostage,* Salerio, *The Merchant of Venice,* Bagot, *Richard II,* Conrade, *Much Ado About Nothing,* Bottom, *A Midsummer Night's Dream,* Sirelli, *Right You Are If You Think You Are,* Sheriff, *The Tavern,* Tartar, *Lower Depths,* all at APA Repertory, NY, 1963; Bottom, *A Midsummer Night's Dream,* Sirelli, *Right You Are If You Think You Are,* Sheriff, *The Tavern,* Tartar, *Lower Depths,* DuCroisy, *Impromptu at Versailles,* Henry Straker, *Man and Superman,* Napoleon Bonaparte, *War and Peace,* Egon, *Judith,* Guide, *Herakles,* Molvik, *The Wild Duck,* Boris Kolenkhov, *You Can't Take It with You* all at APA Repertory, Phoenix, NY, 1964-65; Boris Kolenkhov, *You Can't Take It with You,* Lyceum, NY, 1965.

Sir Oliver, *The School for Scandal,* Sirelli, *Right You Are,* Kolenkhov, *You Can't Take It with You,* Pierre, *War and Peace,* all at APA, Phoenix, NY, 1966; Sir Oliver, *The School for Scandal,* Sirelli, *Right You Are,* both at Royal Alexandra, Toronto, and Lyceum, NY, 1966; Kolenkhov, *You Can't Take It with You,* Napoleon, *War and Peace,* both at Lyceum, NY, 1967; Yepihodov, *The Cherry Orchard,* Royal Alexandra, Toronto, and Lyceum, NY, 1967; Anarchist, *Pantagleize,* Alex, *The Cocktail Party,* Oronte, *The Misanthrope,* all at Royal Alexandra, Toronto, and Lyceum, NY, 1968; Servant, *Cock-a-Doodle Dandy,* Player King, *Hamlet,* both at Lyceum, NY, 1969; *Collision Course,* Pavilion, Pennsylvania State University, PA, 1969; Colonel Mischa Oblenskyk, *A Patriot for Me,* Imperial, NY, 1969; Ned Buntline, *Indians,* Brooks Atkinson, NY, 1969; Napoleon III, *Blood Red Roses,* John Golden, NY, 1970; Captain, Max, George Wague, Reporter, *Colette,* Ellen Stewart Theater, NY, 1970; Prince William of Hesse, Joseph Fouche, Lord Herries, Prince Metternich, *The Rothschilds,* Lunt-Fontanne, NY, 1970.

Keene Curtis in "A Ride Across Lake Constance," Forum, NY, 1972; Curtis Appleby, *Night Watch,* Morosco, NY, 1972; Dr. Isaacs, *Via Galactica,* Uris, NY, 1972; Inquisitor, *Saint Joan,* Ahmanson, Los Angeles, CA, 1974; Joshua, *Ring Round the Moon,* Ahmanson, Los Angeles, CA, 1975; Johnson, *Too Much Johnson,* Lake Forest, IL, 1975; *Life on a Limb,* Elitch Gardens, Denver, CO, 1975; Marquis, *The Baker's Wife,* Dorothy Chandler Pavilion, Los Angeles, CA, 1976; *The Middle Ages,* Mark Taper Forum Laboratory, Los Angeles, CA, 1977; Old Actor, *The Fantasticks,* Dallas Music Hall, TX, 1977; Bert Challenor, *Comedians,* Mark Taper, Los Angeles, CA, 1977; Daddy Warbucks, *Annie,* Curran, San Francisco, CA, Shubert, Los Angeles, CA, 1978; Yugoslavian Revolutionary, *Division Street,* Mark Taper Forum, Los Angeles, CA, 1980, Ambassador, NY, 1981; Gorky, *Checkhov in Yalta,* Feste, *Twelfth Night,* both at Mark Taper Forum Repertory, Los Angeles, CA, 1981; George Thunder, *Wild Oats,* Stratford, Ontario Shakespeare Festival, Canada, 1981; Chandebise and Poche, *Flea in Her Ear,* Oronte, *The Misanthrope,* both at Mark Taper Forum, Los Angeles, CA, 1982; Colonel, *Black Comedy,* Ahmanson, Los Angeles, CA, 1983.

MAJOR TOURS—Stage manager, *Martha Graham's Dance Company,* U.S. cities, 1949-50, European cities; stage manager, *Alvin Ailey-Carmen DeLavallade American Dance Company,* Australian and Far Eastern cities, 1962; Anarchist, *Pantaglaize,* Canadian and U.S. cities, 1967; Albin/Za Za, *La Cage Aux Folles,* U.S. cities, 1985.

PRINCIPAL STAGE WORK—Stage manager, 1950-60: *The Constant Wife, The Male Animal, Mrs. Patterson, The Dark Is Light Enough, Medea, Four Winds, Nude with Violin, Present Laughter, The Firstborn, Look After Lulu, Silent Night Lonely Night,* others.

FILM DEBUT—Lennox, (Orson Welles') *Macbeth,* 1947. PRINCIPAL FILM APPEARANCES—*Blade,* Joseph Green Pictures, 1973; *Heaven Can Wait,* Paramount, 1978; *Buddy System,* 1982.

SIDELIGHTS: RECREATIONS—Carpentry and photography.

ADDRESS: OFFICE—6363 Ivarene Avenue, Hollywood, CA 90068.

*   *   *

CUSACK, Sinead   1948-

PERSONAL: Born February 18, 1948; daughter of Cyril James (an actor) and Maureen (an actress) Cusack; married Jeremy Irons (an actor); children: Samuel James. EDUCATION: Attended Holy Child Convent, Killiney, and Dublin University.

VOCATION: Actress.

CAREER: STAGE DEBUT—Phoebe, *The Importance of Mr. O,* Olympia, Dublin, Ireland, 1960. PRINCIPAL STAGE APPEARANCES—Abbey Theater, Dublin, Ireland; Beatrice, Joanna, *The Changeling,* Gardner Centre, Brighton, 1971; Mirandolina, *The Silence of St. Just,* both 1971; Juliet, *Romeo and Juliet,* Shaw, London, 1972; Grace Harkaway, *London Assurance,* New, London, 1972; Laura Wingfield, *The Glass Menagerie,* Gardner Centre, 1973; Desdemona, *Othello,* Ludlow Festival, 1974; Raina Petkoff, *Arms and the Man,* Oxford Festival, 1976; Lady Amaranth, *Wild Oats,* Piccadilly, London, 1977, then Royal Shakespeare Company, Aldwych, London, 1979; Lisa, *Children of the Sun,* and Isabella, *Measure for Measure,* Royal Shakespeare Company, Aldwych,

London, 1979; Celia, *As You Like It,* Evadne, *The Maid's Tragedy,* Memorial, Stratford-on-Avon, 1980; Roxanne, *Cyrano de Bergerac,* and Beatrice, *Much Ado About Nothing,* London, and Gershwin, NY, 1984.

MAJOR TOURS—Raina Petkoff, *Arms and the Man,* U.K. cities, 1976.

PRINCIPAL FILM APPEARANCES—*Alfred the Great; Hoffman; The Last Remake of Beau Geste.*

PRINCIPAL TELEVISION APPEARANCES—*The Shadow of a Gunman; Trilby; Twelfth Night.*

ADDRESS: AGENT—Hutton Management, 194 Old Brompton Road, London SW5, England.*

*   *   *

CUTHBERTSON, Iain   1930-

PERSONAL: Born January 4, 1930, in Glasgow, Scotland; son of Sir David Paton, CBE, and Jean Prentice (Telfer) Cuthbertson; married Anne Kristen. EDUCATION: Attended Glasgow Academy, Aberdeen, and Aberdeen University.

VOCATION: Actor and director.

CAREER: DEBUT—Radio. STAGE DEBUT—Twins, *The Man Upstairs,* Leven, 1955. LONDON DEBUT—Archibald Gascoyne, *Gay Landscape,* Royal Court, 1958. PRINCIPAL STAGE APPEARANCES—Othello, *Othello,* Proctor, *The Crucible,* Big Daddy, *Cat on a Hot Tin Roof,* all at Citizens' Theatre Company, Glasgow, Scotland, 1958-60; Wallace, *The Wallace,* Edinburgh Festival, Scotland, 1960; Abelard, *Abelard and Heloise,* Friar Antony, *This Way to the Tomb,* both at Arts, London, 1960; Pitlochry Festival, 1961; Armstrong, *Armstrong's Last Goodnight,* Citizen's, Glasgow, 1964; Musgrave, *Serjeant Musgrave's Dance,* Royal Court, London, 1965; Major Domo, *Ariadne Auf Naxes,* Scottish Opera, 1977-78; Boswell, *Boswell's Johnson,* Lyceum, Edinburgh, 1978.

MAJOR TOURS—Angeles, *Dr. Angeles,* 1977.

PRINCIPAL STAGE WORK—Director: Citizens' Theater, Glasgow, 1962-65; associate director, Royal Court, 1965; *Ubu Roi,* Royal Court, London, 1966; Scottish Theater, Perth, 1967-68.

PRINCIPAL FILM APPEARANCES—*The Railway Children,* 1970; *The Assam Garden* (upcoming).

IAIN CUTHBERTSON

PRINCIPAL TELEVISION APPEARANCES—*The Borderers; Sutherland's Law; Destiny; The Story of Darwin; Charlie Endell; Casting the Runes,* many others, 1956-present.

RELATED CAREER—General manager and director of productions, Citizens' Theater, Glasgow, Scotland, 1962-65; rector, Aberdeen University, 1975-78.

WRITINGS: Documentary films.

AWARDS: Honoris Causa, LL.D, Aberdeen University, 1978.

SIDELIGHTS: RECREATION—Sailing.

ADDRESS: AGENT—c/o John French, 26 Binney Street, London W1, England.

D

JACK DABDOUB

DABDOUB, Jack   1925-

PERSONAL: Surname pronounced Dab-du; full name Jack Dabdoub Jr.; born February 5, 1925, in New Orleans, LA; son of Jack (an auto dealer) and Hilda (a fur buyer; maiden name, Bader) Dabdoub; married Rosemary Lynch, November 27, 1959; children: Jack III, Patrick, Alison. EDUCATION: Tulane University, B.E., mechanical engineering, 1944, M.B.A., 1949; studied acting at the American Theatre Wing in New York City with Horton Foote and Alexander Kirkland. MILITARY: U.S. Navy Reserve, Lt. jg, 1943-46.

VOCATION: Actor, singer, and spokesman.

CAREER: STAGE DEBUT—Pirate King, *Pirates of Penzance*, Tulane University, New Orleans, LA, 1946. NEW YORK DEBUT—*Paint Your Wagon*, Shubert, 1951. PRINCIPAL STAGE APPEARANCES—Broadway: Joe Buffalo Dance, *Moose Murders;* Mr. Maclaren and understudy Mr. Lundie, *Brigadoon,* 1980; Governor, Innkeeper,

Man of La Mancha, Vivian Beaumont; Don Quixote (matinees) and Governor, Innkeeper (evenings), *Man of La Mancha,* Martin Beck; *Camelot; Annie Get Your Gun; Her First Roman; Coco; Hotspot; Anya; Guys and Dolls; Happy Hunting; My Darlin' Aida; Baker Street; Paint Your Wagon.*

Off-Broadway: *Dragons; Lola,* York Players; *Of Those Called; Casanova; A Time for the Gentle People; The Peddler and the Dodo Bird; What's Up.*

Summer Stock: Emile deBecque, *South Pacific;* Don Quixote, *Man of La Mancha;* Cesar, *Fanny;* Buffalo Bill, *Annie Get Your Gun;* Beauregard, *Mame;* Wazir, *Kismet;* Count Peppi, *Song of Norway;* Herbie, *Gypsy;* Charlemagne, *Pippin;* H.C. Curry, *110 in the Shade;* Sheriff, *Bloomer Girl;* Old Strauss, *The Great Waltz;* Dr. Engel, *The Student Prince;* Etienne, *Naughty Marietta;* Scaramba, *El Capitan;* Lou Brody, *The Detective Story.*

MAJOR TOURS—Marley, Old Joe, and understudy Scrooge, *A Christmas Carol,* national tour.

PRINCIPAL TELEVISION APPEARANCES—*Ryan's Hope,* ABC; *As the World Turns,* CBS; *Search for Tomorrow; Route 66; Peter Pan; Omnibus; The Beggars' Opera; The Good Years; The Rag Tent; The Hero; Grants Tomb* (pilot); *The Tracer* (pilot); *The Shadow* (pilot).

PRINCIPAL OPERA APPEARANCES—New Orleans Opera Company, two seasons, seven roles; *The Good Soldier Schweik,* Carnegie Hall, NY, Philadelphia, PA; soloist with the New Orlean's Summer Pops and the Erie Philharmonic.

SIDELIGHTS: MEMBERSHIPS—Screen Actors Guild, Actors' Equity Association, American Federation of Television and Radio Artists, American Guild of Variety Artists, American Guild of Musical Artists.

Dabdoub told *CTFT:* "I have been a professional performer since 1948 and have enjoyed every minute."

ADDRESS: HOME—171 W. 79th Street, New York, NY 10024.

*   *   *

DAHL, Arlene   1928-

PERSONAL: Born August 11, 1928, in Minneapolis, MN; daughter of Rudolph S. (a Ford motor dealer and executive) and Idelle (Swan) Dahl; married Fernando Lamas (divorced); married Christian R. Holmes III (divorced); married Rounseville W. Schaum (divorced); married Marc A. Rosen (vice president, Elizabeth Arden Inc.), July

ARLENE DAHL

30, 1984; children: (first marriage) Lorenzo Lamas; (second marriage) Carole Christine; (third marriage) Stephen Schaum. EDUCATION: Studied voice and drama at the Minneapolis College of Music, special business course, Minneapolis Business College at the University of Minnesota; studied drama and speech with Dr. C. Lowell Leeds.

VOCATION: Actress, producer, writer, fashion designer, health and beauty aids designer.

CAREER: STAGE DEBUT—Flouncie, in a Philip Barry play, a women's club theatre, Minneapolis, MN, 1938. NEW YORK DEBUT—*Mr. Straus Goes to Boston*, Century, 1946. PRINCIPAL STAGE APPEARANCES—*Questionable Ladies*, NY; Roxanne, *Cyrano de Bergerac*, City Center, NY, 1952; *I Married an Angel*, Dallas, TX; *Liliom*, Phoenix, AZ; *The King and I*, Boston, MA; *One Touch of Venus*, Chicago, IL; *The Camel Bell*, Chicago, IL; *A Little Night Music*, Chicago, IL; *Life with Father*, Chicago, IL; *Forty Carats*, Delta State University; *Murder Among Friends*, Phoenix, AZ; Margo Channing, *Applause*, Palace, NY, 1972.

MAJOR TOURS—*Roman Candle*, Palm Beach, FL, Detroit, MI, Columbus and Warren, OH; *Blithe Spirit*, Chicago, IL, San Francisco, CA; *Bell, Book, and Candle*, NY, ME, Chicago; *Marriage Go Round*, Detroit, Dallas, Chicago.

FILM DEBUT—Rose, *My Wild Irish Rose*, Warner Brothers, 1947. PRINCIPAL FILM APPEARANCES—*The Bride Goes Wild*, Metro-Goldwyn-Mayer, 1948; *A Southern Yankee*, Metro-Goldwyn-Mayer, 1948; *The Black Book* (originally titled *Reign of Terror*), 1949; *Scene of the Crime*, Metro-Goldwyn-Mayer, 1949; *Ambush*, Metro-

Goldwyn-Mayer, 1949; *The Outriders*, Metro-Goldwyn-Mayer, 1950; *Three Little Words*, Metro-Goldwyn-Mayer, 1950; *Watch the Birdie*, Metro-Goldwyn-Mayer, 1950; *Inside Straight*, Metro-Goldwyn-Mayer, 1951; *No Questions Asked*, Metro-Goldwyn-Mayer, 1951.

Caribbean Gold, Paramount; *Desert Legion*, United Artists, 1953; *Here Come the Girls*, Paramount, 1953; *Sangaree* (first 3-D movie), Paramount, 1953; *Diamond Queen*, Warner Brothers, 1953; *Bengal Brigade*, United Artists, 1954; *Woman's World*, Twentieth Century-Fox, 1954; *Slightly Scarlet*, RKO, 1956; *Wicked As They Come*, Columbia (British), 1957; *She Played with Fire*, Columbia (British), 1958; *Journey to the Center of the Earth*, Twentieth Century-Fox, 1959; *Kisses for My President*, Warner Brothers, 1964; *Les Poneyettes*, Franco-London; *The Way to Katmandu*, Franco-London; *The Big Bankroll*, Saprogee-Filmarco; *The Land Raiders*, Columbia (British), 1970.

PRINCIPAL TELEVISION APPEARANCES—Hostess, *Pepsi Cola Theatre*, ABC; *Chrysler Theatre*, CBS; hostess, *Max Factor Opening Night Theatre*, NBC; hostess, *Model of the Year*, CBS; *Burke's Law*; *Perry Como Show*; *Tonight Show, Starring Johnny Carson*, NBC; *Arlene Dahl's Beauty Spot* (series of 65, five minute color spots), ABC, 1965; *Arlene Dahl's Beauty Happening*, 1970; *Merv Griffin Show*; *Mike Douglas Show*; *Today Show*, NBC; *Good Morning America*, ABC; *Love American Style*, ABC; *Jig Saw John*, NBC; *Arlene Dahl's Starscope*, Time-Life/HBO, 1979-80; *The Love Boat*, ABC; *Night of 100 Stars*, ABC; Lucinda King, *One Life to Live*, ABC, 1980-85; *Fantasy Island*, ABC; *Arlene Dahl's Lovescope*, Hearst/ABC Cable, 1982-83.

RELATED CAREER—President and chief executive officer, Dahlia Productions, 1975-present; president and chief executive officer, Dahlmark Productions, 1978-present.

AWARDS: Bronze Star on Hollywood's Walk of Fame; Bronze Halo, California Motion Picture Council, 1983; Deauville Film Festival tribute, *Coup de Chapeau*, 1983; French Cinematique tribute, Paris, 1983; Woman of the Year in advertising, 1969; Best Coiffed, 1970-72; Heads of Fame, 1973-1983; Mother of the Year, 1979; Today's Woman, 1981; One of the World's Most Elegant Women, 1982.

WRITINGS: BOOKS—*Always Ask a Man*, Prentice-Hall, 1965, Muller (England), 1966; twelve *Beautyscope* books, Simon & Schuster, 1969, revised, 1978; *Arlene Dahl's Secrets of Skin Care*, Arlene Dahl Enterprises, 1971; *Arlene Dahl's Secrets of Hair Care*, Bantam, 1978; *Beyond Beauty*, Simon & Schuster, 1980; *Arlene Dahl's Lovescopes*, Bobbs-Merrill, 1983.

SIDELIGHTS: MEMBERSHIPS—Academy of Motion Picture Arts and Sciences, Academy of Television Arts and Sciences, Le Comanderie du Bontemps de Medoc, Vesterheim & the Norwegian-American Museum, Sons of Norway, Boys Town, Pearl S. Buck Foundation (international director), Ambassador-at-Large for the City of Hope, International Platform Association, American Film Institute, Smithsonian Institute.

According to Dahl's publicity release: "At the age of eight she starred on a children's radio series in her hometown of Minneapolis and danced and sang with a group called the Hollywood Review . She left Minnesota to become a cover girl and photographer's model in New York.

"In addition to her performing career, Dahl designed fashions and in

1980, created the Floating Spa' aboard the Queen Elizabeth II luxury liner. She designed a sleepwear line, including the patented ''Dahl'' boudoir cap and started the ''baby doll'' pajama rage of the 1950's. She has designed a complete fashion line for Vogue Patterns called In Vogue with Arlene Dahl.''

Dahl's business titles include: president and chief executive officer, Dahlia Parfums, 1975-present; vice president, Kenyon & Eckhart advertising agency, 1967-72; president, Woman's World, 1967-72; and director of beauty and health, Sears Roebuck and Company, 1970-75.

ADDRESS: OFFICE—P.O. Box 911, Beverly Hills, CA 90210; P.O. Box 5161, FDR Station, New York, NY 10150. AGENT— Milton Goldman, International Creative Management, 40 W. 57th Street, New York, NY 10019.

*   *   *

DANA, F. Mitchell   1942-

PERSONAL: Born Frank Livingstone Mitchell II, November 14, 1942, in Washington, DC; son of John Daskum (in labor relations) and Elizabeth Francis (a bookkeeper; maiden name, Woods) Mitchell; married Wendy Karen Bensinger (a casting director), December 31, 1967; children: Scott Cameron, Ian Michael. EDUCATION: Utah State University, B.A., 1964; Yale School of Drama, M.F.A., 1967. POLITICS: Republican.

VOCATION: Lighting designer.

F. MITCHELL DANA

CAREER: FIRST NEW YORK STAGE WORK—*Dynamite Tonight*, Martinique, 1967. LONDON DEBUT—*Turandot*, Royal Opera, Covent Garden, 1984 (in repertory). PRINCIPAL STAGE WORK— Broadway (designer unless otherwise indicated): associate designer, *1776*, Shubert, 1969; *Charley's Aunt*, 1970; associate designer, *A Doll's House* and *Hedda Gabler* (repertory), Playhouse, 1972; *Freedom of the City*, 1974; *Man and Superman, The Inspector General, Once in a Lifetime*, all Circle in the Square, 1978; *The Suicide*, ANTA, 1981; *Mass Appeal*, Golden, 1982; *Monday After the Miracle*, 1983; *The Babe*, 1984.

Off Broadway: *The Nuns; Possibilities; Calling in Crazy; One Tiger to a Hill; The Vikings; Songs My Mother Never Sang; Three Acts of Recognition; Monday After the Miracle; A Coupla White Chicks Sittin' Around Talkin'; Mass Appeal; Oh, Coward; Joseph and the Amazing Technicolor Dreamcoat; Hell of a Town; The Philanthropist; Husbandry*, in addition to twelve productions for the BAM Theatre Company, Brooklyn Academy of Music.

Regional: *The Guardsman, The Devil's Disciple*, both at the Ahmanson, Los Angeles, CA; *Guys and Dolls*, Manitoba Theatre Center, Canada; *Richard III, The Torchbearers, Pinocchio, Walsh, Spelling Rhythm*, all at National Arts Center, Ottawa, Canada; *Down at the Old Bull and Bush*, PAF Playhouse, Queens, NY; *Uncle Vanya*, Spreckles; *The School for Scandal, The Importance of Being Earnest, Godspell*, all at Cincinnati Playhouse; *Haven't a Clue, A Perfect Gentleman, Clouds*, all at the Virginia Museum Theatre, Richmond, VA; *Double-Bass*, Syracuse Stage; *Hell of a Town, Billy Bishop Goes to War, Planet Fires*, all at GeVa; *Dear Daddy* and *The Father*, Philadelphia Drama Guild; as well as four productions for Seattle Rep, ten productions for the Mark Taper Forum, eleven productions for the Goodman Theatre including *Richard III*, and *Lakeboat*, seventeen productions for the McCarter Theatre, and fifty-two productions for the American Conservatory Theatre.

MAJOR TOURS—*The Matchmaker* and *Desire Under the Elms*, American Conservatory Theatre/State Department tour of the USSR (Moscow, Lenningrad, Riga), 1976; also *Hello, Dolly!, The Last of Mrs. Cheyney, A Doll's House, The Rothschilds, The Basic Training of Pavlo Hummel*; others.

PRINCIPAL OPERA WORK—*La Traviata*, Juilliard American Opera Center; *The Taming of the Shrew*, Wolftrap; *La Rondine*, New York City Opera; *Harriet: The Woman Called Moses*, Virginia Opera Association; *Orphee*, Stratford, Ontario; *Patria II*, Stratford, Ontario; *Tamu, Tamu*, Chicago Opera; *Turandot*, Olympic Arts Festival, Dorothy Chandler Pavilion, Los Angeles, CA.

PRINCIPAL TELEVISION WORK—Associate lighting designer: *3-2-1 Contact, Sneak Previews, Pinwheel, Slim Goodbody, Take Five, Let's Find Out, ABC in Concert, The Babe, Bravo News Network— Intros and Wrap Ups*.

CONCERT AND CLUB WORK—Lighting designer: *A Soldier's Tale*, Los Angeles Philharmonic, Dorothy Chandler Pavilion, CA; *The Heyday of Rodgers and Hart*, Philharmonic Hall, NY; *The Life of Christ*, Philharmonic Hall, NY; *Anthony Newley at the Waldorf; Black Theatre Festival*, Lincoln Center, NY; others.

RELATED CAREER—Technical director, Columbia School of the Arts, NY, 1967-68; assistant to Jo Mielziner, NY, 1968-69; technical director, Yale Drama School, New Haven, CT, 1970-71; production manager, Pittsburgh Civic Light Opera, PA, 1973-74; associate lighting director, Fred Manning, NY, 1978-present; lecturer: University of Washington, Southern Methodist University, San Francisco State, Rutgers; production properties manager, *Sticks and Bones*, New York Shakespeare Festival (Broadway), 1971; has also worked as a stagehand and stage manager.

AWARDS: Joseph Jefferson Award nominations, Best Lighting, 1978-79, for *Richard III*, 1982, for *Lakeboat;* Dramalogue, 1981, for *The Suicide*.

SIDELIGHTS: MEMBERSHIPS—International Alliance of Theatrical Stage Employees; United Scenic Artists (trustee, 1970-72).

ADDRESS: OFFICE—221 W. 82nd Street, New York, NY 10024.

*   *   *

DANCE, Charles   1946-

PERSONAL: Born October 10, 1946, in Worcestershire, England; son of Walter (a civil engineer) and Eleanor Marion (Perks) Dance; married Joanna Haythorn; children: Oliver, Rebecca. EDUCATION: Widey Technical Schoool, Plymouth, 1958-64; Plymouth College of Art; Leicester College of Art, diploma in graphic design; studied for the theatre privately with Leonard Bennett and Martin St. John Burchardt.

VOCATION: Actor.

CHARLES DANCE

CAREER: STAGE DEBUT—Sven, *It's a Two Foot Six Inches Above the Ground World*, post West End tour of England, 1970. NEW YORK DEBUT—Title role, *Henry V*, Royal Shakespeare Company, at Brooklyn Academy of Music, Brooklyn, NY, 1970's. LONDON DEBUT—Reynaldo and Fortinbras, *Hamlet*, Royal Shakespeare Company, 1975. PRINCIPAL STAGE APPEARANCES—Badger, *Toad of Toad Hall*, Swindon, England; Beaudricourt, *St. Joan*, Oxford; Henry Carr, *Travesties*, Leeds, England; Soliony, *The Three Sisters*, Hotel Manager, *Born Yesterday*, Greenwich, England; understudy Macheath, *The Beggars' Opera*, Chichester Festival, England.

Lancaster, *Henry IV, Parts I and II*, Catesby, *Richard III*, Spanish Envoy, *Perkin Warbeck*, Williams and Scroop, *Henry V*, Oliver, *As You Like It*, Tomazo, *The Changeling*, Truman, *The Jail Diary of Albie Sachs*, all with the Royal Shakespeare Company, England, 1975-79; title role, *Coriolanus*, Odeon Nationale, Paris; Nestor, *Irma La Douce*, West End, London, 1980; Morris Townsend, *The Heiress*, Nottingham Playhouse, England; Frank, *Turning Over*, Bush, England.

FILM APPEARANCES—Klaus, *For Your Eyes Only*, United Artists, 1981; Raymond Brock, *Plenty*, 1985.

PRINCIPAL TELEVISION APPEARANCES—Duke of Clarence, *Edward VII;* Edward Hartford Jones, *Nancy Astor;* Siegfried Sassoon, *The Fatal Spring;* Alan, *Saigon - The Last Day;* Reynaud Callaghan, *Frost in May;* O'Brien, *Father Brown;* Teddy, *Raffles;* Parker, *The Professionals;* Borgheim, *Little Eyolf;* Captain Truman, *Rainy Day Women;* James Lattimer, *This Lightning Strikes Twice;* Charleson, *Thunder Rock;* Guy Perron, *The Jewel in the Crown;* all produced for British television, some seen in the U.S.

AWARDS: Scottish Academy of Television Arts, Best Actor, 1984; British Academy of Film and Television Arts, Best Actor nomination, 1984.

SIDELIGHTS: MEMBERSHIPS—British Actors' Equity.

Dance was an active member of the Royal Shakespeare Company from 1975 until 1979.

ADDRESS: AGENT—Robby Lantz, The Lantz Office, 888 Seventh Avenue, New York, NY 10106 and 9255 Sunset Blvd., Suite 505, Los Angeles, CA 90069.

*   *   *

D'ANGELO, Beverly

PERSONAL: Born in Columbus, OH; father, bass player, mother, violinist.

VOCATION: Actress.

CAREER: NEW YORK DEBUT—Ophelia, *Rockabye Hamlet*. PRINCIPAL STAGE APPEARANCES—Marilyn, *Hey Marilyn*, Charlottestown Festival Repertory Company; *The Zinger*, off Broadway.

PRINCIPAL FILM APPEARANCES—*The Sentinel; Annie Hall; First Love; Hair; Every Which Way But Loose; Coal Miner's Daughter; Honky Tonk Freeway; Paternity; National Lampoon's Vacation; National Lampoon's European Vacation*.

PRINCIPAL TELEVISION APPEARANCE—Stella Kowalski, *A Streetcar Named Desire*, ABC, 1984.

RELATED CAREER—Animator, Hanna-Barbera; singer, Canadian coffee house circuit.*

* * *

DANZA, Tony

BRIEF ENTRY: Born in Brooklyn, NY; attended high school on Long Island and went on to graduate from the University of Dubuque, IA. Actor. Danza entered the New York Golden Gloves and made semi-finals as a lightweight. He returned the next year as a middle-weight and a narrow decision cost him the title. He then turned professional and compiled a 10-3 record in the ring. Danza made his television debut on the series *Taxi*, ABC, then NBC, 1978-83, and currently is the star of *Who's the Boss*, ABC, 1984-present. He also appeared in the television movies *Murder Can Hurt You*, 1981, and *Singles Bars, Single Women*, ABC, 1984. His film credits include *Hollywood Knights*, Columbia, 1980, and *Going Ape*, Paramount, 1981.*

* * *

DAVID, Joanna   1947-

PERSONAL: Born Joanna Hacking, January 17, 1947, in Lancaster, England; daughter of John and Davida Elizabeth (Nesbitt) Hacking; married Edward Fox; children: Emilia. EDUCATION: Elmhurst

JOANNA DAVID

Ballet School, Camberley Surrey; studied acting at the Weber Douglas Academy of Dramatic Art. RELIGION: Church of England.

VOCATION: Actress.

CAREER: DEBUT—*The Importance of Being Earnest*, Scandinavian Theatre Company. PRINCIPAL STAGE APPEARANCES—*Dear Antoine*, Chichester Festival; *Uncle Vanya*, Royal Exchange, Manchester; *Family Reunion*, Royal Exchange, transferred to West End; Miss Giddens, *The Innocents*, Royal Theatre, Northampton; Varya, *The Cherry Orchard*, Haymarket, London; Catherine Sloper, *The Heiress*, London, 1984.

PRINCIPAL TELEVISION APPEARANCES—*When Johnny Comes Marching Home*; Sonia, *War and Peace*; Elinor, *Sense and Sensibility*; Alice Monroe, *The Last of the Mohicans; Colditz*; Princess Alexandra, *Jennie; Ballet Shoes; The Duchess of Duke Street; Within These Walls; Just William; The Dancing Princesses*; Jeanne Marie, *Lillie*; the second Mrs. De Winter, *Rebecca*, BBC; Mary Eleanor Pearcey, *Lady Killers*; Mabel Purdy, *Dear Brutus*; Dora Carrington, *Lytton Strachey; Charlotte and Jane*; Ann, *Fame Is the Spur*, BBC; Christina, *Alexa; The Red Signal; Lady's Maid's Bell*, Granada TV; *Rumpole of the Bailey*, Thames TV; *Brass*, Granada TV; Dolly, *Anna Karenina*, 1984; *Thunder Is the Night*, BBC, 1984; *Murder at Lynch Cross*, Granada TV, 1985.

ADDRESS: AGENT—Peter Browne Management, 13 St. Martins Road, London SW9, England.

* * *

DAVIDSON, Richard M.   1940-

PERSONAL: Born May 10, 1940, in Hamilton, ON, Canada; son of Lou (a clothing merchant) and Lillian (Stoller) Davidson; children: Leslianne, Mary Ellen. EDUCATION: University of Toronto, B.A., 1962; London School of Music and Dramatic Arts.

VOCATION: Actor.

CAREER: STAGE DEBUT—*Coriolanus*, Stratford Shakespeare Festival, Stratford, ON, Canada, 1961. NEW YORK DEBUT—One of an ensemble of seven, *The Beasts*, Direct Theatre, 1978. UNITED KINGDOM DEBUT—Seventeen principal roles, BYRE Theatre, 1964-65. PRINCIPAL STAGE APPEARANCES—Quitt, *They Are Dying Out*, Yale Repertory, 1979; Brother Bill, *The Entertainer*; Guthrie, Minneapolis, MN, 1980; Oscar, *The Survivor*, Morosco, NY, 1981; 1984 Short Play Festival, Actor's Theatre of Louisville, KY.

MAJOR TOURS—Centennial tour, Stratford Shakespeare Festival, Stratford, ON, Canada, 1967.

PRINCIPAL FILM APPEARANCES—Hirsh, *Breaking Point*, Universal, 1977.

SIDELIGHTS: MEMBERSHIPS—British Actors' Equity Association, American Actors' Equity Association, Canadian Actors' Equity Association, Screen Actors Guild, American Federation of Television and Radio Artists, Association of Canadian Television and Radio Artists.

ADDRESS: HOME—330 E. 84th Street, New York, NY 10028. AGENTS—Abrams Artists Inc., 420 Madision Avenue, New York, NY 10017; Noble Talent, 250 W. 57th Street, New York, NY 10019.

*   *   *

DAVIS, Michael   1936-

PERSONAL: Born July 30, 1936, in Little Rock, AR; son of Roy Carlton (an accountant) and Enola Adeline (Neel) Davis. EDUCATION: Attended University of Arkansas; studied acting with David LeGrant, Robert Ravan and Mary Tarsai in NY; studied opera with Carmine Gagliardi and Sarah Lee in NY.

VOCATION: Actor and singer.

CAREER: STAGE DEBUT—Eldest son, *Curious Savage*, Central High, Little Rock, AR, 1954. NEW YORK DEBUT—Ciccio, *Most Happy Fellow*, City Center, 1959. PRINCIPAL STAGE APPEARANCES—Sir Lucius O'Trigger, *All in Love*, Martinque, NY, 1961; understudy Vidal, *Sweet Charity*, Palace, NY, 1966; Dark Glasses, Mike, *The Apple Tree*, Shubert, NY, 1967; prospector, door man, *Dear World*, Mark Hellinger, NY, 1967-68; Bruce, *How Do I Love You*, pre-Broadway, 1969; Tucker, *Look to the Lillies*, Lunt-Fontanne, NY, 1970; Sebastian Baye, *Coco*, Mark Hellinger, NY, 1970; Robert, *Company*, Forum, Chicago, 1973; lead singer, *All Night Strut*, Ford's, Washington, DC, 1975; Kurt Weill, *Berlin to Broadway*, Theatre by the Sea, Portsmouth, NH, also the West-

chester Regional Theatre, 1979; man, *Side by Side by Sondheim*, Syracuse Stage, NY, 1980; Frederick, *A Little Night Music*, Theatre by the Sea, 1980; standby Gerald and others, *Woman of the Year*, Palace, NY, 1981-82; Herod, *Jesus Christ Superstar*, Kansas City Starlight; Henry Higgins, *My Fair Lady*, Wichita Summer, 1985; Ronald Dupre, *The Future of the American Musical*, Musical Theatre Works, 1985.

MAJOR TOURS—*Bells Are Ringing*, National Company, 1959; Marco the Magnificent, *Carnival*, National Company, 1961; Edward Rutledge, *1776*, National Company, 1970-72.

FILM DEBUT—Production singer, *The Producers*, Embassy, 1968. PRINCIPAL FILM APPEARANCES—*Sweet Charity*, Universal, 1969.

TELEVISION DEBUT—*Bell Telephone Hour*, 1960. PRINCIPAL TELEVISION APPEARANCES—*As the World Turns; Days of Our Lives; Ed Sullivan Show; Art Carney Special*.

RELATED CAREER—Literary agent, Sanders Agency, New York.

AWARDS: Joseph Jefferson Award nomination, 1973, for Robert, *Company*.

SIDELIGHTS: MEMBERSHIPS—Actors' Equity Association, Screen Actors Guild, American Federation of Radio and Television Artists.

Davis told *CTFT*, "I believe the salvation of the American theatre lies in the cultivation and nouishment of the American playwright."

ADDRESS: AGENT—Honey Sanders Agency, 229 W. 42nd Street, New York, NY 10036.

*   *   *

DAVIS, Ossie   1917-

PERSONAL: Born December 18, 1917, in Cogdell, GA; son of Kince Charles and Laura (Cooper) Davis; married Ruby Dee (an actress), December 9, 1948; children: Nora, Guy, LaVerne. EDUCATION: Attended Howard University, Washington, DC, 1935-38; trained for the stage with Paul Mann and Lloyd Richards. MILITARY: U.S. Army, 1942.

VOCATION: Actor, playwright, and director.

CAREER: STAGE DEBUT—*Joy Exceeding Glory*, Rose McClendon Players, Harlem, NY, 1941. BROADWAY DEBUT—Jeb Turner, *Jeb*, Martin Beck, 1946. PRINCIPAL STAGE APPEARANCES—Rudolph, *Anna Lucasta*, American Negro Theatre Playhouse, NY, 1948; John Hay, *The Washington Years*, National, 1948; Trem, *The Leading Lady*, Lyceum, NY, 1949; Stewart, *The Smile of the World*, Martin Beck, NY, 1950; Jacques, *The Wisteria Trees*, City Center, NY, 1951; Jo, *The Royal Family*, Broadway, NY, 1951; Gabriel, *The Green Pastures*, Morosco, NY, 1951; Al, *Remains to Be Seen*, Music Box, NY, 1953; Dr. Joseph Clay, *Touchstone*, Barbizon-Plaza, NY, 1953; Jacques, *The Wisteria Trees*, Alvin, NY, 1956; Lieutenant, *No Time for Sergeants*, Imperial, NY, 1957; Cicero, *Jamaica*, Ethel Barrymore, NY, 1959; Walter Lee Younger, *A Raisin in the Sun*, Cort, NY, 1961; Purlie, *Purlie Victorious*, Henry Hudson, NY, 1963; Sir Radio, *Ballad for Bimshire*, Mayfair, NY, 1963; Johannes, *The Zulu and the Zayda*, Cort, NY, 1965; *Take It from the Top*, 1979; *Zora Is My Name!*, Howard University, Washington, DC.

MAJOR TOURS—*A Treasury of Negro World Writing*, 1964.

MICHAEL DAVIS

OSSIE DAVIS

PRINCIPAL STAGE WORK—Stage manager, *The World of Sholom Aleichem*, City Center, NY, 1955; director, *Take It from the Top*, 1979.

FILM DEBUT—*No Way Out*, 1950. PRINCIPAL FILM APPEAR-ANCES—*Fourteen Hours*, 1951; *The Joe Louis Story*, 1953; *The Cardinal*, Columbia, 1963; *The Hill*, Metro-Goldwyn-Mayer, 1965; *The Scalphunters*, United Artists, 1968; *Gone Are the Days (Purlie Victorious)*; *Hot Stuff*, 1979; *Harry & Son*, 1984.

PRINCIPAL FILM WORK—Director: *Cotton Comes to Harlem*, United Artists, 1970; *Kongi's Harvest*; *Black Girl*, Cinerama, 1973; *Gordon's War*, Twentieth Century-Fox, 1973; *Countdown at Kusini*, Columbia, 1976.

PRINCIPAL TELEVISION APPEARANCES—*The Emperor Jones*; *Seven Times Monday*; *The Defenders*; *Bonanza*, NBC; *The Sheriff*; *Name of the Game*; *Hawaii Five-O*, CBS; *A Piece of the Cake*; *King*; *Roots: The Next Generations*, ABC; *All God's Children*, 1980; *Teacher, Teacher*; *With Ossie and Ruby*, PBS; *A Walk through the Twentieth Century*, PBS.

PRINCIPAL RADIO APPEARANCES—*The Ossie Davis and Ruby Dee Story Hour*.

WRITINGS: PLAYS—*Purlie Victorious*, 1961; *Curtain Call*; *Mr. Aldridge, Sir*; *Escape to Freedom*; *Langston*; *Alice in Wonder*; *Last Dance for Sybil*; book for *Purlie* (musical adaption of *Purlie Victorious*).

TELEPLAYS—"School Teacher," *East Side/West Side*; "For Us the Living," *American Playhouse*, PBS, 1983; *Today Is Ours*, CBS.

AWARDS: Emmy Award nomination for *King*; Emmy Award for *Teacher, Teacher*; Jury Award by the Neil Simon Award for *For Us the Living*, 1983; Frederick Douglas Award of the New York Urban League.

SIDELIGHTS: Davis was master of ceremonies for the march on Washington, 1963 and for the Solidarity Poor People's Campaign, 1968.

ADDRESS: OFFICE—P.O. Box 1318, New Rochelle, NY 10802.

*   *   *

DAVIS, R.G.   1933-

PERSONAL: Born July 9, 1933; son of Herman B. (a manufacturer) and Shirely (Gerst) Davis; married Robin Acker (a therapist). EDUCATION: University of New Mexico, B.A., 1955; trained for the theater as a Fulbright Fellow in Paris with E. Decroux. POLITICS: Independent Marxist, pre-Marxist Leninist, Socialist.

VOCATION: Critic, director, and writer.

WRITINGS: PLAYS, PUBLISHED—*We Won't Pay! We Won't Pay!*, Samuel French, 1984. BOOKS—*The San Francisco Mime Troup: The First Ten Years*, Ramparts Press, 1975.

SIDELIGHTS: MEMBERSHIPS—Society of Stage Directors and Choreographers, International Brecht Society.

ADDRESS: HOME—611 Rhode Island, San Francisco, CA 94107.

*   *   *

DEACON, Richard   1923-84

PERSONAL: Born 1923, in Philadelphia, PA; died of a heart attack, August 8, 1984; son of Joseph Deacon. EDUCATION: Studied medicine at Ithaca College, NY.

VOCATION: Actor.

CAREER: PRINCIPAL FILM APPEARANCES—(over 100) *Desiree*; *Abbott & Costello Meet the Mummy*; *My Sister Eileen*; *Good Morning, Miss Dove*; *Hot Blood*; *The Proud Ones*; *The Solid Gold Cadillac*; *The Blackboard Jungle*; *Invasion of the Body Snatchers*; *Decision at Sundown*; *A Nice Little Bank That Should Be Robbed*; *The Remarkable Mr. Pennypacker*; *The Young Philadelphians*; *Everything's Ducky*; *Lover Come Back*; *That Touch of Mink*; *The Birds*; *Critics Choice*; *The Patsy*; *Dear Heart*; *John Goldfarb, Please Come Home*; *Billie*; *That Darn Cat*; *Don't Worry, We'll Think of a Title*; *The Gnome Mobile*; *Enter Laughing*; *Blackbeard's Ghost*; *The One and Only Genuine Original Family Band*; *Lady in Cement*; *The Happy Hooker Goes to Hollywood*.

TELEVISION DEBUT—*The Life of Riley*, 1953. PRINCIPAL TELE-VISION APPEARANCES—Fred Rutherford, *Leave It to Beaver*,

1957-1963; Mel Cooley, *The Dick Van Dyke Show*, 1961-66; *The Beverly Hillbillies; Mister Ed; The Ed Wynn Show; The Donna Reed Show; The Mothers-in-Law*, 1967-68. Also: *The Betty White Show; I Love Lucy; Here's Lucy; The Twilight Zone; The Jack Benny Show; The Love Boat; Trapper John, M.D.; Alice;* was scheduled to appear on *Still the Beaver*.

PRINCIPAL STAGE APPEARANCES—*Hello Dolly!*, Broadway production, 1970.

WRITINGS: BOOKS PUBLISHED—*Richard Deacon's Micro Magic*, cookbook sold over 1,700,000 copies.

SIDELIGHTS: MEMBERSHIPS—Screen Actors Guild, Actors' Equity Association, American Federation of Television and Radio Artists.*

*   *   *

DEDOMENICO, Richard   1936-

PERSONAL: Born March 19, 1936, in Brooklyn, NY; son of John (a tailor) and Elvira (Cardarelli) DeDomenico. EDUCATION: Fordham University, A.B.; trained for the stage at the American Academy of Dramatic Arts. RELIGION: Roman Catholic.

VOCATION: Actor.

CAREER: STAGE DEBUT—Sancho Panza, *Man of La Mancha*, Vineyard Players, Martha's Vineyard, MA, 1975, 15 performances.

RICHARD DEDOMENICO

PRINCIPAL STAGE APPEARANCES—Jack Pinch, *On Again, Off Again*, Cricket, NY, 1976; Reverend Parris, *The Crucible*, Gene Frankel, NY, 1977; Blore, *Ten Little Indians*, Academy Arts Theater Company, NY, 1978; Dr. Rance, *What the Butler Saw*, Academy Arts, NY, 1978; Francois, *Cafe*, A Little Theater, 1979, Dave, *Mulberry Street*, Loretto Theater, NY, 1979; the Wigmaker, *Rashomon*, Shelter West, NY, 1981; Mr. Tyrrell, *A Visit*, Theater for the New City, NY, 1982.

FILM DEBUT—The brother-in-law, *Stardust Memories*. PRINCIPAL FILM APPEARANCES—Chameleon Dancer, *Zelig*.

SIDELIGHTS: RECREATION—Skiing.

DeDomenico is a singer with New York Chorale Society and the West Village Chorale.

ADDRESS: HOME—New York, NY.

*   *   *

DE HARTOG, Jan   1914-

PERSONAL: Born April 22, 1914, in Haarlem, Holland; son of Arnold Hendrik (a university professor) and Lucretia (a univerity professor; maiden name, Meijjes) de Hartog; married Marjorie E. Mein (a photographer), September 29, 1961; children: Arnold H., Sylvia, Nicholas J., Catherine, Eva, Julia. EDUCATION: Attended Amsterdam Naval College, Holland. RELIGION: Quaker. MILITARY: Merchant Marine, World War Two.

VOCATION: Writer.

WRITINGS: PLAYS—*Skipper Next to God*, 1946; *This Time Tomorrow*, 1947; *The Fourposter*, 1951; *William and Mary*, 1964; *I Do, I Do*, 1966. BOOKS—*The Lost Sea*, 1951; *The Distant Shore*, 1952; *The Little Ark*, 1954; *A Sailor's Life*, 1956; *The Spiral Road*, 1957; *The Inspector*, 1960; *Waters of the New World*, 1961; *The Artist*, 1963; *The Hospital*, 1964; *The Call of the Sea*, 1966; *The Captain*, 1966; *The Children*, 1968; *The Peaceable Kingdom*, 1971; *The Lamb's War*, 1979.

SIDELIGHTS: MEMBERSHIPS—Dramatists Guild, Screenwriters Guild.

ADDRESS: AGENT—Robert Lantz, The Lantz Office, 888 Seventh Avenue, New York, NY 10106.

*   *   *

DE LA GIRODAY, Francois   1952-

PERSONAL: Born March 18, 1952, in Oxford, England. EDUCATION: Studied voice with Joy Kane, fencing with Chris Martin, mime with Lewis Gilbert, speech with Majorie Phillips, acting with Bertram Joseph, and movement with Fred Kurchak.

VOCATION: Actor.

CAREER: PRINCIPAL STAGE APPEARANCES—Denis, *Loot*, Caliban, *The Tempest*, Haeman, *Antigone*, the Medium, *Roshomon*,

Queequeq, *Moby Dick,* Lenin, *The Dwarfs,* Andre, *Woyzeck,* all at CSC Repertory Company, NY, 1973-76; Jack Manningham, *Gas Light,* Theatre West Virginia, 1976-77; Michael, *Rats,* Impossible Ragtime, NY, 1977; Renfield, *Dracula,* Soho Repertory, NY, 1977; Wally, *Out to Lunch,* Ensemble Studio, NY, 1978; Ariel, *The Tempest,* Guthrie, Minneapolis, MN, 1981; Lelie, *Sganarelle,* American Repertory, Cambridge, MA, 1981; Rubin/Captain Narvinsky, *Journey of the Fifth Horse,* American Repertory, Cambridge, MA, 1981; Feste, *Twelfth Night,* Alliance, Atlanta, GA, 1982; Austin, *True West,* American Repertory, Cambridge, MA, 1982; Felix, *Paradise Lost,* Mirror Theatre Company, NY, 1983; understudy John Macy, *Monday After the Miracle,* Eugene O'Neill, NY, 1983; Valere, *Tartuffe,* Guthrie, Minneapolis, MN, 1984; the Son, *Six Characters in Search of an Author,* American Repertory, Cambridge, MA, 1984.

MAJOR TOURS—Austin, *True West,* American Repertory summer tour of Europe, 1982.

PRINCIPAL FILM APPEARANCES—*Raging Bull,* United Artists, 1981; *Mr. Mike's Mondo Video.*

PRINCIPAL TELEVISION APPEARANCES—Dr. Wallace, *As the World Turns,* CBS; *The Guiding Light,* CBS; *Love of Life; Search for Tomorrow,* CBS.

ADDRESS: HOME—41-15 51st Street, Woodside, NY 11377. AGENT—c/o J. Michael Bloom Ltd., 400 Madison Avenue, New York, NY 10019.

*   *   *

DELUISE, Dom   1933-

PERSONAL: Born August 1, 1933, in Brooklyn, NY; son of John (a civil servant) and Vicenza (DeStefano) DeLuise; married Carol Arata (professional name, Carol Arthur, the actress), November 23, 1965; children: Peter John, Michael Robert, David Dominick. EDUCATION: Attended Tufts College.

VOCATION: Actor.

CAREER: FILM DEBUT—*Fail Safe,* Columbia, 1964. PRINCIPAL FILM APPEARANCES—*The Glass Bottom Boat,* Metro-Goldwyn-Mayer, 1966; *The Busybody,* Paramount, 1967; *What's So Bad About Feeling Good?,* Universal, 1968; *Norwood,* Paramount, 1970; *The Twelve Chairs,* UMC Pictures, 1970; *Who Is Harry Kellerman and Why Is He Saying Those Terrible Things About Me?,* National General, 1971; *Every Little Crook and Nanny,* Metro-Goldwyn-Mayer, 1972; *Blazing Saddles,* Warner Brothers, 1974; *The Adventures of Sherlock Holmes' Smarter Brother,* Twentieth Century-Fox, 1975; *Silent Movie,* Twentieth Century-Fox, 1976; *The World's Greatest Lover,* Twentieth Century-Fox, 1977; *Sextette,* 1978; *The Cheap Detective,* Columbia, 1978; *The End,* United Artists, 1978; *The Muppet Movie,* Associated Film Distributors, 1979; *Hot Stuff,* 1979; *Fatso,* Twentieth Century-Fox, 1980; *Smokey and the Bandit II,* Universal, 1980; *The Last Married Couple in America,* Universal, 1980; *History of the World - Part I,* Twentieth Century-Fox, 1981; *The Cannonball Run,* Twentieth Century-Fox, 1981; *The Best Little Whorehouse in Texas,* Universal, 1982; voice, *The Secret of Nimh,* Metro-Goldwyn-Mayer/United Artists, 1982;

DOM DELUISE

Benito (upcoming); *Haunted Honeymoon,* Orion (upcoming).

PRINCIPAL FILM WORK— Director, *Hot Stuff,* 1979.

TELEVISION DEBUT—Dominick the Great, *The Garry Moore Show.* PRINCIPAL TELEVISION APPEARANCES—*The Entertainers; The Dean Martin Show; The Tonight Show.* Specials: *The Barrum Bump Show,* 1964; *The Dom DeLuise Variety Show,* CBS. Series: *Lotsa Luck,* NBC, 1973. Movies: *Happy,* 1983.

PRINCIPAL TELEVISION WORK—Producer, *Happy,* 1983.

STAGE DEBUT—Peter, *Peter Rabbit,* grammar school. NEW YORK DEBUT—*Little Mary Sunshine.* PRINCIPAL STAGE APPEARANCES—*School for Scandal, Hamlet, Stalag 17,* and others, Cleveland Playhouse, OH; *All in Love; Half Past Wednesday; Another Evening with Harry Stones; Mixed Company,* Provincetown, MA; *Last of the Red Hot Lovers,* NY, 1968; *The Student Gypsy;* NY; *Here's Love,* NY.

MAJOR TOURS—*Luv,* U.S. cities.

PRINCIPAL STAGE WORK—Director: *Same Time, Next Year,* and *Butterflies Are Free,* Burt Reynolds Dinner Theater, Jupiter, FL.

NIGHTCLUB ACT—*An Evening with Dom DeLuise,* Las Vegas, Atlantic City, etc.

SIDELIGHTS: RECREATION—Furniture refinishing, herb gardening.

ADDRESS: OFFICE—EBM, 132 S. Rodeo Drive, Beverly Hills, CA 90212.

DEMAREST, William   1892-1983

PERSONAL: Born February 27, 1892, in St. Paul, MN; died December 28, 1983; married Lucille Thayer.

VOCATION: Actor.

CAREER: PRINCIPAL STAGE APPEARANCES—*Monkey Business,* 1925; *Sketch Book,* 1929; *Vanities,* 1931.

PRINCIPAL FILM APPEARANCES—*The Jazz Singer,* 1927; *Broadway Melody;* 1929; *Fog Over Frisco; Mr. Smith Goes to Washington; Wedding Present; Fugitive Lady; Diamond Jim; Murder Man; Hands Across the Table; Love on the Run; Charlie Chan at the Opera; Wake Up and Live; Hit Parade; Easy Living; The Great Gambini; Blonde Trouble; Big City; Rebecca of Sunnybrook Farm; One Wild Night; Rosalie; King of the Turf; The Gracie Allen Murder Case; The Great Man Votes,* all 1930's; *The Devil and Miss Jones; The Lady Eve; The Great McGinty; Sullivan's Travels; Hail the Conquering Hero; The Palm Beach Story; The Miracle of Morgan's Creek; My Favorite Spy; Along Came Jones; The Jolson Story; Pardon My Sarong; All Through the Night; Behind the Eight Ball; Salty O'Rourke; Duffy's Tavern; Variety Girl; Whispering Smith; Jolson Sings Again; Sorrowful Jones,* all 1940's; *What Price Glory?; When Willie Comes Marching Home; Riding High; Escape from Fort Bravo; The Private War of Major Benson; Sincerely Yours; Hello on Frisco Bay; The Mountain,* all 1950's; *It's a Mad Mad Mad Mad World,* 1963; *Pepe; King of the Roaring Twenties; Son of Flubber; Viva Las Vegas; That Darn Cat; The McCullocks; Won Ton Ton, the Dog Who Saved Hollywood.*

PRINCIPAL TELEVISION APPEARANCES—*The Millionaire; Love and Marriage,* 1954-60; *Tales of Wells Fargo,* 1961-62; Uncle Charley, *My Three Sons,* 1965-72.

AWARDS: Academy Award nomination, best supporting actor, 1946, for *The Jolson Story;* Emmy Award, best supporting actor, *My Three Sons.*

SIDELIGHTS: MEMBERSHIPS—Actors' Equity Association, Screen Actors Guild, American Federation of Television Arts and Sciences.

Demarest was involved in the William Demarest Foundation and William Demarest Golf Tournament, both charitable organizations.*

*   *   *

DE MORNAY, Rebecca

BRIEF ENTRY: Born in Santa Rosa, CA; has lived for various lengths of time in East Germany, France, Rumania, Mexico, Hungary, Greece, Jamaica, Czechoslovakia and England; graduated from high school in Kitzbuhel, Austria; studied acting with the Lee Strasberg Theater Institute. Actress. De Mornay made her film debut in *One from the Heart,* Columbia, 1982. Her first starring role was in *Risky Business,* Warner Brothers, 1983. She has also appeared in *Testament,* Paramount, 1983, and *The Sluggers Wife,* 1985.*

*   *   *

DENEUVE, Catherine   1943-

PERSONAL: Born Catherine Dorleac, October 22, 1943, in Paris, France; daughter of Maurice and Renee Dorleac; married David

Bailey, 1965 (divorced, 1970); children: Christian Vadim, Chiara Mastroianni. EDUCATION: Attended Lycee La Fontaine, Paris.

VOCATION: Actress.

CAREER: PRINCIPAL FILM APPEARANCES—*Les Petits Chats,* 1956; *Les Collegiennes,* 1956; *Les Portes Claquent,* 1960; *Les Parisiennes,* 1961; *Et Satan Conduit le Bal,* 1962; *Vacances Portugaises,* 1963; *Le Vice et la Vertu,* 1963; *Les Parapluies de Cherbourg,* 1964; *La Chasse a l'Homme,* 1964; *Les Plus Belles Escroqueries du Monde,* 1964; *Un Monsieur de Compagnie,* 1964; *Repulsion,* 1965; *Coeur a la Gorge,* 1965; *Le Chant de Ronde,* 1965; *La Vie de Chateau,* 1965; *Les Creatures,* 1966; *Les Demoiselles de Rochefort,* 1966; *Benjamin,* 1967; *Manon 70,* 1967; *Belle de Jour,* 1967; *Meyerling,* 1967; *La Chamade,* 1968; *The April Fools,* 1968; *La Sirene du Mississippi,* 1968; *Tristana,* 1969; *It Only Happens to Others,* 1971; *Dirty Money; Hustle,* 1975; *Lovers Like Us,* 1975; *Act of Aggression,* 1976; *March or Die,* 1977; *La Grande Bourgeoise,* 1977; *The Last Metro,* 1980; *A Second Chance,* 1981; *Reporters,* 1982; *The Hunger,* 1983.

AWARDS: Golden Palm Award, Cannes Film Festival, 1963, for *Parapluies de Cherbourg;* Golden Lion Award, Venice Film Festival, 1967, for *Belle de Jour.*

ADDRESS: OFFICE—Ufland-Roth Productions, 10201 W. Pico Blvd., Los Angeles, CA 90035.*

*   *   *

DEY, Susan   1952-

BRIEF ENTRY: Born December 10, 1952, in Pekin, IL; daughter of Robert Smith (city editor of *New Rochelle Standard Star*) and Gail (Dey); married Leonard Hirshan. At age 15 she began modeling and was featured on the covers of *Seventeen, American Girl,* and *Simplicity* magazines. Also, she appeared in three television commercials. She began her acting career at age 17 in the television series *The Partridge Family,* ABC, 1970. Later she was one of the stars of the short-lived television series *Emerald Point,* NBC, 1983. Other television series appearances include *Barnaby Jones, Hawaii Five-O, Switch, Little Women, Streets of San Francisco,* and *Loves Me, Loves Me Not.* Dey has appeared in the television movies *Terror on the Beach,* 1973; *Cage without a Key,* 1975; *Mary Jane Harper Cried Last Night,* 1977; *The Comeback Kid,* 1980; *The Gift of Life,* 1982; *Sunset Limousine.* Feature films Dey has starred in are *Skyjacked,* 1972; *First Love,* 1977; *Looker,* 1981; and in the upcoming *Echo Park.**

*   *   *

DIAMOND, Selma   1921-85

PERSONAL: Born 1921, in London, Ontario, Canada; died May 14, 1985. EDUCATION—New York University.

VOCATION: Actress and writer.

CAREER: PRINCIPAL STAGE APPEARANCES—*Come Blow Your Horn; Barefoot in the Park; Follies.*

PRINCIPAL FILM APPEARANCES—Telephone voice of Spencer

Tracey's wife, *It's a Mad Mad Mad Mad World; My Favorite Year; All of Me.*

PRINCIPAL TELEVISION APPEARANCES—*The Tonight Show; Too Close for Comfort;* the Bailiff, *Night Court.*

WRITINGS: COMEDY—(For radio and television) *The Big Show,* NBC radio; *The Sid Caesar Show; The Perry Como Show; The Milton Berle Show; Ozzie & Harriet,* all television variety.*

* * *

DICKINSON, Angie

PERSONAL: Born Angeline Brown, September 30, in Kulm, ND; married Burt Bacharach (divorced); children: Lea Nikki. EDUCATION: Attended Immaculate Heart College and Glendale College.

VOCATION: Actress.

CAREER: PRINCIPAL FILM APPEARANCES—*Rio Bravo,* Warner Brothers, 1959; *Bramble Bush,* Warner Brothers, 1960; *The Sins of Rachel Cade,* Warner Brothers, 1961; *Jessica,* United Artists, 1962; *Captain Newman, M.D.,* Universal, 1964; *The Killers,* Universal, 1964; *The Art of Love,* 1965; *The Chase,* Columbia, 1966; *Cast a Giant Shadow,* United Artists, 1966; *Point Blank,* Metro-Goldwyn-Mayer, 1967; *The Last Challenge,* Metro-Goldwyn-Mayer, 1967; *Sam Whiskey,* United Artists, 1969; *Some Kind of Nut,* United Artists, 1969; *Young Billy Young,* United Artists, 1969; *Pretty Maids All in a Row,* Metro-Goldwyn-Mayer, 1971; *Big Bad Mama,* 1974; *Dressed to Kill,* Filmways, 1980; *Death Hunt,* Twentieth Century-Fox, 1981; *Charlie Chan and the Curse of the Dragon Queen,* 1981.

PRINCIPAL TELEVISION APPEARANCES—Series: *Policewoman,* NBC, 1974-78. Miniseries: *Hollywood Wives,* ABC, 1984. Movie: *A Touch of Scandal,* CBS, 1984.

ADDRESS: AGENT—Black-Glenn Agency, 409 N. Camden Drive, Beverly Hills, CA 90212.*

* * *

DILLON, Matt

BRIEF ENTRY: Born in New Rochelle, NY, Dillon has also lived in Mamaroneck, NY, and was educated in Westchester County. He made his film debut at the age of 14 in *Over the Edge,* 1979, and his next films were *Little Darlings,* Paramount, 1980; *My Bodyguard,* Twentieth Century-Fox, 1980; *Liar's Moon.* Dillon then appeared in the PBS *American Playhouse* presentation of "The Great American Fourth of July . . . and Other Disasters." Since then he has starred in several more feature films: *Tex,* Buena Vista, 1982, in which he played the title role; *The Outsiders,* Warner Brothers, 1982, in which he played the role of Dallas; *Rumble Fish;* and *The Flamingo Kid,* 1984.*

* * *

D'LUGOFF, Art 1924-

PERSONAL: Born Arthur Joshua D'Lugoff, August 2, 1924; son of Raphael (a teacher) and Rachel (Mandelbaum) D'Lugoff; married

ART D'LUGOFF

Avital Achai (a photographer), April 7, 1957; children: Raphael, Sharon, Dahlia, Rashi. EDUCATION: New York University, Washington Square College, B.A., 1949. POLITICS: Democrat. RELIGION: Jewish. MILITARY: U.S. Army Air Force, World War Two.

VOCATION: Producer, director, and designer of cabaret theatres and theatrical properties.

CAREER: PRINCIPAL STAGE WORK—Producer: *One Mo' Time,* Village Gate, NY, 1980-83; *The Golden Land,* Norman Thomas Theater, NY, 1984-85.

SIDELIGHTS: MEMBERSHIPS—Actors Studio, National Trustees and Advisors Group, Community Board Number Two-New York City, Friar's Club.

ADDRESS: OFFICE—Village Gate, 160 Bleeker Street, New York, NY 10012.

* * *

DONENBERG, Benjamin 1957-

PERSONAL: Born March 8, 1957, in Chicago, IL; son of Sheldon Donald (a hardware salesman) and Toby P. (a medical secretary; maiden name, Rosenberg) Donenberg. EDUCATION: Trained for the stage at the Juilliard School of Drama.

VOCATION: Actor, director, producer, and writer.

CAREER: STAGE DEBUT—Rudi Dutchske, *How It All Began,* New

BENJAMIN DONENBERG

WALTER DONIGER

York Shakespeare Festival, NY, 1981, for thirty six performances. PRINCIPAL STAGE APPEARANCES—*Henry IV, Part I*, Delacorte, NY, 1981; *Amadeus*, NY, 1983.

PRINCIPAL STAGE WORK—Director: *Starship Shakespeare*, Lincoln Center, NY, 1983; *Cop-Out*, NY, 1984.

TELEVISION DEBUT—Theo, *The Doctors*, NBC, 1981.

RELATED CAREER—Artistic director, *At Twilight*, Classical Science Fiction Repertory Company; assistant to Robert Lewis, Robert Lewis Theatre Workshop, Los Angeles, CA; voice teacher, American Theatre Arts Conservatory.

SIDELIGHTS: MEMBERSHIPS—Dramatists' Guild, Ensemble Studio Theater, Los Angeles, CA.

ADDRESS: AGENT—c/o Luis San Jurjo, International Creative Management, 40 W. 57th Street, New York, NY 10019.

*   *   *

DONIGER, Walter

PERSONAL: Born in New York City; son of Harry and Roselyn Doniger; divorced; children: Thomas. EDUCATION: Attended Valley Forge Military Academy; Duke University; Harvard Graduate School of Business. MILITARY: U.S. Army Air Force, Motion Picture Unit, World War Two.

VOCATION: Director, producer, and writer.

CAREER: PRINCIPAL FILM WORK—Writer and/or producer: *Rope*

of Sand, 1949; *Tokyo Joe*, 1949; *Cease Fire; Along the Great Divide*, 1951; *Desperate Search*, 1952; *Alaska Seas*, 1954; *Duffy of San Quentin* (also directed), 1954; *Steel Cage* (also directed), 1954; *Steel Jungle* (also directed), Warner Brothers, 1956; *Hold Back the Night*, Allied Artists, 1956; *Guns of Fort Petticoat*, Columbia, 1957; *Safe at Home!* (also directed), Columbia, 1962; *House of Women* (also directed), Warner Brothers, 1962.

PRINCIPAL TELEVISION WORK—Writer, producer, and/or director for: *Delvecchio; Mad Bull; Switch; Movin' On, Baa Baa Blacksheep; McCloud; The Man and the City; Sarge; Owen Marshall; Peyton Place* (200 episodes); *Mr. Novak; The Greatest Show on Earth; Travels of Jaimie McPheeters; Outlaws; Hong Kong; Checkmate; Bat Masterson; The Web; Bold Venture; Tombstone Territory; Maverick; Rough Riders; Captain Grief; Lockup; Dick Powell; The Survivors; Bracken's World; Bold Ones; Kung Fu; Barnaby Jones; Marcus Welby; Lucas Tanner; Kentucky Woman; Roots.*

AWARDS: Writers Guild of America Award nomination, 1984, for *Kentucky Woman.*

SIDELIGHTS: MEMBERSHIPS—Dramatists Guild of America, Writers Guild of America, Academy of Motion Picture Arts and Sciences.

Doniger wrote documentaries for the armed forces during World War Two.

ADDRESS: OFFICE—ITC Productions, 12711 Ventura Blvd., Studio City, CA 91604. AGENT—Triad, 10,100 Santa Monica Blvd., 16th Fl., Los Angeles, CA 90067.

DONOHUE, Jack   1912-84

PERSONAL: Born 1912, in New York City, died of a heart attack, March 27, 1984.

VOCATION: Director, musical director, and dancer.

CAREER: PRINCIPAL STAGE APPEARANCES—Danced in the *Ziegfeld Follies,* 1927; performed in vaudville theatres, 1920-30's.

PRINCIPAL STAGE WORK—Choreographer: *Top Banana,* Broadway production; *Mr. Wonderful,* Broadway production.

PRINCIPAL FILM APPEARANCES—*Babes in Toyland,* 1961; *Marriage on the Rocks,* 1965; *Assault on a Queen,* 1966.

PRINCIPAL FILM WORK—Director: *Close Up* (first film shot entirely on location); *The Yellow Cab Man,* 1950.

Dance Director: *Calamity Jane,* 1953; five Shirley Temple films; *Bathing Beauty; Anchors Aweigh; It Happened in Brooklyn; Neptune's Daughter; The Midnight Kiss; On an Island with You; The Duchess of Idaho; Lucky Me; A Night in Venice; Top Banana.*

PRINCIPAL TELEVISION WORK—Director: 81 Frank Sinatra shows and 42 Red Skelton shows.*

*   *   *

DORWART, David A.   1948-

PERSONAL: Born January 20, 1948; son of Reinhold A. (an author and college professor) and Juanita M. (DeBeauvais) Dorwart; married Mary W. Beckwith, August 21, 1971 (divorced, 1981). EDUCATION: Amherst College, A.B., 1970; Smith College, M.F.A., 1972; trained for the stage at University of Birmingham, England, Royal Shakespeare Company, Juilliard School of Drama, and New York University.

VOCATION: Director and scenic designer.

CAREER: FIRST STAGE WORK—Director, *The Mother of Us All,* Boston Lyric Opera, Boston, MA. FIRST NEW YORK STAGE WORK—Director, *A Moment of Impact,* Circle Repertory, 1982. PRINCIPAL STAGE WORK—Director: *La Boheme, Rigoletto, Amahl and the Night Visitors,* all at Associated Artists Opera, 1975; *Amahl and the Night Visitors, The Mother of Us All,* both at Boston Lyric Opera, 1976; *My Cup Runneth Over, The Wager, Album, A Life in the Theater, The Life That We Lead, Tartuffe, Getting Out,* all at Suffolk Theater Company, Suffolk University, Boston, MA, 1977-82; *Sexual Perversity in Chicago, The Duck Variations,* both at Charles Playhouse, Boston, 1978; *Moving Out,* 1979, *Man of Crete,* 1980, both at Stage West; *The Middleman,* Equity Library, NY, 1982; *A Moment of Impact,* Circle Repertory, NY, 1982.

Scenic designer: *The Play's the Thing,* Portland Stage Company, OR, 1978; *The Gingerbread Lady,* Merrimack Regional Theater, 1979; *The Shadow Box,* Ford's Theater Society, Washington, DC, 1979; *The Shadow Box,* Charles Playhouse, 1979.

PRINCIPAL TELEVISION WORK—*Amahl and the Night Visitors,* 1974, *That Life That We Lead,* 1979, both for WGBH, Boston, MA.

DAVID A. DORWART

SIDELIGHTS: MEMBERSHIPS—Society of Stage Directors and Choreographers, American Theater Association, Theater Communications Group.

ADDRESS: HOME—255 W. 23rd Street, New York, NY 10011. AGENT—c/o William Craver, Helen Merrill Agency, 337 W. 22nd Street, New York, NY 10011.

*   *   *

DOUGLAS, Gordon

VOCATION: Director, writer, and actor.

CAREER: PRINCIPAL FILM WORK—Director: thirty *Our Gang,* shorts; *Saps at Sea,* 1940; *Broadway Limited,* 1941; *Devil with Hitler; First Yank into Tokyo,* 1945; *San Quentin,* 1946; *If You Knew Suzie,* 1948; *Black Arrow,* 1948; *Walk a Crooked Mile,* 1948; *Doolins of Oklahoma,* 1949; *Mr. Soft Touch,* 1949; *The Nevadan,* 1950; *Between Midnight and Dawn,* 1950; *Kiss Tomorrow Goodbye,* 1950; *Great Missouri Raid,* 1950; *Only the Valient,* 1951; *I Was a Communist for the FBI,* 1951; *Come Fill the Cup,* 1951; *Mara Maru,* 1952; *Iron Mistress,* 1952; *She's Back on Broadway,* 1953; *So This Is Love,* 1953; *The Charge at Feather River,* 1953; *Them!,* 1954.

Young at Heart, Warner Brothers, 1955; *McConnell Story,* Warner Brothers, 1955; *Sincerely Yours,* Warner Brothers, 1955; *Santiago,* Warner Brothers, 1956; *The Big Land,* Warner Brothers, 1957; *Bombers B-52,* Warner Brothers, 1957; *Fort Dobbs,* Warner Brothers,

1958; *Yellowstone Kelly,* Warner Brothers, 1959; *Rachel Cade; Gold of the Seven Saints,* Warner Brothers, 1961; *Follow That Dream,* United Artists, 1962; *Call Me Bwana,* United Artists, 1963; *Rio Conchos,* Twentieth Century-Fox, 1964; *Robin and the Seven Hoods,* Warner Brothers, 1964; *Sylvia,* Paramount, 1965; *Harlow,* Paramount, 1965; *Stagecoach,* Twentieth Century-Fox, 1966; *Way Way Out,* Twentieth Century-Fox, 1966; *In Like Flint,* Twentieth Century-Fox, 1967; *Chuka,* Paramount, 1967; *Tony Rome,* Twentieth Century-Fox, 1967; *The Detective,* Twentieth Century-Fox, 1968; *Lady in Cement,* Twentieth Century-Fox, 1968; *Barquero,* United Artists, 1970; *They Call Me Mister Tibbs!,* United Artists, 1970; *Slaughter's Big Rip-Off,* American International, 1973.

PRINCIPAL FILM APPEARANCES—Member of Hal Roach stock company.

PRINCIPAL TELEVISION WORK—Writer/collaborator, *Topper* and *Housekeeper's Daughter.* Director, television movies: *Nevada Smith,* 1975; *Viva Knieval!,* 1977.

ADDRESS: AGENT—Ryder Stilwell Inc. 5900 Wilshire Blvd., Suite 1100, Los Angeles, CA 90036.

*   *   *

DOW, Tony   1945-

PERSONAL: Born April 13, 1945, in Hollywood, CA; son of John Stevens (a designer and general contractor) and Muriel Virginia (Montrose) Dow; married Laura Shulkind, June 16, 1980; children: Christopher T. EDUCATION: Attended University of California at Los Angeles, Columbia College, Sherwood Oaks Experimental College; trained at the Film Industry Workshop. MILITARY: National Guard.

VOCATION: Actor.

CAREER: PRINCIPAL TELEVISION APPEARANCES—Wally, *Leave It to Beaver,* CBS, 1957-58, then ABC, 1958-63; *Mod Squad; Knight Rider; The Love Boat; Square Pegs; Quincy;* host, *Weekday Heroes; Still the Beaver; Four Feet in the Morning; General Hospital; Never Too Young; Merv Griffin Show; Today; Good Morning America.* Movies: *Death Scream,* 1975; *High School, U.S.A.,* 1983;

PRINCIPAL FILM APPEARANCES—*The Carney Case; Kentucky Fried Movie,* 1977; *A New American Tragedy.*

PRINCIPAL STAGE APPEARANCES—*Lovers and Other Strangers; Barefoot in the Park; Come Blow Your Horn.*

MAJOR TOURS—*So Long, Stanley.*

WRITINGS: TELEVISION—"Slumber Party," *Still the Beaver,* 1984.

ADDRESS: AGENT—Phil Gittelman, 1221 N. Kings Road, Los Angeles, CA 90019.

*   *   *

DOWLING, Vincent   1929-

PERSONAL: Born September 7, 1929, in Dublin, Ireland; son of William Francis (a sea captain) and Mary (Kelly) Dowling; married

VINCENT DOWLING

Brenda Mary Doyle (died); married Olwen Patricia O'Herlihy (a theater general manager); children: Bairbre, Louise, Valerie, Rachael, Cian. EDUCATION: Attended Brendan Smith Academy, Dublin.

VOCATION: Director, actor, writer, and teacher.

CAREER: STAGE DEBUT—George, *Our Town,* Peacock Theater, Brendan Smith Academy, Dublin, Ireland, for six performances. NEW YORK DEBUT—*My Lady Luck,* West Side, 1981, for eighteen performances. LONDON DEBUT—Norman, *My Wife's Lodger,* Comedy, 1951, for one thousand performances. PRINCIPAL STAGE APPEARANCES—Abbey Theater, Dublin; Theatre Des Nations Festival, Paris; Great Lakes Shakespeare Festival.

MAJOR TOURS—Ireland, England, Scotland, Wales, Italy.

PRINCIPAL STAGE WORK—Director: Abbey Theatre, Dublin; Great Lakes Shakespeare Festival, Cleveland, OH; PCPA Theater Festival, Santa Maria, CA; Solvang Theater Festival, Solvang, CA.

FILM DEBUT—Norman, *My Wife's Lodger,* Adelphi Films, London, 1952. PRINCIPAL FILM APPEARANCES—*Young Cassidy; Boyd's Shop,* Ardmore Studios.

TELEVISION DEBUT—Producer and director, *Playboy of the Western World,* PBS, 1982.

RELATED CAREER—Deputy artistic director, Abbey Theater, Dublin, Ireland; producing and artistic director, Great Lakes Shakespeare Festival, Cleveland OH, 1976-84; producing and artistic director, PCPA Theater Festival, Santa Maria, CA, 1984-present; producing and artistic director, Solvang Theater Festival, Solvang, CA, 1984-present.

WRITINGS: PLAYS, PRODUCED—*Do Me a Favorite or The Fit-*

Ups, Great Lakes Shakespeare Festival, Cleveland, OH, Old Globe Theater Student Tour; *Cherry Orchard* (translation), *Lysistrata* (translation), both presented at Missouri Repertory. BOOKS—Poetry.

AWARDS: Emmy Award (Cleveland Chapter), for *Playboy of the Western World;* Arts Prize Award, Cleveland City Womens Club, 1983; Honorary Ph.D., John Carroll University, OH, 1984.

SIDELIGHTS: MEMBERSHIPS—Actors' Equity Association, British Actors' Equity Association, American Federation of Television and Radio Artists, Society of Stage Directors and Choreographers, American Theater Association, Theater Communications Group.

ADDRESS: OFFICE—P.O. Box 1700, Santa Maria, CA, 93456. AGENT—c/o Brett Adams Ltd., 448 W. 44th Street, New York, NY 10036.

*   *   *

DRIVAS, Robert   1938-

PERSONAL: Born Robert Choromokos, November 21, 1938, in Chicago, IL; son of James Peter and Hariklia (Cunningham-Wright) Choromokos. EDUCATION: Attended University of Chicago and the University of Miami; trained for the stage with Sanford Meisner, Philip Burton, and at the Actors Studio.

VOCATION: Actor and director.

CAREER: STAGE DEBUT—Danny, *Night Must Fall,* Coral Gables, FL, 1957. NEW YORK DEBUT—Rameses, *The Firstborn,* Coronet, 1958. PRINCIPAL STAGE APPEARANCES—Tom, Jr., *Sweet Bird of Youth,* Actors Studio, Miami, FL, 1957; Tom Lee, *Tea and Sympathy,* Coconut Grove Playhouse, Miami, FL, 1957; *The Lady's Not for Burning, Death of a Salesman, Thieves' Ball, A View from the Bridge,* all at Highland Park Playhouse, Chicago, IL, 1957; Jacko, *One More River,* Ambassador, NY, 1960; Stefan Mazur, *The Wall,* Billy Rose, NY, 1960; Benny Rogers, *Diff'rent,* Mermaid, NY, 1961.

Frankie, *Mrs. Dally Has a Lover,* Cherry Lane, NY, 1962; Giorgio, *Lorenzo,* Plymouth, NY, 1963; Andrew Rankin, *The Irregular Verb to Love,* Ethel Barrymore, NY, 1963; Sigfrid, *And Things That Go Bump in the Night,* Royale, NY, 1965; Young Man, *Sweet Eros,* Gramercy Arts, NY, 1968; Fly Paper, Dracula, *Cops and Horrors,* NY, 1970; Tommy Flowers, *Where Has Tommy Flowers Gone?,* Yale Repertory, New Haven, CT, Eastside Playhouse, NY, 1971; Michael, *A Breeze from the Gulf,* Bucks County Playhouse, New Hope, PA, Eastside Playhouse, NY, 1973; Himself, *The Man Who Had Three Arms,* New World Festival of the Arts, Miami, FL, Goodman, Chicago, IL, and on Broadway; *Julius Caesar,* Yale Repertory, New Haven, CT, 1976; Master, *Jacques and His Master,* American Repertory Theater, Cambridge, MA, 1985.

PRINCIPAL STAGE WORK—Director: *Bad Habits,* Astor Place, NY, 1974; *The Ritz,* Longacre, NY, 1975; *Legend,* Ethel Barrymore, NY, 1976; *Monsters,* Astor Place, NY, 1977; *Cheaters,* Biltmore, NY, 1978; *Little Me; Peg* (Peggy Lee in concert); *Snacks; It Had to Be You,* Los Angeles; *Washington Square,* Athens, Greece; *Clap Trap,* Hasty Pudding, CT.

FILM DEBUT—Loudmouth Steve, *Cool Hand Luke,* Warner Brothers, 1967. PRINCIPAL FILM APPEARANCES—*The Illustrated Man,* Warner Brothers, 1969; *Where It's At,* United Artists, 1969; *Road Movie; Crazy American Girl.*

PRINCIPAL TELEVISION APPEARANCES—*Streets of San Francisco; Cannon; Hawaii Five-0; The F.B.I.;* many others.

PRINCIPAL TELEVISION WORK—Director: Three pilots, including *The Stockard Channing Show,* CBS.

AWARDS: Theater World Award, 1962, for *Mrs. Dally Has a Lover;* National Film Exhibition Award; Carbonel Award, FL, Joseph Jefferson Award, Best Actor, Chicago, both for *The Man Who Had Three Arms;* Obie Award, Best Director, 1974, for *Bad Habits;* Antoinette Perry Award, Best Director, 1975, for *The Ritz.*

ADDRESS: HOME—New York, NY. AGENT—c/o Bruce Savan, Agency for the Performing Arts, 888 Seventh Avenue, New York, NY 10106.

*   *   *

DUDLEY, Carol L.   1949-

PERSONAL: Born July 23, 1949; daughter of Robert Whittier (a lawyer) and Argentina Anselma (Copello) Dudley. EDUCATION: Attended Dartmouth College, 1968-69; Vassar College, B.A., drama, 1971.

VOCATION: Casting director.

CAREER: PRINCIPAL FILM WORK—Casting director: *Eyes of Fire,* Elysian Pictures; *Cross Country,* Film Line Productions.

PRINCIPAL TELEVISION WORK—Casting director: *Santa Barbara,* NBC; *Cutter to Houston,* CBS; *Gavilan,* NBC; *Eleanor, First Lady of the World,* CBS; *But It's Not My Fault,* ABC; *Don't Hit Me Mom,* ABC; *Palmerstown,* CBS; as casting associate: *Call to Glory,* Tisch-Avnet/ Paramount; *Sins of the Past,* ABC; *Shut Down,* ABC; *Cutter to Houston,* CBS; *I Want to Live,* ABC; *Concrete Beat,* ABC; *Farrell for the People,* NBC; *The Jesse Owens Story,* Paramount Pictures; *The A-Team,* ABC; *The Quest,* ABC.

SIDELIGHTS: MEMBERSHIPS—Casting Society of America.

ADDRESS: HOME—1345 N. Hayworth Avenue, Apt. 207, Los Angeles, CA 90046. OFFICE—7083 Hollywood Blvd., Suite 306, Los Angeles, CA.

*   *   *

DUKES, David

PERSONAL: Born in San Francisco; married to first wife, 1965 (divorced, 1975); married Carol Muske; children: (first marriage) Shawn. EDUCATION—American Conservatory Theatre.

VOCATION: Actor.

CAREER: PRINCIPAL STAGE APPEARANCES—Broadway: *Bent; Travesties; The Rules of the Game; Holiday; Chemin de Fer; The School for Wives; Don Juan; The Play's the Thing; The Great God Brown; Love for Love; The Visit; Rebel Woman; Frankenstein; Amadeus.* Appeared in leading roles with the American Conservatory Theatre, San Francisco; The Alley Theatre, Houston; The Center Theatre Group, Los Angeles; Goodman Theatre, Chicago.

PRINCIPAL FILM APPEARANCES—*A Little Romance; The First Deadly Sin; Only When I Laugh; Without a Trace.*

PRINCIPAL TELEVISION APPEARANCES—*Beacon Hill; All in the Family; The Triangle Factory Fire; 79 Park Avenue; Some Kind of Miracle; Winds of War; Sentimental Journey;* "Remembering Melody," *The Hitchhiker; Kane and Abel,* CBS (upcoming).

AWARDS: Los Angeles Drama Critics Award, Outstanding Actor, *Design for Living,* Goodman Theatre; Antoinette Perry nomination, *Bent.**

*   *   *

DUNCAN, Sandy   1946-

PERSONAL: Born February 20, 1946, in Henderson, TX; daughter of Mancil Ray and Sylvia Wynne (Scott) Duncan; married Thomas C. Calcaterra (a doctor; divorced); married Don Correa (an actor and dancer); children: (second marriage) one son. EDUCATION: Attended Lon Morris College; trained for the stage with Wynn Handman, Utah Ground, and Toni Beck.

VOCATION: Actress.

CAREER: STAGE DEBUT—Child, *The King and I,* State Fair Music Hall, Dallas, TX, 1958. NEW YORK DEBUT—Zaneeta Shinn, *The Music Man,* City Center, 1965. PRINCIPAL STAGE APPEAR- ANCES—Louise, *Carousel,* City Center, NY, 1966; Susan Mahoney, *Finian's Rainbow,* 1967; Mary Skinner, *Life with Father,* 1967; Liesl, *The Sound of Music,* 1967; Thulja, *The Ceremony of Inno- cence,* American Place, NY, 1967; Viola, *Your Own Thing,* Orpheum, NY, 1968; Alison, Molly, May, Sweetheart, *Canterbury Tales,* Eugene O'Neill Theater, NY, 1969; April MacGregor, *Love Is a Time of Day,* Music Box, NY, 1969; Maisie, *The Boy Friend,* Ambassador, NY, 1970; Peter Pan, *Peter Pan,* Music Hall, Dallas, TX, 1975; Mary, *Varities,* Mark Taper Forum, Los Angeles, CA, 1976; Peter Pan, *Peter Pan,* Lunt-Fontanne, NY, 1979; *My One and Only,* St. James, NY, 1985.

MAJOR TOURS—Viola, *Your Own Thing,* U.S. and Canadian cities, 1968; *Gypsy; The Music Man, Brigadoon.*

FILM DEBUT—*Million Dollar Duck,* 1970. PRINCIPAL FILM AP- PEARANCES—*The Star Spangled Girl,* 1971; *The Cat from Outer Space.*

PRINCIPAL TELEVISION APPEARANCES—*Funny Face; The Sandy Duncan Show,* 1973; *Laugh-In; The Muppet Show; Roots.*

AWARDS: Gold Medal Award, Photoplay, Golden Apple Award, all 1971.

SIDELIGHTS: FAVORITE ROLES—Louise, *Carousel,* Maise, *The Boy Friend.* RECREATIONS—Needlepoint, plants, gardening, tennis.

ADDRESS: AGENT—William Morris Agency, 151 El Camino Drive, Beverly Hills, CA 90212.*

*   *   *

DUTTINE, John   1949-

PERSONAL: Born May 15, 1949, in Barnsley Yorkshire, England; son of Josef and Caroline Edith (Hampton) Duttine; married Carolyn Margaret Hutchinson; children: Oscar James. EDUCATION: Butter- shaw Comprehensive School; studied acting at the Drama Centre in London.

JOHN DUTTINE

VOCATION: Actor.

CAREER: STAGE DEBUT—Osric, *Hamlet,* Glasgow Citzens, 1970. PRINCIPAL STAGE APPEARANCES—Member of Citizens Theatre Company, two years; Nottingham Repertory Company, Watford Repertory Company, 1970-73; *Hamlet,* Leatherhead, 1984.

TELEVISION DEBUT—Leo, *Pin to See the Peepshow,* BBC, 1973. PRINCIPAL TELEVISION APPEARANCES—Gravedigger, *Lord Peter Whimsey,* BBC, 1974; Able Seaman Scobie, *Warship,* BBC, 1974; *Churchill's People,* BBC, 1974; *Holding On,* six part serial, Lon- don Weekend TV, 1975; Keith Nicholson, *Spend, Spend, Spend,* BBC, 1976; *Coronation Street,* Granada TV, 1977; Federico, *Saturday, Sunday, Monday,* Granada TV, 1977; Archie Carver, *The Avenue,* London Weekend TV, 1977; King John, *The Devil's Crown,* thirteen part series, BBC, 1978; Hindley, *Wuthering Heights,* BBC, 1978; Lennie, *Strangers,* Granada TV, 1978; Donald Radlett, *The Mallens,* Granada TV, 1979; David Powlet-Jones, *To Serve Them All My Days,* BBC, 1980; Alan, *Psy - Warriors,* BBC, 1981; Bill, *Day of the Triffids,* BBC, 1981; "Hit and Run," "Skeleton Item," *Tales of the Unexpected,* 1982; Franit, *The Outsider,* York- shire TV, 1982; *Shades of Darkness: The Intercessor,* Granada TV, 1983; Dave, "Family Man," *Love and Marriage,* London Week- end TV, 1983; Jimmy, *Grounding and the Kite,* BBC, 1983; Joe Lonther, *Woman of Substance,* Portman/Artimes, 1984; Mr. Draite, *Lame Ducits,* BBC, 1984; Alan, *A Still Small Shout,* BBC, 1985.

FILM DEBUT—John, *Jesus of Nazereth,* 1975. PRINCIPAL FILM APPEARANCES—Evan Lloyd, *Who Dares Wins,* White Horse Pro- ductions, 1980.

AWARDS: TV Times Best Actor Award, David Powlett-Jones, *To Serve Them All My Days,* 1980.

SIDELIGHTS: MEMBERSHIPS—Greenpeace, C.N.D.

ADDRESS: AGENT—Peter Browne, 13 St. Martins Road, London SW9, England.

E

EBERSOLE, Christine

PERSONAL: Born in Chicago, IL; married Peter Bergman (an actor; divorced). EDUCATION: McMurray College, two years; studied acting at the American Academy of Dramatic Arts in New York City.

VOCATION: Actress.

CAREER: BROADWAY DEBUT—Guinevere, *Camelot*, Palace, 1979. PRINCIPAL STAGE APPEARANCES—Ado Annie, *Oklahoma!*, revival, NY; *Geniuses*, NY.

PRINCIPAL FILM APPEARANCES—*Tootsie; Amadeus; Thief of Hearts.*

PRINCIPAL TELEVISION APPEARANCES—*Saturday Night Live*, NBC.*

*   *   *

ECKSTEIN, George   1928-

PERSONAL: Born May 3, 1928, in Los Angeles, CA; son of George (a salesman) and Ruth (Wexler) Eckstein; married Ann Guilbert, February 4, 1951 (divorced 1966); married Selette Cole, August 25, 1968; children: Nora, Hallie, Jennifer. EDUCATION: Stanford University, B.A., 1949; University of Southern California, Ll.B., 1953. MILITARY: U.S. Army, 1953-55.

VOCATION: Producer and writer.

CAREER: PRINCIPAL STAGE WORK—Producer, *The Billy Barnes Revue*, York, Golden, Lyceum, NY, 1960, Lyric-Hammersmith, London, 1961.

PRINCIPAL TELEVISION WORK—Producer, series: *Name of the Game; The Fugitive; Banacek; Sara; Sunshine; The Mississippi; Love, Sydney*. Producer, mini-series: *Masada; 79 Park Avenue*. Producer, television movies: *Duel*, 1971; *Sunshine*, 1973; *Amelia Earhart*, 1976; *Tail Gunner Joe*, 1977; *Sunshine Christmas*, 1977; *Where the Ladies Go*, 1980; *Sidney Shorr: A Girl's Best Friend*, 1981; *Victims*, 1982.

WRITINGS: Teleplays—"Jigsaw," *The Untouchables*, 1961; *The Fugitive; Gunsmoke; Dr. Kildare*.

SIDELIGHTS: MEMBERSHIPS—Writers Guild of America, Producers Guild of America (board of directors, 1976-77), Caucus of Producers, Writers, and Directors (chairman, 1977).

ADDRESS: HOME—3201 Oakdell Road, Studio City, CA 91604. OFFICE—4000 Warner Blvd., Burbank, CA 91522. AGENT—Major Talent Agency Inc., 11812 San Vicente Blvd., Suite 510, Los Angeles, CA 90049.

*   *   *

EDEN, Sidney   1936-

PERSONAL: Born Sidney Edelstein, January 5, 1936, in Chicago, IL; son of Sidney and Fay (Quisenberry) Edelstein; divorced; children: Scott. EDUCATION: Attended University of Illinois and Roosevelt University; trained for the stage with Jose Quintero, Jose Ferrer, and John Cassavetes. POLITICS: Democrat. RELIGION: Jewish.

SIDNEY EDEN

VOCATION: Actor, composer, critic, director, producer, writer, and teacher.

CAREER: NEW YORK DEBUT—Sam G. Wood and second committeeman, *Are You Now or Have You Ever Been?*, Century, Promenade, 1978-79. PRINCIPAL STAGE APPEARANCES—Cutler, *Conflict of Interest*, PAF Playhouse, Long Island, NY, Hartman, Stamford, CT, 1979-80; *Sitcom*, St. Nicholas, Chicago; Frank Lippencott, *Wonderful Town*, Brad, *Everybody Loves Opal*, Mike, *Who Was That Lady I Saw You With?*, Harlow Edison, *Gazebo*, LaSalle, *Will Success Spoil Rock Hunter?*, all at Pheasant Run, IL.

Prentice, *What the Butler Saw;* Harry Carson, *Desperate Hours;* Suzie's friend, *Hot L Baltimore*, Ivanhoe Theater; Sir Harry Bumpber, *The School for Scandal*, Robert, *The Assassin*, Nutsy Miller, *Male Animal*, Larry, *Country Girl*, Max, *A Tree Grows in Brooklyn*, Priest, *Twelfth Night*, Sheriff Payne, *Bloomer Girl*, all at Cleveland Playhouse, OH; Nathan Detroit, *Guys and Dolls;* Johnny, *A Hatful of Rain;* Tom, *Glass Menagerie*.

PRINCIPAL STAGE WORK—Director: *Guys and Dolls, You Can't Take It with You, High Button Shoes, A Raisin in the Sun, George Jean Nathan in Revue, Carousel, Decline and Fall of the Entire World as Seen Through the Eyes of Cole Porter, When You Comin' Back Red Ryder, Glass Menagerie, King of Hearts, Song of Norway, Kismet, Say Darling, Country Girl, Plain and Fancy, Confidential Clerk, The Assassin, Student Prince, Fanny, Bells Are Ringing, Kiss Me Kate, Desert Song, Roberta, Pal Joey*, all at theaters including: Cleveland Playhouse, OH; Goodman, Chicago, IL; Brooklyn Academy of Music, NY; Detroit Music Hall for the Performing Arts, MI; University of Massachusetts Fine Arts Center; Tenthouse, Highland Park, IL; Northland Playhouse, Detroit, MI; Brunswick Summer Theater, ME; Lakewood Summer Theatre; Kennebunkport Playhouse; Grand Theatre, Sullivan, IL; First Chicago Center.

Producer: At First Chicago Center, IL: *Hughie, When You Comin' Back Red Ryder?, Sheba; Hughie*, Huntington Hartford, Los Angeles, American Theatre, St. Louis, MO; Golden, NY, 1974.

MAJOR TOURS—Producer and director, *A Raisin in the Sun*, national.

PRINCIPAL TELEVISION APPEARANCES—*One Life to Live*, ABC; *Ryan's Hope*, ABC; narrator, *Wild Kingdom*, NBC.

PRINCIPAL FILM APPEARANCES—*Spook Who Sat by the Door*, United Artists, 1973; *Are You Now or Have You Ever Been?; Chapter Two*, Columbia, 1979; *Conflict of Interest*.

RELATED CAREER—Founder, First Chicago Center Theater, IL; co-founder, Hyatt House Music Theater, Burlingame, CA; chairman, Equity Library Theater, Chicago, IL; vice-chairman, Midwest Advisory Board, Actors' Equity Association; founding director and president, Illinois Theatre Company Foundation; president, Videomonologues; acting teacher, Westwinds Learning Center, Theatre Row, NY; writer and performer, *Broadway Magazine*, Group W Cable Television.

WRITINGS: PLAYS, PRODUCED—*George Jean Nathan in Revue*, Goodman, Chicago, IL, 1977.

SIDELIGHTS: MEMBERSHIPS—Actors' Equity Association, Screen Actors Guild, American Federation of Television and Radio Artists, Society of Stage Directors and Choreographers, Players Club.

ADDRESS: HOME—484 W. 43rd Street, New York NY 10036.

BURT EDWARDS

EDWARDS, Burt   1928-

PERSONAL: Full name Norbert C. Edwards; born January 11, 1928, in Richmond, VA; son of Landon B. (a financier) and Kathleen (Caughy) Edwards. EDUCATION: Attended Virginia University, Richmond, 1945-48; studied acting with Tamara Daykarhanova and Joe Anthony in NY. MILITARY: U.S. Army, 1946-47.

VOCATION: Actor.

CAREER: STAGE DEBUT—Nicky, *Bell, Book, and Candle*, tour of VA and MD, Mason Bliss production, 1952. NEW YORK DEBUT—Oscar, *Another Part of the Forest*, Equity Library, 1957. PRINCIPAL STAGE APPEARANCES—Monty Wooley, Noel Coward, and Clifton Webb, *Red, Hot & Cole*, Variety Arts Center, Los Angeles, 1979; Captain Orton, *The King & I*, Pantages, Hollywood, CA, 1983; performed many major roles at the Virginia Museum Theatre and the Barksdale Dinner Theatre in Richmond, VA.

MAJOR TOURS—Understudy and assistant stage manager, *Tea & Sympathy*, national tour, 1956.

FILM DEBUT—*Marrying Kind*, 1952. PRINCIPAL FILM APPEARANCES—Party-goer, *Stage Struck*, Buena Vista, 1958; *Three Days of the Condor*, Paramount, 1975; *Rollercoaster*, Universal, 1977; *Story of a Patriot; Me Two*.

TELEVISION DEBUT—*Omnibus*, 1954. PRINCIPAL TELEVISION

APPEARANCES—Patrick Henry, *First Continental Congress,* PBS, 1976; Detective Sergeant Sullivan, *General Hospital,* 1984-85; *Dynasty; Trapper John; McClain's Law; Tales of the Gold Monkey; Belle Starr; Dream Merchants; Cagney '& Lacy; The Doberman Gang* (pilot); *Wishhan* (pilot); *Capitol.*

AWARDS: Phoebe Award, Richmond Newsleader, 1976, for Uncle Sid, *Ah! Wilderness.*

SIDELIGHTS: MEMBERSHIPS—Actors' Equity Association, American Federation of Television and Radio Actors, Screen Actors Guild.

Edwards worked as a travel manager for the Automobile Association of America in Richmond, VA, between 1959-79.

ADDRESS: HOME—733 Kings Road, Apt. 358, Los Angeles, CA 90069. AGENT—Mark Levin & Associates, 328 S. Beverly Drive, Suite E, Beverly Hills, CA 90212.

*   *   *

EGAN, Michael   1926-

PERSONAL: Born August 24, 1926, in Washington, PA; son of Arthur (a member of the United States consular service) and Mima (a saleswoman; maiden name, Clark) Egan. EDUCATION: Bucknell University, B.A., 1946. MILITARY: U.S. Air Force, World War Two.

VOCATION: Actor and director.

MICHAEL EGAN

CAREER: STAGE DEBUT—Orsino, *Twelfth Night,* Parr Theater, Pittsburgh, PA, 1943. NEW YORK DEBUT—Tobias and the Angel, *The Father,* Theater de Lys, 1948. PRINCIPAL STAGE APPEARANCES—Pope Leo, *Luther,* St. James, NY, 1963-64; Bird Boot, *Real Inspector Hound,* Kennedy Center, Washington, DC, 1966; George, *Duck Variations,* Cherry Lane, NY, 1976-77; Pozzo, *Waiting for Godot,* Brooklyn Academy of Music, NY, 1978; Angel, *An Angel Comes to Babylon,* PAF Playhouse, NY, 1979; Shamraev, *The Seagull,* Public, NY, 1980; Vivien, *Vivien,* Lincoln Center, NY, 1981; Galileo, *Galileo,* Pittsburgh Public Theater, PA, 1981; standby, *The Dresser,* Biltmore, NY, 1981; The Man, *Tresspassers,* Rutgers University, 1982; Hugh, *Translations,* Centaur, Montreal, Quebec, Canada, 1982; Pischich, *The Cherry Orchard,* Long Wharf, New Haven, CT, 1983; Dr. Dorn, *The Seagull,* Guthrie, Minneapolis, MN, 1983; Colonel Melkett, *Black Comedy,* Philadelphia Drama Guild, PA, 1984; Chebutykin, *Three Sisters,* Guthrie, Minneapolis, MN, 1984; Falstaff, *Henry IV, Part I,* Center Stage, Baltimore, MD, 1984.

PRINCIPAL STAGE WORK—Director: *John L. Lewis, Disciple of Discontent,* Civic Center, Cleveland, OH, 1977, Berkshire Theater Festival, NY, 1978; *My Lady Luck,* Great Lakes Shakespeare Festival, Cleveland, OH, 1980.

MAJOR TOURS—Cromwell, *Man for All Seasons;* Old Man, *Royal Hunt of the Sun,* national.

TELEVISION DEBUT—Sir Humphrey, *Edge of Night,* ABC, 1983.

FILM DEBUT—Zoro, *Square Root of Zoro,* 1962. PRINCIPAL FILM APPEARANCES—Jake, *Two for the Seesaw,* United Artists, 1962; Herbert, *Next Stop, Greenwich Village,* 1976.

ADDRESS: HOME—New York, NY. AGENT—c/o Monty Silver, 200 W. 57th Street, New York, NY 10019.

*   *   *

ELAM, Jack   1916-

PERSONAL: Born November 13, 1916; married Margaret, 1961; children: three. EDUCATION: Attended junior colleges in Modesto, CA. MILITARY: U.S. Navy, World War Two.

VOCATION: Actor.

CAREER: FILM DEBUT—*The Sundowners,* 1950. PRINCIPAL FILM APPEARANCES—*Vera Cruz; Gunfight at the OK Corral; The Comancheros; Firecreek; Once Upon a Time in the West; Support Your Local Sherriff; Rio Lobo; Support Your Local Gunfighter; Rawhide; The Villain; Baby Face Nelson; Hannie Calder; Grayeagle; Hot Lead and Cold Feet; The Norseman; The Apple Dumpling Gang Rides Again.*

PRINCIPAL TELEVISION APPEARANCES—Series: *The Dakotas,* 1963; *Temple Houston,* 1963-64; *The Texas Wheelers,* 1974-75; *Struck by Lightning,* 1979; *The Villain,* 1979. Episodic: *Lacy and the Mississippi Queen; Gunsmoke; Huckleberry Finn; How the West Was Won; Black Beauty; The Ransom of Red Chief; The Daughters of Joshua Cabe.*

ADDRESS: AGENT—Contemporary Korman Artists, Ltd., 132 Lasky Drive, Beverly Hills, CA 90212.*

ELIKANN, Larry   1923-

PERSONAL: Born Lawrence Elikann, August 4, 1923, in New York City; son of Harry (a costume bead importer) and Sadye (Trause) Elikann; married Corinne Schuman (a corporate officer), December 6, 1947; children: Jo Anne Jarrin, Jill Barad. EDUCATION: Brooklyn College, B.A., 1943; Walter Hervey College, E.E., engineering, 1948. MILITARY: U.S. Army, Signal Corps, Staff Seargent, 1943-46.

VOCATION: Television director.

CAREER: FIRST TELEVISION WORK—Cameraman, *Philco Playhouse*, 1950. PRINCIPAL TELEVISION WORK—Director since 1966: ''Rookie of the Year,'' *Afternoon Special*, PBS; ''Heartbeat,'' *Barringer's; Poison Ivy; Knott's Landing; Falcon Crest; Remington Steele; T.J. Hooker; Dallas; Hill Street Blues.*

RELATED CAREER: Technical director, NBC, 1948-64; commercial director, VPI-TV, NY, 1964-66; commercial director, Filmex-TV, 1966-68; director, Plus Two TV, 1968-70; freelance director, 1970-present.

AWARDS: Emmys, National Academy of Television Arts and Sciences, 1973, 1976-79; Christopher Awards, 1972, 1976, 1978; Media Award, Ohio State Film Festival, 1977; Chicago International Film Festival Award, 1977; International Film and Television Festival of New York Award, 1977; Director of the Year, American Center Films for Children, 1978.

SIDELIGHTS: MEMBERSHIPS—Directors Guild of America, American Film Institute, National Academy of Television Arts and Sciences (board of governors), 1961-63.

ADDRESS: OFFICE—100 S. Doheny Drive, Los Angeles, CA 90048. AGENT—Alan Izeman, William Morris Agency, 151 El Camino Drive, Beverly Hills, CA 90069.

*   *   *

ELIZONDO, Hector   1936-

PERSONAL: Born December 22, 1936, in New York City; son of Martin Echevarria and Carmen Medina (Reyes) Elizondo; married Carolee Campbell; children: a son. EDUCATION: Attended Music, Arts, and Commerce High School, NY; prepared for the stage at the Stella Adler Studio with Mario Siletti and with Frank Corsaro.

VOCATION: Actor.

CAREER: STAGE DEBUT—Reber, *Mr. Roberts*, Equity Library Theater, NY, 1961. PRINCIPAL STAGE APPEARANCES— Supervisor, Director, Soldier, Attendant, *Kill the One-Eyed Man*, Provincetown Playhouse, 1965; *Marat/Sade*, Archie, *Armstrong's Last Goodnight*, Oriental manservant, *Candaules*, Commissioner, Vachel Lindsay, *So Proudly We Hail*, the Undertaker, *The Undertaker*, all at Theater Company of Boston, MA, 1966-67; Carl Balicke, *Drums in the Night*, Circle in the Square, NY, 1967; Blackface, *The Great White Hope*, Alvin, NY, 1968; Attendant (God), *Steambath*, Truck and Warehouse, NY, 1970; Antony, *Antony and Cleopatra*, New York Shakespeare Festival, 1972; Mel Edison, *The Prisoner of Second Avenue*, Kurt, *The Dance of Death*, Beaumont, NY, 1974; Simon Able, *Sly Fox*, Broadhurst, NY, 1976.

HECTOR ELIZONDO

FILM DEBUT—*Valdez Is Coming*, United Artists, 1971. PRINCIPAL FILM APPEARANCES—*Born to Win*, United Artists, 1971; *The Taking of Pelham 1, 2, 3*, United Artists, 1974; *Report to the Commissioner*, United Artists, 1975; *Cuba*, United Artists, 1979; *Young Doctors in Love*, Twentieth Century-Fox, 1982; *Flamingo Kid*, Twentieth Century-Fox, 1984.

TELEVISION DEBUT—*The Wendie Barrie Show*, 1947. PRINCIPAL TELEVISION APPEARANCES—*Kojak; The Doctors; The Impatient Heart; Colombo; Baretta; Poppi* (series), 1976; *Freebie and the Bean*, 1980; *Casablanca*, 1983; Commissioner, ''Medal of Honor Rag,'' *American Playhouse*, PBS, 1983; *A.K.A. Pablo*, 1984. Movies: *Out of the Darkness*, CBS; *Death on a Day Pass*, CBS (upcoming).

PRINCIPAL TELEVISION WORK—Director, *A.K.A. Pablo*, 1984.

SIDELIGHTS: MEMBERSHIPS—American Buddhist Academy. FAVORITE ROLES—God, *Steambath;* Mel, *The Prisoner of Second Avenue;* Manservant, *Candaules.* RECREATIONS—Kendo, Zen Buddhism, chess, backpacking, classical guitar playing, cooking.

ADDRESS: AGENT—c/o Peter Kelley, William Morris Agency, 1350 Sixth Avenue, New York, NY 10019.

*   *   *

EMMONS, Beverly   1943-

PERSONAL: Born December 12, 1943; son of Howard W. (a scientist) and Dorothy (Allen) Emmons; married Peter Gombosi,

September 1, 1973 (divorced, 1978); married Peter Angelo Simon (a photographer), October 17, 1980; children: (second marriage) Annie Corinne. EDUCATION: Sarah Lawrence College, B.A., 1965; trained in design at Lester Polakov School of Theatrical Design with Tom Skelton.

VOCATION: Lighting designer.

CAREER: PRINCIPAL STAGE WORK—Lighting designer, Broadway: *Elephant Man; A Day in Hollywood/A Night in the Ukraine; All's Well That Ends Well.*

AWARDS: Antoinette Perry Award nomination, for *Elephant Man;* Obie Award, 1980; Bessie Award, 1984.

SIDELIGHTS: MEMBERSHIPS—United Scenic Artists (executive board).

ADDRESS: HOME—New York, NY. AGENT—c/o John Giroux, 575 Madison Avenue, New York, NY 10022.

*   *   *

ENGEL, Georgia   1948-

PERSONAL: Born Georgia Bright Engel, July 28, 1948, in Washington, DC; daughter of Benjamin Franklin and Ruth Caroline (Hendron)

GEORGIA ENGEL

Engel. EDUCATION: University of Hawaii, B.A., drama, 1969; graduate of the Academy of the Washington Ballet, Mary Day, director. RELIGION: Christian Scientist.

VOCATION: Actress and singer.

CAREER: PRINCIPAL STAGE APPEARANCES—*Lend an Ear,* Equity Library, NY, 1969; Minnie Fay, *Hello, Dolly!,* St. James, 1970; *House of Blue Leaves,* NY, 1971; *Tiptoes,* Goodspeed Opera House, East Haddam, CT, Brooklyn Academy of Music, 1978-79; *My One and Only,* St. James, NY, 1984-85.

PRINCIPAL TELEVISION APPEARANCES—Georgette, *Mary Tyler Moore Show,* CBS, 1972-77; Mitzi, *The Betty White Show,* CBS, 1977; *The Good Time Girls,* CBS, 1980; *Jennifer Slept Here,* CBS, 1983.

PRINCIPAL FILM APPEARANCES—*Taking Off,* Universal, 1971; *The Outside Man,* United Artists, 1973; voice of Love a Lot, *The Care Bears Movie,* 1985.

SIDELIGHTS: MEMBERSHIPS—Actors' Equity Association, Screen Actors Guild, American Federation of Television and Radio Artists.

ADDRESS: AGENT—Bauman & Hiller and Associates, 250 W. 57th Street, Suite 1201, New York, NY 10019.

*   *   *

ENGEL, Lehman   1910-85

PERSONAL: Born September 14, 1910 in Jackson MS; died 1985. EDUCATION: Attended Cincinnati Conservatory of Music, Cincinnati College of Music and the University of Cincinnati; Juilliard School of Music, graduate 1935.

VOCATION: Composer, conductor, and musical director.

CAREER: PRINCIPAL STAGE WORK—Conductor: *Li'l Abner; Shangri-La; Fanny; Wonderful Town; Gilbert & Sullivan Operettas; A Month of Sundays; Bless You All; The Liar; The Consul; Alive and Kicking; That's the Ticket; Macbeth; Bonanza Bound; Call Me Mister; Shadow Play; Der Jasager; Second Hurricane; The Little Dog Laughed; Johnny Johnston; Jamaica.*

PRINCIPAL STAGE WORK—Composer for Broadway productions: *Middle of the Night; The Ponder Heart; Julius Caesar; St. Joan; The Wisteria Trees; Signor Chicago; Uniform of Flesh; Golden Ladder; Anne of a Thousand Days; All the Way Home; The Temporary Island; Me and Molly; A Streetcar Named Desire; Yellow Jack; John Gabriel Borkman; Henry VIII; Thunder Rock; A Kiss for Cinderella; Heavenly Express; The Trojan Women; Trial of a Judge; Horse Play; The Emperor's New Clothes; Mme Capet; Midsummer Night's Dream; Comedy of Errors; Shoemakers Holiday; Robin Landing; A Hero Is Born; The Time of Your Life; Family Portrait.*

Composer and conductor: *Dear Judas; The Birds; Macbeth; Hamlet; Everywhere I Roam; Murder in the Cathedral; Within the Gates.*

Musical director: State Fair musicals, Dallas, TX, 1949-52; *Call Me Madame; The Student Prince; The Wizard of Oz; Carousel; A Tree*

Grows in Brooklyn; Miss Liberty; The Merry Widow; Song of Norway; I Married an Angel; Texas Lil' Darlin; Where's Charlie; Annie Get Your Gun; Desert Song; Roberta; Brigadoon; Maytime; High Button Shoes; Showboat; Chocolate Soldier; Pal Joey; Bittersweet; Look Ma, I'm Dancin'; Bloomer Girl; Rose Marie; Up in Central Park.

RECORDINGS: *Li'l Abner,* Victor; *Carousel,* Victor; *Fanny,* Victor; *Show Boat,* Victor; *Oh Kay,* Columbia; *The Prettiest Girl in the World,* Victor; *Our Common Heritage,* Decca; *The Pied Piper of Hamlin,* Columbia; *The Shoemaker and the Elves,* Columbia; *Barry Wood,* Brunswick; *The Selfish Giant,* Decca; *Bach,* Gamut; *Macbeth,* RCA/Victor; *The Madrigal Singers,* Columbia; *Bing Crosby,* Decca; *Bayou Ballads,* Decca; *Goldilocks,* Columbia; *Rose Marie,* RCA/Victor; *Song Album,* RCA/Victor; *The Chocolate Soldier,* RCA/Victor; *Brigadoon,* Columbia; *Desert Song,* RCA/Victor; three albums with Jeanette MacDonald and Nelson Eddy, RCA/Victor.

PRINCIPAL FILM WORK—*Roogie's Bump,* Republic; *Honduras,* Willard Pictures; *Strategic Attack,* RKO Pathe; *National Defense,* RKO Pathe; *Berlin Powder Keg,* RKO Pathe; for the U.S. Navy during World War Two composed and conducted music for: *The Seventh Fleet, Report to Judy, The Fleet That Came to Stay, Fury in the Pacific, Well Done; Strange Victory,* Target Films; *The Hedgerow Story,* U.S. Department of State.

PRINCIPAL TELEVISION WORK—Composer and conductor: *Taming of the Shrew,* NBC, 1956; "Macbeth," *Hallmark Hall of Fame; The Soul of the Great Bell,* NBC; *The Beggars Opera,* Columbia Workshop; *The Mikado,* Ford Foundation, CBS.

PRINCIPAL RADIO WORK—Composer and conductor: *Hear It Now,* CBS; *The Creation,* CBS; *American Portrait,* CBS; *Brahm's Requiem,* NBC; *This Is War,* Columbia Workshop, all networks; *Michael and Kitty,* Canada Dry; *Gene Autry Program,* CBS; *Texaco,* CBS; *The Beggar's Opera,* CBS; *The Chaplet,* CBS; *Second Hurricane,* CBS; *Madrigal Singers,* all networks.

WRITINGS: BOOKS, PUBLISHED—*Musical Shows: Planning and Producing,* Crown, 1957; *Music for the Classical Tragedy,* Harold Hammer; *Renaissance to Baroque,* Harold Hammer, five volumes; *Folk Songs,* Harold Hammer; *Poor Wayfaring Stranger,* Mercury Music; *Folk Songs,* Theodore Presser. ARTICLES—In *New York Times, New York Times Magazine, New York Herald Tribune, Theatre Arts, Woman's Home Companion, Chicago Tribune, Musical America, Musical Leader, Modern Musical, Dance Observer, Dallas Morning News.*

AWARDS: Honorary Doctor of Music, Bogoslawaki College of Music, Chicago, IL, 1944; Antoinette Perry Awards, Conducting, 1950, for *The Consul,* 1953, for *Wonderful Town,* and for *Gilbert & Sullivan Operettas.*

SIDELIGHTS: MEMBERSHIPS—Arrow Music Press, Inc. (former president); Concert Artists Guild, Inc. (former president).*

*   *   *

ENO, Terry   1948-

PERSONAL: Full name Terry Ross Eno; born June 5, 1948, in Miami, FL; son of Leonard (an airline pilot and architect) and Geraldine Alice (Haddix) Eno. EDUCATION—Attended Dade Junior

TERRY ENO

College and University of Miami, FL; studied acting with Herbert Berghof at Herbert Berghof Studios, NY.

VOCATION: Actor and singer.

CAREER: NEW YORK DEBUT—Absalon, *Canterbury Tales,* Eugene O'Neill, 1969. PRINCIPAL STAGE APPEARANCES—Paris, *Romeo & Juliet, West Side Story, Once Upon a Mattress,* all at Bucks County Playhouse, PA, 1972; singer-dancer, *Irene,* Minskoff, 1973; Windy, *Good News,* St. James, 1974; Potiphar, *Joseph & His Amazing Technicolored Dreamcoat,* Brooklyn Academy of Music, 1978; Bill Calhoun, *Kiss Me Kate,* Wolftrap, VA, 1981; Rooster, *Annie,* Pedro, *Man of La Mancha,* both at Kansas City Starlight, 1982; Riff, *West Side Story,* State Opera of West Germany, Hamburg, soloist, *The Leonard Bernstein Tribute,* Berlin Philharmonic Orchestra, *Das Kleine Mahagonny,* Hamburg Opera of West Germany, all 1979-82; Will Parker, *Oklahoma!,* St. Louis Municipal Opera; Walt, *George M!,* Gubber-Grose Tour Co.; Kenneth, *Call Me Madam,* Coconut Grove Playhouse; Somerset Maugham, *Tallulah,* A.M.D.A.; B. Thomas, *Just Looking,* 21st Street Playhouse, NY; Ken, *Buy Bonds Buster,* Theater de Lys, NY; Brian, *Sing Melancholy Baby;* Jonathan, *Oh Dad, Poor Dad. . .;* Peter, *Forty Carats.*

MAJOR TOURS—Phil Dolan II, *On Your Toes,* National Company, 1984.

FILM DEBUT—Blondell's Son, *Angel Baby,* United Artists, 1958. PRINCIPAL FILM APPEARANCES—Tommy, *Sting of Death,* Allied Artists, 1965; Lifeguard Bill, *Annie,* Columbia, 1982.

TELEVISION DEBUT—Billy, *Everglades,* 1964. PRINCIPAL TELE-

VISION APPEARANCES—*Ed Sullivan Show,* CBS; *Those Comedy Years,* CBS; Bobby and Smitty, *Flipper;* principal, *Special Delivery;* Sergeant Seaview, *All My Children,* 1984.

SIDELIGHTS: MEMBERSHIPS—Actors' Equity Association, Screen Actors Guild, American Federation of Radio and Television Artists, Florida Frogmen's Club.

Eno told *CTFT:* "I started in the theatre with dance, under doctors suggestion to help develop an arch in my left foot. At age seven, I was dancing semi-professionally. My most prominent hobbies are scuba and skin diving and my pet parrots, Herk and Margaret."

ADDRESS: AGENT—Honey Sanders Agency, 229 W. 42nd Street, New York, NY 10036.

*   *   *

ENRIQUEZ, Rene

PERSONAL: Son of Andres (a businessman and politician) and Rosa Emilia (Castillo) Enriquez. EDUCATION: Attended Colegio Centro America, Granada, Nicaragua; City College of San Francisco and San Francisco State Univesity; trained for the stage at the American Academy of Dramatic Art. RELIGION: Roman Catholic. MILITARY: U.S. Air Force, 1955.

VOCATION: Actor and director.

CAREER: TELEVISION DEBUT—*The Defenders.* PRINCIPAL TELEVISION APPEARANCES—*Nurses;* Lt. Ray Calletano, *Hill Street Blues,* NBC, 1980-present; *Imagen.* Movie: Archbishop Romero, *Choices of the Heart* (aka *In December the Roses Will Bloom Again*), NBC, 1983.

FILM DEBUT—*Girl in the Night,* Warner Brothers, 1960. PRINCIPAL FILM APPEARANCES—Colonel Diaz, *Bananas,* United Artists, 1970; Jesus, *Harry and Tonto,* Twentieth Century-Fox, 1974; Somoza, *Under Fire,* Orion, 1983; *The Evil That Men Do,* 1984.

STAGE DEBUT—Mr. A. Ratt, *Camino Real,* Circle in the Square, NY, 1960, 35 performances. PRINCIPAL STAGE APPEARANCES—*Marco Millions,* Lincoln Center Repertory, NY, 1963; *Diamond Orchid,* Henry Miller, NY, 1964; *Truck Load,* NY, 1975.

MAJOR TOURS—*The New Mount Olive Motel,* Westport, Ivoryton, Corning, 1973.

AWARDS: Lulac Theatre Award; Golden Eagle Award; Emmy Award nomination, 1985, for *Imagen.*

SIDELIGHTS: MEMBERSHIPS—Screen Actors Guild (national board of directors, 1984-present), Actors' Equity Association, American Federation of Television and Radio Artists, National Hispanic Arts Endowment (founder and president).

ADDRESS: HOME—Hollywood, CA. AGENT—Henri Bollinger and Associates, 9200 Sunset Blvd., Los Angeles, CA 90069; Sam Gores, 12750 Ventura Blvd., Studio City, CA 91604.

ERICKSON, Mitchell   1927-

PERSONAL: Born June 28, 1927, in Duluth, MN; son of Oscar and May Erickson. EDUCATION: University of Hawaii, B.A., 1948; studied with Uta Hagen at the Herbert Berghof Studio.

VOCATION: Production stage manager, director, and actor.

CAREER: DEBUT—Walk-on, *The Great Waltz,* Philharmonic, Los Angeles. NEW YORK DEBUT—Guard, *Protective Custody,* Ambassador.

PRINCIPAL THEATRE WORK—Production stage manager, Broadway: *Charlotte; Every Good Boy Deserves Favor; Touch of the Poet; The Innocents; Private Lives; Jumpers; Tricks; Vivat, Vivat Regina; The Philanthropist; Child's Play; Play It Again, Sam; Rockefeller and the Red Indians; Rosencrantz and Guildenstern Are Dead; The Astrakhan Coat; Loves of Cass McGuire; Philadelphia, Here I Come; Inadmissible Evidence; Arturo Ui; Luther; Lady of the Camellias; Natural Affection; The Affair; The Best Man; Protective Custody; Lunch Hour; Medea; You Can't Take It with You; Ghosts; Ian McKellan Acting Shakespeare; Pack of Lies.*

Director: *The Best Man; Child's Play; Inadmissible Evidence; Luther; A Streetcar Named Desire.*

MAJOR TOURS—And Kennedy Center productions, as production stage manager: *Home and Beauty; The Last of Mrs. Chaney; Players; Desire Under the Elms; Bed Before Yesterday; Travesties; Souvenir; Texas Trilogy; Present Laughter; The Master Builder; The Day After the Fair; Constant Wife; The Enchanted; Hot September; Sarah in America; Physicists; Toyer.*

ADDRESS: HOME—161 Prince Street, New York, NY 10012.

*   *   *

ESTEVEZ, Emilio

BRIEF ENTRY: Born in New York City; son of Martin (an actor) and Janet Sheen. Actor. Estevez grew up in Los Angeles and attended Santa Monica High School. While in high school he wrote and starred in a play about Vietnam veterans, *Echoes of an Era.* He also acted in a short anti-nuclear film, *Meet Mr. Bomb.* After high school, at age 18, he began acting professionally in *Seventeen Going on Nowhere,* an afternoon television special for teenagers. His other television performances include *Insight,* a program produced by the Paulists (a Catholic order), and *In the Custody of Strangers,* ABC, 1982, with his father, Martin Sheen. On stage Estevez appeared with his father in *Mister Roberts* at Burt Reynold's Theatre.

In Estevez' first feature film, *Tex,* Buena Vista, 1982, he portrayed Johnny Collins. In his next film, *The Outsiders,* Warner Brothers/Zoetrope Studios, 1983, Estevez played Two-Bit Matthews. *Tex* and *The Outsiders* were both based on popular novels by S.E. Hinton. Estevez also acted in a film called *Nightmares* and in 1984's *Repo Man* he played the young punk, Otto. He then played the high school jock, Andrew, in the ensemble cast of *The Breakfast Club,* Columbia, 1985. Next, in *St. Elmo's Fire,* Columbia, 1985, he again co-starred with an ensemble cast. Estevez' first screenplay was an adaptation of S.E. Hinton's novel *That Was Then, This Is Now,* and Estevez stars in the movie, to be released in the fall of 1985.*

F

FAIRCHILD, Morgan

PERSONAL: Born in Dallas, TX.

VOCATION: Actress.

CAREER: TELEVISION DEBUT—*Search for Tomorrow.* PRINCI-
PAL TELEVISION APPEARANCES—Series: *Barnaby Jones; Happy
Days; The Bob Newhart Show; A Man Called Sloane; Police
Woman; Switch; Mork & Mindy; Kojak; Big Shamus, Little Shamus;
Dallas,* Constance Weldon Carlyle, *Flamingo Road; Paper Dolls.*
Movies—*The Memory of Eva Ryker; The Initiation of Sara; Murder
in Music City; Concrete Cowboys; The Dream Merchants; The Zany
Adventures of Robin Hood; Time Bomb.**

*   *   *

FAIX, Anna 1930-

PERSONAL: Born March 23, 1930, in Summit, NJ; daughter of
Frederick (a sheet metal worker) and Anna E. (a bookkeeper and
piano teacher; maiden name, Repasky) Faix. EDUCATION: Trained
for the dance with Madame E. Anderson-Ivantzova, Don Farns-
worth, Aubrey Hitchins, Edward Caton, Peter Gennaro, and Jack
Stanley.

VOCATION: Choreographer and dancer.

CAREER: STAGE DEBUT—Dancer, *Rockettes,* Radio City Music
Hall. NEW YORK DEBUT—Dancer and singer, *Can-Can,* Theater in
the Park, 1959, 14 performances. PRINCIPAL STAGE APPEAR-
ANCES—Electra, *Gypsy,* Canal Fulton Summer Arena, Canal
Fulton, OH, 1973; Tillie, *Redhead,* Nellie, *George M!,* Melba, *Pal
Joey,* all at Gretna Playhouse, Mt. Gretna, PA.

PRINCIPAL STAGE WORK—Choreographer: *Camelot, Promises
Promises, Gypsy,* all at Canal Fulton Summer Arena, Canal Fulton,
OH, 1973; *Once Upon a Mattress,* Country Dinner Theater, Dallas,
TX; *The King and I, Oklahoma!,* both at Playhouse on the Mall,
Paramus, NJ; *George M!, Redhead, On a Clear Day You Can See
Forever, Sweet Charity, Pal Joey, A Funny Thing Happened on the
Way to the Forum,* all at Gretna Playhouse, Mt. Gretna, PA; *Mary
Poppins,* Yates Children's Theatre, Playhouse on the Mall, Paramus,
NJ; *My Fair Lady,* Lake Whalom Playhouse, Fitchburg, MA;
Can-Can, at Ephrata Star Playhouse, Ephrata, PA, Central Park
Theatre, NY, Herb Rogers Music Theatre, Highland Park, IL,
Kansas City Starlight Theater, KS.

ANNA FAIX

MAJOR TOURS—Associate choreographer: *Camelot, My Fair Lady,
How to Succeed,* Rowena Steven Packages; *Once Upon a Mattress,
Can-Can,* U.S. cities.

TELEVISION DEBUT—Dancer, "The Three Hearts," *Bonnie Maid
Versatile Varieties,* NBC, 1949. PRINCIPAL TELEVISION APPEAR-
ANCES—Dancer, *Ed Sullivan Show,* CBS; solo dancer, *Bowery
Music Hall,* WOR, NY.

PRINCIPAL TELEVISION WORK—Choreographer: *Ed Sullivan Show.*

RELATED CAREER—Dance teacher and coach, NY, 1970-81.

SIDELIGHTS: MEMBERSHIPS—Society of Stage Directors and
Choreographers, Actors' Equity Association, Screen Actors Guild.

ADDRESS: HOME—1944 Axton Avenue, Union, NJ 07083.

FARENTINO, James   1938-

PERSONAL: Born James Ferrantino, February 24, 1938, in Brooklyn, NY; son of Anthony and Helen (Enrico) Ferrantino; married Michele Lee Dusick (an actress), February 20, 1966 (divorced); married Deborah Mullowney, June, 1985; children: (first marriage) David Michael. EDUCATION: Trained for the stage at the American Academy of Dramatic Arts.

VOCATION: Actor.

CAREER: PRINCIPAL TELEVISION APPEARANCES—*Death of a Salesman*, 1966; *Vanished*, 1971. Series: *The Bold Ones*, 1970-72; *John Dos Passos: U.S.A.*, 1971; *Cool Million*, 1972; *Dynasty*, 1982-83; *Blue Thunder*, 1984. Movies: *The Elevator*, 1974; *Police Story*, 1974, 1975; *Crossfire*, 1975; *Emily, Emily*, 1977; *Jesus of Nazareth*, 1977; *Eva Peron*, 1981; *The Possessed*, 1978. Miniseries: *Sins*, CBS, 1985-86. Episodic: *Naked City; Laredo; Route 66; The Alfred Hitchcock Hour; Ben Casey; Twelve O'Clock High.*

PRINCIPAL FILM APPEARANCES—*Psychomania*, 1962; *The War Lord*, 1964; *Banning*, 1965; *Ride to Hangman's Tree*, 1965; *The Pad*, 1966; *Rosie*, 1966; *Me Natalie*, 1968; *Story of a Woman*, 1968; *The Final Countdown*, 1980; *Dead and Buried*, 1982.

PRINCIPAL STAGE APPEARANCES—Pedro, *The Night of the Iguana*, Royale, NY, 1961; *The Days and Nights of BeeBee Fenstermaker*, Sheridan Square Playhouse, NY, 1963; Mr. Solares, *In the Summerhouse*, Little Fox, NY, 1964; *One Flew Over the Cuckoo's Nest*, Chicago, IL, 1973; Stanley Kowalski, *A Streetcar Named Desire*, Vivian Beaumont, NY, 1973; *The Best Man*, Chicago, IL, 1974; Biff, *Death of a Salesman*, Circle in the Square, NY, 1975; *The Big Knife*, Chicago, IL, 1976.

MAJOR TOURS—*California Suite*, U.S. cities, 1978.

AWARDS: Golden Globe Award, Most Promising Newcomer, 1966; Best Actor Award, Chicago, 1973; Theater World Award, 1973; Charles MacArthur Award, Chicago Drama League, 1974.

ADDRESS: AGENT—William Morris Agency, 151 El Camino Blvd., Beverly Hills, CA 90212.*

*   *   *

FARWELL, Jonathan   1932-

PERSONAL: Full name Jonathan Kirkpatrick Farwell; born January 9, 1932, in Lansing, MI; son of Arthur George (a composer) and Gertrude Everts (an actress; maiden name, Brice) Farwell; married Joerle Anne Gaines (an actress; professional name Jo Farwell) July 23, 1955 (separated, 1977); children: Alison Beatrice, Elisabeth Evelyn. EDUCATION: Ithaca College, NY, B.F.A., 1958; Yale School of Drama, 1958-59; studied for the theatre at the Tamara Daykarhanova School for the Stage in New York City, 1959-61. MILITARY: U.S. Air Force, 1951-55 (staff sergeant).

VOCATION: Actor.

CAREER: STAGE DEBUT—Shepherd Boy, *Christmas Pageant*, People's Church, Lansing, MI, 1936. NEW YORK DEBUT—Demetrius, *A Midsummer Night's Dream*, New York Shakespeare

JONATHAN FARWELL

Festival, 1961, for twenty-one performances. PRINCIPAL STAGE APPEARANCES—Petruchio, *The Taming of the Shrew*, Arena Stage, Washington, DC, among roles during two years residence with the company, 1963-64; Jack Worthing, *The Importance of Being Earnest*, Seattle Repertory, among roles during four years' residence with the company, 1965-69; Holmes, *Sherlock Holmes* and Chief Bromden, *One Flew Over the Cuckoo's Nest*, Cleveland Playhouse, among roles during five years' residence with the company, 1972-77; standby Wagner, Carson, *Night and Day*, NY, 1979; standby Carl, Thor, David, *Mornings at Seven*, NY, 1980; Von Strack and understudy Salieri, *Amadeus*, NY, 1983; Kralahome, *The King and I*, NY, 1985.

Also played the following roles: Strider, *Strider;* Doc, *Come Back Little Sheba;* Sandor Turai, *The Play's the Thing;* Judge Brack, *Hedda Gabler;* Doc, *Mr. Roberts;* Harry Brock, *Born Yesterday;* Reg, *Norman Conquests;* Count Dracula, *Dracula;* Macbeth, *Macbeth;* John Proctor, *The Crucible;* Mack the Knife, *The Threepenny Opera;* El Gallo, *The Fantasticks;* Charles Condomine, *Blithe Spirit;* Bolingbroke, *Richard II;* at such theatres as Missouri Repertory; Goodman, Chicago; Alley, Houston; Cincinnati Playhouse; Association of Producing Artists; Ahmanson and Mark Taper Forum, L.A. Music Center, Los Angeles; Kennedy Center, Washington, DC; among others.

MAJOR TOURS—Salieri, *Amadeus*, Bus and Truck, 1983-84.

TELEVISION DEBUT—Marine guard, *U.S. Steel Hour*, 1959. TELEVISION APPEARANCES—Judge Marvin Martel, *All My Children*, ABC, 1985; recurring roles on the following soaps: *Search for Tomorrow*, NBC; *The Guiding Light*, CBS; *The Edge of Night; The Doctors; Love of Life;* also appeared on: *The Rogues*, NBC, 1964-65; *Medical Center*, CBS; *Name of the Game*, NBC; *The Duke.*

RELATED CAREER—Directed and taught acting at the University of

North Carolina, Chapel Hill in the M.F.A. program, 1977-78.

RECORDINGS: Talking Books, for Library of Congress through the American Foundation for the Blind.

SIDELIGHTS: RECREATION—Classical piano, real-estate investment; speaks French fairly fluently. FAVORITE ROLES—Chief Bromden in *One Flew Over the Cuckoo's Nest,* Salieri in *Amadeus,* title character in *Sherlock Holmes,* and the title role in *Strider.*

Farwell told *CTFT:* "My actress mother stimulated my interest in theatre in childhood. Acting is an emotional, mental, spiritual sharing with the audience . . . this is most important to me."

ADDRESS: HOME—Long Island City, NY. OFFICE—12-09 Jackson Avenue, Long Island City, NY 11101. AGENT—Richard Astor Agency, 1697 Broadway, Room 504, New York, NY 10019.

*   *   *

FEAST, Michael   1946-

PERSONAL: Born November 25, 1946, in Brighton, England; son of Edward Albert and May Feast; married Kathleen Margaret Merrigan (divorced). EDUCATION: Trained for the stage at the Central School of Speech and Drama.

VOCATION: Actor.

MICHAEL FEAST

CAREER: STAGE DEBUT—Pope, *Galileo,* Phoenix, Leicester, UK, 1968. LONDON DEBUT—Woof, *Hair,* Shaftesbury, 1968. PRINCIPAL STAGE APPEARANCES—Ariel, *The Tempest,* 69 Theatre Company, Manchester, 1969, Nicely-Nicely Johnson, *Guys and Dolls,* '69 Theater Company, Manchester, 1972; *My Sister and I, Skipper, Asides, The Carnation Gang,* 1973-74; *Heads, The Education of Skinny Spew,* both Green Banana Room; *Elizabeth I,* Theatre Upstairs; Harold, *Clever Soldiers,* Hampstead, 1974. At the National Theater, Old Vic (unless otherwise stated): Ariel, *The Tempest,* 1974; Foster, *No Man's Land* (also Wyndham's), 1975; *The Man Himself,* ICA and Young Vic Studio; Raymond, *Watch It Come Down,* 1976. Mercutio, *Romeo and Juliet,* Shaw, London, 1976; Nick, *What the Butler Saw,* Henry, *Skin of Our Teeth,* Teleyeghin, *Uncle Vanya,* Roland Maule, *Present Laughter,* all at Royal Exchange, Manchester, 1976-77; Dave, *On the Out,* Bush and UK tour, 1978; Bobby, *American Buffalo,* National, Cottlesloe, London, 1978; Renfield, *Passion of Dracula,* Queen's, London, 1978; Mayhew, *Dispatches,* Cottesloe, London, 1979; Bernie, *Sexual Perversity in Chicago,* London, 1984; Billy, *Carousel,* Royal Exchange, Manchester, 1984; Peter Verkhovensky, *The Possessed,* Almeida, London, 1985.

PRINCIPAL FILM APPEARANCES—*I Start Counting; Brother Sun, Sister Moon,* Paramount, 1973; *McVicar,* 1980.

PRINCIPAL TELEVISION APPEARANCES—*The Lady from the Sea; Censored Scenes from King Kong; The Chelsea Murders;* Art Markham, *Studio,* Granada, 1983-84.

WRITINGS: PLAYS—*All the Way.*

ADDRESS: AGENT—Kate Feast Management, 43A Princess Road, London NW1, England.

*   *   *

FERRER, Jose   1912-

PERSONAL: Born January 8, 1912, in Santurce, Puerto Rico; son of Rafael and Maria (Cintron) Ferrer; married Uta Hagen, December 8, 1938 (divorced, 1948); married Phyllis Hill, June 19, 1948 (divorced, 1953); married Rosemary Clooney, July 13, 1953 (divorced, 1967); married Stella Magee; children: (first marriage) Leticia Thyra; (third marriage) Miguel, Maria, Gabriel, Monsita, Rafael Francisco. EDUCATION: Attended New York University and Princeton.

VOCATION: Actor, producer, and director.

CAREER: STAGE DEBUT—Showboat performance, Long Island, NY, 1934. NEW YORK DEBUT—Second policeman, *A Slight Case of Murder,* 48th Street Theater, 1935. PRINCIPAL STAGE APPEARANCES—Summer theatre, Suffern, NY, 1935; *Caesar and Cleopatra,* Suffern, NY, 1936; Lippincot, *Spring Dance,* Empire, NY, 1936; Dan Crawford, *Brother Rat,* Biltmore, NY, 1936; Frederick Parsons, *In Clover,* Vanderbilt, NY, 1937; Vergez, *How to Get Tough About It,* Martin Beck, NY, 1938; Billy Gashade, *Missouri Legend,* Empire, NY, 1938; Mr. Wentworth, *Mamba's Daughters,* NY, 1939; Victor d'Alcala, *Key Largo,* Ethel Barrymore Theater, NY, 1939; Lord Fancourt Babberley, *Charley's Aunt,* Cort, NY, 1940.

George Roberts, *Vickie,* Plymouth, NY, 1942; Jerry Walker, *Let's*

Face It, Imperial, NY, 1943; Iago, *Othello,* Shubert, NY, 1943; Cyrano, *Cyrano de Bergerac,* Alvin, NY, 1946; *Design for Living, Goodbye Again,* both at summer theaters, 1947; Volpone, *Volpone,* Mr. Manningham, *Angel Street,* Jeremy and Face, *The Alchemist,* Fat Joe, *The Long Voyage Home,* Yellow Commander, *The Insect Comedy,* all City Center, NY, 1948; Oliver Erwenter, *The Silver Whistle,* Biltmore, NY, 1948; Oscar Jaffe, *Twentieth Century,* ANTA, NY, 1950; Jim Downes, *The Shrike,* Cort, NY, 1952; Cyrano, *Cyrano de Bergerac,* Jim Downes, *The Shrike,* both City Center, NY, 1953-54; Richard, *Richard III,* Lord Fancourt Babberley, *Charley's Aunt,* City Center, NY; Edwin, *Edwin Booth,* 46th Street Theater, NY, 1958; Grand Duke Charles, *The Girl Who Came to Supper,* Broadway, NY, 1963; *Marc Blitzstein Memorial Concert,* Philharmonic Hall, NY, 1964; Dr. Coppelius, *Coppelia,* Royal Poinciana Playhouse, Palm Beach, FL, 1965; *Little Me,* Mineola Playhouse, Long Island, NY, 1965.

Oedipus, *Oedipus Rex,* Salt Lake City, UT, 1966; Don Quixote, *Man of La Mancha,* ANTA, Washington Square, NY, 1966; *You Know I Can't Hear You When the Water's Running,* Coconut Grove Playhouse, Miami, 1968; *The Sunshine Boys,* Geary, San Francisco, CA, 1974; *Gala Tribute to Joshua Logan,* Imperial, NY, 1975; Doctor, *Medal of Honour Rag,* Chichester Festival, UK, 1975; *The Interview,* Pittsburgh Playhouse, PA, 1976; *Long Day's Journey into Night,* Shubert, Boston, MA, 1977; Robert, *A Life in the Theatre,* Harry, *White Pelicans,* both Theater de Lys, NY, 1978; *Home and Beauty,* Eisenhower, Kennedy Center, Washington, DC, 1979; *Paint Your Wagon,* Heinz Hall, Pittsburgh, PA, 1980; *The Dresser,* Coconut Grove Playhouse, FL, 1982; *Life with Father,* Coconut Grove Playhouse, FL, 1983.

JOSE FERRER

MAJOR TOURS—*A Slight Case of Murder,* 1935; *Boy Meets Girl,* 1935; Iago, *Othello,* 1944-45; Sandor, *The Play's the Thing,* Cyrano, *Cyrano de Bergerac,* Richard, *Richard III,* Rajah of Rukh, *The Green Goddess,* all 1946; *Around the World in Eighty Days,* 1965; Don Quixote, *Man of La Mancha,* 1966-67; *A Song for Cyrano,* 1973; Doctor, *Medal of Honor Rag,* 1976.

PRINCIPAL STAGE WORK—Director: *Strange Fruit,* Royale, NY, 1945; *Twentieth Century,* ANTA Playhouse, then Fulton, NY, 1951; *Stalag 17,* 48th Street Playhouse, NY, 1951; *The Fourposter,* Ethel Barrymore, NY, 1951; *The Shrike,* Cort, NY, 1952; *The Chase,* Playhouse, NY, 1952; *My Three Angels,* Morosco, NY, 1953; *Cyrano de Bergerac,* City Center, NY, 1953-54; *Charley's Aunt,* City Center, NY, 1954; *Oh, Captain!,* Alvin, NY, 1958; *Edwin Booth,* 46th Street Theater, NY, 1958; *Juno,* Winter Garden, NY, 1959; *The Andersonville Trial,* Henry Miller's, NY, 1960; *Gianni Schichi,* Sante Fe, NM, 1960; *You Know I Can't Hear You When the Water's Running,* New London, 1968; *The Web and the Rock,* Theatre de Lys, NY, 1972.

A Yard of Sun, Cleveland Playhouse, OH, 1972; *Cyrano de Bergerac,* Chichester Festival, UK, 1975; *Carmelina,* St. James, NY, 1979; *The Interview,* Pittsburgh Playhouse, PA, 1976; *The Living Room,* Herbert Berghof Studio, NY, 1978; *Lewlulu,* Herbert Berghof Studio, NY, 1978; *Home and Beauty,* Eisenhower, Kennedy Center, Washington, DC, 1979; *A Conflict of Interest,* PAF Theater, Huntington, NY, Stamford, CT, 1979; *Off Broadway,* Whole Theater, Montclair, NJ, 1982; *A Destiny with Half Moon, Light Up the Sky, Dancing in the End Zone,* all Coconut Grove Playhouse, FL, 1983; *Glass Menagerie, Sleuth,* both Coconut Grove Playhouse, FL, 1984.

PRINCIPAL FILM APPEARANCES—*Cyrano de Bergerac,* 1950; *Moulin Rouge,* 1952; *The Caine Mutiny,* 1954; *The Shrike,* Universal, 1955; *Cockleshell Heroes,* Columbia, 1956; *I Accuse,* Metro-Goldwyn-Mayer, 1958; *Return to Peyton Place* (also directed), Twentieth Century-Fox, 1961; *Lawrence of Arabia,* Columbia, 1962; *The Greatest Story Ever Told,* United Artists, 1965; *Ship of Fools,* Columbia, 1965; *Cervantes,* 1966; *Enter Laughing,* Columbia, 1967; *Crash!,* 1977; *Forever Young, Forever Free,* 1977; *The Sentinel,* Universal, 1977; *The Swarm,* Warner Brothers, 1978; *The Fifth Musketeer,* 1979; *Fedora,* United Artists, 1979; *Natural Enemies,* Cinema Five, 1979; *The Big Brawl,* 1981; *Midsummer Night's Sex Comedy,* Warner Brothers, 1982; *And They're Off,* 1982; *The Evil That Men Do,* 1983; *To Be or Not to Be,* Twentieth Century-Fox, 1983; *Dune,* 1984.

PRINCIPAL TELEVISION APPEARANCES—Live: *What Makes Sammy Run; A Case of Libel.* Mini-series: *Rhinemann Exchange,* 1977; *French Atlantic Affair,* 1979; *George Washington,* 1984. Movies: *Marcus-Nelson Murders,* 1973; *The Missing Are Deadly,* 1974; *Art of Crime,* 1975; *Exo-Man,* 1977; *Gideon's Trumpet,* 1980; *This Girl for Hire,* 1983; *Samson and Delilah,* 1984. Numerous specials, documentaries, and guest appearances, including *Truman at Potsdam,* 1977; *Quincy,* 1982; *Newhart,* CBS; voice, *Wind in the Willows,* ABC, 1985.

RELATED CAREER—Artistic advisor, Coconut Grove Playhouse, FL, 1983-85.

WRITINGS: PLAYS, PRODUCED—*Oh, Captain!* (co-author), Alvin, NY, 1958.

AWARDS: American Academy and Institute of Arts and Letters Award, Good Speech in the American Theatre, 1949; Academy

Award, 1950, for *Cyrano de Bergerac; Academy of Arts and Sciences of Puerto Rico Award, 1974; Theatre Hall of Fame Award, 1981; National Medal of Arts Award, 1985.*

SIDELIGHTS: MEMBERSHIPS—Players Club (president, 1983-present).

ADDRESS: OFFICE—P.O. Box 616, Coconut Grove, FL 33133.

*   *   *

FIELDS, Judy
See BOHANNON, Judy

*   *   *

FISHER, Carrie Frances   1956-

PERSONAL: Born October 21, 1956; daughter of Eddie Fisher (a singer) and Debbie Reynolds (an actress, singer, and dancer); married Paul Simon (a singer and songwriter).

VOCATION: Actress.

CAREER: PRINCIPAL FILM APPEARANCES—*Shampoo,* Columbia, 1975; *Star Wars,* Twentieth Century-Fox, 1977; *Mr. Mike's Mondo Video,* 1979; *The Blues Brothers,* Universal, 1980; *The Empire Strikes Back,* Twentieth Century-Fox, 1980; *Under the Rainbow,* Warner Brothers, 1981; *Return of the Jedi,* Twentieth Century-Fox, 1983; *The Man with One Red Shoe,* Twentieth Century-Fox, 1985; *Hannah and Her Sisters,* Orion (upcoming).

PRINCIPAL TELEVISION APPEARANCES—Movies: *Come Back, Little Sheba,* 1977; *Leave Yesterday Behind,* 1978.

PRINCIPAL STAGE APPEARANCES—Chorus, *Irene,* Broadway production, 1972; Agnes, *Agnes of God,* Broadway production.*

*   *   *

FLATT, Ernest O.   1918-

PERSONAL: Full name Ernest Orville Flatt; born October 30, 1918, in Denver, CO; son of Ernest Scorrow (a carpenter) and Della May (Allen) Flatt. MILITARY: U.S. Army, 1941-46 (Tech 4 Sergeant).

VOCATION: Choreographer and director.

CAREER: STAGE DEBUT—Dancer, *Oklahoma!,* national company, Biltmore, Los Angeles, 1947. NEW YORK DEBUT—Choreographer, *Fade Out—Fade In,* Mark Hellinger, 1964. PRINCIPAL STAGE WORK—Choreographer: *Kiss Me, Kate,* Los Angeles Civic Light Opera (c. 1960); *It's a Bird! It's a Plane! It's Superman!,* Alvin, NY, 1966; *Lorelei,* Palace, NY, 1973.

Director, *Sugar Babies,* Mark Helinger, NY, 1979.

FILM DEBUT—Dancer, *An American in Paris,* Metro-Goldwyn-Mayer, 1951. PRINCIPAL FILM APPEARANCES—Dancer (and assistant to Gene Kelly), *Singin' in the Rain,* Metro-Goldwyn-Mayer, 1952.

PRINCIPAL FILM WORK—Choreographer, *Anything Goes,* Paramount, 1956.

TELEVISION DEBUT—Choreographer: *Your Hit Parade,* NBC, 1955-58. PRINCIPAL TELEVISION WORK—Choreograher: *The Garry Moore Show,* CBS, 1958-63; *Kiss Me, Kate,* NBC, 1960; *Julie and Carol at Carnegie Hall,* CBS, 1961; *Carol and Co.,* CBS, 1963; *Calamity Jane,* CBS, 1964; *Annie Get Your Gun,* NBC, 1967; *Damn Yankees,* NBC, 1968; *The Carol Burnett Show,* CBS, 1968-77; *Julie and Carol at Lincoln Center,* CBS, 1971.

Director: *Carol and Co.,* CBS, 1963; *Calamity Jane,* CBS, 1964.

Producer: *Julie and Carol at Carnegie Hall* (associate producer), CBS, 1961; *The Jimmy Dean Show,* CBS, 1970.

NIGHT CLUBS—Director and choreographer for a variety of performers including Juliet Prowse, Mitzi Gaynor, Bobby Vinton, and Dorothy Collins.

AWARDS: Christopher Award, *The Garry Moore Show;* Emmy Awards, 1961, for *Julie and Carol at Carnegie Hall,* 1971, for *The Carol Burnett Show;* Golden Rose Award, *Julie and Carol at Carnegie Hall,* 1961.

SIDELIGHTS: MEMBERSHIPS—Actors' Equity Association, American Federation of Television and Radio Artists, Screen Actors Guild, Society of Stage Directors and Choreographers, Directors Guild of America. RECREATION—Avocado cultivation.

ADDRESS: HOME—P.O. Box 8478, Palm Springs, CA 92263. OFFICE—c/o Becker & London, 30 Lincoln Plaza, New York, NY 10023.

*   *   *

FLETCHER, Louise   1936-

PERSONAL: Born 1936, in Birmingham, AL; daughter of Robert Capers Fletcher. EDUCATION: North Carolina State University, B.S., D.D.L.; trained for the stage with Jeff Corey.

VOCATION: Actress.

CAREER: PRINCIPAL FILM APPEARANCES—*Thieves Like Us,* 1974; *Russian Roulette,* 1975; *One Flew Over the Cuckoo's Nest,* 1975; *Exorcist II: The Heretic,* 1977; *Natural Enemies,* 1979; *The Lucky Star,* 1980; *Once Upon a Time in America,* 1982; *Brainstorm,* 1983; *Firestarter,* 1983; *Strange Invaders,* 1983.

PRINCIPAL TELEVISION APPEARANCES—*Maverick.*

AWARDS: Academy Award, Best Actress, 1975, for *One Flew Over the Cuckoo's Nest.*

FONDA, Peter   1940-

PERSONAL: Born February 23, 1940, in New York City; son of Henry Jaynes (an actor) and Frances Sophia (a financier; maiden name, Seymour) Fonda; married Susan Jane Brewer, October 8, 1961 (divorced 1973); married Portia Rebecca Crockett (a writer); children: Bridget, Justin, Thomas. EDUCATION: University of Omaha, 1957-60.

VOCATION: Actor, director, writer, and producer.

CAREER: STAGE DEBUT—Lead, *The Golden Fleece,* Omaha Community Playhouse, Omaha, NE, 1960. NEW YORK DEBUT—Private Oglethorpe, *Blood, Sweat & Stanley Poole,* Morosco, 1961. PRINCIPAL STAGE APPEARANCES—Lead, *Under the Yum Yum Tree,* Mineola Playhouse, NY, 1962, Louisville, KY, 1963.

FILM DEBUT—Dr. Mark Chesnick, *Tammy and the Doctor,* Universal, 1963. PRINCIPAL FILM APPEARANCES—*The Victors,* Columbia, 1963; *Lilith,* Columbia, 1964; *The Young Lovers,* Metro-Goldwyn-Mayer, 1964; *The Wild Angels,* American International, 1966; *Easy Rider,* Columbia, 1969; *The Hired Hand,* Universal, 1971; *Two People,* Universal, 1973; *Dirty Mary, Crazy Larry,* Twentieth Century-Fox, 1973; *Open Season,* 1974; *92 in the Shade,* United Artists, 1975; *Race with the Devil,* Twentieth Century-Fox, 1975; *Fighting Mad,* 1975; *Killer Force,* American International, 1975; *Futureworld,* American International, 1976; *Outlaw Blues,* Warner Brothers, 1977; *High-Ballin',* American International, 1978; *Wanda Nevada,* United Artists, 1979; *Split Image,* Orion, 1982; *Spasms,* 1983; *Dance of the Dwarfs,* 1983; *It's Alright My Friend,* 1983; *Reason to Live,* 1984; *Old Money,* 1985.

PRINCIPAL FILM WORK—Producer and director, *The Hired Hand,* Universal, 1971; director, *Idaho Transfer,* 1971; director, *Wanda Nevada,* United Artists, 1979; producer, *Old Money,* 1985.

TELEVISION DEBUT—*Naked City,* 1961. PRINCIPAL TELEVISION APPEARANCES—''Channing,'' *Alfred Hitchcock Hour; Wagon Train; 12 O'Clock High; The New Breed.*

WRITINGS: SCREENPLAYS—*Easy Rider,* Columbia, 1969; *The Hired Hand* (with Alan Sharp), Universal, 1971.

SIDELIGHTS: MEMBERSHIPS—Actors' Equity Association, Screen Actors Guild, Directors Guild of America, Writers Guild of America.

ADDRESS: HOME—Livingston, MT and Bel Air, CA. OFFICE—Pando Company, 9454 Wilshire Blvd., 4th Floor, Beverly Hills, CA 90212. AGENT—William Morris Agency, 151 El Camino Drive, Beverly Hills, CA 90212.

*   *   *

FONTANA, Tom   1951-

PERSONAL: Born September 12, 1951; son of Charles Louis (a crew coach) and Marie Angelica (a hospital unit coordinator; maiden name, Internicola) Fontana; married Sagan Lewis (an actress), December 18, 1982. EDUCATION: State University College, Buffalo, NY, B.A., speech and theatre arts.

VOCATION: Writer and producer.

CAREER: In addition to playwriting activities below, PRINCIPAL

TOM FONTANA

TELEVISION WORK—Writer and producer, *St. Elsewhere,* NBC, 1982-present; writer, *The Fourth Wiseman.*

WRITINGS: PLAYS, PRODUCED—*Johnny Appleseed: A Noh Play,* Studio Arena, Buffalo, NY, 1970; *This Is on Me,* American Contemporary Theatre, Buffalo, NY, 1971, Williamstown Theatre Festival, MA, 1979; *An Awfully Big Adventure,* Writers Theatre, NY, 1975; *One/Potato/More,* Direct Theatre, NY, 1975; *Nonsense!,* Writers Theatre, NY, 1977; *The Underlings,* Cincinnati Playhouse in the Park, 1978, Writers Theatre, NY, 1979, Williamstown Theatre Festival, 1980, Eisenhower College, Elmira, NY, 1981, Studio Arena, Buffalo, NY, 1982, Thomas More College, KY, 1983, Friends Theatre Company, NY, 1984.

The Overcoat, Williamstown Theatre Festival, MA, 1978, Writers Theatre, NY, 1981; *Old Fashioned,* Chelsea Theatre Center, NY, 1979, Colonnades Theatre Lab, NY, 1981, Linwood Summer Theatre, Linwood, NY, 1980; *The Spectre Bridegroom,* Williamstown Theatre Festival, MA, 1981; *Movin' Mountains,* McCarter, Princeton, NJ, 1981, Writers Theatre, NY, 1982; *Mime,* One Act Theatre, San Francisco, 1982, One Act Theatre, Los Angeles, 1983; *Imaginary Lovers,* American Conservatory Theatre, San Francisco, 1982, One Act Theatre, Los Angeles, 1983, Writers Theatre, NY, 1984.

RELATED CAREER—Playwright in residence, Writers Theatre, 1975-present, Williamstown Theatre Festival, 1979-81.

AWARDS: Emmy, National Academy of Television Arts and Sciences, Outstanding Writing in a Drama Series, 1983-84, for *St. Elsewhere;* three nominations, Humanitas.

SIDELIGHTS: MEMBERSHIPS—National Academy of Television Arts and Sciences, Dramatists Guild, Writers Guild of America,

Authors League of America, American Writers Theatre Foundation (board of directors), 1974-present.

ADDRESS: HOME—304 E. 52nd Street, Apt. 3, New York, NY 10022. OFFICE—MTM Enterprises, 4024 Radford Avenue, Studio City, CA 91604.

*   *   *

FOREMAN, Carl   1914-84

PERSONAL: Born July 23, 1914, in Chicago, IL; died June 26, 1984; son of Isidore and Fanny (Rozin) Foreman; married Estelle Barr (divorced); married Evelyn Smith; children: (first marriage) Carla; (second marriage) Jonathan, Amanda. EDUCATION: Attended University of Illinois, Northwestern University, John Marshall Law School.

VOCATION: Producer, director, and writer.

CAREER: PRINCIPAL FILM WORK—Writer, *Champion*, 1949; writer, *The Men*, 1950; writer, *Young Man with a Horn*, 1950; *Cyrano de Bergerac*, 1950; writer, *High Noon*, 1952; writer, *Bridge on the River Kwai*, 1957; writer and producer, *Guns of Navarone*, 1961; writer, producer, and director, *The Victors*, 1963; producer, *Born Free*, 1965; producer, *Monsieur Le Coq*, 1967; producer, *MacKenna's Gold*, 1969; producer, *The Virgin Soldiers*, 1969; writer and producer, *Young Winston*, 1972; writer, *When Time Ran Out*, 1976; producer and writer, *Force Ten from Navarone;* writer and producer, *The Yellow Jersey*, 1985.

PRINCIPAL TELEVISION WORK—Series: Executive producer, *Born Free*. Movie: Executive producer, *The Golden Gate Murders*.

RELATED CAREER—British Film Institute, board of governors, 1965-71; British National Film School, 1971-75.

AWARDS: Laurel Award, 1969; Best British Screenplay Award, 1971; Variety Club of London Award, Writer of the Year, 1972; Valentine Davies Award, 1977; Royal Order of the Phoenix, Greece; Most Excellent Order of the British Empire.

SIDELIGHTS: MEMBERSHIPS—Writers Guild of America, Writers Guild of Great Britain (president, 1968-76), Israel Screen Writers Guild (founder and president), Saville Club, Garrick Club.*

*   *   *

FORLOW, Ted   1931-

PERSONAL: Full name Clifford T. Forlow; born April 29, 1931, in Independence, MO; son of Clifford Elkington (an insurance representative) and Dorothy Lee (a court reporter; maiden name, Holt) Forlow; married Janet Marie McNearly (a dance teacher), December 29, 1956; children: Mark, Christina, Annette, Denise. EDUCATION: Empire State College, B.P.S., 1981; studied acting and directing with David LeGrant in New York. MILITARY: U.S. Navy, Petty Officer, 2nd Class.

VOCATION: Choreographer, director, actor, and producer.

TED FORLOW

CAREER: PRINCIPAL STAGE WORK—Director and Choreographer: *Sally, George & Martha*, Westchester-Rockland Regional Theatre; *Registered Letter, Hold on Hortense, Man of La Mancha*, 1972-80; *Godspell, Once Upon a Mattress, Carousel, Unsinkable Molly Brown*, Hamilton Theatre, Ontario, Canada, 1975-82; *Last of the Red Hot Lovers, A Funny Thing Happened on the Way to the Forum, The Odd Couple*, all Conway Playhouse, Conway, NH, 1975; *Boys from Syracuse*, University of Wisconsin, Madison Summer Shakespeare Festival, 1981; *Jesus Christ Superstar, Fiddler on the Roof, Sweet Charity, Man of La Mancha*, all Garden City Productions, St. Catherines, Ontario, 1981-83.

Producer, *A Doctor in Spite of Himself*, Masterworks Laboratory Theatre, NY.

PRINCIPAL STAGE APPEARANCES—Broadway productions: David, *Milk and Honey;* Barber, *Man of La Mancha*, 1980; Protean, *A Funny Thing Happened on the Way to the Forum;* Anselmo, *Man of La Mancha;* Bill Lynch, *Cry for Us All;* New Girl in Town; Beg, Borrow or Steal; Subways Are for Sleeping; Destry Rides Again; Wonderful Town, Can Can, Carnival,* last three at City Center, NY. Off Broadway and Regional: Guiseppi, *Man of Destiny*, Masterworks Lab, 1974; Baron, *Salon-Comedie*, Masterworks Lab, 1975; Alec, *The Cat and the Fiddler*, Riverside Church, 1976; Barney, *Does Anybody Here Do the Peabody?*, T. Schriber Theatre, 1976; Strindberg, *A Night at the Black Pig*, Lion Theatre Co., 1976; Dr. Lyman, *Bus Stop*, Westchester Regional, 1977; George, *Pahokee Beach*, St. Clement's, 1983; Silas Phelps, *Down River*, Musical Theatre, 1985. Also: *Hit the Deck*, Jones Beach; Noah, *110 in the Shade;* Harry, *Brigadoon;* Jerry Cohen, *George M!;* Frank, *Showboat;* Rocky, *Damn Yankees;* Floyd the cop, *Fiorello;* Charlie Cowell, *Music Man;* Dillon, *Around the World in Eighty Days;* Jailer, *Redhead;* Arthur, *Take Me Along*.

RELATED CAREER—Co-founder and director, Westchester-Rockland Regional Theatre; teaches acting, yoga, and dance.

ADDRESS: HOME—90 E. Townline Road, Nanuet, NY 10954. AGENT—Nani/Saperstein Management, 1697 Broadway, New York, NY 10019.

* * *

FORSTER, Robert 1941-

PERSONAL: Born Robert Wallace Foster, Jr., July 13, 1941, in Rochester, NY; son of Robert Wallace and Grace Dorothy (Montanarella) Foster; married Marlene, 1964 (divorced, 1965); married June, 1966 (divorced, 1974); married Zivia, 1978 (divorced 1980); children: (first marriage) Robert; (second marriage) Elizabeth, Kathryn, Maeghen. EDUCATION: Attended Heidelberg College, 1959, Alfred University, 1960-61; University of Rochester, B.A., 1963.

VOCATION: Actor.

CAREER: STAGE DEBUT—Buddy, *Come Blow Your Horn*, Rochester Community Theatre, 1963. NEW YORK DEBUT—Frankie, *Mrs. Dally Has a Lover*, Golden, 1965. PRINCIPAL STAGE APPEARANCES—Stanley, *Streetcar Named Desire*, Vivian Beaumont, 1973; *The Glass Menagerie; The Sea Horse; Twelve Angry Men; One Flew Over the Cuckoo's Nest*.

FILM DEBUT—Soldier, *Reflections in a Golden Eye*, Warner Brothers/Seven Arts, 1967. PRINCIPAL FILM APPEARANCES—*The Stalking Moon*, National General, 1969; *Medium Cool*, Paramount, 1969; *Justine*, Twentieth Century-Fox, 1969; *Run Shadow Run* (retitled *Cover Me Babe*), Twentieth Century-Fox, 1970; *Pieces of Dreams*, United Artists, 1970; *Journey Through Rosebud*, Cinerama, 1972; *The Don Is Dead*, Universal, 1973; *Stunts* (retitled *Who Is Killing the Stuntmen?*), 1977; *Avalanche*, 1978; *The Black Hole*, Buena Vista, 1979; *Crunch*, American International, 1980; *Alligator*, 1980; *Vigilante*, 1982; *Walking the Edge*, 1983.

TELEVISION DEBUT—*Banyon*, 1970-72. PRINCIPAL TELEVISION APPEARANCES—*Police Story; Royce; The Clone*. Movies: *Nakia*, 1974 (also the series); *Death Squad*, 1974; *The City*, 1977; *Standing Tall*, 1978.

SIDELIGHTS: MEMBERSHIPS—Actors' Equity Association, Screen Actors Guild.

ADDRESS: OFFICE—Charter Management, 9000 Sunset Blvd., Los Angeles, CA 90069.

* * *

FOSTER, Jodie 1962-

PERSONAL: Born November 19, 1962, in Los Angeles, CA; daughter of Evelyn Foster. EDUCATION: Yale University, B.A., literature.

VOCATION: Actress.

CAREER: TELEVISION DEBUT—*Mayberry R.F.D.* PRINCIPAL TELEVISION APPEARANCES—*The Courtship of Eddie's Father*, ABC; *My Three Sons*; the voice of Annie Chan, *Charlie Chan; Paper Moon. My Sister Hank; Sam; Daniel Boone; The Wonderful World of Disney; Adam 12; Julia; Gunsmoke; Love Story; Kung Fu; The Partridge Family; Bonanza; Ironside; ABC Afternoon Specials:* "Rookie of the Year" and "Alexander." Movies: *Smile Jenny, You're Dead*, 1974; *Svengali*, 1983.

PRINCIPAL FILM APPEARANCES—*Napolean and Samantha*, Buena Vista, 1972; *Menace on the Mountain*, Buena Vista; *One Little Indian*, Buena Vista, 1973; *Tom Sawyer*, United Artists, 1973; *Taxi Driver*, Columbia, 1976; *Bugsy Malone*, Paramount, 1976; *Echoes of a Summer*, Cine Artists, 1976; *Little Girl Who Lives Down the Lane*, American International, 1977; *Freaky Friday*, Buena Vista, 1977; *Il Casotto; Moi Fleur Bleue; Candleshoe*, Buena Vista, 1978; *Foxes*, United Artists, 1980; *Hotel New Hampshire*, Orion Pictures, 1984; *Blood of Others* (upcoming); *Mesmerized* (upcoming).

AWARDS: New York Film Critics, National Film Critics, Los Angeles Film Critics, British Academy Award nomination, Donatello Award, all for Best Supporting Actress, for *Taxi Driver*; Best Actress, British Academy Award and the Italian Situation Comedy Award, for *Bugsy Malone*; Emmy, for *ABC Afterschool Special*, "Rookie of the Year."

SIDELIGHTS: Foster was the original "Coppertone Girl."

She was the only entertainer picked to appear in the Time-Life/BBC documentary, *Americans*, for which she directed and wrote a short film entitled *Hands on Time*.*

* * *

FOX, Michael J.

BRIEF ENTRY: Reared in Vancouver, BC; son of Bill (retired from the Canadian Army) and Phyllis Fox. Fox's television work has included *Leo and Me*, Canadian Broadcasting Corp.; *Palmerstown, U.S.A.;* and he appears as Alex Keaton on the series *Family Ties*, NBC, 1982-present. He has also starred in a television movie, *Poison Ivy*, NBC, 1985. Fox's feature films include *Midnight Madness*, Buena Vista, 1980; Marty McFly in *Back to the Future*, Universal, 1985, and *Teen Wolf*, Atlantic, 1985.*

* * *

FOXX, Redd 1922-

PERSONAL: Born John Elroy Sanford, December 9, 1922, in St. Louis, MO; son of Fred (an electrician) and Mary Alma (a minister; maiden name, Hughes) Sanford; married Evelyn Killibrew (divorced, 1951); married Betty Jean Harris, 1956 (divorced, 1976); married Yunchi Chung, 1978; children: Debraca (stepdaughter). EDUCATION: Chicago Public Schools. RELIGION: Catholic.

VOCATION: Actor and comedian.

CAREER: STAGE DEBUT—Musician, *Bon Bons*, Chicago, 1939-41. PRINCIPAL STAGE WORK—As nightclub comedian, major U.S.

cities, including NY, Baltimore, San Francisco, Los Angeles, Las Vegas, Honolulu, Miami Beach, Chicago, others, 1941-present; teamed with Slappy White, 1947-51.

PRINCIPAL FILM APPEARANCES—*Cotton Comes to Harlem*, United Artists, 1970; *Norman . . . Is That You?*, United Artists, 1976.

PRINCIPAL TELEVISION APPEARANCES—Fred Sanford, *Sanford and Son*, NBC, 1972-77; Fred, *The Best of Sanford and Son*, NBC, 1976; *The Redd Foxx Comedy Hour*, ABC, 1977; Fred Sanford, *Sanford and Son*, NBC, 1980-81.

RECORDINGS: *Laff of the Party*, 1956; and over fifty others, principally for Loma Records, Dooto Records, and King Records, including: *On the Loose, Live—Las Vegas!*, *Bare Facts, Both Sides, Foxx-a-delic, In a Nutshell, Matinee Idol*, and *Pass the Apple, Eve*.

ADDRESS: OFFICE—933 La Brea Avenue, Los Angeles, CA 90038.

*   *   *

FRATTI, Mario   1927-

PERSONAL: Born July 5, 1927, in L'Aquila, Italy; came to the U.S., 1963, naturalized, 1974; son of Leone and Palmira (Silvi) Fratti; married Lina Fedrigo (divorced, 1963); married Laura Dubman (a pianist), September 22, 1964; children: (first marriage) Mirko, Barbara; (second marriage) Valentina. EDUCATION: University of California, Foscari, Ph.D., philology, 1951. MILITARY: Lieutenant, Italian Army, 1951-53. POLITICS: Democrat.

VOCATION: Playwright and educator.

MARIO FRATTI

CAREER: In addition to playwriting activities (see below): professor, Adelphi College, 1964-65, Columbia University, 1965-66, New School, 1965-66, Hunter College, 1967-present, Hofstra University, 1973-74; drama critic for "Paese," "Progresso," 1963-present, "Ridotto," 1963-present, "Ora Zero," 1963-present.

WRITINGS: PLAYS—*The Cage*, Milan, 1963; *The Academy; The Return*, Theatre de Lys, 1963; *Case-Suicide*, 1964; *Mafia*, 1971; *Races*, 1971; *Bridge*, 1971; *Eleven Plays in Spanish*, 1977; *The Refrigerators*, 1977; *Eleanor Duse*, 1982; *Nine*, 46th Street Theatre, 1982; *Birthday; The Third Daughter; Mothers and Daughters; Three Beds; The Young Wife; Six Passionate Women*.

AWARDS: O'Neill, Richard Rodgers, Outer Critics Circle, Drama Desk, Antoinette Perry, 1982, all for *Nine*.

SIDELIGHTS: MEMBERSHIPS—Dramatists Guild, Outer Critics Circle, Drama Desk, American Theatre Critics Association.

Fratti is the subject of Jane F. Bonin's book, *Mario Fratti*, Twayne's Series.

ADDRESS: OFFICE—Hunter College, 689 Park Avenue, Room 1312, New York, NY 10021. AGENT—Bruce Savan, Agency for the Performing Arts, 888 Seventh Avenue, New York, NY 10106.

*   *   *

FRAZER, Rupert   1947-

PERSONAL: Born March 12, 1947, in England; son of Simon Robert (an army officer) and Dawn (a sheep farmer; maiden name, Gwynne-Howell) Frazer; married Jane Cattermull (a television casting agent), March 20, 1975; children: Hugo, Liberty. EDUCATION: Attended Wellington College, Berkshire; trained for the stage at the Drama Centre in London.

VOCATION: Actor.

CAREER: STAGE DEBUT—Sebastian, *Twelfth Night*, Northcott Theater, Exeter, UK, 1970, 21 performances. LONDON DEBUT—Atahualpa, *The Royal Hunt of the Sun*, Round House, 1973, 20 performances. PRINCIPAL STAGE APPEARANCES—The Cook, *Mother Courage*, Montecelso, *The White Devil*, Madame, *The Maids*, Andrea, *Galileo*, all at Citizens Theater, Glasgow, Scotland, 1970-72; Ferdinand, *The Tempest*, National, Old Vic, London, 1974; Ferdinand, *The Duchess of Malfi*, Citizens, Glasgow, 1975; Jonathan Harker, *Dracula*, Shaftsbury, London, 1976; Horseman, *Equus*, Alberry, London, 1979; Hugo and Ferdinand, *Ring Around the Moon*, Royal Exchange, Manchester, 1981; Mirabel, *The Way of the World*, Greenwill Theater, Greenwill, UK, 1984.

MAJOR TOURS—Titus Andronicus, *Titus Andronicus*, Citizens Theater, Weisbaden, West Germany, 1970; Alcibiades, *Timon of Athens*, Citizens Theater, Dublin, 1971; Tamberlane, *Tamberlane*, Citizens Theater, Edinburgh Festival, 1972; Atahualpa, *Royal Hunt of the Sun*, Orsino, *Twelfth Night*, Prospect Theatre Company, Britain, Egypt, Cyprus, 1973; Achilles, *Der Musik*, Prospect Theatre Company, Britain, Egypt, Yugoslavia, Jordan, West Germany, 1977.

FILM DEBUT—Jack, *Hussey*, Don Boyd Productions, 1979. PRINCIPAL FILM APPEARANCES—Blondie, *The Eye of the Needle*,

RUPERT FRAZER

Kings Road Productions, 1980; Clive, *The Wars,* Canadian Production, 1981; Lt. Johnson, *Ghandi,* Indo-British Films, 1982; Wigran Battye, *Far Pavilion,* Goldcrest Films, 1983; Lionel Stevens, *The Shooting Party,* Geoff Reeves Film and Television Production, 1983.

TELEVISION DEBUT—Lord Mark, *The Wings of the Dove,* BBC, 1979. PRINCIPAL TELEVISION WORK—Lord Peter Purley, *Thomas at Seret,* London Weekend Television, 1979; Collins, *The Curse of King Tut's Tomb,* NBC, HTV, 1980; Lt. Roberts, *The Vanishing Arms,* BBC, 1980; Edward Brittail, *Testament of Youth,* BBC, 1980; Philip Castallach, *Permawil,* BBC, 1980; Jack Mallory, *The Schoolmistress,* Yorkshire Television, 1981; Peter Prior, *Aspects of Love,* Granada, 1981; Stephen Tye, *Frost in May,* BBC, 1981; Claude, *The Case of the Middle Aged Housewife,* Thames, 1981; Maurice Bohham-Carter, *No. Ten Asian House,* Yorkshire Television, 1982; Studzinsky, *The White Guard,* BBC, 1982; Octavius, *The Cleopatras,* BBC, 1982; Wigram Battye, *The Far Pavilions,* Geoff Reeves Film and Television, 1983; Stephen Maxim, *Cover Her Face,* Anglia Television, 1984.

SIDELIGHTS: MEMBERSHIPS—British Film Institute.

ADDRESS: HOME—London, England. AGENT—Plant and Froggatt, Four Windmill Street, London W1, England.

*   *   *

FRELICH, Phyllis   1944-

PERSONAL: Born February 29, 1944, in Devil's Lake, ND; daughter of Phillip (a printer) and Esther (Dockter) Frelich; married

Robert Steinberg (an actor), May 17, 1968; children: Reuben, Joshua. EDUCATION: Gallaudet College, B.S.; trained for the stage at the National Theater for the Deaf.

VOCATION: Actress.

CAREER: STAGE DEBUT—Lauretta, *Gianni Schicci,* National Theater of the Deaf, 1967-68. PRINCIPAL STAGE APPEARANCES—Polly Garter, *Songs from Milkwood,* ANTA, NY, 1970; Benjy, *The Resurrection of Jackie Cramer,* New Dramatists' Workshop, NY, 1977; Deaf Woman, *Poets from the Inside,* Public, NY, 1978; The Wall, *The Fantasticks,* URI Summer Festival, 1978; Sarah, *Children of a Lesser God,* Mark Taper Forum, Los Angeles, CA, 1979, then Longacre, NY, 1980-82; Marietta Yerby, *The Hands of Its Enemy,* Mark Taper Forum and Huntington Hartford, Los Angeles, 1984; Frances Walker, *The Debuntane Ball,* South Coast Repertory, Costa Mesa, CA, 1985.

MAJOR TOURS—All with the National Theater of the Deaf: Kasane, *The Tale of Kasane,* 1967-68, Polly Garter, *Songs from Milkwood,* 1969-70, *Journeys,* 1969-70, Marie, *Woyzeck,* European cities, 1970, Canina, *Volpone,* 1970, Fonsia Dorsey, *The Gin Game,* 1979, Sarah, *Children of a Lesser God,* Spoleto Festival, Italy, 1982.

PRINCIPAL TELEVISION APPEARANCES—*The Dick Cavett Show,* 1970; *Good Morning America, Tomorrow, Today, Captain Kangaroo,* 1980; *Night of a Hundred Stars,* 1981; *Barney Miller,* 1981; *Gimme a Break,* 1985.

AWARDS: Antoinette Perry Award, Best Actress, Los Angeles Dramalogue Award, Outer Critics Circle Award, 1980, all for *Children of a Lesser God;* Los Angeles Dramalogue Award, 1985, for *The Hands of Its Enemy.*

ADDRESS: AGENT—Mary Hardin, Bret Adams Ltd., 448 W. 44th Street, New York, NY 10036.

*   *   *

FRIES, Charles

PERSONAL: Children: Charles M., Thomas, Suzanne, Christopher, Diane, Michael, Alice, Jonathan. EDUCATION: Ohio State University, graduate.

VOCATION: Television and film producer.

CAREER: PRINCIPAL TELEVISION WORK—Producer: *Jacques Cousteau's Underwater,* Metromedia Producers Corp.; *Jane Goodall,* Metromedia Producers Corp.; *National Geographic Specials,* Metromedia Producers Corp.

For Fries Entertainment Corp.: *Hey, I'm Alive,* 1975; *Baby, I'm Back; Louis Armstrong: Chicago Style,* 1976; *Francis Gary Powers: The True Story of the U-2 Spy Incident,* 1976; *Call of the Wild,* 1976; *The Amazing Spider Man,* 1977; *The Word; The Greatest Thing That Almost Happened,* 1977; *The Trial of Lee Harvey Oswald,* 1977; *Intimate Stranger,* 1977; *The Martian Chronicles; A Love Affair: The Eleanor and Lou Gehrig Story,* 1978; *And Your Name Is Jonah,* 1979; *High Noon, Part II: The Return of Will Kane,* 1980; *The Children of An Lac,* 1980; *A Cry for Love,* 1980; *Rage,* 1980; *A Rumor of War,* 1980; *Leave 'em Laughing,* 1980; *Bitter Harvest,*

CHARLES W. FRIES

1981; *Ambush Murders,* 1982; *In Love with an Older Woman, 1982;*
Rosie: The Rosemary Clooney Story, 1982; *For Us the Living;*
Cocaine: One Man's Seduction, 1983; *Carpool,* 1983; *Voyeurs;*
Dempsey, 1983; *Memorial Day,* 1983.

PRINCIPAL FILM WORK—Producer, *The Cat People,* Universal,
1982; as vice president in charge of feature films for Columbia:
Lawrence of Arabia, 1962; *A Man for All Seasons,* 1966; *Funny*
Girl, 1968; *Oliver!,* 1968; *Easy Rider,* 1969; *Five Easy Pieces,*
1970; *The Last Picture Show,* 1971.

RELATED CAREER: Vice president in charge of production administration, Screen Gems (Columbia Pictures television); vice president
in charge of feature films, Columbia Pictures; executive vice
president in charge of production, Metromedia Producers Corp.

AWARDS: Humanitas, CINE Golden Eagle, Christopher, Golden
Halo, for *Bitter Harvest;* Golden Halo, Angel, Scott Newman Drug
Abuse Prevention, for *Cocaine: One Man's Seduction;* Golden
Halo, for *Francis Gary Powers: The True Story of the U-2 Spy*
Incident; Film Advisory Board Award of Excellence, for *Intimate*
Strangers; Humanitas, Recommendation by National Education
Administration, for *Leave 'em Laughing;* Christopher, Angel,
American Film Festival Blue Ribbon, Humanitas, for *Memorial*
Day; Film Advisory Board Award of Excellence, for *Rosie: The*
Rosemary Clooney Story; Writers Guild of America Award, for
Rumor of War.

SIDELIGHTS: MEMBERSHIPS—Alliance of Television Film Producers (president), Academy of Motion Picture Arts and Sciences
(served as governor), Producers Guild of America, American Film
Institute (advisory board), Film Industry Workshops (board of
directors), contributor to the Cinema Circulus of the University of
Southern California Cinema School, Caucus of Producers, Writers
and Directors (chairman of the steering committee).

ADDRESS: OFFICE—Fries Entertainment, 9200 Sunset Blvd., Los
Angeles, CA 90069.

*   *   *

FRYER, Robert   1920-

PERSONAL: Born November 18, 1920, in Washington, DC; son of
Harold and Ruth (Reade) Fryer. EDUCATION: Western Reserve
University, Cleveland, OH, B.A.

VOCATION: Producer.

CAREER: PRINCIPAL STAGE WORK—Producer: *A Tree Grows in*
Brooklyn (with George Abbott), Alvin, NY, 1951; *Wonderful*
Town, NY, 1953; *By the Beautiful Sea* (with Lawrence Carr), Alvin,
NY, 1954; *The Desk Set,* NY, 1955; *Shangri-La,* NY, 1955; *Auntie*
Mame, NY, 1956; *Redhead* (with Lawrence Carr), NY, 1959;
Saratoga, Winter Garden, NY, 1959; *There Was a Little Girl,* NY,
1960; *Advise and Consent,* NY, 1960; *A Passage to India,* NY,
1962; *Hot Spot,* Majestic, NY, 1963; *Roar Like a Dove,* NY, 1964;
A Dream of Swallows, NY, 1964; *Sweet Charity* (with Lawrence
Carr and Joseph Harris), Palace, NY, 1966; *Mame* (with Lawrence
Carr and Sylvia and Joseph Harris), Winter Garden, NY, 1966;
Chicago (with James Cresson), 46th Street Theatre, NY, 1975; *The*
Norman Conquests, NY, 1975; *On the Twentieth Century* (with
Harold Prince), St. James, NY, 1978; *Sweeney Todd* (with Richard
Barr, Charles Woodward, Mary Lea Johnson, Martin Richards, and
Dean and Judy Manos), Uris, NY, 1979; *Merrily We Roll Along,*

ROBERT FRYER

Alvin, NY, 1981; *Noises Off*, Brooks Atkinson, NY, 1984; *Benefactors*, NY, 1985. Also between 1971 and 1985 produced fifty-six (56) productions for the Ahmanson Theatre, Center Theatre Group, Los Angeles, CA.

PRINCIPAL FILM WORK—Producer: *The Boston Strangler*, Twentieth Century-Fox, 1968; *The Prime of Miss Jean Brodie*, Twentieth Century-Fox, 1969; *Travels with My Aunt*, Metro-Goldwyn-Mayer, 1972; *Mame*, Warner Brothers, 1974; *The Abdication*, Warner Brothers, 1974; *Voyage of the Damned*, Avco-Embassy, 1977; *The Boys from Brazil*, Twentieth Century-Fox, 1978; *The Shining*, Warner Brothers, 1980.

PRINCIPAL TELEVISION WORK—Producer: *Wonderful Town*, 1959; *Great Expectations*, 1975.

AWARDS: Thirty two Los Angeles Drama Critics' Circle Awards for plays produced at the Ahmanson Theatre; others.

SIDELIGHTS: MEMBERSHIPS—Kennedy Center (board of trustees), American National Theatre (board of directors), President's Committee on the Arts and Humanities.

RECREATION: Music and swimming.

In 1971, Fryer became the artistic director of the Center Theatre Group of the Ahmanson Theatre, Los Angeles Music Center and has currently produced nineteen consecutive seasons (fifty six productions).

ADDRESS: OFFICE—CTG/Ahmanson Theatre, 135 N. Grand Avenue, Los Angeles, CA 90012.

*　　*　　*

FULLER, Janice   1942-

PERSONAL: Born June 4, 1942, in Oakland, CA; daughter of Jack (an actor and artist) and Anna Lee (a singer and actress; maiden name, Hester) Fuller. EDUCATION: San Diego City College, A.A., 1962; studied for the theatre at the Royal Academy of Dramatic Art, 1973, with Eve Shapiro; also with Michael Shurtleff in NY; dancing with Jack Tygett and Carlton Johnson and voice with Ruth Fremont and John McKinney.

VOCATION: Actress.

CAREER: STAGE DEBUT—Miss Freud, *The Girls in 509*, Old Globe, San Diego, CA, 1960. NEW YORK DEBUT—Nurse, *Ice Age*, Chelsea Theatre Center, Brooklyn Academy of Music. PRINCIPAL STAGE APPEARANCES—Ensemble, *Music Hall Spotlights*, Amandine, *Bird in The Hand*, Mama Turk, *Night at the Black Pig*, Jacquenetta, *Loves Labor's Lost*, ensemble, *K—The Trial*, all for Lion Theatre Company, NY; Pup, *Pup*, Playwrights Horizons, NY; Grace, *Bus Stop*, Inez, *In the Summerhouse*, Rosa, *Grand Magic*, all for Manhattan Theatre Club, NY; Georgia, *Marching to Georgia*, off Broadway, NY; Gwen and understudy Alice, *I Can't Keep Running in Place*, off Broadway, NY.

Mistress Quickly, *The Merry Wives of Windsor*, first citizen, *Coriolanus*, Helena and understudy for Titania, *A Midsummer*

JANICE FULLER

Night's Dream, understudy for Portia, *Julius Caesar*, understudy for Lady Anne, *Richard III*, Gwendolyn, *Becket*, all for San Diego Shakespeare Festival, Old Globe; Minnie and Mrs. Borden, *Mourning Becomes Electra*, Mistress Quickly, *The Merry Wives of Windsor*, Juno, *The Tempest*, Maria, *Twelfth Night*, all for American Shakespeare Festival, Stratford, CT; Meg Dillon, *The Hostage*, Old Globe, San Diego; Madame Arcati, *Blithe Spirit*, Mountain Playhouse, PA; Kristen, *Miss Julie*, Indiana Repertory; April, *Hot l Baltimore*, ACT, Seattle, WA; Gertrude, *The Sea Horse*, ACT, Seattle and Theatre-by-the-Sea, Portsmouth, NH; waitress, *Put Them All Together*, Loretto-Hilton, St. Louis, MO; Domina, *A Funny Thing Happened on the Way to the Forum*, Beef 'n Boards Dinner Theatre; Mistress Overdone, *Measure for Measure*, Folger, Washington, DC; Bunny, *Gemini*, Philadelphia Drama Guild, PA; Clara, *Hayfever*, Kenyon Festival, OH; Mrs. Guzzle, *The Virgin Unmasked*, Kennedy Center, Washington, DC.

FILM DEBUT—Duchess of York, *The Goodbye Girl*, Warner Brothers, 1977. FILM APPEARANCES—Granola, *Cry Your Purple Heart Out*.

AWARDS: Atlas, Best Actress, Old Globe Theatre, for Gwendolyn, *Becket*, and Meg, *The Hostage*.

SIDELIGHTS: MEMBERSHIPS—Actors' Equity Association, Screen Actors Guild. RECREATION—Crocheting, canoeing, hiking.

Fuller revealed to *CTFT* that she "once appeared in a Las Vegas revue as a go-go dancer in Mexico City."

ADDRESS: AGENT—Dulcina Eisen, 154 E. 61st Street, New York, NY 10021.

G

MAX GAIL

GAIL, Max   1943-

PERSONAL: Full name Maxwell Trowbridge Gail, Jr.; born April 5, 1943, in Detroit, MI; son of Maxwell Trowbridge (a businessman) and Mary Elizabeth (Scanlon) Gail; married Willie Mae Reese, February 12, 1983; children: India Jade Sun-Ting. EDUCATION: Williams College, B.A., 1965; University of Michigan, M.B.A., 1969.

VOCATION: Actor, director, and musician.

CAREER: DEBUT—Chief Bromdon, *One Flew Over the Cuckoo's Nest,* Little Fox, San Francisco, CA, 1970. NEW YORK DEBUT—Chief Bromdon, *One Flew Over the Cuckoo's Nest,* Mercer Arts Center, 1973. PRINCIPAL STAGE APPEARANCES—Jack Kerouac, *Visions of Kerouac,* Odyssey, Los Angeles, CA, 1976; Babe Ruth,

The Babe, Princess, NY, 1984.

PRINCIPAL TELEVISION APPEARANCES—Detective Sargeant Stanley Wojehowicz, *Barney Miller,* ABC, 1975-82; numerous television movies.

PRINCIPAL FILM APPEARANCES—*The Organization,* 1971; *Distance,* 1975; *D.C. Cab,* 1983; *Heartbreakers; Where Are the Children.*

Gail is president of Full Circle Productions.

RECORDINGS: *Do Something Beautiful.*

SIDELIGHTS: MEMBERSHIPS—American Federation of Radio and Television Artists, Screen Actors Guild, Actors' Equity Association, Directors Guild of America, American Indian Movement.

Gail was a teacher of ancient history and English at the Grosse Pointe University School, MI, 1965-67.

ADDRESS: AGENT—Artists Agency, 190 N. Cannon Drive, Beverly Hills, CA 90210.

*   *   *

GALLOWAY, Don   1937-

PERSONAL: Born July 27, 1937, in Brooksville, KY; son of Paul Smith (a contractor) and Malee (Poe) Galloway; married Linda Robinson (an actress), September 27, 1963; children: Tracy, Jennifer. EDUCATION: University of Kentucky, B.A., 1961; studied acting with Lee Strasberg in NY. MILITARY: U.S. Army, Specialist 3rd Class, 1955-57.

VOCATION: Actor.

CAREER: STAGE DEBUT—Various roles, *Unto These Hills,* Cherokee, NC, 1959. NEW YORK DEBUT—Dan, *Bring Me a Warm Body,* Martinque, 1962.

FILM DEBUT—Jamie, *The Rare Breed,* Universal, 1966. PRINCIPAL FILM APPEARANCES—Richard, *The Big Chill,* Columbia, 1983.

TELEVISION DEBUT—*The Secret Storm,* CBS, 1962. PRINCIPAL TELEVISION APPEARANCES—Ed Brown, *Ironside,* 1967-75. Movie: *Rearview Mirror,* NBC, 1984.

AWARDS: Theatre World, 1962, for Dan, *Bring Me a Warm Body,* 1962.

ADDRESS: OFFICE—BGP Productions Inc., 10637 Burbank Blvd., North Hollywood, CA 91601. AGENT—Beakel and Jennings, 427 N. Canon Drive, Beverly Hills, CA 90210.

*   *   *

GANCE, Abel   1889-1981

PERSONAL: Born October 25, 1889, in Paris, France; died November 10, 1981.

VOCATION: Director, writer, and actor.

CAREER: DEBUT—As a stage actor.

FILM DEBUT—Moliere, *Moliere,* 1909. PRINCIPAL FILM WORK—Director and writer (silent): *La Folie Du Docteur Tube,* 1915; *Les Gaz Mortels,* 1916; *Barberousse,* 1916; *Mater Dolorosa,* 1917; *La Dixieme Symphonie,* 1917; *J'accuse,* 1919; *La Rove,* 1923; *Au Secours,* 1923; *Napoleon,* 1927; *La Fin Du Monde,* 1927. Sound: *Le Maitre De Forges,* 1933; *Poliche,* 1934; *La Dame Aux Camelias,* 1934; *Le Roman Dun Je une Homme Pauvre,* 1935; *Jerome Perreau,* 1935; *Lucrece Borgia,* 1935; *Voleur De Femmes,* 1935; *Un Grand Amour De Beethoven,* 1936; *J'accuse,* 1937; *Louise,* 1938; *Paradis Perdu,* 1939; *Venus Aveugle,* 1940-41; *Le Capitaine Fracasse,* 1942; *La Tour De Nesle,* 1954; *Austerlitz,* 1959; *Bonaparte and the Revolution,* 1960; *Cyrano and D'Artagnan,* 1963.

AWARDS: Association for the Encouragement to Progress Gold Medal Award, 1966.*

*   *   *

GARDENIA, Vincent   1922-

PERSONAL: Born Vincent Scognamiglio, January 7, 1922, in Naples, Italy; son of Gennaro Gardenia and Elisa (Ausiello) Scognamiglio. EDUCATION: Trained for the stage at the Italian Theater, New York City.

VOCATION: Actor.

CAREER: STAGE DEBUT—Shoe Shine Boy, *Shoe Shine,* Brooklyn, NY, 1927. NEW YORK DEBUT—Hugo the Pirate, *In April Once,* Broadway Tabernacle Church, 1955. PRINCIPAL STAGE APPEARANCES—Piggy, *The Man with the Golden Arm,* Cherry Lane, NY, 1956; Corvino, *Volpone,* Rooftop, NY, 1957; Fyodor, *The Brothers Karamazov,* Gate, NY, 1957; Blind Man, *The Visit,* Lunt-Fontanne, NY, 1958; Jim Nightingale, *The Gold Wind and the Warm,* Music Box, NY, 1959; Deputy, *Rashomon,* Music Box, NY, 1959; Mittrich, *The Power of Darkness,* York Playhouse, NY, 1959; Chairman, *Only in America,* Cort, NY, 1959; George H. Jones, *Machinal,* Gate, NY, 1960; Pavel Menkes, *The Wall,* Billy Rose, NY, 1960.

Warden, *Gallows Humor,* Gramercy Arts, NY, 1961; Sergeant Manzoni, *Daughter of Silence,* Music Box, NY, 1961; Hamm,

VINCENT GARDENIA

Endgame, Warden, *Gallows Humor,* both Cherry Lane, NY, 1962; Wilenski, *Seidman and Son,* Belasco, NY, 1962; Mr. Jones and Workman, *The Lunatic View,* ANTA Matinee Series, Theater de Lys, NY, 1962; Eddie Carbone, *A View from the Bridge,* Charles Playhouse, Boston, MA, 1967-68; Carol Newquist, *Little Murders,* Circle in the Square, NY, 1969; Charles Ferris, "The Son Who Hunted Tigers in Jakarta," and Nick Esposito, "The Burial of Esposito," under the overall title of *Passing Through from Exotic Places,* Sheridan Square Playhouse, NY, 1969; Marty Mendelsohn, *Dr. Fish,* Ethel Barrymore, NY, 1970; Father, *The Carpenters,* American Place, NY, 1970; Harry Edison, *The Prisoner of Second Avenue,* Eugene O'Neill, NY, 1971.

Joe Benjamin, *God's Favorite,* Eugene O'Neill, NY, 1974; Marvin, Mort, *California Suite,* Eugene O'Neill, NY, 1977; Foxwell J. Sly, *Sly Fox,* Broadhurst, NY, 1978; *Buried Inside Extra,* Public, NY, and Royal Court, London, 1983; Levine, *Glen Gary Glen Ross,* NY, 1984.

FILM DEBUT—*Murder Inc,* Twentieth Century-Fox, 1960. PRINCIPAL FILM APPEARANCES—*Little Murders,* Twentieth Century-Fox, 1971; *Bang the Drum Slowly,* Paramount, 1973; *Death Wish,* Paramount, 1974; *The Front Page,* Universal, 1974; *Heaven Can Wait,* Paramount, 1979.

TELEVISION DEBUT—1955. PRINCIPAL TELEVISION APPEARANCES—*Studio One; The Untouchables; All in the Family; Maude.* Mini-series: *Hoover; The Kennedys,* 1983.

AWARDS: Academy Award nomination, 1973, for *Bang the Drum Slowly.*

SIDELIGHTS: FAVORITE ROLES—Willie Loman, *Death of a Salesman;* Eddie, *A View from the Bridge;* Carol Newquist, *Little Murders.* RECREATION: Cooking, mountain climbing on 12th Avenue.

ADDRESS: AGENT—Jay Julien, 1501 Broadway, New York, NY, 10036.

*   *   *

GAVIN, John   1932-

PERSONAL: Born April 8, 1932, in Los Angeles, CA; son of Herald Ray and Delia Diana (Pablos) Gavin; married Constance Towers (the actress), 1974; children: Cristina Miles, Maria Della, Maureen Ardath, Michael Ford. EDUCATION: St. John's Military Academy; Villanova Preparatory School, Ojai; Stanford University, B.A., economic history of Latin America, 1952. MILITARY: U.S. Navy, Air Intelligence Officer, Korean conflict; Aide, Flag Lieutenant, Pan American Affairs Officer to the Commandant of Fifteenth Naval District, 1952-55.

VOCATION: Diplomat, ambassador to Mexico, business executive, former actor.

CAREER: NEW YORK DEBUT—*Seesaw*, 1973.

PRINCIPAL FILM APPEARANCES   *A Time to Love and a Time to Die*, Universal, 1958; *Imitation of Life*, Universal, 1959; *Spartacus*,

JOHN GAVIN

Universal, 1960; *A Breath of Scandal*, Paramount, 1960; *Psycho*, Paramount, 1960; *Midnight Lace*, Universal, 1960; *Romanoff and Juliet*, Universal, 1961; *Tammy, Tell Me True*, Universal, 1961; *Back Street*, Universal, 1961; *Thoroughly Modern Millie*, Universal, 1967; *Madwoman of Chaillot*, Warner Brothers, 1969.

SIDELIGHTS: MEMBERSHIPS—Screen Actors Guild (president, 1971-73), Stanford Alumni Association, Omicron Delta Kappa, Chi Psi, Sunset Club (Los Angeles), Villanova Preparatory School (trustee).

Gavin has spent over two decades in government service, first as special advisor to the secretary general of the Organization of American States, from 1961-74 and since 1981 as ambassador to Mexico. Gavin is president of Gamma Services Corp., 1968-present.

ADDRESS: OFFICE—Box 961 Beverly Hills, CA 90213; U.S. Embassy, Box 3087, Laredo, TX 78041.

*   *   *

GEARY, Anthony

BRIEF ENTRY: Born in Coalville, UT. Geary attended Utah University on Utah University's Presidential Award for playwrights. Actor. His big break came when he was cast as Luke Spencer on ABC's *General Hospital.* His stage credits include *The Subject Was Roses.* In 1984, he made a television movie with Billy Dee Williams entitled *The Imposter*, and was also seen on an episode of *Hotel.**

*   *   *

GEORGE, Colin   1929-

PERSONAL: Born September 20, 1929, in Pembroke Dock, Wales; son of Edward Thomas and Helen Mary (Sandercock) George; married Dorothy Vernon. EDUCATION: Surrey and University College, Oxford, M.A.

VOCATION: Director and actor.

CAREER: PRINCIPAL STAGE APPEARANCES—Co-founder and actor, Elizabethan Theatre Company, 1953; actor, Coventry and Birmingham Repertory; Jack Lucas, *Celebration*, Duchess, London, 1961.

PRINCIPAL STAGE WORK—Director: Nottingham Playhouse, 1957; *Romeo and Juliet*, National Children's Theatre, Belgrade, 1959; *Richard III*, Old Vic, London, 1962; *Duchess of Malfi*, Warsaw, 1967; *Vatslav*, Stratford, Ontario, 1968; *The Hostage*, N.A.C., Ottawa, 1968; *Playboy of the Western World*, Abbey, Dublin, 1969; *Strip Jack Naked*, Royal Court, London, 1969; *Oedipus*, 1978; *Mystery Plays of Wakefield*, Adelaide Festival, 1980; *Elisir D'Amore*, State Opera S.A., 1979; *Just Ruth, Too Early to Say, Marx, A Manual of Trench Warfare, Last Day in Wooloomooloo*, all in Australia; *Whale Music*, 1980, *Falstaff*, 1981, both at Haymarket, Leicester; *Servant of Two Masters, The Pearl Fishers, The Magic Flute*, all at Chung Ying Theater Company, Hong Kong, 1981; *Royal Hunt of the Sun, Fidelio*, both at Academy for the Performing Arts, Hong Kong, 1984.

COLIN GEORGE

MAJOR TOURS—Actor, with Elizabethan Theatre Company, U.K. cities, 1953.

RELATED CAREER—Associate director, Nottingham Playhouse, 1957; associate director, Sheffield Playhouse, 1962-64; artistic director, Ludlow Festival, 1964-66; director, Sheffield Playhouse and Crucible, 1965-74; founder, Theatre Vanguard, 1967; advisor and director, Crucible Theatre, Sheffield, 1971; founder, Department of Drama, University of New England, New South Wales, Australia, 1975; artistic director, State Theatre Company, Adelaide, South Australia, 1977-80; director, Haymarket Theatre, 1980-81; head of acting, stage movement, English production, Academy for the Performing Arts, Hong Kong, 1984-present.

ADDRESS: OFFICE—Hong Kong Academy for the Performing Arts, G.P.O. Box 12288, Hong Kong.

*   *   *

GERE, Richard 1949-

PERSONAL: Born August 31, 1949, in Philadelphia, PA. EDUCATION: Attended University of Massachusetts.

VOCATION: Actor.

CAREER: FILM DEBUT—*Report to the Commissioner*, 1975. PRINCIPAL FILM APPEARANCES—*Baby Blue Marine*, 1976; *Looking for Mr. Goodbar*, 1977; *Days of Heaven*, 1978; *Blood Brothers*, 1978; *Yanks*, 1979; *American Gigolo*, 1980; *An Officer and a Gentleman*, 1982; *Breathless*, 1983; *Beyond the Limit*, 1983; *The Cotton Club*, 1984; *The Story of David*, 1985; *Capa* (upcoming); *At Play in the Fields of the Lord* (upcoming); *Power*, Lorimar (upcoming).

PRINCIPAL STAGE APPEARANCES—*Great God Brown*, *Camino Real*, *Rosencrantz and Guildenstern are Dead*, all Provincetown Playhouse; *Killer's Head*, off Broadway production; *Taming of the Shrew*, Broadway production; *Midsummer Night's Dream*, Broadway production; *Habeas Corpus*, Broadway production; *Bent*, Broadway production; *Midsummer Night's Dream*, London.

PRINCIPAL STAGE WORK—Composer, *Volpone*, Seattle Repertory Theatre, Seattle, WA.

SIDELIGHTS: CTFT learned that Gere is an accomplished musician, who plays the trumpet, piano, guitar and bass.*

*   *   *

GERRINGER, Robert 1926-

PERSONAL: Born Robert Geiringer, May 12, 1926, in New York City; son of Arthur Joseph (a surgeon) and Mary Agnes (a teacher; maiden name, Moran) Geiringer; married Patricia Falkenhain (an actress), April 29, 1950. EDUCATION: Fordham University, B.A., 1948; trained for the stage at the Pasadena Playhouse. POLITICS: Democrat. RELIGION: Roman Catholic.

VOCATION: Actor.

CAREER: STAGE DEBUT—Buckingham, *Richard III*, Fordham University Theater, NY, 1946. NEW YORK DEBUT—Towncrier, *Thieves Carnival*, Cherry Lane, 1953. PRINCIPAL STAGE APPEARANCES—Adrian, *In a Garden*, NY, 1948; Maurice, *Obsession*, Women's Club Theater, Waterbury, CT, 1949; Reverend Bronte, *Moor-born*, Hotel Sutton Theater, NY, 1950; Jim, *Separate Rooms*, Mr. Prior, *Outward Bound*, Archibald, *East Lynne*, Sir Paul Martin, *Miranda*, all at Monson Theater, MA, 1950; Don Juan, *Don Juan in Hell*, Mexican, *A Streetcar Named Desire*, both at Kingsbridge Veterans' Hospital, NY, 1952; Caiphas, *His Mother's Promise*, St. Boniface Church, Paterson, NJ, 1953; Lieutenant, *The Man of Destiny*, Kingsbridge Veterans' Hospital, NY, 1953.

Preacher Hagler, *Dark of the Moon*, Stanley Dale, *Here Today*, Bishop, *See How They Run*, Philip Mortimer, *Gently Does It*, Charles, *Blithe Spirit*, John Worthing, *The Importance of Being Earnest*, Reverend Davidson, *Rain*, Geoffrey, *The Two Mrs. Carrolls*, Gene Tuttle, *Personal Appearance*, Joe Morgan, *Ten Nights in a Bar-Room*, all at Canal Fulton, OH, 1954; towncrier, *Thieves' Carnival*, Cherry Lane, NY, 1955; Ligarius, Lepidus, and Casca, *Julius Caesar*, Captain, *The Tempest*, both American Shakespeare Festival, Stratford, CT, 1955; Seyton, *Macbeth*, Shakespearewrights, Jan Hus House Theater, NY, 1955; Friar Laurence, *Romeo and Juliet*, Jan Hus House Theater, NY, 1956; *I Knock at the Door* and *Pictures in the Hallway*, YMHA Theater, NY, 1956.

Gerard Dupuis, *Nina*, Alan Coles, *Oh, Men! Oh, Women!*, Cornelius

Rockley, *You Touched Me*, Josef, *By Candlelight*, McKeever, *The Solid Gold Cadillac*, Starbuck, *The Rainmaker*, Richard Sherman, *The Seven Year Itch*, Bill Reynolds, *Tea and Sympathy*, Bounine, *Anastasia*, all at Canal Fulton, OH, 1956.

Uncle Tom, Jewish Vendor, Minister, and Old Man with cancer of the tongue, *Pictures in the Hallway*, Playhouse, NY, 1956; Third Workman, *Purple Dust*, Cherry Lane, NY, 1956; Duke, *The Two Gentlemen of Verona*, Banquo, *Macbeth*, both at New York Shakespeare Festival, Delacorte, NY, 1957; Father Ambrose, *The Waltz of the Toreadors*, Coronet, NY, 1958; *Guest of the Nation*, ANTA matinee series, NY, 1958; Iago, *Othello*, New York Shakespeare Festival, Delacorte, NY, 1958.

John Wilkes Booth, *Edwin Booth*, La Jolla Playhouse, CA, 1958; Downing, *The Family Reunion*, Phoenix, NY, 1958; Lieutenant, *The Power and the Glory*, Phoenix, NY, 1958; Jasper Culver, *The Andersonville Trial*, Henry Miller's, NY, 1959; *U.S.A.*, John Drew Theater, East Hampton, NY, 1960; first narrator, *Under Milkwood*, Circle in the Square, NY, 1961; Driscoll, *The Long Voyage Home*, Mermaid, NY, 1961; Benedict, *Much Ado About Nothing*, Reverend Chasuble, *The Importance of Being Earnest*, both Antioch Theater, Yellow Springs, OH, 1962; Petruchio, *The Taming of the Shrew*, Phoenix, NY, 1963.

Orgon, *Tartuffe*, stage manager, *Our Town*, Francis Nurse, *The Crucible*, Tobias, *A Delicate Balance*, Pat, *The Hostage*, Poche and Chandel, *A Flea in Her Ear*, all with American Conservatory Theater Repertory, San Francisco, CA, 1967-69; Lord Humphrey, *The Chronicles of King Henry VI, Part I* and *Part II*, Buckingham, *Richard III*, all New York Shakespeare Festival, NY, 1970; Krogstad, *A Doll's House*, Playhouse, NY, 1971; Paycock, *Juno and the Paycock*, Kennedy Center, Eisenhower, Washington, DC, 1971; Paycock, *Juno and the Paycock*, Catholic University, Washington, DC, 1972; Harry, *A Delicate Balance*, Playhouse in the Park, Cincinnati, OH, 1973; Fergus Crampton, *You Never Can Tell*, George Antrobus, *The Skin of Our Teeth*, Arlington Park Theater, Arlington Heights, IL, 1973.

MAJOR TOURS—Gentleman Caller, *The Glass Menagerie*, U.S. summer stock theaters, 1959; Krogstad, *A Doll's House*, Royal Alexandra, Toronto, Canada, 1971; Father Ambrose, *Waltz of the Toreadors*.

FILM DEBUT—Unemployed Man, *Requiem for a Heavyweight*, Columbia, 1962. PRINCIPAL FILM APPEARANCES—Newspaper editor, *Black Like Me*, Walter Reade Pictures, 1964; *Lovely Way to Die*, Universal, 1968; college professor, *The Way We Were*, Columbia, 1973; *The Exorcist*, Warner Brothers, 1973; detective, *The Sentinel*, Universal, 1977.

TELEVISION DEBUT—Mercutio, *Romeo and Juliet*, NBC, 1949. PRINCIPAL TELEVISION APPEARANCES—*Suspense*, CBS; *Danger*, CBS; Skips, "The Lady's Not for Burning," *Omnibus*, NBC; "Men in White," *Dupont Theater*, NBC, 1961; *The 91st Day*, NET, 1964; *The Doctors*, NBC; *Search for Tomorrow*; *A Time for Us*; *A Brighter Day*; the bishop, "Ceremony of Innocence," *NET Playhouse*, PBS, 1970; *Dark Shadows; Texas*; Del Emerson, *The Edge of Night*.

AWARDS: Obie, 1958, for *Guests of the Nation*.

SIDELIGHTS: MEMBERSHIPS—Actors' Equity Association, Screen Actors Guild, American Federation of Television and Radio Actors, Fordham Alumni Association, Players Club.

Gerringer told *CTFT*, "I've been a moderately busy watercolor painter for twenty years and sell my work at the Pemaquid Gallery in Maine."

ADDRESS: HOME—Newcastle, ME 04553. AGENT—Lionel Larner Associates, 850 Seventh Avenue, New York, NY 10019.

*   *   *

GHOSTLEY, Alice   1928-

PERSONAL: Born August 14, 1928, in Eve, MO; daughter of Harry Francis and Edna Muriel (Rooney) Ghostley; married Felice Orlandi. EDUCATION: University of Oklahoma.

VOCATION: Actress, singer, and comedienne.

CAREER: DEBUT—New face, *New Faces of 1952*, Royale, NY, 1952. PRINCIPAL STAGE APPEARANCES—Sheela Cavanaugh, *Sandhog*, Phoenix, NY, 1954; Dinah, *Trouble in Tahiti*, Playhouse, NY, 1955; Miss Brinklow, *Shangri-La*, Winter Garden, NY, 1957; Aunt Polly, *Livin' the Life*, Phoenix, NY, 1957; Lois, *Maybe Tuesday*, Playhouse, NY, 1958; Jeannette Gaines, "She," other parts, *A Thurber Carnival*, ANTA, NY, 1960; Octavia Weatherwax, Kitty Entrail, and Grace Fingerhead, *The Beauty Part*, Music Box, NY, 1962; player, *Gentlemen Be Seated*, City Center, NY, 1963; Mavis Parodus Bugson, *The Sign in Sidney Brustein's Window*, Longacre, NY, 1964; Miss Hannigan, *Annie*, Alvin, NY, 1977.

Also: Bunny Flingus, *The House of Blue Leaves*, Huntington Hartford, Los Angeles, CA; *Come Blow Your Horn*, Burt Reynolds Dinner Theatre, Jupiter, FL; and stock productions of *Take Me Along, Do-Re-Mi, Rose Marie, The Boy Friend, Palm Tree in a Rose Garden, Dig We Must, Stop Thief Stop*.

MAJOR TOURS—*New Faces*, national, 1953-54; *The Sign in Sidney Brustein's Window*, national, 1965; *Love Is a Ball*, 1975.

FILM DEBUT—*New Faces*, 1954. PRINCIPAL FILM APPEARANCES—*To Kill a Mockingbird*, Universal, 1963; *My Six Loves*, Universal, 1963; *The Flim-Flam Man*, Twentieth Century-Fox, 1967; *The Graduate*, Embassy, 1967; *Viva Max*, Commonwealth United, 1969; *Gator*, United Artists, 1976; *Record City*, 1977; *Rabbit Test*, 1978; *Grease*, Paramount, 1978; others.

PRINCIPAL TELEVISION APPEARANCES—Portia, *Rodgers & Hammerstein's Cinderella*, CBS, 1957; Agnes, "Agnes and Arthur," *The Jackie Gleason Show*, CBS, 1962-65; Mrs. Nash, *Captain Nice*, NBC, 1967; Esmerelda, *Bewitched*, ABC, 1969-72; Alice, *Mayberry R.F.D.*, CBS, 1970-71; Bertha, *Nichols*, NBC, 1971-72; *The Julie Andrews Show*, ABC, 1972-73; Edwina Moffatt, *Temperature's Rising*, ABC, 1974. Also: *Art Carney Television Specials; The Jonathan Winters Comedy Hours; Hogan's Heroes; The Odd Couple; Maude; Family; Good Times; What's Happening; One Day at a Time; Madame's Place; Twelfth Night*; others.

AWARDS: Antoinette Perry Award nomination, 1963, for *The Beauty Part*; Antoinette Perry Award, Best Actress in a supporting role, Saturday Review Award, New York Critics Circle Award, Best Performance, 1965, all for *The Sign in Sidney Brustein's Window*.

ADDRESS: OFFICE—c/o AFTRA, 1717 N. Highland Avenue, Hollywood, CA 90028.

*   *   *

GIBSON, William   1914-

PERSONAL: Born November 13, 1914, in New York City; son of George Irving and Florence (Dore) Gibson; married Margaret Brenman (an author and biographer). EDUCATION: College of the City of New York.

VOCATION: Playwright.

WRITINGS: PLAYS, PRODUCED—*I Lay in Zion,* Topeka Civic, Topeka, KS, 1943; *A Cry of Players,* Topeka, KS, 1948, later seen at Berkshire Theatre Festival, Stockbridge, MA, 1968, and Repertory Theatre of Lincoln Center, NY, 1968; *Two for the Seesaw,* NY, 1958; *The Miracle Worker,* Playhouse, NY, 1959; *Dinny and the Witches,* 1959; book for musical, *Golden Boy,* Majestic, NY, 1964; *American Primitive,* 1969; *The Body and the Wheel,* Vineyard Community, MA, 1974; *The Butterfingers Angel, Mary and Joseph, Herod the Nut, Twelve Carols in a Pear Tree,* all 1975; *Golda,* ANTA, NY, 1980; *Monday After the Miracle,* Actors Studio, 1982, revised and seen at the Spoleto Festival, GA, then Biltmore, NY, 1983; *Handy Dandy,* 1984; *Raggedy Ann* (musical), 1984. Also: *John and Abigail,* Berkshire Theatre Festival, Stockbridge, MA, 1960's.

SCREENPLAYS—*The Cobweb,* Metro-Goldwyn-Mayer, 1955; *Two for the Seesaw,* United Artists, 1962; *The Miracle Worker,* United Artists, 1962. TELEPLAYS—*The Miracle Worker,* 1957, then again in 1979.

BOOKS, PUBLISHED—*Winter Crook* (poems), 1947; *The Cobweb* (novel), 1954; *The Seesaw Log* (a chronicle of the original production of *Two for the Seesaw*), 1959; *A Mass for the Dead* (a family chronicle), 1968; *A Season in Heaven* (novel), 1975; *Shakespeare's Game* (criticism), 1978.

AWARDS: Academy Award nomination, Best Screenplay, *The Miracle Worker,* 1962; others.

SIDELIGHTS: MEMBERSHIPS—Dramatists Guild.

During the 1960's Gibson, along with Arthur Penn and Karl Lipsky, assumed leadership of the failing Berkshire Playhouse in Stockbridge, MA, and formed the Berkshire Theatre Festival. It still functions today as a premier summer theatre, attracting new playwrights and top name artists.

ADDRESS: HOME—Stockbridge, MA 01262.

*   *   *

GILBERT, Melissa   1964-

BRIEF ENTRY: Born May 8, 1964, in Los Angeles, CA; daughter Paul (a comedian) and Barbara (a former dancer and actress; maiden name, Crane) Gilbert. Currently attends college at the University of

Southern California. Gilbert first appeared in television commercials at the age of three. She is best known for her role as Laura Ingalls in the long-running television series *Little House on the Prairie,* NBC, 1974-83. She has also appeared on television in *Gunsmoke, Emergency, Tenafly, The Hanna-Barbara Happy Hour, Christmas Miracle in Caufield U.S.A.,* and *The Love Boat.* Gilbert portrayed Jean Donovan in the television movie *Choices of the Heart,* 1983. Other television movies include *Gladiola Girls* (a remake of *The Miracle Worker*), 1979; *The Diary of Ann Frank,* 1980; *Splendor in the Grass,* 1981, and *Family Secrets.* Gilbert's first feature film was *Sylvester,* Columbia, 1985.*

*   *   *

GILBERT, Ronnie   1926-

PERSONAL: Born September 7, 1926, in New York City; daughter of Charles and Sarah Gilbert; married Martin Weg (divorced, 1959); children: Lisa. EDUCATION: Lone Mountain College, M.A., clinical psychology, 1974. POLITICS: Progressive.

VOCATION: Singer and actress.

CAREER: PRINCIPAL STAGE APPEARANCES—*Houdini,* Lambs, NY; *The Man in the Glass Booth,* Royale, NY, 1968; *Specimen Days,* Public Theatre, NY; *Antigone,* Public, NY; *Re-Arrangements, Tourists and Refugees, Trespassing,* all at La MaMa, NY; *The Tempest, The Roundhouse,* both in London; *America Hurrah,* Royal Court, London; *Happy Days,* Waterfront, Vancouver, BC, Canada; *Playgrounds (Dance Play),* Vancouver Playhouse, Toronto Harborfront; *Tourists and Refugees II,* Venezuela Festival, Caracas; *Medea, Tongues & Savage Love,* both at St. Louis Repertory, MO; *A Christmas Carol,* Ford's, Washington, DC.

MAJOR TOURS—*Trio (Lies and Secrets),* NY, London, Edinburgh, Paris; *Three Journeys of Aladdin,* NY, Rennes, Angier, Orleans, Paris, London, Glasgow. Also, as a singer: across the U.S. as member of the Weavers, 1948-1962; solo touring, 1962-64; with Holly Near, 1983-84; with HARP (Holly Near, Arlo Guthrie, Gilbert, and Pete Seeger), 1984; solo, 1985.

PRINCIPAL FILM APPEARANCES—*The Loves of Isadora,* Universal, 1969; *Windflowers; Loin de Vietnam; The Weavers: Wasn't That a Time; Going On; The Hopi: Songs from the Fourth World; Hard Travelin'.*

RECORDINGS: Extensive recording with the Weavers, 1950-81 for Decca, Vanguard and Loom Records, including: *Folk Songs Around the World; Carnegie Hall, Vols. I and II; Fifteenth Reunion; American Folk Singers and Balladeers; Reunion at Carnegie Hall; The Weavers: Together Again;* others. Also: *Legend of Bessie Smith,* RCA Victor; *Alone with Ronnie Gilbert,* Mercury; *The Spirit Is Free,* Redwood, 1985; others.

SIDELIGHTS: Gilbert's press release states that her "work life began at age 13 doing office work in Brooklyn. At 16, she went to Washington, DC for a government job during World War Two. There she joined a folk singing group called the Priority Ramblers which sang songs of social protest and for the war effort, and she met people like Woody Guthrie, Cisco Houston, and Alan Lomax. Her graduation from high school was almost blocked when she refused to participate in the school's minstrel show. How could I do that?,' she remembers. Paul Robeson was my absolute hero.'

RONNIE GILBERT

Photography by Susan Wilson

"Around 1948, the Weavers began as an informal group of eight or ten singers. After a year, they started looking for a way to stay together more seriously. The Weavers, now Gilbert, Pete Seeger, Lee Hays, and Fred Hellerman, were booked at the Village Vanguard in New York, landed a recording contract with Decca, and went on to sell millions of records, making such songs as *Goodnight Irene, On Top of Old Smokey,* and *Kisses Sweeter Than Wine* famous.

"The Weavers overwhelming success was interrupted when they became a target during the McCarthyite era of the early 1950s. In 1952, they recorded their last record for Decca. The Weavers reunited for a Carnegie Hall concert in 1955, and went back into business. Seeger left the group in 1957, and there were three replacements before the group finally disbanded in 1963."

ADDRESS: OFFICE—Redwood Records, 476 W. MacArthur Blvd., Oakland, CA 94609.

*   *   *

GILFORD, Jack   1907-

PERSONAL: Born Jacob Gellman, July 25, 1907, in New York City; son of Aaron and Sophie (Jackness) Gellman; married Madeline Lee Letterman, April 6, 1949; children: Joseph Edward, Lisa, Sam.

VOCATION: Actor and comedian.

CAREER: DEBUT—Comedian, *Amateur Night,* Bronx Opera House, NY, 1934. NEW YORK DEBUT—In revue, *Frank Fay Vaudeville,*

JACK GILFORD

Music Box, 1939. PRINCIPAL STAGE APPEARANCES—In revue, *Meet the People,* Hollywood Playhouse, Los Angeles, CA, then Mansfield, NY, 1940; in revue, *Tommy Dorsey Orchestra,* Paramount, NY, 1941; Barney Snediker, *They Should Have Stood in Bed,* Mansfield, NY, 1942; in revue, *Count Me In,* Ethel Barrymore, NY, 1942; *Meet the People,* Hollywood Playhouse, Los Angeles, 1943; in revue, *Alive and Kicking,* Winter Garden, NY, 1950; Sol Margolies, *The Live Wire,* Playhouse, NY, 1950; Frosch, *Die Fledermaus,* Metropolitan Opera House, NY, 1950 and subsequent revivals, 1958-59, 1962-64, 1966-67; Bontche Schweig, *The World of Sholom Aleichem,* Barbizon-Plaza, NY, 1953; Alexander Gross, *The Passion of Gross,* Theatre de Lys, NY, 1955; in revue, *Once Over Lightly,* Barbizon-Plaza, NY, 1955.

Mr. Dussel, *The Diary of Anne Frank,* Cort, NY, 1955; second soldier, *Romanoff and Juliet,* Plymouth, NY, 1957; Dr. Ullman, *Drink to Me Only,* 54th Street Theatre, NY, 1958; Yacob von Putziboum, *Look After Lulu,* Henry Miller's, NY, 1959; King Sextimus, *Once Upon a Mattress,* Phoenix, NY, 1959; Mr. Zitorsky, *The Tenth Man,* Booth, NY, 1959; *The Desert Song, Can-Can, Cinderella,* all summer stock, 1961; Goddard Quagmire, *The Beauty Part,* Bucks County Playhouse, PA, 1961; Sergeant, *The Policeman,* Phoenix, NY, 1961; Hysterium, *A Funny Thing Happened on the Way to the Forum,* Alvin, NY, 1962; Herr Schultz, *Cabaret,* Broadhurst, NY, 1966; Erwin Trowbridge, *Three Men on a Horse,* Lyceum, NY, 1969; *The Price,* Studio Arena, Buffalo, NY, 1970; Jimmy Smith, *No, No, Nanette,* 46th Street Theatre, NY, 1971; Richard Sherman, *The Seven Year Itch,* Royal Poinciana Playhouse, Palm Beach, FL, 1975; Jethro Couch, *Sly Fox,* Broadhurst, NY, 1976; Arnold, *The Supporting Cast,* Biltmore, NY, 1981; Tevya, etc., *The World of Sholom Aleichem,* Rialto, NY, 1982.

MAJOR TOURS—*Leavitt and Lockwood Revue*, PA, 1934; comedian in vaudeville, 1934-35; *Milton Berle Revue*, 1935-38; *Ina Ray Hutton Revue*, U.S. and Canada, 1937-38; in vaudeville, 1938-39; *Meet the People*, national, 1940; vaudeville, 1940; variety show, *USO in the Pacific*, 1943; vaudeville, 1950; *Anything Goes*, summer tour, 1973; *The Sunshine Boys*, summer tour, 1974.

FILM DEBUT—*Hey, Rookie*, Columbia, 1944. PRINCIPAL FILM APPEARANCES—*The Reckless Age*, Universal, 1944; *Main Street to Broadway*, Metro-Goldwyn-Mayer, 1953; *Mister Budwing*, Metro-Goldwyn-Mayer, 1963; Hysterium, *A Funny Thing Happened on the Way to the Forum*, United Artists, 1966; *Enter Laughing*, Columbia, 1967; *Who's Minding the Mint?*, Columbia, 1967; *The Incident*, Twentieth Century-Fox, 1967; *Harry and Walter Go to New York*, Columbia, 1967; *Catch-22*, Paramount, 1970; *They Might Be Giants*, Universal, 1971; *Save the Tiger*, Paramount, 1972; *Cheaper to Keep Her*, 1980; *Wholly Moses*, Columbia, 1980; *Cave Man*, United Artists, 1981; *Cocoon*, Twentieth Century-Fox, 1985.

TELEVISION DEBUT—Regular, *The Arrow Show* (aka *The Phil Silvers Arrow Show* and *Arrow Comedy Theatre*), NBC, 1948-49. PRINCIPAL TELEVISION APPEARANCES—Ben Dreyfuss, *Paul Sand in Friends and Lovers*, CBS, 1974-75; Grandpa Hollyhock, *Apple Pie*, ABC, 1978; *The Dean Martin Show*, NBC; *The Carol Burnett Show*, CBS; *The Defenders*, CBS; *All in the Family*, CBS; *Rhoda*, CBS; *Soap*, ABC; *Taxi*, ABC; *The Loveboat*, ABC; *Trapper John, M.D.*, CBS; *The Duck Factory*; *Dinah's Place*; ''The World of Sholom Aleichem,'' *Play of the Week*; *Once Upon a Mattress*, CBS; *Of Thee I Sing*, CBS; *The Cowboy and the Tiger*, PBS; *The Very Special Jack Gilford Special*, CBS Cable; Dr. Jelliff, *Anna to the Infinite Power*, cable, 1984. Also well known for ''Cracker Jack'' commercials.

CABARET AND NIGHT CLUBS—At Cafe Society, Downtown, 1939; Cafe Society Uptown, 1946, and many others since 1936.

AWARDS: Antoinette Perry Award nominations, 1963, for *A Funny Thing Happened on the Way to the Forum*, and 1967, for *Cabaret*; Academy of Motion Picture Arts and Sciences nomination, 1972, for *Save the Tiger*.

SIDELIGHTS: With his friend, Zero Mostel, Gilford contributed to the book about their friendship, written by his and Mostel's wives, *170 Years of Show Business*.

ADDRESS: AGENT—International Creative Management, 40 W. 57th Street, New York, NY 10019.

*   *   *

GILL, Peter   1939-

PERSONAL: Born September 7, 1939, in Cardiff, Wales; son of George John and Margaret Mary (Browne) Gill. EDUCATION: Attended St. Illtyd's College, Cardiff.

VOCATION: Director, writer, and actor.

CAREER: PRINCIPAL STAGE WORK—Director: *A Collier's Friday Night*, Royal Court, London, 1965; *The Local Stigmatic*, *The Ruffian on the Stair*, *A Provincial Life*, all Royal Court, 1966; *The*

PETER GILL

Local Stigmatic, *The Dwarfs*, both Traverse, London, 1966; *O'Flaherty VC*, Mermaid, London, 1966; *A Soldier's Fortune*, *The Daughter-in-Law*, both Royal Court, London, 1967; *The Widowing of Mrs. Holroyd*, Royal Court, London, 1968; *Life Price*, *Over Gardens Out*, *The Sleeper's Den*, all Royal Court, London, 1969; *Much Ado About Nothing*, Stratford, Ontario, Canada, 1969; *Landscape and Silence*, Lincoln Center, NY, 1970; *Hedda Gabler*, Stratford, Ontario, 1970; *The Duchess of Malfi*, Royal Court, London, 1971.

Macbeth, Stratford, Ontario, 1971; *Crete and Sergeant Pepper*, Royal Court, London, 1972; *A Midsummer Night's Dream*, Zurich Schauspielhaus, 1972; *The Daughter-in-Law*, Bochum Schauspielhaus, 1972; *The Merry-Go-Round*, Royal Court, 1973; *Twelfth Night*, Stratford-on-Avon, England, 1974; *Fishing*, New York Shakespeare Festival, 1975; *As You Like It*, Nottingham Playhouse, Edinburgh Festival, 1975, Riverside Studios, 1976; *Small Change*, Royal Court, 1976, Riverside Studios, 1977; *The Cherry Orchard*, *The Changeling*, *Measure for Measure*, all Riverside Studios, 1978; *Measure for Measure*, Riverside Studios, 1979; *Julius Caesar*, *Scrape off the Black*, both Riverside Studios, 1980.

At the National Theatre, London: *Don Juan*, *Scrape Off the Black*, *Much Ado About Nothing*, all 1981; *Danton's Death*, *Major Barbara*, *Small Change*, *Kick for Touch*, *Tales from Hollywood*, *Antigone*, all 1983; *Venice Preserv'd*, *Fool for Love*, *As I Lay Dying*, *The Garden of England*, *Up for None*, all 1984; *The Murderers*, 1985; *Twist of Lemon*, *In the Blue*, both National Theater Studio, London, 1985; also: *Fool for Love*, Lyric, London, 1985.

PRINCIPAL STAGE APPEARANCES—Actor, 1957-67.

PRINCIPAL TELEVISION WORK—Director: *Grace*, BBC, 1972; *Girl*, BBC, 1973; *A Matter of Taste, Fugitive*, both BBC, 1974; *Hitting Town*, Thames, 1976.

RELATED CAREER—Associate director, Royal Court Theatre, London, 1970-72; director, Riverside Studios, Hammmersmith, UK, 1976-80; associate director, Riverside Studios, Hammersmith, 1980; associate director, National Theatre, London, 1980; director, National Theatre Studio, London, 1984.

WRITINGS: PLAYS, PRODUCED—*The Sleeper's Den*, 1965; *A Provincial Life*, Royal Court, London, 1966; *Over Gardens Out*, Royal Court, London, 1969; *Small Change, Kick for Touch*, Royal Court, 1976, Riverside Studios, London, 1977; *As I Lay Dying*, 1984; *In the Blue*, National Theater Studio, London, 1985.

AWARDS: Belgrade International Theatre Award, First Prize for a play, 1965, for *The Daughter-in-Law*.

ADDRESS: AGENT—Margaret Ramsay, Ltd., 14a Goodwin's Court, St. Martin's Lane, London WC2N 4LL, England.

* * *

GINGOLD, Hermione 1897-

PERSONAL: Born December 9, 1897, in London, England; daughter of James and Kate (Walter) Gingold; married Michael Joseph (divorced); married Eric Maschwitz (divorced). EDUCATION: Studied acting from Rosina Filippi.

HERMIONE GINGOLD

VOCATION: Actress.

CAREER: LONDON DEBUT—The herald, *Pinkie and the Fairies*, His Majesty's Theatre, 1908. NEW YORK DEBUT—Revue, *John Murray Anderson's Almanac*, Imperial, 1953. PRINCIPAL STAGE APPEARANCES—The page, *Merry Wives of Windsor*, His Majesty's, 1909; Jessica, *The Merchant of Venice*, Old Vic, 1914; Liza, *If*, Ambassador's, 1921; Old Woman, *The Dippers*, Criterion, 1922; *Little Lord Fauntleroy*, the second daughter, *From Morn to Midnight*, Lavinia, *One More River*, Lily Malone, *Hotel Universe*, Vidette, *I Hate Men*, all at the Gate theatre, 1931-33; Camille, *Mountebanks*, Q, 1934; *This World of Ours*, Gate, 1935; *Spread It Abroad*, Saville, 1936; May, *Laura Garrett*, Arts, 1936; the leading lady, *In Theatre Street*, Mercury, 1937; *The Gate Revue*, Gate, Ambassador's, 1939; *Swinging the Gate*, Ambassador's, 1940.

Rise Above It, Comedy, 1941; *Sky High*, Phoenix, 1942; *Sweet and Low*, Ambassador's, 1943; *Sweeter and Lower*, Ambassador's, 1944; *Sweetest and Lowest*, Ambassador's, 1946; *Slings and Arrows*, Comedy, 1948; Mrs. Rocket, *Fumed Oak*, Jane Banbury, *Fallen Angels*, both at Ambassador's, 1949; revue, *It's About Time*, Brattle Theatre, Cambridge, MA, 1951; *The Sleeping Prince*, Huntington Hartford, Los Angeles, 1956; Mrs. Bennet, *First Impressions*, Alvin, NY, 1959; revue, *From A to Z*, Plymouth, NY, 1960; Clara Weiss, *Milk and Honey*, Martin Beck, NY, 1962; Madame Rosepettle, *Oh Dad Poor Dad . . .* , Phoenix, NY, 1963, then Morosco, NY, 1963; Celeste, *Dumas and Son*, Chandler Pavilion, Los Angeles, CA, 1967; *Charley's Aunt*, McCarter Theater, Princeton, NJ, 1968; Agnes Derringdo, *Highly Confidential*, Cambridge, MA, 1969; Mme Armfeldt, *A Little Night Music*, Shubert, NY, Adelphi, London, 1975; *Side by Side by Sondheim*, Huntington Hartford, Los Angeles, 1978.

MAJOR TOURS—Revue, *Sticks and Stones*, U.S., 1956; *Fallen Angels*, U.S., 1957-58; Julia Maltby, *Abaracadabra*, 1960; Madame Rosepettle, *Oh Dad Poor Dad . . .* , National Company, 1963.

PRINCIPAL FILM APPEARANCES—*Around the World in Eighty Days*, United Artists, 1956; *Gigi*, Metro-Goldwyn-Mayer, 1958; *Bell, Book, and Candle*, Columbia, 1959; *The Naked Edge*, United Artists, 1961; *The Music Man*, Warner Brothers, 1962; *Promise Her Anything*, Paramount, 1966.

WRITINGS: BOOKS—*The World Is Square* (autobiography), 1945; *Sirens Should Be Seen and Not Heard*.

AWARDS: Donaldson Award, Hollywood Foreign Press Award.

SIDELIGHTS: RECREATIONS—Interior decoration and collecting china.

ADDRESS: OFFICE—405 E. 54th Street, New York, NY 10022.

* * *

GINTY, Robert 1948-

PERSONAL: Born November 14, 1948, in Brooklyn, NY; son of Michael Joseph (a construction worker) and Elsie M. (a government worker; maiden name, O'Hara) Ginty; married Francine Tacker, May, 1980 (divorced, 1983); married Lorna Patterson (an actress), November 26, 1983; children: (first marriage) James F. EDUCA-

ROBERT GINTY

TION: Harvard University, Yale University, Princeton University, 1966-1970; studied acting with Sanford Meisner at the Neighborhood Playhouse, Lee Strasberg at the Actors Studio, and Herbert Berghof at Berghof Studios.

VOCATION: Actor, writer, producer, and director.

CAREER: PRINCIPAL STAGE APPEARANCES—Broadway: *Great God Brown, Don Juan, Government Inspector.* Off Broadway: *The Indian Wants the Bronx, The Lion in Winter, Once in a Lifetime, Cat on a Hot Tin Roof; Henry IV, Part I, A Midsummer's Night Dream, Macbeth, As You Like It,* all at the New Hampshire Shakespeare Festival; *Silent Partner,* Actors Studio, 1971; *More Stately Mansions, Orpheus Descending, Bring It All Back Home,* all at the Provincetown Playhouse, 1971.

PRINCIPAL FILM APPEARANCES—*To Have Your Cake and Eat It; Incident of October 20th; Children Come Back,* 1971; *Bound for Glory,* United Artists, 1976; *Two Minute Warning,* Universal, 1976; *Coming Home,* United Artists, 1978; *The Exterminator,* 1980; *The Alchemist; Gold Raiders; The Scarab; Bless 'Em All; Warrior of the Lost World; White Fire; Exterminator II,* 1984.

PRINCIPAL TELEVISION APPEARANCES—*Police Story; The Rookies; Gibbsville; Griffin and Phoenix,* 1974; T. J. Wiley, *Baa Baa Black Sheep,* NBC; Anderson, *The Paper Chase,* CBS, 1978-79; Mac Riley, *Hawaiian Heat,* ABC, 1984.

PRINCIPAL DIRECTING WORK—Shorts: *My Father's House,* 1979; *Perfect Master,* 1979.

SIDELIGHTS: MEMBERSHIPS—Actors' Equity Association, Screen Actors Guild.

ADDRESS: AGENT—International Creative Management, 8899 Beverly Blvd., Los Angeles, CA 90048.

*   *   *

GLASS, Ned   1906-84

PERSONAL: Born 1906, in Poland; died June 15, 1984. EDUCATION: Attended City College of New York.

VOCATION: Actor.

CAREER: PRINCIPAL FILM APPEARANCES—Contract player, Metro-Goldwyn-Mayer, 1940's; *He's a Cockeyed Wonder,* 1950; *Storm Warning,* 1950; *The Yellow Tomahawk; The Steel Cage; Hot Rod Rumble; The Rebel Set;* Doc, *West Side Story; Experiment in Terror; Kid Galahad; Who's Got the Action; Papa's Delicate Condition; Charade; A Big Hand for the Little Lady; Blindfold; The Fortune Cookie; Never a Dull Moment; The Love Bug; Lady Sings the Blues; The All American Boy; Save the Tiger; All the Marbles; Street Music.*

PRINCIPAL TELEVISION APPEARANCES—*Studio One; Alcoa Presents; Philco Playhouse; Goodyear Playhouse; Playhouse 90; Gunsmoke; Twilight Zone; Peter Gunn; Phil Silvers Show; Goldie and the Boxer;* Sol Cooper, *Julia,* 1968-71; Uncle Moe Plotnick, *Bridget Loves Bernie,* 1972-73.

PRINCIPAL STAGE APPEARANCES—Broadway: *Street Scene; Counselor at Law.*

WRITINGS: Three Men on a Horse (with Sam Levene).

AWARDS: Emmy Award nomination, 1969, for *Julia.**

*   *   *

GOETZ, Peter Michael   1941-

PERSONAL: Born December 10, 1941; son of Irving A. (a construction engineer) and Esther L. Goetz; married Constance Fleurat, June 11, 1966; children: Michael, Kevin. EDUCATION: University of Miami, FL, Aviation, for two years; State University College, Fredonia, NY, B.A., speech and theatre; Southern Illinois University, Carbondale, M.A., playwrighting and theatre; University of Minnesota, Ph.D, theatre.

VOCATION: Actor.

CAREER: STAGE DEBUT—Joey, *The Homecoming,* Tyrone Guthrie, Minneapolis, MN. NEW YORK DEBUT—*Jail Diary of Albie Sachs,* Manhattan Theatre Club, 1980. PRINCIPAL STAGE APPEARANCES—*The Typist and the Tiger,* 1968; *The Alchemist,* Cricket, Minneapolis, MN, 1968; *Troilus and Cressida* (as guest artist), University of Minneapolis, 1968; Malloy, *A Touch of the Poet,* Mrs. Young's Husband, *The Beauty Part,* both at Tyrone Guthrie, 1969; Sebastian, *The Tempest,* Polly, *A Man's a Man, Love Girl and the*

PETER MICHAEL GOETZ

Innocent, Julius Caesar, Cyrano de Bergerac, Biondello, *The Taming of the Shrew, The Relapse,* Ferdinand, *The Italian Straw Hat,* all at the Tyrone Guthrie, Minneapolis, MN, 1970.

Lenny, *Of Mice and Men,* Snug, *A Midsummer Night's Dream,* Pozzo, *Waiting for Godot,* all at the Guthrie, 1971; Tevye, *Fiddler on the Roof,* Chanhassen Dinner Theatre, Minneapolis, MN, 1972; *Ghost Dancer,* Ekhart, *Baal,* Becket, *Becket,* Bobchinski, *The Government Inspector,* Jerry Devine, *Juno and the Paycock,* all at the Guthrie, 1973; Richard, *Richard III* (guest artist), St. Mary's College, Winona, MN, 1974; Ash, *The National Health,* Ferdinand, *Love's Labours' Lost,* Cleante, *Tartuffe,* all at the Guthrie, 1974; Milo Tindle, *Sleuth,* Fedot, *Chemin de Fer,* both at Chanhassen Dinner Theatre, Minneapolis, 1974.

Mortimer, *Arsenic and Old Lace,* Mitch, *A Streetcar Named Desire,* Elif, *Mother Courage,* Narrator One, *Under Milkwood,* Provost, *Measure for Measure, The Merchant of Venice,* Elder One, *Oedipus,* all at the Guthrie, 1975; Cornelius Hackle, *The Matchmaker,* Gooper, *Cat on a Hot Tin Roof,* Hovstad, *An Enemy of the People,* Polixines, *The Winter's Tale,* Charles Dickens, *A Christmas Carol,* all at the Guthrie, 1976; Creep, *Pantagleize,* Young Marlow, *She Stoops to Conquer,* Bracciano, *The White Devil,* all at the Guthrie, 1977; Fledis and King Skule, *The Pretenders,* Tyrone, *A Moon for the Misbegotten,* both at the Guthrie, 1978; Benson, *Boy Meets Girl,* Podkolyossin, *Marriage,* both at the Guthrie, 1979; six roles, *Eugene O'Neill Playwrights Conference of New Plays,* Waterbury, CT, 1979 and 1980; Balthazar, *Solomon's Child,* Long Wharf, New Haven, CT, 1980; Rudge, *Jerusalem,* Minneapolis Children's Theatre, 1980; Jack (John Barrymore), *Ned and Jack,* Hudson Guild, then Helen Hayes, NY, 1981; Ben, *The Little Foxes,* Berkshire Theatre Festival, Stockbridge, MA, 1981.

Maiden Stakes, Circle in the Square, NY, and White Barn, CT, 1982; Dr. Framingham, *Beyond Therapy,* Brooks Atkinson, NY, 1982; Amos, *The Queen and the Rebels,* Purchase, NY, then Plymouth, NY, 1982; Jack Jerome, *Brighton Beach Memoirs,* Neil Simon, NY, 1983-84 (and pre-Broadway tour); *Miss Lulu Bett,* Berkshire Theatre Festival, Stockbridge, MA, 1984; Starkman, *Before the Dawn,* American Place, NY, 1985; *An Evening with Colleen Dewhurst and Peter Michael Goetz,* Vistaford Lines, at sea, 1985; *Caught,* Berkshire Theatre Festival, Stockbridge, MA, 1985.

FILM DEBUT—*Just Be There,* 1973. PRINCIPAL FILM APPEARANCES—*Jackpot,* 1974; *The Director,* 1975; Selden Ross, *Wolfen,* Warner Brothers, 1981; Charles Delehuth, *Prince of the City,* Warner Brothers, 1981; Jenny's publisher, *The World According to Garp,* Warner Brothers, 1982; Joyner, *Best Defense,* Paramount, 1984; Gramps, *Chud,* 1984; Beer Mr. Feemer, 1984.

PRINCIPAL TELEVISION APPEARANCES—Movies: *Act of Love,* NBC, 1979; Diehms Prosecuting Attorney, *Invasion of Privacy,* ABC, 1980. Series: *One of the Boys,* 1983; Wally Wainwright, *After-M*A*S*H,* CBS, 1984. Also: *Ben Hecht,* PBS, 1981; *Lou Grant; The Phoenix; Nurse; St. Elsewhere;* and pilots for *In Trouble Dad, All Together Now, Braker: Chief of Police;* Tony Award presenter, NBC, 1983.

ADDRESS: HOME—Larchmont, NY. AGENT—J. Michael Bloom, 400 Madison Avenue, NY; J. Michael Bloom, 9200 Sunset Blvd., Suite 1210, Los Angeles, CA 90069.

* * *

GORMAN, Cliff   1936-

PERSONAL: Born October 13, 1936, in New York City; son of Samuel and Ethel (Kaplan) Gorman; married Gayle Stevens, May 31, 1963. EDUCATION: New York University, B.S., 1959.

VOCATION: Actor.

CAREER: FILM DEBUT—*Justine,* 1969. PRINCIPAL FILM APPEARANCES—*Boys in the Band,* 1970; *Cops and Robbers,* 1973; *Rosebud; An Unmarried Woman,* 1978; *Night of the Juggler,* 1979; *All That Jazz,* 1979.

PRINCIPAL TELEVISION APPEARANCES—*Police Story; Paradise Lost; The Trial of the Chicago Seven,* 1970; *Class of 63,* 1973; *The Bunker,* 1981.

STAGE DEBUT—Peter Boyle, *Hogan's Goat,* American Place, NY, 1965. PRINCIPAL STAGE APPEARANCES—Arnulf, *Ergo,* Anspacher, NY, 1968; Emory, *Boys in the Band,* Theatre Four, NY, 1968, then Huntington Hartford, Los Angeles, 1969; Lenny Bruce, *Lenny,* Brooks Atkinson, NY, 1971; Leo Schneider, *Chapter Two,* Ahmanson, Los Angeles, CA, then Imperial, NY, 1977.

MAJOR TOURS—Emory, *Boys in the Band,* U.S. cities, 1970.

AWARDS: Obie Award, 1968, for *Ergo;* Antoinette Perry Award, La Guardia Memorial Award, Show Business Award, Drama Desk Award, all 1972, for *Lenny.*

SIDELIGHTS: MEMBERSHIPS—Honor Legion of New York City

Police Department, Friends of George Spelvin (life).

ADDRESS: AGENT—William Morris Agency, 1350 Avenue of the Americas, New York, NY 10019.*

*   *   *

GOULD, Elliott   1938-

PERSONAL: Born Elliott Goldstein, August 29, 1938, in Brooklyn, NY; son of Bernard and Lucille (Raver) Goldstein; married Barbra Streisand (divorced). EDUCATION: Attended Professional Children's School and Columbia University; trained for the stage with Vladimir Protevitch, Jerome Swinford, Sonya Box, and Bill Quinn.

VOCATION: Actor.

CAREER: PRINCIPAL FILM APPEARANCES—*Bob and Carol and Ted and Alice*, 1969; *M*A*S*H*, 1970; *I Love My Wife*, 1970; *Little Murders*, 1971; *The Long Goodbye*, 1973; *S*P*Y*S*, 1974; *Busting*, 1974; *California Split*, 1974; *Nashville*, 1975; *Whiffs*, 1975; *I Will, I Will . . . For Now*, 1976; *Harry and Walter Go to New York*, 1976; *Mean Johnny Barrows*, 1976; *A Bridge Too Far*, 1977; *Capricorn One*, 1978; *Matilda*, 1978; *The Silent Partner*, 1979; *Escape to Athena*, 1979; *The Lady Vanishes*, 1979; *The Muppet Movie*, 1979; *Falling in Love Again*, 1980; *The Devil and Max Devlin*, 1981; *Over the Brooklyn Bridge*, 1984.

PRINCIPAL TELEVISION APPEARANCES—*Once Upon a Mattress*, 1964; Dr. Howard Sheinfeld, *E/R*, CBS, 1984-present; guest host, *Saturday Night Live*, NBC; *Actors on Acting*, PBS, 1984.

NEW YORK STAGE DEBUT—Chorus, *Rumple*, Alvin, 1957. LONDON DEBUT—Ozzie, *On the Town*, Prince of Wales, 1963. PRINCIPAL STAGE APPEARANCES—Earl Jorgenson, *Say Darling*, ANTA, NY, 1958, then City Center, NY, 1959; Usher, Priest, Warder, *Irma la Douce*, Plymouth, NY, 1960; Harry Bogen, *I Can Get It for You Wholesale*, Shubert, NY, 1962; Bob Purefoy, *Drat! The Cat!*, Martin Beck, NY, 1965; Alfred Chamberlain, *Little Murders*, Broadhurst, NY, 1967; Alex Krieger, *A Way of Life*, ANTA, NY, 1969; *The Guys in the Truck* (previews only), NY, c. 1983.

SIDELIGHTS: MEMBERSHIPS—Actors' Equity Association, American Federation of Television and Radio Artists.

ADDRESS: AGENT—William Morris Agency, 151 El Camino, Beverly Hills, CA 90212.*

*   *   *

GRADY, Don   1944-

PERSONAL: Born Don L. Agrati, June 8, 1944, in San Diego, CA; son of Lou A. (a sausage maker) and Mary B. (a talent agent; maiden name, Castellino) Agrati. EDUCATION: Attended Los Angeles City College. MILITARY: U.S. Army Reserves.

VOCATION: Actor and composer.

CAREER: TELEVISION DEBUT—Mouseketeer, *The Mickey Mouse*

DON GRADY

Club, Disney, 1957. PRINCIPAL TELEVISION APPEARANCES—*Restless Gun; Wagon Train; The Plainsman; Colt .45; Have Gun Will Travel; The Rifleman; Mr. Novak; Eleventh Hour; Ford Star Time; Alcoa Hour;* Robbie, *My Three Sons*, 1960-72; *F.B.I.; Love American Style; Simon and Simon.*

FILM DEBUT—*The Crowded Sky*, Warner Brothers, 1960. PRINCIPAL FILM APPEARANCES—*Cash McCall*, Warner Brothers, 1960; *Ma Barker's Killer Brood*, Film Service, 1960.

STAGE DEBUT—*Love Is a Time of Day*, St. Louis, MO, 1974. NEW YORK DEBUT—Jesus, *Godspell*. PRINCIPAL STAGE APPEARANCES—Pippin, *Pippin;* Tony, *The Boyfriend;* Huck, *Tom Sawyer;* Joe, *Damn Yankees;* Jim, *Pump Boys and Dinnettes.*

MAJOR TOURS—*Pippin*, U.S. cities, 1979.

RELATED CAREER—Composer: For the television show *The Kid-A -Littles*, NBC; "I Can Fly," for the film *Girls Just Want to Have Fun*.

AWARDS: Emmy Award nomination, for *Eleventh Hour*.

ADDRESS: AGENT—MGA, 3575 Cahuenga Blvd., Suite 320, Hollywood, CA 90068.

*   *   *

GRANT, Joyce   1924-

PERSONAL: Born January 23, 1924, in Bloemfontein, South

JOYCE GRANT

Africa; daughter of James Hugh and Magdaline (Kleinhaus) Grant. EDUCATION: University of Cape Town, South Africa; studied for the theatre at the Central School, London.

VOCATION: Actress.

CAREER: STAGE DEBUT—Yellow Ant, *The Insect Play,* Little, Cape Town, 1949. LONDON DEBUT—Mrs. Dawes and Asphynxia, *Salad Days,* Princes, 1961. NEW YORK DEBUT—Mrs. Rockefeller, *Rockefeller and the Red Indians,* Ethel Barrymore, 1968. PRINCIPAL STAGE APPEARANCES—*An Evening of British Rubbish,* Comedy, London, 1963; *Fielding's Music Hall,* Prince Charles, London, 1964; *Four and a Tanner,* New Arts, London, 1964; *Nymphs and Satires,* Apollo, London, 1965, Miss Wheeler, *The Happy Apple,* Apollo, London, 1970.

Three roles, *Tonight at Eight,* Hampstead, then Fortune, London, 1970-71; *Once Upon a Time,* Duke of York's, London, 1972; Mme. Remy, *Doctor Knock,* Oxford Playhouse, 1973; Fairy Godmother, *Cinderella,* Casino, London, 1974; Clara Hibbert, *The Vortex,* Greenwich, 1975; title role, *The Duenna,* Arnaud, Guildford, 1977; Lady Manley-Prowe, *Something's Afoot,* Ambasadors', London, 1977; Algy, *The Club,* Regent, London, 1978; Helga Ten Dorp, *Deathtrap,* Garrick, 1978; Landlady, *Corpse,* Apollo, London, 1984-85; also: roles with the Questors, Ealing, 1950; repertory, High Wycombe, 1952; repertory, Dundee and Guildford, 1953; Amanda Wingfield, *The Glass Menagerie.*

MAJOR TOURS—Mrs. Candour, *The School for Scandal,* Lola,

Come Back, Little Sheba, Emma Hornett, *Sailor Beware,* South Africa, 1954-60, tours and appearances with Nottingham Playhouse, 1964.

TELEVISION APPEARANCES—*The Black Adder,* American television; Caecilie Kurt, *The Dancing Years,* British television, 1979.

SIDELIGHTS: RECREATION—Gardening and motoring. FAVORITE ROLES—Helga Ten Dorp, Amanda Wingfield, and Mrs. Candour.

ADDRESS: HOME—London, England. AGENT—Kerry Gardner Management, 15 Kensington High Street, London W8 5NP, England.

*   *   *

GRAVES, Peter   1911-

PERSONAL: Born October 21, 1911, in London, England; son of Henry Algernon Claud (seventh baron) and Vera Blanche Neville (Snepp) Graves; married Vanessa Lee. EDUCATION: Harrow.

VOCATION: Actor and singer.

CAREER: STAGE DEBUT—*Streamline* (a revue), Opera House, Manchester, England, 1934. LONDON DEBUT—*Streamline,* Palace, 1934. PRINCIPAL STAGE APPEARANCES—(All London unless otherwise noted) Nico, *Glamorous Night,* Drury Lane, 1935; John, *Full House,* Haymarket, 1935; Captain Tarleton, *The Happy Hypocrite,* His Majesty's, 1936; Jimmy Torrence and understudy Michael,

Photography by Rafael

PETER GRAVES

Careless Rapture, Drury Lane, 1936; Donald Thrale, *The Heavenly Passion,* Arts, 1937; Hon. Charles Glenn, *African Dawn,* Daly's, 1937; Lord William Gantry, *The Crest of the Wave,* Drury Lane, 1937; Dauphin, *Henry V,* 1938; Franzel, *The Dancing Years,* 1939; M. Deladier, *Second Helping,* Streatham Hill, 1939 and at the Lyric, 1940, play was retitled *Ladies into Action;* member of the Windsor repertory company, 1941; Franzel, *The Dancing Years,* Adelphi, 1942; Pierre Bachelet, *Arc de Triomphe,* Phoenix, 1943.

Prince Orlofsky, *Gay Rosalinda,* Palace, 1945, also in revival at Prince's, 1946; Max Perry, *Divorce on Tuesday,* Q, 1946; Bill Whittaker, *We Proudly Present,* Duke of York's, 1947; Valentine Brown, *Dear Miss Phoebe,* Phoenix, 1950; Prince Danilo, *The Merry Widow,* Stoll, 1952; John Beaumont, *The Glorious Days,* Palace, 1953; Lord Windermere, *After the Ball,* Globe, 1954; Mr. Bryan, *The Water Gipsies,* Winter Garden, 1955; Lord Ranelagh, *Old Chelsea,* King's, Glasgow, Scotland, 1959; Philip Clair, *Kind Sir,* Connaught, Worthing, 1960; Emperor, *Aladdin,* Hippodrome, Bristol, 1960; Earl of Lister, *The Reluctant Peer,* Duchess, 1965; Charles, *The Last of Mrs. Cheyney,* 1967; Dominique, *Dear Charles,* Duke of York's, 1968; Hartkopf, *The Great Waltz,* 1971; Leslie Bromhead, *No Sex Please, We're British,* Strand, 1977-1983.

MAJOR TOURS—Peter von Hohenburg, *Blossom Time,* 1941; Sir Graham Rodney, *Perchance to Dream,* 1948; Elyot Chase, *Private Lives,* 1949; Evan, *September Tide,* U.S., 1949; Charles, *The Gay Deceiver,* 1956; Lord Ranelagh, *Old Chelsea,* 1959; Captain von Trapp, *The Sound of Music,* Australia, 1961-63; Elyot Chase, *Private Lives,* England, 1964; Earl of Caversham, *An Ideal Husband,* South Africa, 1969; Hubert, *A Boston Story,* 1970; Rupert, *His, Hers and Theirs,* 1970; Moore, *Who Killed Santa Claus?* 1972.

PRINCIPAL FILM APPEARANCES—*Kipps,* 1940; *The Slipper and the Rose,* Universal, 1977.

PRINCIPAL TELEVISION APPEARANCES—*The Duchess of Duke Street; Quiller; Father Brown; Shades of Darkness.*

SIDELIGHTS: Graves was employed in the insurance business and as an estate agent before becoming a successful actor.

ADDRESS: OFFICE—The Spotlight, 42 Cranbourn Street, London WC2, England.

*   *   *

GRAY, Barry   1916-

PERSONAL: Born Bernard Yaroslaw, July 2, 1916, in Red Lion, NJ; son of Manuis Joseph (an insurance broker) and Dora (Horowitz) Yaroslaw; divorced; children: Melodie, Michael. MILITARY: U.S. Army, 1941-44; U.S. Air Force Reserve, 1963-69.

VOCATION: Writer and broadcaster.

CAREER: PRINCIPAL TELEVISION WORK—Newscaster, *Nightly News,* WNEW, NY, 1951-53; newscaster, *Nightly News,* WNET, NY, 1956; *Winner Take All,* CBS; *Songs for Sale,* CBS.

PRINCIPAL RADIO WORK—Daily interviews, WMCA, NY, 1950-present.

STAGE DEBUT—Elwood P. Dowd, *Harvey,* subway circuit, Montclair, NJ, Brooklyn, Bronx, NY.

BARRY GRAY

WRITINGS: BOOKS—*My Night People,* Simon and Schuster, 1974. NEWSPAPER ARTICLES—For *Our Town,* NY. MAGAZINE ARTICLES—For *Smart Living,* NY.

AWARDS: Michael Award, English Speaking Union.

SIDELIGHTS: MEMBERSHIPS—Friars Club.

ADDRESS: HOME—New York, NY. OFFICE—888 Seventh Avenue, New York, NY 10106.

*   *   *

GRAY, Linda

PERSONAL: Born September 12, in Santa Monica, CA; married Ed Thrasher (divorced, 1983); children: Jeff, Kelly. EDUCATION: Trained for the stage with Charles Conrad.

VOCATION: Actress.

CAREER: PRINCIPAL TELEVISION APPEARANCES—Series: *All That Glitters,* 1977; Sue Ellen, *Dallas,* 1978-present. Movies: *The Two Worlds of Jenny Logan; Haywire; Chimps; Not in Front of the Children.* Also *Marcus Welby, M.D.; The Body Human; The Loving Process,* 1981; cohost, *Golden Globe Awards Show,* 1981

PRINCIPAL FILM APPEARANCES—*Dogs.*

AWARDS: Emmy Award nomination, 1981, for *Dallas:* Woman of the Year Award, Hollywood Radio and Television Society, 1982; Bambi Award, Best Actress, Germany, 1982; Il Gato Award, Best Actress, Italy, 1983, 1984.

SIDELIGHTS: CTFT learned Linda Gray is also a professional model and has appeared in over 400 television commercials.

ADDRESS: OFFICE—Richard Grant, Lippin and Grant, 8124 W. Third Street, Los Angeles, CA 90048.*

*　　*　　*

GRAY, Simon　1936-

PERSONAL: Born October 21, 1936, in Hayling Island, Hants; son of James Davidson and Barbara Cecelia Mary (Holliday) Gray; married Beryl Mary Kevern. EDUCATION: Attended Westminster, Dalhousie University, and Trinity College, Cambridge.

VOCATION: Playwright.

WRITINGS: PLAYS—*Wise Child*, 1967; *Dutch Uncle*, 1968; *The Idiot*, 1970; *Spoiled, Butley*, 1971; *Otherwise Engaged*, 1975; *Molly*, 1976; *Dog Days*, 1977; *The Rear Column*, 1978; *Close of Play, Stage Struck*, 1979; *Quartermaine's Terms*, NY, 1981; *The Common Pursuit*, 1984.

TELEVISION PLAYS—*Death of a Teddy Bear; Plaintiffs and Defendants; Two Sundays*. BOOKS—Has written four books.

AWARDS: Writers Guild Award, for *Death of a Teddy Bear*.

ADDRESS: AGENT—Judy Daish Associates Ltd., 83 Eastbourne Mews, London W2 6LQ, England.

*　　*　　*

GREEN, Adolph　1915-

PERSONAL: Born December 2, 1915, in New York City; son of Daniel and Helen (Weiss) Green; married Phyllis Newman (an actress), January 31, 1960; children: Adam, Amanda.

VOCATION: Playwright, lyricist, actor, and entertainer.

CAREER: STAGE DEBUT—Cabaret act, *The Revuers*, Village Vanguard, NY. PRINCIPAL STAGE APPEARANCES—Ozzie, *On the Town*, Adelphi, NY, 1944; *A Party with Betty Comden and Adolph Green* (as a Monday night show) Cherry Lane, NY, then Golden, NY, 1958; *The Cradle Will Rock*, Philharmonic Hall, NY, 1964; with Betty Comden, *Lyrics and Lyricists*, Kaufman Auditorium, 96th St. YM/YWHA, 1971; *A Party with Betty Comden and Adolph Green*, Juilliard School of Music, NY, 1971; *A Party. . .*, Morosco, NY, and tour, 1977; voice over characters, *Phyllis Newman in Vamps and Rideouts*, Berkshire Theatre Festival, Stockbridge, MA, 1982.

PRINCIPAL FILM APPEARANCES—*Simon*, Warner Brothers, 1980; *My Favorite Year*, Metro-Goldwyn-Mayer/United Artists, 1982;

Garbo Talks, 1984; *Lily in Love*, 1985.

WRITINGS: PLAYS, PRODUCED—Sketches, principally in collaboration with Betty Comden and Judy Holliday, *The Revuers*, early 1940's; musical with Betty Comden and Leonard Bernstein, *On the Town*, 1944; musical with Betty Comden and Morton Gould, *Billion Dollar Baby*, 1945; musical with Betty Comden, *Bonanza Bound!*, 1947; sketches and lyrics, with Betty Comden, *Two on the Aisle*, 1951; musical with Betty Comden and Leonard Bernstein, *Wonderful Town*, 1953; additional lyrics with Betty Comden and Jule Styne, *Peter Pan*, 1954; musical with Betty Comden and Jule Styne, *Bells Are Ringing*, 1956; musical with Betty Comden and Jule Styne, *Say, Darling!*, 1958.

Book and lyrics with Betty Comden, *A Party with Betty Comden and Adolph Green*, 1960; lyrics with Betty Comden, *Do-Re-Mi*, 1960; musical with Betty Comden and Jule Styne, *Subways Are for Sleeping*, 1961; *On the Town*, London, 1963; musical with Betty Comden and Jule Styne, *Fade Out-Fade In*, 1964, revised 1965; some lyrics, *Leonard Bernstein's Theatre Songs*, 1965; musical with Betty Comden and Jule Styne, *Hallelujah, Baby!*, 1967; book for musical with Betty Comden, Charles Strause, and Lee Adams, *Applause*, 1970; lyrics, revisions to book, direction with Betty Comden and Jule Styne, *Lorelei*, 1974; book with Betty Comden, *By Bernstein*, 1975; musical with Betty Comden and Cy Coleman, *On the Twentieth Century*, 1978; with Betty Comden, *Peter Pan*, revived 1979; musical with Betty Comden, *A Doll's Life*, 1982.

FILMS—(Screenplays and/or lyrics) *Good News*, Metro-Goldwyn-Mayer, 1947; *The Barkleys of Broadway*, Metro-Goldwyn-Mayer, 1949; *Take Me Out to the Ball Game*, Metro-Goldwyn-Mayer, 1949, *Singin' in the Rain*, Metro-Goldwyn-Mayer, 1952; *The Band Wagon*, Metro-Goldwyn-Mayer, 1953; *It's Always Fair Weather*, Metro-Goldwyn-Mayer, 1955; *Auntie Mame*, Warner Brothers, 1958; *Bells Are Ringing*, Metro-Goldwyn-Mayer, 1960; *What a Way to Go*, Twentieth Century-Fox, 1968.

TELEVISION—*Wonderful Town; Peter Pan; Applause; A Party with Betty Comden and Adolph Green*.

AWARDS: Donaldson Award (with Betty Comden), 1953, for *Wonderful Town;* Academy Award nomination (with Betty Comden), Best Story and Screenplay, 1953, for *The Band Wagon;* Academy Award nomination (with Betty Comden), Best Story and Screenplay, 1955, for *It's Always Fair Weather;* Antoinette Perry Awards, Best Score (with Betty Comden and Jule Styne), best lyrics, *Hallelujah, Baby!*, 1967-68; Antoinette Perry Award (with Betty Comden, Charles Strouse and Lee Adams), Best Musical, 1970, for *Applause;* Antoinette Perry Awards for Best Book (with Betty Comden) and Best Score (with Betty Comden and Cy Coleman), 1978, for *On the Twentieth Century;* Songwriter's Hall of Fame, 1980; Screenwriters Guild Award; A.F.I. voted *Singin' in the Rain*, one of the best American films of all times; *Sight & Sound* magazine named the same film as one of the ten best films of all time (internationally).

ADDRESS: OFFICE—John Springer Associates, Inc., 667 Madison Avenue, New York, NY.

*　　*　　*

GREENE, Lyn　1954-

PERSONAL: Born May 21, 1954, in Newton, MA; daughter of Kermit (a businessman) and Elinore A. (a teacher and author;

maiden name, Ziff) Greene. EDUCATION: Juilliard School, Drama Division, 1972-75; New York University, B.A., Gallatin Division, 1976.

VOCATION: Actress.

CAREER: DEBUT—Lead singer, *Earthlight,* Charles Playhouse, Boston, MA, 1972. PRINCIPAL STAGE APPEARANCES—*Quirks,* Edison, NY; *Say Goodnight Gracie,* Actors Playhouse, NY; *Hi Low,* one woman show staged by Lyn Greene, NY; Michelle Schwartz, *Kid Purple,* Roundabout II, NY, 1984; Hope, *Amateurs,* Michael Bennet Studios, NY.

Nancy, *Oliver,* the Leader, *Zorba,* Sally Bowles, *Cabaret,* Colorado Center for the Performing Arts; Mary Warren, *The Crucible,* Anne Rutledge, *Spoon River Anthology,* Meadowbrook Summer Theatre; Susie La Reve, *The Gang's All Here,* Ralph Freud Playhouse, Los Angeles, CA; Sister Ralph, *Ready or Not,* Pennsylvania Stage Co.; Lina, *Misalliance,* Rosalinde, *As You Like It,* Arizona Theatre Company; lead, *Sprechen Sie Brecht,* White Barn, Westport, CT; lead, *Brecht on Brecht,* St. Louis Rep, Loretto-Hilton, St. Louis, MO; Jenny, *The Threepenny Opera,* Portland Stage Co, OR; Lucy Brown, *The Threepenny Opera,* St. Louis Rep, Loretto-Hilton; Lenny, *Crimes of the Heart,* Portland Stage Co.; Helena, *A Midsummer Night's Dream,* Denver Center Theatre.

MAJOR TOURS—Rotonde, *The Love Cure,* Lincoln Center tour; Lina, *Misalliance,* Rosalinde, *As You Like It,* Arizona Theatre Company.

PRINCIPAL STAGE WORK—Director: *Hi Low,* one woman show, Off Broadway, NY.

LYN GREENE

PRINCIPAL FILM APPEARANCES—Cynthia, *Over the Brooklyn Bridge,* Cannon, 1983.

PRINCIPAL TELEVISION APPEARANCES—Maria Teresa Bonino, *On Our Own,* CBS, 1977-78; various talk shows.

WRITINGS: Sprechen sie Brecht (co-adapted with Swen Swenson).

SIDELIGHTS: MEMBERSHIPS—Actors' Equity Association, American Federation of Television and Radio Artists, Screen Actors Guild.

Lyn Greene writes to *CTFT* that, so far, her "most significant roles have been played in regional theatre."

ADDRESS: AGENT—Kingman-Ganz, 1501 Broadway, Suite 1808A, New York, NY 10036.

*   *   *

GREENFELD, Josh   1928-

PERSONAL: Born February 27, 1928, in Malden, MA; married Foumiko Kometani, 1960; children: Karl Taro, Noah Jiro. EDUCATION: University of Michigan, B.A.; Columbia University, M.A. MILITARY: 1953-55.

VOCATION: Writer.

WRITINGS: BOOKS—*O for a Master of Magic; Harry and Tonto; A Child Called Noah; A Place for Noah,* Holt, Rinehart, and Winston, 1978; *The Return of Mr. Hollywood,* Doubleday, 1984. PLAYS—*I Have a Dream* (produced on Broadway); *Clandestine on the Morning Line* (produced Off Broadway). TELEPLAYS—*Lovey: A Circle of Children, Part II,* 1978. SCREENPLAYS—*Harry and Tonto; Oh God, Book Two.* CRITICISM—Book reviews for "Time," "The New York Times," "Newsweek," "Washington Post," "Chicago Sun-Times," "Commonweal," "The Village Voice," "New York." Contributor to "Life," "The New York Times Magazine," "Esquire," "The Reporter."

AWARDS: Best Magazine Article of the Year, Society of Magazine Writers; Academy Award nomination, Best Screenplay, 1974, for *Harry and Tonto;* Christopher Awards, 1974, 1979, 1980; Guggenheim Foundation fellowship; Ford Foundation fellowship.

SIDELIGHTS: MEMBERSHIPS—Academy of Motion Picture Arts and Sciences, Authors League of America, P.E.N.

ADDRESS: AGENT—William Morris Agency, 151 El Camino Drive, Beverly Hills, CA 90212.

*   *   *

GREGG, Virginia   1916-

PERSONAL: Born March 6, 1916, in Harrisburg, IL; daughter of Edward William (a businessman) and Dewey Alphaleta (a musician; maiden name, Todd) Gregg; married Jaime del Valle (a director); children: Gregg, Jaime, Ricardo. EDUCATION: Trained for the stage at the Pacific Academy of Dramatic Art.

VIRGINIA GREGG

VOCATION: Actress.

CAREER: FILM DEBUT—*Body and Soul*, 1947. PRINCIPAL FILM APPEARANCES—*Casbah*, 1948; *Breaking Point*, 1950; *Dragnet*, 1954; *Love Is a Many Splendored Thing*, Twentieth Century-Fox, 1955; *Crime in the Streets*, Allied Artists, 1956; *I'll Cry Tomorrow*, Metro-Goldwyn-Mayer, 1956; *The Fastest Gun Alive*, Metro-Goldwyn-Mayer, 1956; *Terror at Midnight*, Republic, 1956; *The D.I.*, 1957; *Hound Dog Man*, Twentieth Century-Fox, 1959; *The Hanging Tree*, Warner Brothers, 1959; *Operation Petticoat*, Universal, 1959; *Spencer's Mountain*, 1963; *Two on a Guillotine*, Warner Brothers, 1965; *Joy in the Morning*, Metro-Goldwyn-Mayer, 1965; *A Big Hand for the Little Lady*, Warner Brothers, 1966; *Heaven with a Gun*, Metro-Goldwyn-Mayer, 1969; *A Walk in the Spring Rain*, Columbia, 1970; *Airport '75*, Universal, 1974; *S.O.B.*, Paramount, 1981.

PRINCIPAL TELEVISION APPEARANCES—*Dragnet; Marcus Welby; This Is the Life; Streets of San Francisco; Richie Bronckelman; Baretta; Bronk; Six Million Dollar Man; Bob Hope Specials; State Fair; Rockford Files; Emergency; Adam-12; S.W.A.T.; Police Woman; Happy Days; Cannon; Ironside*, and the television movie, *Dragnet*, 1969.

PRINCIPAL RADIO WORK—*Dragnet; Gunsmoke; Jack Benny; One Man's Family; Let George Do It; Dr. Kildare; Lux Radio Theatre; Screen Guild Theatre; Sam Spade*, others.

ADDRESS: AGENT—Georgia Gilly, 8721 Sunset Blvd., Hollywood, CA, 90046.

GREGORY, Andre

VOCATION: Producer, director, and actor.

CAREER: PRINCIPAL STAGE WORK—Director: *P.S. 193*, Writer's Stage, NY, 1962; *Firebugs*, 1963; *Tartuffe*, 1967; *The Bacchae*, 1969; *Alice in Wonderland*, 1970; *Endgame*, 1974; *The Seagull, Our Late Night*, 1975; *Jinxs Bridge*, 1976.

Producer: *Deirdre of the Sorrows*, Gate, NY, 1959; *The Blacks*, Gate, NY, 1961.

MAJOR TOURS—Producer, *Alice in Wonderland*, U.S. cities and Edinburgh Festival.

PRINCIPAL FILM APPEARANCES—*My Dinner with Andre*.

ADDRESS: OFFICE—The Manhattan Project, c/o the Bunch, 115 Central Park West, New York, NY 10023.*

*   *   *

GROSBARD, Ulu 1929-

PERSONAL: Born January 9, 1929, in Antwerp, Belgium; son of Morris and Rose (Tennenbaum) Grosbard; married Rose Gregorio. EDUCATION: University of Chicago, B.A., 1950; University of Chicago, M.A., 1952; trained at the Yale School of Drama, 1952-53.

VOCATION: Director.

CAREER: FIRST STAGE WORK—Director, *A View from the Bridge*, Gateway Playhouse, Belleport, Long Island, NY, 1957. FIRST NEW YORK STAGE WORK—Director, *The Days and Nights of Beebee Fenstermaker*, Sheridan Square Playhouse, 1962.

PRINCIPAL STAGE WORK—Director: *The Subject Was Roses*, 1964; *A View from the Bridge*, 1965; *The Investigation*, 1966; *That Summer—That Fall*, 1967; *The Price*, 1968; *American Buffalo*, 1977; *The Woods*, 1979; *The Wake of Jamie Foster*, 1982; *Weekends Like Other People*, 1982.

PRINCIPAL FILM WORK—Assistant director, *Splendor in the Grass*, Warner Brothers, 1961; assistant director, *West Side Story*, United Artists, 1961; assistant director, *The Hustler*, Twentieth Century-Fox, 1961; assistant director, *The Miracle Worker*, United Artists, 1962; unit manager, *The Pawnbroker*, Allied Artists/Landau, 1965. Director: *Who Is Harry Kellerman and Why Is He Saying Those Terrible Things About Me?*, National General, 1971; *Straight Time*, Warner Brothers, 1978; *True Confessions*, United Artists, 1981; *Falling in Love*, 1984.

PRINCIPAL TELEVISION WORK—Production manager, *Deadline*, 1959-60; *The Investigation*, 1967.

SIDELIGHTS: RECREATIONS—Chess and swimming.

ADDRESS: OFFICE—29 W. Tenth Street, New York, NY 10011.

PETER GUBER

GUBER, Peter   1942-

PERSONAL: Full name Howard Peter Guber; born March 1, 1942, in Boston, MA; son of Samuel and Ruth Guber; married Lynda Gellis (a film producer); children: Jodie, Elizabeth. EDUCATION: Syracuse University, B.A.; New York University, M.B.A.; New York University School of Law, Juris Doctor, L.L.M.

VOCATION: Producer.

CAREER: PRINCIPAL FILM WORK—Producer: *The Deep,* Columbia, 1977; *Midnight Express; Thank God It's Friday; Missing; Endless Love; An American Werewolf in London; Flashdance,* 1983.

PRINCIPAL TELEVISION WORK—Producer: *Stand by Your Man; Mysteries of the Sea; The Donna Summer Special; The Selling of the President,* 1984; *Dreams,* CBS; *The Toughest Man in the World,* CBS; *Double Platinum; David Steinberg's Hollywood Stars,* Metro-Goldwyn-Mayer/United Artists Television; *Ocean Quest,* 1985.

RELATED CAREER—Production executive, Columbia Pictures, 1968-76; chairman of the board, Casablanca Record and Film Works; chairman, Polygram Pictures, 1980; co-chairman, co-owner, Guber-Peters Entertainment Company, 1983; adjunct professor, University of California at Los Angeles.

AWARDS: Academy Award nomination, Golden Award nomination, both for *The Deep;* six Golden Globe Awards, two Academy Awards, three British Academy Awards, Los Angeles Film Critics

Award, all for *Midnight Express;* Academy Award, Double Platinum Award, for *Thank God It's Friday;* National Association of Theater Owners Award, Producer of the Year, 1971; Palm D'Or Award, Cannes Film Festival, five Golden Globe Award nominations, four Academy Awards, seven British Academy Awards, Christopher Award, Best Picture of the Year, all for *Missing;* Academy Award, for *American Werewolf in London;* Academy Award, two Golden Globe Awards, four Grammy Award nominations, all for *Flashdance.*

SIDELIGHTS: NON-RELATED CAREER—Founder, director, Bel Air Savings and Loan Association.

ADDRESS: OFFICE—4000 Warner Blvd., Bldg. 66, Burbank, CA 91522.

*   *   *

GUETARY, Georges   1915-

PERSONAL: Born Lambros Worlodu, February 8, 1915; son of Georges and Olga Worlodu; married Olga Janspouls; children: two. EDUCATION: Trained for the stage at Rene Simon School of Comedy, Ninon Valin School of Singing.

VOCATION: Actor and singer.

CAREER: STAGE DEBUT—*La Revue,* Alhambra Theater, Paris, 1944. NEW YORK STAGE DEBUT—*Arms and the Girl,* 46th Street

GEORGES GUETARY

Theater, 1949. LONDON STAGE DEBUT—*Bless the Bride*, Strand, 1946, 200 performances. PRINCIPAL STAGE APPEARANCES—Chatelet Theater, Paris, 1950, 1965, 1968; A.B.C., Paris, 1953; London, 1957; New York, 1959.

MAJOR TOURS—*Arms and the Girl*, U.S. cities, 1949.

FILM DEBUT—*Le Cavalier Noir*, Paris, 1944. PRINCIPAL FILM APPEARANCES—*An American in Paris; Baron in Berlin*.

PRINCIPAL TELEVISION APPEARANCES—*Ed Sullivan Show* (five times), 1950.

WRITINGS: BOOKS—*Les Hasards Fabuleux*, La Table Rondi, Paris, 1981.

AWARDS: Drama Critics Award, NY, 1950; Pathe Marconi Award.

SIDELIGHTS: MEMBERSHIPS—The Union of Artists, La Croix Rouge.

ADDRESS: AGENT—Charles and Maurice Marouni, Four Avenue Hoche, Paris, France 75008.

*   *   *

STEVE GUTTENBERG

GUTTENBERG, Steve   1958-

PERSONAL: Born August 24, 1958, in Brooklyn, NY; son of Jerome Stanley (an engineer) and Ann Iris (a surgical assistant; maiden name, Newman) Guttenberg. EDUCATION: Attended Albany State University.

VOCATION: Actor.

CAREER: FILM DEBUT—*The Chicken Chronicles*, Avco, 1977. PRINCIPAL FILM APPEARANCES—*Rollercoaster*, Universal, 1977; *Boys from Brazil*, Twentieth Century Fox, 1979; *Players*, Paramount, 1979; *Diner*, Metro-Goldwyn-Mayer, 1982; *Police Academy*, Warner Brothers, 1984; *Police Academy II*, 1985; *Cocoon*, Twentieth Century-Fox, 1985; *Bad Medicine*, Twentieth Century-Fox, 1985.

TELEVISION DEBUT—*Something for Joey*, Mary Tyler Moore Productions, CBS, 1976. PRINCIPAL TELEVISION APPEARANCES—*Billy*, CBS; *Miracle on Ice*, ABC, 1980; *The Day After*, 1984.

ADDRESS: AGENT—Stan Kamen, William Morris Agency, 151 El Camino, Beverly Hills, CA 90212.

*   *   *

GWYNNE, Fred   1926-

PERSONAL: Full name Frederick Hubbard Gwynne; born July 10, 1926, in New York City; married Jean Reynard, 1952; children: four. EDUCATION: Harvard University, B.A., 1951. MILITARY: U.S. Navy, 1944-46.

VOCATION: Actor and writer.

CAREER: NEW YORK STAGE DEBUT—Stinker, *Mrs. McThing*, Martin Beck, 1952. PRINCIPAL STAGE APPEARANCES—Dull, *Love's Labour's Lost*, City Center, NY, 1953; Luther Raubel, *The Frogs of Spring*, Broadhurst, NY, 1953; Polyt-le-Mou, *Irma La Douce*, Plymouth, NY, 1960; Marvin Shellhammer, *Here's Love*, Shubert, NY, 1963; Abraham Lincoln, *The Lincoln Mask*, Plymouth, NY, 1972; Major Michael Dillon, *The Enchanted*, Estelle R. Neuman Theater, NY, 1973; *More Than You Deserve*, 1973; *Twelfth Night*, and Big Daddy, *Cat on a Hot Tin Roof*, American Shakespeare Festival, Stratford, CT, 1974; Big Daddy, *Cat on a Hot Tin Roof*, ANTA, NY, 1974; Stage Manager, *Our Town*, Autolycus, *The Winter's Tale*, both American Shakespeare Festival, Stratford, CT, 1975; Colonel J.C. Kincaid, *A Texas Trilogy*, Broadhurst, NY, 1976; W. O. Grant, *Angel*, Minskoff, NY, 1978; Jock Riley, *Players*, Lyceum, NY, 1979; Otto Marvuglia, *Grand Magic*, Manhattan Theatre Club, NY, 1979; *Salt Lake City Skyline*, NY, 1982; *Whodunnit?*, NY, 1983.

PRINCIPAL TELEVISION APPEARANCES—*Harvey*, 1958; *The Hasty Heart*, 1958; *The Old Foolishness*, 1961; Officer Francis Muldoon, *Car 54, Where Are You?*, NBC, 1961-63; Herman Munster, *The Munsters*, CBS, 1964-66; *The Lesson*, 1966; *Infancy*, PBS, 1967; *Guess What I Did Today*, NBC, 1968; *Arsenic and Old Lace*, ABC, 1969; *The Littlest Angel*, NBC, 1969; *Paradise Lost*, PBS, 1971; *The Police*, PBS, 1971; *Dames at Sea*, NBC, 1971; *Harvey*, NBC, 1972; *Any Friend of Nicholas Nickleby's Is a Friend of Mine*, PBS, 1982; *Kane and Abel*, CBS, 1985-86.

PRINCIPAL FILM APPEARANCES—*On the Waterfront,* Columbia, 1954; *Munster, Go Home,* Universal, 1966; *Luna,* Twentieth Century-Fox, 1979; *Simon,* Orion, 1980; *Jack-a-Boy,* Phoenix, 1980; *Cotton Club,* 1984; *Off Beat,* Touchstone (upcoming); *The Boy Who Could Fly,* Lorimar Canada (upcoming).

WRITINGS: BOOKS—*Best in Show,* Dutton, 1958; *What's Nude?,* 1960; *God's First World,* Harper, 1970; *The King Who Rained,* Windmill, 1970; *Ick's ABC,* Windmill, 1971; *The Story of Ick,* Windmill, 1971; *The Sixteen-Hand Horse,* Windmill, 1980.

AWARDS: Obie Award, Best Actor, 1979, for *Grand Magic.*

SIDELIGHTS: MEMBERSHIPS—American Federation of Television and Radio Artists, Screen Actors Guild, Actors' Equity Association.

Gwynne was an illustrator of children's books and a copywriter with the J. Walter Thompson Advertising Agency.*

H

HAAS, Charlie 1952-

PERSONAL: Born October 22, 1952, in Brooklyn, NY; son of Philip (an attorney) and Eunice (Dillon) Haas; married Janet Dodson, September 9, 1976 (divorced, 1980); married Barbara K. Moran (a writer and editor), December 23, 1981. EDUCATION: University of California, Santa Cruz, B.A., 1974.

VOCATION: Writer.

WRITINGS: SCREENPLAYS—*Over the Edge* (with Tim Hunter), 1979; *Tex* (with Tim Hunter), Buena Vista, 1982. TELEPLAYS—*Reckless Disregard*, Showtime, 1984; *The Clayton Family* (with Tim Hunter; educational film).

BOOKS—*The Soul Hit* (with Tim Hunter), 1977; *Over the Edge* (with Tim Hunter), 1979; *What Color Is Your Parody?: A Self-Harm Manual for Job-Hunters and Career-Changers*, Price Stern, 1984. MAGAZINES—Contributor to ''New West,'' ''Esquire,'' ''National Lampoon,'' ''Mother Jones.''

AWARDS: First Place, Independent Productions, CEBA Award, World Institute of Black Communications, 1981, for *The Clayton Family* (with Tim Hunter).

SIDELIGHTS: MEMBERSHIPS—Writers Guild of America.

Haas appeared as the second drug dealer in the film of his screenplay *Tex*. He told *CTFT:* ''Always be working on a project and you will never have to live in one.''

ADDRESS: AGENT—Jane Sindell, International Creative 8899 Beverly Blvd., Los Angeles, CA 90048.

*   *   *

HADDRICK, Ron 1929-

PERSONAL: Born April 9, 1929, in Adelaide, South Australia; son of Alexander Norman and Olive May (Gibson) Haddrick; married Margaret Lorraine Quigley. EDUCATION: Studied voice at Adelaide University.

VOCATION: Actor.

CAREER: STAGE DEBUT—Stanislaus, *The Eagle Has Two Heads*, Tivoli, Adelaide, 1948. LONDON DEBUT—Alfred, *Toad of Toad Hall*, Princes, 1954. PRINCIPAL STAGE APPEARANCES—Hubert, *King John*, Tybalt, *Romeo and Juliet*, Antonio, *Twelfth Night*,

RON HADDRICK

Horatio, *Hamlet*, all with Shakespeare Memorial Theatre Company, Stratford-on-Avon, 1954-59; John Tanner, *Man and Superman*, Jamie Tyrone, *Long Day's Journey into Night*, Brutus, *Julius Caesar*, all with Elizabethan Theatre Trust, Sydney, Australia, 1959; Heracles, *The Rape of the Belt*, James Mavor Morell, *Candida*, Monsewer, *The Hostage*, Fourth Tempter and Fourth Knight, *Murder in the Cathedral*, all with Elizabethan Theatre Trust, Sydney, 1960; *Murder in the Cathedral*, Adelaide Festival of Arts, 1960; Alf Cook, *The One Day of the Year*, Palace, Sydney, then Theatre Royal, Stratford, London, 1961; Jacko, *Naked Island*, Union, Sydney, 1962; Dunois, *Saint Joan*, Adelaide Festival of the Arts, 1962.

1963-70, with Old Tote Theatre, Sydney, Australia, roles included: Jamie Tyrone, *Moon for the Misbegotten*, Azdak, *The Caucasian Chalk Circle*, Pinchwife, *The Country Wife*, title role, *Othello*, Claudius, *Hamlet*, Oedipus, Tyrone Guthrie's *King Oedipus*, among others; Nandor, *The Guardsman*, Perth Festival, then

Parade, Sydney, 1971; Foster, *National Health*, Parade, Sydney, 1971, Mayor, *The Government Inspector*, Parade, Sydney, 1971; Ormund, *I've Been Here Before*, Community, Sydney, 1971; Baptista, *The Taming of the Shrew*, Parade, Sydney, 1972; Gov. Lachlan Macquarie, *Macquarie*, MTC, Russell Street Theatre, Melbourne, 1972; Father, *Forget-Me-Not Lane*, Parade, Sydney, 1972; Brigadello, *How Could You Believe Me When I Said I Loved You When You Know I've Been a Liar All My Life*, Parade, Sydney, 1972.

Friar, *Tis Pity She's a Whore*, Octagon, Perth Festival, then Parade, Sydney, 1973; Magistrate, *Lysistrata*, Parade, Sydney, 1973; York, *Richard II*, Ken Collins, *What If You Died Tomorrow*, both with Old Tote Company at Drama Theatre of Sydney Opera House for their opening season, 1973-74, the latter then at Elizabethan, Sydney, and subsequently Comedy, Melbourne, 1974; title role, *Macbeth*, Old Tote Company, Opera Theatre, Sydney Opera House, 1974; Ken Collins, *What If You Died Tomorrow*, Comedy, London, 1974; Button Moulder, *Peer Gynt*, Drama Theatre, Sydney Opera House, 1975; Alan West, *Savages*, Theatre Royal, Hobart, then Princess, Launceston, Australia, 1975; Harry, *Home*, Parade, Sydney, 1975; Ezra Mannon, *Mourning Becomes Electra*, Drama Theatre, Sydney Opera House, 1976; Horace Vandergelder, *The Matchmaker*, Drama Theatre, Sydney Opera House, 1976; Uncle Peter, *The Plough and the Stars*, Drama Theatre, Sydney Opera House, 1977; Logan and Posh Jim, *Unspeakable Acts*, Parade, Sydney, 1977.

Major General Anderson-Green, *The Brass Hat*, Queensland Theatre Company, 1977; Jock, *The Club*, Nimrod, Sydney, then Theatre Royal, 1978; Ernest, *Bedroom Farce*, Theatre Royal, Sydney, 1978; Jardine Leachman, *Lost to the Devil*, Neutral Bay Music Hall, Sydney, 1979; Jock, *The Club*, Hampstead, London, 1980; *Two Gentlemen of Verona, Measure for Measure*, both in Sydney, 1980; Eek and Zeek Perkins, *Man from Mukinupin*, Sydney Theatre Co., 1981; Chebutykin, *The Three Sisters*, Nimrod, Sydney, 1981; Falstaff, *Henry IV, Part I*, Big Daddy, *Cat on a Hot Tin Roof*, Le Bret, *Cyrano de Bergerac*, all with Sydney Theatre Co., 1981; Kalabushkin, *The Suicide*, Nimrod, Sydney, 1982; Casanova, *Camino Real*, Jane Street Theatre, Sydney, 1982; Peppino, *Saturday, Sunday, Monday*, Queensland Theatre Co., 1982; Houses, *Happy & Holy Occasion*, Sydney Theatre Co., 1982; Tom, *Fields of Heaven*, Sir Wilfred Witwood, *The Way of the World*, Van Maibeling, *Gossip from the Forrest*, Firs, *The Cherry Orchard*, Vincent Crummels/Arthur Gride, *Nicholas Nickleby*, all Sydney Theatre Co., 1983; Frank, *Travelling North*, Uncle Harvey, *Seasons Greetings*, both Northside Theatre Co., 1984.

MAJOR TOURS—Dunois, *Saint Joan*, 1962; Jock, *The Club*, 1978; Vincent Crummles and Arthur Gride, *Nicholas Nickleby*, Melbourne and Adelaide.

PRINCIPAL TELEVISION APPEARANCES—Dave Ruben, *Reunion Day*, London; David King, *A Sleep of Prisoners;* Petruchio, *The Taming of the Shrew;* Dr. Redfern, *The Outcasts;* title roles in *Tartuffe* and *The Stranger*.

AWARDS: Member of the British Empire, New Year Honors, 1974.

SIDELIGHTS: FAVORITE PARTS—John Tanner, Azdak, Alf Cook, Jamie Tyrone, Oedipus. RECREATION—Cricket (played for South Australia in 1952).

Before becoming an actor, Haddrick worked as a dental prosthetic technician.

ADDRESS: HOME—17 Kessell Avenue, Homebush West, New South Wales, Australia.

UTA HAGEN

HAGEN, Uta   1919-

PERSONAL: Born June 12, 1919, in Gottingen, Germany; daughter of Oskar Frank Leonard (a doctor) and Thyra Amalie (Leisner) Hagen; married Jose Ferrer (divorced); married Herbert Berghof. EDUCATION: Attended University of Wisconsin; trained for the stage at the Royal Academy of Dramatic Art, London.

VOCATION: Actress and teacher.

CAREER: STAGE DEBUT—Ophelia, *Hamlet*, Eva Le Gallienne's Civic Repertory Company, Dennis, MA, 1937. NEW YORK DEBUT—Nina, *The Seagull*, Shubert, 1938. LONDON DEBUT—Martha, *Who's Afraid of Virginia Woolf*, Piccadilly, 1964. PRINCIPAL STAGE APPEARANCES—Edith, *The Happiest Days*, Vanderbilt, NY, 1939; Alegre d'Alcala, *Key Largo*, Ethel Barrymore, NY, 1939; Desdemona, *Othello*, Cambridge, MA, and Princeton, NJ, 1942; Vickie Roberts, *Vickie*, Plymouth, NY, 1942; Desdemona, *Othello*, Shubert, NY, 1943, and City Center, NY, 1945; Olga Vorontsov, *The Whole World Over*, Biltmore, NY, 1947; Natasha, *Dark Eyes*, 1947; Margaret, *Faust*, Barbizon Plaza, NY, 1947; Mrs. Manningham, *Angel Street*, City Center, NY, 1948; Blanche, *A Streetcar Named Desire*, Ethel Barrymore, NY, 1948, 1949, and City Center, NY, 1950.

Georgia Elgin, *The Country Girl*, Lyceum, NY, 1950; Joan, *St. Joan*, Cort, NY, 1951; Grand Duchess Tatiana Petrovna, *Tovarich*, City Center, NY, 1952; Hannah King, *In Any Language*, Cort, NY, 1952; Grace Wilson, *The Magic and the Loss*, Booth, NY, 1954; *The Affairs of Anatol*, Ann Arbor Drama Festival, MI, 1955; Agata, *Island of Goats*, Fulton, NY, 1955; Natalia Petrovna, *A Month in the Country*, Phoenix, 1956; She Te, *The Good Woman of Setzuan*, Phoenix, NY, 1956; Argia, *The Queen and the Rebels*, Bucks

County Playhouse, New Hope, PA, 1959; Angelique, *Port Royal*, Grace Church, NY, 1960; Leah, *Men, Women, and Angels*, Vancouver Festival, Canada, 1961; Martha, *Who's Afraid of Virginia Woolf?*, Billy Rose, NY, 1962; Madame Ranevskaya, *The Cherry Orchard*, Lyceum, NY, 1968; Charlotte von Stein, *Charlotte*, Belasco, NY, 1980.

MAJOR TOURS—Nina, *The Seagull*, U.S. cities, 1938; *The Admiral Had a Wife*, 1941; Desdemona, *Othello*, 1944-45; Blanche, *A Streetcar Named Desire*, 1948-49; Grand Duchess Tatiana Petrovna, *Tovarich*, 1952; *The Lady's Not for Burning* and *The Deep Blue Sea*, 1954; *The Affairs of Anatol*, 1955; women, *The Affairs of Anatol*, 1957; Charlotte von Stein, *Charlotte*, U.S. regional theaters and universities, 1981-82.

FILM DEBUT—*The Other*, Twentieth Century-Fox, 1972. PRINCIPAL FILM APPEARANCES—*The Boys from Brazil*, Twentieth Century-Fox, 1979.

PRINCIPAL TELEVISION APPEARANCES—*Macbeth; Out of Dust; A Month in the Country*.

RELATED CAREER—Administrator and teacher at the Herbert Berghof Studio, NY, 1947-present.

WRITINGS: BOOKS—*Respect for Acting*, 1973; *Love of Cooking*, 1976; *Sources*, 1983.

AWARDS: Donaldson Award, Antionette Perry Award, New York Drama Critics Award, all 1950, for Georgia Elgin, *The Country Girl;* Antoinette Perry Award, 1962, for Martha, *Who's Afraid of Virginia Woolf?;* honorary doctorates: Smith College, 1978, DePaul University, 1981, Wooster College, 1982; Theater Hall of Fame, 1981, Wisconsin Theater Hall of Fame, 1984.

SIDELIGHTS: RECREATION—Cooking, piano, handicrafts.

ADDRESS: HOME—New York, NY. OFFICE—c/o Herbert Berghof Studio, 120 Bank Street, New York, NY 10014.

*   *   *

HAIGH, Kenneth   1931-

PERSONAL: Born March 25, 1931, in Yorkshire, England; son of William and Margaret (Glyn) Haigh; married Myrna Stephens. EDUCATION: Studied for the stage at Central School of Speech Training and Dramatic Art.

VOCATION: Actor.

CAREER: STAGE DEBUT—Cassio, *Othello*, Drogheda, Ireland, 1952. LONDON DEBUT—Geoffrey Baines, *Dear Little Liz*, New Lindsey, 1954. NEW YORK DEBUT—Jimmy Porter, *Look Back in Anger*, Lyceum, 1957. PRINCIPAL STAGE APPEARANCES—Player, *Shakesperean Season*, Open Air Theatre, Regents Park, London, 1955; Peter Lord, *The Mulberry Bush*, Rev. John Hale, *The Crucible*, Jimmy Porter, *Look Back in Anger*, Beaufort, *Cards of Identity*, all for English Stage Company, Royal Court, London, 1956-57; title role, *Caligula*, 54th Street Theatre, NY, 1960; Jerry, *The Zoo Story*, Arts, London, 1960; Franz von Gerlach, *Altona*, Royal Court, London, then Saville, 1961; the friend, *Playing with Fire*, James, *The Collection* (a double-bill), Royal Shakespeare Company,

KENNETH HAIGH

Aldwych, 1962; Mark Antony, *Julius Caesar*, Royal Shakespeare Co., Stratford-on-Avon, 1963; title role, *Caligula*, Phoenix, London, 1964; Patrick Casey, *Maggie May*, Adelphi, London, 1964.

The burglar, *Too True to Be Good*, Edinburgh Festival, then Strand, London, 1965; Prometheus, *Prometheus Bound*, title role, *Enrico IV*, both Yale University, New Haven, CT, 1967; Governor Endecott, *Endecott and the Red Cross*, St. Clement's Church, NY, 1968; Laurie, *The Hotel in Amsterdam*, Duke of York's, London, 1969; Prometheus, *Prometheus Bound*, Mermaid, London, 1971; Rupert Forster, *Marching Song*, Greenwich, London, 1974; title role, *The Father*, Leicester, London, 1975; Benedict, *Much Ado About Nothing*, 69 Theatre Company, Manchester Cathedral, England, 1976; Dysart, *Equus*, Higgins, *Pygmalion*, both Citadel, Edmonton, Alberta, Canada, 1977; Sidney, *California Suite*, O'Neill, NY, 1977; Henry Jarvis, *The Aspern Papers*, Prince of Salestria, *Look After Lulu*, both Chichester Festival, 1978; Malvolio, *Twelfth Night*, Brutus, *Julius Caesar*, Prospero, *The Tempest*, American Shakespeare Festival, Stratford, CT, 1979; F. Scott Fitzgerald, *Clothes for a Summer Hotel*, Cort, NY, 1980; James Sanders, *Bodies*, Long Wharf, New Haven, CT, 1981; title role, *Othello*, Young Vic, London, 1982; Sir, *The Dresser*, London, 1982.

MAJOR TOURS—Jimmy Porter, *Look Back in Anger*, U.S. tour, 1958-59.

PRINCIPAL STAGE WORK—Director: *Tis Pity She's a Whore*, Yale University, New Haven, CT, 1967.

FILM DEBUT—Entered films in England in 1955. PRINCIPAL FILM APPEARANCES—*My Teenage Daughter*, 1956; *Saint Joan*, United Artists, 1957; *High Flight*, Columbia, 1958; Brutus, *Cleopatra*,

Twentieth Century-Fox, 1963; *A Hard Day's Night*, United Artists, 1964; *The Deadly Affair*, Columbia, 1967; *A Lovely Way to Die*, Universal, 1968; *Eagle in a Cage*, National General, 1972; *The Bitch*, 1979; *Wild Geese II*, Allied Artists, 1985; *Chain Reaction*, 1985.

TELEVISION APPEARANCES—Series: *Man at the Top; Search for the Nile;* McReady, *What the Dickens*, 1983. Specials: Achilles, *Troilus and Cressida*, 1981; *Moll Flanders; Hazlitt in Love*.

SIDELIGHTS: RECREATION—Cricket, literature, and wine.

Haigh has, in addition to the above, been accorded the honor of being created an honorary professor to the Yale Drama School.

ADDRESS: LONDON—c/o Savile Club, 69 Brook Street, London, W1 England. NEW YORK—c/o Yale Club, 50 Vanderbilt Avenue, New York, NY 10017.

* * *

HALE, Georgina 1943-

PERSONAL: Born August 4, 1943, in Essex, England; daughter of George Robert and Dot (Fordham) Hale; married John Forgeham (an actor; divorced). EDUCATION: Studied for the theatre at the Royal Academy of Dramatic Art.

VOCATION: Actress.

CAREER: STAGE DEBUT—Walk-on, Stratford, England. LONDON DEBUT—Nina, *The Seagull*, Duke of York's, 1976. PRINCIPAL

GEORGINA HALE

STAGE APPEARANCES—Repertory, Canterbury, Windsor, Ipswich, others; Gigi, *Gigi*, Juliet, *Romeo and Juliet*, both Liverpool Playhouse, Liverpool, 1967; Liza Doolittle, *Pygmalion*, Thorndike, Leatherhead, 1975; Nina, *The Seagull*, Derby Playhouse, Derby, 1976; Mary Caroline David, *The Tribades*, Hampstead, 1978; Melanie, *Boo Hoo*, Open Space, London, 1978; Bobbi Michele, *Last of the Red Hot Lovers*, Royal Exchange, Manchester, then the Criterion, London, 1979; Josie, *Steaming*, London; *Summit Conference*, Lyric, London; *Lovers Dancing*, Albery, London, 1983; *Phaedra*, Old Vic, London, 1984; *Copperhead*, Bush, London, 1985.

PRINCIPAL FILM APPEARANCES—*The Devils*, Warner Brothers, 1971; Fay, *The Boyfriend*, Metro-Goldwyn-Mayer/EMI, 1971; *Eagle in a Cage*, National General, 1972; Alma, *Mahler*, Mayfair Film Group, 1975; *The World Is Full of Married Men*, 1979; *McVicar*, 1980; *The Watcher in the Woods*, Buena Vista, 1980.

PRINCIPAL TELEVISION APPEARANCES—Ruth Ellis, *The Ladykillers;* Lillian Kirby, *Eden End; Budgie; Upstairs, Downstairs; Electra; Plaintiffs and Defendants; The Seagull;* others.

AWARDS: Best Comedy Performance, Josie, *Steaming*.

ADDRESS: HOME—74A St. John's Wood High Street, London NW8, England.

* * *

HALEY, Jack Jr. 1933-

PERSONAL: Full name John J. Haley, Jr.; born October 25, 1933, in Los Angeles, CA; son of Jack (the actor) and Florence (McFadden) Haley; married Liza Minelli (divorced). EDUCATION: Loyola University, B.S., 1956.

VOCATION: Producer, director, and writer.

CAREER: PRINCIPAL TELEVISION WORK—Producer, *The Race for Space*, 1959; producer and director, *Man in Space*, 1959; producer, *Hollywood: The Golden Years*, 1960-61; producer, *Hollywood: The Great Stars*, 1962; producer, *Hollywood: The Fabulous Era*, 1962; producer, *Biography*, 1962; producer and director, *And Away We Go*, 1963-64; producer, *The Incredible World of James Bond*, 1965; producer, writer, and director, *Hollywood and the Stars*, 1964-65; producer and director, *The General*, 1965; producer, *The Legend of Marilyn Monroe*, 1966; producer and co-writer, *A Funny Thing Happened on the Way to the White House*, 1966; producer, director, and writer, *The Hidden World*, 1967; producer, *The Highlights of the Ice Capades*, 1967; producer, *With Love, Sophia*, 1967; producer and writer, *A Funny Thing Happened on the Way to the White House*, 1967; producer and director, *Movin' with Nancy*, 1967.

Producer and director, *Monte Carlo, C'est La Rose*, 1968; producer, *The Highlights of the Ice Capades*, 1968; producer and director, *The Beat of Brass*, 1968; producer, *The Highlights of the Ice Capades*, 1969; director, *Academy Awards Presentation*, 1969; producer, co-director, and co-writer, *Frank Sinatra, Jr. with Family and Friends*, 1969; producer, *Academy Awards Show*, 1974; producer, *The Mac Davis Special*, 1975; producer, *The Mac Davis Christmas Special*, 1975; producer, *50 Years of MGM*, 1975; producer, *America Salutes Richard Rodgers*, 1976; producer, *Life Goes to the*

Movies, 1976; director, *Life Goes to War: Hollywood and the Homefront*, 1977; producer, *That's Hollywood*, 1977-79; producer, director, and co-writer, *Bob Hope's World of Comedy*, 1976; producer, *Heroes of Rock n' Roll*, 1979; producer, *Academy Awards Show*, 1979; producer, *American Movie Awards*, 1981, 1982; producer, *Hollywood: The Gift of Laughter*, 1982; producer, *Ripley's Believe It or Not!*, 1983-present; producer, *Academy Awards Show*, 1984.

PRINCIPAL FILM WORK—Director: *Norwood*, Paramount, 1970; *The Love Machine*, Columbia, 1970; *That's Entertainment*, United Artists, 1974; *That's Dancing*, 1985.

RELATED CAREER—Board of directors, The Thalians, 1955-65; co-founder, Wolper Productions, 1959; president, Jack Haley Foundation, 1962-present; president, Twentieth Century-Fox Television, 1975-present.

AWARDS: George Foster Peabody Award, 1962, for *Biography;* Silver Lion Award, Venice Film Festival, 1963-64, for *Hollywood and the Stars;* George Foster Peabody Award, Venice Film Festival Award, Silver Lion Award, Grand Prix Monte Carlo International Television Festival Award, all 1967, for *The Hidden World;* Emmy Award, 1967, for *Movin' with Nancy;* Emmy Award nomination, 1975, for *50 Years of MGM*.

ADDRESS: HOME—Los Angeles, CA.

*   *   *

ED HALL

HALL, Ed   1931-

PERSONAL: Full name Edward C. Hall; born January 11, 1931, in Roxbury, MA; son of Ezekiel Robert and Carrie Lee (Corley) Hall. EDUCATION: Howard University. POLITICS: Democrat. RELIGION: Congregationalist. MILITARY: U.S. Army, 1953-56.

VOCATION: Actor.

CAREER: NEW YORK DEBUT—Howard, *The Climate of Eden*. PRINCIPAL STAGE APPEARANCES—Lieutenant, *No Time for Sergeants*, NY, 1956; Joseph Asagi, *A Raisin in the Sun*, NY, 1959; *Death of Bessie Smith*, NY, 1961; *Trumpets of the Lord*, NY, 1963; Counsel for the Bereaved, *Blues for Mister Charlie*, ANTA, NY, 1964; African, *Emmanual Xoc*, Crest, Toronto, Canada, 1965; William, *The Zulu and the Zayda*, Cort, NY, 1965; Blossom, *The Hasty Heart*, Arena Stage, Washington, DC; Sir Walter Blunt, *Henry IV, Part I*, Mark Taper Forum, Los Angeles, CA; *Catch 22*, Hartman, Los Angeles, CA; *The World of Sholom Aleichem*, Roundabout, NY; also: *Wilson in the Promised Land*, Broadway.

With the Trinity Square Repertory Company, Providence, RI: Clay Williams, *The Dutchman*, 1965 and 1967; Streetsinger, *The Three-penny Opera*, 1967 and 1971; John, *Brother to Dragons*, 1968; Hoss, *The Tooth of Crime*, 1974; Joe Mott, *The Iceman Cometh*, 1980; Steve Daniels, *A Lesson from Aloes*, 1981; Scrooge, *A Christmas Carol*, 1982; Diamond Louie, *The Front Page*, 1983; Sebastian, *The Tempest*, 1983; Scott, *Terra Nova*, 1984; Sam, *Master Harold . . . and the Boys*, 1985.

MAJOR TOURS—Asagi, *A Raisin in the Sun*, national tour; narrator, *Black Nativity*, a Trinity Square Production, tour of Edinburgh Festival, India, and Syria.

TELEVISION DEBUT—Howard, "The Climate of Eden," *Play of the Week*, mid-1950's. PRINCIPAL TELEVISION APPEARANCES—Dr. Stan Bricker, *Medical Center*, 1969-76; Col. Wallace Dickey, *Baby, I'm Back*, CBS, 1978; Solomon, *The Road*, CBC, Canada; *The F.B.I.*, ABC; *Barnaby Jones*, CBS; *Here's Lucy*, CBS; *Streets of San Francisco*, ABC; *Another World*, NBC; *Miller's Court; Life Among the Lowly, This House of Mirth*, both Trinity TV Productions.

RADIO APPEARANCES—Tom Pryor, "Outward Bound," *Philip Morris Playhouse on Broadway*.

AWARDS: Foundation for Repertory Theatre of Rhode Island Community Service Award, 1983.

SIDELIGHTS: MEMBERSHIPS—Trinity Square Repertory Company, since 1965.

ADDRESS: OFFICE—Trinity Square Repertory Company, Providence, RI 02903. AGENT—Dennis-Karg-Dennis, 470 S. San Vicente Blvd., Los Angeles, CA 90048.

*   *   *

HALL, Phil   1952-

PERSONAL: Born September 14, 1952, in Durham, NC; son of John Preston (in pharmaceuticals) and Maudie (a retailer; maiden name, Myers) Hall. EDUCATION: University of North Carolina, Chapel Hill, B.A., music, 1974; Indiana University, Bloomington, M.A., music, 1978.

PHIL HALL

VOCATION: Conductor, musical director, pianist, vocal and dance arranger.

CAREER: PRINCIPAL STAGE WORK—Assistant conductor and keyboards, *Mame,* Broadway production, NY; musical director, piano conductor, and vocal arranger, *Play Me a Country Song,* Broadway production, NY; musical director and piano conductor, *Annie Get Your Gun,* Off Broadway production, NY; musical director and piano conductor, *WOR Radio Sixtieth Anniversary,* Carnegie Hall, NY; musical director and vocal arranger, *Some Enchanted Evening,* Terrace Theatre, Kennedy Center, Washington, DC; musical director, *1981 Spring Gala,* Manhattan Theatre Club, NY; assistant musical director and pianist, *The Grass Harp,* York Players, NY; conductor, *Sleeping Beauty,* St. Louis Municipal Opera; conductor, *The Desert Song,* Papermill, Milburn, NJ; musical director and piano conductor, *Great Expectations,* Pennsylvania Stage Company, Allentown, PA; musical director and piano conductor, *The Merry Widow,* Darien Dinner Theatre, CT; musical director and piano conductor, *Joseph and the Amazing Technicolor Dreamcoat;* musical director and piano conductor, *Barnum;* vocal arranger, *Jerry's Girls;* vocal arranger, *Jerome Kern Revue,* Oak Room, Algonquin Hotel, NY.

PRINCIPAL TELEVISION WORK—Musical director and piano conductor, *To Kander and Ebb with Love,* WNYC, NY. PRINCIPAL RADIO WORK—*The Listening Room,* with Robert Sherman.

WRITINGS: ADAPTATIONS—Adapted pre-existing music and created additional music for *Sleeping Beauty,* St. Louis Municipal Opera, 1984. MUSICALS—*First Lady,* (with Tony McDowell), 1984.

SIDELIGHTS: MEMBERSHIPS—BMI Composers and Lyricists Workshop, NY, 1984-85, Affiliated Federation of Musicians, Local 802.

ADDRESS: HOME—752 West End Avenue, New York, NY 10025.

HAMILL, Mark   1951-

PERSONAL: Born September 25, 1951, in Oakland, CA; married Marilou York, 1978; children: Nathan Elias. EDUCATION: Attended Los Angeles City College.

VOCATION: Actor.

CAREER: PRINCIPAL FILM APPEARANCES—Luke Skywalker, *Star Wars,* Twentieth Century-Fox, 1977; *Corvette Summer,* United Artists, 1978; *The Big Red One,* United Artists, 1980; *The Empire Strikes Back,* Twentieth Century-Fox, 1980; *Night the Lights Went Out in Georgia,* Avco Embassy, 1981; *Return of the Jedi,* Twentieth Century-Fox, 1983.

PRINCIPAL TELEVISION APPEARANCES—*General Hospital, Texas Wheelers,* 1975; *The F.B.I.; Owen Marshall; Partridge Family.* Movies: *Eric; 5; Sarah T.: Portrait of a Teen-Age Alcoholic,* 1975; *Delancey Street,* 1975; *The Crisis Within,* 1975; *Mallory: Circumstantial Evidence,* 1976; *The City,* 1977.

PRINCIPAL STAGE APPEARANCES—Renaissance Faire, Agoura, CA; *The Elephant Man,* Booth, NY; Tony Hart, *Harrigan n Hart,* Longacre, NY, 1985.

ADDRESS: OFFICE—Lucas Films, P.O. Box 2009, San Rafael, CA 94912.*

*   *   *

HAMLETT, Dilys   1928-

PERSONAL: Born March 31, 1928, in Tidworth, England; daughter of Sidney and Mary Jane (Evans) Hamlett; married Casper Wrede (divorced); children: a son. EDUCATION: Trained for the stage at the Old Vic School, 1950-52.

VOCATION: Actress and singer.

CAREER: LONDON DEBUT—Lady Ghost, *The Innocents,* His Majesty's, 1952. PRINCIPAL STAGE APPEARANCES—Miss, *Miss Julie,* Edinburgh Festival, Scotland, 1953; first witch, *Macbeth,* Shakespeare Memorial Theatre Company, 1955; Ophelia, *Hamlet,* Mariana, *Measure for Measure,* both Stratford-on-Avon, 1956; Julie, *Danton's Death,* Lyric, Hammersmith, 1959; Agnes, *Brand,* Lyric, Hammersmith, 1959; Miss Quested, *A Passage to India,* Oxford Playhouse, Comedy, London, 1960; Kate Keller, *The Miracle Worker,* Solveig, *Peer Gynt,* both Old Vic, London, 1962; Isabella, *Measure for Measure,* Desdemona, *Othello,* both Old Vic, London, 1963; Rita, *Little Eyolf,* Edinburgh Festival, 1963; Mary Tyrone, *Long Day's Journey into Night,* Marie Louise, *The Ortolan,* Portia, *The Merchant of Venice,* Amanda, *Private Lives,* Widow Quinn, *The Playboy of the Western World,* all at the Century, Manchester, 1966-68.

Gertrude, *Hamlet,* Edinburgh Festival, 1968; *The Trial of Saint Joan,* 1969; the wife, *Country Matters,* 1969; Donna Lucia, *Charley's Aunt,* 69 Theatre Company, Apollo, 1971; Alice, *Tiny Alice,* Theatre Royal, York, 1972; Joan, *The Trial of Joan of Arc,* York Minster, 1973; Rosalind, *As You Like It,* Regent's Park, London, 1973; Catherine Petkoff, *Arms and the Man,* Vera, *Pal Joey,* Northcott, Exeter, 1974; Eleanor, *Thomas and the King,* Her Majesty's, London, 1975; Kate, *Old Times,* Toulouse, 1976;

DILYS HAMLETT

Cleopatra, *Antony and Cleopatra*, Northcott, Exeter, 1976; Joan, *Honegger's St. Joan*, Exeter University, 1976; Mrs. Warren, *Mrs. Warren's Profession*, Theatre Royal, Watford, 1977; Martha, *Who's Afraid of Virginia Woolf?*, York, 1977; Norwegian Lady, *The Ordeal of Gilbert Pinfold*, Royal Exchange, Manchester, 1977; Mary, *Dear Daddy*, Ambassador's, London, 1977.

Paulina, *The Winter's Tale*, Royal Exchange, Manchester, 1978; Alix, *Motherdear*, Northcott, Exeter, 1979; Countess, *The Deep Man*, Madame Ranevskaya, *The Cherry Orchard*, both at Royal Exchange, 1979; Agnes, *A Delicate Balance*, Haymarket, Leicester, 1981; Mother, *Have You Anthing to Declare*, Royal Theater, Manchester, and Milwaukee Repertory, WI, 1981; *Becoming*, The Playhouse, Nottingham, and La MaMa, NY, 1982; Akhmatova, *Hope Against Hope*, Royal Exchange, Manchester, 1983; Miss Moffat, *The Corn Is Green*, Royal Theatre, Northampton, 1983; Judith Bliss, *Hayfever*, Mercury, Colchester, 1984; Mrs. Malaprop, *The Rivals*, Theatre Royal, York, 1984; Mary Tyrone, *Long Day's Journey into Night*, Royal Exchange, Manchester, 1985.

MAJOR TOURS—Eva Hood, *March Hares;* Cleopatra, *Antony and Cleopatra*, 1976; Delia, *Dear Daddy*, South African cities, 1977-78; Paulina, *The Winter's Tale*, European cities, 1978; *Needs and Notions*, Finland and UK cities.

PRINCIPAL STAGE WORK—Director: *The Creditors*, Northcott Theater, Exeter, 1975; *A Man for All Seasons*, Exeter Cathedral, 1978; *Christmas Fun and a Fairy Tale*, Royal Exchange, Manchester, 1979; *Stevie*, The Playhouse, Nottingham, 1980; *Extracts from A Doll's House and Beaux Stratagem*, Rose Bruford College, 1982; *All My Sons*, Royal Theater, Northhampton, 1983; *Romance*,

Orange Theatre, Richmond, 1983; *One for the Road*, Theatre Royal, York, 1984; *Table Manners*, The Playhouse, Nottingham, 1984.

TELEVISION DEBUT—1956. PRINCIPAL TELEVISION APPEARANCES—*Pavlova;* Sonya, *Uncle Vanya;* Viola, *Twelfth Night;* Agnes, *Brand;* Cassandra, *Women of Troy;* Julie, *Dantan's Death;* Wife, *Convalescence; Vicar's Wife; The Last of the Summer Wine; Play for Today*, BBC; *Fire at Magilligan*.

FILM DEBUT—1962. PRINCIPAL FILM APPEARANCES—*What Changed Charlie Farthing?*

ADDRESS: AGENT—David Daly, Personal Management, 68 Old Brompton Road, London SW5, England.

*   *   *

HAMILTON, Margaret   1902-85

PERSONAL: Born December 9, 1902, in Cleveland, OH; died May 16, 1985; daughter of Walter J. and Jennie (Adams) Hamilton; married Paul Boynton Meserv (divorced, 1938); children: Hamilton. EDUCATION: Attended Hathaway-Brown High School, Cleveland, OH and Wheelock Kindergarten Training School, Boston, MA; trained for the stage at the Cleveland Playhouse, OH.

VOCATION: Actress.

CAREER: FILM DEBUT—1933. PRINCIPAL FILM APPEARANCES—Miss Gulch/Wicked Witch of the West, *Wizard of Oz*, Metro-Goldwyn-Mayer, 1939; *My Little Chickadee*, 1940; *George White's Scandals*, 1945; *State of the Union*, 1948; *Brewster McCloud*, Metro-Goldwyn-Mayer, 1970; *The Anderson Tapes*, 1971; *Journey Back to Oz*, 1974.

TELEVISION DEBUT—1950. PRINCIPAL TELEVISION APPEARANCES—Cora, *Maxwell House* commercials.

STAGE DEBUT—*The Man Who Ate the Popomack*, 1923. NEW YORK DEBUT—Helen Hallam, *Another Language*, Booth, 1932. PRINCIPAL STAGE APPEARANCES—Hattie, *Dark Tower*, Morosco, NY, 1933; Lucy Gurget, *Farmer Takes a Wife*, 46th Street Theater, NY, 1934; Gertrude, *Outrageous Fortune*, 48th Street Theater, NY, 1943; Aunt, *On Borrowed Time*, Patio, Los Angeles, CA, 1946; Gwennie, *The Men We Marry*, Mansfield, NY, 1948; Aunt Addie, *Little Boy Blue*, El Capitan, Hollywood, CA, 1950.

Mrs. Hammer, *The Silver Whistle*, Mrs. Fisher, *The Show-Off*, Berkshire Playhouse, Stockbridge, MA, 1951; Lucy Bascombe, *Fancy Meeting You Again*, Royale, NY, 1952; Mrs. Zero, *The Adding Machine*, Phoenix, NY, 1956; Madame Kleopatra Mamaeva, *Diary of a Scoundrel*, Phoenix, NY, 1956; Dolly Tate, *Annie Get Your Gun*, City Center, NY, 1958; Bessie, *Goldilocks*, Lunt-Fontanne, NY, 1958; Grandma, *The American Dream*, Civic, Los Angeles, CA, 1962; Clara, *Save Me a Place at Forest Lawn*, Pocket, NY, 1963; Louise, *The Strangers*, Westport Country Playhouse, CT, 1963.

Mrs. Western, *Tom Jones*, Bucks County Playhouse, PA, 1965; Connie Tufford, *UTBU*, Helen Hayes, NY, 1966; Parthy Ann Hawks, *Show Boat*, New York State, NY, 1966; Madame Arcati, *Blithe Spirit*, Seattle Repertory, WA, 1966; Mrs. Malaprop, *The*

Rivals, Seattle Repertory, WA, 1967-68; Dorinda Pratt, *Come Summer*, Lunt-Fontanne, NY, 1969; Aunt Eller, *Oklahoma!*, New York State, NY, 1969; Mrs. Soames, *Our Town*, ANTA, NY, 1969; Mrs. Dudgeon, *The Devil's Disciple*, American Shakespeare Festival, Stratford, CT, 1970; Madame Arcati, *Blithe Spirit*, Alley, Houston, TX, 1970; *The Nephew*, Studio Arena, Buffalo, NY, 1971.

Madame Desmortes, *Ring Round the Moon*, Seattle Repertory, WA, 1971; Madame Armfeldt, *A Little Night Music*, Forrest, Philadelphia, PA, 1974; Miss Heneage, *The New York Idea*, Anifisa, *Three Sisters*, both BAM Theater Company, Brooklyn, NY, 1977; Mrs. Dudgeon, *The Devil's Disciple*, Ahmanson, Los Angeles, CA, then BAM Theater Company, Brooklyn, NY, 1978; Cleveland Playhouse Company, OH, 1978-79.

Stock: *On the Town; Bells Are Ringing; A Tree Grows in Brooklyn; Bloomer Girl; The Wizard of Oz.*

MAJOR TOURS—Dolly Tate, *Annie Get Your Gun*, U.S. cities, 1958; Stella Livingston, *Light Up the Sky*, U.S. cities, 1972; Madame Armfeldt, *A Little Night Music*, U.S. cities, 1974.

PRINCIPAL STAGE WORK—Producer: At AMAS Repertory Theater, NY, 1973: *An Evening with the Bourgeosie; The Three Sisters; House Party.*

SIDELIGHTS: FAVORITE ROLES—Helen Hallam, *Another Language*, Grandma, *The American Dream*, Margaret, *The Father*, Hattie, *The Dark Tower.*

Hamilton was formerly a kindergarten and nursery school teacher.*

*   *   *

HAMILTON, Neil   1899-84

PERSONAL: Born James Neil Hamilton, September 9, 1899, in Lynn, MA; died September 24, 1984; married Elsa Whitmer.

VOCATION: Actor.

CAREER: PRINCIPAL FILM APPEARANCES—*The Scar; Women; The Restless Sex; The White Rose*, 1923; *America; Isn't Life Wonderful.* As a contract player with Paramount: *Men and Women; The Golden Princess; New Brooms; Desert Hold; Diplomacy; Beau Geste; The Great Gatsby; The Music Master; Ten Modern Commandments; The Joy Girl; The Spotlight; Mother Machree; Don't Marry; Hot News; The Patriot; Three Weekends; What a Night; Why Be Good?; A Dangerous Woman; The Mysterious Dr. Fu Manchu; The Love Trap; The Kibitzer; The Dawn Patrol; The Cat Creeps.*

With Metro-Goldwyn-Mayer: *Strangers May Kiss; Laughing Sinners; The Great Lover; This Modern Age; The Sin of Madelon Claudet; Tarzan, the Ape Man; The Wet Parade; Are You Listening; What Price Hollywood; Payment Deferred; The Animal Kingdom; One Sunday Afternoon; Ladies Must Love; Tarzan and His Mate; Blind Date; Honeymoon Limited; Look Who's Laughing; When Strangers Marry; Brewster's Millions; Batman*, 1966; *Good Neighbor Sam; The Family Jewels; Madame X; Which Way to the Front; Life of General Pershing; The Beast of Berlin; The Iron Kiss; Keeper of the Bees; Torch Song.*

The Studio Murder Case; Darkened Rooms; Lullaby; You Must Get Married; Since You Went Away; She Had to Get Married; Federal Fugitive; Dangerous Lady; X Marks the Spot; Secrets of the Underground.

PRINCIPAL TELEVISION APPEARANCES—*Hollywood Screen Test*, 1948; *U.S. Steel Hour; Kraft Theater; Perry Mason; 77 Sunset Strip; Maverick; The Line-Up; Harrigan and Son; The Real McCoys; Follow the Sun; The Outer Limits; Mister Ed; The Cara Williams Show;* Police Commissioner Gordon, *Batman*, ABC, 1966-68; *Man of Principle.*

PRINCIPAL STAGE APPEARANCES—Stock: *The Better 'Ole; The Charles Blaney Stock Company.**

*   *   *

HAMPSHIRE, Susan   1942-

PERSONAL: Born May 12, 1942, in London, England; married Pierre Granier-Deferre (divorced, 1974); married Eddie Kulukundis, April 4, 1981. EDUCATION: Trained for the ballet.

VOCATION: Actress.

CAREER: STAGE DEBUT—Dora, *Night Must Fall*, Roof Top, Bognor Regis, England, 1957. LONDON DEBUT—Cynthia, *Expresso Bongo*, Saville, 1958. PRINCIPAL STAGE APPEARANCES—Victoria, *Follow That Girl*, Vaudeville, London, 1960; Elaine Musk, Miss Kelly, Gertrude Gentle, and Charlotte Graves, *Fairy Tales of New York*, Pembroke, Croydon, 1960, then Comedy, London, 1961; Marion Dangerfield, *The Ginger Man*, Ashcroft, Croydon, 1963, then Royal Court, London, 1963; Miss Jones, *Past Imperfect*, St. Martins, London, 1964; Kate Hardcastle, *She Stoops to Conquer*, Ashcroft, Croydon, 1966; Helen Hayle, *On Approval*, Arnaud, Guildford, 1966; Mary, *The Sleeping Prince*, St. Martins, London, 1968; Nora, *A Doll's House*, Greenwich, London, 1972; Katherina, *The Taming of the Shrew*, Shaw, London, 1974; title role, *Peter Pan*, Coliseum, London, 1974; Jeannette, *Romeo and Jeannette*, Arnaud, Guildford, 1975; Rosalind, *As You Like It*, Shaw, London, 1975.

Title role, *Miss Julie*, Greenwich, London, 1976; Elizabeth Champion-Cheney, *The Circle*, Chichester, 1976, then Haymarket, London, 1976; Ann Whitefield, *Man and Superman*, Malvern Festival, 1977, then Savoy, London, 1977-78; Siri von Essen-Strindberg, *The Tribades*, Hampstead, London, 1978; Victorine, *An Audience Called Edouard*, Greenwich, London, 1978; Irene St. Claire, *The Crucifer of Blood*, Haymarket, London, 1979; Ruth Carsan, *Night and Day*, Phoenix, London, 1979; Stella Drury, *Houseguest*, Savoy, London.

FILM DEBUT—*During One Night*, 1961. PRINCIPAL FILM APPEARANCES—*The Three Lives of Thomasina*, Buena Vista, 1963; *Night Must Fall*, Metro-Goldwyn-Mayer, 1963; *Wonderful Life*, 1964; *The Fighting Prince of Donegal*, Buena Vista, 1966; *Paris Au Moit d'Aout (Paris in the Month of August)*, Trans-Lux, 1968; *The Trygon Factor*, Warner Brothers/Seven Arts, 1969; *Monte Carlo or Bust*, 1969; *Rogan*, 1969; *A Room in Paris; Time for Loving*, 1971; *Living Free*, Columbia, 1972; *Malpertius; Neither the Sea Nor the Sand; Roses and Green Peppers; David the King*, 1983; *Bang.*

PRINCIPAL TELEVISION APPEARANCES—*David Copperfield*, 1970;

Baffled, 1972; *Andromeda; The Forsythe Saga; Vanity Fair; Katy; The First Churchills; An Ideal Husband; The Lady Is a Liar; The Improbable Mr. Clayville; Dr. Jekyll and Mr. Hyde* (musical); *The Pallisers; Barchester Chronicles; Leaving; Dick Turpin.*

SIDELIGHTS: FAVORITE PARTS—The quartet of roles in *Fairy Tales of New York*. RECREATION—Studying English period design, writing, and music.

ADDRESS: AGENT—Chatto and Linnit, Prince of Wales Theatre, Coventry Street, London WC2, England.

*   *   *

HANCOCK, Sheila   1933-

PERSONAL: Born February 22, 1933, in Blackgang, Isle of Wight, England; daughter of Enrico Cameron and Ivy Louise (Woodward) Hancock; married Alec Ross (died); married John Thaw. EDUCATION: Studied for the theatre at the Royal Academy of Dramatic Art, London.

VOCATION: Actress.

CAREER: STAGE DEBUT—Beth, *Little Women*, Scala, Dartford, England, 1950. LONDON DEBUT—Lily Thompson, *Breath of Spring*, Duke of York's, September, 1958. NEW YORK DEBUT—

SHEILA HANCOCK

Kath, *Entertaining Mr. Sloane*, Lyceum, October, 1965. PRINCIPAL STAGE APPEARANCES—Revue, *One to Another*, Lyric, Hammersmith, 1959, then Apollo, London; Gwen, *Make Me an Offer*, Theatre Royal, Stratford, England, then New, London, 1959; revue, *One Over the Eight*, Duke of York's, London, 1961; Cyrenne, *Rattle of a Simple Man*, Garrick, London, 1962; Praxagora and an Even Older Woman, *The Parliament of Women*, Oxford Playhouse, 1965; Karen, *The Anniversary*, Duke of York's, London, 1966; Lady Dance, *The Soldier's Fortune*, Royal Court, London, 1967; Maggie Harris, *Fill the Stage with Happy Hours*, Vaudeville, London, 1967.

Julia, *A Delicate Balance*, Aldwych, London, 1969; Maggie, *So What About Love*, Criterion, London, 1969; Daughter, *All Over*, Aldwych, London, 1972; Beatrice, *The Effect of Gamma Rays on Man-in-the-Moon Marigolds*, Hampstead, 1972; Marion, *Absurd Person Singular*, Criterion, London, 1973; revue, *Deja Revue*, New London, 1974; Alma, *The Bed Before Yesterday*, Lyric, London, 1976; Hester, *The Deep Blue Sea*, Arts, Cambridge, 1977; Miss Hannigan, *Annie*, Victoria Palace, London, 1978-79; Mrs. Lovett, *Sweeney Todd*, Drury Lane, London, 1980; with Royal Shakespeare Company as actress and director, 1981-84; currently acting and directing for the National Theatre.

PRINCIPAL STAGE WORK—Director: *The Taming of the Shrew*, Bromley, 1964; *The Constant Wife*, 1979 and *In Praise of Love*, 1980, both for Cambridge Theatre Company; various projects for Royal Shakespeare Company and National Theatre.

FILM DEBUT—*Light Up the Sky*, 1958. PRINCIPAL FILM APPEARANCES—*Girl in a Boat*, 1960; *Night Must Fall*, Metro-Goldwyn-Mayer, 1964; Karen, *The Anniversary*, Twentieth Century-Fox, 1968; others.

PRINCIPAL TELEVISION APPEARANCES—*The Rag Trade; Mr. Digby Darling; Now Take My Wife; But Seriously, It's Sheila Hancock;* and many plays.

AWARDS: Order of the British Empire, 1974.

SIDELIGHTS: RECREATION—Music and reading.

ADDRESS: AGENT—John Redway, 16 Berners Street, London W1P 3DD, England.

*   *   *

HANKET, Arthur   1954-

PERSONAL: Born June 23, 1954, in Ft. Belvoir, VA; son of Arthur P. (a business executive and retired U.S. Army officer) and Jimsy Ann (Murphree) Hanket. EDUCATION: U.S. Naval Academy, 1972-74; University of Virginia, B.A., theatre, 1974-76; Florida State University, Asolo Conservatory, M.F.A., acting. MILITARY: U.S. Navy, two years.

VOCATION: Actor.

CAREER: STAGE DEBUT—Ensemble, *Spoon River Anthology*, Yorktown Senior High School, Arlington, VA, 1971. NEW YORK DEBUT—Conleagh, *Cuchulain Cycle*, CSC Repertory, New York, 1979. PRINCIPAL STAGE APPEARANCES—At Florida State University, Asolo Conservatory, Sarasota, FL: D'Artagnan, *Cyrano de*

Bergerac, Dr. Cefercola, *Saturday, Sunday, Monday*, Bentham, *Juno and the Paycock*, Tristan Tzara, *Travesties*, Richmond, *Richard III*, Scapino, *Scapino*; Felix, the Fly, *The Insect Comedy*, Soho Repertory, NY, 1979; Robin, *Doctor Faustus*, 1979, Conlaegh, *The Cuchulain Cycle*, 1979, Pierrot, *Don Juan*, 1980, all at CSC Repertory, NY; Demetrius, *A Midsummer's Night Dream*, Guildenstern, *Hamlet*, both at California Shakespeare Festival, 1980; Faulkland, *The Rivals*, Arizona Theatre Company, 1980; Polynices, *Oedipus at the Holy Place*, Indiana Repertory Theatre, 1981.

At the Alabama Shakespeare Festival: Mortimer, *Henry IV, Part I*, Florinda, *Servant of Two Masters*, 1981, Laertes, *Hamlet*, Feste, *Twelfth Night*, 1983, Mark Dolson, *Mass Appeal*, Grumio, *Taming of the Shrew*, 1983; Ghost, *The Enchanted*, York Theatre Company, 1982; Valentine, *Two Gentlemen of Verona*, Clarence Brown Company, 1982; Valere, *Tartuffe*, Repertory Theatre of St. Louis, 1982; Joey Percival, *Misalliance*, Asolo State Theatre, 1983; Ian Keith, *Flight of the Earls*, Westside Arts, NY, 1983; Ken Talley, *Fifth of July*, Levin, NY, 1984; Patrick Hartie, *Philco Blues*, Westbeth Theatre, NY, 1984 (slated for Broadway, 1985); Fred, *A Christmas Carol*, Pennsylvania Stage Company, 1984.

MAJOR TOURS—Simultaneous translator for La Comedie Francaise: *A Flea in Her Ear, The Misanthrope, Ruy Blas*, Brooklyn Academy of Music, Kennedy Center, American tour, 1979.

WRITINGS: PLAYS, PRODUCED—*Rimbaud: Alchemy of the Word*, Helms Theatre, University of Virginia, 1976; *Saint Genet: A Thief's Journal*, Asolo State Theatre, Sarasota, FL, 1978.

AWARDS: Irene Ryan Scholarship; American College Theatre Festival; National Society of Arts and Letters.

SIDELIGHTS: MEMBERSHIPS—Actors' Equity Association.

ADDRESS: AGENT—The Gage Group, 1650 Broadway, New York, NY 10019.

* * *

HANKS, Tom

BRIEF ENTRY: Born in Oakland, CA; married and the father of two children. Actor. Hanks spent three years with the Great Lakes Shakespeare Festival, Cleveland, OH, and continued with the Riverside Shakespeare Company. His debut was in a Canadian film, *Mazes and Monsters*, 1982. He went on to star in the movies *Splash*, Buena Vista/Touchstone, 1984; *Bachelor Party*, Twentieth Century-Fox, 1984; *The Man with One Red Shoe*, Twentieth Century-Fox, 1985; *Volunteers*, Columbia, 1985; *Nothing in Common*, Tri-Star (upcoming), and *The Money Pit*, Universal (upcoming). On television he appeared on *Happy Days* and played Kip Wilson/Buffy on the ABC series *Bosom Buddies*, 1980-1982.*

* * *

HANLEY, William   1931-

PERSONAL: Born October 22, 1931, in Lorain, OH; son of William Gerald and Anne (Rodgers) Hanley; married Shelley

Post, 1956 (divorced, 1961); married Pat Stanley, 1962 (divorced, 1978); children: Katherine, Nell. EDUCATION: Attended Cornell University, 1950-51; trained for the stage at the American Academy of Dramatic Arts, 1954-55.

VOCATION: Playwright.

WRITINGS: PLAYS, PRODUCED—*Whisper into My Good Ear* and *Mrs. Dally Has a Lover*, both at Cherry Lane, NY, 1962; *Conversations in the Dark*, Walnut Street, Philadelphia, PA, 1963; *Slow Dance on the Killing Ground*, 1964; *Today Is Independence Day* and *Mrs. Dally Has a Lover*, both presented as *Mrs. Dally*, 1965; *Flesh and Blood*, 1968.

SCREENPLAYS—*The Gypsy Moths*, Metro-Goldwyn-Mayer, 1969; *Too Far to Go*, Zoetrope, 1982. TELEVISION MOVIES—*The Family Man*, CBS, 1979; *Father Figure*, CBS, 1980; *Little Gloria . . . Happy at Last*, NBC, 1982; *Something About Amelia*, ABC, 1984. BOOKS—*Blue Dreams*, 1971; *Mixed Feelings*, 1972; *Leaving Mount Venus*, 1976.

AWARDS: Vernon Rice Award, 1962, for *Whisper into My Good Ear* and *Mrs. Dally Has a Lover*; Emmy Award, 1984, for *Something About Amelia*.

ADDRESS: HOME—New York, NY.

* * *

HARRIS, Ed

PERSONAL: Born in Tenafly, NJ. EDUCATION: Columbia University for two years; studied and performed with the summer repertory at California Institute of the Arts for two years.

CAREER: PRINCIPAL FILM APPEARANCES—Billy, *Knightriders*, United Film, 1981; John Glenn, *The Right Stuff*, Warner Brothers, 1983; *Under Fire*, Orion, 1983; *Swing Shift*, Warner Brothers, 1984; *Places in the Heart*, 1984; *Portalana*, 1984; *A Flash of Green*, Spectrafilm, 1985; *Sweet Dreams*, Silver Screen Films (upcoming); *Emerald*, NBC Films (upcoming).

PRINCIPAL STAGE APPEARANCES—*Fool for Love*, Circle Repertory Company, NY, 1983.*

* * *

HARRIS, Julie   1925-

PERSONAL: Born December 2, 1925, in Grosse Point Park, MI; daughter of William Pickett and Elsie (Smith) Harris; married Jay I. Julien, 1946 (divorced 1954); married Manning Gurian 1954 (divorced); married Walter E. Carroll; children: (second marriage) Peter. EDUCATION: Yale University School of Drama, 1944-45; studied for the theatre with Charlotte Perry, Perry-Mansfield Theatre Workshop, Steamboat Springs, CO.

VOCATION: Actress.

CAREER: NEW YORK DEBUT—Atlanta, *It's a Gift*, Playhouse,

JULIE HARRIS

1945. LONDON DEBUT—Emily Dickinson, *The Belle of Amherst*, Phoenix, 1977. PRINCIPAL STAGE APPEARANCES—With Old Vic Company in *Henry IV, Part II* and *Oedipus*, Century, NY, 1946; Nelly, *The Playboy of the Western World*, Booth, NY, 1946; White Rabbit, *Alice in Wonderland*, International, then Majestic, NY, 1947; Weird Sister, *Macbeth*, National, 1948; Ida Mae, *Sundown Beach*, Belasco, NY, 1948; Nancy Gear, *The Young and the Fair*, Fulton, NY, 1948; Angel Tuttle, *Magnolia Alley*, Mansfield, NY, 1949; Delisa, *Montserrat*, Fulton, NY, 1949; Frankie Adams, *The Member of the Wedding*, Empire, NY, 1950; Sally Bowles, *I Am a Camera*, Empire, NY, 1951; Colombe, *Mlle Colombe*, Longacre, NY, 1954; Jeanne D'Arc, *The Lark*, Longacre, NY, 1955; Margery Pinchwife, *The Country Wife*, Adelphi, NY, 1957; Ruth Arnold, *The Warm Peninsula*, Helen Hayes, NY, 1959; Juliet, *Romeo and Juliet*, Stratford Shakespearean Festival, Ontario, Canada, 1960; Brigid Mary Morgan, *Little Moon of Alban*, Longacre, NY, 1960; Josefa Lantenay, *A Shot in the Dark*, Booth, NY, 1961; June (Havoc), *Marathon 33*, ANTA, NY, 1963; Ophelia, *Hamlet*, Delcorte, NY, 1964.

Annie, *Ready When You Are, CB!*, Brooks Atkinson, NY, 1964; Georgina, *Skyscraper*, Lunt-Fontanne, NY, 1965; Blanche du Bois, *A Streetcar Named Desire*, Tappan Zee Playhouse, Nyack, NY, 1967; Ann Stanley, *Forty Carats*, Morosco, NY, 1968; *The Women*, Repertory, New Orleans, 1970; Anna Reardon, *And Miss Reardon Drinks a Little*, Morosco, NY, 1971; Claire, *Voices*, Ethel Barrymore, NY, 1972; Mary Lincoln, *The Last of Mrs. Lincoln*, ANTA, NY, 1972; Mrs. Rogers, *The Au Pair Man*, Vivian Beaumont, NY, 1973; Lydia Crutwell, *In Praise of Love*, Morosco, NY, 1974; Emily Dickinson, *The Belle of Amherst*, Longacre, NY, 1976; Gertie Kessel, *Break a Leg*, Palace, NY, 1979; Ethel Thayer, *On Golden Pond*, Ahmanson, Los Angeles, 1980.

MAJOR TOURS—Sally Bowles, *I Am a Camera*, national, 1952; Jeanne D'Arc, *The Lark*, national, 1956; Anna Reardon, *And Miss Reardon Drinks a Little*, national, 1971-72; Emily Dickinson, *The Belle of Amherst*, national/international tour, 1976-77.

FILM DEBUT—Frankie Adams, *The Member of the Wedding*, Columbia, 1952. PRINCIPAL FILM APPEARANCES—Abra, *East of Eden*, Warner Brothers, 1954; Sally Bowles, *I Am a Camera*, DCA, 1955; *The Truth About Women*, Continental, 1958; *Sally's Irish Rogue* (aka *The Poacher's Daughter*), Show Corp., 1960; Grace Miller, *Requiem for a Heavyweight*, Columbia, 1962; Eleanor, *The Haunting*, Metro-Goldwyn-Mayer, 1963; Betty Fraley, *Harper*, Warner Brothers, 1966; *You're a Big Boy Now*, Seven Arts, 1966; Alison Langdon, *Reflections in a Golden Eye*, Warner Brothers/ Seven Arts, 1967; *The Split*, Metro-Goldwyn-Mayer, 1968; *The People Next Door*, AVCO-Embassy, 1970; *The Hiding Place*, World Wide Pictures, 1975; *Voyage of the Damned*, AVCO- Embassy, 1977; *The Bell Jar*, AVCO-Embassy, 1979.

TELEVISION DEBUT—*Actors Studio*, ABC, 1948. PRINCIPAL TELEVISION APPEARANCES—*Philco Television Playhouse*, NBC, 1948-55; *Starlight Theatre*, CBS, 1950-51; *Goodyear Television Playhouse*, NBC, 1951-60; *Hallmark Hall of Fame*, NBC; Nellie Paine, *Thicker Than Water*, ABC, 1973; Elizabeth Holvak, *The Family Holvak*, NBC, 1975, then CBS, 1977; *Actors on Acting*, PBS, 1984. Appeared in the following plays on television, some in the above mentioned drama-anthology series: *The Lark; Little Moon of Alban; Johnny Belinda; A Doll's House; Anastasia; Pygmalion; The Holy Terror; The Heiress; The Power and the Glory; He Who Gets Slapped; Victoria Regina*. She has also appeared in guest-star slots on many series.

AWARDS: Academy Award nomination, Best Actress, 1952, for *The Member of the Wedding;* Antoinette Perry Awards, 1968, for *Forty Carats*, and 1972, for *The Last of Mrs. Lincoln.*

SIDELIGHTS: MEMBERSHIPS—Actors' Equity Association, Screen Actors Guild, American Federation of Television and Radio Artists.

ADDRESS: AGENT—William Morris Agency, 1350 Sixth Avenue, New York, NY 10019.

*   *   *

HARRISON, John   1924-

PERSONAL: Born June 7, 1924, in London, England; son of George Henry John and Florence Emily (Cockram) Harrison; married Daphne Slater (divorced); married Linda Gardner. EDUCATION: Sir Walter John's School, London; studied for the theatre with Birmingham Repertory Theatre.

VOCATION: Director, writer, and former actor.

CAREER: STAGE DEBUT—As an actor, Birmingham Repertory, 1944. LONDON DEBUT—Benvolio and Chorus, *Romeo and Juliet*, His Majesty's, 1947. PRINCIPAL STAGE APPEARANCES—With Birmingham Rerpertory, 1944-45; Longaville, *Love's Labour's Lost*, Ferdinand, *The Tempest*, Dauphin, *Henry V*, Benvolio and Chorus, *Romeo and Juliet*, all with Stratford Memorial Theatre Company, 1946-47.

MAJOR TOURS—Cassio, *Othello*, Ghost, *Hamlet*, both with Anew

McMaster tour of Australia, 1949.

PRINCIPAL STAGE WORK—Director: *Pericles,* London, 1950; *Hamlet,* London, 1951; *The Easter Man,* 1964; *The Tempest* (Leeds production), 1975; *Every Good Boy Deserves Favour,* Leeds, London, and subsequent U.K. tour, 1979, also Bergen Festival, 1979.

RELATED CAREER—Director of productions, David Garrick Theatre, Lichfield, England, 1949, Nottingham Playhouse, 1952-57; artistic director, Birmingham Repertory Theatre, 1962-66; director, Leeds Playhouse, 1972-present. Also directed plays in Bristol, Zagreb, Chicago, and London.

WRITINGS: PLAYS, PRODUCED—*Gone to Ground,* 1968; *Unaccompanied Cello,* 1970; *Knight in Four Acts,* 1973; *Scene from a Voyage to the Indies,* 1983. TELEPLAYS—*Upstairs, Downstairs; The Collectors* (forthcoming BBC-TV series, 1986). BOOKS, PUBLISHED—*The Cambridge Guide to World Theatre* (contributor), 1986.

SIDELIGHTS: MEMBERSHIPS—British Equity. RECREATION—Music, reading, and doing nothing.

ADDRESS: OFFICE—Leeds Playhouse, Calverley Street, Leeds, England.

*   *   *

HASTINGS, Michael   1938-

PERSONAL: Born September 2, 1938; son of Max Emmanuel Gerald and Marie Katherine Hastings; married Victoria Hardie, 1975; children: (previous marriage) two. EDUCATION: Attended Imperial Service College, Windsor, Dulwich College, and Alleybn's School.

VOCATION: Writer.

WRITINGS: PLAYS—*Don't Destroy Me,* 1956; *Yes and After,* 1957; *The World's Baby,* 1962; *Lee Harvey Oswald: A Far Mean Streak of Independence Brought on by Negleck',* 1966; *The Silence of Saint-Just,* 1971; *The Cutting of the Cloth* (unperformed), 1973; *For the West* (Uganda), 1977; *Gloo Joo,* 1978; *Full Frontal,* 1979; *Carnival War a Go Hot,* 1979; *Midnight at the Starlight,* 1980; *Tom and Viv,* 1984.

BOOKS—*The Game,* 1957; *The Frauds,* 1960; *Rupert Brooke, the Handsomest Young Man in England,* 1967; *Tussy Is Me,* 1968; *The Nightcomers,* 1971; *And in the Forest the Indians,* 1975; *Bart's Mornings and Other Tales of Modern Brazil,* 1975; *Sir Richard Burton: A Biography,* 1978.

TELEVISION—*For the West* (Congo), 1963; *Blue as His Eyes the Tin Helmet He Wore,* 1966; *The Search for the Nile,* 1972; *The Nightcomers,* 1972; *Auntie Kathleen's Old Clothes,* 1977; *Murder Rap,* 1980; *Midnight at the Starlight,* 1980; *Michael Hastings in Brixton,* 1980; *Stars of the Roller State Disco,* 1984.

AWARDS: Arts Council Play Award, 1956, for *Yes and After;* Encyclopedia Britannica Award Medal, 1962, for *The World's Baby;* Evening Standard Comedy of the Year Award, 1978, for *Gloo Joo;* Somerset Maugham Award, 1969, for *Tussy Is Me;* Arts

Council Fiction Award, 1975, for *And in the Forest the Indians;* Emmy Award, 1972, St. Christopher Medallion, and British Screenwriters' Guild Award, 1975, all for *The Search for the Nile.*

ADDRESS: HOME—Two Helix Gardens, Brixton Hill, London SW2, England.

*   *   *

HAWTHORNE, Nigel   1929-

PERSONAL: Born April 5, 1929, in Coventry, England; son of Charles Barnard and Agnes Rosemary (Rice) Hawthorne. EDUCATION: Attended Christian Brothers College and the University of Cape Town.

VOCATION: Actor.

CAREER: STAGE DEBUT—Archie Fellowes, *The Shop at Sly Corner,* Hofmeyr, Cape Town, South Africa, 1950. LONDON DEBUT—Donald, *You Can't Take It with You,* Embassy (Swiss Cottage), 1951. PRINCIPAL STAGE APPEARANCES—Fancy Dan, *Talking to You,* Duke of York's, London, 1962; *Nymphs and Satires,* Apollo, London, 1965; Angry Neighbor, *In at the Death,* Phoenix, London, 1967; Sir Oswald Stoll, *The Marie Lloyd Story,*

NIGEL HAWTHORNE

Theatre Royal, Stratford, 1967; Roy Jenkins, *Mrs. Wilson's Diary*, Criterion, London, 1967; Prince Albert, *Early Morning*, Royal Court, London, 1968; *Total Eclipse*, Count Wermuth, *The Tutor*, both at Royal Court, London, 1968.

Commodore, *Narrow Road to the Deep North*, Prince Albert, *Early Morning*, Lord Touchwood, *The Double Dealer*, Commander Pemberton, *Insideout*, all at Royal Court, London, 1969; Falstaff, *Henry IV*, Macbeth, *Macbeth*, both at Sheffield Playhouse, 1970; Niall, *Curtains*, Traverse, Edinburgh Festival, Scotland, 1970, then Open Space, London, 1971; the Player, *Rosencrantz and Guildenstern Are Dead*, Cambridge Theatre Company, 1971; Christopher, *West of Suez*, Royal Court, London, then Cambridge, London, 1971; Judge, *The Trial of St. George*, Soho Poly, London, 1972.

Face, *The Alchemist*, Baptista, *The Taming of the Shrew*, Brutus, *Julius Caesar*, all at Young Vic, London, 1972; Chairman, *A Sense of Detachment*, Royal Court, London, 1972; Philip, *The Philanthropist*, May Fair, London, 1973; *The Ride Across Lake Constance*, Hampstead, then May Fair, London, 1973; Colonel, *Bird Child*, Theatre Upstairs, London, 1974; Touchstone, *As You Like It*, Mark Hellinger, NY, 1974; Cutler Walpole, *The Doctor's Dilemma*, Mermaid, London, 1975; Stephen, *Otherwise Engaged*, Queen's, London, 1975; Touchstone, *As You Like It*, Riverside Studios, London, 1976; Owen, *Clouds*, Hampstead, 1976; Major Giles Flack, *Privates on Parade*, Royal Shakespeare Company, Aldwych, London, 1977.

Brian, *Blind Date*, King's Head, London, 1977; Abbe de Pradts, *The Fire That Consumes*, Mermaid, London, 1977; Julius Sagamore, *The Millionairess*, Haymarket, London, 1978; Vanya, *Uncle Vanya*, Hampstead, London, 1979; Orgon, *Tartuffe*, Barbican, London, 1983.

MAJOR TOURS—Touchstone, *As You Like It*, North American cities, 1974; Dr. Sloper, *The Heiress*, U.K. cities, 1983.

TELEVISION DEBUT—1956. PRINCIPAL TELEVISION APPEARANCES—*Marie Curie; Edward and Mrs. Simpson; The Tempest; Yes, Minister; Tartuffe; A Woman Called Golda; Jenny's War; John Paul II; Mapp and Lucia; Barchester Chronicles*.

PRINCIPAL FILM APPEARANCES—*Dream Child* (upcoming); *The Chain* (upcoming); *Turtle Summer* (upcoming).

AWARDS: Clarence Derwent Award, SWET Award, both for Best Supporting Actor, 1977, for *Privates on Parade;* Broadcasting Press Guild Award, Best Actor, 1981; British Association of Film and Television Actors Award, Best Actor in Light Entertainment, 1982, 1983.

SIDELIGHTS: FAVORITE ROLES—Falstaff. RECREATION—Drawing, swimming, cycling, gardening, and collecting works by Gordon Craig.

ADDRESS: AGENT—Ken McReddie, 91 Regent Street, London W1, England.

*   *   *

HECKERLING, Amy

BRIEF ENTRY: Born in Bronx, NY; graduate of New York University, 1975; fellow in directing program of American Film Institute.

Director. Heckerling's films include: *High Finance*, a prize-winning short made while she attended NYU; *Getting It Over With*, made while she was at the American Film Institute; *Fast Times at Ridgemont High*, Universal, 1982 (feature directorial debut); *Johnny Dangerously*, Twentieth Century-Fox, 1984; *National Lampoon's European Vacation*, Warner Brothers, 1985; *Permanent Record* (upcoming).*

*   *   *

HEDLEY, Philip   1938-

PERSONAL: Born April 10, 1938, in Manchester, England; son of Leonard and Lois (Gould) Hedley. EDUCATION: University of Sydney; studied acting at East Fifteen Acting School, London.

VOCATION: Director.

CAREER: FIRST STAGE WORK—Director: *The Rivals*, Theatre Royal, Lincoln, England, 1967. PRINCIPAL STAGE WORK—Director: *Live Like Pigs*, Royal Court, 1967; as artistic director of the Lincoln Theatre Royal: *There Is a Happy Land, The Finest Family in the Land, Alice Through the Looking Glass*, 1968-70; as artistic director of the Midlands Arts Theatre Company, Birmingham, works by Henry Livings, David Cregan, 1970-72; *The National Health*, Old Tote, Sydney; assistant director to Joan Littlewood at the Theatre Royal, Stratford East, 1972-74; *Happy as a Sandbag*, West End production, London, 1975; *Leave Him to Heaven*, West End production, London, 1976; *Pump Boys and Dinettes*, West End production, London, 1984.

PRINCIPAL TELEVISION WORK—Director: *Happy as a Sandbag; Leave Him to Heaven; Mother Nature's Bloomers*, 1978.

RELATED CAREER—Hedley resigned as chairman of the board of the Theatre Royal, Stratford East, to become its associate director. He has continued the theatre's policy of presenting mainly new works and has directed premieres by Barrie Keffe, David Cregan, Daniel Mornin, Alan Plater, Michael Abbensetts, Vince Foxall, and David Henry Wilson. He has also taught and directed at a number of drama schools in Britain and abroad.

SIDELIGHTS: MEMBERSHIPS—Arts Council's Drama Panel, England.

ADDRESS: OFFICE—69 Paramount Court, University Street, London WC1, England.

*   *   *

HEIKIN, Nancy   1948-

PERSONAL: Born November 28, 1948, in Philadelphia, PA; daughter of Abraham (in the clothing business) and Judith (Kaplan) Heikin. EDUCATION: Sarah Lawrence, B.A., dance and theatre, 1970; attended Juilliard School of Music, 1981-82; studied for the theatre with Stella Adler and Peter Flood; studied dance and choreography with Bessie Schoenberg, voice with Marge Rivington and Tony Franco, music composition with Heiner Stadler and Ben Johnston, and playwrighting with Wilford Leach, John Braswell, and Crispin Larengiero.

NANCY HEIKIN

VOCATION: Actress, composer, and writer.

CAREER: STAGE DEBUT—The Carrot, *Peter Rabbit,* Children's Theatre, Playhouse in the Park, Philadelphia, 1963. NEW YORK DEBUT—Carmilla, *Carmilla,* LaMa Ma, 1970 (played over one hundred performances since the original production). PRINCIPAL STAGE APPEARANCES—Marlowe, *Forget Him,* NY; Weaver, a Suicide, *A Trilogy,* NY; Debby Specialist –, *C.O.R.F.A.X. (Don't Ask),* NY; Rosemary, *Rat's Mass,* NY; Creusa, *Medea,* NY; the singer and understudy Madonna Sostrada, *The Mandrake,* Violenta, *All's Well That Ends Well,* understudy Mabel, *The Pirates of Penzance,* all at New York Shakespeare Festival; Edith, *The Pirates of Penzance,* Uris, NY; *La Boheme,* New York Shakespeare Festival; Maria, *West Side Story;* Anna I, *The Seven Deadly Sins;* Miss Julie, *Miss Julie;* Serafina, *The Rose Tattoo;* Edna Burge, *Mrs. Farmer's Daughter,* American Music Theatre Festival, Philadelphia, 1984.

MAJOR TOURS—Several tours of Europe for La Ma Ma with Wilford Leach's ETC company and Andrei Serban's company.

TELEVISION DEBUT—*That's the Trouble with Water,* documentary for WCAU-TV, Philadelphia. TELEVISION APPEARANCES—*Saturday Night Live,* NBC; *The Today Show,* NBC.

CONCERTS AND CLUBS—Theatre Gerard-Phillipe and Centre Americain, France; various clubs in New York.

WRITINGS: PLAYS, PRODUCED—*Trio for Two Feet and a Bag,* La Ma Ma, NY, and subsequent tour of European and American cities, 1970; *T.K.O/Arena,* LaMa Ma, NY, and Theatre Gerard-Philipe,

Paris; *Humonic Symphony,* La Ma Ma, NY, and Spoleto Festival, Italy, 1972; *Crumbs,* La Ma Ma, NY, 1973; *Frame,* Washington Square Methodist Church, NY, 1974; *Serenade,* La Ma Ma, NY, 1974-75; *Weeks,* Cubiculo, NY, 1976; *Cloud 9,* Thirteenth Street Theatre, 1976.

MUSICAL WORKS, PRODUCED—*Warsaw Opera,* music-drama, workshop at Actors Studio, NY, 1981-82; *Non Pasquale,* an adaptation of *Don Pasquale* (co-written with Anthony Giles), Delacorte, NY, 1983. MUSICAL WORKS, UNPRODUCED—Carmen Monoxide, commissioned by New York Shakespeare Festival, 1983, completed 1984; No Kidding, optioned by New York Shakespeare Festival for Spring 1985; America Needs a Mom, 1985; Fountain Heads, 1985; Juana, an opera, libretto by Crispin Larangeira.

SCREENPLAYS, UNPRODUCED—About Face; C'est Cheese (co-written with Ellen Kesend).

RELATED CAREER—Dance for Children, Sarah Lawrence College; Head Start program, Philadelphia Board of Education; taught movement for actors, La MaMa, NY; gave master classes in Arts Awareness, Metropolitan Museum of Art, NY; vocal coach, opera division, University of Illinois; teacher, musical theatre, St. Ann's School, NY.

Guest director for two years, *Native American Theatre Ensemble;* taught music, dance and western acting and developed, with the members of the company, a piece on Nez Perce Coyote legends entitled *Coyote Tracks.*

AWARDS: ASCAP Award; Women's Fund, for *Warsaw Opera;* National Endowment for the Arts grant, for choreography; Samuel Rubin Foundation grant, composer/playwright; TCG grant, special travel grant to Indian reservations.

SIDELIGHTS: MEMBERSHIPS—Actors' Equity Association, American Federation of Television and Radio Artists, Screen Actors Guild, ASCAP, Dramatists Guild.

SPECIAL INTERESTS—Piano, balalaika; fluent in French.

Heikin remarked to *CTFT,* "I love to travel and have been fortunate to have spent a lot of time in Europe, particularly France. In 1968, I toured Russia (Leningrad, Moscow and Kiev) with the Sarah Lawrence touring chorus. One of my main musical influences is the melodious folk music of eastern European and Russian Jews. I used to sing and dance with Frank Zappa and the Mothers of Invention at the Fillmore East (a long time ago)."

Coyote Tracks has become the most performed Indian theatre piece in the country. It has toured Indian reservations, colleges and was also seen in West Berlin.

ADDRESS: AGENT—Howard Rosenstock, Rosenstock/Wender, Three E. Fourth Street, New York, NY 10003.

*   *   *

HELLER, Buck

PERSONAL: Born in Brooklyn, NY; son of Joseph (an electrical engineer) and Edith (a teacher; maiden name, Spiegel) Heller;

married Caroline Nova Zettwoch (an actress, singer, and dancer), July 20, 1975; children: Joshua Joseph, Tova Melissa. EDUCATION: High School of the Performing Arts, NY, 1954-57; Julliard School of Music, 1958-60. MILITARY: U.S. Air Force, Air National Guard.

VOCATION: Choreographer and director.

CAREER: PRINCIPAL STAGE WORK—Director and/or choreographer: *Circles*, off Broadway, NY; *Love, Love, Love*, off Broadway, NY; *It's Wilde*, off Broadway, NY; *On a Clear Day You Can See Forever*, Meadow Brook Dinner Theatre; *The Princeton Triangle Show*, 1968; *Gentlemen Prefer Blondes*, Meadow Brook Dinner Theatre; *The Glass Cage*, Julliard School of Music; *A Tree Grows in Brooklyn*, Equity Library; *La Traviata*, Actors Studio; *Funny Girl*, Rockefeller Foundation; *Glass Menagerie*, Foothill, CA.

PRINCIPAL FILM WORK—Choreographer: *A Time for the Professional*.

PRINCIPAL TELEVISION WORK—Director and/or choreographer: *Doug Stevens Special Delivery; Wide-Wide World; Camera Three; Ann Reinking Special; Ben Vereen Special*.

PRINCIPAL INDUSTRIALS—Choreograher: For MacDonalds, 7-Up, International Harvester, Lowenstein Fabrics, Skil Saw, Cotton Inc. (MRA show), Telex Inc., A-C Delco, General Motors, Panasonic, Quaker Oats, Hamms Beer, Johnson Motors, Eaton Yale, Cryovac, A.M.A. show, I.G.A. show, Klopman Inc., Time-Life, IBM, *People* magazine, BMW, Sperry Univac, John Deere.

NIGHT CLUB ACTS—Choreographer for Ed Ames, Rita Gardner, Grace Jones.

RELATED CAREER—Faculty, Herbert Berghof Studio, for thirteen years; faculty, for the New Dance Group, for ten years.

ADDRESS: AGENT—Karen Garber, Honey Sanders Agency Ltd., 229 W. 42nd Street, New York, NY 10036.

*   *   *

HELPER, Stephen Lloyd   1957-

PERSONAL: Born March 8, 1957. EDUCATION: Yale University, B.A., 1979.

VOCATION: Director and manager.

CAREER: FIRST STAGE WORK—Artistic director, Yale Summer Theatre, 1978. PRINCIPAL STAGE WORK—Assistant director, *The Madwoman of Central Park West*, 22 Steps Theater (now Latin Quarter), NY, 1979; assistant director, *West Side Story*, Minskoff, NY, 1980; director, *Fiddler on the Roof*, New York State Theater, Lincoln Center, 1981; director, *Starting Here, Starting Now*, PAF Playhouse, Huntington, NY, 1981; assistant director, *Baby* (in workshop and Broadway productions), NY, 1982-84; director, *The Firebugs*, Actor's Outlet, NY, 1983; director, *They're Playing Our Song*, Zachary Scott Theatre Center, Austin, TX, 1984; director, *Fiddler on the Roof*, Australian Opera Company, Sydney Opera House and Princess Theatre, Melbourne, Australia, 1984; assistant director, *Song and Dance* (in workshop and Broadway productions), NY, 1985.

MAJOR TOURS—Assistant director, *Fiddler on the Roof*, national, 1980.

PRINCIPAL TELEVISION WORK— Assistant to Jerome Robbins, *An Evening of Jerome Robbins' Ballets*, NBC, 1981.

AWARDS: National Opera Institute Apprenticeship Award, 1979-80.

SIDELIGHTS: MEMBERSHIPS—Society of Stage Directors and Choreographers.

Helper told *CTFT:* ''Arthur Laurents gave me my first break. His generosity has been followed by that of Jerome Robbins, Ruth Mitchell, Gerald Freedman, and Richard Maltby, Jr., all of whom continue to be my mentors. I spur myself on daily to match and continue their professionalism and excellence as best I can.''

ADDRESS: HOME—204 W. 88th Street, New York, NY 10024.

*   *   *

HEMINGWAY, Mariel

BRIEF ENTRY: Actress. Married Steve Cresinan, December, 1984. Her film credits include *Lipstick*, Paramount, 1976 (with sister Margeaux); *Manhattan*, United Artists, 1979; *Personal Best*, Warner Brothers, 1982; portrayed Dorothy Stratten in *Star 80*, Warner Brothers, 1983; *Creator*, 1985. Hemingway played an unwed mother in the television movie *I Want to Keep My Baby*, 1976. She made her stage debut in *Place of Amateurs*.*

*   *   *

HENDERSON, Florence   1934-

PERSONAL: Born February 14, 1934, in Dale, IN; daughter of Joseph and Elizabeth (Elder) Henderson; married Ira Bernstein (divorced). EDUCATION: St. Francis Academy, Owensboro, KY; studied acting with Christine Johnson and at the American Academy of Dramatic Arts.

VOCATION: Actress and singer.

CAREER: NEW YORK DEBUT—New girl, *Wish You Were Here*, Imperial, 1952. PRINCIPAL STAGE APPEARANCES— Laurey, *Oklahoma!* City Center, 1953; Resi, *The Great Waltz*, Los Angeles Civic Light Opera, Curran, San Francisco, 1953; title role, *Fanny*, Majestic, NY, 1954; Mary Morgan, *The Girl Who Came to Supper*, Broadway, NY, 1963; *The King and I*, Los Angeles Music Center; Nellie Forbush, *South Pacific*, New York State Theatre, Lincoln Center, 1967.

MAJOR TOURS—Laurey, *Oklahoma!*, 1952-53; Maria, *The Sound of Music*, 1961; Annie Oakley, *Annie Get Your Gun*, 1974; Maria, *The Sound of Music*, Ella, *Bells Are Ringing*, both at Los Angeles and San Francisco Civic Light Opera, 1978-79.

PRINCIPAL FILM APPEARANCES—*The Song of Norway*, Cinerama, 1970.

PRINCIPAL TELEVISION APPEARANCES—Guest panelist, *Hollywood*

FLORENCE HENDERSON

Squares, NBC; guest and guest host, *The Tonight Show,* NBC; Carol, *The Brady Bunch,* ABC.

AWARDS: Sarah Siddon's Award, for *The Sound of Music.*

ADDRESS: AGENT—Katz-Gallin-Morey, 9255 Sunset Blvd., Suite 1115, Los Angeles, CA 90069.

*   *   *

HENIG, Andi

PERSONAL: Full name Andrea Henig; born in Washington, DC; daughter of Sherman and Rita (a real estate broker; maiden name, Himelstein) Henig. EDUCATION: Yale University, B.A.

VOCATION: Actress and singer.

CAREER: STAGE DEBUT—Star of Wonder, *Christmas Play,* St. Cloud, Paris, France. NEW YORK DEBUT—Becky Thatcher, *Adventures of Tom Sawyer,* Brooklyn Academy of Music. PRINCIPAL STAGE APPEARANCES—*The Barnstormers, I Ought to Be in Pictures, The Seagull, Our Town,* all Tamworth Theater, NH, 1981-83; Charlotte and Milkmaid, *Oliver,* Mark Hellinger, NY, 1984; Jo Harper and Joanna Wilkes, *Big River,* Eugene O'Neill, NY, 1985.

MAJOR TOURS—Understudy Wendy and a Lost Boy, *Peter Pan,* U.S. cities, 1982-83.

SIDELIGHTS: MEMBERSHIPS—Actors' Equity Association, Screen Actors' Guild, American Federation of Television and Radio Artists.

ADDRESS: HOME—New York, NY.

*   *   *

HENNER, Marilu

PERSONAL: Born in Chicago, IL; married Frederick Forrest, September 28, 1980 (divorced). EDUCATION: Attended the University of Chicago.

VOCATION: Actress.

CAREER: PRINCIPAL STAGE APPEARANCES—*Grease,* National Company, 1971, then Royale, NY, 1972; *Once Upon a Mattress; The Roar of the Greasepaint, the Smell of the Crowd; Pal Joey,* Broadway production; *Over Here,* Broadway production; *They're Playing Our Song,* Burt Reynolds' Dinner Theatre, 1984.

PRINCIPAL FILM APPEARANCES—*Blood Brothers,* Warner Brothers, 1977; *Between the Lines,* Midwest Film Productions, 1977; *Hammett,* 1983; Agnes, *The Man Who Loved Women,* Columbia, 1983; *Johnny Dangerously,* 1984; *Rustler's Rhapsody,* 1985; *Perfect!,* 1985.

PRINCIPAL TELEVISION APPEARANCES—TV movie: *Dream House,* 1981. Pilots: *The Paper Chase; Off Campus.* Series: Elaine Nardo, *Taxi,* ABC, 1978-82, then NBC, 1982-83.*

*   *   *

HENRITZE, Bette

PERSONAL: Last named pronounced "Hen-writ-C"; born May 23, in Betsy Layne, KY. EDUCATION: University of Tennessee; studied for the theatre at the American Academy of Dramatic Arts.

VOCATION: Actress.

CAREER: NEW YORK DEBUT—Mary Delaney, *Jenny Kissed Me,* Hudson, December 23, 1948. PRINCIPAL STAGE APPEARANCES—Manasquan Theatre, NJ, 1951; Cloyne, *Purple Dust,* Cherry Lane, NY, 1956; peasant woman, *The Power and the Glory,* Phoenix, NY, 1958; Nirodike, *Lysistrata,* Phoenix, NY, 1959; Peer Gynt, Pimple, *She Stoops to Conquer,* Bessie Burgess, *The Plough and the Stars,* all Phoenix, NY, 1960; Mrs. Peyton, *The Octoroon,* Mrs. Gensup, *Giants, Sons of Giants,* both Phoenix, NY, 1961; Margaret, *Much Ado About Nothing,* Duchess of York, *King Richard II,* both New York Shakespeare Festival, 1961; Nerissa, *The Merchant of Venice,* Goneril, *King Lear,* both New York Shakespeare Festival, 1962; Mary Todd, *Abe Lincoln in Illinois,* Anderson, NY, 1963; Cross-Lane Nora, *The Lion in Love,* One Sheridan Square, NY, 1963; Charmian, *Antony and Cleopatra,* Paulina, *The Winter's Tale,* both Delacorte, New York Shakespeare Festival, 1963; Mrs. Hasty Malone, *The Ballad of the Sad Cafe,* Martin Beck, NY, 1963.

Various roles, *The White House,* Henry Miller's, NY, 1964; Emilia,

Othello, Delacorte, New York Shakespeare Festival, 1964; Louise, Maja, Landlady, Young Lady, *Baal,* Martinique, NY, 1965; Mariana, *All's Well That Ends Well,* Mariana, *Measure for Measure,* both Delacorte, New York Shakespeare Festival, 1966; Ermengarde, *The Long Christmas Dinner,* Mlle. Pointevin, *Queens of France,* as part of a triple bill entitled *Thornton Wilder's Triple Bill,* Cherry Lane, NY, 1966; Mrs. Shortley, *The Displaced Person,* St. Clement's Church, NY, 1966; Mary Windrod, *The Rimers of Eldritch,* Cherry Lane, NY, 1967; Bea Schmidt, *Dr. Cook's Garden,* Belasco, NY, 1967; Mrs. Bacon, *Here's Where I Belong,* Billy Rose, NY, 1968; Edna, *The Acquisition,* American Place, NY, 1968; Jessie Mason, *The Erpingham Camp,* Astor Place, NY, 1969; understudy, *Hello and Goodbye,* Sheridan Square Playhouse, NY, 1969.

Margaret Jourdain, *Henry IV, Part I,* Duchess of York, *Henry IV, Part II,* Duchess of York, *Richard III,* all Delacorte, New York Shakespeare Festival, 1970; Anna Ames, *The Happiness Cage,* Estelle Newman, NY, 1970; *Older People,* Anspacher, NY, 1972; Ursula, *Much Ado About Nothing,* Delacorte, then Winter Garden, NY, 1972; Trixie, *Lotta,* Anspacher, NY, 1973; Mother, *Over Here!,* Shubert, NY, 1974; Margaret, *Richard II,* Mitzi E. Newhouse, NY, 1974; Mrs. Soames, *Our Town,* Paulina, *The Winter's Tale,* American Shakespeare Festival, Stratford, CT, 1975; Elizabeth, *Angel Street,* Lyceum, NY, 1975; Nora, *Home,* Long Wharf, New Haven, CT, 1976.

Mrs. Mihaly Almasi, *Catsplay,* Manhattan Theatre Club, then Promenade, NY, 1978; Susan Ramsden, *Man and Superman,* Circle

BETTE HENRITZE

in the Square, NY, 1978; Nurse Guinness, *Heartbreak House,* McCarter, Princeton, NJ, 1979; Anna, *A Month in the Country,* Roundabout, NY, 1979; understudy, *One Night Stand,* Billy Rose, NY, 1980; Essie, *Ah! Wilderness,* Indiana Rep, 1981; Mother Superior, *Agnes of God,* GeVa, Rochester, NY, 1981; Miss Ericson, Monica, *Present Laughter,* Circle in the Square, NY, 1982; Witch, *Macbeth,* Circle in the Square, NY, 1982; Emily Stilson, *Wings,* Center Stage, Baltimore, MD, 1983; the Rebbi's Wife, *The Golem,* Delacorte, New York Shakespeare Festival, 1984; Mary Margaret Donovan, *The Octette Bridge Club,* Music Box, NY, 1985.

MAJOR TOURS—Toured Virginia with the Barter Theatre Company, 1950; Paulina, *The Winter's Tale,* and Mrs. Putnam, *The Crucible,* McCarter, Princeton, NJ, Stratford, CT, 1976; Anna, *A Month in the Country,* and Jenny, *The Torch Bearers,* McCarter, Princeton, NJ, Annenberg, Philadelphia, PA, 1976; Helga Ten Dorp, *Deathtrap,* summer tour, 1979 and 1980 including Royal Poiniciana Playhouse, Palm Beach, FI.

PRINCIPAL FILM APPEARANCES—*The Hospital,* United Artists, 1971; *The Happiness Cage,* Cinerama, 1972; *Rage,* Warner Brothers, 1972; *All That Jazz,* Twentieth Century-Fox, 1979; *The World According to Garp,* Warner Brothers, 1982.

PRINCIPAL TELEVISION APPEARANCES—*Omnibus,* CBS; *The Defenders,* CBS; *The Doctors and the Nurses,* CBS; *East Side, West Side,* CBS; "The Plough and the Stars," *Play of the Week; N.Y.P.D.,* ABC; *Hidden Faces; CBS Repertory Theatre.* Also: *All My Children,* ABC; *The Edge of Night,* ABC; *One Life to Live,* ABC; *Love of Life,* NBC; *Another World,* NBC; *As the World Turns,* CBS; *Ryan's Hope,* ABC.

AWARDS: Obie, 1967, for *The Rimers of Eldritch.*

ADDRESS: AGENT—Triad, 888 Seventh Avenue, Suite 1602, New York, NY 10106.

*   *   *

HERMAN, Danny   1960-

PERSONAL: Born November 2, 1960, in Pittsburgh, PA; son of Bruce B. (a steelworker) and Sara J. (Caliguire) Herman.

VOCATION: Actor, choreographer, and dancer.

CAREER: NEW YORK DEBUT—Juvenile, *Big Bad Burlesque,* Orpheum, NY, 1979. PRINCIPAL STAGE APPEARANCES—Mike, *A Chorus Line,* NY; dancer, *Leader of the Pack,* NY.

MAJOR TOURS—Dancer, *A Chorus Line,* U.S. cities, 1980-81.

PRINCIPAL STAGE WORK—Associate choreographer, *Scandal,* NY.

SIDELIGHTS: Herman told *CTFT,* "I was a competative gymnast and started dancing to improve my gymnastics."

ADDRESS: HOME—430 W. 34th Street, New York, NY 10001.

HEXUM, Jon-Eric   1957-84

PERSONAL: Born November 5, 1957, in Tenafly, NJ; died October 19, 1984, in San Francisco, CA, of an accidentally self-inflicted gun wound; son of Gerta (a secretary and waitress) Hexum.

VOCATION: Actor.

CAREER: PRINCIPAL TELEVISION APPEARANCES—Series: *Voyagers*, NBC; Mac Harper, *Cover-Up*, CBS. Movie: *Making of a Male Model.**

*   *   *

HINGLE, Pat   1923-

PERSONAL: Born July 19, 1923, in Denver, CO; son of Clarence Martin and Marvin Louise (Patterson) Hingle; married Alyce Dorsey (divorced); married Julia Wright; children: Jody, Billy, Molly. EDUCATION: University of Texas, B.F.A., 1949; studied for the theatre at the American Theatre Wing, the Herbert Berghof Studio and at the Actor's Studio. MILITARY: U.S. Naval Reserve, 1942-46, then 1951-52.

VOCATION: Actor.

CAREER: STAGE DEBUT—Lachie, *Johnny Belinda*, Centre Play-

PAT HINGLE

house, Rockville Center, NY, 1950. NEW YORK DEBUT—Harold Koble, *End As a Man*, Theatre de Lys, 1953. PRINCIPAL STAGE APPEARANCES—Joe Foster, *Festival*, Longacre, NY, 1955; Gooper, *Cat on a Hot Tin Roof*, Morosco, NY, 1955; Jules Taggart, *Girls of Summer*, Longacre, NY, 1956; Rubin Flood, *Dark at the Top of the Stairs*, Music Box, NY, 1957; JB, *JB*, ANTA, NY, 1958; Howard Trapp, *The Deadly Game*, Longacre, NY, 1960; Macbeth, *Macbeth*, Hector, *Troilus and Cressida*, both with American Shakespeare Festival, Stratford, CT, 1961; Sam Evans, *Strange Interlude*, Hudson, NY, 1963.

Parnell, *Blues for Mr. Charlie*, ANTA, NY, 1964; Andy Willard, *A Girl Could Get Lucky*, Cort, NY, 1964; Gentleman Caller, *The Glass Menagerie*, Brooks Atkinson, NY, 1965; Oscar Madison, *The Odd Couple*, Plymouth, NY, 1966; Harry Armstrong, *Johnny No-Trump*, Cort, NY, 1967; Victor Franz, *The Price*, Morosco, NY, 1968; Joseph Dobbs, *Child's Play*, Royale, NY, 1970; Senator George Mason, *The Selling of the President*, Shubert, NY, 1972; Coach, *That Championship Season*, Booth, NY, 1973; Hermann Starr, *A Grave Undertaking*, McCarter, Princeton, NJ, 1975; Dr. Wangel, *The Lady from the Sea*, Circle in the Square, NY, 1976; Willy Loman, *Death of a Salesman*, Arena Stage, Buffalo, NY, 1978; lead role, *A Life*, NY, 1980. Also: his one-man show, *Thomas A. Edison: Reflections of a Genius*.

PRINCIPAL FILM APPEARANCES—*On the Waterfront*, Columbia, 1954; *The Long Gray Line*, Paramount, 1955; *The Strange One*, Columbia, 1957; *No Down Payment*, Twentieth Century-Fox, 1957; Ace Stamper, *Splendor in the Grass*, Warner Brothers, 1961; *The Ugly American*, Universal, 1963; Ralph, *All the Way Home*, Paramount, 1963; *Invitation to a Gunfighter*, United Artists, 1964; *Jigaw*, Beverly Pictures, 1965; *Nevada Smith*, Paramount, 1966; *Sol Madrid*, Metro-Goldwyn-Mayer, 1968; *Hang em High*, United Artists, 1968; *Norwood*, Paramount, 1970; *Bloody Mama*, American International, 1970; *WUSA*, Paramount, 1970; *The Carey Treatment*, Metro-Goldwyn-Mayer, 1972; *One Little Indian*, Buena Vista, 1973; *The Super Cops*, United Artists, 1974; *The Gauntlet*, Warner Brothers, 1977; *When You Comin' Back, Red Ryder?*, Columbia, 1979; *Norma Rae*, Twentieth Century-Fox, 1979; *Sudden Impact*, Warner Brothers, 1983; *Bless em All; Running Brave*, Buena Vista, 1983; *Going Berserk*, Universal, 1983; *The Falcon and the Snowman*, 1984; *Brewster's Millions*, 1985.

TELEVISION DEBUT—Cockney panhandler, *Dr. Jekyl and Mr. Hyde*, 1950. PRINCIPAL TELEVISION APPEARANCES—Narrator, *Let Us Now Praise Famous Men;* narrator, *A Texas Romance;* co-star, *Stone;* others.

AWARDS: Antoinette Perry Award nomination, best actor, 1957, for *The Dark at the Top of the Stairs;* honorary Ph.D., Otterbein College, 1974; Clio, Thomas Edison/GE commercials.

SIDELIGHTS: MEMBERSHIPS—Actor's Studio.

Hingle performed at the White House in 1965 and at the Library of Congress in 1984 according to information the actor supplied to *CTFT*.

Before making his living as an actor, Hingle worked as a laborer, waiter, and construction worker.

ADDRESS: HOME—North Hollywood, CA. AGENT—Milton Goldman, International Creative Management, 40 W. 57th Street, New York, NY 10019.

IAN HOLM

HOLM, Ian   1931-

PERSONAL: Born Ian Holm Cuthbert, September 12, 1931, in Goodmayes, Ilford, Essex, England; son of James Harvey (a doctor) and Jean Wilson (Holm) Cuthbert; married Lynn Mary Shaw (divorced). EDUCATION: Studied for the stage at the Royal Academy of Dramatic Art.

VOCATION: Actor.

CAREER: STAGE DEBUT—Spear carrier, *Othello*, Shakespeare Memorial Theatre, Stratford-on-Avon, March, 1954. LONDON DEBUT—Rupert Bliss, *Love Affair*, Lyric, Hammersmith, June, 1956. NEW YORK DEBUT—Lenny, *The Homecoming*, Music Box, 1967.

PRINCIPAL STAGE APPEARANCES—Donalbain, *Macbeth*, Mutius, *Titus Andronicus*, Shakespeare Memorial Theatre, Stratford-on-Avon, 1955; appeared at the Worthing Theatre for six months during 1956; Mutius, *Titus Andronicus*, European tour, Stoll Theatre, 1957; Peter, *Romeo and Juliet*, Sebastian, *Twelfth Night*, Verges, *Much Ado About Nothing*, 1958, Puck, *A Midsummer Night's Dream*, Fool, *King Lear*, 1959, Lorenzo, *The Merchant of Venice*, Gremio, *The Taming of the Shrew*, 1960, all at Shakespeare Memorial Theatre, Stratford-on-Avon; First Judge, *Ondine*, Mannoury, *The Devils*, Little Monk, *Becket*, Gremio, *The Taming of the Shrew*, Trofimov, *The Cherry Orchard*, all at the Aldwych, 1961; Claudio, *Measure for Measure*, Puck, *A Midsummer Night's Dream*, Gremio, *The Taming of the Shrew*, all with Royal Shakespeare Company, Stratford, April, 1962; Troilus, *Troilus and Cressida*, Aldwych, October, 1962.

Ariel, *The Tempest*, Richard, *Edward IV*, Richard III, *Richard III*, all with Royal Shakespeare Company, 1963; Richard, *Edward IV* and *Richard III*, Aldwych, January, 1964; Henry, Prince of Wales, *Henry IV, Parts I and II*, Henry, *Henry V, Edward IV*, and *Richard III*, all with Royal Shakespeare Company, 1964; Lenny, *The Homecoming*, Aldwych, 1965; Henry, Prince of Wales, *Henry IV, Parts I and II*, Henry, *Henry V*, Malvolio, *Twelfth Night*, both with Royal Shakespeare Company, 1966; Romeo, *Romeo and Juliet*, Royal Shakespeare Company, 1967; Manfred, *The Friends*, Round House, London, 1970; Nelson, *A Bequest to the Nation*, Haymarket, London, 1970; Buddy, *Caravaggio Buddy*, Traverse Theatre, Edinburgh, Scotland, 1972; Hatch, *The Sea*, Royal Court, London, 1973; Dave, *Other People*, Hampstead, 1974; Dr. Astrov, *Uncle Vanya*, Hempstead, 1979.

PRINCIPAL FILM APPEARANCES—*A Midsummer Night's Dream*, 1968; *The Fixer*, Metro-Goldwyn-Mayer, 1968; *Events Whilst Guarding the Bofors Gun; The Homecoming*, American Film Theatre, 1973; *Juggernaut*, United Artists, 1974; *Shout at the Devil*, American International, 1976; *Chariots of Fire*, Warner Brothers, 1981; *Dreamchild; Dance with a Stranger; Greystoke: The Legend of Tarzan, Lord of the Apes*, Warner Brothers, 1984; *Langerhouse*, 1984; *Wetherby*, Metro-Golden-Mayer Classics, 1985.

PRINCIPAL TELEVISION APPEARANCES—*The Lost Boys*.

AWARDS: Evening Standard Best Actor Award, 1965, for Henry, *Henry V;* Antoinette Perry Award, Best Supporting Actor, 1967, for *The Homecoming;* Academy Award, Best Supporting Actor, *Events Whilst Guarding the Bofors Gun;* British Association of Film and Television Actors Award, Best Supporting Actor, 1982, for *Chariots of Fire.*

ADDRESS: AGENT—Leading Artists, 60 St. James Street, London SW1, England.

*   *   *

HOOD, Morag   1942-

PERSONAL: Born December 12, 1942, in Glasgow, Scotland; daughter of Thomas and Helen Dallas (Kelso) Hood. EDUCATION: Attended Bellahouston Academy, Glasgow; Glasgow University, M.A. POLITICS—Socialist. RELIGION: Disciple of Charan Singh.

VOCATION: Actress.

CAREER: STAGE DEBUT—*Wedding Fever*, Metropole, Glasgow, Scotland, 1964. LONDON DEBUT—Clarice, *The Servant of Two Masters*, Queen's, 1968. PRINCIPAL STAGE APPEARANCES—Dundee Repertory, Metropolitan Theater, Lyceum Theater, Pitlochry, 1965, Scotland; Liverpool Playhouse, 1966; Alison, *The Lady's Not for Burning*, Bristol Old Vic, 1968; Martirio, *The House of Bernarda Alba*, Greenwich, London, 1973; Elise, *The Miser*, Lyceum, Edinburgh, 1973; Juliet, *Romeo and Juliet*, Liverpool Playhouse, 1973; Stella Kowalski, *A Streetcar Named Desire*, Piccadilly, London, 1974; Kate, *The Flo'ers of Edinburgh*, Edinburgh, 1975; Jane, *Jane*, Theatre Farnham, 1975; *The Fourposter*, Theatre of Vienna, 1975; Annette, *The Bells*, Greenwich, London, 1976.

Gasparina, *Il Campiello*, Celia, *Volpone*, the Shrimp, *The Lady from Maxim's*, Esmeralda, *The Hunchback of Notre Dame*, all

MORAG HOOD

National Theater Company of Great Britain, London, 1976; the Marquise, *The Inconstant Couple,* Chichester Festival, 1978; Isabel, *Then and Now,* Hampstead, 1979; *Lark Rise, Candleford,* both Cottlesloe, National Theatre, London, 1979; Cora, *The Iceman Cometh,* Cottlesloe, National Theater, London, 1980; Constanza, *Amadeus,* Her Majesty's, London, 1981-82; *I Love My Love,* Orange Tree Theatre, Richmond, 1982; *Relative Strangers,* 1984; *Little Lies,* Toronto, Canada, 1984; *A Little Like Drowning,* Hampstead Theatre Club, 1984.

MAJOR TOURS—Kay, *Time and the Conways,* 1976; Annie, *The Real Thing,* 1985.

PRINCIPAL TELEVISION APPEARANCES—Natasha, *War and Peace,* BBC; Breeze, "Breeze Anstey," *Country Matters,* Granada; Mary Musgrove, *Persuasion,* Granada; *The Camerons;* BBC; "Keep Smiling," *Square Mile of Murder,* BBC; *Crown Court,* Granada; *Bully for Cosmo,* Thames; *Jane Eyre,* Thames; *Traveling Man,* Granada. Plays for television: *The Personal Touch,* Scottish television; *Auf Wiedersehen, Pet,* 1985.

PRINCIPAL FILM APPEARANCES—*Wuthering Heights,* 1970; *Diversions,* 1979; *Ill Fares the Land,* 1982.

WRITINGS: RADIO PLAYS—*After Many Cares and Bitter Sorrows,* BBC, 1985.

SIDELIGHTS: FAVORITE ROLES—Stella Kowalski, Gasparina, Isabel.

ADDRESS: AGENT—Patricia Marmont, Langham House, 302-308 Regent Street, London W1, England.

HOUGH, John   1941-

PERSONAL: Born November 21, 1941, in London.

VOCATION: Director.

CAREER: PRINCIPAL FILM WORK—Director: *Twins of Evil,* E.M.I., 1972; *Treasure Island,* National General, 1972; *Legend of Hell House,* Twentieth Century-Fox, 1973; *Dirty Mary, Crazy Larry,* Twentieth Century-Fox, 1974; *Escape to Witch Mountain,* Buena Vista, 1975; *Brass Target,* United Artists, 1979; *Watcher in the Woods,* Buena Vista, 1980; *Eyewitness,* 1981.

PRINCIPAL TELEVISION WORK—Director: *The Avengers; The Saint.*

AWARDS: First Prize, International Film Fantasy, 1973, for *Hell House;* Award of Excellence, California Motion Picture Board, for *Escape to Witch Mountain.*

SIDELIGHTS: MEMBERSHIPS—Directors Guild of America, American Film Institute, ACTT, Directors Guild of Great Britain, British Film Academy.

ADDRESS: OFFICE—Thorn E.M.I. Studios, Borehamwood, Herts., England. AGENTS—John Redway, 16 Berners Street, W1 London, England; Phil Gersh, 222 N. Canon Drive, Beverly Hills, CA 90210.

JOHN HOUGH

HOUSEMAN, John 1902-

PERSONAL: Born Jacques Haussmann, September 22, 1902, in Bucharest, Rumania; son of George and May (Davies) Haussmann; married Joan Courtney. EDUCATION: Attended Clifton College, England.

VOCATION: Actor, director, producer, and writer.

CAREER: PRINCIPAL STAGE WORK—Director: *Four Saints in Three Acts,* Wadsworth Athenaeum, Hartford, CT, and 44th Street Theater, NY, 1934; *The Lady from the Sea,* Valley Forge Theatre Guild, PA, 1935; *Hamlet,* 1936; *Liberty Jones, Anna Christie,* and *Hello Out There,* all 1941; *Lute Song,* NY, 1946; *King Lear,* 1950; *Coriolanus,* 1954; *King John, Measure for Measure,* both 1956, *Othello, Much Ado About Nothing,* 1957, all American Shakespeare Festival, Stratford, CT; *The Devil and Daniel Webster,* City Center, NY, 1959; *The Three Sisters, Six Characters in Search of an Author, Measure for Measure, The Iceman Cometh,* and *King Lear,* all University of California at Los Angeles Professional Theater Group, 1959-64; *Murder in the Cathedral,* 1966, *Macbeth,* 1967, both Stratford, CT; *The Chronicles of Hell, Pantagleize* (with Ellis Rabb), APA Phoenix, NY, 1967-68.

The Country Girl, APA Phoenix, NY, 1972; *Don Juan in Hell,* City Center Company, Good Shepherd Faith Church, 1972; *Measure for Measure, Clarence Darrow,* both at City Center, Billy Rose, NY, 1974; *The Great American Fourth of July Parade,* Carnegie Music Hall, Pittsburgh, PA, 1975; *King Lear,* 1980, *The Cradle Will Rock,* 1983, both with the Acting Company.

Producer: *Panic,* Valley Forge Theatre Guild, PA, 1935; *Haitian*

JOHN HOUSEMAN

Macbeth, Federal Theatre's Negro Theatre Project, 1935; *Doctor Faustus, The Cradle Will Rock, Horse Eats Hat,* all Federal Theater Project 891, 1935; *Julius Caesar, The Shoemaker's Holiday, Heartbreak House, Danton's Death,* all Mercury Theatre, 1937-38; *Native Son* (with Orson Welles), 1941; *Joy to the World* (co-producer), NY, 1948; *The Duchess of Malfi,* Phoenix, NY, 1957; *The Child Buyer, The Egg,* both University of California Professional Theater Group, 1959-64; *The Criminals* (with Ellis Rabb), 1970; *The Robber Bridegroom, Edward II, The Time of Your Life, The Three Sisters,* all with City Center Acting Company at the Rebekah Harkness Theater, 1975.

Operas, director: *The Devil and Daniel Webster,* 1940; *Othello,* 1962; *La Tosca,* 1964; *The Mines of Sulphur,* Dallas Civic Opera, TX, 1968; *Antigone,* 1969; *The Losers,* Juilliard Opera Theatre, NY, 1971.

PRINCIPAL FILM WORK—Producer: *Blue Dahlia,* 1946; *Letter to an Unknown Woman; The Bad and the Beautiful,* 1952; *Julius Caesar,* 1953; *Executive Suite,* 1954; *Lust for Life,* Metro-Goldwyn-Mayer, 1956; *All Fall Down,* Metro-Goldwyn-Mayer, 1962. For the U.S. Government Film Service: *Tuesday in November,* 1944, *Voyage to America,* 1964.

PRINCIPAL FILM APPEARANCES—*Paper Chase,* Twentieth Century-Fox, 1973; *Rollerball,* United Artists, 1975; *Three Days of the Condor,* Paramount, 1975; *The Cheap Detective,* Columbia, 1978.

PRINCIPAL TELEVISION WORK—Producer: *The Seven Lively Arts,* 1957; *Playhouse 90,* 1958-59; *The Dancer's World* and *Three by Martha Graham,* 1969; *Gideon's Trumpet* (also appeared in), 1980.

PRINCIPAL TELEVISION APPEARANCES—*Truman at Postdam; Six Characters in Search of an Author; The Paper Chase; A.D.,* NBC, 1985.

RELATED CAREER—Founder, co-producer, and co-director, Mercury Theater, 1937; editor, Mercury Theater of the Air, 1938-39; artistic director, American Shakespeare Festival, Stratford, CT, 1956-59; artistic director, University of California Professional Theater Group, 1959-64; producing director, APA Phoenix, NY, 1967-68; artistic director, City Center Acting Company, 1972-1975; artistic director, the Acting Company, 1972-present; director of drama division, Juilliard School of the Performing Arts, NY, 1968-76; visiting professor of performing arts, University of Southern California, 1977-79.

WRITINGS: BOOKS—*Run Through,* 1972; *Front and Center,* 1979; *Final Dress,* 1983.

AWARDS: Academy Award, Best Supporting Actor, 1973, for *The Paper Chase;* Alger Meadows Award, Southern Methodist University; Alley Award, Alley Theater, Houston, TX.

ADDRESS: HOME—Los Angeles, CA. AGENT—Artists Agency, 10000 Santa Monica Blvd., Los Angeles, CA, 90067.

*   *   *

HOWERD, Frankie 1921-

PERSONAL: Born March 6, 1921, in York, England. EDUCATION: Attended Eltham and Shooter's Hill Grammar School, London.

MILITARY: Royal Artillery, World War Two.

VOCATION: Actor.

CAREER: STAGE DEBUT—Stage Door Canteen, Piccadilly, London, 1946. NEW YORK DEBUT—John Emery Rockefeller, *Rockefeller and the Indians,* Ethel Barrymore Theater, 1968. PRINCIPAL STAGE APPEARANCES—*Out of This World,* London Palladium, 1950; Idle Jack, *Dick Whittington,* London Palladium, 1952; *Pardon My French,* Prince of Wales, London, 1953; Lord Fancourt Babberley, *Charley's Aunt,* Globe, London, 1955; Bottom, *A Midsummer Night's Dream,* Old Vic, London, 1957; Alister, *Mister Venus,* Prince of Wales, London, 1958; *Glamorama,* Plaza, Jersey, CI, 1963; Prologus and Pseudolus, *A Funny Thing Happened on the Way to the Forum,* Strand, London, 1963; *Way Out in Picadilly,* Prince of Wales, London, 1966; Jack, *Jack and the Beanstalk,* London Palladium, 1973; Billy Crusoe, *Robinson Crusoe,* Alexandra, Birmingham, 1979; Frosch, *Die Fledermaus,* English National Opera, Coliseum, London, 1981.

FILM DEBUT—*The Runaway Bus,* 1954. PRINCIPAL FILM APPEARANCES—*Carry on Doctor; Carry on Up the Jungle; Up the Chastity Belt; Sgt. Pepper's Lonely Hearts Club Band.*

TELEVISION DEBUT—1952. PRINCIPAL TELEVISION APPEARANCES—*The Frankie Howerd Show; That Was the Week That Was; Up Pompeii;* Sir Joseph Porter, *HMS Pinafore,* 1981; Judge, *Trial by Jury,* 1982.

AWARDS: Variety Club of Great Britain, Show Business Personality of the Year, 1967, 1972; Order of the British Empire, 1977.

SIDELIGHTS: RECREATIONS—Reading, walking, music, and tennis.

ADDRESS: AGENT—Tessa Le Bars Management, 18 Queen Anne Street, London W1M 9LB, England.

*   *   *

JANET HUBERT

SIDELIGHTS: MEMBERSHIPS—Actors' Equity Association, American Federation of Television and Radio Artists, Screen Actors Guild.

ADDRESS: AGENT—Jim Weilhelm, Bob Waters Agency, Inc., 510 Madison Avenue, New York, NY 10022.

*   *   *

HUBERT, Janet

PERSONAL: EDUCATION: Juilliard School of Drama; studied acting with Peggy Freeman, Gene Lesser, and Stephen Aaron, voice with Edith Skinner, Liz Smith, and Robert Williams, and dance with Douglas Wassell, Phil Black, Luigi, and Miguel Gidrioux.

VOCATION: Actress, dancer, and singer.

CAREER: DEBUT—Principal, *Dancin',* National tour. NEW YORK DEBUT—Opal, *The First,* Martin Beck, 1981. PRINCIPAL STAGE APPEARANCES—Dancer, *Alvin Ailey Dance Theatre,* 1977-79; Tantomile, *Cats,* Winter Garden, NY; company, *Sophisticated Ladies,* Lunt-Fontanne, NY; *Joseph and the Amazing Technicolor Dreamcoat,* Golden, NY; Carameen, *Sleeping Beauty,* Municipal Opera House, St. Louis, MO; Woman 1, *Home,* Indiana Repertory.

MAJOR TOURS—Afrique, *Sophisticated Ladies,* International tour, including Tokyo and Paris.

FILM DEBUT—*Looking for Mr. Goodbar,* Paramount, 1977. PRINCIPAL FILM APPEARANCES—*The Fury,* Twentieth Century-Fox, 1978; *A Piece of the Action,* 1985.

HUDSON, Rock   1925-

PERSONAL: Born Roy Fitzgerald, 1925, in Winnetka, IL; married Phyllis Gates (divorced, 1958). MILITARY: U.S. Naval Reserve, 1941-46.

VOCATION: Actor.

CAREER: FILM DEBUT—*Fighter Squadron.* PRINCIPAL FILM APPEARANCES—*Giant; Something of Value; A Farewell to Arms; This Earth Is Mine; Pillow Talk; Come September; Lover Come Back; The Spiral Road; A Gathering of Eagles; Send Me No Flowers; Strange Bedfellows; Blindfold; Seconds; Tobruk; Ice Station Zebra; A Fine Pair; Darling Lili; The Hornet's Nest; Pretty Maids All in a Row; Showdown; Embryo; Avalanche; The Mirror Crack'd; The Ambassadors.*

PRINCIPAL TELEVISION APPEARANCES—Series: *McMillan and Wife,* NBC, 1971-76; Daniel Reese, *Dynasty,* ABC, 1984-85. Miniseries: *Wheels,* 1977-78. Movies: *The Starmaker,* 1981; *World*

War 3, 1981; *The Devlin Connection*, 1982; *The Las Vegas Hotel War*, NBC, 1984.

PRINCIPAL STAGE APPEARANCES—*I Do! I Do!*, 1974-75; *John Brown's Body*, 1976; *Camelot*, 1977; *On the Twentieth Century*, 1979.

AWARDS: Academy Award nomination, for *Giant;* King David Award, 1970; Golden Globe Award, World's Favorite Film Actor, 1958, 1960-62; Bambi Award, Germany, 1958-65; Exhibitor Laurel Award, 1958-66; *Look* Magazine Award, 1956.

ADDRESS: AGENT—Creative Artists Agency, 1888 Century Park E, Suite 1400, Los Angeles, CA 90067.*

*   *   *

HURST, Gregory S.   1947-

PERSONAL: Born December 1, 1947, in Oak Park, IL; son of Squire (an executive salesman) and Marcia (an interior designer; maiden name, Tooker) Hurst; married Pamela Baldwin, June 21, 1969 (divorced, 1977); married Joyce Barbara Baum (a theatrical agent and casting director), April 4, 1981; children: Alexander Squire. EDUCATION: Miami University, OH, B.S.; University of Wisconsin, M.A.; University of North Carolina, M.F.A. MILITARY: U.S. Navy.

Photography by Gregory M. Fota

GREGORY S. HURST

VOCATION: Director, producer, and writer.

CAREER: FIRST STAGE WORK—Director, *Funny Girl*, Mule Barn, Tarkio, MO, 1975, 21 performances. PRINCIPAL STAGE WORK—Director: *Hedda Gabler*, Playmakers Repertory, 1972; *Guys and Dolls*, *South Pacific*, both Mule Barn, Tarkio, MO, 1976; *Bells Are Ringing*, Joplin Civic, MO, 1977; *Mary, Mary*, Country Dinner Playhouse, St. Petersburg, FL, 1978; *Kiss Me Kate*, *A Funny Thing Happened on the Way to the Forum*, both Big Fork Playhouse, MT, 1978; with the Pennsylvania Stage Company, Allentown, PA: *The Philadelphia Story*, *The Comedy of Errors*, *That Championship Season*, *Two Gentlemen of Verona*, *Desire Under the Elms*, *All My Sons*, *Stage Struck*, *The Crucible*, all between 1979-85. Premieres at the Pennsylvania Stage Company: *Damon's Song*, 1979, *Feathertop*, 1980, *Great Expectations*, 1981, *Song of Myself*, 1982, *Shim Sham*, 1983, *Copperhead*, 1984, *A Walk Out of the Water*, 1985.

RELATED CAREER—Director of theater, Wayland Academy, 1969-73; acting teacher, University of North Carolina, 1973; associate director, Wayside Theater, 1974; chairman, department of theater, Tarkio College, MO, 1975-77; artistic director, Mule Barn Theater, Tarkio, MO, 1975-77; producing director, Pennsylvania Stage Company, Allentown, PA, 1979-present.

WRITINGS: MUSICALS, PRODUCED—*Terracide*, Wayland Players, 1971; *Song of Myself*, Pennsylvania Stage Company, 1982.

ARTICLES—"Internships: The Sponsor/Employer's View," *1985 Internship Directory*, Writer's Digest.

SIDELIGHTS: MEMBERSHIPS—Missouri Arts Council, 1975-77; Pennsylvania State Council on the Arts, 1983-86; National Endowment for the Arts Opera Musical Program; Playmaker's Repertory Company (founding member), Chapel Hill, NC.

ADDRESS: HOME—140 Riverside Drive, New York, NY 10024; 2223 Allen Street, Allentown, PA 18101. OFFICE—837 Linden Street, Allentown, PA 18101.

*   *   *

HUTTON, Timothy   1961-

PERSONAL: Born 1961, in Malibu, CA; son of Jim (an actor) and Mayline Hutton.

VOCATION: Actor.

CAREER: FILM DEBUT—Conrad, *Ordinary People*, Paramount, 1980. PRINCIPAL FILM APPEARANCES—*Taps*, Twentieth Century-Fox, 1982; *Daniel*, 1983; *Iceman*, Universal, 1984; *The Falcon and the Snowman*, 1984; *Turk 182!*, 1985.

PRINCIPAL FILM WORK—Director: Video of "Drive," for "The Cars," 1984.

PRINCIPAL TELEVISION APPEARANCES—Movies: *Zuma Beach*, 1978; *Young Love, First Love*, 1979; *Baby Makes Six*, 1979; *The Best Place to Be*, 1979; *Friendly Fire*, ABC, 1979; *The Sultan and the Rock Star*, 1980; *Father Figure*, CBS, 1980; *The Oldest Living Graduate*, 1980; *A Long Way Home*, ABC, 1981; *We're Family Again*, 1981.

PRINCIPAL TELEVISION WORK—Director, ''Grandpa's Ghost,'' *Amazing Stories*, NBC, 1985.

PRINCIPAL STAGE APPEARANCES—*Harvey,* summer stock; *Orpheus Descending,* Circle in the Square, NY, 1984.

AWARDS: Academy Award, Best Actor, 1980, for *Ordinary People;* Golden Globe nomination, 1982, for *Taps.**

I

IRONS, Jeremy 1948-

PERSONAL: Full name Jeremy John Irons; born September 19, 1948, in Cowes, England; son of Paul Dugan and Barbara Anne (Sharpe) Irons; married Sinead Moira Cusack (the actress), March 28, 1978; children: Samuel James. EDUCATION: Trained for the stage at the Bristol Old Vic Theatre School.

VOCATION: Actor.

CAREER: PRINCIPAL STAGE APPEARANCES—Simon, *Hay Fever,* Nick, *What the Butler Saw,* Florizel, *The Winter's Tale,* all at Bristol Old Vic, London, 1971; *Diary of a Madman,* Act Inn Lunchtime Theater, 1973; John the Baptist, *Godspell,* Roundhouse, Wyndham's, London, 1973; Don Pedro, *Much Ado About Nothing,* Mick, *The Caretaker,* both at Young Vic, London, 1974; Petruchio, *The Taming of the Shrew,* New Shakespeare Company, Roundhouse, London, 1975; *An Inspector Calls,* Key Theatre, Peterborough, England, 1975; Harry Thunder, *Wild Oats,* Royal Shakespeare Company, Aldwych, Piccadilly, London, 1976-77; James Jameson, *The Rear Column,* Globe, London, 1978; Gustav Manet, *An Audience Called Edouard,* Greenwich, London, 1978; Henry Boot, *The Real Thing,* Plymouth, NY, 1984.

PRINCIPAL FILM APPEARANCES—Mikhail Fokine, *Nijinsky,* Paramount, 1980; Charles Smithson, *French Lieutenant's Woman,* Filmways, 1981; Jerry, *Betrayal,* Twentieth Century-Fox Classics, 1982; Nowak, *Moonlighting,* Universal Classics, 1982; Harold Ackland, *The Wild Duck,* 1983; Swann, *Swann in Love,* 1984; *The Mission* (upcoming).

PRINCIPAL TELEVISION APPEARANCES—Alex Sanderson, *Love for Lydia,* LWT; Otto Beck, *Langrishe Go Down,* BBC; Edward Voysey, *The Voysey Inheritance,* BBC; Charles Ryder, *Brideshead Revisted,* Granada, 1980-81; Alex Hepburn, *The Captain's Doll,* BBC, 1982.

AWARDS: Clarence Derwent Award, Best Actor, 1978, for *The Rear Column;* Variety Artists of Great Britain Award, British Academy of Film and Television Arts Award nomination, Best Actor, both for *French Lieutenant's Woman;* British Academy of Film and Television Arts Award nomination, for *Brideshead Revisited;* Antoinette Perry Award, Drama League Distinguished Performance Award, Best Actor, 1984, for *The Real Thing.*

ADDRESS: AGENT—Hutton Management, 200 Fulham Road, London SW10 9PN, England.

IVANEK, Zeljko

BRIEF ENTRY: Born in Yugoslavia; graduated from Yale and studied at the London Academy of Music and Dramatic Arts. Actor. Ivanek's off Broadway credits include: *The Survivor,* 1980, and *Cloud Nine,* 1981, for which he received a Drama Desk Award. His Broadway credits include *Brighton Beach Memoirs,* for which he received a Antoinette Perry Award nomination. He appeared in the out-of-town run of *Master Harold and the Boys,* with the Yale Repertory Theatre. His films include: *Tex,* Buena Vista, 1982; *The Sender,* Paramount, 1982; *Mass Appeal,* Universal, 1984.*

*   *   *

IVEY, Dana

PERSONAL: Born August 12, in Atlanta, GA; daughter of Hugh

DANA IVEY

Daugherty (a physicist) and Mary Nell (an actress, teacher, and speech therapist; maiden name, McKoin) Ivey. EDUCATION: Rollins College, A.B., theatre; London Academy of Music and Dramatic Art.

VOCATION: Actress.

CAREER: STAGE DEBUT—Palace Guard and Seventh Fairy, *Sleeping Beauty,* Atlanta Children's Theatre, (at age six). NEW YORK DEBUT—Monica Reed, *Present Laughter,* Circle in the Square, July 15, 1982, for 176 performances.

PRINCIPAL STAGE APPEARANCES—*Come Back to the Five and Dime, Jimmy Dean, Jimmy Dean,* Alliance, Atlanta, 1977; Lady Capulet, *Romeo and Juliet,* California Shakespeare Festival, 1979; Kathe ne, *The Taming of the Shrew,* California Shakespeare Festival; gentlewoman and witch, *Macbeth,* NY; Isabel, *A Call from the Fart,* Manhattan Theatre Club, NY; Melanie, *Quartermaine's Terms,* Long Wharf, New Haven, CT, 1983, Playhouse 91, NY, 1983; Madwoman, *Hunchback of Notre Dame,* New York Shakespeare Festival; Nanny and Principal, *Baby with the Bath Water,* Playwrights' Horizons, NY, 1983; Lady Ariadne Underwood, *Heartbreak House,* Circle in the Square, NY, 1983 at the same time as Yvonne in *Sunday in the Park with George,* in workshop at Playwrights Horizons, NY; Yvonne and Naomi, *Sunday in the Park with George,* Booth, NY, 1984; *Pack of Lies,* Royale, NY, 1985.

Also: Antigone, *Antigone,* Lucy Brown, *The Threepenny Opera,* Hartford Stage Company, CT; Claire, *Taking Away of Little Willie,* Mark Taper Forum, Los Angeles, CA; Annie Sullivan, *The Miracle Worker,* Regina, *The Little Foxes,* Elizabeth Proctor, *The Crucible,* Hedda, *Hedda Gabler,* Mistress Quickly, *Henry IV, Part I,* all at Alliance, Atlanta, GA; Alma, *Eccentricities of a Nightingale,* Alaska Repertory; Catherine, *Great Catherine,* Julia, *The Philander-*er, Lucienne, *A Flea in Her Ear,* Shaw Festival, Toronto, Canada; Ruth, *The Homecoming,* Sonya, *Uncle Vanya,* Centaur Theatre, Canada; Stella, *A Streetcar Named Desire,* Manitoba Theatre Center, Canada.

MAJOR TOURS—Miss McCormack and Mimsey, *Plaza Suite,* National Company; Pearl and Dot, *Patio/Porch.*

PRINCIPAL TELEVISION APPEARANCES—Dr. Maria Thompson, *Search for Tomorrow,* CBS; *Spin-Off,* CBC, Montreal, Canada; *Talking about Shakespeare,* BBC; host, *Georgia Forum,* WGTV, Atlanta; *Another World; ABC After School Special; The Beachcomber; From Sea to Shining Sea.*

RELATED CAREER—Director of Drama Tech, Georgia Institute of Technology, Atlanta, GA, 1974-77; classical music disc jockey, interviewer, and programmer, WGKA-AM, Atlanta, GA, 1974-76; private teaching, Atlanta, GA, 1974-77.

AWARDS: Best Actress, Atlanta Circle of Drama Critics, 1977, for *Come Back to the Five and Dime, Jimmy Dean, Jimmy Dean;* Dramalogue, Los Angeles, 1979, for Lady Capulet, *Romeo and Juliet;* Clarence Derwent, 1983; Drama Desk nominations, 1983, for *Present Laughter* and *Quartermaine's Terms;* Obie, 1983, for *Quartermaine's Terms;* Best Supporting Actress, Antoinette Perry nominations, 1983, for *Heartbreak House,* 1984, for *Sunday in the Park with George.*

SIDELIGHTS: MEMBERSHIPS—Actors' Equity Association, American Federation of Television and Radio Artists, Screen Actors Guild, Canadian Actors' Equity Association, Association of Canadian Television and Radio Artists.

ADDRESS: AGENT—Clifford Stevens, STE Representation Ltd., 888 Seventh Avenue, New York, NY 10106.

J

JACOB, Abe J.   1944-

PERSONAL: Born October 7, 1944, in Tucson, AZ; son of Abe T. and Victoria (Shaar) Jacob. EDUCATION: Loyola Univeristy, Los Angeles, CA, B.A., 1966.

VOCATION: Sound designer.

CAREER: FIRST STAGE WORK—Sound designer, *Hair,* Orpheum, San Francisco, CA, 1969. NEW YORK DEBUT—Sound designer, *Jesus Christ Superstar,* Mark Hellinger, 1971. LONDON DEBUT—Sound designer, *A Chorus Line,* Drury Lane, 1974. PRINCIPAL STAGE WORK—Sound designer: *Pippin,* NY; *Chicago,* NY; *Beatlemania,* NY; *The Act,* NY; *Dancin',* NY; *Evita,* NY; *Woman of the Year,* NY; *Seven Brides for Seven Brothers,* NY; *Merlin,* NY; *Cats,* London.

RELATED CAREER—Concert sound designer for the Mamas & Papas, Peter, Paul & Mary, Jimi Hendrix, Peter Allen, Gilda Radner, and Shirley Bassey.

SIDELIGHTS: MEMBERSHIPS—Audio Engineering Society, International Sound Designers, National Academy of Recording Arts and Sciences.

According to his official biography, Jacob is presently serving as audio consultant to the Shubert Organization in New York. He designed the theatre for the Cardinal Newman College in St. Louis, MO, and has been a guest lecturer at the Banff Centre for Continuing Education in Canada. Jacob is now producing and developing his own shows for theatrical presentation.

ADDRESS: OFFICE—130 E. 63rd Street, New York, NY 10021. AGENT—Noel Silverman, Esq., 136 E. 57th Street, New York, NY 10022.

*   *   *

JAMES, Jessica   1931-

PERSONAL: Born October 31, 1931, in Los Angeles, CA; daughter of Jessie (a producer) and Evelyn (a singer and dancer; maiden name, Bauerman) James; children: Bambi Sue, Donald Burke. EDUCATION—University of Southern California; studied acting with Pat Randall and George Morrison and opera with Galli Gurci.

VOCATION: Actress and singer.

CAREER: NEW YORK DEBUT—Bunny, *Gemini,* Little Theatre.

PRINCIPAL STAGE APPEARANCES—Maggie Jones, *42nd Street.*

SIDELIGHTS: MEMBERSHIPS—Actors' Equity Association.

ADDRESS: HOME—305 E. 86th Street, New York, NY 10028. AGENT—Schumer-Oubre Management Ltd., 1697 Broadway, New York, NY 10019.

*   *   *

JARROTT, Charles   1927-

PERSONAL: Born June 16, 1927, in London, England; son of Charles A. (a motor racer) and Ursula Jean (an actress; maiden name, Borlase) Jarrott; divorced, 1983. MILITARY: Royal Navy, 1943-46.

VOCATION: Director and actor.

CHARLES JARROTT

151

COLLEGE OF THE SEQUOIAS

LIBRARY

CAREER: FIRST STAGE WORK—Assistant stage manager, West of England Theatre Company, Exmouth, Devon, England, 1947-59. PRINCIPAL STAGE APPEARANCES—Member of Nottingham and Colchester Repertory Theatres, 1949-53; toured Canada with the London Theatre Company, 1953-54.

FILM DEBUT—Director: *Anne of a Thousand Days,* Universal Pictures, 1969. PRINCIPAL FILM WORK—Director: *Mary Queen of Scots,* Universal Pictures, 1971; *Lost Horizon,* Columbia Pictures, 1972; *The Dove,* Paramount, 1973; *Escape from the Dark,* Disney, 1975; *The Other Side of Midnight,* Twentieth Century-Fox, 1977; *Last Flight of Noah's Ark,* Disney, 1979; *Condorman,* Disney, 1980; *The Amateur,* Twentieth Century-Fox, 1981; *A Married Man,* LWT Films, 1983; *The Boy in Blue,* Regatta/Twentieth Century-Fox, 1984.

PRINCIPAL TELEVISION WORK—Director: *Gallileo,* BBC; *Silent Song,* 1967; *A Case of Libel,* ABC; *Dr. Jekyll and Mr. Hyde,* ABC; *Male of the Species,* ATV; *The Picture of Dorian Gray,* ABC.

RELATED CAREER—Worked for CBC-TV as a director 1957-59, for Armchair Theatre, ABC-TV, London, 1959-63, and for the BBC, 1963-68.

AWARDS: Prix Italia, first prize, *Silent Song,* 1967; BAFTA Best director award, London, England, 1961-62; Golden Globe, Best Director, 1969, for *Anne of a Thousand Days.*

SIDELIGHTS: MEMBERSHIPS—Directors Guild of America, American Academy of Motion Picture Arts and Sciences.

ADDRESS: OFFICE—c/o Jess Morgan & Company, 6420 Wilshire Blvd., 19th floor, Los Angeles, CA 90048. AGENT—Leonard Hirshan, William Morris Agency, 151 El Camino Drive, Beverly Hills, CA 90212.

*   *   *

JELLICOE, Ann   1927-

PERSONAL: Born July 15, 1927, in Middlesborough, Yorkshire, England; daughter of John Andrea and Frances Jackson (Henderson) Jellicoe; married Roger Mayne; children: one daughter, one son. EDUCATION: Polam Hall School, Darlington Co., Durham; Queen Margaret's School, Castle Howard, York; studied for the theatre at the Central School of Speech and Drama.

VOCATION: Playwright, director, and actress.

CAREER: Began as an actress and stage manager in repertory and with the fringe theatre in England.

PRINCIPAL STAGE WORK—Director: *The Sport of My Mad Mother* (with George Devine), 1958; *The Knack* (with Keith Johnstone), 1962; *Skyvers,* 1963; *Shelley,* 1974; *Six of the Best* and *A Worthy Guest,* 1974; *Flora and the Bandits,* 1976; *The Reckoning,* 1978; *The Tide,* 1980; *The Poor Man's Friend,* 1981; *The Garden,* 1982; *The Western Women,* 1984. Also: For the Cockpit Theatre Club/ Open Stage: *The Confederacy, The Frogs, Miss Julie, Saint's Day, The Comedy of Errors,* and *Olympia.*

RELATED CAREER—Teacher of acting, Central School of Speech

and Drama since 1953; literary manager, Royal Court Theatre, 1973-74.

WRITINGS: PLAYS, PRODUCED—*The Sport of My Mad Mother,* 1956; *The Knack,* 1961; *The Rising Generation,* 1964; *Shelley,* 1965; *The Giveaway,* 1969. CHILDREN'S PLAYS, PRODUCED— *You'll Never Guess!,* 1973; *Clever Elsie!,* 1974; *A Good Thing or a Bad Thing,* 1974; *Flora and the Bandits,* 1976; *The Bargain,* 1979. TRANSLATIONS, PRODUCED—*Rosmersholm,* 1959; *The Lady from the Sea,* 1961; *The Seagull,* 1964. "COMMUNITY PLAYS," PRODUCED—(a theatrical form pioneered by Jellicoe) *The Reckoning* (for Lyme Regis), 1978; *The Tide* (for Axe Valley), 1980; *The Western Women* (with Fay Weldon and John Fowles; for Lyme Regis), 1984.

AWARDS: Elsie Fogerty Prize, Central School of Speech and Drama, 1947.

SIDELIGHTS: Founded Cockpit Theatre Club to experiment with the Open Stage, 1951; founded the Colway Theatre Trust, 1980. RECREATION—Reading theatrical biography.

Jellicoe expressed her concern to *CTFT* regarding American ideas of "community" theatre which, unlike the amateur interpretation given it in the States, in England means professional involvement in a new form. "Community plays involve hundreds of people in acting, in helping set up the play, grouped around a small core of professionals who share skills and expertise. A play is specially written and researched by a writer of national standing, the aim being to entertain and celebrate the town. This work is now being taken up and copied all over Britain."

ADDRESS: AGENT—Margaret Ramsay Ltd., 14a Goodwin's Court, St. Martin's, London WC2, England.

*   *   *

JOHNS, Andrew   1935-

PERSONAL: Born December 12, 1935, in Martinez, CA; son of Henry Eudey (an engineer) and Nora Marie (Johnson) Johns; married Evangeline (a writing waitress), June 8, 1957; children: Ariana. POLITICS: "Left of many, but not all." RELIGION: "Unattached, but careful."

VOCATION: Playwright.

WRITINGS: PLAYS, PRODUCED—*Fridays,* Milwaukee Repertory, 1981, Boarshead Theatre, Lansing, MI, 1981, A Contemporary Theatre, Seattle, WA, 1982; *Pigeons on the Walk,* Dallas Theatre Center, 1982, Bayou, Houston, TX, 1982, Stage Arts, NY, 1984; *Countertalk,* Milwaukee Repertory, 1982, Arkansas Repertory, 1983; *Today's Special,* Milwaukee Repertory, 1982; *Why Am I Always Alone When I'm with You,* Theatre Three, Dallas, TX, 1983, Arkansas Repertory, 1983, Chelsea Playhouse, NY, 1985; *Sideshows,* Arkansas Repertory, 1983, Kenyon Theatre Festival, OH, 1983; *Antony and Me,* Milwaukee Repertory, 1984, Actor's Company of Cleveland, 1984.

SIDELIGHTS: MEMBERSHIPS—Actors' Equity Association, Screen Actors Guild, Dramatists Guild.

"I started writing while understudying and working as assistant stage manager on the Broadway production of David Story's play *Home*. Story and Saroyan are the two playwrights I feel closest to. I did not discover I could write until my 30's were almost over. That was dumb, because I've looked and there isn't a pleasure as pleasant as writing."

ADDRESS: HOME—77 Sullivan Street, New York, NY 10012. AGENT—c/o Gilbert Parker, William Morris Agency, 1350 Avenue of the Americas, New York, NY 10019.

*   *   *

JONES, Jeffrey

PERSONAL: Born September 28, in Buffalo, NY; son of Douglas Bennett and Ruth (an art historian; maiden name, Schooley) Jones. EDUCATION: Putney School, Putney, VT, 1961-64; Lawrence University, Appleton, WI, B.A., 1968; trained for the theatre at the London Academy of Music and Dramatic Art.

VOCATION: Actor.

CAREER: DEBUT—Chorus, *The House of Atreus,* Guthrie, Minneapolis, 1967. NEW YORK DEBUT—Limester, *Lotta,* New York Shakespeare Festival, Public, 1973, for sixty performances. LONDON DEBUT—Joseph Surface, *A School for Scandal,* Logan Place, 1970, for six performances.

PRINCIPAL STAGE APPEARANCES—At the Guthrie, appeared in: *Shoemakers Holiday, The Visit, Harpers Ferry, The Second Shepherd's Play;* at the National Theatre of Canada in Stratford, appeared in: *Volpone, Macbeth, The Duchess of Malfi, Much Ado about Nothing, The Merchant of Venice, The Threepenny Opera;* at the Actors Theatre of Louisville: Ivan, *Carmilla;* Kerry, *Noon;* Baron Frank, *Frankenstein;* Matt, *The Threepenny Opera;* Inspector Hound, *The Real Inspector Hound;* Feraillon, *A Flea in Her Ear;* Merlie, *The Ballad of the Sad Cafe;* Sarge, *Female Transport.*

Regional theatre appearances include: Hans Christian Anderson, *Rainsnakes,* Long Wharf, New Haven, CT; Harold, *They're Dying Out,* Yale Rep, New Haven, CT; Chandebise/Poche, *A Flea in Her Ear,* Hartford Stage, CT; Randall Underwood, *Heartbreak House,* Arena Stage; Giles Ralston, *The Mousetrap,* Seattle Repertory, WA; Henry Carver (Leo), *Design for Living,* Tom, *Morrisey Hall,* McCarter, Princeton, NJ; Sergius, *Arms and the Man,* Vancouver Playhouse; Donald, *Porcelain Time,* Berkshire Festival, Stockbridge, MA; Antipholus of Syracuse, *The Comedy of Errors,* Manitoba Theatre Centre; Tony Cavendish, *The Royal Family,* Gentleman Caller, *The Glass Menagerie,* American Stage Festival, NH; Raymond deChelles, *Custom of the Country,* Shakespeare & Co., Lee, MA.

New York theatre appearances include: Sarge, *Female Transport,* New York Shakespeare Festival, Public; Roy, *Scribes,* Phoenix; Francisco, *The Tempest,* Lincoln Center Repertory, Vivian Beaumont; understudy Sherlock Holmes, *Crucifer of Blood,* Booth; Wilson, *Secret Service,* Lincoln Center Repertory; Thompson, *Boy Meets Girl,* Lincoln Center Repertory; Dr. Pinch, *The Comedy of Errors,* New York Shakespeare Festival, Delacorte; Clive and Edward, *Cloud 9,* Theatre de Lys; Captain DeFoenix, *Trelawney of the Wells,* Lincoln Center Repertory; Montjoy, *Henry V,* New York Shakespeare Festival, Delacorte; Bodenschatz, *The Death of Von Richtofen as Witnessed from Earth,* New York Shakespeare Festi-

JEFFREY JONES

val, Public; Lord John, Will, Treves, etc, *The Elephant Man,* Booth; Maurice, *Love Letters on Blue Paper,* Hudson Guild, 1984.

MAJOR TOURS—Lord John, etc., *The Elephant Man,* National Tour (Baltimore, Washington, DC, Chicago, Los Angeles, San Francisco), 1979-80.

FILM DEBUT—Fred, *The Revolutionary,* United Artists, 1970. PRINCIPAL FILM APPEARANCES—Clive Barlowe, *Easy Money,* Orion, 1983; Emperor Joseph II, *Amadeus,* Orion, 1984.

TELEVISION DEBUT—*Kojak,* CBS, 1971. PRINCIPAL TELEVISION APPEARANCES—Wilson, "Secret Service," *Theatre in America,* PBS; *The Adams Chronicles,* PBS; Clifford Connant, *Remington Steele,* CBS; *Interrogation in Budapest; A Fine Romance; Ryan's Hope; One Life to Live.*

AWARDS: Tyrone Guthrie Award, 1971.

SIDELIGHTS: MEMBERSHIPS—Actors' Equity Association, American Federation of Television and Radio Artists, Screen Actors Guild.

In relating highlights from his career for *CTFT,* Jones wrote, "I entered the theater with the encouragement of Tyrone Guthrie, discovered that I enjoyed and respected the profession and decided to pursue it. After a brief post-college retirement' in South America, I attended the London Academy of Music and Dramatic Art. I then spent three years at Stratford, Ontario and other major theatres in Canada. Since then, I have been based in New York City. My involvement in the original production of *Cloud 9* proved to be a major factor in the development of my career.''

ADDRESS: AGENT—J. Michael Bloom, 400 Madison Avenue, New York, NY 10017.

*   *   *

JONES, John   1917-

PERSONAL: Full name John Hayford Jones; born April 26, 1917, in Waukesha, WI; son of Owen L. (a salesman) and Mildred H. Jones; married June Beck (an educator), 1953; children: one son, one daughter. EDUCATION: University of California at Los Angeles, B.Ed., art, 1941, M.A., art, 1948.

VOCATION: Educator, writer, director, and designer.

CAREER: STAGE DEBUT—Mephistopheles, *Doctor Fautus*, UCLA Campus theatre, 1940. PRINCIPAL STAGE APPEARANCES—Danced with Myra Kinch Dancers and toured until 1942.

PRINCIPAL STAGE WORK—Costume designer, Billy Barnes Group, Chi Chi Club, Palm Springs, CA, 1945; designer and director, *The Pearl*, Royce Hall, UCLA, 1954; director, *Montezuma*, Royce Hall, UCLA, 1956; costume designer, *A Game of Gods*, Royce Hall, UCLA, 1959; director, *Allegro*, Theatre 170, Los Angeles, CA, 1959; lighting designer, *Under Milkwood*, Theatre Group Productions, UCLA, 1959; set and lighting designer, *Mother Courage*, Theatre Group Productions, UCLA, 1959; lighting designer, *The Three Sisters, Four Comedies of Despair*, both 1960;

Photography by Johnny Corbin

JOHN JONES

director, *45 Minutes from Broadway*, USO-UCLA Far East tour, 1961; director, *Don Giovanni*, opera workshop, UCLA, 1962.

Director, *Griffin and the Minor Canon*, Little, Los Angeles, CA, 1963; director, *The Infernal Machine*, Magowan Hall, 1963; costume designer, *Peribanez, 'Tis Pity She's a Whore*, both 1963; director and choreographer, *Carousel*, USO-UCLA summer tour, 1964; director, *The Tempest, Noah and a Flood of Other Stuff*, both 1966; director, *El Nino Ha Nacido*, UCLA Latin American Center, 1966; director, *Annabelle Broom*, Huntington Hartford, Los Angeles, 1966; director and costume designer, *Agamemnon*, 1967; director, *Anything Goes*, UCLA, 1968; director, *Celebration*, UCLA, 1968; director, choreographer, and set and costume design, *How to Succeed in Business without Really Trying*, USO-UCLA tour of Germany, 1969; director, *A Funny Thing Happened on the Way to the Forum*, USO-UCLA tour of the Orient, 1973.

PRINCIPAL FILM WORK—Designer and choreographer, *The Highwayman*, 1951.

PRINCIPAL TELEVISION WORK—Producer and photographer, *The Golden Voyage of the Jones Family*, NBC, 1966.

RELATED CAREER—Professor of design, University of California, 1967-present; lecturer at the Film Institute, Cairo, Egypt, 1960-61, 1964-65.

WRITINGS: PLAYS, PRODUCED—*The Pearl*, UCLA, 1954; *Montezuma*, UCLA, 1956; *A Game of Gods*, UCLA, 1959; *Tyger, Tyger*, UCLA, 1970.

AWARDS: Best Collegiate Show, City of Los Angeles; Fulbright teaching grantee, Higher Film Institute, Cairo, Egypt.

ADDRESS: OFFICE—University of California, 405 Hilgard Avenue, Los Angeles, CA 90024.

*   *   *

JORDAN, Glenn

PERSONAL: Born in San Antonio, TX. EDUCATION: Harvard College, Cambridge, MA; Yale University, School of Drama, New Haven, CT.

VOCATION: Director and producer.

CAREER: NEW YORK DEBUT—Director, *Another Evening with Harry Stoones*, Off Broadway. PRINCIPAL STAGE WORK—Director: *The Disintegration of James Cherry*, O'Neill Theatre Center, Waterford, CT, Forum, Lincoln Center Repertory Company, NY; ten new plays at the O'Neill Center, Waterford, CT; *A Delicate Balance*, Williamstown Theatre Festival; *The Glass Menagerie; Rosencrantz and Guildenstern Are Dead; Keep Tightly Closed in a Cool, Dry Place*, La Ma Ma E.T.C.; *A Cry of Players*, Brandeis University; *A Streetcar Named Desire*, Cincinnati Playhouse in the Park; *All My Sons*, FL and Los Angeles; *Actors and Actresses*, Hartman, Stamford, CT, 1983.

FILM DEBUT—Director, *Only When I Laugh*, Columbia, 1981. PRINCIPAL FILM WORK—Director: *The Buddy System*, Twentieth Century-Fox, 1984; *Mass Appeal*, Universal, 1984.

GLENN JORDAN

PRINCIPAL TELEVISION WORK—Director and producer, *Benjamin Franklin*, CBS; producer, *Making Money and Thirteen Other Very Short Plays;* producer, *Dragon Country;* producer, *Paradise Lost;* director, "The Typist," *Hollywood Television Theatre;* director, *Hogan's Goat;* director, *Particular Men;* director, *Eccentricities of a Nightingale;* director, *The Best of Families;* director, "The Displaced Person," *American Short Story;* director, *Frankenstein;* director, *The Picture of Dorian Grey;* director, *A Prowler in the Heart*, ABC; director, *The Oath* (pilot); director, *Family*.

Director of all of the following television movies: Shell Game, CBS, 1975; *One of My Wives Is Missing*, ABC, 1976; *Delta County*, ABC, 1977; *In the Matter of Karen Ann Quinlan*, NBC, 1977; *Sunshine Christmas*, NBC; *The Court Martial of General Custer*, NBC; *Les Miserables*, CBS, 1978; *Son-Rise: A Miracle of Love*, NBC, 1979; *The Family Man*, CBS, 1979; *The Women's Room*, ABC, 1980; *The Princess and the Cabbie*, CBS, 1981; *Lois Gibbs and the Love Canal*, CBS, 1982; *Heartsounds*, ABC, 1984; *Toughlove*, ABC, 1985.

RELATED CAREER: Founding producing director, *New York Television Theatre*, Channel 13, PBS.

AWARDS: Emmy, for producing and directing *Benjamin Franklin;* Peabody, for *Benjamin Franklin;* Emmys for work as producer and director of *New York Television Theatre;* Directors Guild Award, for *Family;* Christopher, Emmy nomination, Directors Guild nomination, *Les Miserables;* Christopher, Humanitas, for *Son-Rise: A Miracle of Love;* Christopher, *Lois Gibbs and the Love Canal*.

ADDRESS: AGENT—c/o Bill Haber, Creative Artists Agency, 1888 Century Park East, Suite 1400, Los Angeles, CA 90067.

JORY, Victor 1902-82

PERSONAL: Born November 23, 1902, in Dawson City, AK; died February 11, 1982; son of Edwin and Joanna (Snyder) Jory; married Jean Innes; children: Jon. EDUCATION: Attended schools in Dawson City, Vancouver, Pasadena, CA, and University of Canada.

VOCATION: Actor.

CAREER: PRINCIPAL FILM APPEARANCES—*State Fair; Madame DuBarry; A Midsummer Night's Dream; The King Steps Out; The Adventures of Tom Sawyer; Dodge City; Each Dawn I Die; Gone with the Wind; The Green Archer; The Shadow; Charlie Chan in Rio; Unknown Guest; State Fair; Gallant Blade; A Woman's Secret; The Highwayman; The Man from the Alamo; The Fugitive Kind; The Miracle Worker; Cheyenne Autumn; Jigsaw; A Time for Dying; Flap; Papillon; The Mountain Men*.

PRINCIPAL TELEVISION APPEARANCES—Det. Lt. Howard Finucane, *Manhunt*, syndication, 1959-61; *King's Row; Banacek; Mannix; Name of the Game; High Chaparral; Ironside; The Virginian; Voyage to the Bottom of the Sea; Heroes of the Bible; Power*.

STAGE DEBUT—1929, Vancouver, British Columbia, Canada. NEW YORK STAGE DEBUT—Geoffrey, *The Two Mrs. Carrolls*, Booth, 1943. PRINCIPAL STAGE APPEARANCES—Mr. Manningham, *Angel Street*, Chicago, IL, 1942; Dale Williams, *The Perfect Marriage*, Ethel Barrymore, NY, 1944; Laurent, *Therese*, Biltmore, NY, 1945; King Henry, *Henry VIII*, John, *John Gabriel Borkman*, Ferrovius, *Androcles and the Lion*, James Carroll, *Yellow Jack*, both American Repertory Theater, International, NY, 1946-47; Anthony Anderson, *The Devil's Disciple*, City Center, NY, then Royale, NY, 1950; *Mrs. Barry's Etchings*, Ford's, Baltimore, MD, 1951; George Crane, *Season in the Sun*, Booth, NY, 1951.

Stock: Elyot Chase, *Private Lives*, 1952; Jeeter Lester, *Tobacco Road*, 1970, Narrator, *Our Town*, 1972, Willy Loman, *Death of a Salesman*, 1972, all Actors Theater of Louisville, KY; James Tyrone, *Long Day's Journey into Night*, 1973; *The Last Meeting of the Knights of the White Magnolia*, 1976; *The Best Man*, 1976; *The Front Page*, 1978.

MAJOR TOURS—U.S. cities: Lt. Commander William Marshall, *Bill Comes Back*, 1945; Laurent, *Therese*, 1945; Jack Rance, *The Girl of the Golden West*, 1947; *The Spider*, 1950; George Crane, *Season in the Sun*, 1952; *Bell, Book, and Candle*, 1953; *My Three Angels*, 1954; Big Daddy, *Cat on a Hot Tin Roof*, 1957-58; *The Happiest Millionaire; The Best Man*, 1964.

PRINCIPAL STAGE WORK—Director: Actors' Theater of Louisville, KY.

SIDELIGHTS: CTFT learned that Jory was a boxer and wrestler and once held the title of Light Heavyweight Champion of British Columbia and won the wrestling and boxing championship of the National Guard in Monterey, CA. His son Jon is the artistic director of the Actors' Theater of Louisville in Kentucky.*

*   *   *

JOUDRY, Patricia 1921-

PERSONAL: Born October 18, 1921, in Spirit River, Alberta, Canada; daughter of Clifford George (a publisher) and Beth (a

Photography by Larry James Fillo

PATRICIA JOUDRY

painter and potter; maiden name, Gilbart) Joudry; divorced from two husbands; children: Gay, Sharon, Stephanie, Melanie, Felicity.

VOCATION: Writer.

WRITINGS: PLAYS, PRODUCED—*Teach Me How to Cry,* NY, 1955; *The Sand Castle,* Margo Jones, Dallas, TX, c. 1956; *Semi-Detached,* NY; *Valerie; Three Rings for Michelle; The Song of Louise in the Morning; A Very Modest Orgy,* Saskatoon, Canada, 1981; *Think Again; O Listen!,* Theatre Calgary, Alberta, Canada, 1984. PLAYS, PUBLISHED—*Teach Me How to Cry, Semi-Detached, The Song of Louise in the Morning,* all Dramatists Play Service. BOOKS, PUBLISHED—*Sound Therapy for the Walkman,* St. Peter's Press, Saskatoon, Canada.

SIDELIGHTS: Joudry informed *CTFT* that there is a doctoral thesis being prepared that deals with her theatrical writing. It is the work of Professor Aviva Ravel of McGill University, Montreal, Canada.

ADDRESS: HOME—Box 78, St. Denis, Saskatoon, SOK 3WO,

Canada. AGENT—Anton Wagner, 201 Shelbourne Street, Suite 2204, Toronto, ON M5A 3X2, Canada.

*   *   *

JURASAS, Jonas R.   1936-

PERSONAL: Last name pronounced You-ray-shas; born June 19, 1936, in Lithuania; son of Jonas (an officer) and Sofia (Jurksaite) Jurasas; married Marita A. Sluckaite (a writer); children: Joris-Christopher. EDUCATION: Department of Theatre, Vilnius State Conservatory; Academy of Moscow Theatre Arts (Gitis-Gosudarstvenny Institut Teatrarnovo Iskusstva Imeni Lunacharskovo).

VOCATION: Director and actor.

CAREER: PRINCIPAL STAGE APPEARANCES—Plays by Chekhov, Gorky, Mayakovsky, Shakespeare, and others, all in the Soviet Union.

PRINCIPAL STAGE WORK—Director: *East-West,* Hartman Conservatory, Stamford, CT, 1976; *A Walk in the Moonlight,* Theatre for the New City, NY, 1978; *Macbeth,* La MaMa, 1977; *Endgame,* Trinity Conservatory, Providence, RI, 1979; *The Suicide,* Trinity Repertory, Providence, RI, then ANTA, NY, 1980; *The Magnificent Cuckold,* Yale Repertory, New Haven, CT, 1981; *Zeks,* Theatre for the New City, NY, 1982; *The Three Sisters,* Japan Performing Arts Center, TOGA Festival, 1984.

Also, in the Soviet Union: *Tango; Moliere; The Mamoth Hunt; Barbora Radvilaite; The House of Terror; Mother's Field; The Bolsheviks; Duel; The Physicists; Macbeth;* others.

PRINCIPAL FILM APPEARANCES—Featured roles in five films produced by MOSFILM, Soviet Union.

RELATED CAREER—Teacher of Stanislavski Method and other theatre-related courses at La MaMa, NY, Yale Drama School, Rhode Island State College, Trinity Conservatory, Hartman Conservatory, Kaunas Drama Theatre, Moscow State University.

AWARDS: For operating and directing, Kaunas State Drama Theatre, 1967-1972.

SIDELIGHTS: MEMBERSHIPS—Society of Stage Directors and Choreographers, Soviet All-Union Theatre Association (1963-72), Lithuanian Theatre Association (1967-1972).

ADDRESS: HOME—Ruemannstrasse 92, 8000 Munchen 40, West Germany. OFFICE—1775 Broadway, Second Flr., RFE/RL, New York, NY 10019.

K

KAHN, Michael

PERSONAL: Born in New York City; son of Frederick Joseph and Adele (Gaberman) Kahn. EDUCATION: Attended Columbia College and Columbia University.

VOCATION: Director.

CAREER: PRINCIPAL STAGE WORK—Director: *The Love Nest,* Writers' Stage, NY, 1963; *Funnyhouse of a Negro, The New Tenant, Victims of Duty, That 5 AM Jazz, Helen, The Owl Answers,* all 1964; *America Hurrah,* Cafe La MaMa, 1964; *The Long Christmas Dinner, Queens of France, The Happy Journey to Trenton and Camden, Measure for Measure,* all 1966; *The Rimers of Eldritch, The Cavern, The Freaking Out of Stephanie Blake,* all 1967; *The Merchant of Venice,* American Shakespeare Festival Theater, Stratford, CT, 1967; *There's Where I Belong, Camino Real, The Death of Bessie Smith,* all 1968.

At the American Shakespeare Festival, Stratford, CT: *Richard II, Love's Labour's Lost,* both 1968, *Henry V, The Three Sisters,* both 1969, *Othello, All's Well That Ends Well,* both 1970, *The Merry Wives of Windsor, Mourning Becomes Electra,* both 1971; *Julius Caesar, Antony and Cleopatra,* both 1972; *Macbeth, Measure for Measure,* both 1973; *Romeo and Juliet,* 1974, *Our Town, The Winter's Tale,* both 1975; *The Crucible, The Winter's Tale, As You Like It,* all 1976.

Crimes of Passion, 1969; *Hough in Blazes,* Philadelphia, PA, 1971; *Women Beware Women,* City Center Acting Company, NY, 1972; *Tartuffe,* Philadelphia Drama Guild, PA, 1972; *Shakespeare and the Performing Arts,* Kennedy Center, Washington, DC, 1973; *The Epic of Buster Friend,* NY, 1973; *The Tooth of Crime,* Goodman, Chicago, IL, 1974; *Cat on a Hot Tin Roof,* Stratford and NY, 1975; *Beyond the Horizon,* McCarter, Princeton, NJ, 1974; *Tis Pity She's a Whore,* Goodman, Chicago, IL, 1974; *Mother Courage, A Grave Undertaking, Section Nine,* all McCarter, Princeton, NJ, 1975; *The Heiress, The Winter's Tale, A Streetcar Named Desire,* all McCarter, Princeton, NJ, 1976; *Eleanor,* Ford's, Washington, DC, 1976; *Angel City, A Wilder Triple Bill,* both McCarter, Princeton, NJ, 1977; *The Night of the Tribades,* NY, 1977; *The Torch-Bearers, Put Them All Together,* both McCarter, Princeton, NJ, 1978; *Grand Magic,* NY, 1979; *A Month in the Country,* McCarter, Princeton, NJ, then NY, 1979; *Showboat,* NY; *Whodunnit?,* NY; *Senorita from Tacna,* NY; *A New Way to Pay Old Debts,* Acting Company, NY.

Producer: *PS 193,* Writers' Stage, NY, 1962.

RELATED CAREER—Head of the Interpretation Department, Drama Division, Juilliard School, NY; artistic director, American Shakespeare Festival, 1969-74, McCarter Theater, Princeton, NJ, 1974, Acting Company, 1978-present; instructor: New York University Tisch School of the Arts, Circle in the Square Theatre School; director, Chautauqua Theatre School.

AWARDS: Antoinette Perry Award nomination, Best Director, for *Showboat.*

ADDRESS: HOME—New York, NY. OFFICE—The Acting Company, 420 W. 42nd Street, New York, NY 10036.

*   *   *

KANE, Carol   1952-

PERSONAL: Born June 18, 1952, in Cleveland, OH.

VOCATION: Actress.

CAREER: FILM DEBUT—*Carnal Knowledge,* Avco-Embassy, 1971; *Wedding in White,* New Line Cinema, 1973; *The Last Detail,* 1974; *Dog Day Afternoon,* Warner Brothers, 1975; *Hester Street,* Midwest Films, 1975; *Harry and Walter Go to New York,* Columbia, 1976; *The Mafu Cage,* 1977; *Annie Hall,* United Artists, 1977; *The World's Greatest Lover,* Twentieth Century-Fox, 1977; *When a Stranger Calls,* Columbia, 1978; *The Muppet Movie,* Associated Film Distributors, 1979; *La Sabina,* 1979; *Les Jeux,* 1980; *Over the Brooklyn Bridge,* Metro-Goldwyn-Mayer, 1984; *Racing with the Moon,* Paramount, 1984.

PRINCIPAL TELEVISION APPEARANCES—Movies: *Many Mansions.* Series: Simka Gravis, *Taxi,* ABC, then NBC, 1981-83; *Cheers,* 1985.

STAGE DEBUT—Age 14.

MAJOR TOURS—U.S. cities: *The Prime of Miss Jean Brodie; Arturo Ui; The Enchanted.*

AWARDS: Academy Award nomination, Best Actress, 1975, for *Hester Street;* Emmy Award, Outstanding Lead Actress in a Comedy Series, 1982, for *Taxi;* Emmy Award, Outstanding Supporting Actress in a Comedy Series, 1983, for *Taxi.*

ADDRESS: AGENT—Creative Artist's Agency, 1888 Century Park E., Suite 1400, Los Angeles, CA 90067.*

KANIN, Garson 1912-

PERSONAL: Born November 24, 1912, in Rochester, NY; son of David M. and Sadie (Levine) Kanin; married Ruth Gordon (the actress and writer), December 4, 1942. EDUCATION: James Madison High School, NY; American Academy of Dramatic Arts. MILITARY: U.S. Army Signal Corps, 1941-42; U.S. Army Air Force, Sergeant, 1942-43; Office of Strategic Services, Europe, Captain, 1943-46.

VOCATION: Writer, director, producer, and former actor.

CAREER: PRINCIPAL STAGE APPEARANCES—Tommy Deal, *Little Ol' Boy*, 1933; young man, *Spring Song*, 1934; Red, *Ladies' Money*, 1934; Al, *Three Men on a Horse*, 1935; Izzy Cohen, *The Body Beautiful*, 1935; Green, *Boy Meets Girl*, 1935; Vincent Chenevski, *Star Spangled*, 1936; as himself, *Remembering Mr. Maugham*, 1966, 1967, and 1969.

PRINCIPAL STAGE WORK—Director: *Hitch Your Wagon*, 1937; *Too Many Heroes*, 1937; *The Rugged Path*, 1945; *Born Yesterday*, 1946; *Years Ago*, 1946; *How I Wonder*, 1947; *The Leading Lady*, 1948; *The Smile of the World*, 1949; *A Month in the Country*, 1949; *The Rat Race*, 1949; *The Live Wire*, 1950; *The Amazing Adele*, 1950; *Fledermaus*, 1950; *The Diary of Anne Frank*, London and NY, 1955; *Into Thin Air*, London, 1955; *Small War on Murray Hill*, 1957; *Hole in the Head*, 1957; *Do Re Mi*, 1960; *The Good Soup*, 1960; *Sunday in New York*, 1961; *A Gift of Time*, 1962; *Come on Strong*, 1962; *Funny Girl*, 1964; *I Was Dancing*, 1964; *A Very Rich Woman*, 1965; *Remembering Mr. Maugham*, 1966; *We Have Always Lived in a Castle*, 1966; *Idiot's Delight*, 1970; *Dreyfus in Rehearsal*, 1974; *Ho! Ho! Ho!*, 1976; *Peccadillo*, 1985.

GARSON KANIN

PRINCIPAL FILM WORK—Director: *A Man to Remember*, RKO, 1938; *Next Time I Marry*, RKO, 1938; *The Great Man Votes*, RKO, 1939; *Bachelor Mother*, RKO, 1939; *My Favorite Wife*, 1940; *They Knew What They Wanted*, RKO, 1940; *Tom, Dick, and Harry*, 1941; *Fellow Americans*, 1942; *Ring of Steel*, OEM, 1942; *Battle Stations*, OWI, 1944; *Salute to France*, OWI, 1944; *The True Glory*, 1945; *Some Kind of Nut*, United Artists, 1969; *Where It's At*, United Artists, 1969.

WRITINGS: PLAYS PRODUCED—*Born Yesterday*, 1946; *The Smile of the World*, 1949; *The Rat Race*, 1949; *The Live Wire*, 1950; *The Amazing Adele* (adapted from a play by Pierre Barillet and Jean-Pierre Gredy), 1950; *Fledermaus* (English version, with Howard Dietz), 1950; *Do Re Mi*, 1960; *The Good Soup* (adapted from play by Felicien Marceau), 1960; *A Gift of Time* (adapted from play by Lael Tucker Wertenbaker), 1962; *Come on Strong*, 1962; *Remembering Mr. Maugham*, 1966; *Dreyfus in Rehearsal* (adapted from a play by Jean-Claude Grumberg), 1974; *Peccadillo*, 1984.

SCREENPLAYS—*Woman of the Year* (in collabaration with Ring Lardner, Jr. and Michael Kanin, but not credited), 1942; *A Lady Takes a Chance* (in collaboration), 1943; *The More the Merrier* (in collaboration), 1943; *From This Day Forward* (in collaboration), 1946; *A Double Life* (with Ruth Gordon), Universal, 1948; *Adam's Rib* (with Ruth Gordon), Metro-Goldwyn-Mayer, 1949; *Born Yesterday*, Columbia, 1950; *Pat and Mike* (with Ruth Gordon), Metro-Goldwyn-Mayer, 1952; *The Marrying Kind* (with Ruth Gordon), Columbia, 1952; *The Girl Can't Help It*, Twentieth Century-Fox, 1957; *High Time* (in collaboration), 1960; *The Rat Race*, Paramount, 1960; *The Right Approach*, 1961; *Some Kind of Nut*, United Artists, 1969; *Where It's At*, United Artists, 1969.

TELEVISION—"Born Yesterday," *Hallmark Hall of Fame* (adapted and co-directed), NBC, 1956; *Mr. Broadway* (also directed pilot of series): "An Eye on Emily," "Something to Sing About," "The He-She Chemistry," 1964; *Hardhat and Legs* (with Ruth Gordon), CBS, 1978; *Josie & Joe* (pilot adapted from *Moviola*, "Scandal"), 1980.

BOOKS, NON-FICTION—*Remembering Mr. Maugham*, Atheneum, 1966; *Tracy and Hepburn: An Intimate Memoir*, Viking Press, 1971; *Hollywood: Stars and Starlets, Tycoons and Flesh-Peddlers, Moviemakers and Moneymakers, Frauds and Geniuses, Hopefuls and Has-Beens, Great Lovers and Sex Symbols*, Viking Press, 1974; *It Takes a Long Time to Become Young*, Doubleday & Company, Inc., 1978; *Together Again! Hollywood's Great Movie Teams*, Doubleday & Company, Inc., 1981.

FICTION—*Blow Up a Storm*, Random House, 1959; *The Rat Race*, Pocket Books, Inc., 1960; *Cast of Characters* (collected short stories), Atheneum, 1969; *Where It's At*, New American Library, 1969; *Adam's Rib* (with Ruth Gordon), Metro-Goldwyn-Mayer Library of Film Scripts, Viking Press, 1972; *A Thousand Summers*, Doubleday & Company Inc., 1973; *One Hell of an Actor*, Harper & Row, 1977; *Moviola*, Simon & Schuster, 1979; *Smash*, Viking Press, 1980; *Cordelia?*, Arbor House, 1982.

SHORT NON-FICTION—*Thanks to Mr. Greely*, 1940; *Letter to a Bewildered Reporter*, 1940; *I Direct*, 1941; *The Bomb and the Parker 51*, 1948; *Trips to Felix*, 1964; *The 49th Street Parallel*, 1965; *I Have Known Ruth Gordon for Something Less Than a Hundred Years*, 1965; *Hollywood: As Was and As Is*, 1967; *My Next Trick Is Great*, 1969; *Feelings in the Presence of a Literary Genius*, 1969; *The Private Kate*, 1970; *A Thornton Wilder Protege by the Skin of His Teeth (Put It in Writing)*, 1971; *I Remember It Well*

(More or Less) 1974; *Trouble on West 46th Street*, 1976; *Anne Frank at 50*, 1979; *Marc Connelly*, 1981; *George Cukor*, 1983; *Jerome Weidman*, 1984.

SHORT FICTION—*A Day at a Time*, 1955; *All Through the House*, 1955; *Faint Heart Etcetra*, 1958; *Something for Susie*, 1959; *Who to Who*, 1961; *The Lady's Maid*, 1962; *An Echo of Love*, 1963; *Define the Word "Wife"*, 1969; *The Money Man*, 1965; *The He-She Chemistry*, 1969; *He Wished Her Dead and Wished Her Dead Until One Day He Died*, 1970; *Another Woman*, 1976.

AWARDS: Academy Award, Best Documentary, 1945, for *True Glory;* the Sidney Howard Memorial Award (shared with Arthur Laurents), Donaldson, Best First Play, Best Director, 1946, all for *Born Yesterday;* Academy Award nomination, Best Original Screenplay, 1947, for *A Double Life* (with Ruth Gordon); Academy Award nomination, Best Story and Best Screenplay, 1950, for *Adam's Rib,* and 1952, for *Pat and Mike* (both with Ruth Gordon); Achievement Award, Academy of Dramatic Arts Alumni, 1958.

SIDELIGHTS: MEMBERSHIPS—Directors Guild of America, Actors' Equity Association, Writers Guild of America, Dramatists Guild Council, Authors Guild, Authors League of America, American Society of Composers, Authors and Publishers, American Federation of Television and Radio Artists, Society of Stage Directors and Choreographers, Academy of Motion Picture Arts and Sciences, Actors Fund of America, Players Club, Friars Club, New York Athletic Club, Century Club, Coffee House Club, PEN.

ADDRESS: HOME—P.O. Box 585, Edgartown Road, Martha's Vineyard, MA 02539. OFFICE—200 W. 57th Street, Suite 1203, New York, NY 10019.

* * *

KANTER, Hal 1918-

PERSONAL: Born December 18, 1918, in Savannah, GA; son of Albert Lewis (a publisher) and Rose (Ehrenreich) Kanter; married Doris Prouder (a writer), September 5, 1941; children: Lisa Kanter Shafer, Donna, Abigail Kanter Jaye.

VOCATION: Writer, producer, and director.

CAREER: PRINICPAL TELEVISION WORK—Producer: *The George Gobel Show*, 1954-57; *Kraft Music Hall*, 1958-59; *Valentine's Day*, 1964-65; *Julia*, 1968-71; *All in the Family*, 1975-76; *Chico and the Man*, 1976-77.

WRITINGS: SCREENPLAYS—*My Favorite Spy*, Paramount, 1951; *Two Tickets to Broadway* (with Sid Solvers), RKO, 1951; *Off Limits* (with Jack Sher), Paramount, 1952; *Road to Bali* (with Frank Butler and William Morrow), Paramount, 1952; *Here Come the Girls* (with Edmund L. Hartmann), Paramount, 1953; *Money from Home* (with James Allardice), Paramount, 1954; *Casanova's Big Night* (with Edmund L. Hartmann), Paramount, 1954; *About Mrs. Leslie* (with Ketti Frings), Paramount, 1954; *Artists and Models* (with Frank Tashlin and Herbert Baker), Paramount, 1955; *Once Upon a Horse*, Universal, 1958; *Loving You* (with Herbert Baker), Paramount, 1958; *Mardi Gras* (with Winston Miller), Twentieth Century-Fox, 1958; *Let's Make Love*, Twentieth Century-Fox, 1960; *Pocketful of Miracles* (with Harry Tugend), United Artists, 1961; *Bachelor in Paradise* (with Valentine Davies), Metro-Goldwyn-Mayer, 1961;

Blue Hawaii (with Harry Allan Weiss), Paramount, 1961; *Move Over Darling* (adaptation; with Jack Sher), Twentieth Century-Fox, 1963; *Dear Brigitte*, Twentieth Century-Fox, 1965.

RADIO SHOWS—*Amos n' Andy; Grand Central Station.*

TELEVISION SHOWS—*Shower of Stars; The Bing Crosby Show; The George Gobel Show; Kraft Music Hall.*

BOOKS, PUBLISHED—*Television and Screen* (contributor), University of California Press, 1958; *Snake in the Glass*, Delacorte, 1971.

AWARDS: Emmy Award, Best Comedy Writer, 1954, for *The George Gobel Show;* Writers Guild Award nominations, Best Screenplay, 1960, for *Let's Make Love*, and 1961, for *Blue Hawaii.*

SIDELIGHTS: RECREATION—Deep sea fishing, travel, philately, public speaking.

ADDRESS: OFFICE—Savannah Productions, 13063 Ventura Blvd., Studio City, CA 91604.

* * *

KAUFMAN, Andy 1949-84

PERSONAL: Born January 17, 1949, in New York City; died May 16, 1984.

VOCATION: Actor and comedian.

CAREER: PRINCIPAL TELEVISION APPEARANCES—*Van Dyke and Company*, NBC, 1976; *Saturday Night Live*, NBC; Latka Gravis, *Taxi*, ABC, then NBC, 1978-83; guest host, *Fridays*, ABC; *The Top*, ABC, 1984; *The David Letterman Show*, NBC; *The Tonight Show*, NBC; *The Merv Griffin Show.*

PRINCIPAL FILM APPEARANCES—*In God We Trust*, Universal, 1980; *Heartbeeps*, Universal, 1981.

PRINCIPAL FILM WORK—Producer, *My Breakfast with Blassie.*

PRINCIPAL STAGE APPEARANCES—*Teaneck Tanzi the Venus Flytrap*, Broadway production, 1983.

SIDELIGHTS: Kaufman was a regular opening act at My Father's Place in Roslyn, NY. He also played a sold out performance at Carnegie Hall, NY, in 1979.*

* * *

KAVNER, Julie 1951-

BRIEF ENTRY: Born September 7, 1951; graduated from San Diego State University. Actress. Kavner's television credits include: Brenda Morgenstern on the series *Rhoda*, CBS, 1974-78; "The Girl Who Couldn't Lose," *ABC Afternoon Playbreak*, 1975; and the television movie *No Other Love*, 1979. Her stage credits include *Particular Friendships*, Astor Place, NY, 1981. She will be seen in *Hannah and Her Sisters*, Orion (upcoming).*

KEATON, Michael

BRIEF ENTRY: Born in Pittsburgh, PA; married Caroline Mac-Williams (an actress). Actor. Keaton's television credits include Lanny Wolf, *All's Fair*, CBS, 1977; *Mary*, CBS, 1978; Kenneth Christy, *The Mary Tyler Moore Hour*, CBS, 1979; Mike O'Rourke in the series *Working Stiffs*, CBS, 1979; Murphy in *Report to Murphy*, CBS, 1981. He is a frequent guest on *The David Letterman Show*. His film credits include *Night Shift*, Warner Brothers, 1982; *Mr. Mom*, Twentieth Century-Fox, 1983; *Johnny Dangerously*, 1984; and *Touch and Go*, 1985.*

*   *   *

KEITH, Brian   1921-

PERSONAL: Born November 14, 1921, in Bayonne, NJ; son of Robert Lee (an actor) and Helena (an actress; maiden name, Shipman) Keith; married Victoria Young (an actress). MILITARY: U.S. Marine Corps, 1941-45.

VOCATION: Actor.

CAREER: PRINCIPAL TELEVISION APPEARANCES—Dramatic: *Studio One*, CBS; *Suspense*, CBS; *Philco Television Playhouse*. Series: Matt Anders, *Crusader*, CBS, 1955-56; Dave Blassingame, *The Westerner*, NBC, 1960; Bill Davis, *Family Affair*, CBS, 1966-71; Dr. Sean Jamison, *The Brian Keith Show*, NBC, 1972-74; Judge Milton G. Hardcastle, *Hardcastle and McCormick*, ABC, 1983-present. Miniseries: Axel Dunmire, *Centennial*, NBC, 1978-79. Movies: *How the West Was Won*, ABC, 1978; *The Seekers*, 1979; *Power*, 1979; *Moviola*, 1980.

STAGE DEBUT—*Heyday*, Shubert, New Haven, CT, 1946. NEW YORK DEBUT—Mannion, *Mister Roberts*, Alvin, 1948. PRINCIPAL STAGE APPEARANCES—Ilyich, *Darkness at Noon*, Alvin, NY, 1951; Lash, *Out West of Eighth*, Ethel Barrymore, NY, 1951; *Moon Is Blue*, Chicago, IL, 1951; Jezebel's Husband, *The Emperor of Babylon*, Boston, 1952; Da, *Da*, Morosco, NY, 1979.

FILM DEBUT—*Arrowhead*, 1952. PRINCIPAL FILM APPEARANCES—*Alaska Seas*, 1953; *Violent Men*, 1954; *Bamboo Prison*, Columbia, 1955; *Five Against the House*, Columbia, 1955; *Storm Center*, Columbia, 1956; *Run of the Arrow*, Universal, 1957; *Dino*, Allied Artists, 1957; *Nightfall*, Columbia, 1957; *Sierra Baron*, Twentieth Century-Fox, 1958; *The Young Philadelphians*, Warner Brothers, 1959; *The Deadly Champions*, Pathe-American, 1961; *The Parent Trap*, Buena Vista, 1961; *Moon Pilot*, Buena Vista, 1962; *Savage Sam*, Buena Vista, 1963; *The Raiders*, Universal, 1964; *A Tiger Walks*, Buena Vista, 1964; *Those Calloways*, Buena Vista, 1965; *The Hallelujah Trail*, United Artists, 1965; *Rare Breed*, Universal, 1966; *The Russians Are Coming, the Russians Are Coming*, United Artists, 1966; *Nevada Smith*, Paramount, 1966; *Reflections in a Golden Eye*, Warner Brothers-Seven Arts, 1967.

With Six You Get Eggroll, National General, 1968; *Krakatoa, East of Java*, Cinerama, 1968; *Gaily, Gaily*, United Artists, 1969; *McKenzie Break*, United Artists, 1970; *Scandalous John*, Buena Vista, 1971; *Something Big*, National General, 1972; *The Yakuza*, Warner Brothers, 1975; *The Wind and the Lion*, United Artists, 1975; *Joe Panther*, 1976; *Nickelodeon*, Columbia, 1976; *Hooper*, Warner Brothers, 1978; *Meteor*, American International, 1979; *The*

Mountain Men, Columbia, 1980; *Charlie Chan and the Curse of the Dragon Queen*, 1981; *Sharkey's Machine*, Warner Brothers, 1982.

SIDELIGHTS: FAVORITE ROLE—Da.

ADDRESS: AGENT—Guild Management, 9911 W. Pico Blvd., Los Angeles, CA 90035; James McHugh Agency, 8150 Beverly Blvd., Suite 303, Los Angeles, CA 90048.*

*   *   *

KELLER, Max A.   1943-

PERSONAL: Born August 29, 1943, in St. Petersburg, FL; son of Joseph David (a shoemaker) and Alma Marie (a bookkeeper; maiden name, Hanken) Keller; married Micheline Herkovic (a film producer), October 31, 1971; children: Nicole, David. EDUCATION: University of San Fernando Valley, Doctorate of Jurisprudence. POLITICS: Republican. RELIGION: Jewish.

VOCATION: Producer, packager, and financier.

CAREER: PRINCIPAL TELEVISION WORK—Producer: *Stranger in Our House*, NBC; *Grambling's White Tiger*, NBC; *Kent State*, NBC; *Now and Forever; Deadly Blessing; Voyage of the Rock; A Summer to Remember*, CBS.

AWARDS: Gold Awards, New York Film Festival, for *Grambling's White Tiger* and *Kent State*.

SIDELIGHTS: MEMBERSHIPS—Television Academy of Arts and Sciences. RECREATION—Racketball, language study.

ADDRESS: OFFICE—14225 Ventura Blvd., Sherman Oaks, CA 91423.

*   *   *

KELLER, Micheline   1948-

PERSONAL: Born Micheline Herskovic, December 19, 1948, in Belgium; daughter of William (a business executive) and Maria (a business executive) Herskovic; married Max A. Keller (an attorney and film executive), October 31, 1971; children: Nicole, David. EDUCATION: University of California at Los Angeles, B.A., 1971; Southwestern University, Juris Doctor, 1974.

VOCATION: Producer.

CAREER: PRINCIPAL TELEVISION WORK—Producer: *Summer of Fear*, 1978; *Kent State*, 1980; *Grambling's White Tiger*, 1981; *Deadly Blessing*, 1981; *Voyage of the Rock Aliens*, 1984; *A Summer to Remember*, 1985.

RELATED CAREER—President, Inter Planetary Pictures, 1976-present; president, Inter Planetary Productions, 1978-present.

AWARDS: Themis Society Gold Award, New York Film Festival Award, 1981 for *Kent State;* Gold Award, New York Film Festival, National Association for the Advancement of Colored People Image

Award, 1982, for *Grambling's White Tiger*.

SIDELIGHTS: MEMBERSHIPS—Academy of Television Arts and Sciences, Women in Film.

Keller is a partner with her husband in the law firm of Keller and Keller.

ADDRESS: OFFICE—Inter Planetary Productions, 14225 Ventura Blvd., Sherman Oaks, CA 91423.

*　　*　　*

KELLMAN, Barnet 1947-

PERSONAL: Born November 9, 1947, in New York City; son of Joseph A.G. (an attorney) and Verona D. (Kramer) Kellman; married Nancy Mette (an actress), June 26, 1982. EDUCATION: Colgate University, B.A., 1969; Yale School of Drama, 1970; Union Graduate School, Ph.D., 1973.

VOCATION: Director.

CAREER: PRINCIPAL STAGE WORK—Director: *Danny and the Deep Blue Sea*, Actors' Theatre of Louisville, KY, Circle in the Square, NY; *Key Exchange*, WPA, NY, Orpheum, NY; *Breakfast with Les and Bess*, Hudson Guild, Lambs, NY; *The Good Parts*, Astor Place, NY; *Friends*, Manhattan Theatre Club, NY; *Eden Court*, Promenade, NY. Has also directed at American Place, NY, Public Theater, NY, Eugene O'Neill Theatre Center, CT, Yale Repertory Theatre, CT; Folger, Washington, DC, and the Williamstown Theatre Festival, MA.

PRINCIPAL FILM WORK—Director, *Key Exchange*, Twentieth Century-Fox, 1985.

PRINCIPAL TELEVISION WORK—Director: *Gemini*, Showtime; *Orphans, Waifs, and Wards*, CBS; *Another World*, NBC; *Hometown*, CBS.

RELATED CAREER—Instructor: Film Division of Columbia University School of the Arts, Leonard Davis Center for the Arts, North Carolina School of the Arts, Circle in the Square Acting School, and the Corner Loft Studio.

AWARDS: Emmy Award nomination, for *Another World*.

SIDELIGHTS: MEMBERSHIPS—Society of Stage Directors and Choreographers (executive board, 1985), Directors Guild of America, Actors' Equity Association.

ADDRESS: AGENT—Samuel Liff, William Morris Agency, 1350 Avenue of the Americas, New York, NY 10019.

*　　*　　*

KEMP, Jeremy 1935-

PERSONAL: Born Jeremy Walker, February 3, 1935, near Chesterfield, Derbyshire; son of Edmund Reginald and Elsa (Kemp) Walker; married Joan Wilson (a television producer, director, and actress; died July, 1985). EDUCATION: Abbotsholme School; studied at the Central School of Speech and Drama, London, 1955-58.

VOCATION: Actor.

CAREER: DEBUT—The landlord, *Misery Me*, Arts Theatre, Felixstowe, Suffolk, England, 1957. LONDON DEBUT—The Orator, *The Chairs*, Royal Court, 1958. PRINCIPAL STAGE APPEARANCES—Malcolm, *Macbeth*, Sgt. Lugg, *The Magistrate*, Oliver, *As You Like It*, all Old Vic, 1958; Frank Broadbent, *Celebration*, Nottingham Playhouse Company, 1960, then Duchess, London, 1961; Hector Barlow, *Afternoon Men*, Arts, 1963; Major, *Incident at Vichy*, Phoenix, 1966; Richard Howarth, *Spoiled*, Haymarket, 1971; Aston, *The Caretaker*, Mermaid, 1972; Buckingham, *Richard III*, Olivier, 1979.

PRINCIPAL FILM APPEARANCES—*Operation Crossbow*, Metro-Goldwyn-Mayer, 1965; *Cast a Giant Shadow*, United Artists, 1966; *The Blue Max*, Twentieth Century-Fox, 1966; *Assignment K*, Columbia, 1968; *Twist of Sand*, United Artists, 1968; *Strange Affair*, Paramount, 1968; *The Games*, Twentieth Century-Fox, 1970; *Darling Lili*, Paramount, 1970; *The Belstone Fox; Saltzburg Connection*, 1972; *Blockhouse*, 1973; *Seven Percent Solution*, Universal, 1976; *A Bridge Too Far*, United Artists, 1977; *East of Elephant Rock; Caravans*, Universal, 1978; *Prisoner of Zenda*, Universal, 1979; *Return of the Soldier*, 1981.

PRINCIPAL TELEVISION APPEARANCES—*Z Cars; Colditz; The Winter's Tale; King Lear; The Winds of War; Sadat; George Washington; St. Joan*.

SIDELIGHTS: MEMBERSHIPS—Lord's Taverners, Stage Golfing Society. RECREATIONS—Bad skiing, pure idleness.

ADDRESS: AGENT—Leading Artists, 60 James's Street, London SW1, England.

*　　*　　*

KESDEKIAN, Mesrop 1920-

PERSONAL: Born March 8, 1920, in Philadelphia, PA; son of Avedis M. (a tailor) and Aznive (Tashjian) Kesdekian. EDUCATION: West Chester (PA) State Teachers College, B.S., 1948; Pennsylvania State University, M.A., 1950; studied for the theatre at the Hedgerow Theatre School with Miriam Phillips. MILITARY: U.S. Air Corps, 1942-45, in China, Burma, and India campaigns.

VOCATION: Director, producer, designer, and teacher.

CAREER: PRINCIPAL STAGE WORK—Director: *Slaughter of the Innocents*, Studio Theatre, Dublin, Ireland, 1954; *The Earth a Trinket*, Studio Theatre, Dublin, Ireland, 1954; *Blood Wedding*, *Saint Joan*, both University Players, Princeton, NJ, 1955; *The Apollo of Bellac*, and *The Browning Version* (a double-bill), Arena Stage, Washington, DC, 1959; *The Beautiful People*, ELT, Lenox Hill Playhouse, NY, 1959; *The Skin of Our Teeth*, ELT, Lenox Hill Playhouse, NY, 1960; *Love's Old Sweet Song*, ELT, Master Institute Theatre, NY, 1961; *The Biggest Thief in Town*, 1961, *Love Among the Platypi*, 1962, *Time Out for Ginger*, 1964, *Tom Jones*, *Mary, Mary*, all at Bucks County Playhouse, New Hope, PA; *The*

MESROP KESDEKIAN

Caretaker, Playhouse-in-the-Park, Cincinnati, OH, 1963; *Thieves' Carnival,* and the double bill *The Typists* and *The Tiger,* Pavilion, Pennsylvania State University, State College, PA, 1964.

You Can't Take It with You, Nature's Way, Arsenic and Old Lace, all for L'Homme Dieu Playhouse, Alexandria, MN, 1975; *The Hot l Baltimore,* Alice Company, Tampa, FL, 1975; *Details without a Map,* Stage Number One, Dallas, TX, 1975; *Da,* 1975, *The Inspector General,* 1977, *Popkin,* 1978, *Uncle Vanya,* 1978, *The Matchmaker,* all at Southern Methodist University, Dallas, TX; *The Hostage,* Eastfield College, Dallas, TX, 1978; *The Glass Menagerie,* North Shore Music Theatre, Beverly, MA, 1979; *Buried Child,* 1979, *The Mound Builders,* 1980, both at Stage Number One, Dallas, TX, 1980; *The Time of Your Life,* 1981, *The Kitchen,* 1981, *Marat/Sade,* 1982, *The Plough and the Stars,* 1983, all at University Theatre, Southern Methodist University, Dallas, TX; *Arsenic and Old Lace,* Granny's Dinner Theatre, Dallas, TX, 1983; *The Tempest,* Dallas Shakespeare Festival, Dallas, TX, 1983; *Charley's Aunt,* University Theatre, Dallas, TX, 1984; *The Dining Room,* Plaza Theatre, Dallas, TX, 1984; *Oh, What a Lovely War!,* University Theatre, Dallas, TX, 1985.

Also: *The Hostage,* Center Stage, Baltimore, MD; *Oasis in Manhattan,* Stage Society, Hollywood, CA; *The Time of Your Life,* Triangle, NY; *The Boy Friend, The Fantasticks, Pygmalion, The Rose Tattoo,* others, all at Green Hills Theatre, Reading, PA, 1952-present.

Designer: Mountain Playhouse, Jennerstown, PA, 1949; *Othello,* Gate Theatre, Dublin, Ireland, 1954; *Summer of the Seventeenth Doll,* Players, NY, Arena Stage, Washington, DC, 1959.

MAJOR TOURS—Director: *The Skin of Our Teeth,* Theatre Guild American Repertory Co., U.S. State Department tour of Latin America and Europe, 1960-61.

RELATED CAREER—Teacher, theatre arts, Pennsylvania State University, 1949-53; American Theatre Wing, 1961-62; Hartford University, CT, 1968; University of South Florida, Tampa, 1969-71; Lawrence University, Appleton, WI, 1969-70, 1972-73; Kalamazoo College, MI, 1974; Southern Methodist University, Dallas, TX, 1976-84 (currently head of professional directing department).

AWARDS: Air Medal with oak leaf cluster, CBI, 1945; American Service Medal; Asiatic-Pacific Service Medal; Distinguished Flying Cross, CBI, 1945.

SIDELIGHTS: MEMBERSHIPS—Actors' Equity Association, Society of Stage Directors and Choreographers, International Institute of Arts and Letters. RECREATION—Collecting sculpture and paintings.

Since 1952, Kesdekian has been the producing-director of the Green Hills Theatre in Reading, PA.

ADDRESS: HOME—6480 Bordeaux, Dallas, TX 75209.

*   *   *

KING, Perry

PERSONAL: Born April 30, in Alliance, OH; son of a physician; separated; children: Louise. EDUCATION: Yale, B.A., theatre; studied acting with John Houseman at the Juilliard School of Drama.

VOCATION: Actor.

CAREER: NEW YORK DEBUT—Lead, *Child's Play,* Morosco. PRINCIPAL STAGE APPEARANCES—*Knuckle,* Phoenix, NY; *Jesse James,* NY; *The Trouble with Europe,* NY; Cassio, *Othello,* Washington, DC; John, *Eccentricities of a Nightingale,* Los Angeles, CA; Bassanio, *The Merchant of Venice,* Old Globe, Los Angeles, CA.

FILM DEBUT—*The Possession of Joel Delaney,* Paramount, 1972. PRINCIPAL FILM APPEARANCES—*Slaughterhouse Five,* Universal, 1972; *The Lords of Flatbush,* Columbia, 1974; *Mandingo,* Paramount, 1975; *The Wild Party,* American International, 1975; *Lipstick,* Paramount, 1976; *Andy Warhol's Bad,* 1976; *The Choirboys,* Universal, 1977; *A Different Story,* Avco Embassy, 1978; *Class of 1984,* 1982.

PRINCIPAL TELEVISION APPEARANCES—*Medical Center,* CBS; *Hawaii Five-O,* CBS; *Apple's Way; Cannon; The Hemingway Play,* PBS; *The Hasty Heart,* Showtime; *The Last Convertible; Aspen;* Rory Armagh, *Captains and the Kings,* NBC, 1976-77; *The Quest,* ABC, 1983-84; *Helen Keller, the Miracle Continues,* Operation Prime Time, 1984; Cody Allen, *Riptide,* NBC, 1984-85; voice of Samson, *Samson and Delilah.*

Television movies include: *The Cracker Factory,* 1979; *Love's Savage Fury,* 1979; *City in Fear,* 1980; *Inmates: A Love Story,* 1981; *Big Truck; Poor Clare; Foster & Laurie.*

PERRY KING

PRINCIPAL RADIO APPEARANCES—Hans Solo, *Star Wars*, National Public Radio; several dramas for *Earplay*, National Public Radio.

AWARDS: Golden Globe nomination, Best Supporting Actor, for *The Hasty Heart*.

SIDELIGHTS: RECREATION—Restoring old cars and motorcycles.

According to his official bio, forwarded to *CTFT* by his agents, King "comes from a long line of celebrated ancestors, including two signers of the Declaration of Independence, General William T. Sherman of Civil War prominence, and the distinguished literary editor Maxwell Perkins, who was his maternal grandfather." Perry "also enjoys writing, a diversion he finds challenging, rewarding and nearly impossible to do well."

ADDRESS: AGENT—PMK, Inc., 8642 Melrose Avenue, Los Angeles, CA 90069.

*   *   *

KLOTZ, Florence

PERSONAL: Born in New York City; daughter of Philip K. and Hannah (Kraus) Klotz. EDUCATION: Attended Parson's School of Design, 1941.

VOCATION: Costume designer.

CAREER: FIRST STAGE WORK—Costume designer, *Oklahoma!*, *Carousel*, *Annie Get Your Gun*, City Center, NY, 1956. PRINCIPAL STAGE WORK—Broadway Productions: *Superman*, 1960; *Never Too Late*, 1960; *Take Her She's Mine*, 1960; *A Call on Kuprin*, 1961; *On an Open Roof*, 1963; *Nobody Loves an Albatross*, 1963; *Everybody Out, The Castle Is Sinking*, 1964; *One by One*, 1964; *The Owl and the Pussycat*, 1964; *The Mating Dance*, 1965; *Best Laid Plans*, 1966; *This Winter's Hobby*, 1966; *It's a Bird . . . It's a Plane . . . It's Superman*, 1966; *Golden Boy* (also coordinator for national tour), 1968; *Norman Is That You?*, 1970; *Paris Is Out*, 1970; *Follies*, 1971; *A Little Night Music*, 1973; *Sondheim: A Musical Tribute*, 1973; *Dreyfus in Rehearsal*, 1974; *Pacific Overtures*, 1977; *Legend*, 1977; *Side by Side by Sondheim*, 1977; *On the Twentieth Century*, 1978; *Harold and Maude*, 1980; *A Doll's Life*, 1983; *The Little Foxes*, 1984; *Peg* (with Peggy Lee), 1984; *Grind*, 1985.

PRINCIPAL BALLET WORK—*Opus Jazz, Eight Lines, Antique Epigraphs, I'm Old Fashioned.*

PRINCIPAL OPERA WORK—*Madam Butterfly*, Chicago Lyric Opera.

PRINCIPAL FILM WORK—Designed costumes for German films; *Something for Everyone; A Little Night Music*, 1977.

AWARDS: Antoinette Perry Awards, 1971, for *Follies*, 1973, for *A Little Night Music*, 1976, for *Pacific Overtures;* Academy Award nomination, 1977, for *A Little Night Music;* Drama Desk, 1978, for *On the Twentieth Century*.

SIDELIGHTS: Klotz designed the costumes for John Curry's 1979 *Ice Dancing*.

ADDRESS: HOME—1050 Park Avenue, New York, NY 10028.

*   *   *

KMECK, George   1949-

PERSONAL: Surname pronounced Kuh-*mek;* born August 4, 1949, in Jersey City, NJ; son of George (a gearcutter and choir director) and Helen (Chabin) Kmeck; married Nora Mae Lyng (an actress), December 29, 1978; children: Phoebe, Max. EDUCATION: Glassboro State College, two years, Fairleigh Dickinson University, one year; studied voice with Ray Buckingham. RELIGION: Byzantine Catholic. MILITARY: U.S. Army, Corporal, 1970-74.

VOCATION: Actor.

CAREER: STAGE DEBUT—Maurauder and lieutenant, *Shenandoah*, stock tour, New England, 1980. NEW YORK DEBUT—Pirate, *Pirates of Penzance*, Uris, 1981. PRINCIPAL STAGE APPEARANCES—Hennesey and Captain, *Dames at Sea*, Neil's New Yorker; Rutledge, *1776*, Ali Ben Ali, *Desert Song*, Jonathan Brewster, *Arsenic and Old Lace*, all at Half-Penny Playhouse, NJ; Sid Sorokin, *Pajama Game*, Gus Esmond, *Lorelei*, Donald, *Irene*, Dr. Kitchell, *Bells Are Ringing*, Herb Miller, *You Know I Can't Hear You When the Water's Running*, all at Surflight Theatre; Johnny Brown, *Unsinkable Molly Brown*, Gaslight and Velvet Dinner Theatres; Innkeeper, *Man of La Mancha*, Village Dinner Theatre; Olin Britt, *Music Man*, Alhambra Dinner Theatre; Terror of Trancus, *Surf City*, Entermedia, NY; Louis Capitaletti, *On Your Toes*, Kennedy Center; Floyd, *Fiorello*, Goodspeed Opera House, 1985.

GEORGE KMECK

TELEVISION DEBUT—Herve Boudin, *One Life to Live*, ABC, 1983.

SIDELIGHTS: MEMBERSHIPS—Actors' Equity Association, American Federation of Television and Radio Artists.

ADDRESS: HOME—2109 Broadway, Apt. 1292, New York, NY 10023. AGENT—Lester Lewis, 110 W. 40th Street, New York, NY 10018.

*   *   *

KONIGSBERG, Frank   1933-

PERSONAL: Born March 10, 1933; son of Bill and Jennifer Konigsberg; married Susanne. EDUCATION: Yale University, B.A., Yale University Law School, 1957.

VOCATION: Producer and attorney.

CAREER: PRINCIPAL TELEVISION WORK—Producer: *Guyana Tragedy: The Story of Jim Jones; The Pride of Jesse Hallam; Dummy; A Christmas without Snow; Before and After; Pearl; Divorce Wars; Coming Out of the Ice; Ellis Island; Bing Crosby: His Life and Legend; Kraft All Star Salute: Pearl Bailey; Bing Crosby: The Christmas Years; Gene Kelly: An American in Pasadena; Bing Crosby's Merrie Olde Christmas; Bing! 50th Anniversary Special; Breaking Away; Dorothy; It's Not Easy; Rituals; The Glitter Dome*, Telepictures Productions; *The Joy of Sex*.

PRINCIPAL FILM WORK—*Wet Gold*, Paramount.

FRANK KONIGSBERG

RELATED CAREER: Admitted to New York Bar, 1957; attorney for CBS, 1957-60; director, Program and Talent Administration, NBC, 1960-65; senior vice president, International Famous Agency - International Creative Management until 1975; executive producer and president, Konigsberg Company which became Telepictures Productions, a division of Telepictures Inc.

AWARDS: Christopher, for *The Pride of Jesse Hallam;* Emmy nomination, for *Dummy;* Humanitarian Award, for *Divorce Wars.*

ADDRESS: OFFICE—Telepictures Productions, 415 N. Crescent Drive, Beverly Hills, CA 90210.

*   *   *

KOPACHE, Thomas   1945-

PERSONAL: Born October 17, 1945, in Manchester, NH; son of Dorothy E. (Sterling) Kopache. EDUCATION: San Diego State University, B.A., theatre, 1971; California Institute of the Arts, M.F.A., acting, 1973; studied acting in NY with Sam Schact. MILITARY: U.S. Navy, 1963-66; served in Vietnam.

VOCATION: Actor.

CAREER: DEBUT—Conrade, *Much Ado About Nothing*, San Diego Shakespeare Festival, 1970. NEW YORK DEBUT—The Emperor, *The Architect and Emperor of Assyria*, La MaMa E.T.C., 1976. PRINCIPAL STAGE APPEARANCES—Macbeth, *Macbeth*, La MaMa,

1977; Scipio, *Caligulia,* Buthcer, the actor, *Arturo Ui,* Wagner, *Faust,* Prospero, *The Tempest,* all at La MaMa, 1978; Morris, *The Bloodknot,* Syracuse Stage, Syracuse, NY, and Walnut Street Theatre, Philadelphia, PA, 1979; Recruiting officer, *Mother Courage,* Center Stage, Baltimore, MD, 1980; Rover, *Hurrah for the Bridge,* La MaMa, 1981; Harry Roat, *Wait Until Dark,* Wye Mills Theatre, 1981; George, *Hunting Scenes from Lower Bavaria,* Manhattan Theatre Club, 1981.

First presser, *The Workroom,* Center Stage, Baltimore, MD, 1982; Macduff, *Macbeth,* Shakespeare & Company, 1982; Ioga, *The Extravagant Triumph . . . ,* Pedro, *The Seniorita from Tacna,* both INTAR, NY, 1982; Kevin Morrow, *Friends Too Numerous to Mention,* Jewish Repertory, NY, 1982; Morris, *The Bloodknot,* New Stage, 1983; Westmoreland, *Henry IV, Parts I and II,* Bob Cratchit, *A Christmas Carol,* Deeley, *Old Times,* all Indiana Repertory Company, 1983; the Dark Man, *The Woman,* Center Stage, Baltimore, MD, 1983; Jack, *Plainsong,* Ensemble Studio, 1984; the waiter and the doctor, *The Danube,* American Place, 1984; Coach, *Baseball Play,* Ensemble Studio, 1984; Jimmy, *Cayuses,* Ensemble Studio, 1985.

MAJOR TOURS—With Camera Obscura, several productions throughout Europe, 1973-76; The Emperor, *The Architect and Emperor of Assyria,* European tour, La MaMa, 1976.

FILM DEBUT—Police officer, *Without a Trace,* Twentieth Century-Fox, 1982. PRINCIPAL FILM APPEARANCES—Highway patrolman, *Strange Invaders,* 1983; truck driver, *Home Free All,* 1983; Cory, *And Then You Die,* 1985.

TELEVISION DEBUT—Cab driver, *Another World,* NBC, 1983.

PRINCIPAL TELEVISION APPEARANCES—Carl, *Guiding Light,* CBS, 1985.

RELATED CAREER—Founding member of Camera Obscura, based in Amsterdam and touring throughout Europe, 1973-76; teacher, movement for actors, University of California at La Jolla and San Diego City College, 1975.

AWARDS: Armed Forces Expedition Army Medal, for landing at Chu Lai.

SIDELIGHTS: MEMBERSHIPS—Actors' Equity Association, Screen Actors Guild, American Federation of Television and Radio Artists.

Kopache told *CTFT:* ''I thank my mother for inspiring me to act, and Ellen Stewart at La MaMa theatre for giving me my start in New York. While stationed in San Diego during my last year in the Navy, I began working in theatre by performing in an on-base production of *South Pacific.* I decided to use my veterans benefits to attend college and remained in San Diego until the early 1970's. I love traveling and deeply love the sea.''

ADDRESS: AGENT—ADM Associates Inc. 165 W. 46th Street, Suite 1109, New York, NY 10036.

*   *   *

KOVENS, Ed   1934

PERSONAL: Born Edward Kovens Jenovese, June 26, 1934, in New York City; son of Patrick Edward (a doctor) and Leone Marsha

THOMAS KOPACHE

ED KOVENS

(a painter and office manager; maiden name, Kovens) Jenovese; married Carmen Presmanes, July 14, 1957 (divorced, 1973); married Susan Miller, December 17, 1974 (divorced, 1980). EDUCATION: Attended New York State Institute and New York University; trained for the stage with Lee Strasberg.

VOCATION: Actor, director, and teacher.

CAREER: STAGE DEBUT—Harry Brock, *Born Yesterday,* Off Park Theatre, Brooklyn, NY, 14 performances. NEW YORK DEBUT—Pozzo, *Waiting for Godot,* New York Theatrical Company, 1959, 21 performances. PRINCIPAL STAGE APPEARANCES—Berto, *Passione,* Morosco, NY; Mr. Marveltine, *42 Seconds from Broadway,* Playhouse One, NY; Bernie Dodd, *Country Girl,* City Center, NY; Handyman, *Three Sisters,* Morosco, NY; Collie, *Deer Park,* Theatre de Lys, NY; Harry, *Bunnie,* Actors Studio Theater, NY; Dr. Frank, *The Last Straw,* American Place, NY; Herod, *Pontius Pilate,* Actors Studio Theater, NY; Big Daddy, *Cat on a Hot Tin Roof,* Rothesay Theater, Canada; Mr. Mattie, *Galileo,* Theater of Living Arts.

MAJOR TOURS—Holy Face, *Fortune and Men's Eyes,* NY, Toronto, Montreal, San Francisco, 1967.

PRINCIPAL STAGE WORK—Director: at Unit Theater, NY; New York Stage Company; Calumet Theater, MI; Encore Theater, San Francisco.

TELEVISION DEBUT—*Jackie Gleason Show,* CBS, 1957. PRINCIPAL TELEVISION APPEARANCES—"One Hand Clapping," *Nurse;* "One Nation Invisible," *Get Smart;* "Murder to Infinity," *N.Y.P.D.;* "Boys Night Out," *N.Y.P.D.; Muggable Mary; Edge of Night; One Life to Live; Search for Tomorrow; Love Is a Many Splendored Thing; 4 Play; Naked City; The Defenders; Car 54, Where Are You?*

FILM DEBUT—*Edge of the City,* Metro-Goldwyn-Mayer, 1957. PRINCIPAL FILM APPEARANCES—*Death Journey; Pursuit of Happiness,* Columbia, 1971; *The Gambler,* Paramount, 1974; *If Ever I See You Again,* Columbia, 1978; *Q* (aka *The Winged Serpent*), 1983.

RELATED CAREER—Instructor: Jack Garfein Theatre Institute, Los Angeles, CA, 1968-69; Lee Strasberg Theater Institute, NY, 1969-74; Performing Group, NY, 1973-74; The Professional Workshop, NY, 1974-present.

SIDELIGHTS: MEMBERSHIPS—Actors' Equity Association, Screen Actors Guild, American Federation of Television and Radio Artists, Society of Stage Directors and Choreographers, Actors Studio.

ADDRESS: AGENT—Richard Cataldi Agency, 180 Seventh Avenue, New York, NY 10011.

L

LACEY, William J. 1931-

PERSONAL: Born October 18, 1931, in Erie, PA; son of William Edward (a municipal employee) and Leona Adelaide (Wykoff) Lacey; married Martha Royce (a dancer and choreographer), July 30, 1951; children: Mary Selene, William Alexander, Timothy Michael. EDUCATION: Boston Conservatory, B.F.A., drama, 1954; graduate studies, Western Reserve University, 1955-56; Boston University, M.A., 1958. RELIGION: Roman Catholic.

VOCATION: Educator, director, and actor.

CAREER: STAGE DEBUT—Tailor, *The Taming of the Shrew*, Erie Playhouse, Erie, PA, 1949. PRINCIPAL STAGE APPEARANCES—Weston Playhouse, VT, twelve summer seasons; Poets Theatre; Boston Drama Quintet; Newton Theatre Company; Old Colony Playhouse; New York City Shakespeare Marathon, No Smoking Playhouse; Erie Playhouse; Playwright's Platform.

PRINCIPAL STAGE WORK—Director: Eighteen professional productions, Weston Playhouse, Boston Shakespeare Company, Piccadilly Playhouse; *The Three Cuckolds*, Boston Bicentennial Celebration, Old North Square, Boston, MA.

TELEVISION DEBUT—*Murder One*, WGBH-TV, Boston, MA. PRINCIPAL TELEVISION APPEARANCES—*The Baxter's*, WCVB, Boston, MA.

PRINCIPAL RADIO WORK—Narrator, actor, casting director, *Yankee Doodle Diary;* director, narrator, *A Child Is Born*, WBCN-FM; interviewer and host, *Authors and Books*, WBCN-FM; actor, *Provincetown Stories*, WWEL.

RELATED CAREER: Associate director, drama department, Boston Conservatory, 1956-60; assistant professor, Northeastern University, 1960-63; faculty, professor, Boston University, 1963-82; director, School of Theatre Arts, Boston University, 1982-present; guest master teacher of voice and speech, Alexander Teacher's Association, London, England; guest master teacher: Loeb Drama Center, Harvard University, Boston Shakespeare Company, Tanglewood Institute, Young Life Institute, Boston University.

AWARDS: An Outstanding Educator of America, 1975.

SIDELIGHTS: MEMBERSHIPS—Actors' Equity Association, American Federation of Television and Radio Artists, American Theatre Association, New England Theatre Conference, League of Professional Theatre Training Programs.

ADDRESS: HOME—89 Sargent Street, Melrose, MA 02176. OFFICE—School of Theatre Arts, Boston University, 855 Commonwealth Avenue, Boston, MA 02176.

LADD, Cheryl 1951-

PERSONAL: Born Cheryl Stoppelmoor, July 2, 1951, in Huron, SD; married David Alan Ladd (an actor; divorced). EDUCATION: Studied acting with Milton Kateselas.

CAREER: TELEVISION DEBUT—Voice of Melody, *Josie and the Pussycats* (animated). PRINCIPAL TELEVISION WORK—Series: As Cheryl Stoppelmoor, *The Ken Berry "Wow" Show*, ABC, 1972; Kris Munroe, *Charlie's Angels, Roots; General Electric All-Star Anniversary; John Denver and the Ladies*, Episodic: *Police Woman*, NBC; *Happy Days*, ABC; *Switch*, CBS; others. Movie: *A New Start*.

PRINCIPAL FILM APPEARANCES—*Jamaica Reef* (unreleased); *Purple Hearts*, Warner Brothers, 1984.

ADDRESS: AGENT—Beakel and Jennings Agency, 427 N. Canon Drive, Suite 205, Beverly Hills, CA 90210.*

* * *

LADD, David Alan 1947-

PERSONAL: Born February 5, 1947; son of Alan Ladd (an actor); married Cheryl Stoppelmoor (an actress, professional name, Cheryl Ladd; divorced).

CAREER: PRINCIPAL TELEVISION APPEARANCES—Episodic: *Zane Grey Theatre*, CBS; *Wagon Train; Playhouse 90*, CBS; *Pursuit*, CBS; *Ben Casey*, ABC; *Gunsmoke*, CBS; *Love, American Style*, ABC; *Kojack*, CBS.

PRINCIPAL FILM APPEARANCES—*Lone Ranger*, Warner Brothers, 1956; *The Big Land*, Warner Brothers, 1957; *Raymie*, Allied Artists, 1960; *Misty*, Twentieth Century-Fox, 1961; *R.P.M.*, Columbia, 1970; *Catlow*, United Artists, 1971; *Deathline; Jamaica Reef* (unreleased); *Day of the Locust*, Paramount, 1975; *Wild Geese*, Allied Artists, 1978.*

* * *

LAGERFELT, Caroline

PERSONAL: Born September 23, in Paris, France; daughter of Baron Karl-Gustav Israel (an ambassador) and Mary Charmian Sara Chapion (de Crespigny) Lagerfelt. EDUCATION: Sigtuna Stiftelsens Humanistiska Larouerket, Sigtuna, Sweden; studied acting at the American Academy of Dramatic Arts.

VOCATION: Actress.

CAROLINE LAGERFELT

CAREER: NEW YORK DEBUT—Liz, *The Philanthropist,* Broadway production. PRINCIPAL STAGE APPEARANCES—Broadway: *Four on a Garden;* Lady Ursula Itchin, *The Jockey Club Stakes;* Marie-Louise, *The Constant Wife;* Beth, *Otherwise Engaged;* Emma, *Betrayal;* Annie, *The Real Thing.* Off Broadway and Regional: Anita, *Quartermaine's Terms,* Playhouse 91, NY, 1983; Gila/Pauline, *Other Places,* Edward/Victoria, *Cloud 9,* both Manhattan Theatre Club; Jean, *The Sea Anchor,* Open Space, NY; Margaret, *Close of Play,* Alison, *Look Back in Anger,* both Manhattan Theatre Club; Ruth Carson, *Night and Day,* Huntington Theatre, Boston, MA; Monika Stettler, *The Physicists,* Kennedy Center for the Performing Arts; Mary, *Vanities,* George Street Playhouse, New Brunswick, NJ; Gwendolyn, *The Importance of Being Earnest,* Pittsburgh Public Theatre, PA; Judith, *The Devil's Disciple,* Meadow Brook, MI; Anita, *Quartermaine's Terms,* Long Wharf, CT; Clarissa, *Spider's Web,* Nassau Repertory.

MAJOR TOURS—Sally Boothroyd, *Lloyd George Knew My Father;* Beatrice, *To Grandmother's House We Go;* Sister Margaret, *The Hasty Heart;* Nia, *The Right Honorable Gentleman.*

FILM DEBUT—Elizabeth Masters, *The Iron Eagle,* 1985.

TELEVISION DEBUT—*Archie Bunker's Place.* PRINCIPAL TELEVISION APPEARANCES—*Do You Remember Love; Twilight Zone; T.J. Hooker; The Guiding Light; Edge of Night.*

AWARDS: Villager Downtown Award, 1982, for *The Sea Anchor;* Obie, 1983, for Anita, *Quartermaine's Terms.*

SIDELIGHTS: MEMBERSHIPS—Actors' Equity Association (coun-cil); American Academy of Dramatic Arts Alumni Association (president); volunteer, Childrens Village, Dobbs Ferry, NY.

ADDRESS: AGENT—Dudley Field Malone Agency, 343 E. 51st Street, Suite 2E, New York, NY 10022; Burton Moss Agency, 113 N. San Vincente Blvd., Suite 202, Beverly Hills, CA 90211.

*   *   *

LAI, Francis   1932-

PERSONAL: Born April 26, 1932, in Nice, France; son of market gardeners; married Dagmar; children: two sons.

VOCATION: Composer.

CAREER: PRINCIPAL FILM WORK—Composer: *House of Cards; Three into Two Won't Go; A Man and a Woman; Vivre Pur Vivre; The Bobo; I'll Never Forget What's His Name; Du Soleil Plein Les Yeux; 13 Jours en France; Mayerling; Hello Goodbye; Hannibal Brooks; The Games; La Louve Solitaire; The Berlin Affair; La Vie l'Amour La Mort; La Lecon Particuliere; Le Soleil Ded Voyous; La Petit Matin; Love Is a Funny Thing; Le Voyou; L'Odeur Des Fauves; Passenger in the Rain; Dans La Poussiere Du Soleil; Smic Smac Smoc; L'Aventure, C'Est L'Aventure; Les Petroleuses; Love Story; La Course Du Lievre A Travers Les Champs; Le Petit Poucet; Un Homme Libre; Les Hommes; A Visit to a Chief's Son; Par Le Sang Des Autres; Un Amour De Pluie; La Ronde; Toute Une Vie; Child Under a Lear; Marriage; Cat and Mouse; La Baby-Sitter; The Good and the Bad; Emmanuelle 2; Le Corps De Mon Ennemi; Ames Perdues; Stip Tease; Si C'etait a Refaire; Bilitis; Un Autre Homme,*

FRANCIS LAI

Une Autre Chance; Widow's Nest; Passion Flower Hotel; Robert and Robert; International Velvet; Les Ringards; Oliver's Story; A Nous Deux; Les Borsalini; Sea Killer; Indian Summer; Le Coueur A L'Envers; Les Uns Et Les Autres; Edith and Marcel; Canicule; Les Ripoux.

PRINCIPAL TELEVISION WORK—Composer: *Les Etoiles Du Cinema.*

AWARDS: Gold Record Award, Triumph Award, Best Original Song Award, 1966, International Festival of Mar del Plata Award, 1967, all for *A Man and a Woman;* Best Music Score Award, 1967, for *Vivre Pour Vivre;* Best Music Score Award, 1969, for *A Man and a Woman;* Gold Record Award, 1969, for *Passenger in the Rain;* Academy Award, Best Music Score, Golden Globe Award, Gold Record Award, all 1970, for *Love Story;* French Film Board Award, Best Music Score, 1972, for *Smic Smac Smoc;* Midem Trophy Award, 1972; Beograd Music Festival Award, 1972; Tokyo Song Festival Award, 1972, for *Pur Un Homme;* Chevalier of the French Order of Arts and Letters Award, 1973; Tokyo Song Festival Award, 1974, for *Et Ce Soir Tu Telephones.*

Broadcast Music Award, 1974, for Live for Life; Anthony Asquity Oscar Award nomination, 1974, for *La Bonne Annee;* Gold Record Award, 1976, for *Francis Lai-The Man and His Music;* Gold Record Award, 1977 for *Les Etoiles Du Cinema;* Yamaha Song Festival Award, Best Foreign Song, 1977 for *Bonsoir Tristesse;* Europe 1 Award, Cesars Award nomination, Gold Record Award, all 1978, for *Bilitis;* Platinum Record Award, Gold Record Award (Switzerland), Platinum Record Award (France), all 1980, for *Bilitis.*

SIDELIGHTS: RECREATION—Electric trains, drawing cartoon strips, football, tennis, skiing.

ADDRESS: OFFICE—23 Rue Franklin, Paris, France 75016.

*   *   *

LANCHESTER, Robert   1941-

PERSONAL: Born August 2, 1941, in Boston, MA; son of Henry Robert (an architect) and Elizabeth Ann (Poole) Lanchester; married Cynthia Jean Maple, August 10, 1974; children: Robert Brian, Kyra Elizabeth. EDUCATION: Massachusetts Institute of Technology, B.A., 1963; University of California at Berkeley, M.A., 1965.

VOCATION: Actor and director.

CAREER: STAGE DEBUT—Spearcarrier, Guthrie, 1967. NEW YORK DEBUT—Soliny, *Three Sisters,* ANTA, 1969. PRINCIPAL STAGE APPEARANCES—Broadway: Osgood, *The Utter Glory of Morrissey Hall;* Camille, *A Flea in Her Ear.* Off Broadway: Cornwall, *King Lear;* Clegg, *Greenwillow;* Baxter, *The Perfect Mollusc;* McDonald, *Johnny Belinda.* Regional: McCarter Theatre, Princeton, NJ; American Conservatory Theater, San Francisco, CA; Asolo State Theater, Sarasota, FL; Guthrie, Minneapolis, MN; Milwaukee Repertory, WI; Syracuse Stage, NY; San Francisco Mime Troupe; Great Lakes Shakespeare Festival, Cleveland, OH; Kennedy Center, Washington, DC; in roles including: Richard, *Richard II;* Malvolio, *Twelfth Night;* Tartuffe, *Tartuffe;* Holmes, *Sherlock Holmes;* Dracula, *Dracula;* General Burgoyne, *The Devil's Disciple;* Wild Bill Hickok, *Indians;* Actor, *The Dining Room;* Weller Martin, *The Gin Game;* Scrooge, *A Christmas Carol.*

ROBERT LANCHESTER

PRINCIPAL STAGE WORK—Director: *Twelfth Night, Brecht on Brecht,* both Guthrie, Minneapolis, MN; *Charley's Aunt, The Matchmaker,* both Asolo State Theater, Sarasota, FL; *The Trial of the Moke, Androcles and the Lion,* both Milwaukee Repertory, WI; *The Day They Shot John Lennon, The Overland Rooms, Putting on the Dog,* all McCarter, Princeton, NJ; *The Life and Adventures of Nicholas Nickleby,* Great Lakes Shakespeare Festival, Cleveland, OH; *True West, Stage Struck,* both Peterborough Players, NH; *Stage Struck, Under Milkwood, Happy Days, The Gin Game,* all McCarter, Princeton, NJ.

RELATED CAREER—Associate director, Theater of the Open Eye, NY, 1978-79; associate artistic director, McCarter Theatre, Princeton, NJ, 1979-present.

AWARDS: Eisner Award for Creativity, University of Minnesota; McKnight Fellowship, 1965-67; Andrews Travelling Scholarship to England.

SIDELIGHTS: MEMBERSHIPS—Society of Stage Directors and Choreographers.

ADDRESS: HOME—Nine Mt. Lucas Road, Princeton, NJ 08540. OFFICE—McCarter Theater, 91 University Place, Princeton, NJ 08540.

*   *   *

LANDES, William-Alan   1945-

PERSONAL: Born April 27, 1945, in the Bronx, NY; son of Sidney Howard (a diamond dealer) and June Dorothy (a writer; maiden

WIlLIAM-ALAN LANDES

name, Heal-Gordon) Landes; children: Wendy Alyn. EDUCATION: Hunter Lehman College, B.A., 1969; California State University at Los Angeles, M.A., 1973. MILITARY: U.S. Air Force, 1963-1967.

VOCATION: Writer, director, and actor.

CAREER: PRINCIPAL STAGE APPEARANCES—Tom, *My Fat Friend;* Jonathan Harker, *Dracula,* Players U.S.A.; Lion, *The Wizard of Oz,* Westwood Playhouse; Lone Eagle, *Indian Tales,* Hollywood Bowl Association; Clarence, *Richard III,* The Group; Brindsley Miller, *Black Comedy,* Gilbert Stock Company; Tranio, *Taming of the Shrew,* C.A.C. Productions; Bill Starbuck, *The Rainmaker,* Westchester Playhouse; Shylock, *Merchant of Venice* and Billy Budd, *Billy Budd,* both Theatre Unique; Arthur, *Blue Denim,* Country Playhouse.

PRINCIPAL STAGE WORK—Director: *The Wizard of Oz,* Westwood Playhouse; *My Fat Friend* and *Robin Hood,* both Players U.S.A.; *No Exit,* Broadway Playhouse; *Rumpelstiltskin,* California State University, Los Angeles; *The Lost Princess,* Arcadia Childrens Theatre; *Ghosts, Taming of the Shrew, King Lear,* all at Theatre Unique; *House of Blue Leaves,* Theatre One.

PRINCIPAL FILM APPEARANCES—Bud, *Campus Capers,* Laureno; Pete, *The Hired Gun,* Scepter; Chuck, *The Last Ride,* Omega; Charles, *Cop Out,* American; Bill, *Encounter,* Psychology Inc; Jack, *Gentlemen, You Have a Race,* Kohler; Gordon, *For Every Action,* Kercheval.

PRINCIPAL FILM WORK—Director: *Billy 'n' the Giant,* L Enterprise; *Glass,* Syncron; *The Man and the Mind,* T.V.I.

PRINCIPAL TELEVISION APPEARANCES—Dave Findlay, *The Camel's Back,* CL-TV & Diamond Inc; host, *Golliwhopper Story-*

book, Players Press; host, *Origins of the Universe, Look Back Time,* Inc; Lone Eagle, *Indian Tales,* Junior Programs; *The Dating Game,* Chuck Barris.

PRINCIPAL TELEVISION WORK—Director: *Indian Tales,* Torrance School District; *Donna Brook's Show,* Tyler; *The Wondrawhopper Storybook,* Empire Entertainment.

WRITINGS: PLAYS, PRODUCED—Childrens músical adaptations: *Rumpelstiltskin,* Players U.S.A., 1973; *Pyramus and Thisbe* (with Mark Lasky), 1973; *Jack 'n' the Beanstalk, Aladdin 'n' His Magic Lamp,* both Players U.S.A., 1974; *The Wizard of Oz,* Westwood Playhouse, 1975; *Alice 'n' Wonderland,* Broadway Playhouse, 1975; *Granpa's Bedtime Story,* 1976; *Peter 'n' the Wolf,* Players U.S.A., 1977; *Rhyme Time,* and *Rapunzel 'n' the Witch,* Players U.S.A., 1978. Also: *Robin Hood, Cinderella, Arthur 'n' the Magic Sword, Androcles 'n' the Loveable Lion, Hansel 'n' Gretel, Fabulous Fables, The Magnificent Toad of Toad Hall, Santa's Littlest Elf, Wendy 'n' the Giant, Indian Tales.*

PLAYS, PRODUCED AND PUBLISHED—*Diary of a Madman,* 1974; *A Pair of Uses,* 1975; *Lunatics,* 1976.

SCREENPLAYS—*Aces and Eights,* 1973; *Cracked Sidewalk,* 1974; *The Baby Maker,* 1979.

RELATED CAREER—Associate producer, IAE/New World Productions, 1971-72; resident director, Players U.S.A., 1975-78 and 1979-present; artistic director, Merrick Studios, 1978-1979.

AWARDS: Best Actor, Players U.S.A., 1975; Best Director, *Showcase* magazine, 1977.

SIDELIGHTS: MEMBERSHIPS—Screen Actors Guild, American Federation of Radio and Television Artists, Actors' Equity Association, Society of Stage Directors and Choreographers, Honor Society of Accounting and Economics.

ADDRESS: OFFICE—P.O. Box 1344, Studio City, CA 91604. AGENT—William Morris Agency, 151 El Camino Drive, Beverly Hills, CA 90212.

*   *   *

LANE, Diane

BRIEF ENTRY: Born in New York City. Actress. At age six, Lane joined the La MaMa Experimental Theatre Group in New York and appeared in Andrei Serban's productions of *Medea, Electra, The Trojan Woman, The Good Woman of Setzuan,* and *As You Like It.* Her other stage credits include *The Cherry Orchard* and *Agamemnon* at Lincoln Center, and *Runaways,* where she created the role of Jackie, the young prostitute. Her television credits include the movies *Touched by Love,* 1980; *Child Bride of Short Creek,* 1981; *Summer; Miss All-America Beauty,* 1982. Lane's film debut was in *A Little Romance,* Orion Pictures, 1979; and has subsequently been seen in *Cattle Annie and Little Britches,* Universal, 1980; *Watcher in the Woods,* Buena Vista, 1980; *Six Pack,* Twentieth Century-Fox, 1982; *The Outsiders,* Warner Brothers, 1983; *Rumble Fish,* Universal, 1983; *Streets of Fire,* Universal, 1984; *The Cotton Club,* 1984. Lane appeared on the August 13, 1979, cover of *Time* magazine.*

LANGE, Jessica   1949-

PERSONAL: Born April 20, 1949, in MN; daughter of Dorothy Lange; married Paco Grande (divorced 1982); children: Alexandra. EDUCATION: Studied dance and mime with Etienne DeCroux in Paris.

VOCATION: Actress and producer.

CAREER: FILM DEBUT—*King Kong*, Paramount, 1976. PRINCIPAL FILM APPEARANCES—*All That Jazz*, Twentieth Century-Fox, 1979; *How to Beat the High Cost of Living*, Filmways, 1980; *The Postman Always Rings Twice*, Paramount, 1981; Frances Farmer, *Frances*, Universal, 1982; *Tootsie*, Columbia, 1983; *Country*, 1984; *Sweet Dreams*, Silver Screen Films (upcoming).

PRINCIPAL TELEVISION APPEARANCES—Television Plays: Maggie, *Cat on a Hot Tin Roof*, Showtime, 1984.

PRINCIPAL STAGE APPEARANCES—*Angel on My Shoulder*, North Carolina, 1980.

RELATED CAREER—Owner, Far West Pictures; dancer, Opera Comique, Paris; model, Wilhelmina Agency, NY.

AWARDS: Academy Award, Best Supporting Actress, 1982, for *Tootsie;* Academy Award nomination, Best Actress, 1982, for *Frances*.

ADDRESS: AGENT—International Creative Management, 8899 Beverly Blvd., Los Angeles, CA 90048.*

*   *   *

LANGTON, Basil   1912-

PERSONAL: Full name Basil C. Langton; born January 9, 1912, in Clifton, Bristol, England; son of Samuel Calvert (a piano tuner) and Esther (Shandel) Langton; married Louise Soelberg, 1938 (a dancer; divorced, 1959); married Nancy Wickwire, 1959 (an actress; divorced, 1969); children: Jessica Louise. EDUCATION: Vancouver Preparatory School, Canada; studied at the School of Dance Mime and Jooss-Leeder School of Dance, Dartington Hall, England.

VOCATION: Actor, director, producer, writer, and teacher.

CAREER: STAGE DEBUT—Dancer, *Let's Go*, Vancouver Theater, Vancouver, Canada, 1930. NEW YORK DEBUT—Director, *Sing Till Tomorrow*, 1953. LONDON DEBUT—*The Hangman*, Duke of York's, 1935. PRINCIPAL STAGE WORK—Actor and director, Vancouver Little Theatre, Canada, 1931; actor, Royal Shakespeare Theatre, Stratford-on-Avon, England, 1935; actor, *The Boy David*, His Majesty's, London, 1936; *Macbeth*, Old Vic, London, 1937; actor, *Judgement Day*, Strand, London, 1937; actor, Phoenix Theatre, London, 1938; *The Moon, Marriage of Blood*, both Phoenix, London, 1939; Yasha, *The Cherry Orchard*, Queen's, London, 1939.

Hamlet, *Hamlet*, Angelo, *Measure for Measure*, Dr. Caius, *Merry Wives of Windsor*, Tranio, *The Taming of the Shrew*, Prince of Arragon, *Merchant of Venice*, Dauphin, *King John*, all at Royal Shakespeare Festival, Stratford, England, 1940; actor, Birmingham

BASIL LANGTON

Repertory, England, 1940; played Hamlet and directed, *Hamlet*, Birmingham Repertory, England, 1942; producer and director, *The Moon Is Down*, Whitehall, London, 1943; producer and director, *Romeo and Juliet, Man and Superman, The Wise Have Not Spoken, Saint Joan*, Theatre Royal, Bristol, England, 1943; producer and director, *Romeo and Juliet, Man and Superman, The Wise Have Not Spoken, Saint Joan, In Time to Come, Electra*, all at Kings, London, 1945.

Artist in residence, Case Western Reserve University, Cleveland, OH, 1947; actor and director, Cleveland Playhouse, OH; actor and director, Catholic University, Washington, DC, Carnegie Tech, Pittsburgh, PA, Antioch College, 1948; actor and director, *Saint Joan*, Group 20, Boston, MA, and Caine Park, Cleveland, OH, 1949; director, *Edwina Black*, NY, 1950; creator, Shaw Festival, Martha's Vineyard, MA, 1951; director, *Heartbreak House*, Brattle Theater, 1952; director, *Peter Pan*, Toronto, Canada, 1952; director, *Sing Till Tomorrow*, NY, 1953; director, *Jalna*, Toronto, Canada, 1953; director, *Creten Woman, Arms and the Man, All My Sons*, Arena Stage, Washington, DC, 1953; actor and director, *The Lady's Not for Burning, School for Scandal, Man and Superman*, Olney Summer Theatre, MD, 1953.

Director, *The Tempest*, Cincinnati Symphony, OH, 1954; director, *Saint Joan*, Puerto Rico, 1954; co-founder (with John Brownlee) of Empire State Music Festival, 1955; director, *Carmen, LaBoheme, Madama Butterfly, La Traviata, A Midsummer Night's Dream*, and producer, *Symphony of the Air*, all at Empire State Music Festival, NY, 1955-56; Macbeth, *Macbeth*, Roof Top, New York, NY, 1957; actor and director, *This Island's Mine*, Bermuda Festival, 1958; director, *The Tempest*, Virginia Festival, 1959; director, *The Machinal, The Tempest*, both at Boston University, MA, 1959;

Dawson-Hill, *The Affair,* Merlin, *Camelot,* both NY, 1964; director and writer, *El Capitan,* Columbia University, NY, 1965; actor, *Manfred,* 1965; narrator, *The Wasteland,* Cincinnati Symphony, OH, 1965; actor, *Unknown Soldier and His Wife,* 1965; actor, *Peg,* 1967; Lord Alanbrooke, *Soldiers,* NY and London, 1968; director, *Ariadne Auf Naxos,* Carnegie Hall, Lincoln Center, NY, 1970.

Director, *Yerma,* Santa Fe Opera, NM, 1971; director, *Boulevard Solitude,* NY, 1972; director, *Don Pasquale,* NY, 1973; director, *Private Lives,* Chicago, IL, 1973; director, *13 Rue de l'Amour,* Chicago, IL, 1974; director, *Hay Fever,* Chicago, IL, 1975; director, *Major Barbara,* Juilliard School of Drama, NY, 1976; director, San Francisco Opera, CA, 1977; director, *13 Rue de l'Amour,* Circle in the Square, NY, 1978, and GeVa, Rochester, NY, 1979; director and adapter, *The Free Lance,* Opera Company of Philadelphia, PA, Iowa State Center, IA, and Academy of Music, Philadelphia, PA, 1979; director, *13 Rue de l'Amour,* Elizabethan Trust, Sydney and Melbourne, Australia, 1980; director, *The Free Lance,* Wolf Trap, VA, 1980.

MAJOR TOURS—Actor and manager, The Traveling Repertory Theater, U.K. cities, 1941; Birmingham Repertory Theater, U.K. cities, mining towns, munition factories, army camps, 1942; actor and director, *Saint Joan,* Germany, Holland, Belgium, France, 1944; Traveling Repertory Theater, U.K. cities, 1946; actor, *Hostile Witness,* U.S. cities, 1966; director, *13 Rue de l'Amour,* U.S. cities, 1978.

TELEVISION DEBUT—BBC, London, 1937. PRINCIPAL TELEVISION APPEARANCES–*Robert Montgomery Presents,* 1952; *Playhouse 90, Omnibus,* 1953; "Macbeth," *Hallmark Hall of Fame,* 1955; "Mallory on Everest," *You Are There,* 1956; "Pygmalion," *Hallmark Hall of Fame,* 1963; *Love's Labour's Lost, Women Beware Women, King Arthur,* all BBC, 1964; "Eagle in a Cage," *Hallmark Hall of Fame,* 1965; *The Secret Storm,* 1968, *Love of Life,* 1968.

RELATED CAREER—Teacher: Manhattan School of Music, Royal Academy of Dramatic Art, London, London Theatre Studio, Case Western Reserve University, Sarah Lawrence College, Carnegie Tech, Boston University, Antioch College, Hunter College, Catholic University, National Theatre School of Canada, Juilliard School of Drama.

WRITINGS: OPERA ADAPTATIONS—*El Capitan, The Free Lance, The Bride Elect.*

AWARDS: Guggenheim Fellowship, 1957; National Endowment for the Arts Grant, 1974, 1975; ASCAP Award, 1982, 1983, 1984.

SIDELIGHTS: MEMBERSHIPS—Actors' Equity Association, Dramatists' Guild, American Society of Composers, Authors, and Publishers, Society of Stage Directors and Choreographers, American Federation of Television and Radio Artists, MacDowell Colony Planetary Citizen.

Langton also worked as a photographer, graphic artist, and print maker.

ADDRESS: HOME—New York, NY; Los Angeles, CA. AGENT—Milton Goldman, International Creative Management, 40 W. 57th Street, New York, NY 10019; The Lantz Office, 9255 Sunset Blvd., Los Angeles, CA 90069.

DANNY LA RUE

LA RUE, Danny

PERSONAL: Born Daniel Patrick Carroll in Cork, Ireland. EDUCATION: Attended schools in London and Exeter. MILITARY: Royal Navy (three years).

VOCATION: Actor and female impersonator.

CAREER: DEBUT—Concert party artist while in the navy. LONDON DEBUT—Revue, Irving Theatre. PRINCIPAL STAGE APPEARANCES—*The Danny La Rue Show,* cabaret theatres in London's West End, 1954-1964; numerous appearances in pantomime for Tom Arnold, 1954-1964; *Come Spy with Me,* Whitehall, London, late 1960's; Queen Passionella, *Queen Passionella and the Sleeping Beauty* (pantomime), Saville, London, late 1960's; *At the Palace,* 1970; *Queen of Hearts* (pantomime), Manchester, England, 1972; season at the Opera House, Blackpool, 1973; *The Danny La Rue Show,* Prince of Wales, London, 1973-1975.

Queen Danniella, *The Exciting Adventures of Queen Danniella,* Casino (now the Prince Edward), London, 1975 (?), Great Yarmouth, 1976, Blackpool, 1977, Scarborough, 1978, Great Yarmouth, 1980, Eastbourne, 1981, Paignton, 1982; *The Danny La Rue Show,* O'Keefe Center, Toronto, Canada, 1976; Merry Widow Twankey, *Alladin* (pantomime), London Palladium, 1978, Hippodrome, Bristol, 1980, Hippodrome, Birmingham, 1981; played at the Royal York, Toronto, Canada, 1983; Dolly Levi, *Hello, Dolly!,* Birmingham Repertory, 1983, Prince of Wales, London, 1984; *The Danny La Rue Show,* Cork, Ireland, 1984.

MAJOR TOURS—*The Danny La Rue Show,* twelve city tour, including Scotland and Wales, 1975, Australia and New Zealand, 1979; subsequent tours of Australia including a cabaret tour in 1981 and a combined theatre and cabaret tour in 1982-83; tour of Canada,

1983; *Danny's Dazzling Rainbow*, Great Britain, 1983; HMS Queen Elizabeth II, 1984; *The Danny La Rue Show*, British Isles, including Ireland, 1984.

FILM DEBUT—*Dear Sir or Madam*, 1970. FILM APPEARANCES—*Our Miss Fred*, 1972.

TELEVISION APPEARANCES—Numerous appearances throughout the 1950's and 1960's on variety programs in England; *Highlights from "At the Palace"*, 1972; *The Good Old Days*, BBC; *Charley's Aunt*, BBC; *Queen of Hearts*, BBC; *Night Out with Danny La Rue; The Ladies I Love; Come Spy with Me; This Is Your Life*, Thames, 1983.

NIGHTCLUB/CABARET APPEARANCES—Churchill's, Winston's, 1954-1964; Danny La Rue's Club, Hanover Square, London, 1964-1972.

RECORDINGS—*On Mother Kelly's Doorstep*, 1968.

AWARDS: Show Business Personality of the Year, Variety Clubs of Great Britain, 1969; Royal Variety Performances, 1969, 1972, 1978; Theatre Personality of the Year, 1970; 25 Years in Show Business Tribute Luncheon, Variety Clubs of Great Britain, 1976; Entertainer of the Decade, 1979; Brinsworth Award, for "his oustanding contribution to the entertainment profession and the community."

SIDELIGHTS: Danny La Rue is the first male performer in many years to make a career, almost solely, on his work in "travesty." He was the first man to play Dolly Levi in the Jerry Herman musical version of the play.

ADDRESS: AGENT—Clifford Elson, International Public Relations, Richmond House, 12/13 Richmond Buildings, Dean Street, London W1V 5AF, England.

*   *   *

LAURENTS, Arthur   1918-

PERSONAL: Born July 14, 1918, in New York City; son of Irving and Ada (Robbins) Laurents. EDUCATION: Attended Cornell University.

VOCATION: Writer and director.

CAREER: PRINCIPAL STAGE WORK—Director: *I Can Get It for You Wholesale*, 1962; *Anyone Can Whistle*, 1964; *The Enclave*, Washington Theater Club, Washington, DC, and Theatre Four, NY, 1973; *Gypsy*, Piccadilly, London, 1973, then Winter Garden, NY, 1974; *Scream*, Alley, Houston, TX, 1978; *The Madwoman of Central Park West*, Twenty-Two Steps, NY, 1979; *La Cage Aux Folles*, NY, 1983.

WRITINGS: PLAYS, PRODUCED—*Home of the Brave*, NY, 1945; *Heart-Song*, NY, 1947; *The Bird Cage*, NY, 1950; *The Time of the Cuckoo*, NY, 1952; *A Clearing in the Woods*, NY, 1956; *West Side Story*, NY, 1957; *Gypsy*, NY, 1959; *Invitation to a March*, NY, 1960; *Anyone Can Whistle*, NY, 1964; *Do I Hear a Waltz*, NY, 1965; *Hallelujah, Baby*, NY, 1967; *The Enclave*, Washington Theatre Club, Washington, DC, Theatre Four, NY, 1973; *The Madwoman of Central Park West*, Twenty-Two Steps Theater, NY, 1979.

SCREENPLAYS—*Rope*, 1948; *The Snake Pit*, 1948; *Caught*, 1949; *Anastasia*, 1956; *Bonjour Tristesse*, 1959; *The Way We Were*, 1973; *The Turning Point*, 1977.

BOOKS—*The Way We Were*, 1972; *The Turning Point*, 1977.

AWARDS: Screenwriters Guild Award; Antoinette Perry Awards for writing and directing; Sidney Howard Playwriting Award; Theatre Hall of Fame Award.

SIDELIGHTS: RECREATION—Skiing and tennis.

ADDRESS: HOME—Dune Road, Quogue, NY 11959.

*   *   *

LAW, Mouzon   1922-

PERSONAL: Born September 17, 1922, in Texarkana, TX; son of Richard Green (an accountant) and Ettie Maria (McWilliams) Law. EDUCATION: University of Texas, B.F.A., 1948; Northwestern University, M.A., 1949; also attended and trained for the stage at Columbia University and New York University. POLITICS: Registered Independent. RELIGION: Methodist. MILITARY: Civilian employee, U.S. Army, World War Two.

VOCATION: Producer, manager, educator, and educational administrator.

CAREER: PRINCIPAL STAGE WORK—Director at: Sharon Playhouse, Sharon, CT, 1954; University of Texas, Austin, Northwestern University, IL, University of Illinois, and Syracuse University, NY, 1949-62.

MOUZON LAW

Producer: *The Crucible,* Martinique, NY, 1958; *Approaching Simone,* Boston University Centennial Theater, MA, 1969, La MaMa E.T.C., NY, 1970; Professional Playwrights Workshop, Berkshire Music Center, Tanglewood, MA, Berkshire Theatre Festival, Stockbridge, MA, 1970; University Theater, Boston University, MA, 1963-79; Summer Professional Repertory, Boston University, 1975.

RELATED CAREER—Assistant professor, Department of Drama, University of Texas, 1949-63; theater manager, University Theater, University of Texas, Austin, TX, 1949-63; guest instructor: Birmingham Southern College, 1950, Tulane University, 1952, Sam Houston State College, 1955, Northwestern University, 1956, Vanderbilt University, 1957-59, University of Illinois, 1960, Syracuse University, 1961; managing editor, *Educational Theatre Journal,* 1953-55; chairman 1963-74, professor, 1963-82, Division of Theatre Arts, producing director, University Theater, 1963-79, director, School of Theatre Arts, Boston University, Boston, MA.

WRITINGS: PERIODICALS—''A Directory of American Colleges and Universities Offering Curricular Programs in Children's Theatre,'' *Educational Theatre Journal,* 1954; ''American Educational Theater Association Reports,'' *Educational Theatre Journal,* 1954-56.

AWARDS: Obie Award, Best Play, Most Distinguished Direction, 1970, for *Approaching Simone;* Outstanding Educator Award, Outstanding Educator of America, 1972, 1975; Professional Achievement Award, University of Texas, 1985.

SIDELIGHTS: MEMBERSHIPS—American Educational Theatre Association (secretary-treasurer, 1953-55); American National Theatre and Academy (assistant executive director, 1957); League of Professional Theatre Training Programs (vice-president, 1971-74); Advisory Council of the American Educational Theatre Association, 1953-58; Children's Theatre Conference of the American Educational Theatre Association, 1953-55; Texas Education Theatre Association (secretary, 1952-53); Southwest Theatre Conference; New England Theatre Conference; National Theatre Conference; Little Flags Theatre Company (chairman, board of directors, 1976-82); National Society of Literature; Players Club.

RECREATION—Reading and gardening.

Law told *CTFT,* ''I was motivated to enter the theatre profession at an early age through participation in oratorical contests, particularly declamation, at which I excelled, while in public schools. I acted in plays in junior high school and senior high school in Texarkana, TX, and in a number of plays produced by the Department of Drama at the University of Texas at Austin. My favorite roles in University Theatre were Biondello, *The Taming of the Shrew,* and an apothecary in *Romeo and Juliet,* both under the direction of B. Iden Payne.

''The causes which interest me are Civil Rights and Affirmative Action.''

ADDRESS: HOME—2215 Wood Street, Texarkana, TX 75501.

*   *   *

LAWFORD, Peter   1923-84

PERSONAL: Full name Peter Sidney Ernest Aylen Lawford; born September 7, 1923, in London, England; died December 24, 1984;

son of General Sir Sidney and Lady Lawford; married Patricia Kennedy, 1954 (divorced, 1966); married Mary Ann Rowan, 1971 (divorced, 1973); married Deborah Gould, 1976 (annuled, 1976); married Patricia Sexton, 1984; children: (first marriage) Christopher, Victoria, Sydney (a daughter), Robin.

VOCATION: Actor.

CAREER: PRINCIPAL FILM APPEARANCES—*Poor Old Bill,* British, 1931; at Metro-Goldwyn-Mayer: *Lord Jeff,* 1938; *Mrs. Miniver,* 1942; *Eagle Squadron,* 1942; *Thunder Birds,* 1942; *A Yank at Eton,* 1942; *Sherlock Holmes Faces Death,* 1943; *Flesh and Fantasy,* 1943; *Someone to Remember; Pan's After Dark; The Man from Down Under,* 1943; *The White Cliffs of Dover,* 1944; *Mrs. Parkington,* 1944; *The Canterville Ghost,* 1944; *The Picture of Dorian Gray,* 1945; *Son of Lassie,* 1945; *Cluny Brown,* 1945.

Two Sisters from Boston, 1946; *It Happened in Brooklyn,* 1947; *Good News,* 1947; *On an Island with You,* 1948; *Easter Parade,* 1948; *Julia Misbehaves,* 1948; *The Red Danube,* 1949; *Please Believe Me,* 1950; *Kangaroo,* 1952; *Just This Once,* 1952; *You for Me,* 1952; *The Hour of 13,* 1952; *Rogue's March,* 1952; *It Should Happen to You,* 1954; *Never So Few,* 1959.

Also *Pepe,* Columbia, 1960; *Exodus,* United Artists, 1960; *Oceans 11,* Warner Brothers, 1960; *Sergeants 3,* United Artists, 1962; *Advise and Consent,* Columbia, 1962; *The Longest Day,* Twentieth Century-Fox, 1962; *Dead Ringer,* Warner Brothers, 1964; *Sylvia,* Paramount, 1965; *Harlow,* Paramount, 1965; *The Oscar,* Embassy, 1966; *A Man Called Adam,* Embassy, 1966; *Skidoo,* Paramount, 1968; *Hook, Line, and Sinker,* Columbia, 1969; *Buena Sera, Mrs. Campbell,* United Artists, 1969; *The April Fools,* National General, 1969; *Body and Soul,* 1971; *Clay Pigeon,* 1971; *They Only Kill Their Masters,* Metro-Goldwyn-Mayer, 1972; *That's Entertainment,* United Artists, 1974; *Rosebud,* United Artists, 1975; *Seven from Heaven; Gypsy Angels; Won Ton Ton,* 1976; *Where Is Parsifal?*

PRINCIPAL FILM WORK—Producer: *Johnny Cool,* United Artists, 1963; *Billie,* United Artists, 1965.

PRINCIPAL TELEVISION APPEARANCES—Bill Hasting, *Dear Phoebe,* NBC, 1954-56; Nick Charles, *The Thin Man,* NBC, 1957-59; *The Doris Day Show,* CBS. Movies: *How I Spent My Summer Vacation,* 1967; *A Step Out of Line,* 1970; *The Phantom of Lot Two; Island of Beautiful Women; Ellery Queen,* 1971; *Highcliffe Manor; Malice in Wonderland,* 1985.

PRINCIPAL TELEVISION WORK—Producer, *The Patty Duke Show,* 1963-66.*

*   *   *

LAZENBY, George   1939-

PERSONAL: Born September 5, 1939; son of George Edward (a film librarian) and Sheila Joan (a shop assistant) Lazenby; married Christina Ross Townson; children: Melanie, Zachary. EDUCATION: Attended public schools in Australia. MILITARY: Australian Army, corporal.

VOCATION: Actor.

CAREER: FILM DEBUT—James Bond, *On Her Majesty's Secret*

GEORGE LAZENBY

Service, United Artists, 1969. PRINCIPAL FILM APPEARANCES—*Universal Soldier,* 1970; *Man from Hong Kong* (aka *The Dragon Flies*), 1975; *Kentucky Fried Movie,* United Film, 1977; *St. Jack,* 1979.

TELEVISION DEBUT—BBC, 1971. PRINCIPAL TELEVISION APPEARANCES—*Rituals; Cover-Up; Masters; General Hospital.*

SIDELIGHTS: RECREATION—Motorcycles.

ADDRESS: AGENT—Light Company, 113 N. Robertson Blvd., Los Angeles, CA 90048.

        *   *   *

LEIBMAN, Ron 1937-

PERSONAL: Born October 11, 1937, in New York City; son of Murray and Grace (Marks) Leibman; married Linda Lavin (divorced); married Jessica Walter, June 26, 1983. EDUCATION: Attended Ohio Wesleyan University; trained for the stage at the Actors Studio.

VOCATION: Actor.

CAREER: NEW YORK STAGE DEBUT—Orpheus, *Legend of Lovers,* 41st Street Theater, 1959. PRINCIPAL STAGE APPEARANCES—Peter Nemo, *Dear Me, the Sky Is Falling,* Music Box, NY, 1963; Rip Calabria, *Bicycle Ride to Nevada,* Cort, NY, 1963; Captain Salzer, *The Deputy,* Theatre of Living Arts, Brooks Atkinson, NY,

1964; Clov, *Endgame,* Astrov, *Uncle Vanya,* Alceste, *The Misanthrope,* Mr. Puff, *The Critic,* all with Theatre of Living Arts, Philadephia, PA, 1965-67; Teddy, *The Poker Session,* Martinique, NY, 1967.

Hermes, *Prometheus Bound,* Solyony, *The Three Sisters,* Mosca, *Volpone,* Sergeant Henderson, *We Bombed in New Haven,* all with Yale Repertory, New Haven, CT, 1967-68; male roles, *Cop-Out,* Cort, NY, 1969; Stan, "Transfers," Bob, "The Rooming House," Galley, "Dr. Galley," all presented as *Tranfers,* Village South, NY, 1970; Gordon Miller, *Room Service,* Edison, NY, 1970; various parts, *Rich and Famous,* Estelle R. Newman Theater, NY, 1976; Herb, *I Ought to Be in Pictures,* Eugene O'Neill, NY, 1980; *Doubles,* Ritz, NY, 1985.

FILM DEBUT—*Where's Poppa?,* United Artists, 1970. PRINCIPAL FILM APPEARANCES—*Slaughterhouse Five,* Universal, 1972; *Your Three Minutes Are Up,* Cinerama, 1973; *The Hot Role,* 1973; *The Super Cops,* United Artists, 1974; *Won Ton Ton: The Dog Who Saved Hollywood,* Paramount, 1976; *Norma Rae,* Twentieth Century-Fox, 1979; *Up the Academy,* Warner Brothers, 1980; *Zorro, the Gay Blade,* Twentieth Century-Fox, 1981; *Romantic Comedy,* Metro-Goldwyn-Mayer/United Artists, 1983; *Rhinestone,* Twentieth Century-Fox, 1984; *Phar Lap,* 1985.

PRINCIPAL TELEVISION APPEARANCES—Martin Kazinsky, *Kaz,* CBS, 1978-79.

AWARDS: Drama Desk Award, for *We Bombed in New Haven;* Ohie Award, Drama Desk Award, both 1970, for *Transfers;* Emmy Award, for *Kaz.*

ADDRESS: OFFICE—27 W. 87th Street, New York, NY 10024.

        *   *   *

LEMMON, Jack 1925-

PERSONAL: Full name John Uhler Lemmon III; born February 8, 1925, in Boston, MA; son of John Uhler and Mildred LaRue (Noel) Lemmon; married Cynthia Boyd Stone, May 7, 1950 (divorced); married Felicia Farr, August 17, 1962; children: (first marriage) Christopher; (second marriage) Courtney. EDUCATION: Phillips Andover Academy, 1943; Harvard University, B.A., B.S., 1947. MILITARY: U.S. Navy Reserve, 1945-46.

VOCATION: Actor.

CAREER: PRINCIPAL STAGE APPEARANCES—Summer stock, 1940-48; *Room Service,* Broadway production, 1953; *Face of a Hero,* Broadway production, 1960; *Idiots Delight,* Los Angeles Music Center, 1970; *Juno and the Paycock,* Los Angeles Music Center, 1975; *Tribute,* 1978 (and subsequent tour); *A Sense of Humor.*

PRINCIPAL FILM APPEARANCES—*It Should Happen to You,* Columbia, 1954; *Phfft,* Columbia, 1954; *Three for the Show,* Columbia, 1955; *My Sister Eileen,* Columbia, 1955; *Mister Roberts,* Warner Brothers, 1955; *You Can't Run Away from It,* Columbia, 1956; *Fire Down Below,* Columbia, 1957; *Operation Mad Ball,* Columbia, 1957; *Cowboy,* Columbia, 1958; *Bell, Book, and Candle,* Columbia, 1959; *It Happened to Jane,* Columbia, 1959; *Some*

JACK LEMMON

Like It Hot, United Artists, 1959; *The Apartment*, United Artists, 1960; *The Wackiest Ship in the Army*, Columbia, 1960; *The Notorious Landlady*, Columbia, 1962; *Irma La Douce*, United Artists, 1963; *Under the Yum Yum Tree*, Columbia, 1963; *Days of Wine and Roses*, Warner Brothers, 1963.

Good Neighbor Sam, Columbia, 1964; *How to Murder Your Wife*, United Artists, 1965; *The Great Race*, Warner Brothers, 1966; *The Fortune Cookie*, United Artists, 1966; *Luv*, Columbia, 1967; *The Odd Couple*, Paramount, 1968; *The April Fools*, Paramount, 1970; *The Out-of-Towners*, Paramount, 1970; *The War Between Men and Women*, National General, 1972; *Avanti*, United Artists, 1972; *Save the Tiger*, Paramount, 1973; *The Front Page*, Universal, 1974; *The Prisoner of Second Avenue*, Warner Brothers, 1975; *Alex and the Gypsy*, Twentieth Century-Fox, 1976; *Airport 77*, Universal, 1977; *The China Syndrome*, Columbia, 1978; *Tribute*, Twentieth Century-Fox, 1980; *Buddy, Buddy*, Metro-Goldwyn-Mayer, 1981; *Missing*, Universal, 1981; *Mass Appeal*, Universal, 1984.

PRINCIPAL TELEVISION APPEARANCES—Series: *That Wonderful Guy*, 1950; *Toni Twin Time*, 1950; *The Adlibbers*, 1951; *Couple Next Door*, 1951-52; *Heaven for Betsy*, 1952. Movies: *The Entertainer*, 1975. Specials: *'S Wonderful, 'S Marvelous, 'S Gershwin*, 1972; host, *1984 Academy Awards*, ABC, 1985; *Macaroni*, HBO, 1985.

AWARDS: Academy Award, Best Supporting Actor, 1955, for *Mister Roberts;* Emmy Award, 1972, for *'S Wonderful, 'S Marvelous, 'S Gershwin;* Academy Award, Best Actor, 1973, for *Save the Tiger;* Emmy Award nomination, 1975, for *The Entertainer;* Best Actor, Cannes, 1981, for *Missing*.

SIDELIGHTS: MEMBERSHIPS—Hasty Pudding Club (president,

1945-46), Delphic (vice president, 1945-46), Harvard University Drama Club, 1945, Players Club.

ADDRESS: OFFICE—Jalem Productions, 141 El Camino Drive, Suite 201, Beverly Hills, CA 90212.

*   *   *

LEVEN, Boris

PERSONAL: Born in Moscow; emmigrated to U.S., 1927, naturalized, 1939; son of Israel and Zinaida (Narkirier) Leven; married Vera Glooshkoff, Feburary 8, 1948. EDUCATION: University of Southern California, B.Arch., 1932; certificate, beaux arts, Institute of Design, NY, 1933. MILITARY: U.S. Army Air Force, 1942-45.

VOCATION: Art director and production designer.

CAREER: PRINCIPAL FILM WORK—Art director: *Alexander's Ragtime Band*, 1938; *Shanghai Gesture*, 1941; *Hello Frisco Hello*, 1942; *Tales of Manhattan*, 1942; *I Wonder Who's Kissing Her Now*, 1946; *The Senator Was Indiscreet*, 1947; *Crisscross*, 1948; *Mr. Peabody and the Mermaid*, 1948; *Sudden Fear*, 1952; *The Star*, 1952; *Silver Chalice*, Warner Brothers, 1955; *Giant*, Warner Brothers, 1956; *Anatomy of a Murder*, Columbia, 1959; *West Side Story*, United Artists, 1961; *Two for the Seesaw*, United Artists, 1962; *The Sound of Music*, Twentieth Century-Fox, 1964; *The Sand*

BORIS LEVEN

Pebbles, Twentieth Century-Fox, 1965; *Star!,* Twentieth Century-Fox, 1968; *A Dream of Kings,* National General, 1969; *The Andromeda Strain,* Universal, 1971; *The New Centurions,* Columbia, 1972; *Jonathan Livingston Seagull,* Paramount, 1973; *Mandingo,* Paramount, 1975; *New York, New York,* United Artists, 1977; *The Last Waltz,* United Artists, 1978; *The King of Comedy,* Twentieth Century-Fox, 1983.

RELATED CAREER—Sketch artist, designer, Paramount Studios, 1933-35; traveled, painted abroad, 1935-36; art director, Twentieth Century-Fox, 1937-38, 1941-42, 1945-46; art director, Universal International Pictures, 1947-48; traveled, sketched in Europe and Russia, 1959-60, 1968, and 1970; exhibited water colors and paintings in private collections.

AWARDS: First Emerson Prize, 1932; First Prize, Beaux Arts Ball, 1932; First Prize, American Institute of Steel Construction, 1932; First Prize, National Scarab Traveling Sketch competition, 1933; First Prize, art direction, American Institute of Decorators, 1947, for *The Senator Was Indiscreet; Photoplay Magazine* medal, 1956, for *Giant;* Academy of Motion Picture Arts and Sciences Award nominations for art direction, 1938, for *Alexander's Ragtime Band,* 1941, for *Shanghai Gesture,* 1956, for *Giant,* 1964, for *The Sound of Music,* 1965, for *The Sand Pebbles,* 1968, for *Star!,* and 1971, for *The Andromeda Strain;* Academy of Motion Picture Arts and Sciences Award, art direction, 1961, for *West Side Story.*

SIDELIGHTS: MEMBERSHIPS—Society of Motion Picture Art Directors, United Scenic Artists, Academy of Motion Picture Arts and Sciences, Scull and Daggar, Delta Phi Delta, Tau Sigma Delta

ADDRESS: HOME—527 Hanley Place, Los Angeles, CA 90049.

*   *   *

LEVIN, Ira   1929-

PERSONAL: Born August 27, 1929, in New York City; son of Charles (a toy importer) and Beatrice (Schlansky) Levin; married Gabrielle Aronsohn, August 20, 1960 (divorced, 1968); married Phyllis Finkel, August 26, 1979 (divorced, 1982); children: (first marriage) Adam, Jed, Nick. EDUCATION: New York University, A.B., 1950. MILITARY: U.S. Army Signal Corps, 1953-55.

VOCATION: Writer.

WRITINGS: PLAYS, PRODUCED—Broadway: *No Time for Sergeants,* 1955; *Interlock,* 1958; *Critic's Choice,* 1960; *General Seeger,* 1962; *Drat! The Cat!,* 1965; *Dr. Cook's Garden,* 1967; *Veronica's Room,* 1973; *Deathtrap,* 1978; *Break a Leg,* 1979.

BOOKS—*A Kiss Before Dying,* Simon & Schuster, 1953; *Rosemary's Baby,* Random House, 1967; *This Perfect Day,* Random House, 1970; *The Stepford Wives,* Random House, 1972; *The Boys from Brazil,* Random House, 1976.

AWARDS: Mystery Writers of America Award; Edgar Allan Poe Award, Best First Novel, 1953, for *A Kiss Before Dying;* Antoinette Perry Award, Best Play, 1980, for *Deathtrap.*

SIDELIGHTS: MEMBERSHIPS—Dramatists Guild (council member, 1981-present), Authors Guild, American Society of Composers, Authors, and Publishers.

ADDRESS: AGENT—Howard Rosenstone, Rosenstone-Wender, Three E. 48th Street, New York, NY 10017.

*   *   *

LEWEY, Todd   1958-

PERSONAL: Born May 27, 1958, in Dorchester, MA; son of Howard Robert (a policeman) and Virginia Beatrice (Rich) Lewey. EDUCATION: Emerson College (two years); New York University (one year); trained for the theatre at the Circle in the Square Theatre School with, among others: Nikos Psacharopoulos, Shirley Nemetz (acting); Stephen Wilson (voice); David Terill (ballet); Marlene Atamanuik (jazz); Mary Jane Brown (tap).

VOCATION: Actor and dancer.

CAREER: NEW YORK DEBUT—Chorus, *Ragged Dick, the Shoeshine Boy,* Theatre for the New City. PRINCIPAL STAGE APPEARANCES—Frankie, *Here's to Sunday,* Fisherman's Players of Cape Cod, toured Boston; Nachum/dancer, *Fiddler on the Roof,* Brooklyn, NY; Barber, *Man of La Mancha,* Tibbits Opera House, Coldwater, MI; Tony Kirby, *You Can't Take It with You,* Baby John, *West Side Story,* Duane Fox, *Applause,* Enoch Snow, Jr., *Carousel,* Manuel, *The Gingerbread Lady,* Officer Klein, *Arsenic and Old Lace,* Bobby Van Heusen, *The Boyfriend,* Rolf Gruber, *The Sound of Music,* Schlemmer, *Mr. Roberts,* all at Town and Country Playhouse, Salem, NH.

TODD LEWEY

TELEVISION APPEARANCES—*Catch a Rainbow,* WCVB-TV, Boston, MA; *Comedienne,* WNET-TV, NY; *The Contest,* PBS; *See How She Runs,* CBS, 1978.

RELATED CAREER—Production assistant, over 25 Broadway and Off Broadway shows, 1978-84.

SIDELIGHTS: RECREATION—Roller skating, all forms of art, bowling, swimming, and horseback riding.

Lewey invented soccer-tennis, using a tennis court and a soccer ball. He is a Blonde American Indian (Micmac tribe).

ADDRESS: HOME—324 W. 43rd Street, Suite 2C, New York, NY 10036.

*   *   *

LEWIS, Geoffrey   1940-

PERSONAL: Born Furth Penscott, September 14, 1940, in Dilbran, Wales; son of Clellon R. (a boiler engineer) and Camaroon (a book binder; maiden name, Helby) Penscott. EDUCATION: Received a high school diploma; special professional training as a telephone repairman by General Telephone. POLITICS: Libertarian. RELIGION: Catholic.

VOCATION: Actor.

CAREER: TELEVISION DEBUT—Junkie, *Night Court,* 1965. TELEVISION APPEARANCES—Frank, *Starsky and Hutch,* ABC; Luke, *Falcon Crest,* 1983.

FILM DEBUT—Sterve, *The Culpepper Cattle Co.,* Twentieth Century-Fox, 1972; Damion, *The Wind and the Lion,* United Artists, 1975; Orville, *Every Which Way but Loose,* Warner Brothers, 1978; lawyer number one, *Ten to Midnight,* Cannon, 1983; Hardcase, *Lust in the Dust,* 1985.

STAGE DEBUT—Myself, *Celestial Navigations,* Matrix, Los Angeles, CA 1984.

SIDELIGHTS: MEMBERSHIPS—Tarzana High Bowlers; Santa Monica Bowling Club. RECREATION—Gardening, fencing, and bowling.

Lewis told *CTFT* that he is "very interested in stopping starvation throughout the world and in backing a female black candidate for president."

ADDRESS: HOME—6120 Shirley Avenue, Tarzana, CA 91356. AGENT—Writers and Artists Agency, 11726 San Vicente Blvd., Los Angeles, CA 90049.

*   *   *

LEWMAN, Lance   1960-

PERSONAL: Born August 8, 1960, in Baltimore, MD; son of Lary Cook (an actor) and Nancy Gail (an actress; maiden name, Posey)

Lewman; married Kristan King (a singer and actress), June 29, 1985. EDUCATION: North Carolina School of the Arts, 1982.

VOCATION: Actor, choreographer, and writer.

CAREER: STAGE DEBUT—Bruce Morse, *The Second Time Around,* Limestone Valley, Cockeysville, MD, 1979. NEW YORK DEBUT—*Losing Battles,* Noel Coward, July 12, 1984, for twelve performances. PRINCIPAL STAGE APPEARANCES—Buddy Layman, *The Diviners,* North Carolina School of the Arts, 1982; Romeo, *Romeo and Juliet,* American Stage Festival, NH, 1984.

TELEVISION DEBUT—David Wilhelm, *Special Needs,* PBS, 1981.

FILM DEBUT—Tom Barnes, *Riot on 42nd Street,* Entertainment Concepts, 1984.

AWARDS: Nancy Reynolds Scholarship, North Carolina School of the Arts, 1981, for Most Outstanding Returning Student.

SIDELIGHTS: MEMBERSHIPS—Actors' Equity Association, American Federation of Television and Radio Artists.

RECREATION—Skiing, swimming, gymnastics, playing guitar and piano, fencing, and writing poetry.

Lewman told *CTFT* that he wants to "put together a screenplay in the near future." He is eager to credit his schooling, saying, "the turning point of my career as an actor had to be the North Carolina School of the Arts. That was when I knew I had come home."

ADDRESS: HOME—449 W. 56th Street, New York, NY 10019. AGENT—Sheldon Lubliner, News & Entertainment Corp., 230 W. 55th Street, New York, NY 10019.

*   *   *

LIBIN, Paul   1930-

PERSONAL: Born December 12, 1930, in Chicago, IL; son of Ely Libin; married Florence A. Rowe. EDUCATION: University of Illinois; Columbia University, B.F.A., 1955.

VOCATION: Producer and theatre executive.

CAREER: FIRST STAGE WORK—Producer (all at Circle in the Square): *The Crucible,* Martinque, NY, 1958. PRINCIPAL STAGE WORK—Producer: *The Time of Vengence,* 1959; *Between Two Thieves,* 1960; *Shadow of Heroes,* 1961; *The Banker's Daughter, The Barroom Monks, A Portrait of the Artist as a Young Man,* all 1962; *Six Characters in Search of an Author,* 1963; *Othello,* 1964; *Baal, In White America, Medea, And Things That Go Bump in the Night, The Royal Hunt of the Sun, The Zulu and Zayda,* all 1965; *Six from La MaMa,* 1966; *Dynamite Tonight, A Midsummer Night's Dream, Iphigenia in Aulis,* all 1967; *A Moon for the Misbegotten, Morning, Noon, and Night,* both 1968; *Trumpets of the Lord, Ah! Wilderness, Seven Days of Mourning,* all 1969; *The White House Murder Case, Chicago 70, Boseman and Lena, Arsenic and Old Lace,* all 1970; *The Last Analysis,* 1971; *Mourning Becomes Electra, Medea, Here Are Ladies, Uncle Vanya,* all 1972-73.

Waltz of the Toreadors, The Iceman Cometh, An American Million-aire, Scapino, all 1973-74; *The National Health, Where's Charley?, All God's Chillun Got Wings, Death of a Salesman*, all 1974-75; *Ah! Wilderness, The Glass Menagerie, The Lady from the Sea, Pal Joey*, all 1975-76; *Days in the Trees, The Night of the Iguana, Romeo and Juliet, The Importance of Being Earnest*, all 1976-77; *Tartuffe, Saint Joan, 13 Rue de l'Amour, Once in a Lifetime*, all 1977-78; *Inspector General, Man and Superman, Spokesong, Loose Ends*, all 1978-79; *Major Barbara, Past Tense, The Man Who Came to Dinner*, all 1979-80; *Candida, Macbeth, Eminent Domain*, all 1980-81; *Present Laughter, The Queen and the Rebels, The Misan-thrope*, all 1981-82; *The Caine Mutiny Court-Martial, Heartbreak House, Awake and Sing*, 1982-84; *Design for Living, The Loves of Anatol, Arms and the Man*, all 1985.

RELATED CAREER—Managing director, Circle in the Square Thea-tre, 1961-present.

AWARDS: Antoinette Perry Award, 1976; recipient, Obie Awards.

SIDELIGHTS: MEMBERSHIPS—League of Off Broadway Theatres and Producers (president), League of New York Theatres and Producers (board of govenors).

ADDRESS: OFFICE—Circle in the Square Theatre, 1633 Broadway, New York, NY 10019.

*　　*　　*

LINDSAY-HOGG, Michael　1940-

PERSONAL: Born May 5, 1940, in New York City; son of Edward and Geraldine (an actress and director; maiden name, Fitzgerald) Lindsay-Hogg.

VOCATION: Director.

CAREER: NEW YORK DEBUT—*Whose Life Is It Anyway?* LONDON DEBUT—*The White Devil*, Old Vic. PRINCIPAL STAGE WORK—*Home*, Long Wharf, New Haven, CT; *The Millionaress*, Hay-market, London; *Agnes of God*, Music Box, NY, 1982; *The Im-portance of Being Earnest*.

PRINCIPAL FILM WORK—*Let It Be*, United Artist, 1970; *Nasty Habits*, Brut Productions, 1977.

PRINCIPAL TELEVISION WORK—*Skin Deep*, BBC; *Mrs. Palfrey at the Claremont*, BBC; *Plaintiffs and Defendants*, BBC; *Two Sun-days*, BBC; *Through the Night*, BBC; *Electra*, BBC; *Professional Foul*, BBC; *Ladies in Waiting*, KCET; *Dr. Fischer of Geneva*, BBC; *Ready, Steady, Go!*, BBC; *Simon and Garfunkel: The Con-cert in Central Park*, 1981; co-director, *Brideshead Revisited*, Granada; *Master Harold . . . and the Boys*, Showtime, 1984.

PRINCIPAL MUSICAL WORK—Directed promotional films for the Who, the Beatles, the Rolling Stones, Wings, Brian Ferry, and Elton John; *Ready, Steady, Go!*, BBC; *Simon and Garfunkel: The Concert in Central Park*, 1981.

ADDRESS: AGENT—c/o Chatto and Linnit, Prince of Wales Theatre, Coventry Street, London W1V 7FE, England.

LINN-BAKER, Mark

BRIEF ENTRY: Born in New York City. Actor. Linn-Baker's film credits include *My Favorite Year*, Metro-Goldwyn-Mayer/United Artists, 1982. He hosted the CBS summer television series *The Comedy Zone*, 1985. He is a member of AIA (Artists in Action), "an activist group whose first order of business is in voter registration."*

*　　*　　*

LION, John　1944-

PERSONAL: Born May 17, 1944, in Baltimore, MD; son of Simon John (an attorney) and Mary Frances (a stenographer) Lion; married Margaret Anne Dunn (a designer), September 10, 1983. EDUCA-TION: University of Chicago, B.A., 1966; University of California, Berkeley, M.A.

VOCATION: Director, producer, writer, and actor.

CAREER: STAGE DEBUT—Tranio, *Taming of the Shrew*, Court Theater, Chicago, IL, 1963, 50 performances. PRINCIPAL STAGE WORK—Director, Magic Theatre, nearly sixty plays since 1967; *Auto Destruct*, Manhattan Theater Club, NY, 1975; director, *La Turista*, Milwaukee Repertory, WI, 1975; producer, *Fool for Love*, Douglas Fairbanks, 1984-present.

MAJOR TOURS—*Fool for Love*, NY, Tokyo.

FILM DEBUT—Larry Bell, *The Right Stuff*, Warner Brothers, 1983. PRINCIPAL FILM APPEARANCES—Chicken Man, *Sudden Impact*, Warner Brothers, 1983.

RELATED CAREER—Founder and general director, Magic Theater, San Francisco, CA, 1967-present; instructor: Stanford University, University of California at Santa Cruz, University of California at Davis, San Francisco State University.

WRITINGS: PLAYS, PUBLISHED—*Rock and Roll Jesus with a Cowboy Mouth*, American Theater Magazine.

AWARDS: San Francisco Art Commission Award, Achievement in Theatre.

SIDELIGHTS: MEMBERSHIPS—Rockefeller Foundation.

ADDRESS: HOME—San Francisco, CA. OFFICE—Magic Theater, Building D, Fort Mason, San Francisco, CA 94123.

*　　*　　*

LIPPS, Ros　1925-

PERSONAL: Full name Roslyn M. Lipps; born June 10, 1925, in New York City; daughter of Morris (creator of Hollywood Bed and Bedding) and Lillian (Goldman) Lipps. EDUCATION: Barnard Col-lege, B.A. 1945, M.B.A. 1952. POLITICS: Liberal Democrat.

VOCATION: Critic and editor.

CAREER: Editor, *Theatrical Calendar,* to 1985; editor, *Theatre World News,* 1985-present; vice president and general manager, Celebrity World News, Inc., 1985-present.

SIDELIGHTS: MEMBERSHIPS—Outer Critics Circle (executive board), Drama Desk.

ADDRESS: HOME—305 W. 52nd Street, New York, NY 10019. OFFICE—Celebrity World Inc., 48 E. 43rd Street, New York, NY 10017.

*　　*　　*

LIVINGSTON, Robert H.   1934-

PERSONAL: Born Robert H. Luria, April 4, 1934; son of Irving M. (a lawyer) and Dorothy N. (Fink) Luria; married Jeanne Epstein, June 2, 1963 (divorced, 1973). EDUCATION: Carnegie Institute of Technology, B.F.A., 1955.

VOCATION: Director and writer.

CAREER: FIRST THEATER WORK—Director, *Gentlemen Prefer Blondes,* Northshore Playhouse, Northport, Long Island, NY, ten performances. FIRST NEW YORK STAGE WORK—Assistant stage manager, *Time Limit,* Booth, 1956, 150 performances. FIRST LONDON STAGE WORK—Director, *Dean,* London Casino, 1977. PRINCIPAL STAGE WORK—Director and adapter, *The Me Nobody Knows,* Orpheum, then Helen Hayes, NY, 1970; director, *Taking My Turn,* Entermedia, NY, 1983.

MAJOR TOURS—Director, *The Effect of Gamma Rays on Man-in-the-Moon Marigolds,* U.S. cities; director and adapter, *The Me Nobody Knows,* Toronto, Baltimore, Chicago, Paris, London, 1984.

FIRST TELEVISION WORK—Director, *It's a Nice Place to Visit,* NET, 1970. PRINCIPAL TELEVISION WORK—*All in the Family,* CBS; *Maude,* CBS; *ABC News; NBC News; CBS News.*

WRITINGS: PLAYS, PRODUCED—*The Me Nobody Knows,* Orpheum, NY, 1970; *Taking My Turn,* Entermedia, NY, 1983.

AWARDS: Obie Award, Antoinette Perry Award nomination, Cohen Award, Knight Award, Strauss Award, all for Best Director, 1970, for *The Me Nobody Knows.*

SIDELIGHTS: MEMBERSHIPS—Directors Guild of America, Society of Stage Directors and Choreographers (executive board).

RECREATION—Custom cabinet making, interior design, photography.

ADDRESS: HOME—New York, NY. AGENT—David Hatfield, Carid Management, 1641 Third Avenue, New York, NY 10028.

*　　*　　*

LOCKE, Sam   1917-

PERSONAL: Full name Samuel David Locke; born January 17, 1917, in Peabody, MA; son of Maurice Harold (Hebrew teacher and

cantor) and Jennie (Sjelizniak) Locke; married June Wallace Thompson (divorced); married Barbara Walters, May, 1959 (divorced, 1962). EDUCATION: City College of New York, B.S., 1937. RELIGION: Orthodox Jewish. MILITARY: U.S. Army Air Force, 1942-46.

VOCATION: Writer.

WRITINGS: SCREENPLAYS—*Deep Sea Monsters,* Adventure Film Company, 1942; *Herblock & Other American Political Cartoonists,* U.S. State Department, 1951; *People of the Forest,* U.S. State Department, 1951; *Voice of the Drum* (also directed), 1953; *Girls on the Beach* (as David Malcom), Paramount, 1964, *Beach Ball,* Paramount, 1965, *Wild Wild Winter,* Universal, 1966.

TELEVISION—Comedy sketches, *Front Row Center,* 1949-50; comedy sketches for Garry Moore and Ed Wynn; *The Web; Sure as Fats; The Westinghouse Summer Theatre,* CBS, 1951; *The Egg and I,* CBS, 1952; *The Red Buttons Show,* CBS, 1952; *Bedroom A,* Schlitz Playhouse, CBS, 1952; *A Matter of Calculation,* Orient Express, CBS, 1953; *The Secret Files,* 1954; "Men of the Clouds," *The Search,* CBS, 1954; *Judge,* 1955; *Charlie Farrell Racquet Club,* 1956; "Woman with Red Hair," *Alfred Hitchcock Presents,* CBS, 1958; *Bachelor Father,* CBS, 1961; *Peter Loves Mary,* NBC, 1962; *McKeever and the Colonel,* NBC, 1962; *McHale's Navy,* ABC, 1964; *Donna Reed Show,* ABC, 1964; "School for Bachelors," *Bob Hope Show,* NBC, 1964; *Gilligan's Island,* CBS, 1966-67; *Green Acres,* CBS, 1966; *Bill Dana Show,* NBC, 1963; *Lucille Ball Show,* CBS, 1966; *It's About Time,* CBS, 1967; *The Flying Nun,* ABC, 1969; *The Ghost and Mrs. Muir,* NBC, 1969; *Julia,* NBC, 1970; *Mayberry RFD,* CBS, 1970; *All in the Family,* CBS, 1972; *Brian Keith Show,* NBC, 1973; *Love American Style,* ABC, 1973.

PLAYS, PRODUCED—*Sunday Night Varieties* (contributor), Club Mirador, NY, 1939; *Straw Hat Revue* (contributor), Ambassador, NY, 1939; *'tis of Thee* (contributor), Maxine Elliot's, NY, 1940; *You Can't Sleep Here* (contributor), Barbizon Plaza, NY, 1941; *Of V We Sing* (contributor), 1942; *Meet the People* (contributor), Los Angeles, CA, 1943; *Tidbits of 1946* (contributor), Plymouth, NY, 1946; *Woman with Red Hair* (with Paul Roberts), Circle Theatre, Los Angeles, CA, 1955; *The Vamp* (with John Latouche), Winter Garden, NY, 1955; *Fair Game,* Longacre, 1957; *W.C.* (with Milton Sperling), Music Fair Inc., 1971.

BOOKS, PUBLISHED—*Your Second Life,* 1976; *Lessons in Loving,* 1978.

RELATED CAREER—Writer and liaison to U.S. State Department, 1951; teacher, adult education, University of California, Northridge, 1977-80.

ADDRESS: AGENT—Chassman-Strick, 6725 Sunset Blvd., Suite 506, Los Angeles, CA, 90028.

*　　*　　*

LOCKLEAR, Heather

BRIEF ENTRY: Actress. Locklear attended UCLA for psychology. She appeared on several television series including *CHiPS,* NBC; *240-Robert,* ABC; *Eight Is Enough,* ABC; *The Beverly Hillbillies*

Special, and in the NBC movies *Twirl,* 1981, and *City Killer,* 1984. She is best known for her roles of Sammy Jo Carrington on ABC's *Dynasty,* and for Stacy Sheridan on ABC's *T.J. Hooker.* She was in the film *Firestarter,* Universal, 1984.*

* * *

LONDON, Jerry   1937-

PERSONAL: Born January 21, 1937, in Los Angeles, CA; son of Micky and Ann (Rae) London; married Marilynn Landau, June 15, 1958; children: Lisa Monet, Todd Mitchell. EDUCATION: Attended University of California, Los Angeles.

VOCATION: Producer and director.

CAREER: PRINCIPAL TELEVISION WORK—Associate producer and director, *Hogan's Heroes,* CBS; associate producer for Bing Crosby Productions, 1965-71; director, *The Bob Newhart Show,* CBS; director, *The Mary Tyler Moore Show,* CBS; director, *Kojak* (two-hour special), CBS, 1976; director, *Wheels,* 1977; director, *Evenings in Byzantium,* 1978; director, *Women in White,* 1979; director, *Shogun,* 1980; director, *Chicago Story* (pilot), 1981; producer and director, *The Ordeal of Bill Carney,* ABC, 1981; producer and director, *The Gift of Life,* ABC, 1982; director, *The Scarlet and the Black,* 1982; producer and director, *Hotel* (pilot), ABC, 1983; supervising producer and director, *Chiefs,* 1983; executive producer, *With Intent to Kill,* ABC, 1984; director, *Ellis Island,* CBS, 1984; producer and director, *MacGruder and Loud* (pilot), ABC, 1984.

JERRY LONDON

RELATED WORK—Film editor, Desilu Productions, 1955-65.

AWARDS: Directors Guild, 1980.

ADDRESS: AGENT—c/o Bruce Vinokour, Creative Artists Agency, 1888 Century Park East, Los Angeles, CA 90067.

* * *

LOONIN, Larry   1941-

PERSONAL: Born January 5, 1941, in Brooklyn, NY; married Rose Rosenblatt (a writer).

VOCATION: Director, writer, and actor.

CAREER: NEW YORK STAGE DEBUT—Director, *The Brig,* Living Theater. PRINCIPAL STAGE WORK—Director of thirty Off Broadway plays; director, *Inserts,* Writers and Directors Lab, NY, 1983.

FILM DEBUT—Acted in *The First Deadly Sin,* Filmways, 1980.

TELEVISION DEBUT—Director, "Golden Honeymoon," *American Short Story,* PBS, 1980.

WRITINGS: PLAYS, PRODUCED—Fourteen produced plays including *Exhausting the Possibilities,* Theatre for the New City, NY; *Inserts* (an adaptation), Actors and Directors Lab, NY, 1983.

RELATED CAREER: College teacher for 18 years; director of theatre, Lehman College, Bronx, NY, 1982-present.

SIDELIGHTS: MEMBERSHIPS—Dramatists Guild, American Federation of Television and Radio Artists, Screen Actors Guild.

ADDRESS: HOME—84 West Broadway, New York, NY 10007. OFFICE—Lehman College, Director of Theatre, Bronx, NY 10468.

* * *

LOVELL, Dyson   1940-

PERSONAL: Born August 28, 1940; son of William (a businessman) and Helen (Lumsden) Lovell. EDUCATION: Attended Rhodesian public schools; trained for the stage at the Royal Academy of Dramatic Art. RELIGION: Church of England.

VOCATION: Producer and former actor.

CAREER: STAGE DEBUT—Understudy, *Henry V,* Old Vic.

TELEVISION DEBUT—Laertes, *Hamlet,* BBC.

PRINCIPAL FILM WORK—*Romeo and Juliet; The Mirror Cracked; Galileo; The Champ; Evil Under the Sun; Endless Love; The Cotton Club.*

ADDRESS: OFFICE—760 N. La Cienega Blvd., Los Angeles, CA 90069. AGENT—William Morris Agency, 1350 Avenue of the Americas, New York, NY 10019.

LOWE, Rob

BRIEF ENTRY: Born in Charlottesville, VA; attended Santa Monica High School. His television appearances have included two *ABC After-School Specials:* "A Matter of Time" and "Schoolboy Father," as well as two series pilots, *Mean Jeans* and *Thrills and Chills*. Also, he acted in the television series, *A New Kind of Family,* ABC, and the television movie *Thursday's Child,* 1983. Lowe made his feature film debut as Sodapop in *The Outsiders,* Warner Brothers, 1982, which was adapted from the S.E. Hinton novel. He then starred in the films *Class,* Orion, 1983; *Oxford Blues; The Hotel New Hampshire* (based on the John Irving novel); *St. Elmo's Fire,* Columbia, 1985, and *Young Blood* (upcoming). Lowe also appeared in the music video *Turn to You,* by the Go-Go's.*

*   *   *

LUBLINER, Sheldon   1950-

PERSONAL: Born March 28, 1950, in Chicago, IL; son of Leo W. and Ruth (Kwiatek) Lubliner; married Velma Anstadt, June 30, 1984. EDUCATION: University of Colorado, B.S., 1972; Brandeis University, M.F.A., 1974.

VOCATION: Producer and talent agent.

CAREER: FIRST STAGE WORK—Producer, *Lenny,* Charles Playhouse, Boston, MA, 1974, 192 performances. FIRST NEW YORK STAGE WORK—Producer, *Spotlight,* Palace, 1978. FIRST LONDON STAGE WORK—Producer, *Lenny,* Criterion, 1975, 72 performances.

PRINCIPAL STAGE WORK—Producer: *Arturo Ui,* Charles Playhouse, Boston, MA, 1975; *Fight for Sight Benefit,* Avery Fisher Hall, NY, 1977; *Scream,* Alley, Houston, TX, 1978.

RELATED CAREER—Vice-President, News and Entertainment Corporation, 1980-present, talent agent.

SIDELIGHTS: MEMBERSHIPS—Variety Club of New York, International Radio and Television Society.

Lubliner told *CTFT,* "My ability to become a producer at age 24 and then to change my profession to being an agent was made possible by my parents who instilled in me the courage, confidence, and support to dream and accomplish those dreams."

ADDRESS: OFFICE—News and Entertainment Corp., 230 W. 55th Street, New York, NY 10019.

*   *   *

LUCAS, Jonathan   1936-

PERSONAL: Born Luca Aco Giarraputo, August 14, 1936, in Salaparuta, Sicily; son of Luca (a stone mason) and Florence Aco (an interpreter; maiden name, McCrady) Giarraputo; children: Peter Lucas. EDUCATION: Southern Methodist University, B.A., Archeology; trained for the theatre for seven years with Balanchine at the American Ballet School; studied at the American Theatre Wing for two years. RELIGION: Buddhist.

VOCATION: Director, producer, and former actor and dancer.

CAREER: STAGE DEBUT—As Lucas Aco: Dancer, *A Lady Says Yes,* Broadhurst, NY, 1945. LONDON DEBUT—Lead role, *Touch and Go,* Prince of Wales, 1950. PRINCIPAL STAGE APPEARANCES—As Lucas Aco: Dancer, *Billion Dollar Baby,* Alvin, NY, 1945; dancing fella, an assistant, Jim, *Around the World,* Adelphi, NY, 1946; first geologist, understudy Og, *Finian's Rainbow,* 46th Street Theatre, NY, 1947.

As Jonathan Lucas: Dancer, *Bloomer Girl,* Shubert, NY, 1948; dancer, *Small Wonder,* Coronet, NY, 1948; Joe, *Me, the Sleeper,* Lenox Hill Playhouse, NY, 1949; featured performer, *Touch and Go,* Broadhurst, NY, 1949; Sam Jenkins, *Of Thee I Sing,* Ziegfeld, NY, 1952; Paris, *The Golden Apple,* Phoenix, then Alvin, NY, 1954; Marco the Magnificent, *Carnival!,* Imperial, NY, 1961.

PRINCIPAL STAGE WORK—Choreographer: *First Impressions,* Alvin, NY, 1959; *Vintage 60* (also director), Ivor, Los Angeles, then Brooks Atkinson, NY, 1960; *The Beauty Part,* Music Box, NY, 1962.

Director: *Season,* Sacramento Music Circus, Sacramento, CA, 1956; *Vintage 60,* 1960; *Upstairs and the Downstairs,* NY, 1961; *4 West,* 1963; Society of Illustrators show, 1963; musical productions, Melodyland, Berkeley, CA, 1963.

Producer: *Hollywood Pavilion,* NY World's Fair, 1964.

MAJOR TOURS—Marco the Magnificent, *Carnival!,* national tour, 1961-62.

JONATHAN LUCAS

PRINCIPAL FILM APPEARANCES—*The Lady from Shanghai*, Columbia, 1948; *Predator*, 1984.

PRINCIPAL FILM WORK—Choreographer: *Happy Go Lovely*, RKO, 1951; *Two Little Bears*, Twentieth Century-Fox, 1961; *Marriage on the Rocks*, Warner Brothers, 1965; *The Trouble with Girls*, Metro-Goldwyn-Mayer, 1969.

TELEVISION DEBUT—*Playhouse 90*, CBS.

PRINCIPAL TELEVISION WORK—Choreographer: *Celebrity Time*, CBS, 1952; *The Martha Raye Show*, NBC, 1953; *The Milton Berle Show*, NBC, 1953; *The Paul Winchell Show*, NBC, 1954; *The Imogene Coca Show*, NBC, 1954; *Melody Tour*, ABC, 1954; *The Jimmy Durante Show*, NBC, 1956; *The Ernie Kovacs Show*, NBC, 1956; *The Walter Winchell Show*, NBC, 1956; *The Eddie Fisher Show*, NBC, 1957; *The Esther Williams Aqua Spectacle*, NBC, 1957; *Cinderella*, CBS, 1958.

Director: *Royal Crown Series*, NBC, 1955; *Esther Williams Aqua Spectacle*, NBC, 1957; *What's Up, America?*, NBC; *A Country Happening*, NBC; *Music Country, USA*, NBC, 1974; *The Dean Martin Comedy Hour*, NBC, 1974.

Producer: *The Lively Ones*, NBC, 1963.

NIGHT CLUB APPEARANCES—With Kay Thompson at Cafe de Paris in London, the Palmer House in Chicago, and the Mocambo, Los Angeles.

WRITINGS: TELEVISION   Sketches for *The Dean Martin Show*, during fourteen years as one of the two directors of these specials.

AWARDS: Donaldson and Theatre World Awards, 1954, for *The Golden Apple*.

SIDELIGHTS: MEMBERSHIPS—Actors' Equity Association, American Federation of Television and Radio Artists, Directors Guild of America, Delta Chi.

ADDRESS: OFFICE—4040 Vineland, Studio City, CA 91604. AGENT—David Sacks, Beverly Hills, CA.

*   *   *

LYNDE, Paul   1926-82

PERSONAL: Born January 13, 1926, in Mount Vernon, OH; died January 9, 1982. EDUCATION: Attended Northwestern University.

VOCATION: Actor, writer, and comedian.

CAREER: PRINCIPAL TELEVISION APPEARANCES—*The Red Buttons Show*, NBC, 1955; Horace Fenton, *Stanley*, NBC, 1956-57; *The Perry Como Show*, NBC, 1961-62; *Dean Martin Presents*, NBC, 1968-69; Claude Pertwee, *Where's Huddles*, CBS, 1970; Uncle Arthur, *Bewitched*, ABC, 1965-72; Paul Simms, *The Paul Lynde Show*, ABC, 1972-73; Dr. Paul Mercy, *Temperature's Rising*, ABC, 1973-74; *Hollywood Squares*; *Donny and Marie*, ABC, 1976; *Flying Nun*; *Burke's Law*; *Colgate Comedy Hour*; *Goldiggers*; *The Martha Raye Show*.

FILM DEBUT—*Bye Bye Birdie*, Columbia, 1960. PRINCIPAL FILM

APPEARANCES—*Son of Flubber*, Buena Vista, 1962; *Under the Yum Yum Tree*, Columbia, 1963; *For Those Who Think Young*, United Artists, 1964; *Send Me No Flowers*, Universal, 1964; *Beach Blanket Bingo*, American International, 1965; *The Glass Bottom Boat*, Metro-Goldwyn-Mayer, 1966; *How Sweet It Is*, National General, 1968; *The Villain*, Metro-Goldwyn-Mayer, 1971.

NEW YORK STAGE DEBUT—Actor and playwright, *New Faces*, 1952. PRINCIPAL STAGE APPEARANCES—*Bye Bye Birdie*, 1960.

PRINCIPAL STAGE WORK—Director and writer, *New Faces*, 1956; writer, *New Faces*, 1960.*

*   *   *

LYON, Milton   1923-

PERSONAL: Born Milton Levine, February 21, 1923; son of Michael (a salesman) and Rose (a piano teacher; maiden name, Wolk) Levine; married Elaine Perry (a director and producer), May 20, 1959 (divorced, 1962). EDUCATION: Carnegie-Mellon University, B.A., 1943; trained vocally with Eva Brown. MILITARY: U.S. Army Air Corps, 1943.

VOCATION: Director, executive, manager, producer, conductor, and actor.

CAREER: STAGE DEBUT—*Uncle Harry*, Woodstock Playhouse, 1945. PRINCIPAL STAGE APPEARANCES—Chapel Playhouse,

MILTON LYON

Guilford, CT, 1946-48; Jake, *Showboat,* City Center, NY, 1954.

PRINCIPAL TELEVISION APPEARANCES—*Armstrong Circle Theater,* 1951; Max, "Burlesque," *Kraft Theater,* 1952.

PRINCIPAL STAGE WORK—Director: *Girl Crazy,* Chapel Playhouse, Guilford, CT, 1948; Equity Library Theater, NY, 1954; Sacramento Music Circus, 1954, 1959, 1962, 1964, 1965, 1966, 1969, 1972, 1980; Flint and Detroit Music Circuses, 1956, 1957; McCarter Theater, 1955-85; *Nightride,* NY, 1971; *Pins and Needles,* Roundabout Theater, NY, 1978; Pittsburgh Civic Light Opera, 1973-75; Chautauqua, 1979; Vancouver Opera, Canada, 1982; Pioneer Memorial Theater, Salt Lake City, 1985.

PRINCIPAL TELEVISION WORK—Director: *Babes in Toyland,* NBC, 1955, 1956; *Naughty Marietta, The Merry Widow, Desert Song, Heidi, The Great Waltz, Dearest Enemy,* NBC, 1956; *Paris in the Springtime, Marco Polo,* NBC, 1957.

RELATED CAREER—General manager, Woodstock Playhouse, Woodstock, NY, 1945; general manager, Chapel Playhouse, Guilford, CT, 1946; founder and executive producer, McCarter Theater for Performing Arts Center, Princeton, NJ, 1960-63; founder and executive director, Foundation for the Extention and Development of Professional Theater, NY, 1964-70; instructor: Princeton University, 1960-63, Columbia University, 1967-72, University of Texas, 1969, Wagner College, 1974, Princeton Theological Seminary, 1983-85; private teacher and vocal coach, 1949-85.

SIDELIGHTS: MEMBERSHIPS—Actors' Equity Association (life member), Screen Actors Guild, American Federation of Television and Radio Artists, Musicians Union, Players Club.

Lyon represented American Theater at the White House Conference on International Peace in 1965.

ADDRESS: HOME—Ten Bayard Lane, Apt. 3, Princeton, NJ 08540.

M

MACADAM, Will   1943-

PERSONAL: Born William MacAdam Hoppe, March 29, 1943, in Uniondale, NY; son of William (an automotive general manager) and Muriel (a welcome wagon hostess; maiden name, MacAdam) Hoppe. EDUCATION: Trained for the stage with Stella Adler. POLITICS: Democrat. RELIGION: Religious Science.

VOCATION: Director and actor.

CAREER: STAGE DEBUT—Prologue, *Hamlet,* American Shakespeare Festival, Stratford, CT, 1964, 70 performances. NEW YORK DEBUT—Policeman and understudy Hal, *Loot,* Biltmore, 1968, 22 performances. PRINCIPAL STAGE APPEARANCES—American Shakespeare Festival, Stratford, CT, 1964, 1967, 1968; *Tom Paine,* Stage 73, NY, 1968; Prince George, *Early Morning,* La MaMa, NY, 1969.

PRINCIPAL STAGE WORK—Director: *A Taste of Honey,* Stagelights, NY, 1977; *The Other Side of the Swamp,* Gallery Theatre, NY, 1978; *The House That Jack Built,* Cubiculo, NY, 1979; *A Life in the Theatre,* Austin Repertory, Austin, TX, 1981; *Gotcha,* New Vic, NY, 1981; *The Cat and the Canary,* Little Theatre of Winston-Salem, NC, 1982; *Frozen Assets,* New York Theatre Ensemble, NY, 1983; *I'm Getting My Act Together and Taking It on the Road,* Studio Theatre of Long Island, NY, 1984; *Who's Afraid of Virginia Woolf?,* American Drama Group, Munich, West Germany, 1985; *Scapino,* Studio Theatre of Long Island, NY, 1985.

TELEVISION DEBUT—Regular student, *Patty Duke Show,* ABC, 1965-66. PRINCIPAL TELEVISION APPEARANCES—Photographer, *Prisoner without a Name;* mental patient, "The People Next Door," *CBS Playhouse;* tree, *Trees,* PBS.

PRINCIPAL FILM APPEARANCES—*Tempest; So Fine; Still of the Night; Cotton Comes to Harlem.*

SIDELIGHTS: MEMBERSHIPS—Society of Stage Directors and Choreographers, Actors Equity Association, Screen Actors Guild.

ADDRESS: HOME—Uniondale, NY. OFFICE—549 E. Twelfth Street, P.O. Box 644, New York, NY 10009.

*   *   *

MALMUTH, Bruce   1934-

PERSONAL: Born February 4, 1934, in Brooklyn, NY; son of Jack (an attorney) and Selma (a dancer and painter; maiden name,

BRUCE MALMUTH

Bloom) Malmuth; divorced; children: Evan James. EDUCATION: Brooklyn College, B.A., 1956; studied film at Columbia University and University of Southern California and trained for the stage at the Actors and Directors Lab with Stella Adler, Peggy Fevry, Milton Katselas, and Jack Garfein. MILITARY: U.S. Army.

VOCATION: Director and writer.

CAREER: FIRST FILM WORK—Director, *Nighthawks,* Universal, 1981. PRINCIPAL FILM WORK—Director: *The Man Who Wasn't There,* Paramount, 1983; *Where Are the Children?,* Rastar-Columbia, 1985.

PRINCIPAL TELEVISION WORK—Director, *Heartbreak Winner,* ABC, 1980.

FIRST STAGE WORK—Director, writer, and producer, *Two Guys, Second Wind,* Century City Playhouse, Los Angeles, CA, 1980, 45 performances.

WRITINGS: PLAYS, PRODUCED—*The Painter and the Dishwasher,* Beverly Hills Playhouse, Los Angeles, CA, 1982; *The Hooky Players,* Zephyr, Los Angeles, CA, 1983.

AWARDS: Clio Award for Best Direction, 1973-75; Emmy Award; Los Angeles Critics Award, 1980, for *Two Guys, Second Wind.*

SIDELIGHTS: MEMBERSHIPS—Motion Picture Academy of Arts and Sciences, Directors Guild of America, Screen Actors Guild, Writers Guild of America.

Malmuth was awarded his Clios for the "Excedrin Headache" campaigns of the mid 1970's.

ADDRESS: AGENT—David Gersh, Gersh Agency, 222 N. Canon Drive, Beverly Hills, CA 90210.

*   *   *

MAMET, David   1947-

PERSONAL: Born November 30, 1947, in Chicago, IL; son of Bernard Morris and Lenore June (Silver) Mamet; married Lindsay Crouse (an actress). EDUCATION: Goddard College; studied for the theatre at the Neighborhood Playhouse.

VOCATION: Playwright and director.

CAREER: Principally known as a playwright; also artistic director, St. Nicholas Theatre Company (also founding member), Chicago, 1973-78; associate director and playwright-in-residence, Goodman Theatre, Chicago, 1978-present; teacher of acting and directing, New York University, University of Chicago, Yale Drama School.

WRITINGS: PLAYS, PRODUCED—*Lakeboat,* also other one-act plays, Marlboro, VT, 1970; *Squirrels,* Chicago, 1974; *Sexual Perversity in Chicago* and *Duck Variations,* double bill produced in Chicago, 1974, St. Clements, NY, 1975; *American Buffalo,* Chicago, 1975, Barrymore, NY, 1977, Cottesloe, London, 1978, Circle in the Square, Downtown, NY, 1981, Booth, NY, 1983-84; *A Life in the Theatre,* Theatre de Lys, NY, 1977; *The Water Engine,* New York Shakespeare Festival, 1977; *Mr. Happiness, Reunion, Dark Pony* (one-acts), *The Woods, Revenge of the Space Pandas, The Poet and the Rent, The Frog Prince,* all Chicago, 1977; *Lone Canoe* (musical book), Chicago, 1979; *Edmond,* NY, 1982; *The Disappearance of the Jews,* Chicago, 1983; *Glengarry Glen Ross,* Goodman Theatre Studio, Chicago, 1984, Golden, NY, 1984, London, 1984.

FILMS, PRODUCED—*The Postman Always Rings Twice,* Paramount, 1981; *The Verdict,* Twentieth Century-Fox, 1982.

BOOKS, PUBLISHED—*Warm and Cold,* a book for children, 1984.

AWARDS: Obie, 1982, for *Edmond;* New York Drama Critics Circle, Pulitzer Prize, Joseph Dintenfass, 1984, for *Glengarry Glen Ross.*

ADDRESS: AGENT—c/o Rosenstone-Wender, Three E. 48th Street, New York, NY 10017.

MANN, Theodore   1924-

PERSONAL: Born Theodore Goldman, May 13, 1924, in Brooklyn, NY; son of Martin and Gwen (Artson) Goldman; married Patricia Brooks. EDUCATION: Attended Columbia University, New York University, and Brooklyn Law School.

VOCATION: Producer and director.

CAREER: FIRST STAGE WORK—Producer, *Alice in Wonderland,* Maverick Players, Woodstock, NY, 1950. FIRST LONDON STAGE WORK—Producer, *Long Day's Journey into Night,* Globe, 1958. PRINCIPAL STAGE WORK—Producer (Circle in the Square Downtown, NY): *Dark of the Moon, Amata, Anouilh's Antigone, The Enchanted,* all 1951; *Bonds of Interest, Yerma, Burning Bright, Summer and Smoke,* all 1952; *The Grass Harp, American Gothic,* all 1953; *The Girl on the Via Flaminia,* 1954; *The King and the Duke, La Ronde, Cradle Song,* all 1955; *The Iceman Cometh,* 1956; *Children of Darkness, The Quare Fellow,* both 1958; *Our Town,* 1959; *The Balcony,* 1960; *Under Milkwood,* 1961.

Producer: *Plays for Bleecker Street, Under Milkwood, Pullman Car Hiawatha,* all 1962; *Desire Under the Elms, The Trojan Women,* both 1963; *The White Devil,* 1965; *Eh?,* 1966; producer and director, *Drums in the Night,* 1967; *Iphigenia in Aulis,* 1967; producer and director, *A Moon for the Misbegotten,* 1968; producer and director, *Seven Days in Mourning,* 1969; *Little Murders,* 1969; *The White House Murder Case, Boesman and Lena,* both 1970; producer and director, *The Last Analysis, F. Jasmine Addams,* both 1971; *Mourning Becomes Electra,* 1972.

At Circle in the Square Uptown, NY: producer and director, *Mourning Becomes Electra,* 1972; producer and director, *The Iceman Cometh,* 1973; producer, *Medea, Here Are Ladies, Uncle Vanya, The Waltz of the Toreadors, Hot L Baltimore,* all 1973; producer and director, *An American Millionaire, Where's Charley?,* both 1974; producer, *Scapino,* 1974; producer, *All God's Chillun Got Wings, Death of a Salesman, Ah Wilderness!,* all 1975; producer and director, *The Glass Menagerie,* 1975; producer and director, *Pal Joey,* 1976; producer, *The Lady from the Sea, Days in the Trees, The Night of the Iguana, The Club,* 1976; producer and director, *Romeo and Juliet,* 1977; producer, *The Importance of Being Earnest, Tartuffe, Saint Joan,* 1977; producer, *13 Rue de L'Amour, Once in a Lifetime, The Inspector General, Man and Superman,* all 1978.

Producer and director, *Past Tense,* 1979; producer, *Spokesong, Loose Ends,* both 1979; producer, *Major Barbara, The Man Who Came to Dinner, The Bacchae, John Gabriel Borkman,* all 1980; producer, *The Father, Scenes and Revelations, Candida,* all 1981; producer, *Macbeth, Eminent Domain, Present Laughter, The Queen and the Rebels,* all 1982; *The Misanthrope, The Caine Mutiny Court Martial, Heartbreak House,* all 1983; producer and director, *Awake and Sing,* 1984; producer, *Danny and the Deep Blue Sea, Design for Living,* both 1984; producer, *The Loves of Anatol, Arms and the Man,* both 1985.

At Ford's Theater, Washington, DC: producer and director, *A Moon for the Misbegotten, Trumpets of the Lord, Ah Wilderness!,* all 1969; producer, *Iphigenia in Aulis,* 1969; producer and director, *Arsenic and Old Lace,* 1970; producer and director, *John and Abigail,* 1971.

Producer (at other theaters): *Long Day's Journey into Night, The Innkeepers,* both 1956; *Camino Real,* 1959; *Smiling the Boy Fell Dead,* 1961; *General Seeger, Great Day in the Morning,* both 1962;

Strange Interlude, Six Characters in Search of an Author, Trumpets of the Lord, all 1963; *Othello, Hughie,* both 1964; *And Things That Go Bump in the Night, The Royal Hunt of the Sun, The Zulu and the Zayda, Baal, Live Like Pigs,* all 1965; *Six from La MaMa,* 1966; *A Midsummer Night's Dream,* 1967; producer and director, *Morning Noon and Night,* 1968; *Trumpets of the Lord,* 1969.

PRINCIPAL TELEVISION WORK—Producer: *The Trojan Women,* 1964; *Six Characters in Search of an Author; Trumpets of the Lord,* others.

SIDELIGHTS: RECREATION—Basketball, tennis, and farming.

ADDRESS: OFFICE—Circle in the Square Theatre, 1633 Broadway, New York, NY 10019.

* * *

MARCOVICCI, Andrea

BRIEF ENTRY: Born in New York City; attended Bennett College in Greensboro, NC, and later studied with Herbert Berghof. Actress. Her stage credits include Ophelia in Joseph Papp's *Hamlet,* Delacorte, New York Shakespeare Festival; *Iphegenias Wedding, Variety Obit,* and *The Seagull* (all off Broadway); *Nefertiti,* 1977, *Chaplin,* and *The Ambassadors* (all Broadway productions) Her television credits include Betsey Chernok on the soap opera *Love Is a Many Splendored Thing,* appearances on *Kojak,* CBS, *Medical Center,* CBS, and *Berringer's,* NBC, 1985; and roles in the television movies *Cry Rape,* 1972, and *Smile Jenny, You're Dead,* 1974. Her films include *The Front,* Columbia Pictures, 1976, *The Hand,* Warner Brothers, 1981; *The Stuff* (upcoming); *White Dragons,* Legend Productions (upcoming). Marcovicci has also appeared at the Reno Sweeny Nightclub in New York City.*

* * *

MARCUM, Kevin 1955-

PERSONAL: Born November 7, 1955, in Danville, IL; son of Roger B. (a superintendent of schools) and Iris J. (a pre-school instructor; maiden name, Nichols) Marcum. EDUCATION: University of Illinois (two years).

VOCATION: Actor and singer.

CAREER: DEBUT—Chorus and understudy, *Carousel,* St. Louis Municipal Opera, MO, 1975. NEW YORK DEBUT—Chorus and understudy, *My Fair Lady,* St. James, 1975-76. PRINCIPAL STAGE APPEARANCES—Dancer, *I Remember Mama,* Majestic, NY; Feldman, *The Magic Show,* Cort, NY; Kevin, *That Remarkable Romberg Ragtime and Romance Review,* Bruno Walter Auditorium, Lincoln Center, NY, 1978; Birdseller, *Sweeney Todd,* Uris, NY; Jeff Douglas, *Brigadoon,* Herman, *The Most Happy Fella,* Darien Dinner Theatre; performer, *Rhapsody in Gershwin,* Kennedy Center, Washington, DC; Lorenzo Fowler, *Song of Myself,* Pennsylvania Stage Company; Brazencourt, *Lock Up Your Daughters,* Goodspeed Opera House, East Haddam, CT; King Louis, *The Three Musketeers,* Hartman Theatre, Hartford, CT; standby for four

KEVIN MARCUM

supporting roles, *A Doll's Life,* Mark Hellinger, NY, 1982; *Going Hollywood* (workshop), 1983; Louis, *Sunday in the Park with George,* Playwrights Horizons, NY, 1983; Old Deuteronomy, *Cats,* Winter Garden, NY, 1984-85.

SUMMER STOCK—Herman, *Sweet Charity;* Mr. Snow, *Carousel;* Sir Simon, *The Canterville Ghost;* Everyman, *Everyman;* Marcellus, *The Music Man;* Doc Parkhurst, *Girl Crazy;* Harry Berlin, *Luv;* Claude, *Hair;* Lion, *The Wizard of Oz.*

MAJOR TOURS—Dap, *Camelot,* National Tour (Richard Burton Company), including New York State Theatre, Lincoln Center, NY; soloist, *An Evening with Sigmund Romberg.*

TELEVISION APPEARANCES—Bartender, *The Drunkard,* cable; Ralph Brooke, *One Live to Live,* ABC.

SIDELIGHTS: MEMBERSHIPS—Actors' Equity Association, American Federation of Television and Radio Artists, Screen Actors Guild.

Marcum's career has permitted him to be included in the *Theatre World* annals every year since 1976, the year of his New York debut.

ADDRESS: AGENT—Barbara Stark, Frontier Booking International Association, 1776 Broadway, New York, NY 10019.

* * *

MARCUS, Donald 1946-

PERSONAL: Born May 22, 1946, in New York City; son of Donald Edwin, Jr. (a business executive) and Eleanor (Hartell) Marcus;

married Lisa Milligan (a singer, actress, and producer), May 25, 1974. EDUCATION: Dartmouth College, A.B., 1968; Smith, M.A., 1969; trained for the stage with Curt Dempster.

VOCATION: Director, producer, and writer.

CAREER: NEW YORK STAGE DEBUT—Horvath, *Charlie the Chicken,* Playwrights' Horizons, 1972. FIRST STAGE WORK—Director, *Mimosa Pudica,* Ensemble Studio, NY, 1973.

PRINCIPAL STAGE WORK—Director: *The Middle Ages,* NY; *Charles Bacon and His Family,* NY.

RELATED CAREER—Founding member, executive committee, Ensemble Studio Theatre, NY, 1971-75; co-founder, co-director, Ark Theater Company, NY, 1978-present.

WRITINGS: PLAYS, PRODUCED—*Parades Shall Follow* (with Gary Nebid), Ensemble Studio, NY, 1974; *Song for Flute and Hermit,* Peterborough Players, 1977; *Lumiere,* Ark Theater Company, 1983.

SIDELIGHTS: MEMBERSHIPS—Alliance of Resident Theatres (board of directors).

ADDRESS: HOME—New York, NY. OFFICE—c/o Ark Theatre Company, 131 Spring Street, New York, NY 10012.

*   *   *

JEFFREY MARCUS

MARCUS, Jeffrey   1960-

PERSONAL: Born February 21, 1960, in Harrisburg, PA; son of Robert (an educator) and Eileen M. (a librarian; maiden name, Issacman) Marcus. EDUCATION: Attended Carnegie-Mellon University for two years; studied acting with Warren Robertson and Mira Rostova in New York.

VOCATION: Actor.

CAREER: STAGE DEBUT—Romeo, *Romeo and Juliet,* New York Shakespeare Company of San Francisco. NEW YORK DEBUT—Billy Spencer, *Almost an Eagle,* Longacre, 1982. PRINCIPAL STAGE APPEARANCES—Shawn Haley, *Almost an Eagle,* American Stage Festival, NH, 1982; *Meals on Wheels, Hot and Cold,* evening of one acts, Back Alley, Los Angeles, 1983; Marc, *Meeting the Winter Bikerider,* Young Playwrights Festival, Public, NY, 1984.

FILM DEBUT—Leonard, *Endless Love,* Universal, 1981. PRINCIPAL FILM APPEARANCES—Schwartzie, *The Chosen,* Twentieth Century-Fox, 1982.

TELEVISION DEBUT—Jon Fullerton, *Senior Trip,* 1981. PRINCIPAL TELEVISION APPEARANCES—Jerry Stein, ''Family Business,'' *American Playhouse,* PBS, 1982; Buzz Roosevelt, *First Lady of the World,* CBS, 1982.

ADDRESS: AGENT—The Gage Group, 1650 Broadway, New York, NY 10019.

MARIN, Richard (Cheech)   1946-

BRIEF ENTRY: Born in Los Angeles, CA, July 13, 1946; California State University, B.A., English. Actor, comedian, and writer. Teamed up with Tommy Chong in an improvisational group and became the comedy duo Cheech and Chong. His film work includes: co-writer and actor, *Up in Smoke,* Paramount, 1978; co-writer and actor, *Cheech and Chong's Next Movie,* Universal, 1980; co-writer and actor, *Cheech and Chong's Nice Dreams,* Columbia, 1981; co-writer and actor, *Things Are Tough All Over,* Columbia, 1982; actor, *It Came from Hollywood,* Paramount, 1982; co-writer and actor, *Still Smoking,* Paramount, 1983; co-writer and actor, *The Corsican Brothers,* Orion, 1984; *After Hours* (upcoming); *Echo Park* (upcoming).*

*   *   *

MARKLE, Christopher J.   1954-

PERSONAL: Born December 16, 1954, in Gary, IN; son of Joseph G. (a physician) and Mary E. (a nurse, maiden name, Kellk) Markle. EDUCATION: Indiana University, B.A., 1976; Yale School of Drama, M.F.A., 1979.

VOCATION: Director, writer, and teacher.

CAREER: FIRST STAGE WORK—Director, *Heartbreak House,* Guthrie, Minneapolis, MN. FIRST NEW YORK WORK—Director,

Issue? I Don't Even Know You!, Playwright's Horizons, 1984. LONDON DEBUT—Assistant director, *The Cradle Will Rock*, Old Vic, 1985. PRINCIPAL STAGE WORK—Director: *Tom Thumb or the Tragedy of Tragedies, The Madman and the Nun, Twelfth Night,* all Yale Summer Cabaret, CT; *The Cloud Dream, Pax De Deux, The Pelican,* all Yale School of Drama; *Trouble Begins at Eight,* Guthrie, Minneapolis, MN, 1981; *A Christmas Carol,* Guthrie, MN, 1982; *The Queen and the Rebels,* Theater in the Round, Minneapolis, MN; *A Midsummer Night's Dream,* The Acting Company; *The Tavern,* ANTA Theater Company; *Miss Julie,* Michigan Ensemble Theater, Ann Arbor, MI; *A Christmas Carol, Hedda Gabler,* both Guthrie, Minneapolis, MN, 1983.

Real Estate, Arena Stage, Washington, DC; *The Matchmaker,* New York University Tisch School of the Arts, NY, 1984; *A Christmas Carol, 'night, Mother,* both Guthrie, Minneapolis, MN, 1984; *Shakespeare Stew: A Fine Sampling of the Heights of Passion,* New York University Tisch School of the Arts, NY, 1984; *The Piggybank,* Guthrie Studio, Minneapolis, MN, 1984.

Assistant director: *The Seagull, Threepenny Opera, Peer Gynt, Summer Vacation Madness, The Tempest, As You Like It, Candide, Eli: A Mystery Play, Our Town, Il Campiello, Elizabeth I,* all Guthrie, Minneapolis, MN.

RELATED CAREER—Associate artistic director, Yale Cabaret, New Haven, CT, 1977-78; staff repertory director, The Acting Company, 1979-81; resident director, Guthrie, Minneapolis, MN, 1981-85; guest artist, New York University, NY, 1984-85.

WRITINGS: PLAYS, PRODUCED—*Caterwaul: A Dire Epic,* Yale Cabaret, New Haven, CT, 1979; *Trouble Begins at Eight,* Guthrie.

AWARDS: Michael Langham Fellowship, 1981.

SIDELIGHTS: MEMBERSHIPS—Actors' Equity Association, Society of Stage Directors and Choreographers, Amnesty International, Oxfam America.

ADDRESS: HOME—209 E. Fifth Street, New York, NY 10003.

*   *   *

MARKOE, Gerald Jay   1941-

PERSONAL: Born March 22, 1941, in Brooklyn, NY; son of Henry Albert (a jewelry mold and die maker) and Florence Marion (Goldstein) Markoe; children: Jeremy, Andra. EDUCATION: Juilliard School of Music, 1960-62; Manhattan School of Music, B. Music, 1962-66, M.M., 1968; studied piano with Amiram Rigai and koto with Fusako Yoshida.

VOCATION: Composer.

CAREER: Markoe has conducted District 12 Orchestra at Lincoln Center, NY, for three years, performed with the New York Philharmonic as well as with the Manhattan School of Music orchestra and chorus. He has led and performed in dance orchestras, including those of Lester Lanin, Meyer Davis, Steven Scott, and the Noblemen as vocalist, guitarist and bassist under the name Jerry Markoe. He has also played in cocktail lounges and piano bars as a one man orchestra.

WRITINGS: MUSICAL STAGE WORKS, PERFORMED—*The Chinese Wall,* Manhattan School of Music, 1968; incidental, one man multitrack tape score, *The Lion in Winter,* Hunter College Auditorium, NY, 1969; *Macbird,* 1976; ragtime score, *Indulgences in the Louisville Harem,* Perry Street, NY, 1976; *Punch and Judy,* Perry Street, NY, 1976; *The Black Princess,* Lincoln Center, NY, 1976-77; incidental, one man multitrack tape score, *Ethan Frome,* St. Clements, NY, 1978; *Alice in Wonderland,* Hartley House, NY, 1978-83; *Cinderella Update,* Hartley House, NY, 1978-80; *The Forgotten Treasure,* Double Image, NY, 1978-80.

Another Time (operetta), Lyric, NY, 1979; *Ludlow Ladd,* Lyric, 1979; *Fair Play for Eve,* American Theatre of Actors, 1979; *C & W* (country-western), American Theatre of Actors, 1980; *Fair Play for Eve,* 3 Muses, NY, 1980, Arena Players, Baltimore, MD, 1981; *Forever Peter Pan* (rock), 3 Muses, NY, 1981; *Ludlow Ladd,* New American, 1982-83; *Charlotte Sweet,* American Theatre of Actors, NY, 1982, Westside Arts Center, 1982-83, Virginia Stage Company, 1983, Chicago, 1984, Theatre Three, Dallas, 1984, Rochester, 1985. MUSICAL STAGE SCORES, PUBLISHED—*The Alchemist's Book,* Samuel French, 1976.

FILMS SCORES, PERFORMED—*Odds Are,* CBS Films, 1982; also educational films for Troll Associates, Eyegate Media, Imperial Films, McGraw-Hill, ABC-TV, Coronet Instructional Media, and the Learning Co-op, 1974-76.

RECORDINGS: *Charlotte Sweet,* Hammond Records, 1984.

AWARDS: Drama Desk nomination, 1983, *Charlotte Sweet;* ASCAP music awards for seven consecutive years.

SIDELIGHTS: MEMBERSHIPS—American Society of Composers, Authors, and Publishers, Dramatists Guild, American Federation of Musicians, National Academy of Recording Arts and Sciences, American Federation of Astrologers (faculty), National Council for Geocosmic Research.

RECREATION: Yoga, meditation, motorcycle riding and mechanics, camping, and nature.

Markoe is the discoverer of astro music which is based on planetary positions and is the founder of astro musical research which produces astrology charts in music. He has published numerous articles and he lectures and gives astro musical concerts. He is currently working on a book on this subject.

ADDRESS: HOME—11 Fort George Hill, 13C, New York, NY 10040. AGENT—Biff Liff, William Morris Agency, 1350 Avenue of the Americas, New York, NY 10019.

*   *   *

MARQUAND, Richard   1937-

PERSONAL: Born September 22, 1937, in Cardiff, Wales; son of Hilary A. (a member of Parliament) and Rachel E. (Rees) Marquand; married Josephine Jones, July 23, 1960 (divorced, 1970); married Carol Bell (a film director), June 19, 1981; children: Hannah Rachel, James Elwyn, Sam Adair, Molly Joyce. EDUCATION: Universite D'Aix, Marseille, 1955; King's College, Cambridge, 1956-59, M.A., 1963. MILITARY: Special Services, Royal Air Force, 1959-61.

RICHARD MARQUAND

VOCATION: Film and television director.

CAREER: FILM DEBUT—Director, *The Legacy,* Universal, 1979. PRINCIPAL FILM WORK—Director: *Birth of the Beatles,* 1980; *Eye of the Needle,* United Artists, 1981; *Return of the Jedi,* Twentieth Century-Fox, 1983; *Until September,* Metro-Goldwyn-Mayer, 1984; *Jagged Edge,* Columbia, 1985; *Capa* (upcoming).

TELEVISION DEBUT—Producer, BBC Television, 1962. PRINCIPAL TELEVISION WORK—Director: *Search for the Nile,* 1975; *Big Henry,* 1977.

AWARDS: Emmy, National Academy of Television Arts and Sciences, Peabody, Christopher, 1975, for *Search for the Nile;* Emmy, Christopher, 1977, for *Big Henry.*

SIDELIGHTS: MEMBERSHIPS—Association of Cinematic and Television Technicians (United Kingdom), Directors Guild of America.

ADDRESS: OFFICE—Hollybush House, Hadley Green, Barnet, United Kingdom. AGENT—Creative Artists Agency, 1888 Century Park E., Los Angeles, CA 90067.

*   *   *

MARTIN, Elliot   1924-

PERSONAL: Born February 25, 1924, in Denver, CO; son of Will H. and Elma A. (Harvey) Martin; married Majorie E. Cuestra. EDUCATION: Attended University of Denver.

VOCATION: Producer and former actor.

CAREER: LONDON DEBUT—Fred, *Oklahoma!,* Drury Lane, 1947. NEW YORK DEBUT—Prospector, neighbor, *Texas, Li'l Darlin',* Mark Hellinger, 1949.

PRINCIPAL STAGE WORK—Assistant stage manager, *Texas, Li'l Darlin',* Mark Hellinger, NY, 1949; executive assistant, Westport Country Playhouse, CT, 1951; manager and director, Bahama Playhouse, Nassau, British West Indies, 1952; production stage manager: *At Home with Ethel Waters, In the Summer House,* both NY, 1953; *The Girl on the Via Flaminia, Home Is the Hero, Portrait of a Lady,* both NY, 1954; *Phoenix '55, The Heavenly Twins,* both NY, 1955; *The Innkeepers, Little Glass Clock, Long Day's Journey into Night,* all NY, 1956.

Co-Producer: *The Painted Days,* Theatre Marquee, NY, 1961; *The Captains and the Kings, Seidman and Son, Never Too Late,* all NY, 1962; *Never Too Late,* Prince of Wales, London, 1963; *Nobody Loves an Albatross,* NY, 1963; *Mating Dance,* NY, 1965; *Dinner at Eight,* NY, 1966; *More Stately Mansions,* NY, 1967; *The Wrong Way Light Bulb,* NY, 1969; *Abelard and Heloise,* NY, 1971; *Emperor Henry IV,* NY, 1973; *A Moon for the Misbegotten, When You Comin' Back, Red Rider?,* both NY, 1974; *Of Mice and Men, Conversations with an Irish Rascal,* NY, 1975; *Dirty Linen and New Found Land, Caesar and Cleopatra, A Touch of the Poet,* all NY, 1977; *The Kingfisher,* NY, 1978; *Clothes for a Summer Hotel,* NY, 1980; *Kingdoms,* NY, 1981; *American Buffalo,* NY, 1982; *Angels Fall,* NY, 1983; *American Buffalo,* Booth, NY, 1983; *Glengarry/ Glen Ross* NY, 1984; *American Buffalo,* Duke of York, London, 1984; *Harrigan n' Hart,* NY, 1985.

MAJOR TOURS—Production stage manager: *The Matchmaker,* U.S. cities, 1957; *Inherit the Wind, The Remarkable Mr. Pennypacker,* both U.S. cities, 1958; *A Majority of One,* U.S. cities, 1959; *The Unsinkable Molly Brown,* U.S. cities, 1960; co-producer: *Morning's at Seven,* U.S. cities, 1976; *Daisy Mayme,* U.S. cities, 1979.

RELATED CAREER—Director, Center Theater Group, Los Angeles, CA, 1966-71.

ADDRESS: OFFICE—152 W. 58th Street, New York, NY 10019.

*   *   *

MARTIN, Pamela Sue

BRIEF ENTRY: Born in Westport, CT; married Manuel Rojas. Martin's television credits include Fallon Carrington Colby on *Dynasty,* ABC, and Nancy Drew in *Nancy Drew Mysteries,* ABC. She was the lead as John Dillinger's girlfriend in the television movie *The Lady in Red,* 1979. Her films include *To Find a Man,* Columbia Pictures, 1972; *The Poseidon Adventure,* Twentieth Century-Fox, 1972; *Buster and Billie,* Columbia Pictures, 1974; *Our Time,* Warner Brothers, 1974; *Torchlight,* 1984.*

*   *   *

MARYAN, Charles   1934-

PERSONAL: Born December 30, 1934, in Chicago, IL; son of Harry Oliver (a doctor) and Hazel (an artist; maiden name, Sinniko)

Maryan; married Sarah Sanders, February 14, 1965 (divorced, 1972); married Lana Fritz (a costume designer), November 20, 1983; children: Abigael. EDUCATION: Dartmouth College, A.B., 1956; trained for the stage at the Neighborhood Playhouse with Stella Adler and Sanford Meisner. MILITARY: U.S. Army, 1957-59.

VOCATION: Director.

CAREER: FIRST STAGE WORK—Director, *The Emperor Jones*, Blue Angel, Chicago, IL, 1959, 40 performances. FIRST LONDON STAGE WORK—Director, *The Typist and the Tiger*, Globe, 1964. FIRST NEW YORK STAGE WORK—Director, *Down in the Valley*, Equity Library, 1965.

PRINCIPAL STAGE WORK—Director: *Mercy Street*, American Place, NY; *Big Broadcast at 53rd*, La MaMa E.T.C., NY; *Let Them Down Gently*, Theatre de Lys, NY; *Playing with Fire*, Counterpoint, NY; *Hamlet*, Everyman Company, NY; *Algonquin Sampler*, Joseph Jefferson, NY; *Crazy Horse*, New Federal, NY; *The First Week in Bogota*, Playwrights Horizons; *Les Bavard*, Lehman Center, NY. Also directed at these NY theatres: St. Clements; New Theatre; New Dramatists; Equity Library; Barr; Wilder; Albee; 78th Street Theatre Lab; Street Theatre; Circle Repertory; Directors' Lab.

Regional: *Plymouth Rock, Playing with Fire, Twelfth Night, Holiday*, all California Actors Theater, 1978-79; *Couple of the Year, Mostly Women, Episode on an Autumn Evening, Algonquin Sampler*, all White Barn Theatre; *The Cage*, Loretto Hilton, St. Louis, MO; *Joe Egg*, Hartford Stage Company, CT; *Sweet Mistress, You Can't Take It with You, Broadway, Male Animal*, Barter, Abingdon, VA. Also directed at these regional theatres: Circle Theatre, Kansas City, MO; Front Street, Memphis, TN; Theatre of the Living Arts, Philadelphia, PA; Virginia Museum Theater, Richmond, VA; Virginia Shakespeare Festival, Williamsburg, VA; Rhinebeck Summer Theatre; American Musical Theatre.

Stock: Mule Barn Theatre, Tarkio, MO; Parker Playhouse, Fort Lauderdale, FL; Green Mansions Theatre, Warrenberg, NY.

Educational: National Theatre Institute, Waterford, CT; Juilliard School of the Theatre, NY; Neighborhood Playhouse, NY; American Academy of Dramatic Art, NY; Yale School of Drama, New Haven, CT; Marymount College, NY; High School of the Performing Arts, NY; Purchase College, NY.

RELATED CAREER—Instructor: O'Neill Theatre Center, National Theatre Institute; Columbia University; Marymount College, 1973-76; also tour manager, Cold Stream Guard and the Royal Scot Dragoon Guards, 1981; Spanish Riding School of Vienna, 1982 and 1984; The Blackwatch and the Scots Guards, 1983.

WRITINGS: BOOKS—*Anne Sexton: The Artist and Her Critics; Reflections: The Poet on the Stage*, Indiana University Press.

AWARDS: Straw Hat Award, Best Director, 1972.

SIDELIGHTS: MEMBERSHIPS—Actors' Equity Association, Society of Stage Directors and Choreographers.

ADDRESS: AGENT—Ray Powers, Marje Fields Agency, 165 W. 46th Street, New York, NY 10036.

MASON, Marsha   1942-

PERSONAL: Born April 3, 1942, in St. Louis, MO; daughter of James Joseph and Jacqueline Helena (Rachowsky) Mason; married Gary Campbell (divorced, 1964); married Neil Simon (playwright), October 25, 1973 (divorced). EDUCATION: Webster College, B.A., speech and drama.

VOCATION: Actress and director.

CAREER: NEW YORK DEBUT—*The Deer Park*, Theatre de Lys, 1967. PRINCIPAL STAGE APPEARANCES—*The Indian Wants the Bronx*, Astor Place, NY, 1968; *Happy Birthday Wanda June*, off-Broadway production, NY, 1970; *Private Lives*, American Conservatory Theatre, San Francisco, CA, 1971; *You Can't Take It with You*, American Conservatory Theatre, San Francisco, CA, 1972; *The Good Doctor*, Broadway production, NY, 1973; *Richard III*, 1974.

MAJOR TOURS—*Cactus Flower*, 1968.

PRINCIPAL STAGE WORK—Director, *Juno's Swans*, Second Stage, NY, 1985.

FILM DEBUT—*Blume in Love*, 1973. PRINCIPAL FILM APPEARANCES—*Cinderella Liberty*, 1973; *Audrey Rose*, 1977; *The Goodbye Girl*, 1977; *The Cheap Detective*, 1978; *Chapter II*, 1979; *Promises in the Dark*, 1979; *Only When I Laugh*, 1981; *Max Dugan Returns*, 1983.

PRINCIPAL TELEVISION APPEARANCES—Specials: *Cyrano de Bergerac*, 1974. Movies: *The Good Doctor*, 1978; *Lois Gibbs and the Love Canal*, CBS, 1981; *Surviving*, ABC, 1984.

AWARDS: Academy Award nominations, for *Cinderella Liberty, Chapter II, The Goodbye Girl, Only When I Laugh;* British Academy Award, for *The Goodbye Girl;* Golden Globe Awards, for *Cinderella Liberty*, 1974, *The Goodbye Girl*, 1978; People's Choice Awards.

SIDELIGHTS: MEMBERSHIPS—Actors' Equity Association, Screen Actors Guild, American Federation of Television and Radio Artists.

ADDRESS: AGENT—Ron Meyer, Creative Artists Agency, 1888 Century Park E., Suite 1400, Los Angeles, CA 90067.

*   *   *

MATSUSAKA, Tom

PERSONAL: Full name Thomas Matsusaka; born August 8, in Wahiawa, HI; son of Edward Minoru (a businessman) and Natsue (Takano) Matsusaka. EDUCATION: University of Hawaii; Michigan State University, B.A.; studied acting with Mary Tareai and voice with Daniel Serra. RELIGION: Metaphysics.

VOCATION: Actor.

CAREER: STAGE DEBUT—Villager, *Chu Chem*, New Locust, Philadelphia, 1966 (pre-Broadway tour which did not come to NY). NEW YORK DEBUT—Ito, *Mame*, Winter Garden, 1968. PRINCIPAL STAGE APPEARANCES—Yoshitsune, *Kanjincho*, Institute for Advanced Studies in Theatre Arts, NY, 1968; Ling, *Anything Goes*,

TOM MATSUSAKA

MCASSEY, Michael   1955-

PERSONAL: Born May 28, 1955, in Wheaton, IL; son of Richard Lee (a men's clothing retailer) and Margaret Orth (Jones) McAssey. EDUCATION: Attended Eastern Illinois University. RELIGION: Catholic.

VOCATION: Actor and dancer.

CAREER: PRINCIPAL TELEVISION APPEARANCES—George, *Guiding Light,* CBS; *Fame.*

PRINCIPAL STAGE APPEARANCES—*I Love My Wife,* Atlantic City, NJ; *Billy Bishop Goes to War,* Sante Fe Festival Theatre; *Silverlake,* Broadway production; *In Gay Company,* off Broadway production.

MAJOR TOURS—Jesus, *Godspell,* U.S. cities; *I Love My Wife,* U.S. cities; *From Broadway to Hollywood,* Paris; *The Argentina Turner Revue* (with Patti LuPone).

PRINCIPAL FILM APPEARANCES—Dancer, *Annie.*

SIDELIGHTS: MEMBERSHIPS—Actors' Equity Association, Screen Actors Guild, American Federation of Television and Radio Artists.

ADDRESS: HOME—150 W. 47th Street, New York, NY 10036. AGENT—Greg Villone, 250 W. 57th Street, Suite 2306, New York, NY 10019.

*　　　*　　　*

Pocono Playhouse, Mountain Home, PA, 1971; Banzo, *Ride the Winds,* Bijou, NY, 1974; Imperial Priest, *Pacific Overtures,* Winter Garden, NY, 1976; Greek Chorus, *Agamemnon,* Vivian Beaumont, NY, 1977; Cheng, *Privates on Parade,* Long Wharf, New Haven, CT, 1979; M. Aung, *Plenty,* Arena Stage, Washington, DC, 1980; *Teahouse,* Pan Asian Repertory, NY, 1983; Imperial Priest, *Pacific Overtures,* York Players, NY, 1984, Promenade, NY, 1984; also: Skinny, *Jungle of Cities,* New York Shakespeare Festival, Public, NY; various plays with Pan Asian Repertory and La MaMa in NY.

FILM DEBUT—Radar operator, *The Private Navy of Sgt. O'Farrell,* United Artists, 1967. PRINCIPAL FILM APPEARANCES—*The President's Analyst,* Paramount, 1967; *Hanky Panky,* Columbia, 1982.

TELEVISION DEBUT—Vietnamese, *Apple Pie,* ABC, 1968. PRINCIPAL TELEVISION APPEARANCES—Bartender, *Texas,* 1981; Mr. Oshita, *Ryan's Hope,* 1984; also: *That's Life,* ABC, 1968-69; *Saturday Night Live; The $45 Billion Connection; Love Is a Many Splendored Thing; Botticelli.*

SIDELIGHTS: MEMBERSHIPS—Actors' Equity Association, American Federation of Television and Radio Artists, Screen Actors Guild.

ADDRESS: HOME—484 W. 43rd Street, New York, NY 10036. AGENT—Jadin Wong, 442 W. 57th Street, Suite 5J, New York, NY 10019.

MCCOWEN, Alec   1925-

PERSONAL: Born Alexander Duncan McCowen, May 26, 1925, in Tunbridge Wells, England; son of Duncan and Mary (Walkden) McCowen. EDUCATION: Attended Skinner's School, Tunbridge Wells; trained for the stage at the Royal Academy of Dramatic Art.

VOCATION: Actor.

CAREER: STAGE DEBUT—Micky, *Paddy, the Next Best Thing,* Repertory Theatre, Macclesfield, UK, 1942. LONDON DEBUT—Maxim, *Ivanov,* Arts, 1950. NEW YORK DEBUT—Messenger, *Antony and Cleopatra,* Ziegfeld, 1951. PRINCIPAL STAGE APPEARANCES—Repertory, 1943-45; repertory, 1946-49, including St. John's Repertory, Newfoundland; George Almaire, *The Mask and the Face,* Kitts, *Preserving Mr. Panmure,* both Arts, London, 1950; *The Silver Box,* Lyric, Hammersmith, 1951; Brian, *The Martin's Nest,* Westminster, London, 1951; Hugh Voysey, *The Voysey Inheritance,* The Announcer, *The Holy Terrors,* both Arts, London, 1952; Daventry, *Escapade,* St. James', London, 1953; Larry Thompson, *Serious Charge,* Repertory Players at the Adelphi, London, 1953; Julian Heath, *Shadow of the Vine,* Wyndham's, London, 1954; Henri de Toulouse-Lautrec, *Moulin Rouge,* New Theatre, Bromley, 1954; Barnaby Tucker, *The Matchmaker,* Haymarket, London, 1954; Vicomte Octave de Clerambard, *The Count of Clerambard,* Garrick, London, 1955; Dr. Bird, *The Caine Mutiny Court Martial,* Hippodrome, London, 1956; Lancelot Berenson, *No Laughing Matter,* Arts, London, 1957; Michael Claverton-Ferry, *The Elder Statesman,* Edinburgh Festival, Scotland, then Cambridge, UK, 1958.

ALEC MCCOWEN

Mr. Brisk, *The Double Dealer*, Touchstone, *As You Like It*, Algernon Moncrieff, *The Importance of Being Earnest*, Ford, *The Merry Wives of Windsor*, Dauphin, *Saint Joan*, Richard, *Richard II*, all Old Vic Company, London, 1959-60; Mercutio, *Romeo and Juliet*, Oberon, *Midsummer Night's Dream*, Malvolio, *Twelfth Night*, Old Vic Company, London, all 1960-61; *Not to Worry*, Garrick, London, 1962; Sebastian, *Castle in Sweden*, Piccadilly, London, 1962; Antipholus of Syracuse, *The Comedy of Errors*, Fool, *King Lear*, both with Royal Shakespeare Company, Stratford-on-Avon and Aldwych, London, 1962; Father Riccardo Fontana, *The Representative*, Aldwych, London, 1963; Antipholus of Syracuse, *The Comedy of Errors*, Fool, *King Lear*, both Aldwych, London, 1964; Ronald Gamble, *Thark*, Yvonne Arnaud Theatre, Guildford, then Garrick, London, 1965; The Author, *The Cavern*, Strand, London, 1965; Arthur Henderson, *After the Rain*, Hampstead Theatre Club, Duchess, London, 1966, then Golden, NY, 1967.

Friar William Rolfe, *Hadrian the Seventh*, Birmingham Repertory, Mermaid, London, 1968, then Helen Hayes, NY, 1969; Hamlet, *Hamlet*, Birmingham Repertory, UK, 1970; Philip, *The Philanthropist*, Royal Court, May Fair, London, 1970, then Ethel Barrymore, NY, 1971; Butley, *Butley*, Criterion, London, 1972; Alceste, *The Misanthrope*, National, London, 1973; Martin Dysart, *Equus*, Old Vic, Albery, London, 1973; Professor Higgins, *Pygmalion*, Albery, London, 1974; Alceste, *The Misanthrope*, St. James', NY, then Old

Vic, London, 1975; Ben Musgrave, *The Family Dance*, Criterion, London, 1976; Martin Dysart, *Equus*, Helen Hayes, NY, 1977; Antony, *Antony and Cleopatra*, Prospect Theatre Company, Edinburgh Festival, Scotland, then Old Vic, London, 1977; *St. Mark's Gospel*, Riverside Studios, Mermaid, Comedy, London, then Marymount Manhattan, Playhouse Theater, NY, 1978; Frank, *Tishoo!* Wyndham's, London, 1979; *The Browning Version and Harlequinade*, National, London, 1980; Hitler, *The Portege to San Christabel of A.M.* Mermaid, London, 1982; *Kipling*, Mermaid, London, then Royale, NY, 1984.

MAJOR TOURS—*Love in a Mist*, ENSA, India, Burma, 1945; Antipholus of Syracuse, *The Comedy of Errors*, Fool, *King Lear*, British Counsul Tour, U.S.S.R., Europe, U.S. cities, 1964.

PRINCIPAL STAGE WORK—Director: *While the Sun Shines*, Hampstead Theatre Club, UK, 1972; *St. Mark's Gospel*, UK and U.S. cities.

FILM DEBUT—*The Cruel Sea*, 1952. PRINCIPAL FILM APPEARANCES—*Time without Pity*, 1956; *Loneliness of the Long Distance Runner*, Continental, 1963; *Agony and the Ecstasy*, Twentieth Century-Fox, 1965; *The Devil's Own*, Twentieth Century-Fox, 1967; *A Midsummer Night's Dream*, 1968; *The Hawaiians*, United Artists, 1970; *Frenzy*, Universal, 1971; *Travels with My Aunt*, Metro-Goldwyn-Mayer, 1973; *Stevie*, 1978; *Hanover Street*, Columbia, 1979; *The Assam Garden* (upcoming).

WRITINGS: BOOKS—*Young Gemini*, 1979; *Double Bill*, 1980; *Personal Mask; Mr. Palfrey of Westminster*, 1984.

AWARDS: Evening Standard Award, Best Actor, 1968, for *Hadrian the Seventh;* Variety Club Award, 1970, for *The Philanthropist;* Evening Standard Award, 1973, for *The Misanthrope*.

SIDELIGHTS: MEMBERSHIPS—The Buckstone Club. FAVORITE ROLES—Astrov, *Uncle Vanya*.

ADDRESS: AGENT—STE Representation, 888 Seventh Avenue, New York, NY 10019.

*   *   *

MCDERMOTT, Tom   1912-

PERSONAL: Born July 20, 1912, in McHenry, IL; son of John M. and Mary (Wegner) McDermott; married Mary F. Hayden (an actress), December 20, 1934; children: Miranda, Deborah, Thomas Jr. POLITICS: Democrat. MILITARY: U.S. Army, World War Two.

VOCATION: Actor.

CAREER: STAGE DEBUT—Four roles, *Merry Go Round*, Adelphi, Chicago, IL, 1932. NEW YORK DEBUT—Lt. Roddey, *The Three Sisters*, 1942, 260 performances. PRINCIPAL STAGE APPEARANCES—*The Best Man; Tiger at the Gates; Much Ado About Nothing; Macbeth*, all NY.

MAJOR TOURS—With the Barter Theater, East coast cities, 1946-47.

PRINCIPAL FILM APPEARANCES—Archbishop, *Ghostbusters; Supercops; The Doctor's Story; Playing for Keeps*.

TELEVISION DEBUT—*Captain Video*, 1950. PRINCIPAL TELEVISION APPEARANCES—*Edge of Night; Love of Life; Hallmark Hall of Fame; Studio One; One Life to Live; Search for Tomorrow*.

SIDELIGHTS: MEMBERSHIPS—Actors' Equity Association (past member of council), Screen Actors Guild, American Federation of Television and Radio Artists.

ADDRESS: AGENT—Bret Adams, 448 W. 44th Street, New York, NY 10036.

*   *   *

MCDOWALL, Roddy   1928-

PERSONAL: Born Roderick Andrew McDowall, September 17, 1928, in London; son of Thomas Andrew and Winifred (Corcoran) McDowall. EDUCATION: St. Joseph's College, London and Twentieth Century-Fox Schoolroom, Hollywood; trained for the stage with Mira Rostova and David Craig.

VOCATION: Actor.

CAREER: FILM DEBUT—1938. PRINCIPAL FILM APPEARANCES—*Man Hunt* 1941; *Confirm or Deny*, 1941; *How Green Was My Valley*, 1941; *Son of Fury*, 1942; *The Pied Piper*, 1942; *On the Sunny Side; Lassie Come Home*, 1943; *My Friend Flicka*, 1943; *White Cliffs of Dover*, 1944; *Macbeth*, 1948; *Kidnapped*, 1948; *Big Timber; Tuna Clipper*, 1949; *Black Midnight; Killer Shark*, 1950; *Steel Fist*, 1952; *The Subterraneans*, 1960; *Midnight Lace*, 1960; *The Longest Day*, 1962; *Cleopatra*, 1963; *Shock Treatment*, 1964; *The Greatest Story Ever Told*, 1965; *That Darn Cat*, 1965; *The Loved One*, 1965; *The Third Day*, 1965; *Inside Daisy Clover*, 1965; *Bullwhip Griffin; Lord Love a Duck*, 1966; *The Defector*, 1966; *It*, 1967; *The Cool Ones*, 1967; *The Planet of the Apes*, 1968; *Beneath the Planet of the Apes*, 1970; *Escape from the Planet of the Apes*, 1971; *Conquest of the Planet of the Apes*, 1972; *Poseidon Adventure*, 1972; *Legend of Hellhouse*, 1973; *Arnold*, 1973; *Battle for the Planet of the Apes*, 1973; *Dirty Mary Crazy Larry*, 1974; *Funny Lady*, 1974; *Embryo*, 1975; *Rabbit Test*, 1977; *The Cat from Outer Space*, 1978; *Laserblast*, 1978; *Scavenger Hunt*, 1979; *Charlie Chan and the Curse of the Dragon Queen*, 1981; *Class of 1984*, 1981; *Evil Under the Sun*, 1982; *Fright Night*, Vista, 1985.

PRINCIPAL FILM WORK—Director: *Ballad of Tam Lin*, 1969; *The Devis's Widow*, 1971.

STAGE DEBUT—Roger Woodley, *Young Woodley*, Westport Country Playhouse, CT, 1946. NEW YORK DEBUT—Bentley Summerhayes, *Misalliance*, City Center, 1953. PRINCIPAL STAGE APPEARANCES—Malcolm, *Macbeth*, Salt Lake City Centennial, UT, 1947; Ninian, *The First Mrs. Fraser*, La Jolla Playhouse, CA, 1948; Walton, *Remains to Be Seen*, Alcazar, San Francisco, CA, 1952; Daventry, *Escapade*, 48th Street Theater, NY, 1953; Louis Dubedat, *The Doctor's Dilemma*, Phoenix, NY, 1955; Ariel, *The Tempest*, Octavius, *Julius Caesar*, Stratford Shakespeare Festival, CT, 1955; Ben Witledge, *No Time for Sergeants*, Alvin, NY, 1955; Yegor Gloumov, *The Diary of a Scoundrel*, Phoenix, NY, 1956; Benjamin, *Good as Gold*, Belasco, NY, 1957; Artie Strauss, *Compulsion*, Ambassador, NY, 1957; Pepe, *A Handful of Fire*, Martin Beck, NY, 1958; Marcel Blanchard, *Look After Lulu*, Henry Miller, NY, 1959; Tarquin, *The Fighting Cock*, ANTA, NY, 1959; Mordred, *Camelot*, Majestic, NY, 1960; Claud, *The Astrakhan Coat*, Helen

RODDY MCDOWALL

Hayes, NY, 1967; Fancourt Babberly, *Charlie's Aunt*, 1976; *Otherwise Engaged*, 1978; Elwood P. Dowd, *Harvey*, 1980.

MAJOR TOURS—Lachie, *The Hasty Heart*, CA and AZ cities, 1949-50; *O Mistress Mine*, 1950-51; Richard, *The Youngest*, 1951-52; *Charley's Aunt*, U.S. cities, 1976.

TELEVISION DEBUT—1948. PRINCIPAL TELEVISION APPEARANCES—*Ah! Wilderness; Heart of Darkness; The Tempest; Planet of the Apes* (series), 1975; *Tales of the Gold Monkey* (series), 1982-83; *Hollywood Wives*, ABC, 1984; voice, *Wind in the Willows*, ABC, 1985; March Hare, *Alice in Wonderland*, CBS, 1986.

WRITINGS: BOOKS—*Double Exposure*, 1966.

AWARDS: American Cinema Foundation Award, 1985.

SIDELIGHTS: FAVORITE ROLES—Artie Strauss, *Compulsion*; Ariel, *The Tempest*.

ADDRESS: AGENT—Phil Gersh Agency, 222 N. Cannon Drive, Beverly Hills, CA 90210.

*   *   *

MCFARLAND, Robert   1931-

PERSONAL: Born May 7, 1931, in Omaha, NE.

VOCATION: Actor.

ROBERT MCFARLAND

CAREER: PRINCIPAL STAGE APPEARANCES—Patterson, *The Butter and Egg Man*, Manhattan Punch Line, NY; Lord Stanley, *King Richard III*, Riverside Shakespeare Co., NY; Mr. Myers, *Witness for the Prosecution*, Apple Corps., NY; General MacKenzie, *Ten Little Indians*, Equity Library, NY; Senex, *A Funny Thing Happened on the Way to the Forum*, Hucklebee, *The Fantasticks*, Cecilwood Playhouse; Merchant, *The Comedy of Errors*, Manhattan Punch Line, NY; Grandfather, *Willie at 40, 60, 90, Promenade, All*, Wolfeboro Playhouse; Dean Damon, *The Male Animal*, Manhattan Punch Line, NY; Germio, *The Taming of the Shrew*, Equity Library, NY; Halske, *When the War Was Over*, IRT, NY; Bromhead, *No Sex Please, We're British*, Canal Fulton Dinner Theatre; Pringle, *Funeral Games*, WPA, NY; Minister, *Marry Me, Marry Me*, Playwrights Horizons, NY; Allen, *Getting Gertie's Garter*, Joseph Jefferson.

PRINCIPAL FILM APPEARANCES—*Serpico*, Paramount, 1974; *The Front*, Columbia, 1976; *The Turning Point*, Twentieth Century-Fox, 1977; *Going in Style*, Warner Brothers, 1979; *Prince of the City*, Warner Brothers, 1981; *Trading Places*, Paramount, 1983; *Zelig*, Warner Brothers, 1983.

PRINCIPAL TELEVISION APPEARANCES—*The Adams Chronicles*, PBS; *The Dain Curse*, PBS; *The Andros Targets; Best of Families; Seventh Avenue; Loving; As the World Turns*, CBS; *The Edge of Night*, ABC; *Another World*, NBC; *All My Children*, ABC; *One Life to Live*, ABC; *Search for Tomorrow*, NBC.

SIDELIGHTS: RECREATION—Swimming, skating, riding, bicycling, modeling, fishing, canoeing, rafting, jazz and tap dancing, piano playing, and singing.

ADDRESS: HOME—400 W. 43rd Street, New York, NY 10036.

*   *   *

MCGOVERN, Elizabeth   1961-

PERSONAL: Born July 18, 1961, in Evanston, IL. EDUCATION: Studied at American Conservatory Theatre in San Francisco and at Juilliard, NY.

VOCATION: Actress.

CAREER: FILM DEBUT—Jeannine, *Ordinary People*, Paramount, 1980. PRINCIPAL FILM APPEARANCES—Evelyn Nesbit, *Ragtime*, Paramount, 1981; *Lovesick*, Warner Brothers, 1983; *Once Upon a Time*, Warner Brothers, 1984; *Racing with the Moon*, Paramount, 1984.

STAGE DEBUT—*To Be Young, Gifted, and Black*, Theatre Off Park, NY, 1981. PRINCIPAL STAGE APPEARANCES—*My Sister in This House*, off Broadway production; *The Hotel Play, Dwarf Man, Master of a Million Shapes*, all in Chicago; *Major Barbara*, Alaska Repertory, 1982; *Painting Churches*, off Broadway production.

AWARDS: Theatre World and Obie Awards, 1981-82, for *My Sister in This House;* Academy Award nomination, Best Supporting Actress, for *Ragtime.**

*   *   *

MCINTYRE, Marilyn

PERSONAL: Born May 23, in Erie, PA; daughter of Roger (an engineer for NASA) and Jeanne Ellen (Corzilius) McIntyre. EDUCATION: North Carolina School of the Arts, B.F.A., 1972; Pennsylvania State University, M.F.A., acting program, 1975; studied at the Rose Bruford College of Speech and Drama, Kent, England.

VOCATION: Actress.

CAREER: STAGE DEBUT—Alexandra, *The Little Foxes*, Penn State Festival, 1977. NEW YORK DEBUT—Meg Roberts, *The Perfect Mollusc*, Players, 1977. PRINCIPAL STAGE APPEARANCES—Judith Hastings, *Gemini*, Little, 1980-81; Millie, *Scenes and Revelations*, Production Company, Circle in the Square, NY, 1981; Amy, *Move*, Virginia Museum, 1981; Lika, *The Promise*, Roundabout, NY; understudy, Juliet, *Measure for Measure*, New York Shakespeare Festival; Lupe, *Action*, Off-Off Broadway, NY; Elvira, *Blithe Spirit*, Off-Off Broadway, NY.

The Happy Hunter, PAF Playhouse, Long Island, NY; at Arena Stage, Washington, DC: *Forever Yours, Marie-Lou, Saturday, Sunday, Monday, Death of a Salesman, Our Town;* at the Penn State Festival: *The Seagull, The Glass Menagerie, The Lower Depths;* at the Utah Shakespeare Festival: *Hamlet, As You Like It, Henry VIII;* Christine, *All the Nice People*, TOMI, Park Royal, NY, 1984.

TELEVISION DEBUT—Dr. Carol Hanley, *Search for Tomorrow,* CBS. PRINCIPAL TELEVISION APPEARANCES—Astrid Collins, *One Life to Live,* ABC; Noreen Donovan, *Loving,* ABC; Sydney Galloway, *Ryan's Hope,* ABC; co-host, *On the Road Again: Baseball 82,* syndicated, Major League Baseball Corporation; female lead, *A Glorious System of Things,* PBS; guest co-host, *A.M. New York,* WABC; guest co-host, *Pittsburgh 2-Day,* WDKA, Pittsburgh, PA.

RELATED CAREER: Teacher, teen division, Weist-Baron Acting Studio, NY, 1980-present.

AWARDS: Nancy Reynolds Merit Scholar, North Carolina School of the Arts; member of the Arena Stage Company, Washington, DC, when it was awarded first special Antoinette Perry Award for outstanding work in the regional theatre.

SIDELIGHTS: MEMBERSHIPS—Actors' Equity Association, American Federation of Television and Radio Artists, Screen Actors Guild, Phi Kappa Phi.

McIntyre told *CTFT:* "I enjoy coaching and especially working with teenagers. I love to ski and scuba diving is a favorite."

ADDRESS: AGENT—Don Buchwald & Associates, Ten E. 44th Street, New York, NY 10017.

MARILYN MCINTYRE

McKERN, Leo   1920-

PERSONAL: Born Reginald McKern, March 16, 1920, in Sydney, New South Wales; son of Norman Walton and Vera (Martin) McKern; married Jane Holland, (an artist). EDUCATION: Attended the Sydney Technical School.

VOCATION: Actor.

CAREER: STAGE DEBUT—Chemist, *Uncle Harry,* Theatre Royal, Sydney, Australia, 1944. LONDON DEBUT—Forester, *Love's Labour's Lost,* with the Old Vic Company at the New Theatre, 1949. NEW YORK DEBUT—Thomas Cromwell, *A Man for All Seasons,* ANTA, 1961. PRINCIPAL STAGE APPEARANCES—(All London unless otherwise noted) With the Old Vic company: Jeremy, *She Stoops to Conquer,* 1949, Guildenstern, *Hamlet,* Simon, *The Miser,* Feste, *Twelfth Night,* Nightingale, *Bartholomew Fair,* all 1950, Nym and Sir Thomas Erpingham, *Henry V,* Nym, *The Merry Wives of Windsor,* messenger, *Electra,* confectioner, *The Wedding,* all 1951, Fool, *King Lear,* Apemantus, *Timon of Athens,* both 1952; with the Shakespeare Memorial Theatre Company, Stratford-on-Avon, England: Ulysses, *Troilus and Cressida,* Grumio, *The Taming of the Shrew,* Quince, *A Midsummer Night's Dream,* Friar Lawrence, *Romeo and Juliet,* all 1954; Toad, *Toad of Toad Hall,* Princes, 1954; Traveller, *The Queen and the Rebels,* Haymarket, 1955; Claggart, *The Good Sailor,* Lyric, Hammersmith, 1956.

Big Daddy, *Cat on a Hot Tin Roof,* Comedy, 1958; Tyepkin, *Brouhaha,* Aldwych, 1958; title role, *Rollo,* Strand, 1959; the Common Man, *A Man for All Seasons,* Globe, 1960; Ferrante, *Queen After Death,* Oxford Playhouse, 1961; with the Old Vic company, London: title role, *Peer Gynt,* Subtle, *The Alchemist,* 1962, Iago, *Othello,* 1963; Menenius, *Coriolanus,* Governor, *The Life in My Hands,* both Nottingham Playhouse, 1963-64; Baron Bolligrew, *The Thwarting of Baron Bolligrew,* Aldwych, 1965; title role, *Volpone,* Oxford Playhouse, Garrick, 1966-67; Governor Bligh, *The Man Who Shot the Albatross,* Rollo, *Patate,* both Melbourne, Australia, 1970-71; Shylock, *The Merchant of Venice,* Oxford Playhouse, 1973; Kelemen, *The Wolf,* Oxford Playhouse then Apollo, Queen's, and the New London, 1973; with the Royal Exchange Company, Manchester, England: *Uncle Vanya, Crime and Punishment,* title role, *Rollo,* all 1978; *The Housekeeper,* Apollo, 1981; *Number One,* Queens, 1983.

PRINCIPAL FILM APPEARANCES—*A Man for All Seasons; Ryan's Daughter; The Chain* (upcoming).

PRINCIPAL TELEVISION APPEARANCES—*Rumpole of the Bailey,* 1984; *King Lear,* 1984.

WRITINGS: BOOKS, PUBLISHED—*Just Resting,* Methuen, 1983; introduction to *Volpone,* Longmans, 1985.

AWARDS: Radio Industries Play of the Year, *Rumpole of the Bailey;* Officer of the Australian Order, A.O.

SIDELIGHTS: MEMBERSHIPS—British Actors' Equity Association, National Trust, Amnesty International, Earthcare.

ADDRESS: AGENT—International Creative Management, 388-396 Oxford Street, London W1N 9HE, England.

LEO MCKERN

MCLAIN, John

PERSONAL: EDUCATION: Attended William and Mary College and Carnegie-Mellon.

VOCATION: Lighting designer.

CAREER: PRINCIPAL STAGE WORK—Lighting designer, Broadway: *On Your Toes; Queen of the Rebels; Night of the Tribades; Leaf People; The Three Sisters; Tiny Alice; A Flea in Her Ear; St. Joan; Major Barbara; The Importance of Being Earnest; Eleanor*. Regional: *Mary Stuart*, Ahmansen, Los Angeles; *Oldest Living Graduate*, Los Angeles; *Mass*, Kennedy Center, Washington, DC; *Peter Allen and the Rockettes*, Los Angeles and NY; *Starmania*, Paris; also worked at the following regional theatres: American Conservatory Theater, San Francisco, CA; Seattle Repertory Company, WA; Old Globe, San Diego, CA; Cincinnati Playhouse in the Park, OH; Hartford Stage, CT; Hartman, Stamford, CT; Guthrie, Minneapolis, MN; Goodman, Chicago, IL; Buffalo Arena, NY; American Shakespeare Festival, Stratford, CT; Trinity Square, RI; McCarter, Princeton, NJ; Milwaukee Repertory, WI; State University of New York at Purchase.

Opera: Washington Opera, Kennedy Center, Washington, DC; Spoleto Festival; Geneva Opera House, Switzerland; Vienna State Opera House, Austria.

MAJOR TOURS—Janis Joplin; Steve Lawrence and Edie Gorme; Harry Belafonte; Robert Goulet.

PRINCIPAL FILM WORK—Lighting designer: *Street Heat; Beat Street*.

SIDELIGHTS: MEMBERSHIPS—United Scenic Artists.

ADDRESS: OFFICE—405 E. 54th Street, New York, NY 10022.

MCSHANE, Ian   1942-

PERSONAL: Born September 29, 1942, in Blackburn, Lancaster, England; son of Harry and Irene (Cowley) McShane; married Suzan Farmer (divorced); married Ruth Post. EDUCATION: Trained for the stage at the Royal Academy of Dramatic Art.

VOCATION: Actor.

CAREER: STAGE DEBUT—Charley, *Infanticide in the House of Fred August*, Arts, London, 1962. NEW YORK DEBUT—Marat, *The Promise*, Henry Miller Theater, 1967. PRINCIPAL STAGE APPEARANCES—Johnnie Leigh, *How Are You, Johnnie?*, Vaudeville, London, 1963; Ralph, *The Easter Man*, Globe, London, 1964; Tom, *The Glass Menagerie*, Haymarket, London, 1965; Marat, *The Promise*, Playhouse, Oxford, then Fortune, London, 1967; John Sutcliffe, *Ellen*, Hampstead, 1971; Jacques, *As You Like It*, Long Beach Theater Festival, CA, 1979; Charlie Castle, *The Big Knife*, Watford Palace Theatre, 1982; Robert, *Betrayal*, Actors for Them selves Theater, CA, 1983; Bill Maitland, *Inadmissible Evidence*, Actors for Themselves Theater, CA, 1984, then Matrix, Los Angeles, 1985.

MAJOR TOURS—Hal, *Loot*, U.K. cities, 1965.

PRINCIPAL TELEVISION APPEARANCES—*A Sound from the Sea*, BBC; *Wuthering Heights*, BBC; *A Month in the Country*, BBC;

IAN MCSHANE

High Tide, BBC; Ken Harrison, *Whose Life Is It Anyway?,* BBC; "Disraeli: Portrait of a Romantic," *Masterpiece Theatre;* Judas, *Jesus of Nazareth; The Letter; Bare Essence; Marco Polo; Evergreen; A.D.; The Grace Kelly Story.* Series: *Lovejoy,* BBC. Movie: *Dirty Money.*

FILM DEBUT—*The Wild and the Willing,* 1962. PRINCIPAL FILM APPEARANCES—*Villain; If It's Tuesday, This Must Be Belgium; Pussycat, Pussycat, I Love You; Freelance; Tam Lin; The Battle of Britain; The Last of Sheila; The Terrorists; Yesterday's Hero; Exposed; Torchlight; Too Scared to Scream; Ordeal by Innocence; Cheaper to Keep Her.*

SIDELIGHTS: FAVORITE ROLE—Bill Maitland, *Inadmissible Evidence.* RECREATION—Football, snooker.

ADDRESS: AGENT—Triad, 888 Seventh Avenue, New York, NY 10019; Triad, 10100 Santa Monica Blvd., Los Angeles, CA 90067.

*   *   *

MEADOWS, Audrey

PERSONAL: Born Audrey Cotter, February 8, in Wu Chang, China; daughter of Francis James (a minister) and Ida Miller (Taylor) Cotter; married Robert F. Six (airline chairman emeritus), August 24, 1961. EDUCATION: Miss Hill's School, Great Barrington, MA.

VOCATION: Actress.

AUDREY MEADOWS

CAREER: PRINCIPAL TELEVISION APPEARANCES—Alice, *The Honeymooners; The Jackie Gleason Show; The Carol Burnett Show; The Lily Tomlin Special; Love Boat; Diff'rnt Strokes; Dean Martin Roasts; Dean Martin Show; Red Skelton Show; Bob and Ray Show; Steve Allen Show; Dinah Shore Show; Perry Como Show; Alfred Hitchcock Hour; Jack Benny Show; Tim Conway Show; Jonathan Winters Show; Wagon Train; Man Against Crime; Checkmate; Robert Cummings Dramatic Special; Play of the Week; Too Close for Comfort; Match Game; Hollywood Squares; Name's the Same; Who'll Buy That; Password.*

PRINCIPAL FILM APPEARANCES—*A Touch of Mink; Take Her She's Mine,* Twentieth Century-Fox, 1963; *Rosie.*

AWARDS: Emmy, for *The Honeymooners;* four Emmy nominations; Sylvania; Cartoonist Society of America.

SIDELIGHTS: MEMBERSHIPS—Pearl Buck Foundation (honorary trustee); Hollywood Park Racing Charities Association (director); First National Bank of Denver (director, eleven years).

ADDRESS: OFFICE—9200 Sunset Blvd., Los Angeles, CA 90069. AGENT—Val Irving, 30 Park Avenue, New York, NY 10016.

*   *   *

MEDAK, Peter   1937-

PERSONAL: Born December 23, 1937, in Budapest, Hungary; son of Gyula (a textile manufacturer) and Elisabeth (Diamounstein) Medak; married Carolyn Seymour, December 9, 1973 (divorced, 1984); children: Christopher, Warren, Joshua, Cornelia. EDUCATION: General education in Hungary.

VOCATION: Director.

CAREER: FILM DEBUT—Associate producer, second unit director, *Kaleidoscope,* Warner Brothers, 1966. PRINCIPAL FILM WORK—Second unit director, *Funeral in Berlin;* associate producer, second unit director, *Fathom,* Twentieth Century-Fox, 1967; director for all of following: *Negatives,* Paramount, 1968; *A Day in the Death of Joe Egg,* Columbia, 1969; *The Ruling Class,* AVCO Embassy, 1971; *Ghost in the Noonday Sun,* Columbia, 1973; *Odd Job,* Columbia, 1978; *The Changeling,* AFD, 1979; *Zorro, the Gay Blade,* Twentieth Century-Fox, 1981.

TELEVISION DEBUT—Associate producer, director, *Court Martial,* 1966. PRINCIPAL TELEVISION WORK—Director: *D.H. Lawrence Stories,* British television, 1975; *The Babysitter,* Filmways, ABC, 1980; *Mistress of Paradise,* Lorimar, ABC, 1981; *Hart to Hart* (four episodes), Fox, ABC, 1982; *Cry for the Strangers,* Metro-Goldwyn-Mayer, CBS, 1982; "Pinnocchio," *Fairy Tale Theatre,* Showtime, 1983; "Snow White and the Seven Dwarfs," "Snow Queen," "The Emperor's New Clothes," *Fairy Tale Theatre,* Showtime, 1984; *The Dark Secret of Black Bayou.*

STAGE DEBUT—Director, *Miss Julie,* Arlington Heights, Chicago, 1975.

RELATED WORK—Trainee with ABPC Studios in England from 1956; cutting room, sound department, camera department, assistant director for Carol Reed, David Lean, Fred Zinneman, Joan Little-

PETER MEDAK

wood; began work for MCA Universal in television, 1963; under contract to Paramount, 1967.

SIDELIGHTS: MEMBERSHIPS—Directors Guild of America, Association of British Film and Television Technicians, Directors Guild of Great Britain.

Medak fled to England during the 1956 Hungarian uprising.

ADDRESS: OFFICE—c/o Fred Altman, 9229 Sunset Blvd., Los Angeles, CA 90069.

*   *   *

MEISTER, Brian 1948-

PERSONAL: Born May 3, 1948, in Hillside, NJ; son of Leo and Mildred (Hoff) Meister. EDUCATION: New York University, B.S., 1970.

VOCATION: Stage manager.

CAREER: PRINCIPAL STAGE WORK—Production assistant, Mineola Theatre, Mineola, NY, 1966-67 season: *Take Me Along, Minsky's Burlesque Follies, Luv, Philadelphia, Here I Come, Wait a Minute!;* stage manager, Repertory Theatre of Lincoln Centre, NY, 1971-72 season: *Play Strindberg, Peope Are Living There, The Ride Across Lake Constance, The Duplex, Mary Stuart;* stage manager, *The Mother of Us All,* Off Broadway, 1972; assistant stage manager, Metropolitan Opera, "Opera at the Forum (Mini-Met)," 1973:

Four Saints in Three Acts, Dido and Aeneas, Syllabaire Pour Phedre.

Production stage manager, *King Oedipus, Midsummer Night's Dream Show,* Composers' Showcase, Whitney Museum, NY, 1973; assistant stage manager, *The Merchant,* Broadway, 1977; stage manager, *Lily Tomlin, Appearing Nitely,* Broadway, 1977-78; assistant stage manager, *Hello, Dolly!,* Broadway, 1978; stage manager, *Wings,* Broadway, 1978-79; production stage manager, *Shirley Bassey on Broadway,* 1979; production stage manager, *Modigliani,* Off Broadway, 1979; assistant stage manager, *West Side Story,* Minskoff, NY, 1980; stage manager, *The Little Foxes,* Martin Beck, NY, 1981; stage manager, *Good,* Golden, NY, 1982-83; stage manager, *Private Lives,* Lunt-Fontanne, NY, 1983.

MAJOR TOURS—Stage manager, 1971-72 season, Repertory Theatre of Lincoln Center, national tour; property master, *La Boheme,* Metropolitan Opera Studio East Coast tour, 1973; production stage manager, *The Rothschilds,* summer stock tour, 1973; assistant stage manager, *The Merchant,* pre-Broadway, 1977; stage manager, *Lily Tomlin Appearing Nitely,* pre-Broadway and national tour, 1977-78; stage manager, *Seven Brides for Seven Brothers,* pre-Broadway, 1978; stage manager, *Wings,* pre-Broadway, 1978-79; stage manager, *The Little Foxes,* pre-Broadway, national tour, and London, 1981-82; stage manager, *Private Lives,* pre-Broadway and national tour.

Directed staged readings of *Cold Manhattan Special, The Safest Place, Cucumber Sandwiches Optional, Lightnin' Bugs an' God an' Things.*

SIDELIGHTS: MEMBERSHIPS—Actors' Equity Association, Stage Managers Association.

Meister told *CTFT* that he "would like to direct and produce in the future."

ADDRESS: HOME—One University Place, New York, NY 10003.

*   *   *

MEKKA, Eddie 1952-

PERSONAL: Born Edward Rudolph Mekjian, June 14, 1952, in Worcester, MA; son of Vaughn V. and Mariam (a presser; maiden name, Apkarian) Mekjian. EDUCATION: Worcester Junior College, Associate Degree; studied dancing for five years with Phil Black.

VOCATION: Actor, dancer, choreographer, and writer.

CAREER: STAGE DEBUT—Chorus dancer and singer, *Promises, Promises,* Chateau de Ville, MA, 1971. PRINCIPAL STAGE APPEARANCES—Chorus, *Jumpers,* Billy Rose, NY, 1972; Manny, *The Magic Show,* Cort, NY, 1973; Lieutenant, *The Lieutenant,* Lyceum, NY, 1974.

MAJOR TOURS—*Damn Yankees.*

TELEVISION DEBUT—Carmine Ragusa, *Laverne and Shirley,* ABC, 1976-83. TELEVISION APPEARANCES—Joey DeLuca, *Blansky's Beauties,* ABC, 1977.

WRITINGS: PLAYS, UNPRODUCED—It's Just a Dream (musical).

AWARDS: Drama Desk Award, Best Actor, 1974, for *The Lieutenant;* Antoinette Perry Award nomination, Best Actor in a Musical, 1974, for *The Lieutenant.*

SIDELIGHTS: Mekka has performed his nightclub act throughout the United States.

ADDRESS: AGENT—Ruth Webb, 7500 DeVista Drive, Los Angeles, CA 90046.

* * *

MERIWETHER, Lee 1935-

PERSONAL: Born May 27, 1935, in Los Angeles, CA; daughter of Greg (an accountant) and Ethel (Mulligan) Meriwether; married Frank Aletter (divorced); children: Kyle Kathleen, Lesley Anne. EDUCATION: City College of San Francisco; studied acting with Lee Strasberg and Curt Conway in NY.

VOCATION: Actress.

CAREER: TELEVISION DEBUT—*Philco Television Playhouse,* 1955. PRINCIPAL TELEVISION APPEARANCES—*The New Andy Griffith Show; The Today Show; The FBI; Twelve O'Clock High; Perry Mason; The Man from U.N.C.L.E.; Mission Impossible; Dragnet.* As a series regular appeared in *Clear Horizon,* 1960-62; *The Young Marrieds,* 1964-65; *Time Tunnel,* 1966-67; *Barnaby Jones,* 1973-80. Television movies: *Cruise into Terror,* 1978; *True Grit,* 1978; *Mirror, Mirror,* 1979; *Tourist,* 1980.

FILM DEBUT—*4-D Man,* Universal, 1958. PRINCIPAL FILM AP- PEARANCES—*The Courtship of Eddie's Father,* Metro-Goldwyn- Mayer, 1963; *Batman,* Twentieth Century-Fox, 1966; *Namu, the Killer Whale,* United Artists, 1966; *The Legend of Lylah Clare,* Metro-Goldwyn-Mayer, 1968; *Angel in My Pocket,* Universal, 1969; *The Undefeated,* Twentieth Century-Fox, 1969.

STAGE DEBUT—*Saddle Tramps,* Fishkill Playhouse, NY. NEW YORK DEBUT—*Talent 59.* PRINCIPAL STAGE APPEARANCES— *Follies,* Town & Gown, Birmingham, AL; Lil, *Last Summer at Bluefish Cove,* San Francisco, CA; Bella, *Angel Street,* Fiesta Dinner Playhouse, San Antonio, TX; *Dial M for Murder; A Hatful of Rain.*

PRINCIPAL STAGE WORK—Producer: *The Lion in Winter,* San Francisco, CA, 1984; *The Artful Lodgers,* Los Angeles, CA, 1985.

AWARDS: Emmy nomination, Best Supporting Actress, for *Barnaby Jones;* Miss San Francisco, Miss California, Miss America, 1955; Genie, American Women in Radio and Television; Woman of the Year and Angel of the Year (honorary member).

SIDELIGHTS: MEMBERSHIPS—Actors' Equity Association, Ameri- can Guild of Television and Radio Artists, Screen Actors Guild.

ADDRESS: OFFICE—P.O. Box 402, Encino, CA 91426. AGENT— Mark Levin Associates, 328 S. Beverly Drive, Suite E, Beverly Hills, CA 90212.

LEE MERIWETHER

MICHAELS, Lorne 1944-

PERSONAL: Born Lorne Lipowitz, November 17, 1944, in Toronto, Canada; son of Florence (Becker) Lipowitz; married Rosie Shuster (divorced); married Susan Forristal (an art gallery owner), 1981. EDUCATION: University of Toronto, 1966.

VOCATION: Writer and producer.

CAREER: PRINCIPAL TELEVISION WORK—Writer, *Rowan and Martin's Laugh-In,* 1968-69; writer and producer, comedy specials, CBC, 1969-72; writer and producer, *Lily Tomlin Special* (four), NBC, 1972-75; writer and producer, *Perry Como,* NBC, 1974; writer and producer, *Flip Wilson,* NBC, 1974; creator, producer, and writer, *Saturday Night Live,* NBC, 1975-80; writer and producer, *Beach Boys,* NBC, 1976; writer and producer, *Paul Simon,* NBC, 1977; writer and producer, *The Rutles: All You Need Is Cash,* NBC, 1978; producer, *Steve Martin's Best Show Ever,* NBC, 1981; executive producer, *Simon and Garfunkel: The Concert in Central Park,* HBO, 1981; producer, *The New Show,* NBC, 1984.

RELATED CAREER—President, Broadway Video, 1979-present.

AWARDS: Emmy Awards, 1973 for *Lily,* 1975 for *Lily Tomlin,* 1976 and 1977 for *Saturday Night Live,* 1978 for *Paul Simon Special;* San Francisco Film Award, 1976; four Writers Guild Awards.

SIDELIGHTS: MEMBERSHIPS—American Federation of Television

and Radio Artists, Writers Guild of America (board member), Beard's Fund, Astoria Foundation.

ADDRESS: OFFICE—Broadway Video, 1619 Broadway, New York, NY 10019.

*   *   *

MICHELL, Keith   1928-

PERSONAL: Born December 1, 1928, in Adelaide, South Australia; son of Joseph (a furniture manufacturer) and Maud Alice (Aslat) Michell; married Jeannette Laura Sterke (an actress and art instructor), October 18, 1957; children: Paul Joseph, Helena Elizabeth Anne. EDUCATION: Port Pirie High School; Adelaide Teachers' College; South Australia School of Arts and Crafts; Adelaide University, qualified as teacher of Art, 1948; studied for the theatre at the Old Vic Theatre School in London.

VOCATION: Actor and artist.

CAREER: DEBUT—Roger, *Lover's Leap*, Playbox, Adelaide, South Australia, 1947. LONDON DEBUT—Charles II, *And So to Bed* (musical), New, 1951. NEW YORK DEBUT—Nestor and Oscar, *Irma La Douce*, Plymouth, 1960. PRINCIPAL STAGE APPEAR-ANCES—Bassanio, *The Merchant of Venice*, Young Vic Company, 1950; appeared in *The Taming of the Shrew*, *A Midsummer Night's Dream*, *Troilus and Cressida*, and *Romeo and Juliet*, Stratford-on-Avon, 1954; MacDuff, *Macbeth*, Master Ford, *The Merry Wives of Windsor*, Orsino, *Twelfth Night*, and Parolles, *All's Well That Ends Well*, Shakespeare Memorial Theatre, Stratford-on-Avon, 1955; Don Juan, *Don Juan*, Royal Court, London, 1956; Benedick, *Much Ado About Nothing*, Proteus, *The Two Gentlemen of Verona*, Antony, *Antony and Cleopatra*, and Aaron, *Titus Andronicus*, Old Vic, 1956; Nestor and Oscar, *Irma La Douce*, Lyric, London, 1958; Vicomte de Valmont, *The Art of Seduction*, Aldwych, 1962; Don John, *The Chances*, Ithocles, *The Broken Heart*, Chichester Festival, 1962; Count, *The Rehearsal*, Royale, NY, 1963; Robert Browning, *Robert and Elizabeth*, Lyric, London, 1964.

Kain Sutherland, *Kain*, Yvonne Arnaud, Guildford, England, 1966; Henry VIII, *The King's Mare*, Garrick, London, 1966; *The Fire of London*, Mermaid, London, 1966; Don Quixote (Cervantes), *Man of La Mancha*, Piccadilly, London, 1968, then at the Martin Beck, NY, 1969; Peter Abelard, *Abelard and Heloise*, Wyndham's, London, 1970, then in Los Angeles and at the Brooks Atkinson, NY, 1971; Hamlet, *Hamlet*, Bankside Globe, London, 1972; Robert Browning, *Dear Love*, Comedy, London, 1973; director, *Tonight We Improvise*, Oidipus, *Oidipus Tyrannus*, Keith Michell in Concert, all Chichester Festival, 1974; Cyrano, *Cyrano de Bergerac*, and Iago, *Othello*, Chichester Festival, 1975 and Hong Kong Arts Festival, 1976; Major Mathieu, *M. Perichon's Travels*, 1976; Magnus, *The Apple Cart*, Becket, *Murder in the Cathedral*, Chichester Festival, 1977; Magnus, *The Apple Cart*, Phoenix, London, 1977; Sherlock Holmes, *The Crucifer of Blood*, Haymarket, London, 1979; Oscar Jaffee, *On the Twentieth Century*, Her Majesty's, 1980; Pete McGynty, *Pete McGynty and the Dreamtime*, Melbourne Theatre Company, 1981; *Captain Beaky Christmas Show*, London, 1981-82; *On the Rocks*, Chichester Festival, 1982; Prospero, *The Tempest*, Brisbane, Australia, 1982; Georges, *La Cage aux Folles*, San Francisco, 1984, Palace, NY, 1984, then Sydney, Australia, 1985.

MAJOR TOURS—Orlando, *As You Like It*, Hotspur, *Henry IV, Part I*, Shakespeare Memorial Theatre Company Australian tour, 1952-53; Thomas, *The Lady's Not for Burning*, New Zealand tour, 1954-55; Nestor and Oscar, *Irma La Douce*, Washington, DC (U.S. debut) and pre-Broadway tour, 1960; *The First Four Hundred Years, in Celebration of the Shakespeare Quatercentenary*, with Googie Withers, toured Australia, New Zealand, 1964; Magnus, *The Apple Cart*, Luxembourg, Brussels, 1977; Othello, *Othello*, Magnus, *The Apple Cart*, with Chichester Festival Company, Australia tour, 1977; Salieri, *Amadeus*, tour, 1983.

PRINCIPAL STAGE WORK—Director: artistic director, Chichester Festival, 1974-present: *Twelfth Night*, 1976; *In Order of Appearance*, 1977. Michell also designed *Twelfth Night* and devised and designed *In Order of Appearance*.

FILM DEBUT—*True as a Turtle*, 1956. PRINCIPAL FILM APPEAR-ANCES—*Dangerous Exile*, Rank, 1957; *The Gypsy and the Gentleman*, Rank, 1958; *The Hellfire Club*, Embassy, 1961; *Seven Seas to Calais*, Metro-Goldwyn-Mayer, 1963; *Prudence and the Pill*, Twentieth Century-Fox, 1968; *House of Cards*, Universal, 1968; *Henry VIII and His Six Wives*, Levitt-Pickman, 1973; *Moments*.

PRINCIPAL TELEVISION APPERANCES—Higgins, *Pygmalion*; Heathcliffe, *Wuthering Heights*; Mark Antony, *Spread of the Eagle* (a series composed of *Julius Caesar* and *Antony and Cleopatra*); Kain Sutherland, *Kain*; Henry VIII, *The Six Wives of Henry VIII*; Robert Browning, *Dear Love*; Captain Beaky, *Captain Beaky and His Band*, and *Captain Beaky, Volume 2*; Robin Oakapple, *Ruddigore*; Grand Inquisitor, *The Gondoliers*; Major General Stanley, *The Pirates of Penzance*; *Act of Violence*; *Mayerling Affair*; *The Bergonzi Hand*; *Ring Around the Moon*; *The Shifting Heart*; *Loyalties*; *An Ideal Husband*; *Keith Michell Special*; *Keith Michell Christmas Show*; *Keith Michell at the Shows*; *Keith Michell in Concert at Chichester*; *Traveller without Luggage*; *Tiger at the Gates*; dual role, *The Great Impersonation*; *The Story of the Marlboroughs*; *The Day Christ Died*.

RECORDINGS: Ancient and Modern; At the Shows; Words, Words, Words; The Sonnets and the Prophet; Captain Beaky and His Band; Captain Beaky, Volume 2.

AWARDS: London Critics, Best Actor in a Musical, *Man of La Mancha*, 1968; Society of Film and Television Arts, Best Actor, 1970; Show Business Personality of the Year (Grand Order of Water Rats), 1971; Sun Television Award, Top Actor, 1971; Royal Variety Club of Great Britain, Special Award, 1971; Royal Academy of Television Arts, Outstanding Single Performance by an Actor, 1971; *Evening News*, British Film Award, 1973; Logie Award, Australia, 1974.

SIDELIGHTS: MEMBERSHIPS—Artistic director, Chichester Festival. RECREATION—Painting, photography, swimming, riding.

Michell was formerly an art teacher. The following works of his have been displayed: *Jamaica*, paintings, 1960; *New York*, 1962; *Portugal*, 1963; *Outback in Australia*, 1965; *Don Quixote*, Wright-Hepburn Gallery, NY, 1969; *Don Quixote*, 1970; *Abelard & Heloise*, 1972; *Hamlet*, 1972; *Self-Portrait, Henry VIII*, screen print edition of 70, Kelpra Studios, 1972; *Piktors Metamorphosis*, lithograph edition of 1000, Curwen Studios, 1973; *Shakespeare Sonnets*, 12 lithographs in portfolio, edition of 100, Curwen Studios, 1974 (published in book form by Landsdowne Press, Melbourne, 1981 deluxe edition of 500); illustrations for *Captain Beaky*, and *Captain Beaky, Volume 2*, 1975; illustrations, *Alice in Wonderland*, for a

BBC presentation; illustrations, *Pete McGynty*, his adaptation of *Peer Gynt*, 1985.

ADDRESS: AGENT—Michael Linnit, Chatto & Linnit, Prince of Wales Theatre, Coventry Street, London W1V 7FE, England.

*   *   *

MILLER, Barry   1958-

PERSONAL: Born February 6, 1958, in Los Angeles, CA; married Marci Phillips, 1983.

VOCATION: Actor.

CAREER: FILM DEBUT—Bobby C., *Saturday Night Fever*, Paramount, 1977. PRINCIPAL FILM APPEARANCES—Ralph Garcy, *Fame*, Metro-Goldwyn-Mayer, 1980; Reuven Malter, *The Chosen*, Twentieth Century-Fox, 1982; Parker, *Natty Gann*, Disney, 1985; Henry "Hub" Palamountin, *The Roommate*, American Playhouse Films, 1985.

NEW YORK STAGE DEBUT—Bernie, *My Mother, My Father, and Me*, W.P.A., 1980. PRINCIPAL STAGE APPEARANCES—Ricky, *Forty Deuce*, Perry Street, NY, 1981; Caliban, *The Tempest*, New York Shakespeare Festival, Delacorte, NY, 1981; Arnold Epstein, *Biloxi Blues*, Neil Simon, NY, 1985.

AWARDS: Villager Award, Best Actor, 1981, for *Forty Deuce;* Outer Critics Circle Award, Drama Desk Award, Antoinette Perry Award, all 1985, for *Biloxi Blues*.

ADDRESS: AGENT—Biff Liff, William Morris Agency, 1350 Avenue of the Americas, New York, NY 10019.

*   *   *

MILLER, David   1909-

PERSONAL: Born November 28, 1909, in Paterson, NJ; son of Samuel Michael (an importer) and Yetta Brondel (Leizerovitz) Miller; married Francis Raeburn (divorced); married Sara Manney; children: Jeffrey, Jessica. EDUCATION: DeWitt Clinton High School. MILITARY: U.S. Army Signal Corps, 1942-46, Major.

VOCATION: Director.

CAREER: FILM DEBUT—Assistant film editor, Columbia, 1931. PRINCIPAL FILM WORK—Director: *Billy the Kid*, Metro-Goldwyn-Mayer, 1941; *Sunday Punch*, Metro-Goldwyn-Mayer, 1942; *Flying Tigers*, Republic, 1942; *Seeds of Destiny*, U. S. War Department, 1946; *Love Happy*, United Artists, 1949; *Top o' the Morning*, 1949; *Our Very Own*, RKO, 1950; *Saturday's Hero*, Columbia, 1951; *Sudden Fear*, RKO, 1952; *Twist of Fate*, United Artists, 1954; *Diane*, Metro-Goldwyn-Mayer, 1955; *The Opposite Sex*, Metro-Goldwyn-Mayer, 1955; *The Story of Esther Costello*, Columbia, 1956; *Happy Anniversary*, United Artists, 1959; *Midnight Lace*, Universal, 1961; *Back Street*, Universal, 1961; *Lonely Are the Brave*, Universal, 1962; *Captain Newman, M.D.*, Universal, 1963; *Hammerhead*, Columbia, 1968; *Hail, Hero!*, Cinema Central, 1969; *Executive*

DAVID MILLER

Action, National General, 1973; *Bittersweet Love*, Embassy, 1976.

PRINCIPAL FILM WORK—Short subjects: director—*Crew Racing*, Metro-Goldwyn-Mayer, 1935; *Table Tennis, Racing Canines, Aquatic Artistry, Dare Deviltry, Trained Hoofs, Let's Dance*, all Metro-Goldwyn-Mayer, 1936; Pete Miller specialties: *Hurling*, Metro-Goldwyn-Mayer, 1936; *Dexterity, Gilding the Lily, Penny Wisdom, Tennis Tactics, Equestrian Acrobatics*, all Metro-Goldwyn-Mayer, 1937, *La Savate, Penny's Party, Modeling for Money, Fisticuffs*, all Metro-Goldwyn-Mayer, 1938; *Crime Does Not Pay* series, "Drunk Driving," Metro-Goldwyn-Mayer, 1939; assisted Frank Capra on the *Why We Fight* series, 1942-44; *The Happiest Man on Earth*.

PRINCIPAL TELEVISION WORK——Director: *The Best Place to Be*, 1979; *Goldie and the Boxer*, 1979; *Love for Rent*, 1979; *Goldie and the Boxer Go to Hollywood*, 1981.

AWARDS: Academy of Motion Picture Arts and Sciences Award, 1937, for *Penny Wisdom*, 1946, for *Seeds of Destiny;* Academy Award nomination, 1939, for *Crime Does Not Pay*, "Drunk Driving," 1939; Dutch Treat Club Award, *The Happiest Man on Earth*.

SIDELIGHTS: MEMBERSHIPS—Directors Guild of America (trustee, foundation committee), Academy of Motion Picture Arts and Sciences.

According to Miller's official biography, he began his long career in motion pictures as a messenger for National Screen Service in New York, then became a writer of "catch lines" for trailers. His Hollywood work began in the editing room as an assistant at

Columbia Pictures, moving on to full-fledged editor with Walter Futter Productions. In 1933 he moved to Metro-Goldwyn-Mayer as a short subjects editor.

His film, *Seeds of Destiny,* is the only film to win an Academy Award without having a commercial theatrical release. Since 1946 it has been shown extensively on a non-theatrical basis and has helped raise $300 million dollars for the United Nations Relief and Rehabilitation Agency.

ADDRESS: OFFICE—1843 Thayer Avenue, Los Angeles, CA 90025.

*   *   *

MILLER, Penelope Ann   1964-

PERSONAL: Born Penelope Andrea Miller, January 13, 1964; daughter of Mark (an actor and filmmaker) and Beatrice (a journalist; maiden name, Ammidown) Miller. EDUCATION: Trained for the stage at Herbert Berghof Studios with Herbert Berghof.

VOCATION: Actress.

CAREER: PRINCIPAL STAGE WORK—Meredith, *The People from Work,* Herbert Berghof Playhouse, NY, 1984; Daisy Hannigan, *Biloxi Blues,* Neil Simon, NY, 1984-85.

PRINCIPAL TELEVISION APPEARANCES—Nancy O'Hara, *The Guiding Light,* CBS, 1984; Lee Melton, *As the World Turns,* CBS, 1984.

SIDELIGHTS: MEMBERSHIPS—Actors' Equity Association, American Federation of Television and Radio Artists.

ADDRESS: AGENT—Robert Beseda, Coleman-Rosenberg Agency, 210 E. 58th Street, New York, NY 10022.

*   *   *

MILLETT, Tim   1954-

PERSONAL: Accent on second syllable of last name, as in Gillette; born December 24, 1954, in Erie, PA; son of Albert N. and Mildred J. (Cassidy) Millett. EDUCATION: Western Kentucky University, B.A., theatre, dance minor, 1976; special training with Dance Educators of America, NY, ballet and musical theatre arts degree, 1975.

VOCATION: Actor, dancer, choreographer, and director.

CAREER: STAGE DEBUT—Dancer, *Irene,* Kenley Players, Warren, OH. NEW YORK DEBUT—Zach, *A Chorus Line,* Shubert, 1981. PRINCIPAL STAGE APPEARANCES—Dancer, *Pal Joey,* Los Angeles, 1978; dancer, *Spotlight,* Washington, DC, 1978; Clifton Webb, *Red, Hot & Cole,* Los Angeles, 1979.

MAJOR TOURS—Don Kerr, *A Chorus Line,* international tour, 1979-80, national tour, 1980, bus & truck, 1980-81.

TIM MILLET

PRINCIPAL STAGE WORK—Choreographer: *Carousel, My Fair Lady, Hello, Dolly!, South Pacific,* Village Dinner Theatre, PA; *Country Gold, Country Jamboree,* Six Flags Mountain Amusement Park, Los Angeles, CA; *The Buck Stops Here,* AMAS Repertory, NY, Arrow Rock Lyceum, MO, Smithsonian Institute, Washington, DC.

Director and choreographer: *A Day in Hollywood/A Night in the Ukraine,* Tommy Brent's Theatre-by-the-Sea, RI; *Prime Time,* 78th Street Theatre Lab, NY; *Hooray for Hollywood, Meet Me in St. Louis,* Three Little Bakers Dinner Theatre, DE; *The Sound of Music,* Three Little Bakers Dinner Theatre, DE, 1985.

TELEVISION DEBUT—Dancer, *Mary,* MTM Productions, CBS, 1978. PRINCIPAL TELEVISION APPEARANCES—*The Mary Tyler Moore Hour,* CBS, 1979; *The Fifth Annual Peoples Choice Awards,* 1979; *The Cheryl Ladd Special-Souvenirs,* 1979.

PRINCIPAL TELEVISION WORK—Choreographer, *Tapdancin',* CBS Cable.

ADDRESS: HOME—796 Ninth Avenue, Apt. 2, New York, NY 10019.

*   *   *

MINEO, John   1942-

PERSONAL: Born October 26, 1942, in New York City; son of

JOHN MINEO

Isidor Jack (a meat packer) and Marie Lucy (a seamstress; maiden name, Danoto) Mineo; children: Bremen Allene, Jarad Damian. EDUCATION: High School of the Performing Arts, NY.

VOCATION: Choreographer, dancer, actor, and director.

CAREER: NEW YORK DEBUT—Baby John, *West Side Story,* Winter Garden, 1960. PRINCIPAL STAGE APPEARANCES—*Bye Bye Birdie,* Shubert, NY; *Henry Sweet Henry,* Palace, NY; Barnaby Tucker, *Hello, Dolly!,* St. James, NY; *George M!,* Palace, NY; *The Rothchilds,* Lunt-Fontanne, NY; *Lolita* (pre-Broadway); *On the Town* (revival); *Sugar;* Executioner, *Pippin,* Imperial, NY; Louis Lementier, *Lorelei,* Imperial, NY; Lucky, *Over Here,* Shubert, NY; Al, *A Chorus Line,* Shubert, NY; *Dancin',* Broadhurst, NY; *One Night Stand,* Nederlander, NY; *Zorba* (revival), Broadway Theatre, NY.

MAJOR TOURS—*West Side Story,* Australian Company, Guber, Gross & Ford circuit; *Bye Bye Birdie,* St. Louis Municipal Opera; *George M!,* national tour; *Zorba,* national tour.

PRINCIPAL STAGE WORK—Choreographer and director: *Becoming,* Circle in the Square, NY; *You Can't Lose,* Dance Theatre Workshop; *Over Here,* Playhouse on the Mall, Paramus, NJ; full length ballet, Dover, Delaware Ballet Company; assistant choreographer for Broadway productions of *Barnum, George M!, Lorelei, Sugar, Over Here.*

PRINCIPAL TELEVISION APPEARANCES—*Naked City; Kraft Music Hall; Andy Williams Show; Perry Como Show; Bob Hope Special; The Ed Sullivan Show; Merv Griffin Show; Mike Douglas Show;* "The Littlest Angel," *Hallmark Hall of Fame; Pippin.*

PRINCIPAL FILM APPEARANCE—*Curse of the Pink Panther.*

SIDELIGHTS: Mineo expressed his feeling about his work to *CTFT* in these words: "This is a business, not show—and don't talk to me about art."

ADDRESS: AGENT—Karen Garber, Honey Sanders Agency Ltd. 229 W. 42nd Street, New York, NY 10036.

*   *   *

MINEO, Salvatore   1939-76

PERSONAL: Born January 10, 1939; died February 12, 1976; son of Salvatore and Josephine Mineo.

VOCATION: Actor.

CAREER: FILM DEBUT—*Seven Bridges to Cross,* 1955. PRINCIPAL FILM APPEARANCES—*Rebel without a Cause,* Warner Brothers, 1955; *Crime in the Streets,* Allied Artists, 1956; *Giant,* Warner Brothers, 1956; *Somebody Up There Likes Me,* Metro-Goldwyn-Mayer, 1957; *The Young Don't Cry,* Columbia, 1957; *Dino,* Allied Artists, 1957; *Tonka,* Buena Vista, 1958; *A Private's Affairs,* Twentieth Century-Fox, 1959; *The Gene Krupa Story,* 1959; *Exodus,* 1961; *Escape from Zahrain,* Paramount, 1962; *Cheyenne Autumn,* Warner Brothers, 1964; *The Greatest Story Ever Told,* United Artists, 1965; *Who Killed Teddy Bear,* Magna, 1965; *Krakatoa, East of Java,* Cinerama, 1969; *Escape from the Planet of the Apes,* Twentieth Century-Fox, 1971.

PRINCIPAL TELEVISION APPEARANCES—*Ellery Queen; Joe Forrester; My Three Sons.*

AWARDS: Academy Award nominations, Best Supporting Actor, 1955, for *Rebel without a Cause,* 1961, for *Exodus.**

*   *   *

MIRREN, Helen   1946-

VOCATION: Actress.

CAREER: STAGE DEBUT—Cleopatra, *Anthony and Cleopatra,* Old Vic, London, 1965. PRINCIPAL STAGE APPEARANCES—Kitty, *Charley's Aunt,* Nerissa, *The Merchant of Venice,* Manchester, UK, 1967; Castiza, *The Revenger's Tragedy,* Diana, *All's Well That Ends Well,* Royal Shakespeare Company, Stratford-on-Avon, 1967; Cressida, *Troilus and Cressida,* Aldwych, London, 1968; Hero, *Much Ado About Nothing,* Aldwych, London, 1968, 1969; Susie Monmican, *The Silver Lassie;* Win-the-Fight Littlewit, *Bartholomew Fair;* Lady Anne, *Richard III,* Ophelia, *Hamlet,* Julia, *The Two Gentlemen of Verona,* Royal Shakespeare Company, Stratford-on-Avon, 1970.

Tatyana, *Enemies,* Harriet, *The Man of Mode,* Miss Julie, *Miss Julie,* Elayne, *The Balcony,* Royal Shakespeare Company, Aldwych, London, 1971; Lady Macbeth, *Macbeth,* Royal Shakespeare Company, Stratford-on-Avon, 1974, then Aldwych, London, 1975; Maggie, *Teeth 'n' Smiles,* Royal Court, London, 1975, then Wyndhams, London, 1976; Nina, *The Seagull,* Ella, *The Bed Before Yesterday,* Lyric, London, 1975; Queen Margaret, *Henry VI, Parts I, II,* and *III,* Royal Shakespeare Company, Stratford-on-Avon, 1977, then Aldwych, London, 1978; Isabella, *Measure for Measure,* Riverside Studio, London, 1974.

PRINCIPAL FILM APPEARANCES—*Age of Consent,* Columbia, 1969; *Savage Messiah,* Metro-Goldwyn-Mayer, 1972; *O Lucky Man,* Warner Brothers, 1973; *Cal,* 1984; *2010,* 1984; *White Nights.*

ADDRESS: AGENT—Al Parker Ltd., 50 Mount Street, London W1, England.*

*   *   *

MITCHELL, Warren   1926-

PERSONAL: Born 1926, in London; married Constance Wake. EDUCATION: Trained for the stage at the Royal Academy of Dramatic Art.

VOCATION: Actor.

CAREER: STAGE DEBUT—Finsbury Park Open Air Theatre, UK, 1950. PRINCIPAL STAGE APPEARANCES—Theophile, *Can Can,* Coliseum, London, 1954; Crookfinger Jake, *The Threepenny Opera,* Royal Court, Aldwych, London, 1956; Mr. Godboy, *Dutch Uncle,* Royal Shakespeare Company, Aldwych, London, 1969; Satan, *Council of Love,* Criterion, London, 1970; Herbert, *Jump,* Queen's, London, 1971; Ion Will, *The Great Caper,* Royal Court, London, 1974; *The Thoughts of Chairman Alf,* Stratford East, UK, 1976; Lear, *King Lear,* Sydney, Australia, 1978; Willy Loman, *Death of a Salesman,* Playhouse, Perth, Australia, 1979, then National Theater, Lyttleton, London, 1979; Davies, *The Caretaker,* National Theater, London; *Ducking Out,* Duke of York's, London.

MAJOR TOURS—*The Thoughts of Chairman Alf,* UK and Australian cities.

PRINCIPAL FILM APPEARANCES—*All the Way Up; Moon Zero Two; Meeting with Remarkable Men; Arrivederci Baby; Charlie Farthing; The Chain; Knights and Emeralds.*

PRINCIPAL TELEVISION APPEARANCES—*Till Death Us Do Part,* BBC; *Moss,* BBC; Shylock, *The Merchant of Venice,* BBC; Davies, *The Caretaker,* BBC. Australian television: *Waterfront; Man of Letters; Dunera Boys.*

AWARDS: SWET Award, Best Actor, 1979, for *Death of a Salesman.*

ADDRESS: AGENT—International Creative Management, 388-396 Oxford Street, London W1, England.

WARREN MITCHELL

MODINE, Matthew

BRIEF ENTRY: Born in Loma Linda, CA; trained with Stella Adler. Actor. Modine initially appeared in several television commercials and in the daytime soap opera, *Texas.* He also had a role in the *ABC After School Special,* "Amy and the Angel."

His first feature film was *Baby, It's You,* Paramount, 1983, and he had a starring role in the movie *Private School,* Universal, 1983. For his performance as Billy in *Streamers,* Modine won the 1983 Venice Film Festival's Best Actor Award. In the film adaptation of John Irving's novel, *The Hotel New Hampshire,* he played two roles: Chipper Dove and Ernst. In *Vision Quest,* Warner Brothers, 1984, he starred as a high school wrestling champion, and he played the role of Jack Biddle in *Mrs. Soffel,* Metro-Goldwyn-Mayer, 1984. He was seen most recently in the film *Birdy,* based on the book by William Wharton.*

*   *   *

MOKAE, Zakes

BRIEF ENTRY: Born in South Africa. Actor and director. Mokae started by playing the sax in the 1950's which led to his appearance in several of Athol Fugard's plays. In 1961, he was in *Blood Knot* in London's West End and shortly after appeared in the BBC production of the same. He enrolled at the Royal Academy of Dramatic Art and British Drama League.

His American debut was in 1969, in *Boesman and Lena*, at Circle in the Square, NY. He enrolled in the American Film Institute and is now a directing fellow there. His other stage credits include: *The Cherry Orchard*, Public, NY; *Fingernails Blue as Flowers* and *Last Days of British Honduras*, both at the American Place, NY; *Trial of Vessay*, New York Dramatists. Other European productions include *Othello, Macbeth, Waiting for Godot, Krapp's Last Tape, Tall Maidens, No Good Friday*, and *The Tempest*. On Broadway, he appeared in *Master Harold . . . and the Boys* and *A Lesson from Aloes. Master Harold . . .* was also presented on Showtime in 1984. Recently he did *Lion and Jewel* and *Brother Jero* at the Inglewood Playhouse, CA. His film credits include: *Darling*, Embassy, 1965; *The Comedians*, Metro-Goldwyn-Mayer, 1967; *Tremor; Dilemma; Legends of Fear; Darkest Africa; The River Niger*, 1976. His directing credits include *Boesman and Lena*, Canada; *Angel Feathers on the Roof*, Johannesburg; *I'm a Come Home Chile*, London. He has taught at the American Conservatory Theatre, San Francisco.*

*   *   *

MONK, Isabell   1952–

PERSONAL: Born October 4, 1952, in Washington, DC; daughter of Henry (a laborer) and Jane Dorothy (a beautician; maiden name, Barnett) Monk. EDUCATION: Towson State University, B.A.; Yale University School of Drama, M.F.A. RELIGION: Catholic.

CAREER: PRINCIPAL STAGE APPEARANCES—At the Yale Repertory: Maxim's girl, *Tales from Vienna Woods*, Ghost, ensemble, *Ubu Rex*, Timandra, *Timon of Athens*, understudy Lena, *Boesman and Lena*, Lady Day, Miss Lady, *The Resurrection of Lady Lester;* Momma, daughter, *Slow Drag Momma*, Actors Theatre of Louisville; at the Guthrie, Minneapolis, MN: Dorine, *Tartuffe*, Baroness, ensemble, *Candide*, Nancy, *Requiem for a Nun; The Tempest*, New York Shakespeare Festival, NY.

MAJOR TOURS—Louisa Mae, *Rupert's Birthday*, Actors Theatre of Louisville, Budapest; Rodeo, French Fries, *Talking With*, Actors Theatre of Louisville, Australia; Antigone, Sister Bea, *The Gospel at Colonus*, Narrator, *Sister Sue Cinema*, United Kingdom, France, Belgium and Brooklyn Academy of Music, NY.

PRINCIPAL FILM APPEARANCES—*The World According to Garp*, Warner Brothers, 1982; *Lovesick*, Warner Brothers, 1983; *Swing Shift*, Warner Brothers, 1984.

PRINCIPAL TELEVISION APPEARANCES—*Benson*, ABC; *Family Ties*, NBC; *Mr. Smith*, ABC; *Isy Monk—We Ain't What We Was*, PBS. Television movies: *Senior Trip*, CBS, 1981; *Girls of the White Orchid*, NBC, 1983; *When She Says No*, ABC, 1984; *Calamity Jane*, CBS, 1984; *Second Sight—A Love Story*, CBS, 1984.

ADDRESS: AGENT—STE Representation Ltd., 888 Seventh Avenue, New York, NY 10106.

*   *   *

MOODY, Ron ˙ 1924–

PERSONAL: Born Ronald Moodnick, January 8, 1924, in London; son of Bernard and Kate (Ogus) Moodnick. EDUCATION: London

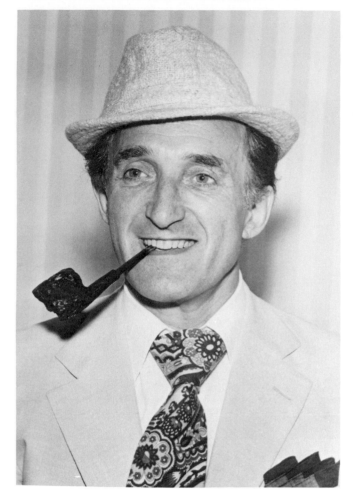

RON MOODY

School of Economics, London University, B.Sc.

VOCATION: Actor.

CAREER: STAGE DEBUT—*Intimacy at Eight*, New Lindsey, London, 1952. PRINCIPAL STAGE APPEARANCES—*Intimacy at 8:30*, Criterion, London, 1954; *For Amusement Only*, Apollo, London, 1956; *For Adults Only*, Strand, London, 1958; Governor of Buenos Aires, *Candide*, Saville, London, 1959; Fagin, *Oliver!*, New, London, 1960; Joey, *Joey, Joey*, Bristol Old Vic, UK, 1962; Mr. Darling and Captain Hook, *Peter Pan*, Scala, London, 1966; Aristophanes, *Liz*, Marlowe Theater, Canterbury, UK, 1968; *Royal Command Performance*, Palladium, London, 1968; Polonius and First Gravedigger, *Hamlet*, Bankside Globe, London, 1971.

MAJOR TOURS—*Move Along Sideways*, U.S. and U.K. cities.

PRINCIPAL STAGE WORK—Director, *Saturnalia*, Belgrade, Coventry, UK, 1971.

Captain Hook, *Peter Pan*, Coliseum, London, 1972; Fagin, *Oliver!*, Los Angeles, and San Francisco, CA, 1973; Mr. Sterling, *The Clandestine Marriage*, Savoy, London, 1975; Captain Hook, *Peter Pan*, Palladium, London, 1975; Showman, *The Showman*, Theatre Royal, Stratford East, UK, 1976; Mr. Darling and Captain Hook, *Peter Pan*, London Casino, 1977; Richard, *Richard III*, Canada,

1978; *Marino Faliero*, Young Vic, London, 1982; Fagin, *Oliver!*, Aldwych, London, 1983, then NY, 1984.

FILM DEBUT—*Davy*, 1953. PRINCIPAL FILM APPEARANCES—*Murder Most Foul;* Fagin, *Oliver!*, 1969; *Dominique; The Spaceman; King Arthur; The Twelve Chairs; Dogpound Shuffle; Wrong Is Right; The Fetchit; Where Is Parsifal?*

TELEVISION DEBUT—1953. PRINCIPAL TELEVISION APPEARANCES—*Is That Your Body, Boy?; Taste; Baden Powell; The Word; Nobody's Perfect; Dial M for Murder*, 1981; *Hart to Hart*, 1981; Iago, *Othello*, 1981; *Other Side of London*, 1983; *Highway to Heaven*, 1984; *Murder, She Wrote*, 1985; *Caucasian Chalk Circle*, Thames, 1985; *Hideaway*, BBC, 1985.

WRITINGS: PLAYS, PRODUCED—Book, music, and lyrics, *Joey, Joey*, Bristol Old Vic, UK, 1962; story and music, *Saturnalia*, Belgrade, Coventry, UK, 1971; book, lyrics, and music, *The Showman*, Theatre Royal, Stratford East, UK, 1976. BOOKS—*The Devil You Don't*, 1979; *Very, Very, Slightly Imperfect*, 1983.

AWARDS: Academy Award nomination, Best Actor, for *Oliver!;* Antoinette Perry Award nomination, Theatre World Award, both 1984, for *Oliver!*

SIDELIGHTS: MEMBERSHIPS—Clowns International (president, 1984). FAVORITE ROLES—Vagabond Student, *For Amusement Only*, Pierrot, *For Adults Only*, governor, *Candide*, Fagin, *Oliver!* RECREATION—Writing, music, painting, theatre history, archaeology.

ADDRESS: OFFICE—Ingleside, 41 The Green, London N14, England.

*   *   *

MOORE, Demi

BRIEF ENTRY: Born Demi Guynes, November 11, in Roswell, NM; daughter of Danny and Virginia Guynes; married Freddy Moore (a songwriter and musician); studied under Zina Provendie. Actress. Since age 16, Moore has worked as a model. In television she appeared on such series as *Kaz*, CBS, and *Vegas*, ABC, and she played the role of Jackie Templeton on the daytime serial *General Hospital*, ABC. Also on television she appeared in *W.E.B.* and in the HBO production of *Bedrooms*. Moore's feature film credits include *Young Doctors in Love; Blame It on Rio; Parasite; No Small Affair; St. Elmo's Fire*, 1985, and *Choices* (upcoming).*

*   *   *

MOORE, Kim   1956-

PERSONAL: Born Kim Moerer, January 11, 1956, in Wheaton, MN; son of Reinhard Arthur (a salesman and farmer) and Marian Marlys (a teacher; maiden name, Dalin) Moerer; married Kathleen McCall (an actress), May 31, 1981. EDUCATION: Moorhead State University, MN, B.A., theatre arts, 1979; completed actors training program, London Academy of Music and Dramatic Art.

VOCATION: Actor and singer.

KIM MOORE

CAREER: PRINCIPAL STAGE APPEARANCES—Andos, *Philemon*, Lucentio, *Taming of the Shrew*, both Center for the Arts, Moorhead, MN, 1977; Will Roper, *A Man for All Seasons*, Straw Hat Players, 1977; Mark, *The Shadow Box*, Center for the Arts, 1978; Alan, *Equus*, Straw Hat Players, 1978; Benedick, *Much Ado About Nothing*, London Academy of Music and Dramatic Art, 1979; Pippin, *Pippin, Side by Side by Sondheim*, both Center for the Arts, 1979; man, *Starting Here Starting Now*, Straw Hat Players, 1980; Rolf, *The Sound of Music*, Chanhassan Dinner Theatre, 1980; Ladvenu, *Saint Joan*, London Academy of Music and Dramatic Art, 1980; Marat, *The Promise*, Chanhassen Courtyard, MN, 1981; Joseph, *Joseph and His Amazing Technicolor Dreamcoat*, Straw Hat Players, 1982; Joe, *Golden Express*, Prometheus, NY, 1983; Chris Halborg, *Iris*, Theatre for the New City, NY, 1983; ensemble, *Shakespeare's Sonnets*, Church of the Ascension, NY, 1983; Callimaco, *Mandrake*, Soho Repertory, NY, 1984; The Boy and The Mute, *The Fantasticks*, Sullivan Street, NY, 1985.

PRINCIPAL TELEVISION APPEARANCES—*Guiding Light; As the World Turns.*

SIDELIGHTS: MEMBERSHIPS—Actors' Equity Association, Screen Actors Guild, American Federation of Television and Radio Artists.

ADDRESS: AGENT—Honey Sanders Agency Ltd. 229 W. 42nd Street, New York, NY 10036.

MOORE, Mary Tyler   1937-

PERSONAL: Born December 29, 1937, in Brooklyn, NY.

VOCATION: Actress.

CAREER: PRINCIPAL TELEVISION APPEARANCES—Series: Sam, *Richard Diamond, Private Eye*, CBS, 1959; Laura Petrie, *The Dick Van Dyke Show*, CBS, 1961-66; Mary Richards, *The Mary Tyler Moore Show*, CBS, 1970-77; *Mary*, CBS, 1978; *The Mary Tyler Moore Hour*, CBS, 1979. Movies: *Love American Style*, 1969; *Run a Crooked Mile*, 1970; *First You Cry*, 1978; *Heartsounds*, ABC, 1984; *Finnegan, Begin Again*, HBO, 1985. Specials: *How to Survive the Seventies*, 1978.

PRINCIPAL FILM APPEARANCES—*X-15*, United Artists, 1964; *Thoroughly Modern Millie*, Universal, 1967; *Don't Just Stand There*, Universal, 1968; *What's So Bad About Feeling Good?*, Universal, 1968; *Change of Habit*, Universal, 1969; *Ordinary People*, Paramount, 1980; *Six Weeks*, Universal, 1982; *Something in Common*, Orion.

PRINCIPAL STAGE APPEARANCES—*Breakfast at Tiffanys; Whose Life Is It Anyway?*

AWARDS: Emmy Awards, 1964, 1965, for *The Dick Van Dyke Show*, 1973, 1974, 1976, for *The Mary Tyler Moore Show;* Golden Globe Awards, 1965, for *The Dick Van Dyke Show*, 1981, for *Ordinary People;* Academy Award nomination, Best Actress, 1981, for *Ordinary People*.

ADDRESS: OFFICE—MTM Enterprises, 4024 Radford Avenue, Studio City, CA 91604.*

*   *   *

MOORE, Robert   1927-84

PERSONAL: Born August 7, 1927, in Detroit, MI; died May 10, 1984; son of Samuel W. and Forrest L. (Rash) Moore. EDUCATION: Attended Catholic University.

VOCATION: Actor and director.

CAREER: NEW YORK STAGE DEBUT—Owen Parkside, *Jenny Kissed Me*, Hudson, 1948. PRINCIPAL STAGE APPEARANCES— Ron Bronson, *Alley of the Tiger*, Jan Hus, NY, 1959; Lewis Cadman, *The Tiger Rag*, Cherry Lane, NY, 1961; understudy F. Sherman, *The Owl and the Pussycat*, ANTA, NY, 1964; Harvey, *Cactus Flower*, Royale, 1965-67; Jack, *Everything in the Garden*, Plymouth, NY, 1967.

PRINCIPAL STAGE WORK—Director: *Ticket-of-Leave Man*, Midway, 1961; *The Boys in the Band*, Theater Four, NY, 1968, then Wyndhams, London, 1969; *Promises, Promises*, NY, 1968; *Last of the Red Hot Lovers*, NY, 1969; *The Gingerbread Lady*, NY, 1970; *Lorelei or Gentlemen Still Prefer Blondes*, NY, 1974; *My Fat Friend*, NY, 1974; *Deathtrap*, NY, 1978; *They're Playing Our Song*, NY, 1979; *Woman of the Year*, NY, 1981.

FILM DEBUT—*Tell Me That You Love Me, Junie Moon*, Paramount, 1970.

PRINCIPAL FILM WORK—Director: *Murder by Death*, 1976; *The Cheap Detective*, Columbia, 1978; *Chapter Two*, Columbia, 1979.

PRINCIPAL TELEVISION WORK—Director: *Thursday's Game*, 1974; *Cat on a Hot Tin Roof; Rhoda*, CBS, 1974-78.

SIDELIGHTS: Moore first appeared on stage under the name Brennan Moore.*

*   *   *

MOORE, Sonia   1902-

PERSONAL: Born Sonia Shatzov, December 4, 1902, in Gomel, Russia; daughter of Evser (an importer) and Sophie (Pasherstnik) Shatzov; married Leon Moore (a diplomat). EDUCATION: Attended Kiev University, Moscow University, Alliance Francaise, Instituto Interuniversitario Italiano, Reale Conservatorio di Musica Santa Cecilia, Reale Academia Filarmonica; trained for the stage at Kiev's Solovtzov Theatre and the Moscow Art Theatre's Third Studio with Vakhtangov.

VOCATION: Actress, director, producer, and teacher.

CAREER: PRINCIPAL STAGE APPEARANCES—Russian Theatre, Berlin, Germany, 1923-26.

PRINCIPAL STAGE WORK—Director: *The Painted Days* (also co-producer), NY; *Sharon's Grave*, Irish Players, NY.

Photography by Drew Jaglom

SONIA MOORE

Producer: At the American Center for Stanislavski Theatre Art: *The Cherry Orchard; Desire Under the Elms; The Crucible; Birdbath; The Man with the Flower in His Mouth; The Slave; This Property Is Condemned; The Indian Wants the Bronx; Look Back in Anger; A Streetcar Named Desire; My Poor Marat; The Stronger; The Marriage Proposal; The Boor; The Anniversary; Long Day's Journey into Night; The Lower Depths,* all 1961-present.

RELATED CAREER—Founder and teacher, Sonia Moore Studio of the Theater, NY, 1961; founder, director, and teacher, American Center for Stanislavski Theatre Art, NY, 1964-present; lecturer: Southeastern Theatre Conference, Birmingham, AL, and Cincinnati, OH; Cultural Department of Alberta, Canada; New York University; South Carolina Theatre Association; American Theatre Association Convention, NY, 1982, Minneapolis, 1983, San Francisco, 1984; Celebration of Women in the Arts, Edmonton, Canada, 1983; visiting professor, University of Missouri, Kansas City, MO, 1981.

WRITINGS: BOOKS—*The Stanislavski Method,* Viking, 1960; *The Stanislavski System,* Viking, 1965, 1974, Greece, 1980, India, 1984, Penguin, 1984; *Training an Actor; The Stanislavski System in Class,* 1968, 1979; *The Logic of Speech on Stage,* 1976; *Stanislavski Today,* 1973. SPECIAL ARTICLES—"The Stanislavski System," *Encyclopedia Britannica.*

SIDELIGHTS: CTFT learned Sonia Moore is convinced if the only existing systematized acting technique—the results of Stanislavski's life work—would become the unified training for actors in the United States, theatre would achieve the high artistic level of the other arts in this country. She is dedicated to bringing into this country Stanislavski's teachings and his final technique, the answer and solution for spontaneity on stage and to artistic theatre in America.

ADDRESS: HOME—New York, NY.

*   *   *

MORAHAN, Christopher   1929-

PERSONAL: Born July 9, 1929, in London, England; son of Thomas Hugo (a film producer and designer) and Nancy Charlotte (a film editor; maiden name, Barker) Morahan; married Joan Murray, October 22, 1954 (died, 1973); married Anna Carteret (an actress), October 12, 1974; children: Ben, Andy, Lucy, Rebecca, Hattie. EDUCATION: Attended Highgate School, London; trained for the stage at the Old Vic Theatre School with Michel St. Denis and George Devine. MILITARY: British Army, 1947-49.

VOCATION: Director and producer.

CAREER: FIRST STAGE WORK—Director, *Little Murders,* Royal Shakespeare Company, Aldwych, London, 1967, 60 performances. PRINCIPAL STAGE WORK—Director: *This Story of Yours,* Royal Court, London, 1968; *Flint,* Criterion, London, 1970; *The Caretaker,* Mermaid, London, 1972; at the National Theatre, London: *The State of Revolution, The Lady from Maxim's,* both 1977; *Brand, The Philanderer, Strife,* all 1978; *The Fruits of Enlightenment, Richard III, The Wild Duck,* all 1979; *Sisterly Feelings,* 1980; *Man and Superman,* 1981; *Wild Honey,* 1984.

PRINCIPAL TELEVISION WORK—Director: *John Gabriel Borkman,*

1960; *Continuity Man,* 1960; *The Hooded Terror,* 1964; *The Brick Umbrella,* 1964; *Progress in the Park,* 1965; *The Orwell Trilogy,* 1966; *Talking to a Stranger,* 1966; *A Month in the Country,* 1967; *A Slight Ache/A Night Out,* 1968; *The Gorge,* 1969; *The Letter, Uncle Vanya,* 1970; *The Common,* 1973; *Old Times,* 1975; *Fathers and Families,* 1977; *Bedroom Farce,* 1980; *The Jewel in the Crown* (also producer), Granada, 1984; *In the Secret State,* BBC2, 1985.

PRINCIPAL FILM WORK—Director: *Diamonds for Breakfast,* 1969; *All Neat in Black Stockings,* Miron Films, 1970; *Clockwise,* Thorn/EMI, 1985.

RELATED CAREER—Head of Plays, BBC Television, 1972-76.

AWARDS: Society of Film and Television Arts Award, Best Play Director, 1969, for *The Letter;* Best Director Award, 1984, for *Wild Honey;* Olivier Award, Standard Award, British Theatre Association Award, Plays and Players Award, British Academy of Film and Television Arts Award for Best Director of a Television Series, Desmond Davis Award for Outstanding Creative Contribution to Television, International Emmy Award, Peabody Award, all 1984, for *Jewel in the Crown.*

ADDRESS: HOME—London, England. AGENT—Leading Artists, 60 St. James's Street, London, SW1, England.

*   *   *

MORNEL, Ted   1936-

PERSONAL: Born December 23, 1936, in New York City; son of Max (a printer) and Ruth (Shoib) Mornel; married Ann Saxman (an actress), March 14, 1964. EDUCATION: Attended City College of New York; trained for the stage at the Herbert Berghof Studio with Bill Hickey.

VOCATION: Director.

CAREER: STAGE DEBUT—Floorwalker, *Auntie Mame,* Putnam County Playhouse, Mahopac, NY, six performances.

PRINCIPAL STAGE WORK—Director: *Touch,* Martinique, NY; *Frankovich,* ATA, NY; *Phantom Limbs, Underbelly Blues,* Re Cher Chez, NY; *Medea,* Troupe, NY; *At Liberty, Sweet Shoppe Miriam, Toploading Lover, Home Free, Night Fever, Grave Robbers, The Tatami, On Trial,* all at Quaigh, NY; *Winter in St. Cloud, They Want Pizza, Leona Is a Funny Name,* all at Theatre for the New City, NY; *Angel Street, A Day in the Life of Ivan Denisovitch, The Harmfulnes of Tobacco,* all at 48th Street Theater, NY; *Icky, Icky, Nye, Nye, Black Robed Entry, Information Please,* all at Samuel Rubin Hall, NY; *San Fernando Valley, Mother's Day, Hippie as a Lark, Bad News, Failed Purposes,* all at Stagelights II, NY.

Sheltered, Cornered, Mirage, Freudian Memoirs of Viola Pickens, Pay Attention to the Ravel, Eli and Emily, The Warhol Machine, all at Playbox Studio, NY; *Transplants, New York Transit Authority,* Theatre 77, NY; *Amen Corner, When Schwartz Meets Goldstein, Magic Time,* University of the Streets, NY; *Down and Out West,* The Assembly, NY; *Souffle of Turbot,* Stagelights I, NY; *The Scavengers,* Theatre for Our Discontent, NY; *Sleeping Bag, The Old Roue and His Icon,* 13th Street Theatre, NY; *Mirage, Haunted Host,* Bastiano's Playwrights, NY; *Night Must Fall,* National Arts

Club, NY.

Stock: *Witness for the Prosecution, Odd Couple, Four Poster, Rainmaker, A Streetcar Named Desire, Bus Stop,* all Georgetown Theatre, Canada; *Hymn, Oh Dad, Poor Dad, Mama's Hung You in the Closet and I'm Feeling So Sad,* both at Plowright Playhouse, PA; *Don Juan in Hell, Angel Street, Oh Dad, Poor Dad, Mama's Hung You in the Closet and I'm Feeling So Sad,* all Greenville Theatre 68, NY; *Touch,* Gaithersburg Theater, MD; *Butterflies Are Free,* Compas Allen Productions.

SIDELIGHTS: MEMBERSHIPS—Society of Stage Directors and Choreographers, Actors' Equity Association.

ADDRESS: HOME—158 W. 15th Street, New York, NY 10011. OFFICE—Quaigh Theatre, 108 W. 43rd Street, New York, NY 10036.

*   *   *

MORRISON, Ann   1956–

PERSONAL: Born April 9, 1956, in Souix City, IA; daughter of Donald Nauman (a music professor) and Elisabeth Scott (a teacher, director, writer, and artist; maiden name, Walker) Morrison; married Blake Walton (an actor and writer), May 18, 1982. EDUCATION: Completed apprenticeship at Burt Reynolds' Dinner Theatre, 1979; studied voice with Marge Rivingston in NY.

CAREER: STAGE DEBUT—Louisa, *The Fantastiks,* Burt Reynolds' Dinner Theatre, Jupiter, FL. NEW YORK DEBUT—Bebe, *Dream Time,* Harold Clurman, 1980. LONDON DEBUT—Peg, *Peg,* Phoenix, 1984. PRINCIPAL STAGE APPEARANCES—Mabel Normand, *Keystone,* GeVa, Rochester, NY, 1981; Mary Flynn, *Merrily We Roll Along,* Alvin, NY, 1981; company member, *Forbidden Broadway,* Palssons, NY, 1983.

MAJOR TOURS—Mrs. Martin, *The Bald Soprano,* Swamp, *Wiley and the Hairy Man,* Vasilisa, *Vasilisa,* Asolo State Theatre tour of southern U. S., 1977-78.

TELEVISION DEBUT—Nurse, *The Doctors,* NBC, 1981. PRINCIPAL TELEVISION APPEARANCES—Mabel Normand, *Keystone,* New Jersey Network, 1983.

AWARDS: Theatre World Award, 1982, for Mary Flynn, *Merrily We Roll Along,* 1982.

SIDELIGHTS: MEMBERSHIPS—Actors' Equity Association, American Federation of Television and Radio Artists, Screen Actors Guild.

Morrison told *CTFT:* ''Theatre is a cooperative effort. It is pure educational joy. There is always something new to bring from any experience. Each role I've done has had a lesson attached. I believe the best way to learn is to do. And most importantly, if you approach anything with a great sense of humor you can't go wrong. I balance my theatre work with esoteric study. This helps give me a broader perspective of the world and my place in it which in turn gives me a sense of contribution and concern for larger issues. So, theatre is not everything to me. I am a curious student and acting is one way I explore my values and especially the way I test myself.''

ADDRESS: AGENT—Lionel Larner Ltd. 850 Seventh Avenue, New York, NY 10019.

ANN MORRISON

MORROW, Vic   1931-82

PERSONAL: Born February 14, 1931, in Bronx, NY; died July 23, 1982; married Barbara Turner (an actress), 1957 (divorced, 1965); children: Carrie, Jennifer. EDUCATION: Attended Honda Southern College; trained for the stage at the Actors Workshop with Paul Mann.

VOCATION: Actor.

CAREER: FILM DEBUT—*The Blackboard Jungle,* Metro-Goldwyn-Mayer, 1955. PRINCIPAL FILM APPEARANCES—*Tribute to Bob Man,* Metro-Goldwyn-Mayer, 1956; *Men in War,* United Artists, 1957; *King Creole,* Paramount, 1958; *God's Little Acre,* United Artists, 1958; *Portrait of a Mobster,* Warner Brothers, 1961; *Cimmarron,* Metro-Goldwyn-Mayer, 1961; *Posse from Hell,* Universal, 1961; *The Babysitter,* Crown International, 1969; *Target: Harry,* 1969; *The Great White; The Treasure of Matecumbe,* Buena Vista, 1976; *Bad News Bears,* Paramount, 1976; *Dirty Mary, Crazy Larry,* Twentieth Century-Fox, 1974; *The Evictors,* 1979; *Humanoids of the Deep,* 1980; *1990-The Bronx Warrior,* United Artists, 1983; *Twilight Zone, the Movie,* Warner Brothers, 1983.

PRINCIPAL FILM WORK—Writer, director, producer, *Deathwatch;* writer, director, actor, *A Man Called Sledge,* Columbia, 1971.

PRINCIPAL TELEVISION APPEARANCES—Sergeant Chip Saunders, *Combat,* ABC, 1962-67; *Step Out of Line,* 1970; *The Glass House,* 1972; *Police Story,* 1973; *Roots; The Seekers; The Last Convertable; Captains and Kings; The Night That Panicked America,* 1975.

PRINCIPAL TELEVISION WORK—Director, *Combat;* director, *The Evil Touch,* Australian television.*

*   *   *

MULHERN, Matt   1960-

PERSONAL: Born July 21, 1960, in Philadelphia, PA; son of William James (a public relations specialist) and Mary Ann (an executive secretary; maiden name, McGowan) Mulhern. EDUCATION: Trained for the stage at the Mason Gross School of the Arts, Rutgers University with William Esper. POLITICS: Republican. RELIGION: Roman Catholic.

VOCATION: Actor.

CAREER: STAGE DEBUT—Fortinbras and soldier, *Hamlet,* American Shakespeare Theatre, Stratford, CT, 1982. PRINCIPAL STAGE APPEARANCES—*Lessons on How to Behave Under Peculiar Circumstances,* Pan Asian Repertory, 28th Street Theater, NY, 1983; Larry McCutcheon, *The Passing of the Shagwine Express,* Church at St. Peters, NY, 1984; Joseph Wykowski, *Biloxi Blues,* Neil Simon, NY, 1985.

MAJOR TOURS—Joseph Wykowski, *Biloxi Blues,* pre-Broadway at Ahmanson, Los Angeles, Curran, San Francisco, 1984-85.

TELEVISION DEBUT—Policeman, *Guiding Light,* CBS, 1984.

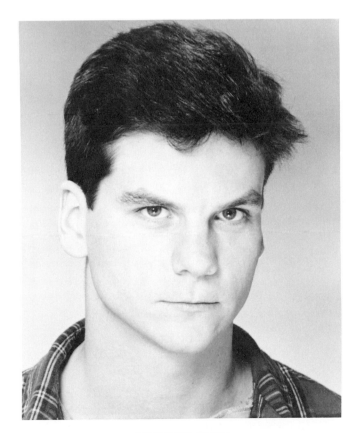

MATT MULHERN

SIDELIGHTS: MEMBERSHIPS—Actors' Equity Association. FAVORITE ROLE—Dan Loggins, *The Mound Builders.*

ADDRESS: AGENT—Dave Liebhart, Don Buchwald Agency, Ten E. 44th Street, New York, NY 10017.

*   *   *

MURIN, David

PERSONAL: EDUCATION: New York University School of the Arts, B.F.A.; apprenticed with Oliver Smith.

VOCATION: Costume designer.

CAREER: PRINCIPAL STAGE WORK—Broadway: *Blues in the Night; Ned and Jack; A Talent for Murder; Devour the Snow; Gorey Stories; The Caine Mutiny Court Martial,* Circle in the Square, 1984.

Off Broadway: *Criminal Minds; Blue Plate Special; The Middle Ages; Jane Avril; The Snow Orchid; The One Act Play Festival at Lincoln Center; Translations; The Chekhov Sketchbook; Styne After Styne, Come Back to the Five and Dime, Jimmy Dean; The Whales of August; Ladyhouse Blues; Chinchilla; The Banana Box; Lulu; Last of the Red Hot Mamas; For the Use of the Hall; The Rehearsal; Heartbreak House, Night of the Black Pig; Mr. and Mrs.; Feathertop,* WPA, 1984.

Regional: *Accent on Youth,* Long Wharf, New Haven, CT; *Rocket to the Moon, A Streetcar Named Desire, Actors and Actresses, The Little Foxes, He Who Gets Slapped,* all at the Hartman, Hartford, CT; *The Magistrate,* Huntington Theatre Co.; *Daughters, Old World, Private Lives, The Last Few Days of Willie Calendar, You Never Can Tell, Summer, Thark, Hobson's Choice, Travesties, Uncle Vanya, The Au Pair Man, Arms and the Man,* all at the Philadelphia Drama Guild; *On Borrowed Time, A Flea in Her Ear,* Hartford Stage Co., Hartford, CT; *Outrage!, Master Class,* Kennedy Center, Washington, DC.

Sherlock Holmes, Design for Living, Williamstown Theatre Festival, MA; *Dramatic License, Sullivan and Gilbert, Feathertop, Dracula, Side by Side by Sondheim, The Royal Family, The Importance of Being Earnest, Sally's Gone, She's Left Her Name, The Man Who Came to Dinner,* all at the American Stage Festival; *The Vinegar Tree, A Loss of Roses,* Berkshire Theatre Festival, Stockbridge, MA, 1984.

PRINCIPAL TELEVISION WORK—*Ryan's Hope,* ABC; *Sherlock Holmes,* HBO; *Dreamhouse,* CBS; *Maid in America,* CBS.

Concerts: Designed stage clothes for Jane Olivor.

RELATED CAREER—Costume design instructor, Temple University, Philadelphia, PA.

AWARDS: Emmy, 1980-81, for *Ryan's Hope.*

SIDELIGHTS: MEMBERSHIPS—United Scenic Artists, Local 829.

ADDRESS: OFFICE—348 E. Ninth Street, New York, NY 10003. AGENT—John Giroux, 575 Madison Avenue, New York, NY 10022.

MURPHY, Eddie   1961-

PERSONAL: Full name Edward Regan Murphy; born April 3, 1961, in Brooklyn, NY.

VOCATION: Actor, comedian, and writer.

CAREER: TELEVISION DEBUT—*Saturday Night Live,* NBC, 1980. PRINCIPAL TELEVISION APPEARANCES—*Saturday Night Live,* NBC, 1980-84; *Joe Piscopo's HBO Special; The Barbara Walters Special; Late Night with David Letterman; Grammy Awards Show; Academy Awards; MTV Awards; The Tonight Show.*

FILM DEBUT—*48 Hours,* Paramount, 1982. PRINCIPAL FILM APPEARANCES—*Trading Places,* Paramount, 1983; Axel Foley, *Beverly Hills Cop,* Paramount, 1984; *A Hell of an Angel,* Paramount (upcoming).

MAJOR TOURS—*Eddie Murphy,* U.S. cities, 1983.

RECORDINGS: Eddie Murphy; Eddie Murphy: Comedian.

AWARDS: Emmy Award nomination, Outstanding Performance, Outstanding Comedy Writing, for *Saturday Night Live;* Grammy Award nomination, for *Eddie Murphy;* NAACP Image Award, Best Actor in a Motion Picture, Golden Globe Foreign Press Award, all 1983, for *Trading Places;* Grammy Award, Best Comedy Album of the Year, 1984, for *Eddie Murphy: Comedian;* Golden Globe Award nomination, Best Actor, Star of the Year Award, People's Choice Award, Favorite All-Around Male Entertainer, all 1985, for *Beverly Hills Cop.*

ADDRESS: AGENT—Entertainment Management Associates, Ltd., 232 E. 63rd Street, New York, NY 10021.

*   *   *

SHARON MURRAY

AWARDS: Drama Desk Award nomination, 1985, for *Grind.*

SIDELIGHTS: MEMBERSHIPS—Actors' Equity Association, Screen Actors Guild.

ADDRESS: AGENT—Diane Cumins, DMI Talent, 250 W. 57th Street, New York, NY 10019.

*   *   *

MURRAY, Sharon

PERSONAL: Born December 13, in Ann Arbor, MI; daughter of Thomas McKelvin (an engineer, retired from U.S. Air Force) and Patricia Madge (a real estate agent; maiden name, Blankenbaker) Murray. EDUCATION: Attended University of Louisville School of Music for three and a half years; studied voice with Joe Scott. RELIGION: Episcopalian.

CAREER: NEW YORK DEBUT—Romaine, *Grind,* Mark Hellinger, 1984. PRINCIPAL STAGE APPEARANCES—Baby Marie, *Babes in Arms,* Coachlight Dinner Theatre, 1983; Harriet, *Whoopee,* Coachlight Dinner Theatre, 1984; Mazeppa, *Gypsy,* Metroversity, Louisville, KY, 1985.

TELEVISION DEBUT—Wife, *Consumer Reports,* HBO, 1983.

MUSSER, Tharon   1925-

PERSONAL: Born January 8, 1925, in Roanoke, VA; daughter of George C. and Hazel (Riddle) Musser. EDUCATION: Berea College, B.A., 1946; Yale University School of Drama, M.F.A., 1950.

VOCATION: Lighting designer.

CAREER: FIRST STAGE WORK—Lighting designer, *The Father,* Provincetown Playhouse, NY, 1949. PRINCIPAL STAGE WORK—Lighting designer (all Broadway productions unless otherwise indicated): *Naked, Lucky Sam McCarver,* Provincetown Playhouse, 1950; dance events, YMHA, NY, 1950-51; *Long Day's Journey into Night,* 1956; *Much Ado About Nothing,* Stratford, CT, 1957; *Shinbone Alley, Monique, The Makropoulos Secret,* 1957; *The Chairs, The Lesson, The Infernal Machine, The Entertainer, The Shadow of a Gunman, Murder in the Cathedral, JB, The Beaux Stratagem, The Rivalry, Once Upon a Mattress,* 1958; *The First-*

THARON MUSSER

born, NY and Tel Aviv, Israel, 1958; *A Midsummer Night's Dream, Romeo and Juliet, A Midsummer Night's Dream, The Merry Wives of Windsor*, all Stratford, CT, 1958; *The Great God Brown, Only in America, Five Finger Exercise*, 1959; *Peer Gynt, The Long Dream, The Tumbler*, 1960; *Twelfth Night, The Tempest, Antony and Cleopatra*, all Stratford, CT, 1960; *As You Like It, Macbeth*, both Stratford, CT, 1961; *The Garden of Sweets*, 1961; *The Turn of the Screw, Anatol, Elizabeth the Queen*, all American Festival, Boston, MA, 1961.

Giants, Sons of Giants, Calculated Risk, Nowhere to Go but Up, HMS Pinafore, 1962; *Androcles and the Lion*, Boston, MA, 1962; *Andora, Mother Courage and Her Children, Here's Love, Marathon '33*, 1963; *King Lear, The Comedy of Errors, Henry V*, all Stratford, CT, 1963; *Much Ado About Nothing, Richard III, Hamlet*, all Stratford, CT, 1964; *Golden Boy, Alfie, Hedda Gabler, Liliom, Any Wednesday*, 1964; *Kelly, All in Good Time, Flora the Red Menace, Minor Miracle*, 1965; *Coriolanus, Romeo and Juliet, The Taming of the Shrew, King Lear*, all Stratford, CT, 1965; *Mais Ouis*, Beirut, Lebanon, 1965; *Malcolm, The Great Indoors, The Lion in Winter, Mame, A Delicate Balance*, 1966; *Falstaff, Murder in the Cathedral, Twelfth Night, Julius Caesar*, all Stratford, CT, 1966; *A Midsummer Night's Dream, Antigone, The Merchant of Venice*, all Stratford, CT, 1967; *Hallelujah, Baby!, The Birthday Party, After the Rain, The Promise, Everything in the Garden*, 1967.

Catch My Soul, Los Angeles, CA, 1968; *Man and the Universe*, Hemis Fair Exhibit, San Antonio, TX, 1968; *Golden Boy*, Palladium, London, 1968; *As You Like It, Androcles and the Lion*, both Stratford, CT, 1968; *House of Flowers, The Lovers, Maggie Flyn*, 1968; *The Fig Leaves Are Falling, The Gingham Dog*, 1969; *Mame*, Drury Lane, London, 1969; *Fedora*, Dallas Civic Opera, TX, 1969; *Blood Red Roses, Applause, The Boy Friend*, 1970; *L.A. Under*

Siege, The Trial of the Catonsville Nine, The Dream on Monkey Mountain, Rosebloom, all Los Angeles, CA, 1970; *The Merry Widow, Madama Butterfly, Il Tabarro, Carmina Burana*, all Dallas Civic Opera, TX, 1970; *Follies, The Trial of the Catonsville Nine*, 1971; *Who Wants to Be the Lone Ranger, Major Barbara*, Los Angeles, CA, 1971; *On the Town, The Prisoner of Second Avenue*, 1971; Los Angeles, CA, 1971; *Fidelio*, Dallas Civic Opera, TX, 1971.

Night Watch, The Creation of the World and Other Business, The Great God Brown, Don Juan, The Sunshine Boys, 1972; *Old Times*, Los Angeles, CA, 1972; *The Dream on Monkey Mountain*, Munich, Germany, 1972; *Applause*, Her Majesty's, London, 1972; *Forget Me Not Lane*, Los Angeles, CA, 1973; *Sondheim: A Musical Tribute, The Orphan, The Good Doctor, A Little Night Music*, 1973; *Andrea Chenier*, Dallas Civic Opera, TX, 1973; *Saint Joan, The Charlatan*, both Los Angeles, CA, 1974; *God's Favorite, Mack and Mabel, Good News, Candide*, 1974; *The Pearl Fishers*, Miami Opera Guild, FL, 1974; *Lucrezia Borgia, Mignon*, both Dallas, TX, 1974.

The Wiz, Same Time Next Year, A Chorus Line, Me and Bessie, 1975; *The Tables of Hoffman*, Dallas, TX, 1975; *The Flying Dutchman*, Miami, FL, 1975; *Othello*, Miami, FL, 1976; *1600 Pennsylvania Avenue, California Suite, Pacific Overtures*, 1976; *A Chorus Line*, London, 1976; *Hooray USA!*, Miami Bicentennial Pageant, 1976; *The Act, Chapter Two, Travesties*, 1977; *A Chorus Line*, Australia, 1977; *The Importance of Being Earnest*, Los Angeles, CA, 1977; *Tribute, Ballroom*, 1978; *Black Angel*, Los Angeles, CA, 1978; *They're Playing Our Song, Whose Life Is It Anyway?, 1940's Radio Hour, Romantic Comedy, Last Licks*, 1979; *Terra Nova*, Los Angeles, CA, 1979; *Children of a Lesser God, I Ought to Be in Pictures, The Road, 42nd Street*, 1980; *I Ought to Be in Pictures*, Mark Taper Forum, Los Angeles, 1980; *Fools, Moony Shapiro's Songbook, Dreamgirls*, 1981; *Hoagy, Bix and Wolfgang*, both Mark Taper Forum, Los Angeles, 1981; *Special Occasions*, 1982; *Tales of Hollywood*, Mark Taper Forum, Los Angeles, 1982; *Merlin, Brighton Beach Memoirs, Private Lives*, 1983; *The Real Thing, Open Admissions*, 1984; *Genius*, NY, 1984; *Biloxi Blues*, NY, 1985.

MAJOR TOURS—*Jose Limon Dance Company*, U.S. cities, Buenos Aires, 1953-54; *The Skin of Our Teeth, The Glass Menagerie, The Miracle Worker*, U.S. State Department, 1961; *Ring round the Moon, The Seagull, The Crucible*, 1963; *She Stoops to Conquer*, National Repertory Theater, 1964; *The Rivals, The Madwoman of Chaillot, The Trojan Women*, National Repertory Theater, 1965; *Tonight at 8:30, A Touch of the Poet, The Imaginary Invalid*, National Repertory Theater, 1966; *John Brown's Body, The Comedy of Errors*, 1967; *Spofford*, 1969.

PRINCIPAL TELEVISION WORK—*Reopening Ford's Theater*, Washington, DC, 1968.

RELATED CAREER—Design consultant, Webb and Knapp, Radcliffe College, American Academy of Dramatic Arts, New York Council on the Arts.

AWARDS: Antoinette Perry Award, for *Follies, A Chorus Line*, and *Dreamgirls;* USITT Art and Technology Award, 1976; honorary doctors of humanities, Berea College, 1979, Emerson College, 1980; Theatre Hall of Fame Award, 1984.

SIDELIGHT: RECREATION—Travel.

ADDRESS: OFFICE—21 Cornelia Street, New York, NY 10014.

N

NAPOLI, Tony 1948-

PERSONAL: Born November 18, 1948, in New York City; son of Anthony (a printer) and Josephine (Krotki) Napoli. EDUCATION: St. Joseph's Seminary, B.A., 1971; City University of New York, M.F.A., 1973.

VOCATION: Director.

CAREER: PRINCIPAL STAGE WORK—Assistant director, *Bojangles,* Broadway production. Director (all off Broadway productions): *Red Rover, Red Rover,* Park Royale; *Sticks and Bones,* Prince Street Playhouse; *Hadrian's Hill, Night Over the Tiber,* both Provincetown Playhouse. Director (all off-off Broadway productions): *Kennedy's Children,* Jason's; *Angelus,* A.T.A.; *Sliphorn Jazz,* Lincoln Center Library; *My Prince, My King,* Actors Studio; *Certain Things About the Trombone, Magic Time, One Day in the Life of Ivan Denisovich,* all Soho Repertory; *Trouble, Pottstown Carnival,* both St. Clement's; *Purgatory,* Direct Theater; *Short Change,* Playwrights Previews; *Nero,* Elysian Playhouse; *Second Shepherd's Play,* Brook; *The Knack, Antigone, The Collection,* all Ward-Nasse Gallery.

University productions: *Tea and Sympathy, House of Blue Leaves,* both St. John's University; *Domenica, Richard II,* both City University of New York; *Venus and Adonis,* University of Bridgeport; *Hadrian VII, Caligula, Royal Hunt of the Sun,* all St. Joseph's Seminary; *Inherit the Wind, Murder in the Cathedral,* both Cathedral College; *Dutchman,* Lincoln.

SIDELIGHTS: MEMBERSHIPS—Society of Stage Directors and Choreographers.

ADDRESS: HOME—68 W. 83rd Street, New York, NY 10024.

*   *   *

NATHAN, Vivian 1921-

PERSONAL: Born Vivian Firko, October 26, 1921, in New York City; daughter of Hipolit and Anna (Marczak) Firko; married Nathan Schwalb. EDUCATION: St. Nicholas Seminary, NY; studied dance with Anna Sokolow, voice with Francis Robinson-Duff, and acting with the Actors Studio.

VOCATION: Actress.

CAREER: STAGE DEBUT—Helen, *Sundown Beach,* Belasco, NY, 1948. PRINCIPAL STAGE APPEARANCES—Mathilde, *Montserrat,*

Fulton, NY, 1949; La Madrecita de los Perdidos, *Camino Real,* National, NY, 1953; Pepina, *The Rose Tattoo,* Martin Beck, NY, 1954; Josefina, *Bullfight,* Theatre de Lys, NY, 1954; Charwoman (Anushka), *Anastasia,* Lyceum, NY, 1954; Clothilde, *The Lovers,* Martin Beck, NY, 1956; Maxine, *The Night of the Iguana,* and Mrs. Crosby, *Tiny Closet,* Festival of Two Worlds, Spoleto, Italy, 1959; Marie Duschene, *Semi-Detached,* Martin Beck, NY, 1960; a Witness for the Prosecution, *The Investigation,* Ambassador, NY, 1966; Margaret Young, the mother, *The Watering Place,* Music Box, NY, 1969; Mary Tyrone, *Long Day's Journey into Night,* Center Stage, Baltimore, MD, 1969-70 season, then at the Actors Studio, NY, 1973; *Golda,* ANTA, 1980; also: *Ascent of Mt. Fuji,* Arena Stage, Washington, DC, for their twenty-fifth anniversary.

FILM DEBUT—Mrs. Kovac, *Teacher's Pet,* Paramount, 1958. PRINCIPAL FILM APPEARANCES—*The Young Savages,* United Artists, 1961; *The Outsider,* Universal, 1961; *Klute,* Warner Brothers, 1971.

PRINCIPAL TELEVISION APPEARANCES—*Playhouse 90,* CBS; *Studio One,* CBS; *The Nurses,* CBS; *Breaking Point,* ABC; *Arrest and Trial,* ABC; *Tyranny,* ABC; *Alfred Hitchcock Presents,* CBS; *Kojak,* CBS; *Hedda Gabler;* witness, *The Investigation,* NBC, 1967.

RELATED CAREER—Teacher, New York Actors Studio.

AWARDS: Finalist, John Golden Auditions, 1948 (led to Actors Studio membership); Clarence Derwent Award for Best Performance in a Non-Featured Role, 1955, for *Anastasia;* voted Best Performance in a Classic on Television for *Hedda Gabler.*

SIDELIGHTS: MEMBERSHIPS—Actors' Equity Association, American Federation of Television and Radio Artists, Screen Actors Guild, Actors Studio (1948-present).

ADDRESS: HOME—New York, NY.

*   *   *

NAUGHTON, David

BRIEF ENTRY: Born in Hartford, CT; graduated with a degree in English literature from the University of Pennsylvania; studied for two years at London Academy of Music and Dramatic Art. Married Denise Stephen, 1977. Naughton's first break came with Joseph Papp's *Hamlet,* New York Shakespeare Festival, in which he played the Player Queen, Francisco, Fortinbras, and various soldiers during each performance. Naughton is well known for his "Dr. Pepper" commercials and his television series, *Makin' It*, ABC, 1979, where he portrayed Billy Manucci. The title song, sung by Naughton, yielded a gold record. His other television credits include *At Ease* and *Planet of the Apes*. His films include: *The Other Side of Victory; Midnight Madness*, Buena Vista, 1980; *Separate Ways; An American Werewolf in London*, Universal Pictures, 1981; *Hot Dog: The Movie*, Metro-Goldwyn-Mayer, 1983; Barry, *Not for Publication*, Thorn-EMI, 1984; *The Boy in Blue* (upcoming). He appeared in the off Broadway production of *Poor Little Lambs*.*

*   *   *

NEDERLANDER, James Morton   1922-

PERSONAL: Born March 31, 1922, in Detroit, MI; son of David T. (a theater owner) and Sarah L. (Applebaum) Nederlander; married Charlene Saunders, February 12, 1969; children: James L., Sharon, Kristina. EDUCATION: Attended Detroit Institute of Technology; University of North Dakota. MILITARY: U.S. Army Air Force, World War Two.

VOCATION: Producer and theater owner.

CAREER: FIRST STAGE WORK—Production staff, *Winged Victory*, 44th Street Theater, 1943.

PRINCIPAL STAGE WORK—Producer: *On a Clear Day You Can See Forever*, Biltmore, NY, 1967; *The Ninety-Day Mistress*, NY, 1969; *Applause, Not Now Darling*, NY, 1970; *Abelard and Heloise*, 1971; *Seesaw*, NY, 1973; *My Fat Friend, London Assurance, Sherlock Holmes*, NY, 1974; *Treemonisha, Habeas Corpus*, NY, 1975; *The D'Oyly Carte Company*, NY, 1976; *Otherwise Engaged, Annie, Caesar and Cleopatra*, NY, 1977; *Hello, Dolly!, Stop the World—I Want to Get Off*, NY, 1978; *Whose Life Is It Anyway?, Peter Pan, Night and Day, Oklahoma!*, NY, 1979; *Hello, Dolly!*, London, 1979. Also, in addition to the above Broadway productions, produced the following Broadway productions: *Betrayal; Woman of the Year; Lena Horne: The Lady and Her Music; The Life and Times of Nicholas Nickleby; The Dresser; Nine; Noises Off; Merlin; Night and Day; Shirley MacLaine on Broadway; La Cage Aux Folles; Strange Interlude; Much Ado About Nothing; Cyrano De Bergerac; Grind; Aren't We All?; Peter Pan; Hello, Dolly!; Porgy and Bess; The Music Man; I Do! I Do!; Oklahoma!; Fiddler on the Roof; West Side Story; Can Can.*

MAJOR TOURS—U.S. cities: *On a Clear Day You Can See Forever*, 1957; *George M!*, 1969; *Spofford!*, 1970; *Applause, Black Girl, The Effect of Gamma Rays on Man-in-the-Moon-Marigolds, Light up the Sky*, 1971; *My Fat Friend*, 1974; *Peter Pan; Hello, Dolly!; Porgy and Bess; The Music Man; I Do! I Do!; Oklahoma!; Fiddler on the Roof; West Side Story; Can Can.*

RELATED CAREER—Chairman of the Board, Nederlander Organization, Inc. Owner of the following theatres—in NY: Brooks Atkinson, 46th Street, Gershwin, Lunt-Fontanne, Mark Hellinger, Minskoff, Nederlander, Neil Simon, New Amsterdam, Portman, Palace; in Los Angeles: Dorothy Chandler Pavilion, Wilshire, Pantages, Greek; in Detroit: Birmingham, Fisher, Masonic Temple; in San Francisco: Curran, Golden Gate, Orpheum; also, Concord Pavilion, Concord, CA; Pacific Amphitheatre, Costa Mesa, CA; Poplar Creek, Chicago; Fox, San Diego; Aldwych, Royal Adelphi, London.

ADDRESS: OFFICE—1564 Broadway, New York, NY 10036.

JEFFREY K. NEILL

NEILL, Jeffery K.   1938-

PERSONAL: Born John Neal Phillips, April 26, 1938, in Indianapolis, IN; son of Audrian Neal (a farmer) and Chloe Zora (a model; maiden name, Jones) Phillips.

VOCATION: Choreographer and director.

CAREER: PRINCIPAL STAGE WORK—Choreographer and director, Tibbits Opera House, Coldwater, MI, 1966-71, 1973-80, and 1984: *Annie Get Your Gun; Anything Goes; Any Wednesday; Babes in Arms; Barefoot in the Park; Bells Are Ringing; Brigadoon; Butterflies Are Free; Cabaret; Carousel; Camelot; Can-Can; Champagne Complex; Dames at Sea; Desert Song; Fantasticks; Fiorello; Funny Girl; George M!; Gigi; Godspell; God's Favorite; Guys and Dolls; Gypsy; H.M.S. Pinafore; Hello, Dolly!; How to Succeed; I Do! I Do!; Jesus Christ Superstar; Joseph and the Amazing Technicolor Dreamcoat; Jubilee; Kiss Me Kate; Luv; Mame; Merry Widow; Mikado; No, No, Nanette; No Sex Please, We're British; Nude with Violin; Odd Couple; Oklahoma!; Oliver!; Owl and the Pussycat; Play It Again, Sam; Promises, Promises; Same Time, Next Year; Showboat; 6 Rms Riv Vu; 1776; Sleuth; The Sound of Music; South Pacific; Stop the World I Want to Get Off; Student Prince; Sweet Charity; The Bat; The King and I; The Mousetrap; Three Men on a Horse; Under the Gaslight; Unsinkable Molly Brown; West Side Story; Write Me a Murder; Wonderful Town; Vanities.*

Choreographer and director: at Enchanted Hills, Syracuse, IN, 1962: Can-Can, Girl Crazy, The Music Man, Silk Stockings, Will the Mail Train Run Tonight?; at Camelback Summer Theater, Tannersville, PA, 1971-72: *Camelot, Charlie Brown, Fantasticks,*

Fiddler on the Roof, Guys and Dolls, I Do! I Do!, Kiss Me Kate, Little Mary Sunshine, Man of La Mancha. Also: *Anything Goes*, 1979, *Side by Side by Sondheim*, 1980, both Bakersfield Community Theater, CA; *Gypsy*, Starlight Theater of Kern, Bakersfield, CA, 1980; *The Mousetrap, Applause*, both Chatham Players, 1981; *Guys and Dolls*, Resorts International Hotel, Atlantic City, NJ, 1981; *Side by Side by Sondheim*, MHB Repertory, Glen Cove, NY, 1983; *Judy: A Garland of Songs*, San Francisco, CA, 1984.

Off and off-off Broadway: *All My Sons*, 1958; *Countdown*, 1959; *Finian's Rainbow*, 1962; *Fiorello*, 1964; *Pajama Game*, 1965; *Sabrina Fair*, 1966; *Bells Are Ringing*, 1966; *Archy and Mehitabel*, 1967; *Once Upon a Mattress*, 1968; *Gentlemen Prefer Blondes*, 1969; *Love and Marriage*, 1969; *Goldilocks*, 1971; *Ernest in Love*, 1971; *First Impressions*, 1972; *Gypsy*, 1972; *One for the Money*, 1972; *Antiques*, 1973; *Company*, 1973; *Mame*, 1973; *Only an Orphan Girl*, 1973; *Kiss Me Kate*, 1974 and 1983; *Can-Can*, 1975; *Ape Over Broadway*, 1975; *Judy: A Garland of Songs*, 1974, 1978, and 1984; *The Pirate*, 1974; *Let's Face It*, 1977; *Happy Hunting*, 1977; *Say It with Music*, 1978-79; *Reunion*, 1978; *Tune the Grand Up*, Lincoln Center, 1978; *The Constant Wife*, 1979; *Anything Goes*, 1979; *Irma La Douce*, 1980; *Carnival*, 1981; *Love and Marriage*, Donnell Library, 1982; *The Women*, 1982; *She Loves Me*, 1983; *Merman: Who Could Ask for Anything More*, Donnell Library, 1983; *Roberta*, 1985.

Dinner Theater: *Eat Your Spinach, Baby*, 1970, *Say It with Music*, 1970, *Darling Eileen*, 1970, all Cookes Tavern, CT; *Judy Garland Story, Kiss Me Kate, Pajama Game*, all Pig n Whistle, NY, 1970; *Hello, Dolly!*, Club Bene, NJ, 1971; *Plaza Suite*, Amber Lantern, NY, 1973; *Unsinkable Molly Brown*, Canal Fulton, Carousel, OH, 1978; *No, No, Nanette, Funny Girl*, Carousel, OH, 1979; *Oklahoma!*, Naples Dinner Theater, FL, 1981; *West Side Story, The King and I, Babes in Arms, Do I Hear a Waltz?*, all 1982, *Once Upon a Mattress, Fiddler on the Roof, Fabulous 40's Radio Show, Annie*, all 1983, *Gypsy*, 1984, all Three Little Bakers Dinner Theatre.

MAJOR TOURS—*Gypsy*, U.S. cities, 1985.

SIDELIGHTS: MEMBERSHIPS—Actors' Equity Association, Society of Stage Directors and Choreographers.

ADDRESS: HOME—57 W. 75th Street, New York, NY 10023.

*   *   *

NEWHART, Bob   1929-

PERSONAL: Born September 5, 1929, in Oak Park, IL; married Virginia Quinn, January 12, 1964; children: four. EDUCATION: Loyola University, B.S., 1952. MILITARY: U.S. Army, 1952-54.

VOCATION: Actor and comedian.

CAREER: PRINCIPAL TELEVISION APPEARANCES—*Dan Sarkin Show*, 1957; *Jack Paar Show*, 1960; *The Bob Newhart Show*, NBC, 1961-62; *The Tonight Show*, NBC, 1962; host, *The Entertainers*, CBS, 1964; *The Hollywood Palace*, ABC, 1964; Bob Hartley, *The Bob Newhart Show*, CBS, 1972-78; Dick Loudon, *Newhart*, CBS, 1982-present.

PRINCIPAL FILM APPEARANCES—*Cool Millions; Catch 22*, Paramount, 1970; *On a Clear Day You Can See Forever*, Paramount,

1970; *Cold Turkey*, United Artists, 1971; *First Family*, Warner Brothers, 1980.

RECORDINGS—*The Button Down Mind of Bob Newhart*, Warner Brothers; *Royal Command Performance*, London.

AWARDS: Emmy Award, Peabody Award, 1961, for *The Bob Newhart Show;* Sword of Loyola Award, 1976.

SIDELIGHTS: Newhart's first job was as a copywriter for the Fred Niles Film company; he was also a law clerk at the U.S. Gypsum Company.

ADDRESS: OFFICE—315 S. Beverly Drive, Beverly Hills, CA 90212.*

*   *   *

NEWMAN, Emil   ?-1984

PERSONAL: Died August 30, 1984.

VOCATION: Composer.

CAREER: PRINCIPAL FILM WORK—Composer: *Sacred Reunion; Rise and Shine*, 1941; *Tall, Dark and Handsome*, 1941; *The Loves of Edgar Allan Poe*, 1942; *Berlin Correspondent*, 1942; *The Magnificent Dope*, 1942; *The Man Who Wouldn't Die*, 1942; *Tonight We Raid Calais*, 1943; *Pin-Up Girl*, 1944; *Bedside Manner; Nob Hill*, 1945; *Behind Green Lights; Texas, Brooklyn and Heaven*, 1948; *Guilty of Treason*, 1949; *Cry Danger*, 1951; *The Lady Says No*, 1951; *The 13th Letter*, 1951; *Big Jim McLain*, 1952; *Japanese War Bride*, 1952; *Rancho Notorious*, 1952; *Hondo*, 1953; *Island in the Sky*, 1953; *The Mad Magician*, 1954; *Ring of Fear*, 1954; *The Naked Street*, United Artists, 1955; *Chicago Confidential*, United Artists, 1957; *Unwed Mother*, Allied Artists, 1958; *Riot in the Juvenile Prison*, United Artists, 1959; *The Great Sioux Massacre*, Columbia, 1965.*

*   *   *

NEWMAN, Phyllis   1933-

PERSONAL: Born March 19, 1933, in Jersey City, NJ; daughter of Arthur and Rachael Newman; married Adolph Green (the playwright, lyricist, and actor), January 31, 1960; children: Adam, Amanda. EDUCATION: Western Reserve University and Columbia University; studied for the stage with Wynn Handman and singing with Keith Davis.

VOCATION: Actress, singer, writer, and director.

CAREER: STAGE DEBUT—Sarah, *Wish You Were Here*, Imperial, NY, 1953. PRINCIPAL STAGE APPEARANCES—Revue, *I Feel Wonderful*, Theatre de Lys, NY, 1954; understudy for Judy Holiday, *Bells Are Ringing*, Shubert, NY, 1956; Jane Bennett, *First Impressions*, Alvin, NY, 1959; Sylvie, *Moonbirds*, Cort, NY, 1959; Martha Vail, *Subways Are for Sleeping*, St. James, NY, 1961; Sura, *Pleasures and Palaces*, Fisher, Detroit, 1965; Eve, Princess Barbara, Ella/Passionella, *The Apple Tree*, Shubert, NY, 1967;

PHYLLIS NEWMAN

Claire, *On the Town*, Imperial, NY, 1971; *Last of the Red Hot Lovers*, Westbury Music Fair, NY, 1972; Edna Edison, *The Prisoner of Second Avenue*, Eugene O'Neill, NY, 1972; *Gala Tribute to Joshua Logan*, Imperial, NY, 1975; *My Mother Was a Fortune Teller*, Hudson Guild, NY, 1978; *The Madwoman of Central Park West*, 22 Steps, NY, 1979; *Vamps and Rideouts*, Unicorn, Berkshire Theatre Festival, Stockbridge, MA, 1982; also: *Red Rover, Red Rover; Rocket to the Moon; Light Up the Sky; Annie Get Your Gun; I Married an Angel*.

MAJOR TOURS—*I'm Getting My Act Together and Taking It on the Road*, Chicago, NY; *Vamps and Rideouts*, 1982.

PRINCIPAL STAGE WORK—Director: *Straws in the Wind*, American Place, NY, 1975; also: *Walking Papers*, Circle in the Square, NY; *Area Code 212*, Public Theatre, NY; *Facade*, for Leonard Bernstein; *Franklin D. Roosevelt Centennial Show*, NY.

FILM DEBUT—Juanita Badger, *Picnic*, Columbia, 1955. PRINCIPAL FILM APPEARANCES—*The Vagabond King*, Paramount, 1956; *Let's Rock*, Columbia, 1958; *To Find a Man*, Columbia, 1972; others.

PRINCIPAL TELEVISION APPEARANCES—Doris Hudson, *Diagnosis: Unknown*, CBS, 1960; regular, *That Was the Week That Was*, NBC, 1964-65; Mary Severance, "Olympus 7-0000," *ABC Stage 67*, ABC, 1967; *The Madwoman of Central Park West; The Tonight Show* (also as guest host).

NIGHTCLUBS AND CABARET—Pfister, Milwaukee, WI, 1974; Freddy's, NY, 1984; others.

AWARDS: Antoinette Perry Award, Best Featured Actress in a

Musical, 1961, for *Subways Are for Sleeping*.

WRITINGS: PLAYS, PRODUCED—*My Mother Was a Fortune Teller*, Hudson Guild, NY, 1978; co-author, *The Madwoman of Central Park West*, 22 Steps, NY, 1979.

SIDELIGHTS: MEMBERSHIPS—Actors' Equity Association.

ADDRESS: AGENT—Harris M. Spylios, The Spylios Agency, 250 W. 57th Street, New York, NY 10107.

*   *   *

NICASTRO, Michelle   1960-

PERSONAL: Born March 31, 1960, in Washington, DC; daughter of Norman Joseph (an opthalmologist) and Carole Rose (Guarino) Nicastro. EDUCATION: Northwestern University, B.F.A., 1982; studied acting with Bud Beyer and Alice Spivak in New York.

VOCATION: Actress and singer.

CAREER: STAGE DEBUT—Chava, *Fiddler on the Roof*, Candlelight Dinner Playhouse, Chicago, IL. NEW YORK DEBUT—Ariadne, *Merlin*, Mark Hellinger, 1982-83.

FILM DEBUT—Darlene, *Body Rock*, New World Pictures, 1984.

TELEVISION DEBUT—Diane Barstow, *Maggie Briggs*, Lorimar, CBS, 1983. PRINCIPAL TELEVISION APPEARANCES—Nurse Susan, *Airwolf*, CBS, 1984; Terry, *Knight Rider*, NBC, 1984.

AWARDS: Sarah Siddons, 1978, for vocal competition.

SIDELIGHTS: RECREATIONS—Singing, foreign travel, French.

Nicastro told *CTFT*: "I play tennis, work out at a gym, love to cook, and garden."

ADDRESS: AGENT—David Shapira and Associates, 15301 Ventura Blvd., Suite 345, Sherman Oaks, CA 91403.

*   *   *

NICHOLAS, Paul   1945-

PERSONAL: Born Paul Beuselinck, December 3, 1945, in Peterborough, UK; son of Oscar (a lawyer) and Marjorie Beuselinck; married Susan (died, 1979); married Linzi Jennings, December 10, 1984; children: Natasha, Oscar, Alexander. EDUCATION: Attended St. Mary's Town and Country School, London.

VOCATION: Actor.

CAREER: LONDON STAGE DEBUT—Claude, *Hair*, Shaftesbury, London. PRINCIPAL STAGE APPEARANCES—*Jesus Christ Superstar*, London; *Grease*, London; *Much Ado About Nothing*, Crete and *Sergeant Pepper*, Young Vic, London; *Pilgrim*, Prospect Theatre Company, London; *The Innocent Bystanders, T. Zee and the Lost Race*, Royal Court, London; *Rum Tum Tugger, Cats*,

PAUL NICHOLAS

London, 1981; *Doubting Thomas*, London; *Starburst*, London; Buttons, *Cinderella*, Wimbledon Theater; Pirate King, *Pirates of Penzance*, London.

PRINCIPAL TELEVISION APPEARANCES—*Season of the Witch; Early Struggles; Two Up Two Down; Chips; The Lady Killers; The Boys from Ipanema; A Little Rococo; Just Good Friends*, BBC.

PRINCIPAL FILM APPEARANCES—*Tommy; Stardust; The Jazz Singer; Listztomania; Sergeant Pepper's Lonely Hearts Club Band; Yesterday's Hero; The World Is Full of Married Men; Alice; Nutcracker; Invitation to the Wedding*.

SIDELIGHTS: MEMBERSHIPS—British Actors' Equity Association, Screen Actors Guild, American Federation of Television and Radio Artists.

ADDRESS: AGENT   Duncan Heath Associates, Paramount House, 167 Wardour Street, London W1, England.

*   *   *

NICHTERN, Claire

PERSONAL: Born Claire Joseph, in New York City; daughter of Fred and Rebecca (Brumer) Joseph; married Sol Nichtern, June 4, 1944 (divorced); married Herbert Kallem (a sculptor); children: Judith, David. EDUCATION: Attended New York University.

VOCATION: Producer.

CAREER: PRINCIPAL STAGE WORK—Producer: *The Banker's*

Daughter, 1961-62; *The Typist and the Tiger*, 1962-63; *Luv*, NY, 1964-67, and London, 1964-65; *Jimmy Shine*, 1968-69; *The Trial of A. Lincoln*, 1971; *I Got a Song*, 1974; *House of Blue Leaves*, 1976; *Absent Friends*, 1977; *Cold Storage*, 1977-78.

RELATED CAREER: Casting director, 1955-58; production coordinator, 1959-60, Phoenix Theater, NY; assistant general manager, Playwrights Company, 1958-59; director of admissions, American Academy of Dramatic Arts, 1970; producer in residence, associate director, Circle in the Square, NY, 1973; director of creative affairs, Warner-Regency, 1978-79; William Morris Agency, 1979; president, Warner Theater Productions, Inc., 1979.

AWARDS: Antoinette Perry Award, 1965.

SIDELIGHTS: MEMBERSHIPS—League of New York Theaters, Association of Theatrical Press Agents and Managers, American Theatre Wing, American Film Institute, Actors Fund.

ADDRESS: HOME—New York, NY. OFFICE—Warner Theatre Productions, Three E. 54th Street, New York, NY 10022.

*   *   *

NORMAN, Maidie   1912-

PERSONAL: Born Maidie Gamble, October 16, 1912, in Lima, OH; daughter of Louis C. (an engineer) and Lila (Graham) Gamble; married McHenry Norman (a real estate broker) December 22, 1937 (died); children: McHenry Norman. EDUCATION: Bennett College,

MAIDIE NORMAN

Greensboro, NC; Columbia University, NY; trained for the stage at the Actors Laboratory, Hollywood, CA. RELIGION: Methodist.

VOCATION: Actress and teacher.

CAREER: STAGE DEBUT—Honey, *Deep Are the Roots*, Mayan, Los Angeles, CA, 1949. PRINCIPAL STAGE APPEARANCES—Mae, *Sugar Hill*, Hollywood, 1950; Lena Younger (Mama), *A Raisin in the Sun*, Hollywood, 1961; title role, *Medea*, CA, 1962; *Purlie Victorious*, CA, 1963; Odessa, *The Amen Corner*, San Francisco, CA, 1964; title role, *Andromache*, Stanford University, Palo Alto, CA, 1968; Mother of the Groom, *Blood Wedding*, Stanford University, Palo Alto, CA, 1969; also: Wendy, *Sty of the Blind Pig*; blind mother, *Kung Fu*; Ju Ju woman, *Carmon*; three seasons with Sombrero Playhouse, Phoenix, AZ.

MAJOR TOURS—Her one woman show, college tour, 1958.

FILM DEBUT—(as Mady Norman) Mother, *Burning Cross*, Somerset-Screen Guild, 1947. PRINCIPAL FILM APPEARANCES—(as Maidie Norman) Mother, *The Well*, United Artists, 1951; Maid, *Torch Song*, Metro-Goldwyn-Mayer, 1953; *Forever Female*, Paramount, 1953; Maid, *Susan Slept Here*, RKO, 1954; *About Mrs. Leslie*, RKO, 1954; Elvira Stitt, *Whatever Happened to Baby Jane?*, Seven Arts-Aldrich/Warner Brothers, 1961; Mother, *Maurie*, National General, 1973; Dorothy, *Airport 77*, Universal, 1977.

TELEVISION DEBUT—*Four Star Playhouse*, CBS, mid-1950's. PRINCIPAL TELEVISION APPEARANCES—*Dragnet*, NBC; *Playhouse 90*, CBS; *Matinee Theatre*, NBC, 1958; *Fireside Theatre*, NBC and ABC; *Cannon*, CBS; *Harry O*, ABC; *Police Woman*, NBC; *Kung Fu*, ABC; *The Jeffersons*, CBS; *Ironside*, NBC; *Marcus Welby, M.D.*, ABC; *Ben Casey*, ABC; *Young Interns*; *Roots, the Second Generation*; "Josh's Run," *Lucas Tanner*, NBC, 1974; *Righteous Apples*; *Matt Houston*, ABC, 1985; *Hotel*, ABC, 1985. Movies and miniseries: *Say Goodbye, Maggie Cole*, 1972; Wendy, *Sty of the Blind Pig*, 1974; *Bare Essence*, 1982; *Secrets of a Mother and Daughter*, 1983.

RELATED CAREER—Administrator of West Coast ANTA Academy, 1961-1964; artist-in-residence, Stanford University, Palo Alto, CA, 1968-69; lecturer, history of black people's theatre, UCLA, Westwood, CA, 1969-77.

AWARDS: Cabrillo Award, 1952; Bennett College Achievement Award, 1953; Author's Study Club, Outstanding Citizen Award, 1955; Woman of the Year, Los Angeles Sentinel, 1964; Black Filmmakers Hall of Fame Inductee, 1977; Maidie Norman Research Award (an annual award presented in Maidie Norman's name to a student at UCLA in theatre arts who presents the best research paper on the history of black people's theatre), 1982-present; member of Olympic Dance Committee, 1984; Professional Artist Award, California Educational Theatre Association, 1985.

SIDELIGHTS: MEMBERSHIPS—Actors' Equity Association, Screen Actors Guild, American Federation of Television and Radio Artists, League of Allied Arts, California Educational Theatre Association. RECREATION—Oil painting and handwork, including hooking rugs, needlepoint, and quilting.

Norman informed *CTFT:* "I have enjoyed every moment of my life as an actress and teacher. It has been most rewarding to play roles written by the great playwrights: Racine's *Andromache*, Baldwin's *Amen Corner*, Phillip Hayes Dean's *Sty of the Blind Pig*, and Hansberry's *Raisin in the Sun*. I have also loved character roles.

"My stint as an artist-in-residence at Stanford University was a real career bonus. It was one of the few opportunities I have had to use my training and skills in classic theater. Also, having the opportunity to develop a course at UCLA in *Black Theatre—Its History and Literature*, was a joy. It remains the only black studies course extant at the university.

"If I were to name a particular highlight it would have to be my induction into the Black Filmmakers Hall of Fame at Oakland, CA. To be so honored by my black brothers and sisters is the highest merit.

"When I can, I travel. I keep in touch with what is happening in the theatre at home and abroad. I spend many hours in community service. I am on the board of the Los Angeles Contemporary Dance Theatre, and am an officer of the League of Allied Arts (a scholarship funding group). I lecture at various universities. I also paint. Landscapes, birds, and animals are my favorite subjects. I feel that as long as I have some project to finish I will never die."

ADDRESS: HOME—4265 Colfax Avenue, Apt. 28, Studio City, CA, 91604. AGENT—Dade-Rosen, 12345 Ventura Blvd., Studio City, CA 91604.

*　　　*　　　*

NORTH, Alex　1910-

PERSONAL: Born December 4, 1910; son of Jesse (a blacksmith) and Bela (Suifer) North; married Annemarie Hollger, March 27, 1940; children: Steven, Elissa, Dylan. EDUCATION: Studied music at Juilliard, Philadelphia, PA, 1929-32, Moscow Conservatory, 1932-35, and Curtis Institute, NY, with Ernst Toch and Aaron Copland. MILITARY: U.S. War Department.

VOCATION: Composer.

CAREER: PRINCIPAL FILM WORK—Composer: *A Streetcar Named Desire*, Warner Brothers, 1951; *The 13th Letter*, Twentieth Century-Fox, 1951; *Death of a Salesman*, Columbia, 1951; *Viva Zapata!*, *Les Miserables*, *Pony Soldier*, all Twentieth Century-Fox, 1952; *The Member of the Wedding*, Columbia, 1953; *Go, Man, Go!*, United Artists, 1954; *Desiree*, Twentieth Century-Fox, 1954; *The Racers*, Twentieth Century-Fox, 1955; *Unchained Melody*, Warner Brothers, 1955; *Man with the Gun*, United Artists, 1955; *The Rose Tattoo*, Paramount, 1955; *I'll Cry Tomorrow*, Metro-Goldwyn-Mayer, 1956; *The Bad Seed*, Warner Brothers, 1956; *The Rainmaker*, Paramount, 1956; *Four Girls in Town*, Universal, 1956; *The King and Four Queens*, United Artists, 1956.

The Bachelor Party, United Artists, 1957; *The Long, Hot Summer*, Twentieth Century-Fox, 1958; *Stage Struck*, RKO, 1958; *Hot Spell*, Paramount, 1958; *South Sea Adventure*, Cinerama, 1958; *The Sound and the Fury*, Twentieth Century-Fox, 1959; *The Wonderful Country*, United Artists, 1959; *Spartacus*, Universal, 1960; *The Children's Hour*, *The Misfits*, both United Artists, 1961; *Sanctuary*, Twentieth Century-Fox, 1961; *All Fall Down*, Metro-Goldwyn-Mayer, 1962; *Cleopatra*, Twentieth Century-Fox, 1963; *The Outrage*, Metro-Goldwyn-Mayer, 1964; *Cheyenne Autumn*, Warner Brothers, 1965; *The Agony and the Ecstasy*, Twentieth Century-Fox, 1965; *Who's Afraid of Virginia Woolf?*, Warner Brothers, 1966; *Africa*, ABC Motion Pictures, 1967; *The Devil's Brigade*,

ALEX NORTH

United Artists, 1968; *The Shoes of the Fisherman,* Metro-Goldwyn-Mayer, 1968; *A Dream of Kings,* National General, 1969; *Hard Contract,* Twentieth Century-Fox, 1969.

Willard, Crosby, 1971; *Pocket Money,* Newman-Forman, 1972; *Once Upon a Scoundrel, Rebel Jesus,* both Independent, 1972; *Lost in the Stars,* Ely Landau, Inc., 1973; *Shanks,* William Castle Productions, 1973; *Journey into Fear,* New World, 1974; *Bite the Bullet,* Columbia, 1975; *Passover Plot,* Atlas Films, 1976; *Somebody Killed Her Husband,* Martin Poll, 1979; *Wiseblood,* Ithaca, 1980; *Carny,* Lorimar, 1980; *Dragonslayer,* Paramount-Disney, 1981; *Under the Volcano,* Ithaca, 1984; *Prizzi's Honor,* ABC Motion Pictures, 1985.

PRINCIPAL TELEVISION WORK—Composer: *Billy Rose Show; Playhouse 90; Nero Wolfe; I'm a Lawyer; F.D. Roosevelt Series; Silent Night,* ABC; *The Man and the City; Rich Man Poor Man; The Word; Sister-Sister.*

PRINCIPAL STAGE WORK—Composer: *Death of a Salesman; The Innocents; Coriolanus; Richard III; The American Clock; Tis of Thee; Queen Sheba; The Great Campaign.*

AWARDS: Guggenheim Fellowship, 1947, 1948; Academy Award nominations, 1951 for *A Streetcar Named Desire,* 1951 for *Death of a Salesman,* 1952 for *Viva Zapata!,* 1955 for *Unchained Melody,* 1955 for *Rose Tattoo,* 1956 for *The Rainmaker,* 1960 for *Spartacus;* Laurel Awards, 1956, 1957, 1966, 1967, 1969, 1971; Academy Award nomination, Composers and Lyricists Guild Award, 1963 for *Cleopatra;* Academy Award nomination, 1965 for *The Agony and the Ecstasy;* Academy Award nomination, 1966 for *Who's Afraid of*

Virginia Woolf?; Academy Award nomination, Golden Globe Award, 1968 for *Shoes of the Fisherman;* Academy Award nomination, 1973 for *Shanks;* Academy Award nomination, Western Heritage Wrangler Award, 1975-76 for *Bite the Bullet;* Academy Award nomination, 1981 for *Dragonslayer,* 1984 for *Under the Volcano.*

SIDELIGHTS: MEMBERSHIPS—American Society of Composers, Authors, and Publishers, Composers and Lyricists Guild, Academy of Arts and Sciences and Films, Affiliated Federation of Musicians, National Academy of Recording Arts and Sciences.

ADDRESS: OFFICE—630 Resolano Drive, Pacific Palisades, CA 90272.

*   *   *

NOVAK, Kim   1933-

PERSONAL: Born Marilyn Novak, February 13, 1933, in Chicago, IL; daughter of Joseph A. and Blanche (Kral) Novak; married Richard Johnson, April, 1965 (divorced); married Robert Malloy, January, 1978. EDUCATION: Los Angeles City College, A.A., 1958.

VOCATION: Actress.

CAREER: FILM DEBUT—1954. PRINCIPAL FILM APPEARANCES—*Man with the Golden Arm,* United Artists, 1956; *Eddy Duchin Story,*

KIM NOVAK

Columbia, 1956; *Picnic,* Columbia, 1956; *Pal Joey,* Columbia, 1957; *Jeanne Eagels Story,* Columbia, 1957; *Bell, Book, and Candle,* Columbia, 1959; *Middle of the Night,* Columbia, 1959; *Strangers When We Meet,* Columbia, 1960; *Boys Night Out,* Metro-Goldwyn-Mayer, 1962; *Notorious Landlady,* Columbia, 1962; *Kiss Me Stupid,* Lopert, 1964; *Amorous Adventures of Moll Flanders,* Paramount, 1965; *The Legend of Lylah Clare,* Metro-Goldwyn-Mayer, 1968; *The Great Bank Robbery,* 1969; *Tales That Witness Madness,* Paramount, 1973; *The White Buffalo,* 1977; *Just a Gigolo,* 1979; *The Mirror Crack'd,* Associated Film, 1980.

PRINCIPAL TELEVISION APPEARANCES—Movies: *Third Girl from the Left,* 1974; *Satan's Triangle,* 1975; *Malibu,* 1982; *Alfred Hitchcock Presents,* 1985.

AWARDS: *Box-Office Magazine* Award, Ten Most Popular Movie Stars, 1956; Brussels World's Fair Award, All-Time Favorite Actress in the World, 1958; All-American Favorite Award, 1961.

SIDELIGHTS: MEMBERSHIPS—Screen Actors Guild.

ADDRESS: AGENT—Leading Artists, Inc., 445 N. Bedford Drive, Penthouse, Beverly Hills, CA 90210.

O

O'BANNON, Dan

VOCATION: Screenwriter, producer, and director.

CAREER: FILM DEBUT—Co-writer, production designer, special effects director and actor, *Dark Star,* Bryanston Productions, 1974. PRINCIPAL FILM WORK—Co-writer, *Alien,* Twentieth Century-Fox, 1979; co-writer, *Blue Thunder,* Columbia, 1983; producer and co-writer, *The Space Vampires,* 1984; writer and director, *The Return of the Living Dead,* 1985; writer, *Lifeforce,* Cannon/Tri-Star, 1985; writer, *Invaders from Mars* (upcoming).

SIDELIGHTS: MEMBERSHIPS—Writers Guild of America, West.

ADDRESS: AGENT—The Morton Agency, 1105 Glendon Avenue, Los Angeles, CA 90024.

* * *

O'BRIAN, Hugh   1930-

PERSONAL: Born Hugh Charles Krampe, April 19, 1930, in New York City; son of Hugh John and Edith Krampe. EDUCATION: University of Cincinnati; City College of Los Angeles. MILITARY: U.S. Marine Corps, drill instructor.

VOCATION: Actor.

CAREER: NEW YORK DEBUT—Title role, *Destry,* Imperial, 1959. PRINCIPAL STAGE APPEARANCES—Romain, *First Love,* Morosco, NY, 1961; Sky Masterson, *Guys and Dolls,* Melodyland, Los Angeles, 1963, revival, New York City Center, 1966; Julian, *Cactus Flower,* Blackstone, Chicago, 1967; Murray Burns, *A Thousand Clowns,* Arlington Park Playhouse, Arlington Heights, IL, 1972; *The Desperate Hours,* Arlington Park Playhouse, 1973; Walter Burns, *The Front Page,* Huntingdon Hartford, Los Angeles, 1974; Alan Baker, *Come Blow Your Horn,* Drury Lane, Chicago, 1974; George Washington, *The Decision,* Walnut Street Theatre, Philadelphia, 1976; also *The Odd Couple, The Tender Trap, The Music Man.*

MAJOR TOURS—Sky Masterson, *Guys and Dolls,* summer, 1965; Julian, *Cactus Flower,* National Company, 1967; *1776,* 1972; Sky Masterson, *Guys and Dolls,* USO, Far East.

HUGH O'BRIAN

PRINCIPAL FILM WORK—Co-producer, *The Country Girl,* Billy Rose, NY, 1972.

FILM DEBUT—*Never Fear,* 1950. PRINCIPAL FILM APPEARANCES—*Little Big Horn; Broken Lance; There's No Business Like Show Business; In Harms Way; Killer Force; Ten Little Indians; The Shootist; Game of Death.*

TELEVISION DEBUT—*Arch Oboler's Mystery Theatre,* 1949. PRINCIPAL TELEVISION APPEARANCES—*90 Minutes; Studio One; Dial M for Murder; Fantasy Island;* appeared as *Wyatt Earp,* six years.

RELATED CAREER—Founder, production company, HOB Inc.; founder, Hugh O'Brian Annual Acting Awards, University of California at Los Angeles.

ADDRESS: OFFICE—10880 Wilshire Blvd., Suite 1500, Los Angeles, CA 90024.

223

O'BRIEN, Edmond   1915-85

PERSONAL: Born September 10, 1915, in New York City; died May 9, 1985; married Nancy Kelly, 1941 (divorced, 1942); married Olga San Juan, 1948 (divorced); children: Bridget, Maria, Brendan.

VOCATION: Actor.

CAREER: FILM DEBUT—*Hunchback of Notre Dame*, 1939. PRINCIPAL FILM APPEARANCES—*A Girl, A Guy and a Gob*, 1941; *Parachute Batallion*, 1941; *Obliging Young Lady*, 1941; *Powder Town*, 1942; *The Amazing Mrs. Holiday*, 1943; *Winged Victory*, 1944; *The Killers*, 1946; *The Web*, 1947; *The Double Life*, 1947; *Another Part of the Forest*, 1948; *For the Love of Many*, 1948; *Fighter Squadron*, 1948; *White Heat*, 1949; *Backfire*, 1950; *D.O.A.*, 1950; *Between Midnight and Dawn*, 1950; *The Admiral Was a Lady*, 1950; *711 Ocean Drive*, 1950.

Two of a Kind, 1951; *The Redhead and the Cowboy*, 1951; *Warpath*, 1951; *Silver City*, 1951; *The Denver and the Rio Grande; The Turning Point*, 1952; *The Hitch-Hiker*, 1953; *The Bigamist*, 1953; *Julius Caesar*, 1953; *Man in the Dark*, 1953; *The Barefoot Contessa*, 1954; *Shield for Murder*, 1954; *The Third Voice*, Twentieth Century-Fox, 1960; *The Great Imposter*, Universal, 1961; *The Birdman of Alcatracz*, United Artists, 1962; *The Man Who Shot Liberty Valance*, Paramount, 1962; *The Longest Day*, Twentieth Century-Fox, 1962.

Seven Days in May, Paramount, 1964; *Sylvia*, Paramount, 1965; *The Viscount*, 1967; *The Love God*, 1969; *The Wild Bunch*, Warner Brothers, 1969; *Dream No Evil; To Commit a Murder*, Cinerama, 1970; *They Only Kill Their Masters*, Metro-Goldwyn-Mayer, 1972; *99 and 44/100% Dead*, Twentieth Century-Fox, 1974.

PRINCIPAL FILM WORK—Producer and director, *Mantrap;* co-director, *Shield for Murder*.

PRINCIPAL TELEVISION APPEARANCES—Movies: *The Hanged Man*, NBC, 1964; Boss Will Varner, *Long Hot Summer*, ABC, 1965; *Doomsday Flight*, NBC, 1967; *The Outsider*, NBC, 1967; *The Intruders*, NBC, 1970; *River of Mystery*, NBC, 1971; *What's a Nice Girl Like You . . .*, ABC, 1971; *Jigsaw*, ABC, 1972. Series: *Name of the Game; Johnny Midnight*, NBC, 1960; Benedict, *Sam Benedict*, NBC, 1962-63. Episodic: *Robert Montgomery Presents; Lux Video Theatre; Playhouse 90; Mission: Impossible; World of Disney; Streets of San Francisco; McMillan and Wife.*

STAGE DEBUT—Broadway: *Daughters of Atrius.* PRINCIPAL STAGE APPEARANCES—Broadway: *Leave Her to Heaven;* Laurence Olivier's *Hamlet;* Mark Anthony, *Julius Caesar; Star Wagon;* John Gielgud's *Hamlet; Parnell; Winged Victory;* Mercury Theatre Players.

PRINCIPAL RADIO APPEARANCE—*War of the Worlds*, 1938.

AWARDS: Academy Award, Best Supporting Actor, 1954, for *The Barefoot Contessa;* Academy Award nomination, Best Supporting Actor, 1964, for *Seven Days in May.**

*   *   *

O'BRIEN, Timothy   1929-

PERSONAL: Born March 8, 1929, in Shillong, Assam, India; son of

TIMOTHY O'BRIEN

Brian Palliser Tieghe and Elinor Laura (Mackenzie) O'Brien. EDUCATION: Attended Wellington College, Cambridge University, and Yale University.

VOCATION: Scenic designer.

CAREER: PRINCIPAL STAGE WORK—Scenic designer: *The Bald Primadonna, The New Tenant*, London, 1956; *Hunter's Moon, Five Finger Exercise*, London, 1958; *The Daring Buds of May*, London, 1959; *Don't Shoot, We're English*, London, 1960; *Henry IV, Part I, Progress to the Park*, London, 1961; *Next Time I'll Sing to You, Licence to Murder, Luv, Poor Bitos*, London, 1963; *Hedda Gabler, Entertaining Mr. Sloane, A Scent of Flowers, Waiting for Godot*, London, *Poor Bitos*, NY, 1964; *Traveling Light*, London, *A Scent of Flowers*, Stuttgart, Germany, 1965.

Royal Shakespeare Company, London and Stratford: *Tango, Days in the Trees, Joey Joey, Staircase*, 1966; *All's Well That Ends Well, As You Like It, Romeo and Juliet*, 1967; *The Merry Wives of Windsor, Troilus and Cressida, The Latent Heterosexual*, 1968; *Pericles, Women Beware Women, Bartholomew Fair*, 1969; *Measure for Measure*, 1970; *The Merchant of Venice, Enemies, The Man of Mode* (with Tazeena Firth), 1971; *The Lower Depths, The Island of the Mighty*, 1972; *Richard II, Love's Labour's Lost*, 1973; *Summerfolk*, 1974; *The Merry Wives of Windsor, The Marrying of Ann Leete*, 1975; *The Zykovs*, 1976.

National Theater of Great Britain, London: *Next of Kin*, 1974; *John Gabriel Borkman*, 1975; *Troilus and Cressida, Force of Habit*, 1976; *Tales from the Vienna Woods, Bedroom Farce*, 1977; *Evita*, London, 1978, NY, 1979.

Royal Opera: *The Knot Garden*, 1970, *Peter Grimes*, 1975, *The*

Rake's Progress, 1979; *The Bassarids*, English National Opera, 1974; *La Cenerentola*, Oslo, Norway, 1972; *Pericles*, Comedie Francaise, Paris, 1974; *The Bassarids*, Frankfurt, 1975; *Wozzeck*, Adelaide Festival, 1976; *Falstaff*, Berlin, 1977; *Cunning Little Vixen*, Gothenburg, 1978; *A Midsummer Night's Dream*, Sydney, 1978; *Peter Grimes*, Gothenburg, 1979.

·*Lulu*, Royal Opera, London, 1981; *La Ronde*, Royal Shakespeare Company, London, 1982; *A Doll's Life*, NY, 1982; *Le Grand Macabre*, English National Opera, London, 1982; *Turandot*, Vienna State Opera, 1983; *Tannhauser*, Royal Opera, London, 1984; *Tramway Road*, Lyric, Hammersmith, 1984; *Samson*, Royal Opera, London, 1985; *Old Times*, Theatre Royal, Haymarket, London, 1985.

PRINCIPAL FILM WORK—Scenic designer, *Night Must Fall*, 1964.

AWARDS: Gold Medal Award, Prague Quadriennale, Best Set Design, 1975.

ADDRESS: OFFICE—33 Lansdowne Gardens, London SW8, England.

*   *   *

ODITZ, Carol   1946-

PERSONAL: Born August 15, 1946, in New York City; daughter of Louis and Doree (Corn) Oditz; married Timothy Phillips (divorced); married David Chapman (a scenic designer), December 31, 1979. EDUCATION: University of South Florida, B.A., 1969; studied with Lester Polokov at the Polokov Studio of Design.

VOCATION: Costume designer.

CAREER: PRINCIPAL STAGE WORK: Costume designer—Broadway: *Monday After the Miracle; Is There Life After High School?; Play Me a Country Song; A History of American Film.* Off-Broadway: *The Wild Duck; How I Got That Story; All's Well That Ends Well; A Midsummer Night's Dream; The Crazy Locomotive; Gimme Shelter; White Pelicans; Medal of Honor Rag; The Heebie Jeebies.* Musicals: *The All Night Strut; Storyville; Lewis J. Stadlen as Groucho; Unsung Cole; Vagabond Stars; I'm Getting My Act Together and Taking It on the Road; Troupers; Day by Day.*

Worked at the following New York and Regional theatres: New York Shakespeare Festival, Kennedy Center, Arena Stage, Long Wharf Theatre, Spoleto, Milwaukee Repertory, American Place, BAM Theatre Company, Chelsea Theatre, Dodger Theatre, PAF Playhouse, Indiana Repertory, Folger Theatre, Ford's Theatre, Berkshire Theatre Festival, Manhattan Theatre Club, Herbert Berghoff Studio, John Drew Theatre, Williamstown Theatre Festival.

PRINCIPAL FILM WORK: Costume designer: *The Lost Boy*, Filmpressions; *Six Characters in Search of an Author; The Renegade*, Filmpressions; *Girlfriends; Medal of Honor Rag; Where Are You Going*, Nepenthe Productions.

AWARDS: Obie Award, Drama Desk nomination, for *The Crazy Locomotive*.

SIDELIGHTS: MEMBERSHIPS—League of Professional Theatre Women, United Scenic Artists, Mensa.

ADDRESS: HOME—New York, NY.

*   *   *

O'KEEFE, Michael

BRIEF ENTRY: Born in Larchmont, NY. He attended the American Academy of Dramatic Arts in Manhattan and went on to New York University for one year. He is married to Alma O'Keefe and they are the parents of twins. Actor. He helped Arthur and Michael Lessac create the Colannades Theatre Lab, an experimental theatre. There he won a Dramatist's Guild Award for his performance in *Moliere in Spite of Himself*. Other stage credits include *Short Eyes*, Second Stage, NY; *Killdeer* and *Ron Rico, Who Are You?*, both at the New York Shakespeare Festival; *Streamers* and *Solomon's Child*, both at the Long Wharf, New Haven, CT; *An American Tragedy*, at the Arena Stage, Washington, DC. His Broadway credits include *Streamers, Fifth of July*, and *Mass Appeal*. His television work includes *Friendly Persuasion*, 1975; *The Dark Secret of Harvest Home*, 1978; *The Oaths; Rumor of War*, 1980. His films include *Gray Lady Down*, Universal, 1978; *The Great Santini*, Warner Brothers, 1979; *Caddyshack*, Warner Brothers, 1980; *Split Image*, Orion, 1982; *Nate and Hayes*, Paramount, 1983; *Finders Keepers*, Warner Brothers, 1984; *The Slugger's Wife*, 1985. In 1979, O'Keefe was nominated for an Academy Award for Best Supporting Actor, for his work in *The Great Santini*. He is currently filming *Captured*.*

*   *   *

OLIVER, Rochelle   1937-

PERSONAL: Born Rochelle Olshever, April 15, 1937, in New York City; daughter of Sol and Bess (Goldsmith) Olshever; married James Patterson, October 15, 1959 (died, 1972); children: John. EDUCATION: Attended Brooklyn College; trained for the stage at the Henry Street Playhouse and the Herbert Berghof Studio with Uta Hagen. RELIGION: Jewish.

VOCATION: Actress.

CAREER: NEW YORK STAGE DEBUT—Lily, *Toys in the Attic*, Hudson, 1960. PRINCIPAL STAGE APPEARANCES—Fenya, *The Brothers Karamazov*, Village Gate, NY, 1956-57; Lolly, *Jackknife*, Village Gate, NY, 1958; Vincent, Cricket, NY, 1959; Lonesome Sally, *Terrible Jim Fitch*, Stage 73, NY; Iris, *Harold*, Cort, NY, 1962; Honey, *Who's Afraid of Virginia Woolf?*, Billy Rose, NY, 1963; Mary, *Happily Ever After*, O'Neill, NY, 1966; standby, *Same Time Next Year*, NY; *The Enclave*, Theatre Four, NY, 1973; *Bits and Pieces*, Manhattan Theatre Club, NY, 1975; Vonnie Hayhurst, *The Roads to Home*, Manhattan Punch Line, 1982.

Summer Stock: *The Cave Dwellers*, Olney Playhouse, MD, 1957; *The Diary of Anne Frank*, Olney Playhouse, MD, 1958; *Summer and Smoke, The Lady's Not for Burning, The Bald Soprano*, all John Drew Theatre, 1961; *Hunger and Thirst*, Stockbridge, MA, 1969; Stella, *A Streetcar Named Desire*, Ivanhoe, Chicago, IL, 1973; Bananas, *House of Blue Leaves*, Adelphi Festival, 1982.

ROCHELLE OLIVER

Regional: *The Maids,* Playwrights at Second City, Chicago, IL, 1961-62; *Solomon's Child,* Longwharf, New Haven, CT, 1980-81; *Goodbye Moscow,* Philadelphia Festival of New Plays, PA, 1983.

FILM DEBUT—*Next Stop Greenwich Village.* PRINCIPAL FILM APPEARANCES—*Lianna;* Mrs. Vaughn, *1918,* 1985; Mrs. Vaughn, *Valentine's Day,* 1985.

PRINCIPAL TELEVISION APPEARANCES—*Naked City; Defenders; Nurses; U.S. Steel Hour.* Movie: *In Defense of Kids.*

RELATED CAREER—Teacher, Herbert Berghof Studio, NY, 1976-present.

AWARDS: Clarence Derwent Award, 1960, for *Toys in the Attic.*

ADDRESS: HOME—New York, NY. AGENT—Richard Astor Agency, 1697 Broadway, New York, NY 10019.

*   *   *

O'MARA, Kate   1939-

PERSONAL: Born Kate Carroll, August 10, 1939, in Leicester, England; daughter of John and Hazel (Bainbridge) Carroll; married Jeremy Young (divorced). EDUCATION: Trained for the stage at the Aida Foster School.

VOCATION: Actress.

CAREER: STAGE DEBUT—Jessica, *The Merchant of Venice,* Flora Robson Playhouse, Newcastle, UK, 1963. PRINCIPAL STAGE APPEARANCES—Shakespeare for Schools Season, Shaftesbury, London, 1964; Lydia Languish, *The Rivals,* Welsh Theatre Company, 1965; Elsa, *The Italian Girl,* Wyndham's, London, 1968; Fleda Vetch, *The Spoils of Poynton,* May Fair, London, 1969; Margaret, *The Holly and the Ivy,* Arnaud, Guildford, 1969; Angelica, *Love for Love,* Palace, Watford, 1970; Curley's wife, *Of Mice and Men,* New, Bromley, 1970; Tamala, *The Silent House,* Thorndike, Leatherhead, 1970; Mrs. Cheveley, *An Ideal Husband,* Palace, Watford, 1971.

Madame Gerda, *The Avengers,* Prince of Wales, 1971; Sybil Merton, *Lord Arthur Savile's Crime,* Sadler's Wells, 1972; Sheila Wallis, *Suddenly at Home,* Fortune, 1972; Elvira, *Blithe Spirit,* Little, Bristol, 1973; Gillian, *Bell, Book, and Candle,* Arnaud, Guildford, 1974; Liza Moriarty, *Sherlock's Last Case,* Open Space, 1974; Louka, *Arms and the Man,* Thorndike, Leatherhead, 1977, then Hong Kong Arts Festival, 1977; Rosaline, *Love's Labour's Lost,* Thorndike, Leatherhead, 1978; Katharina, *Taming of the Shrew,* Ludlow Festival, 1978; Cleopatra, *Antony and Cleopatra,* Thorndike, Leatherhead, 1979.

Lina Szczepanowska, *Misalliance,* Monica Claverton Ferry, *The Elder Statesman,* Malvern Festival, 1979; Irene St. Claire, *The Crucifer of Blood,* Haymarket, London, 1979; Hedda, *Hedda Gabler,* Harrogate, 1981; Beatrice, *Much Ado About Nothing,* New Shakespeare Company, 1981; Katharina, *The Taming of the Shrew,* Nottingham Playhouse, Regents Park, London, 1982; Titania, *The Midsummer Night's Dream,* New Shakespeare Company, 1982; Cleopatra, *Antony and Cleopatra,* Millamant, *The Way of the World,* Nottingham Playhouse, 1982; Hortense, *The Rehearsal,* 1983; Stella, *House Guest,* Greenwich, 1983; Mistress Ford, *The Merry Wives of Windsor,* New Shakespeare Company, Regent's Park, 1984; Lady Macbeth, *An Evening with the Macbeths,* Mercury Studio Theatre, Colchester, 1985.

MAJOR TOURS—Gillian, *Bell, Book, and Candle,* UK cities, 1974; Ann Marsh, *Shock,* UK cities, 1975; Helen Galt, *Double Edge,* UK cities, 1977; Cyrenne, *Rattle of a Simple Man,* UK cities, 1978; Monica Claverton Ferry, *The Elder Statesman,* UK cities, 1979; Ruth Carson, *Night and Day,* UK cities, 1981; Stephanie Abrahams, *Duet for One,* UK cities, 1981-82; Rachel, *The Excorsism,* UK cities, 1983; Elsie, *The Ghost Train,* UK cities, 1985.

FILM DEBUT—1955. PRINCIPAL FILM APPEARANCES—*Great Catherine; The Desperados; The Limbo Line.*

SIDELIGHTS: FAVORITE ROLES—Cleopatra, Stephanie Abrahams. RECREATION—Music, Anglo Saxon history.

ADDRESS: AGENT—Michael Ladkin, Eleven Garrick Street, London WC2, England.

*   *   *

OSWALD, Genevieve   1923-

PERSONAL: Full name Genevieve Mary Oswald; born August 24, 1923, in Buffalo, NY; daughter of Charles T. (a traffic consultant) and Jeannette (Glenn) Oswald; married Dean Johnson, December 7,

1949 (died); children: Anne Pemberton, Charles John Magette. EDUCATION: University of North Carolina, B.S., music, 1945; Juilliard School of Music, 1945-46; New York University, School of Music, 1947; Columbia University, School of Library Science, 1947-48.

VOCATION: Writer and curator.

CAREER: TELEVISION WORK—Consultant, *Dance in America,* PBS, 1975-present.

DANCE EXHIBITIONS—Producer: *French Court and Opera Ballet,* 1948; *British Ballet,* 1949; *Ted Shawn, American Dance,* 1950; *Fanny Elsler,* 1951; *The Magic of Anna Pavlova,* 1956; *The Cia Fornaroli Collection,* 1957; *Marius Petipa,* 1958; *The New York City Ballet,* 1959; *Stravinsky and the Dance,* 1962; *Galina Ulanova,* 1962; *Images of the Dance,* 1967, all at the New York Public Library.

RELATED CAREER—Curator, Dance Collection of the New York Public Library (which she also organized), 1947-present; teacher, *American Dance Heritage,* New York University School of Graduate Studies.

WRITINGS: ARTICLES—Dance editor, *Crowell-Collier Encyclopedia;* contributor, *Dance Encyclopedia;* contributor, *Enciclopedia della Settacolo.* REVIEWS—*Journal of the American Musicological Society, Library Journal, Special Libraries, The New York Times, Dance News, Dance Magazine, Ballet Annual* (London).BOOKS—Editor, *Dance Bibliography,* Smithsonian Institute; co-editor, *Bibliography of Projected Theses and Project Titles for Dance,* American Association for Health, Physical Education and Recreation, 1972; project director, *Dictionary Catalog of the Dance Collection* (ten volumes), 1974 and its supplements, *Bibliographic Guide to Dance,* 1975-82; associate editor, *Research in the Humanities,* 1977.

SPEECHES, PUBLISHED—*Creating Tangible Records for an Intangible Art,* Special Library Association, 1967; *Archive of the Dance: Creating a Resource of Audio-Visual Documentation on the Art of Dance,* Tenth International Congress of Museums and Libraries of the Performing Arts, Brussels, Belgium, 1972; panelist, *Oral History Colloquy,* Eastern Communication Association, Statler Hilton, NY, 1975; *Adventures in the Development of the South East Asian Collection,* fifth CORD Conference, Philadelphia, PA, 1976; *Myth and Legend in the Works of Martha Graham: Night Journey,* American Dance Guild/Committee on Research in Dance Conference, Hawaii, 1978; *The Legend of Bronislava Nijinska* (video program), 1983.

AWARDS: Capezio Award, 1956; American Dance Guild Award, 1970; Dance Masters of America, 1972; honorary doctor of fine arts, University of North Carolina at Greensboro, 1981.

SIDELIGHTS: MEMBERSHIPS—Committee on Research in Dance (board), Dance Notation Bureau (advisory board), American Association for Health, Physical Education, and Recreation, New York State Council on the Arts (dance panel, 1970), Special Libraries Association, American Dance Guild (board), Performing Arts Program of the Asia Society (advisory committee, 1977-79), Dance Chronical (advisory board), 1978, James Waring Dance Foundation (advisory board, 1978-present), Dance Visions '78 (board of advisors), Laban Institute of Movement Studies (advisory council), International Council on Dance (advisory council; president, 1979-81), Brandeis University Creative Arts Awards Commission.

RECREATION—Dance, interior decorating, singing, nineteenth century literature, art.

Oswald's diverse interests and activities, as expressed to *CTFT,* include organizing a program of Asian dance films in 1977 for the Association for Asia Studies, coordinating the International Dance Film and Videotape Conference on the problems of the choreographer in 1981, and developing the dance film archive, which she conceived in 1961, for the New York Public Library's Dance Collection.

She was the U.S. representative to Beijing, China, sponsored by the Chinese Dancers Association, to lecture on the development of American dance and negotiate an exchange agreement in July, 1983.

ADDRESS: OFFICE—Dance Collection, New York Public Library, 111 Amsterdam Avenue, New York, NY 10023.

*   *   *

OWENS, Gary

PERSONAL: Born May 10, in Mitchell, SD; son of Bernard Joseph (the sheriff) and Venetta Florence (the county auditor; maiden name, Clark) Owens; married Arleta Lee Markell, June 26; children: Scott Michael, Christopher Dana. EDUCATION: Dakota Wesleyan University; Minneapolis Art Institute.

VOCATION: Radio and television performer, announcer, and actor, and author.

GARY OWENS

CAREER: PRINCIPAL FILM APPEARANCES—Naval officer, *McHale's Navy Joins the Air Force*, Universal, 1963; *The Love Bug*, Buena Vista, 1969; *The Prisoner of Second Avenue*, Warner Brothers, 1975; *Hysterical*, 1983; *National Lampoon's European Vacation*, 1985.

PRINCIPAL TELEVISION APPEARANCES—War Correspondent, *McHale's Navy*, 1963; announcer, *Rowan and Martin's Laugh-In*, NBC, 1968-73; host, *The Gong Show*, ABC, 1976; host, *Monty Python's Flying Circus*, 1975; performer, *Games People Play*, 1980-81; *Breakaway*, 1983.

Announcer for *Sesame Street*, 1969-present; *The Electric Company*, 1969-present; various animated cartoons, including: *Roger Ramjet*, 1965; *Space Ghost*, 1968; *Dyno-Mutt*, ABC, 1975; *Godzilla's Power Hour*, 1979; *Space Heroes*, 1981.

PRINCIPAL RADIO WORK-since 1955; *The Gary Owens Special Report*, syndicated, 1969-present; *Soundtrack of the 60's*, worldwide syndication, 1981-present; *Biff Owens Sports Exclusive*, 1981-present; *USA Today*, Mutual Broadcasting System, 1982-present; *Gary Owens Supertracks*, world-wide syndication, 1984-present; also was an announcer for *KMPC*, Los Angeles, 1962-82; *KPRZ*, Los Angeles, 1982-present.

WRITINGS: BOOKS, PUBLISHED—*Elephants, Grapes and Pickles*, 1963; *The Gary Owens Know What to Do While You're Holding the Phone Book*, 1973; *A Gary Owens Chresthomathy*, 1980. SCREENPLAYS, UNPRODUCED—*Three Caraway Seeds and an Author's Agent*, 1979. NEWSPAPER COLUMNS—*Hollywood Citizen-News*, 1965-67; *Radio and Records Newspaper*, 1978-present; *Hollywood Magazine*, 1983-present; also: *The Daily News, TV-Radio Mirror*, for the Associated Press, *The Daily Republic, Sodak Sports*.

RECORDINGS: Numerous phonograph recordings for such labels as MGM, ABC, Epic, Warner Bros., RCA, Reprise, and Decca.

RELATED CAREER—Vice-President/Creative Services, Gannett Broadcast Division, since January, 1985.

AWARDS: Billboard's National Gavin Poll, Radio Personality of the Year in the United States, ten time winner, 1965-79; Hollywood Jaycees, Distinguished Service Award, 1966; Man of the Year, All-Cities Employees Association, City of Los Angeles, 1968; International Radio Forum, Toronto, Canada, Top Radio Personality in the World, 1977; David Award, 1978; Hollywood Hall of Fame Award, 1980; star on Hollywood Walk of Fame, 1980; American Award, Cypress College, 1981; honorary member, Northern California Cartoonists Association.

SIDELIGHTS: MEMBERSHIPS—Grammy Awards (board of governors, 1968-present), Pasadena City College (advisory board, 1969-present), Emmy Awards (board of governors, 1972), Sugar Ray Robinson Youth Foundation (1971-present), Multiple Sclerosis Drive, Los Angeles (chariman, 1972), Southern California Diabetes Drive (chairman and grand marshall, 1974-present), National Miracle Committee of the Juvenile Diabetes Foundation (1981-present), Carousel Ball (national committee), Children's Diabetes Foundation (1981-present), Cartoonists and Artists Professional Association.

ADDRESS: OFFICE—6255 Sunset Blvd., Suite 1905, Hollywood, CA 90028.

P

PAGE, Anthony   1935-

PERSONAL: Born September 21, 1935, in Bangalore, India; son of Frederick Charles Graham (a brigadier general) and Pearl Valerie Montague (Hall) Page. EDUCATION: Attended Winchester College, 1948-54; Magdalen College, B.A., 1957; studied with Sanford Meisner and Martina Graham at Neighborhood Playhouse School of Theatre, NY.

VOCATION: Director.

CAREER: PRINCIPAL STAGE WORK—Director: *The Room*, Royal Court, 1958; *The Long and the Short and the Tall* (touring production), 1960; *Coriolanus*, Oxford, 1961; *The Caretaker*, Oxford, 1962; *Nil Carborundum, Women Beware Women*, both Royal Shakespeare Company at the Arts, 1962; *Inadmissible Evidence, A Cuckoo in the Nest, Waiting for Godot, Patriot for Me*, all Royal Court, 1964-65; *Inadmissible Evidence*, NY, 1965; *Diary of a Madman*, London, 1967; *Time Present, The Hotel in Amsterdam, Look Back in Anger*, all 1968; *Uncle Vanya*, 1970; *Hamlet*, Nottingham, 1970, then London, 1971; *The Rules of the Game, West of Suez*, 1971; *Alpha Beta, Hedda Gabler*, 1972; *Not I* and *Krapp's Last Tape* (double bill), 1963; *Cromwell, King Lear*, American Shakespeare Festival, Stratford, CT, 1973.

PRINCIPAL FILM WORK—Director: *Inadmissible Evidence*, Paramount, 1967; *Alpha Beta*, 1970; *I Never Promised You a Rose Garden*, 1976; *Absolution; The Lady Vanishes*, 1980; *Forbidden*, 1985.

PRINCIPAL TELEVISION WORK—Director: *Stephen D*, BBC, 1963; *The Parachute*, BBC, 1967; *The Hotel in Amsterdam; The Missiles of October*, ABC; *Bill*, 1981; *Pat Neal Story*, 1982.

RELATED CAREER—Assistant director, Royal Court Theatre, 1958; artistic director, Dundee Repertory Theatre, 1961-62; artistic director, Royal Court Theatre, 1964-65.

AWARDS: Directors and Producers Guild of England, 1967, for *The Parachute;* Golden Globe Award, 1981, for *Bill*.

ADDRESS: HOME—London, England. AGENT—William Morris Agency, 1350 Avenue of the Americas, New York, NY 10019.

*   *   *

PAIGE, Janis

PERSONAL: Born Donna Mae Tjaden, September 16, in Tacoma, WA; daughter of George and Hazel Leah (Paige) Tjaden; married

JANIS PAIGE

Frank Martinelli (divorced); married Arthur Stander (died); married Ray Gilbert (writer and lyricist; died).

VOCATION: Singer, actress, and music publisher.

CAREER: STAGE DEBUT—Lead, *Desert Song*, Stadium High School, Tacoma, WA. NEW YORK DEBUT—Jody Revere, *Remains to Be Seen*, Morosco, 1951. PRINCIPAL STAGE APPEARANCES—Bebe Williams, *The Pajama Game*, St. James, NY, 1954; Doris Walker, *Here's Love*, Shubert, NY, 1963; Mame, *Mame*, Winter Garden, 1968; Margo, *Applause*, Johannesburg, South Africa, 1971; Helene, *Alone Together*, Music Box, 1985.

MAJOR TOURS—Jody Revere, *Remains to Be Seen*, Chicago, Detroit, Cleveland, 1952; Mame, *Mame*, national tour, 1969; Mama Rose, *Gypsy*, national tour, 1970 and 1974; Bea Asher, *Ballroom*, national tour, 1979; Adelaide, *Guys and Dolls;* Annie

Oakley, *Annie Get Your Gun; High Button Shoes; The Desk Set; Born Yesterday; The Gingerbread Lady.*

FILM DEBUT—*Hollywood Canteen*, Warner Brothers, 1944. PRINCIPAL FILM APPEARANCES—*Please Don't Eat the Daisies; Bachelor in Paradise; Of Human Bondage; Romance on the High Seas; The Caretakers; Follow the Boys; Silk Stockings; Welcome to Hard Times; Wallflower; Two Guys from Milwaukee; Her Kind of Man; The Younger Brothers; The Time, Place, and the Girl; Cheyenne.*

TELEVISION DEBUT—*Milton Berle Comedy Hour*, NBC, 1950. PRINCIPAL TELEVISION APPEARANCES—*The Red Skelton Show; The George Gobel Show; Dinah Shore Show; Bob Hope Vietnam Show*, also in Korea, Japan, Cuba and the Carribean; *Roberta; Perry Como Hour; Hallmark Special; Eight Is Enough; Charlie's Angels; Love Boat; St. Elsewhere; Night Court; Matt Houston; All in the Family.* Movie: *The Other Woman.*

RELATED CAREER—President, Ipanema Music Corporation, 1976-present; president, Janeiro Music Company, 1976-present; president, Rio-Cali Music Company, 1976-present; president, Dindi Music Company, 1976-present; president, Ray Gilbert Music Company, 1976-present; president, Jellybean Productions, 1976-present.

AWARDS: Voted fourth in Motion Picture Exhibitors Poll, Best Newcomers, 1946; Joesph Jefferson Award nomination, 1975, for *The Gingerbread Lady.*

ADDRESS: AGENT—Fred Amsel, 291 S. La Cienega, Beverly Hills, CA 90211.

*   *   *

PAISNER, Dina

PERSONAL: Born April 7.

VOCATION: Actress.

CAREER: PRINCIPAL STAGE APPEARANCES—Broadway: Greek Chorus, *Medea*, Circle in the Square; Mirabehn, *Gandhi*, The Playhouse; The Senora, *Andorra*, Biltmore; Dutchess of Krackenthorp, *Daughter of the Regiment*, Lincoln Center State Opera. Off Broadway: The Mother, *Blood Wedding*, Actors Playhouse; Matilde, *Montserrat*, Gate; Molly, *The Threepenny Opera*, Theatre de Lys; Hagar, *The Cave at Machpelah*, Living Theater; Greek Chorus, *Electra*, New York Shakespeare Festival; Mother, *The Sap of Life*, One Sheridan Square Theater; Spartan Woman, *Lysistrata*, Insane Girl, *Pullman Car Hiawatha*, both Equity Library; Elisa Chrysanthemums, *The Long Valley*, Theatre de Lys; Mother-in-Law, *Blood Wedding*, Intar; Mrs. Jenny Barbalottio, *Amidst the Gladiolas*, Lion.

New York showcases: Flora, *A Slight Ache*, Classic; Susan B. Anthony, *Scandal*, Stage One; Mrs. Kate Mayo, *Beyond the Horizon*, 78th Street Theatre Lab; Mrs. Marjorie Melville, *The Trial of the Catonsville Nine*, Trinity Church; *The Jew Who Defended Hitler*, Manhattan Theatre Club; The Nurse, *Medea*, Cubiculo. Regional: Mrs. Frank, Meadowbrook Playhouse, CT; Priestess, Greek Chorus, *Orestia*, Ypsilanti Greek Theatre, MI; Rebecca Nurse, *The Crucible*, New Jersey Shakespeare Festival.

TELEVISION DEBUT—Mary, Mother of Jesus, *The Saint Matthew Passion*, NBC. PRINCIPAL TELEVISION APPEARANCES—Consuelo,

DINA PAISNER

''The Pearls of Peace,'' *The Saint;* Prison Matron, *Interrogation in Budapest*, NBC; daughter, ''To Confuse the Angel,'' *Prudential on Stage;* ''The Holy Terror,'' *Hallmark Hall of Fame;* Bertha Rochester, ''Jane Eyre,'' *Breck Family Classics.*

FILM DEBUT—The Widow, *Pretty Boy Floyd*. PRINCIPAL FILM APPEARANCES—Dr. Marian Chase, *Lilith;* Gladys, *A Thousand Clowns;* Nurse, *The First Deadly Sin.*

SIDELIGHTS: MEMBERSHIPS—Actors' Equity Association, Screen Actors Guild, American Federation of Television and Radio Artists.

ADDRESS: HOME—New York, NY.

*   *   *

PALMA, Loretta   1946-

PERSONAL: Born July 8, 1946, in Brooklyn, NY; daughter of Anthony and Nettie (Perettini) Palma. EDUCATION—St. John's University, B.A., 1967.

VOCATION: Director, choreographer, actress, and singer.

CAREER: STAGE DEBUT—Ursula and the Sad Girl, *Bye, Bye Birdie*, Sharon Playhouse. PRINCIPAL STAGE APPEARANCES—*Funny Girl*, Village Dinner Theatre, Alhambre Dinner Theatre; *Showboat; South Pacific; The Sound of Music; Camelot; A Funny Thing Happened on the Way to the Forum; Cole Porter by Night and Day; Lil' Abner; The Boyfriend; Pal Joey; Anything Goes; Fanny; Fiorello; Dames at Sea; Hello, Dolly!*

PRINCIPAL STAGE WORK—Director and choreographer: *Jacques Brel Is Alive and Well and Living in Paris, The Amorous Flea, New*

LORETTA PALMA

BETSY PALMER

Girl in Town, Ernest in Love, Scapino, A Midsummer's Night Dream, Play It Again Sam, La Ronde, Exit the King, Private Lives, all at Center for Music, Drama, and Art, Lake Placid, NY; *Family Matters,* Madison Avenue Baptist Church; *Romped Out,* West Side Arts; *For the Sake of Art,* New York City cabarets; *Ms. President,* Troupe Theatre; *Louie the Lech,* Carter Theatre; *The Double Inconstancy,* Meat and Potatoes Theatre.

Also: stage manager, *Move Over Mrs. Markham,* Tidewater Dinner Theatre, *God's Favorite,* Alhambre Dinner Theatre; production stage manager, 1980 Winter Olympic Games, Ceremonies and Awards division.

RELATED CAREER—Associate director, intern program director, public relations director, touring manager, Center for Music, Drama, and Art, Lake Placid.

SIDELIGHTS: MEMBERSHIPS—Actors' Equity Association, Screen Actors Guild, Society of Stage Directors and Choreographers.

Palma worked as an editorial assistant and cartoon editor for *Saturday Evening Post,* 1967; as production manager for McGraw-Hill Publications Company, 1968-71; and as production manager for Harper & Row Publications, 1971-73.

ADDRESS: HOME—109 W. 82nd Street, New York, NY 10024.

*   *   *

PALMER, Betsy   1929-

PERSONAL: Born Patricia Betsy Hrunek, November 1, 1929, in East Chicago, IN; daughter of Vincent R. and Marie (Love) Hrunek;

married Vincent J. Merendino (divorced). EDUCATION: Indiana University, De Paul University, B.A., 1949; studied at the Actors Studio in NY.

VOCATION: Actress.

CAREER: STAGE DEBUT—Summer stock at Lake Geneva, NY, 1950. NEW YORK DEBUT—Kate Wilson, *The Grand Prize,* Plymouth, 1955. PRINCIPAL STAGE APPEARANCES—Sally Mackenzie, *Affair of Honor,* Barrymore, NY, 1956; Lady Dungavel, *Roar Like a Dove,* Booth, NY, 1964; Nellie Forbush, *South Pacific,* City Center, NY, 1965; Stephanie, *Cactus Flower,* Royale, NY, 1967; Nora, *A Doll's House,* Theatre Venture '73, Beverly MA, 1973; *Dark at the Top of the Stairs,* Ivanhoe, Chicago, IL, 1974; *Gala Tribute to Josh Logan,* Imperial, NY, 1975; Nora, *A Doll's House,* Studio Arena, Buffalo, NY, 1975; Alma Winemiller, *Eccentricities of a Nightingale,* Studio Arena, Buffalo, then Morosco, NY, 1976, Doris, *Same Time Next Year,* Brooks Atkinson, NY, 1977; title role, *Countess Dracula,* Studio Arena, Buffalo, NY, 1978-79; *The Shadow Box,* Charles Playhouse, Boston, MA, 1979.

MAJOR TOURS—Lorelei Lee, *Gentlemen Prefer Blondes,* OH, 1962; title role, *Maggie,* 1963; Nellie Forbush, *South Pacific,* 1963; Anna, *The King and I,* 1963; *Wait Until Dark,* 1979; *Life with Father; Gigi,* 1984-85.

FILM DEBUT—*The Long Grey Line,* 1955. PRINCIPAL FILM APPEARANCES—*The Last Angry Man; Mister Roberts; Queen Bee; The Tin Star; Friday the Thirteenth.*

TELEVISION DEBUT—*The Miss Susan Show.* PRINCIPAL TELEVISION APPEARANCES—*Playhouse 90; Studio One; Philco Playhouse; U.S. Steel Hour; Matinee Theatre; Hallmark Hall of Fame;*

panelist, *I've Got a Secret, To Tell the Truth, Masquerade Party;* hostess, *Girl Talk; The Today Show; A.M. America.*

ADDRESS: AGENT—Honey Sanders Agency, 229 W. 42nd Street, New York, NY 10036.

*   *   *

PALMER, Geoffrey   1927-

PERSONAL: Born on April 6, 1927, in London, England; son of Frederick Charles (a chartered surveyor) and Norah Gwendolen (Robins) Palmer; married Sally; children: Charles, Harriet. MILITARY: Royal Marines, Corporal Instructor, 1946-48.

VOCATION: Actor.

CAREER: LONDON DEBUT—*Albertine by Moon Light,* Westminster, 1955. PRINCIPAL STAGE APPEARANCES— Edward, *West of Suez,* Royal Court, London, 1971; Elmer Penn, *Savages,* Royal Court, London, 1973; Victor, *Private Lives,* Globe, London, 1974; Farrant, *Eden End,* National, London, 1974; Richard, *On Approval,* Haymarket, London, 1975; Warwick, *St. Joan,* Old Vic, London, 1978; Layborne, *Tishoo,* Wyndhams, London, 1979; Sir John, *A Friend Indeed,* London, Shaftesbury, 1984.

FILM DEBUT—Basil Keyes, *O Lucky Man,* 1973. PRINCIPAL FILM APPEARANCES—Colonel, *The Outsider;* Belfrage, *The Honorary Consul,* 1983; Fallast, *A Zed and Two Noughts,* 1985; Canford, *Clockwise,* 1985.

GEOFFREY PALMER

TELEVISION DEBUT—*Round Britain,* BBC, 1950. PRINCIPAL TELEVISION APPEARANCES—Ben, *Butterflies,* BBC; Leo, *The Last Song,* BBC; Harry, *Fairly Secret Army.*

ADDRESS: OFFICE—Marmont Management, 308 Regent Street, London W1, England.

*   *   *

PAPAS, Irene   1926-

PERSONAL: Born 1926, in Corinth, Greece. EDUCATION: Trained for the stage beginning at age 12.

VOCATION: Actress.

CAREER: FILM DEBUT—*Lost Angels,* 1951. PRINCIPAL FILM APPEARANCES—*Atilla the Hun,* 1954; *The Unfaithful; Theodora; Whirlpool; Tribute to a Bad Man,* 1955; *Guns of Navarone,* Columbia, 1961; *Antigone; Electra; Zorba the Greek,* International Classics, 1965; *The Brotherhood,* Paramount, 1968; *Z,* Cinema V, 1969; *A Dream of Kings,* National General, 1969; *Anne of the Thousand Days,* 1970; *A Ciascuno il Suo; The Odyssey; The Trojan Women,* Cinerama, 1971; *Moses,* 1976; *Mohammad: Messenger of God,* Tark Film Distributors, 1977; *Iphigenia,* 1978; *Bloodline,* 1979; *Lion of the Desert,* United Films, 1981; *Erendira,* Miramax, 1984.

STAGE DEBUT—Greek Popular Theatre, Athens, Greece, 1958. PRINCIPAL STAGE APPEARANCES—New York: *Iphigenia in Aulis; The Idiot; Journey's End; The Merchant of Venice; Inherit the Wind; That Summer, That Fall; Orpheus Descending,* Circle in the Square, NY, 1984.

PRINCIPAL TELEVISION APPEARANCES—Zipporah, *Moses the Lawgiver,* CBS, 1975.

AWARDS: Salonika Film Festival Award, Best Actress, for *Antigone.**

*   *   *

PARFITT, Judy

PERSONAL: Born November 7, in Yorkshire, Sheffield; daughter of Lawrence Hamilton and Catherine Josephine (Caulton) Parfitt; married Tony Steedman. EDUCATION: Royal Academy of Dramatic Art.

VOCATION: Actress.

CAREER: STAGE DEBUT—Bridesmaid, *Fools Rush In,* Amersham Repertory Company, England, 1954. LONDON DEBUT—Ursula Budgeon, *A Likely Tale,* Globe, 1956. PRINCIPAL STAGE APPEARANCES—(all London unless otherwise indicated) Minnie Gascoigne, *The Daughter-in-Law,* Royal Court, 1967 and 1968; title role, *The Widowing of Mrs. Holroyd,* Royal Court, 1967; Annie, *The Hotel Amsterdam,* Royal Court, New Theatre, Duke of York's, 1968; Gertrude, *Hamlet,* Round House, 1969; Lady Touchwood, *The Double Dealer,* Royal Court, 1969; title role, *The Duchess of Malfi,*

Royal Court, 1971; Mary Queen of Scots, *Vivat! Vivat! Regina!* Piccadilly, 1971; Orinthia, *The Apple Cart*, Theatre Royal, Bristol, 1973; Rachel, *Echoes from a Concrete Canyon*, Theatre Upstairs, 1975; Victoria Musgrave, *The Family Dance*, Criterion, 1976; Ranevsky, *The Cherry Orchard*, Riverside Studios, 1978; *Old Heads and Young Hearts*, Chichester Festival Theatre, 1983; Cleopatra, *Antony and Cleopatra*, Young Vic, 1983; Eleanor, *Passion Play*, Wyndhams, 1984.

FILM DEBUT—*The Mind of Mrs Soames*, 1970. PRINCIPAL FILM APPEARANCES—*Galileo; The Champions*, 1985; *The Chain*, 1985.

PRINCIPAL TELEVISION APPEARANCES—*The Edwardians; Shoulder to Shoulder; Street Orchards;* Mildred Layton, *The Jewel in the Crown; Grand Duo*, play for London Weekend TV; Mrs. Dredger, *Mr. Pye*, 1985.

AWARDS: Best Actress nomination, 1985, for *The Jewel in the Crown*.

SIDELIGHTS: FAVORITE ROLES—Mrs. Holroyd and Content Delville in *The Marriage-Go-Round*. RECREATIONS—Interior decorating, swimming, gardening.

ADDRESS: AGENT—Norman Boyack, Nine Cork Street, London W1, England.

*   *   *

MARILYN PASEKOFF

PARRIOTT, James D.   1950-

PERSONAL: Born November 14, 1950, in Denver, CO. EDUCATION: University of Denver, B.A., 1972; University of California at Los Angeles, M.F.A., 1974.

VOCATION: Writer.

WRITINGS: TELEVISION—*The Incredible Hulk; The Bionic Woman; The Legend of the Golden Gun; From Here to Eternity; Voyagers.*

SIDELIGHTS: MEMBERSHIPS—Writers Guild of America, Directors Guild of America, Producers Guild of America.

ADDRESS: OFFICE—Universal Studios, 100 Universal Plaza, Universal City, CA 91608. AGENT—c/o James Berkus, Leading Artists Agency, 1900 Avenue of the Stars, Suite 1530, Los Angeles, CA 90067.

*   *   *

PASEKOFF, Marilyn   1949-

PERSONAL: Born November 7, 1949, in Pittsburgh, PA; daughter of Sherman and Charlotte Pasekoff. EDUCATION: Boston University, B.F.A., acting; studied acting with Theodore Kazanoff, Robert Hobbs, Maxine Klein; studied speech with Evangeline Machlin, movement with Joseph Gifford and John Wilson, mime with Kenyon Martin; studied voice in New York with Therman Bailey and dance with David Harris.

VOCATION: Actress.

CAREER: PRINCIPAL STAGE APPEARANCES—At Boston University Studio: Lizzie, *The Rainmaker*, Katherine, *A View from the Bridge*, Celia, *Hatful of Rain*, Felice, *After the Fall;* Jane, *The Innocent Party*, Harvard Loeb Drama Center; *Godspell*, Plymouth then Ambassador, NY; principal, *Brainchild*, pre-Broadway try out; *Forbidden Broadway*, Palsson's, NY; *Maybe I'm Doing It Wrong*, Astor Place, NY; *Godspell*, Promenade, NY; *Crosstown/Words*, Equity Library; *Select Any Single*, Production Company, NY; *Snapshots*, Fashion Institute, NY; *Scrambled Feet*, Westwood Playhouse, Los Angeles, CA; *The Odd Couple*, NY, 1985.

MAJOR TOURS—*Godspell*, U.S. and Europe; *Jane Olivor*, West Coast.

PRINCIPAL FILM APPEARANCES—*Disco Fever*.

PRINCIPAL TELEVISION APPEARANCES—*Dinah Shore Show; Days of Our Lives*.

SIDELIGHTS: MEMBERSHIPS—Actors' Equity Association, American Federation of Television and Radio Artists, American Guild of Variety Artists, Screen Actors Guild.

ADDRESS: HOME—215 W. 83rd Street, New York, NY 10024. AGENT—Neiderlitz and Steele, 250 W. 57th Street, New York, NY 10107.

*   *   *

PATACANO, Martino
See CHACKSFIELD, Frank

JAY PATTERSON

PATTERSON, Jay   1954-

PERSONAL: Born August 22, 1954, in Cincinnati, OH; son of James Frank (a construction foreman) and Margaret (a secretary; maiden name, Jones) Patterson. EDUCATION: Ohio University; trained for the theatre at the Terry Schreiber Studio. POLITICS: Democrat.

VOCATION: Actor.

CAREER: STAGE DEBUT—First officer, *Twelfth Night*, Cincinnati Playhouse, for forty performances. NEW YORK DEBUT—Harold, *K-2*, Brooks Atkinson, 1983, for ninety-six performances. PRINCIPAL STAGE APPEARANCES—Lenny, *Of Mice and Men*, Cliff, *The Woolgatherer*, Playhouse by the River; Edwin, *Sons*, Playwrights Lab, Minneapolis, MN; Morris, *The Blood Knot*, Sangoma Ensemble, Minneapolis, MN; Cassio, *Othello*, Antonio, *Twelfth Night*, Monomoy Theatre, MA; Lonnie, *The Taking of Miss Janie*, Penumbra, Minneapolis, MN; Bocardon, *Celimare*, St. Nicholas, Chicago, IL; James Strauss, *Compulsion*, Bradley, *Buried Child*, Doug, *Loose Ends*, Cincinnati Playhouse, Cincinnati, OH; Sgt. Wolff, *Rommel's Garden*, Aspen Playwrights Conference, Aspen, CO; William, *Who They Are, and How It Is with Them*, Center Stage, Baltimore, MD; Andrei, *The Three Sisters*, Guthrie, Minneapolis, MN; Harold, *K-2*, Syracuse Stage, Syracuse, NY.

FILM DEBUT—W.E. Simmons, *Places in the Heart*, Tri-Star, 1984. PRINCIPAL FILM APPEARANCES—Brother Constance, *Heaven Help Us (a.k.a. Catholic Boys)*, Tri-Star, 1984.

TELEVISION DEBUT—Billy Joe Higgins, *Miami Vice*, ABC, 1984. PRINCIPAL TELEVISION APPEARANCES—Officer Beltran, *Another World*, NBC, 1985; *Spectators*, PBS, 1985.

AWARDS: Outer Critics Circle Award nomination, Best Broadway Debut of 1983, for *K-2*.

SIDELIGHTS: MEMBERSHIPS—Actors' Equity Association, Screen Actors Guild.

ADDRESS: AGENT—International Creative Management, 40 W. 57th Street, New York, NY 10019.

*   *   *

PENN, Arthur   1922-

PERSONAL: Born September 27, 1922, in Philadelphia, PA; married Peggy Maurer. EDUCATION: Black Mountain College, Universities of Perugia and Florence, Italy; trained for the stage with Michael Chekhov.

VOCATION: Director.

CAREER: FIRST STAGE WORK—Director, *Two for the Seesaw*, Booth, NY, Haymarket, London, 1958. PRINCIPAL STAGE WORK—Director: *The Miracle Worker*, Playhouse, NY, 1959; *Toys in the Attic*, Hudson, NY, 1960; *An Evening with Mike Nichols and Elaine May*, John Golden Theater, NY, 1960; *All the Way Home*, Belasco, NY, 1960; *In the Counting House*, NY, 1962; *Lorenzo*, NY, 1963; *Golden Boy*, NY, 1964; *Wait Until Dark*, NY, 1966; executive producer, *The Silent Partner*, Actors' Studio, NY, 1972; director: *Felix*, NY, 1972; *Sly Fox*, NY, 1976; *Golda*, NY, 1977.

FIRST FILM WORK—Director: *Left Handed Gun*, Warner Brothers, 1957. PRINCIPAL FILM WORK—*The Miracle Worker*, United Artists, 1962; *Mickey One*, Columbia, 1964; *The Chase*, Columbia, 1965; *Bonnie and Clyde*, Warner Brothers-Seven Arts, 1967; *Alice's Restaurant*, United Artists, 1969; *Little Big Man*, National General, 1971; *Visions of Eight*, 1973; *Night Moves*, Warner Brothers, 1975; *The Missouri Breaks*, 1976; *Altered States*, Warner Brothers, 1980; *Four Friends*, Filmways, 1981.

PRINCIPAL TELEVISION WORK—Director, *Man on a Mountain Top*.

ADDRESS: OFFICE—Florin Productions, 1860 Broadway, New York, NY 10023.*

*   *   *

PENN, Sean   1960-

BRIEF ENTRY: Born August 17, 1960; son of television director and former actor Leo Penn and his wife, former stage actress Eileen Ryan. Penn was educated at Santa Monica High School, and he studied acting with Peggy Feury. He also received training through his apprenticeship with the Los Angeles Group Repertory Theatre. After working a variety of backstage jobs, Penn assisted actor and director Pat Hingle and then directed a one-act play, *Terrible Jim Fletch*. On stage, Penn acted in Albert Innaurato's *Earthworms* and in *The Girl on the Via Flaminia*.

Penn's first professional acting job was in an episode of the television series *Barnaby Jones* in 1979. Other television work has included *Hellinger's Law, The Killing of Randy Webster,* and *Concrete Cowboys.* On the Broadway stage Penn appeared in *Heartland* and *Slab Boys.* He made his film debut in *Taps,* Twentieth Century-Fox, 1981, then played surfer Jeff Spicoli in *Fast Times at Ridgemont High,* Universal, 1982. Other films include *Bad Boys, Crackers,* and *Racing with the Moon.* Penn recently co-starred in *The Falcon and the Snowman,* 1985, playing the role of Daulton Lee in this true story based on a book.*

*   *   *

PENZNER, Seymour   1915-

PERSONAL: Born July 29, 1915, in New York City; son of Simon Arthur (a manufacturer) and Rebecca Gertrude (a singer; maiden name, Smith) Penzner; married Diana Geranios, October 18, 1942; children: Alexa, Jonathan, Marina. EDUCATION—City College of New York, B.A., 1937.

VOCATION: Actor.

CAREER: STAGE DEBUT—Gilbert & Sullivan productions, Cherry Lane Theatre, NY, 1941-42. PRINCIPAL STAGE APPEARANCES—Broadway productions: Dr. Cook, *Dr. Cook's Garden;* Moriarty, *Baker Street;* Jake, *Paint Your Wagon;* Hercule, *Can Can; Finian's Rainbow; Kean; Oklahoma!; Promenade,* Promenade Theatre; *Guitar,* Jan Huss. Stock: Tevye, *Fiddler on the Roof;* Doolittle, *My Fair Lady;* Pseudolus, *A Funny Thing Happened on the Way to the Forum;* Gregory Solomon, *The Price;* Cap'n Andy, *Show Boat;* Ben

Rumson, *Paint Your Wagon;* Panisse, *Fanny;* Wazir, *Kismet; 'Tis a Pity She's a Whore; All My Sons; Caesar at the Rubicon; Show Off;* Sir Toby Belch, *Twelfth Night.*

MAJOR TOURS—Governor and Innkeeper, *Man of La Mancha,* 1968; Peachum, *Threepenny Opera;* Van Helsing, *Passion of Dracula.*

FILM DEBUT—School boy, *Hoosier Schoolmaster,* Whitman Studios, 1924.

PRINCIPAL TELEVISION APPEARANCES—*East Side West Side; Naked City; American Heritage; Cinderella.*

AWARDS: Best Actor of the Season, Tevye, 1971, for *Fiddler on the Roof.*

SIDELIGHTS: MEMBERSHIPS—Actors' Equity Association, Screen Actors Guild, American Federation of Television and Radio Artists, Players Club.

ADDRESS: HOME—680 West End Avenue, New York, NY 10025.

*   *   *

PERKINS, Anthony   1932-

PERSONAL: Born April 4, 1932, in New York City; son of Osgood and Janet Esselton (Rane) Perkins; married Berinthia Berenson.

SEYMOUR PENZNER   **ANTHONY PERKINS**

EDUCATION—Attended Rollins College, FL, and Columbia University.

VOCATION: Actor, director, and writer.

CAREER: NEW YORK DEBUT—Tom Lee, *Tea and Sympathy*, Barrymore, 1954. PRINCIPAL STAGE APPEARANCES—Eugene Gant, *Look Homeward Angel*, Barrymore, NY, 1957; Gideon Briggs, *Greenwillow*, Alvin, NY, 1960; Harold Selbar, *Harold*, Cort, NY, 1962; Andy Hobart, *The Star-Spangled Girl*, Plymouth, NY, 1966, then Huntington Hartford, Los Angeles, 1968; Tandy, *Steambath*, Truck and Warehouse, NY, June 1970; *Sondheim: A Musical Tribute*, Shubert, NY, 1973; Martin Dysart, *Equus*, Plymouth, NY, 1975; Jason Carmichael, *Romantic Comedy*, Ethel Barrymore, NY, 1979.

PRINCIPAL STAGE WORK—Director: *The Star-Spangled Girl*, Huntington Hartford, 1968; *The Unknown Soldier and His Wife*, Playhouse in the Park, Philadelphia, 1968; *The Imaginary Invalid*, 1968, *The Burgermaster*, 1969, both Milwaukee Repertory; *Steambath*, Truck and Warehouse, 1970; *The Wager*, Eastside Playhouse, 1974.

FILM DEBUT—*The Actress*, 1953. PRINCIPAL FILM APPEARANCES—*The Matchmaker; On the Beach; Psycho; Goodbye Again; Friendly Persuasion; Lovin' Molly; Murder on the Orient Express; Winter Kills; Crimes of Passion; Psycho II; Psycho III*, Universal, 1986.

PRINCIPAL FILM WORK—Director: *Psycho III*, 1986.

TELEVISION DEBUT—*Joey*, 1953; numerous television appearances.

WRITINGS: SCREENPLAY—*The Last of Sheila* (with Stephen Sondheim), 1973.

SIDELIGHTS: MEMBERSHIPS—Actors' Equity Association, Screen Actors Guild.

ADDRESS: AGENT—International Creative Management, 8899 Beverly Blvd., Los Angles, CA 90048.

*   *   *

PERKINS, Don   1928-

PERSONAL: Born October 23, 1928, in Boston, MA; married Gittel Tischler, October 11, 1958 (divorced, 1964); married Carol Stevenson (an actress and designer), December 31, 1982; children: (first marriage) Christy, Scott May; (second marriage) David. EDUCATION: Emerson College, B.A. POLITICS: Independent. RELIGION: Catholic. MILITARY: U.S. Marine Corps, corporal, 1951-53.

VOCATION: Actor, singer, and director.

CAREER: STAGE DEBUT—Lieutenant Miller, *Time Limit*, stock production. NEW YORK DEBUT—Prosecutor/priest, *Machinal*, off Broadway, 1959. PRINCIPAL STAGE APPEARANCES—Ed Devery, *Born Yesterday*, Buckingham, *Richard II*, Stage Manager, *Our Town*, Sir George Thunder, *Wild Oates*, Apemantus, *Timon of Athens*, all New Jersey Shakespeare Festival; Touchstone, *As You Like It*, Tom, *The Glass Menagerie*, Mansky, *The Play's the Thing*, Go Go, *Waiting for Godot*, all New Globe; George, *Of Mice and*

Men, Studio Arena, Buffalo, NY; Nathan Detroit, *Guys and Dolls*, Goodman, Chicago; Harry Hope, *The Iceman Cometh*, Martinet innkeeper, *A Flea in Her Ear*, Sgt. Trotter, *The Mousetrap*, Sir Andrew, *Twelfth Night*, George, *Of Mice and Men*, all St. Louis Repertory; the writer, *The Good Doctor*, Westport Playhouse, St. Louis.

Brassett, *Charley's Aunt*, Meadowbrook, MI; Frank Foster, *How the Other Half Loves*, Alfieri, *A View from the Bridge*, both Stage West, Springfield, MA; Peter Quince, *A Midsummer Night's Dream*, Bluntchli, *Arms and the Man*, Brassett, *Charley's Aunt*, Feste, *Twelfth Night*, all Repertory Theatre of New Orleans; Antonio, *The Tempest*, Launce, *Two Gentlemen of Verona*, both San Diego Shakespeare Festival; Lopatkin, *The Cherry Orchard*, Brutus, *Julius Caesar*, Horatio, *Hamlet*, all Seattle Repertory; Reverend Hale, *The Crucible*, New Jersey Shakespeare Festival; *The Lesson*, Wonderhorse, NY; *Fallen Angels, The Rehearsal, Dubliners*, Roundabout, NY; *The Borstal Boy*, Broadway production; *Crossing the Bar*, off Broadway; John Adams, *1776*, New Jersey Shakespeare Festival.

MAJOR TOURS—John Adams, *1776*, National Company, summer package, 1972-73, 1978-79. *The Wake*, National Company, 1978.

PRINCIPAL TELEVISION APPEARANCES—*Best of Families; For Richer for Poorer.*

SIDELIGHTS: MEMBERSHIPS—Actors' Equity Association, American Federation of Television and Radio Artists, Screen Actors Guild, Society of Stage Directors and Choreographers, Players Club.

Perkins informed *CTFT* that he is the only actor on record who has done the Wars of the Roses trilogy twice all the way through.

ADDRESS: HOME—Five Morton Street, New York, NY 10014.

*   *   *

PERRY, Elizabeth   1933-

PERSONAL: Born Rosemary Elizabeth Shein, October 15, 1933, in Cranston, RI; daughter of Howard Cecil (a fireman) and Mary Octavia (a telegrapher; maiden name, Perry) Shein; married Anthony Dalby Call (an actor), April 14, 1965 (divorced, 1982). EDUCATION: Attended Rhode Island School of Design, 1952-53; studied at the American Theatre Wing, NY, 1954.

VOCATION: Actress and playwright.

CAREER: NEW YORK DEBUT—Polly Peachum, *Threepenny Opera*, Theatre de Lys, 1956. PRINCIPAL STAGE APPEARANCES—Catherine Howard, *Royal Gambit*, Sullivan Street Playhouse, 1959; Tatania and Hippolyta, *A Midsummer Night's Dream*, Wendy, *The Farm*, both Folger, Washington, DC; Phoebe, *Move*, Virginia Museum; Lady Macbeth, *Macbeth*, Mistress, *Beckett*, both APA, Ann Arbor, MI; *Did You See the Elephant*, American Renaissance Theatre, NY; Connie, *The Frequency*, WPA, Theatre, NY; Ruby, *Story Time and Majic Time*, American Renaissance Theatre, NY; E.E. Cummings, *Him*, Circle Repertory Company, NY; Mary, *All the Way Home*, Terry Schreiber Theatre, NY; Christina, *Fefu and Her Friends*, American Place Theatre, NY; standby, *Present Laughter*, Circle in the Square, NY; standby, *84 Charing Cross Road*, Nederlander, NY; *The Women*, APA Phoenix Repertory; *Presque Isle*, Theatre of the Open Eye, NY.

PRINCIPAL FILM APPEARANCES—*Taps*.

PRINCIPAL TELEVISION APPEARANCES—Christine, *Nurse*, CBS; *Silent Gun; Banjo Hacket; Gunsmoke; Outer Limits; Bonanza; Perry Mason; Voyage to the Bottom of the Sea; McHale's Navy; Dr. Kildare; Morning Star*.

RELATED CAREER—Associate director, American Renaissance Theatre, NY.

WRITINGS: PLAYS, PRODUCED—*Did You See the Elephant*, American Renaissance Theatre, NY; book and lyrics, *Bags*, Three Muses Theatre, NY; co-author, *A Difficult Borning*, Clark Center, Washington Theatre Club tour.

AWARDS: Mary MacArthur Award, American Theatre Wing presented by Helen Hayes and James MacArthur, 1954; Villager Award, as actress and co-author, 1983, for *A Difficult Borning*.

SIDELIGHTS: MEMBERSHIPS—Actors' Equity Association, American Federation of Television and Radio Artists.

Perry told *CTFT:* ''I am a serious painter and poet, and I enjoy travel and modern Greek. My travels in Judea have enhanced my life.''

ADDRESS: AGENT—Henderson/Hogan Agency, 200 W. 57th Street, New York, NY 10019.

Photography by Timothy Eagan

ROBERT PESOLA

PESOLA, Robert   1949-

PERSONAL: Born August 29, 1949; son of Ernest Ensio (a mechanic) and Janice Mary Pesola. EDUCATION: Attended the Universidad Ibero Americana, Mexico City; Northern Michigan University, B.A., theatre, 1971.

VOCATION: Director and literary manager.

CAREER: PRINCIPAL STAGE WORK—Director: *Butterfly's Evil Spell*, Entermedia Studio, NY, 1974; *Street Jesus*, Peoples Performing Company, NY, 1974; *America and Its People*, Lincoln Center Festival, NY, 1974; *Incident'ly*, Direct Theatre, NY, 1974; *Fiddler on the Roof*, Kaufman Theatre, Marquette, MI, 1974; *Oliver!*, Kaufman, Marquette, MI, 1975; *Dames at Sea*, Vista Summer Theatre, Negaunee, MI, 1975; *Colonization of America*, Theatre for the New City, NY, 1976; *Paper Doll*, Village Writers Festival, NY, 1976; *You're a Good Man Charlie Brown*, Vista Summer Theatre, 1976; *King of Troy Compelled to Ask His Way*, New York Stageworks, 1977; *The Drunkard*, Vista Summer Theatre, 1977.

The Real Inspector Hound, The Great Nebula in Orion, both Academy Arts Theatre, NY, 1978; *How Well I Know*, WPA Theatre, 1978; *Rhinoceros*, Performance Ensemble at Lincoln Center, NY, 1979; *Josephine the Mouse Singer*, Perry Street Theatre, NY, 1979; *The Glass Menagerie*, Clark Theatre, Birmingham, AL, 1980; *The Drunkard*, New Stage Theatre, Jackson, MI, 1981; *The Country Show*, Mid-America Amphitheatre, Hot Springs, AR, 1981; *Bugles at Dawn*, American Theatre of Actors, 1982; *Two by Two*, Clark Theatre, 1982; *On Golden Pond*, Timber Lake Play-

ELIZABETH PERRY

house, Mt. Carroll, IL, 1982; *Carnival*, Clark Theatre, 1983; *Incident'ly*, Judith Anderson Theatre, 1984; *Errand of Mercy*, White Barn Theatre, Westport, CT, 1984; *Mothereddy*, Red Barn Theatre, Key West, FL, 1985.

RELATED CAREER—Dramaturg, Vivian Beaumont Theatre, 1979-80; wrote and directed production for presidential performance at White House, 1980; literary advisor, Circle in the Square, NY, 1983-85; associate producer, *Passion*, Longacre, 1983; co-producer, *Danny and the Deep Blue Sea*, Circle in the Square Downtown, NY, 1984.

WRITINGS: PLAYS, PRODUCED—*Incident'ly*, Direct Theatre, 1974, Manhattan Cable Television, 1975, 18th Street Playhouse, 1976, Judith Anderson Theatre, 1984; *The King of Troy Compelled to Ask His Way*, New York Stageworks, Scrimshaw Theatre, 1977; *Arms Akimbo* (libretto for opera), Manhattan School of Music, 1985.

SIDELIGHTS: MEMBERSHIPS—Society of Stage Directors and Choreographers.

ADDRESS: HOME—319 E. 75th Street, New York, NY 10021. AGENT—Rosenstone/Wender, Three E. 48th Street, New York, NY 10017.

*   *   *

PETERS, William   1921-

PERSONAL: Born August 30, 1921, in San Francisco, CA; son of William Ernest (an advertising executive) and Dorothy Louise (Wright) Peters; married Ann Miller, October 12, 1942 (divorced, 1968); children: Suzanne P. Hilton, Geoffrey W. Peters, Jennifer P. Johnson, Gretchen P. Daniel. EDUCATION: Northwestern University, B.S., 1947. POLITICS: Democrat. MILITARY: U.S. Army Air Corps, Captain, 1942-45.

VOCATION: Writer and producer.

CAREER: PRINCIPAL TELEVISION WORK—Producer, writer, and director for *CBS Reports*, CBS News: "Mississippi and the Fifteenth Amendment," 1962; "Testament of a Murdered Man," 1963; "The Priest and the Politician," 1963; "Storm Over the Supreme Court, Part II: The School Prayer Case," 1963; "Storm Over the Supreme Court, Part III: Bible Reading in the Public Schools," 1963; "Filibuster: Birth-Struggle of a Law," 1964; "Segregation: Northern-Style," 1964; "After Ten Years: The Court and the Schools," 1964.

Writer, producer, and director: *Southern Accents - Northern Ghettos*, ABC, 1967; *The Eye of the Storm*, ABC, 1970; *An Echo of Anger*, ABC, 1972; *Suddenly an Eagle*, ABC, 1976; "Hostage!," *ABC News Closeup*, 1978; *Death of a Family*, PBS; *Bill Moyers' Journal*, 1979; *A Bond of Iron*, South Carolina ETV, broadcast on PBS, 1982; producer and director for the East Africa segments, *Africa*, ABC, 1967; producer and writer, *On Camera* (newsmagazine pilot), ABC, 1977.

PRINCIPAL FILM WORK—Producer, director, and writer: *The Day Before Tomorrow*, VPI Films Inc. for *Newsweek* magazine, 1969; *What Do You Want to Be When You Grow Old?*, DCA Productions

Inc., 1976; *Your Local Station: How Good a Neighbor?*, DCA Productions Inc., 1980.

RELATED CAREER: Fiction staff, *Ladies' Home Journal*, 1951-52; article editor, *Woman's Home Companion*, 1952-53; producer, *CBS Reports*, CBS News, 1962-66; director, Yale University Films, 1982-present.

WRITINGS: BOOKS—*American Memorial Hospital - Reims, France: A History*, American Memorial Hospital, Inc., 1955; *Passport to Friendship: The Story of the Experiment in International Living*, J.B. Lippincott Company, 1957; *The Southern Temper*, Doubleday & Company, 1959; *A Class Divided*, Doubleday & Company, 1971. MAGAZINE ARTICLES—In *Colliers, Coronet, Cosmopolitan, Encounter, Good Housekeeping, Interracial Review, Ladies' Home Journal, Look, McCall's, New Republic, Reader's Digest, Redbook, Reporter, Saturday Evening Post, Saturday Review, Sports Illustrated, This Week*.

AWARDS: George Foster Peabody, 1963, for *CBS Reports*, "Storm Over the Supreme Court, Parts II & III," 1970, for *The Eye of the Storm*, 1976, for *Suddenly an Eagle;* National School Bell from the National Education Association, 1964, for *CBS Reports*, "After Ten Years: The Court and the Schools;" Golden Gavel from the American Bar Association, 1963, for *CBS Reports*, "Storm Over the Supreme Court, Parts II & III;" Writers Guild, 1979, for *Death of a Family*.

SIDELIGHTS: MEMBERSHIPS—Writers Guild of America, Directors Guild of America.

Peters was an account executive for J. Walter Thompson Company, Chicago, IL, between 1947-51.

ADDRESS: OFFICE—Director, Yale University Films, Box 1848, Yale Station, New Haven, CT 06520. AGENT—Perry Knowlton, c/o Curtis Brown Ltd., 575 Madison Avenue, New York, NY 10022.

*   *   *

PETRIDES, Avra

VOCATION: Actress and writer.

CAREER: NEW YORK DEBUT—Susan Fosburgh, *Love Me Little*, Helen Hayes, 1958. PRINCIPAL STAGE APPEARANCES—Electra, *The Oresteia*, Actors Studio, NY, 1960; standby, *A Far Country*, Music Box, NY, 1961; *The Fighting Cock*, ANTA, NY, 1961; Darlene, *Balm in Gilead*, NY, 1964; Honey in the matinee company, *Who's Afraid of Virginia Woolf?*, Billy Rose, NY, 1964; *Measure for Measure*, Theatre Company of Boston; *Arturo Ui*, Annenberg Center, Philadelphia; *The Madwoman of Chaillot*, Royal Poinciana Playhouse, Palm Beach, FL; *The Seagull*, Public, NY, then Amsterdam Theatre Festival, Holland, 1977-79; member, the Manhattan Project, NY, 1977-79; *A Movie Star Has to Star in Black and White*, Public, NY, 1979.

PRINCIPAL TELEVISION APPEARANCES—*The Defenders; U.S. Steel Hour*, 1962-63; Leah, *The Dybbuk*, 1963.

RELATED CAREER—Founder and artistic director of The Bridge, an

AVRA PETRIDES

annual American musical theatre festival in Beziers, France, 1979-present.

WRITINGS: Series of eight plays produced by the Manhattan Theatre Club, WPA Theatre, New Dramatists, and the La MaMa Experimental Theatre, 1970-77.

SIDELIGHTS: MEMBERSHIPS—Actors Studio, New Dramatists.

ADDRESS: HOME—New York, NY. AGENT—Leaverton-Soames, 1650 Broadway, New York, NY 10019.

*   *   *

PEZZULLO, Ralph   1951-

PERSONAL: Born December 27, 1951, in New York City; son of Lawrence (a diplomat) and Josephine (De Mattia) Pezzullo; married Alice Palmisano (a real estate broker), August 8, 1980. EDUCATION: George Washington University, B.A., political science, 1973, M.A., international relations, 1975.

VOCATION: Actor and writer.

CAREER: STAGE DEBUT—Bill Sikes, *Oliver!*, Trinity Theatre, Washington, DC, 1977. NEW YORK DEBUT—Kid Champion, *Kid Champion*, Westside Mainstage, 1981. PRINCIPAL STAGE APPEARANCES—Corky Oberlander, *LuAnn Hampton Laberty Oberlander*,

RALPH PEZZULLO

Westside Mainstage, NY, 1981; Paul, *At Home*, South Street Theatre, NY, 1982; Paul, *Dear Friends*, 13th Street Theatre, NY, 1983; Conde Paso, *On That Day!*, Theater for the New City, NY, 1984; Gorman, *The Education of One Miss February: Sharon Twane*, T.O.M.I., NY, 1985.

WRITINGS: PLAYS, PRODUCED—*Dear Friends*, 13th Street Theatre, NY, 1983; *On That Day!*, 1984, *From Behind the Moon*, 1985, *The Tail of the Tiger*, 1985, all Theater for the New City, NY; *The Education of One Miss February: Sharon Twane*, T.O.M.I., NY, 1985.

SIDELIGHTS: MEMBERSHIPS—Dramatists Guild, Author's League of America, Art Student's League.

Pezzullo worked as a research assistant in the office of Representative Les Aspin, 1975-76; and as a grants specialist for the National Endowment for the Arts, 1976-79.

ADDRESS: HOME—430 E. 65th Street, New York, NY 10021.

*   *   *

PHILLIPS, Peter   1949-

PERSONAL: Born December 7, 1949; son of Almarin (an economics professor) and Dorothy (a nurse) Phillips; married Elaine M. Bromka (an actress); children: Peter Bromka. EDUCATION: Dartmouth, A.B., cum laude, 1971; studied for the theatre at the Royal

PETER PHILLIPS

Academy of Dramatic Art, diploma, 1975. POLITICS: Labor Unionist. MILITARY: Conscientious objector, 1971-73.

VOCATION: Actor and director.

CAREER: THEATRE DEBUT—Bernard, *Death of a Salesman,* American Stage Festival, Milford, NH, 1975. NEW YORK DEBUT—Understudy Henry V, *Henry V,* New York Shakespeare Festival, Delacorte, 1976. LONDON DEBUT—Shannon, *The Night of the Iguana,* VanBrough, Royal Academy of Dramatic Art, 1975. PRINCIPAL STAGE APPEARANCES—Guildenstern, *Hamlet,* Philadelphia Drama Guild; Achilles, *Troilus and Cressida,* Yale Repertory, New Haven, CT; Arthur, *Teeth 'n Smiles,* Folger Theatre Group, Washington, DC.

Horseman and understudy Nugget, *Equus,* Helen Hayes, NY, 1976; Simon Chachava, *The Caucasion Chalk Circle,* Arena Stage, Washington, DC, 1979; John, *Eccentricities of a Nightingale,* Playwrights Horizons, NY; understudy Ben, *Outrage,* Kennedy Center, Washington, DC; Yoshka, *Catsplay,* Manhattan Theatre Club, Promenade, NY; Chris, *Warriors,* American Place, NY; *Warsaw Opera,* Actors Studio, NY; *Five Unrelated Pieces,* Ensemble Studio, NY; ensemble and understudy Trofimov, *The Cherry Orchard,* Vivian Beaumont, NY; Lenox, *Macbeth,* Circle in the Square, NY, 1981; member of the 1979-1980 resident company, BAM Theatre Company, Brooklyn Academy of Music, NY.

MAJOR TOURS—Nugget, *Equus,* bus and truck, 1976; Eilert Lovburg, *Hedda Gabler,* New Globe, 1979.

TELEVISION DEBUT—Extra, *All My Children,* ABC, 1978. PRIN-CIPAL TELEVISION APPEARANCES—Roy Hill, *All My Children,* ABC, 1979; BBC reporter/translator, *Playing for Time,* CBS, 1982; Philip Peters, *All My Children,* ABC, 1983-present.

WRITINGS: ARTICLES—Reviews for *Wagner News,* NY, and *Wagner* (London).

SIDELIGHTS: MEMBERSHIPS—Ensemble Studio Theatre, Actors Studio, Affiliate Artists.

Phillips informed *CTFT* that, in addition to his other accomplishments, he also directed for EST, York Theatre, NY, American Stage Festival, Dartmouth College, Theatre-by-the-Sea, at the University of Michigan and also for New Dramatists. He is currently studying for his law degree at New York University.

ADDRESS: AGENT—Actors Group, 157 W. 57th Street, New York, NY 10019.

*   *   *

PHILLIPS, Sian

PERSONAL: Born in Bettws, Carmarthenshire, Wales; daughter of David and Sally (Thomas) Phillips; married Peter O'Toole (divorced); married Robin Sachs (an actor), December 24, 1979; children: (first marriage) Kate, Pat. EDUCATION: Pintardawe Grammar School, University of Wales; trained for the stage at the Royal Academy of Dramatic Art, London.

VOCATION: Actress.

CAREER: LONDON DEBUT—Hedda, *Hedda,* Duke of York's, 1957. PRINCIPAL STAGE APPEARANCES—(All London unless otherwise indicated) Joan, *St. Joan,* Belgrade, Coventry, 1958; Masha, *Three Sisters,* Nottingham Playhouse, 1958; Princess Siwan, *King's Daughter,* Hampstead Theatre Club, 1959; Katherine, *The Taming of the Shrew,* Oxford Playhouse, 1960; Julia, *The Duchess of Malfi,* Bertha, *Ondine,* Aldwych, first Royal Shakespeare Company season, 1961; Arlow, *The Lizard on the Rock,* Phoenix, 1962; Penelope, *Gentle Jack,* Queen's, 1963; Yolande, *Maxibules,* Queen's, 1964; Hannah Jelkes, *Night of the Iguana,* Ashcroft, Croydon, 1965; Myra, *Ride a Cock Horse,* Piccadilly, 1965.

Ann Whitefield, *Man and Superman,* New Art, Vaudeville, Garrick, 1966; Strange Lady, *The Man of Destiny,* Mermaid, 1966; Edwina, *The Burgler,* Vaudeville, 1967; Alma Winemiller, *Eccentricities of a Nightingale,* Arnaud, Guildford, 1967; Queen Juana, *The Cardinal of Spain,* Arnaud, Guildford, 1969; Ruth Grey, *Epitaph for George Dillon,* Young Vic, 1972; *Alpha Beta,* Palace, Watford, 1973; Virginia Woolf, *A Nightingale in Bloomsbury Square,* Hampstead, 1974; Duchess of Strood, *The Gay Lord Quex,* Albery, 1975; Myra Evans, *Spinechiller,* Duke of York's, 1978; Mrs. Arbuthnot, *A Woman of No Importance,* Chichester Festival, 1978; The Countess, *The Inconstant Couple,* Chichester Festival, 1978; Mrs. Clandon, *You Never Can Tell,* Hammersmith, 1979; *Pal Joey,* Half Moon Theatre, Albery Theatre, 1980-81; *Dear Liar,* Mermaid, 1982; *Major Barbara,* National Theatre, 1982; *Peg,* Phoenix, 1984; *Gigi,* Lyric, 1985.

MAJOR TOURS—Margaret Muir, *The Holiday,* English provincial

SIAN PHILLIPS

tour, 1957; toured for the Arts Council in Wales in original Welsh plays and translations from English classics.

PRINCIPAL FILM APPEARANCES—*How Green Was My Valley; Goodbye Mr. Chips*, 1968; *Dune*, 1984; *Ewoks Again*, 1985; *The Doctor and the Devils*, 1985.

PRINCIPAL TELEVISION APPEARANCES—*I, Claudius; The Oresteia; Crime and Punishment; The Achurch Papers; Lady Windermere's Fan; A Painful Case; Language and Landscape* (bi-lingual Welsh and English); *The Wilderness Clears*.

RECORDINGS: *Pal Joey; Peg; I Remember Mama; Bewitched* (single).

AWARDS: British Academy Awards, Best Actress, *How Green Was My Valley*, and 1978, for *I, Claudius;* Royal Television Society Award, Best Performance, 1978, for *I, Claudius;* Critics Circle Award, New York Critics Award, Famous Seven Critics Award, for *Goodbye Mr. Chips;* made Fellow of Cardiff College; honorary doctor of literature, University of Wales, 1984.

SIDELIGHTS: MEMBERSHIPS—Welsh Arts Council, Governor of the National Theatre of Wales, elected to the Honorary Order of the Druids, National Eisteddfod of Caernarvon in recognition of her services to Welsh Drama.

ADDRESS: AGENT—Saraband Ltd. 153 Petherton Road, London N5, England.

PICKENS, Slim   1919-83

PERSONAL: Born Louis Bert Lindley, Jr., June 29, 1919; died December 8, 1983; married Margaret; children: Maggie Lou, Daryl Ann.

VOCATION: Actor.

CAREER: FILM DEBUT—*Rocky Mountain*, 1950. PRINCIPAL FILM APPEARANCES—*The Sun Shines Bright*, 1953; *Boy from Oklahoma*, 1954; *The Last Command*, Republic, 1955; *Stranger at My Door*, Republic, 1956; *When Gangland Strikes*, Republic, 1956; *The Great Locomotive Chase*, Buena Vista, 1956; *Tonka*, Buena Vista, 1958; *The Sheepman*, Metro-Goldwyn-Mayer, 1961; *One-Eyed Jacks*, Paramount, 1961; *A Thunder of Drums*, Metro-Goldwyn-Mayer, 1961; *Savage Sam*, Buena Vista, 1963; *Dr. Strangelove, or How I Learned to Stop Worrying and Love the Bomb*, Columbia, 1964; *Major Dundee*, Columbia, 1965; *In Harm's Way*, Paramount, 1965; *Up from the Beach*, Twentieth Century-Fox, 1966.

The Glory Guys, United Artists, 1965; *Stagecoach*, Twentieth Century-Fox, 1966; *An Eye for an Eye*, Embassy, 1966; *Rough Night in Jericho*, Universal, 1967; *Will Penny*, Paramount, 1968; *Never a Dull Moment*, Buena Vista, 1968; *The Sweet Creek County War*, Imagery Films, 1969; *The Ballad of Cable Hogue*, Warner Brothers, 1970; *The Honkers*, United Artists, 1972; *The Cowboys*, Warner Brothers, 1972; *The Getaway*, National General, 1972; *Pat Garrett and Billy the Kid*, Metro-Goldwyn-Mayer, 1973; *Blazing Saddles*, Warner Brothers, 1974; *The Apple-Dumpling Gang*, Buena Vista, 1975; *Rancho Deluxe*, United Artists, 1975.

White Line Fever, Columbia, 1975; *Mr. Billion*, Twentieth Century-Fox, 1977; *The White Buffalo; The Swarm*, Warner Brothers, 1978; *Beyond the Poseidon Adventure*, Warner Brothers, 1979; *Spirit of the Wind; 1941*, Universal, 1979; *Tom Horn*, Warner Brothers, 1980; *The Howling*, Avco-Embassy, 1981.

PRINCIPAL TELEVISION APPEARANCES—Episodic: *Wagon Train; Wide Country; Bonanza; Gunsmoke; Alias Smith and Jones; Men from Shiloh; The Mary Tyler Moore Show; Partridge Family; Hawaii Five-O; World of Disney; Baretta; McMillan and Wife; Mannix; Ironside; Name of the Game*. Series: Slim, *The Outlaws*, NBC, 1961-62; California Joe Milner, *The Legend of Custer*, ABC, 1967.*

*   *   *

PIDDOCK, Jim   1956-

PERSONAL: Born April 8, 1956, in Rochester, England; son of Charles Frederick and Celia May (O'Callaghan) Piddock. EDUCATION: Kings College, London University, B.A. (with honors), English; trained for the theatre at the Drama Studio, London.

VOCATION: Actor and screenwriter.

CAREER: DEBUT—Trevor, *Bedroom Farce*, Assembly, Tunbridge Wells, England, for eight performances. LONDON DEBUT—Irish Drunk, *John Bull's Other Island*, Greenwich, 1980, for 56 performances. NEW YORK DEBUT—Fred, *Present Laughter*, Circle in the Square, 1982, for 213 performances. PRINCIPAL STAGE APPEARANCES—John McKenna, *The Boy's Own Story*, Julian, San Francisco, 1981, York, NY, 1983; Colin, *Make and Break*,

JIM PIDDOCK

Kennedy Center, Washington, DC, 1983; Tim, *Noises Off*, Brooks Atkinson, NY, 1983-84.

WRITINGS: SCREENPLAYS—*The Boy's Own Story,* 1984; *The Card,* 1984. TELEPLAYS—*Sisters,* 1984.

AWARDS: Bay Area Theatre Critics, Los Angeles Drama-Logue, 1981, for *The Boy's Own Story;* Drama Desk, 1984, for *Noises Off.*

SIDELIGHTS: MEMBERSHIPS—Rovers Soccer Club, NY; Ulysses Soccer Club, London.

ADDRESS: AGENT—David Lewis, International Creative Management, 40 W. 57th Street, New York, NY 10019.

*   *   *

PIDGEON, Walter   1897-1984

PERSONAL: Born September 23, 1897, in East St. John, NB, Canada; died September 25, 1984, at St. John's Medical Center, Santa Monica, CA, of complications following a series of strokes; married Edna Pickles (died); married Ruth Walker; children: Edna Aitkens. EDUCATION: Attended University of New Brunswick, 1914-15. MILITARY: Royal Canadian Army, World War One.

VOCATION: Actor.

CAREER: STAGE DEBUT—*You Can Never Tell,* Copley Players,

Boston, MA, 1924. NEW YORK DEBUT—*Puzzles,* 1925. LONDON DEBUT—*At Home,* 1925. PRINCIPAL STAGE APPEARANCES— Sheridan Warren, *No More Ladies,* Morosco, NY, 1934; Herbert Gray, *Something Gay,* Morosco, NY, 1935; Guts Regan, *The Night of January 16,* Ambassador, NY, 1935; Leon Nordoff, *There's Wisdom in Women,* Cort, NY, 1935; Anthony J. Drexel Biddle, *The Happiest Millionaire,* Lyceum, NY, 1956; Nat Miller, *Take Me Along,* Shubert, NY, 1959; Frank Michaelson, *Take Her, She's Mine,* 1964; Oliver Jordan, *Dinner at Eight,* Alvin, NY, 1966.

PRINCIPAL FILM APPEARANCES—*Big Brown Eyes,* 1936; *Saratoga,* 1937; *The Girl of the Golden West,* 1938; *The Gorilla,* 1939; *Nick Carter: Master Detective,* 1939; *Man Hunt,* 1941; *How Green Was My Valley,* 1941; *Blossoms in the Dust,* 1941; *Mrs. Miniver,* 1942; *White Cargo,* 1942; *Madame Curie,* 1943; *Youngest Profession,* 1943; *Mrs. Parkington,* 1944; *Weekend at the Waldorf,* 1945; *Holiday in Mexico,* 1946; *Secret Heart,* 1946; *If Winter Comes,* 1947; *Julia Misbehaves,* 1948; *Command Decision,* 1948; *That Forsythe Woman,* 1949; *Red Danube,* 1949; *The Miniver Story,* 1950; *Calling Bulldog Drummond,* 1951; *Unknown Man,* 1951; *The Sellout,* 1952; *Million Dollar Mermaid,* 1952; *The Bad and the Beautiful,* 1952; *Scandal at Scourie,* 1953; *Dream Wife,* 1953; *Executive Suite,* 1954; *Forbidden Planet,* Metro-Goldwyn-Mayer, 1956; *Voyage to the Bottom of the Sea,* Buena Vista, 1961; *Big Red,* Buena Vista, 1962; *Advise and Consent,* Columbia, 1962; *Warning Shot,* Paramount, 1967.

AWARDS: Academy Award nominations, Best Actor, 1942, for *Mrs. Miniver,* 1943, for *Madame Curie.**

*   *   *

PINTER, Harold   1930-

PERSONAL: Born October 10, 1930, in Hackney, London, England; son of Hyman and Frances (Mann) Pinter; married Vivien Merchant, 1956 (divorced, 1980); married Lady Antonia Fraser, 1980. EDUCATION: Attended Hackney Downs Grammer School and the Central School of Speech and Drama.

VOCATION: Playwright, director, and actor.

CAREER: PRINCIPAL STAGE WORK—Director: *The Collection* (with Peter Hall), Aldwych, London, 1962; *The Birthday Party,* Aldwych, London, 1964; *The Lover* and *The Dwarfs,* Arts Theatre, London, 1966; *Exiles,* Mermaid, London, 1970; *Butley,* Criterion, London, 1971; *Next of Kin,* National Theatre, London, 1974; *Otherwise Engaged,* Queens, London, 1975, then NY, 1977; *Blithe Spirit,* 1977; *The Rear Column,* Globe, London, 1978; *Close of Play,* National Theatre, London, 1979; *Quartermaine's Terms,* Queens, London, 1981; *Incident at Tulse Hill,* Hampstead, 1982; *The Trojan War Will Not Take Place,* National Theatre, London, 1983; *The Common Pursuit,* Lyric, London, 1984; *Sweet Bird of Youth,* Haymarket, London, 1985.

WRITINGS: PLAYS, PUBLISHED AND PRODUCED—*The Room,* 1957, produced 1957; *The Birthday Party,* 1957, produced 1958; *The Dumb Waiter,* 1957, produced 1960; *The Hothouse,* 1958, produced 1980; *A Slight Ache,* 1958, produced 1961; *A Night Out,* 1959; *The Caretaker,* 1959, produced 1960; *Night School,* 1960;

Photography by Ivan Kyncl

HAROLD PINTER

The Dwarfs, 1960, produced 1963; *The Collection*, 1961, produced 1962; *The Lover*, 1962, produced 1963; *Tea Party*, 1964, produced 1970; *The Homecoming*, 1964, produced 1965; *The Basement*, 1966, produced 1970; *Landscape*, 1967, produced 1969; *Silence*, 1968, produced 1968; *Old Times*, 1970, produced 1971; *Monologue*, 1972; *No Mans Land*, 1974, produced 1975; *Betrayal*, 1978, produced 1978; *Family Voices*, 1980, produced 1981; *A Kind of Alaska*, 1982, produced 1984; *Victoria Station*, 1982, produced 1982; *One for the Road*, 1984, produced 1984.

SCREENPLAYS—*The Caretaker*, 1962; *The Servant*, 1962; *The Pumpkin Eater*, 1963; *The Quiller Memorandum*, 1965; *Accident*, 1966; *The Birthday Party*, 1967; *The Go-Between*, 1969; *The Homecoming*, 1969; *Langrishe Go Down*, 1970; *A La Recherche Du Temps Perdu*, 1972; *The Last Tycoon*, 1974; *The French Lieutenant's Woman*, 1980; *Betrayal*, 1981; *Turtle Diary*, 1984.

TELEPLAYS—*The Birthday Party*, 1960; *A Night Out*, 1960; *Night School*, 1960; *The Collection*, 1961; *The Lover*, 1962; *Tea Party*, 1965; *The Caretaker*, 1966; *The Basement*, 1967; *Monologue*, 1973; *Old Times*, 1975; *No Mans Land*, 1978; *The Hothouse*, 1981; *A Kind of Alaska*, 1984.

AWARDS: Received Commander of the British Empire in the 1966 birthday honors; honorary doctorate of reading, 1970, from Birmingham, 1971, from Glasgow, 1974, from East Anglia, 1979, from Stirling, and 1982, from Brown University.

ADDRESS: AGENT—ACTAC, Ltd., Sixteen Cadogan Lane, London SW1, England.

PLACHY, William J.   1948-

PERSONAL: Born July 22, 1948, in Cleveland, OH; son of James W. and Erma (Biliczky) Plachy. EDUCATION: Beloit College, B.A., 1970.

VOCATION: Designer.

CAREER: FIRST NEW YORK STAGE WORK—Lighting designer, *Herringbone*, Van Dam, 1976, 12 performances. PRINCIPAL STAGE WORK—Design apprentice, assistant technical director, and lighting designer, Court Theater, Beloit, WI, 1966-70; lighting designer, assistant technical director, Memphis Little Theater, Memphis, TN, 1970-72; technical director, Cecilwood, Fishkill, NY, 1971; lighting designer, New Jersey Shakespeare Festival, 1972; lighting designer, *A Yard of Sun, Romeo and Juliet, Hamlet, Rosencrantz and Guildenstern Are Dead, Sherlock Holmes*, Cleveland Playhouse, OH, 1972-74.

Technical director, lighting designer, Wayside, Middletown, VA, 1973; associate lighting designer, American Heritage Festival, Fulton Opera House, Lancaster, PA, 1974; associate lighting designer, Great Lakes Shakespeare Festival, Cleveland, OH, 1976; lighting designer, *Native Son*, Perry Street Theater, NY, 1977; lighting designer, New York City Stage Company, NY, 1978; lighting designer, *Teeth and Smiles*, IRT Theater, NY, 1979; lighting designer, *Mulatto*, American Theatre Experiment, NY, 1979; lighting designer, Candlewood Area Theater, 1980; lighting designer, *A Tribute to Cheryl Crawford*, Chelsea Theater Center, NY, 1980.

Lighting designer, *The Grass Harp*, Apple Corps, NY, 1982; lighting designer, *Golden Girl*, Theatre for the New City, NY, 1982; lighting designer, *The Primary English Class*, Perry Street Theater, NY, 1983; lighting designer, *Holding Patterns*, Musical Theatre Works, NY, 1984; lighting designer, *Outward Bound*, Apple Corps, NY, 1984.

MAJOR TOURS—Production electrician, Todd Rundgren's Utopia, U.S. cities, 1974; production electrician, Jerry Garcia Band, U.S. East Coast cities, 1978; production electrician, *Elvis, I'll Remember You . . .*, U.S. South coast cities, 1978; lighting designer, production manager, *The Art of the Muppets*, museums in Chicago, Denver, St. Paul, 1980.

RELATED CAREER—Auditorium consultant: Newark public libraries, NJ, Jersey City public libraries, NJ, Poly Preparatory Country Day School, Brooklyn, NY, Harcun Junior College, Bryn Mawr, PA, Fiesta Americana, Guadalahara, Mexico; principal designer, Everett-Plachy Associates, 1980-present; instructor, Parsons School of Design, 1983-present.

WRITINGS: PERIODICALS—"Lighting for: The Art of the Muppets," *Lighting Dimensions* magazine, January, 1982.

AWARDS: Lumen Award Citation.

SIDELIGHTS: MEMBERSHIPS—International Alliance of Theatrical Stage Employees, Illuminating Engineering Society, Designers Lighting Forum.

ADDRESS: OFFICE—115 Court Street, Brooklyn, NY 11201.

DONALD PLEASENCE

PLEASENCE, Donald   1919-

PERSONAL: Born October 5, 1919, in Worksop, Nottinghamshire, England; son of Thomas Stanley and Alice (Armitage) Pleasence; married Miriam Raymond (divorced); married Josephine Crombie (divorced); married Meira Shore. MILITARY: Royal Air Force, 1942-46.

VOCATION: Actor.

CAREER: PRINCIPAL FILM APPEARANCES—*Manuela; Tale of Two Cities; The Man Inside; Look Back in Anger; The Flesh and Fiends; Hell Is a City; Battle of the Sexes; The Great Escape; No Love for Johnnie; The Greatest Story Ever Told; The Horsemasters; The Caretaker; The Story of David; Cul-De-Sac; Dr. Crippen; You Only Live Twice; The Fantastic Voyage; Will Penny; The Eye of the Devil; Matchless; Night of the Generals; The Mad Woman of Chaillot; THX-1138; Soldier Blue; Gold Rod; Tales That Witness Murder; Kidnapped; The Six Wives of Henry VIII; Death Line; Wedding in White; The Rainbow Boys; The Mutation; Dr. Jekyll and Mr. Hyde; Tales from Beyond the Grave; Black Rock; The Black Windmill; Altirment Ci Arabiano.*

Heart of the West; Escape to Witch Mountain; The Count of Monte Cristo; Journey into Fear; I Don't Want to Be Born; The Devils People; The Passover Plot; The Last Tycoon; The Eagle Has Landed; Trial by Combat; Fear; The Uncanny; Oh God!; The Jerusalem File; Outback; The Defection of Simas Kudirka; The Order and Security of the World; Blood Relatives; Goodbye Miss Wykoff; Sgt. Peppers Lonely Hearts Club Band; The Monster Club; Jaguar Lives; Halloween II; Race for the Yankee Zephyr; Night

Trap; Frankenstein's Great Aunt Tilly; Terror in the Aisles; Where Is Parsifal; Treasure of the Amazon; A Breed Apart; Warrior of the Lost; Phenomena; The Hallelujah Trail.

Telefon; The Pied Piper; Innocent Bystanders; All Quiet on the Western Front; Puma Man; Halloween; Labyrynth; Dick Turpin; Dracula; Escape from New York; Alone in the Dark; To Murder a Stranger; Warrior of the Lost; Master of the Game; Power Play; Tomorrow Never Comes; The Ambassador; Black Arrow Wake in Fright.

PRINCIPAL TELEVISION APPEARANCES—*1984; Moment of Truth; Rivals of Sherlock Holmes,* Thames; *Orson Welles Great Mysteries,* Anglia; *Montserrat; One Misalliance; Valuation for the Purposes Of . . . ,* BBC; *The Cafeteria,* BBC; *The Man Outside,* BBC; *The Joke,* BBC; *Future of All Evil,* Thames; *Death,* Canada; *Bi-Centennial; The Life of Jesus of Nazareth,* ATV; *Blade on the Feather,* LWT; *Captain Kopenick,* Canada; *Centennial; Gold of the Amazon Woman; Barchester Chronicles, Falklands Factor,* both BBC; *Witness for the Prosecution; The Corsican Brothers; Occupations; Call Me Daddy.*

STAGE DEBUT—Hareton, *Wuthering Heights,* Playhouse, Jersey, 1939. LONDON STAGE DEBUT—Valentine, *Twelfth Night,* Arts, 1942. NEW YORK STAGE DEBUT—*Caesar and Cleopatra,* and *Antony and Cleopatra,* Sir Laurence Olivier's Company, Ziegfeld, 1951. PRINCIPAL STAGE APPEARANCES—Mavriky, *The Brothers Karamazov,* Hammersmith, 1946; Starkey, *Peter Pan,* Scala, 1946; with Birmingham Repertory, 1948-50; Bristol Old Vic Company, 1951; Sherman, *Right Side Up,* Reverend Giles Aldus, *Saints Day,* both Arts, London, 1951; William Mossop, *Hobson's Choice,* Arts, London, 1952; Huish, *Ebb Tide,* Edinburgh Festival, Royal Court, London, 1952.

Lepidus, *Antony and Cleopatra,* Memorial Theatre, Stratford-on-Avon, then Princes, London, 1953; Maccario, *The Impresario from Smyrna,* Arts, London, 1954; Leone Gola, *The Rules of the Game,* London, 1955; Dauphin, *The Lark,* Lyric, Hammersmith, 1955; Gunner, *Misalliance,* Lyric, Hammersmith, 1956; Monsieur Tarde, *Restless Heart,* St. James', London, 1957; Davies, *The Caretaker,* Arts, then Duchess, London, 1960, then Lyceum, NY, 1961; Bitos, *Poor Bitos,* New Arts, then Duke of York's, London, 1964, then Cort, NY, 1964; Arthur Goldman, *The Man in the Glass Booth,* St. Martin's, London, 1967, then Royale, NY, 1968; Law, *The Basement,* Disson, *Tea Party,* both Duchess, London, 1970; Mrs. Artminster, *Wise Child,* Helen Hayes, NY, 1972; George Greive, *Reflections,* Haymarket, London, 1980.

WRITINGS: PLAYS, PRODUCED—*Ebb Tide,* Edinburgh Festival, Royal Court, London, 1952.

AWARDS: Television Actor of the Year, 1958; Emmy Award for *Call Me Daddy;* London Critics Award, 1960, for *The Caretaker;* Variety Award, 1968; four Antoinette Perry Award nominations; *Time* magazine Award, 1969 for *The Caretaker.*

SIDELIGHTS: MEMBERSHIPS—White Elephant Club. FAVORITE ROLES—Gunner, *Misalliance,* Davies, *The Caretaker.* RECREATIONS—Talking too much.

ADDRESS: AGENT—Joy Jameson Ltd., Seven W. Eaton Place Mews, London SW1, England.

PLUMB, Eve

BRIEF ENTRY: Born in Anaheim, CA; married lighting technician Rick Mansfield. Plumb was one of the stars of the television series *The Brady Bunch*, ABC, playing the role of Jan Brady. Additional series work has included *The Big Valley, It Takes a Thief, Lassie, Mannix, Gunsmoke, Adam 12, Family Affair,* and *Little Women.* She appeared in an ABC Movie of the Week, *In Name Only,* and in the television movies *House of the Green Apple Road,* 1970; *Dawn: Portrait of a Teenage Runaway,* 1976, and *The Brady Brides,* NBC. Plumb has also acted in over 48 television commercials.*

*   *   *

PLUMMER, Amanda

BRIEF ENTRY: Born in New York City to actress Tammy Grimes and actor Christopher Plummer. Studied briefly at Middleburg College, VT. In New York, she held various jobs including riding race horses, ushering in theatres, being a telephone operator, and she was a journeyman for the second company at the Williamstown Theatre Festival, MA, in the late 1970's. Her debut on stage was as Vera in *A Month in the Country,* with her mother, Tammy Grimes. She went on to play Lily Agnes in *Artichokes* at the Manhattan Theatre Club; in regional theatre she was Frankie in *A Member of the Wedding* and Pixrose in *The Wake of Jamie Foster.* She joined *A Taste of Honey,* which ran for a year on and off Broadway and for which she was nominated for a Tony and a Drama Desk Award, and received the Theatre World Award. She played Agnes in *Agnes of God* on Broadway and for that portrayal she won a Tony, a Drama Desk Award, and an Outer Critics Circle Award. She played Laura in *The Glass Menagerie,* with Jessica Tandy on Broadway, and Juliet in *Romeo and Juliet,* CA. She also played in *Orpheus Descending,* Circle in the Square, NY, 1984. On television, she appeared in *The Dollmaker,* ABC, 1984, and was seen in films as Annie in *Cattle Annie and Little Britches,* Universal, 1981; as Ellen James in *The World According to Garp,* Warner Brothers, 1982; as Susan in *Daniel,* 1983, and as Miss Miscarriage in *The Hotel New Hampshire,* Orion, 1984.*

*   *   *

PLYMALE, Trip   1949-

PERSONAL: Born November 15, 1949, in Raleigh, NC; son of Roy F. and Jean O. Plymale. EDUCATION: North Carolina School of the Arts, for two years.

VOCATION: Actor.

CAREER: PRINCIPAL STAGE APPEARANCES—Martin, *What Do I Do About Hemingway?,* New Dramatists, NY; Huck, *Huck Finn,* Greenwich Mews, NY; Billy Dowton, *The Drunkard,* Thirteenth Street Theatre, NY; Christian, *Dance on a Country Grave,* Hudson Guild, NY; Jaybird, *Honky Tonk,* Manhattan Theatre Club, NY; Goat, *The Robber Bridegroom,* Musical Theatre Lab, NY, Biltmore, NY, 1977; ten characters, *Greater Tuna,* Circle in the Square Downtown, NY.

Man 2, *Jacques Brel Is Alive and Well and Living in Paris,*

TRIP PLYMALE

Slade/Switchel, *Ten Nights in a Bar Room,* Red Barn, MI; MC, *The Lost Colony,* NC; Herr Zeller, *The Sound of Music,* Act II Dinner Theatre, SC; Jack Chesney, *Charley's Aunt,* Burt Reynolds Dinner Theatre, FL; Goat, *The Robber Bridegroom,* Mark Taper Forum, Los Angeles, CA, 1976; various roles, *Diamond Studs,* GeVa Repertory, Rochester, NY; Charlie Brown, *You're a Good Man, Charlie Brown,* Ford's Theatre, Washington, DC; Cliff, *Gold Dust,* Actors Theatre of Louisville, KY.

MAJOR TOURS—Dromio of Syracuse, *The Comedy of Errors,* Royal Shakespeare Company/Joe Papp Parks Tour.

TELEVISION APPEARANCES—*Search for Tomorrow,* CBS; as part of singing group, "The Diamonds," on television shows, in nights clubs, on tour, etc. RADIO—Singer, *The Arthur Godfrey Show*

ADDRESS: HOME—250 W. 78th Street, New York, NY 10024.

*   *   *

POINTER, Priscilla   1924-

PERSONAL: Born May 18, 1924, in New York City; daughter of Kenneth K. (an artist) and Augusta Leonora (an artist and illustrator; maiden name, Davis) Pointer; married Jules Irving, December 28, 1947 (died, 1979); married Robert Symonds (an actor and director), January 3, 1981; children: David, Kate, Amy. EDUCATION:

PRISCILLA POINTER

Attended the Professional Childrens' School; trained at the Tamara Daykarhanova School for the Stage.

VOCATION: Actress.

CAREER: STAGE DEBUT—Mildred, *Kiss and Tell*, National Tour, U.S. cities. PRINCIPAL STAGE APPEARANCES—Broadway: *A Streetcar Named Desire; The Time of Your Life; Caucasian Chalk Circle; The Country Wife; Condemned of Altona.* Off Broadway: *Summertree; Scenes from American Life.*

MAJOR TOURS—Lincoln Center Company, Eastern U.S. cities.

FILM DEBUT—Mrs. Snell, *Carrie*, United Artists, 1976. PRINCIPAL FILM APPEARANCES—*Nickelodeon*, Columbia, 1976; *Looking for Mr. Goodbar*, Paramount, 1977; *Gray Lady Down*, Universal, 1978; *The Onion Field*, Black Marble Productions, 1979; *Honeysuckle Rose*, Warner Brothers, 1980; *The Competition*, Rastar, 1980; *Goodbye Cruel World*, NSN Productions; *Mommie Dearest*, Paramount, 1981; *Mickie and Maude*, 1984; *The Falcon and the Snowman*, 1985.

PRINCIPAL TELEVISION APPEARANCES—*The Archer; Judgement Day for Governor Egan*, NBC; *Dallas*, CBS; *Knot's Landing*, CBS; *From Here to Eternity; Stone; Mysterious Two*, NBC; *Mrs. Columbo*, NBC; *Family*, ABC; *Quincy*, NBC; *Studs Lonigan*, CBS; *Rafferty; Mary Jane Harper Cried Last Night; Eleanor and Franklin*, ABC.

RELATED CAREER—Drama instructor, Braille Institute, 1976-79.

AWARDS: Critics Circle Award nomination, for *Eleanor and Franklin;* Drama Desk Award, for *Scenes from American Life.*

SIDELIGHTS: MEMBERSHIPS—Actors' Equity Association, Screen Actors Guild, Women in Film.

ADDRESS: HOME—Hollywood, CA. AGENT—Triad Artists, 10,100 Santa Monica Blvd., 16th Floor, Los Angeles, CA 90067.

*   *   *

POITIER, Sidney   1927-

PERSONAL: Born February 20, 1927, in Miami, FL; son of Reginald (a farmer) and Evelyn (Outten) Poitier; married Juanita Hardy, April 29, 1950 (divorced); married Joanna Shimkus, January 23, 1976; children: (first marriage) Beverly, Pamela, Sherri, Gina; (second marriage) Anika, Sydney (daughters). EDUCATION: Trained for the stage with Paul Mann and Lloyd Richards. MILITARY: U.S. Army, World War Two.

VOCATION: Actor.

CAREER: FILM DEBUT—*No Way Out*, 1950. PRINCIPAL FILM APPEARANCES—Reverend Msinangu, *Cry the Beloved Country*, 1952; *Red Ball Express*, 1952; *Go, Man, Go!*, 1954; *Blackboard Jungle*, 1955; *Goodbye, My Lady*, 1956; *Band of Angels*, 1957; *Something of Value*, 1957; *Edge of the City*, 1957; *The Defiant Ones*, 1958; *The Mark of the Hawk*, 1958; *Virgin Island*, 1958; *Porgy and Bess*, 1959; *All the Young Men*, 1960; *A Raisin in the Sun*, 1961; *Paris Blues*, 1961; *Pressure Point*, 1962; *Lilies of the Field*, 1963; *The Long Ships*, 1964; *The Bedford Incident*, 1965; *The*

SIDNEY POITIER

Slender Thread, 1965; *The Greatest Story Ever Told*, 1965; *A Patch of Blue*, 1965; *Duel at Diablo*, 1966; *To Sir, with Love*, 1967; *In the Heat of the Night*, 1967; *Guess Who's Coming to Dinner*, 1967; *For Love of Ivy*, 1968; *The Lost Man*, 1969; *They Call Me Mister Tibbs!*, 1970; *The Organization*, 1971; *Brother John*, 1971; *Buck and the Preacher*, 1972; *A Warm December*, 1973; *Uptown Saturday Night*, 1974; *The Wilby Conspiracy*, 1975; *Let's Do It Again*, 1975; *A Piece of the Action*, 1977.

PRINCIPAL FILM WORK—Director: *Uptown Saturday Night*, 1974; *Let's Do It Again*, 1975; *A Piece of the Action*, 1977; *Stir Crazy*, 1980; *Hanky Panky*, 1982; *Fast Forward*, 1985.

PRINCIPAL TELEVISION APPEARANCES—"Parole Chief," *Philco Playhouse*, 1952; "A Man Is Ten Feet Tall," *Philco Playhouse*, 1955; "Fascinating Stranger," *Pond Theatre*, 1955; "Tribute to Eleanor Roosevelt on Her Diamond Jubilee," *Sunday Showcase*, NBC, 1959; *The Strollin' 20's*, CBS, 1966; *The New Bill Cosby Show*, CBS, 1972.

STAGE DEBUT—*Days of Our Youth*, American Negro Theatre, NY, 1945. PRINCIPAL STAGE APPEARANCES—Polydorus, *Lysistrata*, Belasco, NY, 1946; *On Striver's Row, Rain, Freight, You Can't Take It with You, The Fisherman, Hidden Horizon, Sepia Cinderella, Riders to the Sea*, all American Negro Theatre, NY; Lester, *Anna Lucasta*, National, NY, 1947; Walter Lee Younger, *A Raisin in the Sun*, Ethel Barrymore, NY, 1959.

PRINCIPAL STAGE WORK—Director: *Carry Me Back to Morningside Heights*, John Golden, NY, 1968.

AWARDS. Academy Award nomination, Silver Bear Award at the Berlin Film Festival for Best Actor, New York Film Critics Award, all 1958, for *The Defiant Ones*; Academy Award, Best Actor, 1968, for *Lilies of the Field*; San Sebastian Film Festival Award, Best Actor, 1968, for *For Love of Ivy*; created Knight Commander, Order of the British Empire.

RELATED CAREER—Formed First Artists' Film Production Company (with Paul Newman, Barbra Streisand, Steve McQueen and Dustin Hoffman), 1969.

SIDELIGHTS: RECREATION—Reading, music, golf, tennis, traveling.

ADDRESS: HOME—Beverly Hills, CA. OFFICE—9350 Wilshire Blvd., Suite 310, Beverly Hills, CA, 90212.

*   *   *

POLLACK, Sydney   1934-

PERSONAL: Born July 1, 1934, in Lafayette, IN; son of David and Rebecca (Miller) Pollack; married Claire Griswold, September 22, 1958; children: Steven, Rebecca, Rachel. EDUCATION: Trained for the stage at the Neighborhood Playhouse. MILITARY: U.S. Army, 1957-59.

VOCATION: Director, producer, and actor.

CAREER: PRINCIPAL STAGE APPEARANCES—Broadway: *The Dark Is Light Enough*, 1954; *A Stone for Danny Fisher*, 1955.

SYDNEY POLLACK

MAJOR TOURS—*Stalag 17*.

PRINCIPAL TELEVISION APPEARANCES—*The Dark Is Light Enough*, 1954; *A Stone for Danny Fisher*, 1955.

PRINCIPAL FILM WORK—Director: *The Slender Thread*, 1965; *This Property Is Condemned*, 1966; *The Scalphunters*, 1967; *Castle Keep*, 1968; *They Shoot Horses, Don't They?*, 1969; *Jeremiah Johnson*, 1972; *The Way We Were*, 1973; *The Yakuza*, 1974; *Three Days of the Condor*, 1975; *Bobby Deerfield*, 1976; *The Electric Horseman*, 1979; *Absence of Malice*, 1981; *Tootsie* (also produced and appeared in), 1982.

PRINCIPAL TELEVISION WORK—Director, *The Chrysler Theatre*, 1960-65.

AWARDS: Nominated for numerous Academy Awards and Emmy Awards.

ADDRESS: OFFICE—Mirage Enterprises, 4000 Warner Blvd., Burbank, CA 91522.

*   *   *

POND, Helen   1924-

PERSONAL: Born June 26, 1924, in Cleveland, OH; daughter of Ralph Herbert and Charlotte Ann (Waters) Pond. EDUCATION:

Ohio State University, A.B., 1949; trained for the stage at Columbia University. POLITICS: Republican. RELIGION: Protestant.

VOCATION: Designer.

CAREER: PRINCIPAL STAGE WORK—Designer: *Lilliom, The Beaver Coat,* 1956; *Idiot's Delight, Right You Are If You Think You Are, A Palm Tree in a Rose Garden,* 1957; *Oklahoma!, Ardele, Hamlet of Stepney Green,* 1958; *She Shall Have Music, Time of Vengeance,* 1959; *Gay Divorce, La Ronde, The Idiot, Man and Superman, Emmanuel,* 1960; *Monteserrat, Five Posts in the Market Place, Smiling the Boy Fell Dead, Oh Marry Me,* 1961; *The Merchant of Venice, Can-Can,* 1962; *I Got Shoes, The Boys from Syracuse, Double Dublin,* 1963; *What Makes Sammy Run?, Roar Like a Dove,* 1964.

Great Scot, 1965; *By Jupiter, The Peddler, The Dodo Bird,* 1967; *Private Lives,* 1968; *Trevor, The Coffee Lace,* 1969; *The Divorce of Judy and Jane,* 1971; *Berlin to Broadway with Kurt Weill, Oh Coward,* 1972; *No Sex Please, We're British,* 1973; *Much Ado About Nothing,* Chicago, Princeton, Stratford, CT, 1978. Also designed at Paper Mill Playhouse, NJ; Cape Playhouse, Dennis, MA; Opera Company of Boston, 1970-present; New York City Opera.

MAJOR TOURS—*On a Clear Day You Can See Forever,* U.S. cities, 1967; *A Community of Two,* U.S. cities, 1974; *A Musical Jubilee,* U.S. cities, 1976; *Showboat,* U.S. cities, 1982.

SIDELIGHTS: MEMBERSHIPS—Old Sturbridge Village Association, Raymond Moore Foundation.

ADDRESS: HOME—316 W. 51st Street, New York, NY 10019; 17 Church Street, Yarmouthport, MA 02675.

*   *   *

PONICSAN, Darryl   1942-

PERSONAL: Last name pronounced ''*Pahn*-a-son''; born May 26, 1942, in Shenandoah, PA; son of Frank G. (a merchant) and Anne (Kuleck) Ponicsan; married Katie Hardison, April 8, 1966 (divorced, 1977); children: Dylan. EDUCATION: Muhlenberg College, A.B., 1959; Cornell University, M.A., 1965. MILITARY: U.S. Navy, 1962-65.

VOCATION: Screenwriter and novelist.

WRITINGS: SCREENPLAYS—*Cinderella Liberty,* Twentieth Century-Fox, 1974; *The Last Detail,* Columbia, 1974; *Taps,* Twentieth Century-Fox, 1981. NOVELS—*The Last Detail,* Dial, 1970; *Goldengrove,* Dial, 1971; *Cinderella Liberty,* Harper, 1973; *The Accomplice,* Harper, 1975; *Tom Mix Died for Your Sins* (biographical novel), Delacorte, 1975; *The Circus from Stoney Flats,* Delacorte, 1977.

RELATED CAREER—Teacher of English, Los Angeles schools, 1965-66; La Canada High School, La Canada, CA, 1966-69.

SIDELIGHTS: MEMBERSHIPS—Authors Guild.

ADDRESS: AGENT—Ned Brown, 407 N. Maple Drive, Beverly Hills, CA 90210.

DARRYL PONICSAN

POWERS, Stephanie   1942-

PERSONAL: Born November 2, 1942, in Hollywood, CA.

VOCATION: Actress.

CAREER: TELEVISION DEBUT—Series: April Dancer, *Girl from U.N.C.L.E.,* NBC, 1966-67. PRINCIPAL TELEVISION APPEARANCES—Toni Feather Danton, *The Feather and Father Gang,* ABC, 1977; Jennifer Hart, *Hart to Hart,* ABC, 1979-84. Movies: *Five Desperate Women,* 1971; *Sky Heist,* 1975; *Return to Earth,* 1976; *Nowhere to Run,* 1978; *Mistral's Daughter,* CBS, 1984; *Hollywood Wives,* ABC, 1985. Miniseries: *Washington: Behind Closed Doors; Deceptions,* NBC, 1985-86. Episodic: *Cannon.*

PRINCIPAL FILM APPEARANCES—*Astral Factor; Mother's Day; Among the Day; Invisible Stranger,* Trans World Entertainment, 1984.*

*   *   *

PRESTON, Robert   1918-

PERSONAL: Born Robert Preston Meservey, June 8, 1918, in Newton Highlands, MA; son of Frank W. and Ruth (Rea) Meservey; married Kay Feltus (the actress Catherine Craig), 1940. EDUCATION: Lincoln High School, Los Angeles.

VOCATION: Actor.

ROBERT PRESTON

CAREER. STAGE DEBUT—*Kearney from Killarney*, Los Angeles, 1932. NEW YORK DEBUT—Oscar Jaffe, *20th Century*, Fulton, 1951 (replacing Jose Ferrer in mid-run). PRINCIPAL STAGE APPEARANCES—*Julius Caesar*, Patia Power Company, Los Angeles, 1936; Shakespearean repertory, and plays *Montezuma, Murder in the Cathedral, Night Over Taos, Ethan Frome, Knights of Song, Idiot's Delight, Star of Navarre,* and *The Girl of the Golden West,* Pasadena Playhouse, CA, 1936-38; Joe Ferguson, *The Male Animal,* City Center, then Music Box, NY, 1952; Peter Hogarth, *Men of Distinction,* 48th Street Theatre, NY, 1953; Clem Scott, *His and Hers,* 48th Street, NY, 1954; George Wilson, *The Magic and the Loss,* Booth, NY, 1954; Joe McCall, *The Tender Trap,* Longacre, NY, 1954; Gil, *Janus,* Plymouth, NY, 1955; Jean Monnerie, *The Hidden River,* Playhouse, NY, 1957; Harold Hill, *The Music Man,* Majestic, NY, 1957-60; Burglar, *Too True to Be Good,* 54th Street Theatre, NY, 1963.

Nat Bently, *Nobody Loves an Albatross,* Lyceum, NY, 1964; Benjamin Franklin, *Ben Franklin in Paris,* Lunt-Fontanne, NY, 1964; King Henry II, *The Lion in Winter,* Ambassador, NY, 1966; Michael (He), *I Do, I Do,* 46th Street, NY, 1966; Mack Sennett, *Mack and Mabel,* Majestic, NY, 1974; Foxwell J. Sly, *Sly Fox,* Broadhurst, NY, 1977 (replacing George C. Scott in mid-run).

MAJOR TOURS—Pancho Villa, *We Take the Town,* pre-Broadway, Shubert, New Haven, CT, 1962; Michael, *I Do, I Do,* First National Company, 1968.

FILM DEBUT—*King of Alcatraz,* Paramount, 1938. PRINCIPAL FILM APPEARANCES—*Illegal Traffic,* Paramount, 1938; *Disbarred,* Paramount, 1938; Dick Allen, *Union Pacific,* Paramount, 1939; Digby Geste, *Beau Geste,* Paramount, 1939; *Typhoon,* Paramount, 1940; Sgt. Jim Brett, *North West Mounted Police,* Paramount, 1940; *Moon Over Burma,* Paramount, 1940; *The Lady from Cheyenne,*

Universal, 1941; *Parachute Batallion,* RKO, 1941; *New York Town,* Paramount, 1941; *The Night of January 16th,* Paramount, 1941; himself, *Star Spangled Rhythm,* Paramount, 1942; Dan Cutler, *Reap the Wild Wind,* Paramount, 1942; Michael Crane, *This Gun for Hire,* Paramount, 1942; Joe Doyle, *Wake Island,* Paramount, 1942; *Pacific Blackout,* Paramount, 1942; *Night Plane from Chungking,* Paramount, 1943; *Wild Harvest,* Paramount, 1947; *The Macomber Affair,* United Artists, 1947; himself, *Variety Girl,* Paramount, 1947; Murray Sinclair, *Whispering Smith,* Paramount, 1948.

Tulsa, Eagle Lion Classics, 1949; *The Lady Gambles,* Universal, 1949; *The Sundowners,* Eagle Lion Classics, 1950; *My Outlaw Brother,* Eagle Lion Classics, 1951; *When I Grow Up,* Eagle Lion Classics, 1951; *Best of the Bad Men,* RKO, 1951; *Cloudburst,* United Artists, 1952; *Face to Face,* RKO, 1952; *The Last Frontier,* Columbia, 1955; Rubin Flood, *The Dark at the Top of the Stairs,* Warner Brothers, 1960; Harold Hill, *The Music Man,* Warner Brothers, 1962; Roger Morgan, *How the West Was Won,* Metro-Goldwyn-Mayer, 1962; *Island of Love,* Warner Brothers, 1963; Jay, *All the Way Home,* Paramount, 1963; *Junior Bonner,* Cinerama, 1972; *Child's Play,* Paramount, 1972; Beauregard Picket Jackson Burnside, *Mame,* Warner Brothers, 1974; *Semi-Tough,* United Artists, 1977; *"S.O.B.,"* Paramount, 1981; Toddy, *Victor/Victoria,* Metro-Goldwyn-Mayer/United Artists, 1982; Recruiter, *The Last Starfighter,* Universal, 1984.

PRINCIPAL RADIO APPEARANCES—Mike Barnett, detective, *Man Against Crime* (substituting for Ralph Bellamy), CBS, June 29 through August 3, 1951.

PRINCIPAL TELEVISION APPEARANCES—Doctor, *Anywhere, U.S.A.,* ABC, 1952; *Plymouth Playhouse,* ABC, 1953; *Medallion Theater,* CBS, 1953-54; *The Chisholms,* 1979; *The Chisholms II,* 1980; *Rehearsal for Murder,* 1982; Finnegan, *Finnegan, Begin Again,* HBO, 1985. Also: *Playhouse 90,* CBS; *Omnibus,* CBS and ABC; *The Ed Sullivan Show,* CBS; *The Man That Corrupted Hadleyburg,* PBS; others.

AWARDS: Antoinette Perry Award, Drama Critics Award, Best Actor in a Musical, 1957, for *The Music Man* and 1968, for *I Do, I Do;* Academy Award nomination, Best Actor, *Victor/Victoria,* 1982.

SIDELIGHTS: MEMBERSHIPS—Actors' Equity Association, Screen Actors Guild, Players Club.

ADDRESS: AGENT—John Springer Associates, 155 E. 55th Street, New York, NY 10022.

*   *   *

PRESTON, William   1921-

PERSONAL: Born August 26, 1921, in Columbia, PA; son of William (a weaver) and Hannah Louise (Hable) Preston. EDUCATION: Pennsylvania State University, B.A., M.A. MILITARY: U.S. Army.

VOCATION: Actor.

CAREER: STAGE DEBUT—Purgon, *The Imaginary Invalid,* Walnut

WILLIAM PRESTON

Street Theatre, Philadelphia, PA, 32 performances. NEW YORK STAGE DEBUT—PFC Joe Carson, *We Bombed in New Haven*, Circle in the Square, 1972, one performance. PRINCIPAL STAGE APPEARANCES—Off Broadway: Mortimer, *The Fantasticks*, Sullivan Street Playhouse; Sick Beggar, *The Golem*, New York Shakespeare Festival. Stock: Martini, *One Flew Over the Cuckoo's Nest*, Old Actor, *The Fantasticks*, Philadelphia, PA, Woodstock, NY, Syracuse, NY; Corbaccio, *Volpone;* Purgon, *The Imaginary Invalid;* Thomas, *The Rivals*.

Regional: Androcles, Androcles and the Lion; Petey, *The Birthday Party;* Herr Schultz, *Cabaret;* Colonel Kincaid, *The Last Meeting of Knights of White Magnolia;* Candy, *Of Mice and Men;* Waffles, *Uncle Vanya;* Lucky, *Waiting for Godot;* Grandpa, Mr. DePinna, *You Can't Take It with You;* Touchstone, Adam, *As You Like It;* Bottom, Peter Quince, *A Midsummer Night's Dream;* Dogberry, *Much Ado About Nothing;* Baptista, Gremio, Grumio, *The Taming of the Shrew;* Toby Belch, Feste, Andrew Aguecheek, *Twelfth Night;* Ghost, First Gravedigger, *Hamlet;* Justice Shallow, *Henry IV, Part II;* Archbishop, King of France, *Henry V;* theatres include Alabama Shakespeare; Alaska Repertory; Arena Stage, Washington, DC; Barter, Abingdon, VA; Coconut Grove, Miami, FL; Cricket, Minneapolis, MN; Folger, Washington, DC; Maine Shakespeare Festival; New Jersey Shakespeare Festival; Hartman, Stamford, CT; Philadelphia Drama Guild, PA; Seattle Repertory, WA; Syracuse Stage, NY; Virginia Museum, Richmond, VA; Woodstock Playhouse, NY.

PRINCIPAL FILM APPEARANCES—Ogden, *Annie Hall;* Desk Clerk, *Gloria;* Sticker, *Carnival of Blood;* Derelict, *Soup for One*.

PRINCIPAL TELEVISION APPEARANCES—Mr. Waterman, *Haunted Mansion;* Bum, *O'Malley;* Tramp, *The Edge of Night; Late Night with David Letterman*.

SIDELIGHTS: MEMBERSHIPS—New York Poetry Forum.

ADDRESS: HOME—New York, NY. AGENT—Pat House, Actors Group, 157 W. 57th Street, New York, NY 10019.

*　　*　　*

PRICE, Don　1933-

PERSONAL: Born May 15, 1933, in College Point, NY. EDUCATION: Los Angeles Community College, A.A.; trained for the stage at the Juilliard School with Lester Horton.

VOCATION: Director and choreographer.

CAREER: PRINCIPAL STAGE WORK—Director: *Marlowe*, Rialto, NY; *Kaboom*, Bottom Line, NY; *The Boys from Syracuse*, Trinity Square, RI; *Dames at Sea*, Meadow Brook, MI, Buffalo Studio Arena, NY; *Anything Goes*, Hartford Stage Company, CT; *Dames at Sea*, Atlanta Theatre of the Stars, GA; *I Do, I Do*, City Island Playhouse; *The Gershwin Years*, Playhouse in the Park, PA; *Dames at Sea*, Fulton Opera House, PA; *Little Mary Sunshine*, Ft. Wayne Civic Theatre, IN; *Time Again*, Troupe Theatre, NY; *Psychedelic Follies*, Caffe Cino; *But Can You Sing*, Playbox, NY; *In One Bed and Out the Other*, Stage Lights Dinner Theater, FL; *Dames at Sea*, Fire Island Pines, NY; *The Member of the Wedding*, Fulton Opera House, PA; *My Fair Lady*, American Musical Theater, New London, CT.

DON PRICE

New York: *Teach Me How to Cry*, Equity Library; *The Merry Wives of Scarsdale*, Baldwin; *Where Have All the Dreamers Gone?*, Open Space; *Painting Distant Men*, Manhattan Theatre Club; *Peace at Hand*, Circle Repertory; *The Occupation of the Grand Canyon*, Playwrites Unit; *The Death of Eagles*, New Dramatists; *Bingo Tonite*, Ansonia Little Theater; *The Middle*, New York Stage Works; *Entre Nous/Things*, Playbox; *The Bundle Man*, Old Reliable; *The Monster*, Theatre in the Streets; *Pinions*, Playwright's Horizon; *Celebrity Suite*, Quaigh; *Beach*, West 42nd Street Studio; *Gianni Schicchi* and *Rita*, Gotham City Opera; *Alice in Wonderland*, Brogue Opera Company.

Foreign: *Dames at Sea*, Playbox, Sydney, Australia; *Tinkle, Tinkle*, Overground Theatre Club, London, England; *Do You Know the Milky Way?*, Arena, Johannesburg, South Africa; *Three American One Acts*, Athol Fugard's Space Theater, Cape Town, South Africa; *The Gingerbread Lady*, Canberra Repertory Society, Australia.

Choreographer: *My Fair Lady*, Atlanta Theatre of the Stars; *She Loves Me*, Mount Gretna Playhouse, PA; *Good News*, Beef and Boards, KY; *Guys and Dolls*, Allenberry Playhouse, PA; *The Boyfriend*, Atlanta Dinner Theater, GA; *Yankee Ingenuity*, Meadow Brook, MI; *Give My Regards to Off Off-Broadway*, La MaMa, NY.

AWARDS: Show Business Award nomination, Best Director, 1969.

SIDELIGHTS: MEMBERSHIPS—Society of Stage Directors and Choreographers, Actors' Equity Association, Screen Actors Guild, American Federation of Television and Radio Artists.

ADDRESS: HOME—260 Riverside Drive, New York, NY 10025.

*   *   *

PRIMUS, Barry   1938-

PERSONAL: Born February 16, 1938, in New York City; married Julie Arenal. EDUCATION: Attended Bennington College and City College of New York.

VOCATION: Actor and director.

CAREER: TELEVISION DEBUT—*The Defenders*. PRINCIPAL TELEVISION APPEARANCES—*Washington Behind Closed Doors; Heart of Steel; Brotherly Love*. Series: Dory McKenna, *Cagney and Lacey*, 1984.

FILM DEBUT—*The Brotherhood*, 1969. PRINCIPAL FILM APPEARANCES—*Been Down So Long It Looks Like Up to Me; The Role; Heartland; Absence of Malice; The River; New York, New York*.

STAGE DEBUT—*The King and the Duke*, Circle in the Square, 1953, 30 performances. PRINCIPAL STAGE APPEARANCES—Broadway: *The Nervous Set*, 1960; *Henry IV, Parts I and II*, New York Shakespeare Festival; *Creating the World*, 1978; *Teibele and the Demon*, 1979.

AWARDS: Birns and Mantel Award, Best Actor in a Dramatic Play, 1968.

SIDELIGHTS: MEMBERSHIPS—Actors Studio (life member).

ADDRESS: HOME—New York, NY. OFFICE—2526 Vasanta Way, Los Angeles, CA. AGENT—Abrams, Harris, and Goldberg, 9220 Sunset Blvd., Suite 101B, Los Angeles, CA 90069.

BARRY PRIMUS

PRINCE, Harold S.   1928-

PERSONAL: Born January 30, 1928, in New York City; son of Milton A. and Blanche (Stern) Prince; married Judith Chaplin. EDUCATION: Attended University of Pennsylvania.

VOCATION: Producer and director.

CAREER: FIRST STAGE WORK—Producer, *The Pajama Game*, St. James', NY, 1954. PRINCIPAL STAGE WORK—Producer, *Damn Yankees*, NY, 1955; producer, *New Girl in Town, West Side Story*, NY, 1957; producer, *A Swim in the Sea*, NY, *West Side Story*, London, 1958; producer, *Fiorello*, NY, 1959; producer, *Tenderloin*, 1960; director, *A Family Affair*, NY, 1962; producer, *A Call on Kuprin, Take Her She's Mine, A Funny Thing Happened on the Way to the Forum*, NY and London, 1963; producer and director, *She Didn't Say Yes*, NY, 1963; producer and director, *She Loves Me*, London, *Fiddler on the Roof, Poor Bitos*, NY, 1964; director, *Baker Street*, producer, *Flora the Red Menace*, NY, 1965.

Producer and director, *It's a Bird . . . It's a Plane . . . It's Superman*, NY, 1966; producer and director, *Cabaret*, NY, 1967; producer, *Fiddler on the Roof*, London, 1967; producer and director, *Zorba*, producer and director, *Cabaret*, London, producer, *The Beggar's Opera*, London, 1968; producer and director, *Company*, NY, 1970; producer and director (with Michael Bennett), *Follies*, NY, 1971; producer, *Company*, London, 1972; producer and director, *The Great God Brown*, producer, *Don Juan, A Meeting by the River*, NY, 1972; producer, *Strike Heaven on the Face, Games, After Liverpool, The Government Inspector*, producer and director, *The Visit*, producer, *Chemin de Fer, Holiday*, NY, 1973.

HAROLD PRINCE

DANIEL PROETT

Producer and director, *A Little Night Music*, NY, 1973; producer, *The Removalists, In the Voodoo Parlor of Marie Leveau, Pretzels, The Rules of the Game*, producer and director, *Love for Love*, New Phoenix, NY, 1974; producer and director, *Candide*, NY, 1974; producer, *A Little Night Music*, London, *The Member of the Wedding, Knuckle, Dandelion Wine, Meeting Place*, New Phoenix, NY, 1975; producer and director, *Pacific Overtures*, NY, 1976; producer, *Side by Side by Sondheim*, NY, 1977; director, *On the Twentieth Century*, NY, *Evita*, London, 1978; producer, *Sweeney Todd*, NY, *Evita*, NY, 1979; producer, *Evita*, Vienna, *Sweeney Todd*, London, 1980; producer, *Merrily We Roll Along*, NY, 1981; producer, *A Doll's Life*, NY, 1982; producer, *End of the World, Diamonds*, NY, 1984; producer, *Grind*, NY, 1985.

Operas: director—*Ashmedai*, New York City Opera, 1976; *The Girl of the Golden West*, Chicago Lyric Opera, 1978, San Francisco Opera, 1979; *Silverlake*, New York Opera, 1980; *Girl of the Golden West, Madame Butterfly*, Chicago Lyric Opera; *Turandot*, Vienna State Opera; *Play Memory*, Princeton, Annenberg Center, Philadelphia, PA; *Girl of the Golden West*, La Scala, Italy, 1983.

WRITINGS: BOOKS—*Contradictions: Notes on 26 Years in the Theatre*, 1975.

AWARDS: Antoinette Perry Award, 1972, for *Company*, 1973, for *A Little Night Music*, 1974, for *Candide*, 1979, for *Sweeney Todd*.

SIDELIGHTS: MEMBERSHIPS—League of New York Theatres (president, 1964-65), National Council for the Arts, National Institute for Music Theatre (chairman).

ADDRESS: OFFICE—1270 Avenue of the Americas, New York, NY 10020.

PROETT, Daniel   1953-

PERSONAL: Born December 27, 1953, in Wakefield, NE; son of Maurice (a baker) and Joann (a florist; maiden name, Powers) Proett. EDUCATION: University of Nebraska at Lincoln, B.F.A.; studied at the Polakov Studios in NY.

VOCATION: Scenic designer.

CAREER: FIRST STAGE WORK—Scenic designer, *Slow Dance on the Killing Ground*. PRINCIPAL STAGE WORK—Regional: Scenic designer—*Hello, Dolly!*, Harlequinn Dinner Theatre, Atlanta, GA; *Night of the Iguana, Loot, Cabaret, The Matchmaker*, all as resident designer at the Nebraska Repertory, Lincoln, 1976-77; *When You Coming' Back Red Ryder?, The Importance of Being Earnest, Prisoner of Second Avenue*, all as resident designer, South Carolina Repertory, Columbia, 1978; *Master Harold . . . and the Boys, A Little Night Music, Tobacco Road, Death of a Salesman, A Streetcar Named Desire, Long Day's Journey into Night*, all as resident designer, George Street Playhouse, New Brunswick, NJ, 1979-85; *Petticoat Lane*, Anneberg Center, Philadelphia, 1980; *Raisin, A Lovesong for Miss Lydia, The Amen Corner, The Bloodknot, American Buffalo, Purlie*, all as resident designer, Crossroads Theatre Company, New Brunswick, NJ, 1981-84; *Talley's Folly, A Coupla White Chicks, On the Razzle, Cap and Bells* (U. S. premier), all as resident designer, Rutgers Theatre Company, New Brunswick, NJ, 1981-84; *West Side Story*, Plays in the Park, Edison, NJ, 1982; *Show Girls*, White Barn, Westport, CT, 1984.

Off Broadway and NY Showcase: Scenic designer—*Comedy of Errors, Simple Stuff, Somersaults, Christmas Almost Passed Us By,* all as resident designer, Lamb's Club, 1980-81; *The Truth,*, Wonder Horse, 1983; *Porch Sole, Saturday Night. . .* , 18th Street Playhouse, 1983; *Children of a Lesser God,* Queens Theatre in the Park, 1983; *Knucklebones,* Nat Horne Musical, 1983; *Family and Friend,* Ensemble Studio, 1983; *Burden's Pie,* Theater 55, 1984; *Ties That Bind,* Amistad World/Intar II, 1984; *Running Time,* Circle Rep, 1984; *American Dreams,* Negro Ensemble, 1984; *Split Second,* Theatre Four, 1984; *Latin Festival,* New York Shakespeare Festival, 1984; *Snow Leopards,* Actor's Outlet, 1985; *Outside Waco,* Hudson Guild, 1985; *Nzinga's Children,* National Black Theatre, 1985.

PRINCIPAL FILM WORK—Assistant designer, *The Flyer,* Smithsonian, 1981.

PRINCIPAL TELEVISION WORK—Scenic designer: *Another World,* NBC; *Late Night with David Letterman,* NBC.

RELATED CAREER—Associate professor, Rutgers University, 1980-84.

AWARDS: Outstanding Design, New Jersey Drama Critics Circle, for *Tobacco Road* and *Talley's Folly.*

SIDELIGHTS: MEMBERSHIPS—United Scenic Artists, Local 829.

ADDRESS: HOME—343 W. 29th Street, New York, NY 10001.

*   *   *

STEVE PUDENZ

PUDENZ, Steve   1947-

PERSONAL: Accent on last syllable of last name; born September 25, 1947, in Sioux City, IA; son of Paul J. and Agnes L. (Goodman) Pudenz. EDUCATION: University of Northern Iowa, B.A., 1969; University of Iowa, M.F.A., 1975.

VOCATION: Actor.

CAREER: NEW YORK DEBUT—*Dona Rosita,* Chelsea. PRINCIPAL STAGE APPEARANCES—*Old Fashioned,* Colonnades, NY; *Saints,* Musical Theatre Lab, NY; *Hijinks,* Chelsea, NY; *Macbeth, Edward*

II, The Adding Machine, Lion, NY; Richard, *Dick Deterred,* West Bank Cabaret, NY; Harold Hill, *The Music Man,* New London Players, NH; also appearances with: Hartwan Theater Company, Indiana Repertory, New Stage, Michigan Ensemble Theatre, Coconut Grove Playhouse.

FILM APPEARANCES—*Blind Alley; Special Effects!*

TELEVISION APPEARANCES—*Search for Tomorrow,* NBC; *Ryan's Hope,* ABC; *As the World Turns,* CBS.

ADDRESS: HOME—New York, NY.

Q

QUAID, Dennis   1954-

BRIEF ENTRY: Born April 9, 1954; son of William Rudy (an electrician) and Juanita (a real estate agent) Quaid; married Pamela J. Soles, November 24, 1978 (separated). He attended the University of Houston. Actor. His film debut was in *September 30, 1955*, Universal, 1978; followed by *Breaking Away*, Twentieth Century-Fox, 1979; *Tough Enough*, Twentieth Century-Fox, 1980; *The Long Riders*, United Artists, 1980; *All Night Long*, Universal, 1981; *Caveman*, United Artists, 1981; *The Night the Lights Went Out in Georgia*, Avco-Embassy, 1981; *Jaws 3-D*, Universal, 1983; *The Right Stuff*, Universal, 1983; *Dreamscape*, Twentieth Century-Fox, 1984. He is currently filming *Enemy Mine*. His television credits include the movies *Bill*, 1981, and *Bill on His Own*, 1983. His stage credits include the off Broadway productions of *The Last of the Knucklemen* and Austin in *True West* (also at L.A. Stage Company, Los Angeles, 1984).*

*   *   *

QUAID, Randy

BRIEF ENTRY: Born in Houston, TX; son of William Rudy (an electrician) and Juanita (a real estate agent) Quaid. He attended the Houston Baptist College and the University of Houston. Actor. Quaid made his debut in the film *The Last Picture Show*, Columbia Pictures, 1971; and has subsequently been seen in *What's Up Doc?*, Warner Brothers, 1972; *Lolly Madonna*, Metro-Goldwyn-Mayer; *Paper Moon*, Paramount, 1973; *The Last Detail*, Columbia, 1974 (received Academy Award and Golden Globe nominations for Best Actor); *The Apprenticeship of Duddy Kravitz*, Paramount, 1974; *Breakout*, 1975; *The Missouri Breaks*, 1976; *The Choirboys*, Universal, 1977; *Bound for Glory*, United Artists, 1977; *Midnight Express*, Columbia, 1980; *The Long Riders*, United Artists, 1980; *Foxes*, United Artists, 1980; *Heartbeeps*, Universal, 1981; *National Lampoon's Vacation*, Warner Brothers, 1983; *The Wild Life*, 1984; *The Slugger's Wife*, 1985. His television credits include *The Guyana Tragedy; Last Ride of the Daltons*, 1979; *Getting Away from It All; Niagara; Raid on Coffeyville; To Race the Wind*, 1980; *Of Mice and Men*, 1981; *Mad Messiah; Inside the Third Reich*, 1982; *Cowboy*, 1983; played Mitch in *A Streetcar Named Desire* (received an Emmy nomination). His stage credits include *The Golem*, New York Shakespeare Festival, Delacorte, and portrayed Lee in the off Broadway production of *True West* (also performed at the L.A. Stage Company, Los Angeles, 1984).*

*   *   *

QUINN, Aidan

BRIEF ENTRY: Born in Chicago, IL, to parents who immigrated from Birr, Ireland. In Quinn's senior year of high school the family moved back to Ireland and he followed, setting up residence in Belfast. At age 19, he moved back to Chicago and worked as a hot tar roofer, but a desire to act made him land a role in *The Man in 605*, Chicago. He continued in *Scheherazade*, voted Best Play of 1984 by the Dramatists Guild; *The Trick; The Irish Hebrew Lesson; Fool for Love* (his NY debut), and *Hamlet*, at Wisdom Bridge Theatre, Chicago. His film debut was as Johnny Rourke in *Reckless*, Metro-Goldwyn-Mayer/United Artists, 1984, followed by *Desperately Seeking Susan*, Orion, 1985, and *The Mission* (upcoming).*

*   *   *

QUINN, Henry J.   1928-

PERSONAL: Born August 6, 1928, in Boston, MA; son of Henry J.

HENRY J. QUINN

255

(a plant manager) and Irene B. (Carlin) Quinn; married Mary T. Weyand, December 20, 1952; children: Irene, Moira, Theresa, Paula. EDUCATION: Catholic University of America, A.B., 1951. RELIGION: Roman Catholic. MILITARY: U.S. Army, 1946-48.

VOCATION: Actor.

CAREER: NEW YORK STAGE DEBUT—Bellamy, *The Fantasticks,* Sullivan Street Playhouse, 1980-82. PRINCIPAL STAGE APPEAR-ANCES—Uncle Stanley, *George Washington Slept Here,* Horace Vandergelder, *The Matchmaker,* Dorset, VT, 1984; Colonel Pickering, *My Fair Lady,* Beef and Boards, Indianapolis, IN, 1984.

TELEVISION DEBUT—*As the World Turns,* 1982. PRINCIPAL TELEVISION APPEARANCES—*All My Children,* 1983; *Edge of Night,* 1984.

RELATED CAREER—Co-founder, Ivy Lane Players, Long Island, NY, 1963.

SIDELIGHTS: MEMBERSHIPS—Actors' Equity Association, Screen Actors Guild, American Federation of Television and Radio Artists, Catholic Actors Guild.

Quinn told *CTFT,* ''What began as an avocational interest lead to extensive on the job training in some 40 roles in community and regional theater and local television until retirement at age 50 signalled the start of a second career.''

Quinn was a special agent for the Federal Bureau of Investigation from 1952-78.

ADDRESS: HOME—Wantagh, NY. AGENT—Lewis Chambers, Bethel Agencies, 513 W. 54th Street, New York, NY 10019.

*   *   *

QUINTERO, Jose   1924-

PERSONAL: Born October 15, 1924, in Panama City, Panama; son of Carlos Rivira and Consuelo (Palmorala) Quintero. EDUCATION: Attended Los Angeles City College and University of Southern California.

VOCATION: Director.

CAREER: FIRST STAGE WORK—Director, *The Glass Menagerie, Riders to the Sea,* Woodstock Summer Theater, NY, 1949. FIRST LONDON STAGE WORK—Director, Globe Theater, 1958.

PRINCIPAL STAGE WORK—Director: At Circle in the Square, NY: *Dark of the Moon,* 1950; *Bonds of Interest, The Enchanted, Yerma, Burning Bright,* 1951; *Summer and Smoke,* 1952; *The Grass Harp, American Gothic,* 1953; *The Girl on the Via Flaminia,* 1954; *La Ronde, The Cradle Song,* 1955; *The Iceman Cometh,* 1956; *Children of Darkness, The Quare Fellow,* 1958; *Our Town,* 1959; *The Balcony,* 1960; *Under Milkwood,* 1961; *Pullman Car Hiawatha, Plays for Bleecker Street,* 1962; *Desire Under the Elms,* 1963.

At other theatres: *In the Summer House,* 1953; *The Girl on the Via Flaminia, Portrait of a Lady,* 1954; *The Innkeepers, Long Day's Journey into Night,* 1956; *Lost in the Stars,* 1958; *The Triumph of Saint Joan,* 1959; *Macbeth,* Cambridge Drama Festival, MA, 1959; *Camino Real, Laurette,* 1960; *Look, We've Come Through,* 1961; *Great Day in the Morning,* 1962; *Strange Interlude,* 1963; *Marco Millions, Hughie,* 1964; *Diamond Orchid, Matty and the Moron and the Madonna,* 1965; *Pagliacci, Cavalleria Rusticana,* Metropolitan Opera Company, 1966; *Pousse, Cafe,* 1966; *More Stately Mansions,* 1967.

The Seven Descents of Myrtle, 1968; *Gandhi,* 1970; *Johnny Johnson,* 1971; *The Big Coca-Cola Swamp in the Sky,* Westport, CT, 1971; *A Moon for the Misbegotten,* 1973; *Gabrielle,* Studio Arena, Buffalo, NY, 1974; *The Skin of Our Teeth,* 1975; *Knock Knock, Hughie,* Lake Forest, 1976; *Anna Christie, A Touch of the Poet,* 1977; *The Human Voice,* Melbourne, 1978; *Faith Healer,* 1979; *Clothes for a Summer Hotel, Welded, Ah! Wilderness,* 1980; *Cat on a Hot Tin Roof,* 1982.

Co-producer: *La Ronde, The Cradle Song,* Circle in the Square, 1955; *Children of Darkness, The Quare Fellow,* Circle in the Square, 1958; *Bleecker Street, Pullman Car Hiawatha,* Circle in the Square, 1962; *Desire Under the Elms,* Circle in the Square, 1963.

PRINCIPAL FILM WORK—Director: *The Roman Spring of Mrs. Stone,* 1961.

PRINCIPAL TELEVISION WORK—Director: *Medea, Our Town,* 1959.

WRITINGS: BOOKS—*If You Won't Dance, They Beat You.* PLAYS, PRODUCED—*Gabrielle,* Studio Arena, Buffalo, NY, 1974.

AWARDS: Antoinette Perry Award, Best Director, 1973, for *Moon for the Misbegotten.*

SIDELIGHTS: MEMBERSHIPS—Directors Guild of America, Society of Stage Directors and Choreographers.

ADDRESS: AGENT—Thomas A. Andrews, Seven E. 67th Street, New York, NY 10021; Paul Kohner Agency, 9169 Sunset Blvd., Los Angeles, CA 90069.

R

RADOSH, Stephen 1951-

PERSONAL: Born January 15, 1951, in New York City; son of Herbert (an engineer) and Marilyn (a school principal; maiden name, Multz) Radosh. EDUCATION: Franklin and Marshall, B.A., 1971; Adelphi University, M.A., 1973.

VOCATION: Director and designer.

CAREER: PRINCIPAL STAGE WORK—Stage manager: *One Flew Over the Cuckoo's Nest; 1776; Man of La Mancha; Look: We've Come Through; Lovers and Other Strangers; Connie Stevens Show; Applause; Bell, Book, and Candle; Merry Wives of Windsor; She Loves Me; The Tiger/The Typists.*

Director and choreographer, The Sound of Music; director, *Promises, Promises;* director, *A Funny Thing Happened on the Way to the Forum;* director and choreographer, *Dames at Sea;* director, *Celebration;* director, *Good News;* director and choreographer, *The Boyfriend;* director and choreographer, *Cabaret;* director and choreographer, *Company;* director, *The Odd Couple;* director, *Tiny Alice;* director, *Two for the Seesaw;* director, *The Sunshine Boys.*

Above work done at North Shore Music Theater, Cape Cod Melody Tent, Gilford Playhouse, South Shore Music Circus, Little Theater on the Square, Carl Hopple's Dinner Theatre, Equity Library, Fulton Opera House, Syracuse Repertory, Showcase Playhouse, Carolina Repertory.

RELATED CAREER—Lighting designer; personal assistant to Barry Manilow; production executive, Manilow Productions; administrative assistant to David Merrick.

SIDELIGHTS: MEMBERSHIPS—Actors Equity Association, American Federation of Television and Radio Artists, Society of Stage Directors and Choreographers.

ADDRESS: HOME—New York, NY. OFFICE—Pasetta Productions, 8322 Beverly Blvd., Los Angeles, CA 90048. AGENT—Dan Schrier, International Creative Management, 8899 Beverly Blvd., Los Angeles, CA 90048.

*   *   *

RAE, Charlotte 1926-

PERSONAL: Born Charlotte Lubotsky, April 22, 1926, in Milwaukee, WI; daughter of Meyer and Esther (Ottenstein) Lubotsky; married John Strauss. EDUCATION: Northwestern University, B.S.

CHARLOTTE RAE

VOCATION: Actress and singer.

CAREER: NEW YORK DEBUT—Tirsa Shanahan, *Three Wishes for Jamie,* Mark Hellinger, 1952. PRINCIPAL STAGE APPEARANCES—Mrs. Peacham, *Threepenny Opera,* Theatre de Lys, NY, 1954; Mrs. Juniper, *The Golden Apple,* Alvin, NY, 1954; *The Littlest Revue,* Phoenix, NY, 1956; Mammy Yokum, *Li'l Abner,* St. James, NY, 1956; Molly Brazen, *The Beggars Opera,* City Center, NY, 1957; Gloria Krumgold, Mrs. Younghusband, Rowena Inchcape, Mrs. Lafacadio Mifflin, *The Beauty Part,* Music Box, NY, 1962; Caretaker, *The New Tenant,* Madeleine, *The Victims of Duty,* Writers Stage, NY, 1964; Mrs. Bardell, *Pickwick,* Curran, San Francisco, CA, then 46th Street Theatre, NY, 1965; Hostess Quickly, *Henry IV, Part I and Part II,* Nurse, *Romeo and Juliet,* New York Shakespeare Festival, 1968; Gertrude, *Morning,* Beryl, *Noon,* Filigree Bones, *Night,* Henry Miller's Theatre, NY, 1968; Charlotte Mendelssohn, *Dr. Fish,* Barrymore, NY, 1970; Lola, *Come Back Little Sheba,* Cincinnati Playhouse in the Park, OH, 1970; Mother Sweet, *Prettybelle,* Shubert, Boston, MA, 1971; Tia Maria, *Whiskey,* St. Clements, NY, 1973; *The Time of the Cuckoo,* Ahmanson

Theatre, 1974; Juno, *Heaven Sent*, New Las Palmas, Los Angeles, 1978.

MAJOR TOURS—Mrs. Bardell, *Pickwick*, national tour, 1965.

PRINCIPAL FILM APPEARANCES—*Hello Down There; Jenny; Hot Rock; Bananas.*

PRINCIPAL TELEVISION APPEARANCES—*Car 54, Where Are You?; The Ed Sullivan Show; Sesame Street; Diff'rent Strokes; The Facts of Life;* "Words by Heart," *Wonder Works Series*, PBS, 1985.

AWARDS: Two Antoinette Perry Award nominations, one Obie nomination, three National Academy of Television Arts and Sciences Awards.

SIDELIGHTS: FAVORITE ROLES—Lola, *Come Back Little Sheba* and Emily, *Othello.*

ADDRESS: AGENT—Kaufman and Bernstein Inc., 1900 Avenue of the Stars, Suite 2270, Los Angeles, CA 90067.

*   *   *

JOSEPH RAGNO

RAGNO, Joseph

PERSONAL: Born in New York City; son of Dominick and Jean (Salvato) Ragno. EDUCATION: Attended Allegheny College, Meadville; studied for the stage with Michael Howard.

VOCATION: Actor.

CAREER: PRINCIPAL FILM APPEARANCES—Maxwell, *Melvin and Howard;* Doorman, *Winterkills;* Mike Pelyg, *Fighting Back;* District Attorney Willens, *Where the Buffalo Roam;* Saul Malone, *The Kidnapping of the President;* Pete, *Law and Disorder;* Freisman, *The Fish That Saved Pittsburgh;* The Interrogator, *The Rehearsal;* Brusco, *They Called Him Don Camillo.*

PRINCIPAL STAGE APPEARANCES—Broadway: Rocky, *The Iceman Cometh;* Spotted Tail, *Indians;* Cornelius, *Cymbeline*, Delacorte. Off Broadway: Billyfred, *Feedlot*, Circle Repertory; Batista, *A Barbershop in Pittsburgh;* David, *A Worm in the Horseradish;* Teddy, *Everyplace Is Newark*, St. Clements; Organvidas, *Interrogation in Havana*, Chelsea Theater Center; Eric, *Economic Necessity*, Actors Studio; Richard, *Richard III*, Assembly Theater; Pontius, *The Memoirs of Pontius Pilot*, Dr. Jivelidian, *Armenians*, Hercules, *The Birds*, all Actors Studio. Regional: Eddie Carbone, *A View from the Bridge*, Hartman, Stamford, CT; Eric, *Nuts for the Underman*, Whitebarn, CT; Billyfred, *Feedlot*, Back Alley; Orestes, *The Chain*, Hartman, Stamford, CT, 1985.

PRINCIPAL TELEVISION APPEARANCES—Schwerb, *Kojak*, CBS; Joe Profaci, *Gangster Chronicles.*

SIDELIGHTS: MEMBERSHIPS—Actors Studio, Ensemble Studio Theatre.

ADDRESS: HOME—New York, NY. AGENT—Kenneth Kaplan Agency, 311 W. 43rd Street, Suite 606, New York, NY 10036.

RAINEY, Ford   1918-

PERSONAL: Born August 8, 1918; son of Archie Coleman (a jack of all trades) and Vyrna (a teacher; maiden name, Kinkade) Rainey; married Sheila Mary Hayden (an actress and artist); children: Robert, James, Kathleen. EDUCATION: Centralia College, Centralia, WA; Cornish School, Seattle, WA; studied acting with Michael Chekhov. MILITARY: U.S. Coast Guard, Boatswain's Mate, second class, 1942-45.

VOCATION: Actor.

CAREER: NEW YORK DEBUT—Reporter, *The Possessed*, Lyceum. PRINCIPAL STAGE APPEARANCES—Toby Belch, *Twelfth Night*, King Lear, *King Lear*, Michael Chekhov Theatre, Ridgefield, CT, 1941-42; *Macbeth*, Las Palmas Theatre, Hollywood, CA, 1948; Danforth, *The Crucible*, Martinque, NY, 1958; title role, *J.B.*, ANTA, NY, 1959; *Naked*, University of California at Los Angeles, 1961; Old Dodge, *Buried Child*, Yale Repertory, New Haven, CT, 1979; Willie Loman, *Death of a Salesman*, Old Dodge, *Buried Child*, Norman, *On Golden Pond*, *Arsenic and Old Lace*, all Trinity Square Repertory Company, Providence, RI, 1979-1982; *Richard III*, *A Month in the Country*, Mark Taper Forum, Los Angeles, CA, 1983; Aslaksen, *An Enemy of the People*, Los Angeles Actors Theatre, 1984; *Hamlet*, Los Angeles Actors Theatre, 1985; King Lear, *Exploring King Lear*, Sound Studio, Hollywood, CA, 1985.

MAJOR TOURS—Old Dodge, *Buried Child*, and *Of Mice and Men*, tour of India, 1982; John Tarleton, *Misalliance*, Dallas, TX, Pittsburgh, PA, and Providence, RI, 1984-85; *Home*, and *In Celebration*, Theatre of Angels, Los Angeles, CA.

FILM DEBUT—*White Heat*, Warner Brothers, 1948. PRINCIPAL

FORD RAINEY

FILM APPEARANCES—*Perfect Strangers,* Warner Brothers, 1948; *Three Ten to Yuma,* 1959; *The Badlanders,* Metro-Goldwyn-Mayer, 1961; *Parrish,* Columbia, 1961; *John Paul Jones,* 1961; *Two Rode Together,* Columbia, 1962; *Kings of the Sun,* 1963; *Sand Pebbles,* Twentieth Century-Fox, 1964; *The Grove,* 1965; *Gypsy Moths; Forty Pounds of Trouble; The Robe; Parallax View; Crow on Junebug; Halloween II.*

TELEVISION DEBUT—Title role, "Abraham Lincoln," *Hallmark Hall of Fame,* NBC, 1953. PRINCIPAL TELEVISION APPEAR-ANCES—*Bonanza; Gunsmoke; Rawhide; The Virginian; The Tall Man; The Richard Boone Repertory; Window on Main Street; Probe; The Six Million Dollar Man; The Bionic Woman; My Sweet Charlie; Beatrice; Strangers; St. Elsewhere; Remington Steele; Bob Newhart Show; General Hospital; Our Town; The Last of Mrs. Lincoln.*

AWARDS: Los Angeles Drama Critics Award, 1978, for *Home;* Dramalogue Awards, 1980, for *In Celebration,* 1982, for *Long Days Journey into Night.*

ADDRESS: AGENT—Progressive Artists, 400 S. Beverly Drive, Beverly Hills, CA 90212.

*   *   *

RAMIS, Harold   1944-

PERSONAL: Full name Harold Allen Ramis; born November 21, 1944, in Chicago, IL; son of Nathan and Ruth (Cokee) Ramis;

married Anne Jean Plotkin (an artist), July 2, 1967; children: Violet Isadora. EDUCATION: Washington University, St. Louis, B.A., 1966.

VOCATION: Actor, director, and writer.

CAREER: STAGE DEBUT—Actor and writer, *The Second City,* Chicago, 1970-1973. NEW YORK DEBUT—Actor and writer, *The National Lampoon Show,* New Palladium, 1975.

PRINCIPAL FILM APPEARANCES—Russel, *Stripes,* Columbia, 1981; Spengler, *Ghostbusters,* Columbia, 1984.

PRINCIPAL FILM WORK—Director: *Caddyshack,* Orion, 1980; *National Lampoon's Vacation,* Warner Brothers, 1983; *Club Paradise,* Warner Brothers (upcoming).

PRINCIPAL TELEVISION APPEARANCES—*Second City Television,* for 26 episodes, 1976-78.

WRITINGS: SCREENPLAYS—*National Lampoon's Animal House* (with Douglas Kenny and Chris Miller), Universal, 1978; *Meatballs* (with Dan Goldberg, Len Blum, and Janice Allen), Paramount, 1979; *Caddyshack* (with Douglas Kenney and Brian Doyle-Murray), Orion, 1980; *Stripes* (with Dan Goldberg and Len Blum), Columbia, 1981; *Ghostbusters* (with Dan Aykroyd), Columbia, 1984; *Armed and Dangerous* (also executive producer), Columbia (upcoming).

TELEVISION SCRIPTS—Headwriter, 39 episodes, *Second City Television,* 1976-78; headwriter and producer, *The Rodney Dangerfield Show,* ABC, 1982.

RELATED CAREER—Associate editor, *Playboy,* 1968-70.

SIDELIGHTS: MEMBERSHIPS—American Federation of Television and Radio Artists, Screen Actors Guild, Writers Guild of America, Directors Guild of America.

ADDRESS: AGENT—Jack Rapke, Creative Artists Agency, 1888 Century Park E., Suite 1400, Los Angeles, CA 90067.

*   *   *

RANDEL, Melissa

PERSONAL: Born June 16, in Portland, ME; daughter of Herbert (a jazz musician) and Myrna Ruth (a dancer; maiden name, Randolph) Randel. EDUCATION: University of California at Irvine, B.F.A., 1976; studied acting with Blair Cutting and Gene Feist in NY.

VOCATION: Actor and dancer.

CAREER: STAGE DEBUT—Anita, *West Side Story,* Long Beach, CA. NEW YORK DEBUT—Judy Turner, *A Chorus Line,* Shubert, 1981-present. PRINCIPAL STAGE APPEARANCES—Dancer, *A Chorus Line,* National and International Bus and Truck Tour, 1980-81; understudy Cassie and Kristine, *A Chorus Line,* Shubert, NY.

PRINCIPAL FILM APPEARANCES—*Purple Rose of Cairo,* Orion, 1985; principal dancer, *A Chorus Line,* Embassy Pictures, 1985.

MELISSA RANDEL

PRINCIPAL TELEVISION APPEARANCES—Comic and entertainer, *The Funniest Joke I Ever Heard,* Dick Clark Productions, 1984; *General Hospital.*

SIDELIGHTS: MEMBERSHIPS—Actors' Equity Association, American Federation of Television and Radio Artists, Screen Actors Guild.

ADDRESS: HOME—New York, NY.

*   *   *

RANDOLPH, John   1915-

PERSONAL: Born Emanuel Cohen, June 1, 1915, in Bronx, NY; son of Louis (a hat manufacturer) and Dorothy (an insurance agent; maiden name, Shore) Cohen; married Sarah Lucie Cunningham (an actress), January 3, 1942; children: Martha, Harrison Henry. EDUCATION: City College of New York, degree, 1935; also attended Columbia University; trained for the stage at the Dramatic Workshop of the New School and with Stella Adler and Erwin Piscator. POLITICS: Left of center. MILITARY: U.S. Army Air Corps, 1942-45.

VOCATION: Actor and writer.

CAREER: FILM DEBUT—Arthur Hamilton, *Seconds,* 1965. PRINCIPAL FILM APPEARANCES—Azenauer, *Pretty Poison,* 1967; Father Harvey, *Gaily, Gaily,* 1969; Coach Jim Southerd, *Number*

JOHN RANDOLPH

One, 1969; Cyrus McNutt, *There Was a Crooked Man,* 1970; Sid Green, *Serpico,* 1973; Angelo Partanna, *Prizzi's Honor,* ABC, 1985.

TELEVISION DEBUT—Jordan, Chief Guard, *Captain Video,* 1947. PRINCIPAL TELEVISION APPEARANCES—John Mitchell, *Blind Ambition;* Junior, *The Bob Newhart Show; Missiles of October; Bonanza; Sandburg's Lincoln; Gathering with All Different Speed.*

STAGE DEBUT—Jacob Engstrand, *Ghosts,* Houston Street Theater, NY, 1935, 81 performances. PRINCIPAL STAGE APPEARANCES—Mac, *Medicine Show,* New Yorker, 1938; radio announcer, *Hold on to Your Hats,* Shubert, NY, 1940; Wozzeck, *Wozzeck,* New School for Social Research, NY, 1941. Broadway: *The Sound of Music; The Visit; A Case of Libel; Come Back Little Sheba; Command Decision.* Off Broadway: *Eulogy,* Ensemble Studio Theater, NY, 1983; *The American Clock,* Mark Taper Forum, Los Angeles, 1984; *Twelve Angry Men,* Henry Fonda Theater, Los Angeles, 1985.

MAJOR TOURS—Jan Erlone, *Native Son,* U.S. cities, 1941-42; Lt. Jake Goldberg, *Command Decision,* U.S. cities, 1948-49; Reverend Jeremiah Brown, *Inherit the Wind,* U.S. cities, 1956-57; *Our Town.*

WRITINGS: TELEVISION—"Stories of Two Worlds," *Camera III,* CBS, 1965. PLAYS, PRODUCED—*Portrait of an Artist* (adapted, with Phoebe Brand and Frederic Ewen), Martinique, NY, 1962; *Magic Mountain,* Manchester, England, 1970.

AWARDS: Stardust Citation Award, New York Post, 1952, for the Milkman in *Come Back Little Sheba;* Hospital Workers Union

Award, 1969; Friends of a Democratic Spain Award, 1972; Paul Robeson Award, German Democratic Republic, 1979; Abraham Lincoln Brigade Award, 1983.

SIDELIGHTS: MEMBERSHIPS—Academy of Motion Picture Arts and Sciences, Actors Equity Association, Screen Actors Guild (board), American Federation of Television and Radio Artists, Actors Fund, American Civil Liberties Union, Abraham Lincoln Brigade, Hospital Workers Union, United States Society for Friendship with the German Democratic Republic.

John Randolph told *CTFT* that one of the highlights of his career was playing the role of the Police Chief in *The Visit* opposite the Lunts.

ADDRESS: HOME—Hollywood, CA. AGENT—Jack Fields and Associates, 9255 Sunset Blvd., Los Angeles, CA 90069.

*   *   *

RANDOLPH, Robert   1926-

PERSONAL: Born March 9, 1926, in Centerville, IO; son of Charles Wilmer and Sadie Mae (Hart) Randolph. EDUCATION: University of Iowa, B.A., M.F.A., 1946-53; MILITARY: U.S. Air Force, 1944-46.

VOCATION: Designer.

CAREER: FIRST NEW YORK STAGE WORK—Designer: Scenery and costumes, *The Saint of Bleecker Street*, Broadway, 1954. PRINCIPAL STAGE WORK—Designer: Costumes, *The Desperate Hours*, NY, 1955; scenery, *Bye Bye Birdie*, NY, 1960; scenery and lighting, *How to Succeed in Business without Really Trying*, NY, 1961, *Bravo Giovanni*, NY, 1962; scenery, *Calculated Risk*, 1962; scenery and lighting, *Little Me*, NY, 1962, *Sophie*, NY, 1963, *Foxy*, NY, 1964; scenery, *Any Wednesday*, NY, 1964; scenery and costumes, *Funny Girl*, NY, 1964, *Something More!*, NY, 1964, *Pleasures and Palaces*, NY, 1965; scenery, *Minor Miracle*, NY, 1965; scenery and lighting, *Christmas in Las Vegas*, NY, 1965; scenery, *Anya*, NY, 1965; scenery and lighting, *Sweet Charity*, NY, 1966, *It's a Bird . . . It's a Plane . . . It's Superman*, NY, 1966, *Walking Happy*, NY, 1966, *Sherry*, NY, 1967, *Sweet Charity*, London, England, 1967, *Henry Sweet Henry*, NY, 1967, *How to Be a Jewish Mother*, NY, 1967, *Golden Rainbow*, NY, 1968.

Scenery, *A Teaspoon Every Four Hours*, NY, 1969; scenery and lighting, *Angela*, NY, 1969; scenery, *Applause*, NY, 1970, *Ari*, NY, 1971; scenery and lighting, *70 Girls 70*, 1971; scenery, *Applause*, London, England, 1972; scenery and lighting, *Gypsy*, London, England, 1973, *No Hard Feelings*, NY, 1973, *Good Evening*, NY, 1973, *The Enclave*, NY, 1973, *Words and Music: Sammy Cahn's Songbook*, London, England, 1974; scenery, *Gypsy*, *The King and I*, Los Angeles, 1974; scenery, *We Interrupt This Program*, Los Angeles, 1975, *How to Succeed in Business without Really Trying*, *Wonderful Town*, Los Angeles, 1975; scenery and lighting, *The Norman Conquests*, NY, 1975; scenery, *Porgy and Bess*, NY, 1976; scenery and lighting, *Annie Get Your Gun*, Los Angeles, 1977; scenery, *Spotlight*, Washington, DC, 1978, *Partridge in a Pear Tree*, *Little Johnny Jones*, *Seven Brides for Seven Brothers*, *Sweet Charity*, 1985.

PRINCIPAL TELEVISION WORK—Scenery: *Antoinette Perry Awards Show*, 1967-84; *That's Life*, 1967-68; *Liza with a Z; Night of 100 Stars*, 1985.

AWARDS: Antoinette Perry Award nominations: *Bye Bye Birdie*, *Little Me*, *Skyscraper*, *Anya*, *Sweet Charity*, *Golden Rainbow*, *Applause*, *Porgy and Bess*.

SIDELIGHTS: MEMBERSHIPS—United Scenic Artists, Local 829.

ADDRESS: HOME—5630 Spreading Oak Drive, Los Angeles, CA 90068.

*   *   *

RAPHAEL, Frederic Michael   1931-

PERSONAL: Born August 14, 1931, in Chicago, IL; son of Cedric Michael and Irene Rose (Mauser) Raphael; married Sylvia Betty Glatt, 1955; children: two sons, one daughter. EDUCATION: Charterhouse, Godalming, Surrey, five years.

VOCATION: Writer.

WRITINGS: SCREENPLAYS—*Nothing but the Best*, 1964; *Darling*, 1965; *Two for the Road*, 1967, *Far from the Madding Crowd*, 1967; *A Severed Head*, 1972; *Daisy Miller*, 1974; *The Glittering Prizes*,

FREDERIC   RAPHAEL

1976. PLAYS—*From the Greek*, Arts Theatre, Cambridge, 1979. TELEPLAYS—*Rogue Male*, 1976; *Something's Wrong* (also directed), 1979; *School Play*, 1979; *The Best of Friends*, 1979; *Richard's Things*, 1981; *Oxbridge Blues*, 1984.

NOVELS—*Obbligato*, 1956; *The Earlsdon Way*, 1958; *The Limits of Love*, 1960; *A Wild Surmise*, 1961; *The Graduate Wife*, 1962; *The Trouble with England*, 1962; *Lindmann*, 1963; *Orchestra and Beginners*, 1967; *Like Men Betrayed*, 1970; *Who Were You with Last Night?* 1971; *April, June, and November*, 1972; *Richard's Things*, 1973; *California Time*, 1975; *The Glittering Prizes*, 1976; *Heaven and Earth*, 1985.

BIOGRAPHIES—*Somerset Maugham and His World*, 1977; *Byron*, 1982. SHORT STORIES—*Sleeps Six*, 1979; *Oxbridge Blues*, 1980; *Comings and Goings*, 1984. TRANSLATIONS—*Poems of Catullus* (with Kenneth McLeish), 1976; *The Oresteia* (televised as *The Serpent Son*, BBC, 1979). ESSAYS—*Bookmarks*, 1975; *Cracks in the Ice*, 1979.

AWARDS: Academy Award, Best Screenplay, 1965, for *Darling;* Writer of the Year, Royal Television Society, 1976, for *The Glittering Prizes;* honorary degree, St. Johns College, Cambridge.

SIDELIGHTS: MEMBERSHIPS—Savile Club.

ADDRESS: AGENT—A.P. Watt Ltd., 26-28 Bedford Row, London WCIR 4HR, England.

*   *   *

GORDANA RASHOVICH

RASHOVICH, Gordana

PERSONAL: EDUCATION: Roosevelt University, B.A.; Royal Academy of Dramatic Art, London, England, diploma; studied stage combat with B.H. Barry, studied with Uta Hagan at the Herbert Berghof Studios in NY.

VOCATION: Actress.

CAREER: PRINCIPAL STAGE APPEARANCES—Marthe, *Watch on the Rhine*, Center Stage, Baltimore, MD; Magda, *Semmelweiss*, Hartman, Stamford, CT; Margorie, *Extremities*, Actor's Theatre of Louisville, American International Theatre Festival; Raina, *Arms and the Man*, McCarter, Princeton, NJ; Laura, *Shivaree*, Rutgers Theatre Company, New Brunswick, NJ; Catherine, *Wuthering Heights*, Actors Theatre of Louisville; Olivia, *Twelfth Night*, Guthrie, Minneapolis, MN; Mrs. Kempler, *Morocco*, Virginia Stage Company, Norfolk, VA; Olivia, *Twelfth Night*, Great Lakes Shakespeare Festival; Rose/Flo, *Algren's Women/Domino Courts*, William Renfield Theatre, NY; Sarah, *Selma*, Theatre for the New City, NY; Emma, *Fefu and Her Friends*, American Place, NY; Jill, *Couple of the Year*, Lambs, NY; Honey, *Who's Afraid of Virginia Woolf?*, Regan, *King Lear*, both Royal Academy of Dramatic Art, London.

PRINCIPAL FILM APPEARANCES—Mrs. Kovach, *Heaven's Gate*.

PRINCIPAL TELEVISION APPEARANCES—Kate Donovan, *Another World*, NBC.

AWARDS: Theatre World Award, for Emma, *Fefu and Her Friends;*

Vanbrugh Theatre Award, for outstanding performance, Royal Academy of Dramatic Art; Derek Ware Prize, for stage swordplay with Shakespeare text, Royal Academy of Dramatic Art.

SIDELIGHTS: MEMBERSHIPS—Actors' Equity Association, Screen Actors Guild, American Federation of Television and Radio Artists.

ADDRESS: AGENT—Leaverton Sames Associates Ltd., 1650 Broadway, New York, NY 10019.

*   *   *

RAVIN, Linda   1956-

PERSONAL: Born Linda Ravinsky, October 21, 1956, in NJ; daughter of Frank and Sophie Genevieve (Adams) Ravinsky. EDUCATION: Jersey City State College, B.A., speech, theatre, and English; studied voice with Ann Countryman, acting with Gene Frankel, and dance with Phil Black and Bob Audy in New York.

VOCATION: Actress and dancer.

CAREER: DEBUT—Dancer, *Salute to Armed Forces*, Mosque Theatre, Symphony Hall, Newark, NJ. NEW YORK DEBUT—*Dance Festival in Park*, Charles Weidman Theatre Dance Company, Delacorte. SPANISH DEBUT—Dancer, Lido Club, Madrid, 1974.

LINDA RAVIN

REAMS, Lee Roy

PERSONAL: Born in Covington, KY. EDUCATION: University of Cincinnati, College-Conservatory of Music, B.A., M.A.

VOCATION: Actor, singer, and dancer.

CAREER: PRINCIPAL STAGE APPEARANCES—Will Parker, *Oklahoma!*, New York State Theatre, Lincoln Center, NY, 1969; Duane Fox, *Applause*, Palace, NY, 1970; Henry Spofford, *Lorelei*, Civic Center Music Hall, Oklahoma City, OK, 1973; Cornelius Hackl, *Hello, Dolly!*, St. James, NY, 1978; Billy Lawler, *42nd Street*, Winter Garden, NY, 1980, 1984-85.

MAJOR TOURS—Henry Spofford, *Lorelei*, nine-month, pre-Broadway tryout tour, ending up at Palace, NY, 1974.

PRINCIPAL TELEVISION APPEARANCES—*The Doctors; Dance Fever; Bonnie and the Franklins; The Loretta Lynn Special; Bob Hope at West Point; American Dance Machine; Eubie* (Kennedy Center); *The Best of Everything; Parade of Stars; Night of 100 Stars (Part II); The Merv Griffin Show; The Tonight Show with Johnny Carson; The Orange Bowl Parade and Half-Time Show.*

CONCERT, GUEST SOLOIST APPEARANCES—*Leonard Bernstein at Wolftrap; Jule Styne and Friends at the Palace; Cy Coleman's "Hey, Look Me Over;" Broadway Salutes New York City Opera with Beverly Sills; The Firefly; One Touch of Venus; Cincinnati Symphony Orchestra.* CABARET APPEARANCES—O'Neal's Time Square, The Grand Finale, The Macambo, Mister Kelly's, The Back Lot.

PRINCIPAL STAGE APPEARANCES—Graciella, *West Side Story*, North Stage Dinner Theatre, 1977; featured in "Sugar Baby Bounce," *Sugar Babies*, Mark Hellinger, NY, 1979-82; Sally, *Funny Face*, Studio Arena Theatre; Theda, *When the Kids Are Away*, New Dramatists, NY; Dee, *Winterfire*, St. Clements, NY; Candy Starr, *One Flew Over the Cuckoo's Nest*, Actors Cafe, Orange, NJ; Lucy, *Dracula*, Cabaret Playhouse, NJ; shoplifter, Mrs. Bagatelle, *Detective Story*, Cabaret Playhouse, NJ; Corrina Stroller, *Afternoons in Vegas*, Theatre by the Sea, Portsmouth, NH; *Telecast*, St. Bart's Playhouse, NY; Bunny, *House of Blue Leaves*.

MAJOR TOURS—Maid, *My Fair Lady;* Baby Doll, *Pippin.*

FILM DEBUT—Dona Inez, *Don Juan*, Jay Wheeler Productions, 1975. PRINCIPAL FILM APPEARANCES—Brenda, *The Cellar*, Jay Wheeler Productions; Jacqueline, *Dino's Case*, Fernando Santos Productions; featured dancer, *Four Friends*, Filmways, 1981.

TELEVISION DEBUT—*Let's Talk to the Stars*, Santos Productions. PRINCIPAL TELEVISION APPEARANCES—Congresswoman, *Ryan's Hope*, ABC; Leigh, *Eddie Capra Mystery*, NBC; *A Little Sex*, MTM Productions, 1982; *The Hamptons*, Cenex Productions.

SIDELIGHTS: MEMBERSHIPS—Actors' Equity Association, American Federation of Television and Radio Artists, Screen Actors Guild.

ADDRESS: AGENT—Vince Cirrincione Associates, 300 W. 55th Street, New York, NY 10019.

LEE ROY REAMS

AWARDS: Antoinette Perry, Best Supporting Actor in a Musical, 1980, for *42nd Street;* Drama Desk nomination, 1980, for *42nd Street.*

SIDELIGHTS: MEMBERSHIPS—Actors' Equity Association, Screen Actors Guild, American Federation of Television and Radio Artists, American Guild of Musical Artists, American Guild of Variety Artists.

ADDRESS: AGENT—Ed Robbins, William Morris Agency, 1350 Avenue of the Americas, New York, NY 10036.

*   *   *

REARDON, John

VOCATION: Singer.

CAREER: PRINCIPAL STAGE APPEARANCES—*New Faces, Do-Re-Mi, The Saint of Bleecker Street,* all NY; Billy Bigelow, *Carousel;* Fred Graham/Petruccio, *Kiss Me Kate;* Hajj, *Kismet;* Debeque, *South Pacific;* Don Quixote, *Man of La Mancha;* Pangloss, *Candide,* Baltimore Opera, Cleveland Orchestra.

Opera: Starring role, *Carmen,* Metropolitan Opera, NY; *L'Italiana in Algeri,* Metropolitan Opera, NY; *Jenufa,* Metropolitan Opera,

NY; Prince Andrei, *War and Peace,* Wolf Trap Farm Park, Washington, DC, Carnegie Hall, NY; *Benvenuto Cellini,* Boston Opera; title role, *Orfeo,* five seasons in NY; title role, *The Last Savage,* Venice, Italy. Operetta: Danilo, *The Merry Widow,* U.S. and Canada.

One Man Show: *Reardon Sings Rodgers & Hammerstein/Hart,* Philadelphia Orchestra, Tucson Opera, Baltimore Opera, Canadian Opera, Pittsburgh Symphony Orchestra, San Diego Chamber Orchestra, Ottawa National Opera.

Concert: *Songfest,* National Symphony Orchestra, Washington, DC, New York Philharmonic, Bayerischer Rundfunk, Germany.

RECORDINGS: On the Town; The Creation; The Rake's Progress. Reardon has recorded extensively and may be heard on the RCA, Deutsche Grammophon, Columbia, Vox, Decca, Seraphim, and Serenus labels.

ADDRESS: AGENT—Sunstone Agency, 239 Johnson Street, Santa Fe, NM, 87501.

*   *   *

RECHT, Ray   1947-

PERSONAL: Born August 9, 1947, in New York City; son of Morton (a C.P.A.) and Lillian F. (an accountant; maiden name, Dembner) Recht; married Claire Des Becker (a ceramic designer), June 27, 1982. EDUCATION: Carnegie-Mellon, B.F.A., 1969; Yale Drama School, M.F.A., 1972; prepared for career as assistant to Ming Cho Lee and Tony Walton. RELIGION: Jewish.

VOCATION: Scenic (set) designer.

CAREER: DEBUT—Scenic, media, and lighting designer, *Happy End* (American premier), Yale Repertory, New Haven, CT, 1972. NEW YORK DEBUT—Set designer, *Medal of Honor Rag,* Theatre de Lys, 1975. PRINCIPAL STAGE WORK—Broadway: Associate designer to Tony Walton, *Woman of the Year,* Palace, 1981; associate designer to David Chapman, *The First,* Martin Beck, 1982; designer, *Trick,* 1982; designer, *Slab Boys,* 1983; designer, *The Babe,* 1984.

Off Broadway: Designer—*The Offering,* Negro Ensemble Co.; *A Backers Audition,* Manhattan Theatre Club; *Black Body Blues,* Negro Ensemble Co.; *Mensch Meier,* Manhattan Theatre Club; *Judgement,* St. Peters, Citicorp Center; *Upstairs at O'Neals,* O'Neals at 43rd Street; *A Hell of a Town,* West Side Arts; *A . . . My Name Is Alice,* Top of the Gate, Village Gate, 1984.

Also: *Anyone Can Whistle,* Berkshire Theatre Festival, Stockbridge, MA, 1981; *Planet Fires,* GeVa, 1985; and many regional theatre productions at Actor's Theatre of Louisville, Barter, Capitol Repertory, Center Stage, Folger, Indiana Repertory, Manitoba Theatre Centre, and McCarter, among others.

Opera: Assistant to David Mitchell, *The Italian Straw Hat,* Santa Fe Opera, NM; designer, *One Christmas Long Ago,* Manhattan School of Music, NY; *The Impressario, Aunt Caroline's Will,* Mannes College, NY; *Werther,* Opera Ensemble of NY; *Song of Norway,* Pittsburgh Civic Light Opera, PA; *Peter Grimes,* Yale Symphony, New Haven, CT.

JOHN REARDON

FILM DEBUT—Assistant to Tony Walton, *All That Jazz,* Columbia,

1978. PRINCIPAL FILM WORK—Assistant art director, *Just Tell Me What You Want,* Warner Brothers, 1980; assistant production designer, *The First Deadly Sin,* Filmways, 1980; art director, *Amityville II: The Possession,* Orion, 1982; art director, *Exposed,* Metro-Goldwyn-Mayer/United Artists, 1983; production designer, *The Hanging Ground,* 1985.

SIDELIGHTS: MEMBERSHIPS—United Scenic Artists, local 829.

'I enjoy working in all three media, film, theatre, and television,'' Ray Recht wrote to *CTFT.* ''I feel each brings new insights which can be applied to the others.''

Recht's works included in exhibition, are *"Contemporary Stage Design, U.S.A."* at the International Theatre Institute and *"200 Years of America Onstage,"* presented by the Kennedy Center and Mobil Corp.

PRINCIPAL TELEVISION WORK—Art director, *French-American Perspective,* Telefrance, cable, 1982; art director, *The Babe,* Corniche Productions, cable; set designer, *Another World,* NBC, 1984.

RELATED CAREER—Lecturer, Goucher College, Baltimore, 1973-76; guest artist, Queensborough Community College, Bayside, NY, 1977-84; adjunct faculty, C.W. Post College, NY, 1981; guest artist, Albright College, Reading, PA, 1983-84.

ADDRESS: OFFICE—267 W 89th Street, New York, NY 10024. AGENT—John Giroux, 575 Madison Avenue, New York, NY 10022.

* * *

REDFIELD, Adam 1959-

PERSONAL: Born November 4, 1959, in New York City; son of William H. (an actor) and Betsy Ann (an actress; maiden name, Meade) Redfield. EDUCATION: Studied for the theatre with Stella Adler.

VOCATION: Actor.

CAREER: DEBUT—Claude, *Swing,* Kennedy Center, Washington, DC, for 30 performances. NEW YORK DEBUT—Desmond, *A Life,* Morosco, 1981, for 88 performances. PRINCIPAL STAGE APPEARANCES—Trinculo, *The Tempest,* Guthrie, Minneapolis, MN, 1981; Trofimov, *The Cherry Orchard,* Whole Theatre, NJ, 1982; Pascal, *Beethoven's Tenth,* Nederlander, NY, 1984.

MAJOR TOURS—Mark Dolson, *Mass Appeal,* Chicago, Toronto, Philadelphia, Baltimore, Washington, 1982-83.

FILM DEBUT—Mr. Fox, *A Midsummer Night's Sex Comedy,* Warner Brothers, 1982.

TELEVISION DEBUT—George Winfield, *Family Reunion,* NBC, 1981. PRINCIPAL TELEVISION APPEARANCES—Bertram Phillips, *The Doctors,* NBC, 1981; Prince Conrad, *Fit·for a King,* NBC, 1982.

AWARDS: Theatre World Award and Antoinette Perry Award

nomination, 1981, for *A Life.*

ADDRESS: AGENT—Lionel Larner, 850 Seventh Avenue, New York, NY 10019.

* * *

REGAN, Sylvia 1908-

PERSONAL: Born Sylvia Hoffenberg, April 15, 1908; daughter of Louis (in the shoe business) and Esther (Albert) Hoffenberg; married James J. Regan (a lawyer), 1936 (divorced); married Abraham Ellstein (a composer and conductor; died, 1963). EDUCATION: Trained for the stage at the American Academy of Dramatic Arts. POLITICS: Democrat. RELIGION: Jewish.

VOCATION: Actress, writer, and institutional theatre promotions manager.

CAREER: NEW YORK STAGE DEBUT—Roumanian girl, *We Americans,* 1927-28. PRINCIPAL STAGE APPEARANCES—Broadway: Elizabeth, *Waltz of the Dogs,* 1928; Marjorie, *Poppa,* 1929; Mexican mother, *Night Over Taos,* 1931.

MAJOR TOURS—Roumanian girl, *We Americans,* U.S. cities, 1927-28.

WRITINGS: PLAYS, PRODUCED—*Morningstar,* Longacre, NY, 1940, then Embassy, London, 1951, under new title, *The Golden Door; Great to Be Alive,* Winter Garden, NY, 1951; *The Fifth Season,* Cort, NY, 1953-55, then Cambridge Theater, London, 1954; *The Golem* (with Abraham Ellstein), New York City Opera, 1961-62; *Zelda,* Barrymore, NY, 1969.

AWARDS: Ford Foundation Grant, 1961; Citation of Merit Award, National Council of Jewish Women, 1953; Citation Award, Federation of Women Zionists of Great Britain, Ireland, and Glasgow, 1953.

SIDELIGHTS: MEMBERSHIPS—Dramatists Guild, Authors League of America, American Jewish Historical Society.

Regan told *CTFT,* ''From 1928 to 1930, I designed hats and headdresses for Broadway shows. Among them were *Dear Jane,* and *Alice in Wonderland.''*

ADDRESS: HOME—55 E. Ninth Street, New York, NY 10003.

* * *

REICH, John 1906-

PERSONAL: Full name Johannes Theodor Reich; born September 30, 1906, in Vienna, Austria; son of Leopold (an industrialist) and Martha (a pianist; maiden name, Baxter) Reich; married Karoline Friederike von Kurzweil, October 23, 1932 (died, February 2, 1945); married Karen Ruth Lasker-Lester, July 8, 1957 (died). EDUCATION: Realgymasium I, B.A., Vienna, Austria, 1928; School of Business, graduate, Vienna, Austria, 1929; Max Reinhardt Seminary of the University of Vienna, directing diploma, 1931; Cornell University, Ph.D., 1944. RELIGION: Roman Catholic.

JOHN REICH

VOCATION: Director, producer, and writer.

CAREER: FIRST STAGE WORK—Director: *Swanwhite,* Theatre in Schoenbrunn Castle, Vienna, Austria, 1930. PRINCIPAL STAGE WORK—Assistant director, *The Robbers,* Burgtheatre, Vienna, Austria, 1931; assistant director, *The Tempest,* Burgtheatre, Vienna, Austria, 1932; director, *As Husbands Go, Measure for Measure,* 1932; *The Passion Play,* Circus Renz, 1933; assistant director, *Faust I,* Salzburg Festival, 1934-35; director, *Tiger at the Gates,* Theatre in der Josefstadt, Vienna, Austria, 1936; director, *The First Legion, Black Limelight, Espionage,* Theatre in der Josefstadt, Vienna, Austria, 1937-38;

Director: *The Imaginary Invalid,* Brander Matthews Theatre, NY, 1945; *The Dream,* Berkshire Festival, MA, 1946; *Faust I,* Equity-Library Theatre, NY, 1946; *Henry IV,* Greenwich Mews, NY, 1947; *Hippolytus,* Lenox Hill Playhouse, NY, 1948; Pirandello's *Henry IV,* Sea Cliff Summer Theatre, NY, 1950; *Mrs. Warren's Profession,* Bleecker Street Playhouse, NY, 1950; *Trial by Jury, Down in the Valley, The Marriage of Figaro, The Magic Flute,* Plymouth Opera Festival, Plymouth Rock Center, MA, 1951-52; *The Sacred Flame,* President, NY, 1952; *The Abduction from the Seraglio,* Caramoor Festival, Katonah, NY, 1953; *Don Giovanni,* Plymouth Opera Festival, 1954; *The Dream,* Brander Matthews, NY, 1957.

As head of Goodman Memorial Theatre and School of Drama, Chicago, IL: producer, *The Merchant of Venice, The Cave Dwellers, Hippolytus,* director, Pirandello's *Henry IV,* producer, *The Good Woman of Setzuan, The Inspector General,* all 1959-60; producer, *The Taming of the Shrew,* director, *Venus Observed,* producer, *Royal Gambit, Under Milkwood, Uncle Vanya, On Borrowed Time,* all 1960-61; producer and director, *Faust,* producer, *The Lark, My*

Heart's in the Highlands, Hedda Gabler, The American Dream, director, *The Caucasian Chalk Circle,* all 1961-62; producer and director, *Becket,* producer, *A Passage to India,* director, *Christopher C.,* producer, *The Lesson, The Rivals,* all 1962-63.

Producer and director, *The Millionairess,* producer, *The Three Sisters, The Glass Menagerie, King Lear, Mother Courage,* director, *A Far Country,* all 1963-64; producer and director, *The Madwoman of Chaillot,* producer, *Macbeth, The Ballad of the Sad Cafe, Rashomon, The Barrets of Wimpole Street, Anna Karenina,* all 1964-65; producer and director, *The Cocktail Party,* producer, *The Winter's Tale, The Pedestrian in the Air, Dylan, The Skin of Our Teeth, Galileo,* all 1965-66; producer and directed, *Tartuffe, A Dream Play,* producer, *Marat-Sade, The Eccentricities of a Nightingale, Much Ado About Nothing, Oh What a Lovely War!* all 1967; producer and director, *The Miser,* producer, *The Balcony, Caesar and Cleopatra, Othello, A Man's a Man, A Flea in Her Ear,* all 1967-68.

Producer and director, *The Salzburg Theatre of the World, The Death and Life of Sneaky Fitch,* producer, *Red Roses for Me, Measure for Measure, Tom Paine, The Recruiting Officer,* all 1968-69; producer, *Soldiers, You Can't Take It with You, The Tempest, The Basement, The Tea Party, The Man in the Glass Booth, Heartbreak House,* all 1969-70; producer, *The Threepenny Opera, Twelfth Night, The Night Thoreau Spent in Jail, Marching Song, Poor Bitos, Lady Audley's Secret,* all 1970-71; producer, *A Place without Doors, Assassination 1865, The Importance of Being Earnest, The Royal Family, The Ruling Class, The Boys from Syracuse,* all 1971-72.

Also, producer, *Amadeus,* Missouri Repertory Theatre, Asolo State Theatre, 1983-84.

PRINCIPAL TELEVISION WORK—Director: Documentary series, *The Doctor Looks,* CBS, 1945; *The Missus Goes Shopping,* CBS, 1945; *Invalid,* CBS, 1946; *Untitled,* CBS, 1946; *The Shelleys,* CBS, 1951.

RELATED CAREER—Distinguished guest artist, University of Miami, University of Wisconsin, University of Kansas, University of Georgia, University of Pennsylvania, Cornell University, State University of New York at Stonybrook; as producing director of Chicago's Goodman Theatre, Reich produced and/or directed 94 major subscription plays in addition to 87 studio plays.

WRITINGS: TRANSLATIONS—*Faust; Mary Stuart; Hannele; Everyman; The Great Salzburg Theatre of the World; In One Night; The Comedy of Words; The Imaginary Invalid; Enrico IV.*

AWARDS: Ford Foundation Award for Producing Directors, 1959; ANTA, Chicago Theatre, Man of the Year, 1960; Governor of Illinois Award for outstanding contribution by a foreign-born American citzen, 1961; received the order, Chevalier des Arts et Lettres, 1964; Grand Badge of Honor, Austria, 1968; honorary doctorate of humane letters, Lake Forest College, IL; Joseph Jefferson Award.

SIDELIGHTS: MEMBERSHIPS—American Theatre Association, Theatre Communications Group, NY (board of directors), National Theatre Conference, Cliff Dwellers Club.

ADDRESS: HOME—724 Bohemia Parkway, Sayville, New York, 11782.

LEE REMICK

REMICK, Lee

PERSONAL: Born December 14, in Boston, MA; daughter of Frank and Margaret (Waldo) Remick; married Bill Colleran, August 3, 1957 (divorced 1969); married Kip Gowans, (a film producer), December 18, 1970; children: (first marriage) Kate, Matthew. EDUCATION—Studied at the Swoboda Ballet School in NY; Barnard College, and with Charles Weidman in NY.

VOCATION: Actress.

CAREER: NEW YORK DEBUT—*Be Your Age*, 1953. LONDON DEBUT—*Bus Stop*, 1974. PRINCIPAL STAGE APPEARANCES—*Anyone Can Whistle*, 1964; *Wait Until Dark*, 1965.

MAJOR TOURS—*Brigadoon; The Seven Year Itch; Jenny Kissed Me; Annie Get Your Gun.*

FILM DEBUT—Betty Lou Heckum, *A Face in the Crowd*, 1956. PRINCIPAL FILM APPEARANCES—*The Long Hot Summer*, 1958; *These Thousands Hills*, 1959; *Anatomy of a Murder*, 1959; *Wild River*, 1960; *Sanctuary*, 1961; *Experiment in Terror*, 1962; *Days of Wine and Roses*, 1963; *The Running Man*, 1963; *The Travelling Lady*, 1963; *The Wheeler Dealer*, 1963; *The Hallelujah Trail*, 1965; *Baby, the Rain Must Fall*, 1965; *No Way to Treat a Lady*, 1968; *Hard Contract*, 1969; *A Severed Head*, 1971; *Sometimes a Great Notion*, 1971; *Loot*, 1972; *A Delicate Balance*, 1973; *Hennessy*, 1975; *The Omen*, 1976; *Telefon*, 1977; *The Medusa Touch*, 1978; *The Europeans*, 1979; *The Competition*, 1980; *Tribute*, 1980; *Emma's War.*

PRINCIPAL TELEVISION APPEARANCES—*The Tempest*, 1960; *And No One Could Save Her*, 1973; *The Blue Knight*, 1973; *Queen's Bench VII*, 1974; *Jennie, Lady Randolph Churchill*, 1975; *A Girl Named Sooner*, 1975; *Hustling*, 1975; *Breaking Up*, 1978; *Wheels*, 1978; *Torn Between Two Lovers*, 1979; *Ike: The War Years*, 1979; *Haywire*, 1980; *The Women's Room*, 1980; *The Letter*, 1982; *The Gift of Love, a Christmas Story*, 1983; *Mistral's Daughter*, 1984; *A Good Sport*, 1984; *Rear View Mirror*, 1984; *The Snow Queen*, 1985.

AWARDS: Academy Award nomination, 1964, for *Days of Wine and Roses;* Golden Globe Awards, 1973, for *The Blue Knight*, 1975, for *Jennie, Lady Randolph Churchill;* doctor of humane letters, Emerson College, Boston, MA, 1975.

ADDRESS: AGENT—International Creative Management, 8899 Beverly Blvd., Los Angeles, CA 90048.

*   *   *

REMME, John   1935-

PERSONAL: Born November 21, 1935, in Fargo, ND; son of Amos Engvald (a laborer) and Solveig Alvina (Ingberg) Remme. EDUCATION: University of Minnesota, 1953-55.

VOCATION: Actor and singer.

JOHN REMME

CAREER: STAGE DEBUT—Teddy Spearing, *The Torch Bearers,* West Side High School, Minneapolis, MN, 1951. NEW YORK DEBUT—Patron in chaps, *The Ritz,* Longacre, 1975. PRINCIPAL STAGE APPEARANCES—Nineteen roles in classic American musicals including: Jim, *Sunny,* Bobby, *Good News,* Rupert, *Sweet Adeline,* Wally, *Lady, Be Good,* Senator Oliver P. Loganberry, *Louisiana Purchase,* all at the Goodspeed Opera House, E. Haddam, CT 1969-1982; Jo, *The Royal Family,* Helen Hayes, NY, 1976; waiter, *Can-Can,* Minskoff, NY, 1981; Patch Riley, *A Touch of the Poet,* Yale Repertory, New Haven, CT, 1983; mouse/Tweedeldee, *Alice in Wonderland,* Virginia, NY, 1983; LeBeau/Hymen, *As You Like It,* Arena Stage, Washington, DC, 1983.

MAJOR TOURS—Budurus, *The Rothschilds,* national tour, Toronto, Washington, DC, Baltimore, September-November, 1972.

TELEVISION DEBUT—Jo, "The Royal Family," *Great Performances,* PBS, 1977.

SIDELIGHTS: MEMBERSHIPS—Actors' Equity Association, Screen Actors Guild, Actors Fund of America.

Remme told *CTFT* that his "numerous roles in the Goodspeed musical revivals helped develop [his] character comedy style, which critics have often found reminiscent of Chaplin, Keaton, Stan Laurel and Victor Moore." His current ambition is to "perform in more dramas, especially those of O'Neill and Ibsen."

ADDRESS: HOME—49 Prince Street, New York, NY 10012. AGENT—Bret Adams, Ltd., 448 W. 44th Street, New York, NY 10036.

*   *   *

RETTURA, Joseph   1953-

PERSONAL: Born October 28, 1953, in Scranton, PA; son of Giovanni and Jeanette (Martelli) Rettura. EDUCATION: University of Scranton, B.A., 1975; New York University, M.F.A. candidate, 1977; studied at the Actors and Directors Lab with Jack Garfein.

VOCATION: Director.

CAREER: PRINCIPAL STAGE WORK—Director: *The Letter,* Quaigh, NY, 1981; *Rockaway Boulevard,* Forum-Italian American Theatre, NY, 1981; *The Hooker and the John,* Quaigh, NY, 1982; *Eleanor,* Quaigh, NY, 1983; *Superior Decision,* Ironbound Theatre, NY, 1985.

SIDELIGHTS: MEMBERSHIPS—Society of Stage Directors and Choreographers, New York Playwriters.

ADDRESS: HOME—Five W. 63rd Street, New York, NY 10023.

*   *   *

REY, Antonia   1927-

PERSONAL: Born Antonia Francesch, October 12, 1927, in Havana, Cuba; daughter of Antonio (a dentist) and Emilia (a nurse; maiden

ANTONIA REY

name, Rangel) Francesch; married Andres Castro (artistic director, Westside Repertory, NY), December 17, 1958. EDUCATION: University of Havana, graduate; studied with Andres Castro in New York City.

VOCATION: Actress.

CAREER: STAGE DEBUT—*Numancia Cervantes,* Havana University, 1948. NEW YORK DEBUT—Lupa, *Bajour,* Shubert, 1964. PRINCIPAL STAGE APPEARANCES—Broadway productions: Lucia, *Mike Downstairs;* Mrs. Murino, *42 Seconds from Broadway;* Mexican woman, *A Streetcar Named Desire.* Off Broadway: Madrecita, *Camino Real,* Lincoln Center; Prisoner, *Poets from the Inside,* Public; Fula Lopez, *In the Summer House,* Manhattan Theatre Club; Maria, *Back Bog Beast,* American Place; Mamita, *The Wonderful Year,* Public; Mother, *Blood Wedding,* INTAR, NY; Mrs. Warren, *Mrs. Warren's Profession,* Ranevsky, *The Cherry Orchard, The Importance of Being Earnest,* all Westside Repertory.

MAJOR TOURS—*Rose Tattoo,* national; *Streetcar Named Desire,* national.

FILM DEBUT—Mrs. Cruz, *Popi,* 1967. PRINCIPAL FILM APPEARANCES—Mother, *Hair,* 1977; Denitza Georgio, *King of the Gypsies,* 1977; Carmelita, *Boardwalk;* Modesta, *To Find a Man;* Mrs. Amador, *Coogan's Bluff.*

TELEVISION DEBUT—*Naked City,* 1962. PRINCIPAL TELEVISION APPEARANCES—Rita Alvarez, *The Marcus Nelson Murders* (pilot for *Kojak* series); Mrs. Profacci, *Honor Thy Father;* Sophie, *Ladies in Waiting,* PBS; Emma, *Dr. Rappaini's Daughter,* PBS; Taxi Driver, *One More Time.*

RELATED CAREER—Assistant to the director, Westside Repertory Theatre.

SIDELIGHTS: MEMBERSHIPS—Actors' Equity Association, Screen Actors Guild, American Federation of Television and Radio Artists.

''I believe acting's primary function is to communicate a thought or emotion to an audience and that freedom is the most important thing in life.''

ADDRESS: HOME—523 W. 112th Street, New York, NY 10025.

*   *   *

RICE, Tim   1944-

PERSONAL: Born November 10, 1944, in Buckinghamshire, England; son of Hugh Gordon and Joan Odette (Bawden) Rice; married Jane McIntosh. EDUCATION: Lancing College, Sussex, 1958-62; Sorbonne University, Paris, 1963; studied law in London, 1963-66.

VOCATION: Lyricist, composer, songwriter, singer, writer, and actor.

CAREER: In addition to his writings (see below). FILM DEBUT—*The Suvivor*, 1980. PRINCIPAL FILM APPEARANCES—*Three Men in a Boat*, BBC, 1982.

PRINCIPAL CONCERT APPEARANCES—Command performance for Her Majesty the Queen Elizabeth, 1981.

ALBUMS—Producer: with Elaine Paige, *Elaine Paige, Stages, Cinema;* with Andrew Lloyd Webber, *It's Easy for You*, recorded by Elvis Presley, 1976.

RELATED CAREER—Part owner and publisher, Pavilion Books; broadcaster for BBC, disc-jockey, quiz show appearances and interview programs.

WRITINGS: MUSICALS—*The Likes of Us* (with Andrew Lloyd Webber), unperformed, 1965; *Joseph and the Amazing Technicolor Dreamcoat* (with Andrew Lloyd Webber), 1967, opened at Colet Court School, Hammersmith, 1968, transfered to NY, 1982; *Jesus Christ Superstar* (with Andrew Lloyd Webber), Mark Hellinger, NY, 1969; *Evita* (with Andrew Lloyd Webber), 1974, opened London, 1978, Broadway Theatre, NY, 1979; *Blondel* (with Stephen Oliver), opened London, 1982; *Chess* (with Bjorn Ulvaeus and Benny Andersson), to be produced 1985.

PRINCIPAL SONGS—Words and music, *That's My Story*, recorded by Nightshift, 1965; collaborated with Marvin Hamlisch; Mike Batt on *A Winter's Tale;* Paul McCartney; Paul Jones; Francis Lai; Vangelis; Rick Wakeman, on *1984, Cost of Living;* Elton John; John Barry, *All Time High*, title song for film *Octopussy*.

BOOKS—*Guinness Book of Hit Singles, British Hit Singles 3* (with Paul Gambaccini, Mike Read, and Jo Read).

SIDELIGHTS: RECREATION: Heads his own Cricket team, Heartaches C.C.

ADDRESS: AGENT—David Land, 118 Wardour Street, London W1, England.

*   *   *

RICHARDS, Paul David   1934-

PERSONAL: Born August 31, 1934, in Bedford, IN; son of Dallis Eugene (a stone cutter) and Ruth Elizabeth (Meglemre) Richards; children: Brian David. EDUCATION: Indiana University, Curtis Institute.

VOCATION: Actor.

CAREER: NEW YORK DEBUT—Minstrel, *Once Upon a Mattress,* Alvin, 1960. PRINCIPAL STAGE APPEARANCES—Understudy, *Camelot,* Majestic, NY, 1961; understudy, *Superman,* Imperial, NY, 1963; Producer, *A Joyful Noise,* Mark Hellinger, NY, 1965; Rutledge and Adams, *1776,* 46th Street Theatre, NY, 1969; *Black Picture Show,* Vivien Beaumont Theatre, Lincoln Center, NY, 1973; Captain John Sutter, *Devour the Snow,* Golden, NY, 1977; *Antigone,* New York Shakespeare Festival, Public, NY, 1977; *My One and Only,* St. James, NY, 1983.

SIDELIGHTS: MEMBERSHIPS—Actors' Equity Association, Screen Actors Guild, American Federation of Television and Radio Artists.

Richards heads his own company, the Paul Richards Management Company (real estate management), 1970-present.

ADDRESS: OFFICE—50 W. 29th Street, New York, NY 10001.

PAUL DAVID RICHARDS

RON RICHARDSON

RICHARDSON, Ron   1952-

PERSONAL: Full name Ronald F. Richardson; born January 27, 1952, in Phildelphia, PA; son of William Franklin and Amanda Florence (Ellison) Richardson. EDUCATION: Temple University.

VOCATION: Actor and choreographer.

CAREER: STAGE DEBUT—Willie Stubbs, *Wake of Man & Line,* touring production, 1969. NEW YORK DEBUT—Chief of Police, *Timbuktu,* Mark Hellinger. PRINCIPAL STAGE APPEARANCES— *Big River,* Eugene O'Neill, NY, 1985.

MAJOR TOURS—*Timbuktu,* national; *Dreamgirls,* Los Angeles; *Porgy and Bess,* Houston Grand Opera, national tour.

AWARDS: Antoinette Perry Award, Drama Desk Award, 1985, *Big River.*

ADDRESS: AGENT—Sheldon Lubliner, News and Entertainment Corporation, 230 W. 55th Street, New York, NY 10019.

*   *   *

RICKLES, Don   1926-

PERSONAL: Full name Donald Jay Rickles; born May 8, 1926, in New York City; son of Max (an insurance salesman) and Etta (Feldman) Rickles; married Barbara Sklar (a secretary), March 14, 1965; children: Mindy Beth, Lawrence Corey. EDUCATION: American Academy of Dramatic Arts, NY, graduate. RELIGION: Jewish. MILITARY: U.S. Navy, World War Two.

VOCATION: Comedian and actor.

CAREER: PRINCIPAL TELEVISION APPEARANCES—*The Tonight Show Starring Johnny Carson; Dean Martin Show; The Merv Griffin Show;* guest host, *Saturday Night Live.* Series: Sharkey, *CPO Sharkey,* NBC; *The Don Rickles Show,* ABC; *The Don Rickles Show,* CBS; host, *Foul-Ups, Bleeps and Blunders,* ABC; *Archie Bunker's Place; Run for Your Life; The Lucy Show; Get Smart; I Spy; The Andy Griffith Show; Dick Van Dyke Show; Bob Hope's Chrysler Theatre; Medical Center; Love on the Run.* Specials: *Don Rickles Is Alive and Kicking,* CBS; *A Couple of Dons,* CBS; *Rickles,* CBS.

PRINCIPAL NIGHTCLUB APPEARANCES—Headliner, Sahara Hotel, Las Vegas, NV; Riviera Hotel, Las Vegas, NV; Resorts International, Atlantic City, NJ; Harrah's Clubs, Reno NV, and Lake Tahoe, NV.

PRINCIPAL STAGE APPEARANCES—Felix, *The Odd Couple,* Ahmanson, Los Angeles, 1967; *The Don Rickles Show,* Mill Run Theatre, Chicago, Westbury Music Fair, Melodyland, Shady Grove Music Fair, Oakdale Music Theatre, O'Keefe Center, Canada.

PRINCIPAL FILM APPEARANCES—*Kelly's Heroes; Enter Laughing; The Rat Race; Run Silent, Run Deep.*

RECORDINGS: ALBUMS—*Hello Dummy!; Don Rickles Speaks.*

DON RICKLES

SIDELIGHTS: MEMBERSHIPS—American Guild of Variety Artists, American Federation of Television and Radio Artists, Screen Actors Guild, Friars Club, Variety Clubs.

ADDRESS: OFFICE—Box 48559, Los Angeles, CA 90048. AGENT— Jerry Braunstein, 1990 Westwood Blvd., Los Angeles, CA 90025.

* * *

RIEGERT, Peter

BRIEF ENTRY: Born in NY. Actor. Riegert graduated from the University of Buffalo with a degree in English. He taught for awhile and did some work as a social worker. His first theatrical training was with an improvisational group known as the "War Babies." His first professional job was as Chico in *Minnie's Boys,* Philadelphia Playhouse in the Park. Other stage credits include: *Sexual Perversity in Chicago,* Cherry Lane Theatre, NY; *Censored Scenes from King Kong; Call Me Charlie,* Performing Garage. He made his Broadway debut in *Dance with Me,* Mayfair Theatre, and was seen off Broadway in *Isn't It Romantic,* Phoenix, and *Sunday Runners,* Public. His film debut was in the award winning short *A Director Talks about His Film.* Riegert went on to do *Animal House,* Universal, 1978; *Head Over Heel,* United Artists, 1979; *Anne and Joey; Local Hero,* Warner Brothers, 1983. His television credits include Groucho Marx in *Feeling Good,* and *Ellis Island,* CBS, 1985.*

* * *

RINGWALD, Mollie

BRIEF ENTRY: Daughter of Bob (a jazz musician) and Adele Ringwald. Ringwald began acting at age five when she appeared in the stage play, *The Glass Harp,* by Truman Capote. She was a guest star on television's *The New Mickey Mouse Club* when she was eight. In 1977, she returned to the stage to play the role of Kate in a west coast production of the musical, *Annie.* Shortly thereafter, Ringwald became a regular on the television series *The Facts of Life,* NBC, and she also appeared in guest spots on television's *Diff'rent Strokes,* NBC, and the *Merv Griffin Show.* Her television movies include *Packin' It In,* 1983, and *P.K. and the Kid.* She made her feature film debut starring in *Tempest,* Columbia Pictures, 1982, then went on to star in the movies *Sixteen Candles,* 1984, *Spacehunter: Adventures in the Forbidden Zone,* Columbia, 1983, *The Breakfast Club,* 1985, and *Pretty in Pink,* Paramount (upcoming).*

* * *

RINKER, Kenneth   1945-

PERSONAL: Born September 4, 1945; son of Thomas and Lillian Rinker. EDUCATION: University of Maryland, B.A., English, 1967; studied dance with Martha Graham, Merce Cunningham, and Twyla Tharp.

VOCATION: Choreographer and dancer.

CAREER: NEW YORK DEBUT—Dancer, *Twyla Tharp Dance Company,* Judson Church, 1970. LONDON DEBUT—*Twyla Tharp Dance Company,* Roundhouse, 1974.

MAJOR TOURS—*Twyla Tharp Dance Company,* dance festivals in Paris, France, 1971, Spoleto, 1975, Edinburgh, Berlin, 1976; *Jacobs Pillow,* 1973-74; *American Dance Festival,* 1975.

FIRST STAGE WORK—Choreographer, *Alice,* New York Shakespeare Festival, Public Theatre, 1979. PRINCIPAL STAGE WORK— Choreographer, *Swing,* Kennedy Center, Washington, DC, 1980.

FIRST FILM WORK—Assistant choreographer, *Hair,* Tri Star, 1979. PRINCIPAL FILM WORK—Choreographer: *Places in the Heart,* Tri Star, 1984; *Murphy's Romance,* Columbia Pictures, 1985.

TELEVISION DEBUT—*Twyla Tharp Dance Company,* CBS, 1973. PRINCIPAL TELEVISION APPEARANCES—"Twyla Tharp Dance Company," *Dance in America,* PBS, 1975.

PRINCIPAL TELEVISION WORK—Choreographer: *42nd Street Variations,* Kenneth Rinker Dance Company, CBS cable, 1981.

RELATED CAREER—Co-founder of Rinker-Cerveitt Dance & Music Inc.

AWARDS: Fulbright Scholarship, Dance, Montevideo, Uruguay, 1985; National Endowment for the Arts Grant for Dance, 1978-1985.

ADDRESS: HOME—96 Park Place, Brooklyn, NY 11217. AGENT— Lisa Booth, 276 Riverside Drive, New York, NY 10025.

* * *

RIPLEY, Patricia Trescott   1924-

PERSONAL: Full name Mary Patricia Ripley; born August 15, 1924, in Evanston, IL; daughter of Charles Trescott (a mechanical engineer) and Mable (a nurse; maiden name, Thomson) Ripley. EDUCATION: Bennington, B.A., 1948; studied for the theatre with Theodore Komisarjevski, Francis Ferguson, Uta Hagen, Harold Clurman, and others. RELIGION: Catholic.

VOCATION: Actress.

CAREER: NEW YORK DEBUT—Jocasta, *The Infernal Machine,* Provincetown Playhouse, June 17, 1948. PRINCIPAL STAGE APPEARANCES—Maolia, *The Seagull,* Olivia, *Twelfth Night,* Brattle, Cambridge, MA, 1948; Catherine Sloper, *The Heiress,* Gwendolyn Fairfax, *The Importance of Being Earnest,* Holiday Stage, Tustin, CA, 1949; Abigail, *Be Your Age,* 48th Street Theatre, NY, 1953; Ellie, *The Ticklish Acrobat,* Amato Opera Theatre, NY, 1954; Queen Isabel, *Henry V,* Betty, *The Beggar's Opera,* Cambridge Drama Festival, Cambridge, MA, 1955; Colonel Baines, *Major Barbara,* Martin Beck, NY, 1956; Cornelia Scott, *Garden District,*

PATRICIA TRESCOTT RIPLEY

York Playhouse, NY, 1958; Beulah Binnings, *Orpheus Descending,* Coconut Grove Playhouse, Miami, FL, 1958; Betty, *The Threepenny Opera,* Theatre de Lys, NY, 1958; Agnes, *A Memory of Two Mondays,* Luisa, *The Purification,* Arena Stage, Washington, DC, 1958; Mrs. Anthony, *The Great God Brown,* Coronet, NY, 1959; the maid, *Sweet Bird of Youth,* Martin Beck, NY, 1959; leader of the chorus, *Lysistrata,* Phoenix, NY, 1959.

Kari, *Peer Gynt,* Phoenix, NY, 1960; Violet, *The Tavern,* Signora Cini, *Right You Are, If You Think You Are,* APA, McCarter, Princeton, NJ, 1960; step-daughter, *Six Characters in Search of an Author,* Arena Stage, Washington, DC, 1961; Miss Gilchrist, *The Hostage,* One Sheridan Square, NY, 1961; Miss Skilton, *See How They Run,* Bucks County Playhouse, New Hope, PA, 1961; Mrs. Shedar, *Hey You, Light Man,* Theatre by the Sea, Matunuck, RI, 1962; photographer, *The Beauty Part,* Music Box, NY, 1962; Mrs. Botting, *Half-a-Sixpence,* Broadhurst, NY, 1965; standby for Colleen Dewhurst, *The Ballad of the Sad Cafe,* Martin Beck, NY, 1963.

MAJOR TOURS—Miss Preen, *The Man Who Came to Dinner,* Max Gordon tour, 1950-51; Marfa, *Romanoff and Juliet,* eight theatre summer package, 1963; Duchess, *Love Match,* pre-Broadway, 1968; *Success in America,* National Humanities tour, 1973; Pauline, *The Prisoner of Second Avenue,* 1973-74; also a tour of *The Children's Hour.*

FILM DEBUT—*Splendor in the Grass,* Warner Brothers, 1961. PRINCIPAL FILM APPEARANCES—*No Way to Treat a Lady,* Paramount, 1968; *Hail to the Chief* (aka *Hail,* aka *Washington, B.C.*), Cine-Globe, 1973; *Detour,* c.1980.

PRINCIPAL TELEVISION APPEARANCES—*The Goldbergs; Mr. Peepers; The Jackie Gleason Show; Car 54, Where Are You?; The Defenders; Felony Squad; The Phil Silvers Show; The Reporter; East Side West Side; Day in Court,* others.

RELATED CAREER—Play reader for the agency Brandt and Brandt; also for William Morris Agency, Flora Roberts Agency, International Famous Agency, The Mark Taper Forum, and many producers.

SIDELIGHTS: MEMBERSHIPS—Actors' Equity Association, Screen Actors Guild, American Federation of Television and Radio Artists, East Harlem Block Association, Association of Producing Artists (APA), 1960; and the executive boards of the following: Taos Historical Society, Friends of Taos Valley, Taos Recycling Center, Women's Chamber of Commerce, Advisory Board of the New Mexico State Parks.

ADDRESS: HOME—P.O. Box 81, Ranchos de Taos, NM 87557. AGENT—Helen Harvey, 410 W. 24th Street, New York, NY, 10011.

*   *   *

RITTER, John   1948-

PERSONAL: Full name Jonathan Southworth Ritter; born September 17, 1948, in Burbank, CA; son of Tex (country and western singer) and Dorothy Fay (Southworth) Ritter; married Nancy Karen Morgan, October 16, 1977; children: Jason, Tyler, Carly. EDUCATION: University of Southern California, B.A., 1971; studied with Stella Adler, Nina Foch and four years at the Harvey Lembeck Comedy Workshop; currently studies at the Mary Carver Studio.

VOCATION: Actor.

CAREER: STAGE DEBUT—Appeared at the Edinburgh Festival, Scotland, 1968-69. PRINCIPAL STAGE APPEARANCES—*Desire Under the Elms,* Berkshire Theatre Festival, Kennedy Center, Washington, DC; *The Glass Menagerie, Butterflies Are Free,* Totem Pole Playhouse, MD; *As You Like It,* First Los Angeles Free Shakespeare Festival; *The Tempest,* Shakespeare Society Production; *Nevada,* Mark Taper Forum Lab.

PRINCIPAL FILM APPEARANCES—*The Barefoot Executive,* Filmex, 1970; *The Other,* Filmex, 1972; *Nickelodeon,* Filmex, 1975; *Americathon,* 1979; *Wholly Moses,* 1980; *Hero at Large,* Metro-Goldwyn-Mayer, 1980; *They All Laughed,* 1981.

TELEVISION DEBUT—*Dan August.* PRINCIPAL TELEVISION APPEARANCES—Series: Jack Tripper, *Three's Company,* ABC, 1975-83; Jack Tripper, *Three's a Crowd,* ABC, 1984-85. Also: *Hawaii Five-O; Medical Center; M*A*S*H; Starsky and Hutch; The Streets of San Francisco; The Rookies; Phyllis; Rhoda;* Reverend Fordwick, *The Waltons.* Specials: Host, *John Ritter: Being of Sound Mind and Body,* ABC; *Mary Tyler Moore Special; Goldie Hawn Special; The Muppet Show; The Secret World of the Very Young,* CBS; *History in the Company of Children,* 60 second vignettes. Movies: *The Comeback Kid; Pray TV; Love Thy Neighbor,* ABC; *In Love with an Older Woman; Sunset Limousine,* CBS; *Letting Go,* ABC, 1985.

JOHN RITTER

JANE MARLA ROBBINS

AWARDS: Honored with a star on the Hollywood Walk of Fame, the 1768th honoree, his star is next to his father's; Golden Globe Award for Best Actor in a Television Series, National Academy of Television Arts and Sciences Award, Best Lead Actor in a Comedy Series, for *Three's Company.*

SIDELIGHTS: MEMBERSHIPS—Actors' Equity Association, Screen Actors Guild, American Federation of Television and Radio Artists, United Cerebral Palsy Association (board of directors).

ADDRESS: OFFICE—Robert Myman, 11777 San Vicente Blvd., 600 Los Angeles, CA 90049.

*   *   *

ROBBINS, Jane Marla   1949-

PERSONAL: Born November 21, 1949, in New York City; daughter of Louis John (an attorney) and Mildred (a consultant for international development; maiden name, Elowsky) Robbins. EDUCATION: Bryn Mawr College, PA, 1965; studied with Sonia Moore and Walter Lott in NY.

VOCATION: Actress, writer, and producer.

CAREER: NEW YORK DEBUT—Ingenue, *Beyond Desire,* 1967. LONDON DEBUT—Fanny Burney, *Dear Nobody,* 1969. PRINCI-

PAL STAGE APPEARANCES—Fanny Burney, *Dear Nobody,* Actors Playhouse, NY, 1968, Cherry Lane, NY, 1974; *Morning, Noon, and Night,* Henry Miller's, NY, 1968; Rosalind, *As You Like It,* Washington, DC, 1969; Lady Anne, *Richard III,* Lincoln Center, 1974; Jane Avril, *Jane Avril,* Provincetown Playhouse, NY, 1982.

MAJOR TOURS—Fanny Burney, *Dear Nobody,* U.S. college tour.

PRINCIPAL STAGE WORK—Co-producer, *Dear Nobody,* 1968, 1974, NY; co-producer, *Jane Avril,* 1974, NY.

FILM DEBUT—Wife, *Coming Apart,* 1969. PRINCIPAL FILM APPEARANCES—*Rocky,* 1975; *Rocky II,* 1978.

TELEVISION DEBUT—Woman, *A Village Wooing,* 1963. PRINCIPAL TELEVISION APPEARANCES—Fanny Burney, "Dear Nobody," *Camera Three,* CBS, 1974; Cousin Trannie, *Park Avenue,* ABC, 1976, 1979; *Betrayal,* 1978; Cheryl Sands, *Victims for Victims,* 1984.

WRITINGS: PLAYS, PRODUCED—*Dear Nobody* (with Terry Berlanger), Actors Playhouse, NY, 1968; *Bat's in the Belfry,* Spoleto Festival, Italy, 1964; *Jane Avril,* Provincetown Playhouse, NY, 1974.

SIDELIGHTS: Robbins has travelled extensively in Europe and the Middle East. She speaks fluent French, German, Italian, and Spanish.

ADDRESS: AGENT—Actors Group, 8285 Sunset Blvd., Los Angeles, CA 90046.

REX ROBBINS

ROBBINS, Rex   1935-

PERSONAL: Full name Rex McNicol Robbins; born March 30, 1935, in Pierre, SD; son of Clarence Edward (a doctor) and Lucy Geraldine (a newspaperwomen; maiden name, McNicol) Robbins; married Patricia Moran (a teacher), February 20, 1961; children: Margaret McNicol, Timothy Thomas Patrick, Mary Victoria Monroe. EDUCATION: Yale University, B.A., 1957; studied for the theatre with Uta Hagen at H.B. Studios in New York City.

VOCATION: Actor.

CAREER: STAGE DEBUT—Dathan, the High Priest, *Black Hills Passion Play,* Spearfish, SD, 1955. NEW YORK DEBUT—In revue, Julius Monks' Plaza-9 and Upstairs at the Downstairs, 1962 (subsequent shows through 1968, four different revues in all). LONDON DEBUT—Lion, *The Play of Daniel,* Westminster Abbey, June, 1960 (on State Department European tour).

PRINCIPAL STAGE APPEARANCES—Dr. Spivey, *One Flew Over the Cuckoo's Nest,* Cort, NY, 1963; *The Changing Room,* NY, 1973; Herbie, *Gypsy,* Winter Garden, NY, 1974; *Sherlock Holmes,* Shubert, NY, 1975; Old Magician, *The Magic Show,* Cort, NY, 1976; *Comedians,* NY, 1976; *An Almost Perfect Person,* Belasco, NY, 1977; *Players,* NY, 1978; *Landscape of the Body,* Academy Festival, Chicago, IL, 1978; *Richard III,* NY, 1979; *Artichoke,* Manhattan Theatre Club, NY, 1979; *The Three Sisters, The Play's the Thing, Julius Caesar,* BAM Theatre Company, Brooklyn Academy of Music, NY, 1980; Mr. Sycamore, *You Can't Take It with You,* Golden, NY, 1983; *The Dining Room,* NY, 1983; *Noises Off,* Brooks Atkinson, NY, 1984; understudy, *A Moon for the*

Misbegotten, NY, 1984; understudy, *An Evening with Richard Nixon,* NY, 1984.

Also: *The Beggars Opera,* Chelsea, NY; *Boy Meets Girl, Secret Service, Memory of Two Mondays,* Phoenix, NY; *The Physicists,* Kennedy Center, Washington, DC; *The Doctor's Dilemma, The Changing Room, Pygmalion, Trelawney of the Wells,* Long Wharf, New Haven, CT; *The House of Blue Leaves,* Adlephi Festival, NY; *Henry IV, Part I,* New York Shakespeare Festival; *Richard II, As You Like It, Androcles and the Lion,* American Shakespeare Festival, Stratford, CT; *The Country Girl, Arturo Ui, A Thousand Clowns,* Williamstown Summer Theatre, Williamstown, MA.

MAJOR TOURS—Cornelius Hackle, *Hello, Dolly!,* national tour, 1966; *The Boys in the Band,* National Company, 1970; Herbie, *Gypsy,* national tour, 1977; *Daisy Mame,* national tour, 1980; *The Lion in Winter, Private Lives,* Long Wharf Theatre on tour, 1981.

FILM DEBUT—Polly, the bartender, *Shaft,* Metro-Goldwyn-Mayer, 1971. PRINCIPAL FILM APPEARANCES—Roger Sherman, *1776,* Columbia/Warner, 1972; *Simon,* Warner Brothers, 1980; *The First Time,* 1983; *Reuben, Reuben,* TLC Films, 1983; *The Man Who Wasn't There,* Paramount, 1983; *Key Exchange,* 1985.

TELEVISION DEBUT—Telephone man, *Armstrong Circle Theatre,* CBS, 1958. PRINCIPAL TELEVISION APPEARANCES—*The Tenth Month,* 1979; *The Day the Women Got Even,* 1980; "The Winning of Mrs. Holroyd," "Secret Service," *Theatre-in-America,* PBS; "The Man that Corrupted Hadleyburg," "The Campaign That Failed," *American Short Story,* PBS; *Nurse* (four episodes), NBC, 1982-83; Dr. Murray Grove, *The Doctors,* NBC, 1982-83; *Love, Sidney,* NBC, 1983; Theodore Sorenson, *Kennedy* (mini-series), NBC, 1983.

AWARDS: Joseph Jefferson Award, 1978, for *Landscape of the Body.*

SIDELIGHTS: Rex Robbins wrote to *CTFT,* "I am interested in versatility in parts, styles, and media. I have belonged to many regional repertory companies. I wish to thank American big business for its commercials, the making of which earns actors enough to keep alive for theatre!"

ADDRESS: AGENT—Richard Astor Agency, 1697 Broadway, New York, NY 10019.

*   *   *

ROBERTS, Doris   1930-

PERSONAL: Born November 4, 1930; daughter of Ann Meltzer; married William Goyen (a novelist); children: (previous marriage) Michael Cannata. EDUCATION: Studied with Sanford Meisner at the Neighborhood Playhouse, NY and with Lee Strasberg at the Actor's Studio, NY.

VOCATION: Actress.

CAREER: NEW YORK DEBUT—A prostitute, *The Time of Your Life,* New York City Center, 1955. PRINCIPAL STAGE APPEARANCES—Miss Rumple, *The Desk Set,* Broadhurst, NY, 1955; The

Nurse, *The Death of Bessie Smith*, York Playhouse, NY, 1961; Mommy, *The American Dream*, Cherry Lane, NY, 1961; *Color of Darkness/Cracks*, Writer's Stage, NY, 1963; Rae Wilson, *Marathon 33*, ANTA, NY, 1963; Miss Punk, *The Office*, Henry Miller's, NY, 1966; Edna, *The Natural Look*, Longacre, NY, 1967; Jeanette Fisher, *Last of the Red Hot Lovers*, O'Neill, NY, 1969; May, *Felix*, Actors Studio, NY, 1972; Miss Manley, *The Secret Affairs of Mildred Wild*, Ambassador, NY, 1972; Dolly Scrupp, "Ravenswood," Becky Hedges, "Dunelawn," under double bill of *Bad Habits*, Astor Place, NY, 1974, then Booth, 1974; Dede, *Ladies at the Alamo*, Actors Studio, 1975; Grace, *Cheaters*, Biltmore, NY, 1978.

MAJOR TOURS—Claudia, *The Opening*, summer tour, 1972; *Morning's at Seven*, national tour, 1976.

PRINCIPAL FILM APPEARANCES—*A New Leaf; No Way to Treat a Lady; The Honeymoon Killers; Little Murders; The Taking of Pelham 1-2-3; Hester Street; The Rose; Such Good Friends; Rabbit Test; An Ordinary Guy.*

PRINCIPAL TELEVISION APPEARANCES—*Look Homeward, Angel; Four by Tennessee Williams; Angie; Remington Steele*, 1984-85.

ADDRESS: OFFICE—6225 Quebec Drive, Los Angeles, CA 90068. AGENT—William Morris Agency, 151 El Camino Drive, Beverly Hills, CA 90212.

*   *   *

ROBERTS, Eric   1956-

BRIEF ENTRY: Born April 18, 1956, in Biloxi, MS. Actor. Robert's father founded the Actor's and Writer's Workshop in 1963, so by the age of five, he was appearing in *The Member of the Wedding, Charlie's Aunt, and The Taming of the Shrew*. In 1973-74 he attended the Royal Academy of Dramatic Art, London, and from 1974-75 he attended the American Academy of Dramatic Arts. He appeared in the plays *Rebel Women*, Public, NY, 1976; *A Streetcar Named Desire*, 1976, and in the Broadway production of *Mass Appeal*. He appeared on the NBC soap opera *Another World*, 1976-77 and was seen in *Paul's Case*, and *Miss Lonely Hearts*, both PBS. His film debut was in *King of the Gypsies*, Paramount, 1978; *Raggedy Man*, Universal, 1981; *Star 80*, Warner Brothers, 1983; *The Pope of Greenwich Village*, Metro-Goldwyn-Mayer, 1984, and *The Coca-Cola Kid*, Cinccom/Film Gallery, 1985.*

*   *   *

ROBERTS, Lance   1959-

PERSONAL: Born December 18, 1959; son of Ambrose C. (Lt. Colonel, U.S. Army) and Theresa E. (a secretary; maiden name, Hogan) Roberts. EDUCATION: Attended Tufts University, two and half years.

VOCATION: Actor, dancer, and singer.

CAREER: DEBUT—Principal, *All Night Strut*, International Company, Royal York Hotel, Toronto, 1979. NEW YORK DEBUT—Featured performer, *America*, Radio City Music Hall, 1981. PRINCIPAL STAGE APPEARANCES—Whizzer Brown, *March of the Falsettos*, Playwrights Horizons, NY, 1981; lead performer, *Get Happy*, Westwood Playhouse, Los Angeles, CA, 1984; standby Old Deuteronomy, *Cats*, Shubert, Los Angeles, CA, 1985.

MAJOR TOURS—Jeff Johnson, *Walls*, Huntington Hartford, Los Angeles, CA, 1983; alter ego/assistant choreographer, *They're Playing Our Song*, Blaisdell Honolulu, HI.

SIDELIGHTS: Roberts told *CTFT:* "My goal in life is to stay happy and I'm happiest when I make people feel joy, sorrow, or other emotions. As long as I'm performing, I'm happy."

ADDRESS: AGENT—Rosenwald and Associates, 250 W. 57th Street, New York, NY 10107.

*   *   *

ROBERTS, Tony   1939-

PERSONAL: Full name David Anthony Roberts; born October 22, 1939, in New York City; son of Kenneth and Norma Roberts; divorced. EDUCATION: Northwestern University.

VOCATION: Actor.

TONY ROBERTS

CAREER: NEW YORK DEBUT—Air cadet, *Something About a Soldier,* Ambassador, 1962. PRINCIPAL STAGE APPEARANCES—Richard Gluck, *Take Her, She's Mine,* Biltmore, NY, 1962; Max, *The Last Analysis,* Belasco, NY, 1964; Charlie, *Never Too Late,* Playhouse, NY, 1964-65; Paul Bratter, *Barefoot in the Park,* Biltmore, NY, 1965; Axel Magee, *Don't Drink the Water,* Morosco, NY, 1966; Charley, *How Now, Dow Jones,* Lunt-Fontanne, NY, 1967; Dick Christie, *Play It Again Sam,* Broadhurst, NY, 1969; Chuck Baxter, *Promises, Promises,* Shubert, NY, 1971; Joe, *Sugar,* Majestic, NY, 1972; appeared with the Yale Repertory Theatre, 1973-74 season; Geoffrey, *Absurd Person Singular,* Music Box, NY, 1974; title role, *Hamlet,* Otterbein University, 1976; Petruchio, *The Taming of the Shrew,* Alliance Theatre, Atlanta, GA 1976; *Serenading Louie,* Academy Festival Theatre, Lake Forest, IL, 1978; Mitchell Lavell, *Murder at the Howard Johnson's,* Golden, NY, 1979; Todd, *Losing Time,* Manhattan Theatre Club, 1979; Vernon Gersch, *They're Playing Our Song,* Imperial, NY, 1979; *Doubles,* The Second Stage, transfered to Broadway, 1985.

FILM DEBUT—*$1,000,000 Duck,* Buena Vista, 1971. PRINCIPAL FILM APPEARANCES—*Star-Spangled Girl,* 1971; *Play It Again, Sam,* Paramount, 1972; *Serpico,* Paramount, 1974; *The Taking of Pelham 1-2-3,* United Artists, 1974; *Annie Hall,* United Artists, 1977; *Just Tell Me What You Want,* Warner Brothers, 1980; *A Midsummer's Night Sex Comedy,* United Artists, 1982; *Amityville III,* Orion, 1983; *Key Exchange,* 1985.

PRINCIPAL TELEVISION APPEARANCES—*Rossetti and Ryan; The Lindbergh Kidnapping Case; The Four Seasons,* CBS, *The Lucy Arnaz Show,* CBS, 1985.

ADDRESS: AGENT—William Morris Agency, 1350 Sixth Avenue, New York, NY 10019.

*   *   *   *   *   *

ROLF, Frederick   1926-

PERSONAL: Born August 14, 1926, in Berlin, Germany; son of Theodor (a physician) and Ilse (Kadisch) Friedrichs; married Roni Dengal (an actress and writer), October 3, 1971.

VOCATION: Actor and director.

CAREER: STAGE DEBUT—Captain Frederick de Foenix, *Trelawny of the Wells,* Grand Theatre, Halifax, England, 1946. NEW YORK DEBUT—Inquisitor, *Saint Joan,* Cort, 1951. PRINCIPAL STAGE APPEARANCES—Arago, *The Strong Are Lonely,* Broadhurst, NY, 1953; First Citizen, *Coriolanus,* Phoenix, NY, 1954; Laomedon and Memnon, *The Immortal Husband,* Theatre de Lys, NY, 1955; Will Shakespeare, *The Dark Lady of the Sonnets,* Cherry Lane, NY, 1956; Pedant, *The Taming of the Shrew,* American Shakespeare Festival, Stratford, CT, 1956; Theophilus, *Time Remembered,* Morosco, NY, 1957; Count, *The Smokeweaver's Daughter,* Fourth Street Theatre, NY, 1959; Judas, *Between Two Thieves,* York, NY, 1960; Gaev, *The Cherry Orchard,* IASTA, 1960; Nicola, *The Burnt Flower Bed,* Westport Country Playhouse, CT, 1960; Judge Brack, *Hedda Gabler,* Fourth Street Theatre, NY, 1960; The Doctor, Raffarad, and Dugommier, *The Egg,* Cort, NY, 1962; Uncle Vanya, *Uncle Vanya,* Charles Playhouse, Boston, MA, 1962; Duncan, *The Day the Whores Came Out to Play Tennis,* Actors'

FREDERICK ROLF

Studio, NY, 1964; Dr. Edward Teller, *In the Matter of J. Robert Oppenheimer,* Vivian Beaumont, NY, 1969.

MAJOR TOURS—Rosencrantz, *Hamlet,* Seyton, *Macbeth,* Margaret Webster touring company, 1948-49; Caesar, *Julius Caesar,* Gremio, *The Taming of the Shrew,* 1949-50; Man from Bellac, *The Apollo of Bellac,* 1950; *Scenes from Great Plays,* 1950.

PRINCIPAL STAGE WORK—Director: *Titus Andronicus,* Joseph Papp's Shakespeare Workshop, NY, 1956; *The Corn Is Green,* Masters Institute, 1961; *The Vegetable,* Masters Institute, 1963; *The Deadly Game,* Playhouse on the Mall, Paramus, NJ, 1964; *Hogan's Goat,* American Place, NY, 1965; *The Bird, the Bear and the Actress,* Eugene O'Neill Foundation, Waterford, CT, 1966; *Fidelio, Aida,* both Atlanta, GA, 1967; *In Search of Dylan,* Richmond, VA, 1969; *Hamlet,* Bucks County Playhouse, PA, 1970; *The Great Waltz,* Atlanta, GA, 1971; *Lake of the Woods,* American Place, 1971; *Die Walkuere,* St. Paul, MN, 1973; *Engagement in San Domingo,* St. Paul, MN, 1974; *Six Characters in Search of an Author,* Juilliard Drama School, NY, 1975; *The Grinding Machine,* American Place, 1978; *Charades,* Wonderhorse, NY, 1979; *Castles,* Westport Country Playhouse, CT, 1981.

PRINCIPAL FILM APPEARANCES—*Daniel,* 1983; *Witness,* 1985.

PRINCIPAL TELEVISION APPEARANCES—King Priam, "The Iliad," *Omnibus,* CBS, 1955; Richard, "Darkness at Noon," *Producers Showcase,* NBC, 1955; Senator James Mason, "The Constitution," *Omnibus,* CBS, 1956; Iago, "A Double Life," *Alcoa Hour,* NBC, 1957; Frederick the Great, "The Craft of Kings," *Camera Three,* CBS, 1957; Dr. Joseph Breuer, "The Wound Within," *U.S. Steel Hour,* CBS, 1958; Adolf Eichmann, "The Adolf Eichmann Story,"

Armstrong Circle Theatre, CBS, 1960; Judas, ''The Death of Judas,'' *Directions '62*, ABC, 1962.

WRITINGS: PLAYS, PUBLISHED—English adaptation of Schiller's drama *Love and Intrigue*, 1962.

SIDELIGHTS: MEMBERSHIPS—Actors' Equity Association, American Federation of Television and Radio Artists, Screen Actors Guild, Society of Stage Directors and Choreographers.

ADDRESS: HOME—177 Midland Avenue, Montclair, NJ 07042.

*   *   *

ROLLINS, Howard E., Jr.

BRIEF ENTRY: Born in Baltimore, MD; the son of a steel worker and a domestic worker. Actor. Rollins' film credits include Colehouse Porter in *Ragtime*, Paramount, 1981 and Davenport in *A Solider's Story*, 1984. His television credits include *Eliza: Our Story*, PBS; Andrew Young in *King*, NBC; George Haley in *Roots; The Next Generation; My Old Man; The Neighborhood; Thornwell; Doctor's Story*, NBC, 1984; Medger Evans in *For Us the Living*, PBS; *He's Fired, She's Hired*, CBS, 1984. His series work includes *Our Street* and *Moving Right Along*, both for PBS; *Another World*, NBC, and *Wildside*, ABC. His theatrical credits include: *Our Street*, Baltimore; *TRAPS*, Players Workshop, NY; *Streamers; Medal of Honor Rag*, Folger, Washington, DC, then Theatre de Lys, NY; *G.R. Point*, Playhouse Theatre, and *The Mighty Gents*, 1978.*

*   *   *

ROSENFIELD, Stephen   1946-

PERSONAL: Born June 4, 1946 in Cincinnati, OH; son of Abe and Eda Rosenfield. EDUCATION—Lawrence University, B.A., 1968; Stanford University, M.F.A., 1972.

VOCATION: Director and writer.

CAREER: PRINCIPAL STAGE WORK—Director: *Awake and Sing, Pins and Needles*, Roundabout, NY; *The Present Tense*, Park Royale; *Fight Song*, Gene Frankel, NY; *Charlie and Algernon*, Pan-Andreas, Los Angeles; *On Such a Night as This, The Subject Was Roses, Scanarelle & Scapin, A Moon for the Misbegotten, Candida*, Main Street Theatre; *Tartuffe, The Country Girl, Arms and the Man*, Intiman Theatre; *This End Up 1980, Take Two*, Next Move Theatre; *Waiting for Godot, Woyzeck*, (Marlowe's) *Edward II, Intermission*, Stanford Repertory Theatre, CA; *Spoon River Anthology, Oh Dad Poor Dad . . . , Room Service, Guys and Dolls, Carousel, Finian's Rainbow*, Cellar Door Theatre; *The Forest of John the Fox*, New York school system tour; *The Taming of the Shrew*, University of Washington.

RELATED CAREER—Artistic director, Cellar Door Theatre, 1964-68, Main Street Theatre, 1979-82; acting teacher, Stanford University and in New York City.

WRITINGS: PLAYS, PRODUCED—*The Present Tense*, Park Royale; *This End Up 1980, Take Two*, Next Move Theatre; *The Forest of John the Fox*, New York City school system tour.

AWARDS: Awarded three fellowships from Stanford Univeristy; Los Angeles Dramalogue Award for directing, *Charlie and Algernon.*

SIDELIGHTS: MEMBERSHIPS—Society of Stage Directors and Choreographers, Dramatists Guild.

ADDRESS: OFFICE—232 E. 58th Street, New York, NY 10022. AGENT—Peter Franklin, William Morris Agency, 1350 Sixth Avenue, New York, NY 10019.

*   *   *

ROSOFF, Barbara   1946-

PERSONAL: Born November 1, 1946, in Philadelphia, PA; daughter of Herbert (an insurance agent) and Estelle (Finkel) Rosoff. EDUCATION: Syracuse University, B.S., 1968; Columbia University, 1968-69.

VOCATION: Director.

CAREER: FIRST STAGE WORK—Actress and wardrobe mistress, La Salle College Music Theatre, Philadelphia, PA, 1962. NEW YORK DEBUT—Director, *Teams*, Cubiculo, 1971. PRINCIPAL STAGE WORK—Director: *Hothouse*, Circle Repertory Company, NY, 1974; *King Humpy*, New York Theatre Strategy, 1975; *Kontraption*, New York Theatre Strategy, 1977; *Becca*, Interart, NY, 1977; *Good Woman of Setzuan*, Lexington Conservatory Theatre, 1979; *Close Ties*, Lexington Conservatory Theatre, 1980; *Alterations, Death of a Miner, Ecco!, Native American, Gardenia, Getting Out, The Threepenny Opera, Terra Nova, Madonna of the Powder Room, Goodbye Freddy, Cloud Nine*, Portland Stage Company, Portland, ME, 1981-85.

PRINCIPAL TELEVISION WORK—Conceived and directed, *We're Still Here*, PBS, Buffalo, 1976.

RELATED CAREER—Resident director and literary manager, Capital Repertory Company, Albany, NY, 1980-81; artistic director, Portland Stage Company, 1981-85.

AWARDS: National Residency Award, CBS New Plays Program 1983, for *Ecco!*

SIDELIGHTS: MEMBERSHIPS—Actors' Equity Association, League of Theater Women (NY), Theatre Panel for the National Endowment for the Arts, Maine State Commission on the Arts, Theatre Communications Group.

ADDRESS: HOME—79 Bay View Avenue, Scarborough, ME 04074. OFFICE—P.O. Box 1458, Portland, ME 04104.

MICHAEL ROSS

ROSS, Michael

VOCATION: Television producer, director, and writer.

CAREER: FIRST TELEVISION WORK—Associate producer to Max Liebman, consultant and program editor, *Caesar's Hour*, NBC, 1954-57. PRINCIPAL TELEVISION WORK—Producer: *Coliseum*, CBS, 1967; *Comedy Is King; All in the Family* (co-producer), CBS, 1971-78; *Maude*, CBS, 1972-78; *The Jeffersons* (co-producer), CBS, 1975-79; *The Dumplings*, NBC, 1976; *Three's Company*, ABC, 1977-83; *The Ropers*, ABC, 1979-80; *Three's a Crowd*, 1984-85.

Director, *The Perry Como Show*, NBC, 1957-63; comedy supervisor and director, *The Garry Moore Show*, CBS, 1964-67; "stager," *Comedy Is King*.

WRITINGS: TELEVISION SCRIPTS—*Comedy Is King; All in the Family* (story editor); *The Jeffersons* (creator); *Maude* (creator); *Chico and the Man* (pilot script); *The Dumplings* (creator).

AWARDS: Emmy, comedy writing, for *All in the Family*.

SIDELIGHTS: Ross formed NRW Productions with Don Nicholl and Bernie West, and as executive producer he developed *Three's Company* and its two spin-offs, *The Ropers* and *Three's a Crowd*.

ADDRESS: OFFICE—The NRW Company, 5746 Sunset Blvd., Hollywood, CA 90028.

ROSSITER, Leonard   1926-84

PERSONAL: Born October 21, 1926, in Liverpool, England; died October 5, 1984, of a heart attack in his dressing room; son of John and Elizabeth (Howell) Rossiter; married Josephine Tewson (divorced); married Gillian Raine (an actress); children: one daughter.

VOCATION: Actor.

CAREER: STAGE DEBUT—Bert, *The Gray Dog*, Repertory Theatre, England, 1954. PRINCIPAL STAGE APPEARANCES—Brennan o' Moor, *Red Roses for Me*, 1962; Fred Midway, *Semi-Detached*, 1963; Corvino, *Volpone*, 1967; Arturo Ui, *The Resistable Rise of Arturo Ui*, 1968; Giordano Bruno, *The Heretic*, 1970; title role, *Richard III*, 1971; Davies, *The Caretaker*, 1972; title role, *Tartuffe*, 1976; Garrand, *Make and Break*, 1980; detective, *Loot*, Lyric, London, 1984.

PRINCIPAL FILM APPEARANCES—*A Kind of Loving*, 1962; *Billy Liar*, 1963; *This Sporting Life*, 1963; *King Rat*, 1965; *Hotel Paradiso*, 1966; *The Devil's Own*, 1966; *Deadlier Than the Male*, 1967; *Oliver!*, 1968; *Diamonds for Breakfast*, 1968; *Deadfall*, 1968; *2001: A Space Odyssey*, 1968; *Bed of Roomers; Waterloo Bridge Handicap; Luther*, 1974; *Barry Lyndon*, 1975; *The Pink Panther Strikes Again*, 1976; *Voyage of the Damned*, 1977; *Trail of the Pink Panther*, 1982; *Britannia Hospital*, 1982; *Water* (upcoming).

PRINCIPAL TELEVISION APPEARANCES—*The Rise and Fall of Reginald Perrin*, 1976; *The Losers; Rising Damp; The Green Tie on the Little Yellow Dog*.

AWARDS: London Critics and Variety Club, Best Actor, 1969, for *The Resistable Rise of Arturo Ui*.*

*   *   *

ROWLES, Polly   1914-

PERSONAL: Born January 10, 1914, in Philadelphia, PA; daughter of Ralph and Mary (Dick) Rowles. EDUCATION—Carnegie Institute of Technology; studied acting with Ben Iden Payne, Elizabeth Kimberly, Chester Wallace, and E. Hickman.

VOCATION: Actress.

CAREER: NEW YORK DEBUT—Calpurnia, *Julius Caesar*, Mercury, 1938. LONDON DEBUT—Natasha Rapanovich, *Dark Eyes*, Strand, 1948. PRINCIPAL STAGE APPEARANCES—Ronnie James, *Carrot and Club*, Shubert, New Haven, 1947; Queen Elizabeth, *Richard III*, Booth, NY, 1949; understudy Lola, *Come Back, Little Sheba*, Booth, NY, 1949; Sophie Kressner, *The Golden State*, Fulton, NY, 1950; Lucy McLean, *The Small Hours*, National, NY, 1951; Candida Kaufman, *Gertie*, Plymouth, NY, 1952; Agnes Carol, *Time Out for Ginger*, Lyceum, NY, 1952; Calpurnia, *Julius Caesar*, American Shakespeare Festival, Stratford, CT, 1955; Clara Dennison, *The Wooden Dish*, Booth, NY, 1955; Anne Rogers, *Goodbye Again*, Helen Hayes, NY, 1956; Vera Charles, *Auntie Mame*, Broadhurst, NY, 1956; Claire, *Look After Lulu*, Henry Miller's, NY, 1959.

Phyllis Clyde, *A Mighty Man Is He*, Cort, NY, 1960; Mollie

Plummer, *No Strings,* 54th Street, NY, 1962; Mrs. Jane Wharton Bondry, *A Remedy for Winter,* Westport Country Playhouse, CT, 1965; Evelyn Hopper, *The Best Laid Plans,* Brooks Atkinson, NY, 1966; Madame Xenia, *The Killing of Sister George,* Belasco, NY, 1966; Mrs. Margolin, *Forty Carats,* Morosco, NY, 1968; *Older People,* Anspacher, NY, 1972; Miss Curtis and Lucy, *The Women,* 46th Street, NY, 1973; Mrs. Fisher, *The Show-Off,* Meadow Brook, Rochester, MI, 1977; Louise Pembley, *Spotlight,* National, Washington, DC, then Roundabout, NY, 1978; Mme. Des Mortes, *Ring Around the Moon,* Meadow Brook, 1978; Mrs. Potter and Madam, *Solitaire Double Solitaire,* Production Company, 1979; *Kudzu,* Playwrights Horizons, NY, 1981; *Steaming,* Brooks Atkinson, NY, 1983.

MAJOR TOURS—Madame Xenia, *The Killing of Sister George,* 1967-68; *Daisy Maye,* 1979-80.

PRINCIPAL FILM APPEARANCE—Lucille De Witt, *Power,* 1985.

PRINCIPAL TELEVISION APPEARANCES—*Playhouse 90; U.S. Steel Hour; Jamies; The Nurses.*

SIDELIGHTS: MEMBERSHIPS—Actors' Equity Association, Screen Actors Guild, American Federation of Television and Radio Artists.

"For the past four years I have been the television spokeswoman for Hanes mens underwear . . . otherwise known as Inspector No. 12."

ADDRESS: AGENT—J. Michael Bloom Agency, 400 Madison Avenue, New York, NY 10022.

*   *   *

RUDRUD, Kristin

PERSONAL: Last name pronounced "Rud Rood;" daughter of Ralph D. (in insurance) and Carol Janice (Anderson) Rudrud. EDUCATION: Moorhead State University, Moorhead, MN; trained for the theatre at the London Academy of Music and Dramatic Art.

VOCATION: Actress.

CAREER: DEBUT—Pablo, *The Tower,* Fargo North High School, Fargo, ND. NEW YORK DEBUT—Peaseblossom, *A Midsummer Night's Dream,* BAM Theatre Company, Brooklyn Academy of Music, for 27 performances, 1980. LONDON DEBUT—Eurysaces, *Ajax,* London Academy of Music and Dramatic Art Theatre. PRINCIPAL STAGE APPEARANCES—Viola, *Twelfth Night,* Riverside Shakespeare Company, NY, 1980; Soubrette, *Cyrano de Bergerac,* Williamstown Theatre Festival, Williamstown, MA, 1980; citizen number 3, *Amadeus,* Broadhurst, NY, 1981.

ADDRESS: AGENT—Hesseltine-Baker Assoc., 165 W. 46th Street, New York, NY 10036.

*   *   *

RUPNIK, Kevin   1956-

PERSONAL: Born February 28, 1956, in Warren, OH; son of Robert and Jenny (Strauss) Rupnik. EDUCATION: Carnegie-Mellon University, B.F.A., 1978; Yale School of Drama, M.F.A., 1981.

VOCATION: Designer.

CAREER: FIRST STAGE WORK—Designed scenery for Pittsburgh Civic Light Opera, 1981. FIRST NEW YORK STAGE WORK—Designer, *Ghosts,* Brooks Atkinson, 1982. PRINCIPAL STAGE WORK—Designed scenery for productions at Alaska Repertory, American Repertory, Hartford Stage Company, Philadelphia Drama Guild, Geva Theatre, Kennedy Center, Coconut Grove Playhouse, Yale Repertory, Williamstown Theatre Festival, Ark Theatre Company; designed off Broadway productions of *Love* and *Greater Tuna.*

MAJOR TOURS—*Greater Tuna,* 1983-85.

RELATED CAREER—Assistant art director, *One Life to Live,* ABC, 1983-84.

AWARDS: Los Angeles Dramalogue award, set design, 1985, for *Greater Tuna.*

ADDRESS: HOME—Eleven and one-half W, 26th Street, New York, NY 10010. OFFICE—Leifer and Youdleman, Three E. 54th Street, New York, NY 10022.

S

SADDLER, Donald 1920-

PERSONAL: Born January 24, 1920, in Van Nuys, CA; son of Elmer Edward and Mary Elizabeth (Roberts) Saddler. EDUCATION: Los Angeles City College. MILITARY: U.S. Army, Sargeant, 1943-45.

VOCATION: Choreographer, dancer, director, and producer.

CAREER: DEBUT—Dancer, *Grand Canyon Suite*, Hollywood Bowl, 1937. NEW YORK DEBUT—Uncle Willie, *High Button Shoes*, Century, 1947. PRINCIPAL STAGE APPEARANCES— Member of Ballet Theatre: *Romeo and Juliet, Billy the Kid, Bluebeard, Swan Lake, Les Patineurs, Peter and the Wolf, Lilac Garden*, 1940-43, 1946-47; dancer, *Dance Me a Song*, Royale, NY, 1950; principal dancer, *Bless You All*, Mark Hellinger, NY, 1950; dancer, *Song of Norway*, State Fair Music Hall, Dallas, TX, 1951.

FIRST STAGE WORK—Choreographer: *Blue Mountain Ballads*, Anton Dolin Dance Company. PRINCIPAL STAGE WORK—Choreographer: *Wonderful Town*, Winter Garden, NY, 1953; *Almanac*, 1953; *Tobia la Candida Spia*, Rome, Italy, 1954; *La Patrona di Raggio di Luna*, Rome, 1955; *Wonderful Town*, Princes, London, then Los Angeles, 1955; *Shangri-La, Buona Notte, Bettina*, Milan, 1956; *L'Adorabile Giulio*, Rome, 1957; as head of his own dance company, Jacob's Pillow, *This Property Is Condemed*, danced in *Winesburg, Ohio; When in Rome*, London, 1959; with Jacob's Pillow, *Macbeth* and *Other Voices, Other Rooms*, 1960; danced, *The Castle Period*, Arts Festival, Boston, MA 1961; *Dreams of Glory*, Joffrey Ballet, 1961; *Milk and Honey*, Joffrey Ballet, 1961; *Sophie, Morning Sun*, 1963; *To Broadway with Love*, New York World's Fair, 1964.

Knickerbocker Holiday, Harkness Ballet, San Francisco, CA, 1971; *No, No, Nanette*, 1971; *Much Ado About Nothing*, 1972; *Berlin to Broadway*, 1972; *Tricks*, 1973; *No, No, Nanette*, London, 1973; *The Merry Wives of Windsor, Miss Moffat*, both Philadelphia, 1974; *A Midsummer Night's Dream*, 1975; *Gala Tribute to Joshua Logan*, 1975; *Rodgers and Hart*, 1975; *The Robber Bridegroom*, 1975; *The Grand Tour*, 1979; *Happy New Year*, 1980; *Pardon, Monsieur Moliere*, Rome, 1982; the tarantella, *A Doll's House*, New York Shakespeare Festival; *On Your Toes*, New York and London; opening of the Roger L. Stevens Center for the Performing Arts, Dallas, TX, 1983; *A Celebration for Sir Anton Dolin*, Royal Opera House, London, 1984; *100 Years of Performing Arts at the Metropolitan*, 1984.

Producer: *New York Dance Festival*, Delacorte, NY, five seasons; *The Dance Collection Gala*, 1972; *The Sol Hurok Birthday Gala*, Metropolitan Opera House, NY, 1973; *The 30th Anniversary of City Center Theatre*, 1975; *The 35th Anniversary of the American Ballet Theatre*, 1975; *Pre-Inaugural Ballet Opera Gala*, Kennedy Center, 1981.

Opera: Choreographer and director—*Abduction from the Seraglio*, Washington Opera; *Aida*, Dallas Civic Opera; *La Perichole*, Metropolitan Opera, NY; *Weiner Blut*, Washington Opera broadcast; *The Student Prince*, New York City Opera, 1980; *The Merry Widow*, New York City Opera, 1982.

PRINCIPAL FILM WORK—Choreographer: *April in Paris; By the Light of the Silvery Moon; Young at Heart; Happy Hooker; Main Attraction*.

PRINCIPAL TELEVISION WORK—Choreographer: *Alice in Wonderland; The Tony Awards Show*, 1973, 1975, 1976, 1977, 1978, 1983; *Much Ado About Nothing; In Fashion; Canzionissima*, Rome; *The Bell Telephone Hour*, three seasons; *Verna the U.S.O. Girl*.

RELATED CAREER—Associate director, Harkness Ballet, four years; executive vice-president, Rebekah Harkness Foundation.

AWARDS: Maschera D'Argento, Italy, for *Tobia la Candida Spia*; Drama Desk Award, *No, No, Nanette*; Antoinette Perry Awards, for *No, No, Nanette* and *Wonderful Town*; Antoinette Perry award nominations, for *On Your Toes* and *Much Ado About Nothing*.

ADDRESS: AGENT—Coleman-Rosenberg Agency, 919 Third Avenue, New York, NY 10022.

* * *

SAINT-JAMES, Susan 1946-

PERSONAL: Born Susan Miller, August 14, 1946, in Los Angeles, CA; daughter of Charles Daniel and Constance (Geiger) Miller. EDUCATION: Attended Connecticut College for women.

VOCATION: Actress.

CAREER: PRINCIPAL TELEVISION APPEARANCES—Movies: *Fame Is the Name of the Game*, 1966; *S.O.S.; Titanic; Night Ones*, 1969; *Scott Free; Magic Carpet*, 1971; *Sex and the Single Parent*, 1979. Series: Peggy Maxwell, *Name of the Game*, NBC, 1968-71; Sally McMillan, *McMillan and Wife*, NBC, 1971-76; Kate McArdle, *Kate and Allie*, CBS, 1984-present. Episodic: *Ironside; It Takes a Thief; McCloud; Love American Style*.

PRINCIPAL FILM APPEARANCES-*Jigsaw*, Beverly Pictures, 1965;

P.J., Universal, 1968; *Where Angels Go . . . Trouble Follows*, 1968; *What's So Bad About Feeling Good?*, Universal, 1968; *Outlaw Blues*, Warner Brothers, 1977; *Love at First Bite*, American Films, 1979; *How to Beat the High Cost of Living*, Filmways, 1980.

AWARDS: Emmy Award, Outstanding Continued Performance by an Actress in a Supporting Role in a Series, 1969, for *Name of the Game*.

ADDRESS: AGENT—International Creative Management, 8899 Beverly Blvd., Los Angeles, CA 90048.*

*   *   *

SAKS, Gene   1921-

PERSONAL: Born November 8, 1921, in New York City; son of Morris and Beatrix (Lewkowitz) Saks; married Beatrice Arthur (divorced). EDUCATION—Cornell University, A.B., 1943; studied at the Actors Studio with Lee Strasberg, Sanford Meisner, and David Pressman, and at the Dramatic Workshop.

VOCATION: Actor and director.

CAREER: STAGE DEBUT—Lord Fancourt Babberly, *Charley's Aunt*, 1939. NEW YORK DEBUT—Joxer, *Juno and the Paycock*, Cherry Lane, 1947. PRINCIPAL STAGE APPEARANCES—Vicar and Poet, *The Dog Beneath the Skin*, 1947; Engineer, *Gas*, 1947; Henry IV, Pirandello's *Henry IV*, 1947; Rene St. Gall, *The Watched Pot*, 1947; the Butler, *Topaze*, Morosco, NY, 1947; Old Shepherd, *The Infernal Machine*, Provincetown Playhouse, NY, 1948; Park Attendant, *Within the Gate*, 1948; *The Doctor Inspite of Himself*, 1948; the German, *Yes Is for a Very Young Man*, Cherry Lane, NY, 1949; Professor of Religion, *Too Many Thumbs*, 1949; Monsieur Jordan, *The Bourgeois Gentleman*, 1949; second discusser, *Marty's Double*, Sam, *All You Need Is One Good Break*, both Mansfield, NY, 1950; the Chauffeur, *Personal Appearance;* Bill Page, *The Voice of the Turtle;* Wilbur, *For Love or Money, Missouri Legend*, both Atlantic City, NJ, 1950-51; Professor, *South Pacific*, Majestic, NY, 1951.

Citizen, servant, *Coriolanus*, Phoenix, NY, 1954; Wicked Duke, *The Thirteen Clocks*, Westport Country Playhouse, CT, 1954; Billy Gordon, *Late Love*, Westchester Playhouse, NY, 1954; Ragnar Brovik, *The Master Builder*, Phoenix, NY, 1955; Charlie Reader, *The Tender Trap*, Westchester Playhouse, NY, 1955; Richard Sherman, *The Seven Year Itch*, Del Rio, *The Gimmick*, both Westchester Playhouse, 1956; various roles, *Johnny Johnston*, Carnegie Hall Playhouse, NY, 1956; First God, *The Good Woman of Setzuan*, Phoenix, NY, 1956; son-in-law, *Middle of the Night*, ANTA, NY, 1957; Captain, *The Infernal Machine*, NY, Phoenix, 1958; the Professor, *Howie*, 46th Street, NY, 1958; various roles, *Album of Leaves*, Spoleto Festival, Italy, 1959; Rabbi, *The Tenth Man*, Booth, NY, 1959; Norman Yarrow, *Love and Libel*, Martin Beck, NY, 1960; Morestan, *A Shot in the Dark*, Booth, NY, 1961; Leo Herman, *A Thousand Clowns*, Eugene O'Neill, NY, 1962; *The Goodbye People*, Berkshire Theatre Festival, Stockbridge, MA, 1971.

MAJOR TOURS—Stefanowski, *Mr. Roberts*, 1950-51.

FIRST NEW YORK STAGE WORK—Director, *Enter Laughing*, Henry Miller's, 1963. PRINCIPAL STAGE WORK—Director: *No-*

body Love an Albatross, NY, 1963; *Half a Sixpence*, NY, 1965; *Generation*, NY, 1965; *Mame*, NY, 1966; *A Mother's Kisses*, NY, 1968; *Sheep on the Runway*, NY, 1970; *How the Other Half Loves*, NY, 1971; *Same Time Next Year*, NY, 1975; *California Suite*, NY, 1976; *I Love My Wife*, NY, 1977; *Home Again*, NY, 1979; *Special Occasions*, NY, 1980; *Supporting Cast*, NY, 1981; *Brighton Beach Memoirs*, Alvin, NY, 1983; *Biloxi Blues*, Neil Simon, NY, 1985; *The Odd Couple*, Broadhurst, NY, 1985.

MAJOR TOURS—Director: *The Millionairess*, 1963; *The Prince of Grand Street*, 1978.

PRINCIPAL FILM APPEARANCES—Leo Herman, *A Thousand Clowns*, 1966; *The Prisoner of Second Avenue*, 1974; *Lovesick; The One and Only; The Goodbye People*.

PRINCIPAL FILM WORK—Director: *Barefoot in the Park*, 1967; *The Odd Couple*, 1968; *Cactus Flower*, 1969; *Last of the Red Hot Lovers*, 1972; *Mame*, 1974; *Brighton Beach Memoirs* (upcoming).

PRINCIPAL TELEVISION APPEARANCES—*The Actors Studio Series*, 1949; *U.S. Steel Hour; You Are There; Playwright 1955-56*.

AWARDS: Antoinette Perry award nominations, 1965, for *Half a Sixpence*, 1966, for *Mame*, 1975, for *Same Time Next Year*, 1975; Antoinette Perry Awards, 1983, for *Brighton Beach Memoirs*, 1985, for *Biloxi Blues*.

ADDRESS: AGENT—William Morris Agency, 1350 Sixth Avenue, New York, NY 10019.

*   *   *

SANDERS, Richard   1940-

PERSONAL: Born August 23, 1940, in Harrisburg, PA. EDUCATION: Carnegie Institute of Technology, B.F.A., 1962; trained for the stage at the London Academy of Music and Dramatic Art on a Fullbright Grant.

VOCATION: Actor and writer.

CAREER: NEW YORK DEBUT—Karl Lindner, *Raisin*, 46th Street Theatre, 1974-75. PRINCIPAL STAGE APPEARANCES—James Joyce, *Travesties*, Mark Taper Forum, Los Angeles, CA, 1976; the man, *Same Time, Next Year*, Tiffany's Attic, Kansas City; *The Boss*, Chelsea Theatre Center, NY; four years with Arena Stage, Washington, DC; also: appearances at: Barter Stage, Abingdon, VA; Center Stage, Baltimore, MD; Front Street Theatre, Memphis, TN; Champlain Shakespeare Festival, Burlington, VT; New York Shakespeare Festival, Lincoln Center, NY; Los Angeles Actors Theatre.

FILM DEBUT—*Billy Jack Goes to Washington*, Warner Brothers, 1976. PRINCIPAL FILM APPEARANCES—*Midway*, 1976; *Nude Bomb*, Universal, 1980; *Valley Girl*, Atlantic, 1983.

TELEVISION DEBUT—Dr. Leale, *Who Killed President Lincoln?*, Wolper Productions, 1973. PRINCIPAL TELEVISION APPEARANCES—Series: Les Nessman, *WKRP in Cincinnati*, CBS, 1978-82; also: *Newhart; Simon and Simon; Goodnight, Beantown; Alice; Gloria; The Rockford Files; McCloud; Barnaby Jones; Lou Grant;*

RICHARD SANDERS

ISABEL SANFORD

Roots, II. Movies: *Found Money; Portrait of an Invisible Woman; Diary of a Teenage Hitchhiker; The Yeagers; Bud and Lou; Alexander—The Other Side of Dawn; Ruby and Oswald.*

WRITINGS: TELEVISION SCRIPTS—Five episodes, *WKRP in Cincinnati*, 1978-82; *Found Money*, NBC, 1983.

SIDELIGHTS: MEMBERSHIPS—Actors' Equity Association, Screen Actors Guild, American Federation of Televison and Radio Artists, Writers Guild of America.

Sanders was a Peace Corps volunteer in Brazil, 1966-69, where he served as director of acting and stage movement for the State Theatre of Paraiba, Brazil, 1966-68.

ADDRESS: AGENT—Bauman, Hiller and Associates, Suite 202, 9220 Sunset Blvd., Los Angeles, CA 90069.

*   *   *

SANFORD, Isabel

PERSONAL: Full name Isabel Gwendolyn Sanford; born August 29, in New York City; daughter of James Edward and Josephine (Perry) Sanford; married William Edward Richmond (deceased); children: Pamela, William Eric, Sanford Keith.

VOCATION: Actress.

CAREER: PRINCIPAL STAGE APPEARANCES—*Shakespeare in Harlem*, NY; *The Egg and I*, NY; *Purlie Victorious*, Los Angeles; *The Blacks*, Los Angeles; *The Amen Corner*, Los Angeles, later Broadway, NY; *And Mama Makes Three*, Little Theatre, Sullivan, IL, 1977.

MAJOR TOURS—*Nobody Loves an Albatross*, national company; *Funny Girl*, national company.

PRINCIPAL FILM APPEARANCES—Tillie, *Guess Who's Coming to Dinner*, Columbia, 1967; *Pendulum*, Columbia, 1969; *Stand Up and Be Counted*, Columbia, 1972; *The New Centurions*, Columbia, 1972; *Love at First Bite*, American International, 1979.

PRINCIPAL TELEVISION APPEARANCES—*The Carol Burnett Show;* Louise Jefferson, *All in the Family*, CBS, 1971-75; Louise Jefferson, *The Jeffersons*, CBS, 1975-present; *Supertrain; The Great Man's Whiskers; The Mod Squad; Bewitched; The Comedy Shop;* others.

AWARDS: Emmy Award, Best Actress in a Comedy Series, 1981, for *The Jeffersons;* Emmy Award nominations, 1982-84, for *The Jeffersons;* March of Dimes Celebrity Mother of the Year, 1984.

SIDELIGHTS: MEMBERSHIPS—March of Dimes, Kwanza Foundation (founding member).

Sanford began her career with the American Negro Theatre (Star Players) which disbanded at the beginning of World War Two. She was later associated with the YWCA drama project in New York City.

In writing to *CTFT*, Sanford said, "If there's anything in life you consider worthwhile achieving—go for it. I was told many times to forget show business, I had nothing going for me. But I pursued it anyway. Voila!"

ADDRESS: AGENT—Sharp Lemack Public Relations, 9157 Sunset Blvd., Los Angeles, CA 90069.

*   *   *

SAUCIER, Claude-Albert   1953-

PERSONAL: Surname pronounced Sew-Cee-Ay; born October 9, 1953, in Berlin, NH; son of Gaston-Louis (a paper production worker) and Germaine Beatrice Saucier. EDUCATION: Dartmouth, B.A., 1975; trained for the stage with the Royal Shakespeare Company at the National Theatre of Great Britain. RELIGION: Roman Catholic.

VOCATION: Actor, director, writer, translator, and voice-over artist.

CAREER: STAGE DEBUT—Sir Nathaniel, *Love's Labour's Lost*, Dartmouth Rep, Hanover, NH. 1972. NEW YORK DEBUT—Deafmute, *The Madwoman of Chaillot*, CSC Repertory, 1977. PRINCIPAL STAGE APPEARANCES—Guildenstern, *Rosencrantz and Guildenstern Are Dead*, Hartford Stage, Hartford, CT, 1979; Horatio, *Hamlet*, Coconut Grove Playhouse, Miami, FL, 1980; *Cyrano de Bergerac*, Long Wharf, New Haven, CT, 1980; young man,

CLAUDE A. SAUCIER

Veronica's Room, Provincetown Playhouse, NY, 1981; Frog footman, Eve LeGallienne's *Alice in Wonderland*, Virginia, NY, 1982; *Plenty*, Boston, MA, 1984; Lucio, *Measure for Measure*, Pittsburgh, PA, 1985.

PRINCIPAL TELEVISION APPEARANCES—*Ryan's Hope*, ABC; *Search for Tomorrow*, NBC; *All My Children*, ABC.

WRITINGS: PLAYS, PRODUCED—*Madwoman of Chaillot* (translation), CSC Repertory, NY, 1977.

SIDELIGHTS: MEMBERSHIPS—Actors' Equity Association, Screen Actors Guild, American Federation of Television and Radio Artists.

Saucier told *CTFT* that his favorite roles are Oberon, Horatio and Andrew Aguecheek in classic theatre; on the contemporary side, he is fondest of the young man in Ira Levin's play, *Veronica's Room*.

ADDRESS: HOME—50 W. 97th Street, New York, NY 10025. AGENT—Lester Lewis Associates, 110 W. 40th Street, Room 2401, New York, NY 10018.

*   *   *

SAVALAS, Telly   1926-

PERSONAL: Born Telly Aristoteles, January 21, 1926, in Garden City, NY; son of Nicholas Constantine and Christina (Kapsallas) Savalas; married Katherine Nicolaides, 1950 (divorced); married Marilyn Gardner, October 28, 1960 (divorced); married Sally Adams, 1974 (divorced); married Julie Hovland, December 22, 1984; children: (first marriage) Christina; (second marriage) Penelope, Candace; (third marriage) Nicholas; (fourth marriage) Christian. EDUCATION: Columbia University, B.S. RELIGION: Greek Orthodox. MILITARY: U.S. Army, World War Two.

VOCATION: Actor.

CAREER: DEBUT—*Bring Home a Baby*, Armstrong Circle Theatre, CBS, late 1950's. PRINCIPAL TELEVISION APPEARANCES—Charles "Lucky" Luciano, *The Witness*, CBS, 1960; Mr. Carver, *Acapulco*, NBC, 1961; *Alcoa Premiere*, ABC, 1961; Lt. Theo Kojak, *Kojak*, CBS, 1973-78. Miniseries: *The French Atlantic Affair; Alcatraz; Alice in Wonderland*. Movies: *The Marcus-Nelson Murders; Hellinger's Law; Kojak: The Belarus File; My Palikari*, PBS.

PRINCIPAL FILM APPEARANCES—*The Young Savages*, United Artists, 1961; Feto Gomez, *Birdman of Alcatraz*, United Artists, 1962; *Cape Fear*, Universal, 1962; Dr. Riccio, *The Interns*, Columbia, 1962; *The Man from the Diners Club*, Columbia, 1963; *The New Interns*, Columbia, 1964; Guffy, *Battle of the Bulge*, Warner Brothers, 1965; Pontius Pilate, *The Greatest Story Ever Told*, United Artists, 1965; *Genghis Khan*, Columbia, 1966; *Beau Geste*, Universal, 1966; *The Slender Thread*, Paramount, 1966; Archer Maggott, *The Dirty Dozen*, Metro-Goldwyn-Mayer, 1967; *The Scalphunters*, United Artists, 1968; *Buona Sera, Mrs. Campbell*, United Artists, 1969; *The Assassination Bureau*, Paramount, 1969; *On Her Majesty's Secret Service*, United Artists, 1969; *Crooks and Coronets* (British), 1969; *MacKenna's Gold*, Columbia, 1969.

Kelly's Heroes, Metro-Goldwyn-Mayer, 1970; *Pretty Maids All in a*

TELLY SAVALAS

SCHAAL, Richard   1928-

PERSONAL: Last name pronounced "Shawl;" born May 5, 1928, in Chicago, IL; son of Victor Cornelius (a machinist) and Margaret Semple (a telephone operator; maiden name, Waddell) Schaal; married Valerie Harper (an actress), September, 1966 (divorced, 1978); married Natasha Warren (a real estate broker), 1980; children: Wendy, Danielle (stepchild). EDUCATION: Institute of Design, Illinois Institute of Technology; Medill School of Journalism, Northwestern University; trained for the stage with Viola Spolin and Paul Sills at the Second City Improvisational Workshop. MILITARY: U.S. Marine Corps., corporal, 1946-48.

VOCATION: Actor.

CAREER: STAGE DEBUT—Charlie Castle, *The Big Knife*, Medill School Drama Department. NEW YORK DEBUT—Farmer in "The Little Peasant," Thief in "Is He Fat?," Man in "Venus and the Cat," Old Man in "The Master Thief," the ass, "Bremen Town Musicians," other roles, *Paul Sill's Story Theatre*, Ambassador, 1970. PRINCIPAL STAGE APPEARANCES—Huey, *Explainers*, Playwrites, Chicago; *Second City Troupe*, Chicago, NY; Jesse James, *Kelly*, Philadelphia, PA; *Something Different*, NY; *Little Murders*, NY; *Same Time, Next Year*, NY.

PRINCIPAL FILM APPEARANCES—*The Russians Are Coming, the Russians Are Coming*, United Artists, 1966; *The Virgin President*, 1968; *Slaughterhouse Five*, Universal, 1972; *Steelyard Blues*, Warner Brothers, 1973; *Corvette Summer*, United Artists, 1978; *Americathon*, United Artists, 1979; *Hollywood Knights*, Columbia, 1980; *O'Hara's Wife*, 1982.

PRINCIPAL TELEVISION APPEARANCES—Leo Heatherton, *Phyllis*,

RICHARD SCHAAL

Row, Metro-Goldwyn-Mayer, 1971; *A Town Called Bastard* (aka *A Town Called Hell*; British-Spanish), 1971; *Pancho Villa* (Spanish), 1972; *Horror Express*, (aka *Panic on the Trans-Siberian Express*; Spanish), 1972; *Inside Out*, Warner Brothers, 1975; *Diamond Mercenaries*, 1975; *Killer Force*, American International, 1975; M.C., *Lisa and the Devil* (aka *The House of Exorcism*; Italian), 1975; *Capricorn One*, Warner Brothers, 1978; *Escape to Athena*, Associated Film Distributors, 1979; *Beyond the Poseidon Adventure*, Warner Brothers, 1979; *The Border*, 1982; *Cannonball Run II*, Warner Brothers, 1984.

PRINCIPAL STAGE WORK—Director, season at Stanford Playhouse, CT, 1958-59.

PRINCIPAL RADIO WORK—Director, *Your Voice of America*, 1955-58.

RELATED CAREER: Senior director, news and special events department, ABC, 1955-58.

AWARDS: Academy Award nomination, Best Supporting Actor, 1962, for *Birdman of Alcatraz;* Emmy Awards, Best Lead Actor in a Television Series, 1973-74, *Kojak;* People's Choice Award, 1975, 1976; Peabody Award; Freedom Foundation Award; The *Sun* (London) Television Award, Top Actor, 1975.

SIDELIGHTS: Savalas served as assistant director for the Near East, South Asia, and Africa, for the Information Service of the Department of State, 1955.

ADDRESS: OFFICE—333 Universal City Plaza, Universal City, CA 91608.

CBS, 1975-76; *The New Yorkers; Second City Reports; Trapper John, M.D.; Just Our Luck,* ABC; *Bachelor at Law; After George; Please Stand By.* Also: *The Mary Tyler Moore Show; Rhoda; The Bob Newhart Show; The Dick Van Dyke Show; The Two of Us; The Window; Harry-O; The F.B.I.; The Rockford Files; Policewoman; Love American Style; The Music Scene; Married Is Better; Harper Valley, P.T.A.; I Dream of Jeannie; It's a Living; The Cube; The Jack Paar Show; The Ed Sullivan Show; The Dinah Shore Show; East Side West Side; The Reporters; Mr. Broadway; The Doris Day Show; Fish,* others. Movies: *Thursday's Game,* 1974; *Let's Switch,* 1975.

SIDELIGHTS: MEMBERSHIPS—Actors' Equity Association, Screen Actors Guild, American Federation of Television and Radio Artists, Directors Guild of America, Writers Guild. RECREATION—Oil painting, writing, sailing, renovating old houses, landscape gardening.

ADDRESS: AGENT—Dan Moulthrope, Don Schwartz Agency, 8721 Sunset Blvd., Los Angeles, CA 90069.

*   *   *

SCHAEFER, George   1920-

PERSONAL: Born December 16, 1920, in Wallingford, CT; son of Louis and Elsie (Otterbein) Schaefer; married Mildred Trares, February 5, 1954. EDUCATION: Lafayette College, B.A.; studied for the theatre at Yale Drama School.

VOCATION: Director and producer.

CAREER: PRINCIPAL STAGE WORK—Director: *Leave It to Smith,* Pastime Players, Oak Park, IL, 1937; fifty productions for the U.S. Army Special Services, Honolulu, HI, 1942-45; *Hamlet,* Columbus Circle Theatre, NY, 1945; *Hamlet,* City Center, NY, 1946; co-director, *Darling, Darling, Darling,* McCarter, Princeton, NJ, 1947; co-director, *Man and Superman,* Alvin, NY, 1947; *The Linden Tree,* Music Box, NY, 1948; *The Teahouse of the August Moon,* Her Majesty's, London, 1954; *The Southwest Corner,* NY, 1955; *Kiss Me Kate,* City Center, NY, 1955; *The Apple Cart,* NY, 1956; *The Body Beautiful,* NY, 1958; *Write Me a Murder,* NY, 1961, then London, 1962; *Zenda,* Los Angeles, 1963; *The Great Indoors,* NY, 1966; *The Last of Mrs. Lincoln,* NY, 1972; *The Student Prince,* tour, 1973; *Ah, Wilderness!,* tour, 1975; *On Golden Pond,* Ahmanson, Los Angeles, 1980; *Mixed Couples,* NY, 1980; *Another Part of the Forest,* Ahmanson, Los Angeles, 1982; and over thirty musicals for State Fair, Dallas, TX.

Producer: At City Center, as executive producer, artistic director and director: *Man and Superman, She Stoops to Conquer,* 1949; *The Corn Is Green, The Heiress, The Devil's Disciple, Captain Brassbound's Conversion,* 1950; *The Royal Family, Richard II, The Taming of the Shrew, Dream Girl, Idiot's Delight, The Wild Duck,* 1951; *Anna Christie, Come of Age, The Male Animal, Tovarich, First Lady,* 1952.

Co-producer, *The Teahouse of the August Moon,* Martin Beck, NY, 1953.

PRINCIPAL FILM WORK—Director: *Macbeth,* 1960; *Pendulum,* Columbia, 1969; *Generation,* Avco-Embassy, 1969; *Doctors'*

GEORGE SCHAEFER

Wives, Columbia, 1971; *Once Upon a Scoundrel,* 1972; *An Enemy of the People,* 1977.

Producer, *An Enemy of the People,* 1977.

PRINCIPAL TELEVISION WORK—Director for *Hallmark Hall of Fame: Hamlet, Richard II, Macbeth, One Touch of Venus, Alice in Wonderland, The Devil's Disciple, Dream Girl, The Corn Is Green, The Good Fairy, The Taming of the Shrew, The Cradle Song,* all 1955-56; *Born Yesterday, Man and Superman, The Little Foxes, The Lark, There Shall Be No Night, The Yeoman of the Guard,* all 1956-57; *Green Pastures, On Borrowed Time, Little Moon of Alban, Dial M for Murder,* all 1957-58; *Harvey, Gift of the Magi, Meet Me in Saint Louis, Johnny Belinda, Kiss Me, Kate, Berkeley Square, Green Pastures,* all 1958-59; *Winterset, A Doll's House, Christmas Festival: The Borrowed Christmas, The Tempest, The Cradle Song, Captain Brassbound's Conversion, Turn the Key Deftly,* all 1959-60.

Shangri-La, Time Remembered, Give Us Barrabas, The Joke and the Valley, Golden Child, all 1960-61; *Victoria Regina, Hour of the Bath, Arsenic and Old Lace,* all 1961-62; *The Teahouse of the August Moon, Cyrano de Bergerac, Pygmalion, The Invincible Mr. Disraeli, The Hands of Donofro,* all 1962-63; *The Patriots, A Cry of Angels, Abe Lincoln in Illinois, Little Moon of Alban,* all 1963-64; *The Fantasticks, The Magnificent Yankee, The Holy Terror,* all 1964-65; *Gideon,* 1970; *Truman at Potsdam,* 1975.

Also: *USA,* PBS, 1971; *A War of Children,* 1972; *F. Scott Fitzgerald and the Last of the Belles,* 1973; *Love Story* (anthology series), NBC, 1973; *Sandburg's Lincoln,* 1974; *In This House of*

Brede, 1975; *Land of Hope*, CBS, 1975; *The Last of Mrs. Lincoln*, PBS, 1975; *Amelia*, NBC, 1976; *Our Town*, NBC, 1977; *Hatter Fox*, CBS, 1977; *The Second Barry Manilow Special*, ABC, 1977; *First You Cry*, CBS, 1978; *Who'll Save Our Children*, CBS, 1978; *Blind Ambition*, CBS, 1979; *The Voyage of the Mayflower*, CBS, 1979; *The Fourth Barry Manilow Special*, ABC, 1980; *The Bunker*, CBS, 1980; *The People vs. Jean Harris*, CBS, 1981; *A Piano for Mrs. Cimino*, CBS, 1982; *The Deadly Game*, BBC/HBO, 1982; *Answers*, NBC, 1982; *Right of Way*, HBO, 1983; *The Best Christmas Pageant Ever*, ABC, 1983; *Children in the Crossfire*, NBC, 1984.

Producer: *Blind Ambition*, 1979; *The Voyage of the Mayflower*, 1979; *The Bunker*, 1980; *The People vs. Jean Harris*, 1981; *A Piano for Mrs. Cimino*, 1982; *Right of Way*, 1983; *The Best Christmas Pageant Ever*, 1983; *The Booth*, PBS, 1983; *Children in the Crossfire*, 1984.

AWARDS: Eight Emmy Awards; Sylvania Award; three Radio Television Daily Awards; three Directors Guild of America Awards; Emmy nomination, 1983, for *The Best Christmas Pageant Ever;* honorary degrees from Lafayette College, 1963, and Coker College, 1973.

SIDELIGHTS: MEMBERSHIPS—Directors Guild of America (president), Phi Beta Kappa Society, Players Club. RECREATION—Duplicate bridge, theatre and film going.

George Schaefer and Merrill H. Karpf, formerly President of Quinn Martin Productions, formed Schaefer/Karpf Productions in 1982, to produce films for television, cable television, and theatrical release.

ADDRESS: OFFICE—Schaefer/Karpf Productions, 12711 Ventura Blvd., Suite 307, Studio City, CA 91604.

*   *   *

SCHEHEREZADE
See ALEANDRI, Emelise

*   *   *

SCHILLER, Bob   1918-

PERSONAL: Born November 8, 1918, in San Francisco, CA; son of Roland E. (a manufacturer) and Lucille E. (Block) Schiller; married Joyce Harris, July 20, 1947 (died, 1965); married Sabrina Scharf (a clean air advocate), May 25, 1968; children: (first marriage) Thomas B., James B.; (second) Abigail R., Sarah M. EDUCATION: UCLA, 1935-39, B.A., economics. MILITARY: 1941-45, Second Lieutenant. POLITICS: Democrat.

VOCATION: Producer and writer.

CAREER: PRINCIPAL TELEVISION WORK—Producer (with Bob Weiskopf), *The Good Guys*, CBS, 1968-70; *Maude*, CBS, 1974-78; *All's Fair*, CBS, 1976-77.

WRITINGS: RADIO AND TELEVISION—*Duffy's Tavern*, NBC, 1947-50; *Mel Blanc Show; Sweeney and March*, CBS; *Abbott and*

Costello, NBC, 1949-54; *Ozzie and Harriet*, ABC Radio, 1949; *The Jimmy Durante Show*, radio, 1950; *The Garry Moore Show*, CBS, 1951; *All Star Revue* (aka *Four Star Revue*), *Danny Thomas* and *Ed Wynn* shows, NBC, 1950-52; *December Bride*, CBS Radio, 1946-50; *The Red Buttons Show*, CBS, 1953.

TELEVISION—(All written with Bob Weiskopf) *That's My Boy*, CBS, 1954; *Professional Father*, CBS, 1955; *It's Always Jan*, CBS, 1955-56; *I Love Lucy*, CBS, 1956-57; *The Lucy—Desi Comedy Hour*, CBS, 1957-60 (seen also 1962-67); *The Ann Southern Show* (pilot), CBS, 1958; *Guestward Ho*, ABC, 1960-61; *Pete and Gladys*, CBS, 1961-62; *The Lucy Show*, CBS, 1962-64; *The Red Skelton Show*, CBS, 1965-68; *The Good Guys*, 1968-70; *The Carol Burnett Show*, CBS, 1970-71; *The Flip Wilson Show*, NBC, 1971-72; *Maude*, CBS, 1972-76; *All's Fair*, CBS, 1976-77; *All in the Family*, CBS, 1978-80; *Archie Bunker's Place*, CBS, 1981-82.

PLAYS, PRODUCED—With Bob Weiskopf, *So Long Stanley*.

AWARDS: Emmy Awards, *Flip Wilson Show, All in the Family;* Writers Guild Awards, *I Love Lucy, The Lucy-Desi Comedy Hour, Maude, All in the Family.*

SIDELIGHTS: MEMBERSHIPS—Writers Guild of America, American Federation of Television and Radio Artists, Riviera Golf Club.

Bob Schiller and Bob Weiskopf have been writing partners for more than thirty-two years. Among their classic television scripts are "Lucy and the Grape Stomping" from *I Love Lucy*, "Attempted Rape of Edith Bunker" and "Cousin Liz" (lesbian episode) from *All in the Family*, and "Maude and the Psychiatrist," a half-hour monologue from the series *Maude*.

ADDRESS: OFFICE—Twentieth Century-Fox TV, Box 900, Beverly Hills, CA 90213. AGENT—Robinson-Weintraub Company, 8428 Melrose Place, Los Angeles, CA 90069.

*   *   *

SCHILLER, Lawrence   1936-

PERSONAL: Born December 28, 1936, in New York City; son of Isidour (a merchant) and Jean (Liebowitz) Schiller; married Judith Holtzer, 1961 (divorced, 1975); married Stephanie Wolf, November 5, 1977; children: (first marriage) Suzanne, Marc, Howard; (second marriage) Anthony, Cameron. EDUCATION: Pepperdine College, B.A.; special training as a photojournalist with Time-Life. POLITICS: Democrat. RELIGION: Jewish.

VOCATION: Director and producer.

CAREER: PRINCIPAL FILM WORK—Producer and director: *The Man Who Skied Down Everest*, 1975; *The American Dreamer;* conceived and executed special still montages and titles for *Butch Cassidy and the Sundance Kid*, Twentieth Century-Fox, 1969, and *Lady Sings the Blues*, Paramount, 1972.

PRINCIPAL TELEVISION WORK—Producer and director: *Hey I'm Alive*, 1975; *The Trial of Lee Harvey Oswald*, 1977; *The Winds of Kitty Hawk*, 1978; *Marilyn*, 1980; *An Act of Love*, 1981; *Raid on Short Creek*, 1981; *The Executioner's Song*, 1981; *Peter the Great*, 1985. Also executive producer, *Death on a Day Pass*, CBS (upcoming).

WRITINGS: BOOKS—*Ladies and Gentlemen, Lenny Bruce* (with Albert Goldman), 1975; *Minamata* (with Eugene Smith), 1976; *The Executioner's Song* (with Norman Mailer), 1979.

AWARDS: Academy of Motion Picture Arts and Sciences Award, 1975, for *The Man Who Skied Down Everest,* 1975; numerous awards in photojournalism, National Press Photographers Association.

SIDELIGHTS: MEMBERSHIPS—Directors Guild of America, Academy of Motion Picture Arts and Sciences, National Press Photographers Association, California Press Photographers Association.

Schiller's career as a photojournalist included work with *Life,* 1959-69, *Look,* 1963-65, *Paris Match,* 1960-69, *London Sun Times,* 1960-69, *Stern,* 1960-69, *Sport,* 1956-60, *Sports Illustrated,* 1956-64.

ADDRESS: OFFICE—P.O. Box 5784, Sherman Oaks, CA 91413.

*   *   *

SCHMIDT, Douglas W.   1942-

PERSONAL: Born October 4, 1942, in Cincinnati, OH; son of Robert W. and Amy Jean (Murdoch) Schmidt. EDUCATION: Boston University.

VOCATION: Set designer.

Photography by Ruffin Cooper, Jr.

DOUGLAS W. SCHMIDT

CAREER: STAGE DEBUT—Designer, *The Caretaker,* Playhouse in the Park, Cincinnati, OH, 1964. NEW YORK DEBUT—Designer, *La Boheme,* Juilliard Opera Theatre, 1965. PRINCIPAL STAGE WORK—Designer: twenty productions between 1964 and 1968 for Playhouse in the Park, Cincinnati; *The Ox Cart,* NY, 1966; *To Bury a Cousin,* NY, 1967; *Father Uxbridge Wants to Marry,* NY, 1967; *King John,* Shakespeare Festival, NY, 1967; *The Memorandum,* Shakespeare Festival, NY, 1968; *Huui-Huui,* Shakespeare Festival, NY, 1968; *Twelfth Night,* Shakespeare Festival, NY, 1969; *Julius Caesar, The Homecoming,* both Tyrone Guthrie, Minneapolis, 1969.

Became resident designer for Repertory Theatre of Lincoln Center, NY, 1969 and his productions there included: *The Time of Your Life,* 1969; *The Good Woman of Setzuan,* 1970; *Operation Sidewinder,* 1970; *The Disintegration of James Cherry,* 1970; *Playboy of the Western World,* 1971; *An Enemy of the People,* 1971; *Antigone,* 1971; *Play Strindberg,* 1971; *Landscape/Silence,* 1971; *Mary Stuart,* 1971; *People Are Living There,* 1971; *Narrow Road to the Deep North,* 1972; *Twelfth Night,* 1972; *The Love Suicide at Schofield Barracks,* 1972; *The School for Scandal,* 1972; *The Hostage,* 1972; *The Lower Depths,* 1972; *Enemies,* 1972; *The Plough and the Stars,* 1973; *A Streetcar Named Desire,* 1973; *The Three Sisters,* 1973; *Measure for Measure,* 1973; *The Time of Your Life,* 1975; *The Three Sisters,* 1975; *Threepenny Opera,* 1976; *Agamemnon,* 1977.

Also designed the following: two productions for the Juilliard Ballet Theatre, 1965-71; *Paris Is Out!,* 1970; *The Losers, Huckleberry Finn,* both Juilliard Opera Theatre, NY, 1971; *The Merry Wives of Windsor,* American Shakespeare Festival, Stratford, CT, 1971; *Pictures in a Hallway,* NY, 1971; *The Wedding of Iphigenia, Iphigenia in Concert,* both Shakespeare Festival, NY, 1971; *Grease,* Golden, NY, 1972; *The Country Girl,* 41st Street Theatre, NY, 1972; *Women Beware Women,* NY, 1972; *Four Beckett Plays: Happy Days, Act without Words I, Krapp's Last Tape, Not I,* NY, 1972.

A Breeze from the Gulf, Eastside Playhouse, NY, 1973; *Veronica's Room,* Music Box, NY, 1973; *Over Here!,* Shubert, NY, 1974; *Fame,* NY, 1974; *Kid Champion,* Shakespeare Festival, NY, 1974; *Who's Who in Hell,* 1974; *Our Late Night,* 1975; *The Robber Bridegroom, Edward II,* both Juilliard (Acting Company), 1975; *Angel Street,* Belasco, NY, 1975; *Truckload,* 1975; *Herzl,* NY, 1976; *The Crazy Locomotive,* 1977; *Sunset,* 1977; *Stages,* 1978; *Runaways,* Shakespeare Festival, NY, 1978; *They're Playing Our Song,* Majestic, NY, 1979; *The Most Happy Fella,* Uris, NY, 1979; *Romantic Comedy,* Ethel Barrymore, NY, 1979.

Samson et Dalilah, San Francisco Opera, 1980; *Aida,* San Francisco Opera, 1981; *Frankenstein,* Palace, NY, 1981; *The Tempest,* 1982; *The Death of Von Richthofen as Witnessed from Earth,* 1982; *The Skin of Our Teeth,* 1983; *Porgy and Bess,* 1983; *Chaplin,* 1983; *Detective Story,* 1984; *Black Comedy,* 1984; *Scapino!,* 1984; *The Loves of Don Perlimpin,* 1984; *Dancing in the End Zone,* Shakespeare Festival, NY, 1985; *Palladium Club Phase I,* 1985.

PRINCIPAL TELEVISION WORK—Designer: *Enemies,* 1974, *The Time of Your Life,* 1976, *The Skin of Our Teeth,* 1983, *Wings,* 1983, *The Rise and Fall of Daniel Rocket,* 1985, all for PBS.

SIDELIGHTS: RECREATION—Transcontinental flying.

ADDRESS: OFFICE—1501 Broadway, Room 1606, New York, NY 10036.

SCHNEIDER, Romy   1938-82

PERSONAL: Born Rosemarie Albach-Retty in Vienna, September 23, 1938; died of a heart attack on May 29, 1982; daughter of Wolf (an actor) and Magda (an actress; maiden name, Schneider) Albach-Retty; married Harry Meyen-Haubenstock (an actor and director; divorced); married Daniel Biasini (divorced); children: (first marriage) David (died, July, 1981).

VOCATION: Actress.

CAREER: FILM DEBUT—*White Lilies*, 1953. PRINCIPAL FILM APPEARANCES—*The Story of Vicki*, 1954; *Monoti*, 1957; *Scampolo*, 1959; *Madchen in Uniform*, 1958; *Forever My Love*, Paramount, 1962; *Montpi; Christine; Boccaccio 70*, Avco-Embassy, 1962; *Fire and Ice; The Trial*, 1963; *The Victors*, Columbia, 1963; *Chimney No. 4; 10:30 P.M. Summer Evening*, 1967; *Triple Cross*, Warner Brothers-Seven Arts, 1967; *The Swimming Pool*, Avco-Embassy, 1970; *Otley*, Columbia, 1969; *Bloomfield; Who?; My Lover, My Son*, Metro-Goldwyn-Mayer, 1970; *Max and the Junkman; La Califfa; The Assassination of Trotsky*, Cinerama, 1972; *Ludwig*, Metro-Goldwyn-Mayer, 1973; *Cesar et Rosalie*, Cinema V, 1972; *The Train; Love in the Rain; Love at the Top; Le Trio Infernal; The Important Thing Is Love; Innocents with Dirty Hands; The Old Gun; Group Portrait with Lady; Made; A Woman at Her Window; A Simple Story*, 1978; *Bloodline*, 1979; *Clair De Femme*, 1979; *Deathwatch*, 1980; *The Female Banker; Phantom of Love; Garde a Vue*, 1981; *La Passante*, 1982.

PRINCIPAL STAGE APPEARANCE—*Tis a Pity She's a Whore*, France.

AWARDS: Two Caesar Awards in France for her performances in *The Important Thing Is Love* and *A Simple Story.**

*   *   *

SCHRODER, Ricky   1970-

BRIEF ENTRY: Born April 3, 1970, on Staten Island, NY; son of Dick (a district manager with New York Telephone) and Diane Schroder. Actor. Schroder's film debut came at nine years of age in *The Champ*, United Artists, 1979. That was followed by *The Last Flight of Noah's Ark*, Buena Vista, 1980; *The Earthling*, Filmways, 1981. He starred in the CBS television remake of *Little Lord Fauntleroy*, 1980; in *Two Kinds of Love*, CBS, and in NBC's *A Reason to Live*, 1985. He is currently seen as Ricky Stratton in the NBC series *Silver Spoons*, which first aired on September 25, 1982.*

*   *   *

SCHWARZENEGGER, Arnold   1947-

BRIEF ENTRY: Born in Braz, Austria, July 30, 1947; son of Karl (a police chief and former champion ice curler) and Aurelia (Barmuller) Schwarzenegger. He came to the United States in 1967, and became a citizen in 1983. He was the "Body Building Champion" from 1965-80. He was the recipient of the "Jr. Mr. Europe" title, Germany, 1965; the "Best Built Man of Europe" title, Germany, 1966; "Mr. Europe" title, Germany, 1966; "International Power-

lifting Champion," Germany, 1966; "Mr. Universe," amateur title, London, 1967; "German Powerlifting Championship," 1968; "Mr. International" title, International Federation of Body Building, Mexico, 1968; "Mr. Universe," amateur title, 1969; "Mr. Olympia" title, 1970-75 and 1980; "Mr. World," Columbus, OH, 1970. He completed his education at UCLA and at the University of Wisconsin where he obtained a degree in Business and International Economics.

In 1976, Schwarzenegger made his film debut in *Stay Hungry*, United Artists, and received the Golden Globe Award for the Best Newcomer. He went on to film *Pumping Iron*, 1977; *The Villian*, 1979; *Scavenger Hunt*, Twentieth Century-Fox, 1979; *Conan, the Barbarian*, Universal, 1982; *Conan, the Destroyer*, Universal, 1984; *The Terminator*, 1984; Kalidor in *The Red Sonja*, 1985; *Commando*, Twentieth Century-Fox (upcoming). His television credits include appearances on *The Merv Griffin Show* and on Lucille Ball's *Happy Anniversary and Goodbye*. He played Mickey Hargitay in *Jayne Mansfield: A Symbol of the '50's*. He has also authored four books: *Arnold: The Education of a Body Builder, Arnold's Bodyshaping for Women, Arnold's Bodybuilding for Men,* and *Arnold's Encyclopedia of Modern Bodybuilding*. He has also produced a videotape entitled: *Shape Up with Arnold.**

*   *   *

SCOTT, Timothy

PERSONAL: EDUCATION: Studied acting at the Royal Academy of Dramatic Arts, London, with David Perry; studied with David Hammond at the American Conservatory Theatre, San Francisco, CA; in New York City, studied with Steven Strimpell and Michael Shurtleff at the Herbert Berghof Studio.

VOCATION: Actor, singer, and dancer.

CAREER: PRINCIPAL STAGE APPEARANCES—Guy Louis, *King of Hearts*, NY; Mark, *A Chorus Line*, Shubert, NY; principal, *Dancin'*, NY; Mr. Mistoffolees, *Cats*, Winter Garden, NY; also, stock appearances at the Sacramento Music Circus, the St. Louis Municipal Opera, and the Long Beach Civic Light Opera.

MAJOR TOURS—Guest Artist, *Shields & Yarnell*, National Company; principal, *Dancin'*; National Company; *No, No, Nanette*, National Company.

PRINCIPAL FILM APPEARANCES *Annie*, Columbia, 1982; *A Chorus Line*, 1985.

ADDRESS: AGENT—Robert Duva Enterprises, Ltd. 277 W. Tenth Street, New York, NY 10014.

*   *   *

SELDES, Marian   1928-

PERSONAL: Born August 23, 1928, in New York City; daughter of Gilbert (critic and author) and Alice (Hall) Seldes; married Julian Claman (divorced); children: a daughter. EDUCATION: Trained for the stage at the School of the American Ballet and at the Neighborhood Playhouse with Sanford Meisner.

MARIAN SELDES

VOCATION: Actress and author.

CAREER: DEBUT—An angel, *Christmas Pageant*, Dalton School, 1935. NEW YORK DEBUT—Dancer, *Petrouchka*, with Ballet Theatre, Metropolitan Opera House, NY, 1942. PRINCIPAL STAGE APPEARANCES—Attendant, *Medea*, National, NY, 1947; Dounia, *Crime and Punishment*, National, NY, 1947; Second Woman of Corinth, *Medea*, City Center, NY, 1949; Anichu, *That Lady*, Martin Beck, NY, 1949; Electra, *The Tower Beyond Tragedy*, ANTA Playhouse, NY, 1950; Nurse Phillips, *The High Ground*, 48th Street, NY, 1951; First Woman in Corinth, *Medea*, Hebbel, Berlin, West Germany, 1951; a close friend, *Come of Age*, City Center, NY, 1952; Nancy, "Oliver Twist" segment of *Highlights of the Empire*, Empire, NY, 1953; Bertha, *Ondine*, 46th Street, NY, 1954; Olivia, *The Chalk Garden*, Ethel Barrymore, NY, 1955; Rachel, *The Flowering Peach*, Cathay Circle, Los Angeles, CA, 1956; Sara, *The Potting Shed*, La Jolla Playhouse, La Jolla, CA, 1957; Romaine, *Witness for the Prosecution*, Player's Ring, Los Angeles, 1957; Symka Berson (later Rachel), *The Wall*, Billy Rose, NY, 1960; Mag, *The Long Voyage Home*, Mermaid, NY, 1961; Emma Crosby, *Diff'rent*, Mermaid, NY, 1961.

Took over the role of Mrs. Patrick Campbell, *A Fig Leaf in Her Bonnet*, Gramercy Arts, NY, 1961; Susan Loring, *A Gift of Time*, Ethel Barrymore, NY, 1962; Miss Frost, *The Ginger Man*, NY, 1963; Blackie, *The Milk Train Doesn't Stop Here Anymore* (revised version), Brooks Atkinson, NY, 1964; postmistress, *All Women Are One*, Gate, NY, 1965; Alice, *Tiny Alice*, for some performances, Billy Rose, NY, 1965; Nurse, *Medea*, Valley Music Theatre, Los Angeles, CA, 1965; Juana, *Juana La Loca*, American Place, NY, 1965; Julia, *A Delicate Balance*, Martin Beck, NY, 1966; Sylvia, *Before You Go*, Henry Miller's, NY, 1968; the woman, *Final*

Solutions, Felt Forum, NY, 1968; *An Evening with James Agee*, Theatre de Lys, NY, 1969; Olga, *The Three Sisters*, American Shakespeare Festival, Stratford, CT, 1969; Daisy, *Mercy Street*, St. Clement's Church, NY, 1969.

Gretchen, *Other People*, Berkshire Theatre Festival, Stockbridge, MA, 1970; Marian, *Father's Day*, John Golden, NY, 1971; Constance, *The Celebration*, Hedgerow, 1971; Katherine Carney, *Remember Me*, Country Playhouse, Westport, CT, 1972; the witness, *Mendicants of Evening* (Martha Graham's ballet), Alvin, NY, 1973; *For the Use of the Hall*, Trinity Square Playhouse, Providence, RI, 1974; Hester Salomon, *Equus*, Plymouth, NY, Oct. 1974, continuing in this part until June 1976, when she took over the role of Dora Strang in the same play; Isadora, *Isadora Duncan Sleeps with the Russian Navy*, American Place, NY, 1977; Rivka, *The Merchant*, Plymouth, NY, 1977; Myra Bruhl, *Deathtrap*, Music Box, NY, 1978; Fanny Church, *Painting Churches*, Second Stage, NY, 1983, and again at the Lambs, NY, 1984; Fanny Church, *Painting Churches*, Birmingham, MI, 1985.

Also in various summer stock theatres since 1945: *Night Must Fall*, *The Late George Apley*, *Peg O' My Heart*, *The Little Foxes*, *The Glass Menagerie*, *The Silver Cord*, *Angel Street*, *Pygmalion*, *The Importance of Being Earnest*, *Lady in the Dark*, *Show Boat*, *Dream Girl*, others.

MAJOR TOURS—Mary, *Who's Happy Now?*, summer, 1968.

FILM DEBUT—*The Lonely Light*, 1951. PRINCIPAL FILM APPEARANCES—*The Young Stranger*, Universal, 1957; *The Big Fisherman*, Buena Vista, 1958; Herodias, *The Greatest Story Ever Told*, United Artists, 1963; *Fingers*, 1978.

TELEVISION DEBUT—*Macbeth*, 1949. PRINCIPAL TELEVISION APPEARANCES—Emilia, *Othello;* Nancy Hanks, *Mr. Lincoln*, others.

PRINCIPAL RADIO APPEARANCES—*CBS Radio Theatre*, appeared weekly, 1974-83, others.

PRINCIPAL STAGE WORK—Director, *Next Time I'll Sing to You*, Good Shepherd-Faith Church, NY, 1972, also in 1974.

RELATED CAREER—Artist in residence, Stanford University, CA, 1955; teacher and director, Drama Division, Juilliard School, NY, 1969, joined the Dance Division, 1972.

WRITINGS: BOOKS, PUBLISHED—*The Bright Lights, A Theatre Life* (a memoir) Houghton-Miflin, 1978; *Time Together* (a novel), Houghton-Miflin, 1981.

AWARDS: Antoinette Perry Award, 1968, for *A Delicate Balance;* mentioned in the *Guinness Book of World Records* for unbroken appearances in a play, *Deathtrap*, February 1978 through July 1983.

SIDELIGHTS: Marian Seldes has had an extraordinary career, almost never unbroken since 1950, with a reputation for remaining loyal to a production from its inception until long after it closes. In her book, *The Bright Lights*, she writes, "We go to the theatre to find moments that are perfect beyond dreaming—even if they are part of someone else's life—knowing that in that place of wonder we will be able to relate all that happens to an imaginary character to our own humanness."

ADDRESS: AGENT—Milton Goldman, International Creative Management, 40 W. 57th Street, New York, NY 10018.

SENICOURT, Roger
    See CHACKSFIELD, Frank

*   *   *

SENN, Herbert   1924-

PERSONAL: Born October 9, 1924, in Ilion, NY; son of Robert Charles (a farmer) and Elizabeth Amelia (a teacher; maiden name, Deutsch) Senn. EDUCATION: Columbia University, 1953-57. MILITARY: U.S. Army, 1949-50.

VOCATION: Designer.

CAREER: FIRST NEW YORK STAGE WORK—Decor designer, *House of Connelly,* Equity Library Theatre, 1955. FIRST LONDON STAGE WORK—Set design: *The Boys from Syracuse,* Theatre Royal Drury Lane, 1963. PRINCIPAL STAGE WORK—Designer: *Liliom, The Beaver Coat,* 1956; *Idiot's Delight, Right You Are (If You Think You Are), The Brothers Karamazov,* 1957; *Oklahoma!, Ardele, Hamlet of Stepney Green,* 1958; *She Shall Have Music, Time of Vengence,* 1959; *Gay Divorce, La Ronde, The Idiot, Man and Superman, Emanuel,* 1960; *Montserrat, Five Posts in the Market Place, Smiling the Boy Fell Dead,* designed lighting for *O Marry Me,* 1961; *The Merchant of Venice,* 1962; *I Got Shoes,* designed lighting for *Double Dublin,* 1963; designed lighting for *What Makes Sammy Run?, Roar Like a Dove,* 1964; *Great Scot!* 1965; *By Jupiter, The Dodo Bird, The Peddler,* 1967; *Private Lives,* 1968; *Little Boxes,* a double bill of *Trevor, The Coffee Lace,* 1969; *The Divorce of Judy and Jane,* 1971; *Berlin to Broadway with Kurt Weill, Oh Coward,* 1972; *No Sex Please, We're British,* 1973; *A Musical Jubilee,* 1975; *Oh Coward,* London, 1975; has designed for 30 seasons at the Cape Playhouse, Dennis, MA.

Opera: at the Boston Opera Company: *Hippolyte,* 1966, *The Trojans,* 1972, *War and Peace,* 1974, *Benvenuto Cellini,* 1975, *Montezuma,* 1976, *Russlan and Ludmilla,* 1977, *The Ice Break,* 1979; at the New York City Opera: *Ariadne and Naxos,* 1975, *Merry Widow,* 1983; *Showboat,* Houston Grand Opera tour, then Gershwin, NY, 1984.

MAJOR TOUR—Set design, *A Community of Two,* 1974.

ADDRESS: OFFICE—316 W. 51st Street, New York, NY 10019.

*   *   *

SEPPE, Christopher   1955-

PERSONAL: Surname pronouced *Se*-pee; born Christopher Sepe, September 19, 1955, in Brooklyn, NY; son of Louis Paul (a beer distributor) and Cynthia Joy (an actress and shopkeeper; maiden name, Muller) Sepe. RELIGION: Buddhist.

VOCATION: Actor and composer.

CAREER: STAGE DEBUT—The Mad Hatter, *Alice in Wonderland,* Baker Elementary School, Darien, CT, for four performances. NEW YORK DEBUT—Matt (the boy), *The Fantasticks,* Sullivan Street Playhouse, for over one thousand performances, June, 1979 to

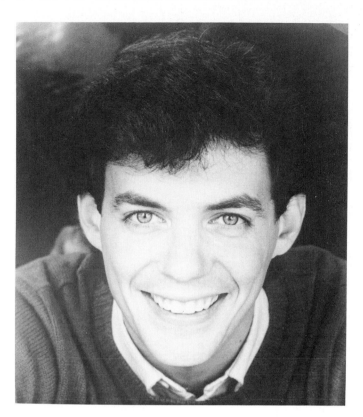

CHRISTOPHER SEPPE

December, 1981. PRINCIPAL STAGE APPEARANCES—Roger, *Everything in the Garden,* Floyd Allen, *Dark of the Moon,* Consortium, Darien/Stamford, CT; Garson, *Norman, Is That You?,* Tony, *The Boy Friend, Jacques Brel Is Alive and Well and Living in Paris,* Gaslight Theatre, Norwalk, CT; Lloyd, *The Me Nobody Knows,* Bridgeport Repertory, CT; Page, *King Lear,* University of Bridgeport, CT; Siro, *The Mandrake,* Center Stage, Baltimore, MD; the Nerd, *Remember Then,* Indiana Repertory, Indianapolis, IN; Ludlow, *Charlotte Sweet,* West Side Arts, Cheryl Crawford Theatre, NY, 1983-84.

Also: featured performer in *Young and on Broadway,* Ambassador, NY; *Broadway Salutes Fordham,* Avery Fisher Hall, NY; *The 1979 Village Voice Obie Awards,* Bottom Line, NY.

FILM DEBUT—Pete Wilson, *Teammates,* International Pictures, 1978.

TELEVISION DEBUT—Singer in medley from *The Fantasticks, 1979 Obie Awards,* WNET, 1979.

WRITINGS: Music and lyrics, *Naughty Girl!* (book by Scott Hayes), Gateway Playhouse, Bellport, NY, 1985.

SIDELIGHTS: MEMBERSHIPS—Actors' Equity Association, American Federation of Television and Radio Artists.

Seppe told *CTFT,* "It seems since I was 17 that I've always been doing a show. Even now, when I'm not actually working in a show, I'm writing or composing and doing every staged reading or backers audition or club review I'm asked to do. I'm known to some people as the King of Staged Readings."

''There are so many facets and areas of theatre, and I try to absorb as much as I can. I find it almost unbelievable when I speak to someone who is in the theatre and around my age about Charlotte Cushman or Laurette Taylor, Bea Lillie, Andre Charlot, George White, the Princess Shows—sometimes even more contemporary names—and I am met with blank stares. This is our history and we should know about it, just as we should know the history of our country.''

ADDRESS: HOME—New York, NY.

*   *   *

SERBAN, Andrei   1943-

PERSONAL: Born June 21, 1943, in Bucharest, Romania; son of George and Elpis (Lichardopu) Serban. EDUCATION: University of Bucharest.

VOCATION: Director.

CAREER: FIRST U.S. STAGE WORK—Director, *Arden of Faversham*, La MaMa, NY, 1970. LONDON DEBUT—Director, *Umbrellas of Cherbourg*, Phoenix, 1980. PRINCIPAL STAGE WORK—Director: *The Trojan Women, Medea, Electra,* La MaMa, and international touring, 1974-76; *The Good Woman of Setzuan,* La MaMa, 1975; *As You Like It,* La MaMa, 1976; *The Cherry Orchard,* Vivian Beaumont, Lincoln Center, NY, 1976; *Agamemnon,* New York Shakespeare Festival, Delacorte, 1977; *The Ghost Sonata,* Yale Repertory Company, New Haven, CT, 1977-78; *An Evening of Moliere Farces,* Yale Repertory Company, New Haven, CT, 1977-78; adapted, *The Master and Margarita,* New York Shakespeare Festival, Public, 1978; *The Umbrellas of Cherbourg,* New York Shakespeare Festival, Public, 1979; *Happy Days,* New York Shakespeare Festival, Public, 1979; *The Sea Gull,* New York Shakespeare Festival, Public, 1980; *The Three Sisters,* 1981-82, *King Stag,* 1985, both at American Repertory Theatre, Cambridge, MA.

Opera: *Eugene Onegin,* Welsh National Opera, 1980; *Puritani, Norma,* Welsh National Opera, 1981; *The Magic Flute,* Paris Opera; *Turandot,* Royal Opera House, London; *Alcina,* New York City Opera; *Marriage of Figaro,* Guthrie, Minneapolis, MN.

ADDRESS: OFFICE—35 E. Tenth Street, New York, NY 10003.

*   *   *

SETRAKIAN, Ed   1928-

PERSONAL: Born October 1, 1928, in Jenkinjones WV; son of Samuel (a businessman) and Agnes (Notalian) Setrakian; children: Whitley Anne. EDUCATION: Concord College, Athens, WV, B.A., B.S.; New York University; studied acting with Lee Strasberg at the Actors Studio.

VOCATION: Actor and writer.

CAREER: NEW YORK DEBUT—Ramon, *Bullfight,* Theatre de Lys, 1953. PRINCIPAL STAGE APPEARANCES—Tom, *There Is No End,* off Broadway, 1957; Montano, *Othello,* New York Shakespeare Festival, 1964; Banquo, *Macbeth,* New York Shakespeare Festival, 1965; Claudius, *Hamlet,* New York Shakespeare Festival, 1969;

ED SETRAKIAN

Captain La Hire, *St. Joan,* Circle in the Square, 1976; Marcel, *Days in the Trees,* Circle in the Square, 1978; Raul, *Seduced,* American Place, 1979.

FILM DEBUT—Officier Belino, *Pursuit of Happiness,* 1968.

PRINCIPAL FILM APPEARANCES—*Three Days of the Condor,* 1972; construction boss, *Dragonfly,* 1975.

TELEVISION DEBUT—Barabbas, *Lamp Unto My Feet,* CBS, 1957. PRINCIPAL TELEVISION APPEARANCES—Recurring roles on many network daytime serials.

WRITINGS: PLAYS PRODUCED—*Mother Was Sober,* La MaMa, 1966; *Macdougal Street,* La MaMa, 1974; *Virility,* Actors Studio, 1974. SCREENPLAYS—*The Growth of Our Children* (documentary).

SIDELIGHTS: MEMBERSHIPS—Actors' Equity Association, Screen Actors Guild, American Federation of Television and Radio Artists, Actors Studio.

ADDRESS: HOME—414 W. 44th Street, New York, NY 10036. AGENT—Fifi Oscard Associates, 19 W. 44th Street, New York, NY 10036.

*   *   *

SHALLO, Karen

PERSONAL: Born in Philadelphia, PA; daughter of Andrew

KAREN SHALLO

Anthony (an artist) and Blanche Ruth (a government worker; maiden name, Walunas) Shallo. EDUCATION: Pennsylvainia State University, B.S., English and speech education, 1968, M.F.A., acting, 1975.

VOCATION: Actress.

CAREER: DEBUT—Monika, *The Physicists*, Pavilion. NEW YORK DEBUT—Laetitia, *Children of Darkness*, Greenwich Mews, 1973. PRINCIPAL STAGE APPEARANCES—Lady Macbeth, *Macbeth*, Arts Company Repertory, 1969-71; Velma, *Birdbath*, Actors Theatre of Louisville, 1970; Elizabeth, *The Crucible*, Arts Company Repertory, 1970; Mary Tyrone, *Long Days Journey into Night*, Studio Theatre, 1970; Mrs. Crowe, *Hadrian VII*, Alley, 1971-72; Madame Dubonnet, *The Boyfriend*, Clark Arts Center, 1971; Masha, *The Three Sisters*, Pavilion, 1971; Stella and Eunice, *A Streetcar Named Desire*, Pavilion, 1973; Luce, *Boys from Syracuse*, Washington Theatre Club, 1973; Doll Tearsheet, *Henry VI, Parts I and II*, Goodman, Chicago, 1974; multiple roles, *Scenes from American Life*, Washington Theatre Club, 1974.

Patsy, *Little Murders*, Pavilion, 1975; Olivia, *Twelfth Night*, Festival, Royal Shakespeare Company, 1975; Vicky, *My Fat Friend*, NY, 1975; Mrs. Malaprop, *The Rivals*, Festival, Royal Shakespeare Company, 1975; Clarisse, *When You Coming Home, Red Ryder?*, Cincinnati Playhouse in the Park, 1976; Ernesta, *Sacraments*, Theatre Off Park, NY, 1976; Madeleine, *Moliere in Spite of Himself*, Colonnades, NY, 1978-80; Rita, *Ballroom in St. Pat's Cathedral*, Colonnades, 1978-80; Martha, *Who's Afraid of Virginia Woolf*, Magus Theatre Centre, 1979; Maggie, *The Shadow Box*, Williamstown Theatre and Boston company, 1979; Valerie, *Carnival Dreams*, Promenade, NY, 1979; Gertrude, *The Sea Horse*, Stage West, 1980; Antonia, *We Won't Pay! We Won't Pay!*, Chelsea Theatre Centre, 1981; Josie, *Moon for the Misbegotten*, Stage West, 1981; Anastasia, *The Overcoat*, Westside Mainstage,

NY, 1981; Dionyza, *Pericles*, NY, 1982; Tina, *Raggedy Ann and Andy*, NY, 1983.

MAJOR TOURS—Standby, *My Fat Friend*, National Tour.

FILM DEBUT—Landlady, *Dana's Time*, Hornbein-Wood, 1970. PRINCIPAL FILM APPEARANCES—Mrs. Aiello, *Once Upon a Time in America*, Regency, 1983; Marlena, *Over the Brooklyn Bridge*, Cannon, 1983; Lina, *The Word Processor*, Laurel, 1984; Harriet, *Garbo Talks*, Metro-Goldwyn-Mayer/United Artists, 1984; Psychic, *Hannah and Her Sisters*, Orion, 1985.

TELEVISION DEBUT—Frosine, *The Miser*, PBS, 1970. PRINCIPAL TELEVISION APPEARANCES—Mrs. Alving, *Ghosts*, PBS, 1970; Wife, *Play*, PBS, 1970; Maggie Green, *The Burgher Family*, PBS, 1981; Louise Adams, *As the World Turns*, CBS, 1982-83; *Saturday Night Live*, NBC, 1984; *Another World*, NBC, 1984.

UPCOMING PROJECTS—*The Rose Tatoo*, Broadway, NY, 1985; Rosa, *About Face*, Off Broadway, NY, 1985-86; currently working on a screenplay.

SIDELIGHTS: MEMBERSHIPS—Actors' Equity Association, American Federation of Television and Radio Artists, Screen Actors Guild.

ADDRESS: AGENT—Bret Adams Ltd., 448 W. 44th Street, New York, NY 10036.

*   *   *

SHANGOLD, Joan

PERSONAL: Born March 28, in Albany, NY; daughter of Benjamin (a psychologist) and Helen (a teacher and writer of childrens textbooks; maiden name, Goldberg) Shangold. EDUCATION: Herbert Berghof Studios, NY.

VOCATION: Actress.

CAREER: STAGE DEBUT—Lady Mortimer/Francis, *Henry IV, Part I*, Croton Shakespeare Festival, Croton-on-Hudson. NEW YORK DEBUT—Betty Paris, *The Crucible*, Equity Library. PRINCIPAL STAGE APPEARANCES—Essie, *The Devil's Disciple*, Equity Library, NY; Moth, *Love's Labour's Lost*, Cherry Lane, NY; Peachblossom, *Under the Gaslight*, SoHo Repertory, NY; Jo, *Thirteen*, Stage Arts, ATA; Gerd, *Brand*, Impossible Ragtime Theatre, NY; Ruth, *Hey Rube*, Interart, NY; Debbie, *Ice*, WPA, NY; Buy, *The Good Woman of Setzuan*, Williamstown Theatre Festival, MA; Toby, *The Shanglers*, O'Neill Playwrights Conference, CT; Joe Egg, *Joe Egg*, Baltimore Center Stage; Christine, *Descendants*; Indiana Repertory Theatre; Lily Agnes, *Artichoke*, GeVa Theatre, A Contemporary Theatre; Monona, *Miss Lulu Bett*, Milwaukee Repertory Theatre; Fan/Martha, *A Christmas Carol*, Milwaukee Repertory; Fan/Ghost of Christmas Past, *Christmas Carol*, Puck, *A Midsummer Night's Dream*, both Alaska Repertory; Laura, *Courtship*, Actors Theatre of Louisville; Jo, *Thirteen*, A Contemporary Theatre.

FILM DEBUT—Policewoman Brady, *The Pope of Greenwich Village*. PRINCIPAL FILM APPEARANCES—The President of America's pencil girl, *American Tickler*.

TELEVISION DEBUT—Anne Turner, *Pity the Poor Soldier*, PBS.

JOAN SHANGOLD

SIDELIGHTS: MEMBERSHIPS—Actors' Equity Association, American Federation of Television and Radio Artists, Screen Actors Guild.

ADDRESS: HOME—New York, NY.

*   *   *

SHEEDY, Ally   1962-

BRIEF ENTRY: Born June 13, 1962; father is an advertising executive and her mother is writer, feminist, and New York literary agent, Charlotte Sheedy. At age seven, Sheedy danced with the American Ballet Theatre, and at age 12 she published a children's book, *She Was Nice to Mice.* She began acting in television commercials when she was fifteen, including ads for Burger King and Clearisil, and she has appeared on *Hill Street Blues,* NBC, as well as other shows. She is currently a senior at the University of Southern California, majoring in acting. In 1983, Sheedy performed in the play *The Majestic Kid,* in Denver, CO. Her first film role was in *Bad Boys,* Universal, 1983; she then co-starred in the movie *War Games,* Metro-Goldwyn-Mayer/United Artists, 1983. She appeared in the film *Oxford Blues* and was a member of the ensemble cast of *St. Elmo's Fire,* Columbia, 1985. Her next film, *Blue City,* is to be released in October 1985.*

MARTIN SHEEN

SHEEN, Martin   1940-

PERSONAL: Born Ramon Estevez, August 3, 1940, in Dayton, OH; son of Francisco and Mary Ann (Phelan) Estevez; married Janet, December 23, 1961; children: Emilio, Ramon, Carlos, Renee. EDUCATION: Graduated high school.

VOCATION: Actor.

CAREER: NEW YORK DEBUT—Ernie, *The Connection,* Living Theatre, 1959. PRINCIPAL STAGE APPEARANCES—Hyllos, *Women of Trachis,* third soldier, *Cavalry,* Living Theatre, NY, 1960; Horace, *Many Loves,* man with turned-up nose, *In the Jungle of Cities,* Living Theater, NY, 1961; Mike, *Never Live Over a Pretzel Factory,* Eugene O'Neill, NY, 1964; Timmy Cleary, *The Subject Was Roses,* Royale, NY, 1964; Vasco, *The Wicked Crooks,* Orpheum, 1967; Hamlet, *Hamlet,* Anspach, New York Shakespeare Festival, 1967; Romeo, *Romeo and Juliet,* Delacorte, New York Shakespeare Festival, 1968; Johnny, *Hello and Goodbye,* Sheridan Square Playhouse, NY, 1969; Reese, *The Happiness Cage,* The Other Stage, NY, 1970; Happy, *Death of a Salesman,* Circle in the Square, NY, 1975.

MAJOR TOUR—Timmy Cleary, *The Subject Was Roses,* national tour, 1965-66.

FILM DEBUT—*The Incident,* 1967. PRINCIPAL FILM APPEARANCES—Timmy, *The Subject Was Roses,* Metro-Goldwyn-Mayer, 1968; *Catch-22,* Paramount, 1970; *No Drums, No Bugles,* Cinerama, 1971; *Rage,* Warner Brothers, 1972; *Pickup on 101,* 1972; *Badlands,* Warner Brothers, 1974; *The Cassandra Crossing,* Avco-

Embassy, 1977; *The Little Girl Who Lived Down the Lane*, American-International, 1977; *Apocalypse Now*, United Artists, 1979; *Eagle's Wing* (British), 1979; *The Final Countdown*, United Artists, 1980; *Loophole* (British), 1980; *Gandhi*, Columbia, 1982; *That Championship Season*, Cannon, 1982; *Enigma*, Embassy, 1983; *Man, Woman and Child*, Paramount, 1983; *The Dead Zone*, Paramount, 1984; *Firestarter*, Universal, 1984.

PRINCIPAL TELEVISION APPEARANCES—Regular role, *As The World Turns;* television movies include: *Then Came Bronson*, 1969; *Mongo's Back in Town*, 1971; *Welcome Home, Johnny Bristol*, 1972; *That Certain Summer*, 1972; *Pursuit*, 1972; *Catholics*, 1973; *Message to My Daughter*, 1973; Slovik, *The Execution of Private Slovik*, 1974; Robert Kennedy, *The Missiles of October*, ABC, 1974; *The California Kid*, 1974; Floyd, *The Story of Pretty Boy Floyd*, 1974; *Sweet Hostage*, 1975; *The Last Survivors*, 1975; *Taxi!!*, 1978; John Dean, *Blind Ambition*, 1979; *The Long Road Home*, 1980; *In the Custody of Strangers;* 1982; *Choices of the Heart*, 1983; John F. Kennedy, *Kennedy*, NBC (mini-series), 1984; *The Atlanta Child Murders*, 1984; *The Guardian*, HBO, 1984; *Actors on Acting*, PBS, 1984; *The Fourth Man*, ABC, 1985; narrator, *Spaceflight*, PBS, 1985; *Consenting Adults*, ABC, 1985; Zigo, *Zigo's Choice*, CBS (upcoming).

Also: *Mannix, The Defenders, Medical Center, Route 66, East Side, West Side, My Three Sons, Mod Squad, Cannon, Columbo, Saturday Night Live*, others.

SIDELIGHTS: Sheen is chairman of Sheen/Greenblatt Productions, an entertainment company formed in 1983.

ADDRESS: HOME—Malibu, CA. AGENT—Kohner-Levy, 9169 Sunset Blvd., Los Angeles, CA 90069.

*   *   *

SHEPHERD, Cybil   1950-

BRIEF ENTRY: Born February 18, 1950, in Memphis, TN; daughter of William Jennings and Patty (Shobe) Shepherd; married David Ford, November 19, 1978. She was a student at Hunter College, 1969; College of New Rochelle, 1970; Washington Square College at New York University, 1971; University of Southern California, 1972; New York University, 1973. Shepherd's stage credits include: *A Shot in the Dark*, 1977; *Picnic*, 1980; *Vanities*, 1982. She was the star of the television series *The Yellow Rose*, 1983-84. Her films include *The Last Picture Show*, Columbia, 1971; *The Heartbreak Kid*, Twentieth Century-Fox, 1973; *Daisy Miller*, Paramount, 1974; *At Long Last Love*, Twentieth Century-Fox, 1975; *Taxi Driver*, Columbia, 1976; *Special Delivery*, American International, 1976; *Silver Bears*, Columbia, 1978; *The Lady Vanishes*, 1978, and *Earthright*, 1980. Her recordings include: *Cybil Does It to Cole Porter*, 1974; *Cybil and Stan Getz*, 1977; *Vanilla with Phineas Newborn Jr., 1978.**

*   *   *

SHERIDAN, Jamey   1951-

PERSONAL: Born July 12, 1951, in Pasadena, CA; son of Marvin Daniel (an actor and stuntman) and Josephine Suzanne (Hayes)

JAMEY SHERIDAN

Sheridan. EDUCATION: University of California, Santa Barbara, B.A. 1976.

VOCATION: Actor.

CAREER: STAGE DEBUT—Hoss, *Tooth of Crime*, Williamstown Theatre Festival (second company), MA, 1978. NEW YORK DEBUT—Spud, *Just a Little Bit Less Than Normal*, Manhattan Theatre Club, 1979. PRINCIPAL STAGE APPEARANCES—Chris, *The Arbor*, Manhattan Theatre Club, 1979; Gately, *Lone Star, Private Wars*, both Baltimore Center Stage, 1979; Mike, two Welsh one-acts, *Two Rooms*, Manhattan Theatre Club, 1980; Sandy, *The Man Who Came to Dinner*, Circle in the Square, NY, 1980; Hoagy, *Hoagy . . . Bix . . .*, Indiana Repertory Theatre, 1980; Fortinbras, *Hamlet*, New York Shakespeare Festival, Public, 1982; Jack, *Homesteaders*, Capitol Repertory Company, Albany, NY, 1983; Mark Antony, *Julius Caesar*, Alliance, Atlanta, GA, 1984.

TELEVISION DEBUT—George Wayne, "Mystery at Fire Island," *CBS Mystery Theatre*, 1980. PRINCIPAL TELEVISION APPEARANCES—Frankie Raimendo, *The Doctors*, NBC, 1981; La Becque, *Another World*, NBC, 1984; Webb Ettlee, *St Elsewhere*, NBC, 1984.

SIDELIGHTS: MEMBERSHIPS—Actors' Equity Association, Screen Actors Guild, American Federation of Television and Radio Artists.

ADDRESS: HOME—519 E. Fifth Street, New York, NY 10009. AGENT—Mary Sames, Leaverton-Sames, 1650 Broadway, New York, NY 10019.

SHERIN, Edwin   1930-

PERSONAL: Born January 15, 1930, in Harrisburg, PA; son of Joseph and Ruth (Berger) Sherin; married Pamela Vevers (divorced); married Jane Alexander (an actress). EDUCATION: Studied acting at Paul Mann's Actors Workshop and with John Houseman at the American Shakespeare Festival Academy. MILITARY: U.S. Navy, served in Korea, 1952-55.

VOCATION: Director and actor.

CAREER: STAGE DEBUT—Citizen, *Measure for Measure*, Phoenix, NY, 1957. PRINCIPAL STAGE APPEARANCES—Tybalt, *Romeo and Juliet*, Malcolm, *Macbeth*, Touchstone, *As You Like It*, Cassio, *Othello*, Sebastian, *Twelfth Night*, all New York Shakespeare Festival, Heckscher Theatre at Belvedere Lake, Central Park, 1957-58; understudy, *Miss Lonelyhearts*, Golden, NY, 1958; Philourgos, *Lysistrata*, Prince Hal, *Henry IV, Parts I and II*, Octavius, *Antony and Cleopatra*, Dr. *Willy-Nilly*, Phoenix Theatre Company, NY, 1959-60; Jonathan Spring, *Face of a Hero*, Eugene O'Neill, 1960; *Diff'rent*, Mermaid, 1961; Theodoric, *Romulus*, Music Box, NY, 1962.

FIRST STAGE WORK—Director, *Deirdre of the Sorrows*, Gate, NY, 1959. FIRST LONDON STAGE WORK—Director, *Find Your Way Home*, Piccadilly, 1974. PRINCIPAL STAGE WORK—Associate director, Arena Stage, Washington, DC, 1961-64; directed: *Joan of Lorraine, Mister Roberts, Galileo, St. Joan, The Inspector General, Billy Budd, The Andersonville Trial, Major Barbara, The Iceman Cometh, Serjeant Musgrave's Dance, The Lonesome Train, Hard Traveling, Project Immortality, The Great White Hope, King Lear*.

Look at Any Man, NY, 1963; *The White Rose and the Red*, NY, 1964; *The Great White Hope; Glory! Hallelujah!*, American Conservatory Theatre, San Francisco, CA, 1968; *Cosi Fan Tutte*, New York City Opera, 1971; *The Time of Your Life*, Washington, DC, 1971; *An Evening with Richard Nixon, Six Rms Riv Vu*, both 1972; *Major Barbara*, Stratford, CT, 1972; *Baba Goya; King Lear; Nourish the Beast*, 1973; *A Streetcar Named Desire; Of Mice and Men*, NY, 1974; *Red Devil Battery Sign*, Boston, 1975; *Sweet Bird of Youth*, Academy Festival Theatre, Lake Forest, IL, also Harkness Theatre, NY, 1975; *Rex*, NY, 1976; *The Eccentricities of a Nightingale*, 1976; *Do You Turn Somersaults; Semmelweiss*, Washington, DC, 1977; *First Monday in October*, 1978; *Losing Time*, 1979; *Goodbye Fidel*, 1980; *Showdown at the Adobe Motel, Hedda Gabler, Rocket to the Moon, Cantorial, Over My Dead Body, The Team*, as producing director, Hartman Theatre, Stamford, CT, 1980-85.

PRINCIPAL TELEVISION APPEARANCES—*Omnibus; Playhouse 90; Studio One; East Side West Side*.

PRINCIPAL TELEVISION WORK—Director: *Deirdre of the Sorrows; King Lear; An American Christmas in Words and Music*.

FIRST FILM WORK—Director, *Valdez Is Coming*, 1969. PRINCIPAL FILM WORK—Director, *My Old Man's Place*.

SIDELIGHTS: MEMBERSHIPS—Actors' Equity Association, American Federation of Television and Radio Artists, Society of Stage Directors and Choreographers.

ADDRESS: HOME—Gordon Road, RD2, Carmel, NY 10512.

SHERMAN, Guy   1958-

PERSONAL: Born January 6, 1958, in New York City; son of Eugene (a financial designer) and Josephine Ann (a dress designer; maiden name, Catenzaro) Sherman. EDUCATION: New York University, B.A., acting, 1979; studied acting at the Lee Strasberg Theatre Institute, and Actors and Directors Lab, NY.

VOCATION: Actor, sound designer, and musician.

CAREER: STAGE DEBUT—The Artful Dodger, *Oliver!*, Florham Park Players, NJ, 1974. NEW YORK DEBUT—Old man, *Bugs*, Harold Clurman Theatre, 1979. LONDON DEBUT—Actor, singer, musician, *The Bottom Line*, revue, 1983.

PRINCIPAL STAGE WORK—Sound designer: *Sister Mary Ignatius Explains It All for You/The Actors Nightmare*, Westside Arts, NY, Boston, San Francisco; *Greater Tuna*, NY; *The Foreigner*, NY; also at Manhattan Punchline and the WPA, NY.

WRITINGS: MUSIC/SONGS—For Stephanie Skura's *Survey of Styles* and *Artbusiness; Doctor Faustus; The Flying Boy*, Boston Childrens Theatre.

ADDRESS: HOME—267 E. Tenth Street, New York, NY 10009.

*   *   *

SHERMAN, Martin

PERSONAL: Born in Philadelphia, PA; son of Joseph T. (an attorney) and Julia (Shapiro) Sherman. EDUCATION: Boston University, B.A., theatre.

VOCATION: Playwright.

WRITINGS: PLAYS, PRODUCED/PUBLISHED—*Fat Tuesday, Next Year in Jerusalem*, Herbert Berghof Playwrights Foundation, NY, 1968; *The Night Before Paris*, published in *Best Short Plays of 1970*, Chilton Books, 1970; *Passing By*, Playwrights Horizons, NY, 1974, Almost Free Theatre, London, 1975, published in *Gay Plays*, Methuen, 1984; *Soaps*, Playwrights Horizons, NY, 1975; *Cracks*, Eugene O'Neill Theatre Center, CT, 1975, Theatre de Lys, NY, 1976, published, *Gay Plays: Volume Two*, Methuen, 1985; *Rio Grande*, Playwrights Horizons, NY, 1976; *Bent*, O'Neill Theatre Center, CT, 1978, Royal Court Theatre, London, 1979, New Amsterdam Theatre, NY, 1979, published Amber Lane Press, London, 1979, Avon, NY, 1980; *Messiah*, Hampstead Theatre, London, 1982, Manhattan Theatre Club, NY, 1984, published Amber Lane Press, London, 1982; *When She Danced*.

AWARDS: Hull-Warrner Award, 1979-80, for *Bent;* Antoinette Perry Award nomination, Best Play, 1980, for *Bent*.

SIDELIGHTS: MEMBERSHIPS—Writers Guild of America, Dramatists Guild.

ADDRESS: HOME—London, England. AGENT—Margaret Ramsay Ltd., 14A Goodwins Court, St. Martins Lane, London WC2, England; Johnnie Planko, William Morris Agency, 1350 Avenue of the Americas, New York, NY 10019.

SYLVIA SHORT

SHORT, Sylvia   1927-

PERSONAL: Born October 22, 1927, in Concord, MA; daughter of Seabury Tuttle (a sugar refiner) and Eleanor (Ballou) Short; married Fritz Weaver, February 7, 1953 (divorced, 1979); children: Lydia, Tony. EDUCATION: Smith College, B.A., 1949; New York University, Ph.D., marine biology, 1974; studied at the Old Vic Theatre School in London.

VOCATION: Actress.

CAREER: STAGE DEBUT—Portia, *The Merchant of Venice*, Barter, Abingdon, VA, 1952. NEW YORK DEBUT—Regan, *King Lear*, City Center, 1956. PRINCIPAL STAGE APPEARANCES—Martha Turner, *Hide and Seek*, Broadway production; standby, Mary, Dolly, *A Life*, Broadway production; standby, Mother, Mrs. Prynne, *Da*, Broadway production; Alicia, *After You've Gone*, NY; Nina, *Stay Where You Are*, NY; Martha, *The Broken Pitcher*, NY; *Milk of Paradise*, American Place, NY; *Just a Little Bit Less Than Normal*, Manhattan Theatre Club; *Nasty Rumours and Final Remarks*, New York Shakespeare Festival, Public, NY; *Says I, Says He* Phoenix, NY.

The Smile of the Cardboard Man, Herbert Berghof Studio, NY; *The Golden Apple*, NY; *The Passion of Gross*, NY; *The Clandestine Marriage*, NY; *Desire Caught by the Tail*, NY; *Chopin in Space*, Ark Theatre; Mother Superior, *Agnes of God*, Theatre by the Sea, Portsmouth, NH; *'84 Shorts*, Actors Theatre of Louisville; Lady Bracknell, *The Importance of Being Earnest*, Guthrie, Minneapolis, MN; Anna, the Pig Woman, *What I Did Last Summer*, Buffalo Studio Arena; Gertrude, *Hamlet*, Mistress Quickly, *Henry IV*, both

American Shakespeare Theatre, Stratford, CT; Lady Alice, *A Man for All Seasons*, Baltimore Center Stage.

PRINCIPAL FILM APPEARANCES—Head nurse, *Endless Love*; Psychiatrist, *The Firm*.

PRINCIPAL TELEVISION APPEARANCES—"Man and Superman," *Hallmark Hall of Fame; The Nurses; U.S. Steel Hour; Another World; Edge of Night; Texas; The Doctors; One Life to Live; All My Children; As the World Turns*.

RELATED CAREER—Teacher and director, Juilliard School Drama Division; reader, *Talking Books*, American Foundation for the Blind.

AWARDS: Fulbright Fellowship to the Old Vic Theatre School, 1949-51; Barter Theatre Award, 1952.

SIDELIGHTS: MEMBERSHIPS—Actors' Equity Association, Screen Actors Guild, American Federation of Television and Radio Artists.

ADDRESS: AGENT—Bret Adams, 448 W. 44th Street, New York, NY 10036.

*　　*　　*

SIEBERT, Charles   1938-

PERSONAL: Born March 9, 1938, in Kenosha, WI; son of Donald E. and Hannah (Rosenblum) Siebert; married Catherine Kilzer, September 8, 1962 (died, 1981); children: Christopher John, Charles Andrew, Gillian Masie. EDUCATION: Marquette University, B.A., speech, 1962; studied for the theatre at the London Academy of Music and Dramatic Art, 1963, and studied musical comedy with David Craig. MILITARY: U.S. Army Reserve, 1962.

VOCATION: Actor and director.

CAREER: STAGE DEBUT—The messenger, *The Bacchae*, London Academy of Music and Dramatic Art Experimental Theatre, London, England, 1963. NEW YORK DEBUT—Richmond, *Richard III*, New York Shakespeare Festival, Delacorte, 1964. PRINCIPAL STAGE APPEARANCES—Oedipus, *Oedipus Rex*, Morris Repertory, Morristown, NJ, 1965; Michael Dean, *Jimmy Shine*, Brooks Atkinson, NY, 1968; Lou Tannes, *The Gingerbread Lady*, Plymouth, NY, 1970; Walsh, *The Changing Room*, NY, 1972.

PRINCIPAL FILMS—*Blue Sunshine*, Cinema Shares, 1976; *The Other Side of Midnight*, Twentieth Century-Fox, 1977; *The Onion Field*, Avco-Embassy, 1979; *And Justice for All*, Columbia, 1979; *All Night Long*, Universal, 1981; *Troubled Times*.

TELEVISION DEBUT—*The Rockford Files*. PRINCIPAL TELEVISION APPEARANCES—Sgt. Cabe, *The Blue Knight*, CBS, 1976; Mr. Davenport, *One Day at a Time*, CBS, 1976-77; Dixon Carter Fielding, *Husbands, Wives & Lovers*, CBS, 1978; Dr. Riverside, *Trapper John, M.D.*, CBS, 1981-present.

SIDELIGHTS: MEMBERSHIPS—Actors' Equity Association, Screen Actors Guild, American Federation of Television and Radio Artists (board member), Directors Guild of America, Academy of Television Arts and Sciences (board member).

ADDRESS: OFFICE—c/o Taylor & Lieberman, 10960 Wilshire Blvd., Suite 908, Los Angeles, CA 90024. AGENT—Smith-Freedman, 123 San Vicente Blvd., Beverly Hills, CA 90211.

*   *   *

SILLIMAN, Maureen   1949-

PERSONAL: Born December 3, 1949; daughter of Russell James (an airline executive) and Eleanor Mathilda (Manzitti) Silliman; married Craig Carnelia (a composer and lyricist), March 8, 1969. EDUCATION: State University of New York at Geneseo; Hofstra University. RELIGION: Catholic.

VOCATION: Actress.

CAREER: STAGE DEBUT—Polly, *The Gingerbread Lady,* Huntington Hartford, Los Angeles, CA, 1971. NEW YORK DEBUT—Jenny, *Shenandoah,* Alvin, 1975. PRINCIPAL STAGE APPEARANCES— Homecoming Queen, *Is There Life After High School?,* Barrymore, NY; Katrin, *I Remember Mama,* Majestic, NY; Emily, *Blue Window,* Production Company, NY; *Notes,* Manhattan Theatre Club; Kathy, *Leaving Home,* Theatre of Riverside Church, NY; Nel, *One Wedding, Two Rooms, Three Friends,* Manhattan Theatre Club; Pooty, *Reckless,* Production Company, NY; Madeleine, *The Umbrellas of Cherbourg,* New York Shakespeare Festival, Public, NY; Terese, *Amerika,* Musical Theatre Lab, Kennedy Center, Washington, DC; Sophie, *Semmelweiss,* Kennedy Center, Washington, DC; Katherine, *A View from the Bridge,* Baltimore Center Stage; Nancy, *The Knack,* Baltimore Center Stage; Homecoming Queen, *Is There Life After High School?,* Hartford Stage Company;

MAUREEN SILLIMAN

Becky, *Hubba Hubba,* Goodspeed Opera House, East Haddam, CT. Stock: Tillie, *Man-in-the-Moon Marigolds;* Laurie, *New Mt. Olive Motel;* Alexandra, *The Little Foxes.*

PRINCIPAL TELEVISION APPEARANCES—*Sanctuary of Fear,* NBC, 1979; *Dixie: Changing Habits,* CBS, 1983; *Six Rms Riv Vu; The Andros Targets,* CBS; *The Guiding Light.*

AWARDS: New Jersy Drama Critics, Best Supporting Actress, *Man-in-the-Moon Marigolds;* Best Supporting Actress, *Umbrellas of Cherbourg.*

ADDRESS: AGENT—Triad Agency, 888 Seventh Avenue, New York, NY 10019.

*   *   *

SINGER, Lori

BRIEF ENTRY: Daughter of Jacques (a symphony orchestra conductor) Singer and his concert pianist wife. Actress. Singer began studying music at age six, and the cello at age nine. At thirteen she made her debut with the Oregon Symphony. In New York she studied with Leonard Rose at the Juilliard School of Music and won the Bergen Philharmonic Competition. During her studies at Juilliard she modelled, which lead to her television debut in the movie *Born Beautiful.* She also appeared in the NBC (now syndicated) series *Fame.* Her movies include *Footloose,* Paramount, 1984; *Falcon and the Snowman,* 1985, and *The Man with One Red Shoe,* Twentieth Century-Fox, 1985.*

*   *   *

SMALL, Neva

PERSONAL: Born November 17; daughter of Selden and Berma Small. EDUCATION: New York University, B.F.A.; Juilliard Drama School; studied with Wynn Handman and Tom Hageman in New York City.

VOCATION: Actress and singer.

CAREER: STAGE DEBUT—*Something More,* O'Neill, NY. PRINCIPAL STAGE APPEARANCES—*Ballad of Baby Doe,* New York City Opera; Chava, *Fiddler on the Roof; Henry Sweet Henry.*

MAJOR TOURS—*Blues in the Night,* East coast.

FILM DEBUT—Chava, *Fiddler on the Roof.* PRINCIPAL FILM APPEARANCES—*Looking Up.*

TELEVISION DEBUT—Hildy, *The Edge of Night.*

RELATED CAREER—Singer with Dizzy Gillespie, Larry Elgart; founder, Neva & Friends Puppet Theatre.

SIDELIGHTS: MEMBERSHIPS—Actors' Equity Association, American Federation of Television and Radio Artists, Screen Actors Guild.

ADDRESS: HOME—New York, NY.

SMALL, Robert Graham   1949-

PERSONAL: Born April 5, 1949, in Spokane, WA; son of Delbert F. (a doctor) and Rosemary (Kendall) Small; married Patricia Lines Shipman (divorced, 1976); married Kathleen Marie Tosco (a managing director and stage manager), May, 1981. EDUCATION: Washington State University, B.A.; Catholic University, M.F.A. POLITICS: Independent.

VOCATION: Manager, director, designer, dramaturg, and teacher.

CAREER: PRINCIPAL STAGE WORK—Production manager: *Strider: The Story of a Horse,* Chelsea Theatre Center, NY; *The Nutcracker Suite,* State University of New York at Purchase; Joyce Festival in Theatre, Dance & Film, State University of New York at Purchase; *Mecca,* Quaigh, NY; production stage manager, Roundhouse Theatre of Washington.

Director: *The Rivals,* Pullman's Summer Palace; *Hagar's Children, House of Bedlam,* both New Playwrights Theatre of Washington; *Mr. Wilson's Peace of Mind,* Quaigh Theatre, NY, and Yale Cabaret; *Houses on the Edge of Good Friday,* Quaigh, NY; *Who's Who in America,* O'Neill Second Step, CT; *A Few Good Men,* Veterans Ensemble Theatre; *Our Town, The Robber Bridegroom,* both New Youth Performing Theatre, Mt. Kisco, NY; *Caucasian Chalk Circle,* Fox Lane Little Theatre; *Lady House Blues,* Stage III, Williamstown, MA; *Fire at Luna Park,* O'Neill National Playwrights Conference, CT; *Hagar's Children,* New York Shakespeare Festival, Public, NY; *The Pond,* Wolf Trap Farm Park, Washington, DC and staged reading, Virginia Museum Theatre.

RELATED CAREER—Production stage manager, Roundhouse Theatre Company, Silver Spring, MD, 1974-75; associate artistic director, Quaigh Theatre, New York City, 1979-80; artistic coordinator and instructor, Yale Repertory Theatre and Yale School of Drama, New Haven, CT; artistic director, New Youth Performing Theatre, Mt. Kisco, NY, 1982-83; resident director and designer, ShenanArts, Staunton, VA, 1983-84; Co-founder, New Playwrights Theatre of Washington, DC.

AWARDS: Directing Fellowship, National Endowment for the Arts, 1980.

SIDELIGHTS: MEMBERSHIPS—Society of Stage Directors and Choreographers, Phi Kappa Phi, National Adjudicator for American College Theatre Festival, 1985.

ADDRESS: HOME—Pennyroyal Farm, Box 167 F, Rt. 5, Staunton, VA 24401.

*   *   *

SMITH, Anna Deavere   1950-

PERSONAL: Middle name pronounced "Duh-veer;" born September 18, 1950, in Baltimore, MD; daughter of Deavere Young (a retired coffee merchant) and Anna (an elementary school principal; maiden name, Young) Smith. EDUCATION: American Conservatory Theatre, San Francisco, M.F.A., 1970. RELIGION: Episcopalian.

VOCATION: Actor, director, and writer.

CAREER: DEBUT—The Savage, *Horatio,* American Conservatory

ANNA DEAVERE SMITH

Theatre, San Francisco, 1974. NEW YORK DEBUT—Marie Laveau, *Alma, the Ghost of Spring Street,* La MaMa, 1976, for twelve performances. PRINCIPAL STAGE APPEARANCES—Company, American Conservatory Theatre, San Francisco, CA, 1974-1976; company, *Mother Courage,* New York Shakespeare Festival, 1980; Doreen, *Tartuffe,* GEVA, Rochester, NY, 1983.

FILM DEBUT—Deborah, *Soup for One,* Warner Brothers, 1982.

TELEVISION DEBUT—Hazel, *All My Children,* ABC, 1983.

WRITINGS: PLAYS, PRODUCED—*On the Road,* Berkeley Rep, Berkeley, CA, 1983; *Aye, Aye, Aye, I'm Integrated,* American Place, NY, 1984; *A Birthday Card and Aunt Julia's Shoes,* one woman show. POETRY, PUBLISHED—With Hard Pressed and Labyris Press.

RELATED CAREER: Assistant professor of theatre, Carnegie Mellon, 1978-79; visiting artist, Yale, 1982; teacher of acting, New York University, 1983-84; visiting teacher, National Theatre Institute, 1984-85.

SIDELIGHTS: MEMBERSHIPS—Directors Guild of America, Dramatists Guild.

Commenting on her own works, Smith told *CTFT,* "I have developed *On the Road* in which I interview people, transcribe the interview and invite the subjects to see themselves performed by myself or other actors. I have developed this into a technique of teaching character to actors based on the linguistic idiosyncrasies of the character/subject.

"I've spent much of the last ten years developing techniques for teaching actors who are outer rather than inner inspired.

"I developed a one woman show, *A Birthday Card and Aunt Julia's Shoes*, which is a combination of original poetry and transcriptions of interviews of real people, the idea being that sometimes people speak their own poetry."

ADDRESS: HOME—349 Amsterdam Avenue, Apt. 4N, New York, NY 10024. AGENT—David Williams, International Creative Management, 40 W. 57th Street, New York, NY 10019.

* * *

SMITH, Derek David   1959-

PERSONAL: Born Derek Smith, December 4, 1959, in Seattle, WA; son of David Warren (a sales representative) and Shirley Yvonne (an interior designer; maiden name, Bakken) Smith. EDUCATION: University of Washington; Julliard, B.F.A., 1984.

VOCATION: Actor.

CAREER: PRINCIPAL STAGE APPEARANCES—As resident member of Juillard Theatre ensemble: Ben Hubbard, *Another Part of the Forest*, Moon, *Blood Wedding*, Hugo and Frederic, *Ring Round the Moon*, Theseus and Oberon, *A Midsummer Night's Dream*, Sganarelle, *The Flying Doctor*, Commandant, *To the Ninth Circle*, Stephan Undershaft, *Major Barbara*, Uncle Vanya, *Uncle Vanya*, Romeo, *Romeo and Juliet;* as resident member of the Acting Company, NY: Bernard, *Pieces of 8*, Fortune Teller, *The Skin of Our Teeth*, Wellborn, *A New Way to Pay Old Debts*, Orlando, *As You Like It*.

MAJOR TOURS—The Acting Company, 1984-85.

TELEVISION DEBUT—*Another World*, NBC, 1984. PRINCIPAL TELEVISION APPEARANCE—*Ryan's Hope*, ABC, 1984.

AWARDS: Richard Rogers Award; Leonard Bernstein's Felicia Montealegre Award; Outstanding Achievement from Julliard.

SIDELIGHTS: MEMBERSHIPS—Actors' Equity Association, American Federation of Television and Radio Artists.

ADDRESS: HOME—111 W. 95th Street, Apt. 1A, New York, NY 10025. AGENT—Abrams Artists Ltd., 420 Madison Avenue, New York, NY 10017.

* * *

SMITH, Jaclyn   1947-

PERSONAL: Born October 26, 1947, in Houston, TX; daughter of Jack and Margaret Ellen Smith; married Dennis Cole (divorced, 1981); married Tony Richmond, August 4, 1981; children: one. EDUCATION: Attended Trinity University.

VOCATION: Actress.

CAREER: PRINCIPAL TELEVISION APPEARANCES—Series: Kelly Garret, *Charlie's Angels*, ABC. Movies: *Escape from Bogen County*, 1977; *The Users*, 1978; *Rage of Angels*, 1980; *Nightkill*, 1980; *Jacqueline Bouvier Kennedy*, 1981; *The Night They Saved Christmas*, 1984; *Sentimental Journey*, CBS, 1984; *My Angry Son*, CBS; *The Nightengale Saga*, NBC, 1985. Miniseries: *George Washington*, 1984. Episodic: *Get Christy Love; McCloud; The Rookies; Love Boat; Switch; World of Disney*.

PRINCIPAL FILM APPEARANCES—*The Adventurers*, Paramount, 1970; *Bootleggers*, 1974; *Deja Vu*, 1984.

SIDELIGHTS: MEMBERSHIPS—American Federation of Television and Radio Artists.

ADDRESS: AGENT—International Creative Management, 40 W. 57th Street, New York, NY 10019.*

* * *

SMITHERS, William   1927-

PERSONAL: Born July 10, 1927, in Richmond, VA; son of Marion Wilkinson (a systems engineer) and Marion Albany (Thompson) Smithers; married Claire Heller, July 13, 1955 (divorced, 1960). EDUCATION: Attended Hampden-Sydney College, 1946-48; Catholic University, 1948-50. MILITARY: U.S. Navy, Seaman 1st Class, 1945-46.

VOCATION: Actor.

CAREER: STAGE DEBUT—Thomas Jefferson, *The Common Glory*, Williamsburg, VA, 1947. NEW YORK DEBUT—Tybalt, *Romeo and Juliet*, Broadhurst, 1951. LONDON DEBUT—David Beeston, *Man and Boy*, Queen's, 1963. PRINCIPAL STAGE APPEARANCES—Broadway: *Legend of Lovers*, 1951-52; *End as a Man*, 1954; *Square Root of Wonderful*, 1957; *Shadow of a Gunman*, 1958; *Man and Boy*, 1963. Off Broadway: Treplev, *The Sea Gull*, 1956; *Who'll Save the Plowboy*, 1962; *The Troublemakers*; Mecurtio, *Romeo and Juliet*, Demetrius, *A Midsummer Night's Dream*, Shakespeare Festival, Stratford, CT, 1959.

MAJOR TOURS—Tom, *The Glass Menagerie*, Doctor, *The Skin of Our Teeth*, Theatre Guild American Repertory Company, 1961.

FILM DEBUT—Lt. Harold Woodruff, *Attack!*, United Artists, 1958. PRINCIPAL FILM APPEARANCES—Police Captain, *Trouble Man*, Twentieth Century-Fox, 1972; Mitchell, *Scorpio*, United Artists, 1973; Commandant at maximum security prison, *Papillon*, Allied Artists, 1973; Professor, *Death Sport*, 1978.

PRINCIPAL TELEVISION APPEARANCES—Laertes, (Maurice Evan's) *Hamlet;* David Schuster, *Peyton Place*, 1965-66; Stanley Norris, *The Guiding Light*, 1970-71; Anderson Galt, *Executive Suite*, 1976; Jeremy Wendell, *Dallas*, 1981, 1984; *The Witness; The Name of the Game; Scarecrow and Mrs. King; Quincy; Julie Farr, M.D.; Lucan; Barnaby Jones; Hawkins; The Six-Million Dollar Man; Lawman; Most Wanted; Marcus Welby; Owen Marshall; Ironside; F.B.I.; Mission: Impossible; Mod Squad; Cade's Country; Star Trek; Judd for the Defense; Felony Squad; The Road West; The Invaders*. Television movies: *The Neon Ceiling*, 1970; *Brotherhood of the Bell*, 1970; *Doctors' Private Lives*, 1978; *The Return of Frank Cannon*, 1980; *Where the Ladies Go*, 1980.

WILLIAM SMITHERS

PEARL SOMNER

AWARDS: Theatre World, for Tybalt, *Romeo and Juliet*, 1951; Obie, Best Performance by an Actor in an Off Broadway Play, Treplev, *The Sea Gull*, 1956.

SIDELIGHTS: MEMBERSHIPS—Actors' Equity Association, American Federation of Television and Radio Artists, Screen Actors Guild, Actors Studio (since 1952).

ADDRESS: AGENT—Beakel & Jennings, 427 N. Canon Drive, Beverly Hills, CA 90210.

*　　*　　*

SOMNER, Pearl   1923-

PERSONAL: Born May 5, 1923. EDUCATION: Art Institute of Chicago; University of Illinois.

VOCATION: Costume designer.

CAREER: FIRST WORK—Commercial/industrial show, 1958. NEW YORK DEBUT—*The Summer of the Seventeenth Doll*, Coronet, 1958. PRINCIPAL STAGE WORK—Broadway: *The Ninety-Day Mistress*, 1967; *But, Seriously*, 1969; *Ulysses in Nighttown*, Winter Garden, 1974; *Shenandoah*, Broadway Theatre, 1974; *The Rocky Horror Show*, Belasco, 1975; *Herzl*, 1976; *The Trip Back Down*, 1977; *Back Country*, 1978; *Angel*, Minskoff, 1978; *Whose Life Is It Anyway?*, Trafalgar, 1979; *Last Licks*, 1979; *Whose Life Is It Anyway?* (Mary Tyler Moore company), Trafalgar, 1980; *The*

World of Sholom Aleichem, 1982; *84 Charing Cross Road*, Nederlander, 1982.

Off Broadway: *Guitar*, 1959; *Oh, Kay!*, 1960; *Billy No-Name*, Truck and Warehouse, 1970; *The Beauty Part*, American Place, 1974; *I'm Getting My Act Together . . . and Taking It on the Road*, Public, then Circle in the Square Downtown, 1978; *O'Neill and Carlotta*, Public, 1979.

Regional: *Room Service*, Theatre-of-the-Living-Arts, Philadelphia, 1966; *Shenadoah*, Wolftrap, VA, 1976; *Dance of Death, Long Day's Journey into Night, Candida*, Massachusetts Center Repertory, Shubert, Boston, MA, 1977; *Guilty Conscience*, Parker Playhouse, FL, 1980.

Europe: *Yankee Doodle Comes to Town*, England; artist-in-residence, *The Berliner Ensemble*, Berlin, East Germany.

MAJOR TOURS—Dance-drama of Henry IV, *The Making of a King*, college tour, 1972; *Shenandoah*, National Company, 1977; *Whose Life Is It Anyway?*, Florida, 1979, Detroit and Washington, DC, 1980, Los Angeles and San Francisco, 1980, Chicago and National Company, 1981.

PRINCIPAL FILM WORK—*The Cross and the Switchblade*, Ross Films, 1969; *Love Story*, Paramount, 1970; *To Avoid a Holocaust*, 1970.

PRINCIPAL TELEVISION WORK—*When Hell Freezes Over, I'll Skate*, WNET-TV, 1979. Also: commercials and industrials, including Westinghouse and Desilu, Hollywood, 1958-1973.

WRITINGS: ARTICLE—"Is Modern Dress a Happening?," *Theatre Crafts,* May/June, 1968 (reissued in *The Theatre Crafts Book of Costume,* as "Modern Dress is No *Accident,"* Rodale Press, 1973).

AWARDS: Best Costumes, Burns Mantle Theatre Yearbook, 1973-74.

SIDELIGHTS: MEMBERSHIPS—United Scenic Artists, Local 829.

ADDRESS: OFFICE—411 West End Avenue, New York, NY 10024.

* * *

SOREL, Theodore 1936-

PERSONAL: Accent on the second syllable of last name; born Theodore Eliopoulos, November 14, 1936, in San Francisco, CA; son of Vassily (a candy maker) and Maria (Piccoulas) Eliopoulos; married Jacqueline Coslow (an actress), December 20, 1964; children: Mariamne, Vassily. EDUCATION: College of the Pacific, B.A., 1958.

VOCATION: Actor.

CAREER: STAGE DEBUT—*The Tender Trap,* Fallon House, Columbia, CA. NEW YORK DEBUT—Sergius, *Arms and the Man,* Sheridan Square Playhouse, 1967. PRINCIPAL STAGE APPEARANCES—*Tartuffe, Death of a Salesman, Six Characters in Search of an Author,* A.C.T., San Francisco, 1967; *The Three Sisters, The*

THEODORE SOREL

Rivals, Once in a Lifetime, Seattle Repertory, 1968-69; *Little Murders, In the Matter of J. Robert Oppenheimer,* The Actors, 1970; *Much Ado About Nothing, A Winter's Tale, Cymbeline,* Old Globe, San Diego, CA, 1970.

Funny Girl, One Flew Over the Cuckoo's Nest, The Best Man, Atlanta, GA, 1973; Captain Crouch, *Sly Fox,* Broadhurst, NY, 1977; *Drinks Before Dinner,* Public, NY, 1979; *A View from the Bridge, Tartuffe, As to the Meaning,* Hartford Theatre, CT, 1979; *The Matchmaker, Flea in Her Ear,* Hartford Stage Company, CT, 1980; *Horowitz and Mrs. Washington,* Lyceum, NY, 1980; *Hedda Gabler,* Roundabout, NY, 1981; Swami, *A Call from the East,* Manhattan Theatre Club, NY, 1981; *The Burnt Flowerbed,* P.A.F. Playhouse, NY, 1981; *The Man Who Could See Through Time,* Yale Repertory, New Haven, CT, 1981; Sal, *A Little Family Business,* Martin Beck, NY, 1982.

Also: *As You Like It, Twelfth Night, King Lear, Julius Caesar,* and other plays, American Shakespeare Festival, Straford, CT, 1961, 1964, 1965, 1974, 1978, 1979.

MAJOR TOURS—American Conservatory Theatre, NY, Westport, CT, Stanford Summer Festival, Palo Alto, CA; Ravinia Festival, IL, 1966.

FILM DEBUT—*Jeremy,* 1973. PRINCIPAL FILM APPEARANCES—*Lenny,* United Artists, 1974; *Network,* United Artists, 1977; *The Killing Hour,* 1982; *Without a Trace,* Twentieth Century-Fox, 1983.

TELEVISION DEBUT—*Shakespeare Variations,* PBS, 1964. PRINCIPAL TELEVISION APPEARANCES—*The Franken Project,* NBC; *Sins of the Father,* NBC; *Riptide,* NBC, 1984; *Scarecrow and Mrs. King,* CBS; *Me and Mom,* ABC; *Fame; Cover Up,* CBS; *Ryan's Hope,* ABC; *As the World Turns,* CBS; *One Life to Live,* ABC; *Falcon Crest,* NBC; *Santa Barbara,* NBC; *General Hospital,* ABC; *Capitol,* CBS; *Dead Wrong,* PBC; *The Tempest, Anthony and Cleopatra,* PBS.

SIDELIGHTS: RECREATION—Sorel told *CTFT* that he spends his spare time restoring the house his grandfather built in the village of Kyparissi, Laconia, Greece, overlooking the Aegean Sea.

ADDRESS: AGENT—Bauman, Hiller, and Associates, 9220 Sunset Blvd., Los Angeles, CA 90069; Bauman, Hiller, and Associates, 250 W. 57th Street, New York, NY 10019.

* * *

SPEAR, David 1953-

PERSONAL: Born November 23, 1953, in Newark, NJ; son of Jack (a producer and director) and Phyllis (a musician and pianist; maiden name, Gomberg) Spear; married Daniele Baranz (a French teacher), May 4, 1980. EDUCATION: University of California, Los Angeles, B.A., music composition, 1975; studied film composition with David Raksin.

VOCATION: Composer, writer, conductor, and orchestrator.

CAREER: STAGE DEBUT—Music director and conductor, *Festival,* Las Palmas, Los Angeles, CA (and subsequent four month tour at

Ford Theatre, Washington, DC, City Center, NY). LONDON DEBUT—Composer and conductor, *Ballet Robotique*, Abbey Road Studio, Royal Philharmonic, 1982. PRINCIPAL STAGE WORK—Conductor and musical director: *Merlin*, Mark Hellinger, NY, 1983; *True Romances*, Mark Taper Lab Production, Los Angeles, CA; *The Sound of Music*, Dorothy Chandler Pavilion, Music Center, Los Angeles, CA.

Also: Music director, *BMI Musical Theatre Workshop*, Mark Taper Forum, Los Angeles, CA; resident music director, *American Academy of Dramatic Arts*, NY.

FILM DEBUT—Composer of source music, *Empire of the Ants*, American International, 1977. PRINCIPAL FILM WORK—Composer of source music, three songs, *Bloodbrothers*, Warner Brothers, 1979; source music, *The Great Santini*, Bing Crosby Productions, Warner Brothers, 1979; complete score, *Fear No Evil*, Avco-Embassy, 1981; *Ballet Robotique* (documentary), 1982; *Exterminator II*, Cannon, 1983; *The Royal Canadian Mounted Police*, Roger Tilton Films.

Orchestrator: *National Lampoon's Animal House*, Universal, 1978; *Bloodbrothers*, Warner Brothers, 1979; *Airplane!*, Paramount, 1980; *Heavy Metal*, Paramount, 1981; *Honky Tonk Freeway*, EMI, 1981; *Force Five*, Jerry Weintraub Productions, 1981; *An Officer and a Gentleman*, Paramount, 1982; *Ghostbusters*, Columbia, 1984. Also: *Misdeal; Mad Shadows* (ballet filmed by Canadian Broadcasting Company); *The Late Great Planet Earth*.

Composer, documentary and education films: *The Ceremony*, UCLA Film Department production; *Mr. Strowger and the Automatic Telephone*, General Telephone Productions; *Soap, Scents, and the Hard, Hard Sell*, Al Higgins Productions; *Let's Do Something for Ecology*, Producers Associates; *It All Goes By So Fast*, Producers Associates.

TELEVISION WORK—Score composer: *Moviola*, Warner Brothers; source music, *Alexander: The Other Side of Dawn*, NBC; *Delta House* (five episodes), Universal Television, ABC; *American Dream*, Universal Television; *The Optimist* (British series); *The Ratings Game*, Showtime; "Golden Honeymoon," *American Short Story*, PBS.

RECORDINGS: Cast album, *Festival*.

AWARDS: Henry Mancini Award, UCLA Music Department Annual Scholarship Award, First Place, 1974, for *Mr. Strowger and the Automatic Telephone*, and *Let's Do Something for Ecology;* Academy Award nomination, Best Documentary, 1982, for *Ballet Robotique*.

SIDELIGHTS: MEMBERSHIPS—American Federation of Musicians, Locals 47 and 802, American Society of Composers and Publishers.

Spear wrote to *CTFT*, saying, "I am deeply grateful to Elmer Bernstein who discovered' me and took me on as his orchestrator and music director."

ADDRESS: HOME—New York, NY. OFFICE—Producers Associates, 7243 Santa Monica Blvd., Hollywood, CA 90046. AGENT—John Hartman, Agency for the Performing Arts, 888 Seventh Avenue, New York, NY 10036; Lou Viola, Agency for the Performing Arts, 9000 Sunset Blvd., Suite 315, Los Angeles, CA 90069.

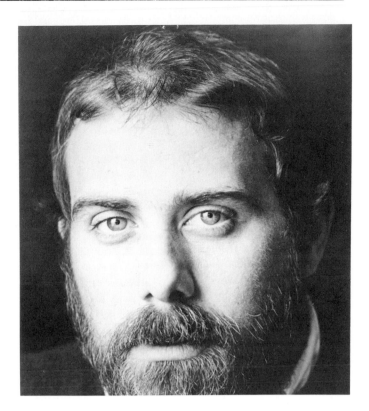

TOM SPILLER

SPILLER, Tom   1949-

PERSONAL: Born June 22, 1949, in Seattle, WA; son of John (an attorney) and Alyce (MacNamara) Spiller; married Tamara Brown (an actress), December 3, 1979. EDUCATION: University of Washington Professional Theatre Training Program, Seattle, B.A. 1973.

VOCATION: Actor.

CAREER: STAGE DEBUT—Fish, *The Resistable Rise of Arturo Ui*, A Contemporary Theatre, Seattle, WA, 1973. NEW YORK DEBUT—Corinthian messenger, *Oedipus*, Classic Stage Company, 1980. PRINCIPAL STAGE APPEARANCES—Von Strohiem, *Ride Across Lake Constance*, Bottom, *A Midsummer Night's Dream*, Crow, *Tooth of Crime*, 1974, Evans, *The Sea*, 1975, all Empty Space Theatre, Seattle, WA; Ralph, *Period of Adjustment*, Advent Theatre, Nashville, TN, 1979; Scroop, *Richard II*, Seattle Repertory Company; Mannion, *Mr. Roberts*, Pittsburgh Public Theatre; Troll King, *Peer Gynt*, Kent, *King Lear*, 1981, Danton, *Danton's Death*, 1983, all Classic Stage Company, NY; Simeon, *Desire Under the Elms*, Roundabout, NY, 1984; Agamemnon, *The Oresteia*, Classic Stage Company, NY, 1984; Stage Manager, *Our Town*, Theatre by the Grove; George Dandin, *George Dandin*, Classic Stage Company, NY, 1985.

SIDELIGHTS: MEMBERSHIPS—Actors' Equity Association, Screen Actors Guild.

Spiller performed as an acrobat and ringmaster with the *Big Apple Circus*, 1976.

ADDRESS: HOME—222 W. 71st Street, New York, NY 10023.

VICTOR SPINETTI

SPINETTI, Victor   1933-

PERSONAL: Born September 2, 1933, in Monmouthshire; son of Giuseppe and Lily (Watson) Spinetti. EDUCATION: Monmouth School; studied at the College of Music and Drama, Cardiff.

VOCATION: Actor and director.

CAREER: STAGE DEBUT—A concert party in Wales, 1953. LONDON DEBUT—A revue, Irving Theatre, 1956. NEW YORK DEBUT—IRA Officier, *The Hostage,* Cort, 1960. PRINCIPAL STAGE APPEARANCES—(All London unless otherwise indicated) Leon, *Fleet Street Editor,* Saville, 1958; Psychiatrist, Parson, Head Waiter, *Expresso Bongo,* Saville, 1958; First Inquistor, Marquis Mileton, *Candide,* Saville, 1959; Sweeting, *Make Me an Offer,* Theatre Royal, Stratford East, then New Theatre, 1959; Brain-Worm, *Every Man in His Humour,* Theatre Royal, Stratford East, 1960; Tosher, *Fings Ain't Wot They Used T'Be,* Theatre Royal, Stratford East, 1963; Drill Sergeant Major, *Oh, What a Lovely War!,* Theatre Royal, Stratford East, then Wyndham's Theatre, 1963; Eartha, *Merry Roosters Panto,* Theatre Royal, Stratford East, 1963.

Glendower, Poins, *Henry IV,* Edinburgh Festival, 1964; Drill Sergeant Major, *Oh, What a Lovely War!,* Broadhurst, NY, 1964; Roger Summerhill, *Skyscraper,* Fisher Auditorium, Detroit, MI, 1965; M Cheri, *La Grosse Valise,* 54th Street, NY, 1965; Felix Unger, *The Odd Couple,* Queen's, 1966; General Irrigua, *Cat Among the Pigeons,* Prince of Wales, 1969; Braham, *The Philanthropist,* Barrymore, NY, 1971; Banquo, *Macbeth,* Bankside Globe, 1973; Samuel Sleary, *Hard Times,* Belgrade, Coventry, 1973; Wizard, Sheriff of Nottingham, *Emu in Pantoland,* Shaftes-

bury, 1976; King Rat, *Dick Wittington and His Wonderful Cat,* Palladium, London, 1980; in his one man show, Edinburgh Festival, 1984.

PRINCIPAL STAGE WORK—Directed: *In His Own Write* (also co-adaptor with John Lennon), National Theatre at the Old Vic, 1968; *Shirley Abicair's Evening,* Arts, 1969; *The Bed,* Royalty, 1970; assisted in production, *Cocky,* 1970; foreign productions of *Hair,* 1970; *Jesus Christ Superstar,* TNP, Paris, 1972; *Off the Peg,* 1974; *Let's Get Laid,* Windmill, 1974; *Deja Revue,* New London, 1974; *Come into My Bed,* Whitehall, 1976; *Don't Bother to Dress,* 1977; *Yes We Have No Pyjamas,* 1979.

PRINCIPAL FILM APPEARANCES—*Help!; The Taming of the Shrew; Under Milk Wood; The Return of the Pink Panther; Voyage of the Damned.*

PRINCIPAL TELEVISION APPEARANCES—*Take My Wife; The Sea; Victor Spinetti Chat Show,* BBC.

AWARDS: Antoinette Perry Award, 1964, for Drill Sergeant Major, *Oh, What a Lovely War!*

ADDRESS: AGENT—Howes & Prior, 66 Berkley House, Hay Hill, London W1, England.

*   *   *

SPRINGFIELD, Rick

BRIEF ENTRY: Born in Sydney, Australia. Singer and actor. Springfield's father was an Australian army career officer. The family moved to England for a brief period at which time Rick joined a group called Jordy Boys and began his musical career. Later he joined a 1950's revival type group and began entertaining in Vietnam. Back in Australia, he joined in with Zoot, which soon became Australia's number one band. In the U.S. he has gone solo and his single *Jessie's Girl* won him a Grammy for Best Male Rock Vocal. On American television he has been seen in *The Six Million Dollar Man; Wonder Woman; California Fever; The Rockford Files;* and *The Incredible Hulk.* He is best known to television audiences for his portrayal of Dr. Noah Drake on the daytime drama *General Hospital,* ABC. He was the star of the film *Hard to Hold,* Universal, 1984.*

*   *   *

SQUIBB, June   1935-

PERSONAL: Born November 6, 1935, in Vandalia, IL; daughter of Louis C. (owned an insurance company) and Joybelle M. (Force) Squibb; married Edward Soster (divorced); married Charles Kakatsakis (an acting teacher); children: (second marriage) Harry. EDUCATION: Studied acting in NY with Robert Lewis, Ken McMillan, and Charles Kakatsakis.

VOCATION: Actress.

CAREER: STAGE DEBUT—Physical education major, *Goodbye My Fancy,* Cleveland Playhouse. NEW YORK DEBUT—Ardis, *Sabie Brush,* Royal, 1956. PRINCIPAL STAGE APPEARANCES—Electra,

JUNE SQUIBB

ARNOLD STANG

Gypsy, Imperial, NY; Mary Rosemarsh, *Gorey Stories,* Booth, NY; Giselle, *The Workroom,* South Street Theatre, NY; Hazel, *Blues for Mr. Charlie,* Amistad Theatre; Mom, Nurse Buchanan, *Funeral March for a One Man Band,* Westbeth; a gypsy, *The Forced Marriage,* South Street Theatre, NY; Mrs. Cooke, *Castaways,* Promenade, NY; Mrs. Salt, laughing lady, Mrs. Moe, *Museum,* Folger, Washington, DC; Mrs. Webb, *Our Town,* Giselle, *The Workroom,* Denise, *Bonjour La Bonjour,* all Baltimore Center Stage; *Sitting and Saving Grace,* Buffalo Studio Arena; Titania, *A Midsummer Night's Dream,* Abigail, *The Crucible,* Ismene, *Antigone,* all Cleveland Playhouse.

MAJOR TOURS—Parthy, *Showboat,* Indianapolis Starlite, Atlantic Civic, St. Louis Municipal Opera; Mrs. Puffy, *The Streets of New York,* Westport Country Playhouse, Laconia, Denver; Helen, *Ballroom,* St. Louis Municipal Opera, Indianapolis, Kansas City Starlite, Tulsa, Atlantic Civic.

PRINCIPAL TELEVISION APPEARANCES—*Search for Tomorrow; The Guiding Light; As the World Turns;* "The Day the Senior Class Got Married," *CBS After School Special.*

PRINCIPAL CLUB APPEARANCES—Upstairs at the Downstairs; Madeira Club, Provincetown, MA; Duplex, NY; various cruise ships.

SIDELIGHTS: MEMBERSHIPS—Actors' Equity Association, Screen Actors Guild.

ADDRESS: AGENT—Henderson-Hogan Agency, 405 W. 44th Street, New York, NY 10036.

STANG, Arnold   1925-

PERSONAL: Born September 28, 1925, in Chelsea, MA; son of Harold L. (an attorney) and Anna (Chest) Stang; married JoAnne Taggart (a writer), September 21, 1949; children: David Donald, Deborah Jane.

VOCATION: Actor, director, and writer.

CAREER: DEBUT—*Horn and Hardart Children's Hour,* NBC (radio), 1934 (at age 9). PRINCIPAL STAGE APPEARANCES—Broadway: Sailor, *Beware; Wallflower,* 1944; *Wedding Breakfast,* 1954; *The Front Page,* Palace, 1969; Hysterium, *A Funny Thing Happened on the Way to the Forum,* 1972; *All in Favor; Same Time Next Week.*

Also, roles in *No Time for Sergeants; Wish You Were Here; The Gazebo; Will Success Spoil Rock Hunter?; Say, Darling; Annie Get Your Gun; Three Men on a Horse; Tobacco Road; Charley's Aunt; The Odd Couple; Rodgers & Hammerstein's Cinderella; Last of the Red Hot Lovers; Play It Again, Sam; You Know I Can't Hear You When the Water's Running; Let 'em Eat Cake,* and others.

FILM APPEARANCES—*Seven Days Leave,* RKO-Radio, 1942; *My Sister Eileen,* Columbia, 1942; *They Got Me Covered,* Goldwyn, 1943; *So This Is New York,* United Artists, 1948; *The Man with the Golden Arm,* United Artists, 1955; *Dondi,* American-International, 1961; *Alakazam the Great,* American-International, 1961; *The Wonderful World of the Brothers Grimm,* Metro-Goldwyn-Mayer, 1962; *It's a Mad, Mad, Mad, Mad World,* United Artists, 1963;

Pinocchio in Outer Space, Universal-International, 1964; *Skidoo,* 1968; *Hello, Down There,* Paramount, 1969.

The Aristocats, Buena-Vista, 1970; *The Gang That Couldn't Shoot Straight,* Metro-Goldwyn-Mayer, 1971; *Raggedy Ann and Andy, a Musical Adventure,* Twentieth Century-Fox, 1977; also: *Hercules in New York; Return of Marco Polo; Spirit of '76; That's Life; We Go Pogo;* over thirty two short films including: *Arnold the Benedict,* Universal; "The Expectant Father," from the *This Is America* series, Warner Brothers, and others.

RADIO APPEARANCES—*Let's Pretend,* CBS, beginning 1934; Seymour Fingerhood, *The Goldbergs,* Blue Network; Gerard, *The Henry Morgan Show,* WOR (for seven years); Joey Brewster, *That Brewster Boy,* NBC (was the second of three to play the role); *The Milton Berle Show,* NBC.

TELEVISION DEBUT—Francis, the badgering stagehand, *The Milton Berle Show,* NBC, 1948, 1953-55. PRINCIPAL TELEVISION APPEARANCES—Regular, *School House,* with Kenny Delmar, Dumont, 1949; regular, *Henry Morgan's Great Talent Hour,* NBC, 1951; Winfield Dell, *Doc Corkle,* NBC, 1952; Top Cat, *Top Cat* (animated), ABC, 1961-62; Ship's Cook First Class Stanley Stubbs, *Broadside,* ABC, 1964-65; also appeared on *Ed Sullivan Show; Hallmark Playhouse; The Jackie Gleason Show; U.S. Steel Hour; Alcoa Presents; Playhouse 90; December Bride; The Jack Benny Show; Batman; Chico and the Man; Love, American Style; The Red Skelton Show; Superjaws & Catfish;* others.

RECORDINGS—*Peter and the Wolf* (with the NY Philharmonic), ABC-Paramount; *Ferdinand the Bull* (with the NY Philharmonic), ABC-Paramount; *Arnold Stang Meets Gus Edwards,* MGM; *Alice in Wonderland,* Disney-RCA; *Winnie the Pooh, Winnie and Baby Rooh,* RCA; *Lots of Luck, Charlie, Where Ya Callin' From, Charlie?,* MGM; *Arnold Stang's Favorite Animal Stories, Arnold Stang's Wonderful World of Comedy,* Peter Pan; *Ivy Will Cling,* MGM; *The Elephant Who Forgot, Percy the Polite Seal, The Clock That Went Tock-Tick, The Happy Hippo,* Coral; *The Front Page,* Theatre Guild; *Chester the Chimp,* Mattel; *Harry the Horse, Further Adventures of Harry the Horse, Beezy the Sneezy Bee, The Car That Couldn't Say Goodbye, Custard the Dragon, Custard the Dragon & the Wicked Knight,* Columbia.

SIDELIGHTS: MEMBERSHIPS—Players Club, Actors Studio.

Stang tells *CTFT* that "his favorite medium is the one he is working in at [that] moment. [He] believes his calm relaxed attitude is a reflection of his unique position on most shows. I am usually called in on a guest star basis. I've worked with practically every star in the business, and I've had all the excitement without any of the crushing responsibilities. The applause that comes at the end of his show means only one thing to the star . . . that it's time to start worrying about next week's show. But I just take a bow, walk off, wash up, and go home.'''

ADDRESS: HOME—P.O. Box 786, New Canaan, CT 06840. OFFICE—349 E. 52nd Street, first floor, New York, NY 10022.

*   *   *

STEINBERG, Roy   1951-

PERSONAL: Born March 24, 1951, in New York City; son of Sy (a salesman) and Flora Joyce (a teacher; maiden name, Matthews)

Steinberg; married Marlena Lustik (an actress), September 8, 1984. EDUCATION: Tufts, B.A., 1973; Yale School of Drama, M.F.A., 1978; studied acting with Michael Howard. POLITICS: Democrat. RELIGION: Jewish.

VOCATION: Actor and director.

CAREER: NEW YORK DEBUT—The Doctor, *Wings,* Lyceum, 1979, 192 performances. LONDON DEBUT—Peachum, *The Beggar's Opera,* Chanticleer at Webber-Douglas School, 1971, three performances. PRINCIPAL STAGE APPEARANCES—Johansson, *The Ghost Sonata,* Yale Repertory, New Haven, CT, 1979; Wilson, *Terra Nova,* Santa Fe Festival, NM, 1982; Ben Sakhov, *Zeks,* Theatre for the New City, NY, 1983. Also: Merchant, *Twilight Crane,* Theatre of the Open Eye, NY; Biedermann, *Firebugs,* John Cocteau Repertory Co., NY; Jack Roots, *After the Rise,* Astor Place, NY; Mumbles, *Our Father,* Colonnades, NY; Krizovec, *In Agony,* Marymount Manhattan Theatre, NY; Lysander, *A Midsummer Night's Dream,* Bouwerie Lane, NY.

Amundsson, *Terra Nova,* Cassius, *Julius Caesar,* Guest, *White Marriage,* Surkkala, *Puntilia,* Friar Peter, *Measure for Measure,* all at Yale Repertory, New Haven, CT; Macbeth, *Macbeth,* Andrew Undershaft, *Major Barbara,* Francisco Pizzaro, *The Royal Hunt of the Sun,* all at Tufts University as Equity guest artist; Lear, *King Lear,* Robert Scott, *Terra Nova,* Canon Chausable, *The Importance of Being Earnest,* Boris Kolenkov, *You Can't Take It with You,* all at Berea College, KY, as Equity guest artist.

MAJOR TOURS—Skelly, *The Rimers of Eldritch,* International Drama Festival, Ireland and subsequent tour of the British Isles, 1972; The Doctor, *Wings,* national tour, 1979; Ben Silverman, *The Sunshine Boys,* Prather Productions tour; Crouch, *Not Now Darling,* Prather Productions tour; Osric and Player King, *Hamlet,* National Shakespeare Company tour.

FILM DEBUT—Taxi hailer, *Manhattan,* United Artists, 1979. PRINCIPAL FILM APPEARANCES—*Going in Style,* Warner Brothers, 1979; *Willie and Phil,* Twentieth Century-Fox, 1980; *Hero at Large,* United Artists, 1980.

TELEVISION DEBUT—Eliezar, *The Wall,* CBS, 1980. PRINCIPAL TELEVISION APPEARANCES—Ticket seller, *As the World Turns,* CBS, 1983; the director, *Private Eye;* Phil, *No Alternative; One Life to Live,* ABC; *Camera Three,* CBS; *Ryan's Hope,* ABC.

RELATED CAREER—Acting teacher, Tufts University, 1978-79, School of Visual Arts, NY, 1983, Berea College, KY, 1983, Lehmann College, Bronx, NY, 1984, University of Rochester, NY, 1984.

AWARDS: Carol Dye Acting Award, Yale School of Drama, 1978.

SIDELIGHTS: MEMBERSHIPS—Actors' Equity Association, Screen Actors Guild, American Federation of Television and Radio Artists, American Theatre Association, Circle Repertory Directors Lab (1983-84), American Place Directors and Dramaturgs Workshop (1983-84). RECREATION: Travel and food.

"My work is a constant education of the world, of myself, and the relationships in the world," Steinberg told *CTFT.*

ADDRESS: HOME—25 Grove Street, New York, NY 10014. AGENT—Bob Tuschman, Lionel Larner, Ltd., 850 Seventh Avenue, New York, NY 10019.

CLARK STERLING

STERLING, Clark   1956-

PERSONAL: Born December 13, 1956, in San Diego, CA; son of George Creighton (a manufacturers representative) and Virginia (a teacher; maiden name, Soper) Sterling. EDUCATION: Stanford University, B.A., political science; studied in Oxford, England, through the Yale School of Drama, and with the American Conservatory Theatre in San Francisco, and the Los Angeles Civic Light Opera training program. RELIGION: Christian.

VOCATION: Actor and singer.

CAREER: STAGE DEBUT—Dancer and singer, *All American College Show*, Walt Disney World, Orlando, FL, 1977. NEW YORK DEBUT—Joel, *Seven Brides for Seven Brothers*, Alvin, 1982. PRINCIPAL STAGE APPEARANCES—Lysander, *A Midsummer Night's Dream*, American Conservatory Theatre Congress; Cliff, *I Am a Camera*, Night Flight Theatre, Los Angeles; Julio, *Paint Your Wagon*, T.U.T.S., Houston, TX; Sebastian, *Twelfth Night*, Morse Center, NY; Bill, *Skyline*, A.T.A., NY; Clark, *Tallulah*, Westside Arts, NY.

MAJOR TOUR—Joel, *Seven Brides for Seven Brothers*, pre-Broadway.

PRINCIPAL TELEVISION APPEARANCE—*Another World*.

PRINCIPAL FILM APPEARANCE—*1941*, Universal/Columbia, 1979.

SIDELIGHTS: MEMBERSHIPS—Actors' Equity Association, Screen Actors Guild, American Federation of Television and Radio Artists, Habitat for Humanity volunteer, vice president, Stanford Club of New York and New Jersey.

ADDRESS: AGENT—Honey Sanders Agency Ltd. 229 W. 42nd Street, New York, NY 10036.

*   *   *

STERN, Daniel

BRIEF ENTRY: Actor. Stern's debut was with the Shakespeare Festival in Washington. He performed in *The Old Glory*, American Playhouse, NY and *Apparitions*, NY. He was first seen on television in *Vegetable Soup*. His films include *Breaking Away*, United Artists, 1979; *A Small Circle of Friends*, United Artists, 1980; *One Trick Pony*, Warner Brothers, 1980; *Diner*, Metro-Goldwyn-Mayer, 1982; *Key Exchange*, 1985, and *Hannah and Her Sisters*, Orion (upcoming).*

*   *   *

STERNHAGEN, Frances   1930-

PERSONAL: Born January 13, 1930, in Washington, DC; daughter of John Meyer and Gertrude (Hussey) Sternhagen; married Thomas A. Carlin; children: six. EDUCATION: Vassar College Drama Department, Perry-Mansfield School of Theatre; studied acting with Sanford Meisner at the Neighborhood Playhouse in NY.

VOCATION: Actress.

CAREER: STAGE DEBUT—Laura, *The Glass Menagerie*, Mrs. Manningham, *Angel Street*, Bryn Mawr Summer Theatre, PA, 1948. NEW YORK DEBUT—Eva, *Thieves Carnival*, Cherry Lane, 1955. LONDON DEBUT—*The War at Home*, Hempstead, 1985. PRINCIPAL STAGE APPEARANCES—At Arena Stage Washington, DC, 1953-54: Margery Pinchwife, *The Country Wife*, Mrs. Webb, *Our Town*, Nancy Stoddard, *The Country Girl*, Phyllis Carmichael, *My Heart's in the Highlands*, Juliette, *Thieves Carnival*, Doto, *A Phoenix Too Frequent*, Ma Kirby, *The Happy Journey from Trenton to Camden*, Muriel, *Ah! Wilderness*, Elvira, *Blithe Spirit;* at the Olney Theatre, MD, 1954 season: Lavina Chamberlayne, *The Cocktail Party*, Ann, *Outward Bound*, Georgie Elgin, *The Country Girl*, Lady Ariadne Utterword, *Heartbreak House*.

Miss T Muse, *The Skin of Our Teeth*, Sarah Bernhardt Theatre, Paris, France, 1955, then ANTA, NY, 1955; Widow Yang, *The Carefree Tree*, Phoenix, NY, 1955; Lydia Carew, *The Admirable Bashville*, Cherry Lane, NY, 1956; Margery Pinchwife, *The Country Wife*, Renata, 1957; Nymph, *Ulysses in Night Town*, Rooftop, 1958; title role, *The Saintliness of Margery Kempe*, York, 1959; Dee Jones, *Viva Madison Avenue!*, Longacre, NY, 1960; Selma Chargesse, *Red Eye of Love*, Provincetown Playhouse, NY, 1960; Gwendolyn, *The Importance of Being Earnest*, McCarter Theatre, Princeton, NJ, 1960; Hypatia, *Misalliance*, Sheridan Square, NY, 1961; Alice McAnany, *Great Day in the Morning*, Henry Miller's, NY, 1962; Mrs. Levi, *The Matchmaker*, Olney, MD, 1962; Sabina, *The Skin of Our Teeth*, Brandeis, MA, 1963; Lois, *A Matter of Like Life and Death*, East End, NY, 1963; Jan, *Play*, Cherry Lane, NY, 1964; Rose, *The Room*, Flora, *A Slight Ache*, both Writers Stage, NY, 1964; Mrs. Ashton Dilke, *The Right Honourable Gentleman*, Billy Rose, NY, 1965; Mrs. Hopewell, *The Displaced Person*, St. Clements Church, NY, 1966.

Lavinia Chamberlayne, *The Cocktail Party,* Jan Loreleen, *Cock-a-Doodle Dandy,* both APA Phoenix, Lyceum, NY, 1968; Widow Quinn, *Playboy of the Western World,* Vivian Beaumont, NY, 1971; Mavis Parodus Bryson, ·*The Sign in Sidney Brustein's Window,* Longacre, NY, 1972; Paulina, *Enemies,* Vivian Beaumont, NY, 1972; various roles, *The Good Doctor,* Eugene O'Neill, NY, 1973; Dora Strang, *Equus,* Plymouth, NY, 1974; Eliza Gant, *Angel,* Minskoff, NY, 1978; Ethel Thayer, *On Golden Pond,* New Apollo, Century, NY, 1979; *The Prevalence of Mrs. Seal,* Manhattan Punchline, 1980; *The Father,* Circle in the Square, NY, 1981; *The Dining Room,* Kennedy Center, Washington, DC, 1981; *Grownups,* Lyceum, NY, 1982; *Summer,* Manhattan Theatre Club, 1982; Miss Prisim, *The Importance of Being Earnest,* John Drew Theatre, East Hampton, NY, 1983; Penny, *You Can't Take It with You,* Royale, NY, 1984; *Laughing Stock,* Manhattan Punchline, 1984; *Home Front,* Royale, NY, 1985; *The Return of Herbert Bracewill,* Chelsea Playhouse, NY, 1985.

MAJOR TOURS—Miss T Muse, *The Skin of Our Teeth,* national tour, 1955; Opal, *The Isle of Cipango,* Postmistress, *Pound on Demand,* national tour, 1958; Miss Madrigal, *The Chalk Garden,* national tour, 1960.

FILM DEBUT—*Up the Down Staircase,* 1967. PRINCIPAL FILM APPEARANCES—*The Tiger Makes Out,* 1970; *The Hospital,* 1971; *Two People,* 1973; *Fedora,* 1977; *Starting Over,* 1979; *Outland,* 1981; *Independence Day,* 1982; *Romantic Comedy,* 1983.

PRINCIPAL TELEVISION APPEARANCES—Toni, *Love of Life,* 1968; Phyllis Corrigan, *Doctors,* 1970; *Who'll Save Our Children,* 1978; *Prototype,* 1983; *Under One Roof,* 1985.

AWARDS: Clarence Derwent Award; Obie awards; Antoinette Perry Award, 1973, for *The Good Doctor.*

SIDELIGHTS: MEMBERSHIPS—Actors' Equity Association, Screen Actors Guild, American Federation of Television and Radio Artists.

FAVORITE ROLES—Margery Pinchwife, Sabina, Dora in *Equus,* Ethel, *On Golden Pond.* RECREATIONS—Caring for her six children, singing, painting.

Sternhagen was a teacher at Milton Academy, MA.

ADDRESS: HOME—New Rochelle, NY. AGENT—Triad Agency, 888 Seventh Avenue, New York, NY 10019.

*   *   *

STEVENS, K.T.   1919-

PERSONAL: Born Gloria Wood, July 20, 1919, in Los Angeles, CA; daughter of Sam (a film director) and Clara (Roush) Wood; married Hugh Marlow (an actor), 1946 (divorced, 1967); children: Jeffrey Wood, Chris. EDUCATION: University of Southern California; trained for the theatre for two years.

VOCATION: Actress.

PERSONAL: DEBUT—Alice, *You Can't Take It with You,* road company. NEW YORK DEBUT—Walk-on role, *Summer Night.* PRINCIPAL STAGE APPEARANCES—*Nine Girls,* NY, 1944; Sally,

The Voice of the Turtle, Selwyn, NY, 1944-46; Laura, *Laura,* Chicago and NY, 1947; Sylvia, *The Tender Trap,* Chicago and NY, 1955.

The Land Is Bright; The Man Who Came to Dinner; My Sister Eileen; Yankee Point; Rebecca; Amphytrion 38; Who Was That Lady I Saw You With; The Mousetrap; The Women; Bell, Book, and Candle; Time Limit; Once More, with Feeling; The Best Man; Janus; Critics Choice; And Perhaps Happiness; Invitation to a March; Kind Sir; Saint Joan.

FILM DEBUT—*Peck's Bad Boy,* Fox, 1934. PRINCIPAL FILM APPEARANCES—*Navy, Blue, and Gold,* Metro-Goldwyn-Mayer, 1937; Molly, *Kitty Foyle,* RKO-Radio, 1940 (as Katherine Stevens); *The Great Man's Lady,* Paramount, 1942; *Address Unknown,* Columbia, 1944; *Port of New York,* Eagle Lion Classics, 1949; *Harriet Craig,* Columbia, 1950; *Vice Squad,* United Artists, 1953; *Tumbleweed,* Universal, 1953; *Missle to the Moon,* Astor, 1959; *Bob & Carol & Ted & Alice,* Columbia, 1969.

PRINCIPAL TELEVISION APPEARANCES—*Schlitz Playhouse,* CBS; *Cross-Roads,* ABC; *Thriller,* NBC; *Lux Video Theatre,* CBS and NBC; *I Love Lucy; Wagon Train; The Real McCoys; Rifleman; The Patty Duke Show; Bronk; Matinee Theatre; The Millionaire; Mannix; Panic; Manhunt; Divorce Court; Buck Rodgers; Alfred Hitchcock Presents; State Trooper; The Big Valley; Line-up; The Brothers Brannagan; Adam-12; Little House on the Prairie; M-Squad; The Perry Mason Show; Marcus Welby, M.D.*

Also: The Young and the Restless; Paradise Bay; Days of Our Lives; General Hospital.

SIDELIGHTS: MEMBERSHIPS—Actors' Equity Association, American Federation of Television and Radio Artists (vice president, local), Screen Actors Guild.

ADDRESS: AGENT—Lew Sherrell Agency, 7060 Hollywood Blvd., Suite 610, Hollywood, CA 90028.

*   *   *

STEVENS, Leslie   1964-

PERSONAL: Born August 10, 1964, in Elmhurst, IL; daughter of James William (a real estate broker) and Carole Janice (a real estate broker; maiden name, Fetz) Stevens. EDUCATION: Parkway Central Senior High School, Chesterfield, MO.

VOCATION: Actress and dancer.

CAREER: STAGE DEBUT—Greta and chorus, *Carnival,* St. Louis Municipal Opera, St. Louis, MO, 1980. NEW YORK DEBUT—Anne, *La Cage aux Folles,* Palace, 1983. PRINCIPAL STAGE APPEARANCES—Neapolitan and soloist, *Swan Lake,* Missouri Concert Ballet, Powell Hall, St. Louis, 1981; flower girl, *Robert and Elizabeth,* Papermill, Milburn, NJ, 1982.

MAJOR TOURS—Chorus, *Sugar Babies,* Sally Rand tour, March to July, 1982, National Tour (Eddie Bracken company), 1982; girl in pink tights, *A Chorus Line,* 1984.

TELEVISION DEBUT—Justine Calvert, *Search for Tomorrow,* NBC, 1984.

LESLIE STEVENS

LARRY STEWART

SIDELIGHTS: MEMBERSHIPS—Actors' Equity Association, Screen Actors Guild, American Guild of Variety Artists, New Dramatists, American Cancer Society, UNICEF.

ADDRESS: AGENT—Richard Rosenwald, 250 W. 57th Street, Suite 722, New York, NY 10107.

*   *   *

STEWART, Larry J.   1951-

PERSONAL: Born November 10, 1951, in Little Rock, AR; son of Reverend Frank James and Oia Faye (a teacher; maiden name, McTyer) Stewart; children: Shawn Darnell Michael. EDUCATION: Attended Texas Southern University, Houston, TX; studied with Earle Hyman at the Herbert Berghof Studio, NY.

VOCATION: Actor, dancer, and singer.

CAREER: NEW YORK DEBUT—Larry, *It's So Nice to Be Civilized,* Martin Beck, 1980. PRINCIPAL STAGE APPEARANCES—Preacher, *Jam,* off Broadway production; Preacher, *Dunbar,* off Broadway production; multiple standby roles, *Dreamgirls,* Imperial, NY, 1981-85.

MAJOR TOURS—Papa Du, *One Mo' Time,* national tour, 1980; MC, Mr. Morgan, *Dreamgirls,* national tour, 1981.

FILM DEBUT—Singer, *The Cotton Club,* 1984.

TELEVISION DEBUT—*All My Children,* ABC.

SIDELIGHTS: MEMBERSHIPS—Actors' Equity Association, Screen Actors Guild, American Federation of Television and Radio Artists.

ADDRESS: HOME—243 W. 99th Street, New York, NY 10025.

*   *   *

STING   1951-

BRIEF ENTRY: Born Gordon Matthew Sumner, 1951, in Newcastle-upon-Tyne, England. Actor and singer. He was educated at Warwick University. After graduation, he began teaching nine year olds in a small mining village in Northumberland. His musical career began when he met Stewart Copeland and Andy Summer and they formed the new-wave British rock band *The Police.* Their first record, *Roxanne,* sold thirty million records since 1979, and their album *Synchronicity* has received four Grammies. His first film role was as a homosexual who called Sex Pistol singer Johnny Rotten "a faggot." The role was later cut from the film, but it got him a role as a maruding, street-fighting, "Ace Face" in The Who's *Quadrophenia.* Subsequent roles were as a gas station attendant obsessed with 1950's rock singer Eddie Cochran in *Radio On;* an angel in *Artemus 81,* for the BBC; as Martin in *Brimstone and Treacle,* 1982; as Feyd-Rautha in *Dune,* 1984; in *The Bride,* Columbia, 1985; and in the upcoming film version of *Plenty.* He also appeared in the concert films, *The Secret Policeman's Other Ball,* 1982; *Urgh! A Music War,* and *The Police—Synchronicity Concert Film.* Sting was a featured performer in the recent "Live Aid" benefit at Wimbley Stadium, London, 1985, and is selling out arenas across the U.S. on his 1985 solo tour. His nickname comes from a black and yellow striped sweater he always wore.*

STORCH, Arthur   1925-

PERSONAL: Born June 29, 1925, in Brooklyn, NY; son of Sam and Bessie (Goldner) Storch; married Virginia Kiser (divorced); married Cynthia Martin; children: Max, Alex. EDUCATION: Brooklyn College; New School for Social Research, B.A., 1949; studied with Lee Strasberg at the Actors Studio in NY.

VOCATION: Actor and director.

CAREER: STAGE DEBUT—Stock production, Deertrees, ME, 1951. NEW YORK DEBUT—Maurice Maynall Simmons, *End as a Man*, Theatre de Lys, then Vanderbilt, 1953. PRINCIPAL STAGE APPEARANCES—Lt. Mike Livingston, *Time Limit!*, Booth, NY, 1956; Gene Mitchell, *Girls of Summer*, Longacre, NY, 1956; Luke Gant, *Look Homeward, Angel*, Barrymore, NY, 1957; Businessman, *Night Circus*, Golden, NY, 1958; Mr. McWilliams, *The Long Dream*, Ambassador, NY, 1960; Emmett, *The Enemy Is Dead*, Bijou, NY, 1973.

FIRST STAGE WORK—Director, *Two by Saroyan*, East End, NY, 1961. FIRST LONDON WORK—Director, *Talking to You* and *Across the Board on Tomorrow Morning*, Duke of York's, 1962. PRINCIPAL STAGE WORK—Director: *The Typists* and *The Tiger*, 1963; *The Owl and the Pussycat*, 1964; *The Impossible Years*, 1965; *Under the Weather*, 1966; *Golden Rainbow*, *Waiting for Godot*, Charles Playhouse, Boston, MA, 1968; *The Local Stigmatic*, *The Rose Tattoo*, Hartford, CT, 1969; *Hunger and Thrist*, Berkshire Theatre Festival, 1969; *The Chinese, Dr. Fish, Hay Fever*, Seattle Repertory Theatre, 1970; *The Gingerbread Lady*, Buffalo Studio Arena, 1971; *Promenade All!*, 1972; *The Milliken Breakfast Show*, 1972; *42 Seconds form Broadway*, 1973; *Tribute*, 1978.

As producing and artistic director, Syracuse Stage, NY: *Waiting for Lefty, Noon, Of Mice and Men*, 1973-74; *La Ronde, The Butterfingers Angel*, 1974-75; *Morning's at Seven, Dynamo*, 1975-76; *A Quality of Mercy, The Seagull*, 1976-77; *Love Letters on Blue Paper, The End of the Beginning*, 1977-78; *The Butterfingers Angel, Loved*, 1978-79; *Naked*, 1979-80; *Old World, Twice Around the Park* (transferred to the Cort, NY), *A Christmas Carol, The Impromptu of Outremont, Cyrano de Bergerac, Arms and the Man, Clarence, Handy Dandy*, all 1980-85.

FILM DEBUT—*The Strange One*, 1957. PRINCIPAL FILM APPEARANCES—*The Mugger; Girl of the Night; The Exorcist*.

TELEVISION APPEARANCES—*Sharon: Portrait of a Mistress*.

PRINCIPAL TELEVISION WORK—Director: *Harry Belafonte Special; 100 Years of Laughter;* "George Washington Crossing the Delaware," "The Exhaustion of Our Son's Love," both presented by *Robert Brustein Theatre; Calucci's Department*.

RELATED CAREER—Teacher, Stella Adler Studio, NY, 1962-64; teacher in the playwriting unit, actors unit, and directors unit, Actors Studio, NY, 1963-present; appointed producing and artistic director, Syracuse Stage Company, NY; chairman, Syracuse University Drama Department, 1973.

AWARDS: Shubert Chair in Theatre, Syracuse University, 1977.

SIDELIGHTS: MEMBERSHIPS—Actors Studio, Society of Stage Directors and Choreographers.

ADDRESS: OFFICE—Syracuse Stage, 820 Genesee Street, Syracuse, NY 13210.

JERRY STRICKLER

STRICKLER, Jerry   1939-

PERSONAL: Born December 4, 1939, in Goose Creek, TX; son of Bill and Lucille Strickler; divorced. EDUCATION: Southwestern University; studied for the theater at the American Theatre Wing with Herbert Machiz; served an apprenticeship at the Alley Theatre in Houston, TX.

VOCATION: Actor and writer.

CAREER: STAGE DEBUT—*Bye Bye Birdie*, national company. NEW YORK DEBUT—Larry Henderson, *Mr. President*, St. James, 1962. PRINCIPAL STAGE APPEARANCES—*Love and Kisses*, NY; *Venus Is*, NY; *Rate of Exchange*, Players, NY; *Daffodils and Daisies*, La MaMa, NY; *Harvey*, Windmill Dinner Theatre, Houston, TX; *6 Rms Riv Vu, The Tender Trap*, both Barn Dinner Theatre, Albuquerque, NM; *Wait Until Dark*, Corning Summer Theatre, Corning, NY; *How to Succeed in Business without Really Trying*, Roanoke, VA; *Oklahoma!, 110 in the Shade, Mr. President*, all Kansas City Starlight; *Mr. President*, St. Louis Municipal Opera, St. Louis, MO; *Tender Loving Care*, Coconut Grove Playhouse, Miami, FL; *Wizard of Oz*, Alley, Houston, TX.

MAJOR TOURS—*The Sound of Music*, Cape Cod Circuit; *Make a Million*, national company; *Mr. President*, national company.

FILM APPEARANCE—*The House of Seven Corpses*, 1973.

PRINCIPAL TELEVISION APPEARANCES—*Police Story; Cannon; Mannix; The Magician; Mod Squad; Night Gallery; The Smith Family; San Francisco International; Lancer; The New People; The Defenders; Patty Duke Show; The Edge of Night; Love of Life;*

Amateur's Guide to Love.

WRITINGS: PLAY—*The Alamo Family.*

ADDRESS: HOME—444 Hudson Street, New York, NY 10014.

*   *   *

STROUD, Don   1943-

PERSONAL: Born September 1, 1943, in Honolulu, HI; son of Claude (a comedian, member of the "Stroud Twins") and Ann (a blues singer; maiden name, McCormack) Stroud; married Linda Hayes (a flight attendant), September 11, 1982.

VOCATION: Actor.

CAREER: FILM DEBUT—*Games,* Universal, 1967. PRINCIPAL FILM APPEARANCES—*Madigan,* Universal, 1968; *What's So Bad About Feeling Good?* Universal, 1968; *Coogan's Bluff,* Universal, 1968; *Bloody Mama,* American International, 1970; *Explosion,* American International, 1970; *. . . Tick . . . Tick . . . Tick,* Metro-Goldwyn-Mayer, 1970; *Von Richthofen and Brown,* United Artists, 1971; *Joe Kidd,* Universal, 1972; *Scalawag,* Paramount, 1973; *The Killer Inside Me,* 1976; *The Choirboys,* Universal, 1977; *The House by the Lake,* American International, 1977; *The Buddy Holly Story,* Columbia, 1978; *The Amityville Horror,* American International, 1979; *The Night the Lights Went Out in Georgia,* AVCO Embassy, 1981; *Search and Destroy,* 1981 (filmed in 1978,

DON STROUD

released in 1981); *Striking Back; Sweet Sixteen,* Aquarius Films Releasing, 1984.

TELEVISION DEBUT—Surfing stand-in for Troy Donahue, *Hawaiian Eye,* ABC, 1962-63. PRINCIPAL TELEVISION APPEARANCES—*Hawaii Five-0,* CBS; *Trapper John, M.D.,* CBS; *Matt Houston,* ABC; *The A-Team,* NBC; *Knots Landing,* CBS; *Knight Rider,* NBC; *The Fall Guy,* ABC; *Fantasy Island,* ABC; Captain Pat Chambers, *Mickey Spillane's Mike Hammer,* CBS, 1984; and over one hundred more.

SIDELIGHTS: RECREATION—Surfing, playing bongo drums, sailing, traveling.

According to his press release, "at nineteen, Stroud was the fourth-ranked surfer in the world. He had a black belt in karate while still in his teens and played bongos with many native Hawaiian musical groups. He worked as a towel boy at the Kahala Hilton, as a Waikiki beach lifeguard, and as a surf boarding and catamaran sailing instructor. He parked cars at Scandia, in Los Angeles and was the doorman, later manager, for Whiskey-a-Go-Go."

ADDRESS: HOME—Bel Air, CA; Santa Barbara, CA; Hawaii. OFFICE—The Garrett Co., 6922 Hollywood Blvd., Los Angeles, CA 90028. AGENT—Abbey Gressler, 9200 Sunset Blvd., Suite 909, Los Angeles, CA 90069.

*   *   *

STRUTHERS, Sally Anne   1948-

PERSONAL: Born July 28, 1948, in Portland, OR; daughter of Robert Alden and Margaret Caroline (Jernes) Struthers. EDUCATION: Trained for the stage at the Pasadena Playhouse.

VOCATION: Actress.

CAREER: PRINCIPAL TELEVISION APPEARANCES—Series: Gloria, *All in the Family,* CBS, 1971-78; Gloria, *Gloria,* CBS, 1982-83. Specials: *Summer Brothers Smothers Show; The Tim Conway Comedy Hour.* Movies: *Aloha Means Goodbye,* 1974; *Hey, I'm Alive,* 1975; *The Great Houdinis,* 1976; *Intimate Strangers,* 1977; *And Your Name Is Jonah,* 1978; *A Gun in the House,* 1980.

PRINCIPAL FILM APPEARANCES—*The Sphynx,* Warner Brothers, 1970; *Five Easy Pieces,* Columbia, 1970; *The Getaway,* National General, 1972; *Charlotte,* Gamma III, 1975.

PRINCIPAL STAGE APPEARANCES—Florence, *The Odd Couple,* Broadhurst, NY, 1985.

ADDRESS: AGENT—Segal-Goldman, 9348 Santa Monica Blvd., Beverly Hills, CA 90210.*

*   *   *

SULLIVAN, Susan

PERSONAL: Born November 18, in New York City; daughter of Brendan and Helen (Rockett) Sullivan. EDUCATION: Hofstra

SUSAN SULLIVAN

University, B.A., theatre and psychology, 1966; studied at the American Academy of Dramatic Arts, NY.

VOCATION: Actress.

CAREER: STAGE DEBUT—As a member of resident company, Cleveland Playhouse, 1966-68, *Mary, Mary; Macbeth.* NEW YORK DEBUT—Elizabeth, *Jimmy Shine,* Broadway production, 1968. PRINCIPAL STAGE APPEARANCES—*The Beauty Part,* American Place, NY, 1974; *She Stoops to Conquer,* National Repertory Theatre Company, Ford's, Washington, DC; *The Fifth of July,* Mark Taper Forum, LA, 1979; *Last Summer at Blue Fish Cove,* Theatre-on-the-Square, San Francisco, CA, 1983.

TELEVISION DEBUT—Three Shakespeare plays for WNET, NY, 1968. PRINCIPAL TELEVISION APPEARANCES—*A World Apart,* ABC; *Another World,* NBC, four years; *S.W.A.T.; Kojak; Taxi; Medical Center;* Maggie Porter, *Rich Man, Poor Man,* ABC; title role, *Julie Farr M.D.* ABC, 1978-79; *The Incredible Hulk,* CBS, 1978; *It's a Living,* ABC, 1981; Maggie Gioberti, *Falcon Crest.* Movies: *Midway,* 1976; *The Comedy Company,* CBS, 1977; Julie Farr, *Having Babies II,* 1977, then *Having Babies III,* 1978; *The New Maverick,* ABC, 1978; *Panic on Page One,* ABC, 1979; *The Ordeal of Dr. Mudd,* 1980; *Marriage Is Alive and Well,* 1980.

AWARDS: Emmy Award nominations, *Rich Man, Poor Man, Julie Farr, M.D.;* fellowship, Cleveland Playhouse.

SIDELIGHTS: MEMBERSHIPS—Actors' Equity Association, Screen Actors Guild, American Federation of Television and Radio Artists, National Hospice Organization, Women in Film Association, Muscular Dystrophy Association (vice president, 1983-84).

RECREATIONS—Literature, travel, music, skiing, analyzing her friends, and collecting art.

ADDRESS: AGENT—S.T.E. Representation Ltd., 211 S. Beverly Drive, Beverly Hills, CA 90212.

*　　　*　　　*

SULLIVAN, Tom   1947-

PERSONAL: Born March 27, 1947, in Boston, MA; son of Thomas J. (a saloon owner) and Marie C. (Kelly) Sullivan; married Patricia M. Steffen, May 17, 1969; children: Blythe, Thomas J. III. EDUCATION: Providence College, RI, 1965-67; Harvard University, B.S., clinical psychology, 1969. POLITICS: Republican. RELIGION: Catholic.

VOCATION: Singer, actor, writer, and composer.

CAREER: PRINCIPAL FILM APPEARANCES—Singer of the National Anthem, *Black Sunday,* 1976; *Airport '77,* 1977.

PRINCIPAL TELEVISION APPEARANCES—*Love's Dark Ride,* 1978; *M*A*S*H,* 1978; special correspondent, *Good Morning America,* ABC, 1979-81; *Mork & Mindy,* 1981; *Fame,* 1980-81; *WKRP in Cincinnati,* 1982; *Search for Tomorrow; Mike Douglas Show, Dinah Shore Show, Merv Griffin Show, The Tonight Show Starring Johnny Carson.*

TOM SULLIVAN

PRINCIPAL CONCERT APPEARANCES—Opening act for Liza Min-neli, Las Vegas, NV, 1976; toured Japan with Shirley Bassey, 1976; opening act for Helen Reddy, Las Vegas, NV, 1978; opening act for Don Rickles, Las Vegas, NV, 1980; performed National Anthem at Super Bowl X.

WRITINGS: BOOKS—*If You Could See What I Hear* (with Derek Gill; autobiography), Harper & Row, 1976, released as a motion picture, 1982; *Adventures in Darkness* (young adult version of *If You Could See What I Hear*), Ideals Publishing, 1976; *You Are Special*, Ideals Publishing, 1981; *Common Senses* (children's book), Ideals Publishing, 1982. SONGS/MUSIC—For the film version of his autobiography, *If You Could See What I Hear*.

AWARDS: Most Outstanding Performance, Yamaha Music Festi-val, Tokyo, Japan, 1976; Fellowship Award, California Museum Foundation, 1978; Americana Award, Cyprus College, CA, 1981; Los Angeles Bicentennial Salute, Los Angeles Human Relations Commission, 1981; honorary doctor of humane letters, D'Youville College, Buffalo, NY, 1983; CIL'S Man on the Move award, San Francisco, CA 1983.

SIDELIGHTS: MEMBERSHIPS—American Federation of Television and Radio Artists, Screen Actors Guild, American Society of Composers, Authors, and Publishers, Boston Musicians Associa-tion, Braille Institute (board of directors), Famous People Players, Up with People, Blind Children's Center, Los Angeles, CA (development committee), Muscular Dystrophy Association (vice president), NCAH Artists Committee, Torrance Memorial Hospital (board of trustees), Sunshine Kids Winter Games (honorary chairman).

Sullivan told *CTFT*, "Handicaps are inconveniences, and everyone has one. I believe that disadvantages can be turned into advantages. Because of my blindness since birth, I am frequently asked to speak motivationally and have been doing so extensively for the last two years."

ADDRESS: OFFICE—P.O. Box 7000-117, Redondo Beach, CA 90277. AGENT—Jack Rose Agency, 6430 Sunset Blvd., Suite 1203, Hollywood, CA 90028.

*   *   *

SUNDE, Karen   1942-

PERSONAL: Born July 18, 1942, in Wausau, WI; daughter of John E. (a retail manager) and B. Marie (Schoen) Sunde; children: John, Paul. EDUCATION: Iowa State University, B.S., English and speech, 1963; Kansas State University, M.A., dramatic literature, 1965.

VOCATION: Director, actress, and writer.

CAREER: STAGE DEBUT—Helena, *A Midsummer Night's Dream*, New Shakespeare Company, San Francisco, 1967. NEW YORK STAGE DEBUT—Artist, *Portrait of the Artist*, Playbox, 1970; with the CSC Repertory Comapny, NY: Alice, *Dance of Death*, Lotte, *Big and Little/Scenes*, Ranevskaya, *The Cherry Orchard*, Mother Aase, *Peer Gynt I/II*, Jocasta, Antigone, *Oedipus Cycle*, Portia, *The Merchant of Venice*, Madwoman, *The Madwoman of Chaillot*, Irma, *The Balcony*, Ruth, *The Homecoming*, Hesione, *Heartbreak House*, Celestina, *La Celestina*, Hedda, *Hedda Gabler*, Antigone, Anouilh's *Antigone*, Isabel, *Measure for Measure;* created and performed, *Poems from Finland*, New York and Minneapolis;

KAREN SUNDE

Photography by Gerry Goodstein

performed for the Circle Repertory Company's playwright's work-shop, McCarter Theatre staged readings program, at the Colorado Shakespeare Festival, and the Arrow Rock Lyceum Theatre.

PRINCIPAL STAGE WORK—Director: *Balloon, Leonice and Lena*, both CSC Repertory; *Exit the King, Philoctetes*, both Jean Cocteau Repertory Theatre; co-director, *Ghost Sonata*, CSC Repertory.

TELEVISION DEBUT—Mary Brewster, *Mayflower*, CBS, 1979.

PRINCIPAL FILM APPEARANCE—Narrator, *Image Before My Eyes*, 1981.

RELATED CAREER—Associate director, actress, playwright, CSC Repertory, 1971-85.

WRITINGS: PLAYS PRODUCED/PUBLISHED—Radio play, *The Sound of Sand*, Iowa State University Players, 1963; *Day Before Noon*, NY, 1970; *The Running of the Deer*, CSC Repertory Theatre, 1978; *D'Eon* (libretto for Andrew Thomas); *Philoctetes* (transla-tion), Jean Cocteau Repertory, 1983; *Balloon*, workshop, 1980, CSC Repertory, 1983, published by Broadway Play Publishing, 1983; *Dark Lady*, Requested-Jeu de Lumiere, Avignon. TELE-PLAY—*Deborah: The Adventures of a Soldier*, O'Neill Center.

AWARDS: Bob Hope Award, 1963, for *The Sound of Sand;* Outer Critic's Circle Award nomination, Villager Award, 1983, for *Balloon;* grants from the Scandinavian Foundation Finnish Litera-ture Center.

SIDELIGHTS: MEMBERSHIPS—Actors' Equity Association, Screen Actors Guild, New Jersey State Council on the Arts (theatre panel).

ADDRESS: HOME—New York, NY. AGENT—Michael Imison, 28 Almeida Street, London N1, England.

SYDOW, Jack 1921-

PERSONAL: Full name John David Sydow; born October 7, 1921, in Rockford, IL; son of John David (a corporate executive and photo engraver) and Ida Beulah (Hoover) Sydow. EDUCATION: University of Illinois, B.S., 1947; Yale University School of Drama, M.F.A., 1950. MILITARY: U.S. Army Air Force, 1942-45.

VOCATION: Director, actor, playwright, and teacher.

CAREER: FIRST STAGE WORK—Co-director, *Hump Happy,* a revue, Air Transport Command, Bamboo Music Hall, Chabua, India, 1943. PRINCIPAL STAGE WORK—Director: *Ladies in Retirement,* Little Theatre, Rockford, IL, 1946; *Outward Bound, Arsenic and Old Lace, East Lynne, John Loves Mary, Blithe Spirit, My Sister Eileen, The Man Who Came to Dinner, The Philadelphia Story, The Glass Menagerie, You Can't Take It with You, Peg o' My Heart, The Late Christopher Bean,* all Town Hall Theatre, Sturbridge, MA, 1948-49; *Come What May,* Weidman Studio, NY, 1950; *The Enchanted, The Respectful Prostitute,* both Woodstock Playhouse, 1951; *Trial by Jury, Ruddigore, The Gondoliers,* all Hunter College Playhouse, 1952-53; assistant director, *Babar the Elephant, Ariadne auf Naxos, Hansel and Gretel, L'Enfant et les sortileges,* all Little Orchestra Society, NY, 1953-55; *Two for Fun,* Greenwich Mews, NY, 1955; *The Emperor's New Clothes,* pre-Broadway at Tamiment, PA, 1957.

Once upon a Mattress, pre-Broadway at Tamiment, PA, 1958; assistant director, *Once upon a Mattress,* Alvin, NY, 1959; *The Sudden End of Anne Cinquefoil,* East End Theatre, NY, 1961; *The Turn of the Screw, Elizabeth the Queen,* both American Festival at the Boston Arts Center, 1961; *Chrysanthemum, Brigadoon,* Royal Poinciana Playhouse, 1962; *Here Today, Ring 'Round the Moon, The Miracle Worker,* Sombrero Playhouse, Phoenix, AZ, 1963; *The Matchmaker,* Royal Poinciana Playhouse, 1963; *Sophie,* Winter Garden, NY, 1963; *The Amorous Flea,* East 78th Street Theatre, NY, 1964; *The Giant's Dance,* Cherry Lane, NY, 1965; *Annie Get Your Gun,* revival, State Theatre, Broadway, 1966; *The Imaginary Invalid, A Touch of the Poet, Still Life,* all ANTA, 1967; *John Brown's Body,* National Repertory Theatre at Ford's Theatre, 1968; *Sganarelle,* National Theatre of the Deaf at the ANTA, 1970.

At the University of Washington, Seattle, WA: *The Adding Machine, A Thurber Carnival,* 1971, *The Madwoman of Chaillot, A Comedy of Errors,* 1974, *A Resounding Tinkle, Was He Anyone?, The Good Person of Szechuan,* 1975, *Company,* 1976, *Dinner at Eight, The Sunday Promenade, Hay Fever,* 1977, *The Matchmaker,* 1978, *A Midsummer Night's Dream, The Warrior's Husband,* 1979, *The Chalk Garden,* 1980, *The Threepenny Opera,* 1981, *And Miss Reardon Drinks A Little,* 1982, *Arms and the Man,* 1983, *Agnes of God,* 1984; *The Boor, The Marriage Proposal, The Anniversary,* 1973; *Oh, Coward!* 1975, all A Contemporary Theatre, Seattle, WA; *The Guardsman,* University of California at Berkeley, 1976; *A Christmas Sampler,* Intiman Theatre, 1979.

MAJOR TOURS—Director: *Hump Happy,* Air Transport Command, U.S. Army Air Force tour of Africa, Arabia, Egypt, 1943; *Once upon a Mattress,* bus and truck tour, 1960, national tour, 1960-61; *Mary Stuart, Elizabeth the Queen,* National Repertory Theatre tour of the U.S., 1961-62; *Here Today, Kismet, Kiss Me Kate, Call Me Madam,* stock tours, 1963; *The Rivals,* National Repertory Theatre tour, 1965; *The Music Man, Major Barbara, Misalliance,* stock tours, and Westport Country Playhouse, 1966; *Luv, On a Clear Day You Can See Forever,* stock tours, 1967; two tours for the Little Theatre of the Deaf, 1968-69.

PRINCIPAL STAGE APPEARANCES—Wagner, *Room Service,* Beverly Carlton, *The Man Who Came to Dinner,* Town Hall Theatre, Sturbridge, MA, 1948-49; Harry Holland, *The Live Wire,* Bohun,

JACK SYDOW

You Never Can Tell, Inspector, *An Inspector Calls,* Walter Channing, *Invitation to a Murder,* Cuthbertson, *The Philanderer,* Lt. Commander Challee, *The Caine Mutiny Court Martial,* Lord Summerhays, *Misalliance,* all Woodstock Playhouse, NY, 1951-53; Adolphus Cusins, *Major Barbara,* Greenwich Mews, NY, 1954; various roles, *The Brothers Karamazov,* Gate, NY, 1957-58; Pozzo, *Waiting for Godot,* Penthouse Theatre, Seattle, WA, 1979; Uncle Willie, *Bent,* Empty Space Theatre, 1981; title-role, *Paphnutius,* Showboat Theatre, Seattle, WA, 1982; Merwin Saltzman, *There Must Be a Pony,* John Drew Theatre, East Hampton, NY, 1982; Duncan, Porter, *Macbeth,* Old Globe Theatre, San Diego, 1983.

TELEVISION DEBUT—*Omnibus,* CBS, 1954. PRINCIPAL TELEVISION APPEARANCES—*Armstrong Circle Theatre; Goodyear Playhouse; Kraft Theatre; Look Up and Live; Philco Playhouse.*

RELATED CAREER—Professor of acting and directing, School of Drama, University of Washington, Seattle, WA, 1970-1986; founder with Eve La Gallienne, National Repertory Theatre, 1961.

WRITINGS: PLAYS, PRODUCED—*The Brothers Karamazov* (adapted with Boris Tumarin), Gate, NY, 1957; *The Idiot* (adapted with Boris Tumarin), Gate, NY, 1960.

AWARDS: Received a King Gustave V Fellowship from the American Scandinavian Foundation to study theatre in Sweden, 1950-51; Obie Award, with Boris Tumarin for Best Play Adaptation, 1957, for *The Brothers Karamazov;* Antoinette Perry Award nomination, Best Director of a Musical, 1967, for *Annie Get Your Gun.*

SIDELIGHTS: MEMBERSHIPS—Actors' Equity Association, Society of Stage Directors and Choreographers, American Federation of Television and Radio Artists, American Guild of Musical Artists.

ADDRESS: AGENT—Richard Bauman, Bauman, Hiller & Associates, 9220 Sunset Blvd., Hollywood, CA 90069.

T

IRENE TEDROW

TEDROW, Irene   1910-

PERSONAL: Born August 3, 1910; daughter of Harry Beecher (an attorney) and Camilla (an elocutionist; maiden name, Roberts) Tedrow; married William Edward Kent (an insurance broker), August 26, 1939 (died); children: Enid Lavinia, Roger Thomas. EDUCATION: Carnegie Mellon University, B.A., drama.

VOCATION: Actress.

CAREER: PRINCIPAL STAGE APPEARANCES—Appeared at the Mark Taper Forum in four productions, 1969-83; all star revival, Mrs. Webb, *Our Town,* 1969-70; member of the resident company for five years at the Cleveland Playhouse; played eighteen roles in various Shakespeare plays with the Maurice Evans Company (first company) and at the Old Globe Theatre, San Diego, CA; *Catsplay,* Old Globe, 1984; *Foxfire,* Old Globe, 1984-85.

PRINCIPAL FILM APPEARANCES—Featured in over 45 films since 1940.

PRINCIPAL TELEVISION APPEARANCES—Mrs. Ruggles, *The Ruggles,* 1949; Mary Hall, *Eleanor and Franklin; James at Sixteen; Quincy; Mary Tyler Moore Show; Three's Company; House Calls; Centennial; Streets of San Francisco; Little House on the Prairie; Remington Steele,* 1984; *Paper Chase,* 1985.

PRINCIPAL RADIO APPEARANCES—Mrs. Archer, *Corliss Archer,* eleven years; *Aunt Mary,* eight years.

AWARDS: Emmy Award nominations: Best Supporting Actress, for Mary Hall, *Eleanor and Franklin,* for Best Leading Actress, *James at Sixteen.*

ADDRESS: AGENT—Century Artists Ltd., 9744 Wilshire Blvd., Beverly Hills, CA 90212.

*   *   *

THURM, Joel

PERSONAL: EDUCATION: Hunter College, B.A.; Sorbonne, Doctorate, Russian literature.

VOCATION: Casting director.

CAREER: PRINCIPAL FILM WORK—Casting director: *Grease,* Paramount, 1978; *Airplane!,* Paramount, 1980; *Altered States,* Warner Brothers, 1980.

PRINCIPAL TELEVISION WORK—Thurm is vice president of talent for NBC.

ADDRESS: HOME—Los Angeles, CA. OFFICE—NBC Entertainment, 3000 W. Alameda Blvd., Burbank, CA 91523.

*   *   *

TILLY, Meg

BRIEF ENTRY: Born in California and raised in Victoria, BC. Actress. Tilly's debut in film was a few lines in *Fame,* United Artists, 1980, most of which ended up on the cutting room floor. She went on to portray Jamie in *Tex,* Buena Vista, 1982; *One Dark Night,* 1983; Chloe in *The Big Chill,* Columbia, 1983; Jennifer in *Impulse,* Twentieth Century-Fox, 1984; Agnes in *Agnes of God,*

Columbia (upcoming); *Off Beat,* Touchstone (upcoming). On television she has appeared in *Hill Street Blues* and "The Trouble with Grandpa," an *After School Special.**

*   *   *

TILTON, James F.   1937-

PERSONAL: Born July 30, 1937, in Rochelle, IL; son of Norval B. and Magdeline (Ripplinger) Tilton; married Helga Strang (divorced). EDUCATION: University of Iowa, B.A., 1959. MILITARY: U.S. Army, Special Services, 1959-62.

VOCATION: Designer.

CAREER: FIRST STAGE WORK—Decor designer, *Stage Door,* West High School auditorium, Rockford IL, 1954. FIRST NEW YORK STAGE WORK—Designer, *Scapin,* Phoenix, 1964. PRINCIPAL STAGE WORK—Designer: For the John Drew Theatre, East Hampton, NY, 1963: *Finian's Rainbow, Carousel, Brecht on Brecht, Come Blow Your Horn, Irma la Douce, Brigadoon, Write Me a Murder;* for the APA Phoenix Theatre Company, NY, 1964: *Right You Are If You Think You Are, The Lower Depths, Impromtu de Versailles, Herakles.*

For the Front Street Theatre, Memphis, TN, 1964-66: *Ah! Wilderness, The Seven Year Itch, My Fair Lady, Damn Yankees, The Country Wife, The Sound of Music, The Little Hut, The Taming of the Shrew, Misalliance, My Three Angels, You Can't Take It with You, The Tavern, A Midsummer Night's Dream, The Music Man, Roberta, The School for Scandal, We Comrades Three, Guys and Dolls, The Wild Duck, War and Peace, Pantagleize, The Show Off,* and lighting for *Exit the King;* for the Professional Theatre Program, University of Michigan, 1967-69: *Escurial, The Cat and the Moon, Sweet of You to Say So, The Flies, The Cherry Orchard, The Cocktail Party, The Misanthrope, Ballad for a Firing Squad, The Latent Heterosexual, Chronicles of Hell, Macbeth, Play.*

Cock-a-Doodle Dandy, Hamlet, Private Lives, Oh! Calcutta! NY, Los Angeles, San Francisco, 1969; *Love-In,* Kansas City Opera, 1969; *The Doctor's Dilemma,* 1969; *Harvey, The Merchant of Venice, Siamese Connections,* San Francisco, 1970; *The Selling of the President, Antony and Cleopatra, Caesar and Cleopatra,* American Conservatory Theatre, San Francisco; *Charley's Aunt, Rainbow, The Matchmaker,* Asolo State Theatre, Sarasota, FL, 1971-72; for John Drew Theatre, East Hampton, NY, 1972-73: *The American Dream, The Long Christmas Dinner, What the Butler Saw, The Palace at 4 A.M., Dudes, The Government Inspector, The Merchant of Venice; That Championship Season,* Flint, Buffalo Studio Arena, 1974; for the Phoenix at John Drew Theatre, East Hampton NY, 1973-74: *End of Summer, The Private Ear and the Public Eye, The Rehearsal, Tonight at 8:30.*

Death of a Salesman, Buffalo Studio Arena, 1976; *The Cat and the Fiddle,* Cleveland Playhouse, 1976; *Vieux Carre, Galileo, The Auction Tomorrow, Flying Blind,* Hartman Theatre Company, Stamford, CT, 1977-79; for the Phoenix, NY, 1975-78: *Twenty Seven Wagons Full of Cotton, A Memory of Two Mondays, They Knew What They Wanted, Boy Meets Girl, Secret Service, Ladyhouse Blues, American Modern/Canadian Gothic, Marco Polo, A Sorrow Beyond Dreams, GR Point, Scribes, Hot Grog, Uncommon Women, The Elusive Angel, One Crack Out, City Sugar, Big and*

Little, Later; Pagliacci, University of Iowa, 1979; *Clari, or The Maid of Milan,* 1980; *Light Up the Sky, Rogues to Riches, The Importance of Being Earnest,* John Drew Theatre, East Hampton, 1981-82; *Twice Around the Park,* Cort, 1983-84; *You Can't Take It with You,* Broadway production, 1983-84; for the Mirror Theatre Company, NY, 1985: *The Madwoman of Chaillot, Clarence, Vivat! Vivat Regina!;* lighting, *The Loves of Anatol,* Circle in the Square, 1985.

MAJOR TOURS—Designer: *Butterflies Are Free, The Age of Shaw, A Connecticut Yankee in King Arthur's Court,* National Theatre Company, 1973; *The Miracle Worker; Declaration; Knuckle; Seascape; Shakespeare Is Alive and Well and Living in America; Chaplin and His Time.*

PRINCIPAL TELEVISION WORK—Designer: *Secret Service,* PBS, 1977; *Uncommon Women & Others,* PBS, 1978; *A Conflict of Interest,* PBS, 1981; *You Can't Take It with You,* PBS, 1984.

PRINCIPAL FILM WORK—Designer, *Dear Dead Delilah,* 1970.

RELATED CAREER—Resident designer, Frankfurt Playhouse, Frankfurt am Main, West Germany, 1959-62; artist in residence, University of Michigan and University of Iowa; principal designer, APA Phoenix, NY and at John Drew Theatre, East Hampton.

ADDRESS: OFFICE—726 Eighth Avenue, New York, NY 10036.

*   *   *

TOM, Lauren   1959-

PERSONAL: Born August 4, 1959, in Chicago, IL; daughter of Chan (in Chinese frozen foods) and Nancy (Dare) Tom; married Glenn Lau-Kee (an attorney), October 23, 1982. EDUCATION: Northwestern University, 1977; New York University, B.A.

VOCATION: Actress and singer.

CAREER: STAGE DEBUT—Connie Wong, *A Chorus Line,* international touring company, 1978-79. NEW YORK DEBUT—Aki Sakata, *The Music Lessons,* New York Shakespeare Festival, Public, 1980. PRINCIPAL STAGE APPEARANCES—Connie, *A Chorus Line,* Shubert, NY, 1980-81; Jenny, *Family Devotions,* New York Shakespeare Festival, Public, 1981; Honey, *Doonesbury,* Biltmore, NY, 1983-84; understudy Donna, *Hurlyburly,* Barrymore, NY, 1985.

FILM DEBUT—Eloi, *Nothing Lasts Forever,* Metro-Goldwyn-Mayer, 1982.

TELEVISION DEBUT—Miko (guest appearance), *The Facts of Life,* NBC, 1982. PRINCIPAL TELEVISION APPEARANCES—"Mom's on Strike," *ABC Afterschool Special,* 1984; "Foreign Exchange," *CBS Afterschool Break,* 1984.

SIDELIGHTS: MEMBERSHIPS—Actors' Equity Association, Screen Actors Guild, American Federation of Television and Radio Artists; supports the Asia Institute in Washington, DC.

Tom told *CTFT,* "I am interested in playing roles that do not perpetuate the Asian stereotype and also in finding ways to create more opportunities for Asian actors."

ADDRESS: AGENT—Marie Pastor, P.O. Box S, New Rochelle, NY 10802; Kass & Woo, 156 Fifth Avenue, New York, NY 10010.

*   *   *

TOMLIN, Lily 1939-

PERSONAL: Born September 1, 1939, in Detroit, MI. EDUCATION: Attended Wayne State University; trained for the stage with Paul Curtis.

VOCATION: Actress and comedian.

CAREER: PRINCIPAL FILM APPEARANCES—*Nashville*, Paramount, 1975; *The Late Show*, Warner Brothers, 1977; *Moment by Moment*, Universal, 1978; *Nine to Five*, Twentieth Century-Fox, 1980; *The Incredible Shrinking Woman*, Universal, 1981; *All of Me*, Universal, 1984.

PRINCIPAL TELEVISION APPEARANCES—Host, *Music Scene*, ABC, 1969-70; *Rowan and Martin's Laugh-In*, NBC, 1970-73; *Lily Tomlin* (specials), CBS, 1973, 1981, 1982, then two for ABC, 1975; guest host, *Saturday Night Live*, NBC; *Who's Who*, CBS, 1977; host, *Late Show*.

PRINCIPAL STAGE APPEARANCES—In cabarets and nightclubs; *Appearing Nightly*, Broadway production, 1977.

WRITINGS: Comedy writer for herself, Paul Simon, and Carol Burnett, among others.

AWARDS: Antoinette Perry Special Award, Grammy Award, 1971; Emmy Award, Outstanding Writing Achievement in Variety or Music, 1973, for *The Carol Burnett Show;* Emmy Award, Best Writing in Comedy-Variety, 1974, for *Lily;* Emmy Award, Outstanding Writing in a Comedy-Variety or Music Special, 1976, for *Lily Tomlin;* Emmy Award, Outstanding Writing in a Comedy-Variety or Music Special, 1978, for *The Paul Simon Special;* Emmy Award, Outstanding Variety, Music or Comedy Program, 1981, for *Lily Sold Out.*

ADDRESS: OFFICE—P.O. Box 27700, Los Angeles, CA 90027.*

*   *   *

TRAVOLTA, John 1954-

PERSONAL: Born 1954, in Engelwood, NJ; son of Salvatore and Helen Travolta.

VOCATION: Actor.

CAREER: PRINCIPAL FILM APPEARANCES—*Carrie*, 1976; *Saturday Night Fever*, 1977; *Grease*, 1978; *Moment-by-Moment*, 1978; *Urban Cowboy*, 1980; *Blow Out*, 1981; *Staying Alive*, 1983; *Two of a Kind*, 1983; *Perfect!* 1985.

PRINCIPAL TELEVISION APPEARANCES—Vinnie Barbarino, *Welcome Back Kotter*, ABC, 1975-79; *The Boy in the Plastic Bubble*, 1976.

RECORDINGS: Saturday Night Fever, 1976; *Grease,* 1977.

AWARDS: Billboard Award, Best New Male Vocalist, 1976; Record World Award; Music Retail Magazine Award; Women's Press Club Award nomination, Best New Male Star, 1976; National Board of Review Award, Best Actor, National Film Critic's Award, New York Film Critics Circle Award, Golden Apple Award from *New York Magazine,* Academy Award nomination, Best Actor, all 1977, for *Saturday Night Fever;* Hasty Pudding Club Award, Man of the Year, Harvard University, 1981.

ADDRESS: OFFICE—c/o Edwards, 4810 Woodley Avenue, Encino, CA 91436.

*   *   *

TRIPP, Paul 1916-

PERSONAL: Born February 20, 1916, in New York City; son of Benjamin (an actor and singer) and Esther Tripp; married Ruth Enders (an actress and journalist), August 8, 1943; children: Suzanne, David. EDUCATION: City College of New York, B.A.; studied law at Brooklyn College. POLITICS: Independent. MILITARY: U.S. Army, Signal Corps, Sergeant, four years during World War Two.

VOCATION: Actor, writer, director, and lyricist.

CAREER: STAGE DEBUT—Second Marquis, *Cyrano de Bergerac,*

PAUL TRIPP

Hartford Auditorium, Hartford, CT, 1936. NEW YORK DEBUT—Second Marquis, *Cyrano de Bergerac,* Walter Hampden's Company, New Amsterdam, 1936. PRINCIPAL STAGE APPEARANCES—*Enemy of the People,* 1937; *Jeremiah,* 1939; *Temper the Wind,* 1946; *The Forty-Ninth Cousin,* 48th Street Theatre, NY, 1959; *Echoes,* Bijou, NY, 1975.

MAJOR TOURS—Ben Franklin, *1776,* national tour, 1971-72; one man show, *Will Rogers, U.S.A.,* national tour, 1974.

PRINCIPAL STAGE WORK—Director: *The Army, Play by Play,* U.S. Army production; *Seeds in the Wind,* Empire, NY.

PRINCIPAL CONCERT PERFORMANCES—As narrator of his own works: Philadelphia Orchestra, New York Philharmonic Orchestra, Worcester Music Festival, New Haven Symphony Orchestra, Reading Symphony, National Orchestra, American Youth Orchestra.

FILM DEBUT—*The Christmas That Almost Wasn't,* 1966.

PRINCIPAL TELEVISION APPEARANCES—*Mr. I. Magination,* CBS, 1949-1953; *On the Carousel,* CBS, 1954-59; *Birthday House,* NBC, 1963-68; *Edison,* one man show, PBS, 1980; host, *Wheel of Fortune,* CBS; also: *The Dick Van Dyke Show; Perry Mason; The Defenders; The Real McCoy's; Philco Playhouse; The Dupont Show of the Month; Imogene Coco Show; Studio One; You Are There; Jamie.*

PRINCIPAL TELEVISION WORK—Producer and director: *Mr. I. Magination; On the Carousel; Birthday House.*

WRITINGS: TELEVISION—Head writer, *Freedom Rings;* special material, *Omnibus,* CBS; scripts, *The Verdict Is Yours,* CBS; *Lamp unto My Feet; Tales of Tomorrow; A Paul Tripp Christmas,* WNBC; *Christmas Tree Lighting Ceremony at Rockefeller Plaza,* WNBC, NY, also served as host; *Thanksgiving Day Parade,* NBC, also served as host; "Under the Christmas Tree," *Bell Telephone Hour,* CBS; *Little Star of Bethlehem,* ABC; *Orange Bowl Parade,* NBC, 1971; *Children's Television Around the World,* CBS.

SCREENPLAYS—*The Christmas That Almost Wasn't,* Childhood Productions; *Rapunzel,* 1971; *Tubby the Tuba,* Paramount, 1983.

RADIO—*Plymouth Rock '49.*

LYRICS—*Tubby The Tuba,* record album, 1945, animated film, 1983; *The Christmas That Almost Wasn't,* 1966.

CHILDREN'S BOOKS—*The Strawman Who Smiled by Mistake,* Doubleday, 1967; *The Little Red Flower,* Doubleday, 1968; *Tubby the Tuba,* Vanguard Press; *Minnie the Mump,* Corinthian, 1969; *The Tail That a' Went Looking,* Doubleday, 1971.

RECORDINGS: *Story of Celeste,* Golden Records, Signature Records; *Pee Wee the Piccolo,* RCA; *Billy on a Bike,* RCA; *Mr. I. Magination,* Columbia and Musicor; *The Little Star of Bethlehem,* Columbia; *Instrument Songs,* Columbia; *Good Night Dear Lord,* recorded by Johnny Mathis, Columbia; *Birthday House,* albums one and two, Musicor; *Paul Tripp's Partytime,* Musicor; *Plymouth Rock to Moon Rock.*

AWARDS: Peabody, original *Look* award, Ohio State University award, Variety Showmanship award, all for *Mr. I. Magination;* three Ohio State University awards, Emmy Award, for *On the Carousel;* National Academy of Television Arts and Sciences Special Governor's Citation, for *Birthday House;* National Academy

of Motion Picture Arts and Sciences nomination, Best Short Subject, *Tubby the Tuba;* National Academy of Recording Arts and Sciences nomination, Best Children's Record Album, for *The Christmas That Almost Wasn't;* Galaxy Science Fiction award, *Tales of Tomorrow.*

SIDELIGHTS: MEMBERSHIPS—Actors' Equity Association, American Federation of Television and Radio Artists, Screen Actors Guild, Writers Guild of America, American Society of Composers, Authors, and Publishers, National Academy of Television Arts and Sciences (govenor, 1957-61, 1964-68), ATVAS (national trustee, 1960-62), Players Club; New York City Youth Board, 1954-59; social worker for Christodora House, 1935-42.

ADDRESS: HOME—New York, NY. AGENT—Lester Lewis Associates, 110 W. 40th Street, New York, NY 10018.

*   *   *

TRUFFAUT, Francois   1932-84

PERSONAL: Born February 6, 1932, in Paris, France; died 1984; son of Rol and Janine (de Monferr) Truffaut; married Madeline Morgentern, October 29, 1957 (divorced); children: Laura, Eva.

VOCATION: Director, scriptwriter, and actor.

CAREER: PRINCIPAL FILM WORK—Director: *Une Visite,* 1955; *Une Histoire d'eau,* 1958; *Four Hundred Blows,* 1959; *Mississippi Mermaid,* 1969; *The Last Metro,* 1980.

Director and co-writer: *Les Mistrons,* 1958; *Shoot the Piano Player,* 1960; *Jules and Jim,* 1961; *The Soft Skin,* 1966; *Farenheit 451,* 1966; *Bed and Board,* 1970; *Two English Girls,* 1971; *Such a Gorgeous Kid Like Me,* 1973; *The Story of Adele H.,* 1975; *Small Change,* 1976; *The Man Who Loved Women,* 1977; *Love on the Run,* 1979; *Confidentially Yours,* 1983.

Director and actor, "Antoine and Colette," episode of *Love at 20.*

Director, writer, and actor: Dr. Jean Ilfard *The Wild Child,* 1969; Ferrand, *Day for Night,* 1973; Julien Davenne, *The Green Room,* 1978.

Actor: French scientist, *Close Encounters of the Third Kind,* Columbia, 1977.

WRITINGS: SCREENPLAY—In addition to above, *A Bout de Souffle,* 1959 (Jean-Luc Godard's first film).

BOOKS—*Le Cinema Selon Hitchcock,* 1966; *Les Aventures d'Antoine Doinel,* 1970; *La Nuit Americaine et la Journal de Farenheit,* 1974; *Les Films de Ma Vie,* 1975; *L'Argent de Poche,* 1976; *The Man Who Loved Women,* 1977.

AWARDS: Best Director, Cannes Festival 1959, for *Four Hundred Blows;* Prix Luis Delluc and Best Director, National Society of Film Critics, 1969, for *Stolen Kisses;* Academy Award for Best Foreign Language Film, Best Direction from New York Film Critics, Best Direction from British Academy Award and Best Director from National Society of Film Critics, all 1973, for *Day for Night.*

Truffaut's first job was as a reporter and motion picture critic for *The Movie Journal and Arts,* from 1954-58.*

TULL, Patrick 1941-

PERSONAL: Born July 28, 1941, in Bexhill, England; son of Richard (a soldier) and Phillida (an actress; maiden name, Pantlin) Tull; married Pamela Exton-Jones (divorced, 1974); married Nancy Butler (divorced, 1978); married Suellyn M. Dennis (an executive), December 10, 1979; children: Katharine, Siobhan. EDUCATION: London Academy of Music and Dramatic Arts. RELIGION: Episcopalian.

VOCATION: Actor.

CAREER: STAGE DEBUT—The Caretaker, *Rhinoceros, Nottingham Playhouse, England, 1961.* LONDON DEBUT—Cookson, *Peter Pan,* Scala, 1962. NEW YORK DEBUT—Sergeant Harris, *The Astrakhan Coat,* Helen Hayes, 1967. PRINCIPAL STAGE APPEARANCES—England: Nottingham Playhouse, 1961-62, 1964-65; Harrogate, York, Cramer, Sidmonth, Salisbury, and Canterbury repertory companies; Vanhattan, *The Apple Cart,* Mermaid, 1969; Window-washer, *Witness,* King's Head; *Macbird, The Provok'd Wife, The Marie Lloyd Story,* Captain Cat, *Under Milkwood,* Dublin. United States: Priest, *Amadeus,* Broadhurst, NY; Blore, *Ten Little Indians;* Petey, *The Birthday Party,* YM/YWHA; Montague, *Romeo and Juliet,* 28th Street Playhouse; Andrew Wyke, *Sleuth,* Tennessee Williams Fine Arts Center; Giles Corey, *The Crucible,* NY; Seamus Shields, *Shadow of a Gunman,* Syracuse Stage; Chasuble, *Importance of Being Earnest,* Clarence Brown Theatre, Knoxville, TN; *A Christmas Carol,* Greeley Street Theatre, Chappaqua, NY; Van Helsing, *Dracula,* Baptista, *The Taming of the Shrew,* St. Mary's Festival, MD; Clocker, *Goodman Clocker;* First Voice, *Under Milkwood.*

FILM DEBUT—First Accountant, *Life at the Top,* Romulus Productions, 1965. PRINCIPAL FILM APPEARANCES—Cecil, *Parting Glances;* Templeton, *Mosquito Squadron;* bearded student, *Tomorrow; All Neat in Black Stockings; The Inn Way Out.*

TELEVISION DEBUT—*Z Cars,* BBC, 1963. PRINCIPAL TELEVISION APPEARANCES—George Thorp, *Jamestown: Beware of the People of the Sunrise,* Corinthian Productions; Terry, *Murder Motel,* ABC; Charlie Modryb, *Progress to the Park,* BBC; *No Hiding Place; Dad's Army; Softly Softly; Hugh and I; Lieutenant Tenant; Londoners; To the Frontier; Thirty Minute Theatre; Sentimental Education.*

PRINCIPAL RADIO APPEARANCES—BBC repertory.

PATRICK TULL

WRITINGS: RADIO—Adaptation of Isaac Asimov's *Foundation Trilogy,* BBC.

SIDELIGHTS: MEMBERSHIPS—Actors' Equity Association, American Federation of Television and Radio Artists, Screen Actors Guild.

Tull recorded several monster voices for *Dr. Who.*

ADDRESS: AGENT—Stephen Draper, 37 W. 57th Street, New York, NY 10019.

U

SHARON ULLRICK

ULLRICK, Sharon   1947-

PERSONAL: Born March 18, 1947, in Dallas, TX; daughter of Edward Bunker and Clara Frances (Ray) Ullrick. EDUCATION: Southern Methodist University, B.A., 1969; studied acting with Stella Adler.

VOCATION: Actress.

CAREER: STAGE DEBUT—Nurse, *Romeo and Juliet*, Harlequin Players, Dallas, 1965. NEW YORK DEBUT—Joanne, *Vanities*, Chelsea Westside Theatre. PRINCIPAL STAGE APPEARANCES—Mrs. Malaprop, *The Rivals*, Maria, *Twelfth Night*, both STARCO, Ft. Worth; Lady Teazle, *School for Scandal*, Pacific Conservatory, Santa Maria, CA, 1968; *Pursuit of Happiness, Secret Service*, both Diamond Circle Theatre, Durango, 1969; Susan Walker, *Once in a Lifetime*, Mark Taper Forum, Los Angeles, 1975; Ada, *Jones/Bailey Circus*, Mark Taper Forum Lab, 1975; Avra, *Cross Country*, Mark Taper Forum, 1976; Faith, *To See the Elephant*, Mark Taper Forum Lab, 1976; Joanna, *Home Free*, Cast Theatre, 1977; Clayton, *Gringo Planet*, La MaMa, Hollywood, 1977; Faith/Clarice, *Purse Strings*, La MaMa, Hollywood, 1978; Julia, *Fefu and her Friends*, Los Angeles, 1979; Carnelle, *The Miss Firecracker Contest*, New Stage Theatre, Jackson, MI, 1980; Chick Boyle, *Crimes of the Heart*, Golden, NY, 1981-82; Aunt Sally, *Adventures of Huck Finn*, Seattle Repertory Company, 1983; Catherine, *Standing on My Knees*, Stage One, Dallas, 1984.

MAJOR TOURS—Mary, *Vanities*, 1981; Chick Boyle, *Crimes of the Heart*, 1983.

FILM DEBUT—Charlene Duggs, *Last Picture Show*, 1970. PRINCIPAL FILM APPEARANCES—Barbara, *The Harrad Experiment*, 1972.

TELEVISION DEBUT—*The F.B.I*, ABC, 1971. PRINCIPAL TELEVISION APPEARANCES—*All in the Family*, CBS, 1977; *Doc*, CBS, 1977; *Flying High*, CBS, 1977; *The Rockford Files*, NBC, 1977; *Baa Baa Blacksheep*, NBC, 1977; *Flying High*, CBS, 1978; *On the Rocks*, CBS, 1978; *Studs Lonigan*, NBC, 1978; *Billy Peoples*, NBC, 1978; *The Beasts Are in the Streets*, NBC, 1978; *Fast Lane Blues*, ABC, 1978.

AWARDS: Dramalogue Award, 1979, for *Fefu and Her Friends;* best actress, Dallas *Morning News* and Dallas *Times Herald*, 1984, for Catherine, *Standing on My Knees*.

SIDELIGHTS: MEMBERSHIPS—Actors' Equity Association, American Federation of Television and Radio Artists, Screen Actors Guild, Actors Fund.

ADDRESS: AGENT—Michael Thomas Agency, 22 E. 60th Street, New York, NY 10022.

V

VACCARO, Brenda 1939-

PERSONAL: Born November 18, 1939, in Brooklyn, NY. EDUCATION: Trained for the stage at the Neighborhood Playhouse, NY.

VOCATION: Actress.

CAREER: PRINCIPAL FILM APPEARANCES—*Midnight Cowboy,* United Artists, 1969; *Where It's At,* United Artists, 1969; *I Love My Wife,* Universal, 1970; *Summer Tree,* Columbia, 1971; *Going Home,* Metro-Goldwyn-Mayer, 1971; *Once Is Not Enough,* Paramount, 1975; *Airport '77,* Universal, 1977; *Capricorn One,* Warner Brothers, 1978; *First Deadly Sin,* Filmways, 1980.

PRINCIPAL TELEVISION APPEARANCES—Episodic: *The Greatest Show on Earth,* 1963; *Fugitive,* 1963; *The Defenders,* 1965; *Doctors and Nurses,* 1965; *Coronet Blue,* 1967; *The F.B.I.,* 1969; *The Psychiatrist,* 1971; *Name of the Game,* 1971; *Marcus Welby, M.D.,* 1972; *Banacek,* 1972; *McCloud,* 1972; *The Shape of Things,* 1974; *McCoy,* 1976; *Streets of San Francisco,* 1976. Series: Sara Yarnell, *Sara,* CBS, 1976; Kate Hudson, *Dear Detective,* CBS, 1979; Julia Blake, *Paper Dolls,* ABC, 1984. Movies: *Travis Logan, D.A.,* 1971; *What's a Nice Girl Like You,* 1971; *Honor Thy Father,* 1973; *Sunshine,* 1973; *The Big Ripoff,* 1975; *Julius and Ethel Rosenberg,* 1978; *Guyana Tragedy—The Story of Jim Jones,* 1980.

STAGE DEBUT—*The Land of Dreams Come True,* Ursuline Academy, Dallas, TX, 1946. NEW YORK DEBUT—Gloria Gulock, *Everybody Loves Opal,* Longacre, 1961. PRINCIPAL STAGE APPEARANCES—Angelina, *The Willow Tree,* Margo Jones Theatre, Dallas, TX, 1961; Miss Novick, *The Tunnel of Love,* Westbury Music Fair, Long Island, NY, 1962; Laura Howard, *The Affair,* 1962; Melissa Peabody, *Children from the Games,* Morosco, NY, 1963; Toni, *Cactus Flower,* Royale, NY, 1965; Reedy Harris, *The Natural Look,* Longacre, NY, 1967; Cynthia, *How Now, Dow Jones,* Lunt-Fontanne, NY, 1967; Nancy Scott, *The Goodbye People,* Ethel Barrymore, NY, 1968; Louise, *Fathers Day,* John Golden, NY, 1971.

AWARDS: Theatre World Award, 1961-62; Emmy Award, Best Supporting Actress, 1974, for *The Shape of Things;* three Antoinette Perry Award nominations; two Hollywood Press Association Award nominations.

ADDRESS: AGENT—William Morris Agency, 151 El Camino, Beverly Hills, CA 90212.*

JOHN C. VENNEMA

VENNEMA, John C. 1948-

PERSONAL: Last name is pronounced with accent on first syllable; born August 24, 1948; son of Ame (an executive) and Catherine Grace (Silvernale) Vennema; married Maureen Jo Missner (a marketing director for a furniture and fabric company), September 1, 1979. EDUCATION: Princeton University, B.A., politics, 1970; trained for the theatre at the London Academy of Music and Dramatic Arts.

VOCATION: Actor.

CAREER: STAGE DEBUT—Truscott, *Loot,* C.S.C. Repertory, NY, 1973. PRINCIPAL STAGE APPEARANCES—Gunga, *The Royal Family,* Helen Hayes, NY, 1976; Stephen Hench, *Otherwise Engaged,* Plymouth, NY, 1977; Lt. Wilken, *The Biko Inquest,* Theatre Four, NY, 1978; Lord John, *The Elephant Man,* Booth, NY, 1979-80; Cassius, *Julius Caesar,* Actor's Theatre of Louisville, KY, 1982; Colin, *In Celebration*, Manhattan Theatre Club, NY, 1984; Tuzenbach, *The Three Sisters*, Actors Theatre of Louisville, KY, 1984.

Also: Lovborg, *Hedda Gabler*, Orsino, *Twelfth Night*, Lenny, *The Homecoming*, all at C.S.C. Repertory, NY; Barnabus, *A Slight Ache*, Law, *The Basement*, Jimmy Flynn, *Ballymurphy*, White Actor, *Scenes from Soweto*, Det. J. de Prees, *Statements. . .*, five roles, *No End of Blame*, all at Manhattan Theatre Club, NY; Johnny, *Misalliance*, Marley's Ghost, *A Christmas Carol*, Frank Falzon, *Execution of Justice*, all at Actors Theatre of Louisville, KY; Edgar Evans, *Terra Nova*, the other part, *Ashes*, Pittsburgh Public, PA; Gary, *Patrick Henry Lake Liquors*, P.A.F. Playhouse, NY; Straker, *Man and Superman*, Vladimir, *Waiting for Godot*, Dr. Rance, *What the Butler Saw*, all at George Street Playhouse, New Brunswick, NJ; and roles in the 1983 and 1984 New Plays Festival, Philadelphia Festival for New Plays, Annenberg Center, Philadelphia, PA.

TELEVISION APPEARANCES—*Ryan's Hope; Another World.*

ADDRESS: HOME—246 E. 48th Street, New York, NY 10017. AGENT—Mary Harden, Bret Adams, Ltd. 448 W. 44th Street, New York, NY 10036.

*   *   *

BEN VEREEN

VEREEN, Ben   1946-

PERSONAL: Born October 10, 1946, in Miami, FL; married Nancy; children: Ben Jr., Malakia, Naja, Kabara, Karon. EDUCATION—High School of the Performing Arts, NY.

VOCATION: Actor.

CAREER: STAGE DEBUT—*The Prodigal Son*, Greenwich Mews, NY, 1965. PRINCIPAL STAGE APPEARANCES—Brother Ben, *Sweet Charity*, Caesar's Palace, Las Vegas, 1966; Daddy Sebastian Brubeck, *Sweet Charity*, Shubert, Boston, 1967; Flight Announcer, *Golden Boy*, Auditorium, Chicago, 1968; Claude, *Hair*, Biltmore, NY, 1968; alternated roles of Hud and Berger, *Hair*, Aquarius, Los Angeles, 1968; Johnny Williams, *No Place to Be Somebody*, National Shakespeare Company, 1970; Judas Iscariot, *Jesus Christ Superstar*, Mark Hellinger, NY, 1971; Leading Player, *Pippin*, Imperial, NY, 1972; *Grind*, Mark Hellinger, NY, 1985.

PRINCIPAL FILM APPEARANCES—*Funny Lady*, 1975; *All That Jazz*, 1979; *The Zoo Gang.*

PRINCIPAL TELEVISION APPEARANCES—Movies: *Louis Armstrong—Chicago Style*, 1976; Chicken George, *Roots; The Jessie Owens Story; Ellis Island*, CBS. Series: Tenspeed, *Tenspeed and Brownshoe*, ABC, 1980; Uncle Phillip, *Webster*, ABC; ''Puss n' Boots,'' *Faerie Tale Theatre*. Specials: *Ben Vereen—His Roots; Night of a 100 Stars*, NBC, 1983; *Here's Television Entertainment*, 1984; *Salute to the USA Olympic Team*, NBC; *Lynda Carter Special*, CBS; *Antoinette Perry Awards*, CBS; *Two-Hour Love Boat Musical Special*, ABC, *Statue of Liberty Special.*

PRINCIPAL CLUB APPEARANCES—Las Vegas, Atlantic City, Reno, Lake Tahoe, England, France, Monaco, Hong Kong, Portugal, Mainland China.

AWARDS: Antoinette Perry and Drama Desk Awards, for *Pippin;* Entertainer of the Year, Rising Star and Song and Dance Star from American Guild of Variety Artists, 1978; Image Award from National Association for the Advancement of Colored People, 1978 and 1979; honory doctorate, Emerson College, 1977; Israel's Cultural Award, 1978; Israel's Humanitarian Award, 1979; Eleanor Roosevelt Humanitarian Award, 1983.

SIDELIGHTS: MEMBERSHIPS—Actors' Equity Association, American Guild of Variety Artists, American Federation of Television and Radio Artists, Screen Actors Guild, American Heart Association's Dance for Heart campaign (chariman), Sudden Infant Death Syndrome (international chairman).

ADDRESS: AGENT—William Morris Agency, 1350 Avenue of the Americas, New York, NY 10019.

*   *   *

VERNACCHIO, Dorian   1953-

PERSONAL: Born May 18, 1953, in Philadelphia, PA; son of Edward (a dancer) and Joy (an artist; maiden name, Freman) Vernacchio; married Deborah Raymond (a scenic designer), September 8, 1984. EDUCATION: Temple University, B.A., theatre, 1978; New York University, M.F.A., scenic design, 1981.

VOCATION: Scenic and lighting designer.

CAREER: FIRST STAGE WORK—Scenic designer, *Cabaret,* Cockpit in Court, Baltimore, MD, 1974. NEW YORK DEBUT—Scenic designer, *Henry IV, Part I,* Riverside Shakespeare Co., 1979. PRINCIPAL STAGE WORK—Scenic designer: *La Traviata,* Chesapeake Opera Co., Baltimore, MD, 1975; *George M!,* Music Theatre of Abington, PA, 1976; *The Sunshine Boys,* Inn of the Four Falls Dinner Theatre, 1976; *Finian's Rainbow,* Music Theatre of Abington, PA, 1977; *Children of Our Mother's,* Theatre Center of Philadelphia, PA, 1977; *South Pacific,* Music Theatre of Abington, PA, 1978; *Saved,* New York University, NY, 1980; *The Desparate Hours,* Wonderhorse, NY, 1981; *The Three Cuckolds,* Riverside Shakespeare Co., NY, 1981; *Dark of the Moon,* Monmouth College, NJ, 1981.

The Architect and the Emperor of Assyria, Medicine Show Theatre, NY, 1981; *Romeo and Juliet,* Monmouth College, NJ, 1981; *H.M.S. Pinafore,* Monmouth College, NJ, 1981; *Pig Jazz,* Actors' Playhouse, NY, 1981; *Pippin,* Monmouth College, NJ, 1982; *The Unseen Hand,* Cafe La MaMa ETC, NY, 1982, then Provincetown Playhouse, NY, 1982; *Edward II,* Riverside Shakespeare Co., NY, 1982; *The Comedy of Errors,* Riverside Shakespeare Co., NY, 1982; *Robin Hood,* Band Wagon, NY, 1982; *The Nutcracker,* John Drew, NY, 1982; *The Boyfriend,* John Drew, NY, 1982; *Kid Twist,* Repertory Theatre, NY, 1983; *South of Show Business,* New Vic, 1983; *Jacques Brel Is Alive and Well and Living in Paris,* Downtown Cabaret, Bridgeport, CT, 1983; *They're Playing Our Song, Showboat, Annie, Barnum,* all at Theatre by the Sea, Matunuck, RI, 1983; *The Three Cuckolds,* Cubiculo, NY, 1983; *From Here to Hester Street,* Robert N. Strauss Drama Workshop, NY, 1983.

Lighting designer: *Auntie Mame, Rain,* Vagabonds, 1974; *Rosencrantz and Guildenstern are Dead,* E.C.C.S.T.A., 1975; *The Bald Soprano,* Randall Lab, Temple University, PA, 1976; *What's My Motivation,* Randall Lab, 1977; *Angel City,* Wonderhorse, NY, 1982; *CiCi,* Il Teatro Italio-Americano, NY, 1983; also, several productions with lighting and scenic design, including *George M!, South Pacific, Saved, Pippin, The Nutcracker,* others.

Assistant scenic designer: To Sandro LaFarla, *Hitinks,* Chelsea Theatre Center, 1980; to Deborah Raymond, *Tea House of the August Moon,* Cumberland County Playhouse, 1984; to Jon Terzis, the Cars ''Drive,'' music video, Picture Music International, 1984; others.

SIDELIGHTS: MEMBERSHIPS—United Scenic Artists.

ADDRESS: HOME—74 Winter Avenue, Staten Island, NY 10301. AGENT—Ginny Raymond, Writers and Artists, 11726 San Vicente Blvd., Los Angeles, CA 90049.

*   *   *

VERNON, David   1959-

PERSONAL: Full name David Lyle Vernon; born February 7, 1959, in Greensboro, NC; son of Brenda K. (a legal secretary; maiden name, Richardson) Vernon.

VOCATION: Actor, dancer, and choreographer.

DAVID VERNON

CAREER: STAGE DEBUT—Rusty Charlie, *Guys and Dolls,* Northwest Players, Greensboro, NC, five performances. NEW YORK DEBUT—Ribbando, *Robin Hood,* Band Wagon, Larry Richardson Dance Gallery, eight performances, 1982. PRINCIPAL STAGE APPEARANCES—Dream Curly, *Oklahoma!;* Pippin, *Pippin;* James, *Shenandoah;* George, *George M!,* all in stock or dinner theatre.

MAJOR TOURS—Soloist and dance captain, *Cole Porter,* Romanian tour; Sascha, *A Day in Hollywood/A Night in the Ukraine,* First National Company.

FILM DEBUT—*9 1/2 Weeks.*

TELEVISION APPERANCES—*The Guiding Light; Search for Tomorrow; As the World Turns; One Life to Live.*

RELATED CAREER—Artist in residence, teacher, Dayton Dance Theatre, Dayton, OH, 1981-82.

SIDELIGHTS: MEMBERSHIPS—Actors' Equity Association, Screen Actors Guild, American Federation of Television and Radio Actors. RECREATION—Psychology, hypnotism, collecting Marilyn Monroe memorabilia.

ADDRESS: HOME—236 W. 52nd Street, Apt. 2A, New York, NY 10019.

VOGEL, Paula A.   1951-

PERSONAL: Born November 16, 1951; daughter of Donald Stephen (in advertising) and Phyllis Rita (a secretary; maiden name, Bremerman) Vogel. EDUCATION: Bryn Mawr College, 1969-72; Catholic University, B.A., 1974; Cornell University, 1974-77.

VOCATION: Playwright and teacher.

WRITINGS: PLAYS, PUBLISHED/PRODUCED—*Meg*, 1976, produced at Cornell University, 1976, New Playwrights Theatre, Washington, DC, 1976, Kennedy Center, 1977, Toneel Academie, Maastricht, Netherlands, 1978 (in translation), ANTA-West, Los Angeles, CA, 1978, Lexington Conservatory Theatre, 1978, McGill University, Montreal, Canada, 1978, Central Florida Civic Theatre, 1979, Production Company, NY, 1979, Agustana College, 1981; published by Samuel French, Inc. *Desdemona*, 1977, finalist, Great American Play Contest, Actors Theatre of Louisville; produced at Cornell University, 1978, American Lyric Theatre Workshop, NY, 1978, Lexington Conservatory Theatre, NY, 1978, State University of New York, Binghamton, 1981.

The Last Pat Epstein Show Before the Reruns, 1979; finalist, O'Neill Theatre Center's New Playwrights Conference; produced at University of Regina, Canada, 1979, Central Casting Theatre, 1982. *Apple-Brown Betty*, 1979, commissioned and produced by Actors Theatre of Louisville. *The Oldest Profession*, 1980, finalist, O'Neill Theatre Center's Playwrights Conference, 1981, produced at Hudson Guild, NY, 1981, Theatre Matrix, NY, 1982, Alaska Perserverance Theatre, 1982, University of Regina, Canada, 1982, Little Theatre, NY, 1982. *And Baby Makes Seven*, 1982, staged reading, University of Regina, 1982. *Heirlooms*, 1984.

RELATED CAREER—Visiting guest artist, McGill University, 1979; lecturer, Cornell University, 1977-78; instructor, Cornell University, Theatre Arts, 1979-80; instructor, Theatre Workshop in Playwriting, University of Alaska, Juneau and Perseverance Theatre, 1981; visiting guest artist, University of Regina, 1982; writer of league audition scenes, New York University, 1983; reader, Manhattan Theatre Club; educational co-ordinator, American Place Theatre; chairman, Forbes-Heermans Playwriting Contest, 1979-82; professor of playwriting, Brown University, 1984-85; faculty, Writers Voice, NY, 1984-85.

AWARDS: Samuel French Award; American College Theatre Festival National Playwriting Award; ANTA-West Playwriting Award; National Endowment for the Arts Playwriting Fellowship, 1979-80; MacDowell Colony Fellow.

SIDELIGHTS: MEMBERSHIPS—Dramatists Guild, MacDowell Fellow, Cornell University Theatre Festival Committee.

"I owe a great deal to the encouragement and advice of three people: Beth Eisenberg, Gordon Edelstein, and David Savran. My writing has benefitted from working with them enormously."

ADDRESS: OFFICE—Graduate Writing Program, Brown University, Providence, RI 02912.

*   *   *

VOIGHT, Jon   1938-

PERSONAL: Born December 29, 1938, in Yonkers, NY; son of Elmer and Barbara Voight; married Marcheline Bertrand, December 12, 1971; children: James Haven, Angelina Jolie. EDUCATION: Graduated from Catholic University; prepared for the stage at the Neighborhood Playhouse and with Sanford Meisner.

VOCATION: Actor and writer.

CAREER: PRINCIPAL FILM APPEARANCES—*Hour of the Gun*, United Artists, 1967; *Fearless Frank*, American International, 1967; *Out of It*, United Artists, 1969; *Midnight Cowboy*, United Artists, 1969; *Catch 22*, Paramount, 1970; *The Revolutionary*, United Artists, 1970; *Deliverance*, Warner Brothers, 1972; *The All-American Boy*, Warner Brothers, 1972; *Conrack*, Twentieth Century-Fox, 1974; *The Odessa File*, Columbia, 1974; *End of the Game*, Twentieth Century-Fox, 1976; *Coming Home*, United Artists, 1978; *The Champ*, United Artists, 1979; *Looking to Get Out*, Paramount, 1982; *Table for Five*, Warner Brothers, 1983; *Desert Bloom*.

PRINCIPAL TELEVISION APPEARANCES—*Cimarron Strip*, CBS; *Gunsmoke*, CBS.

STAGE DEBUT—*O Oysters Revue*, Village Gate, NY, 1961. PRINCIPAL STAGE APPEARANCES—Rolf Gruber, *The Sound of Music*, Lunt-Fontanne, NY, 1961; Rodolpho, *A View from the Bridge*, Sheridan Square Playhouse, NY, 1965; Romeo, *Romeo and Juliet*, Ariel, *The Tempest*, Thurio, *Two Gentlemen of Verona*, all National Shakespeare Festival, San Diego, CA, 1966; Steve, *That Summer—That Fall*, Helen Hayes, NY, 1967; *The Dwarfs*, Theatre Company of Boston, MA, 1967; Stanley Kowalski, *A Streetcar Named Desire*, Ahmanson, Los Angeles, CA, then Studio Arena, Buffalo, NY, 1973; Hamlet, *Hamlet*, Levin Theater, Rutgers University, NJ, 1976.

PRINCIPAL STAGE WORK—Co-producer: *The Hashish Club*, Bijou, NY, 1975.

WRITINGS: SCREENPLAYS—Co-writer, *Lookin' to Get Out*, Paramount, 1982.

AWARDS: Cannes International Film Festival Award, Best Actor, Academy Award nomination, Best Actor, both 1969, for *Midnight Cowboy;* Academy Award, Best Actor, Golden Globe Award, Cannes International Film Festival Award, Best Actor, all 1978, for *Coming Home;* Golden Globe Award, Best Actor, 1979, for *The Champ*.

ADDRESS: OFFICE—Screen Actors Guild, 7750 Sunset Blvd., Los Angeles, CA 90046.*

*   *   *

VOLAGE, Charlotte

PERSONAL: Born August 1, in Waterbury, CT; daughter of Peter John (a crane operator) and Viola Linnea (Johnson) Volage. EDUCATION: Wagner College, B.A.; Pennsylvania State University, M.S.; trained for the theatre with George Morrison and at H.B. Studio, NY.

VOCATION: Actress, stage manager, and writer.

CAREER: DEBUT—Margaret, *Kind Sir*, Worcester Foothills Theatre,

CHARLOTTE VOLAGE

Worcester, MA. NEW YORK DEBUT—Maryanne, *Amidst the Gladiolas,* South Street, 1981, for three performances. PRINCIPAL APPEARANCES—Mrs. Cratchit, *A Christmas Carol;* Margaret, *Kind Sir;* Mrs. Boyle, *The Mousetrap;* Sister, *Damn Yankees;* Mrs. Hedges, *Born Yesterday;* Ethel, *Seesaw;* Mrs. Loomis, *Inherit the Wind;* Maude, *The Music Man;* Carmen, *The Pajama Game;* Whore, *Jesus Christ, Superstar;* Gemini Twin, *A Funny Thing Happened on the Way to the Forum;* Manicurist, *Born Yesterday;* Connie, *South Pacific;* Wife, *The Fisherman's Wife;* Ethel, *The Eternal Circle;* Alice, *The Final Act of Love.*

Isabella, *Turandot;* Anna, *The Wedding;* Nurse, *The Doctor in Spite of Himself;* Miss Prism, *The Importance of Being Earnest;* Janet, *Witness for the Prosecution;* Crissie, *Ex-Miss Copper Queen;* Fran Doris, *Littlest Wild West Fighter;* Waitress, *Sophie;* Mary, *Dreams;* Hen, *The Ugly Duckling and the Swan;* Kate, *The Taming of the Shrew;* all performed at the following theatres: Westport Country Playhouse, Worcester Foothills, Thomaston Opera House, Revival, Clockwork Repertory, Theater-by-the-Sea, Children's Theatre Company, Three Muses, The Glines, Trinity Players, New Media Repertory, HighStar Playhouse, Director's Workshop, Thirteenth Street, Actor's Playhouse.

PRINCIPAL STAGE WORK—Stage manager: *Witness for the Prosecution,* HighStar; *Alfred the Dragon,* Children's Improv Company; *Story Theatre, Godspell,* Thomaston Opera House; *Voices from the Past,* Chelsea Westside, NY; *Swak,* Phoenix, NY.

Director: *Housepainters,* Loft; *Curt's Mime Show,* Macy's Christmas Window, NY; *Littlest Wild West Fighter, Born Yesterday,* Thomaston Opera House.

Has also worked as assistant to executive director, Hartman, Stamford, CT, 1983 season; sound technician, New Media Repertory; prop mistress, Ensemble Studio, NY; caretaker, Manhattan Theatre Club, NY; mask designer and costumer, Thomaston Opera House; box-office treasurer, Bill Baird Puppet Theatre, NY; casting director, Prism; producer, *Bullpen,* Prism; assistant to the producers, *Goodtime Charley,* Palace, NY, 1975.

PRINCIPAL FILM APPEARANCES—*The Fan,* Paramount, 1981; Mary, *The Marriage.*

PRINCIPAL TELEVISION APPEARANCES—Dr. Cranbarn, *Axiotis;* midwife, *FYI,* ABC.

RELATED CAREER—Entertainment correspondent, *Our Town;* certified to teach drama in New York City public schools.

WRITINGS: PLAYS, UNPRODUCED—The Toast of New York.

SIDELIGHTS: MEMBERSHIPS—Actors' Equity Association, Screen Actors Guild.

Volage has been a social worker in the child abuse department in Connecticut and was assistant editor for *The Host Magazine.*

ADDRESS: HOME—157 E. Second Street, Apt. 5A, New York, NY 10009. OFFICE—Four Washington Square Village, Apt. 17L, New York, NY 10012.

*   *   *

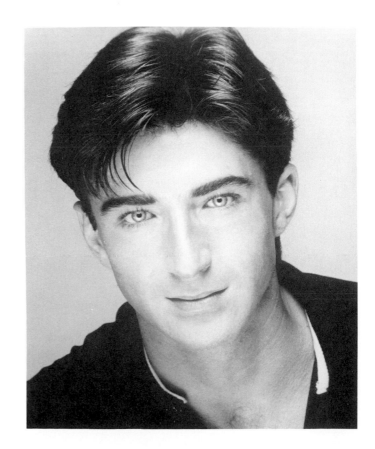

LENNY VON DOHLEN

VON DOHLEN, Lenny   1959-

PERSONAL: Born December 22, 1959, in Augusta, GA; son of L.H. the III (a car dealer) and Gay (Aoueille) Von Dohlen. EDUCATION: Loretto Heights College in Denver; University of Texas, Austin; trained for the theatre with Blair Cutting at the Michael Chekhov Studio.

VOCATION: Actor.

CAREER: STAGE DEBUT—Romeo, *Romeo and Juliet,* May Bonfils Center, Denver, CO, 1977. NEW YORK DEBUT—Robert Wesner, *Twister,* Academy Arts Players, February, 1980, fifty performances. PRINCIPAL STAGE APPEARANCES—Hal, *Loot,* Oregon Contemporary Theatre, Portland, OR, 1981; Betty/Gerry, *Cloud 9,* Lucille Lortel, NY, 1982; Tom, *Asian Shade,* WPA, NY, 1983; Eben, *Desire Under the Elms,* Roundabout, NY, 1984.

Regional theatre appearances: Tom, *Tea and Sympathy,* Richard, *Ah, Wilderness!,* Gustave, *Thieves Carnival,* Bus Riley, *Bus Riley's Back in Town,* Fortinbras, *Hamlet,* first player, *Rosencrantz and Guildenstern Are Dead,* King and Judge, *King Ubu,* Charles, *School for Scandal,* all at University of Texas; Japheth, *The Flowering Peach,* May Bonfils Center, Denver, CO; Richard, *The Chinese Viewing Pavilion,* Board Head, Michigan Public Theatre.

MAJOR TOURS—Don Baker, *Butterflies Are Free,* Grand Lake Colorado Summer Theatres.

FILM DEBUT—Robert Dennis, *Tender Mercies,* Universal, 1983. PRINCIPAL FILM APPEARANCES—Miles Harding, *Electric Dreams,* Metro-Goldwyn-Mayer, 1984.

TELEVISION DEBUT—Cal, *Kent State,* NBC, 1980. PRINCIPAL TELEVISION APPERANCES—Knoleton Whitney, *Under the Biltmore Clock,* PBS; Erik Crimpley, *How to Be a Perfect Person in Just Three Days,* PBS; Ricky, *Mother, May I?* PBS, 1981; Paulie, *Sessions,* NBC, 1982; Richard, *Miami Vice,* NBC, 1985.

SIDELIGHTS: MEMBERSHIPS—Actors' Equity Association, Screen Actors Guild, American Federation of Television and Radio Artists.

ADDRESS: HOME—New York, NY. OFFICE—c/o Dale Davis & Company, 1650 Broadway, Suite 1005, New York, NY 10019. AGENT—The Lantz Office, 888 Seventh Avenue, New York, NY 10106.

W

WAJDA, Andrzei 1927-

PERSONAL: Born March 6, 1927, in Suwalki, Poland. EDUCATION: Attended Educated Fine Arts Academy, Krakow, Poland, 1945-48; High School of Cinematography, Lodz, Poland, 1950-52.

VOCATION: Director.

CAREER: FIRST FILM WORK—Director, *While You Sleep* (short), 1950. PRINCIPAL FILM WORK—Director: *The Bad Boy* (short), 1950; *The Pottery of Zlza* (short), 1951; *The Generation*, 1954; *I Go to the Sun* (short), 1955; *Kanal*, 1957; *Ashes and Diamonds*, 1958; *Lotna*, 1959; *Innocent Sorcerers*, 1960; *Samson*, 1961; *Fury Is a Woman*, 1962; "Warsaw, Poland" segment of *Love at Twenty*, 1962; *Ashes*, 1965; *Gates to Paradise*, 1967; *Everything for Sale*, 1968; *Hunting Flies*, 1969; *Landscape After Battle*, 1970; *The Wedding*, 1972; *Promised Land*, 1974; *The Shadow Line*, 1976; *Man of Marble*, 1977; *Without Anesthesia*, 1978; *The Young Maids of Wilko*, 1979; *The Orchestra Conductor*, 1980; *Man of Iron*, 1981; *Danton*, 1982; *A Love in Germany*, 1983.

PRINCIPAL TELEVISION WORK—Director, Polish television: *Roly-Poly*, 1968; *The Birch Wood*, 1971; *Pilate and the Others*, 1972; *The Dead Class*, 1978; *November Night*, 1980.

AWARDS: The Golden Palm, Cannes Film Festival 1981, for *Man of Iron*.

SIDELIGHTS: During the occupation of Poland by Germany, Wajda worked at odd jobs including assistant in the restoration of paintings in a church in Radom. In 1942, he joined the A.K. (Home Army Resistance) led by the Polish government in Exile. He was the head of the filmmaker's association, but under the government's demands he had to resign in return for allowing continued existence of the organization. His Studio X Film Production Group was dissolved by the government in 1983.

Wajda's *A Generation*, 1954, *Kanal*, 1957, and *Ashes and Diamonds*, 1958, were a prime force in the "Polish school" of poetic realism, helping to establish Polish cinema internationally.*

*   *   *

WALDEN, Stanley 1932-

PERSONAL: Born December 2, 1932, in Brooklyn, NY; son of Herman and Henrietta (Brody) Walden; married Barbara Dolgin (a dance therapist), September 4, 1955; children: Matthew, Joshua. EDUCATION: Queens College, B.A., music, with honors; studied composition with Ben Weber, clarinet with David Weber.

VOCATION: Composer.

CAREER: PRINCIPAL THEATRE WORK—Incidental music: *Scuba Duba*, 1967; *Pinkville*, American Place, NY, 1970; *The Kid*, American Place, NY, 1972; *Sigmunds Freude*, Bremen Stadt Theater, Bremen, West Germany, 1975; *American Days*, Manhattan Theatre Club; *Horseman Pass By*.

Complete scores: *Oh! Calcutta!*, NY and London, 1969; *The Caucasian Chalk Circle*, Arena, Washington, DC, 1978; *Back Country*, Wilbur, Boston, 1978; *Improvisations Over Shylock*, 1979; *My Mother's Courage*, 1979; *Untergang der Titanic*, 1980; *Hamlet*, 1980; *Death & Co.; Der Voyeur*, Berlin Festival, 1981; *Jubilaeum*, Bochum Schauspielhaus, 1983; *Dr. Faustus Lights the Lights*, Cologne Schauspielhaus, West Germany, 1983; *Peepshow; Die Beteleroper (The Beggars Opera)*, Rennaisance Theater, West Berlin, West Germany, 1984.

Also scores for: *The Serpent, The Mutation Show, The Winter Project*, all at the Open Eye; *The Tommy Allen Show*, Actors Studio; *(We've Each Got a Reason for) Bein' Here Tonight*, Theatre Center, Philadelphia, PA, also Vienna, Austria; *Paradise Lost*, Temple University, Philadelphia, PA.

CONCERT MUSIC—*Love's Proper Exercise*, written for Jan De-Gaetani; *Circus*, Louisville Orchestra; *Stretti*, the Group for Contemporary Music; *Some Changes*, for Jan DeGaetani; *Fandangle*, Bennet College; *Primer*, Lincoln Center Institute; *Jacks or Better, Legno*, for M. Kupferman; *Three Ladies*, for Jan DeGaetani and G. Kalish; *Symphony—After Ausschwitz*, Musica Nova, Eastman School, Rochester, NY.

FILM MUSIC—*La Fille d'Amerique*, Greenwich Films, Paris, 1975; *Frohes Fest*, ZDF; *Desperado City*, Atossa Film, Munich, 1980; *All by Myself*.

BALLET MUSIC—*Dance Sonata*, for Daniel Nagrin; *Untitled*, for Anna Sokolow; *Image*, Harkness Ballet; *Weewis*, Margo Sappington for the Joffrey Ballet, 1971.

RELATED CAREER—Teacher: Juilliard School, NY, 1965-71, SUNY-Purchase, 1973-78, Sarah Lawrence, NY, 1973-75, Max Reinhardt-Schule, Berlin, C.W. Post, NY; Guest lecturer: University of Wisconsin, Yale Drama School, Eastman School of Music, Rochester, NY, Southern Methodist University.

Pianist for Martha Graham Dance Company and Anna Sokolow Dance Company; musical director for Tamaris-Nagrin Dance Company.

RECORDINGS: *The Open Window,* Vanguard; *Circus,* First Edition; *Oh! Calcutta!,* Aidart; *Die Betteleroper (The Beggars Opera),* Renaissance Theater, Berlin.

ADDRESS: HOME—Route 7, Box 356, Hopewell Junction, NY 12533.

* * *

WANSHEL, Jeff 1947-

PERSONAL: Full name Jeffrey M. Wanshel; born August 24, 1947, in White Plains, NY; son of Jerome Nelson (an attorney) and Sylvia (a social worker and real estate agent; maiden name, Greenwald) Wanshel. EDUCATION: Wesleyan University, Middletown, CT, B.A., English, 1969; studied at Yale University School of Drama, 1969-70.

VOCATION: Playwright.

WRITINGS: PLAYS PUBLISHED/PRODUCED—*The Disintegration of James Cherry,* produced at Repertory Theatre of Lincoln Center, NY, 1969-70; American Conservatory Theatre, San Francisco, CA, 1971; on BBC Radio, 1972; Manhattan Theatre Club, NY, 1972; Hudson Guild, NY, 1976. *The Rhesus Umbrella,* produced at Yale Repertory Theatre, 1970. *Auto-Destruct,* produced at Magic Theatre, San Francisco, CA, 1972-73; Manhattan Theatre Club, 1973;

JEFF WANSHEL

Theatre Genesis, NY, 1976. *Fog and Mismanagement,* produced at Circle Repertory Company, NY, 1976. *Parade,* National Theatre of the Deaf, U.S. and international tour, 1975-76.

Isadora Duncan Sleeps with the Russian Navy, produced at American Place, NY, 1976-77. *The General Brutus,* produced on "Earplay," National Public Radio, 1978. *The Wild Goose,* produced at Magic Theatre, San Francisco, CA, 1978. *Holeville* (with songs and direction by Des McAnuff), produced at Dodger Theatre, Brooklyn Academy of Music, 1979. Adaptation of Kafka's *A Metamorphosis in Minature,* Music Theatre Group/Lenox Arts Center and the Cubiculo, NY, 1982. Adaptation of Landolfi's *Gogol's Wife,* Music Theatre Group/Lenox Arts Center, 1983. *Times and Appetites of Toulouse-Lautrec; Fun in Nuclear Park.*

TELEPLAYS—Adaptation of James Thurber's "The Greatest Man in the World," *American Short Story,* PBS, 1980; adaptation of Faulkner's "The Bear," *American Masterworks,* PBS, 1985.

AWARDS: Audrey Wood Fellowship, Rockefeller Fellowship, O'Neill Fellowship, 1971; Rockefeller Playwriting Award, 1972; CAPS Grant, New York State Council on the Arts, 1977; National Endowment for the Arts Creative Writing Fellowship in Screenwriting, 1982; Obie, Best New American Play, 1982, for *A Metamorphosis in Minature.*

SIDELIGHTS: MEMBERSHIPS—Writers Guild of America East, Dramatists Guild.

ADDRESS: AGENT—Luis Sanjurjo, International Creative Management, 40 W. 57th Street, New York, NY 10019.

* * *

WARREN, Jennifer Leigh

PERSONAL: Born August 29, in Dallas, TX; daughter of Ruby Ruth Warren. EDUCATION: Dartmouth College, B.A., theatre.

VOCATION: Actress and singer.

CAREER: DEBUT—Lutiebelle, *Purlie,* Center Theatre, Hanover, NH. NEW YORK DEBUT—Crystal, *Little Shop of Horrors,* Orpheum then WPA, 1982. PRINCIPAL STAGE APPEARANCES—Alice's daughter, *Big River,* O'Neill, 1985.

TELEVISION DEBUT—Karen Jones, *All My Children,* ABC, 1985.

AWARDS: Marcus Heiman Award for excellence in theatre, Dartmouth College.

SIDELIGHTS: MEMBERSHIPS—Actors' Equity Association, American Federation of Television and Radio Artists, Screen Actors Guild.

ADDRESS: AGENT—Ambrose Company, 1466 Broadway, New York, NY 10036.

JENNIFER LEIGH WARREN

DAVID WARRILOW

WARRILOW, David   1934-

PERSONAL: Born December 28, 1934, in England; son of Charles Kenneth (a shoe retailer) and Ellen (Cregg) Warrilow. EDUCATION: University of Reading, England, B.A., French, 1957.

VOCATION: Actor.

CAREER: STAGE DEBUT—*The Red Horse Animation*, Mabou Mines, Guggenheim Museum, NY, 1970. LONDON DEBUT— Three roles, *Three Samuel Beckett Plays*, Donmar Warehouse, 1984. PRINCIPAL STAGE APPEARANCES—*Animations, Cascando, Play, The Lost Ones, Dressed Like an Egg, Southern Exposure*, all at Mabou Mines, NY, 1970-79; Jacques, *As You Like It*, Almaviva, *The Marriage of Figaro*, Hector, *Heartbreak House*, Judge Brack, *Hedda Gabler*, Norman, *Hang on to Me, Kudos*, all at the Tyrone Guthrie, Minneapolis; psychiatrist, *Penguin Touquet*, New York Shakespeare Festival, Public, NY; speaker, *A Piece of Monologue*, LaMaMa ETC, NY, 1979; protagonist, *Catastrophe, What Where* (two Beckett plays), Harold Clurman, NY; Reb Ellis, *Messiah*.

MAJOR TOURS—Reader, *Ohio Impromptu*, OH, Chicago, Paris, NY, Edinburgh, London.

FILM DEBUT—Mr. Sutherland, *La Ferdinanda*, 1981.

TELEVISION DEBUT—Voice, *Samuel Beckett: Silence to Silence*, RTE (Irish television), 1984.

AWARDS: Obie Awards, 1976, for *The Lost Ones*, 1979, for *Southern Exposure;* Twin Cities Critics Award, 1982, for *Kudos*.

SIDELIGHTS: MEMBERSHIPS—Actors' Equity Association.

Warrilow told *CTFT*, that Samuel Beckett wrote *A Piece of Monologue* expressly for him to play. Warrilow has toured extensively throughout the United States, Europe and Australia, and was trained as a magazine editor, at *Realites*, in Paris, France.

ADDRESS: HOME—428 E. Ninth Street, New York, NY 10009.

*   *   *

WASSON, Susanne

PERSONAL: Born September 19, in Searcy, AR; daughter of C.R. (an insurance broker) and Viva Mac (worked for the Arkansas Revenue Department; maiden name, Lanier) Wasson. EDUCATION: Texas Women's University, B.A., theatre; trained for the theatre with Lee Grant and Stella Adler (acting), Carolyn Tannen (voice), and Ron Clairmont (vocal coach).

VOCATION: Actress.

CAREER: DEBUT—Julie, *The Tender Trap*, North Hatley Playhouse, Canada, 1960. NEW YORK DEBUT—Sue Easton, *Whitsuntide*, Martinique, February, 1972 for twenty-five performances. PRINCIPAL STAGE APPEARANCES—Joanna, *Present Laughter*, Piggery, Quebec, 1961; Viola, *Twelfth Night*, Totem Pole, PA; Gittel, *Two for the Seesaw*, Horseshoe, Los Angeles, CA, 1962; Gloria, *The Tiger*, Desilu, Los Angeles, CA, 1964; Claire, *There's a Girl in My Soup*, Alhambra, Jacksonville, FL, 1970; Ruth, *Blithe*

SUSANNE WASSON

Spirit, Alhambra, 1971; understudy, *Cracks,* Theatre de Lys, NY, 1973.

Elizabeth, *Catch Me If You Can,* Hayloft, VA, 1973; *My Daughter Is X-Rated,* Kenley Players, OH, 1973; Elizabeth, *Catch Me If You Can,* Westgate, OH, 1974; *Under the Yum Yum Tree,* Kenley Players, OH, 1974; Ellie, *A Late Snow,* Playwrights Horizons, NY, 1974; Jennifer, *A Nestless Bird,* New Dramatists, NY, 1974; Doris, *Same Time, Next Year,* Theatre New Brunswick, Canada, 1979; Chelsea, *On Golden Pond,* Ann, *Free at Last,* Theatre New Brunswick, Canada, 1980; Dorothy, *Smile of the Cardboard Man,* Sara Lee Cutter, *The Natives Are Restless,* No Smoking Theatre, NY, 1984.

MAJOR TOURS—Leila Tree, *Panama Hattie,* pre-Broadway tryout, Ft. Lauderdale, FL, Papermill, Milburn, NJ, Syracuse, NY, OH, 1976.

FILM DEBUT—Judith Bradley, *Stitches,* Marcucci/Kerr Productions, 1985.

TELEVISION DEBUT—*Alfred Hitchcock Presents,* 1962. PRINCIPAL TELEVISION APPEARANCES—*Mannix,* CBS; *Mission: Impossible,* CBS; *Star Trek,* NBC; *Women in Chains,* 1971; *Hart to Hart,* CBS; *The A-Team,* ABC; *Crazy Like a Fox,* CBS, 1985; *Filthy Rich; Middle Earth* (pilot); *The Young and the Restless; One Life to Live; As the World Turns; General Hospital; All My Children.*

SIDELIGHTS: MEMBERSHIPS—Actors' Equity Association, American Federation of Television and Radio Artists, Screen Actors Guild, Canadian Actors' Equity Association.

Since 1979, Wasson has taught in her own theatre workshop.

ADDRESS: AGENT—Roxy Horen Management, 300 W. 17th Street, Suite 2E, New York, NY 10011.

WEAVER, Fritz   1926-

PERSONAL: Full name Fritz William Weaver; born January 19, 1926, in Pittsburgh, PA; son of John Carson and Elsa W. (Stringaro) Weaver; married Sylvia Short, February 7, 1953; children: Lydia Charlotte, Anthony Ballou.

VOCATION: Actor.

CAREER: STAGE DEBUT—As member of the Barter Theatre, Abingdon, VA, 1952-54. NEW YORK DEBUT—Fainall, *The Way of the World,* Cherry Lane, 1954. PRINCIPAL STAGE APPEARANCES—With the Group 20 Players, Wellesley, MA: Petruchio, *The Taming of the Shrew,* Sir Francis Chesney, *Charley's Aunt,* Preacher, *Dark of the Moon,* Oberon, *A Midsummer Night's Dream,* Caesar, *Androcles and the Lion,* Edward II, *Carnival King;* Secretary, *The Doctor's Dilemma,* and Flamineo, *The White Devil,* both at the Phoenix, NY, 1955; Casca, *Julius Caesar,* and Antonio, *The Tempest,* both at the American Shakespeare Festival, Stratford, CT, 1955; Maitland, *The Chalk Garden,* Barrymore, NY, 1955.

Philip Faulconbridge, *King John,* and Gremio, *The Taming of the Shrew,* both at the American Shakespeare Festival, 1956; Marc Bradley, *Protective Custody,* Ambassador, NY, 1956; a boy, *Miss Lonelyhearts,* Music Box, NY, 1957; title role, *Hamlet,* American Shakespeare Festival, 1958; Harry, Lord Monchensey, *The Family Reunion,* and the Priest, *The Power and the Glory,* both at the Phoenix, NY, 1958; Malvolio, *Twelfth Night,* Cambridge Drama Festival, MA, 1959; Dion Anthony, *The Great God Brown,* Coronet, NY, 1959; title role, *Peer Gynt,* title role, *Henry IV, Part I* and *Part II,* Cambridge Drama Festival, and at the Queen Elizabeth, Vancouver, BC, 1961; Mark, *Men, Women, and Angels,* Winter Garden, NY, 1962; Henderson, *All American,* NY, 1962; M. Beaurevers, *A Shot in the Dark,* Booth, NY, 1962; Van Miessin, *Lorenzo,* Plymouth, NY, 1963; Phileas Fogg, *Around the World in Eighty Days,* Jones Beach, NY, 1963; various roles, *The White House,* Henry Miller, NY, 1964.

Sherlock Holmes, *Baker Street,* Broadway, NY, 1965; Fredrick the Great, *The Sorrows of Fredrick,* Mark Taper Forum, LA, 1967; Henry Higgins, *My Fair Lady,* City Center, NY, 1968; Jerome Malley, *Child's Play,* Royale, NY, 1970; Patrick Power, *Patrick's Day,* Long Wharf, New Haven, CT, 1973; title role, *Macbeth,* American Shakespeare Festival, Stratford, CT, 1973; Ronald, *Absurd Person Singular,* Music Box, NY, 1975; one man show, *Lincoln,* Chelsea Theatre Center, NY, 1976; Sidney Kentridge, *The Biko Inquest,* Theatre Four, NY, 1978; *Dialogue for Lovers,* Symphony Space, 1980; *A Tale Told,* Circle Repertory Company, NY, 1980, Mark Taper Forum, Los Angeles, 1981; *Angel's Fall,* Circle Repertory Company, NY, 1982, then Longacre, NY, 1982-83; *Beethoven's Tenth,* Ahmanson, Los Angeles, 1983.

MAJOR TOURS—Father Day, *Life with Father,* summer tour, 1974; *Beethoven's Tenth,* five city tour, 1983-84.

PRINCIPAL FILM APPEARANCES—*The Crimson Curtain,* 1955; *Fail-Safe,* 1964; *The Guns of August,* Universal, 1965; *The Maltese Bippy,* Metro-Goldwyn-Mayer, 1969; *A Walk in the Spring Rain,* Columbia, 1970; *The Day of the Dolphin,* Avco-Embassy, 1973; *Marathon Man,* 1976; *Black Sunday,* Paramount, 1977; *The Demon Seed,* United Artists, 1978; *The Big Fix,* Universal, 1979; *Creepshow,* Warner Brothers, 1982.

PRINCIPAL TELEVISION APPEARANCES—*Kraft Television Theatre; U.S. Steel Hour; Studio One; She Stoops to Conquer; A Tale of Two*

Cities; The Potting Shed; Jane Eyre; The Crucible; The Power and the Glory. Also: *The Borgia Stick, 1966; The Berlin Affair,* 1970; *The Hunter,* 1971; *Heat of Anger,* 1971; *The Snoop Sisters* (retitled *Female Instinct),* 1972; *Antigone,* 1973, *A Touch of the Poet,* both PBS, 1974; *Legend of Lizzie Borden,* 1975; *Captains Courageous,* 1977. Mini-series: *Holocaust; The Martian Chronicles; A Death in California,* 1985.

AWARDS: Antoinette Perry Award, Variety Critics Poll Drama Desk, 1971, all for his portrayal of Jerome Malley, *Child's Play.*

ADDRESS: HOME—New York, NY. AGENT—Lucy Kroll Agency, 390 West End Avenue, New York, NY 10023.

*   *   *

WEINER, Zane David   1953-

PERSONAL: Born July 11, 1953, in Holyoke, MA; son of Mathew (a retailer) and Helen Marie (a nurse; maiden name, Bernstein) Weiner. EDUCATION: University of New Hampshire, B.A., theatre, 1975. POLITICS: Democrat. RELIGION: Jewish.

VOCATION: Stage manager, production manager, and writer.

CAREER: FIRST STAGE WORK—Production stage manager, *Tuscaloosa's Calling Me,* Village Gate, NY. PRINCIPAL STAGE WORK—Stage manager and production stage manager: *Salt Lake City Skyline,* off Broadway production; *Coriolanus, Julius Caesar, Othello, Curse of the Starving Class, Ashes,* all New York Shakespeare Festival; *Happy New Year,* Morosco, NY; *A Chorus Line,* Shubert, NY; *Bosoms and Neglect,* Longacre, NY; *Ballroom,* Majestic, NY; *Pirates of Penzance,* New York Shakespeare Festival, Delacorte, then Uris, NY; *Dreamgirls,* Imperial, NY.

MAJOR TOURS—Stage manager, *A Chorus Line,* international tour.

PRINCIPAL FILM WORK—Musical production coordinator, *The Cotton Club,* Orion Pictures, 1984.

WRITINGS: PLAYS, UNPRODUCED—Firetown; Lottery; Bad Luck Charlie; The American Spirit.

SIDELIGHTS: MEMBERSHIPS—Actors' Equity Association.

Weiner told *CTFT,* "I enjoy putting together technically complex productions, dealing with people, and being challenged. My one big hobby is that I am a professional fisherman."

ADDRESS: OFFICE—253 W. 72nd Street, New York, NY 10023.

*   *   *

WEISKOPF, Bob

VOCATION: Producer and writer.

CAREER: PRINCIPAL TELEVISION WORK—Producer (with Bob Schiller): *The Good Guys,* CBS, 1968-70; *Maude,* CBS, 1974-78; *All's Fair,* CBS, 1976-77.

WRITINGS: RADIO AND TELEVISION—*The Eddie Cantor Show,* 1940-41; *Rudy Vallee, John Barrymore, Joan Davis Show,* 1941-42; *The Fred Allen Show,* 1942-50.

TELEVISION—(All written with Bob Schiller) *That's My Boy,* CBS, 1954; *Professional Father,* CBS, 1955; *It's Always Jan,* CBS, 1955-56; *I Love Lucy,* CBS, 1956-57; *The Lucy—Desi Comedy Hour,* CBS, 1957-60 (seen also 1962-67); *The Ann Southern Show* (pilot), CBS, 1958; *Guestward Ho,* ABC, 1960-61; *Pete and Gladys,* CBS, 1961-62; *The Lucy Show,* CBS, 1962-64; *The Red Skelton Show,* CBS, 1965-68; *The Good Guys,* CBS, 1968-70; *The Carol Burnett Show,* CBS, 1970-71; *The Flip Wilson Show,* NBC, 1971-72; *Maude,* CBS, 1972-76; *All's Fair,* CBS, 1976-77; *All in the Family,* CBS, 1978-80; *Archie Bunker's Place,* CBS, 1981-82.

PLAYS, PRODUCED—With Bob Schiller, *So Long Stanley.*

AWARDS: Emmy Awards, 1971, for *Flip Wilson Show,* 1978, for *All in the Family;* Writers Guild Awards, for *I Love Lucy, The Lucy—Desi Comedy Hour, Maude, All in the Family.*

SIDELIGHTS: MEMBERSHIPS—Writers Guild of America, American Federation of Television and Radio Artists.

Bob Schiller and Bob Weiskopf have been writing partners for more than thirty years. Among their classic television scripts are "Lucy and the Grape Stomping" from *I Love Lucy,* "Attempted Rape of Edith Bunker" and "Cousin Liz" (lesbian episode) from *All in the Family,* and "Maude and the Psychiatrist" a half-hour monologue from the series, *Maude.*

ADDRESS: AGENT—Robinson-Weintraub Company, 8428 Melrose Place, Los Angeles, CA 90069.

*   *   *

WEISS, Joel   1953-

PERSONAL: Born September 21, 1953; son of Charles (an actor) and Beatrice Weiss. EDUCATION: Bronx Community College, A.A.; Lehmann College, B.A., theatre; studied for the stage with Joan Matiessen at the Herbert Berghof Studios. RELIGION: Jewish.

VOCATION: Actor.

CAREER: STAGE DEBUT—Third westerner, *Pony Express,* fifth grade class at P.S. 33, Bronx. NEW YORK DEBUT—Bear, *Shooting Gallery,* 13th Street Theatre, 1976, 27 performances.

FILM DEBUT—Cropsey, *The Warriors,* Paramount, 1979. PRINCIPAL FILMS—*Subway Fantasy; Housing Project U.S.A.; The Bargain;* Johnny Able, *A Block in the Bronx,* Bronx Film Project, 1983; *The Flamingo Kid,* 1984; *Brewster's Millions,* 1985, Universal.

TELEVISION DEBUT—Headwaiter, *Another World,* NBC, 1978. PRINCIPAL TELEVISION APPEARANCES—Wilson Carter, *CHiPS,* NBC; *Senior Trip,* 1981.

JOEL WEISS

SIDELIGHTS: MEMBERSHIPS—Actors' Equity Association, Screen Actors Guild, American Federation of Television and Radio Artists, Waiter's Union, Locals 6, 11, and 100, Actor's Fund.

Weiss wrote to tell *CTFT*, that is his favorite part was "my role as Cropsey in Walter Hill's *The Warriors*, because I had such a good time and made money." The two films in which Mr. Weiss starred, *The Bargain* and *A Block in the Bronx*, were selected for inclusion at the 1984 New York Film Festival.

ADDRESS: HOME—3340-5 Bailey Avenue, Bronx, NY 10463. AGENT—Leonetti Talent Agency, 6526 Sunset Blvd., Hollywood, CA 90028.

*   *   *

WEISS, Marc B.

VOCATION: Designer, producer, and director.

CAREER: FIRST STAGE WORK—Set designer: Washington Ballet, Arena Stage, Washington, DC. PRINCIPAL STAGE WORK—Lighting designer (all Broadway productions): *6 Rms Riv Vu*, 1972; *Find Your Way Home*, *Cat on a Hot Tin Roof*, *Words and Music*, all 1974; *Hughie/Duet*, 1975; *The Eccentricities of a Nightingale*, 1976; *Ladies at the Alamo*, 1977; *Deathtrap*, 1978; *Once a Catholic*, 1979; *The First*, 1981; *Othello*, 1982; *Zorba*, 1983; *A Moon for the Misbegotten*, *The Rink*, both 1984.

MAJOR TOUR—Lighting designer, *My One and Only*, international tour, 1985.

MARC B. WEISS

PRINCIPAL FILM WORK—Special lighting, *Four Friends*, 1983.

ADDRESS: HOME—225 W. 90th Street, New York, NY 10024.

*   *   *

WELLER, Michael   1942-

PERSONAL: Born September 26, 1942; son of Paul and Rosa (Rush) Weller. EDUCATION: Brandeis University, B.A., 1965; studied at Manchester University.

VOCATION: Playwright and screenwriter.

WRITINGS: PLAYS PUBLISHED/PRODUCED—*How Ho-Ho Rose and Fell* (also music), produced at Manchester University, 1966; *Happy Valley*, produced at Edinburgh Festival, 1969; *The Body Builders*, *Now There's Just the Three of Us* (one acts), Open Space, 1969; *Cancer*, Royal Court, 1970, produced in the U.S. as *Moonchildren*, Royale, 1972; *Grant's Movie, Tira Tells Everything There Is to Know about Herself* (one acts), 1971; *Twenty Three Years Later*, Los Angeles, 1973; *Fishing*, 1975; *Split* (one act), 1978; *Loose Ends*, 1979; *Dwarfman*, 1980; *The Ballad of Soapy Smith*, Seattle Repertory Company, New York Shakespeare Festival, 1983-84; *Ghost on Fire*, La Jolla Playhouse, 1985.

LYRICS—With Jim Steinman, *More Than You Deserve*, 1973.

SCREENPLAYS—*Hair*, 1979; *Ragtime*, 1980.

ADDRESS: HOME—New York, NY.

WELLMAN, Wendell   1944-

PERSONAL: Born December 20, 1944, in Waterloo, IA; son of Wendell (a businessman) and Leah (a teacher; maiden name, Voight) Wellman. EDUCATION: Pasadena College, B.A., 1967; University of California, Los Angeles, M.A., 1970; studied for the theatre at the Actors Studio and the UCLA Film School.

VOCATION: Actor and screenwriter.

CAREER: FILM DEBUT—*The Klansman,* Paramount, 1974. PRINCIPAL FILM APPEARANCES—*Sudden Impact,* Warner Brothers, 1983.

TELEVISION DEBUT—*The New Land,* ABC, 1974.

RELATED CAREER—Guest teacher, screenwriting, UCLA.

WRITINGS: SCREENPLAYS—*Firefox,* Warner Brothers, 1983; *End of the World Weekend,* New World Pix; *Fair Game,* Warner Brothers, 1984.

SIDELIGHTS: MEMBERSHIPS—Screen Actors Guild, Screen Writers Guild.

ADDRESS: HOME—Santa Monica, CA. AGENT—Mike Simpson and Lenny Hipshan, William Morris Agency, 151 El Camino Drive, Beverly Hills, CA 90212.

*   *   *

THOMAS EDWARD WEST

WEST, Thomas Edward   1954-

PERSONAL: Born May 11, 1954, in Mansfield, OH; son of Edward Elden (a university administrator) and Doris Miriam (a teacher; maiden name, Peat) West; married Alana Stackhouse (an actress), September 10, 1977. EDUCATION: Ashland College, B.A., theatre, 1975; Florida State University, M.F.A., directing, 1977.

VOCATION: Director, manager, and writer.

CAREER: PRINCIPAL STAGE WORK—Director: *Godspell,* Ashland Summer Theatre; *A Funny Thing Happened on the Way to the Forum,* Venice Little Theatre; *The Sound of Music,* Festival of American Theatre, Ogden, UT; *Timesteps,* Encompass Theatre, NY; *Wiley and the Hairy Man, Plain Folk,* both Asolo Touring Theatre, Sarasota, FL; *In This Golden Land, A History of the American Film,* Asolo State Theatre; *Golden Land,* 78th Street Theatre Lab, NY; *A Life in the Theatre, What the Butler Saw,* both New Stage Theatre, Jackson, MS; *Rosencrantz and Guildenstern Are Dead,* Boston Shakespeare Company; *The Matchmaker, Inner Grace,* both Fulton Opera House, Lancaster, PA; *Alice and Fred,* New York Theatre Bridge; *Period of Adjustment,* Ten Ten Repertory, NY; *Scapino, The Tragedy of Macbeth,* Asolo Touring Theatre; *The School for Wives,* Asolo State Theatre, *The Comedy of Errors,* Virginia Shakespeare Festival, Williamsburg, VA; *Othello,* Boston Shakespeare Festival; *The Changeling,* Equity Library Theatre, NY.

PRINCIPAL TELEVISION WORK—Writer and producer, *A Dream Coming True,* WXLT, Sarasota, FL; host and producer, *Film Forum,* WRDL, Ashland, OH; Writer, director, and producer, *Meshugana!,* WRDL, Ashland, OH.

RELATED CAREER—Associate managing director, Ashland Summer Theatre, 1975; associate artistic director, Asolo State Theatre, 1977-80; artistic director, Asolo Touring Theatre, 1977-80; guest professor, Lawrence University, Appleton, WI; instructor, Asolo Conservatory, Sarasota, FL.

WRITINGS: PLAYS, PRODUCED—*O. Henry's Christmas,* Pittsburgh Public Theatre; *The Tragedy of Macbeth,* adapted from Shakespeare for Asolo Touring Theatre; *The Inspector General,* translated from Gogol for Asolo State Theatre; *Plain Folk,* Asolo Touring Theatre; *Mark Twain: Member-at-Large for the Human Race,* adapted from Mark Twain's writings and speeches.

SIDELIGHTS: MEMBERSHIPS—Society of Stage Directors and Choreographers.

ADDRESS: HOME—326 Columbus Avenue, New York, NY 10023. OFFICE—Rialto Theatrical, P.O. Box 1516, New York, NY 10023.

*   *   *

WESTON, Jack   1915-

PERSONAL: Born in 1915. EDUCATION: Trained for the stage at the Cleveland Playhouse, OH, and at the American Theatre Wing, NY. MILITARY: U.S. Army, World War Two.

VOCATION: Actor.

CAREER: PRINCIPAL FILM APPEARANCES—*Please Don't Eat the Daisies,* Metro-Goldwyn-Mayer, 1960; *All in a Night's Work,* Paramount, 1961; *The Honeymoon Machine,* Metro-Goldwyn-Mayer, 1961; *It's Only Money,* Paramount, 1962; *Palm Springs Weekend,* Warner Brothers, 1963; *The Incredible Mr. Limpet,* Warner Brothers, 1964; *Mirage,* Universal, 1965; *The Cincinnati Kid,* Metro-Goldwyn-Mayer, 1965; *Wait Until Dark,* Warner Brothers-Seven Arts, 1967; *The Thomas Crown Affair,* United Artists, 1968; *The April Fools,* National General, 1969; *Cactus Flower,* Columbia, 1969; *A New Leaf,* Paramount, 1971; *Fuzz,* United Artists, 1972; *Marco,* Cinerama, 1973; *The Ritz,* Warner Brothers, 1976; *Gator,* United Artists, 1976; *Cuba,* United Artists, 1979; *Can't Stop the Music,* Associated Film, 1980; *The Four Seasons,* 1981; *Desert Bloom.*

PRINCIPAL TELEVISION APPEARANCES—Series: Chick Adams, *My Sister Eileen,* CBS, 1960-61; Walter Hathaway, *The Hathaways,* ABC, 1961-62; Danny Zimmer, *The Four Seasons,* CBS, 1984. Guest appearances: *The Carol Burnett Show,* CBS; *Red Browning of the Rocket Rangers; Gunsmoke,* CBS; *Philco Playhouse,* NBC; *Studio One,* CBS; *Twilight Zone,* CBS; *The Untouchables,* ABC.

NEW YORK STAGE DEBUT—Michael Lindsey, *Season in the Sun,* Cort, 1950. PRINCIPAL STAGE APPEARANCES—Stewpot, *South Pacific,* Majestic, NY, 1952; Francis, *Bells Are Ringing,* Shubert, NY, 1956; *The Trouble with People . . . and Other Things,* Coconut Grove Playhouse, Miami Beach, FL, 1974; Gaetano Proclo, *The Ritz,* Longacre, NY, 1975; Marvin Michaels, "Visitor from Philadelphia," Mort Hollender, "Visitors from Chicago," *California Suite,* Eugene O'Neill, NY, 1976; Sam, *Cheaters,* Biltmore, NY, 1978; Dietrich Merkenschrift, *Break a Leg,* Palace, NY, 1979.

MAJOR TOURS—Rudy "Baby" Filbertson, *Crazy October,* U.S. cities, 1958-59; Pfancoo, *The Office,* U.S. cities, 1966; Barney Cashman, *The Last of the Red Hot Lovers,* U.S. cities, 1970-71.*

*   *   *

WHITEHEAD, Robert   1916-

PERSONAL: Born March 3, 1916, in Montreal, Canada; son of William Thomas and Selena (Labatt) Whitehead; married Virginia Bolen (died); married Zoe Caldwell (an actress and director). EDUCATION: Trinity College School; Lower Canada College; studied for the theatre at the New York School of the Theatre with Benno Schneider.

VOCATION: Producer and former actor.

CAREER: DEBUT—(As an actor) At the Barter, Abingdon, VA. NEW YORK DEBUT—(As an actor) *Night Must Fall,* Barrymore, 1936. LONDON DEBUT—(As a producer) *Bequest to the Nation,* 1970.

PRINCIPAL STAGE WORK—Producer: *Medea,* National, NY, 1947; *Crime and Punishment,* National, NY, 1947; *The Member of the Wedding,* 1950; *Night Music,* 1951; *Desire Under the Elms, Mrs. McThing, Golden Boy, Four Saints in Three Acts, Sunday*

Breakfast all for ANTA, 1952; all Broadway productions: *The Time of the Cuckoo,* 1952; *The Emperor's Clothes,* 1953; *The Remarkable Mr. Pennypacker,* 1953; *The Confidential Clerk,* 1954; *The Flowering Peach,* 1954; *Bus Stop,* 1955; *Tamburlaine the Great,* 1956; *Major Barbara,* 1956; *Separate Tables,* 1956; *The Sleeping Prince,* 1956; *The Waltz of the Toreadors,* 1957; *A Hole in the Head,* 1957; *Orpheus Descending,* 1957; *The Day the Money Stopped,* 1958; *The Visit,* 1958; *A Touch of the Poet,* 1958; *Goldilocks,* 1958; *The Cold Wind and the Warm,* 1958; *Much Ado About Nothing,* 1959; *The Conquering Hero,* 1961; *Midgie Purvis,* 1961; *A Man for All Seasons,* 1961; *Banderol,* 1962; *The Physicists,* 1964.

After the Fall, Marco Millions, But for Whom, Charlie, The Changeling, Incident at Vichy, all for Lincoln Center for the Performing Arts at ANTA, Washington Square, 1964; all Broadway productions: *The Prime of Miss Jean Brodie,* 1968; *The Price,* 1968; *Sheep on the Runway,* 1970; *The Creation of the World and Other Business,* 1972; *Old Times,* 1972; *Finishing Touches,* 1973; *A Matter of Gravity,* 1975; *No Man's Land,* 1976; *1600 Pennsylvania Avenue,* 1976; *A Texas Trilogy,* 1976; *The Prince of Grand Street,* 1978; *Bedroom Farce,* 1979; *Betrayal,* 1979; *Lunch Hour,* 1980; *The West Side Waltz,* 1981; *Death of a Salesman,* 1984; *Lillian,* 1985.

PRINCIPAL STAGE WORK—Director: *Medea,* NY, 1982; *Lillian,* NY, 1985.

For the Kennedy Center, Washington, DC: *The Prodigal Daughter,* 1973; *Semmelweis,* 1978.

MAJOR TOURS—Producer: *Saint Joan,* 1954; *The Skin of Our Teeth* (Salute to France Program), 1955; *Foxy,* 1962.

PRINCIPAL TELEVISION WORK—Producer: *The Skin of Our Teeth,* 1956.

RELATED CAREER—Managing director, ANTA, 1951; executive producer, Producer's Theatre, 1953; consultant, Lincoln Center for the Performing Arts, 1958; joint producing-director (with Elia Kazan) of the Repertory Theatre of Lincoln Center, 1960-64. Whitehead has also maintained a close producing relationship with the Kennedy Center in Washington, DC.

AWARDS: Critics Circle Award, 1950, for *The Member of the Wedding,* 1957, for *The Waltz of the Toreadors,* 1958, for *The Visit,* 1961, for *A Man for All Seasons;* Sam S. Shubert Foundation Gold Medal Award, 1973.

SIDELIGHTS: MEMBERSHIPS—League of New York Theatres (past president and, in 1967, treasurer), Century Club, Players Club. RECREATION—Fishing.

For a time, Whitehead was a commercial photographer.

ADDRESS: OFFICE—Whitehead-Stevens Associates, 1501 Broadway, New York, NY 10036.

*   *   *

WHITELAW, Billie

PERSONAL: Born June 6, in Coventry, England; daughter of Gerry and Frances Mary (Williams) Whitelaw; married Peter Vaughan (divorced); married Robert Muller.

VOCATION: Actress.

CAREER: STAGE DEBUT—*Pink String and Sealing Wax,* Princes, Bradford, 1950. LONDON DEBUT—Victoire, *Hotel Paradiso,* Winter Garden, 1956. NEW YORK DEBUT—Woman, *Rockabye,* La MaMa ETC, 1982.

PRINCIPAL STAGE APPEARANCES—(All London unless otherwise indicated) Mag Keenan, *Progress to the Park,* Theatre Royal, Stratford, England, 1960, then Saville, London, 1961; revue, *England, Our England,* Princes, London, 1962; Sara Melody, *A Touch of the Poet,* Dublin and Venice Festivals, 1962; second woman, *Play,* National Theatre Company, Old Vic, 1964; Francischina, *The Dutch Courtesan,* Desdemona, *Othello,* both National Theatre Company, Chichester Festival, 1964; Francischina, Old Vic, London, 1965; Maggie Hobson, *Hobson's Choice,* Old Vic, 1965; Avonia Bunn, *Trelawney of the Wells,* Chichester Festival, 1965, also Old Vic, 1965; Clare, *After Hagerty,* Royal Shakespeare Company, Criterion, 1971; Mouth, *Not I,* Royal Court, 1973 (revived, 1975); Lucy, *Alphabetical Order,* Hampstead, 1975, then Mayfair, London, 1975; May, *Footfalls,* Royal Court, London, 1976; Molly, *Molly,* Comedy, London, 1978; Winnie, *Happy Days,* Royal Court, London, 1979; Andromache and Athene, *The Greeks,* Aldwych, London, 1980; Eleanor, *Passion Play,* Aldwych, London, 1981, then National, 1982; Nellie Mann, *Tales from Hollywood,* National, 1983; *Rockabye, Enough, Footfalls,* all Samuel Beckett, NY, 1984.

MAJOR TOURS—June Hodge, *Where There's a Will . . . ,* 1954; National Theatre Company tour of Moscow and Berlin, 1965.

PRINCIPAL FILM APPEARANCES—*Bobbikins,* 1959; *Hell Is a City,* 1960; *Make Mine Mink,* 1960; *No Love for Johnnie,* 1961; *Payroll,* Allied Artists, 1961; *The Comedy Man,* 1961; *Charlie Bubbles,* Regional, 1968; *Twisted Nerve,* National General, 1969; *The Adding Machine,* 1969; *Leo the Last,* 1970; *Start the Revolution without Me,* Warner Brothers, 1970; *Gumshoe,* Columbia, 1972; *Frenzy,* Universal, 1972; *Eagle in a Cage,* National General, 1972; Sarah Cooke, *Night Watch,* Avco-Embassy, 1973; *The Omen,* Twentieth Century-Fox, 1976; *The Water Babies,* (British/Polish) 1978; *Leopard in the Snow,* (Canadian/British), 1978; Ogra, *The Dark Crystal,* Universal, 1981; *Slayground,* Universal, 1984; *The Chain* (upcoming); also: *An Unsuitable Job for a Woman, Shadey, Tangier, A Tale of Two Cities,* others.

TELEVISION APPEARANCES—*A World of Time; Sextet; The Withered Arm; Happy Days; The Serpent Son;* WNET documentary on the creation of Samuel Beckett's play, *Rockabye; No Train to Lime Street; Lady of the Camellias; The Pity of It All; You and Me; Resurrection; Dr. Jekyl and Mr. Hyde; Poet Game; Wessex Tales; The Fifty Pound Note; Supernatural; Three Plays by Samuel Beckett; Eustace and Hilda; The Oresteia of Aeschylus; The Haunted Man; Private Schulz; Jamaica Inn; Camille,* CBS, 1984; others.

AWARDS: Variety Club Actress of the Year, 1960; British Film Academy Award, Best Supporting Actress, 1969, for *Charlie Bubbles;* SFTA Best Actress of the Year Award, 1960 and 1972; U.S. National Society of Film Critics Award, Best Supporting Actress; Variety Club Award, 1977; *Evening News,* Best Film Actress, 1977; Television Actress of the Year Award; regents professor, University of Santa Barbara, 1985.

SIDELIGHTS: MEMBERSHIPS—National Theatre of Great Britain, 1964-1967. RECREATION—Do-it-yourself.

ADDRESS: AGENT—Joy Jameson Ltd., Seven W. Easton Place Mews, London SW1, England.

*   *   *

WHITMORE, James   1921-

PERSONAL: Born October 1, 1921, in White Plains, NY; son of James Allen and Florence (Crane) Whitmore; married Nancy Mygatt (divorced); married Alldra Lindley. EDUCATION—Yale University, B.A., 1944; studied for stage at the American Theatre Wing, 1947.

VOCATION: Actor.

CAREER: STAGE DEBUT—Appeared with the Players, Peterboro, NH, summer, 1947. NEW YORK DEBUT—Sergeant Harold Evans, *Command Decision,* Fulton, 1947. PRINCIPAL STAGE APPEARANCES—Peer Gynt, *Peer Gynt,* University of California, Los Angeles, 1953; Starbuck, *The Rainmaker,* La Jolla, CA, 1954; Mr. Antrobus, *The Skin of Our Teeth,* 1957; Barney, *Summer of the 17th Doll,* Bucks County Playhouse, New Hope, PA, 1958; Tom Willard, *Winesburg, Ohio,* National, NY, 1958; Narrator, *Under Milk Wood,* University of California, 1959; leading role, *Brand,* Fresno State College, CA, 1961; leading role, *Gideon,* Playhouse on the

JAMES WHITMORE

Mall, Paramus, NJ, 1963; Emanuel Block, *Inquest,* Music Box, NY, 1970; Will Rogers in the one man show *Will Rogers' USA,* Ford's, Washington, DC, 1970, then Helen Hayes, 1974; President Harry S. Truman, *Give 'em Hell Harry!,* Ford's, Washington DC, 1975; *The Magnificent Yankee,* Eisenhower, Washington, DC, 1976; Theodore Roosevelt in the one man show *Bully,* Forty-Sixth Street, NY, 1977; *Handy Dandy,* John Drew, East Hampton, NY, 1985.

MAJOR TOURS—Will Rogers, *Will Rogers' USA,* 1970-72, 1974, 1977; President Harry S. Truman, *Give 'em Hell Harry!,* 1975.

FILM DEBUT—*Battleground,* 1949. PRINCIPAL FILM APPEARANCES—*Next Voice You Hear,* 1950; *Asphalt Jungle,* 1950; *Mrs. O'Malley and Mr. Malone,* 1950; *Outriders,* 1950; *Please Believe Me,* 1950; *Across the Wide Missouri,* 1951; *It's a Big Country,* 1951; *Because You're Mine,* 1952; *Above and Beyond,* 1952; *Girl Who Had Everything,* 1953; *All the Brothers Were Valiant,* 1953; *Kiss Me Kate,* 1953; *The Command,* 1954; *Them!,* 1954; *Oklahoma!,* Magna, 1955; *Battle Cry,* Warner Brothers, 1955; *McConnell Story,* Warner Brothers, 1955; *Eddy Duchin Story,* Columbia, 1956; *Face of Fire,* Allied Artists, 1959; *Who Was That Lady?,* Columbia, 1960; *Black Like Me,* Reade-Sterling, 1964; *Chuka,* Paramount, 1967; *Waterhole 3,* Paramount, 1967; *Nobody's Perfect,* Universal, 1968; *Planet of the Apes,* Twentieth Century-Fox, 1968; *Madigan,* Universal, 1968; *The Split,* Metro-Goldwyn-Mayer, 1968; *Guns of the Magnificent Seven,* United Artists, 1969; *Chato's Land,* United Artists, 1972; *Where the Red Fern Grows,* 1974; *Give 'Em Hell Harry,* Theatre Television, 1976; *Serpent's Egg,* Paramount, 1978; *First Deadly Sin,* Filmways, 1980.

PRINCIPAL TELEVISION APPEARANCES—Abraham Lincoln Jones, *The Law and Mr. Jones,* ABC, 1960-62; *Celebrity.*

AWARDS: Antoinette Perry Award, 1948, for Sergeant Harold Evans, *Command Decision.*

SIDELIGHTS: MEMBERSHIPS—Actors' Equity Association, American Federation of Television and Radio Artists, Screen Actors Guild.

ADDRESS: AGENT—Abrams-Rubaloff & Lawrence, 8075 W. Third Street, Suite 303, Los Angeles, CA 90048.

*　　*　　*

WHITTON, Margaret

PERSONAL: Also known as Peggy Whitton; born November 30, in Philadelphia, PA; daughter of James Richmond and Margaret Eleanora (Brown) Whitton.

VOCATION: Actress.

CAREER: DEBUT—Elf, *Elves and Shoemaker,* school play. NEW YORK DEBUT—Sylvia, *Baba Goya,* American Place. PRINCIPAL STAGE APPEARANCES—Bianca, *Othello,* New York Shakespeare Festival, Delacorte, 1978; Lady Percy, *Henry V, Part I,* New York Shakespeare Festival, Delacorte, 1981; Camille, *Camille,* Guthrie, Minneapolis, MN, 1982; Jane, *Steaming,* Brooks Atkinson, NY, 1983; *Don Juan,* New York Shakespeare Festival, Delacorte, 1983.

MARGARET WHITTON

MAJOR TOURS—Lucy, *Dracula,* Washington, DC, Baltimore, Los Angeles, Chicago; Corinna Stroller, *The House of Blue Leaves,* East Coast tour.

FILM DEBUT—Jackie Steinberg, *Lovechild,* Alan Ladd Co./Warner Brothers, 1982. FILM APPEARANCES—Molly, *9 1/2 Weeks,* Metro-Goldwyn-Mayer/United Artists, 1984; Darlene, *The Best of Times,* Kings Road Productions, 1985.

TELEVISION DEBUT—Claire Hart, *Search for Tomorrow,* CBS, 1974. PRINCIPAL TELEVISION APPEARANCES—Mother, *Motherlove,* Film Boston, PBS.

SIDELIGHTS: MEMBERSHIPS—Actors' Equity Association, American Federation of Television and Radio Artists, Screen Actors Guild.

ADDRESS: AGENT—Jeff Hunter, Triad, 888 Seventh Avenue, New York, NY 10106.

*　　*　　*

WICKES, Mary

PERSONAL: Born Mary Isabella Wickenhauser, June 13, in St. Louis, MO; daughter of Frank August (a banker) and Mary Isabella (a civic leader; maiden name, Shannon) Wickenhauser. EDUCA-

TION: Washington University, St. Louis, MO, B.A.; UCLA, graduate studies toward a Masters in theatre arts. RELIGION: Episcopalian.

VOCATION: Actress and teacher.

CAREER: STAGE DEBUT—Berkshire Playhouse, Stockbridge, MA. PRINCIPAL STAGE APPEARANCES—*Biography*, Berkshire Playhouse, Stockbridge, MA, 1934; Mary McCune (Little Mary), *Stage Door*, Music Box, NY, 1936; *Father Malachy's Miracle*, NY, 1937; Miss Preen, *The Man Who Came to Dinner*, Music Box, NY, 1939; *Jackpot*, NY, 1944; *Hollywood Pinafore*, NY, 1945; *Park Avenue*, NY, 1946; *Town House*, NY, 1948; Aunt Eller, *Oklahoma!*, Palace, NY, 1979; Mistress Quickly, *Henry IV, Part I*, American Shakespeare Festival, Stratford, CT, 1982; Rosemary, *The Palace of Amateurs*, Berkshire Theatre Festival, Stockbridge, MA, 1982; *Light Up the Sky*, Coconut Grove Playhouse, Miami, FL, 1983; *Detective Story*, Ahmanson, Los Angeles, CA, then Auditorium, Denver, 1984.

With the American Conservatory Theatre: Penny, *You Can't Take It with You*, Goody Nurse, *The Crucible*, Mrs. Noah, *The Fourteenth Century Mystery Cycle;* also her one-woman show, Geary, San Francisco, CA; Juno, *Juno & the Paycock*, Mark Taper Forum, Los Angeles; *Wonderful Town*, Los Angeles Civic Light Opera, Dorothy Chandler Pavilion, Los Angeles; Madame Arcati, *High Spirits*, Los Angeles and Houston; Eulalie McKechnie Shinn, *The Music Man*, Parthy Ann, *Show Boat*, Clothilde, *The New Moon*, all at St. Louis Municipal Opera, St. Louis, MO; Elizabeth, *Elizabeth the Queen;* Lady Jane, *Patience; Danton's Death*.

She has appeared in plays and musicals at the Cape Playhouse, Bucks County Playhouse, Woodstock Playhouse and the Houston Music Theatre as well. Also: Lady Bracknell, *The Importance of Being Earnest*, William and Mary College; Amanda, *The Glass Menagerie*, Washington University.

MAJOR TOURS—Aunt Eller, *Oklahoma!*, pre-Broadway tour and in Miami, Ft. Lauderdale, Palm Beach, and St. Louis, for nine months.

FILM DEBUT—Miss Preen, *The Man Who Came to Dinner*, Warner Brothers, 1941. PRINCIPAL FILM APPEARANCES—*The Mayor of 44th Street*, RKO, 1942; *Private Buckaroo*, Universal, 1942; Dora Pickford, *Now, Voyager*, Warner Brothers, 1942; *Who Done It?*, Universal, 1942; *How's About It?*, Universal, 1943; *Rhythm of the Islands*, Universal, 1943, *Happy Land*, Twentieth Century-Fox, 1943; *My Kingdom for a Cook*, Columbia, 1943; *Higher and Higher*, RKO, 1943; Rosemary, *June Bride*, Warner Brothers, 1948; *The Decision of Christopher Blake*, Warner Brothers, 1948; *Anna Lucasta*, Columbia, 1949; *The Petty Girl*, Columbia, 1950; Stella, *On Moonlight Bay*, Warner Brothers, 1951; *I'll See You in My Dreams*, Warner Brothers, 1951; *The Will Rogers Story*, Warner Brothers, 1952; *Young Man with Ideas*, Metro-Goldwyn-Mayer, 1952.

Stella, *By the Light of the Silvery Moon*, Warner Brothers, 1953; *The Actress*, Metro-Goldwyn-Mayer, 1953; *Half a Hero*, Metro-Goldwyn-Mayer, 1953; *Destry*, Universal, 1954; Emma, *White Christmas*, Paramount, 1954; *Good Morning, Miss Dove*, Twentieth Century-Fox, 1955; *Dance with Me, Henry*, United Artists, 1956; Janie, *Don't Go Near the Water*, Metro-Goldwyn-Mayer, 1957; *It Happened to Jane*, Columbia, 1959; *Cimarron*, Metro-Goldwyn-Mayer, 1960; *The Sins of Rachel Cade*, Warner Brothers, 1961; Mrs. Squires, *The Music Man*, Warner Brothers, 1962; *Who's Minding*

MARY WICKES

the Store?, Paramount, 1963; *Fate Is the Hunter*, Twentieth Century-Fox, 1964; *Dear Heart*, Warner Brothers, 1964; Harold's secretary, *How to Murder Your Wife*, United Artists, 1965; Sister Clarissa, *The Trouble with Angels*, Columbia, 1966; Sister Clarissa, *Where Angels Go, Trouble Follows*, Columbia, 1968; *Napoleon and Samantha*, Buena Vista, 1972; *Snowball Express*, Buena Vista, 1972; *Touched by Love*, Columbia, 1980.

RADIO APPEARANCES—Irma Barker (the second of three in the role), *Lorenzo Jones*, NBC, c.1940.

TELEVISION DEBUT—Mary, "Mary Poppins," *Studio One*, CBS, 1946. PRINCIPAL TELEVISION APPEARANCES—Regular, *Inside U.S.A. with Chevrolet*, CBS, 1949-50; housekeeper, *The Peter Lind Hayes Show*, NBC, 1950-1951; Martha, the maid, *Bonino*, NBC, 1953; Alice, *The Halls of Ivy*, CBS, 1954-55; girl friday, *Make Room for Daddy;* Miss Cathcart, *Dennis the Menace*, CBS, 1959-60; Maxfield, *The Gertrude Berg Show (a.k.a. Mrs. G. Goes to College*, CBS, 1961-62; Miss Preen, "The Man Who Came to Dinner," *Hallmark Hall of Fame;* Mrs. Chegley, *Julia*, NBC, 1968-71; Miss Tully, *Doc*, CBS, 1975-76; plant lady, *Sesame Street*, PBS; *M*A*S*H*, CBS; Zelda, *Sigmund and the Sea Monsters;* "First the Egg," *After School Special*, ABC, 1985.

Also appearances on: *The Waltons; The Love Boat; Matt Houston; Trapper John, M.D.; Punky Brewster;* many *Lucy* shows, including Lucille Ball's last television special; others.

RELATED CAREER—Acting and comedy teacher, seminars at Washington University, College of William and Mary, and American Conservatory Theatre in San Francisco.

AWARDS: Emmy nomination, Best Supporting Actress in a Series, *Mrs. G. Goes to College;* Emmy nomination, *M*A*S*H;* Honorary Doctor of Arts degree, Washington University; Outstanding Actress Award, St. Louis Variety Clubs, 1967; awards for volunteer work from Hospital of the Good Samaritan, UCLA, School of Medicine of the University of Southern California; Humanitarian Award, Masons; Brass Tack Award, St. Louis Junior Chamber of Commerce; Missouri Society for Crippled Children Award; Outstanding St. Louisan Award, St. Louis Globe-Democrat; Missouri Woman of Achievement Award.

SIDELIGHTS: MEMBERSHIPS—Actors' Equity Association, American Federation of Television and Radio Artists, Screen Actors Guild, Academy of Motion Picture Arts and Sciences, Phi Mu, Cancer Research Associates.

According to Mary Wickes' official biography, she holds the "unique distinction of having played and created roles in five Broadway productions directed and/or written by George S. Kaufman who described her as my favorite comedienne, and those are not just polite words, by the way.'''

ADDRESS: AGENT—Artists Agency, 10000 Santa Monica Blvd., Los Angeles, CA 90067.

*　　*　　*

WILDER, Gene   1935-

PERSONAL: Born Gene Silberman, June 11, 1935, in Milwaukee, WI; son of William J. and Jeanne (Baer) Silberman; married Mary Joan Schutz, October 27, 1967 (divorced); married Gilda Radner; children: (first marriage) Katharine Anastasia. EDUCATION: University of Iowa, B.A., 1955; trained for the stage at the Bristol Old Vic Theatre School, London. MILITARY: U.S. Army, 1956-58.

VOCATION: Actor, director, and writer.

CAREER: PRINCIPAL FILM APPEARANCES—*Bonnie and Clyde,* Warner Brothers, 1966; *The Producers,* Embassy, 1967; *Start the Revolution without Me,* Warner Brothers, 1968; *Quackser Fortune Has a Cousin in the Bronx,* UMC, 1969; *Willy Wonka and the Chocolate Factory,* Paramount, 1970; *Everything You Wanted to Know About Sex, but Were Afraid to Ask,* United Artists, 1971; *Rhinoceros,* American Film Theater, 1972; *Blazing Saddles,* Warner Brothers, 1973; *The Little Prince,* Paramount, 1974; *Silver Streak,* Twentieth Century-Fox, 1976; *The Frisco Kid,* Warner Brothers, 1979; *Stir Crazy,* Twentieth Century-Fox, 1980; *Hanky Panky,* Columbia, 1981; *Woman in Red,* Orion, 1984; *Haunted Honeymoon,* Orion (upcoming).

PRINCIPAL FILM WORK—Director, writer, actor: *The Adventures of Sherlock Holmes' Smarter Brother,* Twentieth Century-Fox, 1975; *The World's Greatest Lover,* Twentieth Century-Fox, 1977; *Sunday Lovers,* United Artists, 1980; actor and co-writer, *Young Frankenstein,* Twentieth Century-Fox, 1974.

PRINCIPAL TELEVISION APPEARANCES—*The Scarecrow,* 1972; *The Trouble with People,* 1973; *The Marlo Thomas Special,* 1973;

Thursday's Games, 1973.

PRINCIPAL STAGE APPEARANCES—Broadway: *The Complaisant Lover,* 1962; *Mother Courage; Luv.*

AWARDS: Clarence Derwent Award, 1962, for *Complaisant Lover;* Academy Award nomination, 1974, for *Young Frankenstein.*

ADDRESS: OFFICE—9350 Wilshire Blvd., Apt. 400, Beverly Hills, CA 90212.*

*　　*　　*

WILLIAMS, Ann   1935-

PERSONAL: Born May 18, 1935, in Washington, DC; daughter of John (a scientist) and Alys (Gott) Williams; married Robert D.P. Welch (died, September 19, 1964); children: Amanda, Elizabeth, Daniel, Diana Rebecca. EDUCATION—George Washington University, A.A., 1956. RELIGION—Episcopalian.

VOCATION: Actress.

CAREER: STAGE DEBUT—Miss Weston, *Damn Yankees,* national tour, 1957-58. NEW YORK DEBUT—Understudy lead role, *New Girl in Town,* Forty-Sixth Street, 1958-59. PRINCIPAL STAGE APPEARANCES—Blackie, *Milk Train Doesn't Stop Here Anymore,* Morosco, NY, 1963; Karen, *Applause,* Palace, NY, 1970.

TELEVISION DEBUT—Lead role, *Last of the Belles,* Kraft Theatre. PRINCIPAL TELEVISION APPEARANCES—*Young Dr. Malone,* 1961-62; Maggie, *The Doctors,* 1963-65; Eunice, *Search for Tomorrow,* 1965-77; Margot, *Edge of Night,* 1978-81; June Slater, *Loving,* 1983-4.

AWARDS: Fanny Kemble Award from the Charlotte Cushman Club, for Blackie, *The Milk Train Doesn't Stop Here Anymore.*

SIDELIGHTS: MEMBERSHIPS—Actors' Equity Association, Actors Studio.

ADDRESS: AGENT—Ann Wright Representatives, 136 W. 57th Street, New York, NY 10022.

*　　*　　*

WILLIAMS, Billy Dee   1937-

PERSONAL: Born April 6, 1937, in New York, NY. EDUCATION: Attended High School of Music and Art, NY; trained for the stage at the National Academy of Fine Arts and the Actor's Workshop, NY, with Paul Mann and Sidney Poitier.

VOCATION: Actor.

CAREER: FILM DEBUT—*The Last Angry Man,* Columbia, 1959. PRINCIPAL FILM APPEARANCES—*The Out of Towners,* Paramount,

1970; *The Final Comedown; Lady Sings the Blues,* Paramount, 1972; *Hit!,* Paramount, 1973; *Mahogany,* 1975; *The Bingo Long Travelling All-Stars and Motor Kings,* Universal, 1976; *The Empire Strikes Back,* Twentieth Century-Fox, 1980; *Nighthawks,* Universal, 1981; *The Return of the Jedi,* Twentieth Century-Fox, 1983; *Marvin and Tige,* 1983; *Fear City.*

PRINCIPAL TELEVISION APPEARANCES—Movies: Gayle Sayers, *Brian's Song,* 1971; *The Glass House,* 1972; *Scott Joplin: King of Ragtime,* 1977; *The Imposter,* ABC, 1985. Episodic: *The Mod Squad; The Jeffersons; The Interns; The F.B.I.; Mission: Impossible; Police Woman.* Miniseries: *Chiefs,* CBS, 1983. Series: Brady Lloyd, *Dynasty,* ABC, 1984-present.

AWARDS: Emmuy Award nomination, 1972, for *Glass House.*

ADDRESS: AGENT—Star Direction, 605 N. Oakhurst Drive, Beverly Hills, CA 90210.*

*   *   *

WILLIAMS, Treat

VOCATION: Actor.

CAREER: PRINCIPAL STAGE APPEARANCES—Broadway: Danny Zuko, *Grease; Once in a Lifetime; Some Men Need Help;* Utah, *Over Here;* Pirate King, *Pirates of Penzance.* Off Broadway: Bo Decker, *Bus Stop.* Repertory: Zeppo, *Picnic on the Battlefield;* Prince Hal, *Henry IV;* Sam Jenkins, *Of Thee I Sing;* Lysander, *A Midsummer Night's Dream;* Captain Jinks, *Captain Jinks of the Horse Marines;* Jack, *Charley's Aunt;* Nicholas and Alan, *Canterbury Tales;* Malvolio, *Twelfth Night.* Stock: Dick, *Play It Again Sam;* Danny Zuko, *Grease; Servant of Two Masters.* Cabaret: *Maybe I'm Doing It Wrong.*

PRINCIPAL FILM APPEARANCES—Michael Brick, *The Ritz,* Warner Brothers, 1976; Billings, *Deadly Hero,* Avoc-Embassy, 1976; Captain Clark, *The Eagle Has Landed,* Columbia, 1977; Berger, *Hair,* United Artists, 1979; *1941,* Universal, 1979; *Why Would I Lie?,* United Artists, 1980; Danny Ciello, *Prince of the City,* Warner Brothers, 1981; D.B. Cooper, *Pursuit of D.B. Cooper,* Universal, 1981; Jimmy O'Donnell, *Once Upon a Time in America,* 1984; *Napoli; Flashpoint.*

PRINCIPAL TELEVISION APPEARANCES—Jack Dempsey, *Demsey;* Stanley Kowalski, *A Streetcar Named Desire.*

SIDELIGHTS: MEMBERSHIPS—Actors' Equity Association, Screen Actors Guild.

ADDRESS: AGENT—William Morris Agency, 1350 Avenue of the Americas, New York, NY 10019.

*   *   *

WILLIAMSON, Nicol   1938-

PERSONAL: Born September 14, 1938, in Hamilton, Scotland;

married Jill Townsend (divorced).

VOCATION: Actor and director.

CAREER: STAGE DEBUT—Dundee Repertory Theatre, 1960-61. LONDON DEBUT—I-ti, *That's Us,* Royal Court, 1961. NEW YORK DEBUT—Bill Maitland, *Inadmissible Evidence,* Belasco, NY, 1965. PRINCIPAL STAGE APPEARANCES—I-ti, *That's Us,* Arts Theatre, Cambridge, 1961; Flute, *A Midsummer Night's Dream,* Malvolio, *Twelfth Night,* both Royal Court, 1962; SAC Albert Meakin, *Nil Carborundum,* Royal Shakespeare Company at the New Arts, 1962; Satin, *The Lower Depths,* 1962; Leantio, *Women, Beware Women,* 1962; man at the end, *Springs' Awakening,* Royal Court, 1962; Kelly, *Kelly's Eye,* Royal Court, 1963; Sebastian Dangerfield, *The Ginger Man,* Ashcroft, Croydon, 1963; Bill Maitland, *Inadmissible Evidence,* Ashcroft, Croydon, 1964; Peter Wykeham *A Cuckoo in the Nest,* 1964; Vladimir, *Waiting for Godot,* 1964.

Bill Maitland, *Inadmissible Evidence,* Wyndham's, 1965; Joe Johnson, *Miniatures,* Royal Court, 1965; Sweeney, *Sweeney Agonistes,* in a program of homage to T. S. Eliot, Globe Theatre, 1965; Alexei Ivanovitch Poprichtchine, *Diary of a Madman,* Duchess, 1967; played three roles in *Plaza Suite,* Plymouth, 1968; Hamlet, *Hamlet,* Round House, 1969, then Lunt-Fontanne, NY, 1969; Uncle Vanya, *Uncle Vanya,* Circle in the Square, NY, 1973; Coriolanus, *Coriolanus,* Royal Shakespeare Company, Aldwych Theatre, 1973; Malvolio, *Twelfth Night,* Stratford, Aldwych, 1974-75; *Macbeth,* Stratford, Aldwych, 1974-75; Uncle Vanya, *Uncle Vanya,* Other Place, 1975; Henry VIII, *Rex,* Lunt-Fontanne, NY, 1976; Bill Maitland, *Inadmissible Evidence,* Royal Court, 1978, then Roundabout, NY, 1980; *Macbeth,* Circle in the Square, NY, 1982; *The Entertainer,* Roundabout, 1983; Henry Boot, *The Real Thing,* Plymouth, NY, 1985.

PRINCIPAL STAGE WORK—Director: *Uncle Vanya,* Other Place, 1975; *Macbeth,* Circle in the Square, NY, 1982.

MAJOR TOURS—Black Will, *Arden of Faversham,* 1961; Hamlet, *Hamlet,* 1969.

PRINCIPAL FILM APPEARANCES—*Inadmissible Evidence; The Bofors Gun; The Reckoning; Laughter in the Dark; The Jerusalem File; The Seven Per Cent Solution; Hamlet; The Wilby Conspiracy; Robin and Marian; The Human Factor; The Goodbye Girl; The Cheap Detective; Excalibur; I'm Dancing as Fast as I Can; Return to Oz.*

PRINCIPAL TELEVISION APPEARANCES—Pierre, *War and Peace;* Warwick, *The Lark;* Arturo Ui, *Arturo Ui;* Richard Nixon, *I Know What I Meant;* King Ferdinand, *Christopher Columbus,* Mountbatten, *Mountbatten: The Last Viceroy.*

AWARDS: New York Drama Critics Award, 1966, for Bill Maitland, *Inadmissible Evidence;* Best Actor, *Evening Standard,* 1969, for *Hamlet.*

ADDRESS: AGENT—International Creative Management, 22 Grafton Street, London W1, England.

ELIZABETH WILSON

WILSON, Elizabeth   1921-

PERSONAL: Born April 4, 1921, in Grand Rapids, MI. EDUCA-TION—Grand Rapids Junior College; trained for the stage at the Neighborhood Playhouse, NY.

VOCATION: Actress.

CAREER: NEW YORK DEBUT—Christine Schoenwalder, *Picnic,* Music Box, 1953. PRINCIPAL STAGE APPEARANCES—Miss Warriner, *The Desk Set,* Broadhurst, NY, 1955; Miss McCracken, *The Tunnel of Love,* Royale, NY, 1957; Hilda Rose, *Big Fish, Little Fish,* ANTA, 1961; Constance, *Yes Is for a Very Young Man,* Players, NY, 1963; Liz Cantriss, *Rich Little Rich Girl,* Walnut Street, Philadelphia, PA, 1964; Mrs. Murray, *Eh?,* Circle in the Square, 1966; Marjorie Newquist, *Little Murders,* Circle in the Square, NY, 1969.

Martha Wilkins, *Sheep on the Runway,* Helen Hayes, NY, 1970; took over for one week from Maureen Stapleton as Karen Nash, Muriel Tate and Norma Hubley, *Plaza Suite,* Plymouth, NY, 1970; Mrs. Shin, *The Good Woman of Setzuan,* Vivian Beaumont, NY, 1970; Harriet, *Sticks and Bones,* Anspacher, NY, 1971, then John Golden, 1972; Helen Wild, *The Secret Affairs of Mildred Wild,* Ambassador, NY, 1972; Sonya, *Uncle Vanya,* Circle in the Square, NY, 1973; Mrs. Peachum, *Threepenny Opera,* Vivian Beaumont, 1976; Lady Bracknell, *The Importance of Being Earnest,* Circle in the Square, NY, 1977; *The 75th,* Public, NY, 1978; Countess of Roussillon, *All's Well That Ends Well,* Delacorte, NY, 1978; Aunt Helen, *Taken in Marriage,* New York Shakespeare Festival, Newman, 1979; Aaronetta Gibbs, *Morning's at Seven,* Lyceum, NY,

1980; Penny, *You Can't Take It with You,* Royale, NY, 1984; Enid, *Salonika,* New York Shakespeare Festival, Newman, 1985.

PRINCIPAL FILM APPEARANCES—*Little Murders; Day of the Dolphin; Man on the Swing; The Graduate; Catch 22; Prisoner of Second Avenue; The Happy Hooker; Picnic; Tunnel of Love; Patterson; The Goddess; The Birds; A Child Is Waiting; Jenny; The Incredible Shrinking Woman; 9 to 5; The Ultimate Solution of Grace Quigley; Where Are the Children.*

PRINCIPAL TELEVISION APPEARANCES—*East Side, West Side; Doc.*

AWARDS: Antoinette Perry and Obie Awards, for Harriet, *Sticks and Bones;* Drama Desk Award, for Mrs. Peachum, *Threepenny Opera;* Obie Award, for Aunt Helen, *Taken in Marriage.*

SIDELIGHTS: MEMBERSHIPS—Actors' Equity Association, Screen Actors Guild.

ADDRESS: AGENT—STE Representation, 888 Seventh Avenue, New York, NY 10019.

*   *   *

WINDOM, William   1923-

PERSONAL: Born September 28, 1923, in New York City; son of Paul (an architect) and Isobel (Peckham) Windom; married Patricia Veronica Tunder (a writer), December 31, 1975; children: Rachel, Heather Juliet, Hope, Rebel Russell. EDUCATION—Williams College, The Citadel, Antioch College, University of Kentucky, Biarritz American University, Fordham University, Columbia University. MILITARY—U.S. Army, 1943-46.

VOCATION: Actor.

CAREER: STAGE DEBUT—Duke of Glouster, *Richard III,* Biarritz, France, 1937. NEW YORK DEBUT—Surrey, *Henry VIII,* Columbus Circle Theatre, 1940. LONDON DEBUT—One man show, *Thurber I,* New London Theatre, 1975. PRINCIPAL STAGE APPEARANCES—Broadway: *John Gabriel Borkman; What Every Woman Knows; Androcles and the Lion; Yellowjack; Alice in Wonderland; Time Remembered; Candide; Hotel Paradiso; Madamoiselle Colombe; Fallen Angels; Viva Madison Avenue; A Girl Can Tell; The Greatest Man Alive; The Grand Prize; The World of Suzie Wong; Double in Hearts; Come Blow Your Horn,* all 1946-61. Off Broadway productions: *Career; Twelfth Night; USA; Drums Under the Windows; Rules of the Game; When The Bough Breaks.* Also: *Period of Adjustment, The Child Buyer,* California, 1962-63.

MAJOR TOURS—*Bell, Book, and Candle,* national tour; one man shows, *Thurber I, II, Ernie Pyle I, II, Famous Poems Illustrated.*

FILM DEBUT—District attorney, *To Kill a Mockingbird,* 1962. PRINCIPAL FILM APPEARANCES—*For Love or Money,* 1963; *Cattle King,* 1963; *One Man's Way,* 1964; *The Americanization of Emily,* 1964; *Hour of the Gun,* 1967; *The Detective,* 1968; *The Angry Breed,* 1969; *The Gypsy Moths,* 1969; *Brewster McCloud,* 1970; *Echoes of a Summer,* 1974.

TELEVISION DEBUT—Duke of Glouster, *Richard III,* NBC, 1947.

PRINCIPAL TELEVISION APPEARANCES—Series: Congressman Glen Morley, *The Farmers Daughter*, ABC, 1962-65; *My World and Welcome to It*, NBC, 1969-70. Episodic: "They're Tearing Down Tim Riley's Bar," *Night Gallery*, NBC; Commodore Decker, "Doomsday Machine," *Star Trek*, NBC; many others.

AWARDS: Emmy award, 1970, for *My World and Welcome to It*.

SIDELIGHTS: MEMBERSHIPS—Actors Equity Association, Screen Actors Guild, American Federation of Television and Radio Artists, Players Club, Catboat Association.

Windom told *CTFT*, "Sailing has been my hobby since 1937, and I have owned seven different small boats since 1953. My goal is to acquire a New England Catboat with standing headroom. Currently, I command a Windsurfer No. 1210."

ADDRESS: AGENT—Mike Livingston, The Artists Agency, 10,000 Santa Monica Blvd., Los Angeles, CA 90067.

*   *   *

WINGER, Debra   1955-

BRIEF ENTRY: Born 1955, in Cleveland, OH. Actress. In 1972, after finishing high school, Winger went to Israel, applied for citizenship, and enrolled in the army for three months. After her return to the U.S., she majored in sociology at California State, Northridge. While working at Magic Mountain amusement park in California, she suffered a serious head injury and spent the following year in and out of hospitals. Her first role was as Wonder Girl in the series *Wonder Woman*, and she was seen in episodes of *Police Woman*, and the television film *Special Olympics*, 1978. Her first major film was *Thank God It's Friday*, Columbia, 1978; followed by *French Postcards*, Paramount, 1979; *Urban Cowboy*, 1980; *Cannery Row*, Metro-Goldwyn-Mayer, 1982; *An Officer and a Gentleman*, Paramount, 1982; *Terms of Endearment*, Paramount, 1983, and *Mike's Murder*, Warner Brothers/Ladd Co., 1984. She was nominated for an Academy Award for her role in *Terms of Endearment*.*

*   *   *

WINKLER, Henry   1945-

PERSONAL: Full name Henry Franklin Winkler; born October 30, 1945, in New York City; son of Harry Irving (a lumber company executive) and Ilse Anna Maria (Hadra) Winkler; married Stacey Weitzman, May 5, 1978; children: Zoe Emily, Max; (stepson) Jed. EDUCATION: Emerson College, B.A.; Yale University, School of Drama, M.F.A., 1970. RELIGION: Jewish.

VOCATION: Actor, director, and producer.

CAREER: PRINCIPAL STAGE APPEARANCES—*Defender of the Faith*, Yale Repertory Company; story theatre, Yale Repertory

HENRY WINKLER

Company in East Hampton, NY; *Off the Wall*, off Broadway comedy revue; *42 Seconds from Broadway*, Broadway production, 1973; *Incident at Vichy*, Cincinnati Playhouse in the Park, 1973.

MAJOR TOURS—*Room Service*, Kenley Players circuit.

PRINCIPAL FILM APPEARANCES—*The Lords of Flatbush*, 1972; *Crazy Joe*, 1973; *Heroes*, 1977; *The One and Only*, 1977; *Night Shift*, 1983.

PRINCIPAL TELEVISION APPEARANCES—*The Bob Newhart Show; Mary Tyler Moore Show; Paul Sand Show; Rhoda;* Arthur Fonzarelli ("The Fonz"), *Happy Days*, ABC, 1974-84. Specials: *Richard Rogers; Henry Winkler Meets William Shakespeare*. Movies: *Katherine; An American Christmas Carol*, ABC, 1979; *When Your Lover Leaves*, NBC, 1983.

PRINCIPAL TELEVISION WORK—Director: *Joanie Loves Chachi* (one episode), ABC, 1982.

Producer: *Who Are the Debolts and Where Did They Get Nineteen Kids; Run, Don't Walk*, 1981; *Ryan's Four*, ABC, 1983; *All the Kids Do It*, CBS, 1984; *Mr. Sunshine; Macgyver*, 1984-85.

RELATED CAREER—President and founder, Fair Dinkum Productions Inc.; drama teacher, adult extension, University of California at Los Angeles.

AWARDS: Photoplay Magazine Award, Best Actor in a Comedy Series, *Happy Days*, 1976-77; Golden Globe Awards, Best Actor, *Happy Days*, 1975, 1976, 1978; Emmy Award nominations, 1975,

1976, 1977; King Baccus Award, Mardi Gras, New Orleans, 1977; Golden Plate Award, American Academy of Achievement, 1980; Sorrisi e Canzoni Telegatto Award, Italian Television Award, 1980; Honorary Doctor of Humane Letters, Emerson College, 1978; honored with a star on the Hollywood Walk of Fame; presented ''Fonzie's'' leather jacket to the Smithsonian Institute, Washington, DC.

SIDELIGHTS: MEMBERSHIPS—Actors' Equity Association, Screen Actors Guild, American Federation of Television and Radio Artists, Epilepsy Foundation (honorary youth chairman), Toys for Tots (honorary chairman), 1977-present, Arts for the Handicapped (national committee), Special Olympics.

ADDRESS: OFFICE—Paramount Pictures, 5451 Marathon Street, Hollywood, CA 90038. AGENT—Lippin & Grant, 8124 W. Third Street, Suite 204, Los Angeles, CA 90048.

*   *   *

WINNER, Michael Robert   1935-

PERSONAL: Born October 30, 1935, in London, England; son of George Joseph (a company director) and Helen (Zloty) Winner. EDUCATION: Downing College, Cambridge, 1953-56, M.A.

VOCATION: Director, producer, and writer.

CAREER: PRINCIPAL THEATRE WORK—Producer: *Nights at the Comedy,* Comedy, London, 1960; *The Silence of St. Just,* Gardner, Brighton, England, 1971; *The Tempest,* Wyndham's, London, 1974; *A Day in Hollywood/A Night in the Ukraine,* Mayfair, London, 1978.

MICHAEL WINNER

PRINCIPAL FILM WORK—Producer and director: *Shoot to Kill,* 1960; *The System* (U.S. title, *The Girl Getters*), A.I.P., 1963; *You Must Be Joking,* Columbia, 1965; *The Jokers,* United Artists, 1966; *I'll Never Forget What's 'Isname,* Regional, 1967; *Hannibal Brooks,* United Artists, 1968; *The Games,* Twentieth Century-Fox, 1969; *Lawman,* United Artists, 1970; *The Nightcomers,* Avco-Embassy, 1971; *Chato's Land,* United Artists, 1971; *Scorpio,* United Artists, 1972; *The Stone Killer,* Columbia, 1973; *Death Wish,* Paramount, 1974; *Won Ton Ton, the Dog That Saved Hollywood,* Paramount, 1975; *The Sentinel,* Universal, 1976; *The Big Sleep,* United Artists, 1977; *Firepower,* Associated Film Distributors, 1978; *Death Wish II,* Filmways, 1981; *The Wicked Lady,* Metro-Goldwyn-Mayer/United Artists, 1982; *Scream for Help,* 1983; *Death Wish III,* Cannon (upcoming).

Director: *Haunted England,* 1961; *Play It Cool,* Allied Artists, 1962; *The Cool Mikado,* 1962; *West Eleven,* 1963; *The Mechanic,* United Artists, 1972.

PRINCIPAL TELEVISION WORK—Involved with the British television series *White Hunter* and the American series, *Dick and the Duchess,* CBS, 1957-58.

WRITINGS: SCREENPLAYS—*The Cool Mikado,* 1962; original story, *You Must Be Joking* (with Alan Hackney), 1965; original story, *The Jokers,* 1966; original story, *Hannibal Brooks* (with Tom Wright), 1968; *The Sentinel* (with Jeffrey Konvitz), 1976; *The Big Sleep,* 1977; *The Wicked Lady* (with Leslie Arliss), 1982.

RELATED CAREER—Writer for Fleet Street Newspapers, London, 1956-58.

AWARDS: Venice Film Festival Award, 1971, for *The Nightcomers;* special award from the School of Visual Arts, NY, for aiding education, 1976.

SIDELIGHTS: MEMBERSHIPS—Directors Guild of Great Britain (council member and chief censorship officer), Police Memorial Trust (U.K., chairman).

ADDRESS: OFFICE—Scimitar Films Ltd., 6/8 Sackville Street, London W1X 1DD, England.

*   *   *

WINNINGHAM, Mare

BRIEF ENTRY: Born May 16, in CA. Winningham's television debut was made at the age of sixteen on *The Gong Show* as the result of a ''dare''. Her television movies include *Off the Minnesota Strip,* 1980; *Operation Runaway; Amber Waves,* 1980 (received an Emmy Award); *The Women's Room,* 1980; *Special Olympics* (aka *A Special Kind of Love*), 1980; *Freedom,* 1981, and *Helen Keller— The Miracle Continues.* She appeared in the television miniseries *Studs Lonigan.* Her films include: *One Trick Pony,* Warner Brothers, 1980; *Threshold,* Twentieth Century-Fox, 1983; *St. Elmo's Fire,* Columbia, 1985.*

*   *   *

WISE, Robert E.   1914-

PERSONAL: Born September 10, 1914, in Winchester, IN; son of Earl W. (a meat packer) and Olive R. (Longenecker) Wise; married

ROBERT WISE

Patricia Doyle, May 25, 1942 (deceased, 1975); married Millicent Franklin, January 29, 1977; children: Robert A. EDUCATION: Franklin College, IN, one year.

VOCATION: Film director.

CAREER: PRINCIPAL FILMS—Director: *The Curse of the Cat People* (co-directed with Gunther von Fritsch), RKO, 1944; *Mademoiselle Fifi*, RKO, 1944; *The Body Snatchers*, RKO, 1945; *A Game of Death*, RKO, 1945; *Criminal Court*, RKO, 1946; *Born to Kill*, RKO, 1947; *Mystery in Mexico*, RKO, 1948; *Blood on the Moon*, RKO, 1948; *The Set-up*, RKO, 1949; *Three Secrets*, Warner Brothers, 1950; *Two Flags West*, Twentieth Century-Fox, 1950; *The House on Telegraph Hill*, Twentieth Century-Fox, 1951; *The Day the Earth Stood Still*, Twentieth Century-Fox, 1951; *Captive City*, 1952; *Something for the Birds*, Twentieth Century-Fox, 1952; *Destination Gobi*, Twentieth Century-Fox, 1953; *The Desert Rats*, Twentieth Century-Fox, 1953; *So Big*, Warner Brothers, 1953; *Executive Suite*, Metro-Goldwyn-Mayer, 1954; *Helen of Troy*, Warner Brothers (made in Italy), 1955 (released in U.S., 1956).

Tribute to a Bad Man, Metro-Goldwyn-Mayer, 1956; *Somebody Up There Likes Me*, Metro-Goldwyn-Mayer, 1956; *This Could Be the Night*, Metro-Goldwyn-Mayer, 1957; *Until They Sail*, Metro-Goldwyn-Mayer, 1957; *Bannon* (uncompleted), 1957; *Run Silent, Run Deep*, United Artists, 1958; *I Want to Live!*, United Artists, 1958; *Odds Against Tomorrow*, United Artists, 1959; *West Side Story* (co-directed with Jerome Robbins), United Artists, 1961; *Two for the Seesaw*, United Artists, 1962; *The Haunting*, Metro-Goldwyn-Mayer, 1963; *The Sound of Music*, Twentieth Century-Fox, 1965; *The Sand Pebbles*, Twentieth Century-Fox, 1966; *Star!*, Twentieth Century-Fox, 1968 (re-edited and released as *Those Were the Happy Times*, 1969); *The Andromeda Strain*, Universal, 1971; *Two People*,

Universal, 1973; *The Hindenburg*, Universal, 1975; *Audrey Rose*, United Artists, 1977; *Star Trek—The Motion Picture*, Paramount, 1979.

RELATED CAREER—First job, film porter, RKO editing department, 1933; sound cutter, assistant editor, film editor, RKO 1939-43 (edited *Citizen Kane*, 1941; *All That Money Can Buy* a.k.a. *The Devil and Daniel Webster*, 1941; *The Magnificent Ambersons*, 1942).

AWARDS: Academy of Motion Picture Arts and Sciences, nomination, Best Editing, 1941, for *Citizen Kane*, nomination, Best Director, 1958, for *I Want to Live!*, Best Director award, 1962, for *West Side Story*, 1965 and for *The Sound of Music*, 1965; Irving G. Thalberg Memorial Award, 1967; Honorary D.F.A., Franklin College, 1968; Torch of Freedom Award from the State of Israel, 1984.

SIDELIGHTS: MEMBERSHIPS—Directors Guild of America (president, 1971), National Endowment for the Arts (council member, 1970-76), American Film Institute Study Center, Motion Picture Academy (chairman, board of trustees), Beverly Hill Tennis Club, Regency Club, Lotos Club (NY).

Wise is a partner in the Filmmakers Group and the Tripar Group.

ADDRESS: OFFICE—Sunset-Gower Studios, 1438 N. Gower Street, Suite 562, Hollywood, CA 90028. AGENT—Phil Gersh Agency, 222 N. Canon Drive, Beverly Hills, CA 90210.

*   *   *

WOJTASIK, George   1935-

PERSONAL: Surname pronunced "Voi-ta-shiek;" born January 17, 1935, in Milwaukee, WI; son of Nick Thomas (a butcher) and Adeline (Rydzewski) Wojtasik; married Susan Pond, May 10, 1958 (divorced, 1984); children: Ann Elizabeth, Nicholas Paul. EDUCATION: Ripon College, B.A., 1956.

VOCATION: Director, manager, producer, and actor.

CAREER: DEBUT—The Angel, *Fancy Meeting You Again*, Lakes Region Playhouse, Gilford, NH.

PRINCIPAL STAGE WORK—Director: Advance director, *A Thousand Clowns*, 1964; assistant director, *The Dead Survivors*, Jan Hus, NY, 1964; *A Lesson in Understanding*, Judson Poet's Theatre, NY, 1965; *A Porch and Wide Verandah*, IASTA, NY, 1965; *Music, Wit, and Manners*, Ars Antiqua, Rochester, NY, 1966; *Invitation to a March*, Equity Library Theatre, 1967; *A Small Expectation*, Lambs Club, NY, 1971; *Kind Lady*, Monomoy Theatre, Chatham, MA, 1973; *The Portable Geranium*, Rollins College, Winter Park, FL, 1974; *Light Up the Sky*, Alhambra Dinner Theatre, 1974; *Kind Sir (Indiscreet)*, Firehouse Dinner Theatre, NE, 1976; *Dear Richard, Private Lives*, Sharon Playhouse, CT, 1977; *The Perfect Mollusc*, Players Theatre, NY, 1977.

RELATED CAREER—Managing director, Equity Library Theatre, 1967-present; guest lecturer on theatre, Rollins College, University of Miami, Marywood College; guest artist and director, Rollins College, Ohio University.

GEORGE WOJTASIK

RUTH WOLFF

AWARDS: Show Business Special Award, 1970; Outer Critics Circle Award, 1972; Special Theatre World Award, 1975; Special Antoinette Perry Award, 1977.

SIDELIGHTS: MEMBERSHIPS—Society of Stage Directors and Choreographers, Actors' Equity Association, Stage Directors and Choreographers Foundation (board).

ADDRESS: HOME—New York, NY. OFFICE—Equity Library Theatre, 165 W. 46th Street, New York, NY 10036.

*   *   *

WOLFF, Ruth   1932-

PERSONAL: Born December 17, 1932, in Malden, MA; married Martin Bloom (an architect), August 7, 1955; children: Evan Todd. EDUCATION: Smith College, B.A., 1953; Yale University School of Drama, 1954-55.

VOCATION: Playwright.

WRITINGS: PLAYS PRODUCED/PUBLISHED—Adaptation, *The Golem*, off Broadway production, 1959; *Folly Cove*, O'Neill Theatre Center, 1967; *Still Life with Apples*, O'Neill Theatre Center, 1968; *Arabic Two*, New Theatre workshop, 1969; *Eden Again*, Kennedy Center Commission, 1976; *Eleanor of Aquitane*, staged

reading, Playwrights Horizons; *The Abdication*, Bristol Old Vic, 1971, Italian production touring Italy, Eureka Theatre, San Francisco, 1979, productions in Massachusetts, Illinois, Kansas, Missouri, California, and De Haagse Comedie, Holland, 1985; published in *The New Women's Theatre*, Random House, 1977; *Sarah in America*, Kennedy Center, Washington, DC, 1981, seen on *Kennedy Center Tonight*, PBS; *George and Frederic*, staged reading, Williamstown Theatre Festival, MA, 1982, stage reading, Playwrights Horizons; *Empress of China*, Pan Asian Repertory Theatre, NY, 1984, Cincinnati Playhouse in the Park, 1984; *The Perfect Marriage*, 1983.

SCREENPLAYS—*The Abdication*, Warner Brothers, 1974; *The Incredible Sarah*, 1976.

RELATED CAREER—Wolff read from and discussed her work at the Manhattan Theatre Club's *Evening with Women Playwrights;* spoke on ''A Playwright's Life'' at the conference *Critical Stages: Women in American Theatre;* wrote article, ''The Aesthetics of Violence'' for *MS Magazine.*

AWARDS: Rockefeller Foundation Playwrighting Fellowship, Wesleyan University; Kennedy Center Bicentennial Commission; MacDowell Colony residency.

SIDELIGHTS: MEMBERSHIPS—Dramatists Guild, Writers Guild of America West.

Wolff told *CTFT*, ''While I often seem to be dealing with the past, with history, to me it is the present. For me, it is too limiting to be bound by this minute, this place. I feel my province is any time, all places. Even hell and heaven. That is because I feel human nature never changes. Attitudes change. Surfaces change. The basic verities don't. If there is any theme which runs through all my plays, it is the insistence of each of these heroines on taking life into her own hands and making as much as she can of it. If there is any subject which is common to all the plays, it is, in one variation or another, the baffling, exciting, infuriating, inexhaustible, impenetrable subject of love."

ADDRESS: AGENT—Rick Leed, Hesseltine-Baker Associates, Ltd., 165 W. 46th Street, New York, NY 10036.

*   *   *

WOLPER, David Lloyd   1928-

PERSONAL: Born January 11, 1928, in New York City; son of Irving S. and Anna (Fass) Wolper; married Margaret Dawn Richard (divorced, 1974); married Gloria Hill, June 11, 1974; children: (first marriage) Mark, Michael, Leslie. EDUCATION: Attended Drake University and University of Southern California.

VOCATION: Producer.

CAREER: PRINCIPAL TELEVISION WORK—Producer: Specials— *Biography; Race for Space; The Making of the President; The Yanks Are Coming; Berlin; Kaiser to Khruschev; December 7: Day of Infamy; The American Woman in the Twentieth Century; The Rise and Fall of American Communism; Legend of Marilyn Monroe; Four Days in November; Krebiozen and Cancer; National Geographic Series; Undersea World of Jacques Cousteau; China: Roots*

DAVID L. WOLPER

of Madness; The Journey of Robert F. Kennedy; Say Goodbye; George Plimpton; Appointment with Destiny; They've Killed President Lincoln; Sandburg's Lincoln; Primal Man; The First Woman President; Collision Course; Judgement; Roots; Roots: The Next Generations; Moviola; Agatha Christie movies; *The Thorn Birds; North and South.* Series: *Chico and the Man; Welcome Back Kotter.*

PRINCIPAL FILM WORK—Producer: *The Hellstrom Chronicle; The Devil's Brigade; Four Days in November; The Bridge at Remagen; If It's Tuesday This Must Be Belgium; Willy Wonka and the Chocolate Factory; Visions of Eight.*

RELATED CAREER—Vice-president, treasurer, Flamingo Films, 1948-50; vice-president, Motion Pictures for Television, 1950-54; chairman of the board and president, Wolper Productions, Los Angeles, 1958-present; president, Fountainhead International, 1960-present; Wolper Sales Company, 1964-present; vice-president, chairman of the board, Metromedia Inc., 1956-58; president, chairman of the board, Wolper Pictures Ltd., 1968-79; Wolper Productions Inc., 1970-71; consultant to Warner Brothers and executive producer, 1979-present; president, David L. Wolper Productions Inc., 1979-present.

AWARDS: National Academy of Television Arts and Sciences, forty awards, 138 nominations; International Emmy Award; National Academy of Motion Picture Arts and Sciences, two awards, eleven nominations; five Peabody Awards; seven Golden Globe awards.

SIDELIGHTS: MEMBERSHIPS   Academy of Motion Picture Arts and Sciences, Academy of Television Arts and Sciences, American Film Institute, Producers Guild, Caucus for Producers, Writers and Directors, Los Angeles County Museum of Art (board of trustees), American Film Institute (board of trustees), American Federation of the Arts (board of trustees), Los Angeles Olympic Committee Athletic Foundation (board of directors), Los Angeles Olympic Organizing Committee (vice-chairman, board of directors, executive committee), Cedars-Sinai Medical Center (board of governors), President's Council on Physical Fitness, American Revolution Bicentennial Administration.

ADDRESS: OFFICE—Warner Brothers, 4000 Warner Blvd., Burbank, CA 91522.

*   *   *

WONSEK, Paul   1948-

PERSONAL: Born July 2, 1948, in Springfield, MA; son of Paul F. Jr. (a welder) and Virginia (a college professor; maiden name, Albanese) Wonsek. EDUCATION: University. of Massachuetts, B.A., 1970, M.F.A., 1973.

VOCATION: Designer.

CAREER: FIRST STAGE WORK—Set designer, *A Penny for a Song,* Repertory Theatre of St. Louis, 1978. NEW YORK DEBUT—Set and lighting designer, *Knuckle,* Hudson Guild, 1981. PRINCIPAL STAGE WORK—Scenery and lighting design: *My Fair Lady, Brigadoon, The Wiz, Sugar, Bye Bye Birdie, Bubblin' Brown Sugar, Al Jolson Tonight,* all Starlight Theatre, Kansas City, MO, 1978-1980; *Showboat, George M!, Camelot, Annie Get Your Gun, Hans*

Christian Andersen, Grease, Gigi, West Side Story, They're Playing Our Song, Sound of Music, Pirates of Penzance, Pal Joey, Man of La Mancha, The King and I, Can-Can, Sugar Babies, Sleeping Beauty, The Music Man, all St. Louis Municipal Opera, St. Louis, MO, 1981-84.

The Three Sisters, Repertory Theatre of St. Louis, 1979; *A Man for All Seasons,* Baltimore Center Stage, 1981; *Write Me a Murder,* Buffalo Studio Arena, 1981; *House Music,* American Jewish Theatre, NY, 1981; *Deathtrap,* Buffalo Studio Arena, 1982; *Robert and Elizabeth,* Paper Mill Playhouse, NJ, 1982; *Of Mice and Men,* Buffalo Studio Arena, 1982; *Sleep Beauty, Wonderland, Hooters,* all Hudson Guild, NY, 1982; *Weapons of Happiness,* Buffalo Studio Arena, 1983; *Blood Relations, Sus, Sand Dancing,* all Hudson Guild, 1983; *I Am a Camera,* American Jewish Theatre, NY, 1983; *Mornings at Seven,* Walnut Street Theatre, Philadelphia, 1984; *The Dresser,* Buffalo Studio Arena, 1984; *Hay Fever,* Cincinnati Playhouse in the Park, 1984; *Foxfire,* Alliance Theatre, Atlanta, GA, 1984; *Doom of Frankenstein,* Buffalo Studio Arena, 1984; *Love Letters on Blue Paper, Brownstone,* both Hudson Guild, 1984; *Losing It,* Provincetown Playhouse, 1984; *Quartermaine's Terms,* Walnut Street Theatre, Philadelphia, 1985; *My Old Friends,* American Jewish Theatre, NY, 1985; *Jesus Christ Superstar, Evita, Dorothy Hamill Ice Show,* all St. Louis Municipal Opera, 1985.

MAJOR TOURS—Scenic designer: *Guys and Dolls,* national tour, 1979; *Anything Goes,* national tour, 1980.

PRINCIPAL TELEVISION WORK—Lighting director, *Cable Network News,* 1983.

RELATED CAREER—Assistant professor: Moorhead State University, 1973-74, Wright State University, 1974-77, Boston University, 1977-78, Webster College, 1978-79.

WRITINGS: PLAYS, PRODUCED—*The Doom of Frankenstein* (co-author), Buffalo Studio Arena.

AWARDS: Manhattan Award nomination for scene design, 1981, for *Knuckle;* Villager Award for lighting design, 1982, for *Blood Relations.*

ADDRESS: OFFICE—302 W. 76th Street, New York, NY 10023.

*   *   *

WOODBRIDGE, Patricia   1946-

PERSONAL: Born August 9, 1946; daughter of J. Eliot (a research chemist) and Carol (an antique dealer; maiden name, Coburn) Woodbridge. EDUCATION: Bennington College, B.A.; New York University School of the Arts, M.F.A.

VOCATION: Set designer.

CAREER: PRINCIPAL STAGE WORK—Set design: *The Runner Stumbles,* Golden, NY; *How I Got That Story,* Chelsea Westside Theatre, NY; *Triple Feature,* Manhattan Theatre Club, NY; *Dispatches,* New York Shakespeare Festival; *Nightclub Cantata,* Village Gate, NY; *Fishing,* Public Theatre, NY; *The Other Half,* Acting Company, NY; *The Blood Knot,* Manhattan Theatre Club; *Acrobatics, Crab Quadrille,* both at Interart Theatre, NY; *A Midsummer Night's Dream,* New York Shakespeare Festival.

The Road, Goodman, Chicago, IL; *Fallen Angels,* Portland Stage Company, Portland, ME; *The Contest,* Philadelphia Drama Guild, PA; *Threads,* Playmakers Repertory Company, NC; *Ladyhouse Blues,* American Stage Festival, NH; *Death of a Salesman,* Syracuse Stage, NY; *How I Got That Story,* Kennedy Center, Washington, DC; *I'm Getting My Act Together and Taking It on the Road,* Ford's, Washington, DC; *Of Mice and Men,* Philadelphia Drama Guild, PA; *Loose Ends,* Cincinnati Playhouse, OH; *A Safe Place,* Berkshire Theatre Festival, CT; *Nightclub Cantata,* Arena Stage, Washington, DC; *Crucifer of Blood,* Stage West, Springfield, MA.

PRINCIPAL DANCE WORK—*Bilitis Esseulee,* Ruth Mayer, choreographer, at the Joyce Theatre; *Paris/Chacon/Venice/Milan,* Meredith Monk, choreographer.

PRINCIPAL OPERA WORK—*Cavalleria Rusticana,* and *I Pagliacci,* Teatro Colon, Bogota, Columbia; *Carmen,* and *Lucia Di Lammermoor,* Tri Cities Opera; *Pauvre Matelot,* Philadelphia Music Academy.

PRINCIPAL TELEVISION WORK—Art director, *Saturday Night Live,* NBC; art director, *The News Is the News,* NBC; draftsman, *Dick Cavett Special;* draftsman, *The Dining Room,* WNET, NY; draftsman, *Media,* Metropolitan Pittsburgh Broadcasting.

PRINCIPAL FILM WORK—Draftsman, *Year of the Dragon,* De Laurentiis.

RELATED CAREER—Instructor, design department, New York University, Tisch School of the Arts, 1977-present.

SIDELIGHTS: MEMBERSHIPS—United Scenic Artists, Local 829, League of Professional Theatre Women, New York City.

ADDRESS: OFFICE—530 West End Avenue, New York, NY 10024. AGENT—Jonathan Sand, Writer & Artists Agency, 162 W. 56th Street, New York, NY 10019.

*   *   *

WOODS, Richard

PERSONAL: Born May 9; son of Norman Edward (a business man) and Henrietta Johanna (Erftenbeck) Woods. EDUCATION: Ithaca College, B.F.A., theatre, 1949; studied with Herbert Berghof at the American Theatre Wing, 1950-51. MILITARY: Served three years during World War Two.

VOCATION: Actor.

CAREER: NEW YORK DEBUT—*My Heart's in the Highlands,* Equity Library Theatre, 1950. PRINCIPAL STAGE APPEARANCES—*Summer and Smoke,* Circle in the Square Downtown, NY, 1953; *American Gothic,* Circle in the Square Downtown, NY, 1954; *The Crucible,* Martinique, NY, 1959; *Beg, Borrow or Steal,* Martin Beck, NY, 1960; *Sail Away,* Broadhurst, NY, 1961; performed with the APA-Phoenix Repertory Company at the Lyceum Theatre, NY, and on national tours, 1962-69; *Caesar and Cleopatra,* American Shakespeare Festival, Stratford, CT, 1963; *The Year Boston Won*

RICHARD WOODS

JO ANNE WORLEY

the Pennant, Forum, Lincoln Center, NY, 1969; *Coco*, Mark Hellinger, NY, 1969-70; at the Alliance, Atlanta, GA, 1972 season: *Pygmalion, The Prime of Miss Jean Brodie, Hamlet.*

At the Civic Light Opera of Pittsburgh, PA, summers, 1972-74: *The Music Man, Sound of Music, South Pacific, Camelot, Brigadoon, The King and I, Kiss Me Kate, Showboat, Applause, West Side Story; The Last of Mrs. Lincoln*, ANTA, NY, 1973; *Gigi*, Uris, NY, 1974; *Murder Among Friends*, Biltmore, NY, 1975; *Sherlock Holmes*, Broadhurst, NY, 1975; *The Royal Family*, Helen Hayes, 1976; *Deathtrap*, Music Box, NY, 1978; *Man and Superman*, Circle in the Square, NY, 1978-79; *The Man Who Came to Dinner, The Father*, both Circle in the Square, NY, 1980; *Present Laughter*, Circle in the Square, NY, 1982; *Alice in Wonderland*, Virginia, NY, 1982; *You Can't Take It with You*, Plymouth, NY, 1983; *Design for Living*, Circle in the Square, NY, 1984-85.

MAJOR TOURS—*Coco*, national tour, 1971; *The Royal Family*, national tour, 1976.

TELEVISION DEBUT—*Armstrong Circle Theatre*, 1958. PRINCIPAL TELEVISION APPEARANCES—*Ryan's Hope; Don Juan in Hell; A Peculiar Treasure; Sherlock Holmes; You Can't Take It with You; Edith Wharton Looking Back; Bob Hope in Central Park.*

SIDELIGHTS: MEMBERSHIPS—Actors' Equity Association, American Federation of Television and Radio Artists. Screen Actors Guild.

ADDRESS: AGENT—S.T.E. Representation, 888 Seventh Avenue, New York, NY 10019.

WORLEY, Jo Anne   1939-

PERSONAL: Born September 6, 1939, in Lowell, IN; daughter of Joseph F. (a farmer) and Rose I. (Gardner) Worley; married Roger Perry (an actor), May 11, 1975. EDUCATION: Attended Midwestern University in Witchita Falls, TX, for two years; studied at the Pasadina Playhouse and with Richard La Pour. RELIGION: Christian.

VOCATION: Actress, comedienne, and singer.

CAREER: STAGE DEBUT—Talking woman, *Laugh Capades*, Le Grande Comedy Theatre, Hollywood, CA, 1953. NEW YORK DEBUT—*Billy Barnes People*, Royale, 1961. PRINCIPAL STAGE APPEARANCES—Standby, *Hello, Dolly!*, Broadway production; *Second City Revue, The Mad Show, Hotel Passinato, That Thing at the Cherry Lane*, all off Broadway productions.

Opera: *Die Fledermaus.*

MAJOR TOURS—National companies: *Carnival, Pirates of Penzance, Gypsy, Mame, Hello, Dolly!, They're Playing Our Song, Annie Get Your Gun, Once Upon a Mattress, Anything Goes, Can-Can, Gentlemen Prefer Blondes, Wizard of Oz, Most Happy Fella, Wonderful Town, The Mikado, Same Time Next Year, Lovers & Other Strangers, Luv, Murder at the Howard Johnsons, Goodbye Charlie.*

FILM DEBUT—Beatnik, *Moonpilot*, Buena Vista, 1960. PRINCIPAL FILM APPEARANCES—*The Shaggy D.A.; Nutcracker Fantasy.*

TELEVISION DEBUT—Mrs. Farrintino, *Dobbie Gillis*. PRINCIPAL TELEVISION APPEARANCES—*Rowan & Martin's Laugh-In*. Specials: *Bob Hope Specials, Tom Jones Specials, Engelbert Humper-*

dink Specials, Andy Williams Specials, Jerry Lewis Show, Robert Goulet Special, Tony Orlando Special, Jackson 5 Special, The Ed Sullivan Show, Hollywood Palace, Circus of the Stars. Game shows: *Super Password, Body Language, Hollywood Squares, Match Game, $25,000 Pyramid, Cross Wits, It Pays to Be Ignorant, It Takes Two.* Talk shows: *The Tonight Show, Hour Magazine, Merv Griffin Show, John Davidson Show, Jim Nabors Show, Don Ho Show, Mike Douglas Show.* Childrens shows: *Captain Kangaroo, Kids Are People Too, New Zoo Review, Disney's 25th Birthday.* Series: *Hot Dog, Mouse Factory.* Movies: *What's a Nice Girl Like You, Feminist & the Fuzz, Don't Miss the Boat, Through the Pyramid, Gift of the Magi.* Episodic: *Murder She Wrote, Love Boat, Night Gallery, Emergency, Adam 12, Chips, Love American Style, Hawaii Five-O.*

PRINCIPAL CLUB APPEARANCES—Sands Hotel, Las Vegas, NV; Royal Box, NY; Bimbo's, San Francisco, CA; The Cave, Vancouver, BC; Royal York, Toronto; Sahara, Lake Tahoe, CA; Regency Hyatt, Atlanta, GA; Statler Hilton, Los Angeles, CA; Chateau Madrid, Ft. Lauderdale, FL.

RELATED CAREER—Spokesperson for Kleenex Tissues, four years; spokesperson, Ralston Purina.

AWARDS: Dramalogue Award, for *Gypsy.*

SIDELIGHTS: MEMBERSHIPS—Actors' Equity Association, Screen Actors Guild, American Federation of Television and Radio Artists, American Guild of Musical Artists, Actors and Others for Animals (board of directors).

ADDRESS: OFFICE—Perry & Neidorf, 315 S. Beverly Drive, Beverly Hills, CA 90212.

Y

YALE, Kathleen Betsko   1939-

PERSONAL: Born Kathleen Yale, May 6, 1939, in Coventry, England; daughter of George (a factory worker) and May (a bus conductress; maiden name, Langford) Yale; married Stephen Betsko, 1959 (divorced, 1967); married Robert Saunders, 1969 (divorced, 1973); children: Candy May, Stephen Glenn. EDUCATION: University of New Hampshire, B.A., theatre, 1974; studied with Herbert Berghof in NY. POLITICS: Left.

VOCATION: Playwright and actress.

CAREER: STAGE DEBUT—Meg, *The Birthday Party,* University of New Hampshire, 1973. NEW YORK DEBUT—Nurse, *Equus,* Plymouth, 1976. PRINCIPAL STAGE APPEARANCES—Mrs. Pearce, *My Fair Lady,* Chateau Deville Dinner Theatre, circuit, 1975; Mother, *Ring Round the Moon,* Gramercy Park Theatre, NY, 1975; Flora, *A Slight Ache,* Manhattan Theatre Club, 1976; Helen, *A Taste of Honey,* NY, 1977.

MAJOR TOURS—Nurse, *Equus,* national tour, 1976-77.

WRITINGS: PLAYS, PRODUCED/PUBLISHED—*Beggar's Choice,* staged reading, Herbert Berghof Studios, 1977; O'Neill Theatre Center Playwright's Conference, 1978; "Earplay," National Public Radio, 1980; Australian Public Radio, 1983. *Johnny Bull,* reading, Herbert Berghof Studios, 1980; O'Neill Theatre Center Playwrights Conference, 1981; reading, Long Wharf Theatre, 1981; produced, Mark Taper Forum, Los Angeles, CA, 1981; produced, Yale Repertory Company, 1982; published by Dramatists Play Service, 1985. *Stitchers and Starlight Talkers,* staged reading, Ensemble Studio Theatre, 1981; O'Neill Theatre Center, Playwrights Conference, 1982; readings, Forum of Italian-American Playwrights, 1983; Matrix Theatre, NY, 1983; Playmakers Repertory Company, NC, 1983; Circle Repertory Company, NY, 1983. PLAYS, UNPRODUCED—Evacuee; The Hanging of Ruth Blay; Starlings; In a Similar Vein. TELEPLAYS—*Daisy's Gang; Bad Guy* (with Rosalyn Drexler). BOOKS—*Interviews with Contemporary Women Playwrights,* William Morrow, 1986.

AWARDS: Selected as a playwright fellow, O'Neill Theatre Center, National Playwrights Conference, 1978, 1981, 1982; Creative Artists Public Service Grant, New York State, 1982.

SIDELIGHTS: MEMBERSHIPS—Dramatists Guild, Authors League of America, Actors' Equity Association, Writers Bloc, Actors Studio Playwrights and Directors Unit, Columbia Pictures Writers Television Workshop.

Yale told *CTFT,* "I look forward to the time when women playwrights no longer have to work twice as hard and be twice as good for half the praise and only 10% of the grant monies accorded male writers. I look forward, with hope, to the time when women are free to speak the unvarnished truth on stage, not just of their own experiences as mothers, workers, daughters, wives, lovers, and artists, but also of the experiences of dispossessed men, women, and children everywhere whose suffering is ignored and whose voices are silent. When women stop modifying their words in order to spare men's feelings (or for fear of public humiliation at pens of the reviewers), the theater will be rocked to its foundations by the reverberations. Far from destroying the theatre, this upheaval will revitalize it, will allow meaning and feeling to surge back to the stage. The way can then be paved for a more honest cameraderie with men, will create deeper possibilities for compassion and love between the sexes, between nations, rather than—as is now the case—endless overt and covert battles caused by fear of intimacy and the struggle for absolute power."

ADDRESS: AGENT—Jonathan Sand, Writers and Artists Agency Inc., 162 W. 56th Street, New York, NY 10019.

*   *   *

YALMAN, Tunc   1925-

PERSONAL: First name pronounced "Toonch;" born September 9, 1925, in Istanbul; son of A. Emin (an editor and publisher) and Rezzan (a writer; maiden name, Korle) Yalman. EDUCATION—Yale University, M.F.A., 1950.

VOCATION: Director.

CAREER: STAGE DEBUT—Eilert Lovborg, *Hedda Gabler* (also directed), Dormen Theatre, Istanbul, Turkey. NEW YORK DEBUT—Director: *The Trial of Lee Harvey Oswald,* ANTA, 1967. PRINCIPAL STAGE WORK—Director: *Arms and the Man,* Dormen, Istanbul; *Coriolanus, Timon of Athens, The Women, Roots, Both Your Houses, The Mayor of Zalamea, The Winslow Boy,* all Municipal Theatre, Istanbul, 1959-66; *Electra, Medea, A Doll's House, The Skin of Our Teeth, Design for Living, The Lesson* and *The Chairs, Oh Pioneers,* all Milwaukee Repertory, 1966-71; *Stuck, The Executioners, A Disturbance of Mirrors,* all O'Neill Theatre Center, 1972; *The Liar,* Cleveland Playhouse, 1972; *A Conflict of Interest,* Urgent Theatre, NY, 1973; *Joe Egg, The Trial of the Catonsville Nine,* both American Conservatory Theatre, Seattle, 1973-74.

Young Osman, International Arts Festival, Istanbul, 1973; *Entertaining Mr. Sloane,* Urgent Theatre, NY, 1974; *The Devil's General,* Asolo Theatre, 1974; *In the Well of the House,* Missouri

Repertory, 1974; *Misalliance,* Loeb Theatre, 1975; *Othello,* National Theatre of Turkey, 1978; *Ghosts,* Playmakers Repertory Company, NC, 1979; *Hedda Gabler,* Monomoy Theatre, Cape Cod, 1980; *Queen After Death,* Angiers Festival, France; *The Duchess of Malfi, The Lower Depths, The Bald Soprano, The Chairs,* all University of Washington; *The Three Sisters, The Man of Mode, The Provoked Wife, A Midsummer Night's Dream, The Merchant of Venice, Tartuffe, The Willard Case,* all North Carolina School of the Arts; *Modigliani,* Istanbul City Theatre, 1985; *The Country Girl,* Trinity Square Repertory Company, 1985.

RELATED CAREER—Artistic director, Milwaukee Repertory Theatre, 1966-71; resident director and faculty member, North Carolina School of the Arts, 1976-present.

WRITINGS: PLAYS, PRODUCED—*A Ball for the Imaginative,* Yale University, and off Broadway, 1949; *The Myrmidons,* Yale University, 1950; *The Liar* (adapted from Goldoni), 1971.

AWARDS: Rockefeller Foundation fellow, 1957; Rockefeller Foundation grantee, 1962.

SIDELIGHTS: MEMBERSHIPS—Stage Society of Directors and Choreographers, National Theatre Conference, ANTA, Eugene O'Neill Theatre Center, and Milwaukee Repertory Company (honorary board member).

ADDRESS: OFFICE—North Carolina School of the Arts, Winston-Salem, NC, 27107.

TUNC YALMAN

Z

MARK ZIMMERMAN

ZIMMERMAN, Mark 1952-

PERSONAL: Born April 19, 1952, in Harrisburg, PA; son of Marlin E. and Winifred E. (Spahr) Zimmerman; married Nancy Johnson (an actress), March 6, 1984. EDUCATION: University of Pennsylvania, B.A., political science.

VOCATION: Actor and singer.

CAREER: PRINCIPAL STAGE APPEARANCES—Jeff, *Brigadoon,* Majestic, NY; Max Jacobs, *On the Twentieth Century,* St. James, NY; understudy James, *Shenandoah,* Mark Hellinger, NY; Raleigh, *Elizabeth & Essex* and Starbuck, *110 in the Shade,* both at York Theatre Company, NY; *Rodgers & Hammerstein,* King Cole Room, St. Regis Hotel; Mark, *On a Clear Day You Can See Forever,* Steve Canfield, *Silk Stockings,* card dealer, *Fiorello!,* all at Equity Library; Ace, *Two Over Easy;* Charles, the manservant, *Man with a*

Load of Mischief, Asolo State Theatre, Sarasota, FL; Lenadro, *Scapino* and Ernest, *Ernest in Love,* both at CMDA, Lake Placid, NY.

PRINCIPAL TELEVISION APPEARANCES—Sargeant Li Ducca, "Private Contentment," *American Playhouse,* PBS; FBI agent, *A Question of Honor,* 1982; *How To. . . ,* USA Network; *Search for Tomorrow; Ryan's Hope; Another World; One Life to Live; As the World Turns.*

SIDELIGHTS: MEMBERSHIPS—Actors' Equity Association, Screen Actors Guild, American Federation of Television and Radio Artists, Friars Club, Penn Players, Mask and Wig.

*   *   *

ZIMMERMAN, Paul D. 1938-

PERSONAL: Born August 3, 1938, in New York City; son of William (a lawyer) and Hedda (in public relations; maiden name, Liverman) Zimmerman; married Barbara Jacobson, June 26, 1965; children: Ian Andrew, Kirsten Scott. EDUCATION: Amherst College, B.A., 1960; University of California, Berkley, M.A., literature, 1962; Columbia University, B.S., journalism, 1964. POLITICS: Anti-nuclear. RELIGION: Quaker (Jewish background).

VOCATION: Writer.

WRITINGS: SCREENPLAY—*The King of Comedy,* Twentieth Century-Fox, 1983. BOOKS PUBLISHED—*The Open Man,* Random House; *The Year the Mets Lost Last Place,* New American Library; *The Marx Brothers at the Movies,* Putnam.

RELATED CAREER—Film critic, *Newsweek,* 1972-77.

AWARDS: British Academy Award, Best Screenplay, 1983, for *The King of Comedy.*

SIDELIGHTS: MEMBERSHIPS—Alliance for Nuclear Disarmament (president).

Zimmerman was a delegate to the Republican National Convention in 1984.

ADDRESS: HOME—Stonybrook Road, Newton, PA 18940. AGENT—International Creative Management, 40 W. 57th Street, New York, NY 10019.

ZIPPRODT, Patricia

PERSONAL: Born in Evanston, IL; daughter of Herbert Edward (an advertising executive) and Irene (Turpin) Zipprodt. EDUCATION: Wellesley College, B.A.; Art Institue of Chicago; New School, NY; Art Students League of NY; Fashion Institute of Technology, NY; served as assistant to Rouban Ter-Artunian, William and Jean Eckart, Boris Aronson, Robert Fletcher, and Irene Sharaff.

VOCATION: Costume designer.

CAREER: FIRST STAGE WORK—Costume design, *The Potting Shed*, Bijou, NY, 1957. PRINCIPAL STAGE WORK—Broadway, plays: *A Visit to a Small Planet*, 1957; *The Rope Dancers*, 1957; *Back to Methusalah*, 1958; *The Gang's All Here*, 1959; *The Night Circus*, 1960; *Laurette*, 1961; *The Garden of Sweets*, 1961; *Sunday in New York*, 1961; *Step on a Crack*, 1962; *A Period of Adjustment*, 1962; *The Little Foxes*, 1967; *Plaza Suite*, 1968; *Scratch*, 1971; *All God's Chillun' Got Wings*, 1975; *Poor Murderer*, 1976; *Stages*, 1978; *Charlotte*, 1979; *Kingdoms*, 1981; *Fools*, 1981; *Whodunnit*, 1982; *Brighton Beach Memoirs*, 1983; *The Glass Menagerie*, 1983; *Accidental Death of an Anarchist*, 1984.

Broadway, musicals: *She Loves Me*, 1963; *Fiddler on the Roof*, 1964; *Anya*, 1965; *Pousse Cafe*, 1966; *Cabaret*, 1966; *Zorba*, 1968; *1776*, 1969; *Georgy*, 1970; *Pippin*, 1972; *Mack and Mabel*, 1974; *Chicago*, 1975; *King of Hearts*, 1978; *Swing*, 1979; *One Night Stand*, 1980; *Alice in Wonderland*, 1982; *Sunday in the Park with George*, 1984.

Regional and Off Broadway: *The Crucible* and *The Quare Fellow*, both Circle in the Square, NY, 1959; *Our Town* and *The Balcony*, both Circle in the Square, 1960; *Madame Aphrodite* and *Camino Real*, both Circle in the Square, 1961; *Don Perlimplin*, Cincinnatti Playhouse in the Park, OH, 1962; *The Blacks, Oh Dad, Poor Dad . . . , The Matchmaker, The Dragon*, and *Next Time I'll Sing to You*, all at the Phoenix, NY, 1962; *Calvary*, Princeton Experimental, 1963; *A Man's a Man* and *Mornin' Sun*, both at the Phoenix, NY, 1963; *Too Much Johnson* and *The Tragical History of Dr. Faustus*, both at the Phoenix, NY, 1964; *Tales of Kasane*, National Theatre of the Deaf, 1969; *Waiting for Godot*, Tyrone Guthrie, Minneapolis, 1973; *Dear Nobody*, Cherry Lane, NY, 1974; *Four Saints in Three Acts*, National Theatre of the Deaf, 1976; *Don Juan*, Tyrone Guthrie, 1982; *Sunset*, Village Gate, NY, 1983; *Anna Christie*, Central Theatre Institute, Beijing, China, 1984.

MAJOR TOURS—*Bette Midler*, 1976; *Ben Vereen*, 1983.

PRINCIPAL FILM WORK—*The Graduate*, Embassy, 1967; *The Last of the Mobile Hotshots*, Warner Brothers, 1969; *1776*, Columbia, 1972.

PRINCIPAL TELEVISION WORK—*Anne Bancroft Special*, CBS, 1970; *June Moon*, PBS, 1973; *The Glass Menagerie*, ABC, 1973; *Pippin*, HBO; *Alice in Wonderland*, PBS, 1983.

PRINCIPAL OPERA WORK—*La Boheme* and *Madame Butterfly*, Boston Opera Company, 1962; *Hippolyte E Aricie*, Boston Opera Company, 1966; *Katerina Ismailova*, New York City Opera Company, 1967; *The Flaming Angel*, New York City Opera Company, 1968; *The Rise and Fall of the City of Mahagonny*, Boston Opera Company, 1972; *The Mother of Us All*, Guggenheim Museum, NY, 1972; *Lord Byron*, Julliard Opera, 1973; *Don Giovanni*, Metropolitan Opera, NY (designed but not produced due to lack of funds), 1973; *Tannhauser*, Metropolitan Opera, NY,

1977; *Naughty Marietta*, New York City Opera, 1978; *The Barber of Seville*, Metropolitan Opera, NY, 1982; *The Loves of Don Perlimplin*, San Francisco Opera and State University of New York, Purchase, 1984.

PRINCIPAL BALLET WORK—*La Sonnamnbula*, National Ballet of Washington; *L'Histoire Du Soldat*, Israel Cultural Foundation, 1967; *Les Noces*, American Ballet Theatre, 1969; *The Poppet*, Joffrey Ballet, NY, 1970; *Watermill*, New York City Ballet, 1972; *Lord Byron Ballet*, Alvin Ailey, 1973; *Dumbarton Oaks*, New York City Ballet, 1973; *Dybbuk Variations*, New York City Ballet, 1974; *The Leaves Are Fading*, American Ballet Theatre, 1975; *Tres Cantos*, Ballet Hispanico, 1976; *Caprichos*, Ballet Hispanico, 1976; *Estuary*, American Ballet Theatre, 1983; *Llamada*, Ballet Hispanico, 1983; *Tito on Tambales*, Ballet Hispanico, 1984.

RELATED CAREER—Teacher of master classes and lecturer at: Yale School of Drama, Harvard, Wellesley, Brandeis, Smith, Northwestern, University of Rhode Island, New York University School of the Arts, Pratt Institute, U.S. Institute of Theatre Technicians, Martha's Vineyard Sculpture Gallery series, Brooklyn Museum; adjunct professor of theatre design, University of Utah.

WRITINGS: ARTICLES—"Designing Costumes," *Contemporary Stage Design, U.S.A.*, 1974; interviews and articles in *Theatre Crafts*, 1971, 1973, 1974, 1977.

AWARDS: Antoinette Perry Awards, 1964, for *Fiddler on the Roof*, 1966, for *Cabaret*, 1984, for *Sunday in the Park with George;* Antoinette Perry Award nominations, 1968, for *Zorba*, 1972, for *Pippin*, 1974, for *Mack and Mabel*, 1975, for *Chicago*, 1983, for *Alice in Wonderland;* Drama Desk Awards, 1968, for *Zorba*, and *1776*, 1972, for *Pippin*, 1978, for *King of Hearts;* Emmy, National Academy of Television Arts and Sciences, 1969, for *Anne Bancroft Special;* Wellesley College Alumnae Achievement Award, 1971; Special award, New England Theatre Conference, 1973, "For creative excellence;" Ritter award, Fashion Institute of Technology, 1977; Joseph P. Maharam Awards, 1969, for *1776*, 1983 for *Alice in Wonderland* and *Don Juan*, 1984, for *Sunday in the Park with George;* Joseph P. Maharam Award nomination, 1981, for *Fools;* Distinguished Career Award, Southeastern Theatre Conference, 1985.

SIDELIGHTS: Zipprodt has had sketches and drawings exhibited at: Wright-Hepburn, London, for *Fiddler on the Roof*, 1966; Capricorn Gallery, NY, 1968; theatre collection, Museum of the City of New York, 1972; University of California at San Diego, 1974; Toneelmuseum, Amsterdam, "International Stage Design," 1975; U.S. International Theatre Institute, traveling Stage Design Exhibition assembled for the Prague Quadriennale, Lincoln Center Library, Smithsonian Institute, 1974-78; American Ballet Theatre, traveling exhibit, 1976-78.

ADDRESS: HOME—29 King Street, New York, NY 10014.

*   *   *

ZORICH, Louis   1924-

PERSONAL: Born February 12, 1924, in Chicago, IL; son of Christ and Anna (Gledi) Zorich; married Olympia Dukakis (an actress),

LOUIS ZORICH

VILMOS ZSIGMOND

November 30, 1962; children: Christina, Peter, Stefan. EDUCA-TION—Roosevelt College, B.A.; Goodman School of Drama. MILI-TARY—U.S. Army, 1943-45.

VOCATION: Actor.

CAREER: STAGE DEBUT—*Springtime for Henry,* Tenthouse Thea-tre, Rhinelander, WI. NEW YORK DEBUT—*Shadow of Heroes,* York Theatre, 1959. PRINCIPAL STAGE APPEARANCES—Broad-way: *Becket; Moby Dick; Fun City; Moonchildren; Herzl; Hadrian VII; Blau & Irving; Death of a Salesman; Arms and the Man; They Knew What They Wanted.*

MAJOR TOURS—*A View from the Bridge,* 1958-60; First Baron, *Becket,* 1961-62;

FILM DEBUT—Constable, *Fiddler on the Roof,* United Artists, 1970. PRINCIPAL FILM APPEARANCES—*Made for Each Other; For Pete's Sake; The Don Is Dead; Newman's Law; Where Are the Children?*

TELEVISION DEBUT—*DuPont Show of the Week,* 1958.

AWARDS: Antoinette Perry Award, for *Hadrian VII;* Drama Desk Award nomination, for *They Knew What They Wanted.*

SIDELIGHTS: MEMBERSHIPS—Actors' Equity Association, Screen Actors Guild, Whole Theatre Company, Montclair, NJ (trustee).

ADDRESS: HOME—222 Upper Mountain Avenue, Upper Mont-clair, NJ 07043.

ZSIGMOND, Vilmos   1930-

PERSONAL: Name pronounced "Vilmosh Gigmond;" born June 16, 1930; son of Vilmo (soccer goalie and coach) and Bozena (an administrator; maiden name, Illichman) Zsigmond; married Eliza-beth Fuzes (divorced); children: Julia, Susi. EDUCATION: State Academy of Motion Picture and Theatre Arts, Budapest, Hungary, M.A., Cinematography.

VOCATION: Cinematographer.

CAREER: PRINCIPAL FILM WORK—Cinematographer: *The Time Travelers,* American International, 1964; *The Sadist; The Name of the Game Is Kill,* Fanfare, 1968; *Futz,* Commonwealth Interna-tional, 1969; *Picasso Summer,* 1969; *The Monitors,* Common-wealth United, 1969; *Red Sky at Morning,* Universal, 1970; *McCabe and Mrs. Miller,* Warner Brothers, 1971; *The Hired Hand,* Universal, 1971; *The Ski Bum,* Avco-Embassy, 1971; *Deliverance,* Warner Brothers, 1972; *Images,* Columbia, 1972; *The Long Good-bye,* 1973; *Scarecrow,* Warner Brothers, 1973; *Cinderella Liberty,* Twentieth Century-Fox, 1974; *The Sugarland Express,* Universal, 1974; *The Girl from Petrovka,* Universal, 1974; *Obsession,* Colum-bia, 1976; *Sweet Revenge,* United Artists, 1977; *Close Encounters of the Third Kind,* Columbia, 1977; *Winter Kills,* Avco-Embassy, 1979; *The Deer Hunter,* Universal, 1979; *The Rose,* Twentieth Century-Fox, 1979; *Heaven's Gate,* United Artists, 1980; *Blow Out,* Filmways, 1981; *Jinxed,* Metro-Goldwyn-Mayer/United Artists, 1982; *Table for Five,* Warner Brothers, 1983; *The River,* 1984; *No Small Affair; Real Genius,* Tri-Star, 1985.

PRINCIPAL TELEVISION WORK—Documentaries for Wolper productions for CBS; television commercials through Cinematic Directions Inc. and Filmfair.

RELATED CAREER—Formed own company, Cinematic Directions Inc., 1985.

AWARDS: Academy of Motion Picture Arts and Sciences Award, for *Close Encounters of the Third Kind;* Academy of Motion Picture Arts and Sciences Award nominations, for *The Deer Hunter, The River;* British Academy of Motion Picture Arts and Sciences, for *The Deer Hunter.*

SIDELIGHTS: MEMBERSHIPS—American Society of Cinematographers, Academy of Motion Picture Arts and Sciences, International Alliance of Theatrical Stage Employees Local #659, Directors Guild of America.

ADDRESS: OFFICE—9229 Sunset Blvd., Suite 700, Los Angeles, CA. AGENT—Smith-Gosnell Agency, 3872 Las Flores Canyon Road, Malibu, CA 90265.

Cumulative Index

To provide continuity with *Who's Who in the Theatre*, this index interfiles references to *Who's Who in the Theatre*, 1st-17th Editions, with references to *Contemporary Theatre, Film, and Television*, Volumes 1-2. Only those deceased or inactive individuals whose *Who's Who in the Theatre* entries are included in Gale's *Who Was Who in the Theatre* are not listed in this index.

References in the index are identified as follows:

Number only—*Contemporary Theatre, Film, and Television*, Volumes 1-2
WWT and edition number—*Who's Who in the Theatre*, 1st-17th Editions

Cumulative Index

COLLEGE OF THE SEQUOIAS

REFERENCE

LIBRARY